"This fine introductory volume does precisely what it sets out to do: it presents readers with an outline of what to look for as they make their way through the biblical text. The commentary does not overpower the reader with scholarly theories; instead it allows the reader to confront the text as it stands."

— GARY A. ANDERSON
University of Notre Dame

"Onto the crowded shelf of introductions to the Bible comes this welcome addition. Acknowledging that much of the Bible is narrative witness to a people's experience of God, the authors add two things that set this textbook apart from others. They incorporate narrative criticism into their approach to the biblical texts, without, however, neglecting the results of historical-critical methods; and they identify the theological claims made by each biblical book.

"Those attentive to the pedagogical challenges of teaching Bible to undergraduates will appreciate the organization and standard elements of each chapter: 'Getting Started' exercises by which to pique student interest in the text; a concise 'Walk Through' the content of the particular biblical book; introduction to the 'Critical Issues' in studying the particular book; and identification of the book's 'Theological Themes.' A 'Glossary of Terms,' 'Questions for Review and Discussion,' and recommendations for 'Further Reading' are also provided.

"Not likely to sit on an office shelf collecting dust, this volume, with its useful pedagogical features and its attention to the Bible as theological witness, has much to offer for those teaching introductory Bible courses in theology departments and seminaries."

— SUSAN A. CALEF
Creighton University

An Introduction to the Bible

Robert Kugler and Patrick Hartin

WILLIAM B. EERDMANS PUBLISHING COMPANY
Grand Rapids, Michigan / Cambridge, U.K.

Published 2009 by
Wм. B. Eerdmans Publishing Co.
2140 Oak Industrial Drive N.E., Grand Rapids, Michigan 49505 /
p.o. Box 163, Cambridge cb3 9pu U.K.
www.eerdmans.com

Printed in the United States of America

14 13 12 11 10 09   7 6 5 4 3 2 1

Library of Congress Cataloging-in-Publication Data

Kugler, Robert A.
    An introduction to the Bible / Robert Kugler and Patrick Hartin.
       p.   cm.
    isbn 978-0-8028-4636-5 (cloth: alk. paper) 1. Bible — Introductions.
    I. Hartin, P. J. (Patrick J.)   II. Title.
    BS475.3.K84   2009
    220.6′1 — dc22

                                        2008035221

Contents

Introduction to the New Testament

Maps

Abbreviations

ABD	*Anchor Bible Dictionary*, ed. David Noel Freedman	NIGTC	New International Greek Testament Commentary
ABRL	Anchor Bible Reference Library	NRSV	New Revised Standard Version
AnBib	Analecta biblica	OBT	Overtures to Biblical Theology
ANET	*Ancient Near Eastern Texts Relating to the Old Testament*, ed. James B. Pritchard	OTG	Old Testament Guides
		OTL	Old Testament Library
BAR	*Biblical Archaeology Review*	*OTP*	*The Old Testament Pseudepigrapha*, ed. James H. Charlesworth
BRS	Biblical Resource Series	OTS	Old Testament Studies
BTB	*Biblical Theology Bulletin*	*RevQ*	*Revue de Qumrân*
BZAW	Beihefte zur Zeitschrift für die alttestamentliche Wissenschaft	SNTSMS	Society for New Testament Studies Monograph Series
DSD	*Dead Sea Discoveries*	WBC	Word Biblical Commentary
ECB	*Eerdmans Commentary on the Bible*, ed. James D. G. Dunn and John Rogerson		
ECC	Eerdmans Critical Commentary		
EDB	*Eerdmans Dictonary of the Bible*, ed. David Noel Freedman		
FCB	The Feminist Companion to the Bible		
FOTL	The Forms of the Old Testament Literature		
GBS	Guides to Biblical Scholarship		
GNS	Good News Studies		
HBD	*HarperCollins Bible Dictionary*, ed. Paul J. Achtemeier		
ITC	International Theological Commentary		
JSOTSup	Journal for the Study of the Old Testament: Supplement Series		
KJV	King James Version		
LXX	Septuagint		
NCBC	New Century Bible Commentary		
NICOT	New International Commentary on the Old Testament		

Biblical Books

Old Testament/Hebrew Bible

Gen	Genesis
Exod	Exodus
Lev	Leviticus
Num	Numbers
Deut	Deuteronomy
Josh	Joshua
Judg	Judges
Ruth	Ruth
1–2 Sam	1–2 Samuel
1–2 Kgs	1–2 Kings
1–2 Chr	1–2 Chronicles
Ezra	Ezra
Neh	Nehemiah
Esth	Esther
Job	Job
Ps, Pss	Psalms

Prov	Proverbs
Eccl	Ecclesiastes
Song	Song of Songs
Isa	Isaiah
Jer	Jeremiah
Lam	Lamentations
Ezek	Ezekiel
Dan	Daniel
Hos	Hosea
Joel	Joel
Amos	Amos
Obad	Obadiah
Jonah	Jonah
Mic	Micah
Nah	Nahum
Hab	Habakkuk
Zeph	Zephaniah
Hag	Haggai
Zech	Zechariah
Mal	Malachi

Apocrypha/Deuterocanonicals

Tob	Tobit
Jdt	Judith
Add Esth	Additions to Esther
Wis	Wisdom
Sir	Sirach (Ecclesiasticus)
Bar	Baruch
Ep Jer	Epistle of Jeremiah
Add Dan	Additions to Daniel
Pr Azar	Prayer of Azariah
Sg Three	Song of the Three Jews
Sus	Susanna
Bel	Bel and the Dragon
1–2–3–4 Macc	1–2–3–4 Maccabees
1–2 Esdr	1–2 Esdras
Pr Man	Prayer of Manasseh

New Testament

Matt	Matthew
Mark	Mark
Luke	Luke
John	John
Acts	Acts
Rom	Romans
1–2 Cor	1–2 Corinthians
Gal	Galatians
Eph	Ephesians
Phil	Philippians
Col	Colossians
1–2 Thess	1–2 Thessalonians
1–2 Tim	1-2 Timothy
Tit	Titus
Phlm	Philemon
Heb	Hebrews
Jas	James
1–2 Pet	1–2 Peter
1–2–3 John	1–2–3 John
Jude	Jude
Rev	Revelation

Other Ancient Works

1 En	*1 Enoch*
b. B. Bat.	Babylonian Talmud *Baba Batra*
m. Yad.	Mishnah *Yadayim*
4QMMT	Qumran *Miqṣat Maʿaseh ha-Torah*
Josephus *C. Ap.*	*Contra Apion*
Philo *Contempl.*	*On the Contemplative Life*
Mos.	*On the Life of Moses*

Glossary of Terms

This Glossary contains only the major terms that are important for understanding the material of the Hebrew Bible and the New Testament. For a much fuller and more detailed explanation of these and other terms, refer to any Dictionary of the Bible.

Among the more important Dictionaries of the Bible we mention the following:

Evans, Craig A., and Stanley E. Porter, eds. *Dictionary of New Testament Background.* Downers Grove: InterVarsity, 2000.

Freedman, David Noel, Allen C. Myers, and Astrid B. Beck, eds. *Eerdmans Dictionary of the Bible.* Grand Rapids: Wm. B. Eerdmans, 2000.

Achtemeier, Paul J., ed. *HarperCollins Bible Dictionary.* Rev. ed. San Francisco: HarperSanFrancisco, 1996.

Freedman, David Noel, ed. *The Anchor Bible Dictionary.* 6 vols. New York: Doubleday, 1992. [*ABD*]

Metzger, Bruce M., and Michael D. Coogan, eds. *The Oxford Companion to the Bible.* New York: Oxford University Press, 1993.

Aaronites   Priestly descendants of Aaron (brother of Moses and ancestor of the priesthood in Israel) (see Ps 115:10). Both Zechariah and Elizabeth, parents of John the Baptist, were descendants of Aaron (Luke 1:5).

Acropolis   A precipitous hill in northwest Athens on which stood the famous temple, the Parthenon, dedicated to the goddess Athena, patroness of the city of Athens.

Acrostic   A technique of Hebrew poetry by which each successive line begins with the following letter of the Hebrew alphabet (see Psalm 119).

Adonai   (Hebrew, "Lord"). A title of majesty applied to Israel's God. Since the Israelites considered God's name Yahweh too sacred to pronounce, they used the word Adonai. The name Jehovah is a combination formed by introducing the vowels of Adonai into the consonants of Yahweh.

Alexander the Great   (356-323 B.C.E.). Son and successor of Philip of Macedonia. He became ruler in 336. After first unifying Greece under his control, he conquered the Persian Empire and extended his rule as far as India. Mentioned in 1 Macc 1:1-9 and 6:2. His empire diffused the Greek language, thought, and culture (see **Hellenism**) throughout the world.

Alexandria   An Egyptian seaport founded by Alexander the Great in 332 B.C.E. Famous for its lighthouse that was counted among the seven wonders of the ancient world. Together with Rome and Antioch, it was one of the major cities of the Roman Empire with an estimated population of about half a million. It was the major intellectual center of the Hellenistic world with a museum and two libraries. The largest Jewish population in the world outside of Palestine was here. Jews were influenced by Greek thought and culture, and some Jewish scholars tried to harmonize their own wisdom and law with that of Greek philosophy (e.g., Philo). The Septuagint, the Greek translation of the Hebrew Scriptures, emerged here.

Allegory   An extended metaphor presented in the form of a story in which people, things, and events all have a hidden meaning. Some Jewish scholars of Alexandria and other Jewish population centers interpreted the Hebrew Bible in an allegorical way, just as Paul did in his interpretation of the narrative of Abraham, Sarah, and Hagar (Gal 4:21-31). Many early church writers interpreted the Bible allegorically by identifying moral principles in almost every part of the Bible (see **Parable**).

Amen (Hebrew, "it is true; so be it"). Used especially as a way of giving agreement to what has been said (1 Kgs 1:36). In the New Testament it is often used at the conclusion to a prayer (e.g., 1 Cor 14:16).

Angel (Greek *angelos* [Hebrew *mal'ak*], "messenger"). Throughout the ancient Near East, angels were understood as messengers of the deity. Many scholars see Israel's belief in angels originating with the Persians. Gabriel and Michael are named in the Scriptures, and other names such as Raphael occur in other writings. In the Christian writings angels play an important role in the Infancy stories about Jesus (Matt 1–2; Luke 1–2).

Annunciation Term given to the account in Luke 1:26-38, where Mary learns from the angel Gabriel that she is to be mother of the Messiah.

Anointed Ritualistic use of oil was very common in the ancient Near East. The purpose was to make the person or object sacred. Priests, the tent, the ark, the furniture of the tent were all anointed (Exod 30:22-33). Kings were anointed (Saul [1 Sam 10:1]; David [1 Sam 16:13]; Solomon [1 Kgs 1:39]). In Isa 61:1 the prophet says that he has been anointed to proclaim the good news to the poor. In this instance (as well as others such as 1 Sam 16:13) anointing is seen to confer the gift of God's Spirit so that the person could carry out God's plan. In the New Testament Jas 5:14 (as does Mark 6:13) speaks about anointing the sick with oil (see also **Christ**; **Messiah**).

Anthropomorphism Attribution of human qualities or characteristics to something that is not human. This applies especially to the description of God in human terms.

Antinomianism (Lit., "opposed to the law"). In early Christianity it refers to those groups claiming that faith in Jesus Christ absolved them from following any moral laws. Paul vehemently opposed them (see Gal 5:13–6:10; see also 1 and 2 John).

Antioch Two important Hellenistic cities bore this name. (1) *Antioch in Syria:* The royal city of the Seleucid kings. It had been founded by Seleucus I in 300 B.C.E. on the Orontes River where it runs through the Lebanon and Taurus mountain ranges. It was approximately 17 miles inland from the sea. Originally a Greek military colony, it soon expanded to become one of the largest cities in the Roman Empire with an estimated population about half a million. When the Romans captured this city in 64 B.C.E., they made it the capital of the Province of Syria (to which Palestine belonged) and it became an important intellectual center. This city continued to exercise this important intellectual role during Christian times. From the 4th to the 6th century C.E. some significant theological schools flourished there. (2) *Antioch in Pisidia:* A major city in Galatia (central Asia Minor). A Christian church was founded here by Paul and Barnabas (Acts 13:14-50).

Antiochus IV Epiphanes (Greek *epiphanes,* "manifestation [of god]"). A Seleucid ruler who tried to force the Jews to adopt Greek culture. His actions in imposing Greek ways and religion on his people were largely responsible for the outbreak of the Maccabean revolt in 167 B.C.E.

Aphorism A short, pithy saying that challenges conventional wisdom. Jesus proclaimed his message in the mold of sayings that were easily remembered and handed on by his followers.

Apocalypse (Apocalyptic/Apocalyptic literature) (Greek *apokalypsis* ("to reveal, to uncover"). A type of literature popular between the 2nd century B.C.E. and the 2nd century C.E.) largely written for people experiencing persecution and opposition because of their faith. It was expressed in the form of visions and symbols that only people of that particular culture and worldview could understand. Examples of such literature are the books of Daniel, Enoch, 2 and 3 Baruch, 2 Esdras as well as Revelation in the New Testament. Ultimately Good will triumph over Evil, the Messianic Kingdom will be established by God's Messiah, and the world will be transformed (see also Matthew 24; Mark 13; Luke 21).

Apocrypha (Greek, "hidden"). Books not incorporated into the Hebrew or Protestant canons, rejected because they were considered not to express the faith of all the communities.

Apodictic Law Laws expressed through direct unconditional demands. E.g., "Thou shalt not kill" (Exod 20:13) states unequivocally that one is not to commit murder.

Apology (Greek *apologia,* "defense"). A well-reasoned explanation for one's beliefs and actions. In the Greek world Plato produced an "Apology" for Socrates. Justin Martyr (an early Christian philosopher) produced a defense of the Christian faith in the early 2nd century C.E.

Apostasy (Greek *apostasia,* "rebellion"). The rejection of a religious faith.

Apostle (Greek *apostellein,* "to send out"). In early Christianity the term referred to those followers of Jesus who had seen the risen Christ and had been sent out on a mission to preach the same message that Jesus preached.

Apostolic Fathers   A collection of extracanonical writings by Christian leaders of the 2nd century C.E. considered to be followers of the apostles. They continued to write to communities just as had the Apostles. In areas of the Christian world some of these writings (such as the *Didache*) were considered Scripture.

Aramaic   The language of the Aramaeans (the Syrians). A West Semitic language used in Mesopotamia from *ca.* 1000 B.C.E., it became the official language of the Persian Empire from 500 onwards. The Jews continued to speak it when they returned from exile in Babylon. Some parts of the Old Testament were written in Aramaic, and it was the mother tongue of Jesus.

Areopagus   (Greek *areios pagos,* "hill of Ares" ["Mars Hill"]). Before the 5th century B.C.E. the Supreme Council of Athens met here before being transferred elsewhere. The name continued to refer to either the place or the Supreme Council. Hence, when Acts 17 mentions that Paul was taken to the Areopagus, it is not certain whether he is brought to the place or before the Council.

Ark of the Covenant   (also known as "ark of the testimony"). A small portable box or chest (Exod 25:10–22) made of acacia wood overlaid with gold inside and outside, about 3 feet 9 inches × 2 feet 3 inches in size. The ark contained the two stone tablets representing the Ten Commandments, traced back to Moses. It could be carried into battle (Josh 6:4-11; 1 Sam 4) and was finally brought to Jerusalem and placed in the holy of holies in Solomon's Temple of Jerusalem. After the destruction of this temple, the Ark disappeared from history. The top of the ark contained a gold plate referred to as the "mercy seat," or the "propitiatory." Here God received the acts of atonement of the people and bestowed mercy upon Israel. Above all, the ark symbolized God's presence among God's people. Modern archaeological studies have demonstrated the existence of portable shrines among the people of Arabia prior to the emergence of Islam.

Armageddon   (Greek transliteration of Hebrew *Har Megiddo* ["Mountain of Megiddo"]. Site of many battles in biblical times because this hill overlooked the Plain of Jezreel, through which ancient armies had to pass when they moved from north to south. The book of Revelation situates the final battle against the forces of evil here (Rev 16:16).

Ascension   The return of the risen Jesus to heaven (Acts 1:6-11).

Asclepius   Greek god of medicine. Son of Apollo (god of the creative arts and of health). Renowned as a doctor, he was acclaimed to be able to raise the dead. After death he was considered a god and shrines were erected to him throughout the Mediterranean world, where his powers were invoked and cures acknowledged.

Asherah   (Hebrew for Canaanite goddess *Asherat*). Wife of El, chief Canaanite god.

Assyria/the Assyrians   An empire and people that ruled the ancient Near East from the 11th to the 7th centuries B.C.E.

Athanasius   Bishop Athanasius of Alexandria (Egypt) wrote his Easter Letter to his community in 367 C.E. in which he listed the 27 New Testament writings. This is the first evidence for such a listing of the 27 books together.

Athens   Cultural capital of Greece. Paul interacted with the intellectual world of this city according to Acts 17:15-34.

Augustus   First Roman Emperor (29 B.C.E.–14 C.E.). He established peace throughout the Roman world (the "Roman peace" [Latin, *pax Romana*]). Jesus was born during his rule (Luke 2:1).

Babylon/Babylonians   Capital city of the people who bear this name, situated in Mesopotamia between the two Rivers, the Tigris and Euphrates. The Babylonians created an empire extending throughout the ancient Near East from 625-539 B.C.E.

Babylonian Captivity/Exile   In 587 B.C.E. the Babylonians destroyed the Southern Kingdom of Judah and brought the leaders of the Israelite community into captivity in Babylon (hence the name *"Babylonian Captivity/Exile"*). When Cyrus, king of the Persians, captured Babylon in 539, he allowed the Jews to return to their homeland.

Balaam   A prophet from outside Israel, hired by the king of Moab, Balak, to curse the Israelites when they tried to cross Moab on their journeys to the land of Canaan. The God of Israel caused Balaam's cursing to turn into a blessing for Israel (Numbers 22–24). Another tradition blames Balaam for corrupting the Israelites (Num 31:8, 15-17), and another lies behind the references to Balaam in Revelation and the letters of Jude and 2 Peter (Rev 2:14; Jude 11; 2 Pet 2:15-16).

Ban   A practice that dedicated the spoils of victory to the god of the conquering nation.

Baptism   A ritual whereby water is poured over the head of the individual. In the New Testament this ritual is connected with John the Baptist (Matt 3:6; Mark 1:4; 11:30; Luke 7:29). Jesus was baptized (Matt 3:13-17; Mark 1:9-11; Luke 3:21-22; John 1:29-34), and the early

Christian church used baptism as a way of initiating converts into their movement (Acts 2:38-41), replacing the Jewish ritual of circumcision. Its exact origins are disputed. Some scholars see it originating within the community of the Dead Sea Scrolls, the Essenes, while others see it developing from the ritual baths of purification that have recently been excavated in Israel.

Barabbas A bandit, condemned to death, but released by Pontius Pilate instead of Jesus at his trial (Matt 27:15-23; Mark 15:6-15; Luke 23:18-25; John 18:39-40).

Barnabas An apostle and important leader of the early Christian church sent by the Jerusalem church to care for the Christian community of Antioch. He was a traveling companion of Paul on his first journey (Acts 9:26-30; 11:22-30; 13:1-3; 13:42-52; 14:1–15:4; 15:22-40; 1 Cor 9:6; Gal 2:1-13: Col 4:10).

Baruch Jeremiah's secretary who recorded the prophet's message. These notes probably became the core of the message of the scroll of Jeremiah (Jer 32:9-15; 36; 43:6). The book of Baruch was attributed to him as well as the apocalypses of 2 and 3 Baruch.

Bathsheba Wife of Uriah, a Hittite soldier. David committed adultery with Bathsheba. To cover it up, he ensured that Uriah was killed in battle. David then married her (2 Sam 11:1-4). Nathan condemned David's actions (2 Sam 12:1-23). She was Solomon's mother and manipulated events so her son would succeed David as king (1 Kgs 1:15-17).

B.C.E./C.E. Abbreviations for "Before the Common Era/Common Era," equivalent to the Christian designations B.C. ("before Christ") and A.D. (*Anno Domini,* lit., "in the year of the Lord," meaning "after Christ").

Beatitudes (Latin *beati,* "Blessed"). The phrase "Blessed are. . ." opens each of Jesus' nine sayings introducing Matthew's Sermon on the Mount (Matt 5:3-11).

Behemoth A beast that probably derived from Mesopotamian mythology (Job 40:15-24).

Bel A common name for Marduk, the patron deity of the Babylonians (Isa 46:1-4).

Belial The common English rendition of Greek *Beliar* (2 Cor 6:15), a demon found often in apocalyptic literature. The name is a corruption of Hebrew *beliyyaal* which means "malice" or "wickedness." In the intertestamental period some Jewish (and also Christian) groups attributed the origin of evil to angels (e.g., 1 En 1–36). Among these groups the name Belial was given to the chief demon (the devil). The Dead Sea Scrolls provide the first evidence for this personal usage of Belial for the devil (see 1QH, 1QS and 1QM).

Benjamin Youngest son of Jacob and second son of Rachel (Jacob's favorite wife). He features in the narrative of Joseph (Genesis 42–44). The tribe that bears his name was given their territory adjacent to that of Judah. When Israel split into two kingdoms, Benjamin sided with Judah against the other 10 tribes and formed the Southern Kingdom (1 Kgs 12:21).

Bethel (Hebrew *beth El,* "house of El [God]"). A place *ca.* 14 miles north of Jerusalem associated with the patriarchs Abraham (Gen 12:8) and Jacob (Gen 28:11-22). Jeroboam I built a sanctuary here close to Judah's northern border (1 Kgs 12:32). It became a center of prophetic activity: Amos (3:14; 4:4; 5:5) denounces activities here, especially worship of the image of a calf.

Bethlehem (Hebrew *beth lehem,* "house of bread" or "house of [the god] *Lahm*"). A village 5 miles south of Jerusalem, home to David's family (1 Sam 16:4) where Samuel anointed David king (1 Sam 16:1-5; see also 20:6). The prophet Micah (5:1-2) extols this town because of its ties to the line of David — he foresees that the future ruler of the Israelites will come from this town. According to the Gospel narratives, it was the birthplace of Jesus (Matt 2:5-6; Luke 2:4; John 7:42).

Bethsaida Town on the northern shore of the Sea of Galilee from which Peter, Andrew, and Philip came (John 1:44; 12:21). One of the towns cursed by Jesus (Matt 11:21; Luke 10:13).

Blasphemy Language that is contemptuous or defamatory directed against God or holy things or places. In the Holiness Code it is punished by stoning (Lev 24:16). The Sanhedrin brought this charge against Jesus (Matt 9:3; 26:65; John 10:36).

Boanerges (Aramaic, "Sons of Thunder"). A nickname given by Jesus to the sons of Zebedee, James and John. It probably indicated that they had a fiery temperament (Mark 3:17; see also Luke 9:52-56).

Boaz A wealthy landowner of Bethlehem (Ruth 2:1) who married Ruth and an ancestor of Jesus (4:21-22). Both Boaz and Ruth are identified in Jesus' genealogy as his ancestors (Matt 1:5).

Booths, Feast of An agricultural festival celebrated in the Fall for the purpose of thanking God for the wine harvest. The participants constructed booths or shelters that reminded them of the time in the desert when Israel journeyed from Egypt to Canaan. Also known as the Feast of Tabernacles or the Feast of Sukkoth (Lev 23:39-43; Neh 8:13-18).

ca. Lat. *circa,* "about," "around."

Caesar Family name of Gaius Julius Caesar (100-44 B.C.E.) who became dictator of Rome and laid the foundations for the imperial government of Rome. Succeeded by Octavian (or Augustus, the first Roman emperor) who adopted this name of Caesar. Henceforth, the name Caesar became an official title for the emperor. Three Caesars are mentioned in the New Testament: Augustus, Tiberius, and Claudius.

Caesarea City on the Palestinian coast built by Herod the Great on the site of Strato's Tower and named in honor of Augustus Caesar. It was the main port of Palestine and seat of the Roman procurator. It was the port for the arrival and departure of many missionary journeys (Acts 9:30; 18:22; 21:8). Paul was imprisoned here for two years before he was sent to Rome (Acts 23:23; 24–26).

Caesarea Philippi Town in the far north of Palestine situated at one of the sources of the Jordan River in the southern foothills of Mount Hermon. Built by Philip, one of the sons of Herod the Great, as the capital of the territory over which he ruled (4 B.C.E.–34 C.E.). He named it in honor of Tiberius Caesar and added his own name to distinguish it from other cities also named Caesarea. The area or villages around this town were the scene for Peter's confession of Jesus as the Messiah (Matt 16:13; Mark 8:27).

Caiaphas High priest in Jerusalem during the reign of Tiberius Caesar (Matt 26:3, 57-66; John 18:13-28; Acts 4:6). He was son-in-law to the previous high priest, Annas. He was appointed high priest by the procurator, Valerius Gratus, in 18 C.E. and deposed by Vitellius in 36 C.E. He presided over Jesus' trial before the Sanhedrin.

Calvary (see **Golgotha**)

Canaan The land between Syria and Egypt where the Israelites settled. The name appears in both Egyptian and cuneiform records from the 2nd millennium B.C.E. It was the territory that God promised Abraham for his descendants (Gen 15:7-21; 17:1-8).

Canon (Greek *kanon,* "reed," used as an instrument of measurement). A measure or rule that offers a standard. In the context of the biblical writings it refers to those writings that serve as a standard or measure against which the faith, morality, and way of life of the community (Hebrew or Christian) can be measured. Any books that are excluded from the canon are referred to as *extracanonical* books.

Capernaum Town on the northern shore of the Sea of Galilee. In the Synoptic Gospels it is the headquarters for the activity of Jesus and his followers. Matthew 4:13 says that Jesus "made his home" here, and in Matt 9:1 it is referred to as "his own town."

Casuistic Law (or Case Law) Law expressed in terms of cases or situations. Generally introduced in conditional terms: "If someone. . . then. . ." (e.g., Deut 21:18-21). It was the common way of expressing laws in the ancient Near East (see by contrast **Apodictic Law**).

Christ (Greek *Christos,* Hebrew *Mashiaḥ,* "Anointed One"). This term comes from the practice of anointing kings at their coronation. The hoped-for Messiah or Christ was to be a descendant of David (see **Anointed**; **Messiah**).

Christology The theological understanding of the nature and person of Christ, including the extent of the union of his humanity and divinity as well as the implications of Jesus' own self-understanding. Though the New Testament portrays Jesus Christ in various ways, the church's reflection on these issues did not arise until well into the 1st century C.E.

Circumcision Custom of cutting off the foreskin of the male organ. Performed when the boy was eight days old, its purpose was as an initiation ceremony into the community and religion of Israel. Its origin in Israel is attributed to Abraham as a sign of God's covenant with God's people (Gen 17:10-14). In the early Christian church the first dispute was whether those pagans who joined the Christian community had first to be circumcised. Paul championed the freedom of the Christian from this custom (Phil 3:2-6), and his position won the day.

Code of Hammurabi The Laws of Hammurabi (sixth king of the First Amorite dynasty of Babylon [1728-1686 B.C.E.]) were engraved on a stela found at Susa in Elam in 1902. Now housed in the Louvre in Paris, it stands about 6 feet high. Some of the laws on this stela anticipate those of the Mosaic Torah. These laws are all formulated as casuistic laws.

Codex Earliest book form of ancient biblical manuscripts. Originally, biblical texts were written on scrolls of papyrus, usually about 9 inches wide and 35 feet long. In the 2nd century C.E. Christians invented the modern book form in order to replace the unmanageable scrolls.

Covenant A bond or contract entered into between two parties. In the Bible it refers to that bond that establishes a relationship between God and humanity.

Covenant Code The collection of laws found in Exod 20:23–23:33. Also referred to as the Book of the Covenant (Exod 24:7).

Cult A particular system of religious worship or practices that pertains to a group expressed through rituals, rites, or ceremonies.

D Scholarly abbreviation for the Deuteronomistic Document or Tradition (see **Deuteronomic**).

Day of Atonement (Yom Kippur) Annual ritual in which Israel's high priest offered "sin offerings" to reconcile God and the people (Leviticus 16). The priest lays upon a "scapegoat" the collective guilt of the people of Israel and banishes it into the desert. On this day too the High Priest enters the most holy place in the temple ("the holy of holies") and sprinkles blood from the sin offerings in atonement for his sins and those of his people, Israel.

Day of the Lord (Day of Yahweh) Day of judgment for God's people and for all humanity, a popular theme of the prophets who considered that day when God will destroy evil and bring humanity to account. Also a day of salvation when the nations will rise against Israel, but God will intervene and overcome the nations. In the later prophets Israel will survive the judgment and destruction, not just because she is God's chosen people, but also because she has led a morally good existence.

Dead Sea Scrolls Manuscripts containing biblical and other religious writings dating from the 2nd century B.C.E. to the 1st century C.E. The first of these discoveries was in 1947 in caves on the northwest shore of the Dead Sea. Since that initial discovery, other caves and sites along the western shores of the Dead Sea have revealed more than 800 manuscripts (see **Essenes; Qumran**).

Decalogue (Greek *deka*, "ten" + *logos*, "word"; "the ten words"). The Ten Commandments, referring to the list of 10 laws that were inscribed on stone tablets given by God to Moses (see Exod 20:1-17; Deut 5:6-21).

Dedication, Feast of Jewish festival lasting eight days to commemorate the rededication of the temple of Jerusalem and the consecration of the altar in 165/164 B.C.E. under Judas Maccabeus (see 1 Macc 4:36-61) after Antiochus IV Epiphanes had desecrated it. The Hebrew name for this feast is Hanukkah. It is also known as the Feast of Lights and is referred to in John 10:22-38.

Deuterocanonical (Lit., "second canon"). Those books (or parts of books) found in the Septuagint (the Greek translation), but not part of the Hebrew Bible. These books were accepted into the Latin Vulgate and are hence part of the Roman Catholic Bible, while most non-Catholics do not accept them as Sacred Writings. Among these writings are the books of Tobit, Wisdom, Ben Sirach, Judith, 1 and 2 Maccabees, Baruch, as well as additions to the books of Daniel and Esther.

Deuteronomic/Deuteronomistic History/Deuteronomic Collection In 621 B.C.E. King Josiah (of Judah) undertook reforms of the Israelite religion based on a book that was discovered in the temple. This book has come to be associated with parts of the book of Deuteronomy (Deuteronomy 12–26). Not only did it inspire Josiah's reforms, but it also stressed that God alone could be worshipped in the one temple in Jerusalem. The persons who edited the book of Deuteronomy are called the Deuteronomists. Other writers formed a school of thought influenced by the Deuteronomist and produced a history that we term "Deuteronomistic History," comprising the books of Joshua, Judges, Samuel, and Kings. Its religious worldview influenced the historical perspective that inspires these documents.

Diaspora (Lit., "scattering"). Those Jews living outside Palestine. Jewish communities were found throughout the Greco-Roman world.

Didache ("Teaching of the Twelve Apostles"). An early Christian writing from *ca.* 120 C.E. containing instructions for Christian rituals and way of life.

Disciple (Lit., "one who engages in learning through instruction from another"). The New Testament uses this term to refer to Jesus' followers and embraces more than just the Twelve. It refers to all those associated with Jesus.

Documentary Hypothesis A theory presented to explain the growth and development of the Pentateuch. This scholarly hypothesis (associated in origin with Julius Wellhausen) sees the first five books of the Hebrew Scriptures growing out of four distinct documents: J (the Yahwist, dating to *ca.* 950 B.C.E.); E (the Elohist, *ca.* 850); D (the Deuteronomist, between 650 and 621) and P (the Priestly document, between 550 and 450).

Domitian Roman Emperor (81-96 C.E.), son of Vespasian and brother of Titus (both Emperors before him). He persecuted Christians because of their refusal to offer worship to him as divine. The book of Revelation emerges from the context of his reign.

Doxology Concluding formula of praise that offers glory to God.

Dualism System of thought that argues for the existence of two separate worlds, a physical world of matter and an invisible world of the spirit. Moral dualism pictures the world divided into a struggle between two powers or entities: Good and Evil, Light and Dark. Humanity is caught up in this primordial struggle for allegiance.

E   Scholarly abbreviation for the Elohist source of the Pentateuch (see **Elohist**).

Egypt   Nation situated southwest of Palestine and centered around the Nile River in North Africa. In the biblical story its importance began when Abraham went there (Gen 12:10-20); Joseph and his brothers migrated there during a famine, staying for the next four hundred years (Exod 12:40). The prophets warn their kings not to place their trust in the power of the Egyptians (Isa 30:1-7).

El/Elohim   The generic West Semitic word for a god and name of the chief Canaanite god. In the Hebrew Bible the name El usually occurs in conjunction with another phrase: El Shaddai (God of the mountain); El Bethel (God of the house of God); El Elyon (God Most High). The plural Elohim is used to refer to Israel's God (Gen 1:1; 2:5) or to foreign gods (Exod 15:11).

Elijah   Prophet of the Northern Kingdom (*ca.* 9th century B.C.E.), vehemently opposed to the inroads that the Canaanite god Baal had made into the culture of the people. Elijah's struggles influenced the lives of his people greatly. He was reportedly carried off to heaven in a fiery chariot (2 Kings 1–2), which led to the hopes that he would return one day to prepare for the coming Day of the Lord. In the context of the New Testament John the Baptist is identified with Elijah (see Luke 1:17; Mark 9:12-13) because his role was to prepare the way for the coming Messiah.

Elisha   One of the great prophets of the Northern Kingdom Israel in the 9th century B.C.E. He continued the prophetic ministry of Elijah.

Elohist   In the context of the Documentary Hypothesis the compiler of the traditions of the Pentateuch known as **E** (probably coming from the Northern Kingdom of Israel). This name comes from the characteristic use of the word **Elohim** to refer to Israel's God.

Enuma Elish   (Lit., "When on high"). The opening words of the Babylonian Creation Epic.

Epicureanism   The philosophical system of Epicurus (a Greek philosopher, *ca.* 342-270 B.C.E.) that taught that the world is a chance combination of atoms. The greatest good is pleasure, understood as freedom from disturbance or pain (see **Stoicism**).

Epiphany   The making known or manifestation of a divine being especially by means of extraordinary natural phenomena. In the Old Testament, also called "theophany."

Eponym   A real or imaginary person from whom some group or some thing is said to derive its name (see Gen 36:1).

Eschatology   (Greek *eschatos,* "last" + *logos,* "word"; "the last words"). Teaching regarding the expectations of the end times dealing with death, judgment, the afterlife. Apocalyptic literature gave much attention to eschatological concerns.

Essenes   A religious movement within Second Temple Judaism, especially from *ca.* 146 B.C.E. until 70 C.E. According to Josephus, together with the Pharisees and the Sadducees, they constituted the three major groups within Judaism in the late Second Temple period. They formed a communal association which they entered through a ritual initiation. The Essenes considered themselves to be the true remnant faithful to God's law and had their own interpretation of the Torah and the Prophets. They are identified with the Qumran community that produced the Dead Sea Scrolls (see **Dead Sea Scrolls; Qumran**).

Etiology   The study of the causes postulated for something. In the biblical context it refers to a narrative that is told to explain, among other things, the origins of a social practice, or a ritual, or even the name of a place.

Eucharist   (Greek *eucharistia,* "thanksgiving"). The ritual initiated by Jesus when he celebrated his Last Supper (Mark 14:22-25; Matt 26:26-29). The word does not occur in the New Testament, but is first found in the Didache (9:1-5) (see **Passover**).

Eusebius   First historian of the Christian church (*ca.* 260-339 C.E.). He was commissioned by Constantine to produce 50 manuscripts of the Bible in order to promote unity throughout the Roman Empire.

Evangelist   (from Greek *evangelion,* "good news"). The authors of the Gospels.

Exegesis   The critical analysis and interpretation of a biblical text. The Greek word means literally "to lead out." Hence the explanation is a "leading out" of the meaning of the biblical text by following scholarly accepted and established methods and procedures. Exegesis is to be distinguished from *eisegesis,* in which the reader of the biblical text reads his/her own interpretation into the text itself.

Exile   The period when the Israelites were led into captivity in Babylon (587-538 B.C.E.).

Exodus   The period when the Hebrews escaped from slavery in Egypt under the leadership of Moses (*ca.* 1280-1250 B.C.E.). For the biblical narrative this event is God's central saving action whereby God formed a group into God's own chosen people (see Exod 15; 20:1-2).

Fertile Crescent   Semicircle or crescent of fertile land stretching from the Persian Gulf in the northeast to Egypt on the southwest. It includes Mesopotamia, Syria, and Palestine.

Form Criticism   (German *Formsgeschichte*). A method of biblical criticism that focuses on the identification and classification of the individual units (called forms) which make up a literary text. This method also attempts to identify the oral form of these units before they made their way into the literary text. Finally, it attempts to trace the history of the development of these units (forms) from the oral stage to the final literary stage.

Former Prophets   The books of the Hebrew Bible that comprise Joshua, Judges, 1 and 2 Samuel, and 1 and 2 Kings. According to Hebrew tradition these books were attributed to the early prophets Joshua (book of Joshua), Samuel (Judges, 1 and 2 Samuel), and Jeremiah (1 and 2 Kings). Christian tradition refers to these writings as the historical books.

Fragment Hypothesis   The hypothesis that the Pentateuch came together as a result of various fragments of narrative and legal material being edited together into a whole.

Genre   A literary form, referring to the ways in which something can be classified (e.g., a poem, essay, short story, novel, narrative). The New Testament books represent three major genres: narrative; letters; apocalypse. Threefold characteristics of a genre include form, content, and function.

Gentile   A person not a Jew; someone who belongs to the "nations" of the world. The distinction is made clear when all humanity is referred to by phrases such as "Jews and Gentiles" or "Jews and Greeks" (see 1 Cor 1:22-24).

Gilgamesh   Hero of the Babylonian *Epic of Gilgamesh.* Fragments of this epic date to *ca.* 3000 B.C.E. The narrative tells of this legendary king of Uruk who seeks immortality and strives to overcome evil. The epic also includes a Flood Story narrated by Utnapishtim, an ancestor of Gilgamesh.

Gnosticism   Religious-philosophical movement of the 1st to the 6th centuries C.E. which held that God could be apprehended only by *gnosis* ("knowledge"). This movement produced a large body of writings in which it tried to explain some of the biblical narratives through their own philosophical viewpoints. Salvation is not attained through the death of Jesus, but rather through accepting the enlightenment that his teachings brought.

Golgotha   (Aramaic, "[place of a] skull"). Synonymous with Calvary (Latin, *calvaria* which translated Greek *kranion,* "skull"), it refers to the place where Jesus was crucified outside the city walls of Jerusalem (see Matt 27:33; Mark 15:22; Luke 23:33; John 19:17). Many explanations have been given for the name of this place: Origen suggested that it got its name because Adam's skull was buried beneath Jesus' cross. Jerome argued that its name came from the numerous skulls of executed prisoners that could be seen everywhere. There is no literary or archaeological evidence for the popular belief that the place of execution was on a hill. The topography of the land has changed much in the past two thousand years. The traditional identifications for the place of Jesus' death and subsequent burial are still considered by archaeologists to be as close as one can come to situating them.

Gospel   (Anglo-Saxon *Godspell, "good news,"* which translates Latin *evangelium*). The good news or the message of salvation preached either by Jesus or by his disciples about Jesus (what he said or did). The term does not refer to a literary genre, but rather to the content of these writings which can be expressed by means of many different genres: such as *narratives* about Jesus (our canonical Gospels: Matthew, Mark, Luke, and John); *sayings collections* (Gospel of Thomas); *collections of deeds* (Jesus' miracles, as found in the first part of John's Gospel).

Greek   Language spoken by the inhabitants of Greece. After the conquests of Alexander the Great (died 323 B.C.E.), Greek culture and the Greek language spread throughout the Mediterranean world. When the Romans conquered this area, the Greek language remained the *lingua franca.* Even in Palestine, especially Galilee, people were conversant with Greek.

Hades   The Greek word for the place where the dead go, the realm of the Underworld, ruled by the Greek god Hades. The Septuagint uses Hades to translate the Hebrew concept of *Sheol,* which refers to that place under the earth where all the good and evil go. In the New Testament the usual term for the place of the dead is Hades.

Hanukkah   (see **Dedication, Feast of**)

Hasmoneans   Jewish dynasty from Modein founded by the Maccabees, who undertook a successful revolt in 167 B.C.E. against the rule of the Seleucid king of Syria, Antiochus IV Epiphanes. They are named after Hasmon, ancestor of Mattathias, father of the Maccabee brothers.

Their rule ended with the conquest of Palestine by the Romans under the General Pompey in 63 B.C.E.

Hebrew   (1) A northwestern Semitic people. (2) The language (Semitic) spoken by the Israelites in which the Old Testament was written.

Hellenism   Modern term to describe the interaction of Greek culture, language, and thought with the cultures of peoples from other regions especially around the Mediterranean Sea that occurred from Alexander the Great until the battle of Actium (336-31 B.C.E.). See 2 Macc 4:13 for a reference to the adoption of this "Greek way of life."

Henotheism   Worship of one God while accepting the existence of other gods. See Psalm 82 and Exodus 15, which reflect this understanding.

Hierocracy   Rule or government that is controlled by religious leaders, especially priests. The period beginning with the return from the Babylonian exile onwards reflects such a rule in which the high priests were in control of the nation, representing the people before other rulers and nations.

Historical Criticism   Method of interpreting the biblical writings whereby the text is situated and understood against the background of the time, place, and circumstances in which it was written.

Holiness Code   The section of religious and cultic laws in Leviticus 17–26. They concentrate on the call to holiness (separateness) that the lives of the Israelite people must demonstrate which set them apart from other nations: "You shall be holy to me; for I the LORD am holy" (Lev 20:26). Thought by some to form a source of the Pentaeuch like J, E, D, or P.

Horeb   Mountain in the Sinai Desert where Moses received God's Law. It is referred to by this name in the E and D traditions (see Exod 17:6; Deut 1:2,6). In J and P this mountain is referred to as Mount Sinai (see Exod 19:11; 34:29) (see **Sinai**).

Idumea   Name given by the Greeks and Romans to the territory south of Judea, formerly called Edom, the home of Herod the Great (Mark 3:8).

Immanuel   (Hebrew, "God is with us"). The name given to a child whose birth symbolized God's presence. It first appears in Isa 7:14; 8:8 and is taken up by Matt 1:23 *(Emmanuel)* as a prophecy that is being fulfilled by the birth of Jesus.

Israel   Name first given to Jacob by an angel when he wrestles with him at night in the Transjordan region: "You shall no longer be called Jacob, but Israel, for

you have striven with God and with humans, and have prevailed" (Gen 32:28). God confirms this name change at Bethel (Gen 35:10) and goes on to tell Jacob that many nations and kings will descend from him, recalling the promises made to Abraham (Gen 17:5-6). Henceforward, the term *Israel* also applies to the "children of Israel," namely, the descendants of the 12 sons of Israel taking on the designation of God's chosen people. Finally, the name is also used in a restrictive sense to refer to the people of the Northern Kingdom in the time of the divided monarchy.

J   Scholarly abbreviation for *Yahwist,* the name given to the person who produced the document or the document itself that is the oldest and the foundation for the whole Pentateuch (see **Yahwist**).

Jesus   English transliteration of the Latin rendition of Greek *Iesous,* which in turn translated the Hebrew name *Joshua* ("Yahweh will save").

Jew   Originally, a member of the tribe of Judah or one who lives in the Southern Kingdom of Judah, the Judaeans (see 2 Kgs 16:6). After the return from exile, the term referred to all the inhabitants of the Persian province of Judah. With time this term was used to refer to any member of God's covenant people wherever they may be living (including those outside the Promised Land).

Josephus, Flavius   Jewish historian (*ca.* 37-100 C.E.) who wrote two important works in Greek for the Greco-Roman World, *The Antiquities of the Jews* and *The Jewish Wars,* which comprise about 30 volumes. These writings are significant because they provide a source of information for our understanding of the context of the world in which Christianity was born.

Jubilee   The Year of Jubilee (derived from Hebrew *yobel,* "ram's horn" or trumpet), the 50th year in a series of seven Sabbatical Years described in Lev 25:8-24. It was proclaimed by a trumpet blast on the Day of Atonement. During a Jubilee Year land was to be returned to its original owners and all debts were canceled (see **Sabbatical Year**).

Judaism   Term used to refer to the religion of the people of Judah, especially from the return from the Babylonian Exile onwards (538 B.C.E.).

Judea   Greek designation *(Ioudaia)* for the territory of Judah after the Exile (538 B.C.E.). In the New Testament it refers to that region of Palestine in distinction to the other regions (Samaria, Galilee, Perea, and Idumea).

Kerygma   (Greek, "proclamation"). The oral preaching of the early witnesses to the message of Jesus.

Ketubim   "The Writings," the third division of the Hebrew Bible (after the Torah and the Prophets, or **Nebi'im**).

Kingdom of God   The concept of God's kingdom is based upon the Old Testament hopes in the establishment of a future rule of God. In the New Testament God's rule refers not so much to a spatial dimension, but rather to the relationship established between God and humanity where God's power works on behalf of those in that relationship. This image is central to Jesus' ministry and his message. Jesus inaugurated God's kingdom in his ministry, but it will only come to completion in the future eschatological end times.

Koine   Major dialect spoken throughout the Hellenistic and later Roman worlds. Called Koine (or "common") Greek, it was based on 4th-century Attic Greek, the language spoken in Athens, the cultural and political dominant Greek city-state of the 5th century. The Septuagint and the New Testament were all written in Koine Greek.

L   Scholarly abbreviation for that special material in the Gospel of Luke not found in any of the other Synoptic Gospels.

Latter Prophets   The group of prophetical books comprising Isaiah, Jeremiah, Ezekiel, and the Twelve Minor Prophets. They are also otherwise known as "the writing prophets." This grouping of writings is to be distinguished from the **Former Prophets.**

Levites   Members of the tribe of Levi, one of the 12 tribes of Israel. This tribe was entrusted with priestly duties in place of being given land at the time of the conquest of Canaan (Deut 18:1-8). However, only descendants of Aaron were allowed to be priests who serve in the sanctuary (according to the P tradition). Numbers 18:1-7 offers a clear distinction between the functions of the descendants of Aaron and the descendants of Levi.

Lex Talionis   (Latin, "The Law of Talion"). The law of retribution which is summed up in the phrase: "If any harm follows, then you shall give life for life, eye for eye, tooth for tooth, hand for hand . . ." (Exod 21:23-25). It was rejected by Jesus (Matt 5:38-39).

Literary Criticism   A means of analyzing the biblical text according to its literary features, including such aspects as the sources behind the text (also called "source criticism") and the type (or genre) of the writing. In recent decades this term has been expanded from its original concern with sources and genre to include analyses based upon rhetorical features of the text.

Logos   (Greek, "word"). The Gospel of John alone uses this term to refer to the pre-existent Son of God, identified with Jesus of Nazareth: "In the beginning was the Word . . ." (John 1:1). There is a long Greek history behind the usage of this term. For the Greek Stoic philosophers, *logos* was the rational element that pervades the entire universe controlling order and life. The Jewish philosopher Philo of Alexandria used it to refer to the rationality of God's mind. The Gospel of John's usage is distinctive in that *logos* now refers to a person, Jesus, not just to a force.

LXX   (Lit., *"seventy"*). An abbreviation for the word *Septuagint,* which refers to the Greek translation of the Hebrew Scriptures made in Alexandria, Egypt, from the 4th to 1st centuries B.C.E. This term reflects the legend found in the Letter of Aristeas that 72 (or 70) Jewish elders translated the Torah (or Pentateuch) from Hebrew into Greek.

M   Scholarly abbreviation for that special material in the Gospel of Matthew not found in any of the other Synoptic Gospels.

Maccabees   Name given to that family of religious fighters who took up arms against the might of the Seleucid Empire to win independence for the Jewish state when their religion was being persecuted by the ruler Antiochus IV Epiphanes (175-163 B.C.E.). Judas, the son of Mattathias, led the revolt against the Seleucids. Judas was given the nickname *Maccabeus* ("the hammer") and the term Maccabees was applied to himself and his brothers who succeeded him. The name Maccabee is not found in rabbinic literature, where "Hasmonean" is used instead. This dynasty lasted until 63 B.C.E., when the Romans conquered Palestine under Pompey.

Marcion   An early Christian living in Rome *ca.* 140 C.E. who first asked: "What are the authentic books that make up the canon of scripture?" He was highly anti-Semitic and rejected from his list of Sacred Books any that were favorable toward the Jews. Hence, he excluded the entire Old Testament from the canon. He was excommunicated from Rome in 144 C.E. because of his views.

Masoretes   The *Masorah* are the traditional rules that directed the copying of Biblical Hebrew manuscripts. Consequently, *Masoretes* refers to those scholars whose task it was to hand on the tradition governing the copying of Biblical Hebrew manuscripts. Besides ensuring the fidelity of the text to the tradition, they also made a major contribution to the biblical language by introducing vowel signs into the consonantal text.

Masoretic Text   (Abbreviation *MT*). The standard text of the Hebrew Bible, produced and established by the

Masoretes or scholars entrusted with the faithful transmission of the biblical texts (*ca.* 600-950 C.E.).

Mesopotamia   (Greek, "land in the middle of the rivers"; Hebrew *'aram naharayim,* "land within the two rivers"). Territory between the two rivers, the Tigris and Euphrates (modern Iraq). Home to the great civilizations and powers of the Sumerians, Akkadians, Assyrians, and Babylonians (see 1 Chr 19:6; Acts 2:9; 7:2).

Messiah   (Hebrew, "Anointed One"; translated into Greek as **Christ**). Refers to the hope of the Jews that in the future God would raise up someone and anoint that person with God's power to liberate the Jews from the oppression of their enemies and establish God's kingdom, God's rule, over the world (see **Anointed; Christ**).

Minor Prophets   Twelve short prophetic books in the Hebrew Scriptures that were written on a single scroll (Hosea through Malachi). Also called the Book of the Twelve.

Monotheism   Belief in and worship of only one god with a denial of the existence of other gods (see **Henotheism**). Deutero-Isaiah (or "Second Isaiah," Isaiah 40–55) is a staunch proponent of monotheism.

Muratorian Fragment   Portion of an 8th-century C.E. manuscript that discusses and lists the books of the New Testament. It was found in the library of Milan in 1740 C.E. by the librarian Ludovico Antonio Muratori. Its origin dates back to the second half of the 2nd century C.E. and is the second oldest (after Marcion's list) canon or list of New Testament books.

Mystery   (Greek *mysterion,* "something revealed by God"). In the Greek world religious rituals or cults that flourished throughout the Hellenistic and Roman sphere. In the Gospels this term is used only in Matt 13:11; Mark 4:11; Luke 8:10 to refer to "the mystery of the kingdom of God/heaven" that is revealed to the disciples by Jesus, but to others it is revealed in parables. Paul connects this term with the crucified Jesus (1 Cor 2:1). For Paul the mystery is "God's plan of salvation for humanity."

Myth   (Greek *mythos,* "story"). A story or narrative that attempts to make sense of the personal, social, or cosmic world by providing explanations as to why things are the way they are whether in the natural, cosmic world, or in the institutions of society, or the relationships among peoples within that society. While the modern world tends to discard myths as fictitious legends, myths have a vital role to play even within our own society. Every society has its own distinctive myths that struggle to provide explanations for the same aspects. Myths have a power

to construct a worldview that provides legitimacy for the customs, institutions, and identities of the specific society.

Mythology   The systematizing of the narratives and stories within a particular society that attempts to provide explanations for the way things are. Every mythology is specific to each culture, such as the Greeks, the Romans, the Norse, etc., but every mythology battles with the same challenge: to offer explanations for similar questions.

Nabi   (Hebrew, "prophet"). A Hebrew and Christian prophet is someone who acts as God's spokesperson, interpreting events within the world according to God's will and God's Law (Torah), and utters judgments and praise insofar as people's lives conform to God's Law.

Narrative Criticism   A literary approach to interpreting the Bible, assessing the three elements of author, text, and reader to view the biblical books as narratives. This method distinguishes between actual authors and the implied authors of texts (the picture of the author deduced from the text itself) as well as three levels of readers: the actual first-time reader, the implied reader(s) (for whom the author appears to or claims to have been writing), and present-day readers.

Nebi'im   (Hebrew, "prophets"). The second section of the Hebrew Scriptures, the Prophetical Writings (see **Torah,** Law; **Ketubim,** Writings).

New Year Festival   (Hebrew, *Rosh Hashanah*). A time of celebration and renewal through ritual. The celebration of the New Year is greatly discussed among scholars. Apparently, a shift took place in Israel regarding its celebration. Before the Exile the New Year was celebrated in the fall. After the Exile Israel adopted the Babylonian calendar and celebrated the New Year in the spring month of Nisan (March-April). It began a 10-day period that led up to Yom Kippur (see **Day of Atonement**).

Omega   The 24th and final letter of the Greek alphabet. It is used figuratively in the New Testament in combination with the first letter of the alphabet, Alpha ("the Alpha and the Omega") to describe *God* (Rev 1:8; 21:6) as well as *Jesus* ("I am the Alpha and the Omega, the first and the last, the beginning and the end" [Rev 22:13; see also 1:17]).

P   Scholarly abbreviation for the Priestly tradition or document behind the Pentateuch (see **Priestly Document**).

Palestine   The land bordered by the Mediterranean Sea on the west, Syria to the north, the Arabian desert to the east, and the Sinai Peninsula to the south. During the time of the Patriarchs it was known as the land of Canaan (Gen 12:5-6). The name *Palestina* is the Greek form of the Hebrew word, which is derived from **Philistine,** the inhabitants of five cities along the coastline. The name *Palestina* is attested as early as the Greek historian Herodotus (*ca.* 450 B.C.E.) and also in the writings of Philo and Josephus (1st-century C.E.).

Parable   (Greek *parabole,* "something placed alongside" another thing to explain it). In the New Testament a short fictitious narrative whereby one unknown thing is explained by means of something well known. It was Jesus' usual method of teaching. He took his images largely from agricultural scenes familiar to his audience to explain the kingdom of God. In contrast to an **allegory,** a parable focuses on one point of comparison and generally the story leads to or culminates in that point (see Matthew 13; Mark 4). The Hebrew Bible also contains a number of well-known parables such as Nathan's "poor man's ewe lamb" (2 Sam 12:1-14) and Isaiah's "Song of the Unfruitful Vineyard" (Isa 5:1-7).

Parousia   (Greek *parousia,* "arrival" or "presence"). In the Hellenistic world the arrival of a ruler or important person. Paul adopts this word to speak about the future "coming" of Jesus at the end of time (1 Cor 15:23; 1 Thess 2:19). This coming is described in apocalyptic terms that include judgment of the wicked and the destruction of the world in cataclysmic terms.

Parthenon   A temple dedicated to the goddess Athena erected on the top of the Acropolis in Athens.

Passion   (Latin *passio,* "suffering"). The suffering and death of Jesus (Acts 1:3).

Passover   One of three major pilgrimage feasts of Israel (together with the **Feast of Booths** or Tabernacles and **Pentecost** or the Feast of Weeks) when the Israelites were encouraged to journey to Jerusalem for the celebration of the festival. Observed on the 14th day of Nisan (April-May), this festival celebrates God's deliverance of the people of Israel from slavery in Egypt. The ritual included the slaughter of a lamb and the celebration of a family meal in which the lamb was eaten. This feast was joined to the Festival of Unleavened Bread, a week-long celebration beginning on the 15th of Nisan. The celebration of Passover is evidenced throughout the Hebrew Scriptures: e.g., Joshua 5:10; Josiah (2 Kgs 23:21-23); the exiles returning from Babylon (Ezra 6:19). Jesus and his disciples also celebrated this feast. According to the Synoptic Gospels, the last meal Jesus celebrated with his disciples was a Passover meal (see Matt 26:17-30; Mark 14:12-25; Luke 22:7-23) (see **Eucharist**).

Pastoral Epistles   (Latin *pastor,* "shepherd"). The letters of 1 and 2 Timothy and Titus, written to leaders (shepherds) of the Christian churches. While they present Paul as writing to his fellow workers Timothy and Titus, modern scholars judge these letters to have been written after Paul's death by some of his followers, probably toward the end of the 1st century C.E.

Pentateuch   (Greek *pente teuchos,* "[the book of] five volumes"). The first of the threefold division of the Hebrew Scriptures, referred to as the Torah (the Law) in Hebrew.

Pentecost   (Greek *pentekoste,* "the 50th [day]"). Originally an agricultural feast celebrating the spring harvest occurring 50 days after the firstfruits were offered at the Feast of Passover and Unleavened Bread. Also referred to as the Feast of Weeks (Exod 34:22; Deut 16:10), the Feast of Harvest (Exod 23:16), and the Day of the First Fruits (Num 28:26). Together with the Passover (Unleavened Bread) and Tabernacles, it is one of the three pilgrimage festivals. Later the festival became associated with the giving of the law to Israel and the covenant of Sinai. In the early Christian community Pentecost is associated with the descent of the Holy Spirit upon the Apostles (Acts 2). Just as God's people were inaugurated at Sinai, so the writer of Luke sees the Christian community inaugurated as God's people by the gift of the Spirit.

Persia   Ancient Near Eastern power that had conquered the world from the shores of Asia Minor as far as India. Cyrus established its might by uniting the Medes and the Persians in 549 B.C.E. The Jews were allowed to return from captivity in Babylon in 538. The Persians referred to their kingdom as *Aryana,* meaning "noble."

Pharaoh   Title for the ruler of Egypt. Originally the term referred to the royal palace, but then was used to designate the royal authority that resided in the Egyptian king. Generally, in the Hebrew Scriptures the Egyptian ruler is designated simply by this title without reference to his name (see, e.g., Gen 12:14-20).

Pharisees   An important Jewish group within Second Temple Judaism (especially *ca.* 2nd century B.C.E.–1st century C.E.). Because they left behind no writings of their own, the reconstruction of who they are depends upon Christian sources (the New Testament), the Jewish historian Josephus, and later rabbinic scholars. It is difficult to say with certainty anything about their origins. They were a lay group of experts in the Law (the Torah) who upheld as well the oral law, those interpretations of the Torah that had been handed on orally over time. Their influence was exercised in the synagogue.

Of significance in their thought is a strong belief in the resurrection of the dead.

Philistines   Sea-faring people who migrated to the southern coast of Palestine from the Aegean Sea in the 13th and 12th centuries B.C.E., just before the Exodus of the Israelites from Egypt. They established a league of five cities along the coast — Ashdod, Ashkelon, Ekron, Gaza, and Gath — and were the Israelites' chief opponents during the 12th century.

Philo of Alexandria   (also known as **Philo Judaeus**). A Jewish philosopher (*ca.* 20 B.C.E.-50 C.E.) well educated in Greek, living in Alexandria, Egypt. His prolific writings are a wonderful source illuminating the thought and culture of Hellenistic Judaism. His most noteworthy approach was an allegorical interpretation of the Hebrew Scriptures which influenced Christian scholars (e.g., Clement of Alexandria, Origen, Ambrose, Augustine). Survival of his writings is largely attributed to early Christian interest in this form of interpretation. However, there is little or no record of Jewish scholars reading or using his writings before the 16th century C.E. His possible influence upon New Testament writers is highly disputed among scholars. The thought process and methodology of the Letter to the Hebrews reflect the methodological approach of Philo. The use of the term *logos* is also found in both Philo and the Gospel of John. Despite these similarities, it is difficult to argue conclusively that these Christian writers were influenced directly by Philo. More likely they are using Hellenistic Jewish traditions to which Philo also attests.

Polytheism   Belief in and worship of many gods. The whole Greco-Roman world was a polytheistic world (see **Henotheism**; **Monotheism**).

Priestly Document   Final addition to the Pentateuch, characterized by genealogical material as well as statistical and legal information put together during the Babylonian Exile. It is thought to have begun in circles associated with the priests somewhere in the course of the 8th century B.C.E.

Pseudepigrapha   (Greek, "falsely [attributed] writings"). Writings emerging from *ca.* 250 B.C.E. until *ca.* 200 C.E., whose authorship was attributed to ancient heroes from the past, such as Enoch, Moses, Isaiah. They do not form part of the Hebrew Scriptures.

Pseudonymity   A common literary practice in the Hellenistic world (200 B.C.E.–200 C.E.) where writings would be attributed to famous figures from the past. E.g., in the New Testament the Pastoral Epistles as well as the letters of Peter and Jude all seem to belong to this category because their content and style betray a period long after that of the Apostle Paul.

Ptolemy   The founder of the Hellenistic dynasty that ruled Egypt after the death of Alexander until the battle of Actium (323-31 B.C.E.). His successors all used the name Ptolemy.

Purim   (Hebrew *purim,* "lots"). A Jewish feast celebrating the defeat of Haman and the survival of the Jews as narrated in the book of Esther. It is held on the 14th of Adar in the springtime.

Q   (Abbreviation for German *Quelle,* "source"). A hypothetical written collection of Jesus' sayings used by the authors of the Gospels of Matthew and Luke. It contains only sayings and was written in Greek before 70 C.E. It does not contain an account of the Resurrection of Jesus.

Qumran   Ruins of an Essene community located on the northwest shore of the Dead Sea some 8.5 miles south of Jericho and situated near the caves where the Dead Sea Scrolls were discovered (see **Essenes**; **Dead Sea Scrolls**).

Rabbi   Title of respect meaning "teacher" or "master." Jesus is so designated in the Gospels of Matthew, Mark, and John. In the Gospel of Luke the title is lacking because Luke's Gentile audience would see no meaning in the use of a title so strongly rooted in Jewish culture.

Rabbinic   Pertaining to rabbis or to their learned writings. In Judaism, after the destruction of the temple in 70 C.E., the title rabbi was used as an official term for outstanding scholars recognized by the Jewish community. The teachings of these rabbis are recorded in the rabbinic literature known as the Mishnah and Talmud. Only after the era of the destruction of Jerusalem are scholars referred to as "rabbi" (e.g., Rabbi Akiba).

Redaction Criticism   Scholarly method applied to the study and interpretation of the biblical texts which aims at determining and identifying the contribution made by the authors (or "redactors," from the German) to the Gospels in compiling their texts from the various sources that they used.

Revelation   Making known or disclosing something that had been hidden. In the context of the biblical writings, it refers to the making known of God and God's will for humanity.

Rhetorical Criticism   Scholarly method of biblical interpretation that examines the form, structure, and stylistic properties of a given work. In addition, this method tries to ascertain the purpose for these stylistic features as well as the effect they have upon the reader.

Roman Empire   Rule exercised by Rome over the whole Mediterranean world extending from Gaul (France and southern Germany) in the north to Egypt in the south. The Jewish homeland became part of the Roman Empire in 63 B.C.E. when it was conquered by the Roman general Pompey. It remained subject to Roman rule until the second Jewish war in 135 C.E., when the Jewish homeland ceased to exist.

Sabbath   (Hebrew *Shabbat,* referring to the seventh day in a week of seven days). According to the Ten Commandments, one of the fundamental commandments of the nation of Israel (see Exod 20:8-11; Deut 5:12-15). A theological reason is given for this day of rest based upon God's action in creation: God rested on the seventh day after having created the world. Consequently, all Jews must hold this day sacred in imitation of God.

Sabbatical Year   The seventh year in a seven-year cycle, intended to be a "year of resting" and a "year of release." During this year fields were meant to be left fallow. Those Israelites that had been sold into slavery were to be released and all debts were to be canceled (see Lev 25:1-19).

Sadducees   An important Jewish group (alongside the Pharisees) within Second Temple Judaism (especially *ca.* 1st century B.C.E. until the 1st century C.E.). Because they left behind no writings of their own, the reconstruction of who they are depends upon Christian sources (the New Testament), Josephus (the Jewish historian), and later rabbinic scholars. It is very difficult to say with certainty anything about their origins. They are not as important in the New Testament writings as the Pharisees. The Sadducees were the priestly aristocracy of the land and extremely wealthy, hence they were conservative both politically and religiously. Because of their status and wealth they wanted the status quo to continue without change. Religiously they accepted only the first five books of the Torah and did not accept belief in the resurrection of the dead.

Salvation   Act of protection from every form of evil, whether physical, moral, or political. In the context of the New Testament it implies a deliverance from sin, alienation from God, and eternal punishment.

Samaria   Capital of the Northern Kingdom of Israel. Founded by King Omri (876-869 B.C.E.), it was destroyed by the Assyrians in 721. People from outside the nation of Israel were repopulated into this region, and the descendants of this mixture of Israelites and non-Israelites became known as the Samaritans.

Samaritans   Religious group situated in Samaria, a territory in the middle of Palestine, placed between the regions of Galilee in the north and Judea in the south. Since they were a mixed race, mainstream Judaism shunned them. They had their own temple as a place of worship as well as their own copy of the Pentateuch. In the New Testament Jesus goes out of his way to embrace Samaritans as positive role models (see the parable of the Good Samaritan, Luke 10:29-37). Jesus' discussion with the woman of Samaria gives an example of how he leads someone to faith (namely a Samaritan [John 4:5-42]).

Sanctuary   A holy place whose main function is to provide a place of worship for believers. It also provided a place of safety for those who sought refuge there.

Sanhedrin   Council of Jewish leaders operating from the 3rd century B.C.E. until the end of the Roman rule in 70 C.E. The high priest was the leader of the council. Jesus was tried before the Sanhedrin (Matt 26:59; Mark 14:55; Luke 22:66; John 11:47). Stephen was stoned as a result of its verdict (Acts 6:12-15). Paul was brought before the Sanhedrin and charged with violating the Mosaic law (Acts 22:30–23:11).

Satan   Adversary who takes the side of another and acts in their defense. In the book of Job Satan appears as a prosecutor and adversary of God (Job 1–2). In the New Testament Satan is the leader of the forces of evil who wants the destruction of all people, especially the Messiah (Matt 4:1-11; Luke 4:1-13). Satan is also described as "the evil one" (Matt 6:13; 13:19), "the devil" (Matt 4:1; 13:39; John 8:44), as well as the serpent who tempted Eve (Rev 12:9).

Savior   Someone who frees from danger. God is referred to as Savior (Ps 106:21; Isa 43:1-7; Luke 1:47; 1 Tim 4:10; 2 Tim 1:8-9), as is Jesus (Luke 2:11; John 4:42).

Scriptures   (Latin *Scripturae,* "Writings"). The Sacred Writings of either Judaism or Christianity.

Second Temple Period   Period embracing Judean history from the rebuilding of the temple of Jerusalem in 515 B.C.E. to the destruction of this temple by the Romans in 70 C.E. During this period Judea was under the domination of foreign powers (Persians, Greeks, and Romans).

Seleucids   One of the kingdoms created after the dissolution of Alexander's empire upon his death. Founded by Seleucus I (hence the name) (312-280 B.C.E.), its center was Syria with its capital at Antioch. Because it was such a vast territory (the largest division of Alexander's empire), its population was very diverse with a decentralized area that made it difficult to govern. The Seleucids defeated the Ptolemies in 198 and took over control of Palestine until 165, when the Maccabees revolted against the Seleucids.

Septuagint   (see **LXX**).

Sinai   The name for both a wilderness area and the mountain at which God entered into a covenant with God's people and where they received the Decalogue (Ten Commandments). The mountain is called Sinai by J and P, while E and D refer to it as Mount Horeb (see **Horeb**).

Sitz im Leben   German phrase designating "life situation." It was especially used in **Form Criticism** to refer to the context out of which a particular unit grew and developed.

Son of Man   (Hebrew *ben ʾadam;* Aramaic *bar ʾenash*). A term with many different nuances of meaning:

In the Old Testament the term occurs as a designation for "humanity" or "human beings." In the prophet Ezekiel it is used 93 times as a reference to the prophet in order to contrast the mortality of the prophet to the divine sovereignty of God. The New Revised Standard Version of the Bible translates it as "mortal" (see Ezek 2:1; 3:1; 4:1; 5:1).

Daniel 7:13-14 speaks about "one like a son of man." This is variously interpreted as referring either to the nation of Israel or to a person who receives from God the power to rule over all peoples of the world and is given the promise of an eternal kingship (Dan 7:14-18).

In 1 Enoch 37–71 (the so-called parables of Enoch) the titular and messianic dimensions of this term are stressed. He is God's agent in the coming day of judgment.

In the Gospels the phrase "Son of Man" is an almost exclusive self-designation of Jesus and is used as a title for Jesus. Jesus uses it in three ways, showing his indebtedness to the tradition:

It refers to Jesus' earthly ministry ("The sabbath was made for humankind, and not humankind for the sabbath; so the Son of Man is lord even of the sabbath" [Mark 2:27-28]).

It refers to Jesus' future coming in glory to bring judgment and salvation ("You will see the Son of Man seated at the right hand of the Power, and 'coming with the clouds of heaven'" [Mark 14:62]).

It refers to Jesus' suffering and death ("Then he began to teach them that the Son of Man must undergo great suffering, and be rejected by the elders, the chief priests, and the scribes, and be killed, and after three days rise again" [Mark 8:31]).

Source Criticism   Scholarly method of biblical interpretation that analyzes a biblical document in order to determine the sources that the author used in compiling his narrative. Source criticism established the hypothesis that the Pentateuch was formed from the sources **J, E, D, P**. With regard to the Synoptic Gospels it has been shown that these three Gospels have two major documents as their basic sources, namely the Gospel of Mark and the Q Sayings Source.

Stoicism   A Greek philosophy very popular in Roman times, characterized above all by a life of self-control in which one strives to avoid all pain and all pleasure. It stressed the performance of one's duty to the gods, one's family, and the state, and believed in a divine force that gave direction to the destiny of each person. Acts 17:18-34 mentions Paul's encounter with the Stoics when he preached in Athens (see **Epicureanism**).

Sukkoth   (see **Booths, Feast of; Tabernacles**).

Synagogue   A place of assembly within the Jewish communities used chiefly for worship. There is no reference to the synagogue in the Old Testament, but the New Testament refers to it frequently. While its origin is much discussed, scholars think that the synagogue began during the Babylonian Exile when no temple existed. Archaeological excavations have provided more evidence for the existence of synagogues outside of Israel. Synagogue worship revolved around the singing of hymns, the continuous reading of passages from the Scriptures (the Torah and the Prophets), and the delivery of a sermon explaining the readings.

Syncretism   The combining or joining of different religions in which opposing principles and practices are brought together. E.g., scholars use this term to refer to the incorporation of many Canaanite practices within the Israelite faith. This practice is sternly condemned by the prophets (see 1 Kgs 16:31).

Synoptic   (Greek *syn,* "with" + *optikos,* "sight"). "Taking a comprehensive view." The term is applied to the Gospels of Matthew, Mark, and Luke, which share so much material in common. They can be placed in parallel columns and an overall picture of the life and ministry of Jesus can be attained.

Tabernacles, Feast of   (see **Booths, Feast of**).

Tanak   Modern designation for the Hebrew Bible. This term is constructed from the first consonants that make up the three divisions of the Hebrew Bible, namely the Torah, the Prophets, and the Writings (Hebrew *Torah, Nebiʾim, Ketubim*), giving T, N, K.

Tetrateuch   A designation for the first four books of the Hebrew Bible: Genesis, Exodus, Leviticus, and Numbers.

These books comprise material taken from the sources J, E, and P, with little contribution from the Deuteronomist (D) that is largely found in the fifth book.

Textual Criticism   A scholarly and scientific analysis of all the existing manuscripts bearing witness to the various biblical texts. The aim is to establish as far as possible the original reading of a particular text by trying to account for the differences and errors that have crept into the manuscript tradition in the process of its transmission.

Theodicy   (Greek *theos,* "God" + *dike,* "justice"). The attempt to explain how a God of goodness and justice can tolerate a world of evil and suffering. It is the issue with which the book of Job struggles.

Theophany   (from Greek *theos,* "god," *phanein,* "appear"). An appearance of God, to individuals (see Gen 12:7) or groups (Exod 19:16-25). Often accompanied by earthquakes, thunder and lightning, trumpet blasts, and darkness or extreme light (e.g., Judg 5:4-5), theophanies are occasions of awe and fear (see Gen 16:13; Exod 3:6).

Thomas, Gospel of   A collection of 114 sayings of Jesus discovered at Nag Hammadi, Egypt (1945). While written in Coptic *ca.* 4th century C.E., their origins go back to the end of the 1st century C.E.

Torah   (Hebrew, "instruction, guidance, law"). The first five books of the Hebrew Scriptures, otherwise referred to as the Books of Moses or the Pentateuch. These books contain God's instruction, God's will, according to which the people of Israel were to live their lives.

Tradition Criticism   Scholarly approach to studying the biblical texts in order to discover the origin, growth, and development of a particular religious theme or thought (such as the concept of God, the Exodus, or the kingdom of God).

Transfiguration   (Latin *transfiguratio,* "change of shape"). An episode narrated in the Synoptic Gospels in which Jesus appears clothed in white on a mountain together with Elijah (who represents the prophetic tradition of the Old Testament) and Moses (who represents the Law/Torah in the Old Testament). This event is witnessed by Jesus' three closest disciples, Peter, James, and John. A voice from heaven speaks (as at the baptism), confirming Jesus to be God's Son. In this symbolic way, Jesus is identified as the one to whom the Law and the Prophets lead — he brings them together and is superior to them.

Twelve   The 12 Apostles whom Jesus specifically chose to be his closest followers (Matt 10:1-5; Mark 3:16-19; Luke 6:12-16; Acts 1:12-26). The number 12 is symbolic of the 12 tribes of Israel. Hence, Jesus shows his intent of reconstituting a new people of God around himself.

Vulgate   Jerome's Latin translation of the Bible (4th century C.E.). It became the official translation of the Roman Catholic church.

Weeks, Feast of   (see **Pentecost**).

Yahwist   The name given to the composer of the J document, the oldest tradition behind the Torah according to the **Documentary Hypothesis**.

Yom Kippur   (see **Day of Atonement**).

Zealots   (Greek *zelotes,* "one who shows zeal and enthusiasm"). A group of 1st-century C.E. Jewish political fanatics who wished to liberate Palestine from Roman oppression by all necessary means, including force. While they were not operative at the time of Jesus, their importance grew after the middle of the 1st century C.E. They incited a number of uprisings, eventually succeeding in the final revolt of 66-70 C.E., which was crushed by the Romans when Jerusalem and the temple were destroyed.

Chapter 1

General Introduction

Preliminary Comments

For many who teach the Christian Scriptures, an often troubling aspect of Introductions to the Bible is their tendency to focus less on making the content of the Bible clear to readers than on clarifying current critical theories *about the Bible*. While such information is interesting, and does have a place in introductory texts like this one, it should not predominate to such an extent that readers do not first receive an adequate introduction to what is *in the Bible*. Likewise, scholarly interest in theories regarding the Bible's origin and history has long forced to the sidelines discussion of the Bible's basic interest, theology, reflection on the nature of God and of humanity in relationship with God.

We hope to have produced an Introduction that avoids this twofold error. To do so we have brought to the forefront of our Introduction the neglected practice of guiding readers carefully and completely through the biblical text. With very few exceptions, the chapters of this textbook provide section-by-section surveys of the biblical text called "A Walk through [Name of Book]." We hope that these relatively leisurely strolls through the books of the Bible will serve as roadmaps for students as they read the Bible itself. We have found this to be a helpful tool in our own teaching, and we suspect it will serve our readers well too.

We also place in bold relief reflections on the theological implications and claims of the biblical books. For each biblical book we offer a section titled "Theological Themes in [Name of Book]." Here too we hope to give our readers something they often miss in contemporary Introductions. For a variety of reasons, this aspect of the Bible has been left aside altogether or relegated to separate, "specialized" introductions. We understand the Bible as an intrinsically theological book, one that begs to be read as such, just as much as instructions for assembling a child's new toy demand being read as technical writing. To us, it makes no sense to introduce students to the Bible merely as history, literature, a record of political or ideological history, or a testimony to societies living or dead. The Bible may be read with all those questions and concerns in mind, but it must first and foremost be read as the text it presents itself as, a theological witness.

Lest readers expecting the more typical fare be disappointed, we also provide between our walks through the biblical books and our surveys of their theological themes a section titled "Critical Issues in [Name of the Book]." These include coverage of the most significant issues, theories, and hypotheses that modern critical scholarship has developed in studying the Bible. In this regard, though, we confess to having practiced restraint, providing students with only an introduction to the topics evoked by the last centuries' study of the Bible, not a comprehensive survey of those topics.

In treating the books of the Bible according to these three simple headings we hope to please a greater number of readers than those we vex. We also hope to have given our Introduction some distinction that sets it apart from others, that saves it from joining the ranks of the common.

Our Approach to Writing This Book and a Framework for Using It

Having distanced ourselves from the norm of privileging reports of historical criticism's results over rehearsing the biblical text and its theological implications, we hasten to reiterate that we have not ignored the fruits of critical scholarship, and to point out that they do not appear only in the "Critical Issues" section of each chapter; we have integrated the fruits of critical scholarship into the walks through the biblical books and the discussions of theological themes. In the following paragraphs we explain how we did that, and in doing so we provide readers with a framework for appreciating more fully the contents of this book.

Biblical scholarship's many critical methods — most of which we introduce you to in the course of this Introduction — have yielded results that can appear daunting in their complexity to those who are not professional scholars, who just want to understand the Bible better. The good news, though, is that it is possible to reduce most of that complexity to two basic angles of vision from which to make sense of the Bible, those of its "implied authors" and "implied readers."

In general, biblical scholarship has been concerned to determine what authors intended in writing the texts that have come down to us, as well as to establish the meaning that their audiences derived from receiving those texts. To be sure, there are many other issues that concern scholarship: when and where a text was written, what editorial processes it underwent, what earlier sources it incorporates, and so on; but the answers to virtually all of these questions stand in service of elucidating the texts' authors and audiences. As a consequence, whenever one speaks straightforwardly of a biblical text's author or its recipients, one is synthesizing much of the complex evidence produced by critical scholarship. Likewise, inasmuch as our walks through the books of the Bible, surveys of critical issues, and discussions of theological themes entail in large part

talk about the Bible's authors and recipients, we pass on to our readers the results of modern historical criticism in the simplest form possible.

That said, it is also important to be clear about what we mean when we write in the pages that follow about texts' authors and earliest readers. In reading the Introduction it will quickly become apparent that the authors and audiences we speak of are only approximations of the actual authors and earliest recipients of the biblical texts. Indeed, we cannot speak of named authors for Genesis, Exodus, Leviticus, Numbers, or even Deuteronomy (where Moses might be a good candidate, but for the fact that the book narrates his death in ch. 34!). Nor is it possible to make anything of the much later attributions of the Gospels to Matthew, Mark, Luke, and John. And although we know Paul's name, the tensions between the little he reveals of himself in his letters and the accounts of him in Acts confuse critics as much as they enlighten them. Clearly, then, to reconstruct the authors of any of these texts in any substantial way requires primary reliance on the texts they produced. We must "imply" the authors from the texts they wrote.

Just so, although we can know something of Paul's audiences in Corinth, Rome, Philippi, Galatia, and so forth from archaeological and historical sources, we have to rely mostly on the clues left in Paul's letters to grasp his target audiences' concerns and interests. This is all the more true with respect to texts where we are altogether uncertain as to who were their intended addressees (the Gospels, the books of the Torah, the prophetic books, etc.). Just as we must imply authors from texts, we have to imply the authors' target audiences from the books they wrote. For example, when we read First and Second Kings we imagine an author who was a historian, a collector and redactor of tales and traditions, but one who had a clear agenda in retelling the past (e.g., to suggest that the failure of Israel and Judah resulted from faithlessness vis-à-vis their God). Likewise, we can infer that his audience may have wondered about the question his history answers, why God allowed the chosen people to fail utterly as nation-states. When we read the Gospel of John we construct an implied author who is meditative in the telling of Jesus' story, who reflects upon events, and we infer an audience able to appreciate the text's subtle dependence on larger intellectual and religious traditions in this account of Jesus (e.g., "proto-Gnosticism"). When we read the Gospel of Matthew we imply an author who wants to link Jesus closely to the major traditions of Judaism, and we imagine an audience that knew those traditions and would somehow appreciate that Jesus could be tied so closely to them. And so on goes the story of the Bible from this perspective.

Examples of Implied Readers from Proverbs 1-9 and 1 Corinthians

The books of the Bible come in widely varying genres. Does this approach work well for all of them? Examples from such different genres as Proverbs in the Old Testament and Paul's letters in the New Testament help us here.

After introductory verses that attribute the proverbs to Solomon and describe their purpose as service to the wise and the simple in living their lives, a speaker announces, "Hear, my child, your father's instruction and do not reject your mother's teaching; for they are a fair garland for your head and pendants for your neck" (Prov 1:8-9). The speaker implies that his readers are youth requiring instruction, and the masculine gender of the word for "my child" makes it plain they are sons. Moreover, the speaker indicates that heeding the instruction that follows will bring honor and recognition to his readers. Reading the rest of Proverbs 1-9 lets us understand that the speaker is also fearful that sons will *not* listen to their parents, but to the alluring voices of women who tempt them to go a different way. But of course, we see this temptation from the perspective of the implied author of the text who understands himself to be in a competition for the souls of the young!

Paul's letters also give some good examples of "implied readers" in non-narrative texts. For example, in 1 Corinthians Paul makes this appeal to the readers: "Now, I appeal to you, brothers and sisters, by the name of our Lord Jesus Christ, that all of you be in agreement and that there be no divisions among you, but that you be united in the same mind and the same purpose" (1 Cor 1:10). Paul implies that his readers are having disputes among themselves. What are these disputes? By reading the letter we can build up a mental picture of the disputes and concerns among the readers. We also see the picture of the dispute solely from Paul's perspective. The actual readers of the first century could have understood the dispute differently (and probably did).

We share this framework for understanding the Bible with our readers at the start not only because it shaped how *we* synthesize and present the results of critical scholarship. We do so because we think it is also a convenient framework for *you* as a reader to make sense of the Bible and of the Introduction you hold in your hands. It is easy to be put off by the uncertainties expressed by scholars regarding the date, provenance, authorship, audiences, and meaning of biblical texts. But if readers keep in mind the vagaries we have just described in attending to these matters and embrace the

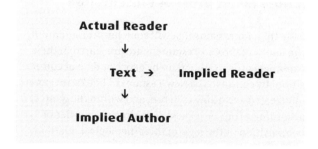

reality that we may only imply or infer authors and audiences, the uncertainties are not only more understandable, but the interpretive possibilities that come with such a freer approach to assessing the text are positively enriching to our contemporary theological imagination.

Putting it All Together, and a Word of Advice on Using the Introduction

Throughout this Introduction we put the approach explained here to use. Do not expect, however, repeated references to "implied authors" and "implied readers." Instead, readers of the Introduction can trust that especially our walks through the biblical text have been informed by this approach, and are reflections of its fruits. We hope this way of coming to know the Bible is as useful to our readers as it has been to us, and to our students.

To instructors and students we offer this additional encouragement. We realize the size of this book can be daunting. However, we hope users — especially students taking direction from their instructors! — will feel free to use only parts of the book as they wish. One option for reducing the amount of time spent reading the Introduction for the sake of increasing time spent with the Bible itself is to omit for some or all books one or more of the three parts devoted to each. Occasionally the walk-through section will be unnecessary, at other times the critical issues section can be ignored, in other instances the discussions of theological themes can be overlooked, and in some cases two sections can be omitted. Another way to reduce the burden of the book, of course, is not to treat in a single- or two-semester course on the Old and New Testaments every book of the Bible. Another way to make the Introduction less daunting lies in recognizing that readers can start anywhere their reading of it and do fairly well; cross-references abound, and most chapters stand alone well in any case.

A Note about Order of Presentation

Note that, for reasons that will soon become apparent, the books of the Old Testament are presented in their canonical order, rather than by genre or date of composition. By contrast, the New Testament books are generally treated according to genre, and within the genres, according to our best guess regarding their order of composition or the logic of their theological relationships.

Review and Discussion Questions

1   Cut out the same story from two different newspapers. Compare the two articles and try to discern the sources that they used. Can you identify the viewpoint of each writer as well as what had been omitted from each article? What sort of authors and readers do the two articles imply?

2   Examine the accounts of creation in Genesis 1–2. Identify what is similar and what is different. How do the viewpoints of the two accounts differ, and what do they suggest about implied authors and readers?

Framework for Reading the Old Testament

Chapter 2

What Is the Old Testament?

Getting Started

1 Take a look at a table of contents for the Old Testament in your Bible. How many of the book names do you recognize? Can you describe the content of any of them? Do any of them fit into general categories of literature with which you are familiar?

2 Consider the conventions of modern composition: authors identify themselves, they are required to cite their use of another author's material, they aim in history writing for factual and "true" accounts of the past, and in fiction writing they seek to entertain. Keep these basic modern conventions in mind as you read through the description of the Hebrew Bible's composition history. Pay close attention to the differences you already begin to see between the modern and ancient ways of writing, and especially of writing texts intended to have religious authority.

Our Context as Readers of the Old Testament

As college students approach the Old Testament (or Hebrew Bible) they bring with them a wide array of expectations and interests. Some students come to the text having already encountered some or all of the Old Testament through their experience as Christians, Jews, or Muslims. Other students do not identify with any of these religions and have encountered the Hebrew Bible only indirectly through its stories that have become a part of popular culture. (For instance, how many times have you seen Adam and Eve used to peddle one thing or another?) Some hold the Bible in relatively high esteem, either for its religious value or its cultural influence. Others regard the Bible less appreciatively, thinking it outdated, surpassed by the concerns of a new age.

No matter their differences, all of these readers share one thing in common: they all live in a world which remains indelibly imprinted by images, ideas, themes, and specific passages of the Hebrew Bible. Even in our "postmodern world," where diversity is thought to have replaced dominant perspectives with a multitude of conflicting viewpoints, the ideas of the Hebrew Bible remain a powerful influence. The advice of the preacher of Ecclesiastes to enjoy the good in life and endure the ill looms large in the postmodern imagination. Deuteronomy's notion that the righteous are rewarded and the wicked punished pervades contemporary culture, either as a dominant ethos or one that is scorned or challenged. And the voices of the prophets condemning injustice are echoed in the speeches of many social activists. There is no escaping the reach of the Old Testament. Thus one can hardly go wrong devoting some energy to its study!

The Context of the Hebrew Bible

The Hebrew Bible itself comes from a context like the one we just described, a world in ferment but nonetheless under the influence of ancient traditions. As we shall see, the Old Testament was mostly composed between the 6th and 2nd centuries B.C.E., a time of enormous change for the people of Israel. During that period they endured exile in Babylon and the destruction of their holy city Jerusalem and the temple on Zion, their place of worship. They saw the defeat of Babylon and the rise of the Persian Empire, and they experienced Persian rule with all of its demands. They saw in turn the rise of the great power from the west, the Macedonian Alexander and his armies bringing Greek culture with them. Later they endured the rule of Alexander's successors, the Ptolemies and Seleucids, and all of the new experiences — good and bad — that they brought to the people of Israel. Yet for all the changes they faced, the authors of the Hebrew Bible remained under the sway of ancient traditions about ancestors, liberators, war heroes, kings, prophets, and priests. The authors of the Bible constructed texts from these traditions that were intended to set their world in order and explain their relationship with their God. Understood in this way, the texts and compositional processes we examine in this Introduction have remarkable resonance with our own experience: we too make sense of our contemporary confusion with resources from the past, including the Old Testament! So for all of the separation in time and culture between us and the days of the Old Testament, we shall see that we stand in remarkable continuity with that text and its world.

The Contents of the Old Testament/ Hebrew Bible

So just what is this thing we are talking about, the Old Testament? One way to define it is by simply *listing* its contents. (We come below to a *description* of the Old Testament's contents.) However, that is not as easy

"Before the Common Era" and the "Common Era"

We are accustomed to the acronyms B.C. and A.D., which stand for "Before Christ" and "Anno Domini" ("in the year of the Lord"). However, such Christian ways of dividing time fail to account for the diverse religious perspectives that are a fact of human existence from time immemorial. Therefore many have adopted the more neutral terms "Before the Common Era" (B.C.E.) for B.C. and "Common Era" (C.E.) for A.D. This depends on the worldwide use of the Common Western Calendar. We use B.C.E. and C.E. throughout this book.

as it sounds, since the Old Testament of Protestant Christians is different from that of Catholic Christians or Christians of the Eastern churches. And there is still another "canon" among Jews.

The lists on page 10 reveal the content differences among the Jewish, Orthodox (Greek and Russian), Roman Catholic, and Protestant canons. Some items require explanation. First, note that the Jewish canon counts among the "prophetic books" the prophetic *and* historical books of the Roman Catholic and Protestant canons and divides them between the "Former" and "Latter Prophets." The Jewish canon also makes the so-called Minor Prophets (Hosea to Malachi) one book among the Latter Prophets. Second, the Orthodox canon understands the Torah or Pentateuch as just another part of a collection of Historical Books and names the Samuel and Kings books 1-4 Kingdoms. The Orthodox canon's 2 Esdras is a rough approximation of Ezra and Nehemiah, and its editions of Esther, Psalms, and Daniel contain additional material beyond that found in the Jewish or Protestant editions of those books. Psalm 151 is added in the Orthodox canon, and Daniel includes four distinct additional episodes: the Prayer of Azariah, the Song of the Three Young Men, Susanna, and Bel and the Dragon. Third, in the Roman Catholic canon Esther and Daniel are similarly supplemented, while Baruch also includes the Orthodox canon's Letter of Jeremiah. In addition, the Roman Catholic canon embraces other books excluded from one or more of the other collections: Tobit, Judith, 1-2 Maccabees, Wisdom of Solomon, and Ecclesiasticus. Finally, the Protestant canon excludes the additions to Esther and Daniel found in the Orthodox and Roman Catholic canons, as well as the Apocrypha of the Roman Catholic collection: Tobit, Judith, 1-2 Maccabees, Wisdom of Solomon, Ecclesiasticus, and Baruch. This exclusion came from Martin Luther's decision that without the "true Hebrew" of these texts — he knew them only in Greek — they could not be used in the colloquial translation he prepared for German Christians.

Terms for the Old Testament and the Idea of Canon

You have probably noticed already that we use two terms interchangeably, "Old Testament" and "Hebrew Bible." Old Testament is the Christian title for a collection of books that begins with Genesis and concludes with Malachi (see the full listing of the Protestant and Catholic Old Testament collections on p. 10). Hebrew Bible is the term used chiefly by scholars as a more neutral designation, one that avoids indication of religious affiliation and especially the Christian bias of the title Old Testament. This is not an entirely satisfactory alternative, since parts of the "Hebrew" Bible are in fact composed in Aramaic, nor is it as neutral as some think, since the word Bible connotes religious commitments. Another ostensibly neutral term has developed its own following: "First Testament."

Two other titles commonly used by Jews should be noted as well. One is "Tanak," really an acronym for the Hebrew words Torah (Law), Nebi'im (Prophets), and Ketubim (Writings) (see below, p. 10), and the other is "Mikra," which means "Scripture."

The word "canon" requires some explanation. The term comes from a Greek word for "measuring rod" or "ruler." When applied to religious texts, it refers to a body of literature acknowledged by one or another religious group as authoritative. Thus the canon of the Old Testament refers to those books accepted among Christians as authoritative, just as the canon of the Jewish Scriptures refers to those embraced by Jews as binding on thought and action. As we see below (p. 10) canons are not defined only by their contents, but also by their arrangement of accepted texts. For more on the process that led to the canons of the Old and New Testaments, see Chapters 44 and 63.

It is not just a matter of content that determines a canon's meaning; the arrangement of books within a canon can have a significant impact on how recipients understand their collections of authoritative books. For example, as noted above, Jews count as the "Former Prophets" Joshua to 2 Kings, and as the "Latter Prophets" Isaiah, Jeremiah, Ezekiel, and Hosea to Malachi (The Twelve). Thus "prophecy" in the Jewish canon includes the history of the people of Israel under God's promise and covenant (Joshua to 2 Kings) and the speech of God's "servants the prophets" (Amos 3:7) as God's commentary on that history (Isaiah to Malachi). By contrast the Protestant and Roman Catholic canons reserve the term "Prophets" for Isaiah to Malachi and add to the list Daniel, an *apocalyptic* work placed among the "Writings" in the Jewish canon. Apocalyptic litera-

ture portrays the present as an age of enduring conflict between the powers of good and evil and foretells the future when God will intervene on the side of good to bring history to an end and vindicate the righteous. As a consequence, the "Prophets" in the Christian canons are not so much about history as the future and history's conclusion. In the shadow of Daniel, Isaiah and his compatriots become foretellers of the Christian messiah, who in turn is a harbinger of the apocalyptic conclusion to history.

A Description of the Contents of the Old Testament

A further way to answer the question "What is the Old Testament?" is to provide a brief description of the contents of each of the major portions of the Hebrew Bible. This overview should also help readers who are new to the Bible to navigate its story line as we work through each of the books individually.

The Pentateuch

Genesis 1–11 tells stories from "before time began," including the stories of creation, the sin of Adam and Eve in the garden, Cain's murder of Abel, the flood and Noah's ark, and the tower of Babel. These seem to argue that while humanity sins without end, God is just as relentless in mercy. Yet, at the end, in the story of the tower of Babel, God's patience has worn out, and there is no divine mercy at the conclusion of the story; instead all of humanity is dispersed to the corners of the earth, and God seems irreconcilably alienated from creation.

Genesis 12–50 contains the stories of the ancestors (or the "Patriarchs") of Israel — Abraham, his son Isaac, Isaac's son Jacob, and Jacob's 12 sons, along with their spouses, and other women of renown. These stories begin with God deciding not to remain alienated from humanity (as God was at the conclusion of ch. 11); instead God signals his desire to remain in touch with humanity by choosing Abraham to be the father of a great people, through whom God will bless all creation. Thus this section tells the story of how God's chosen people had their origins in Abraham and Sarah and their descendants. At the conclusion of this set of stories Jacob and his sons and their families are in Egypt. There one of his sons, Joseph, has become a powerful leader among the Egyptians.

Exodus 1–18 picks up the story many years after Jacob and his sons and their families were gone from the scene. By this time Pharaoh, the ruler of Egypt, had enslaved the descendants of Abraham. These chapters tell of how God chooses Moses from among the descen-

Jewish, Orthodox, Roman Catholic, and Protestant Canons

JEWISH	ORTHODOX	ROMAN CATHOLIC	PROTESTANT
Torah	**Historical Books**	**Pentateuch**	**Pentateuch**
Genesis	Genesis	Genesis	Genesis
Exodus	Exodus	Exodus	Exodus
Leviticus	Leviticus	Leviticus	Leviticus
Numbers	Numbers	Numbers	Numbers
Deuteronomy	Deuteronomy	Deuteronomy	Deuteronomy
	Joshua		
Former Prophets	Judges	**Historical Books**	**Historical Books**
Joshua	Ruth	Joshua	Joshua
Judges	1-4 Kingdoms	Judges	Judges
1-2 Samuel	1-2 Chronicles	Ruth	Ruth
1-2 Kings	1-2 Esdras	1-2 Samuel	1-2 Samuel
	(Ezra, Nehemiah)	1-2 Kings	1-2 Kings
Latter Prophets	Judith	1-2 Chronicles	1-2 Chronicles
Isaiah	Tobit	Ezra	Ezra
Jeremiah	Esther (with Additions)	Nehemiah	Nehemiah
Ezekiel	1-3 Maccabees	Tobit	Esther
The Twelve		Judith	
Hosea	**Poetic and**	Esther (with Additions)	**Wisdom Books**
Joel	**Didactic Books**	1-2 Maccabees	Job
Amos	Psalms (with Psalm		Psalms
Obadiah	151)	**Wisdom Books**	Proverbs
Jonah	Prayer of Manasseh	Job	Ecclesiastes
Micah	Job	Psalms	Song of Songs
Nahum	Proverbs	Proverbs	
Habakkuk	Ecclesiastes	Ecclesiastes	**Prophetic Books**
Zephaniah	Song of Songs	Song of Songs	Isaiah
Haggai	Wisdom of Solomon	Wisdom of Solomon	Jeremiah
Zechariah	Sirach	Ecclesiasticus	Lamentations
Malachi			Ezekiel
	Prophetic Books	**Prophetic Books**	Daniel
Writings	Hosea	Isaiah	Hosea
Psalms	Amos	Jeremiah	Joel
Proverbs	Micah	Lamentations	Amos
Job	Joel	Baruch (with Letter of	Obadiah
Song of Songs	Obadiah	Jeremiah)	Jonah
Ruth	Jonah	Ezekiel	Micah
Lamentations	Nahum	Daniel (with Additions)	Nahum
Ecclesiastes	Habakkuk	Hosea	Habakkuk
Esther	Zephaniah	Joel	Zephaniah
Daniel	Haggai	Amos	Haggai
Ezra	Zechariah	Obadiah	Zechariah
Nehemiah	Malachi	Jonah	Malachi
1-2 Chronicles	Isaiah	Micah	
	Jeremiah	Nahum	
	Baruch	Habakkuk	
	Lamentations	Zephaniah	
	Letter of Jeremiah	Haggai	
	Ezekiel	Zechariah	
	Daniel (with Additions)	Malachi	
	4 Maccabees in		
	Appendix		

dants of Abraham to confront Pharaoh and demand that he let God's people leave that they might go to the Promised Land (Palestine). After many attempts on Moses' part, Pharaoh relents and lets Moses lead his people away from Egypt, only to go back on his word and chase them through the Red Sea, where he and his army are destroyed. By the end of ch. 18 the people have arrived at Mount Sinai, in the desert north of Egypt.

According to **Exodus 19–Numbers 10** (this includes all of **Leviticus**) the people remained at Sinai, where God gives Moses the law that would govern the people as they wander in the wilderness before they can enter the Promised Land, and that will govern their life in the land as well. Apart from a few stories, almost all of this section is made up of laws dealing with everything from the punishment to be meted out to a murderer to what foods the people can and cannot eat. The giving of the law takes place at Mount Sinai.

Numbers 11–36 portrays the people as they wander in the wilderness after they leave Mount Sinai and before they arrive at the edge of the Promised Land on the Plains of Moab. The stories in this section show how the people rebelled against God and God's chosen leader, Moses, time and time again. At the same time it shows how God was forgiving over and over again, and how God chose to continue in a relationship with the people in spite of their sin.

Deuteronomy begins as the people finally arrive at the edge of the Promised Land, on the Plains of Moab. The entire book is devoted to Moses' sermon to the people before they enter the land. His sermon amounts to new laws that govern their life in the Promised Land, and the assurance that if they follow those laws they will prosper in the land; but if they break the laws, they will be driven out of the land by their enemies. At the end of the book Moses dies and the people are ready to enter the Promised Land.

The Historical Books

The story of the people's conquest of the land is told in **Joshua** and **Judges 1:1–2:5**. Joshua recounts the people's glorious victories in taking the land from its residents. In Judg 1:1–2:5 the account is quite different insofar as it depicts the conquest as a difficult battle to win and control the land, a struggle that only achieves limited results.

The rest of **Judges** and **1 Samuel 1–7** relate the story of the people's life in the land as tribes, without a king. (**Ruth**, the tale of a Moabite woman who becomes a faithful Israelite, is positioned between Judges and 1 Samuel in the Christian canon. Although the book is not part of the "Deuteronomic Collection" that encompasses Deuteronomy to 2 Kings, it is placed after Judges because it begins with the words, "In the days when the judges ruled.") Judges tells over and over again the story of the people's failure to keep the law, the suffering they endured at the hands of enemies as a result of their disobedience, their cry to God that they be delivered, and God's response in raising up a war hero (a "judge") to deliver them.

1 Samuel 8–15 relates how the people — tired of relying on "judges" to deliver them — ask for a king. After hesitating, God obliges them with the appointment of Saul, the first king in Israel. His reign is successful at first, but then he fails to follow God's law and he loses God's favor.

In **1 Samuel 16–1 Kings 11** we hear the story of David's rise as a replacement for Saul. Eventually David becomes king, and at first rules with success and honor. But eventually his mistakes produce disaster for him, his family, and his kingdom. After David, Solomon rules, and he too makes his own errors by marrying foreign women, allowing the worship of other gods, and alienating his people.

In **1 Kings 12–2 Kings 17** the story continues with the division of the kingdom into two parts (because the north rebelled against Solomon's and his son's tyrannical rule), Israel in the north and Judah in the south. These chapters narrate the reigns of the kings in the two kingdoms and remind the reader how almost all of those kings abandoned God's demand that they worship God and God alone and that they rely on God alone. Thus these chapters tell the story of the kings' failure to obey God's law. They set the stage for what happens at the end of this section, namely the destruction of the northern kingdom, Israel, by the imperial army of Assyria. 2 Kings 17 explains that destruction as God's punishment for the kings' failure to keep the law. We know that the destruction took place *ca.* 722 B.C.E.

The account of Judah as the remaining kingdom is told in **2 Kings 18–25**. It is the story of a number of kings who carry on the tradition of disobedience, and of one in particular who tried to do otherwise. The obedient king, Josiah, seeks to return the people to observance of the law. But, as the story goes, it is too late; Judah also must suffer the punishment for its failure to follow God's law. So, the final chapters of 2 Kings tell of Judah's defeat by Babylon. The nation is utterly destroyed and its people are taken into captivity in Babylon. This occurred in 586 B.C.E.

There is almost nothing in the Old Testament that tells the story of the people's life in captivity in Babylon. Only a small part of **2 Kings 25** narrates how they lived in exile and how the last king of Judah, Jehoiachin, was eventually allowed at least the privilege of eating at the table of the king of Babylon.

In the Christian canon 1 and 2 **Chronicles** follow 2 Kings. These books recount events from Adam to Saul via genealogies (1 Chronicles 1–9), then linger at length over David's reign (1 Chronicles 10–29), and cover more quickly the history from Solomon to the exile (2 Chronicles).

The story picks up again at the end of the Exile, in 538 B.C.E., in the books of **Ezra** and **Nehemiah**. These books tell of how the people were allowed to return to the Promised Land by Cyrus, king of Persia, when he defeated Babylon (an event mentioned already in 2 Chr 36:22-23). They also narrate the struggles they had in rebuilding the city of Jerusalem, its fortifications, and the temple, the people's house of worship.

The book of **Esther** follows Ezra and Nehemiah. It tells the story of an Israelite woman who becomes a wife of the king of Persia and who uses her role to save the people of Israel from destruction at the hand of the king's prime minister.

The Writings

Coming second in Christian collections, these books are often described as "wisdom literature" and/or poetry and hymns. There is some truth to this description inasmuch as Job and Ecclesiastes, for instance, seem to offer indirect and direct instruction on "how to live life" and Psalms is a collation of 150 hymns. But as our survey here shows (and our fuller description of each of the books in Chapters 20–25 proves), there is much more to these texts than mere instruction and hymnody.

The first book in this category is **Job**, the well-known tale of the righteous Israelite who is the unwitting victim of a wager between God and Satan, a member of God's heavenly council (whose name means only "Adversary" in the book of Job). But more significantly, it contains the speeches of Job, his friends, and God contending with the question of God's justice.

A second book in this category is **Psalms**, essentially Israel's and early Judaism's hymnbook. The psalms in this collection address the full range of human emotions and religious sentiments relative to God.

Proverbs is a "wisdom" book inasmuch as it offers advice to its readers on all kinds of human activities, from childrearing to doing business to courting to farming.

Ecclesiastes also fits into the category of "wisdom" since it too offers advice of a very practical nature. Its author gives us the famous dictum "Eat, drink, and be merry," not as counsel to hedonism, but to enjoyment of the rare goodness that comes one's way in an otherwise difficult existence.

Last is **Song of Songs**. It is essentially erotic poetry, love songs shared between a man and a woman. It is

The Masoretic Text

The "Masoretic Text" refers most broadly to any of the Hebrew manuscripts of the Bible prepared by the Masoretes, scribes whose activity commenced perhaps as early as the 6th century C.E. and continued through the 16th century C.E. The hallmarks of a Masoretic Text are fourfold: the letters, Masoretic vowel signs and accents, and marginal notes meant to guard the integrity of the text as it was repeatedly copied and recopied by hand. The letters were likely set firmly in place at the beginning of the Masoretic period, and the Masoretes developed their vowel and accent system in the 6th and 7th centuries C.E. Their sign system is called the "Tiberian" system (while the other ancient system was dubbed the "Babylonian" system). Because of the Masoretes' long tradition of maintaining absolutely consistent vowel and accent systems, they produced a very stable text regarded by many as the best text available for contemporary critical study, as well as for devotional and liturgical use in the synagogue. Indeed, the Leningrad Codex (1009 C.E.) is the text used in the standard critical edition, *Biblia Hebraica Stuttgartensia;* and the Blomberg (or "Second Rabbinic") Bible (1524-25 C.E.), a corrected version of an earlier (incompletely preserved) Masoretic manuscript called the Aleppo Codex (*ca.* 915 C.E.), is the traditional text used among Jews.

read, though, as the poetry of the love shared between God and God's people.

Prophetic Books

The Christian collection of prophetic books — the Latter Prophets of the Jewish canon plus one (Daniel; on the impact of adding Daniel to the Latter Prophets, see above) — reports the words of Israelite, Judean, and Jewish prophets from the 8th century to as late as the 4th century B.C.E.

Books that preserve prophecies from the 8th century B.C.E., the period covered by 1 Kings 12–2 Kings 17, include **Isaiah, Amos, Micah,** and **Hosea. Jonah** reports a story that ostensibly took place in that period (see 2 Kgs 14:25), but was almost certainly composed in the Persian period. The others are dominated by oracles of condemnation for Israel and Judah and for the nations that opposed them, as well as occasional passages anticipating a better future for God's people. Books that relate prophecies from the late 7th and early 6th centuries, the period covered by 2 Kings 18–25, are **Jeremiah, Lamentations, Nahum, Habakkuk,** and **Zephaniah**. These too are dominated by messages of doom either for Judah or the foreign nations. (Lamentations, though, is not actually a prophetic book, but rather a collection of laments over the fall of Jerusalem to the Babylonian conquerors. It is placed immediately after Jeremiah because it is attributed to him.) Books that relate prophecies from the period of the Exile are **Ezekiel**, **Obadiah**, and **Daniel** (and portions of Isaiah 40–66; see our treatment of Isaiah in Chapter 27). Ezekiel explains the Exile as the result of the people's disobedience, and then condemns the nations for exceeding their divinely appointed task of punishing God's people, and finally offers visions of hope for Israel's future. Obadiah is devoted entirely to a tirade against Edom for its sacking of Judah after the Babylonian conquest. Daniel, as we have seen, is not a prophetic book at all, but rather a late apocalyptic work. Finally, prophecies from the postexilic period are **Haggai**, **Zechariah**, **Malachi**, and **Joel** (and portions of Isaiah 40–66; see our treatment of Isaiah in Chapter 27). These are divided in their focus between supporting the new temple-centered hierarchy and economy of the Persian period and attacking it for its abuses.

The Language, Text, and Translation of the Old Testament

The Old Testament is also called the Hebrew Bible for good reason: it is composed almost exclusively in Hebrew, the language of ancient Israel. Portions of it, though, appear in a related language, Aramaic. They are Dan 2:4–7:28; Ezra 4:7–6:18; 7:12–28; Jer 10:11; and two words in Gen 31:47. Both Hebrew and Aramaic are members of the Northwest Semitic family of languages. Hebrew is the older of the two. Around 600 B.C.E. Aramaic, the official language of the Persian Empire, had supplanted Hebrew as the language spoken day-to-day among the people of Israel, but Hebrew continued to be written, especially to record "sacred" stories. So if you date the composition of most of the Old Testament to the Babylonian period and later, as is the tendency among many scholars these days, it appears to have been written in an "archaizing" language, that is, a tongue that was revered as a sacred language, not the language of everyday speech.

The text of the Old Testament used most widely as the basis for contemporary modern-language translations is called the Masoretic Text (MT), named for the Jewish scribes, the Masoretes, who produced manuscripts of the Hebrew Scriptures during the 9th and 10th centuries C.E. The Masoretes carefully controlled transmission of the text to assure its stability; they did so by introducing marginal marks called the masorah.

Other texts are used in creating contemporary translations. The Greek translation of the Old Testament, called the Septuagint or LXX, is thought occasionally to preserve older, more reliable readings of the Masoretic Text inasmuch as it was translated from Hebrew texts before the turn of the eras, making it a much older text than the one produced by the Masoretes. For instance, the Masoretic Text of 1 and 2 Samuel appears in some places to be corrupted by scribal mistakes while the Septuagint of the Samuel books appears to be much more reliable. (However, as our treatment of 1 and 2 Samuel below proves, not all share this view of the LXX and the MT of those books; see also Chapter 4 below on text criticism.) Other parts of the Septuagint, though, are not so helpful in creating a "more original text" inasmuch as they reflect the cultural sensibilities of the translators as much as they do the meaning of the original Hebrew text. One example of this is the Greek of the book of Proverbs.

Another important resource for preparing translations of the Old Testament is the Dead Sea Scrolls. The Scrolls form the library of an ancient Jewish sect, the Essenes. These "biblical" manuscripts from Qumran — dating from as early as the late 3rd century B.C.E. — are a treasure trove for scholars who work with the text of the Old Testament to surmise its oldest forms. (We call these scholars text critics; see further in Chapter 4 below.) For example, the *Hebrew* manuscript 4QSamuel[a] (the first manuscript of Samuel identified in Cave 4 at Qumran) has many readings in common with the *Greek* translation of 1 and 2 Samuel that has long been preferred to the readings in the ostensibly corrupt Masoretic Text! So you can see how important the Scrolls are for understanding the text of the Old Testament and preparing translations of it.

What about translations? People often wonder which are the most "reliable" or most "authentic" with respect to the original text. By now you should already have some understanding of how hard it is to say that we have in any of the ancient texts that survive evidence of the "original" text. Does that mean that translations end up being a mixture of readings from the various ancient witnesses? It does! For example, if you pay close attention to the textual notes in the New Revised Standard Version of the Bible — the italicized notations at the bottom of the page that correspond to raised letters in the text itself — you quickly discover that it reads with the MT in some places, the LXX in other places, and the Qumran manuscripts in still other places. Your Bible translation, in other words, is actually an amalgam of readings from the Bibles of many other readers before you. Of course, the hope of those who provided the NRSV translation is that their mixed text is closer to a more original form of the text than any of the ancient witnesses we touched on above.

The Septuagint

The term Septuagint refers to those writings in Greek that translate the books of the Hebrew Bible, together with additions to some books, as well as a number of writings that originally appeared in Greek and were not incorporated into the Hebrew Bible. A legend describes the origin of the translation in this way: Seventy-two Jewish scholars translated the Torah into Greek at the request of the Egyptian ruler Ptolemy II (285-247 B.C.E.), who wished to collect copies of all the books of the world for his library in Alexandria. These scholars completed their task at the end of 72 days. The number 72 (nearly!) accounts for the origin of the name Septuagint (from Latin *septuaginta* meaning 70). The commonly used abbreviation is LXX. While the story is fictitious, there is undoubtedly much truth behind it, namely that the Hebrew Torah was the first part of the sacred writings to be translated into Greek somewhere in the course of the 4th century B.C.E. to accommodate the needs of Jews in the Diaspora who no longer understood Hebrew. Over time the other sacred writings were also translated into Greek. Alongside these were other writings that the Jews in Alexandria judged to be authoritative in addition to those being acknowledged in Palestine. For an interesting account of the legend, read the Epistle of Aristeas, a writing that appeared somewhere *ca.* 150 B.C.E. in Alexandria.

The Growth and Development of the Old Testament

But what preceded the *text* of the Old Testament? That is, what was the process of the Hebrew Bible's composition? While the answers to this question vary widely because not all scholars agree especially on the timing of the Pentateuch's formation, the following account is one that commands increasing respect, and it is the one we will tend to favor throughout the rest of the Introduction.

According to this approach, the story of the Bible's composition begins in the Exile, when many Judeans found themselves in the land of Babylon as deportees, victims of war between nations. It was among those people that the first generation of religious texts that would later form the heart of the Hebrew Bible came into existence. It is true that already by this time the 8th-century prophets (Isaiah, Hosea, Amos, Micah, and Zephaniah) had passed from the scene, along with still others who were active in the 7th and early 6th centuries. It is also likely that by then many of the stories incorporated into Genesis to Deuteronomy had long been shared from memory among the people as stories

The Essenes and the Dead Sea Scrolls

From late in the 2nd century B.C.E. to around 68 C.E. a group of separatist Jews — dubbed "Essenes" by Philo, Josephus, and Pliny — maintained a religious retreat center at the northwest corner of the Dead Sea. There they gathered to indulge their interest in interpreting the law, rephrasing the received traditions, and singing God's praises (1QS 6:7). Their source material for this endeavor, as far as we can tell, included nearly all of what we know to be the Hebrew Bible (only Esther and Nehemiah are completely absent among the surviving Scrolls). As a consequence their library has provided us with the oldest known texts of the Old Testament, a resource of inestimable worth for Bible critics and readers. For more on the Essenes and the Dead Sea Scrolls, see Chapter 44 below.

of their heroes, of their past, and of their origins. But it was in the Exile — under the pressure to explain the enigma of their expulsion from the Promised Land — that the people's disparate memories and the words of the prophets began to be gathered together to answer a serious question: why had God permitted them to end up in exile if they were God's chosen people?

Answering the latter question generated significant parts of the Hebrew Bible. The first response may well have been what we read in **Deuteronomy**, **Joshua**, **Judges**, **1 and 2 Samuel**, and **1 and 2 Kings**. These books constitute a theological history of the people from the days when they were about to enter the Promised Land and were instructed on how to live in God's sight until the days when God drove them from the land to Babylon. These books explain the Exile as God's punishment for the people's failure to meet their obligations (Joshua to 2 Kings) under a covenant that God graciously initiated with them (Deuteronomy). It is also possible that the authors of these books collected and edited much of the material we find in **Isaiah 1–39**, along with the words of **Hosea**, **Amos**, **Micah**, and **Zephaniah** and perhaps **Obadiah**, **Nahum**, and **Habbakuk** to support their claims. After all, these prophets foretold the Exile in God's name long before it happened! However, the authors and editors of this massive work were not completely without hope. Woven into their account of the people's failure are speeches which promised that if the people called to God from exile, even then God would permit them another chance at living according to the covenant made through Moses.

It seems certain that some recipients of Deuteronomy to 2 Kings, the "Deuteronomic Collection," were unimpressed by its theological claims. They responded with their own accounts of why the Exile happened and what the future would bear. One such response comes in the "Yahwist Work," spread out over **Genesis 2–50**, **Exodus 1–24, 32–34**, and **Numbers 11–36**. The Yahwist writer (so named because he calls God by the divine name "Yahweh" from the beginning of his account) told the story of God's dealings with all of humanity in Genesis 2–11, with the ancestors in Genesis 12–50, and with the people of Israel as a whole in Exodus 1–24, 32–34 and Numbers 11–36. He did so to prove over and over again that God made a unilateral promise to give the chosen people land and descendants, and that no matter how many different ways the people could find to sabotage that promise through their sin and disobedience, God would still fulfill it. True enough, they would often have to suffer the natural consequences of their foolish actions, but God was always there to redeem them and direct them back again to the fulfillment of those promises. Thus the Yahwist's response to the Deuteronomists is to suggest that even before God made the covenant with the people through Moses (notice that the Yahwist Work was composed as a prologue to the Deuteronomic Collection) God had made a unilateral promise that, being more ancient, superseded the Mosaic covenant of Deuteronomy! The people could expect rescue from their self-imposed exile precisely because that was God's plan for them.

The book of **Job** was also probably composed in this period as another answer to the difficulty of the Exile. When we come to it we will see that it does not so much reject the Deuteronomic or Yahwist views as raise them, as well as several others, as possible ways of explaining the extraordinary fact of being God's chosen people in exile and suffering.

A section of the Great Isaiah Scroll (1QIsaᵃ). The only one of the Dead Sea Scrolls to survive virtually complete, the scroll contains many variant readings that provide greater understanding of the biblical text. (Courtesy of the Israel Antiquities Authority)

The Great Isaiah Scroll (1QIsaiah)

From late in the 2nd century B.C.E. to around 68 C.E. a group of separatist Jews — dubbed "Essenes" by Philo, Josephus, and Pliny — maintained a religious retreat center at the northwest corner of the Dead Sea. There they gathered to indulge their interest in interpreting the law, rephrasing the received traditions, and singing God's praises (1QS 6:7). Their source material for this endeavor, as far as we can tell, included nearly all of what we know to be the Hebrew Bible (only Esther and Nehemiah are completely absent among the surviving Scrolls). As a consequence their library has provided us with the oldest known texts of the Old Testament, a resource of inestimable worth for Bible critics and readers. For more on the Essenes and the Dead Sea Scrolls, see Chapter 44 below.

Lamentations was composed during the Exile by someone dwelling in Jerusalem. The book's Jerusalem provenance is evident from its description of the brutal conditions that prevailed in the city and the rest of Judah after the Babylonian devastations of the region in 597, 586, and 582. Lamentations is deeply touching testimony to the uncertainty that God, having permitted such total destruction, had anything more to do with the people at all.

In Babylon the prophet **Ezekiel** was active from 597 to 573. His prophecies also explain the Exile, but in a very different way: he suggests that it was merely an exercise in God's sovereignty, executed because of the sin of the people. No law or covenant guided the relationship between God and people, only common sense and justice, both things the people lost sight of. However, Ezekiel is not without hope either: he anticipates the day when God, seeing the shame of the people for their sin, would restore them to a wonderful new Jerusalem and an even more wonderful new temple.

Lastly in the Exile we hear from the author of **"Second Isaiah,"** Isaiah 40–55. While others surely contributed to this part of the book of Isaiah and the author of most of this contributed to aspects of Isaiah 1–39 (and perhaps 55–66), much of these 16 chapters clearly reflect the experience of Judeans in the Babylonian Exile after 546 B.C.E. By then it had become certain that Cyrus of Persia would soon liberate the Judeans in exile and demand that they return home to rebuild their temple and its economy so as to make that land profitable for his empire. Second Isaiah looked forward to this day, but knew that, because of the comfortable life many Jews had made in Babylon, few would want to return to Judah. So

Second Isaiah was not concerned so much to explain the Exile as to reveal why God decided to bring it to an end and restore the people to their land.

The period of Persian rule was the next era to produce a great deal of Jewish religious literature. Persian policy granted limited religious autonomy to subject peoples so long as their priests collected taxes satisfactory to the empire. Thus when Cyrus decreed that Jews in Babylon should return to Judah and rebuild the temple, the race was on to determine the shape of the Judaism that would take root back in the land. This was the first major issue faced in the Persian period. The Priestly Work — made up of selected passages in **Genesis 1–50** (e.g., chs. 1, 5, 17, 23), parts of **Exodus 1–24**, all of **Exodus 25–31, 35–40, Leviticus**, and **Numbers 1–10**, and parts of **Numbers 11–36** — was one major contribution to this effort. Some think it may have been authored while Jews were still in Babylon, preparing for their anticipated return to Judah, while others suggest it was created once the people had made their way back to Judah. In either case, it provides a blueprint for an orderly society and temple cult by showing that God's mandates for proper Jewish practice (e.g., observance of the Sabbath and Passover, circumcision, and the Day of Atonement), the authority of Aaronite priests, and the structure and activities of the temple were all provided to Israel in the days of the ancestors and Moses. The antiquity and authority of the ancestors and Moses offered powerful support for the Priestly Work's view of how things should be in the Persian period (also referred to as the Second Temple period after the restored sanctuary in Jerusalem).

A number of prophetic texts clearly came into existence during this period too. Some of those supported the Priestly Work's eagerness to see priests in charge of Jewish life, while others condemned the priests' hegemony over Jewish life. **Haggai** and **Zechariah 1–8** are the words of two prophets who advocated the speedy reconstruction of the temple under Persian rule and the recognition of priestly authority over Jewish affairs in Judah. **Malachi** preserves the voice of a prophet who was quite concerned about the corruption of the ruling priestly class, but this did not mean he wanted to see priestly rule end; rather he was eager to see its purification so that proper sacrifices would be offered to God. **Isaiah 55–66**, on the other hand, expresses the views of a prophet who was so dissatisfied with the priests after the temple's reconstruction that he found no use at all for them and their leadership. He anticipated a day when God would intervene to bring their corruption to an end and elevate those who had been oppressed by their rule to new stature in the Jewish community. **Joel** stands somewhat apart from this Persian-period tradition of prophetic critique or approval regarding the temple

and the priests, revealing how some prophets preached in service of the temple; for this they are often called "cult prophets." Joel's words are perhaps the language spoken in a temple service to explain a recent crop devastation as God's punishment for communal sin and to describe God's coming and final judgment.

A second major issue that Jews in the Persian period had to confront was how to handle the new experience of cultural and ethnic diversity in Judah. Should Jews seek to convert their neighbors or steer clear of them altogether? The author(s) of **1 and 2 Chronicles** and **Ezra-Nehemiah**, considered by many to be one person or a group of thinkers from the same school of thought, seemed to think the isolationist option most suitable. The final compilers of the book of **Proverbs** seemed to share this view, as is evident from the passages warning young men against the "stranger woman" in Proverbs 1–9. By contrast the authors of **Ruth** and **Jonah** clearly desired a more open attitude toward non-Jewish neighbors.

A third concern for Jews in this period was how to make their own voice heard in the temple liturgy, and how to give expression there and elsewhere in their day-to-day life to their yearning for a Davidic king without offending their Persian rulers. The book of **Psalms** answers the first matter, providing a hymnbook for the temple. It is also one among several Persian-period biblical texts which may subtly give expression to the royalist, Davidic hopes of the people. For some scholars its five-book structure rehearses the rise and fall of the Davidic royal line and anticipates its restoration in the future (see also 1 and 2 Chronicles for some of the same pro-David sentiments).

Alexander the Great brought the Persian Empire to a sudden and ignominious end, and beginning in 333 B.C.E. Jews in Judah were under Greek rule. From that period we have two books in the Hebrew Bible and a wealth of other Jewish texts that did not make it into the canon, although some do appear in the Deuterocanonical books of the Roman Catholic canon (e.g., *1 Enoch, Jubilees,* Tobit, Judith, Sirach). **Ecclesiastes** was written by a Jew reflecting on the futility of trying to change one's lot under the rule of the Ptolemies, Alexander's successors who ruled Judah from 301 to 198. The author of Ecclesiastes suggested that all of life is futile, and that we should simply enjoy what good comes to us, suffer stoically through the bad, and die unburdened by regret. Later, when the Ptolemies yielded Judah and the rest of Palestine to the other major successors to Alexander, the Seleucids, Antiochus IV Epiphanes went so far as to ban Judaism and its practice. This brought a variety of responses, one of which was the passive resistance advocated by the book of **Daniel**. Daniel's vision was literally of the end of the world and the beginning of a new one, an apocalyptic vision. The book looks forward to the day when God's cataclysmic intervention into human affairs would break the oppressive rule of the Seleucids and vindicate the Jews who remained faithful in spite of the opposition. The book of **Esther** may come from roughly the same period. If so, its story counsels a very different response to oppressive foreign rule: if the opportunity presents itself to destroy your enemies, do so!

Even before Daniel was written Jews had begun to interpret the books that would become their Bible and the Christian Old Testament. They wrote new texts that reflect those interpretive interests. For instance *1 Enoch* was developed from the biblical notion that Enoch was taken up to heaven by God before he died; thus he could well have seen heavenly secrets which he then reported back to humanity. Another example of this early interpretive tradition is *Jubilees,* a rewriting of Genesis 1 to Exodus 14 that tells "the rest of the story" in the form of an angel's account to Moses. It interprets and expands much of Genesis and Exodus with the aim of establishing the authority of Hellenistic-era Jewish law not found otherwise in the Bible. These and many other texts provide us with important insight into how interpretation opened up and expanded the Hebrew Bible. This, too, is part of the Hebrew Bible's compositional history, at least in an extended sense of the term.

Canonizing the Old Testament/ Hebrew Bible

How did the collection of books that grew over such a long time come to be the Hebrew Bible/Old Testament we know today? The one-word answer is "canonization."

The answer to the question "What does that mean?" comes in Chapters 44 and 63, where we treat the topic as it pertains to both the Old and New Testaments.

Questions for Review and Discussion

1   What does the word "canon" refer to, and how many different canons of the Old Testament/Hebrew Bible did we cover above?

2   How does the arrangement of material within a canon of the Hebrew Scriptures impact the Bible's meaning?

3   What were the major periods in the formation of the Old Testament? What were some of the concerns that drove the process of the Bible's formation?

Further Reading

Freedman, David Noel. "The Earliest Bible." In *Backgrounds for the Bible,* ed. M. P. O'Connor and Freedman. Winona Lake: Eisenbrauns, 1987, 29-37.
Freedman offers a defense of the view that much of the "first Bible" derived from the late monarchic and exilic periods.

Van Seters, John. *The Pentateuch: A Social-Science Commentary.* Sheffield: Sheffield Academic, 1999.
Van Seters provides a good overview of the different approaches to explaining the Pentateuch's compositional history, especially the one that dominates our discussion in the ensuing chapters, and provides the basis for the compositional history rehearsed above.

Chapter 3

The World of the Old Testament

Getting Started

1   Read Amos 1:1. What names and events are mentioned in this single verse? Suggest some ways in which identifying these might improve one's understanding of Amos's words.

2   How might archaeology be helpful in clarifying the date of Amos's activity, inasmuch as Amos 1:1 dates it relative to an earthquake? Besides evidence of an earthquake, what other evidence would be necessary to assign a date to Amos's ministry?

3   Read Amos 1:2. How would understanding the locations and topography of Zion, Jerusalem, and Carmel help in understanding this verse? How would appreciation of the social and cultural contexts of those locations add to one's appreciation of the verse, as well as the rest of Amos?

Preliminary Comments

Understanding the Hebrew Bible requires some awareness of the contexts that produced it, and contexts, as it turns out, are complex realities. Our knowledge of contexts comes from what we know of history, archaeology, geography, and ancient religions, societies, and cultures. The following chapter provides just enough information about each of these to help you navigate the rest of this Introduction to the Hebrew Bible.

The World of the Old Testament: History

We begin our historical survey with the first literate people to appear on the scene in the Near East, the Sumerians. Their population centers — the city-states Eridu, Uruk, Nippur, and Ur — were concentrated in southern Mesopotamia, extending northwest from the Persian Gulf for nearly 250 miles to Nippur. The Sumerians — whose name derives from the Babylonian name for southern Babylonia, Sumer — probably migrated from the north or east, perhaps Iran or northern India. They arrived in the region sometime after the middle of the 4th millennium B.C.E. The Sumerians are especially notable for the history of the Hebrew Bible because they were some of the first peoples in the ancient world to use writing as a communication medium, and their mythic flood stories served as models for the account of a world flood in Genesis 6–9.

The Sumerians settled among the Akkadians, a Semitic population that had its roots in the west, in Arabia, Syria, and perhaps Palestine. Only *ca.* 2400 B.C.E. did these people's ruler, Sargon of Akkad, overtake the Sumerians and subjugate their lands. Sargon and his successors established a short-lived empire that substantially extended northward the scope of urbanized Sumerian Mesopotamia. Around 2180 the Gutians, from the Zagros Mountains to the east, seriously compromised Akkadian hegemony in the region. Akkadian control of the region was broken completely by a Sumerian resurgence from 2050 to 1950, and after that the northern region, dubbed Assyria for the most significant power in the area, developed separately from the south (called Babylon after the chief city of the region). Semitic peoples controlled both areas.

It had long been thought that during the 3rd millennium B.C.E. Syria-Palestine remained in the prehistoric age, that is, none of its inhabitants had writing. But with the discovery of written records at Tell Mardikh (Ebla) in 1975-76 minds changed overnight. We now know that the people of this land, whom we call Canaanites, had also established city-states and that the city at Tell Mardikh may have been the center of an empire that reached as far east as Mesopotamia and as far west as Cyprus. Late in the 3rd millennium this region was conquered by outsiders whose identity remains a mystery, although the Amorites (see below) are strong candidates.

During this period Egypt experienced greatness, decline, and a restoration to greatness. The Old Kingdom (*ca.* 2900-2200) reached its full efflorescence in the middle of the millennium and then experienced a sudden decline due to social and political unrest. This produced the First Intermediate Period (*ca.* 2200-2000), an era of decline which concluded with the beginning of the Middle Kingdom. Notably, the Old Kingdom laid the foundations for the rich cultural heritage subsequent Egyptian kingdoms would enjoy.

The ancient Near Eastern history that interests us most begins in earnest with what some have called the "Patriarchal" or "Ancestral Age" (*ca.* 2000-1500 B.C.E.). The name comes from the idea that this is when Abraham and his descendants, whose story is in Genesis 12–50, appear on the scene. As we shall see, most scholars question the reliability of this notion. In any case, it was during these years that Assyria and Babylon, two powers to figure significantly in Bible history, first come to our attention. Assyria, the northern part of Mesopotamia,

was ruled by Akkadians from around 1900 to 1750. Then the Amorites, a people who also appear around this time in Syria-Palestine, conquered the region and took control of it. Amorites founded the city of Mari, now an archaeological site that has yielded important literary evidence for the life of the region in antiquity. Babylon, the southern part of Mesopotamia, also fell under Amorite control in this period. Hammurabi, a ruler of the city of Babylon from *ca.* 1725-1685, is especially well known for his law code that is often thought to bear close resemblance to the code in Exodus 21–23. The Amorite dominance of Mesopotamia came to an end early in the 17th century with the rise of the Hurrians (also called the Mitanni), a non-Semitic people from the northwest. Around 1500, when we have good epigraphic (written) evidence again, it appears that the Hurrians had become the dominant power from east to west in Mesopotamia and may even have influenced Syria-Palestine. They ruled over the Assyrians and Babylonians. Meanwhile, in Asia Minor another non-Semitic people, the Hittites, were emerging as a powerful force in the ancient Near East. In fact, they would soon clash with the Hurrians.

Since we have virtually no epigraphic remains from Syria-Palestine for this period, the identity of the people who did establish an urban culture there in the 2nd millennium B.C.E. remains a mystery. Because pottery styles found at Syro-Palestinian sites are comparable with those in known Amorite cities elsewhere, some speculate that the urbanizers were Amorite. In any case, it is clear that by 1600 urban centers did exist in places like Aleppo, Hazor, and Jerusalem.

Egypt, meanwhile, enjoyed the best years of the Middle Kingdom (2100-1800 B.C.E.). The Middle Kingdom's decline, however, ushered in the Second Intermediate Period, the chief characteristic of which was the arrival of the Hyksos, a group whose identity otherwise remains a mystery, although most observe that they came from Syria-Palestine and were likely Amorite. The Hyksos drove the native Egyptian rulers to the south and seized control of the northern region. At the end of this period Egypt reasserted itself and set out to defend its territory against future incursions from the north by extending its influence into Syria-Palestine. This policy brought empires into serious conflict for the first time and established a pattern of using Palestine as a highly-contested land bridge between the great imperial centers of Egypt and Mesopotamia. As we shall see, over the centuries that followed this imperial regard for Syria-Palestine would have serious consequences for the people of that land — including the people of Israel and Judah.

The next period, 1500-1200 B.C.E., saw increasing conflict among the Hurrians, Hittites, and Egyptians, with the Assyrians becoming the benefactors of the tensions. Circumstances made the Hurrians and Egyptians allies against the Hittites, at least so long as the relationship was mutually beneficial. But because of Egyptian inattention to foreign policy — Amenophis III was preoccupied with his building projects and his successor Akhenaten engaged in ill-advised religious innovations — and the Hurrians' weakening grip on power, the Hittites soon gained the upper hand. In the middle of the 14th century they brought the Hurrian kingdom to an end, permitting Assyria to reassert itself in the northeast under Asher-uballit. The Hittites then became embroiled in renewed war with Egypt, a sporadic conflict that continued until the middle of the 13th century, when Hittite concern for the Assyrian threat to the east and Egyptian worry over the incursion of the Sea Peoples (tribes from the Aegean and Crete) required the two weary powers to make peace. Soon the Sea Peoples took Asia Minor and the major Hittite landholdings, and by 1200 the Hittites had vanished. The Egyptians, for their part, were driven back to their own land, never

Stela depicting Hammurabi receiving symbols of authority from the sun-god Shamash. Below are listed 282 laws exemplifying the ideals of royal justice. (Louvre)

to seriously threaten anyone else's hegemony in Syria-Palestine again. This period also witnessed the rise and fall of the great civilization at Ugarit, near the Mediterranean coast in Syria. This highly civilized urban culture seems to have been a center point for the region, as is evident from the texts discovered there from the 14th century (see the section on Archaeology below).

It is in the later part of this period amidst its population shifts that many scholars speculate the Exodus (or something like it) of the Hebrew people from Egypt took place. The Assyrians, for their part, took advantage of the shifting balance of power to increase their own strength. Indeed, they became the dominant power in the region.

From 1200 to 721 the Assyrians controlled the region. Also during the early centuries of this period the people of Israel went from being a collection of tribal groups occupying Palestine to a single nation-state ruled first by Saul, then by David and Solomon, and finally to a nation divided in two, Israel in the north and Judah in the south. At this point, then, our story is no longer one that has two or three different centers — Mesopotamia, Syria-Palestine, and Egypt — but involves all parties at once. And since we will return to much of the story later in covering the biblical books, we may move with more speed from here to the end.

As for Assyria, beginning already in 1276 with the accession of Shalmaneser to the throne, its greatness as a military power was clear. Under Tiglath-pileser I, who took the throne in 1115, Assyria might have reached all the way to the Mediterranean, affecting the Sea Peoples (Philistines) who had settled there, as well as the Israelite tribes located close by. As for the people of Israel, they existed without kings until *ca.* 1020 when Saul came to power. David (*ca.* 1000-960) and Solomon (*ca.* 960-922) succeeded Saul and overtook his hope for dynastic succession. Solomon's successor, Rehoboam, failed to keep the kingdom together, and it divided into the two nation-states, Judah and Israel, with the Davidic dynasty continuing to rule in the south and the Omride and Jehu dynasties dominating the history of the Northern Kingdom.

The two kingdoms lived with cold and hot war for two centuries. Perhaps the lowest point in their relations came in 733 when Syria and Israel tried to force Judah into a doomed alliance against Assyria — all three of the minor states had by then become subject to that empire to varying degrees. Judah refused to join and sought protection from Assyria, a move that only deepened Judean dependence on the imperial power and worsened the status of Israel relative to Assyria. The Assyrians finally campaigned against Israel in 722-21, utterly defeating it and deporting its citizenry. Assyrian conquest was particularly brutal and resulted in the near eradication of the northern tribes.

From 721 to 586 Judah struggled to survive as Assyria applied increasing pressure and used the Palestinian land bridge to move against Egypt, aiming to make Egypt part of its own empire. Clearly, this made life difficult for the people of Judah. But Assyria's fascination with Egypt was also its downfall, for as it looked toward the Nile it ignored the resurgence of Babylon to the south. Indeed, in 626 Babylon regained independence under Nabopolassar, and with the help of the Medes and Scythians, the Babylonians defeated the Assyrians, putting an end to their long imperial reign. The effect for Judah, however, was insubstantial: it merely changed the address to which the annual vassalage fee was sent. No wiser from the experience of others, the Judean kings rebelled against Babylonian rule, prompting the empire to attack in 597, 586, and 582. The deportations associated with the first two Babylonian incursions produced the Judean exile in Babylon, the second invasion destroyed the temple and the city of Jerusalem, and the third left the countryside in ruins as well.

Many of the people of Judah dwelt in exile from 586 to 538 while others remained in Palestine. During those years the Babylonian Empire grew weak, and Persia developed as the new imperial power. In 538 Cyrus of Persia completed his conquest of the Babylonian Empire by entering the city of Babylon itself. Cyrus's policy of permitting religious autonomy to conquered nations, so long as priests collected taxes from worshippers for the Persian coffers, made him particularly popular not only among priests, but also among laity who attached great importance to the proper worship of their chosen gods. Because Cyrus had also taken the land of Israel in his conquests, and because the best and brightest of that region had been deported decades before to Babylon, Cyrus encouraged the exiled Judeans to return to Palestine and rebuild their temple so that a vital agrarian economy there would generate income for the Persian Empire as well.

The Persian period lasted from 538 to 333. We know little about the era from Jewish texts, but the Persians kept good imperial records that give some idea of the conditions Jews faced. They indicate that while the middle period of Persian rule over the region was relatively peaceful and prosperous, the beginning and end were turbulent times at best. Especially during the late Persian period the tax burden on Judea and Samaria increased to very difficult levels. When we come to biblical texts associated with the Persian period we shall delve into some of the other details of Jewish life in this period. For now, though, it is enough to say that when the next challenger for imperial rule, Alexander the Great, appeared in the late 4th century, his advent was welcomed by many who hoped for an end to Persian rule and relief from its increasingly oppressive policies.

Alexander's armies took control of Palestine *ca.* 333 B.C.E. When he died in 323 and left his kingdom to be divided among his generals, many hoped for a peaceful transition. Their hope was soon disappointed, for Alexander's successors, Ptolemy in Egypt, Antigonus in Asia Minor, and Seleucus in Syria, were determined to overcome one another for possession of all of Alexander's empire. Their battleground was too often too close to the land of Israel to permit any stability in the region. Only *ca.* 300 did a degree of peace finally break out, with Antigonus largely passing from the scene and Ptolemy and Seleucus dividing what remained of Alexander's empire. Ptolemy, based in Alexandria, took control of the Promised Land.

The Ptolemaic era lasted until 198 B.C.E. During that time Jews in Palestine suffered under the highly burdensome tax policies of the Ptolemies, as well as five wars waged between the Ptolemies and Seleucids for control of the region. Only *ca.* 200, when the Seleucid leader Antiochus III promised tax relief to the Jews in exchange for their help in fighting the Ptolemies, did the Seleucids win the land for themselves. But Antiochus's ambition soon brought him into conflict with the emerging power in the ancient world, Rome. He was defeated in the battle of Magnesia in 190, and rather than depose him, Rome asked only that he pay an annual vassalage fee to remain in power. To make his annual payment and remain in good standing as a client to his Roman patrons Antiochus had to steal from the nations subject to his rule, and that meant raiding temples, which often served as banks for community wealth in antiquity. Antiochus was killed in one of those raids and was succeeded by his son Seleucus IV (187-175). A second son, Antiochus IV, came to power in 175. Antiochus IV added to his name the title "Epiphanes" ("manifestation [of god]") to emphasize his royal pretensions to divine status. Perhaps it was this that brought him into such severe conflict with the Jews. In any case he soon criminalized the practice of Judaism and even desecrated the temple in 167.

Antiochus's oppressive policies provoked a Jewish rebellion known as the Maccabean Revolt, after the surname of Judas Maccabeus, the rebellion's first leader. (We also call it the Hasmonean Revolt, after the family name of Judas.) Initially this was a guerilla war waged from the hills of Judea, but in time enough sympathy attached to the Maccabean cause that they could muster an army. In 164 they recaptured the temple in Jerusalem and rededicated it, and by 141 they succeeded in driving the last Seleucid soldiers from the land. In 152

Archaeology and the Hebrew Bible

Recent Uses of Archaeology in Biblical Scholarship.

Archaeology as an adjunct to the study of the Bible has a varied history. Through the middle of the last century its use was characterized by the moniker "biblical archaeology." In fact, only a few biblical scholars actually engaged in archaeological research (among them Wiliam F. Albright and his student G. Ernest Wright); others were "armchair archaeologists," digesting the results of other scholars' excavations. The hallmark of this phase of biblical scholarship's interest in archaeology was a desire to find the material evidence that would help "prove the Bible true," that is, corroborate in some way the accuracy of the biblical narrative at least from the stories of the ancestors onward. After the middle of the 20th century, though, professional archaeologists who are not primarily interested in the Bible, but in the archaeology of the region in general (Syro-Palestinian archaeology), entered the debate. Instead of focusing so much on buildings, city walls, and other such evidence that purportedly corroborates the political history reported in much of the Bible, these archaeologists devote attention to understanding the realities of day-to-day life in the ancient world. Their efforts may have moved away from the grand aims of the biblical archaeology movement, but they have certainly added to our understanding of the world in which the Bible was created and received. So while one might say that the earlier phase of archaeological endeavor sought to re-create the political history of the biblical world, the more recent phase seeks to better comprehend its social and cultural realities.

Archaeological Method.

Here is a brief description of the chief methods Syro-Palestinian archaeologists use to do their work.

Survey archaeology locates the most promising place to begin an excavation of an archaeological site (or tell, from *tel,* the Arabic word for a mound under which the remains of an ancient city or settlement can be found). The method entails what its name implies: the archaeologist seeks traces of ancient civilizations on the surface of the tell and directs her colleagues to the location that provides the most promising evidence.

Stratigraphy entails digging down into a tell at the spot determined by the survey archaeologist so as to leave standing walls ("balks") within the ever-growing cavity. The habitation and destruction layers discerned in the balks and on the outer walls of the cavity provide a chronological record of the settlement or city's past.

Ceramic typology is one of the chief means by which the destruction and habitation layers of a tell are dated. Through long experience of unearthing and categorizing ancient pottery, archaeologists have developed a typology of pottery styles one expects to find in particular periods of the ancient world. This is a particularly useful method of dating layers because pottery was so widely used in everyday life, it was rarely recycled, and it survives the decay that overtakes most other remains of human habitation.

Numismatics, the study of coins, is another method of dating layers in the tell. When currency finally made its appearance in the ancient Mediterranean world as a means of economic exchange, coins were also often used to denote a ruler's control over a region or to commemorate events of importance. Thus their usefulness in dating a layer is obvious, and like potsherds, they do not decay with the passage of time.

New methods relying on the natural sciences have become ever more a normative component of archaeological research in the Syro-Palestinian region. New scientific technologies have made it possible to analyze the composition and nature of things so diverse as the clay used to make a piece of pottery and human fecal remains discovered at the bottom of ancient latrines. These technologies permit researchers to know where the clay of a pot came from and what a resident of a region ate — not insignificant pieces of information since they can determine whether people relied on available resources or engaged in far-flung trade! Archaeologists can employ many new scientific techniques like this in their quest to understand the human past in its fullest richness through material evidence.

Kinds of Archaeological Evidence.

Already it should be obvious that the character of archaeological evidence varies considerably. One way to distinguish among the types of evidence is to classify it according to three broad categories. This oversimplifies matters, but is sufficient for our interests.

Artifact evidence encompasses, for our purposes, anything from city walls, the ruins of ancient homes, palaces, or temples to broken pottery and buried coin caches. Any object made by human beings is an artifact, and each artifact has its own story to tell. Note, though, that all such evidence is, without some inscription, mute; it depends on modern interpreters for meaning in the ancient context. For instance, the value of the remains of a village — home foundations, cooking installations, pottery kilns, and the like — is at least somewhat limited when we have no written testimony that identifies the village with a particular site we know of otherwise from the ancient world.

Thus *epigraphic evidence* is very important to archaeologists. "Epigraphic" refers to written evidence and includes such obvious textual discoveries as the Dead Sea Scrolls or, from the New Testament period, the Nag

Hammadi codices. But other kinds of epigraphic evidence also serve archaeologists well. For instance, the Tel Dan inscription is little more than the etchings of a king's scribes on a stone. Similarly, a few words etched on potsherds found at Lachish and Qumran reveal a great deal about the lives of Israelites in different places and times in the ancient world. Epigraphic remains are emphatically not mute, precisely the characteristic that makes them so important to archaeologists and historians.

"Dirt archaeology" is a rough-and-ready term for the third kind of archaeological evidence. Included here is anything that is not an artifact — an object crafted by human beings — and is not inscribed in any way.

For instance, an important kind of "dirt" is human fecal remains discovered in ancient latrines. As noted above, analyzing the substance of such remains often tells archaeologists the diet of the people who left them behind. This is especially important when we learn from such analysis that a given community was eating a grain or other food not indigenous to their own region; this proves trade between that community and the one that produced the "imported" food. Obviously, human skeletal remains, which modern science can make speak volumes about the life patterns of the people whose bodies they supported, are another kind of evidence that falls under this heading.

the Maccabees had usurped the Jewish high priesthood and so gained complete religious and political control over the land of Israel. As a result their rule was not welcomed by all Jews, especially inasmuch as they were perceived by many to be too liberal in their economic, cultural, and foreign policies. They also faced the difficult task of maintaining some national autonomy in the face of Rome in the west, the remains of the Seleucid Empire and the rising Parthians in the east, and their own internal dissension. As a result, by the beginning of the 1st century B.C.E. independent Jewish rule was endangered, and Rome, still lurking on the horizon, prepared to take over. In 63 B.C.E. Rome did just that through the leadership of Pompey, and so began the period of Roman rule in the land of Israel.

The World of the Old Testament: Archaeology

How do we know about the world of the Bible? What permits us to speak of the culture, religion, and society of the peoples who pass across the stage of this long period in history? The Bible provides some information, as do other ancient writings ranging from royal records of the ancient Mesopotamian powers to the works of Josephus, the Jewish historian active in the 1st century C.E. But if we relied on written evidence alone, we would know far less than we do. Archaeology — the practice of retrieving evidence from the soil of the Near East — has added much to our understanding of the past. Admittedly, there are methodological problems with using the mute evidence of undated, uninscribed objects associated with ancient peoples. Indeed, the most significant problem is that all such evidence is dependent on modern interpreters for its meaning and significance! With that said, archaeological evidence still provides insight

on the Bible and its world that we would otherwise not have. To demonstrate the value of archaeology we offer a sampling of some of the most significant discoveries relating to the Old Testament and its world. As for the practice and methods of archaeology in relation to the Bible, see page 22.

Among finds from the Early Bronze Age (*ca.* 3000-2000 B.C.E.) are the Ebla tablets found at Tel Mardikh in Syria. The tablets reveal that Semitic peoples very early on adapted the Sumerian cuneiform script. The tablets also reveal the vital economic life this city enjoyed, a commercial existence that entailed substantial trade with other parts of the region, which in turn proves the early cross-fertilization of cultures in the Near East. Tell Mozan, a site dating from the 22nd century, underscores this observation: it yielded tablets containing Hurrian, Sumerian, and Akkadian proper names written in Akkadian (which uses Sumerian cuneiform characters). Also dating to this period is Tell Hariri (Mari), another city site that produced much commercial epigraphic evidence (and some of religious significance as well).

Another important site, Jericho, reveals that in the Middle Bronze Age (*ca.* 2000-1550 B.C.E.) there was considerable urban culture in Palestine. The ruins of Jericho also prove that there was significant violence in the land. In the Middle Bronze Age Jericho clearly endured violent destruction, perhaps at the hands of the Hyksos as they fled Egypt (*ca.* 1550). However, together with the tell identified as the ancient city of Ai, Jericho of the Late Bronze Age (*ca.* 1550-1200) and Iron Age I (1220-1000) also provides important evidence contradicting the book of Joshua's account of the conquest of the land of Israel: neither city was fortified at the time, as is required by the account in Joshua 6–8, and the sort of destruction one might expect given the biblical record is not to be found. Not unrelated are the el-Amarna tablets from Egypt (named after the Bedouin tribe that found

Cuneiform tablets from the palace library at Tel Mardikh (ancient Ebla) in Syria documenting the diplomatic and economic activities of an extensive third-millennium empire. *(Biblical Archaeologist)*

doubt the archaeological record throws on the substantive nature of David's kingdom, another discovery, the Tel Dan Inscription, seems to offer undeniable proof of a dynasty that bore David's name, regardless of the significance of his own rule. The inscription, from the middle of the 9th century, is an Aramaean victory stela that records the victory of a king of Aram over a "king of Israel" and a "house of David" (see below). While some still question whether the phrase "house of David" is the best way to read the line on the stela, most now accept this

them). Among the tablets are letters between Pharaoh Akhenaten and his fellow "great kings" as well as correspondence with his vassal-kings. Of particular interest, correspondence with vassals in Canaan proves that nonurban rebels against the city-states of the region, called *'apiru,* were plaguing the urban dwellers. Some scholars think that these *'apiru* were related to, or even identical with, the cause of diminished urban culture in Canaan around the middle of the 2nd millennium and that they might be identified with the "Hebrews" who came into the land after a journey from Egypt, according to the biblical record.

Thanks to the discovery of ancient Ugarit at Tel Ras Shamra near the Mediterranean coastline, we also have a wealth of texts written in Ugaritic, Akkadian, Hurrian, Egyptian, and Hittite. The subject of the texts ranges from administrative and business documentation to mythological works such as the Baal-Anat Cycle and the Legend of Aqhat. The particular significance of the discoveries at Ugarit is the evidence they provide for a vibrant urban culture in Canaan long before Israel arose as a power in the Levant, as well as their testimony to the considerable commercial and intellectual trade between the two ends of the Fertile Crescent, Egypt and Mesopotamia (see the discussion of religion below).

For the period of the United Monarchy (*ca.* 1000 to 925 B.C.E.) we cite the excavations in Jerusalem that indicate the "City of David" was far less than the Bible might lead one to believe. Nonetheless, with the reign of David's son, Solomon, some of the building structures typical of royal power began to appear. In spite of the

reading and acknowledge the importance of the find for proving the historical existence of a Davidic dynasty.

A noteworthy archaeological find from the Northern Kingdom during the years of Israel's and Judah's coexistence (*ca.* 925-722) are the 33 Samaria ostraca. The ostraca — inscribed potsherds — were discovered in what appears to have been an administrative building in the Samaria acropolis. They provide the most substantial

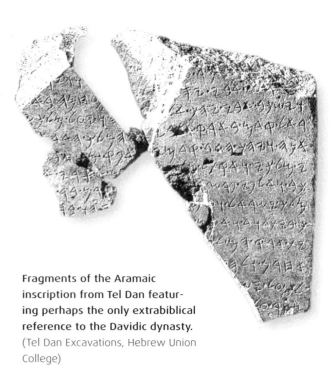

Fragments of the Aramaic inscription from Tel Dan featuring perhaps the only extrabiblical reference to the Davidic dynasty. (Tel Dan Excavations, Hebrew Union College)

From the last days of Judah's independence we have ostraca from Lachish, an important city and military installation that served in part as a buffer for Jerusalem and the heartland of the Judean kingdom. The ostraca preserve military correspondence that provides tantalizing evidence of the situation commanders and citizens alike faced as Babylon drew ever closer to conquering Judah.

Little to nothing remains of the archaeological record in Judea for the period of Babylonian domination, and the evidence for the Persian period is nearly as scant. However, in both eras evidence for Jewish life in the Diaspora is available. For instance, from Babylon we have the Murashu Documents, the records of a family real estate and personal loan business. Although the documents are later than the period of the Exile, the presence of Jewish names in records of transactions involving large sums and substantial properties confirms that life for the Judean community in exile was eventually made quite good by the Babylonian practice of generously integrating deported peoples into the

Ostracon from Samaria recording the transfer of commodities between outlying villages and the northern capital in the early 8th century B.C.E. (David Harris)

epigraphic remains of the Northern Kingdom, casting particular light on the kingdom's commercial practices.

In this same period Jerusalem, the capital of the Southern Kingdom, was at its height of power, occupying as much as 150 acres (as compared to the 20 acres covered by Lachish, Judah's second largest city). An especially noteworthy "public utility" that served Jerusalem in this period was Hezekiah's Tunnel, a channel for bringing water into the city even in the event of a siege (2 Kgs 20:20).

The Yavneh-Yam ostracon is another important discovery. It dates from the last decades of the 7th century B.C.E. and was found near Joppa, a seacoast location. It records the complaint of a farm laborer against his overseer, who had taken his cloak in payment for his apparent failure to meet his daily harvest quota. The laborer complains that he had indeed met his quota and that the supervisor, Hoshaiah, should return the cloak. There is also a hint that the laborer is appealing to the law in Exod 22:26-27 (cf. Deut 24:12-13) which requires a creditor to return the cloak of a debtor before sunset, lest the debtor suffer unnecessarily from the cold of the night.

The pool of Siloam, a reservoir within Jerusalem for water carried through Hezekiah's Tunnel from the Gihon Spring outside the city. (Phoenix Data Systems, Neal and Joel Bierling)

homeland economy. From the Persian period Aramaic papyri from a Jewish military colony on Elephantine, an island in the Nile River, reveal much about that Diaspora colony's customs and practices. In particular, two papyri demonstrate that the colonists had their own temple, in competition with the one in Jerusalem, and yet they sought somehow to coordinate their festivals, including Passover, with the calendar kept in Jerusalem.

We conclude our survey of especially noteworthy finds with the Dead Sea Scrolls (noted already in Chapter 2; see p. 14) and the associated Qumran site. The Scrolls are the literature of a community of separatist Jews who maintained a center of study in the Judean Desert from sometime near the end of the 2nd century B.C.E. through the time of the war between Rome and the Jews in 66-70 C.E. The Dead Sea Scrolls are considered by many to be one of the most significant discoveries of the 20th century. Not archaeologists, but a Bedouin combing the caves by the Dead Sea, perhaps in hopes of finding saleable antiquities, first made this discovery! The Scrolls provide tremendous insight into the devel-

opment of the biblical text, the nature of early Judaism in the Greco-Roman period, and even the Jewish roots of various elements of early Christianity. As for the Qumran site itself, most scholars accept the view that it offers abundant evidence for the life of the Essenes, the people linked to the Scrolls by Philo, Josephus, and Pliny. An ostracon recently discovered at Qumran supports this linkage between the Scrolls and the Qumran site. We know from the Community Rule, a "community charter" among the Scrolls, that members were required to share their property in common. The ostracon, found in a deposit next to a wall in the Qumran site, is apparently a member's pledge of personal property to the community.

The World of the Old Testament: Geography

It often surprises students to discover the significant role geography played in shaping the Old Testament. That the people of Israel found themselves at the crossroads of competing imperial powers (Egypt to the south, the great powers of Mesopotamia to the east, and finally Alexander and his successors from the northwest) assured them a long history of conflict and struggle, the results of which show up abundantly in the biblical record. That the land of Israel itself is geographically divided also impacted the shape of the Bible: we see, for instance, varying versions of similar stories in the Pentateuch that seem to differ mostly on the basis of geographical affiliation. Clearly, it will be important to know something of the lay of the land in the world of the Old Testament.

We begin with the land of Israel itself (see p. 28 for a discussion of the names used for the territory). The natural regions of the land are most easily understood by dividing it into four north-south oriented strips of land: the Coastal Plain, the Central Highlands, the Jordan Rift, and the Transjordan.

The Coastal Plain is the westernmost strip of land. Its northernmost portion, the Plains of Phoenicia and Acco, extends north nearly to Sidon and terminates at the foot of Mount Carmel, which plunges almost directly into the Mediterranean. Immediately below Mount Carmel are the Plains of Dor and Sharon, which are divided from one another by Wadi Zerqa. The Plain of Sharon terminates where the Valley of Aijalon reaches the Mediterranean, near the city of Joppa. Below this is the Plain of Philistia, named for the people who inhabited its environs in much of the Old Testament period. This part of the Coastal Plain is home to particularly cultivable rolling hills, which in antiquity nurtured crops of barley

Lachish ostracon containing correspondence regarding the military situation as the Babylonians advanced on Judah in 587 B.C.E. (Courtesy of the Israel Antiquities Authority)

Names for the Land of Israel

Thus far we have used several terms to refer to the region where much of the Hebrew Bible developed and where most of its narratives are set. This land situated between Syria in the north, Egypt in the south, the Mediterranean Sea on the west, and the Jordan River on the east is routinely referred to by different names with equally differing origins. The phrases "land of Israel" and "Promised Land" relate to the biblical claim that God promised the territory to the people descended from Jacob. "Palestine" derives from the Greek form of "Philistine," the name given to the sea-coast peoples encountered there. "Canaan" is also used to designate the same territory, although it is a term mostly used by historians; it is also the name given to the region in Mesopotamian, Egyptian, and Phoenician writings from as early as the 15th century B.C.E. "Levant" is yet another name for the region, which refers somewhat neutrally to the lands bordering the eastern Mediterranean. All four terms are used in this book rather interchangeably, though with some respect for the logic of usage where the context requires it. In any case, our rather random use of terms is meant in part to avoid the possibility of endorsing any of the political or nationalist views that some attach to one or the other of these names for the land.

Overview of the Qumran site settlement and the surrounding area, facing northwest. Across the face of the ravine (lower left), which leads to the Wadi Qumran, are four of the caves where the Dead Sea Scrolls were found. (Werner Braun)

and wheat. The rainfall necessary for crops diminishes farther south and all but disappears at the southern end of the plain, where it merges with the Negeb and the Coastal Plain comes to an end.

The Central Highlands are actually two elevated regions separated from one another by the Valley of Jezreel and the Plain of Megiddo. In the north are Upper and Lower Galilee and in the south are the hill countries of Ephraim and Judah. The Upper Galilee is home to the highest peaks in Palestine, topping out on Jebel Jermaq at 3962 feet (1208 meters). Sharply rising and falling mountains characterize the region, making it barely habitable or cultivable. Lower Galilee's peaks are much more squat, their descents gentler, and the valleys between them much broader. Thus the Lower Galilee supported a great deal more habitation and agriculture than the Upper Galilee. The Plain of Megiddo and the Valley of Jezreel form the natural break between the Galilee and the hill countries of Ephraim and Judah. The Kishon River runs through the Valley of Jezreel and the Plain of Acco, making the latter one of the most fertile regions in the land. At the southern edge of the valley is a gradual rise into the hill country of Ephraim, an upland of gentle hills and fertile valleys which accommodated olive and fig cultivation and wheat and barley

Elephantine Island, a Jewish military garrison and asylum for refugees after the Babylonian conquest of Jerusalem in 587 B.C.E. (Phoenix Data Systems, Neal and Joel Bierling)

farming respectively; it also served as a crossroads for trade routes running north and south and east and west. The hill country of Judah is differentiated from that of Ephraim because of its slightly different topography, and not by any natural dividing line between them. Unlike the gentle hills of Ephraim, Judah's are more rugged, featuring more rock outcroppings, which make cultivation and habitation more difficult, but defense easier. Also, because of its physical attributes the hill country of Judah was less welcoming to trade routes, and consequently less prone to attack by enemies. Also distinguishing Judah from Ephraim is the Shephelah, a foothill region to the west, set apart by a series of north-south valleys. The Shephelah was arable and extends from Aijalon in the north to Beer-sheba in the south. The Shephelah also offered a remarkably effective buffer against the Philistine threat from the Plain of Philistia. Below the Shephelah the heights at the southern end of the Judean hill country achieve nearly 3000 feet (914 meters) and then drop away suddenly to the Valley of Salt and the northern edge of the Negeb.

The third strip of land is the Jordan Rift, a deep depression situated between two geological faults. Part of it constitutes the lowest open surface on earth. At its northern end, near the Old Testament city of Dan, are the headwaters of the Jordan River. South of Dan is Lake Huleh, a swamp in biblical times, but now a dry basin. To the south of Lake Huleh was the city of Hazor. Still farther south the Jordan empties into the Sea of Galilee, more than 500 feet (152 meters) below sea level. This lake plays an important role in the New Testament, but hardly features at all in the Old Testament. Below the Sea of Galilee the Jordan descends ("Jordan" in Hebrew means

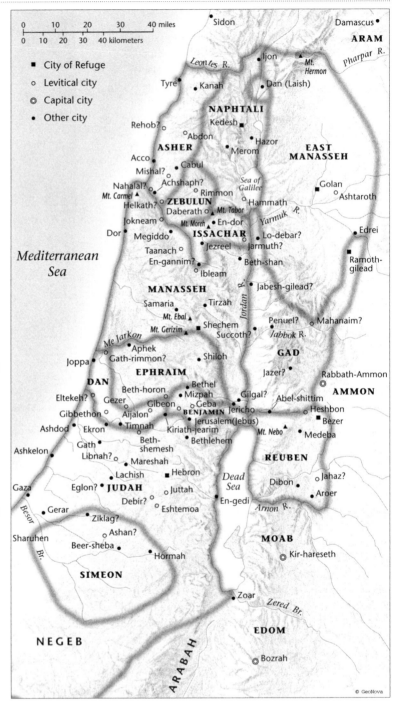

THE LAND OF ISRAEL

"to go down") on a tortuous path to about 1300 feet (396 meters) below sea level where it empties into the Dead Sea. The 65 miles between the Sea of Galilee and the Dead Sea are barely habitable and provide refuge only for Jericho near its southern end. By contrast modern archaeological excavations prove that the region surrounding the Dead Sea and the "Wilderness of Judah" to

its west were home to various desert dwellers, including John the Baptist and the people of the Dead Sea Scrolls.

The easternmost region, the Transjordan, is largely mountainous, often rising up suddenly from the Jordan Rift to stunning heights. At its northern end — just east of the Upper Galilee, Dan, and Luke Huleh — is Bashan, an area well suited to farming and cattle ranching (Deut

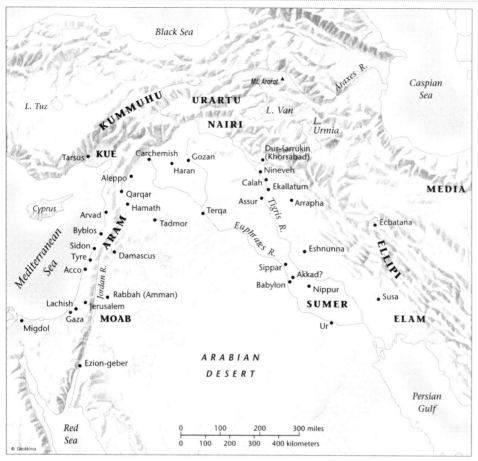

THE FERTILE CRESCENT

land of Israel will help us read the Bible more profitably, so too an understanding of the "international" context of the ancient world deepens our comprehension of the Bible.

We begin with the Fertile Crescent, that arc-shaped strip of land that has its western terminus in Egypt and its eastern tip in Mesopotamia and the outflow of the Tigris and Euphrates Rivers into the Persian Gulf. Egypt, located to the south of the land of Israel, was capable of producing a succession of imperial powers because of the Nile Delta, a narrow but extremely productive river basin. Surrounded by desert lands, the Nile literally permits riches to grow in wastelands. From those riches great civilizations and empires were able to develop. A succession of Egyptian dynasties ruled from the upper part of the Nile Delta. In keeping with their character as imperial powers, these dynasties sought to increase their territory, and the most logical direction in which Egyptian rulers sought to expand was north and east toward Mesopotamia, taking in their wake the land of Israel. However, because of its more restrained imperial policies and diminished strength over time, Egypt exercised less influence on the people of the Old Testament than did the Mesopotamia-based nations.

At the other end of the Fertile Crescent the riches deposited by the annual flooding of the Tigris and Euphrates enriched the farmlands of Mesopotamia. The resulting agricultural wealth permitted great empires to take root in the region; the Sumero-Akkadians and Babylonians were followed by the Assyrians, the Neo-Babylonians, and, at the edge of the Mesopotamian region, the Persians. Beginning with the Assyrian Empire these international powers made their presence felt in telling ways in the land of Israel. Assyria's hegemonic ambitions brought Israel, the Northern Kingdom, to its bitter end in 722 B.C.E. Then the Neo-Babylonian Empire's desire to stave off threats from foes in the

32:14; Ps 22:12; Amos 4:1). The River Yarmuk marks the boundary between Bashan and Gilead. Situated to the east of the Jordan as it runs between the Sea of Galilee and the Dead Sea, Gilead was inhabited by members of the tribe of Ephraim and was home to Jephthah and his late, lamented daughter (Judges 11). Bisecting Gilead is the River Jabbok, an important tributary to the Jordan. South of Gilead and slightly to the east was Ammon, and still further to the south, adjacent to the Dead Sea, was Moab. The latter two nation-states — according to Gen 19:30-38 descended from the illicit union between Lot and his daughters — provided their share of troubles for the people of Israel, but according to Ruth 1:1 also offered occasional refuge from famine. Still farther to the east and below the Dead Sea was Edom, home of Esau's descendants (Genesis 36) and Judah's mortal enemy (see Obadiah).

At its greatest extent, the wider context within which the Bible developed and was interpreted stretches from North Africa in the south to Asia Minor in the north, from Macedonia and Greece in the west to Media in the east. Just as comprehending the local context of the

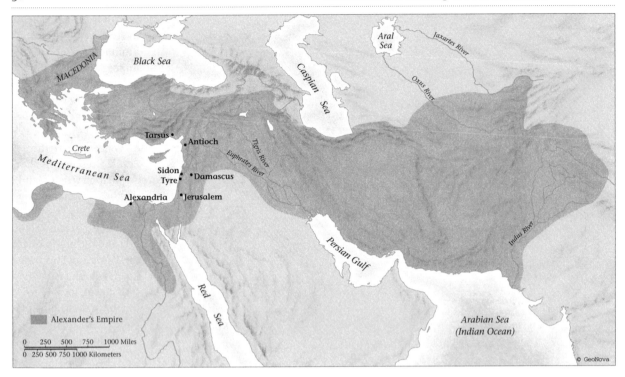

Alexander's Empire

0   250   500   750   1000 Miles

0 250 500 750 1000 Kilometers

© GeoNova

ALEXANDER'S EMPIRE

neighborhood of Judah and from Egypt led to the destruction of Judah in successive incursions and the exile of Judeans to Babylon in 597 and 586. And the imperial aspirations of Cyrus of Persia produced the defeat of the Neo-Babylonian Empire and rise of the Persian Empire in 538. Persian imperial policy that permitted subject peoples religious autonomy in their homelands brought the return of the exiles from Babylon, especially because Judah was considered an important buffer zone against encroachment on Persian imperial landholdings from the west.

Persia's greatest rival was Alexander of Macedonia. Alexander eventually succeeded in defeating the Persians (333 B.C.E.). Before his untimely death in 323 he managed to build an astounding empire that stretched from Greece and Macedonia in the west to the western edge of India in the east. Thus the geographical context in which the Bible developed expanded to include lands much farther to the west and east, as well as the peoples and cultures of those regions. Moreover, Alexander exported the culture of his neighbors, the Greeks, to all the regions he conquered. (Some call this intentional mixture of Greek culture with the cultures of the east "Hellenism.") No longer was the land of Israel caught only between the competing interests of Egyptian and Mesopotamian powers; it was now at the crossroads between imperial contenders located to its northwest, south, and northeast.

At his death Alexander's empire passed into the hands of his generals, who established separate Hellenistic kingdoms. Ptolemy established his kingdom in Egypt, North Africa, and parts of the Mediterranean and Aegean, and, for the first century or so of its existence, the land of Israel. Antigonus controlled much of Asia Minor at first, but was eventually restricted to Macedon itself. And Seleucus established his kingdom in Asia Minor, Syria, Mesopotamia, and east to the edge of Alexander's holdings; his successors were in control of all or part of the land of Israel from 198 to 141. The results of this division of Alexander's empire had important implications for Palestine and for the Bible's development: as the generals vied for sole control of Alexander's lands (323-301), the Ptolemies and the Seleucids fought over Palestine itself (301-198), and the Seleucids exercised tenuous control of Palestine (198-141), they all sought to "Hellenize" their holdings to varying degrees, and some fought ceaselessly over control of the remains of Alexander's empire. As a consequence, the land of Israel especially suffered from their antics, often finding itself at the center of their militaristic adventures. And because of their interest in exporting Greek culture to the rest of the world, cultural and religious developments in all regions, especially Palestine, were inevitably impacted.

Macedonian rule of the land of Israel came to an end with the rise of the Maccabees. The Maccabees' rebellion against the oppressive policies of the Seleucids succeeded in restoring independent Jewish rule in Judea beginning in 166 B.C.E. and continuing to 63 B.C.E.

when Rome took over. So as the composition of the Old Testament drew to a close and the stage was set for the New Testament era, there was a brief period of independent Jewish rule which eventually encompassed much of Palestine from well north of the Sea of Galilee to the southern tip of the Dead Sea and from the Mediterranean to the eastern edge of the Transjordan.

The World of the Old Testament: Religion, Culture, and Society

Our survey of the history, archaeology, and geography of the Old Testament world has prepared us to address some interrelated elements that were most influential for the development of the Hebrew Bible and early Israelite and Jewish religion: political organization, social and economic structures, religious systems, and cultural expressions.

An essential pair of factors in the rise of ancient Near Eastern societies, religions, and cultures was the mutually dependent development of political and economic organizations. A key component permitting settled communities in the ancient Middle East was the introduction of stepped and/or irrigation agriculture. With the skills necessary to cultivate land, population groups were able to settle in a single place, and with that, of course, came political organization. In the ancient Near East political organization often entailed simple and complex states governed by central figures, from tribal leaders to kings. For example, at the relatively simple end of the spectrum is Rezin, the last king of Aram-Damascus (Syria) before Assyria subsumed it into its empire in 732 B.C.E. Rezin was unquestionably a king — he is recognized as such in the biblical record (2 Kgs 15:37; 16:5) — but the extent of his power was typical of other "kings" ruling minor states caught between the great imperial powers. From as early as 739 Rezin was paying tribute to Tiglath-pileser III of Assyria to retain power over his own country, and the utter failure of his attempt with Pekah of Israel to force Judah into an alliance against Assyria further proves the fundamental limitations on his power. At the other end of the spectrum is the king who defeated Aram and executed Rezin (2 Kgs 16:9), Tiglath-pileser. This highly successful king of Assyria ruled over an empire that expanded at an alarming rate under his direction and succeeded in overwhelming virtually all of the small nation-states in Syria-Palestine. These two ancient foes provide a good sense of the range of power held by the rulers of ancient Near Eastern states.

This mutual dependence between agricultural economies and nascent political structures engendered socio-economic and religious structures as well. Usually in the ancient world agrarian economies overseen by centralized political structures engendered a relatively consistent social hierarchy. Closely affiliated with the central authority was a landed and leisure class, the "elites" of ancient agrarian societies. These elites achieved their landed status by acquiring property from laborers after loaning so much capital to the landed poor that they could no longer repay their debt and had to give up their land to their creditors. The landed elite then also became a leisure class by permitting the former landowners to remain on the farm as tenant farmers; these former landowners become renters and peasant workers who provided the labor that produced the wealth that allowed the new landowners their leisure. In other words, this process created an enormous landless laborer class that existed to provide the much smaller landowner leisure class all that they required to sustain their lifestyle. Between these two deeply polarized classes were the few who provided goods and services that were not agricultural in nature (e.g., pottery, glassware, materials for clothing). Given the narrow concentration of expendable wealth among the landed elite, it is not surprising that this tiny "middle class" saw most of its labor and goods consumed by the leisure class.

Our best examples of this particular socioeconomic structure come from 8th-century Israel and Judah, for which the biblical record and archaeological evidence provide ample evidence. The 8th-century prophets make clear that these dynamics were at work. Micah unequivocally condemned the greedy few who used their wealth and power to dispossess small landholders:

> Alas for those who devise wickedness and evil deeds on their beds! When the morning dawns, they perform it, because it is in their power. They covet fields, and seize them; houses, and take them away; they oppress householder and house, people and their inheritance. (Mic 2:1-2; see also Isa 5:8)

Similarly, Amos decries the elite's habit of gorging themselves on the occasion of various feasts with the livestock, wine, and oils of their poor laborers.

> Alas for those who lie on beds of ivory, and lounge on their couches, and eat lambs from the flock, and calves from the stall; who sing idle songs to the sound of the harp, and like David improvise on instruments of music; who drink wine from bowls, and anoint themselves with the finest oils, but are not grieved over the ruin of Joseph! Therefore they shall now be the first to go into exile, and the revelry of the loungers shall pass away. (Amos 6:4-7)

That the lambs, calves, wine, and oils came from the laborers is certain: the elite produced none of those themselves! (The archaeological record also confirms this practice; excavations have recovered the remains of ivory beds, as well as the rudimentary homes of the laborers that included stalls on the first floor for livestock.) Further, some of these feasts were "pagan" in nature, perhaps even *marzeach*s, feasts for the dead. The special difficulty with this would have been the occasion's capacity to render the celebrant impure with relation to the God of Israel, and therefore duty bound to sacrifice in God's temple. Of course, to do so required another theft of livestock from the landless laborer!

To be sure, this social divide was not to be found universally across the ancient world. It was especially unlikely to develop in the great imperial centers of the Nile Delta and the Tigris-Euphrates basin because the agricultural riches produced by those two regions spared ordinary farmers the need to take on debt simply to survive day to day. The socioeconomic structures in the imperial centers were therefore much less polarized, and it was possible for a much larger "middle class" to emerge. This made life in the heartlands of the great empires very attractive compared to eking out an existence from the land in places like Canaan. Particular evidence of this truth are the Murashu Documents from Babylon and the Elephantine Papyri from Egypt, described above. Both caches of epigraphic evidence prove that Judeans who were taken into exile or fled to Egypt found much better lives for themselves in worlds where a middle class could flourish, resource-rich worlds that provided real opportunities for even the least privileged.

In virtually all regions religious phenomena were closely intertwined with political and socioeconomic structures. From the days of the Sumero-Akkadian Empire to Alexander's short rule over the ancient world, from Egypt to Babylon rulers legitimated their control through appeal to one or more gods who were credited with creating the regnant political and socioeconomic order. Not only that, the wishes of the gods were said to be served by sustaining the prevailing order and it was thought that to neglect the gods' wishes could lead to dire results for the whole community. Further, rulers themselves came to be identified with gods or goddesses and were thus given the authority of divine beings in their task of maintaining the socioeconomic order. Especially important to such religious systems were sacrificial cults overseen by priests. The demand for animal and grain sacrifices stimulated agrarian economies, and the need for priests to oversee citizens' sacrifices established a bureaucracy that also had an important hand in promoting the mutually reinforcing political, socioeconomic, and religious structures. Of course, gods were associated not only with the socioeconomic and political structures, but also with a range of phenomena including the origins of the cosmos, the natural elements (particularly weather), war, and procreation.

Again, examples of all of these religious characteristics abound in the ancient world. Religion in Canaan, where for a long time the nation-states were not so well organized as to engender a full-blown hierarchy of deities associated with political structures, exhibited a pantheon most closely tied to natural and human phenomena. Gods were worshiped at "high places" (the name given to pagan sanctuaries by the Hebrew Bible; e.g., 2 Kgs 17:9, 11, 29, 32). These gods included most prominently Hadad, a storm-god named in the Bible with the title "Baal" (which means "lord"). The Baal Epic from Ugarit (*ANET*, 129-42) records Baal's defeat of Mot ("death") in a story that echoes the weather, agricultural, and human life cycles from beginning (rain, sowing, life) to end (drought, harvest, death) and round again. Baal also is depicted in combat with Yamm, the sea-god in Canaan, but the particular combat myth can also be compared favorably with the Mesopotamian myth of creation that entails the defeat of primeval chaos embodied by the chaotic waters of that region's annual floods. The chief deity at Ugarit and the progenitor of Baal, El, also appears in these Philistine texts, along with his consort, Asherah. The chief god, Dagon, was associated with the corn harvest and he too had a consort, Ashtart, the goddess of war.

By contrast, the pantheon in Babylon, where the state was more highly organized, was in fact multiform. The deities associated with the state were Anu, god of heaven, Enlil, a weather-god, and Ea, god of water and wisdom. The king was annually re-enthroned by the god in the *akitu* festival, which may also have commemorated creation by acting out the combat myth of creation (wherein the murder of one god by another produces the elements of creation). Another set of deities was associated with each city, and sacrifice to them was essential both for the denizens' confidence that their deity would take care of them and for the local economy, which depended on the priestly and commercial hierarchy and economic exchanges that are attendant upon a sacrificial cult. Finally, at the level of popular religion, Babylon produced a host of minor gods to whom one could make appeal regarding all manner of life exigencies.

Finally we turn to the cultural expressions of these ancient Near Eastern peoples. We begin by noting that much of the literature and art produced then had similar origins to those of today's cultural products: they responded to the political, socioeconomic, and religious dynamics of their own world, either to describe them, laud them, question them, or even reject them. To be sure, some ancient world cultural expressions emerged for purposes of entertainment, just as some do today. But even our entertainments today are shaped by the larger world that produced them, just as were those of ancients.

So what do we find? We cite first a particularly fine example from the visual arts of the relationship between cultural products and a people's wider political, socio-economic, and religious sensibilities. The Black Obelisk of Shalmaneser III bears reliefs depicting the homage of kings whom Shalmaneser defeated, among them Jehu, king of Israel. On one panel of the obelisk we see the Israelite king bowing to the ground before an upright Shalmaneser. The relief is a powerful political and religious statement: Jehu's prostration before the Assyrian emperor graphically depicts not only the subjection of one king and nation state to another, but also the deference of one "sponsoring" divinity to another. The relief also betrays an inescapable truth about Assyrian economic power, that it depended on conquest and tribute to sustain its might. The preference in Assyrian reliefs for military scenes and their outcomes (see also the Sennacherib relief from the palace in Nineveh depicting the conquest of Lachish [Isa 36:1-2]) rather than fields of waving grain and farmers working their crops testifies to an imperial policy that, though celebrated in art, was disastrous for imperial survival. One loots an enemy once, but fields can be harvested time and again!

Surely the most significant cultural artifacts of ancient Near Eastern civilizations are their literary creations. We begin our brief survey with a series of myths and epics. The first, the Atrahasis Epic of ancient Sumer, explained how the gods created humanity to do the labor of land cultivation and how humanity then developed its own civilization, which became too noisy and disruptive to the gods' rest. The gods then devised unsuccessfully to destroy all of humanity by means of plagues and other natural disasters, finally completing the job — save for Atrahasis and his family, who were warned by the god Enki — by a flood. As the epic closes, the gods agree on less devastating means of population control, including barrenness for some women, celibacy for a class of priestesses, and the natural phenomenon of maternal and infant mortality. Like other myths and epics, this one operates at several levels. It provides an explanation for the origin of humanity, for the rise of civilization, and for the floods and other natural disasters that plague humanity. It also depicts a human family, Atrahasis and his clan, as a model of human existence in the face of struggle and triumph, life and death. And it provides aspects of the religious and political order that prevailed in ancient Sumer.

Very much similar in function was the *Enuma Elish*,

Black Obelisk of Shalmaneser III, which shows the Assyrian emperor receiving tribute from the Israelite king "Jehu, son of Omri." (Oriental Institute, University of Chicago)

a Babylonian myth that explains the origin of Marduk's ascendancy among the gods. It begins with a theogony — the begetting of the deities — by the primal duo, Tiamat and Apsu. The myth continues with a complex conflict among the gods that leads to the ascendancy of one, Marduk, and to the death of Tiamat, the primal goddess. The conflict is at once an explanation of the power of natural disasters, a legitimation of Babylonian royal authority, and an explanation of how social order is established. Also from Mesopotamia is the Epic of Gilgamesh. Gilgamesh was a semi-divine figure who sought immortality after witnessing the premature death of his best friend and comrade, Enkidu (with whom he shared many adventures among the gods). His search led him to Utnapishtim, the immortal survivor of a world flood (see Atrahasis above). Utnapishtim reminds Gilgamesh that death is inevitable for human beings, but directs him to a plant that would at least provide youth to the old. But after going to great lengths to obtain the plant, Gilgamesh loses it to a serpent. And so he returns reconciled to his inevitable demise. Here too the connection between literature and the order of things in the world — from how the gods work to the nature of human existence — is obvious.

Finally, while these myths and epics of Mesopotamia *reflect* much of the socioeconomic, political and religious reality of the groups that authored them, other literature of the ancient world *critiques* its world. For instance, some Egyptian texts (*The Dispute Between a Man and His Ba* [*ANET,* 405-7]; *The Admonitions of Ipu-wer* [*ANET,* 441-44]) and a Canaanite work, the Epic of Keret (*ANET,* 142-49), along with the Sumerian work *A Man and His God* (*ANET,* 589-91) all take on, in one way or another, the widely prevailing view that the gods reward the righteous and punish the wicked. An especially clear example of this basic questioning of the logic of the relationship between the gods and humanity (and implicitly, between kings and their subjects) is the Babylonian Theodicy (*ca.* 1100 B.C.E.; *ANET,* 601-4). In this work a complainant takes up the matter of his god's injustice with a friend, and the sufferer bluntly questions the righteousness of his god (and king?).

Questions for Review and Discussion

1 Using a Bible atlas (see below for a reliable collection of maps), locate the "land of Israel," the Fertile Crescent, and major cities of the ancient world such as Jerusalem, Damascus, Babylon, and Alexandria.

2 What are the kinds of archaeological evidence described above, and what is their use relative to "biblical archaeology" and "Syro-Palestinian archaeology"?

3 How might one understand the interplay among political and economic structures, society, religion, and culture in the ancient world? Be careful to observe whether our study of the Old Testament conforms to our understanding of this interplay of factors.

Further Reading

Barton, John, ed. *The Biblical World.* 2 vols. London: Routledge, 2002.
Hallo, William W., ed. *The Context of Scripture.* 3 vols. Leiden: Brill, 1997-2003.
    A collection of ancient Near Eastern texts relating to the Old Testament.
May, Herbert G. *Oxford Bible Atlas.* 3rd ed. Oxford: Oxford University Press, 1984.
Pritchard, James B., ed. *Ancient Near Eastern Texts Relating to the Old Testament.* 3rd ed., with suppl. Princeton: Princeton University Press, 1969. *(ANET) The authoritative collection of ancient Near Eastern texts such as* Enuma Elish, *the Code of Hammurabi, and much, much more.*

Chapter 4

Interpreting the Old Testament

Getting Started

1 Read Amos 9:11-12. What approach might you take to understand the meaning of the phrases "booth of David" and "remnant of Edom"?

2 In general, Amos 9:11-15 contains some of the most hopeful rhetoric in the book; in fact, it sharply contradicts the mood of the other speeches of Amos, and introduces David for the first time. What does this suggest about this passage and how might you go about testing your hypothesis?

3 Do you know of any literary forms from your own experience with which to compare the genre of these two verses?

Preliminary Comments

In Chapter 1 we observed that the basic elements of narrative criticism would guide our approach to reading the Bible in this Introduction. That approach entails close attention to the author and readers implied by the text and to the narrative voices that move the text forward.

It also requires due consideration of what we can know about the actual author and readers.

In this chapter we introduce some of the critical methods that support the requirements of a narrative-critical approach to reading the Old Testament. Our introduction to these methods is necessarily brief, and through the course of the Introduction we will not often speak explicitly in their terms. All the same, what is presented in the Introduction derives in great part from the results these methods have achieved. For now, in this chapter we provide an overview of the methods as an important aspect of understanding how modern critics understand the Bible.

Methods Focused on Establishing the Best Text

Scholars face some basic textual hurdles in making sense of the Hebrew Bible. The fullest Hebrew manuscript tradition of the Old Testament comes from Hebrew scribes in Tiberias, called Masoretes. Their name derives from the notations they appended to their texts of the Hebrew Bible to maintain its integrity, the Masorah (see p.12 above). For critical study and modern translations scholars depend on two major Masoretic

An Illustration of Old Testament Text Criticism

In 1 Samuel 1 we read that Hannah, the mother of Samuel, was at first barren and even suffered the indignity of her husband, Elkanah, taking a rival wife to make up for her shortcoming. In response she prayed to God in the sanctuary at Shiloh during the family's annual pilgrimage that she be given a child whom she would dedicate to service in that sanctuary. God heard her prayer, and she conceived and bore a son, Samuel. Thus when the time for the annual pilgrimage came around again, Elkanah urged her to fulfill her vow. Following are the verses from the NRSV of 1 Samuel 1 that relate the ensuing exchange between Hannah and Elkanah, and the events that followed their conversation.

The Text: 1 Samuel 1:21-25

²¹The man Elkanah and all his household went up to offer to the LORD the yearly sacrifice, and to pay his vow. ²²But Hannah did not go up, for she said to her husband, "As soon as the child is weaned, I will bring him, that he may appear in the presence of the LORD, and remain there forever; I will offer him as a nazirite for all time." ²³Her husband Elkanah said to her, "Do what seems best to you, wait until you have weaned him; only — may the LORD establish his word." So the woman remained and nursed her son, until she weaned him. ²⁴When she had weaned him, she took him up with her, along with a three-year-old bull, an ephah of flour, and a skin of wine. She brought him to the house of the LORD at Shiloh; and the child was young. ²⁵Then they slaughtered the bull, and they brought the child to Eli.

A Discussion of the Variants

1:22. The sentence, *I will offer him as a nazirite for all time,* is not attested in any Hebrew or Greek manuscripts, but the line is present in a fragmentary manuscript of the Samuel books from Qumran (4QSamᵃ [Cave 4 at Qumran, the "a," or first, manuscript of Samuel from cave 4]). Josephus, a Jewish historian who rewrote most of the Hebrew Scriptures for his 1st-century C.E. Roman audience, provides a similar phrase in retelling Samuel's birth narrative. This combination of very early witnesses — the scroll dates from the first half of the 1st century B.C.E., and Josephus wrote in the 1st century C.E. — convinced text critics responsible for the NRSV that the sentence, whether a gloss by a later scribe or not, merits inclusion in a modern translation.

1:23. Elkanah's admonition upon departing for Shiloh and leaving Hannah and Samuel behind, *"may the LORD establish his word,"* appears in the Masoretic Text of Samuel, but is contradicted by a Greek manuscript that agrees with the Hebrew of 4QSamᵃ. The latter two give the equivalent of *"may the LORD establish what comes from your mouth."* Within the story of Samuel's birth alone it is clear that the Qumran text and the Greek translation provide the least difficult reading; after all, Hannah is the one who made a vow to turn Samuel over for service at Shiloh. But on the principle of *lectio difficilior* the NRSV translation committee presented the Masoretic Text! (Note, though, that at least one scholar has argued that the Masoretic Text is the *less* difficult of the two inasmuch as Elkanah is referring to *God's promise* in Deut 18:15 to raise up a prophet like Moses!)

1:24. The phrase *"three-year-old bull"* in v. 24 appears in the Qumran manuscript, Greek translations, and a Syriac "daughter translation" (a translation that derives not from the Hebrew text, but a first translation, in this case Aramaic). However, the Masoretic Text reads *"three bulls,"* providing what appears to be the more difficult reading. So why not follow the Masoretic Text according to the rule observed in 1:23? Apparently, the comment following in 1:25 that *"then they slaughtered the bull"* permitted text critics to ignore the rule of *lectio difficilior* in favor of the view that the Masoretic Text is corrupt.

This brief example reveals how eclectic modern translations can be. Just in the scope of 1 Sam 1:22-24 the NRSV relies on a Qumran manuscript (with the support of Josephus), the Masoretic Text, and a Greek text!

manuscripts, the Aleppo Codex and the Leningrad Codex, dated to 915 and 1009 C.E., respectively. But because scribes transmitted the text of the Old Testament manually for generations before the Masoretes began their efforts, mistakes and intentional changes naturally crept in over the centuries. Additionally, the text of the Old Testament also comes down to us in the form of ancient translations, many of which depended on Hebrew texts quite unlike the Masoretic tradition. (The most important translations are in Greek, Aramaic, and Latin.) Together these different Hebrew manuscripts and translations present scholars with equally varying options for reading and translating into modern languages the text of the Old Testament.

The question naturally arises: Which variant forms of the text should we trust and translate for today's readers? The answer comes from **text criticism,** the critical method that sets out to ascertain the "best" text of the Old Testament. By "best text" most scholars mean the most original, the form closest to the original author's composition. Text criticism sets out to achieve this objective by comparing the variants among textual witnesses and using some basic rules of thumb to judge among those variants. For example, the premise that scribes clarify difficulties rather than add them to the texts that they copy engenders the rule of *lectio difficilior,* "the more difficult reading." This rule holds that the more difficult of two variants is usually the older one. When applied repeatedly in the process of preparing a critical edition or a modern translation of the Hebrew Bible, this rule and others produce texts that are eclectic, that is, composites of the readings available in a variety of different Hebrew manuscripts and translations. On page 36 we provide an example of such a text from the New Revised Standard Version.

Of course, not all text critics are persuaded that comparing variants will draw us that much closer to an "original" text, and some even doubt that we may speak of an original text. Still others even acknowledge in the existence of the different textual families evidence that from the beginning there were variant editions of the biblical books.

"Grammatical" Criticism

Few in biblical studies these days would assign much meaning to the phrase **"grammatical criticism."** We use it, nonetheless, because it is a useful way to name what all readers of the Bible must do, whether they are professional scholars or lay readers: everyone has to make sense of the language, grammar, and syntax of the text and understand something of its structure. This is the simple process of understanding the biblical books *as literature.*

For the most part, the vocabulary of the Hebrew Bible is clear to scholars. However, some books possess more than their share of peculiar terms, the most challenging of which are called *hapax legomena,* words that occur only once and thus have no comparisons by means of which their meaning can be determined. The book of Job, for example, contains such a great number of these and other difficult-to-translate terms that modern translations can often differ a great deal, depending on the varying judgments of translators.

Hapax legomena are not the only words that require special consideration. Other repeated terms that refer to broad concepts must be treated with special care. For instance, the Hebrew word we translate as "covenant," *berit,* occurs in Gen 15:18, where God's unilateral promise is the sole term of the covenant God makes with Abraham. The same word also appears throughout Deuteronomy to name an agreement between God and the people that is explicitly bilateral. The same word appears in Hosea, but in reference to the marriage agreement between him and Gomer. Clearly, understanding the shifting meaning of this central word and concept in the Old Testament is integral to understanding the text as a whole.

Another aspect of grammatical analysis is determining the organization of a text: the flow of a narrative, the structure of a homily, the verses of a hymn, etc. This is not usually a terribly difficult task, but it is one of the most important. Indeed, there is a reason that scholars squabble over the precise outlines of books like Ecclesiastes, which is difficult to map out clearly, or Deuteronomy, which provides hints enough to engender differing, equally valid proposals. The reason this is such a disputed topic, of course, is the way decisions about structure shape our reading experience of a text.

Finally, there is the simple matter of establishing the grammar and syntax of the text. It is not only necessary to define words and establish structures; it is also incumbent on thoughtful readers to understand how the grammar and syntax of a text work, for these too contribute significantly to a text's meaning. This is all the more necessary when dealing with texts written in a language foreign to us, and in an ancient form of that language. Add to that the absence of any sort of consistent and complete vowel and punctuation system in the text of the Hebrew Bible until the Masoretes began their work — a fact that permits considerable variation along these lines between the earlier Greek translations and the Masoretic Text — and the question of syntax especially requires careful consideration.

Methods Focused on the History of the Text

Other methods of Old Testament study hone in on the history of the text. A text's history can include many things: its date of composition, its author's general identity and location, its intended audience, the oral and written sources it includes, the history of editorial changes it underwent, its precise form upon completion, its inclusion among other biblical books, and even its career among later interpreters. Note how many of these are related in different ways to our overarching concern to treat texts with attention to their implied and actual authors, their actual and implied readers, and the narrative voices in them.

Before explaining some of the methods used to get at this long list of issues, we should also note that some scholars are more interested in the history *in* the text than the history *of* the text. These are historians who seek to reconstruct the history narrated in parts of the Bible or the periods to which we assign parts of the Bible. For example, 1 and 2 Kings often provide our only written record of events in the history of Israel and

Judah, and Ezekiel, though in general not a (historical) narrative at all, sheds a sliver of light on the otherwise quite poorly understood lives of the Judean exiles in Babylon. Significantly, historians who wish to use the Old Testament for this purpose are quite dependent on the work of scholars who attend to the issues outlined in the previous paragraph. Clearly, to use 1 and 2 Kings reliably to reconstruct the history of Israel and Judah, one must first submit the biblical books to critical assessment to determine what in their narrative may be trusted as an account of what actually happened and what of the text reflects the interpretive views of much later thinkers and writers, or of even later redactors. In this Introduction we set aside, for the most part, concern for the history *in* the text to focus on the prior issue, the history *of* the text. We turn now to a quick survey of the basic methods associated with this scholarly preoccupation.

Source Criticism

Chapter 5 deals in detail with this method, so we provide now only a brief statement of its basic form and uses.

Readers of the Pentateuch, Genesis through Deuteronomy, have long observed the presence of double versions of narratives, contradictions of fact, and variations in vocabulary and style. We will examine examples of these variations in Chapter 5. For now we only observe that they prompted readers to suspect that these books were composed not of one, but several "sources." To test that suspicion scholars developed **source criticism**, a method that catalogues the variations in style, repetitions, and contradictions to delineate the contours of distinct sources within the Pentateuch. As we shall see, the dominant hypothesis that emerged from the first generation of source critics is the Documentary Hypothesis, which assigns to the Pentateuch four separate sources and posits four corresponding authors or groups of authors.

Form Criticism

Source criticism was borne not so much from Bible readers' suspicions about sources; such inklings had been on their minds since antiquity. Rather, it was part of their response to the Enlightenment's challenge to Jewish and Christian faith that both religions' canonical Scriptures were unreliable, fanciful, composite works. Enlightenment thinkers charged that the Bible's key narratives, from Genesis to the Gospels, were merely the fanciful creations of well-meaning but pre-rational human beings; with the rise of reason such literature was outmoded and its authority no longer tenable. Source criticism was a first attempt to respond to this perceived attack on faith; it was intended to get back to the origins

of the text, to show that the authors were not irrational, deluded tale-weavers, but rather historiographers and thinkers with rational pedigrees as good as any Enlightenment philosopher. However, source criticism did not accomplish this task; it only proved that the tale-weavers were greater in number than previously thought!

In part, **form criticism** arose as a response to source criticism's "failure" to answer the Enlightenment challenge. A new suspicion about the text, that the sources of the Pentateuch were composed from numerous smaller portions of text that were in turn the written manifestations of oral forms at home in specific human contexts, offered hope to those who wanted to get back to the origins of the Bible. Form criticism developed in large part to address this possibility. As we shall see in later chapters, it sets out to classify the oral genres that survive in written form in the Old Testament and then to assign each oral genre to a specific human context (*Sitz im Leben,* "setting in life," is the now commonplace term early German form critics assigned to the human context). Although rooted in study of the Pentateuch, this method soon became significant in the critical study of the history of nearly all kinds of Old Testament texts.

Redaction Criticism

Just as source criticism failed to live up to the hopes of those who sought chiefly to answer the Enlightenment challenge to the Bible's credibility, form criticism also fell short. Nonetheless, source and form criticism had uncovered far more interesting questions about the text's history than the issue of its "authenticity." As a result, additional methods developed less out of the interest to respond to the Enlightenment, and more as a result of deepening fascination with the history and development of the Bible in its own right.

One such critical method is **redaction criticism.** Traditionally associated with the study of the Synoptic Gospels, redaction criticism's interest in clarifying the interests and intentions of the writers who drew sources and forms together to create the text we have now has served study of the Old Testament too. This method interprets the results produced by source and form critics from the perspective of the human author who finally produced the texts now available in the Hebrew Bible. For instance, many recognize traces of several stages of development in the book of Jeremiah. The redaction critic considers how one or more "editor-authors" assembled the various elements that predated the final form of Jeremiah to create the book as a whole. As is the case in studying the Synoptic Gospels, redaction critics are particularly interested in discerning material unique to these late editor-authors, and in determining as precisely as possible how they adjusted the sources and forms they inherited from their predecessors.

Tradition Criticism

Redaction critics, along with source and form critics, also noticed that very different books of the Old Testament share certain traditions in common (e.g., traditions about the Exodus from Egypt can be found in many places outside the book of Exodus, including Isaiah 40–55, the Psalms, and the Wisdom of Solomon). **Tradition criticism** developed as a means of tracing these traditions from their first appearance through their various reappearances in various books of the Old Testament.

The approach of the tradition critic is as elementary as it seems: he or she isolates occurrences of repeated traditions in the Old Testament and compares them to see how the basic tradition is used and reused time and again by ancient authors and thinkers. Notice, though, that tracing the development of a tradition requires answering a question about texts that we have yet to address in our survey: when — and concomitantly, where, by whom, and for whom — were the books of the Bible written? Without some rudimentary judgments on these issues, it is impossible for the tradition critic to address fully the ways in which traditions were handed on and redeveloped by biblical authors.

Historical Criticism

The rather nebulous term **"historical criticism"** covers for many observers the endeavor entailed in answering the set of questions with which we concluded the preceding paragraph. Historical critics who take up these questions work according to some very simple procedures.

First, historical critics are responsible to gather evidence pertinent to the issue at hand. For instance, if their concern is the date of a text, scholars collect comparative literary evidence, the date of which *is known,* as well as any other nonliterary evidence that may be of assistance. For example, various Assyrian royal records can be dated definitively and provide good comparative evidence for assessing some of the narratives in Kings about Israel and Judah. And, as we shall see in Chapter 13, the archaeological evidence regarding Jericho and Ai (two cities conquered by the people of Israel according to Joshua 6–8) provide significant evidence for considering the date of the book of Joshua relative to the events it narrates.

Second, historical critics submit their evidence to critical scrutiny. To use the preceding example, they understand that Assyrian records that allude to events otherwise mentioned in Kings are *imperial* documents pertaining to a relatively *insignificant subject state.* Conversely, Kings records events from the perspective of the *insignificant subject state* that hardly viewed itself in that way! Further, historians understand that the results of source, form, redaction, and tradition critics must be taken into account in determining the date of a text, its likely author, or its intended audience. Citing the example of Kings once more, application of those methods to studying Kings proves that the books were not completed until the period of the Exile, that they include a variety of source materials (some of which are explicitly mentioned by the author), and that their authors utilized a wealth of genres and traditions to compose them. These simple observations play a key role in answering the questions of Kings' date, authorship, and audience.

Third, historical critics formulate and articulate a hypothesis on the basis of their critical assessment of the evidence they have gathered. Returning yet again to Kings, most view the present form of the two books to have taken shape in the Exile and to be the product of the same author or authors who produced all of Deuteronomy to 2 Kings in its present form. As for the intended audience, most agree that they were Judeans either in exile or still in Judah during the exilic period who, in any case, demanded an explanation for the fate that befell their nation.

Finally, historical critics submit their hypotheses to criticism from other historical critics and from the source, form, redaction, and tradition critics upon whose work they draw. From this critique usually come a variety of competing hypotheses. To take a particularly stark example, some scholars reject the explanation of Kings given above (and more fully in Chapters 12 and 17) and argue instead that the two books were composed in the Hellenistic period and that they record few or no real historical events at all!

More Recent Methodological Developments

The preceding observation regarding the disagreement over the actual date of Kings typifies the state of critical analysis of the Old Testament: it has produced far less consensus than it has expanded the debate. This failure to achieve consensus using the traditional historical-critical methods outlined above has engendered a relatively recent blossoming of new approaches and methods. Some, represented here by social-science criticism, seem intended to make up for the failure of the traditional methods to achieve certainty regarding the history of the biblical text. Others despair of reaching any degree of certainty regarding the history of the text and resolve to treat instead the text as it is received without regard for the story of its growth and composition; these are characterized as "literary-critical" in nature.

And still others see in the traditional methods and the rise of new approaches like social-scientific criticism and literary-critical analysis a continuing avoidance of the real issue of unacknowledged bias in interpretation; these scholars urge critics to acknowledge and *privilege* their particular subjective perspectives instead of trying uselessly to overcome them.

Social-scientific criticism grows out of the judgment that traditional methods fail to achieve consensus because they *lack sufficient objectivity.* More precisely, this approach views the older methods as imposing anachronistic assumptions on our attempts to understand biblical texts and the worlds that engendered them. Practitioners of this approach adopt models, methods, and paradigms from the social sciences and cultural anthropology that they consider capable of helping them to overcome their own cultural and historical biases. Using such concepts as **honor-shame** and **patron-client** relationships to analyze the ancient text and its world, these critics claim to achieve at least some of the certainty about this history of the text that traditional methods have not reached.

Literary-critical approaches, on the other hand, have taken root especially among those who feel the failure thus far to reach consensus only proves that we will never achieve that goal. They contend that a more fruitful approach to study of the biblical text is one that deals in the certainty of the text as we know it, rather than the mystery of the text's life before it attained its present shape. The collection of criticisms that have sprung up around this general insight include certain brands of the **narrative criticism** that informs our own treatment of the text in this Introduction, as well as numerous other approaches such as **structural criticism** and **reader-response criticism**. The hallmark that unites all of these is their focus on the text and its reception in the present context.

Advocacy exegesis and **ideological criticism** are characterized by open acknowledgement of bias in interpretation. Advocacy exegesis rests on the premise that biblical interpretation *should not be value free,* but should instead read the text to *support the causes of underprivileged groups.* What sets ideological criticism apart from advocacy exegesis is its slightly more aloof posture regarding the impact of interpretation. Ideological critics focus less on making their interpretation "work" than on making clear that all interpretive efforts are ideological, expressions of the horizons of interpreters.

All of these alternative approaches have made their mark on the study of the Old Testament. We will have occasion to see the impact some of them have made on our appreciation of the Bible in the chapters that follow.

Theological Interpretation and the Variety of Approaches

Our survey of modern critical approaches to the Old Testament must conclude with a very brief explanation of another way to read the text, the one that has been around the longest, and that also governs a large part of our discussion of the Old and New Testaments in this Introduction: theological interpretation.

There was a time when theological interpretation was done to the exclusion of the other critical methods surveyed here. For many centuries that was necessary, inasmuch as the critical methods did not yet exist. And even after the rise of the critical methods some have continued to hold theological interpretation of the Bible apart from the impact of any modern critical approaches. In any case, theological interpretation focuses on eliciting from the text its own speech about the nature of God and about the nature of being human in relationship to God. Aquinas, Augustine, Luther, Calvin, Barth, Bultmann — these and many others were to varying degrees and at different times in their careers exclusively theological interpreters of this sort. But Bultmann especially, along with other major figures in 20th-century biblical scholarship such as Gerhard von Rad and more recently Brevard Childs, consciously blended the critical enterprise with concern for the fundamental theological thrust of the Bible. They learned from critical scholarship so as to deepen and broaden the Bible's voice as it speaks of God. In a very modest way the rest of this book aims chapter after chapter to accomplish something of the same. By rehearsing the text and touching on the critical issues that it has evoked in scholarly readers we hope to have enriched our discussion of the theological issues of the Old (and New) Testament(s), to have broadened and deepened the Bible's word about God for our readers.

Questions for Review and Discussion

1 What prompted the development of textual criticism as a method for studying the Old Testament? Likewise, what triggered critics' interest in sources and forms? How did an interest in "getting back to beginnings" and basic intuitions about the text engender these three methods?

2 How did redaction and tradition criticism develop? Were their origins the same as those of text, source, and form criticism?

3 How might you describe the relationship between the traditional historical-critical methods and the

alternative methods classified under the terms "social-scientific criticism," "literary criticism," and "advocacy exegesis" or "ideological criticism"?

Further Reading

Barton, John. *Reading the Old Testament: Method in Biblical Study.* Rev. ed. Louisville: Westminster John Knox, 1996.

Harrisville, Roy A., and Walter Sundberg. *The Bible in Modern Culture: Baruch Spinoza to Brevard Childs.* 2nd ed. Grand Rapids: Wm. B. Eerdmans, 2002.

Hayes, John H., and Carl Holladay. *Biblical Exegesis: A Beginner's Handbook.* Rev. ed. Atlanta: John Knox, 1987.

The Pentateuch

Introduction to the Pentateuch

This chapter serves to introduce the contents of the Pentateuch and the standard and alternative approaches to understanding its compositional history. Along the way we provide a fuller explanation of source criticism than was provided in Chapter 4, and we have occasion to see how form and tradition criticism have also functioned in the story of the Pentateuch. We leave discussion of the theological themes of the Pentateuch to our discussions of the individual books.

A Summary of the Pentateuch

The Pentateuch, the first five books of the Old Testament (also called the Torah among Jews), moves from an account of creation to the arrival of the people on the Plains of Moab under Moses' leadership. It narrates the story of God's relationship with God's people from before the time they existed until the moments before they came into possession of the land God promised them.

Genesis 1–11 is often called the "Primeval History" because it tells stories of origins: the creation of the world (told twice in Genesis 1–2), the source of alienation between the God of Israel and the human race (ch. 3), the beginning of violence in the world (ch. 4), the power of human corruption to bring God's wrath (chs.

6–9), and the beginning of many languages (11:1-9). Interspersed among these narratives are some genealogies (ch. 5; 11:10-32) and a "Table of Nations" (ch. 10).

Genesis 12–50, dubbed the "Ancestral Narrative," tells the tale of Israel's ancestors, Abraham and Sarah, Isaac and Rebekah, Jacob and Leah and Rachel, and Jacob's 12 sons. There are two large story cycles, one for Abraham and Sarah (12:1–25:11) and another for Jacob and Leah and Rachel (25:19–35:29); these are linked and concluded by two genealogies (25:12-18; 36), and a handful of stories about Isaac are inserted into them (see especially chs. 21; 22; 26). In Genesis 12–36 the action moves from "Ur of the Chaldees" (ch. 12) to the land of Canaan (ch. 35) with excursions into neighboring lands along the way (e.g., Egypt in ch. 12). Then Genesis 37–50 completes the story of the ancestors with a novella about Joseph, who is sold into slavery in Egypt by his brothers and whose success in the foreign land ensures his family's survival. Thus Genesis ends with the ancestors of Israel comfortably settled in the land of Egypt.

Exodus 1–18 picks up the story of the people of Israel many years later. Their descendants had been enslaved by the rulers of Egypt, but were so numerous as to provoke Pharaoh's concern that they would overwhelm Egypt entirely. Thus Pharaoh attempted to limit the Hebrews' growth in numbers and made the conditions

The accounts of Israel's ancestors suggest a setting much like contemporary Bedouin society, characterized by the interaction of nomadic peoples, populations settled in towns and villages, and seasonal migrants. (Phoenix Data Systems, Neal and Joel Bierling)

of their enslavement more severe (ch. 1). From these actions came Moses' rise to prominence and his eventual leadership in delivering the people from their Egyptian bondage (chs. 2–15). After a number of trials in the wilderness Moses and the people arrived at Mount Sinai (chs. 16–18).

Exodus 19–Numbers 10 (including all of Leviticus) reports how at Sinai (also called Horeb) God gave to Moses and the people the law that would govern them in their wilderness wanderings and their life in the land. Exodus 19–24 relates a theophany (an appearance of God; ch. 19; 20:18-21), the Ten Commandments (20:1-17), a law code (commonly referred to as the "Covenant Code"; 20:22-23:33), and a ceremony to ratify a covenant between God and the people (ch. 24). Exodus 25–31 and 35–40 report God's instructions to Moses for building a mobile sanctuary (the "tent of meeting") and the carrying out of those instructions. Placed between the instructions and their execution is the account of the people's worship of a golden calf and the consequences that befell them for this apostasy (Exodus 32–34). Leviticus 1–7 is God's instruction to the people regarding proper sacrifice. Leviticus 8–10 dictates the selection and ordination of priests to serve in the sanctuary and relates a cautionary tale of priestly apostasy and its consequences. Leviticus 11–15 provides purity regulations pertaining to kinds of animals acceptable for consumption (ch. 11) and the impurities resulting from childbirth (ch. 12), skin disease (chs. 13–14) and genital discharges (ch. 15). Leviticus 16 stipulates observances for the Day of Atonement. Leviticus 17–26 offers a potpourri of legal stipulations that together constitute the "Holiness Code." Leviticus 27, an appendix to the book of Leviticus, details the cost of redeeming vows and offerings owed to God. Finally, Numbers 1–10 reports the census of the tribes of Israel

to order them for their march from Mount Sinai to the Promised Land, as well as other measures made preparatory for the people's departure from Sinai.

Numbers 11–36 relates the people's wandering in the wilderness after they left Mount Sinai and before they arrived at the edge of the Promised Land on the Plains of Moab. Numbers 11–21 reports their travel to Kadesh and an unsuccessful attack on Canaan in the south. Numbers 22–36 records their journey through the Transjordan to prepare for an attack from the east. Along the way from Sinai to Kadesh and from Kadesh to the Plains of Moab Numbers also recounts the people's frequent uprisings against God and Moses (e.g., chs. 11, 16, 25), as well as the provision of some additional laws (e.g., chs. 15 and 19).

Deuteronomy begins as the people finally arrive at the edge of the Promised Land. In a first address to the people before they enter the land Moses recites their experience from the time they left Egypt to their arrival on the Plains of Moab (chs. 1–4). In a second address Moses expounds the meaning of life in God's sight in the land they were about to occupy (chs. 5–11). At the heart of Deuteronomy is the "Deuteronomic Law Code" (chs. 12–26). Deuteronomy 27–28 reports the curses and blessings that God promised the people if they obeyed the law or broke it. Deuteronomy 29–30 concludes Moses' speeches to the people before entering the land with Moses' further exhortation that the people keep the law and with God's assurance that, if they fail and are punished, God will nonetheless renew the covenant with them. Deuteronomy 31–34 reports the closing events of Moses' life, his blessings for the tribes, and his death before entering the Promised Land.

Two Accounts of Loading the Ark

Genesis 6:18-22	Genesis 7:1-5

Genesis 6:18-22

[18]"But I will establish my covenant with you; and you shall come into the ark, you, your sons, your wife, and your sons' wives with you.

[19]And of every living thing, of all flesh, you shall bring two of every kind into the ark, to keep them alive with you; they shall be male and female.

[20]Of the birds according to their kinds, and of the animals according to their kinds, of every creeping thing of the ground according to its kind, two of every kind shall come in to you, to keep them alive.

[21]Also take with you every kind of food that is eaten, and store it up; and it shall serve as food for you and for them."

[22]Noah did this; he did all that God commanded him.

Genesis 7:1-5

[1]Then the LORD said to Noah, "Go into the ark, you and all your household, for I have seen that you alone are righteous before me in this generation.

[2]Take with you seven pairs of all clean animals, the male and its mate; and a pair of the animals that are not clean, the male and its mate;

[3]and seven pairs of the birds of the air also, male and female, to keep their kind alive on the face of all the earth.

[4]For in seven days I will send rain on the earth for forty days and forty nights; and every living thing that I have made I will blot out from the face of the ground."

[5]And Noah did all that the LORD had commanded him.

Who Wrote the Pentateuch?

Relying in part on references in the Hebrew Scriptures (e.g., Exod 17:14; Deut 4:44; 31:24; Neh 8:1), Jews (Babylonian Talmud, *Baba Bathra* 14b) and Christians (Matt 8:4; Mark 1:44; Luke 5:14; John 7:19) have long viewed Moses as the Pentateuch's author. Yet for nearly as long readers have nonetheless puzzled over its authorship, and for good reason. Even the preceding summary of the Pentateuch's contents might convey something of its vast variety in terms of genre: indeed, it entails creation narratives, genealogies, travel itineraries, sermons, law codes, etiologies, cultic legends, novellas, and more. And as we begin to study the Pentateuch's contents more closely, its occasionally repetitive and self-conflicting testimony will also become clear. For instance, the name for God is sometimes "God" (*Elohim* in Hebrew) and other times "Lord" (*Yahweh* in Hebrew); two creation accounts differ substantially (Genesis 1–2); God commands Noah to load the ark twice, and in two different ways (Gen 6:18-22; 7:1-5); Abraham gives Sarah away to a foreign king twice (Genesis 12; 20), and Isaac repeats the act with Rebekah (Genesis 26); and the laws regarding sacrifice in Exodus 20, Deuteronomy 12, and Leviticus 17 are not easily reconciled. Likewise, careful readers quickly recognize that vocabulary and style differ from portion to portion in the Pentateuch. For instance the pair of passages on loading the ark provide good evidence in this regard. Compare especially the parallel command and execution sayings in 6:18 and 7:1 and 6:22 and 7:5, as well as the different contents of the ark in 6:19-21 and 7:2-3. It is hard to miss the contradictions and repetitions.

Taken together, these literary characteristics make it difficult to accept the traditional view that Moses was the author of the Pentateuch, a notion already placed in question by the fact that Deuteronomy 34 itself narrates Moses' death, and by various anachronisms in the Pentateuchal account, comments Moses could not have made (e.g., "until this day" [Deut 3:14], "at that time" [Gen 13:7], or "These are the kings . . . of Edom, before any king reigned over the Israelites" [Gen 36:31]).

Source Criticism

Observing these literary characteristics provided scholars in the 18th and 19th centuries with the fundamentals of a method for sorting out the different sources — and thus, different authors — of the Pentateuch. We call this method source or literary criticism (for more on the method, see Chapter 4). By cataloguing the variations in style and vocabulary (especially the usage of the different divine names, *Elohim* and *Yahweh*), the double traditions, and the contradictory narratives, scholars developed profiles of authors, sources, or portions of the Pentateuch.

From the use of this very simple critical method came three competing explanations for the diversity in the Pentateuch. One, labeled the Fragment Hypothesis, held that the Pentateuch was composed of large tradition units (e.g., the Primeval History, the Ancestral Narrative, the Sinai Pericope) that developed separately but were brought together by one or more "redactor-authors." A rudimentary form of tradition criticism was important in the formulation of this hypothesis, as was form criticism in helping to identify genres that characterized "tradition units."

A second explanation, the Supplementary Hypothesis, suggested that the Pentateuch grew by additions to an original narrative whole. Source criticism mixed with a sort of redaction criticism played an important part in the development of this hypothesis, as the focus was on determining the characteristics of particular authors who did not work to compose distinct works so much as editorial additions to existing works.

The third explanation, the Documentary Hypothesis, had its own long history of development that began with the work of an 18th-century Scottish Roman Catholic priest and culminated with the publication of a series of essays by Julius Wellhausen in 1876-77 and his disciples' elaboration of his formulation of the hypothesis. Because this hypothesis dominated scholarly imagination throughout much of the 20th century it demands further explanation.

The Documentary Hypothesis

Wellhausen and his intellectual heirs produced the "Documentary Hypothesis." The hypothesis identifies four separate documents that were merged with one another to create the Pentateuch. Each of the four is assigned to a different period in Israelite history.

The first document is called the **Yahwist Source** (for the name its author gives to God, *Yahweh*), or simply **"J"** (because German scholars devised the title and *Yahweh* is spelled in German with a "J," *Jahweh*). J is also characterized by, among other things, an anthropomorphic view of God, naming the mountain where Moses received the law Mount Sinai, and a dramatic writing style. J encompasses most of the Primeval History, the Ancestral Saga, the escape from Egypt and travel to Sinai, God's appearance to Moses at Sinai and the revelation of a law code, and some of the narratives of wilderness wandering in Numbers. A few scholars think J extends into Joshua, Judges, and Samuel, but the majority holds to the more conservative view that J is found only in Genesis, Exodus, and Numbers.

As for its origin, J's focus on locales in the south (especially places associated with David's kingdom; e.g., the land promised to Abraham in Gen 15:18-21 reflects the shape of David's kingdom) suggests to some a Judean derivation. This and other indicators such as the emphasis on the Davidic line's ancestor, Judah, have prompted scholars to date J to the reign of David or Solomon, and to view it as an effort to legitimate and/or celebrate the Davidic monarchy and its hegemony over Israel.

The second document is called the **Elohist Source** (for the name its author gives to God, *Elohim*), or simply **"E."** In contrast to J, E is characterized by, among other things, an abstract view of God, naming the mountain where Moses received the law Mount Horeb, and the use of the phrase "fear of God" (e.g., Gen 20:11). E begins with an Ancestral Saga thought to parallel that of J and continues with roughly parallel accounts of the remainder of what J also records.

As for its origin, E's habit of locating ancestral stories in places situated in the north, especially Ephraim, sug- gests to some a derivation from the Northern Kingdom. Since the Northern Kingdom came into existence in 921 B.C.E., the Documentary Hypothesis holds that E must have been composed some time after that date, perhaps in the second half of the 9th century.

The Documentary Hypothesis next theorizes that these two competing histories were woven together by a redactor, or editor, after the fall of the Northern Kingdom in 721 B.C.E. The intent was to preserve both sagas, although the J account dominates. The desire to safeguard both accounts resulted in some of the most prominent double traditions in the Pentateuch (see Gen 12:10-20; 20:1-18; but see also 26:1-11).

The third document is called **"D"** after its major content, the book of Deuteronomy. Some scholars also think D redactors added **Deuteronomic** fragments to the combined JE saga to bring it into line with their own theological perspective. Deuteronomy is characterized by its law code (Deuteronomy 12–26), at the beginning of which is the requirement that Israel worship one God in the one place God chooses (which in the course of the Deuteronomistic History [see Chapter 12] proves to be Zion). Success in observing that central law assures God's blessing for Israel; failure to keep it leads to Israel's expulsion from the land. In addition to the law code, the book of Deuteronomy provides Moses' sermonic introduction and conclusion to the law, the curses and blessings attached to its keeping or rejection, and an account of the end of Moses' life and the commissioning of Joshua to succeed him.

Although it is possible that Deuteronomy was composed in the Northern Kingdom and brought to the south by refugees after the Assyrian conquest of Israel, what is nearly certain is that it came into use in the south only when Josiah's temple repair led to its "discovery" in 621 B.C.E. The discovery and the reforms Josiah instituted in light of its central law are narrated in 2 Kings 22–23. The elements of that reform match key elements of the Deuteronomic law code (e.g., centralization of worship in Jerusalem and the requirement of a national Passover feast), leaving little doubt about the connection between the law code Josiah discovered and the core of Deuteronomy.

Documentarians also explain the presence of Deuteronomic rhetoric in passages that would otherwise be assigned to J or E as the result of Deuteronomists' editorial efforts. For instance, Exodus 32–34 appears in many ways to belong to the Yahwist's narrative structure, but it contains language more familiar from the Deuteronomic Collection. Scholars explain this inconcinnity by positing a D redactor of J and E, or assigning the bulk of this and other pre-Deuteronomy Deuteronomic texts (!) in their entirety to the Deuteronomists.

The fourth source for the Pentateuch is labeled the **Priestly Source, "P,"** for its strong interest in matters related to the temple and its religious leaders. Marked not only by such sacerdotal interests (e.g., P expands Aaron's role considerably in the Exodus-Sinai story), P uses highly formulaic language, introduces genealogies, and makes provision for maintaining Israelite identity apart from Jerusalem and the temple. The Priestly Source, thought by Documentarians to have once been a separate and complete document, was woven into the JE saga so that parts of it appear in Genesis, Exodus, and Numbers. In one way or another the Priestly writers are credited with providing all of Leviticus as well.

As for P's date and origin, it is assigned either to the late exilic period in Babylon or to the early postexilic era in Persian-period Judea. In either case, its purpose was to establish communal and cultic order for restored Israel and to legitimate the leadership of Aaronites in Persian-period Judah.

According to the Documentary Hypothesis, Priestly editors completed the Pentateuch when they wove their original composition into the existing JE saga and appended to that a revised form of Deuteronomy (which they adjusted mostly by rewriting Moses' death account to provide a suitable conclusion to the whole). Most think this process must have been concluded by the time Ezra read the "Book of the Law" to the people gathered in Jerusalem (Nehemiah 8); the supposition is that the "Book of the Law" was roughly the Pentateuch as we know it today.

Revisions to the Documentary Hypothesis

In recent decades the Documentary Hypothesis has been subject to vigorous critique, leading in some cases to its refinement and revision and in others to its rejection and replacement with alternative hypotheses. Refinements have largely taken the form of ever more precise definitions of the sources and their authors' interests. In some cases, rather dogmatic uses of source criticism have produced much too refined accounts of what belongs to the various sources; and in a few instances this doctrinaire use of the method has produced not one or two Yahwist, Priestly, Elohist, or Deuteronomic writers each, but multiple J's, P's, E's, and D's!

The most significant revisions to the Documentary Hypothesis, however, have entailed rejecting the existence of E as a separate source and the substitution of a Priestly *Redaction* for the Priestly *Source*. In the case of E, scholars have long observed its truncated shape compared with J, as well as the paucity and weakness of indicators distinguishing texts as belonging to it. As closer scrutiny steadily diminished the scope of E, and the earmarks announcing its presence lost their

significance, fewer and fewer scholars saw it as a literary stratum that is in any way distinct from J. Eventually, many scholars simply dismissed the idea of a separate E document and assigned its parts to a J document that incorporated northern and southern traditions and so embraced its own doublets.

As for replacement theories, they are generally of two types, renewals of the Fragment and Supplementary Hypotheses. The Fragment Hypothesis has experienced a revival chiefly through the work of Rolf Rendtorff and his student Erhard Blum. These two scholars have mostly rejected the Documentary Hypothesis as a way to understand the formation history of the Pentateuch. Instead, relying on aspects of tradition and form criticism, they suggest that explaining the formation of large units of text such as the Primeval History or the Ancestral Saga takes priority over tracing sources through the whole of the Pentateuch. Thus Rendtorff and Blum reject traditional source criticism in favor of form criticism (to analyze and define those large units of text) and tradition history (to theorize about the units' development from oral tradition to text). Blum especially has elaborated this approach. He theorizes that sizable chunks of text — chiefly Genesis 12–50, the Ancestral Saga, and a history of Moses in Exodus and Numbers — developed over time and were first linked by a Deuteronomic composer-redactor by introducing to both the promise to the ancestors. This "KD" (the *D-Komposition* in German) began with Genesis 12:1-3 and continued through the stories of wilderness wandering. Subsequently Priestly composer-redactors added the Primeval History and other material routinely identified as Priestly (e.g., Exodus 25–31; 35–40; Leviticus) to create "KP" (the *P-Komposition* in German).

The work of John Van Seters best reflects the revival of the Supplementary Hypothesis. Van Seters accepts the two major revisions offered by the Documentarians, that there never was an Elohist Source and that the Priestly contribution to the Pentateuch is no more than a redaction. His major contribution is to redate the Yahwist Work (which in his approach includes what was once thought to be the remains of the Elohist Work). Van Seters places J in the Exilic period and conceives of it as a response and *supplement* to Deuteronomy and the Deuteronomistic History (on the latter, see Chapter 12). He dates the completion of Deuteronomy and the Deuteronomistic History (which we will call, along with some prophetic books, the "Deuteronomic Collection") to the Exilic era as well, treating it as an answer to the question of why the Exile occurred. The answer the Deuteronomic Collection provided was that the people had broken God's bilateral covenant with them and so they were experiencing the divinely-ordained consequences attendant to a breach of the covenant's terms (see Deut 29:25-29). According to Van Seters, the Yahwist Work is a reply to the Deuteronomic explanation of the Exile. As a supplementary prologue to Deuteronomy — 2 Kings, the Yahwist Work argues that before God made a bilateral covenant with the people, God promised land and descendants unilaterally (e.g., Genesis 12; 15, etc.). Thus, on this view the Yahwist Work is a "confessional reformulation" that not only works as a literary supplement to Deuteronomy to 2 Kings but also as a theological corrective. Subsequent to the formulation of the Yahwist Work, Priestly writers added their contribution to the Pentateuch. Additional editorial adjustments to the Pentateuch in the form of supplements and modest revisions continued until the end of the 4th century B.C.E.

Not one of these newer approaches to understanding the formation of the Pentateuch has achieved the same sort of consensus status the Documentary Hypothesis once enjoyed among critics. However, a careful reader of this book will no doubt observe a tendency in what follows to favor the revised Supplementary Hypothesis of Van Seters. But no matter the hypothesis one favors, careful readers of the Pentateuch itself will also soon realize that regardless of the precise nature of its composition history, it is, in its complete form, an enormously rich collection of theological perspectives.

Questions for Review and Discussion

1   Be prepared to rehearse the basic story line of the Pentateuch so that as we launch into the material itself you have an easy time in tracking the story line.

2   What method was key to sorting out the compositional history of the Pentateuch, and what theory or theories about the Pentateuch's history did its use produce?

3   Which of the methods we surveyed in Chapter 4 played a part in producing the alternatives to the Documentary Hypothesis? How might you explain the rise of alternative hypotheses as the result of new intuitions about the text like those that produced source criticism and the Documentary Hypothesis in the first place?

Further Reading

Blenkinsopp, Joseph. *The Pentateuch.* ABRL. New York: Doubleday, 1992.

Van Seters, John. *The Pentateuch: A Social-Science Commentary.* Sheffield: Sheffield Academic, 1999.

Whybray, R. N. *Introduction to the Pentateuch.* Grand Rapids: Wm. B. Eerdmans, 1995.

Chapter 6

Genesis 1–11

Getting Started

1 What are the main elements of Genesis 1:1–12:3? According to the story what are the contours of God's relationship with humanity: ever expanding, ever decreasing, or a bit of both?

2 As you read Genesis 1–11, look for signs of more than one authorial hand. What are some of those signs, and what do they indicate about the chapters' compositional history?

3 Consider the possibility that Genesis 1–11 is concerned in particular with themes of chaos and order, with God's relationship to humanity, and with the nature of God and of human beings as "characters" in a story. What do these chapters suggest regarding those topics?

Preliminary Comments

The first book of the Bible is aptly named: the word "genesis" is a transliteration of the Greek word for "beginning." The title actually derives from the first words of the Greek translation of Genesis, *en te genesei,* "In the beginning" (which is a translation of the Hebrew of the same phrase, *bere'shit*). And just as the title is apt, the book's contents also reflect its name. Chapters 1–11 record "primeval history," the story of the world before time began, from creation to when humanity flourished upon the face of the planet. Likewise, the remainder of the book, chs. 12–50, tells how God began to make a people for himself from one family among the many that populated earth. So it is, indeed, a story of beginnings.

A Walk through Genesis 1–11

Genesis begins with two accounts of creation. The first, 1:1–2:4a, relates that "in the beginning" God systematically organizes the watery chaos he encounters in the cosmos. He opens and illuminates a space within the waters so that above is a firmament and below is the sea. In the midst of the sea he causes dry ground to appear; he affixes to the firmament the sun, the moon, and the stars to determine the passing of the times and seasons; and he fills the sea with fishes, the air with birds, and the earth with plants and living animals. And on the sixth day God creates humanity in God's own image to rule over the earth and all that is in it. Deeming all of this to be good, on the seventh day God rests from his labors. The account closes with the declaration, "These are the generations *(toledot)* of the heavens and the earth" (2:4a).

In addition to naming God differently — as "Lord God" — 2:4b-25 provides a sharply contrasting creation story. Even before there is vegetation God creates the first man, Adam, from a mixture of the dust of the earth and God's own breath. Then the Lord God creates a garden of delightful things and waters it with a river that becomes four tributaries, including the Tigris and the Euphrates. The Lord God places Adam in the garden along with the trees of life and of the knowledge of good and evil, and God commands Adam to eat only plant life, but not from the tree of knowledge, lest he die. Then the Lord God creates the animals and birds as companions and helpers for Adam, but Adam deems none of them a suitable partner. So the Lord God puts Adam to sleep and removes a rib from him to form a woman. Adam finds her to be very pleasing indeed, and together they dwell innocently in the garden.

According to 3:1-24 little time passes before Adam and the woman corrupt the goodness of creation and their own innocence. The cunning serpent informs the woman that eating of the tree of knowledge of good and evil would not bring death, but rather the divine power of discrimination. Trusting the serpent's word, the woman eats of the tree to become wise, and she shares its fruit with Adam: indeed, their innocence, represented by their unconcern over being naked before one another, vanishes, but in its place comes shame at their nudity. When the Lord God discovers their disobedience the serpent proves correct once more: they do not die, but instead God assigns to each of them specific consequences (enmity between the serpent and humanity, pain in childbirth for the woman, and difficulty in horticulture for the man). Then God expels them from

the garden and seals it against re-entry, lest humanity eat from the tree of life. In an act of mercy the Lord God sews clothing for Adam and Eve.

The denigration of God's creation deepens in the next episode, 4:1-26. Adam and Eve's sons, Cain and Abel, till the soil and tend flocks, respectively. Each makes offerings to the Lord from the fruits of their labors, but the Lord has regard only for Abel's gift. Cain becomes angry, and though the Lord exhorts him to master the sin "lurking at the door and desiring him," he lures his brother to the open field where he kills him. (Seth was born to Adam and Eve to replace Abel.) Confronted by the Lord as were his parents before him, Cain dissembles and upon being discovered, is, like his parents before him, driven into exile. But in another act of mercy, the Lord marks Cain so that no one would commit murderous violence against him. Cain goes forth, builds a city, marries, and produces sons. Cain's descendants are the founders of culture, establishing in particular pastoralism, music, and smithery. But also in keeping with Cain's reputation, his descendant Lamech increases violence in the earth.

Genesis 5:1-32 provides a genealogy from Adam to Noah as an interlude in the narrative account of how humanity degraded the Lord's good creation. The genealogy is notable not only for using the same word for "generations" as the one used in 2:4a, but also for the longevity assigned to its members (900-1000 years) and the peculiar fate of Enoch, who is taken up to heaven to walk with God without experiencing a human death.

The story of creation's decline resumes in 6:1-4, the strange account of how the sons of God descend to earth to mate with human women and produce the Nephilim, the "heroes of old, warriors of renown." Whether a consequence of this divine-human mixture or not, the Lord observes in 6:5-8 that the inclination of the human heart is evil and that therefore all should be drowned in a global flood, the humans together with the creatures of the earth and the birds of the air. In the ensuing story only Noah and his family are preserved on an ark, along with sufficient numbers of the animals to ensure each species' survival. Notably the story seems at times redundant and even self-contradictory. For example, the narrator explains that God condemns creation because of the evil inclination of human hearts (6:5-8), but again because of earth's corruption and violence (6:11-12). Likewise, once God commands Noah to fill the ark with one male-female pair of every kind of animal (6:18-22), but again the Lord requires him to equip it with one pair each of the unclean animals and seven pairs each of the clean (7:1-5). As for the flood itself, it seems to last either 150 days (8:3) or 40 days (8:6). And when Noah disembarks, God promises never to curse the ground again because every inclination of the human heart is irreconcilably evil (8:20-22), but in 9:1-17 God offers no reason for making the same promise (sealed this time with the sign of the rainbow), and adds to it permission to eat not just plants, but animal life as well, along with the prohibition against shedding human blood.

Genesis 9:20-28 renews the theme of human corruption. As the world's first vintner, Noah consumes too much of his own produce and lies naked and drunk in his tent. Ham enters the tent and sees "the nakedness of his father" and compounds his sin by gleefully reporting the encounter to his brothers, Shem and Japheth. Once sober, Noah curses Ham (in the person of Ham's son, Canaan), and blesses Shem and Japheth, assigning Canaan's descendants as slaves to the descendants of Shem and Japheth.

The Table of Nations in 10:1-32, a record of how Noah's descendants populated the earth, echoes the rhetoric of Genesis 5. It explains that the descendants of Japheth inhabit Asia Minor; those of Ham reside in the region of Egypt and Canaan; and Shem's descendants, the Hebrews, are located throughout the land. The Table of Nations' implication that all people speak one language provides the basis for 11:1-9, the story of the Tower of Babel. The narrator reports that the peoples coming from the east settled in what was the Tigris-Euphrates basin (home to the great Mesopotamian cultures of antiquity), and there they conspire to build a city and a tower reaching to the heavens to make a reputation for themselves, lest they be scattered across the earth. The Lord observes humanity's renewed inclination to transcend human bounds (cf. ch. 3) and responds by scattering the people, as they had feared, and multiplying their languages.

Genesis 11:10-32 provides another genealogy (similar in language and form to the ones in chs. 5 and 10) that leads from Shem to Terah and his three sons, one of whom is Abram.

Critical Issues in Genesis 1–11

Two related critical issues occupy our attention. The first, the frequent echoes of ancient Near Eastern creation and etiological myths, provides some insight on how one views the second, the authorship, date, and provenance (origin) of the Primeval History.

Ancient Near Eastern Backgrounds

Critics have long observed the many resonances Genesis 1–11 shares with ancient Near Eastern myths of creation and the origin of human personality, culture, technology, and society. Cataloguing those parallels was the pas-

What do we mean by "myth"?

In the modern person's imagination, the word "myth" is usually employed to denigrate what someone says or claims. For an account to be a "myth" it must be untrue, fantastical. But that is not the meaning we give the term in the study of the Hebrew Scriptures. Myths are the tales told by ancient speakers and writers to explain basic truths about the human condition, the natural world, the divine beings, and the relationships among all three entities. Myths explain the origin of the world, the cause of evil in the world, the power of nature to destroy, and the ways of the gods. The authors of the Hebrew Bible regularly used widely known myths shared by many cultures and religions to explain their unique views on these basic questions of human existence in the world. Much of Genesis 1–11 reflects this practice, as do many other parts of the Old Testament we are yet to explore in this book.

sion of some of the earliest historical critics of the Old Testament (e.g., James Henry Breasted). We list some of these below.

The first creation account, Genesis 1:1–2:4a, borrows rhetoric and themes from the creation account ensconced in the classic Babylonian myth, *Enuma Elish* (a tale that seeks to legitimate the ascendancy of Marduk among the gods).

- The temporal clause in Gen 1:1 recalls the opening words of *Enuma Elish* (*ANET,* 60).
- The "deep" (Hebrew *tehom*) that God must restrain to bring order from chaos echoes the name *Tiamat,* the sea-goddess of *Enuma Elish* who is likewise the chaos that the high god Marduk must control.
- Genesis 1:6 posits a cosmology that matches the one achieved in *Enuma Elish* (p. 54; *ANET,* 67).
- The concern for calendar reckoning through the creation of astral bodies in 1:14-19 likewise reflects the interests of *Enuma Elish* (*ANET,* 67).
- The account of the creation of humanity in the image of God and as sovereign over nature in Gen 1:26 echoes Mesopotamian tales where humanity is formed to serve as a regent for God over creation.
- And the very way in which God creates — through speech — recalls the Egyptian Memphis Theology that tells how the god Ptah created through utterances of the tongue (*ANET,* 4-6).

The second creation account, the stories of humanity's earliest rebellion, the Cain genealogy and its members' founding of civilization, and the Adam to Seth genealogy with its reference to Enoch's journey to the heavens (Genesis 2–5) also reiterate elements of ancient Near Eastern myths.

- The formation of man from the dust of the earth is known from the Atrahasis Epic (*ANET*, 104-6).
- According to a Sumerian account the god and goddess Enki and Ninhur-sag enjoyed goodness so long as they remained in the presence of a tree of life (*ANET*, 37-41).
- The serpent in Genesis 3 recalls the water-god Apsu of *Enuma Elish* (*ANET*, 67).
- Recalling Cain and Abel, Dumuzi and Enkimdu, Mesopotamian shepherd- and farmer-gods respectively, compete for the love of the goddess Inanna (*ANET*, 41-42).
- The Sumerian King List provides a rationale for the origin of elements in civilization, as does Cain's genealogy (*ANET*, 265-66).
- Enoch and his journey to the heavens (Gen 5:21-24) seem to be modeled on Mesopotamian traditions concerning a king, Enmeduranki, and a corresponding sage, Utu'abzu, who are also seventh on king and sage lists and dwelt before the gods.
- The Sumerian King List also mentions a flood and uses it to divide between the age when humans lived to a very great age and when their life spans were more like ours.
- The flood itself is routinely recounted in the ancient Near Eastern myths, although the cause in the Atrahasis Epic is nothing so momentous as the gods' judgment that all humanity is depraved, but rather their annoyance at the noisiness of humans (*ANET*, 104-6).
- Like the Genesis account, the Gilgamesh Epic (*ANET*, 93-95) and the Deluge Tablet (*ANET*, 44) both provide for humanity's survival through one hero and his family (Utnapishtim and Ziusudra, respectively).

Finally, even though it is not an ancient Near Eastern myth we mention the Babylonian practice of building *ziggurats*, stepped towers, to bring human worshippers closer to the gods. There is a wide consensus that this Mesopotamian architectural feature provides the background for the Tower of Babel story in Genesis 11.

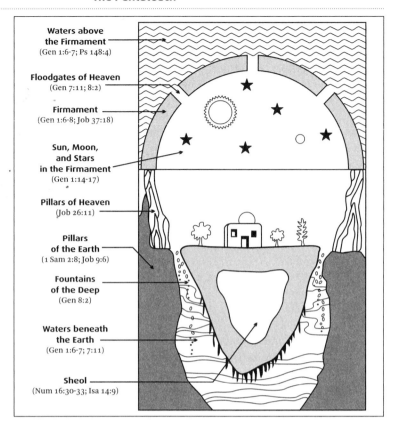

THE COSMOS IN THE ANCIENT IMAGINATION

Waters above the Firmament (Gen 1:6-7; Ps 148:4)

Floodgates of Heaven (Gen 7:11; 8:2)

Firmament (Gen 1:6-8; Job 37:18)

Sun, Moon, and Stars in the Firmament (Gen 1:14-17)

Pillars of Heaven (Job 26:11)

Pillars of the Earth (1 Sam 2:8; Job 9:6)

Fountains of the Deep (Gen 8:2)

Waters beneath the Earth (Gen 1:6-7; 7:11)

Sheol (Num 16:30-33; Isa 14:9)

The Authorship, Date, and Provenance of Genesis 1–11

The Documentary Hypothesis divides the Primeval History between the Yahwist and the Priestly Writers.

According to the Documentary Hypothesis Genesis 1–11 came to be in this way: First, the Yahwist material was composed in the early monarchy as part of a larger

Steps leading to the top of the ziggurat at Ur, constructed by Ur-nammu, founder of the Third Dynasty of Ur. (Jack Finegan)

The Yahwist and Priestly Works in Genesis 1–11

Yahwist Material	Priestly Material
	1:1–2:4a, Creation
2:4b-25, Creation	
3:1-21, Garden of Eden	
4:1-16, Cain and Abel	
4:17-26, Cain's descendants	
	5:1-24, Adam's genealogy
6:1-4, Sons of God	
6:5-8, Reason for the flood	
	6:9-13, Reason for the flood
6:14–7:24, Flood (J)	
	6:14–7:24 Flood (P)
8:1-22, Post-Flood Renewal (J)	
	8:1-22, Post-Flood Renewal (P)
	9:1-17, Covenant with Noah
9:18-27, Noah and Ham	
10:1-32, Table of Nations (J)	
	10:1-32, Table of Nations (P)
11:1-9, Tower of Babel	
	11:10-32, Genealogy of Shem and Terah

work explaining the origins of the Davidic dynasty, and the Priestly material was added to it later, in the late Exilic or early Persian period. This simple explanation has long been relied on to account for the thoroughly mixed character of parts of the Primeval History, especially the flood and post-flood narratives in Genesis 6–9.

However, on the assumption that a Priestly editor would have been concerned for at least a modicum of coherence and logic, some have observed that the Priestly material is not always best explained as an addition to earlier Yahwist material (e.g., 7:11-12, attributed to P, announces the beginning and duration of the flood, while only in 7:16 does J announce that the Lord shut Noah, his family, and his menagerie into the ark!). So the priority of the Yahwist in the Primeval History has come into question. Likewise, the thematic coherence of the supposed J material in Genesis 1–11 with the J material in Genesis 12–50 has also been questioned. Taking these and other indications into account, some have recently posited the late formation of the Primeval History as a whole and its subsequent attachment to what we know as Genesis 12–50 as an independent prologue. Still others have argued that the Primeval History is a single, seamless composition, including the flood story, and therefore provides evidence against sources in the Penta-

teuch altogether. In short, the compositional history of the Primeval History is a touch point for those who wish to dispute the basic tenets of the Documentary Hypothesis.

Quite apart from the foregoing issues, among those who accept the existence of Yahwist source material in the Primeval History there are some who question whether it can be so easily dated to the Davidic or Solomonic era, as proponents of the Documentary Hypothesis insist. Its unflattering portrait of human beginnings and its recurring theme of expulsion from the land cannot have been particularly popular themes for kings and their courts. But if not in the early monarchy, when was this composed? The reliance on Mesopotamian mythic traditions in Genesis 1–11 argues strongly for an exilic date and provenance for its contents, especially since the Neo-Babylonian Empire responsible for the Judean Exile was unique in its desire to cultivate among its citizens the ancient myths of Mesopotamia. On this reading the Yahwist material in Genesis 1–11 may have been composed with an eye to capitalizing on the myths' familiarity to and authority over residents in the Babylonian Empire, but also to signaling the hegemony of the God of the Judeans. After all, the Primeval History proves their God to be the true creator and director of all reality. At the same time, by using the myths to explain the origin of human disobedience and resulting alienation from creation the author offers an explanation for the Exile and extends his effort to co-opt the Babylonian myths for Israelite use. If we accept this dating of the Yahwist, the portrait of God in the Primeval History is also quite interesting relative to the exilic experience. Note how God, though perplexed and unsettled by human rebellion, nonetheless provides mercy for sinners while dealing out consequences as well: God sews clothing for Adam and Eve, marks Cain to protect him, and forswears total annihilation after the flood because he knows the natural, unyielding human inclination to do evil (Gen 6:5-8). And as we shall see, the grace note that

God provides after the Tower of Babel incident is the new start on blessing all creation through the agency of one man and his family, Abraham, a man who *comes from Mesopotamia to receive the blessing of the Promised Land!* Altogether such evidence suggests quite strongly an exilic, Babylonian origin for the Yahwist Work.

Assuming still the accuracy of the Documentary Hypothesis (as well as that of the Supplementary Hypothesis), the addition of the Priestly material to the Yahwist's narrative seems likely to have been accomplished in the late Exilic or early Postexilic period. The orderly account of creation in 1:1–2:4a can be understood as a response to the certainty among returnees to Judah under Persian rule that they faced enormous chaos: the author announces as when God encountered cosmic chaos he effortlessly ordered it; just so, sorting out the chaos of postexilic Judah would be that much easier for God. Likewise, the introduction of the genealogies, the additional explanation of the flood, the flood chronology, the covenant with Noah, and the Table of Nations provide to the account of Primeval History structure and order characteristic of the Priestly Writer. We return to a fuller description of that author and audience's interests in Chapter 9 below.

Theological Themes in Genesis 1–11

A survey of Jewish and Christian interpretive traditions rooted in the Primeval History signals its enormous fecundity for theological reflection. Some of these traditions, though, began as little more than the response of later readers to curiosities in the grammar, syntax, or rhetoric of the text. Since this was such a popular enterprise in early Judaism and Christianity — solving exegetical puzzles in the Torah especially — we will sample such motifs in our "Theological Themes" sections of this chapter and Chapters 7-11.

Early Jewish and Christian Interpretive Traditions

For instance, because the Hebrew of Gen 1:1 lacks punctuation, it is not clear whether it is an independent clause or an introductory clause to v. 2. If it is an independent clause ("In the beginning God created the heavens and the earth"), it may support the notion of *creatio ex nihilo,* creation from nothing. But if v. 2 is read with v. 1 ("In the beginning *when* God created the heavens and the earth, the earth was a formless void . . .") God began the creative process with some raw material ready to hand. Even if the ancient Near Eastern parallels that the creation account is in part modeled on do not espouse the notion of *creatio ex nihilo,* there is nonetheless a long tradition of reading Genesis 1 as promoting

that view. The Septuagint's unequivocal treatment of v. 1 as a main clause has helped the cause, perhaps leading to the embrace of *creatio ex nihilo* in 2 Macc 7:28; Philo of Alexandria, *On Dreams* 1:76; Augustine, *City of God* 11:4.

Another example of interpreters responding to the simple grammar of the text is the interpretive tradition associated with 1:26-27 and the reference to God in the first person plural. Not surprisingly early Christian readers understand the plural to refer to God's cooperation with Jesus (and the Holy Spirit in some cases) to create humanity (Augustine, *On the Trinity* 12.6.6; Gregory of Nyssa, *On the Origin of Man;* Prudentius, *Poems*). Jewish interpreters had other ways of contending with this curious verse: some rabbis emend the text to read a singular verb in place of the plural; Philo says God's "lieutenants" assisted at creation so as to release God from responsibility for human sin (*Confusion of Tongues* 179); and Josephus simply asserts that, regardless the language of the text, God created alone (*Against Apion* 2.192).

God's Passion for Order

There are in addition at least two larger theological themes more intimately related to what the authors may have intended in composing Genesis 1–11. The first theme is God's passion for order where there is chaos. Speaking against the idea that 1:1–2:4a authorizes notions of *creatio ex nihilo* is the fact that the story moves from disorder in creation to perfect order, capped by God's self-declared day of rest in observance of the *good* work accomplished. In similar fashion 5:1-24; 10:1-32; and 11:10-32 provide order to the progression of early human developments narrated in the rest of the Primeval History. Especially the Priestly explanation for the flood (6:9-13) emphasizes that the introduction of disorder in the form of violence and corruption was the reason for God's decision to permit watery chaos to work its woe. And finally, upon the completion of the flood God restrained the waters of chaos again and sealed the promise not to permit chaos its full power again with a covenantal promise (9:1-17).

On God, Humanity, and the Relationship between the Two

In addition to revealing God's concern for order, particularly the Yahwist portion of the Primeval History casts early light on the nature of God and humanity and the relationship between them. This set of stories characterizes that relationship as one where, in spite of God's yearning for peaceful affiliation, humanity consistently acts against God's blessing. Consider how Genesis 2 proves that from the moment of his creation, Adam, made by God to be God's companion, yearns for camaraderie with any other being but God. Genesis

3 seems to argue that Adam and Eve not only had no regard for God as a companion, but they wanted even more, to transcend God's place over them. Genesis 4 is a story of God seeking to assist humanity to come to grips with its inclination for evil — see God's encouraging advice to Cain in 4:7 — but humanity's inability to appreciate that help. Genesis 6:1-13 provides a threefold explanation of the ways in which humanity instigated or participated in deeds corrupting God's good creation, and the flood signals God's impatience at last with human rebellion. Noah's drunkenness and Ham's indiscretion after the flood (9:18-27) illustrate the incorrigibility of humanity even when placed under the most severe discipline, and the Tower of Babel story proves the abiding desire of humans to exceed God in knowledge and power (11:1-9).

Yet for all of that, the same set of stories reveal God to be an educable divinity, a God who learns by the mistakes of creation, and who throughout is determined to bless creation, even in the wake of its most rebellious moments. At first God punishes human disobedience directly (3:14-19; 4:10-12; 6:5-13), though providing in each instance a "grace note," a sign of God's continuing desire to bless humanity (3:21; 4:15). But realizing that the inclination of the human being is to disobedience, sin, and evil (6:5; 8:21), God resolves to step aside from the business of punishing humanity toward more perfect obedience (8:21-22; 9:14-17) and in most instances treats discipline for evil action as a matter to be handled among human beings (9:18-27).

And yet again, for all that God learned from experience with humanity through the first 10 chapters of Genesis, God's patience seems to run out with the Tower of Babel incident and the recrudescence of human pride and arrogance in relation to God. In an act that is more prophylactic than punitive, God confuses the language of the tower builders and spreads them across the earth, lest the human desire to be like God — even transcend God — finally be realized (11:1-9). As the Primeval History draws to a close with the genealogy that leads from Shem to Abram, one wonders if perhaps God has simply given up on creation and all that is in it. But as we shall see, Genesis 12 makes clear God still has plenty in store for creation after all.

In closing it is worth noting again that these two major theological themes, God's passion for order where there is chaos and the relationship between a God bent on blessing and humanity bent on rebellion, would not be out of place in the Exilic and Postexilic periods. The latter theme might work well to explain the Exile and suggest that, in spite of that experience, God sought even in the Exile to bless the people who brought their fate upon themselves. And the concern for order in the midst of chaos would be an especially poignant theme for the people of restored Judah under Persian rule: as the historical survey in Chapter 3 proves, the early Postexilic period was marked by the threat that chaos posed to the people's survival.

Questions for Review and Discussion

1 In what ways does Genesis 1–11 show the influence of ancient Near Eastern myth on Israelite religious imagination?

2 How was myth understood in the ancient world, and how was that understanding put to use by the authors of Genesis 1–11?

3 What are the dominant theological themes of Genesis 1–11, to which sources (J and P) are they assigned, and how do they still work together through Genesis 1–11 as a whole?

Further Reading

Blenkinsopp, *The Pentateuch;* Van Seters, *The Pentateuch;* Whybray, *Introduction to the Pentateuch.*
Carr, David M. *Reading the Fractures of Genesis: Historical and Literary Approaches.* Louisville: Westminster/ John Knox, 1996.
Kugel, James L. *The Bible As It Was.* Cambridge, MA: Belknap, 1997.
Virtually all of the early Jewish and Christian interpretive traditions cited in this chapter and the rest of our treatment of the books of the Torah come from this important book by Kugel. Kugel also produced a longer version of the work, *The Traditions of the Bible* (Cambridge, MA: Harvard University Press, 1998). It is perhaps the more desirable of the two works for its greater completeness. In any case, it is a terrific resource for anyone interested in pursuing other exegetical motifs related to the Pentateuch like those cited here and in Chapters 7 through 11.
Matthews, Victor H., and Don C. Benjamin. *Old Testament Parallels.* 3rd ed. New York: Paulist, 2006.
Rogerson, J. *Genesis 1–11.* OTG. London: T. & T. Clark, 2004.
Wenham, Gordon J. "Genesis." In *Eerdmans Commentary on the Bible,* ed. James D. G. Dunn and John W. Rogerson, 32-47. Grand Rapids: Wm. B. Eerdmans, 2003. *(ECB)*

Chapter 7

Genesis 12–50

Getting Started

1   Read Genesis 12:1-3. Does God's promise to Abram require nothing of Abram in return? Compare this passage to 15:1-21. Does Genesis 15 require anything of Abram in return for the fruits of God's promises? How about Genesis 22?

2   Read Genesis 12:10-20, along with 20:1-18 and 26:1-11. How are these stories similar and/or different from one another? What do the similarities suggest about the authorship of these stories?

3   Glance through Genesis 37–50 and consider how those chapters differ in the character of their story-telling from the passages assigned to you in questions 1 and 2.

Preliminary Comments

Just as Genesis 1–11, the Primeval History, aptly reflects the biblical book's title, Genesis 12–50, the Ancestral Saga, is also about beginnings. It tells how God began to bless all creation by starting with one family among the many that populated earth. Like the Primeval History, the Ancestral Saga is a story of new realities. But, while Genesis 1–11 narrowed from God's concern for all creation in Genesis 1 to a seeming abandonment of the whole project in 11:1-9, Genesis 12–50 seems to move in the opposite direction, from but one man and his family toward offering blessing for all humankind.

A Walk through Genesis 12–50

Genesis 12–50 is organized as three saga collections related to Abraham, Jacob, and Joseph separated by brief genealogies. (A saga is a legendary narrative about an eponymous ancestor. An eponym is an ancestor's name that is also the name of the people that preserve his or her stories.) The Abraham and Jacob cycles are in fact loose collections of narratives held together in part by itineraries (travel notices), while the Joseph "cycle" is a novella, perhaps one of the earliest in world literature. A further set of stories associated with Isaac is sometimes deemed a saga cycle as well, but as we see below, the few stories of Isaac alone are integrated into the sagas assigned to his father and his son.

Genesis 12:1–25:18: The Abraham Cycle
The story of Abraham dominates Genesis 12:1-25:18.

The account begins in chs. 12–13 with a series of promise passages, a heroine-in-jeopardy account, and etiologies, all strung together by itinerary notices. After God promises Abraham land and descendants and commands him to travel to the place he would inherit, Abraham journeys to Canaan where God shows him the Promised Land. Abraham builds an altar there between Ai and Bethel, establishing the site of a later sanctuary. On account of a famine Abraham then moves on to Egypt where he forfeits his wife to Pharaoh, passing her off as his sister, lest Pharaoh kill him to have the beautiful Sarah. God afflicts Pharaoh, prompting Sarah's return to Abraham, and Abraham leaves Egypt for Canaan enriched by his sojourn in Egypt. When Abraham returns to Canaan, Lot reports the tension between their herders over pasturage, so Abraham and Lot agree to divide the land; Lot receives the territory to the east (home to Sodom and Gomorrah, and later to Ammon and Moab), and Abraham settles in Canaan, where God reaffirms the covenant promise to Abraham.

In a curious interlude Genesis 14 reports a war story that temporarily converts Abraham into a military hero and brings him into contact with one of the Hebrew Bible's most mysterious characters. After a coalition of kings sack Sodom and Gomorrah and capture Lot and his possessions, Abraham pursues and defeats the enemies and returns Lot to his home. Upon his triumphant return, the mysterious King Melchizedek of Salem, "priest of the God Most High," meets Abraham, and Abraham exchanges a tithe for a blessing from Melchizedek. Apart from a perplexing reference in Ps 110:4, we never encounter Melchizedek again in the Hebrew Bible, and while Genesis 14 is itself difficult to assign (thus the question mark placed next to it on page 65), Melchizedek *of Salem* (= Jerusalem) probably serves in the story to root Jerusalem's sacred status in greatest antiquity.

Next, Genesis 15:1–18:15 poignantly sandwiches the story of Ishmael's birth and God's promise of heirs to him between episodes reporting and confirming God's covenantal relationship with Abraham. In ch. 15 God comes to Abraham in a dream akin to those received by prophets (cf. 15:1 and Hos 1:1). God assures Abraham of his favor and tells him that his descendants would be more numerous than the stars; when Abraham believes this, God "reckons it to him as righteousness," signaling that faith alone elicited God's positive judgment, where normally a deed was required. And when Abraham also asks for assurance that he would obtain land, God performs a covenant ceremony that normally entailed both parties passing between the halves of slain animals to signal the contractors' fate if they failed to honor their agreement (cf. Jer 34:17-20). Notably, in the theophany that is at the heart of the ceremony God alone passes through the parts (as a smoking fire pot and flaming torch), making clear the unilateral nature of the covenant God initiated with Abraham in Genesis 12 and confirmed in this episode (see p. 60 for a discussion of types of covenants in the ancient world). But ch. 16 reports that because Abraham still has no heirs by Sarah (since she is barren; cf. 11:30), she provides her maid, Hagar the Egyptian, as a surrogate. But when Hagar conceives, Sarah's mood darkens so severely that Hagar flees to the wilderness where God commands her to return to Sarah and promises that her son, Ishmael, will become the ancestor of a great nation. Finally, in a departure from the unilateral covenant of Genesis 15 (and 12:1-3), ch. 17 reports God's promise of land and descendants on the condition that all males in the covenant be circumcised. Also on this occasion God calls Abraham and his wife Sarah by those names for the first time. (Until this point they are called Abram and Sarai.) Furthermore, God requires all male parties to the covenant to be circumcised, and decrees that Sarah will have a son of her own, and that she will "give rise to nations, kings shall come from her." As if to put an exclamation point on God's promise of a child to Abraham and Sarah, 18:1-15 reports the visit of three travelers to the couple as they dwell by "the oaks of Mamre." One of the strangers is the Lord. In the course of a shared meal the travelers inform Abraham that Sarah will bear a son to him, at which Sarah, who eavesdrops from the family tent, sniggers derisively. The Lord's response is to assure the couple that the promise will be fulfilled.

From there the narrative shifts focus in 18:16–19:38 to the fate of Sodom and Gomorrah and Lot and his family. First, in a dramatic encounter with the Lord, Abraham bargains to save Sodom, persuading the Lord that for the sake of even 10 righteous people in the city it should be spared God's wrath. However, 19:1-29 reports that in the meantime the Lord's two companions have gone on to Sodom only to find it an inhospitable city. Although Lot receives the two divine visitors sociably, the men of the city seek to abuse them sexually. Perhaps on account of this lack of hospitality God resolves to destroy Sodom (cf. Ezek 16:48-49), sparing only Lot and his family (although Lot's wife dies too because she peers back at the burning city). Genesis

Parity, Suzerainty-Vassal, and Unilateral Covenants

Treaties between nations in the ancient world had some influence on the covenants we encounter in the Pentateuch. Between nations there were two basic types of ancient Near Eastern treaties: parity treaties and suzerain-vassal treaties. Few examples of the former survive, and do seem to have been the least-often used. A parity treaty entails agreement between two equal parties, usually to avoid aggression between each other. The most widely cited example of a parity treaty is the one executed between the Hittite Hattusilis III and the Egyptian Ramses II after a battle between the two powers in the early 13th century B.C.E. (see *ANET,* 199-203 for the Hittite and Egyptian versions).

Much more common was the suzerain-vassal treaty that entailed an agreement between two unequal parties. The superior power, the suzerain, used the treaty to consolidate its power and put the vassal at a permanent disadvantage so as to ensure continued subjugation. Here the best-known example comes from the Assyrians. The Vassal-Treaties of Esarhaddon (*ANET,* 534-41) date from the 7th century B.C.E. The form of the suzerain-vassal treaty generally included: (1) a preamble that identifies the parties; (2) a historical review of the relationship between the two parties; (3) the stipulations of the treaty (laws); (4) provision for the treaty's publication; (5) a calling out of witnesses; (6) blessings and curses attendant upon keeping or breaking the agreement; and (7) in some cases provision for covenant continuity after its makers pass from the scene.

The relationship between these different types of treaties and the covenants we encounter in the Hebrew Bible has long been debated. However, it should be clear that the suzerain-vassal treaty is *not* at the heart of the covenant God makes with the ancestors in Genesis 12–50. This "covenant" is more like a unilateral promise (or covenant) whereby one party obliges itself to the other without requiring any commitments in return. That said, however, the suzerain-vassal treaty was influential on the form we encounter in Deuteronomy, as we shall see below in Chapter 11. Nor is the parity treaty an adequate model for what appears in Genesis. This leaves open the possibility that our author was tinkering with the treaty form to announce something new and different for which God was responsible.

19:30-38 concludes with the story of Lot's daughters seducing their father to gain offspring by him, on the mistaken assumption that the conflagration that consumed Sodom has destroyed all humankind. In a none-too-subtle critique of Israel's neighbors, the narrator reports that from these incestuous unions between Lot and his daughters come the forefathers of all of Moab and Ammon.

According to Genesis 20, after traveling to Mamre to settle between Kadesh and Shur, Abraham endangers the matriarch of Israel once more by giving her away to King Abimelech of Gerar, this time for no apparent reason apart from his certainty that because there was "no fear of God" in Gerar the Gerarites would kill him on account of his wife. Afflicted for wrongfully possessing the patriarch's wife like Pharaoh before him, Abimelech returns Sarah untouched to Abraham along with gifts of livestock and slaves, and the invitation to settle in his land. In return Abraham prays as a "prophet" for Abimelech's healing.

Genesis 21 reports that at last Abraham and Sarah have a son, whom they name Isaac, "he laughs," after his mother's joy at his birth (and perhaps her earlier derision at hearing that she would conceive and bear him!). Because she fears her child will not be favored, Sarah demands that Abraham cast out Hagar and Ishmael. He does so with God's assurance that Ishmael will survive to father a great nation himself. Thus God protects the mother and son in the wilderness and grants them success apart from Abraham and his clan. The same chapter narrates a brief conflict between Abraham and Abimelech over the well at Beer-sheba, a dispute that is settled when Abraham purchases the water source and makes a covenant with Abimelech that permits him to dwell there "as an alien [for] many days."

In one of the most evocative episodes in all of world literature, Genesis 22 reports God's unexplained command that Abraham sacrifice his son, Isaac. Abraham responds unflinchingly to God's command, gathering wood for the sacrifice, and traveling to the appointed mountain site (Moriah, a place not to be located geographically, although 2 Chr 3:1 lists it as the location of Solomon's temple). He even prepares the sacrifice to the point of binding his son upon the altar. (The episode is called the *Akedah* in Jewish tradition, using the verb for binding to describe it. Only at the last moment does God spare Isaac, providing in his place a ram for the sacrifice. The episode concludes with another expression of God's promise of land and descendants to Abraham and his descendants, one that recalls the promise in Gen 13:16 and 15:5 in particular, with its reference to the innumerability of the sand and stars. After this Abraham travels to Beer-sheba.

Genesis 23:1–25:18 concludes the Abraham cycle with accounts of Sarah's death and the purchase of land at Machpelah for her burial place (ch. 23), Eliezer's trip to Haran to find a wife — Rebekah — for Isaac (ch.

24), and Abraham's death (25:1-11). Genesis 25:12-18 records the descendants of Ishmael.

Genesis 25:19–36:43: The Jacob Cycle

The next cycle of stories in Genesis 25:19–35:29 unexpectedly features Jacob rather than Isaac (on this see "Critical Issues" below). In fact, the few narratives dealing exclusively with Isaac — getting a wife for him in ch. 24 (with a promise passage), a heroine-in-jeopardy story (cf. chs. 12 and 20), and an account of Isaac's tensions with Abimelech of Gerar in ch. 26 — have been absorbed mostly into his father's and son's story cycles.

Indeed, surrounding the small collection of Isaac stories in ch. 26 is the first part of the Jacob cycle, an account of the rivalry between Esau and Jacob that focuses on Jacob. Genesis 25:19-28 reports Rebekah's troubled pregnancy and God's explanation that it is two nations warring in her womb (Jacob and Esau are the eponymous ancestors of Israel and Edom, respectively), and that against the law of primogeniture (which mandates that the older receive the birthright) the younger of the two would rule over the older. Genesis 25:29-34 adds the tale of Jacob purchasing the birthright from his hungry brother for nothing more than a bowl of porridge; ch. 27 recounts how Rebekah and Jacob trick an aging Isaac into granting to Jacob the blessing owed to Esau, and

The Sacrifice of Isaac, Rembrandt Harmensz van Rijn (1655), engraving and drypoint. (Bildarchiv Preussischer Kulturbesitz/Art Resource, NY)

how Esau's understandable rage forces Jacob to flee to Aram and forego the pleasures attendant to having the birthright. (Many note the further irony of Jacob's purchase and theft of the birthright: God promised it to him apart from such actions even before his birth!) Genesis 28 explains, though, that on his way to Aram Jacob encounters God in a dream that confirms God's promise to Rebekah that Jacob, the younger of the twins, would receive the benefits of God's blessing and promise (cf. 12:3; 13:16). Jacob commemorates the site by erecting a sacred pillar or standing stone, thus establishing what later becomes the northern sanctuary, Bethel (cf. 1 Kgs 12:28-29).

Genesis 29–31 recounts Jacob's experiences with Laban, the father of the women Jacob married, and a trickster worthy to rival Jacob. Jacob falls in love with Rachel, Laban's younger daughter, and is required by Laban to work seven years to earn her hand in marriage. On the wedding night, Laban slips his older daughter, Leah, into the wedding tent so that Jacob mistakenly consummates a marital relationship with the wrong woman (but, as 29:26 reveals, the right one from Laban's perspective as the father; note the irony given Jacob's own record as a *younger* brother). Thus he is required to work yet another seven years to earn the right to marry Rachel. With these two wives and their maids, Zilpah and Bilhah, Jacob fathers many children and grows prosperous in his exile. Thus Laban tries to defraud Jacob of his earnings as a partner in the clan's sheep ranching business, but through a peculiar instance of animal husbandry Jacob outwits Laban. Then at God's behest Jacob prepares to take his wives and family back to his homeland. As they depart, Rachel pilfers the gods of her father's household, prompting one last (peacefully resolved) confrontation between Jacob and his father-in-law.

Genesis 32–33 then narrates Jacob's return to Canaan and his reconciliation with Esau. As he approaches his brother's land, Jacob divides his property and entourage in parts and sends the majority on ahead — either as peace offerings to his brother or a buffer to protect himself, depending on Esau's disposition. As this staged return draws to a close, Jacob has a further encounter with God at Peniel, an encounter that matches the one he had at Bethel on his way to Laban. This time he wrestles with God to a draw in the night, and demands God's blessing. He receives the blessing in the form of a new name, Israel, a sign that he has "struggled with God and men and overcome," and that he will be the ancestor of the nation state that is to bear his name. After this Jacob meets and reconciles with Esau and settles his clan in Shechem.

Genesis 34–35 concludes the Jacob cycle with a series

of loosely related episodes. Chapter 34 recounts the incident of Dinah's rape at Shechem and the vengeance wreaked against the Shechemites by Jacob's sons, Simeon and Levi (after they had tricked the Shechemites into accepting circumcision so they could make peace and do business together). Chapter 35 relates Jacob's journey from Shechem to Mamre to be present when Isaac dies, observing that along the way Jacob's clan strike terror in the hearts of the neighboring people, permitting them safe passage. Also along the way, at the sacral site of Bethel, God appears to Jacob again to reveal for a second time his new name, Israel; Rachel bears the last of Jacob's children, Benjamin; and Rachel dies (in childbirth) and is buried in the area of Bethlehem. When the clan stops briefly short of their destination, Reuben, one of Jacob's sons, sleeps with Jacob's concubine, Bilhah. Finally Jacob completes the last leg of the journey to reach Mamre just in time to be with his father Isaac in his last moments.

Genesis 36 serves as the bridge between the Jacob cycle and the Joseph novella. It provides a list of the descendants of Esau by his three wives (taken in opposition to his father's wish that he marry within the clan), a list that proves him to be the father of the nation of Edom. The chapter even includes a list of kings who ruled Edom before Israel arose.

Genesis 37–50: The Joseph Novella

At first glance, Genesis 37–50 takes up the story of but one of Jacob's sons, Joseph. But while this nearly self-contained tale of Joseph's sale into slavery in Egypt and his rise to power in Pharaoh's court keeps the rest of his family on the sidelines most of the time, it is ultimately about them as well: their responsibility for landing Joseph in this situation, their unmerited profit from it when Joseph brings them to Egypt to survive a famine in their own land, and the way in which God's promise to bless all nations through them (12:1-3) is nonetheless sustained. So although the novella lacks the direct references to God and occasions of divine intervention so prominent in the Abraham and Jacob cycles, it still serves the larger theological agenda they pursue.

The story begins with a young Joseph, favored son of Jacob, dreaming of his ascendancy over his older brothers and foolishly recounting his visions to his brothers. For this miscalculation they plot against him and only stop short of killing him for his arrogance when the opportunity presents itself to Judah to convince the brothers to sell Joseph instead to passing traders, who in turn sell him into slavery in Egypt (ch. 37).

After an interlude that recounts Judah's own indiscretion with his daughter-in-law, Tamar (ch. 38), Joseph's story continues with an account of how his master's wife's attempts to seduce him, and the master — Potiphar — has Joseph jailed because he believes his wife who, caught in the act, claims Joseph is the seducer (ch. 39). In prison, Joseph reveals his skill not only for dreaming, but for interpreting dreams, a gift which wins his release from Pharaoh's prisons to the royal courts when Joseph rightly interprets Pharaoh's dreams of seven fat cows and seven lean cows as predictions of feast and famine.

In Pharaoh's court Joseph quickly rises to power as the vizier who controls Egypt's food production so the nation can survive and flourish in the impending famine (chs. 40–41; 47:13-26). When Egypt does become the world's food source during the famine, Joseph's brothers are compelled to travel there to seek food, and as it happens they have to deal with him directly to get it. They do not recognize Joseph, and over the course of their two trips to Egypt for food he tests them unmercifully before identifying himself and reconciling with them (42:1–47:12).

As Genesis concludes, the narrative relates that Jacob and his sons and their families are thus gathered safely together in Egypt, a land of abundance in the famine that rages otherwise through their world. Jacob dies there in peace after adopting Joseph's twin sons, Ephraim and Manasseh, and blessing all his sons in varying ways. At the very last we read that Joseph's brothers are concerned that he will deal with them harshly after their father's death. Joseph replies that they have nothing to fear, for though they meant it all for evil against him, God meant it for good (47:13–50:26).

Critical Issues in Genesis 12–50

As is the case with the Primeval History, great uncertainty plagues attempts to sort out the compositional history of the Ancestral Saga and to assign to its various portions authors, dates, and provenances. Dependent in part on the outcome of the debate about compositional history is a second critical issue, the relationship of these stories to actual historical events.

History and the Ancestral Narratives

Establishing some measure of historicity for the Ancestral Saga has concerned various kinds of Bible readers, especially since the rise of historical criticism and its natural skepticism regarding the biblical narrative's reliability. From Israelis who want documentary support for their claim to parts of the Levant, to Christian fundamentalists who want to prove the Bible an accurate historical record, to historians seeking to write credible accounts of the ancient world, this pastime has long

Caravan of "Asiatics" bearing goods to Egypt; wall painting from the tomb of Khnum-hotep III at Beni Hasan, ca. 1890 B.C.E. (Oriental Institute, University of Chicago)

been a major preoccupation. We share this interest, at least insofar as attending to it gives us some idea of the implied author and audience of Genesis 12–50.

For all of the interest in the topic, though, the personal and particular nature of the stories wards off attempts to prove the historical authenticity of the specific events and persons in the Ancestral Saga. Instead, the focus has been on linking the ancestral period with known times, places, and cultures from the ancient world. Such efforts, however, have also achieved little success, not least of all because the Ancestral Saga references no known historical events or personages, nor are there any references to Israel's ancestors in literature outside the Bible. But these impediments have not foreclosed attempts to link the saga to particular contexts.

For instance there is a popular theory that the designation of Abraham as an *'ibri* in Gen 14:13 marks him as one of the *'apiru*, a semi-nomadic people described in a number of ancient Near Eastern sources from the 2nd millennium B.C.E. However, in addition to the difficulty associated with dating Genesis 14 and integrating it with the rest of the Ancestral Saga (see the discussion of that chapter above), the fact that the *'apiru* are present for so long in the sources — throughout the entire 2nd millennium — makes the equation only modestly helpful, even if it holds true.

A second possibility, the "Amorite hypothesis," correlates archaeological evidence for a de-urbanization of city culture in the early 2nd millennium with roughly contemporaneous references in Akkadian texts to "Amorites" who may have infiltrated the cities from the countryside (recall our survey of the historical back-

ground to the biblical world above). The hypothesis links Abraham and his descendants with these Amorites (even suggesting that some of the individual names in the Ancestral Saga are Amorite in origin). But without any real evidence in the biblical record for this Amorite hypothesis, it holds little broad appeal.

The mid-2nd millennium Mari records from the Euphrates region have also been used to date and locate the ancestors. They reflect a *dimorphic* society — one that includes both nomadic peoples and sedentary populations in interaction with each other — like the one evident in the stories of the ancestors. The problem, of course, is that dimorphic societies can be found throughout history in the Middle East (e.g., contemporary Bedouin culture as it interacts with village, town, and city), so the Mari evidence is also of little help.

The Nuzi tablets found in northern Iraq, also from the mid-2nd millennium, have likewise been suggested to provide evidence of the culture shared by the ancestors, but in this case too there are insurmountable problems with the evidence. For instance, on first analysis it was thought that the Nuzi tablets advocated a form of sister marriage that parallels the explanation Abraham offers to Abimelech for having called Sarah his sister (Genesis 20). However, closer study has suggested that when we read the Nuzi tablets in their own right — apart from the wishes of biblical scholars seeking to confirm the existence of the ancestors' culture — the practice of sister marriage and other supposed parallels to ancestral culture vanish.

While the evidence for dating the ancestral stories to a very early era turns out to be problematic at best, there are also indications in the text itself that the stories are in any case much later than the period they refer to. Indeed, the Philistines, who enter the world stage only in the 12th century B.C.E., are featured in Gen 21:32, 34; 26:1, 14-15, 18. Likewise, the use of the phrase "to this day" with reference to place names or practices (e.g., 19:38; 26:33; 32:32) indicates that the stories' narrators lived long after the events they narrate. And perhaps most telling is the fact that the saga begins with the announcement that God called Abraham from "Ur of the Chaldeans." This particular way of referring to Ur, a 3rd-millennium Mesopotamian city, first appeared in the Neo-Babylonian Empire of the late 7th and early 6th centuries B.C.E.! On even this partial list of the evidence for a later date, it seems wise not to ask the ancestral stories to relate reliable history from the period they narrate. Rather more intriguing is the possibility that they cast light on the concerns of Israelites from a much later time, perhaps as late as the Exile.

The Authorship, Date, and Provenance of Genesis 12–50

So when did the Ancestral Saga make its debut? What were its authors' interests and those of its audience? Form critics observe that substantial portions of it were oral creations long before they became written texts, "legends" developed to explain the origins of everything from daily life practices to the existence of particular peoples. For instance, Hermann Gunkel, an early practitioner of form criticism, observed that the ancestral stories embrace, among other oral genres, etiologies (e.g., why Israelites don't eat the thigh muscle; Gen 32:29-32) and ethnologies (e.g., where peoples like the Ammonites and Moabites came from; 19:30-38). Later scholars extended Gunkel's approach to suggest that clusters of such legends formed around named figures — Abraham and Jacob in particular — who were the eponymous ancestors of the peoples who collected and retold the legends to reflect and define their identity.

This approach, however, still does not provide insight into the author and audience of the Ancestral Saga as a whole. But source criticism and its progeny, the Documentary Hypothesis, do move in that direction, positing the combination of legend collections to form the "sources" of the Pentateuch. The hypothesis' results for the Ancestral Saga are depicted below on page 65. Because the Elohist is now widely believed to have been no source at all, but rather northern traditions incorporated by the Yahwist Writer, we simplify the table by assigning all formerly Elohist material to the Yahwist. We also do not subdivide passages in such minuscule portions as some Documentarians are wont to do. Only the general parameters are provided.

Even a cursory glance at the table reveals the central role played by the Yahwist in creating the Ancestral Narrative. Thus understanding that author and his audience — dating his activity and locating it in a particular place — is important if we are to comprehend the Ancestral Saga as clearly as possible.

As noted in Chapter 5, the Documentary Hypothesis places the Yahwist in Judah during the halcyon days of the United Monarchy. Documentarians cite a number of indicators favoring such a date and provenance. For instance, the boundaries of the land God promised to Abraham in Gen 15:18 are those of the Davidic kingdom according to 1 Kgs 4:21, and the assertion that Abraham's descendants would be as numerous as the "sand of the seashore" (Gen 13:16; 15:5; 22:17) sees its fulfillment in the description of Solomon's kingdom in 1 Kgs 4:20. On this view, by telling the story of the ancestors, the Yahwist Writer offers an explanation of the origins of the glorious Davidic-Solomonic kingdom.

Of course, this approach does not explain what we observed above, that the name for Abraham's place of origin, Ur of the Chaldeans, was known only from the period of the Exile on. Nor does it take into account the tenor of the story narrated in the Ancestral Saga. Like the record of early human behavior in the Primeval History, the stories of the ancestors are hardly flattering: both Abraham and Isaac give their wives away to strangers to save their own skin; Jacob takes advantage of his dimwitted brother, deceives his father and father-in-law, and takes no umbrage at the rape of his daughter by a stranger; and Joseph is an arrogant, thoughtless brother and his siblings return the favor with their own acts of double-dealing. It is hardly believable that these are the exemplars an author would wish to share with the royal court to explain the origins of the monarchy and its great possessions! But just as the evidence points to an exilic date for the Yahwist material in the Primeval History, the language, content, and themes of the Ancestral Saga also match the period closely. And by dating the Yahwist to the Exile, Abraham's origin in the (Neo-Babylonian named!) Ur of the Chaldeans makes perfect sense: his departure from there to receive the gift of the Promised Land gives expression to the exiles' anticipation that they would one day return home. Likewise, the portrait of the ancestors as people afflicted by the evil inclination that God observed in humanity in the Primeval History (Gen 6:5; 8:21) extends the Primeval History's implicit explanation for the Exile: it was the natural outcome of human arrogance and willfulness. At the same time, God's steadfast adherence to the promises he had made — even to the egregiously sinful Jacob — refines the Primeval History's portrait of God as blessing creation, no matter its rebellion against him. God has devised in his special

The Yahwist and Priestly Works in Genesis 12–50

Yahwist Material	*Priestly Material*
12:1-3, Promise to Abraham	
12:4-9, Abraham's journey	
12:10-20, First wife-sister episode	
13:1-18, Abraham and Lot divide land	
14:1-24, War with the four kings (?)	
15:1-21, Abrahamic covenant	
16:1-16, Birth of Ishmael	
	17:1-27, Abrahamic covenant
18:1-33, Three travelers	
19:1-38, Sodom and Gomorrah	
20:1-18, Second wife-sister episode	
21:1-7, Birth of Isaac	
21:8-21, Hagar and Ishmael	
21:22-34, Abraham and Abimelech	
22:1-24, Binding of Isaac, covenant	
	23:1-20, Purchase of cave at Machpelah
24:1-67, Rebekah	
25:1-6, Sons of Keturah	
	25:12-18, Genealogy of Ishmael
25:19-26, Birth of Jacob and Esau	
25:27-34, Jacob purchases the birthright	
26:1-11, Third wife-sister episode	
26:12-35, Isaac and Abimelech	
27:1-45, Jacob and Rebekah trick Isaac	
	28:1-9, Jacob blessed, Esau marries
28:10-22, Covenant promise at Bethel	
29:1-30, Jacob, Laban, Leah and Rachel	
29:31–30:24, Jacob's children	
30:25-31:55, Jacob and Laban	
32:1-21, Jacob's return	
32:22-32, God renames Jacob	
33:1-20, Jacob reconciles with Esau	
34:1-31, Shechem incident (?)	
35:1-8, Return to Bethel	
	35:9-15, God renames Jacob
35:16-21, Rachel's death	
35:22, Reuben's sin with Bilhah	
	35:23-29, Jacob's children, Isaac's death
	36:1-30, Esau's genealogy
36:31-43, Edomite king list	
37–50, Joseph novella	

relationship to Abraham and his descendants a more manageable means of blessing all creation; through this man and his descendants God would bless all creation (12:3). Indeed, not only *in spite of*, but even *through* the evil inclinations of Abraham's descendants God worked out the fulfillment of his promise (50:20). From this thematic perspective the Yahwist's account of the ancestors is dated most easily to the Exilic period.

To this the Priestly Writer added the covenant of circumcision, the purchase of the cave at Machpelah, as well as some genealogical notices. As we observed in Chapter 5, there is much less dispute about the date and authorship of the Priestly Work. It seems certain to have been the creation of Aaronite priests (as we will most clearly see in treating Exodus to Numbers) and to have been written around the time the Persian Empire replaced Babylon as the region's great power. As such, the covenant of circumcision may reflect in part the Priestly Writer's desire to provide a way for Judeans living apart from the land of Israel to mark themselves as adherents to the cult of Yahweh; the story of the purchase of the Cave at Machpelah buttresses the returnees' claim to the land of Israel as they returned under Persian mandate to rebuild the temple and renew its activities; and the genealogical notices provided order to the human communities in and around Persian-period Judea.

Theological Themes in Genesis 12–50

Like the Primeval History the Ancestral Saga evokes two kinds of theological reflection: musings related to large and small curiosities in the text and consideration of the major themes that are woven throughout it.

Addressing Curiosities in the Ancestral Saga
Among the many curious elements in the stories of the ancestors, several stand out for their ability to stir the imagination of interpreters.

Ancient interpreters were fond of using the mystery surrounding Melchizedek's sudden and peculiar appearance as a priest-king in Genesis 14 as the seed for larger narrative and theological speculation. Not surprisingly, an early Christian writer saw in him a suitable model for understanding Jesus (Hebrews 5–7), and one of the Dead Sea Scrolls that reflects the Qumran community's eschatological imagination assigns him the tasks of proclaiming release and expiation for the Sons of Light and wreaking God's vengeance on the Sons of Darkness in the last days (11QMelchizedek).

Clearly the most provocative episode for ancient interpreters in the Ancestral Saga was the near-sacrifice of Isaac in Genesis 22. The burning question was — and remains for many readers today — why God would command such a thing. A wide variety of texts suggest that, just as Satan tempted God to test Job, the Evil One provoked God by suggesting Abraham was not as faithful as he seemed (4QPseudo-Jubilees[a]; *Jubilees* 17:15–18:19; *b. Sanhedrin* 89b; *Genesis Rabbah* 56.4).

Joseph's marriage to "Asenath daughter of Potiphera, priest of On" (Gen 41:45, 50; 46:20) raised more than a few eyebrows in antiquity. How could Joseph, a model for all Israelites (see, e.g., *Testament of Joseph*), have married a foreigner, and the daughter of an idol's minister, no less? The charming pseudepigraphic romance *Joseph and Asenath* offers an extended answer to this question that explains how Joseph's purity of faith actually led to Asenath's conversion!

Anthropology and Theology: God, the Ancestors, and the Relationship between Them
While the Primeval History reveals a God who is engaged in the process of learning the contours of his own creation — especially its capacity for good and evil — the God of the Ancestral Saga requires no further education: from the first moment of this story God makes promises and works diligently to fulfill them. From the initial promise to Abraham in Genesis 12, to the renewal of it in ch. 15, to the start on fulfilling it in the birth of Isaac in ch. 21, to the use of Joseph to protect and extend it in chs. 37–50, the story of the ancestors is a story of God's faithfulness, in spite of the ancestors' often willful contempt for his overtures.

Indeed, while the portrait of God may be different in the Primeval History and the Ancestral Saga, the substantive characterization of humanity in Genesis 12–50 simply applies the principles developed in the Primeval History to telling the story of Abraham and his family: like Adam and Eve, Cain, Ham, and the builders of the tower, with few exceptions the inclination of the ancestors' heart is evil (almost) continually. While there are moments of fidelity such as Abraham's response to God's command that he sacrifice his son, they count for little in the balance against the other missteps committed by the ancestors. Even Joseph, the paragon of virtue in later Jewish literature, is at first arrogant and then vengeful as he relates to his brothers. Seemingly every moment of the story is weighed down with the possibility that the selfish, arrogant choices of the ancestors would nullify God's promise to them.

Election, Promise, and Covenant
This curious relationship between God and humanity is highlighted by the dynamics of election, promise, and covenant at work in the Ancestral Narrative. While Abraham is elected to receive God's unilateral promise in Genesis 12, the reader perceives a hint of bilateralism: after all, Abraham must leave his home to receive the fruits of God's promises, land and progeny. But Genesis 15, with its covenant of the pieces, seems to erase any equivocation on God's part: only God seems bound by the ceremony of the pieces. In its complete form — including the Priestly Writer's contribution — the Ancestral Narrative offers another proviso regarding the fulfillment of God's promises in Genesis 17 by introducing the covenant of circumcision. Then Genesis 22 seems to undercut seriously the notion of God's pure promise by announcing that Abraham had to prove his faithfulness in the near sacrifice of his son Isaac. Yet by the time one comes to the end of the story, it seems clear that ultimately God intends to bless God's people no matter their actions. Joseph's reply to

his brothers' anxiety in Gen 50:20 leaves little doubt on this score.

So what explains this vacillation between unequivocally unilateral promise and hints of bilateralism on God's part? In at least one instance, Genesis 17, the swing toward bilateralism can be explained by the combination of somewhat disparate sources, J and P. But even within the Yahwist portions of the Ancestral Narrative there still seems to be some inconsistency. As we shall see, one possible explanation is that the Yahwist Writer was responding to what we will come to know as the Deuteronomic tradition, evident in Deuteronomy to 2 Kings. According to most scholars of the Pentateuch's compositional history, that massive work explained the Exile to Babylon as the result of the people's failure to keep the law that God had established in a bilateral covenant (announced in Deuteronomy). The Yahwist's response may have been to say that before God forged the bilateral agreement, God made unilateral promises that endured even into the Exile, assuring the people of God's abiding promise. We shall soon see plenty more evidence that Genesis to 2 Kings gives voice to these two competing theological perspectives.

Questions for Review and Discussion

1 In what ways does Genesis 12–50 show the influence of ancient Near Eastern treaty forms on the authors of the Ancestral Narrative?

2 How were treaties understood in the ancient world, and how do you think that understanding was put to use by the authors of Genesis 12–50?

3 What are the dominant theological themes of Genesis 12–50, and how do the two sources present there give expression to them separately and together?

Further Reading

Blenkinsopp, *The Pentateuch;* Van Seters, *The Pentateuch;* Whybray, *Introduction to the Pentateuch.*

Carr, David M. *Reading the Fractures of Genesis: Historical and Literary Approaches.* Louisville: Westminster/ John Knox, 1996.

Moberly, R. W. L. *Genesis 12–50.* OTG. Sheffield: JSOT, 1992.

Wenham, Gordon J. "Genesis." In *ECB,* 47-71.

Chapter 8

Exodus

Getting Started

1. Read Exodus 1. What amount of time has passed since the days when Joseph and his family descended into Egypt? What does the narrator tell you about the changed conditions of the people of Israel?

2. Read Exodus 12–15 and 32. What events do these passages narrate? How does God's action in these events measure up to the ways of God in Genesis?

3. Skim Exodus 25–31. How does this material differ from the other parts of Exodus you have read so far? To which material in Genesis does it bear most resemblance?

Preliminary Comments

From the very beginning the book of Exodus makes clear that much time has passed since Jacob and his family descended to Egypt to dwell there with Joseph, and Exod 12:40 confirms it, saying that "the time that the people of Israel dwelt in Egypt was four hundred and thirty years" (but compare Gen 15:13). During the interval Jacob's descendants went from being welcome guests to

slaves of Pharaoh. The book of Exodus tells the story of the people's escape from their bondage in Egypt, their flight into the wilderness and on to Sinai, their rebellion along the way, and their receipt of laws for life together before God. As we shall see, although Exodus relates an entirely new chapter in Israel's early history, it continues the themes in Genesis: here too we find God's command to the people to be fruitful and multiply and God's promise to them of unilateral blessing. Also, Exodus elaborates the theme first sounded in Gen 12:3, that God will bless those who bless God's chosen people and curse those who curse them.

A Walk through Exodus

Exodus is organized into several major parts that bring the people from slavery in Egypt under Moses' leadership to a long stay at Sinai.

Exodus 1–18: From Slavery in Egypt to Freedom at Sinai

Exodus 1 announces that, because the pharaohs who favored Israel ceased to reign in Egypt, the descendants of Jacob find themselves enslaved and forced to work on royal building projects in Pithom and Rameses (see the map on page 70). Pharaoh imposes especially oppressive policies because he deems the Israelites' increasing numbers and strength to be a threat to Egyptian power (1:7, 10). As Israel continues to flourish even under harsh oppression, Pharaoh adopts yet stiffer measures: first he (unsuccessfully) recruits midwives to kill sons born to Israelites; when that measure fails he demands that every son born to Jacob's descendants be thrown into the Nile to drown (1:12, 15-22).

This command from Pharaoh sets off the chain of events that eventually bring Moses before him as a foe (chs. 2–4). Responding to the fear that her son would be drowned in the Nile, one mother seeks to save him by sending him down the river in a basket to be found by Pharaoh's daughter. Her plan succeeds and the child grows to adulthood and becomes in time a member of Pharaoh's household as his daughter's son, Moses. But when Moses slays a harsh taskmaster of the Hebrew slaves and his murderous deed becomes known to Pharaoh, Moses is forced to flee to Midian. There he meets Jethro, a priest of Midian, and he marries Zipporah, one of Jethro's daughters. All the while, the Hebrews continue to suffer the degradations imposed on them by Pharaoh. Thus God appears to Moses at Sinai (also called Horeb) to call him to service as God's instrument for liberating the people from their bondage. Moses responds with great reluctance to God's election of him, arguing that he would be unable to explain who sent him on this errand: God's response is to reveal the divine name *(YHWH,* or *Yahweh),* to assure Moses of the eventual success of his mission, to provide Moses with magical skills to match those of Egypt's sorcerers, and to promise Aaron as Moses' partner in the task. So after parting with his father-in-law, Moses and his family set out for Egypt, encountering an inexplicably murderous God along the way (4:24-26), but nonetheless arriving safely.

Exodus 5–11 reports Moses' struggle to persuade Pharaoh to release the Israelites from slavery. After a first unsuccessful attempt to persuade Pharaoh to let God's people go, there is a fresh account of Moses' call (cf. ch. 3). Then follows a series of plagues announced by Moses and inflicted by God. The Nile turns to blood, its waters are made undrinkable, frogs invade the land, there are plagues of gnats and flies, farm animals take ill, humans and animals break out with boils, hail and locusts destroy crops, and darkness covers the land. But these are not enough to convince Pharaoh to release the people, for when he fails to harden his own heart against the Israelites (7:13, 22; 8:15; 9:35), God sees to it for him (9:12; 10:20, 27; 11:10). Thus God announces the final plague, the death of the firstborn of Egypt.

Exodus 12:1–13:16 mixes a narrative of the 10th plague and Israel's departure from Egypt with instructions for observing Passover, the Feast of Unleavened Bread, and the mandate to consecrate to God all the firstborn of Israel. The narrative explains that the Israelites escape the 10th plague's effects by each household slaughtering a lamb and daubing its blood on the doorframe of their dwelling so that God would know to cause the plague of death to pass over their house. The cultic instructions included in this section transform what was probably a springtime shepherd's feast into a ceremonial meal commemorating Israel's deliverance from Egypt. The instructions also join this Passover meal of a slaughtered lamb and bitter herbs to the Feast of Unleavened Bread (originally an agricultural festival associated with barley harvest). Likewise, the account also links instructions for the consecration to God of all Israel's firstborn to Israel's deliverance through the 10th plague; the same instructions provide for the redemption of firstborn humans.

Exodus 13:17–14:31 explains that because of the 10th plague Pharaoh finally lets the people go. But as soon as they are on their way God hardens Pharaoh's heart so that he will pursue Israel and God can gain glory by defeating Pharaoh and his might. Indeed, it is on account of the circuitous route God takes the people by leading them by a pillar of cloud by day and of fire at night that Pharaoh is able to catch up with them at the edge of a sea. Seeing their predicament, the people rebel for the first (and certainly not the last) time against Moses' leadership. But as Pharaoh and his army are about to overtake the people, God instructs Moses to part the sea by raising his hand over it so that the people can pass through dry-shod. In a scene recalling the ancient Near Eastern battle myths of creation, the parted waters permit Israel to pass safely and then return to their place to destroy the army of Pharaoh. Safe on the other side, Moses and Miriam sing songs of victory (15:1-21).

Exodus 15:22–18:27 reports the difficulties of the people's journey toward Mount Sinai. Almost immediately they rebel against Moses because their water is bitter; in response God instructs Moses to cast a stick of wood into the pool to make the water sweet. The people complain

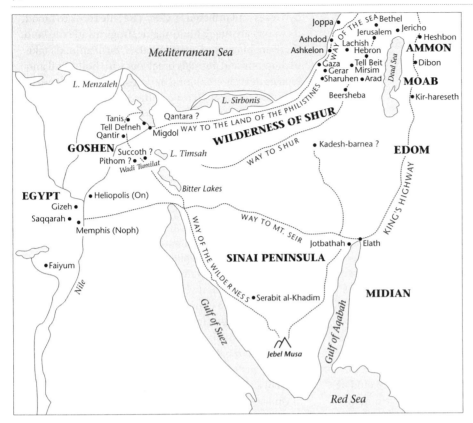

ROUTE OF THE EXODUS

associated with Sinai.) God immediately sets about inviting them into a covenantal relationship through the mediation of Moses. The people accept the invitation and are then instructed on observing proper boundaries in relation to God and God's holiness. The chapter concludes with a theophany — an appearance of God — to all the people in the form of what is best described as a violent thunderstorm. The (somewhat confused) frequency with which Moses travels up and down the mountain to establish this new relationship between God and people indicates something of the highly composite character of this chapter.

Before the theophany concludes, God speaks the "Ten Commandments" to the people. An "Ethical Decalogue" that is repeated in Deut 5:6-21, it is made up of apodictic laws, that is, absolute, or unconditional commands. They are formed as simple positive or negative commands. The enumeration of the commandments differs among Christian and Jewish traditions, but perhaps the division most reflective of the text itself counts the first four commandments as Israel's obligations to God, and the remaining six as the Israelites' responsibilities to one another. In any case, when the announcement of the commandments is completed, the theophany concludes with the people eschewing direct contact with God, requesting instead that Moses henceforth be their mediator.

The next section, 20:22–23:33, is known as the Covenant Code. This body of case, or casuistic, law begins, like other law codes in the Hebrew Bible, with cultic law (cf. Leviticus 17; Deuteronomy 12). It stipulates that wherever Israelites choose to worship God, they must only make an earthen altar or one of unhewn stones without steps up to it. (By contrast, Deuteronomy 12 centralizes worship in "the place the Lord . . . will choose" [Jerusalem], and Leviticus 17 presumes centralized sacrifice and goes further still to prohibit profane slaughter.) The code then treats the rights of slaves and regulates a variety of human behaviors affecting the

against Moses that they are hungry and that they would have been better off back in Egypt; in response God provides manna from heaven for food and commands that the people gather twice the normal amount on the sixth day so they can rest on the seventh. The people thirst and rebel once more against Moses; in response, God instructs Moses to strike a rock to produce water to satisfy the people. As if this were not enough trouble, the Amalekites then become the first people to attack Israel (making them forevermore Israel's archetypal enemy). Throughout the battle the people are victorious so long as Moses stretches his hands over the battle scene, but when he grows weary and lowers his hands, Amalek prevails. Thus Aaron and Hur have to prop up his outstretched arms to ensure Israel's victory. Following this, Moses' father-in-law, Jethro, arrives and makes sacrifice to God in thanksgiving for Israel's deliverance from Egypt. And seeing the stress Moses suffers in leading the people, Jethro convinces Moses to appoint assistants, elders over the people.

Exodus 19–24: A Theophany, Law Code, and Covenant Ceremony at Sinai

According to Exodus 19 the people finally arrive at Mount Sinai. (See p. 71 for a picture of the mountain typically well-being of others and their personal and real property, and society as a whole. It also includes cultic laws and a cultic calendar. The structure of the case laws is as one would expect it to be. For example, Exod 23:4 reads "When you come upon your enemy's ox or donkey going astray, you shall bring it back": a case is posited (the finding of an enemy's lost livestock) and a proper response is mandated (the return of the lost livestock to its owner). One odd feature of the Covenant Code noted by many readers is the way it occasionally seems incomplete. For instance, the law just cited addresses only the lost livestock of the *enemy*. What about the livestock of one's neighbor, friend, or relative? We return to this issue below in "Critical Issues."

Aerial view of Jebel Musa (Arab. "Mountain of Moses"), traditionally associated with Mount Sinai. (Werner Braun)

After the Covenant Code, Exodus 24:1-15 relates the covenant confirmation ceremony. This complex chapter provides two traditions regarding the ratification ritual. According to 24:1-2, 9-11 Aaron and his sons Nadab and Abihu, along with 70 elders of Israel ascend the mountain. There they actually see God and share a covenant banquet in God's presence to confirm the covenant. An alternate tradition in 24:3-8 indicates that all the people make sacrifice through Moses to confirm their commitment. Finally, in 24:12-14 Moses ascends the mountain again to receive the two stone tablets containing the covenant document, and according to 24:15-18 he remains on the mountain to receive the instructions for the construction of the tent of meeting, the tabernacle, and the other cultic accoutrements.

Exodus 25–31, 35-40: Providing Order for the Cultic Space

Exodus 25–31 reports the instructions God gives Moses for the design of the moveable worship center, the tabernacle that the people would use on their journey toward the Promised Land. First God instructs Moses to ask the people for the resources necessary to construct the holy place and its accoutrements. Then God provides detailed instructions for fabricating the ark of the covenant, the table to hold the holy bread and the sacred vessels, and the seven-branched lampstand (ch. 25); the tabernacle or the tent of meeting (ch. 26); the altar of the burnt offering and the court in which it is situated (ch. 27); and the priests' vestments (ch. 28). Then God provides instructions for ordaining the priests who will serve in the tabernacle (ch. 29). Finally, Exodus 30–31 reports that God addresses other priestly matters as well, such as the offering of incense, the collection of taxes to support the sanctuary, the purifying ablutions priests are required to undertake, the consecratory anointing for the sanctuary and its contents (including the priests), and the appointment of craftsmen to execute the plans. The section concludes with God's reminder to the Israelites that they are to keep the Sabbath holy.

After the account of the golden calf episode (chs. 32–34; see below) Exodus 35–40 in large part repeats chs. 25–31, but to report that the instructions given in the earlier chapters are carried out. For example, 36:8-38 essentially reiterates the instructions for the pattern of the tabernacle with its curtains and structural supports given in ch. 26, but this time as a report of what the artisans actually accomplish.

In addition to the structure proposed by these "temple blueprints" (see p. 72 for a sketch of the structure proposed in chs. 25–31; 35-40), one of the more noteworthy elements of this massive description of how the cultic space and its accoutrements are put in order is its literary symmetry with the story of creation in Genesis 1. Just as God methodically established cosmic order where there was chaos, God commands Moses to oversee the ordering of the cult. Indeed, while Genesis 2:2 reports that "God had finished all the work he had done" at the end of the creation account, Exod 40:33 reports that "Moses finished the work" to conclude this episode.

Exodus 32–34: The Golden Calf Episode

The golden calf episode in Exodus 32–34 separates the reports of the plan for the traveling worship center and its actual construction. Ironically, this incident reveals how the people rebel against God by worshipping other gods precisely while Moses receives the designs for the cultic center. According to ch. 32, Moses' long delay on the mountaintop leads some among the people to fear that he has perished, so they urge Aaron to provide for them a new god to worship. Aaron obliges by fashioning their offerings of jewelry and fine metals into a golden calf that they then worship. When God sees this he determines to destroy the people and establish a new nation through Moses. Moses intercedes for the people. He observes that the Egyptians would be vindicated by such an act on God's part, and echoing Genesis 15, he reminds God of the sworn oath God made to provide land and descendants "like the stars of heaven" to Abraham, Isaac, and Jacob. With that God repents of the plan to destroy the people. Moses then descends from the mountain, sees the people's apostasy, and angrily destroys the tablets on which the commandments have

been inscribed. He then questions Aaron about the incident, and Aaron disingenuously claims his innocence in the affair. Then Moses summons the Levites who have remained faithful in spite of the golden calf's presence in their midst and sets them to the task of destroying the apostates; for their zeal the Levites are rewarded with ordination to God's service. Then Moses intercedes for the people yet again, and God spares them complete destruction, sending instead a punishing plague on the apostates.

Exodus 33–34 begins with God announcing his decision not to accompany the people to the Promised Land lest he destroy them in anger over the golden calf incident and their abiding capacity for disobedience. Moses intercedes again for the people, this time in the tent of meeting pitched at a distance from the camp. He begs God not to let the people continue on their way unless the divine presence goes with them. God relents, and then Moses demands to see God face to face; God relents to this request as well, arranging to reveal only his backside to Moses on the mountain. Thus Moses ascends the mountain once more to receive his vision of the Lord and obtain new engraved stone tablets. This time the tablets are inscribed with a different set of "Ten Commandments," a "Ritual Decalogue," so named because of the stipulations' focus on matters of worship. As ch. 34 closes Moses descends the mountain with the new tablets of stone to meet the people and begin the construction of the tabernacle.

The Old Testament Tabernacle

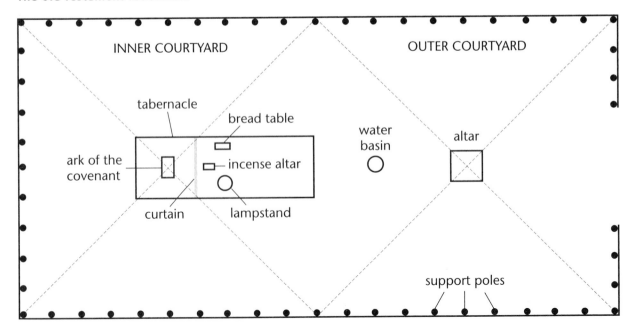

Critical Issues in Studying Exodus

Among the myriad critical issues associated with the study of Exodus we may address only four. Because it is such a constitutive event for Judaism and Christianity, the historicity of the Exodus from Egypt has been the subject of enormous interest among professional scholars and lay readers alike. A not unrelated issue is the apparent influence of some ancient Near Eastern myths on the material in Exodus. Of additional note is the attitude toward Aaron and the Levites in the golden calf episode and its implications for competition among priestly factions in Israel's history. And because Exodus, like Genesis, is clearly composite in nature, questions of authorship, date, and provenance are of signal importance as well.

History and the Exodus from Egypt

For Jews and Christians, the story of the Exodus has always been much more than fodder for a Hollywood blockbuster. Rather, it was a foundational event for Israelite religion and remains so for Judaism to this day; and it has always been a paradigmatic episode for Christian theology, modeling God's desire to liberate his people that Christians identify in the story of Jesus. So it is no wonder that verifying the historical authenticity of the Exodus from Egypt has long fascinated scholars and lay readers alike. And it is not as though the fascination is unsupported by the evidentiary record. Quite apart from attempts to rationalize the escape through the sea — by suggesting that it was the *Reed* Sea that parted, or that meteorological or oceanographic phenomena unique to the region created the conditions reported in Exodus — there are some genuine indicators that may be cited as evidence of the Exodus's historicity.

As for the obvious prerequisite to the Exodus — the presence of the Hebrews in Egypt from the time of Joseph — a variety of ancient witnesses (*ANET*, 230-34) testify to the dominance in Egypt of "Shepherd Kings" from Asia, the Hyksos, from the 18th to the 16th centuries B.C.E. Many commentators link these Hyksos with the Hebrews and explain the tradition of Joseph's gubernatorial stint as evidence of that dominance. Likewise, the renewal of Egyptian hegemony through the campaigns of Ahmose I may account for the enslavement of the Hebrews.

It is also certain that there were forced-labor projects in Egypt in the middle of the 13th century B.C.E., when most scholars date the Exodus, and that some slaves fled to obtain their freedom from such projects. Indeed, Pithom and Rameses (see the map on p. 70), the supply cities the Hebrew slaves were required to build for Pharaoh according to Exod 1:11, are both known to have been occupied in the 1200s B.C.E. Papyri texts indicate that in the same era ʿapiru made up part of the labor force and that at least once the Egyptians had to mount an expedition to recover runaway slaves.

Another piece of evidence cited in favor of the general historicity of the story related in Exodus is the religious policy of Pharaoh Akhenaton (reigned *ca.* 1380 to 1362 B.C.E.). Whether the perception was accurate or not, Akhenaton's devotion to the sun-god Aton seems to have been viewed as an unusual expression of monotheism. Some think that this policy may have influenced Moses, producing in him his devotion to one God. Indeed, Moses' name may be of Egyptian origin, meaning "to be born" (compare the pharaonic titles Ah*mose*, Tut*mose*, etc.).

As tantalizing as each of these hints may be, not one piece of the evidence just cited actually proves the historicity of the Exodus reported in the Bible. Moreover, no Egyptian source datable to the time of the Hebrews' enslavement in Egypt or from the suggested time of their escape from the land mentions them by name, nor do Egyptian texts record plagues such as the ones reported in the Bible or anything like the people's miraculous escape through the Red Sea. There is also no archaeological evidence of Israelite occupation in Egypt from the pertinent period (and by comparison the physical evidence of the settlements in the Levant that might be associated with early Israelite culture is basically Canaanite — indigenous — in character). Also, one must admit that the biblical record of the events from Moses' birth to the Exodus itself hardly exudes verisimilitude. It lays claim to extraordinary numbers of Israelite refugees (six hundred thousand *men* alone according to Exod 12:37) and conjures fabulous images of miracles, from Moses' staff-cum-snake to the parting of the sea. As we see below, it more often resembles ancient Near Eastern mythic traditions than historical narrative.

To sum up, perhaps the most judicious thing to say is that just as there is no unequivocal evidence for the historicity of the Exodus, there is also no explicit proof against it. That being said, it also seems unlikely that the event could have been fabricated entirely by ancient writers. It is possible, as some suggest, that a series of slave rebellions and escapes from Egypt were merged by those who experienced them into one grand story of deliverance from bondage. It is also possible that even just a single experience of oppression and deliverance was magnified to create the biblical story of the Exodus. In any case, as the discussion that follows shows, the size or significance of the historical kernel that lies behind this biblical story is ultimately of less importance than what became of it, a witness to the powerful intention of the One God to redeem God's people.

Ancient Near Eastern Myths and Traditions and the Book of Exodus

Although relative to the occurrences in Genesis they are few in number, the echoes of ancient Near Eastern myths in Exodus are critical in understanding the book's thrust as a whole. Three instances in particular tend to support the view that much of Exodus may have been formulated in the Babylonian Exile, and that in all of its parts it was intended as a story-form expression of Israel's special place in the sight of God.

The narrative of Moses' birth and miraculous deliverance from a greater power's evil intentions stands in a long line of such accounts that extends all the way to the New Testament and Revelation 12. But its closest congener in the ancient Near East is the Mesopotamian story of the birth of King Sargon, the legendary founder of Akkad. Not surprisingly, the oldest known version of this threatened-hero story comes from the antiquarian-obsessed Neo-Babylonian Empire. Sargon reports,

> My mother . . . conceived me, in secret she bore me.
> She set me in a basket of rushes, with bitumen she
>   sealed my lid.
> She cast me into the river which rose not over me.
> The river bore me up and carried me to Akki, the drawer
>   of water.
> Akki, the drawer of water lifted me out as he dipped
>   his ewer.
> Akki, the drawer of water took me as his son and
>   reared me. (*ANET,* 119)

Though there are obvious differences between this story and that of Moses' birth — Sargon's mother concealed the birth not out of fear for her child's life but to conceal the illegitimacy of his parentage and save her own position, and the child's savior is a man, not a woman — the parallels between the two are equally obvious. It would seem that the author sought to trade on the ancient prestige of Sargon — something one would expect to find in Mesopotamia, not Egypt! — to enhance Moses' reputation.

The story of the Exodus itself also resonates with the Mesopotamian myths of which the Neo-Babylonian Empire was so fond. Readers familiar with the Mesopotamian creation myths that involve watery chaos and divine warriors recognize motifs from these sagas in the Exodus story. The parting of the sea to permit the emergence on the other side of God's new people recalls the division of chaotic waters to provide dry land on which new life comes forward. Likewise, the tradition in *Enuma Elish* that the high god Marduk slew the watery goddess Tiamat to give birth to something new resonates with the Exodus story. Add to this the popular the-

ory that the Hebrew name for the sea Moses parts, *yam suf,* is best understood from the standpoint of ancient Near Eastern mythology as a "sea of chaos," and the case for reading the Exodus story as an idealized, mythology-fortified account of what might have been a real incident of escape and liberation grows quite strong. We have more to say on this when we come to theological themes in Exodus below.

Also notable are the similarities between the Covenant Code and one of the most famous ancient Near Eastern law collections, the Code of Hammurabi. While other Mesopotamian law codes bear some similarity to the laws in Exod 20:22–23:33 (see *ANET,* 159-98), this one is most similar both in content *and* structure; and conspicuously, like the tale of Sargon's birth, the Code of Hammurabi was preserved by the antiquarians of the Neo-Babylonian Empire. The example on page 75 below provides a glimpse into the similarities shared between the two law codes, as well as an instance of the ways in which the Covenant Code sets itself apart from the Mesopotamian law. Also noteworthy is a similar law in the Code of Eshnunna (likewise known in the Neo-Babylonian period) that some speculate may have provided the very wording that we find in the Covenant Code version of the law on the goring ox.

Lastly it is worth noting the possibility of a connection between the Egyptian *Tale of Sinuhe* and the story of Moses' flight to Midian. By the measure of the surviving manuscript evidence, this Middle Egyptian tale was enormously popular from the 18th to 11th centuries B.C.E. It relates the experiences of an Egyptian official who went into voluntary exile in Asia, where he prospered greatly, but who then returned at the invitation of a pharaoh and took up duties in the royal court where he experienced his true successes. There are some obvious, if only very general, parallels between this and Moses' experience, and it is difficult to say how echoing this tale might have been helpful to the author of the story of Moses.

Priestly Conflict in Ancient Israel and Exodus 32

The history of the priesthood in ancient Israel — from the time of the First Temple through the Second Temple's existence — is shadowy and quite difficult to sort out. However, one thing is clear: there was considerable competition among parties for the ascendant role of service as altar priests, the ones who actually offered to God the sacrifices of Israel.

Evidence of this conflict appears in Exodus 32. Careful reading of the account demonstrates that when he was asked by the people to provide them with an alternative to the God of Israel, Aaron obliged them by making for them the golden calf. This alone impugns Aaron's honor, whom the Priestly Writer regards as the ancestor

The Code of Hammurabi and the Covenant Code Compared

Code of Hammurabi

251. If an ox be a goring ox, and it is shown that he is a gorer, and he (the owner) does not bind his horns, or fasten the ox up, and the ox gore a free-born man and kill him, the owner shall pay one-half a mina in money.
252. If he kill a man's slave, he shall pay one-third of a mina.

Covenant Code

21:29 If the ox has been accustomed to gore in the past, and its owner has been warned but has not restrained it, and it kills a man or a woman, the ox shall be stoned, and its owner also shall be put to death.
21:32 If the ox gores a male or female slave, the owner shall pay to the slaveowner thirty shekels of silver, and the ox shall be stoned.

of all true priests. But the situation grows far worse for Aaron's reputation when Moses questions him about the incident and Aaron boldly states that the calf simply emerged from the fire of its own accord; and anyway, argues Aaron, he was only doing the bidding of stiff-necked Israel (32:24)! Then Moses calls upon the people to avenge the travesty, and the narrator reveals that the Levites — the clan from which Aaron came, the non-altar, hard-labor priests of the Priestly Writer's imagination! — are the ones who heed Moses' call, and for that they are rewarded with ordination to God's service and a special blessing (32:25-29).

However this episode fits into the larger history of the priesthood, it provides unequivocal evidence that there was an ongoing debate among claimants to the highest form of the office, the altar priesthood. It also indicates that the debate likely lasted from the first days of the First Temple to the last days of the Second Temple. We will see more evidence of this running debate in Leviticus and Numbers.

The Authorship, Date, and Provenance of Exodus

We provide on page 76 the division of sources in Exodus from the perspective of the Documentary Hypothesis, but with the usual provisos: the Yahwist and Elohist are merged in keeping with the widespread rejection of a separate Elohist Work, and minuscule assignments to one or the other of the sources within larger units are not recorded.

With only a few significant exceptions, the major portions of Exodus marked off by our "Walk through Exodus" above are easily assigned in their entirety to the Yahwist or Priestly Writers. Exodus 1–18 (the story from Israel's bondage in Egypt to her arrival at Sinai), chs. 19–24 (the account of God's appearance to Israel at Sinai to give law and make a covenant with Israel), and chs. 32–34 (the story of the golden calf incident and its fallout) are all from the Yahwist Writer. The Priestly Writer, on the other hand, authored the instructions for making the tabernacle, as well as the narrative of its fabrication in chs. 25–31 and 35–40.

The Priestly Writer provides the significant exceptions to this general outline. The call of Moses in 6:2-25 is from the Priestly Writer, as is the following episode involving Aaron, Moses, and Pharaoh and Pharaoh's magicians in 7:1-13. The Priestly Writer also added plagues to those already described by the Yahwist Writer (gnats in 8:16-19 and boils in 9:8-12). The instructions for Passover observance in 12:1-20 are also Priestly, as is probably the section on manna collection and Sabbath observance in the wilderness in 16:2-36. The usual understanding of these literary relationships is that the Priestly material was added to an existing Yahwist Work. It is also important to note that a corollary of the Documentary Hypothesis' early date for the Yahwist is that the Covenant Code was Israel's first law code and a source for later collections, including the Deuteronomic Code in Deuteronomy 12–26.

An important revision of this compositional history comes from the perspective of the Supplementary Hypothesis. The revisionist view does not deny the priority of the Yahwist material over the Priestly additions. But as in the case of Genesis, it does question the early date of the Yahwist material for several good reasons.

First, proponents of the Supplementary Hypothesis observe that the Covenant Code's designation as the earliest Israelite legal collection depends on the priority the Documentary Hypothesis assigns to the Yahwist Work. But the abbreviated character of the Code raises suspicions that it is, in fact, a supplement to an existing collection. And comparing it with other Hebrew Bible law codes reinforces that suspicion and makes it difficult to date it so early. For instance, Exod 23:4, the law cited above regarding lost livestock, does appear to *supplement* Deut 22:1-3 (p.76): the law in Deuteronomy concerns itself with the *neighbor's* livestock, and the directive in Exodus simply adds concern for the *enemy's* livestock as well. And notably the word for "enemy" here is the same one used repeatedly in Lev 26:34-45 for the neighbors of Israelites in exile!

A second indication of the post-Deuteronomic character of the Yahwist material in Exodus is the

The Yahwist and Priestly Works in Exodus

Yahwist Material	*Priestly Material*
1–18*, From Israel in Bondage to Arrival at Sinai	6:2-25, The Calls of Moses
	7:1-13, Aaron, Moses, and Pharaoh's Magicians
	8:16-19; 9:8-12; Plagues of Gnats and Boils
	12:1-20, The Passover Meal
	16:2-36, Manna Collection and Sabbath Observance
19–24, Theophany, Covenant Code, and Covenant	
	25-31, Blueprints for the Traveling Sanctuary and Its Accoutrements
32–34, Golden Calf Episode	
	35-40, Completion of the Traveling Sanctuary and Its Accoutrements

*Indicates that much, but not all, of the material so marked belongs to the author noted.

language of 32:7-14. Because this passage "sounds" so Deuteronomic to most readers, Documentarians deem it a late Deuteronomic redaction of the original Yahwist composition. (As we have seen already, this is the Documentary Hypothesis' explanation for other instances of Deuteronomic rhetoric in Genesis as well; see Chapter 5 above.) The problem with this argument is the anti-Deuteronomic theology of the passage: as we shall see, the Deuteronomists held strongly to the view that God responds retributively to apostasy, yet 32:7-14 subverts that understanding of God's way of dealing with humanity, saying that when the people worshipped the golden calf, God checked his wrath out of (albeit grudging!) faithfulness to the unilateral promise he made to Abraham, Isaac, and Jacob. The Supplementary Hypothesis plausibly explains this seemingly contradictory set of circumstances as the consequence of a Yahwist author writing after the Deuteronomist tradition had been formulated; the Yahwist author mimics the style of

Deuteronomy while contradicting its theology! Thus, we have in the Deuteronomic rhetoric in Exodus further evidence for the Supplementary Hypothesis and its post-Deuteronomy, exilic date for the Yahwist.

No matter how one dates the Yahwist material in Exodus, nearly all agree that the Priestly material was added to the narrative either late in the Exile or in the Postexilic period when Judeans had been repatriated to Judah by the Persian Empire. Speaking at least in part for the view that the Priestly material was composed while Israel was still in exile is the concern in Exodus 12 to provide a means of observing Passover in the absence of the temple. But the same concern could persist even into the restoration era since Israelites were scattered far and wide in the Diaspora from the Exile onward. In that case the Priestly Writers seem to have built a list of ways Israelites living in diaspora could maintain their identity even when apart from the temple and its sacrifices and the land of Israel: Sabbath observance, circumcision,

The Law of Lost Livestock in the Covenant and Deuteronomic Codes

Exodus 23:4	*Deuteronomy 22:1-3*
⁴When you come upon your enemy's ox or donkey going astray, you shall bring it back.	¹You shall not watch your neighbor's ox or sheep straying away and ignore them; you shall take them back to their owner. ²If the owner does not reside near you or you do not know who the owner is, you shall bring it to your own house, and it shall remain with you until the owner claims it; then you shall return it. ³You shall do the same with a neighbor's donkey; you shall do the same with a neighbor's garment; and you shall do the same with anything else that your neighbor loses and you find. You may not withhold your help.

and now Passover observance were all rites provided by the Priestly Writer as means of expressing one's Israelite identity in the absence of access to priests or temple sacrifices. The other major Priestly contribution to Exodus, the plans for and the construction of the tabernacle and its accoutrements, reinforces the view that this was a postexilic work: the "portable" sanctuary and its accessories described in Exodus 25–31 and 35–40 hardly seem portable; instead they look like the blueprints for a temple, perhaps the Second Temple conceived and constructed during Persian rule of Judah.

Theological Themes in Exodus

Like the Primeval History the Ancestral Saga evokes two kinds of theological reflection: musings related to large and small curiosities in the text and consideration of the major themes its authors sought to convey.

Addressing Curiosities in Exodus

Thoughtful readers of Exodus 1:16 are struck by the illogic of Pharaoh's command that all infant Hebrew *boys* be murdered at birth: if his goal was to limit the growth of the Israelite population, it would have made more sense to kill the daughters of Israel, the future bearers of additional children. Thus Philo suggests that the real purpose behind this command was not population reduction, but rather reduction of the number of available combatants against Egypt, should the two peoples ever come to blows (*Life of Moses* 1:8). Pseudo-Philo speculates that Pharaoh also wanted to preserve the women of Israel to serve as slaves to the women of Egypt (*Biblical Antiquities* 9:1).

Even more troubling to ancient — and modern! — interpreters is God's hardening of Pharaoh's heart so as to necessitate the murder of *all firstborn* in Egypt to secure the freedom of Israel. Some interpreters dealt with the difficulty by imagining how much worse it could have been: God might have commanded the death of *all Egyptians* but restricted himself to only the firstborn (Philo, *Life of Moses* 1:134). *Jubilees* 49:2 took a different tack, passing off the actual murderous act on the Evil One (called Mastemah in *Jubilees;* cf. 4QPseudo-Jubilees 1:3).

Another example of later interpreters wondering about the destructive elements of the Exodus story involves the puzzle of God's three forms of punishment for those who worshipped the golden calf. The rabbis observed that even though God repented of the decision to destroy all of Israel (32:14), he nonetheless disciplined some with the forced consumption of ashen water (32:20), some through slaughter administered by the Levites (32:28), and others with a plague (32:35). Why,

asked the rabbis, did God utilize such diverse modes of punishment? The Babylonian Talmud explains that the methods corresponded to the manner in which the apostates worshipped the calf: different punishments for different acts (*b. Yoma* 66b)!

Anthropology and Theology: God and the Chosen People Together

As you will recall, Genesis 1–11 proved time and again that humanity in general is inclined to disobedience whenever boundaries are imposed: on the hope that it would make them like God, Adam and Eve ate from the tree they were instructed to leave untouched (Genesis 3); Cain gave in to the sin that God exhorted him to resist (Genesis 4); the daughters of humankind made love with the angels of heaven (Genesis 6:1-4); Noah overindulged in strong drink, and Ham took advantage of his father's condition and open nudity (Genesis 9:20-27); and all of humanity sought like Adam and Eve to transcend its limitations by building a tower to the heavens (Genesis 11:1-9). And Genesis 12–50 showed that God's chosen people differed from that generic pattern of disobedience only in refining it to include a penchant for acting solely for one's own self-interest, regardless of the consequences for others: Abraham gave his wife away to foreigners twice to save his own skin (Genesis 12; 20), and his son Isaac committed the same deed once for the same reason (Genesis 26); Jacob conned his brother out of the family's inheritance in exchange for a bowl of porridge and then stole it outright through deceit (Gen 25:29-34; 27:1-29), and later he endangered his family rather than himself to test his wronged brother's capacity for forgiveness (Genesis 32); Joseph was an arrogant, coddled, favored son, and later a vengeful brother; and Joseph's jealous brothers were would-be cold-blooded killers and the (only!) accessories to kidnapping (Genesis 37; 39-50).

Exodus, as it happens, simply carries this portrait of humanity forward and develops it with respect to the earliest Israelites as well. Although Moses stands above the fray — and why not, since he is twice referred to as a god (Exod 4:16; 7:1)! — the rest of the book's cast of characters are subject to the same foibles as those in Genesis. From the moment of their liberation from Egypt to the last we hear of them as a community in Exodus, the people rebelled against their God and the man God chose to lead them (cf. 16:2; 32). As for Aaron, the future priest, he proved as easily lured away from true worship of the God of Israel as any of the lay Israelites (32:1-6), and when he was confronted with his apostasy he dissembled in fear and trembling, blaming it on the laity (32:21-24).

Meanwhile, the God of Exodus is less a copy of the

God we encounter in Genesis than the logical successor to him; the resulting relationship between God and people is hardly surprising. For in Exodus, God appears to have taken to heart the lessons about the human penchant for sin learned in Genesis 1–11 and reinforced by Genesis 12–50: this God anticipates the people's apostasy and responds with measured discipline, but also with mercy that permits a continued relationship between himself and the chosen people. Only once is God tempted to void the promises he made, and he is saved from that temptation and its possible consequences when Moses reminds him of the way he bound himself to those promises (32:7-14). At the same time, the God of Genesis also proved himself to be passionate about order where there is chaos and about providing a way for God's people to mark themselves as his, no matter where in the world they might be: thus cosmic chaos was replaced with creation's order and the Sabbath was instituted as a time of rest for those who honor God. Just so, in Exodus God provided to the people enough imperishable food in the wilderness on the sixth day that they could show themselves to be his by resting from gathering on the seventh day (Exodus 16). To Sabbath observance God added Passover as yet another way to prove oneself a part of God's kingdom of priests anywhere in the world (Exodus 12). And to prove his abiding passion for order, God commanded Moses to complete the ordering of the cultic space and its appurtenances.

Promise and Covenant

The foregoing portrait of God and humanity together is very much what one expects, given the way the Yahwist's themes of promise and covenant in Genesis are continued so faithfully in Exodus. We hear at the very beginning of Exodus that the people heartily fulfilled the covenantal requirement to be fruitful and multiply, so much so that they were deemed a threat by Pharaoh to his success and power (Exod 1:8-10; cf. Gen 1:28; 9:1; 17:2; 28:3; 35:11). Intertwined with this is the Priestly Writer's emphasis on God's passion for order: the people's success in achieving great numbers according to God's commission is threatened by Pharaoh's hostility, and as the story appears in its Yahwist-Priestly mix, God responds to that threatening chaos by first making clear who is truly in charge, and then by vanquishing it utterly and finally granting to God's people the cultic space and order necessary to celebrate their chosen status.

Indeed, if one reads from the end of Genesis straight on to the narrative in Exodus, it is hard to miss that this is a story of how God upheld, against the threat of an oppressive foreign power, the promise of land and descendants characteristic of the Yahwist Work. The account begins with the memory of the oppression that

followed years of prosperity and success in Egypt, an oppression that endangered the fulfillment of God's promise in both of its aspects. It continues with God electing Moses to help God defend his promise and see to its fulfillment. The call of Moses is redolent with the rhetoric and themes of the promise: God self-identifies as the God of Abraham, Isaac, and Jacob (Exod 3:6, 15, 16), God recalls the promise of a glorious land (3:8, 17), and God's purpose in Moses to save the Israelites from Pharaoh is nothing less than an expression of God's commitment to provide descendants. Then, just as in the Ancestral Saga, God reveals a profound steadfastness to the promise, not veering from course even when the people rebel (14:10-12; 15:23-25; 16:2-8; 17:1-7), and when finally God is pushed to the limits by their rebellion, it is Moses' reminder of the profoundly unilateral and binding nature of the promise that draws God back from the abyss (32:1-14), and leads God to add new dimensions to the promissory relationship whereby the people might mark themselves out as God's own people through religious observances (34:6-27).

It was not difficult for the Priestly Writers to append to this narrative an affirmation of the covenant to be fruitful and multiply and an expression of their concern that the people have a way to express their identity wherever they might be (ch. 12) and that there be order where there is chaos (chs. 25–31, 35–40). By adding to the beginning of the J narrative the list of Jacob's sons and the statement that Israel was fruitful and multiplied greatly in Egypt (1:1-7) the Priestly Writer noted both the orderly nature of Israel even in Egypt and its success in fulfilling the command to be fruitful and multiply in a foreign land. Whether it was intended to function in this way or not, the Priestly Writer's addition of instructions for Passover observance in Exodus 12 not only provided another outlet for Jewish self-definition in a diverse world; it also provided another way for God's people to express the order God desires for creation and the liberation he promises them.

God and the Nations

A last theme surfaced by Exodus is that of God and the nations. In Gen 12:1-3 God promises to bless those nations that bless Abraham's descendants but also to curse those that curse the people. The fate of Egypt and its leader-god, Pharaoh, illustrates this theme clearly. Egypt does not bless God's chosen ones, but rather chooses to curse them, oppress them, and even seek their annihilation. The account of Egypt's fate, embodied by the death of the firstborn and the sea of chaos overcoming the pursuing army, signals clearly God's intention to honor this promise, even its negative side. One wonders if this, a part of the Yahwist Writer's account, does not reflect still more of the exilic context. Could it be that Egypt is a cipher for Babylon and the promise is made that the oppressive power that exiled Israel would in time pay the price of cursing God's people? Finally, the contemporary theological challenge of this particular promise from God and its narrative fulfillment in the Exodus story cannot go unnoticed.

Questions for Review and Discussion

1   In what ways does Exodus show the influence of ancient Near Eastern — especially Neo-Babylonian—traditions, and what does that suggest to Supplementarians about the possible date of the Yahwist Writer?

2   What is the result of sidestepping the question of the Exodus' historicity and focusing instead on what the text seems to convey about God's intentions toward the people of Israel?

3   What are the dominant theological themes of the Yahwist and Priestly Writers' contributions to Exodus, and how do they work together in Exodus as a theological witness?

Further Reading

Blenkinsopp, *The Pentateuch;* Van Seters, *The Pentateuch;* Whybray, *Introduction to the Pentateuch.*

Batto, Bernard F. "Red Sea or Reed Sea: How the Mistake Was Made and What *yam sûp* Really Means." *BAR* 10/4 (1984): 57-63. Suggests that the Hebrew translated as "Red Sea" actually refers to "chaos" and thus has symbolic meaning for what God overcomes for the people's sake.

Johnstone, William. *Exodus.* OTG. Sheffield: Sheffield Academic, 1990.

Van Seters, John. *A Law Book for the Diaspora: Revision in the Study of the Covenant Code.* Oxford: Oxford University Press, 2003.

Chapter 9

Leviticus

Getting Started

1 Skim Leviticus 1–9. What is the focus of these chapters? What sort of "real world" seems to stand behind these regulations?

2 Read Leviticus 11–12. Can you discern any organizing principle for the material in these two chapters? If you are intrigued enough, read on through chapters 13–15 and try to answer the question again!

3 What do Leviticus 19:1-2; 20:7 suggest about God's holiness? Does this contrast in any way with what you discovered in looking through Leviticus 1–9, 11-12?

Preliminary Comments

It is routine to begin an introductory discussion of Leviticus with an apology to the student for the book's supposedly dull character. After all, instructions for religious practices long ago left behind — sacrifices, priestly ordinations, and purity regulations — can hardly hold much interest for contemporary readers. But we offer no such apology in this Introduction, for no matter how antiquated the detailed instructions provided by Leviti-

cus may seem, the book remains enormously interesting as an expression of the religious vision of the Priestly Writer (and perhaps of a second theologian responsible for the inclusion of Leviticus 17–26, the so-called Holiness Code). Likewise, its testimony to the ways humans relate to God and organize their lives before God was not just of interest to the first-time actual readers, but may also be of concern to modern readers.

A Walk through Leviticus

One of the most striking things about Leviticus is its nearly complete lack of narrative passages. Only Leviticus 8–10 and 24:10-23 record "happenings"; the rest of the book provides instructions for cultic practice, rules for purity, and the like. (Note that the words "cult" and "cultic" are technical terms used to refer to practices and personnel associated with the temple. This understanding should not be confused with the contemporary use of both words to refer to unusual, often unsavory religious groups and practices.) As for the "narrative world" of Leviticus, its instructional and regulatory material is part of what Moses received from God on behalf of the people at Sinai; thus it is but a portion of a longer sequence of material that stretches from Exodus 19 to

Numbers 10. Likewise, the two narrative episodes noted above take place at Sinai.

Leviticus 1–7: Providing a Means for Relating to God

Leviticus begins with God summoning Moses to the tent of meeting to instruct him regarding proper sacrificial procedures in the new sanctuary. Chapters 1–7 are devoted to relating those instructions. Leviticus 1:1–6:7 systematically describes how the five types of offering are to be made; 6:8–7:38 supplements those instructions with further directives mostly addressed to the priests responsible for carrying out the actual sacrifice. (Some speculate that this material is a sort of "priest's manual" for sacrifices used in the days when the temple stood. [Note that the continued use of the "historical present" in narrating this part of the text does not mean that the sacrifices described are still made today.])

The burnt offering or "holocaust" (from the Greek word meaning "wholly burned") entails, as its name suggests, the incineration of the animal offered, apart from the blood dashed on the altar by the priest (a practice associated with the peace offering and the guilt offering, too). Depending on one's means, the offering could be a bull, a male sheep or goat, or a bird. The burnt offering is brought to fulfill a vow, as a freewill offering, as a purification offering, as a daily offering, or for the celebration of festivals. The offering is made holy by priestly consecration of it for sacrifice.

The grain offering is thought by some to follow the burnt offering because it could substitute for the latter if one's means are so limited as to prohibit even the purchase of a bird. It requires burning a portion of the grain and oil brought by the layperson; the remainder, made holy like the burnt offering through priestly consecration, is left for the priests to consume. Grain offerings function in the same ways the burnt offerings do and could be offered independently or accompany another kind of sacrifice.

The peace offering is less holy than the last two offerings, and it functions to fulfill vows or serve as a freewill offering. The sacrificial animal could be a male or female from the flock, but in any case has to be unblemished. Unlike the prior two offerings, the portions of the peace offering not consumed by the fire could be eaten by the layperson who makes the offering.

The purification offering is made to overcome unintentional sins and incursions of severe impurity, the effects of either of which are thought to impact the sanctuary to varying degrees by polluting it. Depending on one's status in the community's hierarchy, the offering could be anything from a bull (for the priest) to a pigeon (for a layperson of limited means). Here too the portions not consumed by the fire on the altar are given to the priests to consume.

The guilt offering is for those who have polluted a holy item, feel they have done something wrong which they cannot identify, or have made a false oath to a neighbor. This offering entails the sacrifice of a ram, and the priests consume any part of it not destroyed by the altar fire.

All of these sacrifices, no matter their specific purpose, function to facilitate the layperson's contact with God. In particular the "pleasant odor" of the cooked meat or grain offering draws God's attention to the person who brings the sacrifice. Another common feature among the offerings that entail the death of an animal is the laying of a hand by the layperson upon the sacrificial animal's head. This apparently effects the transfer of a person's sin to the sacrificial animal. As we shall see in "Theological Themes in Leviticus" below, yet another common feature among the offerings is their function as a means of mediation between a broken humanity and a holy God.

Types of Offering in Leviticus 1–7

Passage	Offering type	Item offered
1:1–17 (6:8–13)	Burnt offering	Whole animal
2:1–16 (6:14–23)	Grain offering	Flour and oil
3:1–17 (7:11–38)	Peace offering	Unblemished animal
4:1–5:13 (6:24–30)	Purification offering	Various kinds of animals
5:14–6:7 (7:1–10)	Guilt offering	Ram

Leviticus 8–10: Providing (and Limiting) Priests as Mediators between God and Humanity

Leviticus 8–10 narrates the consecration and early practices of the priests who facilitates the contact made between God and laypeople through offerings. Leviticus 8 describes how Moses carries out the instructions for consecrating the priests provided in Exodus 28–29. First, Moses assembles the people and the sacrifices required for the consecration. Then he washes and vests (clothes in priestly garb) Aaron and his sons, and then he makes purification and burnt offerings, as well as a special ordination offering. This process is to be repeated each day for seven days. Then Leviticus 9 reports that to complete the consecration process, on the eighth day Aaron and his sons assume their priestly roles and perform for the people the sacrifices described in Leviticus 1–7. Leviticus 10 relates how later, Nadab and Abihu, two of Aaron's sons, bring "strange fire" into the sanctuary — perhaps the wrong sort of incense, a type utilized in the worship of another god — and are consumed by the fire that comes from the presence of the Lord. This prompts God's judgment that improper priestly practice will be punished no matter the privileges priests enjoyed. The following story of further priestly malpractice and its consequences (improper consumption of sacrificial offerings) underscores the claim that priests are subject to restrictions. Altogether, then, these chapters concern themselves with the institution of the altar priesthood as an Aaronite privilege, but one that also carries with it responsibilities that are quite costly to disregard.

Leviticus 11–15: Purity Laws

Leviticus 11–15 turns attention from the priests and their responsibilities to laypeople and what is required of them, at least with respect to the maintenance of purity in their daily life. In what is best described as an unusual set of rules, Leviticus 11 labels certain kinds of animals as clean for consumption and rejects others as unclean. For instance, animals that are cloven hoofed *and* chew the cud (e.g., cows) may be used for food, but ones that possess only one of these features are unclean (e.g., pigs), and only animals of the sea with fins *and* scales may be consumed. If there is a unifying element to these and the other food regulations, it is that any dead animal — clean or unclean — makes the person who comes into contact with it unclean. Thus from the beginning of this section, contact with death appears to be most threatening to a person's purity (and concomitant capacity to approach God and to remain a part of the larger community).

Oddly, the next chapter dealing with childbirth may confirm the centrality of death as the chief cause

Four-horned altar from Beer-sheba (reconstructed). Dismantled following the reforms of Hezekiah, the stones were incorporated into a storehouse wall. (Phoenix Data Systems, Neal and Joel Bierling)

of impurity. Leviticus 12 declares that a woman who gives birth to a male infant is "ceremonially unclean" (i.e., may not approach holy things or places) for seven days, and remains impure for another 33 days during which time her impurity subsides. By contrast, the woman who bears a female infant is impure for 14 days and 66 more days must pass before her impurity has subsided entirely so that she may approach holy things and places, especially the sanctuary, its personnel, and accoutrements. That childbearing makes a woman impure at all surely has to do with the fact that it was in antiquity a bloody business (and remains so even in our more antiseptic age). Inasmuch as blood was deemed by the inhabitants of the ancient world to be life force, and so much of it appeared to be lost in childbirth, it is not surprising then that a life-giving experience such as this was nonetheless seen as being fraught with death as well. Thus a daughter's birth may have been determined to be doubly polluting because the infant would one day grow to be a woman whose body and bodily functions would also bear impurity for the community. We will return to this possibility below when we consider the various explanations critics have offered for the purity regulations as a whole.

Leviticus 13–14 addresses the "skin disease" that humans, buildings, and garments suffer. With respect to humans, a variety of skin eruptions and imperfections are addressed. In each case the priest is required to examine the person to determine whether the lesions are active and spreading, and often whether they are open and oozing or closed and dormant. The criterion for determining that a skin disease is unclean is often whether the lesion permits the loss of blood or bodily fluids, reinforcing the notion that the central issue throughout

Leviticus 11–15 is the loss of life force. However, this is not exclusively the case in the treatment of skin disease, nor is it easy to argue that when the mildew on walls and garments — the "skin disease" that involves structures and clothing — meets certain requirements it is somehow a loss of life force from those objects.

Lastly, Leviticus 15 addresses genital discharges. Here the sense that the loss of life force is the interpretive key to Leviticus 11–15 reasserts itself. For instance, a woman's recovery from the impurity of normal menses requires her only to wait for a specific time and then wash; but if her menses is out of phase, that is, if it entails an extraordinary loss of blood, she must wait, wash, *and make sacrifice.* Likewise, a man who has an abnormal discharge from his penis — what we know to be a symptom of gonorrhea, but the ancients apparently thought was an extraordinary loss of semen, another form of *life force* — was required to wait, wash, *and make sacrifice*. Note also that any of these people suffering from the loss of life force would render any persons or things they came into contact with impure. Again, we will return below to the possible explanations for these purity requirements.

Leviticus 16: The Day of Atonement

Leviticus 16 addresses the Day of Atonement and so seems to be a continuation of the developments in Leviticus 8–10. God instructs Moses that Aaron and his sons should not enter the holy of holies just anytime, but rather only once during the year, and then only to undertake very special sacrifices, ones intended to cover for the sins of all Israel everywhere throughout the prior year. One sacrifice, of a bull, is for the sins of the priests. Another, of a goat, is for the sins of the laypeople. The priest is also to lay hands on the head of a third beast, another goat, to transfer to it the sins of the people: it is then sent into the wilderness to the mysterious "Azazel" (who may be a desert demon; see below in "Critical Issues"). At the conclusion of the entire rite the priest is to exit the tent of meeting and put off the garments worn for the rite, bathe, put on new vestments, and offer a whole burnt offering for himself and the people, apparently in recognition of the fact that contact with holiness, like contact with impurity, requires one to cleanse oneself afterwards.

At the end of this section it is perhaps helpful to imagine the world constructed by Leviticus 1–16 spatially. It is a world populated by "profane" (i.e., not holy) laypersons and sanctified (i.e., holy) priests, people who are at different times pure and impure. Notably, when laypersons incur impurity for one reason or another they are required to keep their distance from the holiness of the priests and the temple; their impurity must not come into contact with the sacerdotal world's holiness. That said, an impure "profane" person (a layperson) can be restored to proximity to the temple's and the priests' holiness through waiting, washing, and oftentimes sacrifice.

Leviticus 17–26: The Holiness Code

Leviticus 17–26 is commonly called the "Holiness Code" because of the insistence that the people of Israel be as holy as their God. In fact, this command to be holy does not appear that often (19:1-2; 20:7); but the title observers have given to these chapters is proper nonetheless since the code as a whole concerns itself extensively with the consequences of dispersing holiness among the people. Just how much these chapters may be distinguished from the surrounding Priestly material is an issue we return to below.

Like the beginning of other legal codes in the Hebrew Bible (cf. Exod 20:22-26; Deuteronomy 12), the first chapter of the Holiness Code concerns itself with sacrifice. But the scope of the law in Leviticus 17 is startling by comparison with the others: it seems to prohibit profane slaughter, the killing of an animal for food, apart from sacrifice in the temple. Of course, in the story world of the text the people were wandering in the wilderness and lived constantly in the presence of the mobile sanctuary; requiring that every slaughter take place as a sacrifice at the tent of meeting was not problematic under those conditions. But, as we shall see, the law code in its present literary form was almost certainly meant for postexilic Judah, and thus required slaughter at the temple in Jerusalem; this was a considerable challenge to anyone living more than a few kilometers from Jerusalem and raises questions about the legislation's real aim. We return to this issue below. In any case, the chapter closes with a stern prohibition against eating the blood of animals offered for sacrifice.

Leviticus 18 abruptly shifts the focus to forbidden sexual relations. The premise at the outset is that these are relations engaged in by the people of Canaan, but it is hard to imagine that provides the rationale for this long list of proscribed sexual unions. The chapter addresses intercourse among family relations, between a man and a woman in menses, between a man and another man's wife, between two males, and between humans and beasts. The single non-coital act prohibited by this chapter is offering a child to the god Molech, a sacrifice that required immolation of the gift. Violation of any of these prohibitions incurred the penalty of being "cut off from the people," perhaps a reference to capital punishment.

Only in Leviticus 19 do we finally come to the rhetoric that earns Leviticus 17–26 its moniker. The chapter begins with the simple declaration that Israel shall be holy because its God is holy. It goes on to blend cultic law with ethical regulations as an expression of how Israel could demonstrate its holiness. At the heart of the collection is the well-known command that every Israelite should "love your neighbor as yourself" (19:18).

Leviticus 20 then provides a list of the penalties incurred by those who violate the community's standards of holiness, including the prohibition against worshipping Molech, consulting mediums and wizards, cursing one's parents, and engaging in proscribed sexual relations (cf. ch. 18). It concludes with an exhortation remarkably similar to the one that appears at the end of the Covenant Code (Exod 23:23-33), except that here there is also the command to be holy as God is holy.

Leviticus 21 is concerned with the priests in two particular respects: how they may behave when they are called upon to mourn and what defects are acceptable in their own bodies. In the first instance, severe limitations are placed on priests because ancient mourning practices entail physical changes that would be defiling, such as shaving the head or mutilating the body. Likewise, because of the code's high demand for holiness, priests are not permitted to have any physical deformities.

Chapter 21's theme leads naturally to that of ch. 22, the proper use of holy offerings. The first part of the chapter makes clear that priests in a state of uncleanness are prohibited from eating the proceeds of sacrifices, and no layperson is permitted to consume them either. The rest of the chapter provides further details about the required qualities of the sacrifices legislated in chs. 1-7.

Leviticus 23-25 continues the focus on religious observances and cult. Leviticus 23 offers a sacred calendar that more or less parallels those known from Exod 23:14-17; 34:18-24 and Deut 16:1-17. Leviticus 24:1-9 makes provision for the sanctuary lamp's oil and the bread of the presence. Leviticus 24:10-23 departs from pure instruction to narrate the case of a blasphemer and then lists a series of crimes for which direct restitution was required (as if to indicate that the reason blaspheming was punished by death was that it took life from God and had to be repaid by a human life). Finally, ch. 25 makes provision for the Sabbatical and Jubilee Years, the seventh and 49th years in seven-year cycles when debts were to be released, slaves set free, land permitted its rest, and so on. These acts associated with the Sabbatical and Jubilees Years are characterized by their literary context as the acts of a holy Israel.

Finally, Leviticus 26 makes clear the choice that lay before Israel: the people could either choose to embrace the laws and experience enormous blessings, or they could reject the laws and endure horrible punishments, the most stinging of which was expulsion from the land.

Leviticus 27, a disparate (and probably late) chapter, draws the book to a close by addressing things and persons dedicated to the Lord and the ways in which someone was able to redeem vows rather than fulfill them.

Critical Issues in Studying Leviticus

Among the issues that attract the interest of ancient and modern readers of Leviticus, three stand out for attention. First, there is particular interest in the rationale behind the rules regarding purity in Leviticus 11-15. Second, the legislation on same-gender sexual intercourse in Leviticus 18 and 20 also demands our attention. And third, the date, provenance, and authorship of Leviticus provoke interest, particularly because of the uncertain relationship between the Holiness Code and the rest of the book (let alone the rest of the Priestly Writer's contribution to the Pentateuch as a whole).

Theories Regarding the Rationale for the Purity Rules of Leviticus 11–15

Beginning in the Middle Ages, some explained the purity regulations in Leviticus 11-15 as an attempt to ensure proper hygiene; these chapters were, on this reading, a sort of ancient health code. For example, pigs carry trichinosis, thus they were forbidden for consumption. Likewise, people with skin diseases, and particularly with open sores, were thought to be contagious, and so they required quarantining. But even though this explanation is still preferred by some readers, so little as a glance back at our survey of Leviticus shows that this would be an incomplete health code at best, and certainly a very whimsical one at that. Only where it addresses food and skin disease can it remotely be said to be concerned with health issues. As for how quarantining a woman after childbirth, making a judgment about mildew in houses or garments, or marginalizing people with ordinary genital discharges are public health matters, one is at a loss for explanations.

A slightly more sophisticated approach observes that the purity laws have to do largely with chaos, with things that seem out of place: chewing the cud and cloven hooves go together, so where one is present and the other is missing in an animal, something is out of place; or where a person's skin is blemished in extraordinary ways, a woman's menstrual cycle is out of phase, a man experiences a steady penile discharge, or a woman experiences the violent pain of childbirth, there is physical disorder. But while this explanation seems to cover more of what we find in Leviticus 11-15 — and it meshes well with what we have already learned of the Priestly Writer's interests — it does not address key elements in the purity legislation. In particular, it is difficult to see how the birth of a daughter is more disordering than the birth of a son.

This leads to a third possible explanation, one that blends well with the last. As we noted in our survey above, a unifying element in Leviticus 11–15 is the concern throughout with death, or the loss of life force (blood or semen). While the food laws appeal to order over disorder, it is the dead animal that is most certain to pollute. While skin disease violates the order of the body, it is the open and oozing sore that permits the loss of blood that is most polluting. While a normal menstrual cycle requires a woman to go through a period of purification, an abnormal cycle that entails an extraordinary loss of blood requires a sacrifice as well. In short, all of these purity rules concerned not only the maintenance and/or restoration of order for the community; they also aimed to hem in or fence off incursions of death into the community as a whole. This sort of explanation makes sense of the childbirth legislation as well. For childbirth was surely perceived not only as a disordering experience in antiquity, but in light of infant and maternal mortality rates associated with the event, it was also considered a moment when life and death clashed violently with one another, using the woman's body as the battlefield. Surely this was viewed as a particularly intense incursion of death and its polluting power into the life of the community. On this reading, it is no wonder that a woman was considered impure for a long time afterward, and especially so in the case of a daughter's birth, as she too would one day be the bearer of such peril for the community concerned with incursions of death and the loss of life force. We return to the significance of this for the theological themes of the Priestly Writer below. For now it is enough to observe that this concern to symbolically constrain death fits well into the Priestly Writer's interest in promoting order in place of chaos.

Condemnations of Male-to-Male Intercourse

Especially in light of 21st-century debates regarding homosexuality it is not surprising that the condemnation of intercourse between males in Lev 18:22; 20:13 has drawn considerable interest. Relying also on New Testament passages that address the same issue (among them Rom 1:27), contemporary readers have argued that the Bible condemns homosexuality. But do these passages in Leviticus really address sexual orientation?

To answer that question entails addressing the prior question of what this legislation aimed to address in its own right, and that issue remains a bit of a puzzle.

One proposal observes that the single act condemned in Leviticus 18 that is not sexual in nature is the sacrifice of a child to Molech. Also, the framing verses provided in 18:3 and 30 indicate that the chapter addresses practices of Egypt and Canaan that are to be avoided by the people of Israel. These two observations suggest to some that the chapter as a whole addresses idolatrous practices that entail sexual unions for the sake of worshipping fertility gods. The evidence for this is uncertain, though, and so this tantalizing explanation has not prevailed in most discussions of the chapter. Moreover, it does not easily explain the prohibition of intercourse between males in Lev 20:13, where the surrounding material seems to serve interests broader than idolatry.

Perhaps a more fruitful approach begins by observing that Leviticus 18 and 20 may have been most concerned to fend off potential disruptions of an orderly world, especially ones that entailed mixing kinds in disruptive ways. Indeed, any intercourse outside of a marital relationship was likely to disrupt the good order of the family or the community. Likewise, intercourse between human beings and animals involved a mixing of kinds that violated the obvious order in creation. In this light, intercourse between men might also be seen as a violation of order: the penetration of one male by another graphically disrupted the apparent order in human sexual relations permitted by the biology of man and woman; it may also have been seen as an improper mixing of kinds (which is a concern expressed elsewhere in the Holiness Code; cf. 19:19). This might explain why sexual expressions between women were not condemned as well; they did not involve penetration, the graphic breaking of accepted boundaries.

In any case, on any of these readings it seems unwise for contemporary opponents of homosexuality to rely on Leviticus 18 and 20 for support, especially inasmuch as these passages are not about sexual *orientation,* but rather sexual *practice.* Moreover, modern interpreters almost universally forget that Leviticus addresses the issue chiefly out of theological, not psychosexual interests.

The Authorship, Date, and Provenance of Leviticus

The question of who wrote Leviticus is for most readers a non-issue: the vast majority of commentators assign the entirety of the book to the Priestly Writer. We shall see in a moment that the Holiness Code presents some challenges to this position, but first, we summarize the reasons for assigning the rest of Leviticus to the Priestly Writer and observe how Leviticus adds to our understanding of the Priestly Writer's interests.

The consistent concern for temple-related issues in

Leviticus 1–10 — sacrifice and the ordination of temple personnel — provides abundant evidence of the Priestly Writer's hand. As for the section on purity concerns in Leviticus 11–15, its preoccupation with restraining chaos in favor of order is typical of the Priestly Writer, although this treatment refines the notion of chaos to include in it the reality of death. And finally, Leviticus 16 and its treatment of the Day of Atonement as an occasion for the forgiveness of the sins of all Israelites in all places adds to the list of ways in which Israelites can be assured of their identity even if they live apart from Jerusalem, the temple, and its sacrifices.

The concerns of the Priestly material just surveyed reinforce those who assign the Priestly contribution to the Pentateuch to the Persian period. Only in the presence of an operational temple does it make sense to lay out in such detail the modes of making sacrifice and of appointing and ordaining priests. Also it seems likely that an active priesthood is the prerequisite to generate the concern about priestly malpractice implied by the stories in Leviticus 10, and this too was only the case again under Persian rule. Finally, like Sabbath observance, circumcision, and Passover observance, the Day of Atonement reflects an interest in ensuring Israelite identity for Jews living in diaspora, a concern that would have fit in the Postexilic era as well. Thus Leviticus strengthens the case for a Persian-era date for the Priestly Writer.

As for the place of the Holiness Code in the Priestly material, most observers account for its obviously different character by saying that it was an older legal collection that the Priestly Writer found attractive and amenable to his purpose; thus it was simply taken up into the larger Priestly contribution to the Pentateuch. There are, however, some problems with this view. From a literary perspective, there is evidence of the Holiness Code not only in Leviticus 17-26, but also in scattered passages otherwise assigned to the Priestly Writer; see, for example, Exodus 31:12-17; Leviticus 11:43-45; Numbers 15:40-41. According to the standard view, these passages are the result of a Priestly editor having spread about scraps of the Holiness Code like fertilizer on soil needful of enrichment. But one naturally asks why a Priestly editor might have held such a poor view of his own work, and such a high estimate of the Holiness Code. And from a thematic or theological perspective, the problem is even more difficult. While the Holiness Code "democratizes" God's holiness, making it a trait of the people of Israel too (19:1-2), the Priestly Writer confines God's holiness within the temple and even within the holy of holies, permitting only the priests to make contact with God's holiness. So while these literary and theological characteristics do support the notion that the Holiness Code did not come directly from the hand

of the Priestly Writer, they also speak against the view that its incorporation into the Priestly material was particularly friendly. For instance, introducing Leviticus 11:43-35, with its democratization of holiness, into the middle of Priestly material that is concerned chiefly to *separate the pure from the impure,* and that reflects the larger Priestly perspective that holiness is the domain of God and the priests, seems a hostile literary and theological move. From this perspective the Holiness Code appears to be a later addition to the Priestly material in the Pentateuch. But why would the Holiness Code have been introduced into the Pentateuch in this way?

One clue may lie in the close association of the Holiness Code with Deuteronomy and the prophetic book of Ezekiel, which date to the late preexilic and exilic era. Leviticus 17 presupposes the cult centralization we see in Deuteronomy 12, the festival calendar of Leviticus 23 depends on the one in Deuteronomy 16, and the law of the Sabbatical Year in Lev 25:2-7 relies on the seven-year cycle of Deut 15:1. Likewise, the Holiness Code shares with Ezekiel language that appears nowhere else in the Hebrew Bible, and the two books also share some of the same visions of the future promised to an obedient Israel (e.g., Ezek 34:25-31 echoes Lev 26:3-13). Additionally, the Holiness Code seems to draw off Deuteronomy's call to strict accountability before God and Ezekiel's demand for justice between human beings and righteousness between God and people. Thus, there is reason to suspect that the Holiness Code was added to the Priestly material to offer an ethical supplement — even corrective — to its nearly exclusive concern for cultic matters in postexilic Israel.

Theological Themes in Leviticus

Like the rest of the Pentateuch that we have studied so far, Leviticus has evoked two kinds of theological reflection: musings related to curiosities in the text and consideration of the major themes its implied authors perhaps sought to raise. Again we begin by examining how ancient Jewish and Christian interpreters dealt with some of the more eye-catching aspects of the book.

Addressing Curiosities in Leviticus
Many readers of Leviticus have been struck by the oddity of Nadab and Abihu's death in Leviticus 10. What was it, precisely, that made the fire they brought before God so provocative? Josephus notes that Lev 10:1 describes their offering as not being in accord with what God had commanded; thus he concludes that they mistakenly used the incense that they had used *before* Moses provided God's new instructions (*Antiquities* 3.209).

The rabbis, though, noticed that as a follow-up to the incident 10:9 required that priests entering the sanctuary eschew strong drink; thus the rabbis concluded that Nadab and Abihu were drunk, and so stirred God's wrath (*Leviticus Rabbah* 12:1). Philo employs a sharply contrasting strategy to make sense of the two priests' deaths, suggesting that God's cryptic comment about showing himself holy through those who are near him (10:3) indicates that Nadab and Abihu's demise was not a punishment, but an exaltation to the heavens (*On Dreams* 2.67).

Ancient interpreters were also struck by the quirkiness of the food legislation in Leviticus 11. From the many attempts to provide a logic for the rules, we cite but one, Philo's clever explanation of the Bible's preference for cud-chewing animals (11:3-8): it means to promote a student's cogitation on what he or she learns from a teacher inasmuch as, like the animal that chews and re-chews its food as a cud, the good student holds new lessons in mind for a long time to ensure that they take strong hold (*Special Laws* 4.106-107).

While these two oddities in Leviticus are plain to modern readers as much as they were to ancient recipients of the book, other peculiarities were picked up on by ancient readers that we miss, in part because we do not read the Bible as closely as they did. An example of this is the twist 4 Macc 2:10 provides to an interpretation of God's double commandment in Lev 19:3 to "revere your mother and father and keep my Sabbaths." Capitalizing on the (otherwise inexplicable) juxtaposition of the command to honor one's parents with the requirement to observe the Sabbath, the writer of 4 Maccabees converted the conjunction "and" into an adversative "but" (a perfectly acceptable conversion as the same expression in Hebrew works for both words). Thus the author of 4 Maccabees argued that the law that required honor to God prevails even over fondness for one's parents!

Embracing the Yahwist's View of the Human: Providing a Means of Relating to God

One way to understand the laws for sacrifice and the provision of a sanctified priestly leadership in Leviticus 1–10 is to see it as the Priestly Writer's acknowledgement of the accuracy of the Yahwist Writer's judgment on human beings: apart from some assistance people are hopelessly alienated from God through their undyingly willful disobedience. But the elaborate systems of sacrifice and priestly leadership also signal the Priestly Writer's reluctance to accept unreservedly the Yahwist Writer's solution to this problem, dependence solely on God's promises.

By providing a system of atoning sacrifices, the Priestly Writer acknowledges the need for reconciliation between God and humanity. While some offerings had nothing to do with atonement (e.g., sacrifices made to fulfill vows or given as freewill offerings), others were designated specifically as atonement for known *and* unknown sins (the purification and guilt offerings). Especially the provision of sacrifice that atones for unintentional or unknown sins suggests the Priestly Writer's acute awareness of the Yahwist's judgment regarding the depth of human corruption.

By the same token, though, the Priestly Writer rejects both the Yahwist Writer's conclusion that humanity has no avenue of approach to God as a result of the alienation from God humanity suffered and the insistence that Israel must therefore rely on God's initiative alone. Just as the sacrifices indicate the Priestly Writer's awareness of human sinfulness, they also confirm his insistence that humanity still can draw near to God and please God, and not only to atone for sin. In the eyes of the Priestly Writer, the sacrificial system's facilitation of contact between God and humanity in the absence of sin is equally valuable. Freewill offerings, thank offerings, and vow fulfillment offerings do not entail human disobedience, but rather the exercise of human initiative in reaching out to God. These sacrifices clearly contradict the Yahwist Work's judgment that humanity is so alienated from God by its disobedience that it depends entirely on God to renew their relationship.

But in a renewed nod to the Yahwist Writer's anthropology, Leviticus 8–10 reflects the Priestly Writer's awareness that even though humanity may, according to his judgment, approach God of its own accord, mediation is nonetheless required. Even in the more optimistic anthropological worldview of the Priestly Writer humans may not approach God directly. They depend, instead, on the mediating power of sanctified priests. The ritual of ordination, prescribed in Exodus 28–29 and carried out in Leviticus 8–9, entails setting Aaron and his sons apart for altar service. By their consecration they receive sufficient sanctified status to approach the Lord on behalf of the people. In this way, the contact between sinful, disobedient humanity and the holy God is made possible. And perhaps just to show that, in spite of their consecrated status the priests are also still only human beings before God, the Priestly Writer records the story of Nadab and Abihu's bad taste in incense and consequent punishment. Even consecrated priests are subject to the human penchant for disobedience toward God. Thus the last word in this unit on priests from the Priestly Writer settles on agreement with the Yahwist Writer regarding the human capacity for good and ill.

Controlling Death, the Chief
Expression of Chaos: The Purity Laws

In our study of the Priestly Writer's contribution to the Pentateuch we have repeatedly seen his concern to convey God's interest in creating order where there is chaos and in sustaining order where it exists. God's commitment to creating cosmic order was evident in Gen 1:1–2:4a, and God's desire for cultic order was clear in Exodus 25–31, 35–40. Now God's concern for communal order is made clear in Leviticus 11–15.

We have already seen that the best explanation for the strange set of purity laws in Leviticus 11–15 combines two explanations: the section is about restraining disorder or the improper mixing of kinds, *and* it is preoccupied with fencing off incursions of death into the community. In fact, these are not two different explanations so much as two parts of a single account of the passage's rationale. Recalling our developing argument that the Priestly Writer was active in Judah during the Persian period, this makes particular sense, especially if we add detail to our earlier portrait of Persian-period Judah.

We already learned in Chapter 3 that the Israelite community that the Persians restored to Judah was struggling to organize its life. Several factors engendered these difficulties. First, the returnees faced enormous pluralism borne from the influx of various refugee groups during the Babylonian period; the challenge of sustaining a clearly defined communal identity was itself a terrific challenge. Second, the Babylonian attacks on Judah in the late 6th century B.C.E. had left a completely broken infrastructure for commerce and daily life. Third, the economic, political, and cultural interests of the parties Persia sponsored to return to Judah were not always in harmony. For instance, the priests were eager to see the restoration of the temple, but many laypeople resisted its reconstruction because its completion entailed turning the proceeds of sacrifices and taxes for Persia over to the priests housed by a temple. Others fought over how the people who remained in the land during the Exile should be treated by the returnee community. In short, it is not hard to imagine that under such conditions chaos, not order, governed daily life. And as we shall see in our study of Proverbs, Ezra and Nehemiah, and Haggai and Zechariah, the leaders of the restored community had legitimate concerns over the possible loss of community members to other ethnicities, along with the land apostates may have possessed.

Under these conditions, the death of the community as a whole could soon become the anticipated outcome of the chaos that reigned. Thus the Priestly Writer's interest in expressing God's concern to constrain chaos in favor of order could also be expressed as a divine interest in restraining the power of death. That, more than anything else, seems to be the point of the purity rules that we encounter in Leviticus 11–15. Moreover, cultural anthropologists have taught us that in some cultures the human body can be read as a metaphor for the community as a whole. With that in mind, the theological logic of Leviticus 11–15 becomes even clearer: the purity regulations focused on restraining chaos and protecting members of the community against unnecessary contact with bodies infected with death are symbolic of the greater concern to protect the community as a whole against extinction through loss of its life force, its citizens. With these regulations the Priestly Writer proclaims that, just as God responded to cosmic and cultic chaos by ordering creation and the temple, God responds to communal chaos and the threat of extinction by providing boundaries that ensure the community's survival.

Holiness as a Transcendent Responsibility

However one judges the relationship between the Holiness Code and the Priestly material in Leviticus, there can be no doubt that the Holiness Code supplies a distinctive theological voice that must be given its due.

As noted above, that theological voice democratized God's holiness, endowing all of God's people with its quality. While this seems laudable at first, bringing as it does God and humanity into closer association, its further consequence is to intensify the demands placed on human beings to avoid impurity and sinful action. Indeed, recalling the worldviews of the Priestly Work and the Holiness Code, we see that the Holiness Code produces a different set of dynamics. While it accepts the idea that holiness and impurity are to be kept out of contact with one another, it changes the reality proposed by the Priestly Work. Instead of holiness being fenced off inside the temple and confined to the priestly class, the Holiness Code views it as a state of being that affects all of Israel. As a result, in the Holiness Code's worldview the "profane" layperson's reality is also "holy," and thus all Israel is required to exercise extraordinary vigilance against incursions of impurity and certainly to avoid intentional transgressions.

Understood in this way, the Holiness Code does seem to be a theological reply to the Priestly Writer. It works especially against the possibility of abuses of the priestly system. Indeed, priests stood to gain a great deal from the repeated movement of laypeople from a pure state to an impure state and back again when the restoration of purity entailed a sacrifice in the temple. Likewise, laity may have seen an advantage in incurring some degree of impurity if it benefited them in practical terms, such as they might have thought possible through the (temporary) worship of another god. The Holiness Code removed this possibility by its insistence that all Israel was holy: intentional transgressions under such conditions could lead to being "cut off" from one's people (Leviticus 18:29).

Perhaps the Holiness Code was meant as a real alternative to the Priestly worldview, or it might have been intended only as a utopian vision to be compared with the Priestly worldview to reveal its potential abuses. In any case, the Holiness Code enters into the Pentateuch's variety of theological perspectives one that gives to the human audience an extraordinary responsibility in relation to God's holiness. As such it is nearly unique among the theological perspectives in the Hebrew Bible, and it played a significant role in later Jewish and Christian thought. Indeed, the Jesus traditions to be surveyed in this Introduction often seem to have taken into account this variant theological tradition.

Questions for Review and Discussion

1   What is the "standard" view of the relationship between the Priestly Writer's contribution to Leviticus and the Holiness Code in Leviticus 17–26? What alternative is suggested in this chapter? How do the two views differ?

2   Regardless of the compositional history of Leviticus, when it is read as a whole, what does it suggest about the concerns of its author and its readers? How does it work as a complete text?

3   As you draw closer to completing your study of the Pentateuch, take this occasion to begin to consider how the Torah works as a whole. If you take all of Genesis to Leviticus into consideration, what theological themes stand out? How does the text as a whole bear those out?

Further Reading

Blenkinsopp, *The Pentateuch;* Van Seters, *The Pentateuch;* Whybray, *Introduction to the Pentateuch.*
Grabbe, Lester L. *Leviticus.* OTG. Sheffield: JSOT, 1993.
Houston, Walter J. "Leviticus." In *ECB,* 101-24.
Knohl, Israel. *The Sanctuary of Silence: The Priestly Torah and the Holiness School.* Minneapolis: Fortress, 1995. A defense of the view that the Holiness Code comes from a different author than the Priestly Writer.

Chapter 10

Numbers

Getting Started

1 Glance through Numbers 1–10. What is the nature of this material? Could you assign it a genre? Which work does this most resemble, that of the Yahwist or the Priestly Writer?

2 Read Numbers 16–18; 25:1-13. What seems to be the chief issue addressed by this collection of stories and regulations? How does this passage relate to what you saw in Exodus 32:20-29?

3 Read Numbers 22–24. What are the most peculiar features of this story? Which work does the whole of Numbers 22–24 (but especially the blessing Balaam speaks) most resemble, that of the Yahwist or the Priestly Writer?

Preliminary Comments

Like Leviticus, Numbers often receives little attention in standard introductions. But unlike Leviticus, Numbers may be less popular than other books of the Hebrew Bible not because its concerns are often esoteric in nature — which they are from time to

time — but rather because it is such a diverse and (by many measures) disorganized collection of materials. Once more, though, we hope to dispute the common wisdom, and point out how Numbers should at least be appreciated as the work that effectively draws to a close the theological arguments made by the Yahwist and Priestly Writers. As such it is a rich resource for theological imagination.

A Walk through Numbers

For all of the complaints among some observers about this book's dislocated narrative, it can be divided neatly into three major parts. As the following survey shows, the reason many see Numbers to be disjointed lies in the disparate material that appears particularly in the last two portions of the book.

Numbers 1:1–10:10: Last Things at Sinai

This large section of continuous Priestly material is in some ways more closely connected to Leviticus than to what follows in Numbers. Its concerns are typically Priestly and seem in many ways to take up where Leviticus 16 left off: it reports a census, regulations regarding purity and Nazirite vows, the Aaronic benediction, the consecration of Levites, further rules for Passover observance, and details of the pillar of fire and cloud that would lead the people and of the trumpets used to summon them to the sanctuary.

Numbers 1 provides a census of the tribes as they are stationed at Sinai, counting only men "from twenty years old and upward, everyone able to go to war." The total population, even under these limited terms that exclude females and anyone under twenty, reaches 603,550 men! The number is not widely accepted at face value and has elicited a variety of speculative explanations (e.g., that the word "thousand" refers to a part of the tribe, but not literally to one thousand men; or the census is actually of Israel at the time of the monarchy). Whatever the actual number, the large figure does seem designed to convey the divinely-ordained superiority of the people even in the wilderness. As we shall see, this stands in sharp contrast with the people's lack of confidence in their capacity to take the land that God promised them.

Numbers 2 next provides the people's physical arrangement in their encampment and their marching formation as they travel toward their destination. Notably, the Levites are arranged around the sanctuary, and the tribe of Judah obtains the privileged position on the east of the camp. The remaining tribes are arranged in sections radiating out from the tabernacle at the center of the encamped and marching assembly. This symbolic layout indicates a desire to privilege the tribes that gave rise to priests and kings. The concern for priests is hardly surprising from the Priestly Writer, while the interest in kings is not altogether expected.

Attention turns in Numbers 3 to the setting apart of the Levites and a census of all the males a month old and upward. The census divides the Levites into the households of Gershon, Kohath, and Merari and assigns to each household responsibility for different aspects of the tabernacle and its appurtenances. Concluding the chapter is a new census of all Israel, this time to determine the firstborn of each tribe. Numbers 4 continues the theme of census-taking by focusing on a count of the Levites of age relative to their priestly duties.

Numbers 5–6 deals with an assortment of issues that are loosely connected by theme or concern. The unit begins with a ruling that people who have been impure by reason of leprosy, genital discharge, or contact with the dead should be put outside the encampment lest they pollute it. Perhaps picking up on the notion that impure people can damage the encampment by their presence, ch. 5 continues with a ruling on the importance of accompanying guilt offerings with restitution for those wronged. It closes with a lengthy prescription for determining whether a woman has wronged her husband through infidelity. Perhaps building on the theme of determining infidelity or fidelity, the text then moves on to address the characteristics of a Nazirite vow, at the heart of which is strict fidelity to the terms of the vow (which include avoidance of strong drink, not cutting one's hair, and remaining free of contact with the dead). Numbers 6 concludes (somewhat inexplicably) with the Aaronic benediction.

To commemorate the completion of Moses' consecration of the tabernacle (see Exod 40:17; Lev 8:10-13) Numbers 7 reports in great detail and at length that the leaders from each of the tribes bring elaborate offerings to the sanctuary. Numbers 8 relates that when the offerings are concluded, God then instructs Moses to consecrate the Levites for their special service to the sanctuary.

The final preparations for departing from Sinai are reported in 9:1–10:10. First, in association with the observance of the feast before they set out from Sinai, God communicates to Moses additional instructions regarding Passover observance. The instructions permit someone who is impure or away from the sanctuary at the appointed time to observe the feast a month later during a "second Passover." The new legislation also grants to willing sojourners the right to observe Passover. Following this new legislation are a (premature; cf. 10:11-36) description of how the pillar of cloud and fire lead the people on their journey away from Sinai and a prescription for the fabrication and use of the trumpets that sound the alarm to all the people to gather at the tent of meeting.

Numbers 10:11–25:18: The Last Generation Before the Promised Land

This section of text, like the one that follows in chs. 26–36, is episodic, much as one might expect, given that it is essentially a travel itinerary with narratives attached to it. It begins in 10:11-36 with a narrative of when and how the people set out from Sinai: following the cloud-guide provided by God they leave 11 months after arriving at the mountain (cf. Exod 19:1), marching according to the plan laid out in Numbers 2–3.

Numbers 11 proves that no sooner than they are on the road do the Israelites resume complaining as they had in their travels from Egypt to Sinai. (Indeed, some see a parallel structure between the journey toward Sinai and away from it that places mirrored accounts of grumbling and rebellion in the center.) In this case the people are dissatisfied with the manna God provides to them for food. In response, God feeds and punishes them in one act by raining down quail in such superabundance that the people overeat and consume overripe meat so that they suffer the consequences of gluttony. Intertwined with this rebellion story is an account of how Moses complains of bearing the people's difficulties, and how in response God appoints for him elders who will support him in his work.

Numbers 12 reports a quite separate rebellion, this time by Miriam and Aaron against Moses, ostensibly for his marriage to a Cushite woman (Zipporah?), but also because they are jealous of his authority. God's response to their murmuring against Moses is to make Miriam leprous for seven days; oddly Aaron receives no more punishment than the natural fear he experiences at seeing Miriam's affliction. In any case, the episode ends with Moses' authority strengthened and affirmed, rather than weakened as Miriam and Aaron may have hoped.

The spy story that follows in Numbers 13–14 provides a turning point in the story. Moses sends out 12 men, a spy from each tribe, to check out the land the people are destined to conquer. On their return only Joshua of the tribe of Ephraim and Caleb of the tribe of Judah express confidence that they can take the land, and this because they are living under the promise of God; the remaining spies express reluctance because they are fearful of the "giants" they see in the land. The people have respect only for the negative report, and so they cry out against Moses and God for leading them out of Egypt. In response, God suggests, as he has already in Exodus 32 at the sight of the golden calf, that he destroy the people altogether for their faithlessness. And as in the earlier episode, Moses dissuades God from his plan by saying it would only vindicate the Egyptians. But this time, rather than also remind God of the promise to Abraham as a trump card, Moses recalls God's own self-definition offered in the wake of the calf episode as "slow to anger, and abounding in steadfast love" (14:18; Exod 34:6). This works to bring God back from the brink of utter annihilation, but God determines nonetheless to punish the people by letting the present generation pass away before bringing the people into the Promised Land and by killing the spies who spoke against attempting conquest. The remainder of Numbers 14 reports that the people try, nonetheless, to take the land from the south; they fail miserably for lack of the Lord's assistance.

Numbers 15 offers a mix of legal stipulations and a story illustrating a law in action. God first commands Moses to share with the people sacrificial regulations concerning the grain and drink offerings that can accompany a whole burnt offering, the firstfruit offering, and the purification offering. Immediately following is the story of a man found gathering sticks on the Sabbath: in keeping with the law already articulated in Exod 31:14-15; 35:2, God commands the man to be stoned for his violation of the prohibition against labor on the Sabbath. Perhaps in light of what may have been a simple case of forgetfulness gone horribly wrong, God follows this episode with the instruction to the Israelites to wear fringes on their garments that will remind them of the commandments.

In Numbers 16 two rebellion stories involving challenges to Moses' and Aaron's authority are woven into one. Following that in chs. 17–18 is an account of how the matter of Aaron's authority is settled at last, and as a consequence, the Aaronites are assigned responsibilities to the people and the people are required to provide a tithe to support the Aaronites (and Levites). The rebellion stories entail a lay rebellion led by Dathan and Abiram against Moses and a priestly rebellion led by Korah and other Levites of Kohathite descent against Aaron. Moses responds to the challenges from both parties by inviting especially Korah and his followers to a contest of censers with Aaron. The result, as expected, is poor for the rebels: they are destroyed along with their families, and the metal of the Kohathites' censers is fashioned into covering plates for the altar to warn non-Aaronites not to approach the altar with incense, lest they suffer the Kohathites' fate. Seeing this, the people rise up against Moses and Aaron again, fearing that they too might suffer a similar fate as the rebels Korah, Dathan, and Abiram. For this God punishes them with a plague that is stemmed, ironically, by Aaron offering atoning incense to the Lord in the people's midst. Then according to ch. 17 God orders a staff from each tribe to be placed overnight before God in the "tent of the covenant"; in the morning, the blossoming staff will signal which tribe should have priestly leadership. Aaron lacks a staff since he is of the tribe of Levi; so Moses gives to him alone the staff of the tribe of Levi, and in the morning his staff has not only blossomed, it has even put forth ripe almonds! This is taken as proof that God chooses Aaron and his descendants to lead Israel in its sacral life. The section concludes in ch. 18 with God's instructions that affirm resoundingly the ascendant position secured by the Aaronites: the Levites are assigned to assist the Aaronites in their priestly duties, Israelites are mandated to provide tithes to support the Aaronites and Levites, but Levites are required in turn to tithe their income to the Aaronites.

Numbers 19 hearkens back to Leviticus 11–15 with its concern for the impurity of those who have come into contact with a corpse. Not only does it offer a list of the ways in which one might incur corpse contamination, it also more famously details the procedures for purifying those who have become polluted. This entails the slaughter of a red heifer and the mixing of its ashes with water to prepare a purifying compound for sprinkling on the impure.

Numbers 20–21 returns to the travel narrative that drives the book's narrative. The people arrive at Kadesh. Along the way, the people complain again that there is not enough water and God provides it again from a rock that Moses strikes with his staff. Although there is no indication in the text of their distrust, God condemns Moses and Aaron because, says God, "you did not trust me" in the matter of water from the rock (20:12). As a result they are both forbidden entry into the Promised Land. Next the people seek passage through Edom from Kadesh, but are refused the right by the king of the land. Thus they have to travel the long way around. When they come to Mount Hor, Aaron dies and is buried there, and the Israelites mourn him at the place for 30 days. After this, the people are attacked by a Canaanite king who dwells in the Negeb; they respond by waging divinely assisted war against his army to wipe him out. Then they set out to travel around Edom, but again the people weary and rebel, and as a result they are punished with biting serpents. They are saved from utter destruction only by Moses' intercession by means of a bronze serpent, the sight of which protects them from the ill effects of the snakebite. Then a brief passage reports their itinerary until they reach "the region of Moab" where they request passage through the land of King Sihon of the Amorites; Sihon responds to their request with an attack and once more Israel prevails, and this time some of them settle in their defeated foes' lands. Finally, King Og of Bashan opposes the people and he too is defeated. The path to the plains of Moab is cleared.

Numbers 22–24 reports the well-known story of the prophet Balaam and his encounter with Israel and its God. The king of Moab, Balak, hears of Israel's military prowess and fears the annihilation of his countrymen by the Israelites. So he seeks to hire Balaam, a prophet respected for the effectiveness of his blessings and curses, to curse the people of Israel that they might fail in their all-but-certain attack on his lands. Visited by Balak's agents, Balaam receives a vision from God that he should not go, so he refuses the commission. But again Balak's agents implore Balaam, and Balaam relents only after God grants him permission in a dream to go with Balak's agents. As he travels to the appointed location, though, Balaam's donkey sees the angel of the Lord blocking their way and refuses to continue along the road. Unaware of the angel, Balaam's irritation with his donkey escalates, and he strikes it. At this God gives speech to the donkey, which rebukes his master for striking him and points out that only his obstinacy saved Balaam from the sword-bearing angel of the Lord. Upon hearing (without evident surprise!) the words of his talking donkey, Balaam is able to see the angel. Curiously, the angel rebukes Balaam for consenting to the task Balak asked of him, and Balaam apologizes and offers to demur from his appointed prophecy. But once again, God reverses course and prods Balaam on to speak as Balak requested. And so finally Balaam is positioned to see the people and direct a curse against them on behalf of Balak: but each time he does so — a total of four times — he speaks only Yahwist Writer–style blessings over the people, even providing in his fourth speech the prophecy of a star and scepter that will come from Jacob, an apparent reference to the royal line of David. Thus by the end of ch. 24 it is plain to the reader of Numbers that this people is destined to receive the patrimony long guaranteed them from God, in spite of their obdurate ways.

And yet, as this long section of Numbers draws to a close in ch. 25 we read that in spite of the affirmation of the promise, the people continue to reveal their alienation from God: immediately after the Balaam episode they marry the women of Moab and sacrifice to the foreign god, Baal of Peor. For this God's wrath comes upon them in the form of a plague that is stemmed only by the intervention of Phinehas, grandson of Aaron. When Phinehas sees an Israelite bring a Midianite woman into the camp, perhaps as a cultic prostitute or even as his wife, Phinehas slays the man and the woman out of concern for the community's purity. Not only does this stem the plague, it also wins Phinehas God's promise of a covenant of perpetual priesthood, a reaffirmation of God's commitment to the line of Aaron as Israel's priestly leadership.

Numbers 26–36: The New Generation Travels Toward the Promised Land

Apparently the plague reported in Numbers 25 and other devastations that strike the people between Sinai and Shittim manage to eliminate the generation that has traveled from Egypt (apart from Moses, Joshua and Caleb). Thus a new census is ordered to determine the number of men over 20 years of age available for war. As in the first census, the number arrived at is extraordinary, coming to 601,730 men. Like the count in Numbers 1, this one in ch. 26 is also meant mostly to convey the superiority of God's people, even in spite of their relentless apostasy!

With the exception of the second half of ch. 27 that narrates the appointment of Joshua as Moses' eventual successor, Numbers 27–30 provides more legal material directed by God through Moses to the people. Issues addressed include: whether women may inherit property (they may in unusual circumstances); offerings for the daily offering and the Sabbath sacrifice and for observances linked to the appearance of the new moon, the feasts of Unleavened Bread, Pentecost, and New Year, and the Day of Atonement and Festival of Booths; and when vows made by women must be honored.

Next Numbers 31 recounts in vivid detail the war that God commands Moses to wage against Midian in retribution for its part in the Baal of Peor incident (cf. ch. 25). While the incident report illustrates the implementation of the rules for holy war theory and for purification from corpse contamination (cf. Exod 17:8-16 and Numbers 19), it seems also to function as a narrative context for the law of war booty distribution. It also conveniently provides a context for punishing not only Midian, but also seeing to the elimination of Balaam! The prophet whose speech offered only blessing for Israel in chs. 23–24 is blamed nonetheless for inciting the women of Midian to marry with Israelites, requiring not only his execution in war, but also the demise of the women who participate in his stratagem.

After reporting the war against Midian, Numbers at last moves swiftly to a close: ch. 32 relates the allotment of land in the Transjordan to Reuben, Gad, and Manasseh for their help in the battle for Canaan; ch. 33 rehearses in summary form Israel's itinerary from Egypt to the edge of Canaan (and includes warnings about Canaanite religious practices); ch. 34 lays out the idealized boundaries of the Promised Land; ch. 35 provides a plan for Levitical cities and cities of refuge and relates the law for dealing with premeditated and unpremeditated murder; and ch. 36 prescribes laws to avoid the alienation of tribal property through inheritance.

Critical Issues in Studying Numbers

Scholars frequently address a range of historical questions associated with Numbers, not the least of which is its significance for tracing the itinerary of the people in the wilderness. However, our focus is not on dealing with biblical texts as historical records, so we set that issue aside. Instead we focus once more on literary and source-critical questions as they help us appreciate the theological themes of the work, as well as on the author and audience suggested to us by the text itself. To begin, though, we note the reappearance of some ancient Near Eastern influences. Then we consider the difficult question of source division in the book of Numbers, and finally make some comments on the structure that the Priestly editors provided for the book.

Ancient Near Eastern Traditions in Numbers

The narrative that entails the bronze serpent Moses used to save the people in Numbers 21 and the Balaam episode in chs. 22–24 both reflect notable ancient Near Eastern influences on Numbers. Numbers 21:4-9 reports the people's rebellion at the prospect of the long trip required to skirt Edom (because the king of Edom would not permit them safe passage through his land). God punishes them with poisonous serpents, and when they acknowledge their sin and beg Moses to implore God on their behalf, God instructs Moses to mount a bronze serpent on a pole, the sight of which saves the serpent-bitten Israelites. The question that naturally arises in many readers' minds is where such an apparently idolatrous act could have come from. In fact, serpents were frequently used as a religious symbol across the ancient world, and they could play negative and positive roles. A serpent plays a negative role in the Gilgamesh Epic, stealing and swallowing the plant that would have granted Gilgamesh eternal life. Some cultures associated serpents with their deities (e.g., Baal's consort, Asherah, was often pictured with a serpent; see p. 95 for an example). Also, the healing cult of Asclepius connected the serpent with healing. So it is not altogether surprising that the serpent appears this way in Numbers.

It is even less surprising when we take into account the references to serpents in Deut 8:15 and 2 Kgs 18:4, especially if we accept the Supplementary Hypothesis's view that the Yahwist Writer simply expanded Deuteronomy's account of the wilderness wanderings and developed further details by playing off themes in the Deuteronomistic History (see Chapter 12 for an introduction to the Deuteronomistic History). Deuteronomy 8:15 uses the same phrase used in Numbers 21 to describe the creatures as Moses reminds the people that serpents plagued their journey through the wilderness, and 2 Kgs 18:4 reports that when Hezekiah reformed the temple cult he "broke in pieces the bronze serpent that Moses had made, for until those days the people of Israel had made offerings to it; it was called Nehushtan."

Notably, the serpent of Numbers 21 recurs in John 3 in Jesus' monologue that grows out of his encounter with Nicodemus. Jesus likens the Son of Man, who will be lifted up, to the serpent Moses lifted up in the wilderness (John 3:14). It may be that the serpent of Revelation 12 and 20 is also intended to echo the biting ones of Numbers 21.

Another instance of ancient Near Eastern influence on Numbers appears in the Balaam episode. An 8th-century B.C.E. inscription from Deir ʿAlla in the Transjordan details the activities of an apparently well-known prophet-for-hire, Balaam of Peor. It appears that Numbers 22–24 is a play on what must have been a widely-known tradition that Balaam was an effective prophet, a sort of "hired gun in the old Near East." Since there is no reason to date Balaam earlier than the 8th century, we are forced once more to consider a later date for the Yahwist Work than the Documentary Hypothesis's 10th-century date. And like the serpent incident in Numbers 21, this one too may have roots in the Deuteronomic tradition inasmuch as the Yahwist Writer's adaptation of Balaam makes of him the Deuteronomists' ideal prophet, someone who speaks only the words that God puts in his mouth (Deut 18:18).

Authorship, Date, and Provenance

Although the division of Numbers into Yahwist and Priestly strands is more complex than the summary on p. 97 lets on, this suffices to provide a general sense of the source division in Numbers. The first 10 chapters of the book are almost exclusively Priestly material. From there on the two sources sometimes alternate providing large portions of text. At other times they are woven together, often so tightly they are nearly impossible to separate.

In the date of the Deir ʿAlla inscription we have already seen evidence that favors dating the Yahwist Writer's contribution to Numbers later than the 10th-century date assigned by the Documentary Hypothesis. In addition, the connections shared between the Balaam episode and the reference to the bronze serpent and traditions in Deuteronomy and the Deuteronomistic History indicate a post-Deuteronomic date for this material. Another instance of the Yahwist Writer's possible reliance on Deuteronomy may appear in Numbers 32, which in many ways looks like an expansion of Deut 3:12-20. Taken together, these indications offer indirect support to the view that the Yahwist Writer worked during the Exile, or at least after the Deuteronomists concluded their work. We also note the tenor of the Balaam episode as further indirect evidence of an exilic provenance: called by a foe of Israel to oppose Israel as it stood ready to receive the patrimony of the Promised Land, Balaam could only bless Israel and promise its eventual possession of the land. Further, Balaam spoke in language reminiscent of Second Isaiah's rhetoric, an author we know to have been active in the Exile (Isaiah 40–55; on identifying and dating Second Isaiah, see Chapter 27). And what better image to offer the exiles than a foreign prophet speaking against his will God's

Votive stela with Tanit (Punic goddess identified with Asherah) holding a serpent. (Réunion des Musées Nationaux/Art Resource, NY)

blessing for Israel, especially in light of the earlier Yahwist material's emphasis on God's unbendable will to bless Israel with land and descendants?

As for the Priestly material in Numbers, once more it is easy to see how it fits in a postexilic context. The censuses in Numbers 1 and 26 are typical of this writer's concern for order and perhaps even provide some insight on the ideals the postexilic Judean community sought to uphold as it faced the difficult task of reconstituting itself. The material dealing with the arrangement of the tribes around the tabernacle in Numbers 2 also may reflect an idealized notion of how Persian-period Judah should be arranged. Of course, the extensive legislative material relating to the sacrificial system and purity issues is quite suited to the Second Temple period when concerns of that sort would have been at the forefront of people's imaginations. Finally, the passages legitimating Aaronite authority and cautioning against challenges to it (chs. 16–18; 25) clearly reflect an author's interest in settling the question of who would be in charge in a temple-centered commonwealth.

Oblivious to the angel of the Lord, the seer Balaam strikes his donkey, who refuses to continue in the face of the divine agent (Num 22:20-35). (Nuremberg Bible, 1493; Victoria and Albert Museum, London; ArtResource, NY)

Structure in Numbers

Because the structure of Numbers is so notoriously vexing to critics the topic deserves some comment. The difficulty of this issue stems in large part from the addition of Priestly material to the earlier Yahwist narrative. But that is perhaps also the key to solving the problem, for the present form of Numbers is the result of the Priestly Writer adding his material to the existing Yahwist narrative at points suitable to his own purposes. The difficulty in deciphering the actions of a Priestly redactor stem largely from our uncertainty as to the reasoning that motivated the Priestly Writer's placement choices.

It should be clear by now that Num 1:1–10:28 is the last portion of an enormous Priestly insertion into the Yahwist narrative that likely moved from the aftermath of the golden calf episode in Exodus 34 to the preparations for departure from Sinai in Num 10:29-36 and continued then with further stories of rebellion in chs. 11–14, 16, and 21. These were followed in the Yahwist narrative by the Balaam episode and its affirmation of God's promise in spite of the people's apostasy, just as it is followed by further apostasy in the Yahwist's account of the Baal of Peor incident (25:1-5).

Further Priestly material was inserted into this Yahwist narrative at often discernibly strategic points. Num-

bers 15 was likely intended to confirm that, even though the Exodus generation would not enter the land, their offspring would; therefore they needed to know the rules designed specifically for new inhabitants of Canaan, how to manage Sabbath law violators, and the value of wearing tassels as a reminder of the law. The addition of Korah's rebellion to that of Dathan and Abiram (ch. 16) and the insertion of the blossoming rod episode and tithe regulations (chs. 17–18) also have their own logic: they all build on the existing Yahwist story of rebellion against Moses and its negative outcome for the rebels to indicate revolt against Aaron's descendants was equally doomed to failure. By contrast, the placement of ch. 19, the red heifer rite, is genuinely inexplicable, as are the reasons for locating in ch. 20 travel stories and the account of Moses and Aaron's rejection. On the other hand, the Priestly Writer's effort to sew his account of Phinehas' zeal into the existing rebellion story reported in ch. 25 is a move that once more clearly capitalized on the Yahwist Writer's unwitting provision of strong foundations for the Priestly Writer's effort to legitimate Aaronites against other rebellious priestly factions. As for the remaining Priestly material in chs. 26–36, the organizing principle for those insertions seems impossible to discern.

The Yahwist and Priestly Works in Numbers

Yahwist Material

10:29-36, Departure from Sinai

11–12, Rebellion Stories

13–14, Spy Story and Rebellion

16*, Dathan and Abiram's Revolt

21, Conflicts and the Serpent Incident

22–24, The Balaam Episode

25*, Rebellion at Moab

32, Land for Reuben, Gad, and Manasseh

*Contain both Yahwistic and Priestly material

Priestly Material

1–4, Census and Arrangement of the Tribes

5–6, Legal Rulings

7–8, Sacrifices and Consecration of Levites

9–10:28, Final Preparations to Leave Sinai

15, Sacrificial Legislation

16*, Korah's Revolt

17–18, Securing Aaron's Role

19, The Red Heifer Rite

20, Travel Stories and Rejection of Moses

25*, Zimri, Cozbi, and Phinehas' Zeal

26, A New Census

27–30, Appointment of Joshua, Legal Matters

31, Midianite War

33, Itinerary from Egypt to Canaan

34, The Scope of the Promised Land

35, Levitical Cities and Cities of Refuge

36, Protecting Tribal Lands

Theological Themes in Numbers

Our task in this section is twofold. We offer first a survey of the ways in which early Judaism and Christianity contended with some of the peculiarities of the book of Numbers and of the theological themes evoked by the book itself. Second, we use this occasion to conclude our look at the Yahwist and Priestly Works, since by most accountings they do not extend into Deuteronomy.

Addressing Curiosities in Numbers

In part because it is such a concatenation of different episodes that produce their own seeming incongruities, Numbers drew a great deal of interest from early Jewish and Christian interpreters. We only rehearse three instances here.

Commentators have long noted the intensity of God's response to Aaron and Miriam's query as to why the Lord God chose to speak through Moses and not through them (12:2). God's reply is that he reveals himself to prophets in visions, but to Moses he speaks mouth to mouth and he reveals himself to Moses in his full form, all because Moses "is entrusted with all my house" (12:6-8). In particular, the notion that Moses was entrusted with (or "in" as the Hebrew preposition may also be translated) all God's house attracted attention and expansion. One particularly interesting reuse of this motif appears in Heb 3:5-6. There the writer plays with the preposition to suggest something about the incomparable nature of Jesus in relation to Moses: "Now Moses was faithful in all God's house as a servant, to testify to the things that would be spoken later. Christ, however, was faithful over God's house as a son, and we are his house if we hold firm the confidence and the pride that belong to hope."

Another puzzling characteristic of Numbers that elicited its share of responses was the depiction of Balaam as an equivocating instrument of God when it came to accepting Balak's call to curse God's people (chs. 22–24). Just how should one construe his unwillingness, his commission from God, God's later reluctance and rebuke, and finally Balaam's seemingly unwitting blessing for Israel? 2 Peter 2:15-16 solves the problem with a judgment against Balaam, saying that he "loved the wages of doing wrong" but was rebuked by God through the talking donkey. Revelation 2:14 goes a step further, accusing Balaam of being the one who first encouraged Balak in his opposition to the people!

Finally, one can hardly ignore the use to which Balaam's most famous prophecy was put: A star shall come out of Jacob, and a scepter shall rise out of Israel" (24:17). Combined with the closely-related blessing Jacob offered Judah in Gen 49:10 (which states that the "scepter shall not depart from Judah"), Jews and Christians alike took this prophetic speech as a reference to a future ruler, a messiah. By associating the star of 24:17 with the scepter-cum-king of Gen 49:10, the light source itself took on messianic significance. Thus we hear an echo of Balaam's prophecy in a text from Qumran, 4Q Apocryphon of Levi[b] ar 9 i 3-4. The scroll announces that the anticipated eschatological high priest's "eternal sun will shine, and its brightness will warm all the corners of the earth." Likewise, in Rev 22:16 Jesus announces, "It is I, Jesus, who sent my angel to you with this testimony for the churches. I am the root and the descendant of David, the *bright morning star.*"

Theological Witness in Numbers

Just as the structure of Numbers seems unruly to interpreters (or perhaps because of that), its theological witness has remained elusive to most readers as well. All the same, there are some clear, if still somewhat subtle outcomes from the melding of Priestly and Yahwist material in this book.

One outstanding example is the way the Priestly Writer's "piggybacking" of rebellion stories on existing revolt accounts affirms the Yahwist's view of humanity and the people as broken and mutinous. Yet the outcome of these stories — see especially ch. 16, followed by chs. 17 and 18, and ch. 24, followed by 25:1-13 — is to go a step further and show that God provided a means of protecting the people from themselves that the Yahwist did not take into account: a true and faithful priesthood that could mediate between sinful humanity and the Almighty God by means of cultic activity. In that sense, one of the recurring and exceptional themes throughout Numbers is the significance

of the priesthood for the well-being of Israel. Numbers 19 provides clear testimony to the importance of priestly participation in ritual actions that restore balance between God and humanity, even under the extreme conditions of corpse contamination.

Another theme that stands out in Numbers is God's fidelity to his covenant. Again, the blend of Yahwist and Priestly material has wrought something quite complex and wonderful: the Yahwist narratives permit no doubt about God's unrelenting choice of the people, no matter their behavior (so Balaam's blessing in ch. 24), and the Priestly emphasis on sacerdotal and cultic matters shows how God has provided an ongoing means of expressing that fidelity.

Finally, we suggest that Numbers' compositional technique of placing the genesis of specific statutes in narrative frameworks is perhaps partly responsible for the theology of the law that sees it as God's response to human needs encountered in daily life (cf. 15:32-41; 31). Whether its author adhered to this particular theology of the law, *Jubilees'* generous use of Numbers' compositional technique certainly reinforced its theological implications. Thus, by the time we come to Jesus and Paul of early Christian tradition, the theology is fully articulated. Indeed, Jesus ascribes the law of divorce in Deut 24:1 to God's concession to the hardness of human hearts (Mark 10:4-5), and Paul assigns the origin of the law to God's aim to dominate and then nurture human will (see especially Romans and Galatians).

Summarizing the Yahwist and Priestly Works

As we close our investigation of the books of the Tetrateuch — Genesis, Exodus, Leviticus, and Numbers — it is fitting that we summarize the basic themes we have encountered in them through the separate and combined writings of the Yahwist and Priestly Writers, both of whose work probably concludes in Numbers.

Taking the Yahwist Work first, we observe that the heart of its concern throughout was to define clearly human capacities and the divine response. From the beginning of the Primeval History the Yahwist Writer makes clear his judgment on the human capacity for behavior pleasing to God: It simply is not within humankind's grasp. In fact, the Primeval History, the Ancestral History, and the Ancestral Saga all show time and again that human beings are more inclined to rebel against God and God's promises than to cooperate with him and his plan. By contrast, God learns quickly the human penchant for sin and the importance of living in relationship to his creation with due respect for that penchant: if God is to make his way with them, God must take a path of persistent mercy. At the same time, the Yahwist Writer reveals God's occasional impatience with this situation (see, e.g., Exodus 32), but also makes clear that God, having bound himself to fulfill his promises, remains steadfast to the end, even making a foreign prophet speak God's blessing on the people, announcing God's special favor for them against all odds and reason.

With respect to the nations, the Yahwist Writer also has something interesting to say. The Yahwist announced this theme already in Gen 12:1-3: the people who bless Israel, God will bless; the people who curse Israel, God will curse. In other words, where nations were willing to be included in the promises of God, they would be included in the people of God; but wherever they became a stumbling block to God's promises, God would remove them as an obstacle to God's will. The two-part story of Egypt and the people of God provides the clearest illustration of this perspective. Because of Pharaoh's positive reception of Joseph and favor for his family, Egypt prospered, savoring success and wealth even during the great famine. But when Egypt later turned on God's people and sought to destroy them in the story of the Exodus, God's curse in the form of the overwhelming waters of the Red Sea could hardly have been plainer.

The Priestly Work was added, in time, to this narrative structure. Its themes are somewhat more expansive than those taken up in the Yahwist Work. The Priestly Writer was interested in reassuring a postexilic audience that the cosmic, communal, and cultic chaos they faced upon their return to Judah would not last, thanks to God's will to put all things in order. Cosmic chaos, reflected in the demolished infrastructure of postexilic Judah, would surely be put right by God who created order from the most primal cosmic chaos imaginable (Gen 1:1–2:4a). Communal chaos, a natural concomitant to the competing interests of the returnees and those who remained in the land during the Exile, would be met with the ordered concern for community integrity symbolized in the Priestly view of the human body, its boundaries, and its experiences of purity and impurity (Leviticus 11–15). And cultic chaos was the easiest disorder to treat: the plan for the new temple in the design God offered for the tent of meeting and the tabernacle (Exodus 25–31; 35–40), the rules for sacrifice (Leviticus 1–7), and the stories of priestly selection, discipline, and conflict (Leviticus 8–10; Numbers 16–18; 25:1-13) gave proof from the days of Moses how God wanted the cultic life of the Second Temple to be ordered.

The Priestly Writer was also concerned to address the interests of God's people who were not so lucky as to live in the Promised Land and near the Second Temple. For them he revealed the ancient instructions for being a Jew in diaspora: keep the Sabbath (Genesis 1; Exod 31:14-15; 35:2) and the covenant of circumcision (Genesis 17), observe the Passover (Exodus 12), and trust in the efficacy of the high priest's sacrifice for them on the Day of Atonement (Leviticus 16). These things ensured one's Jewish identity anywhere in the world.

What happened when these two viewpoints were merged? What do we have in Genesis to Numbers as a whole? What sort of author or audience emerges from the Tetrateuch? We have already glimpsed an answer to this question in our closing discussion of Leviticus. There we observed that through the marriage of the Yahwist and Priestly worldviews, the steadfast and merciful God who makes and fulfills promises, even in spite of the obstinate opposition of humanity (the Yahwist Work), goes yet further and provides an earthly means of being present to his willful and rebellious creation. Through priests, a sacrificial cult, and order imposed on the multiform chaos from which God engendered creation, God sees to delivering on his promises of mercy and redemption, of life where there is death (the Priestly Writer). The story told in Genesis to Numbers, then, is one of mercy and goodness from a steadfast God for a broken humanity.

Questions for Review and Discussion

1   Take this opportunity to review the treatments offered of Genesis to Numbers and make your own assessment of the "author" and "audience" of the text as a whole. Does it match the brief proposal made above? Is it different? If it is different, what elements in your view set your proposal apart?

2   Also take this opportunity to review the basic notion of how Genesis to Numbers emerged. What is the view of the Documentary Hypothesis? What is the perspective of the Supplementary Hypothesis (the one represented in this book)? Keep these differences in mind as we take up the book of Deuteronomy, and consider this question: Do the two hypotheses treat Deuteronomy in substantially different ways?

3   From literary and theological perspectives, how is Numbers different from the three books that precede it? What does the likely compositional history of the Pentateuch have to do with the distinctive character of Numbers in relation to Genesis to Leviticus?

Further Reading

Blenkinsopp, *The Pentateuch;* Van Seters, *The Penta-
teuch;* Whybray, *Introduction to the Pentateuch.*
Budd, Philip J. *The Book of Numbers.* WBC 5. Waco:
Word, 1984.

Sakenfeld, Katherine Doob. *Journeying with God: A Commentary on the Book of Numbers.* ITC. Grand Rapids:
Wm. B. Eerdmans, 1995.

Chapter 11

Deuteronomy

Getting Started

1   Read Deuteronomy 1–3, and as you do try to recall
how the same or similar episodes in the people's
past were narrated in Exodus and Numbers. How
might one explain the relationship between this brief
account of the people's wandering in the wilderness
and the longer version of it in Exodus and Numbers?

2   Read Deuteronomy 4:1-43. What does Moses seem
to presume about the future of the people as they are
about to enter the land promised to them? What does
he indicate lies in their future? How does he anticipate God responding to their future actions?

3   Read Deuteronomy 12:5-14, and compare its stipulations regarding sacrifice to those articulated in
Exodus 20:22-26 and Leviticus 17:1-9. How does Deuteronomy differ from Exodus and Leviticus on the
question of where one sacrifices and/or slaughters
animals?

Preliminary Comments

The title "Deuteronomy" derives from the Septuagint
translation of Deut 17:18, the instruction to the kings
of Israel to have always at hand "a copy of the law." The
Septuagint translated the phrase as *deuteronomion,*
"second law." Meanwhile, the Jewish canon names the
book with a single word from its first phrase, "These
are the words [of Moses]" ("words," Hebrew, *debarim*).
Neither title is completely without merit. Deuteronomy
12–26 provides what some would describe as the *second*
law code in the Hebrew Bible after the Covenant Code in
Exod 20:22–23:33 (although others might argue that Leviticus 17–26 is really the *second* code!). And as a whole,
the book is largely a collection of words from Moses in
the form of sermons and laws.

Apart from its name, a more significant marker of
Deuteronomy's character is its most natural affiliation
with the material on either side of it in the canon. Although it is classified as part of the Pentateuch in Christian circles and as the last book of the Torah among
Jewish readers, its content links it more closely with the
six books that follow it, Joshua, Judges, 1 and 2 Samuel,
and 1 and 2 Kings. (In Christian canons a seventh book,
Ruth, follows Judges, but only because it begins with the
words "In the days of the judges . . ."). Like those books,

Reading Guide to Deuteronomy

Historical Recollection and Anticipation as
     Prologue (1:1–4:43)
Sermon on the Purpose of the Law (4:44–11:32)
Deuteronomic Law Code (12:1–26:15)
Curses and Blessings as Explanation of the Law's
     Purpose (26:16–28:68)
Moses' Final Discourse as Epilogue (29–30)
Moses Appendix (31–34)

Deuteronomy focuses on cultivating a theology that has at its center a bilateral covenant between God and the people. In fact, as we see in the section on critical issues in studying Deuteronomy, it is the first book of a larger compositional unity that continues with Joshua and concludes with 2 Kings, a composition that we call the "Deuteronomic Collection." For now, however, we focus on the content of Deuteronomy in its own right.

A Walk through Deuteronomy

While there are a variety of competing proposals regarding the structure of Deuteronomy, it rather boldly exhibits its own hints, providing clear section headings in 1:1; 4:44; 12:1; 29:1, and distinct sections in 26:16–28:68 and chs. 31–34.

Deuteronomy 1:1–4:43: The Prologue

This first portion of Deuteronomy recalls the events that led to the people's arrival at the edge of the Promised Land. It also records Moses' first substantial sermon, a discourse on the second commandment that is designed to encourage faithfulness to the covenant, but also to anticipate the time when the people would fail in their covenantal obligations and suffer the stipulated consequences.

The first five verses of Deuteronomy establish the physical and temporal context of the book: poised to take the land promised to them, the people are stationed somewhere on the Plains of Moab to the east of the Jordan River, and the time is the "fortieth year, on the first day of the eleventh month" since they departed from Egypt, not long after they had defeated King Sihon of the Amorites (Num 21:21-35). Notably, this "contextualizing" prologue permits Deuteronomy to stand quite apart from any preceding material; it begins as though it is an independent work.

Deuteronomy 1:6–3:29 is Moses' summary of the people's experience from the time of their departure from Sinai (called Horeb in Deuteronomy). One would expect a repetition of Numbers 12–36, but that is not strictly the case. For instance, the report of travel from Sinai to Kadesh in Deut 1:19-45 differs from the corresponding material in Num 12–19, not only in length but also with significant variation. To cite but one example, Deut 1:37 suggests that Moses was not permitted to enter the Promised Land because he shared the people's fear of the land's inhabitants after hearing the spies' report; by contrast Num 20:10-13 assigns blame to Moses' (apparent) lack of trust in the matter of the waters of Meribah. Similarly, Deut 2:1-8a contradicts Num 20:14-21 by declaring that the people carefully crossed Edom so as not to provoke conflict, while Num 20:14-21 indicates that they asked permission to traverse Edom, but were refused. Deuteronomy 2:8b-25 also departs significantly from its parallel in Num 20:22–21:14, omitting the death of Aaron and the serpent episode and giving a different travel itinerary. The account of the victories over Sihon and Bashan follow in both Deut 2:26–3:10 and Num 21:21-35, but once more they differ in significant ways. Next, Deut 3:12-22 narrates differently the distribution of lands reported in Numbers 32. Finally, Deut 3:23-29 records God's reproachful reply to Moses' plea to see the land: Moses is commanded to transfer power to Joshua so that he, not Moses, would behold the land by leading the people into it. By contrast, Num 27:12-23 depicts Moses accepting God's judgment without argument and urging Joshua's appointment to succeed him.

Deuteronomy 4:1-43 presents Moses' first real sermon. While in some respects it seems to be little more than an address on the commandment prohibiting idols, it actually serves as an exhortation on obedience to all of God's commandments. It draws several contrasts: obedience versus disobedience; remembering God's requirements versus forgetting them; and God versus mere idols. To ensure the audience's attention, the address begins by recalling the incident at Peor (Num 25:1-13). Conspicuously, the author follows this by denying not only the validity of idols as objects worthy of worship — in fact people of the ancient Near Eastern world saw the objects only as representations of the gods they worshipped — but also the existence of the gods themselves (see esp. 4:15-20); therefore there was no earthly reason to violate by idolatrous worship the covenant God had made with the people. Nonetheless, said Moses, his audience would grow complacent, forget the covenant, and fail to heed the admonition against idolatry; as a consequence they would be driven into exile. But from there they could cry out to God and be heard, and receive a second chance at living within the covenant's terms. The sermon concludes with Moses observing the wondrousness of God in providing such a relationship with the people and urging them one more time to faithfulness.

Deuteronomy 4:44–11:32: The Purpose of the Law

The second part of Deuteronomy is devoted to elaborating the essence of the law that stands at the heart of the covenant between God and the people. The focus in this section is threefold. First, it epitomizes the law for the Israelites in the Ten Commandments and the "Great Commandment" of 6:5. Next, it explains through repetition and refrain that Israel has the law and its antecedent, the covenantal relationship, not through its own merit, but as a result of God's choice. And finally, it sketches out the two choices before Israel — faithfulness or apostasy — and articulates the consequences of following one path or the other (with illustrations from Israel's past).

In a surefire indicator of Deuteronomy's composite nature, this new section opens with a paragraph (4:44-49) that echoes 1:1-5 by setting the context of Moses' speech a second time. The difference is that this new section lacks the temporal definition provided by 1:1-5, and what follows is identified as the law that Moses spoke to Israel, not simply the words he shared with them. (Note that some would treat the heading, "These are the laws that Moses spoke . . ." as indication that this second discourse should extend all the way to 26:19.)

In Deuteronomy 5 the second discourse begins in earnest with Moses contemporizing his audience's experience with the covenant-making event on Sinai: the covenant made there and then was meant also for the present generation. Then Moses launches into a repetition of the Ten Commandments given on Sinai and a recollection of how he was then appointed by God as the people's mediator so they would not have to face God themselves.

Next Deuteronomy 6 reports Moses' sermon on the first commandment. The homily is characterized by the repeated refrain, "Hear, O Israel!" and the famous command, "You shall love the Lord your God with all your heart, and with all your soul, and with all your might" (6:5). The contrast to this, Moses explains, is worship of other gods. Obeying the commandment will bring blessing and prosperity, and its violation will evoke God's wrathful destruction, such as the people experienced at Massah. The sermon closes with Moses admonishing his audience to explain to their descendants that the statutes they observe are given out of God's desire to mark the people indelibly as his own people after having brought them from bondage in Egypt.

Deuteronomy 7–11 shifts focus to the theme of how Israel should relate to the peoples in the land they are about to possess. Deuteronomy 7 makes clear by repetition and refrain that Israel is to destroy the people of the land and their gods so as to ensure that they will not ensnare Israel in idolatrous worship or intermarriage

that also could lead to apostasy. Moreover, God reminds them that they were chosen not because of their numbers or strength, but because God has regard for the oath he swore to their ancestors and because he loves them, small in number and weak though they are.

In 8:1–10:11 the sermon moves on to consider the possibility that Israel might grow prideful and forget its history with God: Moses warns against this, reminding the people by another historical review (that differs from the others by its non-linear account) that God chose them for no merit of their own and brought them safely — even comfortably! — through their wilderness wandering, providing their every need even when they complained without reason. Moses cites in particular the golden calf episode and its aftermath (see Exodus 32–34) as testimony to God's resolute commitment to his promise, in spite of the people's rebellious nature.

Finally, the last discourse before the law code closes with a final speech (10:12–11:32) in which Moses begins with the question: what does the Lord require of you? The answer to the question, says Moses, lies in keeping God's commandments. Then Moses reminds the people that the cost of opposing God is considerable; they should recall the fate of Pharaoh and his army, and of Dathan and Abiram. By contrast, those who heed the commandment, argues Moses, will prosper, nature itself will bless them, and the land will be cleared of its inhabitants to make way for them. At the heart of obedience, argues Moses, is love of the Lord God above all else, loyalty to the Lord.

Deuteronomy 12:1–26:15: The Law Code

This law code, like the ones in Exod 20:22–23:33 and Leviticus 17–26, begins with stipulations pertaining to proper sacrifice and then moves on to other matters, including many that are also covered in the other two law codes. However, unlike the other two collections, this one not only governs the actions of ordinary Israelites but also the acts of various "office holders" in Israelite life, such as judges, kings, priests, and prophets. This concern for Israel's leaders not only sets the Deuteronomic Code apart from the Covenant and Holiness Codes (although the latter does deal with priests), it is also a significant indication of the code's composite character (in spite of the admonition in 4:2 and 12:32 not to take away from or add to the law code!).

Deuteronomy 12 commands Israel to worship the Lord God alone and to worship him in but one place. Within the narrative world of Deuteronomy, of course, the commandment to worship in one place cannot name Jerusalem — the people had not yet encountered the holy city — but the referent of the repeated phrase, "the place that the Lord your God will choose," is plain enough. Particularly striking is the additional provision in this chapter for profane slaughter. Unlike Leviticus 17, which insists that all slaughter is sacrifice, the framers of this law were concerned about the implications of centralization for using livestock for food. They addressed this concern by making specific provision for profane slaughter in 12:15-28.

The seriousness of the commandment to worship the Lord God alone is made clear in Deuteronomy 13, which requires the execution of prophets and diviners, and even friends and family members, who lead Israel into idolatry. Likewise, if a town or city has turned to idolatrous worship it is subject to the ban (extermination) and should be consumed entirely as though it were a whole burnt offering.

Deuteronomy 14-15 turns attention to various ways in which the people exhibit their peculiar status as God's chosen: avoidance of pagan customs for mourning the dead; observance of food laws like those promulgated in Leviticus 11; setting aside tithes from harvests and flocks for offerings at the annual harvest festival and every third year for the Levites, sojourners, widows and orphans; and observance of the Sabbatical Year in all respects, including the release of slaves. While many of these laws have parallels in the Covenant Code, the Holiness Code, or in other legal stipulations that turn up in Leviticus 1–16 or Numbers, they are modified to reflect the peculiar interests of the Deuteronomic Code. For instance, the law of firstlings in Deut 15:19-23 is incorporated into the centralization of worship by the commandment that the firstborn of the flock be offered and consumed at the central sanctuary (cf. Exod 22:29-30). The same customizing of laws for the Deuteronomic Code's interests can be seen in the festal calendar that follows in Deut 16:1-17. Providing for the Passover and the concomitant Feast of Unleavened Bread, the Feast of Weeks, and the Feast of Booths, Deuteronomy mandates that for each of these — three times a year — Israelite males should appear to make offering to God at the place that God chooses.

Deuteronomy 16:18–18:22 provides stipulations regarding judges and the administration of justice, kings and their function, the rights and responsibilities of and the provision and authenticity of prophets. While this legislation's variety regarding Israelite officials is apparent even from the foregoing list, there is a unifying element: while Israel's leaders are charged with oversight of the people, the real intent of the laws for leadership is to secure *God's rule* over the people. The clearest evidence for this is in the law of the king in 17:14-20: rather than behave as a typical ancient Near Eastern monarch, he should not acquire horses (to build an army), marry many wives (to make alliances with foreign kings), or acquire great wealth (to purchase a strong military and win the hands of the daughters of foreign kings). Instead, he is to have a "copy of this law" (i.e., Deuteronomy) close at hand to read and keep so that he leads the nation in observing God's law. In short, the laws of institutional leadership aim toward a theocracy.

Deuteronomy 19-20 provides the last two substantial legal formulations before the rest of the code is devoted to a sort of legal miscellany in chs. 21-25. Chapter 19 addresses the administration of justice in cases of unintentional and intentional murder and dictates the provision of cities of refuge for unintentional murderers. The same chapter makes stipulations regarding witnesses to a crime, insisting that two or three are necessary to sustain a charge against an accused person and that false witnesses are to be punished according to the harm their mendacity caused. This last ruling prompts a recitation of the *lex talionis,* the decree that judgments should trade an eye for an eye, a tooth for a tooth. This may in turn be the prompt for addressing in ch. 20 the law of holy war as an exception to the *lex talionis:* when the people of Israel approach a town they are to offer it terms of peace, but if those terms are refused they are to destroy it utterly, taking booty only from towns outside of Canaan. An ancient environmentalist sentiment imbues the remaining stipulation, that in the event of holy war only fruitless trees are to be used as instruments in battle, and in no case are trees to be wantonly destroyed.

As noted, Deuteronomy 21-25 is a miscellany of stipulations governing the Israelites' life together. Here are just a few of the many things addressed in this section.

- The treatment of the bodies of criminals executed for capital crimes (21:22-23).
- Who may be excluded from the assembly of the Lord (23:1-8).
- Prohibition of cultic prostitution or the use of profits from it for the Lord's sanctuary (23:17-18).
- Laws regarding economic exchanges between private parties (24:10-15).
- The law of levirate marriage that requires the brother of a deceased man to marry the widow to provide offspring who can carry on the name of his brother (25:5-10).

Notably it is this medley of laws that often prompts observers to claim that the Deuteronomic Code is especially humane relative to other ancient Near Eastern law collections, and even the Covenant Code. Whether that is true or not, by contrast with much of the rest of the

Deuteronomic Code, this disparate collection is marked by its particular interest in the quality of relationships between human beings.

In 26:1-15, a liturgy for the offering of firstfruits at the central sanctuary during the Feast of Weeks (see 14:22-29) concludes the law code. The liturgy includes a confession of faith in story form that was long thought to be an ancient creedal formula, but is now acknowledged to be a Deuteronomic composition. In a sense it is a fitting conclusion to the code, drawing attention back to the beginning and the collection's overarching interest in mandating centralized worship of the Lord God. With this passage the motive for loyalty to the one God is made clear once more: it is this one God who saw to the people's freedom from bondage and their eventual possession of the Promised Land.

Deuteronomy 27 and 26:16-19; 28:1-68: The Shechem Ceremony and Covenantal Blessings and Curses

The next major section of Deuteronomy is plainly composite. Deuteronomy 26:16-19 provides Moses' exhortation to keep the laws in light of the covenantal relationship between God and the people, and 28:1-46 extends that motif by announcing and explaining the curses and blessings that would come to Israel in the event of covenant apostasy or loyalty. Deuteronomy 27, however, appears to interrupt the flow of this material: not only does it offer a second set of blessings and curses, and specify for them a ceremonial context at Shechem, it also changes to third-person speech. Deuteronomy 28:47-68 is also probably an editorial addition, since its commentary on the curses in 28:15-19 demonstrates an awareness of the circumstances of the Babylonian Exile.

Deuteronomy 29-30: Moses' Final Discourse

Although we encounter further speech from Moses in his blessings for the tribes in ch. 33 (as well as in his report of the song God assigned him to pass on to the people in ch. 32), Deuteronomy 29-30 constitutes Moses' last discourse related to the law. Its flavor is much like that encountered in 28:47-68, at least inasmuch as it too seems to be aware of the Exile that eventually befell Israel.

Deuteronomy 29 is Moses' speech to the assembled people in which he recalls once again how God delivered them from their enemies and transported them to the edge of the Promised Land. He also observes that, although God gave them much through the covenant, they are already beginning to imagine the ways in which they will violate the covenant. For this, Moses, says, the people will suffer the curses already announced to them,

and in time they will find themselves uprooted and scattered to the corners of the earth.

Then in 30:1-10 Moses, presupposing the certainty of the Exile, exhorts the people to remember to cry out in those days to God to appeal for restoration (cf. 4:29-31). When they do, God will restore them and etch the law into their hearts so that they can live according to the Great Commandment without needing so much as a reminder (6:5). In that day the people will prosper again.

Deuteronomy 30:11-20 concludes the section — and probably an early form of Deuteronomy altogether — with a poignant plea. Moses points out that, in spite of the possibility that the people will fail, the covenant and its terms are not so challenging that they should *necessarily* fall short. Indeed, says Moses, the word of the covenant is "very near to you; it is in your mouth and in your heart for you to observe." Thus Moses concludes by challenging the people to choose between the life offered through the keeping of the covenant and the death that comes from ignoring it.

Deuteronomy 31-34: Epilogue

The content, rhetoric, and themes of Deuteronomy 31-34 vary widely and are also distinctive in relation to the rest of the book. Thus most think it likely that these chapters were sources incorporated by the Deuteronomic authors of the book as a whole or perhaps, in the case of ch. 34, added by a later editor (who may have been from the Priestly school). In any case, the section as a whole functions as a sort of epilogue to Deuteronomy.

Deuteronomy 31 rehearses key events at the conclusion of Moses' life: the commissioning of Joshua; Moses' writing of the law (that had to this point in the narration of Deuteronomy been only oral!); and the giving of instructions regarding the disposition of the Book of the Law in the ark of the covenant in the sanctuary. Furthermore, God commands Moses in ch. 31 to teach Israel the song preserved in 32:1-43. In 32:44-52 Moses commands the people to hand down his words from generation to generation and he narrates his vision of the land. Next ch. 33 gives Moses' blessing for the tribes of Israel — a piece that parallels Jacob's blessings for his sons in Genesis 49 — and Deuteronomy 34 reports Moses' death.

Critical Issues in Studying Deuteronomy

Deuteronomy has long been fertile territory for biblical scholars, especially since 1805 when W. M. L. de Wette demonstrated that Deuteronomy 12–26 constitutes the "Book of the Law" that Josiah used to legitimate the religio-political reform reported in 2 Kings 22–23.

Late Bronze fortress temple at Shechem featuring a great standing-stone *(masseba)* in the forecourt. Mount Gerizim lies in the background to the south. (Phoenix Data Systems, Neal and Joel Bierling)

Thanks to de Wette's discovery, Deuteronomy has become the "Archimedean point" in Pentateuchal studies, the set piece around which others are positioned in terms of chronology and literary relationships. Since de Wette, Deuteronomy has been linked with the Historical Books that follow it, with the Wisdom literature of the Hebrew Bible, and even with nonbiblical sources such as the vassal treaties of the Assyrian Empire. We can only touch on some of the most important topics that have attracted scholarly attention, and we focus especially on ones that relate to our larger interest in comprehending the theological agenda of the book.

Literary Questions
Critical imagination relative to Deuteronomy was stirred early on by the abundant evidence for its composite character. For instance, the frequent shift between the singular and plural of the second person suggests the incorporation of diverse sources. Even the central chapter on cult centralization is divided along these lines into two parts: 12:1-12 uses the second person plural, while 12:13-31 employs the second person singular. However, this particular case points up the promise and peril in making much of the change in number: to some it plausibly indicates the work of more than one hand in creating Deuteronomy, but for others

it is just as easily explained as a stylistic device used by a single author.

The multiple section headings contained within the book offer more compelling evidence of a compositional history. We listed the major instances of this at the beginning of our survey of Deuteronomy's content. They include 1:1-5; 4:44-49; 12:1; and 29:1. These suggest to some readers that an author, acting mostly as a redactor, gathered and wove together a variety of sources to create Deuteronomy. Others argue that these section headings reflect editorial expansions made by different redactor-authors over the course of time. And of course, still others argue that the section headings are the work of a single author who meant them as section divisions and are therefore not evidence of a compositional history at all.

Least arguable as evidence of Deuteronomy's composite nature is the difference in content and character of various portions of the book. While it is possible to argue that the awareness of the Exile exhibited in chs.

4, 29–30, and 28:47-68 is in fact genuinely anticipatory in nature, it seems more likely that these passages were added to an existing work in light of the Judeans' deportation to Babylon. And few defend the common authorship of the legal core of Deuteronomy and the poetry we encounter in chs. 32 and 33. These and other such obviously different sections of Deuteronomy assure us that it is in significant ways a composite work.

Deuteronomy's genre, a question that is related to the compositeness of the book, has also occupied its share of scholarly attention. The most obvious literary analog is the valedictory speech. Indeed, even within the Deuteronomistic History that follows Deuteronomy we find close, if considerably abbreviated parallels to Moses' speech: Joshua 23 presents the valedictory of the book's namesake; 1 Samuel 12 is Samuel's departing speech; and although it is not, strictly speaking, his valedictory, Solomon's speech at the dedication of the temple is similar in form and character. The Apocrypha and New Testament demonstrate the abiding popularity of the genre as well; see, for example, the speeches of Judith, Mattathias, and Stephen (Jdt 8:11-27; 1 Macc 2:49-68; and Acts 7:2-53). The genre was known in classical literature as well and was particularly popular with Thucydides and Herodotus.

All that being said, Deuteronomy encompasses so much more than Moses' end-of-life discourses as to elude classification only as a valedictory speech. Indeed, by embracing legal material, covenantal rhetoric, and ceremonial language it has also been linked with the vassal or suzerainty treaties known from the ancient Near East, and especially with that of Esarhaddon of Assyria (see p. 60 for a discussion of the different kinds of ancient Near Eastern treaties). These treaties entailed expressions of mutual obligation between two parties, one of which was a conqueror (the suzerain) and the other the conquered kingdom (the vassal or client). The weight of obligation, of course, fell on the vassal, and in the case of Esarhaddon, the treaties were in fact loyalty oaths. As such, the documents were probably instruments for ceremonies in which the vassal expressed loyalty to the suzerain with the language of total love and devotion. The treaty or loyalty oath often included the following elements: a preamble that identifies the parties; a historical review of the relationship between the two parties; the stipulations of the treaty (laws); provision for the treaty's publication; a calling out of witnesses; blessings and curses attendant upon keeping or breaking the agreement; and in some cases, provision for covenant continuity after its makers pass from the scene. The figure provides a listing of the elements of Esarhaddon's treaty and the corresponding parts as they appear in Deuteronomy. Yet our survey of Deuteronomy

Deuteronomy and Esarhaddon's Treaty
Preamble: 1:1-5
Historical Review: 1:6–4:43
Stipulations: 4:44–26:15
Publication: 27:1-10
Calling of Witnesses: 30:19 ("I call heaven and earth to witness against you today that I have set before you life and death, blessings and curses.")
Blessings and Curses: 27:11–28:68
Covenant Continuity: 29–30

above proves that even the suzerainty treaty form is at best an imperfect parallel.

Another genre possibility presents itself when we realize that Deuteronomy is the "prologue" to the Deuteronomistic History (Joshua, Judges, 1 and 2 Samuel, and 1 and 2 Kings). It provides the theoretical framework for understanding the historiographic record presented in those books. While this hardly matches any known form from the ancient world out of which Deuteronomy came, it may provide a hint at what was intended by the authors of the book: they sought to provide a *new* genre to introduce their theological history of Israel in the land, but to do so they needed to marshal the resources of forms their audience would recognize so as to gain the audience's attention in the first place. And what better form to imitate and twist than the loyalty oath! The suzerain in *their* world was not merely a human king (indeed, see 17:14-20), but the one, Almighty God.

A final literary feature of interest is the structure of the canonical form of Deuteronomy. Although generally viewed as too simplistic, the following organization of the whole is often suggested and retains enough merit to work in this context.

First discourse with historical review that "anticipates" the Exile, 1–4

Second discourse as an exhortation to keep the law, 5–11

Deuteronomic Code, 12–26

Blessings and curses as exhortation to keep the law, 27–28

Third discourse with historical review that "anticipates" the Exile, 29–30

Epilogue of additional material, 31–34

Organized in this way Deuteronomy appears as a ring composition that has additional material appended to it (chs. 31–34). As we see below, this has implications for how some view the compositional history of the book and, later, of the Deuteronomistic History as a whole.

Thematic and Content Affiliations Between Deuteronomy and Other Parts of the Hebrew Bible

Another critical issue that attracts interest is Deuteronomy's affiliation with other parts of the Hebrew Bible. We discuss here three of those: the Yahwist material in the Tetrateuch, speeches by major figures and the narrator in Joshua to 2 Kings, and wisdom traditions.

The Documentary Hypothesis explains the relationship between the historical reviews in Deuteronomy and the corresponding portions of the Yahwist narrative in Numbers as a result of the Deuteronomic writers' reliance on the Yahwist. But two things about this explanation have long puzzled interpreters. First, as we saw in our survey of Deuteronomy, its account of Israel's travel from Sinai to the plains of Moab flatly contradicts Numbers at times. Second, many observe Deuteronomic rhetoric in Numbers, as well as in the Yahwist portions of Exodus. How do we explain these things if Deuteronomy was written *after* the Yahwist Work? Documentarians say that authors of Deuteronomy introduced the differences by severely telescoping the Numbers account and retouching the Tetrateuch with their own Deuteronomic rhetoric. The Supplementary Hypothesis, on the other hand, suggests that Deuteronomy was composed first, and that the Yahwist expanded and adapted Deuteronomy's brief account of the wilderness wandering to fit his own agenda. As for the Deuteronomic rhetoric scattered throughout the Yahwist material, this approach explains it as the result of an author's conscious effort to affiliate his *alternative* theological agenda with the dominant religious perspective articulated already in Deuteronomy to 2 Kings. For the most vigorous proponent of the Supplementary Hypothesis, John Van Seters, this also means that the Covenant Code was not composed first among the Pentateuch's legal collections, but rather after the Deuteronomic Code and in dependence on it (and on Babylonian law codes known to the Yahwist Writer in exile, see Chapter 8).

We have already mentioned the most important affiliation Deuteronomy shares with other Hebrew Bible material: the Deuteronomistic History in Joshua, Judges, 1 and 2 Samuel, and 1 and 2 Kings. Since Martin Noth identified the Deuteronomistic History in 1943, there has been near unanimity among scholars that Deuteronomy serves as the introduction to the history that runs from Joshua to 2 Kings and that the history demonstrates Israel's initial success and ultimate failure in keeping the covenant laid out in Deuteronomy. We return to a fuller discussion of this affiliation

Seal of vassal treaty of the Assyrian king Esarhaddon (672 B.C.E.) from the temple of Nabu, Nimrud, listing covenant terms imposed on his subjects, including "Manasseh, king of Judah." (Iraq Museum, Baghdad)

between Deuteronomy and Joshua to 2 Kings in the following chapter.

Finally, critics have also observed a relationship between Deuteronomy and some Israelite wisdom literature. A number of commands in Deuteronomy have parallels in Proverbs. For instance, the prohibition against removing boundary markers in Deut 19:14 and 27:17 also appears in Prov 22:28 and 23:10. In addition to other precise parallels such as this one, Deuteronomy understands the law in much the way wisdom literature understands human wisdom: as a guide to life lived well, and something that, when possessed and appreciated, marks a person as wise in his or her own right (Deut 4:6). This affiliation turns out to be significant in considering the character of the authors of Deuteronomy.

Authorship, Date, and Provenance of Deuteronomy

The questions of when and where Deuteronomy was written and who wrote it are closely connected to the observation that the core laws were likely the "Book of the Law" on which Josiah based his reform of the cult according to 2 Kings 22–23. We date that effort to around 621 B.C.E., so we know at least that the law code was in existence by then. Opinions vary as to when and by whom the law code was first composed, but the most widely accepted hypothesis is that it was developed by Levites of the Northern Kingdom who brought it with them to Jerusalem as they fled the Assyrian conquest.

Opinions also differ regarding the compositional process that eventually produced the book of Deuteronomy we know today from the seeds of the law code. Although we have no way of being certain, one plausible process is suggested by the "ring structure" we noted above. First, to support Josiah's reform (roughly) chs.

5–11 and 27–28 may have been added to the law code to provide it with a sermonic framework and conform it more or less to the vassal treaty pattern we observed above. Then, when the reform eventually failed and the people were driven into exile and the rest of the Deuteronomistic History was composed, chs. 1–4 and 29–30 were added to express recognition of that event and hope for the future (see esp. 4:29-31; 30:1-10).

Theological Themes in Deuteronomy

Deuteronomy lays down the basic theological insights that shape the following books (Joshua to 2 Kings). It announces that God freely elected Israel to possess the land and imposed the keeping of the law as a requirement for maintaining possession of the land. The sermonic material surrounding the law code also functions to express through historical recollection and outright proposition some basic understandings of the nature of God and of the people, and of the shape of their relationship with one another. And while the law code provides rules for a wide spectrum of human conduct, the sermonic material already gives pride of place to the regulations for proper worship of the God of Israel. Before turning to these theological themes let us one last time examine some attempts by early Jews and Christians to contend with puzzling aspects of one of the books of the Pentateuch. This time we limit ourselves to two exegetical motifs.

One of the more striking contradictions in Deuteronomy centers on its central character, Moses. In 18:15, 18 God announces to the people through Moses that he will in time raise up for them a prophet like Moses, apparently referring to the mediator's role Moses has played for them. Yet 34:10 says unequivocally, "Never since has there arisen a prophet in Israel like Moses, whom the Lord knew face to face." This seems to undercut the possibility that 18:15, 18 referred to any of the prophets who did follow Moses in the biblical record. So who is announced in ch. 18? For early Judaism and Christianity one answer was to continue anticipating the promised prophet, but also to exalt him and treat him as a forerunner of the messiah. Thus 1QS (the *Community Rule* for the Essenes, the people of the Dead Sea Scrolls) 9:11 speaks of the coming of "*the* prophet" before the arrival of the messiahs of Aaron and Israel. Likewise, in John 1:21 the priests and Levites sent to question John the Baptist ask him if he is "*the* prophet," and in the same gospel the people mistake Jesus for "*the* prophet" on more than one occasion (6:14; 7:40, 52); in both instances the Gospel of John seems to treat "*the* prophet" as the forerunner of the messiah, the fulfillment of

God's promise in Deut 18:15, 18 and the explanation of 34:10.

Like the other law codes in the Pentateuch, the Deuteronomic Code has its share of rules that drew the interest of later interpreters. An example is 25:4, which decrees that "You shall not muzzle an ox while it is treading out the grain." The intention, obviously, is to permit the ox sustenance while it does the work of the farmer. But the temptation to read this not so much as a rule for humane treatment of farm animals, but as an admonition regarding just payment to human laborers was too great for ancient readers. Thus, Paul argues for the right of apostles to work for their living by citing this passage (1 Cor 9:9; cf. 1 Tim 5:18). But James Kugel (see "Further Reading" in Chapter 6) has also pointed out that the same passage was also used in the *Apostolic Constitutions* 2.4.25 to argue against gluttony on the part of church leaders, who were apparently taking undue advantage of their positions of authority and control over community wealth; just as an ox naturally avoids overindulgence when treading out the grain, the bishop should use restraint in his use of church resources for his own purposes!

God Elects Israel from among the Nations to Possess the Land

A striking feature in Deuteronomy is the way Moses reminds the people that they take possession of the land by God's initiative alone, and that the people of the land are dispossessed of it "because of their wickedness" (see esp. chs. 8–9). The insistence that the relationship between God and people was not based, at its initiation, in any way on the people's merit, or especially their keeping of the law, is a feature of Deuteronomy and its accompanying theology that is often overlooked. Deuteronomy goes out of its way to make clear that God's decision to place Israel in the land came before the giving of the law and the relationship founded on it. There is, therefore, a clearly unilateral characteristic to God's relationship with the people in Deuteronomy: it lies at the beginning of the relationship, in God's election of Israel.

The Character of God in the Covenantal Relationship

Deuteronomy as a whole makes clear that in addition to electing Israel freely and bringing them into the land, God promises to the people of Israel blessing and prosperity if they obey the law of God in the land, but wrath and condemnation if they reject the law (28:15-68). But already in Deuteronomy it is clear that the single most important law requires the worship of the one God of Israel in the one place God chooses. Deuteronomy 8:1-20 epitomizes this complete perspective:

This entire commandment that I command you today you must diligently observe, so that you may live and increase, and go in and occupy the land that the LORD promised on oath to your ancestors. . . .

Keep the commandments of the LORD your God, by walking in his ways and by fearing him. For the LORD your God is bringing you into a good land. . . .

Take care that you do not forget the LORD your God, by failing to keep his commandments, his ordinances, and his statutes, which I am commanding you today. . . .

Remember the LORD your God, for it is he who gives you power to get wealth, so that he may confirm his covenant that he swore to your ancestors, as he is doing today. If you do forget the LORD your God and follow other gods to serve and worship them, I solemnly warn you today that you shall surely perish. Like the nations that the LORD is destroying before you, so shall you perish, because you would not obey the voice of the LORD your God.

Deuteronomy also reveals another dimension to God as a covenantal partner. On several occasions, God acknowledges through the speech of Moses that the people may well indeed fail in keeping the law, and especially in obeying the command to worship the one God of Israel. As a consequence they will be driven into exile, and realizing there the mistake they made they will call out to the Lord who will hear them and respond with a renewal of the covenantal relationship (4:25-31).

The evidence of Deuteronomy, then, is that while God makes a bilateral agreement with the people regarding their life in the land, they receive it first by divine election, and should they lose it by violating the terms of the covenant, even then God will not annul the relationship altogether, but will remember his election of Israel if Israel calls out to him for mercy. As we shall see, these generous terms for the covenantal relationship are much needed, given the story that follows in Joshua to 2 Kings.

The Character of the People in the Covenantal Relationship

It is a good thing that God takes such a generous posture in Deuteronomy, for when we turn to examine the character of the people with whom God has made the covenant, Deuteronomy already reports a past that indicates how much they will require God's mercy. The people's rebellion is a recurring motif in Moses' recitation of the people's history with God and a major theme of the future they will share together. Indeed, the verb "to rebel" (Hebrew *marah*) appears frequently in the

historical recitations that describe Israel's conduct in the wilderness generation (1:26, 43; 9:7, 23, 24), and it is the word Moses uses to describe the behavior he anticipates from the people after he has left them in the care of Joshua (31:27). Our survey of the Deuteronomistic History in the following chapters will show that, in spite of the people's assurances to the contrary, they do not disappoint Moses in this respect!

The Centrality of the Command to Worship One God in One Place

Finally, we must note the singular importance of the centralization of worship in "the place that the Lord will choose." This centralization of the cult in one place and its focus on the one God are announced in ch. 12, which is then followed by laws governing a wide range of conduct, religious and "secular" in character. But when Moses addresses the people regarding their future failure in the land, he speaks almost exclusively of their idolatry. Both of the lengthy passages above make this clear, and they exemplify what we read throughout Moses' speeches in Deuteronomy. Here too, the Deuteronomistic History matches the anticipation of the future announced in Deuteronomy.

Questions for Review and Discussion

1 How does the theology of Deuteronomy compare with the theology implied by the Yahwist Writer? The Priestly Writer? The Tetrateuch as a whole?

2 What is the nature of the covenant worked out between God and humanity in Deuteronomy? How is it like the one we see in the Yahwist Work? How does it differ from that covenant?

3 What is the most likely explanation for the origin of the book of Deuteronomy, and how can this explanation be related to the final shape of the book?

Further Reading

Blenkinsopp, *The Pentateuch;* Van Seters, *The Pentateuch;* Whybray, *Introduction to the Pentateuch.*

Nelson, Richard D. *Deuteronomy.* OTL. Louisville: Westminster John Knox, 2002.

Rofé, Alexander. *Deuteronomy: Issues and Interpretations.* OTS. London: T. & T. Clark, 2002.

The Historical Books

Introduction to the Historical Books

Given modern notions of historiography — the writing of history — readers often expect biblical "Historical Books" like Joshua or 2 Kings or Nehemiah to recount without bias what actually happened in the ancient world. But we shall soon see that such an approach seriously misjudges the nature of ancient historiography. As it turns out, ancient writers of history were more interested in persuading audiences to particular theological, political, or social agendas than in communicating an unadorned account of past events.

A Survey of the Historical Books

The Historical Books in all Christian canons include Joshua, Judges, Ruth, 1 and 2 Samuel, 1 and 2 Kings, 1 and 2 Chronicles, Ezra-Nehemiah, and Esther. To this list Catholic readers add further books from the Apocrypha (or Deuterocanonical books): Tobit and Judith are placed after Nehemiah, additions are made to Esther, and 1 and 2 Maccabees follow Esther (see p. 10 for the different canonical collections).

In terms of content, Joshua takes up the story where Deuteronomy left off, relating the people's conquest of the land that God promised to them. Judges recounts the life of the tribes of Israel in the land when they relied on the periodic intervention of tribal war heroes for leadership to deliver them from oppression by the Canaanites who remained in the land. Placed after Judges because it begins with the words, "In the days of the judges . . . ," Ruth is a short story about a foreign woman's faith in the God of Israel and her role in providing the lineage that produced David. 1 and 2 Samuel then relate the rise of kingship and the days of a united kingdom under the rule of Saul and then David. 1 and 2 Kings tell the story of Solomon's rule, the division of the kingdom into two parts (Judah and Israel), the defeat of the Northern Kingdom (Israel) by the Assyrian Empire, and finally the defeat of the Southern Kingdom (Judah) by Babylon.

1 and 2 Chronicles follow with a renewed recital of Israel's history from Adam to the Babylonian destruction of Judah and the repatriation of Judeans to the land of Judah by Cyrus of Persia. In fact, the "recital of history" from Adam to David is accomplished by means of genealogical lists (1 Chronicles 1–9). Then 1 Chronicles 10–29 retells the story of David as it appears in the Samuel books, but without the sordid details of David's moral, parental, and royal failures best known from 2 Samuel 11 onward. Solomon's reign is likewise sanitized in 2 Chronicles 1–9, and 2 Chronicles 10–36 reviews the remainder of the kings of Judah. Ezra 1–6 picks up where

2 Chronicles 36 left off, relating in greater detail the circumstances surrounding the exiles' return to Judah under Zerubbabel. Then, in a strange division of materials, Ezra 7–10 and Nehemiah 8–9 report Ezra's experience in dealing with the postexilic Judean community, while Nehemiah 1–7 and 10–13 deal with Nehemiah's experiences in the same capacity.

Esther follows Nehemiah in all Christian collections, and in the Roman Catholic canon two additional books come after Esther, Tobit and Judith. All three books are like Ruth in that they have the trappings of historical narratives but are in fact early Jewish novellas. Esther, the story of a Jewish woman saving her people from destruction under the rule of a Persian king, logically follows Nehemiah as a matter of chronology. Though not sharing in the same synchronicity, the tales of Tobit and Judith may have been placed next because they too are accounts of Israelites who were faithful in the face of oppressive foreign rulers. Tobit is the story of the title character and his family and their tribulation and triumph under Assyrian rule, and Judith is the story of that title character's courageous deliverance of her Israelite village from the threat of a foreign army.

Finally, the Roman Catholic canon includes two further "historical" works, 1 and 2 Maccabees. These actually continue the tale of Jewish experience long after the end of Persian rule detailed in Ezra and Nehemiah, picking up the story again only with the last decades of Seleucid rule over Judea at the end of the first half of the 2nd century B.C.E. (Thus, the Hebrew Bible has no direct accounts of Jewish experience during the time of Alexander's conquest of the Persian Empire in the late 4th century, the contest between Alexander's successors — especially the Ptolemies and the Seleucids — at the end of the 4th century, Ptolemaic rule over Judea in the 3rd century, and the beginning of Seleucid dominance in the first half of the 2nd century!) Both books focus on the Maccabean rebellion against the Seleucids and on Maccabean (Hasmonean) rule in Judea until late in the 2nd century B.C.E.

An Approach to Studying the Historical Books of the Hebrew Bible

As the foregoing survey already shows, there are two different kinds of material among the "historical books" of the Hebrew Bible. There are, first, roughly continuous historical narratives in Joshua to 2 Kings (excepting Ruth) and 1 Chronicles to Nehemiah, and parallel historical narratives in 1 and 2 Maccabees. The remaining books — Ruth, Tobit, Judith, and Esther — are novellas. In the scope of this Introduction as a whole we treat

Joshua to Esther in their canonical order as they appear in the Protestant collection (for the full list and a discussion of the different canons see Chapter 2 and page 10), and we discuss 1 and 2 Maccabees and Tobit and Judith in a chapter devoted to the Apocrypha or Deuterocanonicals. However, as a matter of convenience, in introducing the Historical Books in this chapter we consider them according to their thematic and genre associations, beginning with the Deuteronomistic History (Joshua, Judges, 1 and 2 Samuel, and 1 and 2 Kings) and continuing with the Chronicler's History (1 and 2 Chronicles and Ezra-Nehemiah), the parallel histories of 1 and 2 Maccabees, and finally the novellas (Ruth, Tobit, Judith, and Esther).

The Deuteronomistic History

We have already seen that the continuous account of ancient Israel's history from the conquest to the Babylonian Exile in Joshua, Judges, Samuel, and Kings shares much in common with Deuteronomy. Indeed, it is history narrated from Deuteronomy's theological perspective — an excellent example of the ancient historiography we described in the opening paragraph of this chapter. As a result, scholars have come to call these books the "Deuteronomistic History."

Notably, it was not until Martin Noth suggested the connection in 1943 that Deuteronomy was associated in this manner with Joshua to 2 Kings, and the idea of the Deuteronomistic History was first proposed. Noth observed the similarities among the speeches of Moses in Deuteronomy and those of major figures and the narrator in the Deuteronomistic History (which include, among others, Joshua 23; Judg 2:11–3:6; 1 Samuel 12; 1 Kings 8; 2 Kgs 17:7-18, 20-23). What linked all these speeches was a shared theological perspective that is characterized by the assertion that, although Israel possessed the land of Israel by virtue of God's election, it would retain the land and have prosperity only by keeping the law provided by God, especially the law requiring Israel to worship the one God in one place, Jerusalem. Failing that, Israel could expect to be expelled from the land by a wrathful God.

Noth argued that there was one edition of the entire Deuteronomistic Collection that emerged after the beginning of the Babylonian Exile. Its purpose, he insisted, was to explain the Exile as the result of Israel's relentless apostasy. However, other scholars observed signs in Deuteronomy and the Deuteronomistic History that suggested a more complex history behind the collection's composition. For instance, the mixed attitude toward kingship and the Davidic dynasty — compare the dynastic promise in 2 Samuel 7 and the frequent echoes of it (e.g., 1 Kgs 11:12-13, 32, 34; 2 Kgs 8:19; 19:34; 20:6) with the long narrative of David's troubles in 2 Samuel 11–20! — prompted one major revision of Noth's hypothesis by Frank Moore Cross. Cross suggested a first edition of the Deuteronomistic History was produced during Josiah's reign to coincide with Josiah's centralization effort and to glorify the Davidic dynasty. Cross posited a second edition in the Exile that introduced the less glamorous view of kingship in light of the kings' role in bringing down Judah. Hans Walter Wolff also observed tensions within the Collection that suggested to him a compositional history more complex than the one proposed by Noth. Wolff noticed that, in addition to predicting the people's expulsion from the land if they failed in their covenant obligations (a first edition), some of the Deuteronomistic speeches assume that exile would come to pass but also address its remedy as well (a second edition): the people should cry out to God in repentance and God would heed their plea and restore them to the covenantal relationship (Deut 4:29-31; 30:1-10; 1 Kgs 8:46-53). Still others have identified three editions with separate historical, prophetic, and nomistic (legal) interests. As was the case in source-critical study of the sources of the Tetrateuch, the dogmatic pursuit of an intuition about the authorship of Joshua to 2 Kings has tended to proliferate authors and redactors where at one time there was but one author!

For our purposes, speculation about multiple editions is best avoided. Instead we begin with the assumption that the Collection was completed in the Exile. This end date for the Collection's composition is well justified by the conclusion of the Deuteronomistic History that narrates the invitation of Jehoiachin, the exiled king of Judah, to share meals at the emperor's table in Babylon (2 Kings 25). Thus, we presume that our author wrote from the perspective of the exilic experience. We also assume, given the different textures and emphases of the narrative, that the author employed vastly diverse sources to compose his work, and that he was contending with a wide variety of perspectives on the two questions that most occupied the interest of his readers: How did God's chosen people end up in exile? And what was their future beyond the experience of exile and with the God who had elected them? Thus we should expect a diversity of perspectives within the Collection, not only because of the many sources used, but also because the author no doubt felt compelled to contend with what were surely many competing answers to these two key questions.

This set of assumptions and expectations has implications for how we approach the Deuteronomistic History. First, we must shed any modern notions of "objective history" when it comes to reading Joshua to 2 Kings. This is clearly an account that was meant by its author to persuade his audience to a certain view of their ancestors' history. And that it involves judgments about the nature of God and his relationship with the people makes clear that the author was engaged in theological persuasion: he was not writing history so much as doing theology.

Second, the foregoing account of what an author intended in creating the Deuteronomic Collection also makes clear that it is polemical, that is, it argues its own view of history in competition with other interpretations of the same events. As we shall see, the author had little positive regard for kingship, for human wisdom, and for prophecy. Moreover, he was perfectly willing to shape his arguments to combat the proponents of those human institutions and offices. So, not only was this author a theologian, he was also an apologist, an argumentative theologian, as it were.

Finally, we must acknowledge that there probably was a longer compositional history for the Deuteronomic Collection than that implied by our presupposition of a single, exilic-era author. Indeed, there was almost certainly not only a compositional history, but also multiple authors who brought to bear multiple sources in creating this massive work. It seems quite likely that the Deuteronomistic view of kings, wisdom, prophets, and covenant developed over a long period of time that extended at least from the days of Josiah, well into the Exile and beyond, and that the attitude toward those realities changed over time. All the same, for sake of simplicity we will focus attention on the single moment in the compositional history that brought the Deuteronomic Collection to completion, one we may reliably place in the Exilic period. As a consequence, while we will, in passing, take note of the sources that were used to create the Deuteronomistic History and some possible stages in its development, we will speak mostly (albeit artificially) of a single Deuteronomist rather than many Deuteronomists in our discussion of Joshua, Judges, Samuel, and Kings below, and we will focus on the last stage in the Collection's compositional history. (We note, in closing, that a further minority view of the Collection's origin places it in the Hellenistic period, and treats virtually all of the "history" narrated in Joshua to 2 Kings as the work of fabulists bent on legitimating a Hellenistic-era Jewish state. This explanation of the Deuteronomistic History has won very few followers.)

The Chronicler's History

Since the early 19th century, scholars have argued that a single author or school of authors composed Chronicles and Ezra and Nehemiah. There are several pieces of evidence supporting this view. First, the end of the Chronicler's account, 2 Chr 36:22-23, is repeated by Ezra 1:1-3a. Second, a related book of the Apocrypha, 1 Esdras, contains 2 Chronicles 35–36; Ezra 1:1-11; Nehemiah 8. Third, Chronicles and Ezra and Nehemiah share some otherwise unusual terminology and genres (e.g., "house of God" and the extensive use of lists and genealogies). And finally, they have in common some distinctive themes, including the Jerusalem temple, the priesthood, and Levites and their functions. More recent scholarship, however, has questioned the association of Chronicles with Ezra and Nehemiah. Some of the evidence for this alternative view includes: the intense concern for retributive justice in Chronicles that is largely absent in Ezra and Nehemiah; differing attitudes toward the northern tribes in the two works; and the focus on the Davidic dynasty in the Chronicler's work and the absence of interest in it in Ezra and Nehemiah. These and other indicators have cast doubt on the once rock-solid notion that the same author (or authors) was (were) responsible for Chronicles *and* Ezra and Nehemiah; as a result there is little consensus on the precise relationship between the Chronicler's work and Ezra and Nehemiah.

For our purposes, though, the matter can be simplified somewhat. Inasmuch as we are chiefly interested in an implied author — that is, the one that the text as we receive it conveys — as well as that author's audience, it seems best to read these books as closely related. The overlap between the conclusion of 2 Chronicles and the beginning of Ezra compels recipients to read them together, rather than separately. Likewise, the books' common interests are stronger and more numerous than the differences, and the divergences in some cases are not unexpected due to the different periods narrated by the two bodies of work. For example, a lack of concern for the Davidic dynasty is not surprising in Ezra and Nehemiah since they are books about Judah in the Postexilic period, when Persian imperial policy prohibited the renewal of the monarchy let alone the restoration of a royal dynasty! In light of this, and other common interests shared between the two bodies of work that we will see in the course of our study of them, we speak in this Introduction — again, somewhat artificially — of a single Chronicler in dealing with 1 and 2 Chronicles and Ezra and Nehemiah.

Finally, we note that, just as the Deuteronomistic History is less history than theology, the same will be evident of the Chronicler's History when we come to it. And just as the theology in the Deuteronomistic History was polemical in character, it seems likely that the Chronicler's theological stance was rooted, at least in part, in opposition to alternative visions for postexilic Israel. In any case, we shall see that like the Deuteronomist, the Chronicler also had the ancient historiographer's zeal for theological or ideological bias.

The Books of the Maccabees

When we come to the two books that bear the name of the Jewish rebels who arrayed themselves against Seleucid rule, we will encounter a much less unified body of literature than what we see in the Deuteronomistic History and the Chronicler's History. In fact, there is no doubt about the separate authorship and intentions of 1 and 2 Maccabees. It suffices for now to say that 1 Maccabees was likely intended in large part as a defense of the Maccabees' rule over Judea in the late 2nd century B.C.E. against accusations of apostasy from the true faith; on the other hand, 2 Maccabees was probably interested in promoting that "true faith" especially among Jews of the Diaspora and particularly in encouraging them through historiography and martyrology to embrace Hanukkah as a feast of liberation. All the same, these two works may be treated together, for they both engage in their different political and theological agendas by narrating (to admittedly different degrees) events from the same period in Jewish history.

Ruth, Esther, Judith, and Tobit (and Jonah too)

As noted above, we treat Ruth and Esther in their canonical order, even though Ruth, in fact, interrupts the Deuteronomistic History to follow the book of Judges (see above) and Esther seems to have been placed after Nehemiah only because it tells a tale from the Persian period. In the Roman Catholic canon, Tobit and Judith are placed between Nehemiah and Esther, but are treated in this Introduction in the chapter that covers the Apocrypha (Chapter 44). What these books *do* share in common, though, is their genre, the historical novella. One other biblical book, Jonah, fits this description as well. We take a moment here to consider briefly this genre and how these five books evince it.

A historical novella is an account that takes as its starting point a known past event, context, or personage and builds around that a (fictional) tale that works not just to entertain but also to persuade its audience. For instance, Jonah is a book that satirizes its namesake, a figure who is named only in passing in 2 Kgs 14:25; but in doing so the book challenges a whole mindset about the accessibility of God's mercy to no one but Israel. Likewise, Tobit places its namesake in the "Assyrian diaspora," a historical context about which little was known, in order to highlight the difficulties Tobit faced in remaining faithful to the God of Israel and to encourage others who faced similar difficult circumstances in their faith. Note that, in this way, these overtly fictional accounts — not history at all like that offered in the Deuteronomistic History — are deeply akin to the other "Historical Books" addressed in this chapter: together, both sets of books work to persuade, to cajole, to convince, and to transform their audiences. That is what all of the texts we turn to now in greater detail have in common.

Further Reading

We include here only some general discussions of the Deuteronomistic History and the Chronicler's Work.

Bibliography related to 1 and 2 Maccabees and the historical novellas is to be found at the end of the relevant chapters.

Ackroyd, Peter R. *The Chronicler in His Age*. JSOTSup 107. Sheffield: JSOT, 1991.

Schearing, Linda S., and Steven L. McKenzie, eds. *Those Elusive Deuteronomists*. JSOTSup 268. Sheffield: Sheffield Academic, 1999.

Grabbe, Lester L., ed. *Did Moses Speak Attic? Jewish Historiography and Scripture in the Hellenistic Period*. JSOTSup 317. Sheffield: Sheffield Academic, 2001.

Chapter 13

Joshua

Getting Started

1   Read Joshua 3–4. Does this account of the crossing
of the Jordan remind you of an episode from the
Pentateuch? How is it like that episode? How is it different?

2   Read Joshua 6–8. While the story of Jericho is likely
familiar to you, the conquest of Ai is just as likely
relatively unfamiliar. How does a continuous reading
of the two episodes — the conquest of Jericho and
the eventual defeat of Ai — change your perception of
the first episode?

3   Read Joshua 23–24. In what ways do some of the parts
of these two chapters recall Deuteronomy? Can you
identify particular phrases and ideas that are familiar
to you already from your reading of Deuteronomy?

Preliminary Comments

Stories of military conquest fill the first part of Joshua.
Indeed, it is in this book that we hear the familiar account of the walls of Jericho falling at the sound of the
people of Israel shouting. But a closer look at Joshua reveals that there is far more to it than a collection of battle accounts. It also relates the events leading up to the
Conquest, the division of the land among the tribes after
their successful campaign, and a "covenant episode"
that affirms the people's relationship to the Lord God.
There is still more, for underlying the simple narrative is
the first chapter in the Deuteronomist's account of how
the covenantal relationship between God and people established in Deuteronomy actually worked out. Behind
the tales of war and daring lies a theological claim about
the land, that it belonged to God's chosen people, and
that God was the one who secured their possession of it.
But just so, if, having come into control of the land, they
failed to live according to God's design for them in it, the
land could just as quickly be taken from them as it was
given to them. In short, Joshua makes clear, right at the
beginning of the Deuteronomistic History, the curious
tension between God's lordship over Israel's destiny and
Israel's own responsibility for her destiny.

A Walk through Joshua

As we already noted, there is more to Joshua than war stories. In fact, contrary to popular imagination, military campaign accounts make up less than half of the book (chs. 6–12).

Joshua 1–5: Preparing to Take the Land

The book begins with a new commission to Joshua from the Lord God. He promises to Joshua success at every turn in taking the land, saying, "from the wilderness and the Lebanon as far as the great river, the river Euphrates, all the land of the Hittites, to the Great Sea in the west shall be your territory" (1:4; cf. Deut 11:24). But with this comes a double warning that hearkens immediately back to the admonitions in Deuteronomy: Joshua and the people should carefully keep the law, never turning "from it to the right hand or the left" (1:7; cf. Deut 5:32; 17:11, 20; 28:14), and like kings who live according to the Deuteronomic prescription, Joshua should meditate upon the law day and night to act in accordance with all its stipulations, for that will ensure success (1:8; cf. Deut 17:19-20). Thus, from the first words of the Deuteronomistic History, God's appointed leader of the people is commissioned according to the law as a king might be, and the people are instructed to remain true to the law. In short, from the beginning it could hardly be clearer: God is the ruler of this people through his law. Joshua 1 closes then with Joshua reminding the men of the tribes of Reuben, Gad, and Manasseh that they are obliged to assist in the Conquest according to their prior agreement (cf. Num 32:1-33; Deut 3:13, 18-20).

Joshua 2 then recounts Joshua's attempt to reconnoiter the land by sending two spies to Jericho. In an act that hardly requires explanation — although pious commentators have certainly tried — the two men go straight to "the house of a prostitute whose name was Rahab, and spent the night there" (2:1). Although not prohibited by the Deuteronomic Code, the spies' choice of activities upon entering the city is hardly what one would expect, given their assignment; and if, as some suspect, Rahab was a cult prostitute, the spies' visit foreshadows Israel's later penchant for worshipping

foreign gods. Further, if the episode is taken to foreshadow the way of the people in the land, it is an inauspicious beginning, at least for them: for the true hero of the story is a heroine, and a foreign one at that! Rahab, the (cultic?) prostitute, recognizes the power of the spies' God and offers to protect them and their people. To sweeten the deal Rahab agrees, along with her whole household, to worship the God of Israel. While the people of the covenant turn from the path laid out for them "to turn to the right hand and the left," it is a non-Israelite who exhibits the greatest faith in the story. It is as if the storyteller wants to underscore from the very beginning the nature of this people with whom God has made an agreement.

Joshua 3–4 records the people's crossing of the Jordan near Jericho. The episode recalls the people's escape from Egypt through the parted sea (Exod 14:5-31; Deut 11:3-4), but it also includes significant differences. In this case the priests, instructed by Joshua, hold the ark of the covenant in the middle of the Jordan to cause the dry land to appear. As the priests stand there, the people pass between the stayed waters. Next, God commands Joshua to select 12 men, one from each tribe, to return to the dry ground around the priests to retrieve one large stone each to be set up on the shore. (Notably, there seems to be a second tradition about the standing stones woven into this account; it is most obvious in 4:9, where we hear that Joshua sets the stones up _in the middle of the river!_) Joshua decrees that the standing stones are there to remind future generations of the miraculous crossing of the Jordan and its forerunner, the crossing of the sea. (Many scholars observe, in addition, that the episode probably also recalls some cultic practice at Gilgal associated with a memory of the Exodus; standing stones were often used by ancient Near Eastern cultures to mark sacral sites.)

A series of episodes in Joshua 5 completes the cycle of stories that lead to the conquest of the land. After learning that upon hearing of the crossing at Gilgal the kings of the Amorites and of the Canaanites by the sea lose all heart before the advancing Israelites, the reader encounters two double-edged etiologies. Not only do they explain the origin or reason for a landmark or a practice (the function of an etiology), they also underscore Deuteronomic theological claims. The first is God's instruction for Joshua to see to the circumcision of all remaining uncircumcised male Israelites. The account explains the name given to the place (Gibeath Haaraloth, "hill of foreskins"), but it also emphasizes the Deuteronomist's assertion that, for all of the blessings God offers the people, they are prone even from the time before they entered the land toward lawlessness: that God has to make this request of Joshua indicates

Nahr Hasbani, longest of the four sources of the Jordan River. (W. S. LaSor)

that the wilderness generation has erred not only in faithlessly fearing the people of the land (Numbers 13; Deut 1:22-40) but also in failing in their obligation to circumcise their sons! The next brief notice that the people then eat unleavened bread and roast grain for the Passover near Jericho is also an etiology, clarifying why the manna ceases at that time: it is no longer necessary, as the land itself begins to provide for the people. This etiology, too, serves one of the Deuteronomist's larger theological aims, to affirm the intrinsic bounty of the land that God promised and gave to Israel.

The final event at Gilgal reported in ch. 5 is as strange as it is significant to understanding the account of conquest that follows. Near Jericho Joshua encounters a man with a drawn sword, and when Joshua asks whose side he will be on in the upcoming battles, the man answers that he is on neither side, but that he has come as commander of the Lord's army. When Joshua then asks what message the Lord intends, the sword bearer simply tells him to remove his sandals, for he stands on holy land. With that the episode ends. Its role in the Deuteronomic account seems to be twofold: to announce that the land the Israelites are about to move into belongs to God and is subject to the rules of holiness (thus the command to go shoeless, as Moses did before the burning bush); and to emphasize that the taking of the land will not be so much by the human act of warfare, as by God's intervention on behalf of whom he chooses. The last point is equally promising and ominous, and should be read with reference not only to the Conquest stories that immediately follow, but with

reference to the whole Deuteronomic story that ensues, all the way to the end of 2 Kings where God's might no longer favors Israel, but rather her enemies.

Joshua 6–12: Conquest of the Promised Land

In any case, the stories of conquest that follow in Joshua 6–8 undeniably illustrate the ritual character of warfare aimed at taking the Promised Land. Purified and prepared, the people follow to the letter God's instructions for the conquest of Jericho (ch. 6), instructions that would madden any commander of military forces. Marching in circles, blowing trumpets, and shouting loudly hardly seem to be adequate military tactics. But they are precisely what bring Jericho's walls down and permit the people to enter the city and carry out the ban (*herem* in Hebrew), the destruction of all living things and the dedication of the defeated people's wealth to God.

The conquest of Jericho illustrates the principle that God wins battles for those whom he favors. The ensuing episode in Joshua 7 further affirms that principle, for when the people attack Ai with reduced forces because the advance team determines it to be a poorly defended city, they are turned back and 36 Israelites are slain. Joshua responds by accusing God of misleading the people into a disastrous situation, and God replies that he let them suffer defeat because someone in their midst has withheld some of the wealth of Jericho for himself. Israel is bound to identify the covenant breaker and destroy him. The lot falls to Achan and his family, and they are stoned (thus explaining an apparently well-known mound — another etiology, gruesome as it may be!). With the breach in Israel's covenant loyalty repaired, God sends Israel against Ai a second time with a battle plan that entails considerably more cooperation between God and people, and this time they experience enormous success, routing Ai as they had Jericho, making of it a heap of ruins visible "to this day" (8:28) and burying its defeated king under a separate pile of stones which also "remains to this day" (8:29). To conclude the episode and reaffirm the Israelites' covenantal relationship to God, Joshua builds an altar at the important site of Shechem on Mount Ebal (another stone memorial!) and makes a sacrifice to God. He also cuts a new copy of the law in stone to commemorate the occasion and reads the law to the assembled people as they stand in two groups before Mount Ebal and Mount Gerizim.

Having established a "theology of conquest," the remaining account of the taking of the land is narrated in relatively quick order. First, hearing of the Israelites' reputation, the Gibeonites deceive Israel into making a mutual defense treaty by disguising themselves as travelers from afar who come to make peace with Israel

Standing stones in the Middle Bronze III high place at Gezer, possibly a covenant-renewal sanctuary for a ten-city league. (Phoenix Data Systems, Neal and Joel Bierling)

(Joshua 9). The deceit succeeds, and so Israel is obliged to come to Gibeon's defense when other Canaanite city-states hear of the deception and decide to punish their neighbor for joining forces with Israel. The result is Israel's divinely-aided defeat of the five southern city-states occupying what would be Judah, including Jerusalem (ch. 10). Word travels once more of Israel's success, this time to the north, where Jabin of Hazor (a powerful city-state in northern Canaan in the period of the conquest) organizes a coalition to fight Israel. Israel achieves victory once more and conquers the northern territory as well (ch. 11). Joshua 12 then lists the conquests to indicate the totality of Israel's occupation of the land.

Joshua 13–21: Establishing Tribal Territories
This seldom-read section of Joshua is a dry account of the distribution of territories to the tribes. In spite of the tedium associated with it, though, it does further the theological agenda pursued by the author. In Joshua 13–19 the lands are distributed among the tribes mostly by lots, a further indication of the fact that God is its true owner: they are divided according to divine will! The provision of Levitical cities in ch. 21 (ch. 20 assigns cities of refuge for accidental murderers) may also have been used to advance the author's agenda. Assuming that the Deuteronomists were themselves instructors of the Torah, reporting God's provision of property in hoary antiquity for personnel who were charged with the same

duty, the Levites, is a none-too-subtle Deuteronomic claim to ownership privilege in their own day.

Joshua 22–24: Covenantal Conclusion
The conclusion of Joshua approaches the issue of covenantal fidelity from several different angles. First, Joshua 22 narrates the return of the Reubenites, Gadites, and half-tribe of Manasseh to their territory on the other side of the Jordan and their construction of an altar there. The other tribes perceive sacrifice apart from the ark of the covenant as a violation of covenantal loyalty (thus foreshadowing the centralization of worship in Jerusalem so important to the Deuteronomists). So they send a delegation to complain and threaten civil war. The three Transjordanian tribes reply that they have erected the altar only to signal their connection to the other tribes in Canaan, and that they too belong to the God of Israel. To avoid war they agree to forego sacrifice and retain the altar as (another) stone heap that will memorialize their relationship to the other tribes and God.

Joshua 23 reports that after the passage of quite some time Joshua gathers the people to address them. In a speech that borrows from Moses' sermons in Deuteronomy (and foreshadows others from key figures in the Deuteronomistic History) Joshua reminds the people that God has fulfilled the promise of land, and that now they should be faithful to their role in the covenantal relationship. But like Moses before him, Joshua also warns the Israelites that if they take up the practices of the survivors of the Canaanite peoples whom they drove out, God will punish them with exile from the land.

Finally, Joshua 24 takes on the issue of covenant loyalty from one more perspective, reporting that Joshua gathers the people at Shechem to renew the covenant in what amounts to another treaty-signing ceremony. After a historical review from the days of Abraham to the present the people are challenged to be faithful to the one God. They reply that they will serve God alone, and Joshua reminds them that vowing such loyalty and not honoring the vow will bring destruction. Still they make the vow, and Joshua records the agreement on (yet another) memorial stone. The chapter closes with Joshua's death and the interment and the burial of Joseph's bones at Shechem (cf. Gen 50:25; Exod 13:19).

Critical Issues in Studying Joshua

Among the many we can choose from, we treat just two critical issues in the study of Joshua, namely the sources used in its composition (especially etiological narratives) and the trustworthiness of Joshua as an account of the land's conquest. Treating these two issues prepares us well to address the theological themes the Deuteronomist pursues in Joshua.

But before turning to our more detailed consideration of sources and history in Joshua, it is worth noting at least in passing an issue that our survey of Joshua's contents may have raised. It is hard to miss the similarities between the story of the crossing of the Jordan and the escape story in Exodus. This and other echoes of content and rhetoric in the Tetrateuch prompted an earlier generation of scholars to wonder if Yahwist or Priestly material stretched into Joshua, requiring one to speak not of a Tetrateuch or Pentateuch, but instead, of a Hexateuch. That hypothesis, once popular, has lost nearly all of its supporters over the past decades as it becomes ever more apparent that Joshua is a thoroughly Deuteronomic composition. And a closer look at Joshua 5 indicates that in addition to the absence in particular of a pursuing army that is destroyed by the waters, this is a very "priestly" account of the crossing, unlike the story in Exodus 14. Although this last observation has prompted some scholars still intent on finding some of the Tetrateuch in Joshua to suggest that at least the Priestly Writer's hand can be detected in the book, that too is an idea that founders on the evidence: Joshua's "sacerdotal" passages do not match the stipulations found in the Priestly material of the Tetrateuch. All of this has led others to suspect that, while the Deuteronomist knew an independent tradition of the Exodus and sought to mimic it in Joshua 5, he also had access to a variety of sources rooted in a certain priestly tradition (different from the one that produced so much of the Tetrateuch) that he found useful in composing Joshua in particular. This observation leads us to address the issue of sources in Joshua.

Etiologies and Other Sources in Joshua

It is hard to miss in even a casual reading of Joshua that its creator was more of a collector-redactor than an author in the strictest sense of the word. As the figure indicates, even an incomplete list of the episodes that appear to have been built from inherited tales and traditions is impressively long.

The list reveals that very little of Joshua came solely from the hand of a Deuteronomic author. Instead, he relied on a large array of source material that ranged from tales of encounters between human beings and angelic soldiers to lists of tribes and the lands assigned to them. But especially notable are the many etiologies among the sources, stories that explain a variety of phenomena such as communal conditions and relationships and physical features of the Promised Land. Communal conditions and relationships explained in Joshua include the presence of Rahab's descendants among the

---

Episodes Built From Sources in Joshua

2, The spies in Jericho and the inclusion of Rahab's family in the people of Israel

3, The crossing of the Jordan

4, Two explanations for standing stones at Gilgal

5, Explanations for the names Gibeath Haaraloth and Gilgal, and for the cessation of manna; the encounter with the angelic warrior

6, The legend of the fall of Jericho (and an explanation for a *tel* at the site?)

7, An explanation for a stone heap in the Valley of Achor

8, Explanations for the *tel* at Ai, a stone heap at the site, and the sanctuary at Shechem

9, An explanation of the Israelites' relationship with Gibeon

13–21, Lists and other genres as explanations for tribal locations in the land and the existence of cities of refuge and scribal training centers

22, An explanation of a stone heap in the Transjordan

---

people of Israel (ch. 2), the cessation of manna (ch. 5), the presence of Gibeonites among the people of Israel (ch. 9), and the affiliation of certain tribal groups with particular places in the land and of some cities with special functionaries (chs. 13–21). However, the length of the list of stories that explain physical features in the land — virtually everything else on the list in the figure — suggests this author's special fondness for such etiologies, and especially for offering reasons for the existence of stone heaps and *tel*s (a *tel* is a mound that contains below its surface, layer by layer [each of which is called a stratum], the remains of human settlements over the course of hundreds or even thousands of years). Below we shall see what this latter observation indicates about the reality of Israel's conquest of the land, and we saw already in our survey of Joshua the role some of these etiologies play in the Deuteronomist's larger theological agenda. In any case, the prevalence of such stories in Joshua suggests the author's access to a collection of "physical feature" etiologies that came in handy in composing his account of the people's conquest of the land.

In stark contrast to this heavy use of sources in Joshua, very little of it seems to have come directly from the pen of the Deuteronomist; but what little there is of such distinctive material is quite efficient in accomplishing the purpose of making the book as a whole an unequivocally Deuteronomic composition. The first chapter, the commissioning of Joshua, bears many of the hallmarks of a Deuteronomic composition (e.g., "servant of the Lord," "act in accordance with the law," etc.), as do the closing chapters 23–24. Both sections of text frame the work as a whole with their clear determination that the land is possessed by God's people, not by their own might but by God's will and determination, but that to remain in the land the people must obey the law God gave them through Moses and that Joshua read aloud to them. Moreover, to fail with respect to the law would risk expulsion from the land. There is little about this that is *not* Deuteronomic in tone!

The clever use of sources in Joshua does not stop with the provision of framing chapters. On numerous other occasions the collector-redactor has strategically arranged and redacted source material. For instance, by juxtaposing the story of God's propitious use of the spies' choice of activities in Jericho with the divinely-directed defeat of Jericho, the failed attack on Ai, and the discovery and correction of Achan's sin, the editor makes a typically Deuteronomic point: God is determined to give this people the land in spite of their own foibles and will even welcome outsiders into the covenant if they trust in the God of Israel (the spies and Rahab). Where the people violate God's commandments they will pay a price (the defeat at Ai), yet they can also experience renewed success if they correct their ways and eliminate their sin (the punishment of Achan and his family and the second, successful attack on Ai). Likewise, by adding just a little to these cleverly arranged sources, the Deuteronomic editor-redactor makes of them a thoroughly Deuteronomic work. By reporting the inscription of the law as a celebratory act after the defeat of Ai (ch. 8) the meaning of the preceding string of stories is crystal clear: they prove the significance of the law for Israel now that the land promised has been granted.

The Historical Reliability of Conquest Narrative

Already readers may have doubts about putting too much stock in Joshua's account of the Conquest; for our discussion of sources in Joshua certainly suggests the author had less concern for history than for theology. Not only that, the narrative of the Conquest in Joshua 6–11 does little to support the occasional claims for complete conquest of the land (e.g., 10:40-43). For instance, the places mentioned in chs. 6–10 (and in 2–5 as well) focus attention almost exclusively on Benjaminite tribal territories in the south, and the ostensible evidence for Israel's conquest of the north in ch. 11 provides evidence of only a limited engagement in that region. Meanwhile, inconsistencies between Joshua and Judges abound, and there are a few within Joshua as well. For instance, Judges 1 lists a host of places where Canaanites persisted in the land and Josh 23:7 has the book's namesake warn the people against associating "with these nations left here among you," yet the Joshua

Conquest account suggests a completeness gainsaid by these elements. Also, according to Joshua 11 Hazor and its allies were soundly defeated by Joshua's army, but Judges 4–5 tells a tale of Canaanite power in the same city many years later. The evidence against the biblical record's reliability is considerable.

As a consequence, historians have turned attention to the material evidence, archaeology, to construct a more accurate picture of the rise of Israel in the land. Regrettably, the archaeological record is as ambiguous and diffident about yielding sure results as the Bible! So rather than a single alternative to the Bible's accounting of the Conquest we have as many as four other explanations.

One model that relies only modestly on the archaeological record and heavily on a critical reading of the text comes from the German scholars Albrecht Alt and Martin Noth. On the basis of the archaeological evidence they observed that, while urban centers persisted on the plains in the 2nd millennium B.C.E., the highlands of that era exhibited less developed population centers and fewer numbers of inhabitants. Relating this to the claim in Judges 1 that the residents of the lowland cities survived after the initial Israelite conquests, Alt and Noth suggested that the newcomer Israelites initially inhabited the highlands and only later immigrated into the lowland country. Thus Alt and Noth grant no historical reliability to the Conquest account in Joshua (and their model also suggests that some of the ancestral stories in Genesis originated from the later lowland encounters with the people of Canaan).

In sharp contrast to the German school, the American "biblical archaeology" movement of the mid-20th century was confident of the biblical account and that archaeology could verify its accuracy (for more on "biblical archaeology," see Chapter 3 above). These scholars hoped that with the excavation of the *tel*s in the region that correspond with the sites mentioned in the biblical account, the biblical account would be confirmed. And indeed, initial work proved that in the 1200s and 1100s — the period to which the Conquest is usually assigned — there were violent disruptions of some cities in Canaan. But the problem is that the destructions did not occur in places corresponding with the biblical narrative. Numbers 21:21-35 reports that the Israelites fought successful battles in the Transjordan even before entering the land, but excavation of the corresponding sites tells a different story, revealing that all the Israelites would have found were *tel*s, not inhabited cities. The same is true of Jericho and Ai, the conquests featured in Joshua 6–8. And to make matters worse, Hazor did suffer destruction at the right time, but as we have already seen, Judges 4–5 admits Canaanite possession of the city at a much later time. Ironically the biblical archaeology movement's effort to prove the Bible "true" accomplished quite the opposite. It developed impressive evidence that the Joshua accounts of conquest could not be taken at face value as a report of what actually transpired. On one hand, the stories appear as (more) etiologies targeted at explaining large stone heaps, the *tel*s that no doubt dotted the land as the people began to establish themselves there (e.g., Num 21:21-35; Joshua 6–8). On the other hand, further stories appear to have been adaptations of real conquests carried out by indigenous Canaanites, not outsider Israelites (e.g., Joshua 11 on Hazor).

An alternative hypothesis, also originating among American scholars, provides a slightly different use of the archaeological evidence. The archaeology of the region actually suggests a long period of sporadic violent destructions of Canaanite city-states and a transition over time in the lowlands to a less developed urbanized culture. This hypothesis also takes special note of the brigands mentioned in the el-Amarna Letters from the 14th century B.C.E. (on the nature of these letters, see Chapter 3 above), the *ʿapiru*. Reading the evidence of the letters and the archaeological record together, this hypothesis suggests that the rebels were indigenous Canaanite peasant-nomads weary of Egyptian taxation and the concomitant oppressive actions vassal city-states took against them. The Israelites who escaped from Egypt joined these *ʿapiru* under the banner of the liberator God of Israel, and together they carried out a long guerilla war against the city-states and their kings. Clearly this theory is attractive for its open embrace of the archaeological evidence that points to a long period of conquest and a transition to a "lower culture," but it also suffers from some obvious drawbacks. The first is textual: there is no evidence in the biblical record that Joshua and the Israelites were part of a "liberate Canaan" movement. Second, that the hypothesis is built as much on Marxist political theory as it is on the textual and archaeological evidence understandably makes critics wary. One is left wondering — with considerable justification — if the theory trumps the evidence.

A last explanation dubbed the "gradual emergence" model is nowadays perhaps the most popular. Proponents of this approach depend on a variety of evidence, little to none of which is biblical. First, they take seriously the recent observation that during the 13th to 11th centuries numerous unwalled villages sprang up all around the central highlands, especially in places later identified particularly with the emerging nation-state of Israel. Notably, though, the four-room houses and collared-rim jars that distinguish these sites are not distinctively "Israelite" as once thought, but rather reflect a somewhat diminished version of the culture found in Canaanite city-states of the lowlands. Thus the influx of population to the central highlands appears to have originated from within Canaan, perhaps as a movement of poor, disaffected city-state residents to the countryside. Second, this approach also acknowledges the evidence of the late-13th-century victory stela from the Egyptian Pharaoh Merneptah claiming victory over Israel in Canaan: this proves that there was by that time some group in the land that went by the name "Israel." Together these pieces of evidence suggest that Israel was an entity that arose from (slave?) flight out of Canaanite city-states to the central highland. In short, Israel was an indigenous Canaanite development. Advocates of this approach do acknowledge that the unique worship of Yahweh may have come from escaped slaves from Egypt who joined the settlements or from Midianite traders who brought to the region their storm-god. But of course, we cannot be certain of either possibility.

Regardless which of the preceding approaches one favors, it should be clear that not one of them matches well with the story told in Joshua. This leaves us conceding once again that Joshua is more theology than history. So we turn now to its witness as theology.

Theological Themes in Joshua

Throughout our treatment of the books of the Deuteronomistic History we will focus mostly on the major theological theme that can be found in all of them: the way the covenant relationship actually worked out in history and what it proved about the nature of God and humanity and the relationship between the two. We will also trace the effort of the Deuteronomist to answer what appeared to have been competing theological perspectives grounded in kingship, wisdom, and prophecy.

The Covenant in Joshua

The opening verses of Joshua set out plainly the terms of the covenant between God and Israel announced already in Deuteronomy and their implication for taking and remaining in the land.

The elements of God's commission to Joshua set the stage not only for the Conquest account that follows but also for the entirety of the Deuteronomistic History. First, we read that God *gives* the land unilaterally to Israel. Second, we understand that no one shall be able to stand against Joshua, and by extension, the people of Israel whom he leads into the land. But third, the taking of the land given as a gift *does* require strength and courage and the keeping of the law. And last, retaining the

Detail of the Merneptah stela (ca. 1210-1207 b.c.e.) containing the earliest extant reference to Israel outside the Bible. (Service de Musées, Cairo)

land in prosperity also requires careful keeping of the law given by God.

Key elements of the story that follows prove the accuracy of these propositions. First, at the crossing of the Jordan the power of God's presence to separate the waters and permit the people to pass underscores God's commitment to securing the land (chs. 3–4). Second, Joshua's encounter with the angelic commander of God's army in 5:13-15 confirms that, much as God intended Israel to possess the land, God remained free to take whichever side God might choose. Third, the sequence of events from the miraculous taking of Jericho, to the failed conquest of Ai, to the discovery of Achan's sin, to the successful conquest of Ai proves that even with God's commitment to Israel's possession of the land, the people must still live by the laws God provided to receive the fulfillment of that promise. Finally, Joshua's valedictory speech and the covenant ceremony at Shechem in chs. 23–24 articulate clearly — even doubly — the absolute necessity of faithfulness to the laws for maintaining possession of the land.

The Emerging Portrait of
God and Humanity Together

While Deuteronomy provides only a theoretical sketch of how God would behave in a covenantal relationship and only the evidence of the wilderness generation for how the people of Israel would act, Joshua begins to add much more substance to this picture.

As for the people of Israel, we learn that in spite all of the warnings regarding the necessity of courage and strength and heedfulness of the law, they fail almost immediately and in a wide spectrum of ways. The spies' choice of the (cultic?) prostitute's house to visit upon entering the city of Jericho signals a certain dereliction of duty and even perhaps provides the first sign of Israel's penchant for worshipping the gods of the people in the land. Joshua's overblown response to the loss of some Israelites in the first attack on Ai — after having utterly eradicated the population of Jericho! — is surely an instance of loss of courage and strength. The Achan incident reveals a dangerous lack of regard for God's direct command. And the exchange with the Gibeonites heralds the people's occasional vulnerability to a certain dimwittedness that undercuts their chances of success in the land. By contrast, when the people do live according to the law, they experience the success that God promised them: they take the city of Jericho by trusting in very unusual battle plan instructions; they cooperate with God in the eventual defeat of the city of Ai; and the rest of their successful conquests in the book come through faithful adherence to God's directions for war.

The portrait of God that emerges from this first portion of the Deuteronomistic History possesses some nuance that is not present in Deuteronomy. When confronted with the people's first failure, God becomes a didact rather than a vengeance-seeking deity, offering Joshua instruction on how to redeem Israel's relationship with God. Further evidence of that instructional role comes in the first verses of the book, as well as in the rhetoric of the last two chapters. And clearly, God evinces in this, the first unit of the Deuteronomistic History, a corresponding penchant to that exposed in the people for worship of foreign gods: a will to offer second and third chances to a people forewarned of the consequences of lawbreaking. Moreover, the Rahab episode proves God's willingness to embrace all who confess him as Lord and submit themselves to the laws of God.

Finally it is important to note that Joshua makes clear the centrality of the land to the Deuteronomic vision:

it is what God promises to provide to his elect people, it is what they must exert their strength and courage to take possession of in cooperation with God, and it is the keeping of it that their law-keeping is intended to achieve. As we turn to Judges, 1 and 2 Samuel, and 1 and 2 Kings we see how that remains a focus for the people and for God in the Deuteronomist's imagination.

The Violence of the Conquest in Joshua: A Theological Problem?

One additional issue requires our attention here, namely the disturbing violence of the Conquest narrative in the book of Joshua. Its overwhelming, categorical character has long troubled readers. The fact that God mandates the slaughter of innocents — though this is hardly the only place in the Old or New Testaments where that is the case — has given more than a few cause to look askance at the God of the Bible. What "explains" this bloody account? Is it not a "theological problem"?

Some have sought solace in pointing out the parallels between what is described in Joshua and a wider ancient Near Eastern practice. For instance, it was in fact customary across the ancient Near Eastern world to obliterate one's defeated foe. Indeed, the Moabite Stone of King Mesha from the 9th century B.C.E. describes his use of the ban against Nebo, and in bloodier fashion than most biblical accounts of destruction. Others have tried to soften the offense to some extent by noting that the ban was in fact a religious act, a way of dedicating by sacrifice all life to the Lord of the winners, and this too was a common ancient Near Eastern practice.

One might also explain the problem away by observing how this narrative works, given its implied audience. That is, perhaps thinking of this from the perspective of the Deuteronomist, who writes in exile and with a sense of the narrative flow, overcomes some of the moral objections one might raise against the God of Joshua. From that writer's perspective it was Israel's divine right to possess the land, whether anyone occupied it or not. The way to maintain possession of that land was by eliminating the temptations within it, by carrying out God's beneficent instructions for cleansing it. But the story the exilic Deuteronomist tells is one of the persistence of the natives in the land — see Joshua's admission in 23:7! This proves that for all of their fine intentions, Israel did not succeed in the cooperative effort to possess the land entirely. They failed in realizing in cooperation with God the ideal of a land purified of other influences. And as we shall see, this fact is further underscored by the refrain in Judg 1:1–2:5, "and they did not drive out the people in the land," and by the angelic speech that condemns the people for their faithlessness to the enduring presence of the people of the land to plague them (Judg 2:1-5). In short, from this perspective the violence of the Conquest is not a theological *problem* so much as it is part of a larger theological *lesson.*

Having said that, full disclosure requires one to admit that still, after all things are considered, the account in Joshua crystallizes for the reader an aspect of the God of the Bible that remains deeply troubling to readers of all times and places. And no matter what we may say to explain it away, the God of these stories, and still others we are yet to encounter even within the Deuteronomistic History, remains a mysterious and often threatening power.

Questions for Review and Discussion

1 What does the book of Joshua suggest about the conquest of the land by the people of Israel? How does that account compare with the archaeological evidence? What four models have been developed to reconcile (or dismiss!) the biblical record in relation to archaeological evidence?

2 Setting aside the question of just how Israel came into possession of the land, what seems to be the thrust of the "theological history" that we read in Joshua 1–12? How does this fit into a larger Deuteronomic agenda?

3 As noted in the closing section of this chapter, the violence God mandates of the people of Israel in taking the land has long troubled readers. We noted some attempts to understand that violence of God. Do you find any of them convincing, or does the issue remain one of concern? What contribution to theology — an understanding of God — does this pattern, and others like it in the Bible, make?

Further Reading

Dever, William G. "Israel, History of: Archaeology and the Israelite 'Conquest.'" *ABD* 3:545-58.

Nelson, Richard D. *Joshua.* OTL. Louisville: Westminster John Knox, 1997.

Younger, K. Lawson, Jr. "Joshua." In *ECB,* 174-89.

Chapter 14

Judges

Getting Started

1   Read Judges 1:1–2:5. How does this account of the conquest of the land compare with Joshua 1–12? What might account for the differences you notice?

2   Read Judges 2:11–3:6 and 3:12-30. Can you identify the rhetoric and ideas in 2:11–3:6 with anything you have read in Deuteronomy and Joshua? How about the ideas and rhetoric of 3:12-30? How are they different from what you have seen thus far in your reading of the Old Testament?

3   Read Judges 9. How does this account of Israel's first experiment with kingship compare with its experience of judges as you know it already from 3:12-30?

Preliminary Comments

The title "Judges" conjures images of men and women in black robes making decisions on issues brought before them. While some of that is done by one of the "judges" in this book (without black robes, and in the person of a woman, Deborah), their predominant role is that of military heroes, saviors of the people in their time of need. And not all of them even live up to that billing, at least not in the way we would expect. One delivered the people by killing his foe in the bathroom (Ehud), another came by his military skills through a career as a bandit (Jephthah), and another was a profoundly disobedient Nazirite (Samson). However, what they all had in common, as we shall see, were a place in a tribe's memory, a role to play in the Deuteronomic writer's story of the days when "there was no king in Israel," and election by the God of Israel to perform their tasks.

A Walk through Judges

The book of Judges begins as though much of the Conquest narrated in Joshua never occurred. After recounting a more limited taking of the land, it lays out the pattern of life in the place thereafter for the people: peace, followed by apostasy, followed by oppression by the people of the land, followed by cries for deliverance and God's provision of it through a "judge," a war hero for Israel. The rest of the book, more or less, recounts how that pattern repeated itself time and again in the days of the judges.

Reading Guide to Judges
An Account of the Taking of the Land (1:1–2:5)
The Death of Joshua and the Deuteronomic
    Prologue (2:6–3:6)
The First Five Judges and a Failed Royal
Experiment (3:7–9:57)
Seven More Judges (10:1–16:31)
First Illustrative Epilogue (17–18)
Second Illustrative Epilogue (19–21)

Judges 1:1–2:5: The First Prologue

Judges 1:1–2:5 reports the taking of the land again —
almost as though it never happened as described in
Joshua 6–12 — and this time the conquest is explicitly
incomplete. The three southern tribes are not successful in completely securing the sole possession of the
land demanded by God (1:1-21), and the six northern
tribes fail even more miserably (1:22-36). Indeed, the
reader hears no fewer than nine times that the tribes
failed to drive out the Canaanites from the land. The
concerns Joshua expresses in his valedictory speech
are, as it turns out, well founded. So it is not surprising that the section closes in 2:1-5 with the angel of the
Lord announcing in unmistakably Deuteronomic terms
God's disappointment with Israel's performance and
determination to use the remaining peoples in the land
to plague the Israelites.

Judges 2:6–3:6: The Second Prologue

The second prologue begins with the death of Joshua
and the passing of the generation that had entered the
land with him (2:6-10). The passage ominously observes
that the dying generation constitutes the people who
knew the deeds God did for Israel in its wilderness
wanderings, but that the new generation does not. This
leads to the Deuteronomic introduction to the stories
of the judges (2:11–3:6). The introduction establishes
a clear pattern to which the diverse stories more or less
conform: doing "what was evil in the sight of the Lord,"
the people abandon the Lord for the Canaanite gods of
their neighbors (e.g., Baal and Astarte); God becomes
angry and delivers the people into the hands of their
enemies; when the people cry out, God raises up judges
to deliver them from their enemies; and so long as the
judge is alive (40 years each according to the Deuteronomic report) the people continue to be protected from
their foes; but when the judge dies they relapse and the
cycle starts all over again. Notably the introduction also
observes that precisely because of the people's eagerness for apostasy God refuses to drive out the last of the
indigenous Canaanites so as to provide a constant test
by which Israel can prove herself loyal or apostate.

Judges 3:7–9:57: The First Five Judges and a King

With the pattern established clearly at the outset, the
Deuteronomic writer next strings together a series of
tribal hero stories, providing only the slightest editorial
assistance to integrate them into his theologized recollection of the days before kings ruled Israel. A judge's
career is preceded by the refrain, "And the people did
what was evil in the sight of the Lord" so that the Lord
delivered them into the hands of their enemies. Next
the narrator repeatedly states that, "when the Israelites
cried out to the Lord, the Lord raised up for them a deliverer," and then follows the judge's story of deliverance
for Israel (and often the remark that while he ruled [rou-
tinely for 40 years] the people knew peace in the land).

"Baal of the Lightning," stela from Ras Shamra/Ugarit.
The small human figure may be a deity or a person in
the god's care. (Louvre)

The first judge is Othniel. Apart from learning that he is Caleb's nephew, and that he delivered Israel from a king of Aram-naharaim, we know nothing else of him (3:7-11). The record of the third judge, Shamgar, who delivered Israel from the Philistines, is even briefer (3:31). So it is left to the second judge, Ehud, to provide us with a first sense of just how tribal and folkloristic these tales were (3:12-30). Although Ehud is called upon to deliver all Israel from King Eglon of Moab, he is in fact merely the Benjaminite chosen to deliver his tribe's tribute to Eglon after Moab captured their city, Jericho. It would seem this is a matter between Benjamin and Moab, not Israel and Moab. Not only that, this story takes on considerable color. First, Ehud is left-handed, a sign of strangeness, mystery, or even inborn idiocy in the ancient world; thus he is, as it were, a wolf in sheep's clothing. We also learn that Ehud wins his tribe's freedom largely by making what might be read as a rather salacious suggestion to Eglon, that he has a secret message for him to be shared in the palace bathroom. There Ehud stabs the eager Eglon to death with one thrust, losing his dagger in the fat of the Moabite king. And because Eglon's servants are too embarrassed to disturb him while relieving himself, they discover the murder far too late to catch the perpetrator and stop the onslaught of emboldened Benjaminites.

The fourth judge's tale and *her* song of victory also underline these stories' tribal derivation and enchanting character. Under the power of King Jabin of Hazor (cf. Joshua 11!), Israel cries out and is delivered by a curiously mixed force. First is Deborah, the prophetess *qua* judge; second is Barak who, at Deborah's command, gathers the forces of the tribes of Naphtali and Zebulun to attack Jabin's general Sisera and his army; and third is the Kenite woman Jael, a disinterested bystander to the dispute who nonetheless murders the fleeing Sisera with a tent peg through the temple (4:1-24). It hardly comes as a surprise when the ancient song of Deborah (5:1-31) adds further color to the account by observing that Barak experienced such

success against the fearsome chariots of Sisera because a sudden rain mired their wheels in mud.

The last judge before the trial run for kingship is Gideon. Here we encounter one of the lengthiest and most peculiar judge accounts, further confirmation of their vast independence (6:1-8:35). Called to defeat Midian, Gideon has to be convinced of his role by fiery rocks (6:19-24), dewy and dry fleeces (6:36-40), and reports of the dreams of enemy soldiers (7:9-14). His battle name is theophoric (containing all or part of a divinity's name) of the enemy's god, Baal (Jerubbaal). And as for choosing an army from the tribes of Asher, Zebulun, Naphtali, and Manasseh, he is commanded to take only the three hundred who refresh themselves by lapping water like dogs! Once he has made the inevitable conquest of his foe (7:15-8:3) he goes on to deal brutally with people who refuse to support him and his army (8:4-21). And after (honorably) refusing an offer of kingship from his neighbors, he (dishonorably) transforms the gifts they give to him in lieu of a throne into an object of worship, ensnaring himself and the people in the same apostasy that began his story in the first place (8:22-35).

In Judges 9, Gideon's son Abimelech (whose name, with certain irony, means, "My father is king") provides an ominous glimpse of Israel's future with kingship. Perhaps remembering the people's willingness to have his father as king, he seizes the role for himself, and to make sure that he has no competition he kills all his 70 brothers but the youngest, Jotham, who escapes. After a brief and brutal rule inaugurated by his remaining brother's curse on him and marked by bloody discord with his subjects, Abimelech's skull is crushed by an enemy woman's well-directed toss of a millstone; he escapes the final indignity of death at the hands of a woman only by having his sword bearer slay him instead. Israel's first experience with kings is foreboding, at best.

The Canaanite fertility-goddess Astarte, consort to Baal. Bronze figurine from Nahariya. (Courtesy of the Israel Antiquities Authority; photo David Harris)

Judges 10:1–16:31:
Seven More Judges

After reporting the experiment with kingship the book presents seven more judges, five of whom are dealt with in perfunctory fashion (perhaps a sign that they were added only to make the total come to 12 in correspondence with the number of Israelite tribes). They are Tola and Jair (10:1-5) and Ibzan, Elon, and Abdon (12:8-15). Sandwiched between the first two and the last three is the account of Jephthah (10:6–12:7), and after the last three comes the best-known judge of all, Samson (13–16).

Once more, the full measure of a judge, Jephthah, proves the collection to contain diverse and legendary tales only lightly edited by a Deuteronomic collector-redactor. In this case, the collector-redactor has provided an introduction, perhaps authoring much of 10:6-16, where we hear that the Israelites act faithlessly again, are oppressed by the Philistines and Ammonites, and cry out to God, but receive an unexpected reply: God suggest this time they seek help from the gods they have come to worship in his place. And unlike other instances, there is never any explicit divine commissioning of Jephthah. Instead, Jephthah's kinsmen recruit him to deliver them on account of his legendary military skills. They do so in spite of the fact that, until his special skills make him necessary to them, they have ostracized him because he is the son of a prostitute. Ironically, their unkind treatment has engendered his unusual military prowess, because as an outcast he has survived by banditry. He agrees to return to his tribe as a commander of the army only on the condition that he become the tribe's leader, a demand readily granted. After an attempt at diplomacy, Jephthah asks God's help to defeat the Ammonites, vowing to sacrifice whatever crosses the threshold of his house first upon his victorious return. Unfortunately, it is his daughter who first exits the household as the victorious Jephthah returns, and so he is compelled to sacrifice his daughter after allowing her time to bewail her virginity (as it was a disgrace to die childless). And as if to add insult to injury, Jephthah is forced to stave off an attack from men of Ephraim who are perhaps jealous for the spoils of war to which they are not entitled, having not taken part in the battle.

The final judge is Samson, from the tribe of Dan. His story is surely best known of all (Judges 13–16). This account's most curious elements once more demonstrate the distinct and folkloristic character of the judges' stories. According to ch. 13, Samson was born miraculously to a barren woman and was destined through the instruction of an angel from birth to be a Nazirite (someone dedicated to God's service who is marked as such by taking no alcoholic drink and never cutting his hair; cf. Num 6:1-21). In ch. 14 we hear of his strange choice of brides — a daughter of the enemy, a Philistine woman — and his even stranger barehanded killing of a lion, eating of honey from its carcass, and deadly riddle contest with his new wife's kinsmen. Judges 15 relates his foxtail-on-fire revenge against the Philistines who take his wife from him, the Philistines' retaliatory slaughter of his wife and her father, his slaughter of the Philistines with the jawbone of an ass, and the satisfaction of his thirst after such a spate of exhausting activity. Finally, ch. 16 relates Samson's dalliance with a prostitute of Gaza, his escape from his enemies who lay in wait for him, and his ill-fated marriage to Delilah that leads to his death, but also the destruction of the Philistines at their own victory party. Just this laundry list of elements in Samson's story proves it to be the richest of all of the accounts of the judges in folkloristic elements.

Judges 17–18: The First Epilogue

The two epilogues are framed by the repeated judgment, "In those days there was no king in Israel; all the people did what was right in their own eyes" (17:6; 21:25). As a survey of their content shows, the point seems to be that what "was right in their own eyes" was hardly the best thing for all concerned, and was certainly not what was right by Deuteronomic standards.

The first epilogue, Judges 17–18, explains the origin of the cult center at Dan that later violated the Deuteronomic sensibilities regarding centralized worship (cf. Deuteronomy 12; 2 Kings 22-23). It also reveals the common practice of "private home religion" in ancient Israel, another offense to the Deuteronomic tradition.

The first story in ch. 17 is of a wandering Levite who freelances his way into the service of Micah, a man who steals money from his own mother, returns it to her, and then receives it back to make an idol, ephod, and teraphim. The pairing of the two is somehow appropriate inasmuch as they are both "irregular" in their practices and produce together an irregular pattern of conduct according to the Deuteronomic writer, namely domestic worship of an idol with the sacerdotal mediation of a family member. However, as we shall see below in "Critical Issues," this was probably not irregular conduct in popular practice, thus the Deuteronomic writer's interest in recording the story and condemning the practice.

In ch. 18 the second story relates the migration of the Danites from the south (where the Philistine incursions plague them endlessly) to the far north, in Galilee. What links this tale to the previous chapter is the Danites' sojourn along the way at Micah's house where they persuade the Levite to abandon his master and life as a domestic priest in favor of service to them as an entire tribe's priest; they persuade him to take the idol, ephod, and teraphim as well, and with these things he establishes the northern shrine at the new city of Dan. Thus the story is an etiology.

Judges 19–21: The Second Epilogue

The second epilogue offers further chilling proof that when people "do what is right in their own eyes" things go badly. Here we encounter a Levite who is estranged from his concubine. She flees her husband's house to return to her father's home. He tenderly seeks her out and persuades her to return home with him. On their way back they have to pause overnight, and they choose an Israelite city, Gibeah, over Jebus (Jerusalem), thinking the former to provide safer lodgings. Gibeah provides no resting place at all until a citizen of the city offers his home to them. They take his offer, but are soon beset by the men of the city who wish to have intercourse with the Levite. In a disturbing move he turns his once much-sought concubine over to the rapists to save himself from abuse. After a night of terror she crawls to the threshold of their host's home to be found there by the Levite in the morning. He says only to his near-dead concubine, "Get up, we are going," and receiving no response takes her home and dismembers her and sends her body parts to the tribes of Israel as a summons to join him in meting out justice to the Benjaminites of Gibeah. After several pitched battles the men of Israel defeat the tribe of Benjamin and realize that in killing all the women of the tribe, Israel would soon be at a loss for a twelfth of its population. And so when the men of Israel realize in turn that Jabesh-Gilead does not respond to the call for soldiers in the war against Benjamin, they go and exterminate all of that place, leaving only the virgin women as wives for Benjamin that the tribe might survive in spite of its sin against the Levite's concubine. In a second version of how Benjamin is repopulated, the men of Israel grant the Benjaminites the right to kidnap unprotected women from the women of Shiloh when they "come out to dance the dances." On that note the epilogue illustrating the judgment of men in Israel ends.

Critical Issues in the Study of Judges

Perhaps most striking among the critical issues that have attracted scholarly attention with respect to Judges is one that is less significant than one might expect: a concern to establish the "historicity" of the events narrated in the book. In large part because of these stories' disparity and folkloristic qualities few have tried to make of them a blow-by-blow, reliable account of Israel's early days in the land, and most understand that it is at most an impressionistic portrait of that age. (And we add, the book itself contradicts Joshua on several counts: see, for

example, the incompleteness of the conquest and the persistence of Jabin of Hazor, who though once defeated according to Joshua 11, remains a plague to Israel in Judges 4–5. Likewise, archaeological evidence, where it is available, does not square well with the accounts in Judges.) As a result, other questions have concerned readers, such as the identity and nature of the religions and cultures that tempted Israel so in Canaan; the critical, and often unhappy role women are made to play in the book; the sources and traditions used in Judges; and the extent and nature of the Deuteronomic writer's contributions to the book.

What Was So Tempting?
The Cultures and Religions of Canaan

One might ask in reading Judges what was so tantalizing about the local cultures and religions that they constantly lured Israel away from worship of the God of Israel. From a historian's point of view, though, forming the question this way is misguided, for a closer look suggests that the people did not arrive in the land with a fully-developed Yahweh cult that was then infected by the local cults. Instead, reverence for Yahweh alone seems to have evolved through interaction with the local religions, taking on elements from them through a process of syncretism (the mixture of different systems of religious belief).

A look at activities around Shechem, a central site for some of the action in Judges, provides a glimpse of just how true this claim is. First, that Israel did not arrive in Canaan devoted solely to the Lord is already clear from the speech Joshua gives at the Shechem ceremony: he commands them even then to "put away the gods that your ancestors served beyond the River and in Egypt, and serve the Lord" (Josh 24:14). Ironically, he makes his speech at a site where Jacob had long before built an altar to honor a certain "El, God of Israel" (Gen 33:18-20). You will recall from Chapter 3 above that El was the progenitor of Baal in the religion of the ancient Canaanite city, Ugarit. But in the days of the short-lived King Abimelech we hear that Shechem was also the site of a temple (or temples?) of "El-berith" (God of the Covenant) and of "Baal-berith" (Baal of the Covenant). Thus the Israelite God, it seems, was not the first to dwell there, and in fact he may have derived some of his passion for covenant from the site's older divine residents. Another oft-recognized indication in Judges of how Yahweh absorbed some of his character not only from Canaanite gods, but also from the wider region, is found in Deborah's song when she speaks of Yahweh setting out from Seir (Edom; cf. Gen 36:1) like a storm from the east (5:4-5). The phrase recalls Hadad (also called Baal), a storm-god known across the ancient Near East. There

Hebrew inscription and drawing from Kuntillet 'Ajrud depicting "Yahweh of Samaria and his Asherah." (Courtesy Ze'ev Meshel)

is still more: Gideon was called Jerubbaal, a name that valorizes Baal as the name-bearer's protector, and he had to be converted (repeatedly, so it seemed) to trust in the Lord of Israel; the same judge worships an ephod at the end of his career; Jephthah reflects the practice of human sacrifice, a feature not unheard of among other ancient Near Eastern religions and one that no doubt was a part of Yahwism for a time (cf. Genesis 22; 2 Kgs 16:3; 17:17; 21:6; 23:10); and Micah worships an undefined idol at home with the help of a family priest. These and other indications make clear the irony of Judges: while telling tales that rail against syncretistic practices, they also reveal the diverse origins of the God of Israel and the variegated practices of the earliest Israelites in the land.

But who were the main gods that exercised such a powerful influence over Israel's identity and that of its own God? Judges 10:6 provides a tidy answer to this question: "the Baals and the Astartes, the gods of Aram, the gods of Sidon, the gods of Moab, the gods of the Ammonites, and the gods of the Philistines."

To the names Baal and his consort Astarte we may add another consort, Asherah, as well as Hadad, the storm-god, Dagon, the god of the Philistines, and El, the *Ur*-god known from Ugarit (see pp. 128–129 for depictions of Baal and Astarte; see above for images of the some of the other named gods). While it vastly oversimplifies the situation, the attraction of many of these gods was surely in part their role as fertility and weather divinities; as masters and mistresses of the natural world, worship of them could secure for their devotees good crops, abundant flocks, and favorable climatic conditions. Thus it is

hardly any surprise at all that they should have been attractive to people trying to make their way in a land that does not easily yield its fruits and that depends so heavily upon stable weather patterns for the moisture necessary for successful farming and ranching. The God of Israel clearly had serious competitors in ancient Canaan.

Women in Judges

The women of the book of Judges are many and varied in character: Deborah, the prophetess and judge, and Jael, the Kenite murderess of Sisera, combine forces to deliver Israel (chs. 4–5); Jephthah's daughter suffers a bitter fate for the sake of the people's rescue, but needlessly so inasmuch as the Lord fought for her father *before* he made his sacrificial vow (11:29-30); the charms of Delilah (and still other Philistine women) lure Samson into Philistine hands and to agony *and* glory for Israel (chs. 14–16); and the Levite's once strong-willed concubine (ch. 19) suffers an unspeakable fate at the hands of foe (the men of Gibeah) and friend (her husband, the Levite) alike (ch. 20).

These varied feminine portraits have drawn much interest especially in recent years as feminist readings of the Hebrew Scriptures have gained in popularity. Some scholars have speculated on the reasons for the concentration of such tales in one book. The simple answer seems to lie in the nature of Judges as a whole. It is, after all, a collection of tribal folklore and memories of the acts of their people, and as such it is only a matter of common sense that the tribes revered not just their men, but also their women, for both genders surely contributed to the life of the people.

Other readers have been more interested in contending with the implications of reading some of these stories as "authoritative" for modern religion and culture. Especially difficult from this perspective are the "texts of terror," the stories of Jephthah's daughter and the Levite's concubine. The fate of women in those stories understandably raises important questions about the capacity of such texts to be normative, and if they retain that quality, just how they should exercise it in contemporary imagination. Some resolve this difficulty by denying the texts in question any authority, but that solution is not available to all faith communities. As a result the interpretive discussion rightfully continues unabated.

Sources and Traditions Incorporated in Judges

By now it should be abundantly clear to readers that Judges was composed from a variety of legends and folklore traditions. But where did they come from? The answer is likely also clear by now: they seem to have derived from the traditions and memories of the tribes and regional groupings within Israel. This may most easily be observed in the figure, which lists each of the judges,

Judges, Tribes, and Texts

Judge	Home/tribal affiliation	text
Othniel	Judah (?)	3:7-11
Ehud	Benjamin	3:12-30
Shamgar		3:31
Deborah	Ephraim	4:1-5:31
Gideon	Manasseh	6:1-8:35
Tola	Issachar	10:1-2
Jair	Gilead	10:3-5
Jephthah	Gilead	10:6-12:7
Ibzan	Bethlehem	12:8-10
Elon	Zebulun	12:11-12
Abdon	Ephraim	12:13-15
Samson	Dan	13:1-16:31

their home or tribal affiliation, and the part of Judges that tells their story (see also the map of the judges and their locations on p. 134).

Viewed this way, the stories of the judges look very much like the sort of tales parents and elders shared with their young around the fire at night to entertain, instruct, and inspire them. For instance, Ehud's story from the tribe of Benjamin was likely all of these at once: its charming combination of curious, gory, and humorous details (3:16, 22, 24-25) entertained listeners; its portrait of Ehud as a (deceptively) left-handed sharer of salacious secrets (3:15-16, 19) instructed listeners in the virtue of concealing one's true strength and character from enemies; and the account of the glorious victory won by the Benjaminites over the powerful Moabite army (3:27-30) inspired pride among tribal members. A similar accounting with obvious variations might be given about each of the other judges included in the book. The biblical book we read today, it would seem, had its beginnings in the traditions of separate tribes of Israel.

The Deuteronomic Writer's Contribution to Judges

This last observation leads to the final critical issue we want to touch upon in the study of Judges, namely the Deuteronomic writer's editorial contribution to its present shape. There are clearly two elements to this: the collection of stories about judges and the melding of them into a single coherent *Deuteronomic* account of the people's life in the land before there were kings.

The first element can be seen in the number of judges presented, 12 in all. While they do not cover every tribe of Israel (see above) — perhaps the Deuteronomic writer

did not have available to him legends from every tribe of Israel — their number probably signifies the collector's intention to claim that this is illustrative of *all Israel's experience,* of *every tribe* in the federation that became in time the nation-state of Israel (and later Israel and Judah separately). Indeed, the merely token mention of seven judges, Othniel, Shamgar, Tola, Jair, Ibzan, Elon, and Abdon, seems to underscore this point; they appear to have been added merely to fill out the Deuteronomic writer's dozen-line dance card!

How did the Deuteronomic writer meld these into a coherent whole that served his particular interests? Apart from a few more substantial additions (e.g., 10:6-16) the approach was quite simple. First, he introduced the whole collection with a fresh account of the conquest of the land that, unlike Joshua, left Canaanites there to tempt Israel (1:1–2:5). Then he provided an initial, substantial explication of the pattern to which he bent all of the judges' stories to one degree or another (2:11–3:6). From there he only had to add the editorial touches that made the judges conform to the blueprint: with sufficient regularity to make his point, he announced in the course of relating the judges' experiences that the people were apostate, God delivered them into the hands of their enemies, they cried out to God for help, God raised up a judge to deliver them, the judge performed his or her function for the people, and they had rest while the judge ruled.

But conforming the judges to his theologized view of history did not exhaust the Deuteronomic writer's editorial effort. He also cleverly framed the unhappy stories in the double epilogue with his formulaic phrase, "In those days there was no king in Israel; all the people did

The 12 Judges and Their Victories

1. Othniel of Judah (3:9):
   victory against Cushan-rishathaim.
2. Ehud of Benjamin (3:15):
   victory against Eglon of Moab.
3. Shamgar (3:31): victory against the Philistines.
4. Deborah (Ephraim) and Barak (Naphtali) (4:4-6);
   victory over Jabin and Sisera.
5. Gideon of Manasseh (6:15):
   victory over the Midianites and Amalekites.
6. Tola of Issachar (10:1).
7. Jair of Gilead (10:3).
8. Jephthah of Gilead (11:11):
   victory over the Ammonites.
9. Ibzan of Bethlehem (12:8).
10. Elon of Zebulun (12:11).
11. Abdon of Ephraim (12:13).
12. Samson of Dan (13:2):
    victory against the Philistines.

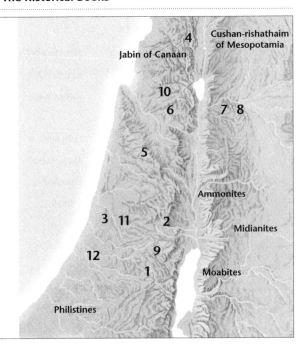

what was right in their own eyes" (17:6; 21:25), and inserted earlier between two clusters of judges an account of Israel's first miserable experience with kingship. The conclusions the writer seemed to want readers to draw from this about the judgment of ungoverned human beings *and* about kingship as an alternative are, as we see in "Theological Themes," ominous indeed.

Theological Themes in Judges

By virtue of its simple formula (2:11–3:6) and the conformity of the stories of the major judges to the formula, the book of Judges adds depth to the basic claims already established in Deuteronomy and underscored by Joshua regarding the nature of God and the people in their covenantal relationship. In it the Deuteronomic writer also begins to make his argument against kingship as an acceptable form of leadership for the people.

God and Humanity Together in Covenantal Relationship

After observing that Israel incompletely conquered the land and that the people of the land and their gods remained as a temptation to Israel (1:1–2:5), the Deuteronomic writer states in 2:11-23 the pattern that would repeat time and again throughout Judges.

The people do "what was evil in the sight of the Lord."

The people abandon the Lord for the Canaanite gods of their neighbors.

God becomes angry and delivers the people into the hands of their enemies.

When the people cry out, God raises up judges to deliver them from their enemies.

So long as the judge is alive the people continue to be protected from their foes.

When the judge dies they relapse, and the cycle starts all over again.

This passage reflects almost perfectly the portrait of Israel and God and their relationship already articulated in Deuteronomy and illustrated in Joshua: the people demonstrate their penchant for covenantal infidelity, and God demonstrates his commitment to punish their sins according to the terms of the covenant, but also his willingness to restore them and provide in response to their pleas for help new opportunities to live faithfully in the covenant.

Judges adds another dimension to this basic description of the relationship between Israel and her God. By naming a total of 12 instances in which judges were required to deliver Israel — even though all but five are present in little more than name only — the Deuteronomic writer signals that *all Israel* suffered from the weaknesses that led to its eventual downfall. It is as if the Deuteronomic writer were perhaps answering the claim on the part of some in the wake of the Exile that not everyone shared in responsibility for the catastrophe. His answer was unequivocally to the contrary: 12

times, corresponding to the number of the tribes, Israel required deliverance. All Israel bore responsibility for the Exile, the failure to keep God's covenant.

Judges also refines the Deuteronomic writer's portrait of the people of Israel. Not only are the rank-and-file members of the community prone to faithless behavior, but we also discover with the judges that even God's elected leaders behave with disregard for the law of God. The two chief witnesses to this come at the end of each of the two separate sequences of judges arranged around Israel's first experiment with kingship. Gideon, the last judge before Abimelech, first forces God to affirm repeatedly that his use of Gideon will be successful, but becomes a much more obviously problematic figure when he concludes his career as judge over Israel by making of the people's gifts an idol and worshipping it in violation of the central Deuteronomic legal stipulation. And Samson is anything but a model of human virtue, succeeding at his appointed task largely through exercising his own willfulness toward his neighbors! Thus the Deuteronomic writer emphasizes his fundamentally negative judgment on the people's capacity to do what was right in God's sight: even the sort of leaders God preferred were subject to the same weaknesses and foibles as the rest of Israel.

Beginning the Deuteronomic Polemic against Kingship

Anyone familiar with the stories from 1 and 2 Samuel and 1 and 2 Kings knows that the Deuteronomic writer had competition when it came to explaining the relationship between God and the people of Israel. Fondness for kingship and for the Davidic line was at the heart of a "David-Zion" theology that appears in the positive stories of David and especially in the dynastic promise to David in 2 Samuel 7. Instead of the Deuteronomic writer's insistence on the righteousness of all Israel relative to the cult, the David-Zion theology depends on the fidelity of the Davidic descendant who holds the throne in Zion. It was clearly an appealing theology, as we will see in the chapter on 1 and 2 Samuel, and it certainly provided a stiff challenge to the Deuteronomic perspective. Perhaps because of its popularity, the Deuteronomic writer did not simply erase it from his history. Instead he embraced the David traditions and the account of the promise, but in the end carefully hemmed them in with subtle, as well as outright, critiques of the concept of kingship. (Remember, we make no argument here that this move came at the beginning, middle, or end of the process of Deuteronomic composition; we only observe that in its final form the Deuteronomistic History seems to treat kingship at best with severe ambivalence; for more on this, see Chapter 12 above.) We encounter the first of

these critiques in Judges 9. The experience with Abimelech's test of kingship was unambiguously negative: he murdered all but one of his brothers in an unsuccessful effort to assure the security of his throne, and he ruled, albeit only briefly, with equal brutality until he experienced his own violent death. With that, Israel's first experiment with kingship came to a bitter conclusion, and the people gratefully returned to the leadership of judges. As it turns out, the Deuteronomic writer used this as a harbinger of things to come from kings. His polemic against kingship and defense of God's rule through occasional human agents was underway, and more of this we shall see in our treatment of 1 and 2 Samuel and 1 and 2 Kings.

Questions for Review and Discussion

1 Summarize the attitudes in Judges toward human leadership. Who, according to the author of Judges, should be in charge of Israel's fate and future?

2 Why do women play such a prominent role in the book of Judges? How do you judge these varying narratives? Should their authority be denied because many of them hold very outdated — indeed repulsive — views of how women can be treated? Or should these texts remain authoritative and their value somehow be sustained without taking their treatment of women as exemplary? If so, how might one do that?

3 Keeping in mind the basic Deuteronomic claim beginning in Deuteronomy that the faithlessness of Israelites in the land would result in their expulsion from it, how do you read the series of events narrated in Judges? What does this account do toward adding nuance and fullness to the Deuteronomic portrait of God?

Further Reading

Brenner, Athalya, ed. *Judges: A Feminist Companion to the Bible*. FCB 2/4. Sheffield: Sheffield Academic, 1999.
Guest, P. Deryn. "Judges." In *ECB*, 190-207.
Mayes, A. D. H. *Judges*. OTG 8. Sheffield: JSOT, 1995.
Trible, Phyllis. *Texts of Terror: Literary-Feminist Readings of Biblical Narratives*. OBT 13. Philadelphia: Fortress, 1984.

Chapter 15

Ruth

Getting Started

1 Since it is such a brief book, read Ruth straight through in one sitting, and as you do, try to construct an outline of the book as a whole.

2 What view of women dominates this small book? How are they depicted as actors and ones who are acted upon? What differences are there between Israelite and non-Israelite women in this book, especially in terms of their hopes, expectations, and initiative? And how do the women of Ruth compare to the women you encountered in the book of Judges?

3 Does God play any role in the book of Ruth, and if so what role does God play? Is there much "theology" in the book of Ruth?

Preliminary Comments

It is surely clear to readers that the book of Ruth does not "fit" the Deuteronomic mold. It lacks the rhetoric and ideas of the Deuteronomic writer, and even might be seen to contradict one of its tenets, that one should never permit a Moabite to enter the assembly of God's

people (cf. Deut 23:3). Indeed, this is not part of the Deuteronomic Collection.

So why does it come between the book of Judges and 1 and 2 Samuel, interrupting the very consistent and clear narrative thread of the Deuteronomistic History? As noted above in Chapter 2, in the Christian canons Ruth is placed here because the book begins with the words, "In the days when the judges ruled." The collectors and canonizers of the Christian Bible took that temporal marker seriously: they placed Ruth "in the days when judges ruled" by putting her story after the book of Judges. Note that by contrast the book of Ruth is among the Writings of the Jewish canon (see p. 10 for the different canonical lists).

A Walk through Ruth

The book of Ruth divides neatly into four parts corresponding to its four chapters. Some are wont to treat the four parts as acts in a play.

Ruth 1: Ruth Meets Her New Family, God, and Nation

The book of Ruth opens with no mention of its heroine. Instead, we hear that her future parents-in-law and husband and his brother feel compelled to flee the land of Israel for fear of famine. Not long after arriving in Moab, Elimelech has the bad taste to die and leave his wife a widow in a foreign land. His sons, having married Moabite women themselves, likewise exhibit poor taste in dying and leaving their wives, Orpah and Ruth, widows in their own land, and undesirable to others by their marriage to foreigners. In view of this sad situation Naomi chooses to return to where she came from, Bethlehem, apparently with little hope for anything more than the privilege of ending her existence in her hometown. As for her daughters-in-law, she instructs them to return to their mothers' homes with the hope of finding new husbands to care for them. Orpah accepts Naomi's judgment and returns, but Ruth will have nothing to do with such a proposal. Instead, she announces in 1:16-17 a poignant pledge of loyalty that effectively means Ruth gives up her identity as a Moabite, trading it for that of an Israelite, and taking with it in the bargain Naomi's God and all that comes with faith in that God.

> Do not press me to leave you, or to turn back from following you! Where you go, I will go; where you lodge, I will lodge; your people shall be my people, and your God my God. Where you die, I will die — there I will be buried. May the Lord do thus and so to me and more as well, if even death parts me from you!

It is important to note the sharp contrast in mood evinced by Naomi, the native-born Israelite. She accepts her daughter-in-law's decision in silence and, upon arriving home with Ruth in tow, ignores her companion and greets her old neighbors who call her by her name, Naomi (which means "pleasant"), with these words (1:20-21):

> Call me no longer Naomi, call me Mara [which means "bitter"], for the Almighty has dealt bitterly with me. I went away full, but the Lord has brought me back empty; why call me Naomi when the Lord has dealt harshly with me, and the Almighty has brought calamity upon me?

It is hard to miss the implication that Ruth, the foreigner from Moab, not Naomi, the home-born Israelite, is the woman of faith and trust, the one who grasps the possibilities God permits.

Ruth 2: Ruth Meets Boaz and New Possibilities Emerge

As the second chapter begins the reader is informed that Naomi "had a kinsman on her husband's side, a

---

> **Reading Guide to Ruth**
> Ruth Meets Her New Family, God, and Nation (1)
> Ruth Meets Boaz and New Possibilities Emerge (2)
> Naomi Devises a Plan to Secure Her and Ruth's Survival (3)
> Men Meet and Secure the Fate of Ruth and Naomi (4)

prominent rich man, of the family of Elimelech, whose name was Boaz" (2:1). Apparently unaware of this, but obviously savvy to the laws of the land of Israel, Ruth asks permission to glean in the fields to ensure her and her mother-in-law's sustenance (see p. 138 for the law of gleaning), and receiving permission, she fortuitously chooses the fields of Boaz.

No sooner than Ruth begins to glean does Boaz appear to survey his workers and the produce of his field. Seeing Ruth, he inquires about her and learns who she is and that her work as a gleaner is without parallel for its zeal. He then addresses Ruth directly, encouraging her to glean always in his fields and to drink from his waters to refresh herself. Her response is obeisance before Boaz and to question why he honors her, a foreigner, with such kindness. He responds that he knows of her care for her mother-in-law and the sacrifices she has made of her own identity to see to Naomi's well-being. For this, he says, she should be rewarded by the God of Israel, "under whose wings you have come for refuge" (2:12). Apparently Boaz sees himself as the agent of God's favor.

The chapter continues with Ruth and Boaz sharing the midday meal. He instructs his overseers to permit Ruth to "glean" among the standing, un-harvested sheaves of grain and even to make sure she is successful by spreading some of the harvested grain in her way as she gleans. The result for Ruth is a bounty that day not normally realized from gleaning.

When Ruth arrives home Naomi wonders who has been so kind to Ruth. Learning that it is Boaz, Naomi instructs Ruth to continue gleaning in his field, for he "is a relative of ours, one of our nearest kin" (2:20). Perhaps somewhat disingenuously Naomi adds that it would be good to continue in Boaz's field, lest Ruth be molested in a less friendly setting. Thus Ruth continues in this pattern through the barley and wheat harvests.

Ruth 3: Naomi Devises a Plan to Secure Her and Ruth's Future

Perhaps because the harvest season — and the time for gleaning — is drawing to a close, Naomi begins to consider a long-term solution to her and Ruth's security. Her proposal to Ruth is that she go to Boaz in secret at night when he would be working alongside his hired laborers to bring in the harvest in good time. The sexual

When you reap the harvest of your land, you shall not reap to the very edges of your field, or gather the gleanings of your harvest. You shall not strip your vineyard bare, or gather the fallen grapes of your vineyard; you shall leave them for the poor and the alien: I am the Lord your God. (Lev 19:9-10; cf. Lev 23:22; Deut 24:19-22) (Phoenix Data Systems, Neal and Joel Bierling)

overtone in Naomi's proposal is difficult to overlook — she instructs Ruth to go and uncover Boaz's "feet" (understanding that "feet" can be a euphemism for "genitals" in Hebrew) and lie down (3:4). Even the most cautious readers will admit that this sounds like instructions for a seduction.

Boaz's response to this approach is at first not even to notice Ruth's presence. "At midnight," though, "the man was startled, and turned over, and there, lying at his feet was a woman!" (3:8). In the ensuing exchange Ruth recalls Boaz's wish for Ruth — that the Lord God, under whose wings she sought refuge, would reward her — by asking him to spread his cloak/wing over her, for, she says, he is her next-of-kin redeemer. (That is to say, he has a claim in marriage on her.) Boaz's response is to treat Ruth as the one who deserves honor, for in this act she risks a great deal to see once more to the comfort of her mother-in-law. To this Boaz declares his intention to serve as her "redeemer" — to marry her — but only if a more immediate claimant relinquishes his right to "redeem" Ruth and receive the patrimony of land left by Elimelech. Then he bids her stay the night, but leave early enough to avoid being seen. As she departs for home Boaz gives her six measures of barley in the bargain.

Arriving home, Ruth tells her mother-in-law all that has happened, curiously adding that the six measures of barley were given for Naomi (perhaps to further enhance Boaz's image in Naomi's eyes). Hearing that there is another claimant to be dealt with, Naomi speaks with wry appreciation of the ways of men: "Wait, my daughter, until you learn how the matter turns out, *for the man will not rest,* but will settle the matter today" (3:18).

Ruth 4: Men Meet and Secure the Fate of Ruth and Naomi

The final section of the book relates the man's confirmation of Naomi's jaded view of his gender — he is indeed restless for a resolution of the matter — and the blessed consequences for Ruth and Naomi, and ultimately for all of Israel.

Boaz gathers men in the city gate to witness the consultation between himself and the other legitimate claimant to the land that Elimelech left. After informing the other man that he has first right to the land purchase and hearing the man agree to the purchase, Boaz adds that Ruth will come in the bargain. To this the unnamed man responds unfavorably, indicating that (somehow) accepting Ruth would damage his own inheritance. Thus the lot falls to Boaz, and his right to the land and Ruth is confirmed ceremonially.

As the chapter closes we learn that the marriage between Boaz and Ruth provides a son. Curiously, Ruth all but disappears from the narrative for the remaining nine verses of this brief book. Instead, the women of the village determine this to have been a birth *to Naomi,* and it is Naomi who nurses the child, and she and her neighbors name him (Obed). Finally, in the last six verses we learn how Obed is (a necessary) part of the lineage that leads in time to the birth of David, king of all Israel.

Critical Issues in the Study of Ruth

The chief critical issue in studying the book of Ruth has long been establishing its date (and concomitantly, its provenance). In addition we take up the question of the book's attitude toward women and the possibility that its author was a woman.

The Date and Provenance of the Book of Ruth

There are two basic positions on this question. Some, observing the interest in establishing the lineage of David, place the book in the Solomonic period, and suggest its aim was to add to the glory of the nascent Davidic dynasty. While this is an interesting suggestion, there are several difficulties with it. First, if the book was meant to glorify the Davidic line, it seems odd to explain part of its history as the fortuitous byproduct of women seeing to their survival. Even accounting for the positive themes of loyalty and faithfulness as additional reasons for the extension of David's line, such an approach also seems to render the increase in David's lineage as little more than chance, and chance created by the ancient world's "lesser gender," women. But second, and more to the point, there are Aramaisms (Hebrew expressions using Aramaic syntax and idiom) in the book that would probably have been linguistic possibilities only in the Exilic or Postexilic period. It is possible that these Aramaisms were introduced by later editors, and that the original story came into being in the Solomonic era, but in the end we are still compelled to deal with the text we have, not one we might imagine having once existed.

The other option for dating the book of Ruth has been the Postexilic period. On this view the book is a response to the Ezra-Nehemiah reforms that rejected all marriages between Israelite men and non-Israelite women. This easily accounts for the Aramaisms because Aramaic was the imperial language of the Persians. It is also a rather logical way of explaining the book's interest in validating foreign marriage. To this last point, though, some object, saying that the book shows no sign of being concerned over foreign marriage. Yet the answer to such a complaint is twofold. It is, in the first place, a wise strategy *not* to problematize in a narrative defense of it a practice that is already under fire; the foes have already made enough of its vices; the storyteller is compelled to reveal instead all of its virtues (such as, in this case, the restoration of land to productivity in a temple economy and the extension of the line that led to David). Second, one should not forget the unnamed claimant's attitude toward taking over Elimelech's land when he learns that he would be required to marry a foreigner; his sudden change of heart surely signals an acknowledgement that some in the author's and audience's world regarded intermarriage with considerable distaste. And third, it is interesting that for all of its glorification of Ruth, the woman of Moab, it is the true Israelite woman who, though the least trusting and loyal character in relation to the God of Israel, is said to have the child who extends the line leading to David, and who nurses him to toddlerhood. One might explain this as the author's sly concession to the naysayers, a morsel thrown their way to satisfy them.

Even more significant for dating and locating Ruth is a consideration of the circumstances that prevailed in Persian-period Judah. As we learned in Chapter 3, Persian policy was to permit subject peoples religious autonomy so long as they collected and paid reasonable tax revenues through healthy temple economies. So, inasmuch as temple economies depended on land — its produce and its importance for raising flocks and herds — such a policy engendered an intense interest on the local leaders' part in retaining exclusive possession of land in the hands of their own co-religionists. Thus we hear in Ezra 9–10 and Neh 13:23-30 that when intermarriage did raise the possibility of land passing into the hands of generations not loyal to the God of Israel, leaders reacted by mandating divorce and child abandonment on the part of the Israelite men who had "erred." Intermarriage *was* a concern in this period (see also Proverbs 1–9 and the possible context for it proposed in Chapter 23). At the same time, there were others who were clearly deeply disappointed at the failure to restore the Davidic line to direct rule over Judah in spite of Persian rule; we will hear their voices indirectly in the oracles of Haggai and Zechariah, two early Persian-period prophets to the postexilic Judean community.

These two postexilic Judean dynamics — the prohibition of exogamy, marriage with persons not a part of one's own community, and the yearning for a restored Davidic monarchy — may provide just the background one expects for the book of Ruth. On one hand, the tale makes absolutely clear the *value* of marriage to a foreign woman when it comes to maintaining a man's patrimony for service to the temple economy: who more than Ruth is loyal to the God of Israel in this story? Indeed, by her marriage to Boaz, land that apparently all the while lay unused was brought back into the temple economy by transfer of ownership to Boaz, a faithful Israelite. On the other hand, for those who worried that the line of David had come to an end forever, this story shows how faithful and loyal Israelites managed to see to its continuation under difficult conditions once before. This tale invites readers to imagine that the same could happen again. For these reasons it seems most likely that Ruth was composed in postexilic, Persian-era Judah.

Who Wrote the Book of Ruth?

The question posed in the heading above is perhaps better stated this way: Could anyone but a woman have authored this book? The answer given by most readers, including important feminist critics like Phyllis Bird, is that, as much as one might think a woman wrote it, most likely a man composed it, especially given the standard conventions regarding advanced literacy in the ancient world.

But to many readers that seems too trite a response to the possibility of a woman author. After all, female scribes were known in the ancient world, and to exclude the possibility out of hand is to ignore much about the literary artistry of the book that argues heavily in favor of a woman author. First, the characterization of Boaz, though clearly making him an honorable and deeply sympathetic character, also shows him to be less an actor in his own right than an instrument of God and the women. It is by chance and/or divine providence that Ruth chooses his field to glean, but from then on his actions are largely engineered by the plans and actions of the women. Even when the women take the risk that he would reveal Ruth's seductive behavior in ch. 3, they seem to know already that there is in fact little risk at all: this man has shown himself already to be deeply enamored with Ruth and a man of extraordinary kindness. Second, in this regard it is also particularly noteworthy that in Ruth 4 we witness the seriousness of *men* choosing to meet to decide the fate of land, when in fact they have been forced together by women who want most of all to engender a favorable judgment on *their fate!* Third, Naomi's wry remark about the behavior of men in 3:18 — that they are restless beings who cannot have the patience to let a matter lie for a time — should not be ignored, nor should one miss her corresponding commentary on her own gender in the same verse: though the men may rush, she and Ruth would *wait* for the outcome of the events. Altogether, these three observations make it difficult to imagine an ancient Israelite male composing the book of Ruth. Such self-conscious reflection on male foibles and exaltation of feminine insight and power would have required a very "liberated" male, a figure who is much less plausible in the ancient world than a female scribe and intellectual!

What if we still exclude the possibility of female authorship? What sort of man could have written such a gender-sensitive work? The likeliest answer, it seems, must be a man who had married against the mandates of Ezra and Nehemiah and their fellow leaders. A man who sought to defend his marriage to a non-Israelite — and to preserve his right to parent the children from such a union — could well have composed this little book. Such a man might even have the sort of "feminist insight" suggested by the characterization of Boaz, the woman-directed nature of the book's action, and Naomi's sardonic observation on male behavior.

Theological Themes in the Book of Ruth

Some might insist that few, if any, theological themes appear in the book of Ruth. After all, God is hardly present in the story, for the most part being mentioned only in passing. But a closer look reveals a surprising richness in the book's theological insight. We take up a few of the theological themes the book invokes in its recipients.

Loyalty, Family, and God

The interplay among these three in the book of Ruth — loyalty, God, and family — is unmistakably present. The disloyalty of Elimelech to God is little remarked upon, but present nonetheless. Assuming for a moment that this author and audience knew the Deuteronomic worldview — as most certainly would have been the case if the book is dated to the Postexilic period — the idea that Elimelech should flee the Promised Land for a foreign place to avoid a famine is tantamount to heresy. Such action signals disloyalty to the God of Israel who promised the land and prosperity to those who kept the law and trusted in God. Fleeing to Moab, a nation whose citizens are banned from entry into the congregation of the Lord according to Deut 23:3, could hardly be taken as an act of loyalty. Under such Deuteronomic conditions Elimelech's loyalty to his family is also placed in serious question, as is his permission to his sons to marry women of Moab; by taking his family with him into exile and allowing these marriages he implicates his family in his own disloyalty and allows his sons to engage in exogamy, an act prohibited by Deut 7:2-3!

By contrast we have Ruth. Her loyalty to her family-by-marriage, even in the absence of her husband, is astoundingly portrayed in her confession (1:16-17). It is important to note that Ruth has, in fact, *nothing to gain* in making this confession of fealty to Naomi. And that this familial loyalty produced in turn new national and religious loyalties — the two went inextricably together in the ancient world — only further marks Ruth off from her father-in-law, and in large degree from her mother-in-law as well. For while Ruth continues to seek the best for herself and her mother-in-law (even to the extent of unflinchingly taking enormous personal risks in seducing Boaz at her mother-in-law's suggestion), Naomi only slowly awakens to the possibilities for survival that Ruth eagerly embraces; prior to that Naomi plays the role of the fatalistic, faithless soul. And when she does finally see the opportunities, she assigns all the risks to Ruth, never taking any herself.

A further contrasting figure is Boaz. His loyalty is to a woman with whom he is enamored, and to the rules by which one played fairly in his world. He is the model of kindness and uprightness, and to his credit he steps up to the task when Ruth asks him to fulfill his own wish for her that the God of Israel protect her (2:12) by marrying her (3:9). His circumspection in how he treats Ruth and the possibility of purchasing Elimelech's land and marrying Ruth (3:10–4:12) also proves his loyalty to standards of good conduct.

But most of all we see in Ruth an exemplary instance of loyalty to God and family. Her care for Naomi has been observed time and again, and her complete transformation from a woman of Moab worshipping the gods of Moab to a heroine of Israel worshipping the God of Israel is well known. Her confession of faith in 1:16-17, made with *nothing to gain for herself,* is testimony enough to the way she, the foreign woman, evinces best of all the quality of loyalty. A convert to the covenant, she is unmatched in her fidelity to it.

The Land of Israel

The theme of the Promised Land pervades this book. In the first verse we hear that Elimelech is content to abandon "the land" for greener pastures in Moab. Assuming some awareness on the part of our author and audience of the tradition of God's land promise, it is hard to miss the fact that Elimelech demonstrates bad faith in this action. Throughout the Pentateuchal traditions we saw the strength of the promise to Israel: they would inherit a land that would serve them well, and they could trust God to see to that, especially if they remained faithful to God. Elimelech shows nothing but disdain for that promise.

By contrast, Ruth seems to understand from her first moment in her adopted land that its produce was meant by God to sustain those who trust in him. Thus she boldly gleans from the land according to the laws God gave for its use. Even though the pervasive term for land in the middle of the book is "field," the fact that Ruth shows a superior appreciation of the land promise relative to her Israelite family members ensures that recipients continue to have that promise in sight.

At the end of the book the theme returns in full force when the question of the disposition of Elimelech's land comes up for decision between Boaz and the other, unnamed claimant to the field and Ruth's hand in marriage. And here again the theme of the land promise is echoed. For as we read to the conclusion of the book we see that Ruth's and Naomi's actions not only attend to their future well-being, but also to the restoration of some of the Promised Land to productivity for the people of God.

The Line of David

The theme of God's promise to provide human leadership through the line of David is also raised by this book, and not only in the closing chapter where we learn that Ruth was essential to extending the family line that produced David and his descendants. The theme is struck already in the first verse when we learn that Elimelech and his kin are from Bethlehem, the place of David's family (1 Sam 16:1-5). So from the beginning of the book this author signals one further theological theme, that of the promise to David and Israel of rule through the line of David.

Women in the Fulfillment of God's Plan

This theme ties all the rest together. Obviously, Ruth is the cause of restoring a part of the Promised Land to service of God's people; without her the line of David would not have been extended; and she is the epitome of loyalty to God and family. But on closer examination we see that the book goes even further in making this claim regarding the centrality of women to fulfilling God's plans.

In the speech of the neighbors blessing Boaz's marriage to Ruth (4:11-12), they pray that Ruth be to him as Rachel and Leah were to Jacob and as Tamar was to Judah! They make no mention of Jacob/Israel in founding the nation: it is Rachel and Leah who have pride of place in their address. And they cite Tamar — the strong-willed seducer of her stingy father-in-law, Judah, and a key player in sustaining the line of David — as a model for Ruth. It is as if the author wants to signal one last time for the audience the fact that *women* were as important as men, if not more so, in cooperating with God to bring Israel its glory. They were the ones who knew how to create the conditions for the nation to be born and the line of David to continue. Without them neither reality would have come to pass.

Questions for Review and Discussion

1   What are the two views of the date of the book of Ruth, and what are the arguments for each? Which do you find more persuasive, and why?

2   What are the arguments for and against a woman as author of Ruth? Which view do you find most persuasive, and why?

3   The role of women in the life of Israel and in establishing its glory seems plain enough in Ruth. How does this story compare with the women of the Pentateuch? With Esther from the book of Esther? With Deborah and Jael of the book of Judges? What does the existence of these various "women's stories" in the Hebrew Bible suggest about the attitudes toward women in ancient Israel?

Further Reading

Brenner, Athalya, ed. *Ruth and Esther: A Feminist Companion to the Bible*. FCB 2/3. Sheffield: Sheffield Academic, 1999.
Fewell, Dana Nolan, and David Miller Gunn. *Compromising Redemption: Relating Characters in the Book of Ruth*. Louisville: Westminster John Knox, 1990.
Larkin, Katrina J. A. *Ruth and Esther*. OTG. Sheffield: Sheffield Academic, 1996.
West, Gerald. "Ruth." In *ECB*, 208-12.

Chapter 16

1 and 2 Samuel

Getting Started

1 Read 1 Samuel 1–2 in a study Bible with good text-critical notes at the bottom of the page. Get acquainted with the sigla (e.g., "Q," "MT," etc.) by consulting the appropriate introductory section in your Bible. What do you notice about the translation of 1 Samuel 1–2 that you have in your Bible? (Recall our earlier survey of text criticism in Chapter 4.) Does it represent only one text of the Old Testament, or are multiple witnesses evident in your translation? What does your answer to this question suggest about the *nature* of your translation as a "text" of 1 Samuel in its own right?

2 Read 2 Samuel 6–7 and compare the depictions of David in both chapters. How would you characterize David's regard for his wife and his own honor in ch. 6? By comparison, how would you describe God's regard for David in ch. 7?

3 Read 2 Samuel 11–12 and add the information from these chapters to your portrait of David. How does his image appear to a fresh, relatively unbiased reader in light of this further information?

Preliminary Comments

The two books bearing Samuel's name are not only curiously named — Samuel features in them hardly at all — but their division into two books also seems illogical, at least from a content perspective. In fact, they were likely one book in their original Hebrew form (together they occupy a single scroll from Cave 4 at Qumran), and only in Greek (and later Latin) manuscripts were they divided into two books for convenience' sake. It is best to remember as well that these were part of the much larger whole that we are surveying in these chapters, the Deuteronomistic History; thus even the separation of a single "book of Samuel" from the account that begins in Joshua and ends in 2 Kings 25 is an artifice not fully intended by an implied (and almost certainly "original") author!

That being said, we set out to treat 1 and 2 Samuel in a separate, single chapter. Although it makes for a lengthy chapter, we think it best to treat the Samuel books as a whole, for together they narrate a single critical passage in the Deuteronomic writer's history: the transition to kingship and the emblematic reigns of its first two representatives, Saul and David. The account of kingship's rise and initial manifestations in Saul and David, though seemingly fraught with contradictions, proves to work as a whole to deliver the Deuteronomic judgment on the institution that is then reflected time and again in the stories of subsequent kings of Israel and Judah.

A Walk through 1 and 2 Samuel

Even a casual overview of 1 and 2 Samuel proves its coherence as a whole, even if it is also apparent that, like Joshua and Judges before, it is a thoroughly composite work. Together, though, the many pieces assembled by the Deuteronomic collector and editor work to address some themes central to the Deuteronomic imagination, the most important of which is the nature of human kingship. As we shall see, the judgment on this institution is not altogether favorable, even — or perhaps especially — in the case of Israel's great hero, David.

1 Samuel 1–7: The Birth and Early Career of Samuel and the Ark Narrative

1 Samuel 1 begins appropriately enough with the story of Samuel's birth. His father, Elkanah, has a barren wife, Hannah. As a consequence Elkanah takes a rival wife, Peninnah (polygamy was common in ancient Israel and the practice probably endured into the early rabbinic period). In near despair over her situation, Hannah visits the sanctuary at Shiloh during her family's annual pilgrimage there to sacrifice and promises God the service of her son if only God would give her a child. (Shiloh was an important cult center before the monarchy, and perhaps remained so even after Josiah's centralization of the cult; see Josh 18:1; Judg 21:12; Jer 7:12; Ps 78:60). Granted her prayer, Hannah bears Samuel, whom she eventually delivers to Eli, the priest of the sanctuary. The episode closes with Hannah's song on the occasion of handing Samuel over to Eli (1 Sam 2:1-11). The song is an individual hymn of thanksgiving adapted for use here (and adapted again later for use in Mary's "Magnificat" in Luke 1:46-55). Its theme is God's exaltation of the lowly and reduction of the mighty, a premise suited not only to Hannah, but also ultimately to the people of Israel as the Deuteronomic writer's story continues.

1 Samuel 2:12-36, an account of the priestly misconduct of Eli's sons Hophni and Phinehas, provides the necessary backdrop both for the continuation of Samuel's story with his prophetic call and the story of the ark's loss

> ### Reading Guide to 1 and 2 Samuel
> The Birth and Early Career of Samuel and the Ark Narrative (1 Samuel 1–7)
> The Rise of Kingship (1 Samuel 8–12)
> Saul's Early Career as Proof of Kingship's Dangers (1 Samuel 13–15)
> David's Rise and Saul's Demise (1 Samuel 16–31)
> David Consolidates His Kingdom (2 Samuel 1–8)
> The "Succession Narrative" (2 Samuel 9–20)
> A "David Appendix" (2 Samuel 21–24)

into Philistine hands in 1 Samuel 4. First, we hear that after some years of service at Shiloh, Samuel has an auditory visit from God — much like the one that ordained Jeremiah (Jeremiah 1) — who calls him and informs him that Eli's house will fall for the sins of Eli's sons (1 Sam 3:1-4:1a). Then the story of the ark follows (4:1b-7:2). When Israel sees that the Philistines are a threat, they decide to take the ark of the covenant with Hophni and Phinehas accompanying it into battle against the enemy to ensure their success. But unexpectedly — or at least unexpected to the Israelites, though the reader can hardly be surprised! — the brothers are killed and the ark is captured by the Philistines, for Israel's faithlessness has offended God. But as soon as the Philistines take home the "god" of the enemy, the traditional prize of war in the ancient Near East, their god Dagon is to be found face down before the ark of the covenant every morning and they experience plagues of "tumors" (likely hemorrhoids) and, according to the Greek translation of 6:4, plagues of mice as well! After this happens in village after village, the Philistines return the ark to the Israelites by placing it and a guilt offering of five golden hemorrhoids and five golden mice on a cart pulled by two milch cows. The cows return the ark to Beth-shemesh turning "neither right nor left" as they go (as Israel was instructed to do in keeping the law!). For their trouble on behalf of Israel the cows are slaughtered and sacrificed as a whole burnt offering; the ark is transferred to Kiriath-jearim.

The remaining episode before the story of kingship's rise, an account of Samuel acting as a judge (7:3-17), contrasts sharply with the failed war effort in ch. 6 and with the battle Saul wages against Nahash in ch. 11. In an episode reminiscent of the defeat of Jericho, Israel succeeds not because of military might or the leadership of a king, but because it expresses complete fidelity to God through ritual means. We shall see below in considering the way the Deuteronomic writer has marshaled his resources in the Samuel books that this likely was meant to underscore the author's preferred form of leadership: judges as God's occasional human instruments and in complete dependence on God.

Relief showing a wheeled structure, possibly the ark of the covenant, from the Capernaum synagogue (early 4th century c.e.). (Erich Lessing/ArtResource, NY)

that he will experience that day several signs indicating his election as king, the last of which will entail spirit possession and ecstatic prophecy. At the fulfillment of the last sign Saul realizes the truth of Samuel's word and he returns home with the private knowledge of his future.

A second, Deuteronomic account of Saul's selection follows in 10:17-27a. Samuel's warning speech to the people at Mizpah echoes classic Deuteronomic rhetoric, and his inscription of the rules of kingship in a book recalls the law of the king in Deut 17:14-20. This is followed by the proof of Saul's legitimacy provided by his zeal to take on and defeat Nahash, the eye-gouging king of Ammon who has it in mind to make all the people of Jabesh-gilead monophthalmic (1 Sam 10:27b–11:15). (Note how Saul summons the tribes to join him in the defense of Jabesh-gilead in virtually the same way the Levite summoned help in Judg 19:29-30.)

The introduction of kingship in Israel concludes with Samuel's farewell address, one of the characteristic speeches of the Deuteronomistic History (ch. 12). Samuel refrains from scolding the people directly for their desire for a king, but in an oblique reprimand he does remind them of God's faithfulness to them. Then he places kingship and the people's relationship to the institution squarely within the framework of the Deuteronomic covenant: if the king and the people live together in harness to God's law, all will go well for them; but ominously Samuel adds, "if you . . . do wickedly, you shall be swept away, both you and your king" (12:25). On that note, the Deuteronomic writer closes his introduction of kingship in Israel.

1 Samuel 8–12: The Rise of Kingship

These five chapters reflect a complex mix of traditional material inherited by the Deuteronomic writer and the Deuteronomic writer's own compositions that together provide a conflicted assessment of the rise of kingship in Israel. As we see below in "Critical Issues" and "Theological Themes," the weight of the evidence indicates the Deuteronomic writer's negative judgment on the new institution, but for now we merely survey the text's contents.

No sooner than Samuel finishes demonstrating the abiding capacity of judges to save and protect Israel from her enemies (7:3-17) do the people make their appeal to him for kings, using his age and his sons' ineffectualness as an excuse for the request: "You are old and your sons do not follow in your ways; appoint for us, then, a king to govern us, like other nations" (8:5). Samuel's response is to complain to God that they are rejecting him, and God's response to Samuel is that they are rejecting God. Not only that, according to Samuel's ensuing speech kings would make the people forget their God and they would be insatiable in their desire for the people's resources, gobbling up their children, livestock, crops, and land to feed the royal apparatus. But the warning falls on deaf ears, and the people plead even more intensely for a king.

What follows, then, is the story of Saul's selection, or better the double account of that event. The first account is fablelike (9:1–10:16). Saul and one of his father's servants set out to find lost donkeys and hit upon the idea of visiting a (seemingly obscure!) seer named Samuel for advice. Meanwhile, forewarned of the visit by God, Samuel knows he is to meet that day the future king of Israel. Upon meeting Saul, Samuel instructs Saul

1 Samuel 13–15: Saul's Early Career as Proof of Kingship's Dangers

As soon as he begins to reign, Saul proves the difficulties of managing the royal office under God's law, and in the bargain loses all hope of establishing a dynasty.

1 Samuel 13 relates the beginning of Saul's war against the dreaded Philistines, who are the ostensible reason for the people's eagerness to have a king. We read that when he has prepared to engage the Philistines in a critical battle, Saul only needs the pre-engagement sacrifice to be offered by Samuel, the duly appointed sacerdotal functionary. But because Samuel is late and Saul is concerned that his troops will lose their edge, or even desert, he performs the sacrifice in Samuel's place. Just then Samuel arrives and flies immediately into a rage, condemning Saul for worrying more about human skill and numbers (cf. Gideon in Judges 7) than ritual done rightly for God (cf. Israel against Jericho in Joshua 6; and Samuel against the Philistines in 7:3-17). For his apostasy, says Samuel, Saul will not enjoy dynastic succession.

As if to underscore how dim-witted kings can be about religious matters (and military strategy, as well) 1 Samuel 14 relates that just as the troops of Israel have the Philistines decisively on the run, Saul perplexingly declares a fast that soldiers must keep on pain of death. Of course, this weakens them so much that they lose their strength to finish off the enemy. And when his own son, unaware of his father's declaration, eats during the fast, Saul is determined to follow through with the sentence he has decreed, death. Only the good sense and protective custody of the soldiers save Jonathan from his father's senseless declarations.

1 Samuel 15 narrates the completion of Saul's fall from grace, providing a second reason for the loss of dynastic succession. He is commanded to destroy all the Amalekites, to carry out the ban against them. He does defeat them, but spares some of the best livestock and King Agag of the Amalekites, much as a wise ancient Near Eastern monarch might do to husband scarce and valuable resources. But such behavior is nonetheless a violation of God's decree that the people of the land should be utterly eliminated, and so after killing Agag himself, Samuel again declares Saul without hope. And with that Saul's long, slow descent toward his eventual ignominious death begins.

1 Samuel 16–31: David's Rise and Saul's Demise

If the stories of Saul's early failures as king seem to answer the question of kingship's value in the negative, the next large portion of text clouds the issue once more; for while Saul continues his long decline, David steps forward as a new hope for the office. Notably, a variety of traditions about David are woven together throughout this long portion of text, providing abundant evidence that David's positive reputation in Israelite memory generated its full share of legends and traditions.

1 Samuel 16 provides two accounts of the discovery of David as a royal or extraordinarily attractive figure. The first half of the chapter tells the story of Samuel divining David's destiny to rule from among Jesse's sons and his anointing him; the second half relates how an evil spirit descends on Saul and how, requiring a musician to soothe his spirit, Saul elects David for the task on the advice of one of his servants who describes him as a talented musician and great warrior. But then ch. 17 introduces David again in the story of David and Goliath, an account that is clearly composite in the Hebrew text (e.g., David is introduced to Saul in 17:32-38, yet Saul seems not to know him in 17:55-58; for more on this, see the discussion of the text of the Samuel books in "Critical Issues" below). In a tale filled with folkloric features (e.g., David sheds the gift of Saul's armor because he is too small to bear it), David alone is willing to stand against the Philistine giant. Reflecting the tradition's glorification of David, he declares in 17:45-47 that while Goliath comes with weapons of war, David trusts in the Lord God of Israel. And of course, his trust is well founded; like Israel against Jericho, Gideon against the Midianites, and Samuel against the Philistines, fighting for the Lord's cause ensures success.

The result of David's success is twofold: he wins the loyalty of the people of Israel and of Saul's son Jonathan (18:1-8) but he also provokes Saul's jealousy and earns his enmity (18:9). As a result, while Israel glorifies David and Jonathan transfers to him the mantle of succession to Saul's throne, Saul seeks to assassinate him and, failing that, assure his demise in battle. But Saul has no success, with the further consequence that Jonathan and Michal, Saul's daughter, become even stauncher allies of David against their father (18:10–19:24). Indeed, ch. 20 narrates Jonathan's covenant with David to secure David's safety from Saul under all circumstances. And so it is that on Jonathan's advice David flees Saul's ambit. 1 Samuel 21–27 then narrates how in his exile David comes under the care of the priests of Nob (whom Saul murders for their trouble); deceives the Philistines at first by playing the madman in their midst and then by pretending to ally himself with them and lead his band of brigands against Israel (when in fact he is raiding Israel's other enemies in the region); hides out in Adullam and Keitah and meets Abiathar, who gives him oracular advice; and twice has the chance to kill his nemesis Saul but resists out of honor for the royal office. All the while Saul's fortunes fall, so that finally in ch. 28, as he and the Philistine army prepare to meet each other in a decisive battle, he seeks advice — against his own rules — from a witch at Endor. Her vision of the future foretells Saul's death that day in battle against the Philistines (ch. 31). Meanwhile, David is spared the deadly battle against Saul because the Philistine lords distrust him. Given the

THE EXTENT OF DAVID'S KINGDOM ACCORDING TO THE SAMUEL BOOKS

commission to Saul in 1 Samuel 15 to carry out the ban against Amalek, it is somewhat ironic that David spends that time instead sacking the Amalekites in vengeance for their attack on his people and his family at Ziklag (chs. 29–30).

2 Samuel 1–8:
David Consolidates His Kingdom

This section takes up the story of how David takes control of Saul's former holdings. It begins in 2 Samuel 1 with David learning of the deaths of Saul and Jonathan and the dirge he sings in their honor. 2 Samuel 2–5 then narrates the tensions and violence that break out between Saul's and David's houses and David's eventual subjection of all to his will. Chapter 5 concludes with David's defeat of the pesky Philistines. This tidying up of old scores sets the stage for two episodes that provide contrasting perspectives on David.

The first episode, 2 Samuel 6, is unflattering to David, even if it begins somewhat favorably. It reports that David takes advantage of the respite from battle to bring the ark of the covenant to his new home in Jerusalem. But as he and his men transport the ark on the first leg of their journey, one of those tending it, Uzzah, reaches out to steady the ark and upon touching it is struck dead. David's response is fear, and the declamation, "How can the ark of the Lord come into my care?" Thus he leaves it to languish halfway to Jerusalem. But when David sees that the presence of the ark prospers those who have charge of it, he overcomes his fear and brings it the

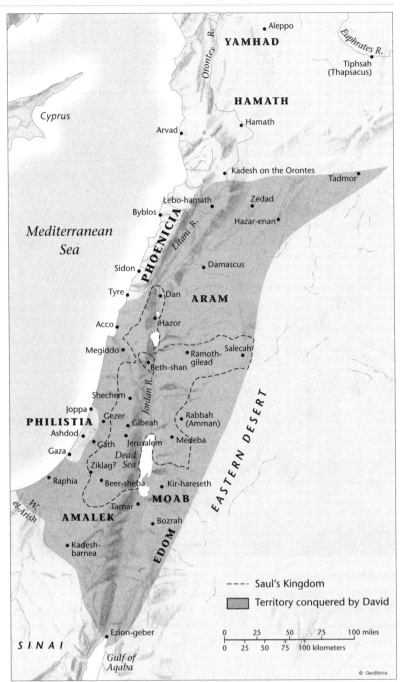

rest of the way to Jerusalem, dancing before it all but naked as it approaches the city. Seeing this, David's wife Michal, the daughter of Saul, scolds David for acting immodestly before the people and especially the women in the crowd. David's response is anything but kind: returning scold for scold, he promises to make himself even more contemptible in Michal's eyes and his own, effectively promising to provide her no offspring, thus ending the line of Saul.

2 Samuel 7 offers a sharp contrast to the unflattering portrait of David provided in ch. 6 (as well as a key passage not only for what can be called the "David-Zion" theology, but also for Jewish and Christian imagination regarding messianic figures; see below). When David recognizes that although he has his own palace, the presence of God in the ark is housed in nothing more than a tent, he announces his plan to build a temple (Hebrew *bayit*, "house") for God. God rejects the offer in Nathan's oracle that promises instead an eternal

Rembrandt Harmenszoon van Rijn, *Biblical Scene with Two Figures* (1642); variously interpreted as David's farewell from Jonathan and the reconciliation of David and Absalom. (Hermitage, St. Petersburg; Scala/ArtResource, NY)

to the throne after David rather than any of David's older sons. While that may have been the narrative's aim at least in part, it hardly accounts for it entirely. In fact, it also provides a dismal account of David's behavior as a king, parent, and subject of the God of Israel.

In a prelude 2 Samuel 9–10 relates how David attends (kindly) to Saul's surviving grandson, Mephibosheth, and then consolidates some remaining territories. As ch. 10 closes we read that David has subdued the majority of his enemies, though the Ammonites remain a threat. Thus the episode with Bathsheba in chs. 11–12 begins with the ominous notice, "In the spring of the year, the time when kings go out to battle, David sent Joab with his officers and all Israel with him; they ravaged the Ammonites, and besieged Rabbah, but David remained at Jerusalem." And things only worsen, and quickly, for in the very next verse we hear that David stays home to spy on an attractive neighbor, Bathsheba, and take her as his mistress and impregnate her. To cover his sin he arranges for her husband Uriah, a Hittite serving in his army, to be killed in battle so that David could marry the grieving widow. But God makes Nathan wise to all of this and sends him to confront David with a tale of another man's injustice; when David expresses outrage at the tale, Nathan identifies him as the offender and condemns the child from the illicit union to die. David's response is to mourn prematurely, hoping to change God's mind, and when that fails David gives up his fast precisely when one would have expected it to begin. As the chapter closes we hear that David and Bathsheba conceive another child, Solomon, and that David finally goes to battle and completes the conquest of the Ammonites.

The next unit of text, chs. 13–14, relates the difficul-

dynasty (Hebrew *bayit*, "house") for David. Indeed, even if David's descendants sin against the Lord and are punished, God will still provide unilaterally for the continuation of the line. 2 Samuel 8 then completes this portion of the story describing how David secures the larger borders of his territory by subduing the eastern regions and then sees to an appropriate administrative structure for the kingdom.

2 Samuel 9–20: The "Succession Narrative"
Scholars have long conceived of this section of text as a narrative explanation for the accession of Solomon

ties among David's children that sow the seeds for Absalom's full rebellion against his father. First, Amnon, getting advice from a "wise" friend, acts on his desire for his sister Tamar and rapes her. Then, seeing that David is not inclined to discipline Amnon, Absalom sees to the murder of Amnon. Absalom then flees to Geshur, apparently in part because his murderous behavior could be construed as a move toward usurping his father's rule, and remains there for three years during which time David grows wistful for Absalom. Thus Joab, David's commander, uses the tale-telling of a (wise!) woman from Tekoa to gain David's acquiescence to Absalom's return to the kingdom.

The return of Absalom is the first in a cascade of events that leads to David's ignominious exodus from Jerusalem and eventual restoration to power (chs. 15–20). After building support for his cause, Absalom enters into open rebellion against his father and seeks even to rout his army and kill him. But with the aid of a spy in Absalom's camp, David is able to foil his son's plans. But even then David acts against all the rules of ancient Near Eastern kingship and commands that the usurper not be slain. Thus when David learns that Absalom is dead — Joab kills him — David mourns so publicly as to prompt Joab to rebuke him and insist that he reassure the people of his satisfaction at defeating the foe. Indeed, even that is not enough, for David has at the end of this section to put down another revolt led by the Benjaminite Sheba.

2 Samuel 21–24: A "David Appendix"

2 Samuel 21–24 functions as a sort of appendix of "other David traditions" inserted before the conclusion of the so-called Succession Narrative in 1 Kings 1–2. It amounts to a concatenation of traditions that relate the execution of Saul's heirs, stories of the Philistine wars, a psalm of praise, the last words of David (given prematurely), a list of David's heroes, and David's census that results in his acquisition of Araunah's threshing floor as a place to make sacrifice to God and legendarily the site of Solomon's temple.

Critical Issues in the Study of 1 and 2 Samuel

We treat here three critical issues in the study of 1 and 2 Samuel: the books' text-critical status; the Deuteronomic writer's use of sources; and the evidence of the books for the rise of kingship in ancient Israel.

The Textual Witnesses to 1 and 2 Samuel

Even the earliest critical analyses of 1 and 2 Samuel recognized the significant differences between the Masoretic and Septuagint texts of the two books. The variants are great in number and vary widely in scope, from differences over single, small phrases to whole sections of text. The consequence, in any case, is that the two textual traditions function as virtually distinct witnesses to the Samuel books. For instance, at one end of the spectrum we encounter in the story of Samuel's birth (1 Samuel 1–2) numerous small differences, few of which alone are significant, but that together make the Masoretic Text and Septuagint accounts fundamentally different stories. In the Septuagint Hannah is unflinchingly obedient to the vow she makes to relinquish Samuel to service at Shiloh, but Hannah may be read in the Masoretic Text account as dragging her feet and seeking ways to escape her vow (see p. 36 for the NRSV of 1 Sam 1:21-25 with text-critical notes and explanations). At the other end of the spectrum, the story of David and Goliath is different in the two textual traditions in much more immediately obvious ways: the Septuagint lacks the Masoretic Text's 17:12-31, 50, 55-58; 18:1-5, and as a consequence reads somewhat more smoothly (the additions in the Masoretic Text provide contradictory elements in the narrative).

Before discovery among the Dead Sea Scrolls of Hebrew manuscripts of Samuel, text critics argued vigorously for the primacy of the Septuagint or Masoretic Text witness. Some held that, though a translation of the Hebrew, the Septuagint was generally more coherent within itself than the Masoretic Text and deserved priority in reconstructing an "original" Samuel. Others held to the view that the Masoretic Text, a *Hebrew* text preserved with care by the Masoretes for centuries, should be most highly honored even if its readings are at times more difficult. Indeed, such critics note that the text-critical principle of preferring the *lectio difficilior,* the more difficult reading, demands prizing the Masoretic Text above the Septuagint in many instances. But the discovery of the Dead Sea Scrolls produced a very early *Hebrew* manuscript that compares more favorably with the Septuagint than the Masoretic Text, as well as other manuscripts that go their own direction. Thus it appears increasingly likely that the differing textual witnesses to Samuel are not evidence of a single textual tradition that changed over time thanks to scribal errors and intentional adjustments, but of alternate "editions" of the books. Clearly this is an important lesson for textual criticism of the Hebrew Scriptures.

The Deuteronomic Writer's Use of Sources in 1 and 2 Samuel

The Samuel books, in part by sheer size and complexity, offer much more obvious evidence of the Deutero-

Examples of Sources in 1 and 2 Samuel

According to 1 Samuel 1 Hannah turns Samuel over to Eli for service in the sanctuary at Shiloh: "For this child I prayed . . . therefore I have lent him to the Lord; as long as he lives, he is given (Hebrew *shaul*) to the Lord" (1 Sam 1:27-28). Her declaration explains Samuel's name, but as the quotation makes clear, it is properly an explanation of Saul's name. Thus it appears that the Deuteronomic writer assigned the standard miraculous birth story provided for royal figures to Samuel instead (perhaps as part of a larger effort to discredit kingship in general; see below in "Theological Themes").

The conclusion to the same episode, Hannah's song on turning Samuel over to Eli (1 Sam 2:1-10), is widely understood to be a freestanding psalm of individual thanksgiving employed for this occasion as a poetic expression of the Deuteronomic writer's insistence that God is ultimately in control of history, raising up the lowly and bringing down the lofty.

1 Samuel 4–6 and 2 Samuel 6 are generally thought to be part of an originally independent "ark narrative." The first installment, 1 Samuel 4–6, works to demonstrate at a critical point in the story the sovereignty of the God of Israel not only over other gods and peoples (Dagon and the Philistines), but also over the people of Israel when they think they can manipulate God for their own uses, or turn, as they do in the following section (1 Samuel 8–12), to kings for the things only God provides. It is, after all, God who chooses to go into exile among the Philistines, who gives Israel victory and assigns her to defeat.

2 Samuel 6, the second installment of the ark narrative, is used to foreshadow the disreputable behavior of David not only toward others (Michal), but God as well (through his open manipulation of God in the self-interested, staged transfer of the ark to Jerusalem).

1 Samuel 7:3-17, a tradition about Samuel as a judge, is introduced after the first installment of the ark narrative to reveal the proper way to wage war against Israel's enemies. Perhaps it is also placed before the story of kingship's rise in Israel to demonstrate what appears to be the Deuteronomic writer's preferences for judges.

The careful integration of stories related to the election of Saul as Israel's first king and his function in that office (1 Sam 9:1–10:16; 10:27b–11:15; 13-15) with material mostly composed by the Deuteronomic writer functions to convey the author-redactor's plain dislike for kingship. The episode begins in 1 Samuel 8 with a Deuteronomic composition: the request to Samuel for a king, God's judgment that the people are rejecting him, and Samuel's warning about the practical dangers of kingship. Then, following the legend of God's election of Saul for the office (9:1–10:16) and before Saul's military validation of his claim to the office (10:27b–11:15), the Deuteronomic writer inserted his own less sanguine account of Saul's appointment (10:17-27a). Next, following the battle against the Ammonites and the people's acclamation of Saul as king (10:27b–11:15), Samuel delivers his Deuteronomic valedictory speech that warns again of the theological and practical dangers of kingship and subjects kingship to the law of God (12). And to make certain that readers do not miss the point of Samuel's warning, chs. 13–15 prove that the monarchy worked just as he had predicted.

Finally we observe (only in the broadest sense) how positive traditions about David are balanced by stories that undercut his credibility, again probably so as to weaken the argument that kingship was good for Israel. After all, how better to undermine the office than tarnish the reputation of its greatest holder in Israelite memory? Thus the Deuteronomic writer's record of David in 1 Samuel begins extraordinarily well: the author weaves into the story of Saul's gradual demise the tales of David's military might and musical genius as a young man, his honor for his elders even though they seek to vex him, and his wiliness as a leader of soldiers and as a budding politician (1 Samuel 16–31). Then 2 Samuel 1–8 extends the positive record regarding David, but places just before the high point of the dynastic promise (2 Samuel 7) a foreboding tale of David's willfully arrogant, self-interested, and theologically tone-deaf behavior (2 Samuel 6). And then with the Succession Narrative the Deuteronomic writer delivers a body blow to David's reputation: the tales included there prove him to be a shirker of his royal duty, an adulterer, a disdainer of God's laws, an overly indulgent parent, and an incompetent king. As we shall see in "Theological Themes" below, when at last David relinquishes his grip on power it is as a man without any manly characteristics let alone royal qualities.

nomic writer's erudite use of sources than do Joshua and Judges. What we see in 1 and 2 Samuel over and over again is a clever blending and bending of existing sources to the Deuteronomic writer's aims. Some examples of this are found on p. 150. We elaborate more fully on these in "Theological Themes" in this chapter and the next.

The Rise of Kingship in Israel: Ancient Near Eastern Royal Ideology and the David-Zion Ideal

As is clear from their request to have monarchs "like all the other nations" (Deut 17:14; 1 Sam 8:5, 20), the people of Israel did not draw their notion of kingship as a desirable form of leadership from thin air. Indeed, the Deuteronomic writer had to contend with this form of government in spite of his clear distaste for it precisely because it was rooted in a powerful ideology that spanned the ancient Near Eastern world and that had been adapted by Israel to form the basis of the David-Zion ideology.

The idea of kingship in Mesopotamia was thought literally to have fallen from the heavens as an earthly manifestation of the gods and their sphere of influence. In Egypt, kings were thought to be incarnations of the god Horus, and after death the pharaohs were linked to Osiris, father of Horus and lord of the afterlife. Lesser nation states between the two great imperial centers readily imitated this pattern. So when Israel developed into a petty kingdom in the midst of these monarchies it is no surprise that her people eventually wanted to be governed by kings as well, nor should it be hard to imagine that when they looked to kings they also sought to link their monarch to Israel's God. All the evidence suggests that early Israel negotiated this difficulty by stopping short of making the king a manifestation of God, providing him instead with an especially close relationship with the God of Israel. This special relationship was embodied in the dynastic promise to David in 2 Samuel 7 (see also 2 Samuel 23; Psalms 2; 110) that unilaterally assured God's blessing to David and his descendants as faithful kings over Israel. Through that blessing all Israel could experience prosperity and success. Because the blessing entails a faithful Davidide holding the throne in Zion, we may call this constellation of ideas the "David-Zion theology."

Of course, this dynastic promise, as popular as it surely was among the people, could hardly have been an attractive concept to the Deuteronomic writers when they arrived on the scene. Their understanding of God's relationship with the people entailed an *entire people's responsibility* to the divine; the David-Zion theology required only God's recognition of *one individual.* So it is hardly surprising that the Deuteronomic writer, though acknowledging the David-Zion theology by including the dynastic promise and the many stories of David's glorious beginnings, worked so hard to undercut the royal ideology with doubts about its justice (1 Samuel 8) and its reliance on weak human beings (2 Samuel 11–20). And of course, the fact of the Exile — which brought to an end the dynastic succession in Zion — made it possible to engage in an effective critique of the theology. Thus we will see in the next chapter that the Deuteronomic writer's story ends with only a hollow validation for Jehoiachin, the heir to the throne in exile, an invitation to eat at another king's table.

But the royal ideology did not disappear so easily from the Israelite imagination. Psalm 89 is powerful testimony to one response to the Exile: it demands that God exercise proper justice and demonstrate his character in relation to other gods by renewing and bringing to fruition his promise to David. And better known is the transformation of the Davidic promise in the Greco-Roman period into messianic expectation, the hope that God would one day raise up a deliverer to lead Israel in victory over her imperial rulers. In time this was adapted in early Christian circles to understand Jesus as a Messiah.

Theological Themes in 1 and 2 Samuel

As in Joshua and Judges, the Deuteronomic writer continues in 1 and 2 Samuel to hone his portraits of God, the people of Israel, and their relationship under the terms of the covenant with a variety of telling episodes, one of which (the ark narrative) we will address. But most of all, the Deuteronomic writer illustrates the covenantal relationship between God and people by means of a study of the problem of kingship. The Deuteronomic writer also uses 1 and 2 Samuel to introduce a polemic against what we might call "wisdom theology."

God and Humanity Together in Covenantal Relationship

Throughout 1 and 2 Samuel the Deuteronomic writer reaffirms his view that God was essentially committed to bringing the terms of the covenant to bear in response to Israel's actions, but that God was also willing to provide Israel mercy repeatedly to sustain the relationship when it might otherwise have ended. Likewise, where the Deuteronomic writer is not engaged solely in repeating the most positive traditions about David, he uses the story of kingship's rise (see below) to illustrate the people's abiding penchant for ignoring their covenantal obligations. But he also takes up in 1 and 2 Samuel another dimension of this portrait of God in the covenantal relationship. Although we cannot be certain, the ark narrative in 1 Samuel 4–6 seems to have been used to reply to those who may have doubted God's covenantal loyalty in light of the exilic experience. The answer 1 Samuel 4–6 offers is simple: whenever it occurred, exile was entirely God's choice, and it functioned as punishment for the people of Israel for *their* covenantal disloyalty, not as a display of God's weakness or failure in the covenant. The obeisance of the Philistine god Dagon to the ark of the covenant and the plagues on the Philistine people proved from village to village who was in charge, and with some humor. And the return of the ark by milch cows that neither turned to the left or the right — as the people were called to do with respect to keeping the law — surely also added some wry humor to an otherwise accusatory tale. In any case, by the end of the story there could be no mistaking its point: anyone who saw the people's exile in Babylon as a sign of the weakness of the God of Israel was quite mistaken; the Exile, in fact, was a demonstration of God's power.

Extending the Polemic against Kingship

From the very beginning of 1 Samuel the Deuteronomic writer seems to have been engaged in critiquing kingship. As we noted above, it seems likely that the miraculous birth story traditionally provided to a king was taken from Saul and assigned instead to Samuel, the last of the judges. Notably, the Deuteronomic writer left the evidence that the story belonged originally to Saul in plain sight (1 Sam 1:28), so his audience could not miss what had been done.

The critique continues in the arrangement of the narrative pieces that constitute the account of kingship's rise in Israel. As we noted above, the positive traditions regarding kingship's first sanctioned appearance in Israel (1 Samuel 9–11) are framed by negative judgments on it (chs. 8, 12). And once the first king actually begins to exercise his power over Israel, Saul confirms that all the difficulties anticipated in kingship come to pass: he usurps the role of Israel's legitimate religious leader (ch. 13), ignores God's law (ch. 15), and is completely tone deaf to the correct use of religious rites when he does legitimately proclaim them (ch. 14).

It would seem to the casual reader that for all of the Deuteronomic writer's animosity toward kingship he nonetheless held David in high esteem, for 1 Samuel 16 begins a long section of text that presents the "best of David." In 1 Samuel 16–2 Samuel 8 David proves to be a great musician, a mighty warrior, an able statesman, an honorable foe, and a generous patron. But the Deuteronomic writer was merely biding his time and (perhaps) reverencing for some in his audience a figure *they* held in particularly high regard. For just before we come

to the high point of the traditions glorifying David, 2 Samuel 7, we encounter in 2 Samuel 6 his disgraceful behavior over bringing the ark of the covenant to Jerusalem: he only wants it when he thinks it might benefit him, and when he is rebuked for his dance before the ark by his wife he treats her with utter contempt (and perhaps unwittingly prophesies his own ignominious end; cf. 1 Kings 2 and comments in the next chapter). We hardly need to rehearse the elements of the Succession Narrative to show how they further underscore David's failures as a parent, adherent to the laws of the God of Israel, king, and human being. In spite of his mercy for his enemies — which in itself was ironically a sign of his weakness as a king! — David failed in all other respects in this story. In light of such a narrative, the David-Zion theology surely endured some hard scrutiny by even its most zealous defenders. And as we shall see, the Deuteronomic writer was not done with his critique of kingship with this account. 1 and 2 Kings completes the polemic in impressive and decisive fashion.

The Beginning of the Polemic against Wisdom Theology

The Deuteronomic writer may have had another competitor for people's religious imagination, something we might call "wisdom theology." It is clearly evident in 1 Kings with the sections that acknowledge Solomon's reputation for wisdom, and as we shall see, it may have been a target of critique in the well-known story of Solomon, the two women, and the single child.

But even before 1 Kings we see hints of this polemic particularly in 2 Samuel in the roles assigned to "wise" and "insightful" people. Twice the term "wise" (Hebrew *hakam*) is used to describe persons whose wisdom facilitates disaster. In 13:3 we read that Jonadab, Amnon's "wise" friend, provides the plan that facilitates Amnon's rape of his sister, an act that eventually leads to Amnon's own death at the hands of his vengeful brother, Absalom. And David permits Absalom to return from exile after murdering Amnon only after listening to the tale of the "wise" (Hebrew *hakam[ah]*) woman recruited from Tekoa by Joab to persuade David (14:2). From these and several other occurrences of the term in 2 Samuel it is already apparent that whatever its value, wisdom should also make one wary.

Questions for Review and Discussion

1   What seems to be the view of human leadership for ancient Israel in 1 and 2 Samuel? Did the Deuteronomic writer's hopes necessarily match the reality that Israel experienced in terms of leadership patterns?

2 In what ways did the Deuteronomic writer express
   his regard for kings? What literary strategies did he
   employ to do this?

3 How do the Samuel books fit into the larger agenda
   of the Deuteronomic writer as we described it in
   Chapter 12? Can you think of any way in which to
   argue that 1 and 2 Samuel stand on their own and
   should *not* be read as a part of the Deuteronomistic
   History?

Further Reading

Auld, Graeme. "1 and 2 Samuel." In *ECB,* 213-45.

Cartledge, Tony. *1 & 2 Samuel.* Macon: Smith and Helwys, 2001.

Gordon, Robert P. *1 & 2 Samuel.* OTG. Sheffield: Sheffield Academic, 1999.

Schniedewind, William M. *Society and the Promise to David: The Reception History of 2 Samuel 7:1-17.* Oxford:
   Oxford University Press, 1999.

Chapter 17

1 and 2 Kings

Getting Started

1   Read 1 Kings 1–2. How does the story of the transition from David to Solomon end? What portrait of David emerges from this account? How does Solomon's reign begin?

2   Read 1 Kings 3:16-28. How does this well-known story of Solomon's wisdom support the idea that he was a particularly insightful person? Would it make any difference to your reading of the story if, in fact, when Solomon instructed his servants to give the child to one of the women, he did not actually name the woman, but merely said to them, "Give it [the child] *to her?*"

3   Read 2 Kings 17. According to this anonymous speech, what was the reason for the defeat of the Northern Kingdom, Israel? Does the rhetoric of this speech sound at all familiar? If so, to what does it best compare?

Preliminary Comments

In 1 and 2 Kings the Deuteronomic writer completes his story of Israel's struggle to keep to the covenant made between Israel and God in Deuteronomy. The books are aptly named, not only because they concentrate on the reigns of the kings of Israel and Judah, but also because in doing so they lay at the kings' doorstep all blame and honor for Israel's failures and successes. It is, as we shall see, a narrative that suggests the blame for Israel's and Judah's fall to imperial conquest lay squarely — even exclusively — on the shoulders of the kings.

Also we note that this chapter is somewhat lengthier than its predecessors because we end it with a retrospective look at the entire Deuteronomistic History and Deuteronomic Collection.

A Walk through 1 and 2 Kings

After taking a relatively sedate pace in recounting Solomon's rule, the narrative quickly summarizes and judges according to a Deuteronomic standard each king's rule down to the Exile. It only slows occasionally, chiefly to give more detailed attention to the ministries of the prophets Elijah and Elisha and to the reigns of Ahab in the north and Hezekiah and Josiah in the south.

1 Kings 1–11: Solomon's Accession to the Throne and His Reign

Many read 1 Kings 1–2 as the conclusion of the Succession Narrative that begins in 2 Samuel 9–20. On this reading 2 Samuel 21–24 was an editorial insertion — perhaps by the Deuteronomic writer — to include other traditions about David. But whatever the history of this unit's composition, in its present form it does explain how Solomon, and not the surviving older son of David named Adonijah, inherited the throne from his father.

1 Kings 1 makes clear that David is by this point a shadow of the major figure we read about in 1 and 2 Samuel. In what may be an ironic echo of David's taunt of Michal in 2 Samuel 6 — that he would shame himself even more than she could imagine with the handmaids who saw him nearly nude as he danced before the ark — he is supplied with a handmaid, Abishag the Shunammite, to ignite his passions; but the text reports that though she served him, he did not "know her sexually" (1 Kgs 1:4).

And so the jostling for David's throne begins, with Bathsheba, a king's counselor named Benaiah, and Zadok the priest lined up on the side of Solomon and Joab and Abiathar, the priest, on the side of Adonijah. The outcome is well known; Solomon ascends to the throne and deals harshly with those who oppose him, having Adonijah and Joab killed and Abiathar exiled. Though a mostly bare-bones sort of storytelling, this account of the beginning of Solomon's reign demonstrates from the beginning Solomon's conformity to typical and rather brutal norms of exercising kingship in the ancient Near Eastern world.

The next major segment covering Solomon's reign accounts for his reputation for wisdom. Clearly, already in the Exile wisdom had come to be associated with Solomon. That it was associated with him later is obvious from the subsequent attribution to him of Proverbs, Ecclesiastes, the Wisdom of Solomon, and the Song

of Solomon. 1 Kings 3–4 tells us that he prayed for this gift when God offered him a blessing, and that he then demonstrated it in settling the dispute between the two prostitutes over the single surviving child between them (1 Kgs 3:16-28) and through his administration of the kingdom, composition of proverbs and psalms, and classification of the natural world (ch. 4). It is worth noting, however, that throughout this narrative of his great wisdom is a certain ambiguity, exemplified most clearly in the fact that when he judges between the claims of the two women to the surviving child he actually says to his servants only, "Give the child *to her*." His instruction provides no indication that he actually understood the outcome of his own trial of the two women! We return to this possible reading of Solomon's behavior in "Critical Issues" and "Theological Themes" below.

1 Kings 5–8 recounts how Solomon then built the temple of the Lord in Jerusalem. He made it an elaborate home for Israel's God that was matched only by the palace he built for himself. Indeed, he became so indebted to his builder, Hiram of Tyre, that he had to pay off his debt to the foreign king with land in the northern part of the kingdom. Tinged by this episode of over-budget construction though it may have been, this building effort is otherwise portrayed positively by the Deuteronomic writer, who after all was concerned especially that Israel offer sacrifice to God in the proper place, Jerusalem. The account is capped by Solomon's oration at the dedication of the temple that is another of the Deuteronomic writer's distinctive speeches. Solomon recounts God's blessings to Israel, recalls the covenant made through Moses, reminds the people of the cost of not honoring the covenant, and (signaling the exilic-era composition of the speech) acknowledges that Israel might fail and be exiled. If so, argues Solomon, they should cry out to God for deliverance and he will hear them and renew them in their covenantal relationship.

The next section of text, 1 Kings 9–11, begins to narrate in earnest the path that led to the exile Solomon's speech foresaw. We read first in 9:1-9 that the unilateral Davidic covenant was "conditionalized" by God's expression of it to Solomon: so long as he obeyed the laws of God his line would endure on the throne in Jerusalem. The poignancy of this reframing of the Davidic covenant at this point can hardly be missed, for almost immediately we read that Solomon begins to violate the most basic law governing him, that of the king in Deut 17:14-20. 1 Kings 9:11–11:40 reports that in violation of it Solomon acquires from Egypt horses for his army (Deut 17:16), amasses enormous amounts of wealth (Deut 17:17b), and marries foreign wives in great number (and permits the worship of their gods; Deut 17:17a). Of course, in doing all of these things he is acting as a "wise" monarch

Six-chambered gate and casement wall at Hazor, representative of Solomon's building activity. (L. T. Geraty)

of the ancient world: he needs a well-equipped cavalry to defend his lands; alliances with foreign kings through arranged marriages were critical to a successful foreign policy; and wealth was necessary to realize both of the prior objectives. Solomon well illustrates the tension between kingship as it had to be practiced in the ancient world and as the Deuteronomic writer's theology permitted it to be practiced. Indeed, the prophet Ahijah anticipates the division of Solomon's kingdom at the hand of God in recompense for the king's violation of the Deuteronomic law of kingship. His story, then, is the template for those of most of the kings who followed him.

1 Kings 12–16: The Division of the Kingdom

This long section on the kings of Israel and Judah that also includes the careers of Elijah and Elisha is marked most obviously by a Deuteronomic formula that is applied to each of the kings. For the formula as it is adapted to the kings of the north and south, see p. 157.

The story begins with an account of the division of the United Kingdom in 1 Kings 12. Upon Solomon's death Rehoboam rules in his place and refuses to ease up in his use of corvée labor from the northern tribes to continue his father's building projects. As a result, Jeroboam, who has served Solomon as the overseer of the laborers from the tribe of Joseph, leads a rebellion that results in establishment of the Northern Kingdom of Israel. We also learn in 1 Kings 12 that Jeroboam, lacking access to Jerusalem as a place to worship the God of Israel, establishes shrines in Dan and Bethel. There he places golden calves, probably with the intention that they would depict what the God of Israel rested upon in those places. But the Deuteronomic writer reports the events so as to indict Jeroboam for promoting worship of foreign gods. And in any case, Jeroboam promotes worship apart from Jerusalem, a violation of Deuteronomy 12.

Note also the parallel between this historical recollection and the golden calf incident in Exodus 32. It is easy to see why some suggest that the latter story was built from a recollection of these events.

1 Kings 13 reports a truly strange incident that falls here largely because the man of God who acts in the account prophesies against Jeroboam's sanctuaries in the north. (As we shall see he reminds one of Amos, another prophet who traveled from the Southern to the Northern Kingdom to preach for God.) The real action in the story, though, centers on God's command that the man of God do his business in the north and return home without delay, and on a local prophet's knowing persuasion of the man of God to pursue a contrary line of conduct (by offering him food and drink in his home). Sure enough, the man of God is killed for his violation of God's command and in an odd and belated act of magnitude the old prophet of the north sees to the burial of the southern prophet's body. We shall return to this curious episode below in "Critical Issues" and "Theological Themes."

1 Kings 14 then relates how Jeroboam sought counsel from the prophet who appointed him over Israel, Ahijah, regarding his line's fate as rulers in the north. Ahijah prophesies that Jeroboam's son will die, that he will not found a dynasty, and that all the kings of Israel that follow him are likewise doomed because of his sin in leading the people to worship wrongly in the land of Israel. This sets the stage for the long succession of failed rulers in the north that includes the Omride and Jehu dynasties and the parallel history of Davidic kings in the south. The beginning of the succession is narrated in

1 Kings 15–16 with the succession from Abijam to Asa in Judah and Nadab to Ahab in Israel. (For lists of the kings of Israel and Judah, see p. 158; we provide dates only for the most significant kings, as establishing a fairly precise chronology is notoriously difficult. The dates provided are based on indications in the biblical text, as well as best scholarly guesses; see, e.g., Michael D. Coogan, ed., *The Oxford History of the Biblical World* [Oxford: Oxford University Press, 1998], 597-601.)

1 Kings 17–2 Kings 1: The Elijah Cycle

Readers have probably recognized that to this point in the Deuteronomistic History prophets function largely to call kings to account for their misdeeds (especially relative to Deuteronomic standards of conduct) and occasionally foretell the fate of a king relative to his conduct. The cycle of stories about Elijah, though departing in many ways from what one would expect of a good prophet in Deuteronomic imagination, seems to confirm that role for prophets. Indeed, the Deuteronomic notion of a particularly good prophet is one who stood firm against any infection of full-blown ancient Near Eastern royal ideology, who announced God's control over human affairs in spite of any king's aspirations to the contrary. Elijah is certainly a model of that practice, and he adds to it the consistent claim that the gods worshipped most aggressively in the Northern Kingdom, Baal and Asherah, were no competition for the God of Israel.

The cycle of stories includes a series of discrete episodes. In 1 Kings 17–18 a divinely-ordained drought gives Elijah the opportunity to show the Omride Ahab the power of the God of Israel over Baal and his prophets. While Elijah as a single prophet can successfully call upon the God of Israel to bring rain to the land, the many frenzied prophets of Baal who serve Ahab not only fail miserably in the same effort, but are also easy prey for Elijah and his God. Stitched into this larger story is Elijah's encounter with the widow of Zarephath, who

hungers and thirsts and is fed miraculously by Elijah and whose dead son is revived by him; this insertion into the drought story serves to demonstrate the power the God of Israel shows for those whom he favors, a sharp contrast with his posture toward those whom he does not favor, such as Ahab.

1 Kings 19 then tells the well-known tale of Elijah's frightened journey to Horeb. Because of his divinely directed and deadly contest with the prophets of Baal who are dear to Ahab and especially his wife Jezebel, his life is endangered. Fearful for his life, Elijah flees to the mountain and there encounters God in the famous "still small voice" (KJV). Punctuating the story line's basic claim that God — not kings or other gods or their prophets — controls all of history, the God of Israel instructs Elijah to have no fear and to return to action so as to anoint God's chosen rulers of Aram and Israel, as well as his own successor, Elisha.

1 Kings 20–22 closes out 1 Kings by narrating the war between Ben-hadad of Aram and Ahab of Israel. According to ch. 20 God devotes Ben-hadad to destruction, but Ahab spares him, securing the announcement from an unnamed prophet that Ahab will die for his transgression. 1 Kings 21 then tells the tale of Ahab's longing for the vineyard of one of his subjects, Naboth, Jezebel's counsel that facilitates Ahab's theft of the vineyard and Naboth's death, and Elijah's announcement that for this (too) Ahab's line will be terminated (though thanks to Ahab's penance the end of the Omrides is delayed until the reign of Jehoram). 1 Kings 22 finally tells the tale of a new engagement between Aram (Syria) and Israel and Ahab's divinely directed death in battle.

The last act of Elijah before leaving his duties to Elisha is narrated in 2 Kings 1. Ahab's successor on the throne, Ahaziah, falls from his window and is gravely injured. Seeking to know if he will die of his injuries Ahaziah queries not the God of Israel, but Baal-zebul, "God of the exalted" (called mockingly in the story Baal-*zebub*,

Deuteronomic Formulae Summarizing the Reigns of the Kings of Judah and Israel

Kings of Judah

1. The date when the king began to reign relative to the king(s) of Israel

2. The length of the king's reign

3. The name of the king's mother

4. An evaluation of the king relative to David as the comparative standard

5. Reference to a full account of the king in the Book of the Annals of the Kings of Judah

Kings of Israel

1. The date when the king began to reign relative to the king(s) of Judah

2. The length of the king's reign

3. A negative evaluation of all the kings (because they had no access to the proper place of worship)

4. Reference to a full account of the king in the Book of the Annals of the Kings of Israel

The Kings of Israel and Judah

Israel and Judah

Saul (1025-1005?)
David (1005-965?)
Solomon (968-928)

Israel	Judah
Jeroboam (928-907)	Rehoboam
	Abijah
Nadab	Asa
Baasha	
Elah	
Zimri	
Omri (882-871)	Jehoshaphat (867-846)
Ahab (873-852)	
Ahaziah	
Jehoram	Jehoram
Jehu	Athaliah
	Joash
Jehoahaz	
Jehoash	Amaziah
Jeroboam II (788-747)	Uzziah
Zechariah	
Shallum	
Menahem	
Pekahiah	Jotham
Pekah	Ahaz
Hoshea	
Fall of Israel to Assyria (722)	Hezekiah (727-698)
	Manasseh (698-642)
	Josiah (641-609)
	Jehoahaz (609)
	Jehoiakim (608-598)
	Jehoiachin (597)
	First Deportation to Babylon
	Zedekiah (597-586)
	Fall of Judah to Babylon (586)

"lord of the flies"). For his error Elijah announces in place of the foreign god that Ahaziah will die, and so he does. Once again the stories of Elijah illustrate the sovereignty of the God of Israel over history and the gods.

2 Kings 2–10: The Elisha Cycle and Dynastic Change in Israel

This peculiar collection of stories about Elijah's successor, Elisha, focuses in part on Elisha's oversight of the events prompted by Elijah's prophecies and proves further God's control over history, kings, and gods. But it also demonstrates that prophets *as the Deuteronomic writer understands them* were forth-tellers of God's law

and were otherwise much like the other ecstatic prophets of the ancient world, figures who did miracles and unusual deeds more or less at will. Later, in considering the Deuteronomic writer's attitude toward figures like Isaiah, Amos, Hosea, Micah, and Jeremiah we will have occasion to suggest an explanation for this posture on the part of the Deuteronomic writer.

2 Kings 2 narrates the transfer of power from Elijah to Elisha. Notably, Elijah is taken up into the heavens without experiencing death. As a consequence, his return came to be an event thought to anticipate a new age, even the dawning of a messianic era (see Mal 4:4-6; Mark 9:2-13). In any event, the story functions here to

further demonstrate the submission of the prophet to God's will. The chapter concludes with two demonstrations of Elisha's power, the "curing" of a poisoned well and the destruction by she-bears of children who insult his coiffure!

Elisha's career begins in earnest with his oversight of the Israelite conquest of Moab in 2 Kings 3. But immediately following is perhaps the best-known collection of stories about Elisha. In chs. 4–8 Elisha deals in turn with a widow in need of debt relief and a Shunammite woman who desires to bear a child and then requires his services to revive the child when he dies as a youth; makes poisonous food edible and multiplies loaves to feed 100 men; heals Naaman the Syrian of his leprosy; miraculously retrieves an axe-head lost in the Jordan; and blinds the army of Aram to lead them to defeat. In all of this Elisha demonstrates the qualities of a typical Near Eastern prophet and miracle worker; he assures the Deuteronomic writer's readers as to what a prophet should indeed be if not engaged in foretelling God's plans.

2 Kings 9–10 completes Elisha's career as he works to support the overthrow of the last of the Omrides and inaugurate the beginning of the Jehu dynasty. He anoints Hazael king over Aram (Syria) as a foe for Israel and sets Jehu to the task of destroying the remnants of the Omride dynasty. By the end of 2 Kings 10 the deed is done and God's judgment against Ahab and Jezebel — and the Omrides as a dynasty — has been executed, and we even hear God's typical judgment on Jehu himself: though God's faithful instrument of vengeance against the Omrides, he too did not turn from Jeroboam's sin — how could he without access to Jerusalem? — and so he too is condemned at the last.

2 Kings 11–17: The Assyrian Crisis and the Fall of Israel

2 Kings 11 narrates a brief episode in which Athaliah, from the line of Ahab, usurps control in Judah and attempts to eliminate the Davidic line. Joash, the surviving heir, is protected by the priests and is soon restored to the throne. Then 2 Kings 12–15 provides a Deuteronomic summary of the careers of kings in Israel and Judah from Jehoahaz (Israel) and Joash (Judah) to Pekah (Israel) and Jotham (Judah). The period covered runs from 837 to 732 B.C.E. The end of this period was when Israel and Judah first experienced the prophets whose words we know from books like Isaiah, Amos, Hosea, and Micah. We will discuss below in "Critical Issues" the conditions this period produced that engendered in turn the activity of these prophets.

2 Kings 16–17 narrates the "Assyrian crisis" that led in time to the conquest of Israel by Assyria. Tiglath-pileser III of Assyria campaigns westward, pressuring Aram (Syria) and Israel. The kings of the latter two countries, Rezin and Pekah, join forces to fend off the Assyrian, and pressure Ahaz of Judah to join them. Ahaz chooses instead to seek protection from Tiglath-pileser, who then succeeds in subjugating Damascus, the capital of Syria, placing Israel under serious threat, but also making Judah into a vassal. It is not long, then, before Israel also falls to the Assyrians (ruled by then by Sargon II) and its people are dispersed to the corners of the Assyrian empire to dilute their capacity to renew their resistance to Assyria. The bulk of 2 Kings 17, then, presents the Deuteronomic writer's judgment on Israel, that her doom comes as a result of her failure to honor the God of Israel as she should have and her zeal instead for the gods of her neighbors. The speech also warns Judah: be careful lest this too become your fate.

2 Kings 18–25: Judah Alone to the Babylonian Exile

These final chapters of 2 Kings narrate the last century and a half of Judah's existence. The first part of the narration, 2 Kings 18–20, covers the reign of Hezekiah, a king judged by the Deuteronomic writer to have been particularly good. (We shall see below in the chapter on Isaiah that 2 Kgs 18:13, 17–20:19 reappears in Isaiah 36–39.) We hear at the beginning of the section that Hezekiah sought to eliminate the worship of other gods in his kingdom and perhaps aimed to centralize worship in Jerusalem. He also tried to reverse the policy of his predecessor Ahaz of relying on Assyrian protection. When Assyria besieges Jerusalem and all seems lost, Hezekiah prays to the Lord and receives assurance through the prophet Isaiah that the city will be spared. The biblical account tells us that an angel of the Lord attacked Sennacherib's soldiers that very night, forcing them to flee for home. In fact, we know that the Assyrians did besiege Jerusalem and that they did permit the city to survive; but history provides nothing to contradict the Bible's account of things with more "natural causes" for Sennacherib's sudden retreat! In any case, after the siege lets up Hezekiah falls ill and consults the Lord once more, this time to ask if he will survive. Through Isaiah a positive answer is provided, but Isaiah also prophesies the Babylonian Exile to come nearly a century later.

2 Kings 21 then narrates the (for the Deuteronomic writer, troublingly) long reign of Manasseh, Hezekiah's son. Manasseh is remembered for having reversed his father's good policies and having encouraged the worship of the many gods, not the one Lord alone. Because of his wanton apostasy the Deuteronomic writer delivers the judgment that Judah would suffer defeat. Neither the good done by his father nor by Josiah his grandson

could overcome the evil he did. His son Amon ruled after him for about one year.

Thus Josiah's reform, recounted in 2 Kings 22–23, though an honorable course of action that won him some of the Deuteronomic writer's most glowing reviews, was doomed to provide only a respite for Judah before it faced its fate. As is well known, Josiah sought to reform the cult in Jerusalem on the basis of a "book of the law" that temple cleaners discovered in the course of their work. This book of law, almost certainly the core laws of Deuteronomy 12–26, demanded that the Lord be worshipped only in Jerusalem and that all worship of foreign gods cease from the land. Josiah consults Huldah, a prophetess, regarding the significance of the find and learns that his own efforts will not save the kingdom from the doom already announced for it, but that he will be rewarded for his efforts with a peaceful death (though that hardly turns out to be true, as he dies in battle against the Egyptians). Then Josiah sends his soldiers out to execute the commands of the book of the law by eliminating the worship of any god but the Lord and centralizing in Jerusalem all such worship (thus forcing the country priests to come to the city). Josiah also sees to the observance of Passover in the city according to the law. But this is all for naught, as Josiah meets his own death leading the forces of Judah against Egypt at Megiddo, attempting to cut short an Egyptian-Assyrian alliance against Babylon.

2 Kings 24–25 then narrates in quick succession the remaining days of Judah's existence. Josiah's successor, Jehoiakim, seeks to ally himself with varying imperial powers, settling finally and fatefully on Egypt. As Babylon approaches Jerusalem to discipline Jehoiakim and his kingdom for the poor choice of allies, Jehoiakim dies, and so when Babylon takes Jerusalem the first time in 598/7 his son, Jehoiachin is the unlucky steward of the kingdom. He and other elites are deported to Babylon according to Babylonian imperial policy. (The Babylonians anticipate prospering from the skills and commerce of the deportees.) His Babylonian-appointed successor, Zedekiah, is compliant for only a short time, and when he too rebels against the Babylonian yoke, the imperial army returns in 587/6 to do the job right this time: besides torturing and executing the Judean royal family they destroy the temple and much of the city, as well as the surrounding region's agricultural infrastructure. The governor whom the Babylonians appoint to oversee their new holdings, Gedaliah, is also led astray by rebellious forces, and so the Babylonians return one more time, in 582, to inflict even more damage. As the story told by the Deuteronomic writer closes we survey a devastated land of Judah, emptied of the people whom God gave the land in the first place. They have failed

their covenantal obligations with stunning results. The only faint note of hope at the end is that Jehoiachin is invited by the king of Babylon to join him at the royal meals.

Critical Issues in the Study of 1 and 2 Kings

In treating the critical issues associated with studying 1 and 2 Kings, one stands out, in addition to the questions of sources and the Deuteronomic writer's unique contributions to the account. The issue is that of the history behind the story told in such cursory fashion in these two books.

History and 1 and 2 Kings

With only a few exceptions, 1 and 2 Kings constitute all the evidence we have of the political and social history of the kingdoms of Israel and Judah. For instance, apart from a famous inscription discovered at Tel Dan in 1992, there is no evidence outside of the biblical record for the reign of David, to which nearly 40 percent of the biblical narrative about kings over Israel and Judah is dedicated! (Note that the inscription actually provides only direct evidence for the existence of a Davidic line, not for David or his own reign; see p. 24 and the accompanying comments in Chapter 3 on the abiding uncertainty among some about the inscription's significance.) Moreover, archaeology typically contradicts the biblical claims for the vast reach of David's and Solomon's holdings, suggesting instead that they ruled over petty kingdoms at most, and according to some historians perhaps even less. In fact, one school of thought rejects any notion of the Kings books' historical reliability, arguing that they are late literary constructions meant to project legitimation for later political organizations into the ancient past.

So when does the historical record provide good evidence to parallel the biblical account? With some irony we admit that it is in the 8th century B.C.E. — when the biblical account becomes most cursory in character! — that archaeology and other historical indicators offer something to go on. The evidence indicates that in the years covered so summarily by 2 Kings 11–15 Israel and Judah experienced a delusory prosperity: under their respective rulers they seemed to have expanded their military and commercial influences and to have developed relatively healthy trade relations. But the affluence was deceptive because it was not shared widely among the populations of both countries. Instead, the wealth from such enterprises was concentrated in the hands of a few, while the vast majority of Judeans and Israelites fell into ever deeper debt to the wealthy few as they tried

Assyrian soldiers lead away prisoners of war. Alabaster relief from Ashurbanipal's palace at Nineveh. (Louvre)

to scratch out a living in a land that could at times be extremely harsh to its inhabitants. We shall come back to these disparate economic conditions when we consider the words of the 8th-century prophets who announced the doom of Israel and Judah in part because of this state of affairs. For now it is enough to observe that as a result of this imbalanced economy, both nations grew ever more vulnerable to threats from beyond their borders. Unfortunately for both kingdoms, this coincided with intensified Assyrian interest in the western regions and led to the troubles narrated above in our survey of 2 Kings 16–17, as well as those encountered later by Judah at the hands of Babylon.

Another matter of historical interest that must be addressed in considering 1 and 2 Kings is the nature of Josiah's reform. While 2 Kings 22–23 presents it as a religious reform born of Josiah's desire to honor the demands of the God of Israel as made evident to him by the "book of the law," it is apparent that he was motivated by political interests as well. Josiah surely understood that the Assyrian Empire was growing weaker by the day and was vulnerable to defeat. He also seemed to be realistic enough to understand that under such circumstances Judah could only hope to situate itself most favorably with respect to whichever nation-state took Assyria's place as

the preeminent power on the world stage. He apparently concluded — rightly, as it turns out — that the power soon to replace Assyria would be Babylon. Thus one interpretation of his centralization of the cult in Jerusalem and his demand that the people of Judah come to the city regularly to observe feasts is that by doing so he was able to cull from a wider population by census and taxes resources and personnel for a military machine strong enough to provide tangible assistance to the emerging new imperial power. Thus we find Josiah at the end of 2 Kings 23 attempting to foil Egypt's alliance with Assyria against Babylon by ambushing the Egyptian army on its way to join the Assyrians. But as we saw in our survey of the text, his effort only brought death to him and defeat to his army. Thus his geopolitical objectives were not achieved. But his religious reform movement, motivated though it may have been by politics, did achieve real religious change: it likely was coincidental with, if not also the reason for, the rise of the movement that produced our Deuteronomic writer, a religious reform movement that saw Israel's salvation in living by the law God gave as a gift to Israel long before.

Sources in 1 and 2 Kings

As in all the other books produced by the Deuteronomic writer, we find in 1 and 2 Kings plenty of evidence of sources, but here what was only apparent before is now explicit: in addition to citing the "Book of the Acts of Solomon" (1 Kgs 11:41), the narrator tells the reader time and again that he also relied on the "Books of the Annals of the Kings of Judah" (1 Kgs 14:29; 15:7, 23; 22:45; 2 Kgs 8:23; 12:19; 14:18; 15:6, 36; 16:19; 20:20; 21:17, 25; 23:28; 24:5) and the "Books of the Annals of the Kings of Israel" (1 Kgs 14:19; 15:31; 16:5, 14, 20, 27; 22:39; 2 Kgs 1:18; 10:34; 13:8; 12; 14:15, 28; 15:11, 15, 21, 26, 31). We have no other evidence of these books, but given the ancient Near Eastern practice of keeping official records of a king's reign we have no reason to doubt the existence of these sources used by the Deuteronomic writer.

In addition, the Deuteronomic writer clearly incorporated cycles of stories and traditions about Elijah and Elisha as northern prophets. That they were sources and not compositions of the Deuteronomic writer is clear enough from the elements in them that contradict that author's sensibilities. To cite but one example, Elijah makes sacrifice on Mount Carmel in his battle with the prophets of Baal (1 Kings 18) in violation of the Deuteronomic writer's passionate concern that sacrifice take place only in Jerusalem. That the Deuteronomic writer edited these stories is not all that clear to observers, and some critics even argue that the Elijah cycle, with its greater emphasis on the theme of retributive justice that is so dear to the Deuteronomic writer, might have been composed after the Elisha cycle, perhaps even by the Deuteronomic writer. It is more likely, though, that these two story collections developed almost entirely in the north long before the Deuteronomic writer wrote and that he incorporated them with only some light redactional touches. His aim may have been to portray Israel's prophets as typical ancient Near Eastern prophetic figures (see p. 163 for a brief discussion of ancient Near Eastern prophecy) who were distinguished from other prophets by their service to the Deuteronomic agenda of speaking God's word directing recipients to worship the one God of Israel alone (Deut 13:1-5; 18:15-22). Thus it is also possible that 1 Kings 13, the story of the man of God and the old prophet, was also a source adapted by the Deuteronomic writer to serve his purpose, namely to suggest that true prophets were assigned to speak God's word against false worship, but that they too were subject entirely to God's word.

The Deuteronomic Writer's Contribution to 1 and 2 Kings

The Deuteronomic writer made a variety of his own distinctive contributions to these two books, some of which we discuss here.

The most obvious contribution is the repeated refrain regarding the quality of each of the kings' reigns (see p. 157 above). These formulaic passages are an unquestionably Deuteronomic innovation, for they function to render that author's theological judgment on each king.

A second obvious contribution from the Deuteronomic writer is found in Solomon's speech at the temple's dedication (1 Kings 8) and the narrator's judgment over Israel in 2 Kings 17. The rhetoric of these passages recalls that of Moses in Deuteronomy, Joshua, and Samuel in their valedictory speeches (Joshua 23; 1 Samuel 12) and the "pattern passage" in Judg 2:11–3:6. Especially unmistakable as a Deuteronomic passage composed in exile is Solomon's musing that the people might indeed fail in their covenant obligations and be scattered to a foreign land and need God's deliverance from the hand of their enemies (1 Kgs 8:46-53).

Finally, we note that perhaps the Deuteronomic writer's most important contribution was the arrangement of the source material used in 1 and 2 Kings. To cite but one example, the positioning of the story of the man of God and the old prophet in 1 Kings 13 between Jeroboam's inauguration of the cult centers at Bethel and Dan and his consultation of Ahijah works well to serve the Deuteronomic writer's larger purpose of condemning worship at any sanctuary but the one in Jerusalem and portraying prophets as preachers of the law, foretellers of God's plan, and yet themselves subject to the law that they preach. Again, as we shall see in "Theological Themes," this is a particular interest of the Deuteronomic writer.

Theological Themes in 1 and 2 Kings

1 and 2 Kings caps the theological argument of the Deuteronomic writer, so it is hardly surprising that one encounters here all the themes we have tracked thus far, and more.

God and Humanity Together in Covenantal Relationship

Interestingly, this dimension of the Deuteronomic writer's theological pedagogy is curtailed in 1 and 2 Kings. While up to this point in the Deuteronomistic History the people as a whole have been an important part of the story of covenantal failure and occasional success, here the responsibility for fidelity falls almost entirely on the shoulders of the kings. From Solomon's infidelity especially in marrying many wives, to Manasseh's massive betrayal of the covenant's terms, to Hezekiah's and Josiah's attempts to take a different approach, the narrative attaches almost singular significance to the kings' choices and actions. And the kings' actions that count have almost exclusively to do with how they behave relative to worship of the one God in the right place. Without access to Jerusalem the northern kings cannot ever manage to satisfy the "right place" criterion, and so they all fall into "Jeroboam's sin" and are all doomed, regardless of their best intentions (few though those may have been). And the kings of Judah from the line of David disappoint more often than not by their embrace of the worship of foreign gods, with only Hezekiah and Josiah receiving the most favorable reviews. The people's responsibility in all of this was to have followed the lead of their kings; their culpability for violating the covenant arose from the kings' misdeeds.

The Polemic against Kingship

From the foregoing and our survey of the two books above, it is clear how the polemic against kingship builds toward its conclusion in 1 and 2 Kings. From Solomon onward the kings of Israel and Judah made fatal mistake after fatal mistake in their leadership of the people, and it was especially the kings' promotion of cultic infidelity that led to the fall of both kingdoms. Given the outcome of the story in 2 Kings 25 the Deuteronomic writer can even include the repeated refrain with respect to the kings of Judah that God preserved something to them "for the sake of David" (e.g., 1 Kgs 11:13; 2 Kgs 19:34) without concern: all that remained was an invitation to the king's table in Babylon, hardly the glorious reward that proponents of the David-Zion theology imagined would come to Judah's kings.

1 and 2 Kings does add another component to the polemic, and it provides the rationale for God's promise to David being disappointed at the end. In a number of passages we see that the dynastic promise to David was made unequivocally conditional on the king's observance of God's law. 1 Kings 9:1-9 is perhaps the clearest example of this move.

It is true that 2 Sam 7:14 reports a similar condition on kingship, but there it amounts to a passing reference, perhaps from the Deuteronomic writer's hand. But with this passage and its clear statement of the requirements imposed on kings for the dynastic promise to remain in force there can have been no question by the end of the story why God seemed to have abrogated that promise: the kings were egregiously heedless of the condition on their reception of God's blessing and, so says the

Prophecy in the Ancient Near East

In the ancient Near East prophets varied in their role and function from place to place and even within particular contexts. In Egypt prophets were priestly in their function, in Syria-Palestine they were often technical diviners (especially for royalty), and across the ancient Near Eastern world they were thought to speak for or under the direction of gods and goddesses. In these roles they served as social critics, diviners of the future, political consultants, and ecstatic mediators of the gods' wishes or directions.

A particularly significant resource for understanding prophecy in non-Israelite cultures of Syria-Palestine is the Deir 'Alla inscription that mentions Balaam, who has a vision from heavenly beings (see Numbers 22–24). From Mesopotamia, the Mari finds provide by far the richest vein of evidence for prophetic activity in the ancient Near East. Here the "prophet" played such a wide variety of roles — from seer to ecstatic to divine intermediary to cult functionary — that prophets at Mari are best described as all-purpose servants of royalty and nonroyalty alike.

Deuteronomic writer, Manasseh's outrageous disregard for the condition was irreversible. Kingship, says the Deuteronomic writer, was the cause of Israel's failure in the land.

The Polemic against Wisdom Theology

Since Solomon was the hero of wisdom, the Deuteronomic writer's polemic against wisdom theology as an alternative to the Deuteronomic agenda understandably escalates in the account of Solomon's reign. This appears at first to be a subtle argument, but once the evidence is assembled, its persuasive power seems undeniable. Recall our explanation of the language in the test of Solomon's wisdom in 1 Kgs 3:16-28 and how it hinted at Solomon's failure to see the outcome of his own test. When one adds to this the indication in the text that it is precisely Solomon's exercise of his gift for wisdom that led to his accumulation of wealth and his pursuit of the typical policies of an ancient Near Eastern king (making alliances through marriage and acquiring resources for making defense and war making purposes), the case against human wisdom's capacity to contribute to a proper relationship between God and people seems clear.

The Deuteronomistic History and the Deuteronomic Collection: A Look Back

The end of 2 Kings brings the Deuteronomistic History to a close. It is fitting, then, that we pause at this point to summarize what we have seen in this portion of our study. By taking a step back we can see what the Deuteronomic writer — or at least the implied author of Deuteronomy, Joshua, Judges, 1 and 2 Samuel, and 1 and 2 Kings — accomplished, and what the implied audience of this work might have understood from encountering the whole of the Deuteronomic Collection.

With respect to this author's view of God and a corresponding anthropology, the Deuteronomic Collection leaves little doubt: God elected Israel unilaterally, but once that relationship was established God imposed a bilateral covenant on Israel, one not unlike an ancient Near Eastern suzerain-vassal treaty. Through keeping the law that God expounded, Israel remained the beneficiary of God's blessing in the land. If, however, Israel failed in its legal obligations — most especially the requirement that Israel worship the one God in the place God chooses — God was permitted to punish Israel by the withdrawal of the blessing and expulsion from the land. In short, God in the view of the Deuteronomic writer is a God of retributive justice. Correspondingly, the Deuteronomic writer posits a fairly "muscular" anthropology, at least inasmuch as it presumes the human capacity to cooperate with God in achieving God's plan for creation and the chosen people. The people are made accountable to God and to God's plan for creation.

In addition to this positive agenda, the Deuteronomic writer engaged in a multi-front polemic against potentially competing theological visions. The most obvious polemic is against the David-Zion theology, the view that God made a unilateral covenant with David and his descendants to maintain them on the throne in Jerusalem (Zion) forever, and that under these conditions Israel would be blessed (see esp. 2 Samuel 7). It is true that some have viewed the Deuteronomic writer to be positive rather than negative on this score, especially in light of the refrain found throughout the Deuteronomistic History that God preserved something of the line of David in spite of the Davidides' apostasy, "for the sake of my servant David whom I chose and who did keep my commandments and my statutes" (1 Kgs 11:34). Yet a careful reading of the entire Deuteronomistic History shows this to be an illusion: as the story closes the only thing that can be said positively of the remnant of David's line is that Jehoiachin gets to join the Babylonian king's table merriment as a guest, a king in exile dependent on the good will of his conqueror (2 Kings 25). Moreover, it is hard to overlook the sustained narrative-style polemic against David himself beginning with the Bathsheba incident (2 Samuel 11) and concluding with David's own ignominious demise (1 Kings 1–2). And that the Deuteronomic writer should be opposed to the David-Zion theology is hardly surprising: it proposes that

through the righteousness of one, the people of Israel would be blessed, while the Deuteronomic worldview insists on the righteousness of all with respect to God's demand for worship and honor. The final blow to any notion that the Deuteronomic Collection in its present form glorifies kingship comes in its penchant, in spite of its interest in the righteousness of all, for blaming the Exile ultimately on kings and their failure to lead the people in righteousness.

The Deuteronomic writer also seems to have it in for proponents of the view that exercising one's God-given intelligence — wisdom — would suffice to sustain humanity in relationship to God. Just as it is difficult to overlook the animosity expressed toward kings, one is hard pressed to see anything positive in this author's view of human wisdom as an alternative to the law of God as a guide for living. Already in the story of David's family troubles one senses the polemic. It is a "wise" friend of Amnon, Jonadab, who gives him the plan to rape his sister, Tamar (2 Sam 13:3). It is the "wise" woman from Tekoa who persuades David to let Absalom return from exile (2 Sam 14:2), and her own use of the term to describe David's power of decision-making in the same incident can only be read as deeply ironic (14:20). With a slightly different slant that still entails a violent outcome, a "wise" woman of Bichri counsels Joab and her fellow citizens in a plan that results in Sheba, the last rebel against David, losing his head. And as if to foreshadow the ultimately destructive nature of Solomon's wisdom, David is the first to refer to him with the term when he counsels Solomon from his deathbed to deal violently with David's surviving enemies (1 Kgs 2:9). Then, when Solomon, famed man of wisdom comes to ask God for the gift of wisdom, God grants it, but with the proviso that his life would be lengthened — the gift would have value — only if Solomon would walk in God's ways, "keeping my statutes and my commandments, as your father David walked" (1 Kgs 3:12-14). Again, the irony of such a claim is hard to miss: David is hardly a righteous keeper of God's law when he violates Bathsheba, overlooks her impurity, sees to her husband's death, and so on. And we have already noted the ambiguity in the demonstration of Solomon' wisdom in 1 Kgs 3:16-28; he does not seem to known, in fact, which of the two women should receive the child in light of the trap he sets. Lastly, his wisdom proves impotent when it counts most; rather than recall the legal proviso God places on enjoyment of wisdom's fruits (1 Kgs 3:12-14), Solomon marries many foreign women and mistreats the citizens of the northern part of his kingdom, paying for his *lack of wisdom* with half of his kingdom (1 Kings 11–12). Human wisdom, apart from the law, it seems, is not all what it is said to be, at least according to the

Deuteronomic writer. As demonstrated by the case of Solomon, it has to be tempered by the God-given law to be of any value.

One final polemic stance taken by the Deuteronomic writer may have been directed against the traditions of the "prophets." In particular Isaiah, Hosea, Amos, Micah, and Jeremiah likely posed a bit of a challenge for the Deuteronomic theology. The first four prophets were active in the 8th century B.C.E., long before the rise of the Deuteronomic movement (if we date its beginnings to sometime around the reforms of Josiah in 621 and following). But their words clearly had cogency for the Israelite imagination, surviving them by a century and more by the time the Deuteronomic Collection came into being. And as we shall see, Jeremiah was a contemporary of the early days of the Deuteronomic movement, perhaps even competing with them as evidenced by Jer 8:8-9 where the prophet speaks these words.

How can you say, "We are wise,
    and the law of the LORD is with us,"
when, in fact, the false pen of the scribes
    has made it into a lie?
The wise shall be put to shame,
    they shall be dismayed and taken;
since they have rejected the word of the LORD,
    what wisdom is in them?

Many scholars think the targets of Jeremiah's scorn are representatives of the Deuteronomic theology, and in light of what was said above about the Deuteronomic view of wisdom, there seems to be considerable logic to this. Jeremiah quotes a Deuteronomic writer as claiming wisdom through his guardianship of the law, precisely what one would expect of the Deuteronomic movement given its depiction of wisdom in the case of Solomon. But Jeremiah's view is that such a perspective is a perversion of the law, and that concomitantly the wisdom of such claimants is not wisdom at all.

But what did Jeremiah say that placed him at such odds with the Deuteronomic movement? And what did Jeremiah share with the 8th-century prophets that may have made them also a target of Deuteronomic polemic? As we shall see more fully in our treatment of the books named for Isaiah, Jeremiah, Hosea, Amos, and Micah (see Chapters 27, 28, 32, 34, and 37), almost certainly what disturbed our Deuteronomic writer of the Exile was the insistence of these prophets that God's judgment was made against the people of Israel, not on the basis of a covenant that entailed the keeping of a code of law (which was perhaps mediated by the Deuteronomic movement), but in light of their disregard for ordinary conventions of just human conduct and for simple

honor of the God of Israel. Moreover, the prophets presented themselves as the simple mouthpieces for divine speech to the people, speech that could issue in many different messages for God's people. It was perhaps threatening to the Deuteronomic movement to encounter such an approach to relating God to the people, since it contrasts sharply with the Deuteronomic notion that God's essential speech was restricted to the law code and the mediation of that code through its agents. Notably, when prophets do appear in the Deuteronomistic History they are either restricted mostly to doing miracles and stating the importance of observing God's law and the consequences for failing to do so (Elijah and Elisha), or to demonstrating that prophets themselves are subject to God's decrees (the man of God of 1 Kings 13) and can be very subversive, deceitful, and dangerous characters (the old prophet of 1 Kings 13).

On this view some are led to the conclusion that the Deuteronomic movement found as much offense in the memory of the 8th-century prophets and their own contemporary, Jeremiah, as they did in the David-Zion theology and wisdom theology. The prophetic speakers' message was a direct challenge to them, suggesting that it was not the law (mediated by the Deuteronomists?) that determined God's relationship to the people, but rather God's own direct and recurring speech (mediated by the prophets) that set the agenda for human-divine relations. Thus some perceive in the Deuteronomic stories of Elijah and Elisha as miracle workers and speakers of God's law in specific cases an attempt to constrain the office of the prophet, and the story of the man of God and the old prophet in 1 Kings 13 as commentary on the prophets' personalities and their subjection to the law of God. Some others, as we shall see, go further and see in the final editions of at least Jeremiah and Amos, if not also Micah, Hosea, and Isaiah, the evidence of a Deuteronomic editorial hand, one that sought perhaps to make the prophets into allies, not enemies of the Deuteronomic movement.

We cannot close this summary of the Deuteronomic perspective without observing a strange irony inherent in the Deuteronomistic History. Even if it holds to such a clear-eyed view of God as a God of retributive justice and of humanity as capable of cooperating with God in achieving God's plan, it tells a story that seems to contradict at every turn both premises. From the very beginning God backtracks on the promise to expel the people of Israel from the land if they fail in their keeping of the law, providing instead myriad less severe punishments and a corresponding number of second chances. As for the human capacity to cooperate in God's plan of retributive justice, here too the story line contradicts the basic premise. From the failure at Ai (Joshua 7), to the expulsion of Israel from its land (2 Kings 17), to the exile of Judeans from their homes (2 Kings 24–25), the people proved time and again a profound *incapacity* for cooperation in the divine plan. Instead their greatest capacity was for apostasy from true worship of the God of Israel, and for willful reverence for the gods of Canaan.

This recognition regarding the story line's contradiction of the basic theological premises of the Deuteronomic Collection leads one to wonder what it truly did accomplish theologically. True, its historical author may have intended it to promote the Deuteronomic agenda. And whatever his *intentions,* we shall see in much of the rest of this book that the basic ideas of the Deuteronomic Collection made a deep and lasting impact on Jewish and Christian theology. To name but a few of the books that build upon its principles we cite only Haggai and Zechariah 1–8 (Chapters 41 and 42), Daniel (Chapter 31) and James (Chapter 61). Yet at the same time, there can also be no doubt that the curiously contradictory story line of the Deuteronomistic History opened the door to challenges to the Deuteronomic writer's premises about God and humanity. As we shall see below in Chapters 21 and 24, the wisdom books of Job (perhaps) and (most certainly) Ecclesiastes were in part reactions to the theology we find in the Deuteronomic agenda. And if one accepts the Supplementary Hypothesis's dating of the Yahwist Work after the Deuteronomic Collection, the Yahwist Work is a direct response to the Deuteronomic writer's notions about God and humanity (see the relevant portions of Chapters 5, 6, 7, 8, and 10 above). Some aspects of the New Testament witness seem to make a point of challenging the notions of a God of retributive justice and humanity capable of cooperating in achieving God's plans for creation (see esp. Romans and Galatians, Chapter 57). And there are certainly many other texts of early Judaism that are not part of the canon that seem to have taken seriously the implications of the Deuteronomistic History for the notions of a God of retributive justice and a humanity possessed of robust powers of cooperation with God (see Chapter 44 for a discussion of some of these). In short, the Deuteronomistic History itself seems to have sown the seeds for a reconsideration of its agenda. And as we shall see more fully in our treatment of Jeremiah (Chapter 28), the epitome of the tendency to reconsider the powerfully articulated claims of the Deuteronomic writer may have come from the hand of a follower who knew the language of the movement, but despaired of the theology's capacity to prescribe accurately *or even describe* the human condition as it relates to the One God (Jer 31:31-34).

Questions for Review and Discussion

1 How does 1 Kings characterize the reign of Solomon, from his accession to the throne to the time of his death? How does the Deuteronomic writer handle Solomon's reputation as a man of renowned wisdom? How does the Deuteronomic writer "grade" Solomon as a king?

2 How might one explain the function of Elijah and Elisha in the Deuteronomistic History? What do they do for the Deuteronomistic portrait of "prophets" as a religious force in ancient Israel?

3 Summarize the themes and accomplishments of the Deuteronomic Collection and relate them to the perspective offered by the Yahwist Work as we surveyed it in the chapters on Genesis, Exodus, and Numbers. What difference does it make to take the view of the Supplementary Hypothesis or the Documentary Hypothesis with respect to the formation of the Pentateuch and the Deuteronomistic History?

Further Reading

Nelson, Richard D. *First and Second Kings*. Interpretation. Atlanta: John Knox, 1987.
Provan, Iain. *1 and 2 Kings*. OTG 11. Sheffield: Sheffield Academic, 1997.
Tomes, Roger. "1 and 2 Kings." In *ECB*, 246-81.

Chapter 18

The Chronicler's History: 1 and 2 Chronicles and Ezra-Nehemiah

Getting Started

1 Glance through 1 Chronicles 1–9. What genre dominates this long section of text? Which two tribes of Israel seem to receive the greatest attention in this section? Why do you think these two come in for such intense focus?

2 Glance through 1 Chronicles 10–29 and 2 Chronicles 1–9. Who are the two figures most prominent in this long section of text? How do the accounts of them match with what you know from 2 Samuel and 1 Kings?

3 Read Ezra 9–10 and Nehemiah 13:23-30. What do these two passages have in common? What does the issue addressed in each of them suggest about the concerns of Judeans living in postexilic, Persian-period Judah?

Preliminary Comments

1 and 2 Chronicles and Ezra and Nehemiah follow the Deuteronomistic History in the Christian canon. (Included among the Writings [Hebrew *Ketubim*], they

are the last books in the Hebrew Bible in reverse order, with 1 and 2 Chronicles following Ezra and Nehemiah.) They provide a renewed recital of Israel's history from Adam to the Babylonian destruction of Judah, and they add the story of the Judeans' repatriation to the land of Judah by Cyrus of Persia under the leadership of Judeans who included Ezra and Nehemiah. As we shall see in "Critical Issues" below, the question of common authorship for Ezra and Nehemiah, on the one hand, and 1 and 2 Chronicles, on the other hand, is far from settled. We treat them together, in any case, as they do form an identifiable block of material in the Old Testament, especially if we consider them from the perspective of an implied author and his readers.

It is also worth noting at the outset that one concern does hold these four books together, whether or not they were authored by one person or community of authors: the interest in providing a blueprint for the postexilic community situated in Judah after the end of the Babylonian Exile. As we shall see, it is a pattern that aimed to legitimate the temple and its functionaries as the center of that restored community and to do so by rooting their origins in the glory of the Davidic monarchy of the Preexilic period.

A Walk through 1 and 2 Chronicles and Ezra-Nehemiah

The shape of the Chronicler's Work betrays what we just observed: at its heart are extended treatments of the reigns of David and Solomon, the latter the founder of the temple and the former the root of the Davidic monarchy.

1 Chronicles 1–9: Genealogies

The genealogies in 1 Chronicles 1–9 move quickly from Adam to Abraham and his sons (1:1-34), then treat in the remainder of ch. 1 the descendants of Esau. Then 2:1-2 resumes the Abraham line with a list of the sons of Jacob/Israel, and 2:3–9:1 gives genealogies for the tribes of Israel. Though he was born fourth, Judah's genealogy comes first and he receives the lion's share of attention (2:3–4:23). This is surely due to the Chronicler's great interest in the line of David, and proof of that lies in the fact that ch. 3 is entirely devoted to the Davidic line, tracing it down to several generations after Zerubbabel. Another tribe that plays a prominent role is Levi (6:1-81), and this too gives away another of the Chronicler's interests, namely the Levitical line as the suppliers of temple functionaries. Also notable is the inclusion of the northern tribes, even though in the Postexilic period they were all but nonexistent. This signals the "all Israel" sensibility of the Chronicler, his desire to say that the restored community was no mere fragment of the nation that it once was.

1 Chronicles 9 lists those who returned after the Exile. This list includes people from the tribes of Judah, Benjamin, Ephraim, and Manasseh. The last two might be included because they reflect the northern contingent and confirm the Chronicler's view that all Israel reconstituted the Judean community in the Postexilic period. That being said, the list is, in fact, mostly a litany of temple personnel who made the journey back to Judah, including priests, Levites, temple singers, and gatekeepers. The chapter concludes, though, with a segue back to Saul's story (his genealogy from 8:29-40) so as to permit the narrator to begin the recitation of David's story with the last chapter of Saul's.

1 Chronicles 10–29: David's Reign

1 Chronicles 10 essentially repeats 1 Samuel 31, the story of Saul's demise. This sets the stage for an account of David's accession to the throne that is very different from the one we read in 2 Samuel wherein he is acclaimed by all Israel as king because of his successful service to Saul (1 Chronicles 11). Of course, this is a correction of the Samuel narratives where David first has to engage in a prolonged conflict with Saul, and then has

to gradually unify the twelve tribes under his leadership, at times by force. Also in this first chapter on David's reign we read that he takes Jerusalem immediately (a sign of the city's primacy for this author), and that he establishes his chiefs and warriors (cf. 2 Samuel 23) to consolidate his power. Then 1 Chronicles 12 narrates the growth in David's prestige and power with material that has virtually no parallels with Samuel narratives.

1 Chronicles 13 and 15, an account of how David brought the ark of the covenant to Jerusalem, provides further evidence of the author's special interest in Levites and his desire to sanitize David's reign. (Chapter 14 underscores David's success in Jerusalem and provides an explanation of his preparation of a place for the ark.) Chapter 13 repeats 2 Sam 6:1-11 (the first attempt to bring the ark and Uzzah's death on touching it) with much faithfulness, but when we come to the conclusion of the episode in 1 Chronicles 15, the author notably adds a careful account of David's appointment of Levites to transport the ark to Jerusalem. The author explains that Uzzah's death results from the wrong personnel being assigned to the task: God prefers Levites. Likewise, once the ark arrives in Jerusalem, the author omits Michal's rebuke of David and David's churlish response to her.

The rest of the account of David's reign may be summarized quickly. The Chronicler reports the staffing of the sanctuaries with Levites (ch. 16), the dynastic promise to David and David's prayer (ch. 17), an account of how David's kingdom expanded (chs. 18–20), David's census of Israel (ch. 21), David's preparation for the construction of the temple (ch. 22), the establishment of a national administration (ch. 23), David's priestly appointments of the Levites (ch. 24), and the establishment of temple singers, gatekeepers, and treasurers, and of military leaders and other administrators (chs. 25–27). With the administrative organization of the kingdom established, the text then recounts the people's ratification of David's notice to them that Solomon should follow him on the throne in Jerusalem and David's provision of a plan and endowments for the temple that Solomon would build (ch. 28; 29:1-9). Finally, the remainder of 1 Chronicles 29 relates David's farewell prayer, his death, and the transfer of power to Solomon.

It is most important to observe several things about this lengthy treatment of David's reign. First, it sanitizes the version of David's reign in Samuel by omitting the worst elements of it, including such things as David's conflict with Saul, the Bathsheba affair, David's alliance with the Philistines, and other such difficult episodes. And where it was necessary to narrate something problematic — the census from 2 Samuel 24 because it resulted in David's possession of the site for the temple! — the Chronicler makes the cause of David's sin to be Satan the "Adversary," not the Lord. (See the discussion of Satan in the Hebrew Bible.) Second, as we have seen, Levites take a privileged position in the Chronicler's account of David's reign, while in Samuel they are barely mentioned. And last, the Chronicler transfers primary responsibility for the founding of the temple in Jerusalem from Solomon to David so as to root the institution in the glory days of the monarchy and under the rule of its greatest representative (from the Chronicler's perspective).

2 Chronicles 1–9: Solomon's Reign

This section focuses mostly on Solomon's construction and dedication of the temple. In ch. 1 we read of Solomon's early reign and prosperity, and chs. 2–4 narrate his preparation for and actual construction of the temple. Chapter 5 recounts the transfer of the ark of the covenant to the temple, and ch. 6 reproduces Solomon's prayer at the dedication of the temple from 1 Kings 8 (with some changes typical of the Chronicler's interests). Likewise, ch. 7 provides God's reply to Solomon from 1 Kgs 9:1-9 that makes the dynastic promise conditional on Deuteronomic terms, but the Chronicler adds further material to exalt the temple and ensure that it is the only place to offer petitions to God. Finally 2 Chronicles recites approvingly deeds and events from Solomon's reign, including his great wealth. With David his father, Solomon ruled over the most glorious period of Israel's existence.

Here too the Chronicler has to sanitize the Deuteronomist's account he inherited. He omits Solomon's purge of Adonijah and those who oppose him (1 Kings 2), his marriage to foreign women and construction of shrines to other gods (1 Kgs 11:1-13), and the prophecy of Ahijah regarding the consequences of Solomon's mistakes (1 Kgs 11:26-40). It is a matter of some interest that the Chronicler also omits Solomon's judgment between the two women over their single child (1 Kgs 3:16-

Satan in the Hebrew Bible

Although the name Satan occurs more than 20 times in the Old Testament, he actually appears in only four books: in Numbers 22; 1 Chronicles 21; Job 1-2; and Zechariah 3. In no one of these cases is Satan anything more than a member of the heavenly council, albeit a problematic member. In Num 22:22, 32 it is the "angel of the Lord" who comes to oppose Balaam the prophet; here he seems to play a positive role, although one must admit that the story makes it somewhat ambiguous. In 1 Chr 21:1 we only hear that he, not God, incites David to count the people of Israel. In Job 1–2 he is "one of the heavenly beings" (1:6), whose job apparently it is to patrol the earth (1:7). It is his questioning of Job's righteousness that provokes God to test Job (for more on this episode, see Chapter 21). And in Zech 3:1, 2 he is a heavenly council member who urges the purification of the high priest, Joshua, and the reinvestment of Joshua with pure priestly garments (for more on this episode, see Chapter 42). Satan's reputation, then, is that of a heavenly being who is a bit mischievous. That his name derives from a verb root meaning "to accuse" and is related to a noun meaning "opponent, accuser" is hardly surprising. Thus it should also hardly be surprising that in later Jewish texts he comes to play the role of full-fledged opponent to God and all things belonging to God. This dichotomy between the heavenly realm and its beings and an evil realm and its inhabitants ("Satan" is not the only name for demonic beings; see, e.g., Asmodeus in Tobit [see Chapter 44]) may have had its roots in exposure to Persian dualism (Zoroastrianism is a possibility) or simply in the Jewish experience of evil so complete that it became necessary to spare God responsibility for it. In any case, remember that within the Hebrew Scriptures, Satan is just an ornery council member!

28). One wonders if the Chronicler also understood that this might not have been such a complimentary tale for Solomon (see Chapter 17 above).

2 Chronicles 10–36: The Kings of Judah

While 1 Kings 12–2 Kings 17 narrates the succession of kings in Israel and Judah until the fall of the Northern Kingdom, 2 Chronicles ignores the northern kings entirely, except for when events in the north impact the story in Judah. This section may be divided as follows: 2 Chronicles 10–16 relates events from Rehoboam to Asa, chs. 17–25 cover the period from Jehoshaphat to Joash, chs. 26–32 account for the period from Uzziah to Hezekiah, and chs. 33–36 recount events from Manasseh to the Exile.

The Chronicler's account of Judah engages in the same sanitizing of royal records that it did in retelling the reigns of David and Solomon, especially on matters of cultic fidelity. For example, Abijah is described negatively in 1 Kgs 15:1-8, but 2 Chronicles 13 makes him a heroic guardian of the Davidic kingdom. Jehoshaphat, whose reign is only briefly summarized in 1 Kgs 22:41-44, receives sustained attention in 2 Chr 17:1–21:1 to serve a variety of the Chronicler's special interests, including ch. 20, which demonstrates how ritualized battle that depends on priestly leadership is the successful mode of war-making. And most significantly, the account of Hezekiah's rule is expanded to make him as great as or even greater than Josiah in his zeal for cultic purity; indeed, says the Chronicler, Hezekiah cleanses the temple before Josiah, celebrates Passover before Josiah, and sees to it that the Levites attend to their appointed liturgical tasks like David before him (2 Chronicles 29–32).

One of the more peculiar twists is the Chronicler's handling of Manasseh (2 Chr 33:1-20). He adds an episode in which the king is made captive in Babylon where he repents for his apostasy in Jerusalem. He is then returned to Jerusalem where he undoes the evidence of his earlier sin and prays to God (a reference that engendered the Prayer of Manasseh of the Septuagint and some editions of the Apocrypha). This story of Manasseh's sojourn in Babylon was inserted perhaps to explain the length of Manasseh's rule and his peaceful death in spite of the record of his apostasy in 2 Kings.

This section of 2 Chronicles concludes with an updated version of Josiah's reign (chs. 34–35) and a summary account of the last four kings of Judah and the Babylonian conquest (ch. 36). Interestingly, blame for the Exile falls not on Manasseh, but on a larger collection of people including kings, priests, and people for their religious infidelity.

Ezra 1–6: Return to Judah and Reconstruction of the Temple

The first four verses of Ezra are critical for understanding much of what follows. They provide a recitation of Cyrus' decree that the Judeans in Babylonian exile return to Jerusalem to rebuild their temple (Ezra 1:1-4).

> In the first year of King Cyrus of Persia, in order that the word of the Lord by the mouth of Jeremiah might be accomplished, the Lord stirred up the spirit of King Cyrus of Persia so that he sent a herald throughout all his kingdom, and also in a written edict declared: "Thus says King Cyrus of Persia: The Lord, the God of heaven, has given me all the kingdoms of the earth, and he has charged me to build him a house at Jerusalem in Judah.

> Any of those among you who are of his people — may their God be with them! — are now permitted to go up to Jerusalem in Judah, and rebuild the house of the Lord, the God of Israel — he is the God who is in Jerusalem; and let all survivors, in whatever place they reside, be assisted by the people of their place with silver and gold, with goods and with animals, besides freewill offerings for the house of God in Jerusalem."

The first two verses are also the last verses of 2 Chronicles 36, a sign of the conjoined nature of 1 and 2 Chronicles with Ezra-Nehemiah. Then follows a copy of the decree issued by Cyrus of Persia in 538 B.C.E. It reflects his policy of recognizing the gods of his subject peoples and encouraging them to worship their gods through sacrifice. He only asks that priests collect taxes to help fund the empire's other activities.

The enlightened imperial policy not only provided for the restoration in Judea, but also prompted the activities reported in the rest of Ezra-Nehemiah. The first of these are reported in Ezra 1. At the behest of the Persian Empire Sheshbazzar returns with a first wave of émigrés and the temple vessels to commence the temple's reconstruction. Some believe that Sheshbazzar and his compatriots were only able to establish the foundations of the new temple before their work broke off.

Ezra 2 then lists a group of returnees under the leadership of Zerubbabel, suggesting a second repatriation (dated usually to 522). Reflecting the author's interest in bloodline purity, this congregation of returnees is constituted by Israelites (laity), priests, and Levites as separate and distinct groups. Next, Ezra 3 relates the activities of this group in rebuilding the altar and founding the Second Temple (the first being Solomon's sanctuary).

Ezra 4–6 then narrates the opposition locals provide to the rebuilding effort and the eventual resolution of conflict between the returnees and the people already in the land through the intervention of Persian officials. The sequence of events is this. First, the locals ask to join in the rebuilding effort because they say they worship the same God as the returnees (thus they may have been descendants of those who remained in Judah after the Babylonian defeat). Then the returnees reject the offer of assistance, perhaps out of further concern for purity, although the text observes that it is a matter of obeying Cyrus's decree. The people of the land then complain to the Persian ruler that the rebuilders are actually refortifying the city toward the goal of rebelling against Persian rule, and that if the records were to be checked the king would know that these people have a long history of rebellion; the king's reply confirms what the locals have suggested and reconstruction efforts are halted. (Some speculate that this letter about wall-rebuilding is out of place and belongs later, with the Nehemiah mission.) But the prophets Haggai and Zechariah (whom we shall meet at greater length later in Chapters 41 and 42) exhort the returnees to renewed building efforts, and when they are questioned by the Persians regarding the legitimacy of their work, they appeal to Cyrus's original decree and are then permitted by the emperor to continue their work on the temple. After this series of letter exchanges is reported, Ezra 6 completes the story with the finalization of the rebuilding effort, a temple dedication and celebration of Passover.

Ezra 7-10; Nehemiah 8-9: The Ezra Memoirs

Ezra 7–10 and Nehemiah 8–9 recount Ezra's mission in Jerusalem. Although other explanations are offered for this arrangement of the material, it seems most likely that Nehemiah 8–9 was somehow misplaced. In any case, Ezra 7 gives Ezra's pedigree (which connects him to the best scribal and priestly bloodlines) and the royal letter authorizing him to oversee the religious and daily life of Jerusalem and the temple. Then Ezra 8 narrates Ezra's extensive preparations to depart for Jerusalem, which entail gathering the entourage and ritual preparation of the entourage as its members would serve the temple upon arrival there. Finally, the text narrates the group's departure and celebrated arrival in the city. As we shall see below in "Critical Issues," many date these events to 458, although there is no certainty on this matter nor on the question of how it conflicts with what we know of Nehemiah's mission.

Ezra 9–10 tells of the discovery that some men of Judah were marrying women not from among their own people and of Ezra's and the community's response. The explanation the text offers for why this is problematic comes in Ezra's penitential prayer or sermon that recalls the consequences of intermarriage in the days before the Exile: the people worshiped the gods of their foreign spouses and thus were apostate. For fear of a repetition of the Exile, Ezra decrees that the foreign wives and their children should be divorced and sent away and that those who refuse to follow this decree will lose their property in the new temple community. The result of the decree and the attendant threat is communal compliance.

Assuming that Nehemiah 8–9 completes Ezra's memoirs and was simply misplaced, it appears that the people respond to this crisis with a renewal of their dedication to the Torah. They gather together in Jerusalem to hear the Torah read aloud (and translated into Aramaic, the common language of the Persian Em-

pire). Then they celebrate the Feast of Booths, and Ezra recites to them in yet another prayer the history of God from creation to their present moment.

Nehemiah 1–7; 10–13: The Nehemiah Memoirs

Again, assuming that the present state of Ezra-Nehemiah is somewhat confused due to an error in transmission, it seems likely that Nehemiah 1–7; 10–13 recounts the missions of the book's namesake, the first beginning around 445 B.C.E. and ending in 433 and the second coming some years later. Like Ezra, Nehemiah receives a commission to serve Persia in Judea and sets out with a prayer to undertake his task. Upon arrival, Nehemiah discovers that the city's walls need attention and he sets out immediately to attend to the matter. However, as Nehemiah 2 draws to a close we learn that Nehemiah is opposed by Sanballat, the Horonite, and Tobiah, the Ammonite, apparently because they fear a too-powerful Jerusalem. Nonetheless the restoration work goes forward and boundaries of Jerusalem in all four directions are restored (Nehemiah 3). Then Nehemiah 4–6 narrates the obstacles to reconstruction that Nehemiah faces: threats from outsiders, economic difficulties, and plots against Nehemiah. For all of that, the close of ch. 6 still announces that the walls are completed. Nehemiah 7 then records how Nehemiah sets up gatekeepers into the city, and it reiterates the list of returnees that appears first in Ezra 2, as if to say that the end of the reconstruction effort stands in continuity with its beginning.

The Nehemiah memoir resumes in Nehemiah 10 with a list of signatories to agreements regarding various religious obligations. Among others they include the agreement not to intermarry with the people of the land, not to do business on the Sabbath, to forego crops and the exaction of debt in the Sabbatical Year, and to provide yearly a one-third shekel tax for the temple, the wood offering for the altar, gifts of the firstfruits and firstborn, and tithes for temple personnel. Nehemiah 11 continues with the assignment of people to towns and villages for repopulation and a census of the repopulated city and surrounding settlements. Nehemiah 12:1-26 provides another list, this time a review of the priestly and Levitical genealogies. Then Nehemiah reports in 12:27–13:3 that the people gather to dedicate the wall, even purifying the wall itself to make the city holy.

Nehemiah 13 closes out the memoir with a report of events that occur on Nehemiah's second mission to Jerusalem after he had returned to Artaxerxes. While he was away the community had violated some of the stipulations made in ch. 10, including housing Tobiah the Ammonite in the temple, failing to see to the portions

Hasmonean tower built on a portion of the wall of Nehemiah, traces of which can be seen in the lower courses of the tower and in other portions of the wall behind and beside the tower. (W. S. LaSor)

assigned to the Levites and temple singers, violating the Sabbath, and engaging in intermarriage. Nehemiah responds to each matter according to the laws of the Torah (e.g., Tobiah is evicted from the temple precincts on the basis of Deut 23:3).

Critical Issues in the Study of the Chronicler's Work

Several critical issues have attracted scholarly attention to 1 and 2 Chronicles and Ezra-Nehemiah, not the least of which is the relationship between the Chronicles

books and Ezra and Nehemiah, that is, whether the two pairs of books come from the same author or school of thought. Also of note are the sources that were used in creating all four books, ranging from the Samuel and Kings books in 1 and 2 Chronicles to Persian imperial correspondence in Ezra and Nehemiah. Finally, there is some natural interest in the historical context and circumstances surrounding the missions of Ezra and Nehemiah as well as the efforts of their predecessors, Sheshbazzar and Zerubbabel.

The Relationship Between 1 and 2 Chronicles and Ezra and Nehemiah

As we noted in Chapter 12 on the "Historical Books," since the early 19th century, scholars have argued that Chronicles and Ezra and Nehemiah were all composed by a single author or at least by authors who hailed from the same school of thought. Several arguments are usually cited in favor of this view. First, the end of the Chronicler's account, 2 Chr 36:22-23, is repeated by Ezra 1:1-3a. Second, a related deuterocanonical book, 1 Esdras, contains 2 Chronicles 35–36; Ezra 1–10; Nehemiah 8. Third, the books share some otherwise unusual terminology and genres (e.g., "house of God" and the extensive use of lists and genealogies). Finally, they have in common distinctive themes, including particular concern for the temple in Jerusalem, the priesthood, and the Levites and their functions. More recent scholarship, however, has questioned the association of Chronicles with Ezra and Nehemiah. Among the arguments for this view scholars note that the clear concern for retributive justice throughout Chronicles is absent in Ezra and Nehemiah; the two works take differing views of the northern tribes; and the Chronicler is intensely interested in the Davidic dynasty while David's rule is of little interest in Ezra-Nehemiah. In short, there is little consensus on the precise relationship between the Chronicler's work and Ezra-Nehemiah.

Whatever the truth about the common authorship of Chronicles and Ezra-Nehemiah, the matter can be simplified somewhat. If one is mostly interested, as we are, in the implied author — that is, the one that the text as we receive it conveys — as well as that author's audience, it seems best to read these books as at least very closely related. The overlap between the conclusion of 2 Chronicles and the beginning of Ezra invites recipients to read them together, rather than separately. Likewise, their common interests are stronger and more numerous than the differences just listed. Anyway, the divergences cited above are for the most part expected due to the different periods narrated by the two bodies of work. For example, a lack of concern for the Davidic dynasty is not surprising in Ezra-Nehemiah as it is a

Cyrus cylinder (536 B.C.E.) permitting release of captives back to their own lands and aiding the restoration of their temples. (British Museum)

work about Judah in the Postexilic period, when Persian imperial policy prohibited the renewal of the monarchy, let alone the restoration of a royal dynasty! Thus the most sensible option remains that of considering all four books as projecting a relatively common perspective and agenda.

Sources in 1 and 2 Chronicles

There is clear evidence of "intertextuality" in 1 and 2 Chronicles. The genealogical notices in 1 Chronicles 2–8 depend on Genesis, Exodus, Numbers, Joshua, Samuel, and Ruth. Allusions to prophetic texts and Psalms are apparent as well (e.g., Jer 25:11-12; 29:10 in 2 Chr 36:21; Psalms 96, 105, 106 in 1 Chr 16:7-36). But obviously the most prevalent source from the Hebrew Scriptures is Samuel-Kings, as is evident from the occasional references above in our survey of the books' contents. What is perhaps most remarkable in this is the way the Chronicler has sanitized his source, eliminating embarrassing episodes in the reigns of David and Solomon and even embellishing the reigns of others who receive little attention in the Deuteronomistic History. Observers also note that the Chronicler rearranged source material from the Deuteronomistic History, an example of which is the transfer of the list of David's great men in 2 Samuel 23 to the beginning of David's reign in 1 Chronicles 11.

The question of whether the Chronicler had other sources than those already mentioned is unsettled.

The choice is generally between assigning material not paralleled in the Deuteronomistic History to the Chronicler or to other sources. The Chronicler does refer to other sources from time to time (e.g., 2 Chr 9:29), but he may have been referring to the Deuteronomistic History itself on those occasions.

Sources in Ezra-Nehemiah

It is clear that the author of Ezra-Nehemiah also had sources, most particularly Ezra's and Nehemiah's memoirs. These may have been similar to reports from Persian appointees to their imperial overlords. A convenient comparison is found in the record of Udjahoresnet, an Egyptian priest who was brought by Cambyses, an earlier Persian ruler, to Persia to learn the imperial style of government. Educated accordingly, Udjahoresnet returned to his own land as an indigenous ruler employing local patterns and religious practices to implement Persian policy. Ezra and Nehemiah's memoirs at times have the aura of reports providing evidence that they are accomplishing just that task.

Other sources in Ezra-Nehemiah are the Persian decrees and letter exchanges, including the Cyrus decree (Ezra 1:2-4) and various letters sent between Persia and Judah (e.g., Ezra 5:6-17, the letter from Tattenai to Darius). That these are in some degree authentic is evident from the fact that they are preserved in Aramaic, the language of the empire.

Scholars speculate that still other sources were used by the author of Ezra-Nehemiah to compose the two books. We cannot be certain of these, nor of where they begin or break off.

The History of the Return and the Evidence of Ezra-Nehemiah

The history of the return under Ezra and Nehemiah and their predecessors can be reconstructed from the two books with some certainty. We hear first of Sheshbazzar returning with an entourage under the Edict of Cyrus (538 B.C.E.). His period of influence seems to have been brief, and he failed to reconstruct the temple, as mandated by Persia, for we next encounter Zerubbabel in Ezra 3:2, 8; 5:2 and Neh 12:1. Thanks to a reference in the dated speech of the postexilic prophet Zechariah (4:9; see Chapter 42 below), we know that Zerubbabel (and the accompanying high priest Joshua) were active in Jerusalem around 521/520, and they were the ones who saw to the rebuilding of the temple. Thus there appears to have been a nearly two-decade delay in accomplishing what Persia had ordered, apparently in part due to neglect on the part of the returnees (Haggai, Zechariah's contemporary, notes that people were more intent on building their paneled homes than reconstructing the Lord's house), and, as Ezra explains it, because of conflict with people who occupied the land when the returnees arrived. The delay may also have been possible because the Persian Empire was undergoing considerable internal turmoil that may have permitted regions on the empire's periphery — such as Judah — to ignore imperial demands without too much consequence. But with the rise of Darius as emperor in 521 the turmoil came to an end, and delays in carrying out Persian policy were no longer acceptable.

The next moment we can isolate is the beginning of Ezra's mission. The beginning of his activity is assigned to the seventh year of the reign of Artaxerxes, and most scholars assume the reference is to Artaxerxes I, who governed from 465 to 424. Thus Ezra commenced his mission in 458. He was most probably sent by Persia to function as a Judean Udjahoresnet (see above), to help win the loyalty of locals by his indigenous leadership and by his promulgation of laws the Judeans accepted (the Torah). Ezra's concerns included, as we saw, the issue of intermarriage and its potential impact on the postexilic Judean community.

That Nehemiah had to deal with the issues surveyed above in his mission some 13 years after Ezra's activity indicates something of the weakness with which Ezra's reforms took hold. In any case, most calculate that Nehemiah was active from 445 to 443, returned to Persia for a few years, and came back again to attend to the issues detailed in Nehemiah 13. It is this last account in particular that echoes the sort of reports we might expect an Udjahoresnet to have been sending back to the imperial rulers.

In closing this section it is worth recalling what we observed in Chapter 3 above regarding the socio-historical dynamics in Persian-era Judah as a way of understanding the fixation of Ezra and Nehemiah on the question of intermarriage. True, they were anxious to avoid repeating the sins of Solomon in encouraging the worship of foreign gods through marriage to non-Israelite women (Neh 13:26-27) and to ensure the continued use of their own language and the culture it bore (13:24). But especially noteworthy is the fact that Ezra 10:8 mandates that men who fail to give up their foreign wives and the children born of those wives *forfeit their land.* The fear was apparently that through intermarriage and the eventual transfer of property to children who may have chosen to honor the god of the non-Israelite parent land would be removed from the temple economy. And given the truly pluralistic conditions experienced by returning Judeans during the early Persian period, such fears were perhaps not unfounded. This was a community that, though given charge over the land, could just as easily lose control of it through assimilation with the local population. So whatever the exact chronology of the material preserved in Ezra and Nehemiah, we can be relatively certain of its association with the postexilic effort to sustain order in potentially chaotic conditions, an endeavor not unlike that of the Priestly Writer.

Theological Themes in the Chronicler's Work

The theological themes in the Chronicler's Work are largely focused on the line of David and the temple, its personnel, and its operation. In many ways it looks to be an apologetic for David and his line and an elaboration of details associated with the temple cult. Thus the Chronicler's Work is, in a sense, derivative of earlier traditions such as the David-Zion theology and the Priestly Work; or perhaps it is better to say that it is deeply influenced by them. Also key for the Chronicler was the Torah, which he linked intimately with the first two interests mentioned. As a result what emerges in reading the Chronicler's Work are three theological foci: the line of David, the temple, and the Torah. Likewise, what we discover in the Chronicler's Work is an intense interest in the offices of the king and the priest, fascinations of some note in the Postexilic period when the work came into existence, at least inasmuch as we do not expect a postexilic author to dare show such interest in kings (see our discussion of Persian imperial policy above in Chapter 3). But as it turns out, the dual focus is, in fact, one that works toward directing most attention to the temple and its leaders.

The Covenant with David

In that so much space is devoted to the line of Judah from early on (see esp. 1 Chr 2:3–4:23), the Chronicler's focus on the covenant with David is evident. The further evidence of this interest is plain in the Chronicler's concern to tell extensively the story of David's and Solomon's reigns (1 Chronicles 10–29; 2 Chronicles 1–9) and sanitize them and to do the same to a lesser extent for other Davidic descendants whose records in the Deuteronomistic History were also somewhat questionable. Of course, it is easy to see in all of this the influence of the David-Zion theology we saw being critiqued in parts of the Deuteronomistic History and that we will see exalted by figures like Isaiah of Jerusalem. At first glance, the Chronicler looks to have been an ardent fan of the Davidic line, even as an author writing for a Persian-era audience, one that did not dare entertain the restoration of kingship lest the Persian authorities find in that cause to rescind the privileges of self-rule through religious leaders.

But for all of this, a closer look suggests that the real focus of the Chronicler's concern for the covenant with David is on its role in legitimating and establishing the temple and its cult. By pushing the founding of the temple and the establishment of the cultic personnel back to David's reign (not just Solomon's rule; see esp. David's temple-construction charge to Solomon in 1 Chronicles 22) the Chronicler ties the two realities together. Just so, in the Chronicles account of the kings of Judah and Israel their success or failure hinges on their adherence to the patterns established in David's reign. So Israel's kings are doomed from the outset and are of no real interest to the Chronicler, and southern kings are judged accordingly. Thus the Chronicler is not, as one might suppose, counseling rebellion against Persia with his interest in kingship; rather he is laying the basis for the importance of the temple on the solid foundation of the Davidic tradition, calling perhaps on widespread fondness for it in spite of its absence in practice.

The Temple Cult

Further evidence of this author's more intense interest in the temple cult is plain enough from the survey of Chronicles' and Ezra's and Nehemiah's contents given above. In 1 Chronicles 1–9 one lengthy chapter is devoted to the genealogy of the line of Levi (6:1-81) to show where the temple personnel came from. In 1 Chronicles 9 we read a listing of the returnees from exile that is dominated with an enumeration of priests, Levites, temple singers, and gatekeepers. Evidence of the author's particular interest in Levites is the adjusted retelling of the first, failed attempt by David to have the ark brought to Jerusalem: Uzzah's death upon touching the ark stemmed, in fact, from the failure to have proper Levite personnel carrying the ark! More indication of a fascination with the temple is the material in ch. 22 detailing *David's* preparation for the construction of the temple, as well as the appointment of Levites and other temple personnel in chs. 24–27. 2 Chronicles 1–9 focuses mostly on Solomon's preparation for and construction of the First Temple.

In Ezra and Nehemiah the focus is likewise placed on the temple. Ezra 1–6, though on the surface all about the return to the land of Judah, tells of events that were entirely directed at creating the conditions necessary for the temple's restoration. Ezra 1 tells of how the return was engineered by the Persians explicitly to establish the temple and its operations. Ezra 2, in listing the returnees, focuses in particular on the supply of temple personnel who returned. Ezra 4–6 hones in on the conflict between the returnees and the people who had remained regarding participation in the temple's reconstruction. Ezra 9-10 is concerned to address the problems posed for worship of the God of Israel (in the temple!) when men married foreign women. And Nehemiah 8–9 (perhaps the completion of Ezra's memoirs; see above) gathers the people in Jerusalem before the temple for a hearing of the Torah and then a celebration of a feast that entailed temple activity. Nehemiah 10 returns to the focus on the temple with agreements regarding religious obligations, at the center of which stands a variety of responsibilities to the temple and its personnel. Nehemiah 12:1-26 reviews rather abruptly the priestly and Levitical genealogies, and at the last, in ch. 13 Nehemiah sees to the purity of the temple precincts by expelling Tobiah the Ammonite from within its boundaries and ensuring once more that men not marry foreign women and threaten the community with failure to worship God properly in the temple.

This rehearsal of the temple-centered material in Chronicles and Ezra-Nehemiah speaks clearly about the temple's centrality to these four books and in part holds them together as a single work, whether authored by one person or not. But we also observe in this the influence of the Priestly worldview articulated so clearly in the Tetrateuch (esp. in Genesis 1; 17; 23; Exodus 12; 25–31; 35–40; Leviticus 1–16; and Numbers 1–10; 16–18; 25). The keen interest of the Chronicler's Work in highlighting a temple and the economy it engenders, the personnel it employs, and the religious interests of purity and clear communal identity it serves can hardly be missed and likewise cannot be understood apart from the agenda of the Priestly Writer in the Tetrateuch. While aspects of the Chronicler's agenda may diverge from those found in the Priestly traditions, there can be no doubting that they are related phenomena and that in the books discussed here the imprint of the Priestly Writer can be plainly seen.

The Torah

When one notes that nearly 20 percent of all occurrences of the word "Torah" in the Hebrew Bible appear in 1 Chronicles to Nehemiah, it is already apparent that the true heart of this author's concern is something like what we have come to know as the Pentateuch. Indeed, the Chronicler's first use of the word Torah in 1 Chr 16:40 indicates that David charged Zadok with offering "burnt offerings to the Lord on the altar of burnt offering regularly, morning and evening, in accordance with everything written in the *Law of the Lord, which he had given Israel." The Chronicler's pressing concern for temple and sacrifice and for its personnel, it seems, came from the Torah.* Similarly, in David's commission to Solomon in 1 Chronicles 22 he admonishes Solomon to "keep the *Law of your Lord God."* This is an expansion of Solomon's own speech at the dedication of the temple in which he recalls his father's admonition regarding temple construction, *but without reference to the Torah.* We could multiply many times over examples of this elevation of Torah in the Chronicler's rewriting of source material, and they would repeatedly signal what we see here: the Chronicler's "Torah sensibility," his implicit claim that his driving interests in the line of David and the temple and its operation derive from the Torah and its instructions. The Chronicler, in this sense, signals the early triumph of the Torah in postexilic Judaism, its growing influence over virtually all religious imagination.

Questions for Review and Discussion

1   What do we mean in this chapter by the term the "Chronicler's Work"? Is it universally agreed that the books we assign to this are genuinely from a single author or school of authors?

2   What are the key interests of the Chronicler? How do those interests square with Persian imperial policy? What do they indicate about the author's principal theological interests?

3   What seems to be the source of the Chronicler's interests? What does your answer to this question indicate about the Old Testament as a "self-referencing" work? Is this something one might call "intertextuality"?

Further Reading

1 and 2 Chronicles

Coggins, Richard J. "1 and 2 Chronicles." In *ECB*, 282-312.

Endres, John C., William R. Millar, and John Barclay Burns, eds. *Chronicles and Its Synoptic Parallels in Samuel, Kings, and Related Biblical Texts.* Collegeville: Liturgical, 1998.

Graham, M. Patrick, Steven L. McKenzie, and Gary N. Knoppers, eds. *The Chronicler as Theologian.* JSOTSup 371. London: T. & T. Clark, 2003.

Jones, Gwilym H. *1 & 2 Chronicles.* OTG. Sheffield: JSOT, 1993.

Ezra and Nehemiah

Grabbe, Lester L. "Ezra." In *ECB,* 313-19.
———. "Nehemiah." In *ECB,* 320-28.
Williamson, H. G. M. *Ezra and Nehemiah.* Sheffield: JSOT, 1987.

Chapter 19

Esther

Getting Started

1 Read Esther 1. Given the tenor of this account of the king's banquet and his own behavior, what might you conclude about the story's view of Gentiles?

2 Read Esther 2. What does this chapter indicate regarding the character assigned to Jews in this story?

3 On the basis of your reading of Esther 1–2, what are the indications regarding the book's quality as historiography?

Preliminary Comments

The book of Esther, placed after Nehemiah because it is set in the Persian period, is in fact a novella or "court tale" surely written many years after the time in which its story is placed. As a matter of genre it is most closely associated with texts like Daniel 1–6, another collection of court tales, or the story of Joseph in Pharaoh's court in Genesis 37–50. While this says little about the date of the book of Esther, it does indicate quite a bit about how we should approach it — as a tale told to instruct and cultivate in its recipients certain attitudes toward the world around them, *not* as history. And yet, as we shall see, the book of Esther is also the ostensible basis for the Feast of Purim.

A Walk through the Book of Esther

The book of Esther takes the shape of an ancient "court tale," an entertaining story from the halls of royalty.

Esther 1–2: The Persian King's Harem and Court; Esther and Mordecai

The story begins with an account of how King Ahasuerus of Persia (= Xerxes I, 485-465 B.C.E.) throws a lavish festival and feast lasting 180 days for his friends and fellow nobility, and how at the same time his Queen, Vashti, likewise gives a party for the women of the palace (1:1-9). That such parties actually took place in the Persian Empire is highly likely, since Greek writers mention sumptuous festivals and feasts associated with Persian kings, but the 180 days of Ahasuerus' party reflects the hyperbole typical of the book. In any case, 1:10-22 reveals that on this particular occasion the king grows intoxicated by the seventh day of merriment and calls for Queen Vashti to dance before him and his intoxicated guests; she refuses, and for her refusal is dethroned as Ahasuerus' queen. All in the kingdom are informed of this and an unchangeable law commanding wifely submission to husbands is decreed!

We learn first about Mordecai and Esther in the following chapter. As it turns out, Mordecai is a Benjaminite who has been delivered into exile under Babylonian rule, and Esther is his cousin for whom he cares in the absence of her deceased parents. (This fact alone makes clear the nonhistorical character of the book; Mordecai could hardly have been part of the Babylonian deportation and still alive to tell about it in the period of Persian kings.) When King Ahasuerus decides it is necessary to replace Vashti, Esther turns up in the kingdomwide search for the most beautiful woman. Thus she is taken into the king's harem and there she is prepared over the course of a year for her audience with the king. When that audience comes, if the king finds pleasure in the young woman of the occasion, she will be invited back to his presence; otherwise her relationship with the king ends then and there. Esther, for her part, not only finds favor with him, but is determined to be so perfect as to fulfill the role of Vashti's replacement. While all this transpires, Mordecai keeps watch over his cousin by loitering at the king's gate, where he overhears a plot against the king, informs on the conspirators, and so saves the king's life.

Esther 3–5: Haman and Mordecai; Esther and Mordecai; Esther and the King

While these events are transpiring, King Ahasuerus promotes Haman, an Agagite, to the post of something like Prime Minister. In honor of his status Haman expects all to bow as he passes, something Mordecai, the Benjaminite, will not do. Esther 3:4 merely indicates that as a Jew Mordecai will not do this; perhaps the text hints as well that the old enmity between the tribe of Benjamin and the people of Agag has something to do with Mordecai's reticence to do obeisance (1 Sam 15:7-9). In any case, Haman's rage at this slight — and perhaps at Saul's defeat of his ancestors! — is apparently without bounds, as he seeks and gains the king's approval to destroy all Jews in the kingdom as recompense for Mordecai's lack of respect for him; notably, Haman does not explain who the people are that he seeks to destroy, only that their laws differ from the king's and they do not keep his law (Esther 3).

Hearing of Haman's plans, Mordecai sends word to Esther that she should intercede with the king to save her people. Her reply through an intermediary is that under the law anyone who seeks an audience with the king and is not welcomed by him will die. Mordecai's reply through the same mediator is that Esther will suffer the same fate as all Jews, even if she is within the walls

of the king's house. This eliminates her reticence and, in sharp contrast to the king's feast and the banquets that Esther soon requests, she implores Mordecai to call a fast on her behalf as she prepares herself to request an appointment with King Ahasuerus to plead for her people's lives (ch. 4). (Note that the fast the people and Esther and her maidens take up is not accompanied by prayer, as one might expect from other descriptions of the practice in the Hebrew Bible; yet the Additions to the Book of Esther solves that problem, by providing a prayer in this spot; see "Critical Issues" below.)

Esther 5 then narrates Esther's anxious, but successful, approach to the king. Upon seeing her he raises his scepter to her and announces his willingness to fulfill her every request. At this point she only asks the king to attend, with Haman, a banquet that she will prepare. They do, and when asked again by the king what she wants, she invites both men for a second banquet. Haman, feeling particularly gratified by supping not once, but twice with the king and queen, is nonetheless still irked by Mordecai's customary refusal to bow to him as he leaves the palace; thus his glee turns to gloom as he passes through the palace gate. Seeing his discontent, Haman's wife and counselors advise him to vent his spleen by setting up a gallows especially for Mordecai to be used on the day of the Jews' destruction in Persia.

Esther 6–7: Haman Falls and the Jews Are Saved

In Esther 6 we hear that while Haman is being persuaded by family and friends to design a special death for Mordecai, the king, unable to fall asleep, is apparently resorting to royal records as a soporific. But rather than being lulled to sleep, he is surprised to find an account of his near assassination and deliverance through the good offices of Mordecai. Discovering this, he calls Haman to his side, as Haman has just returned to the palace to arrange with the king the special fate he plans for Mordecai. Before Haman can make his gruesome intentions known, the king announces joyfully his discovery and declares that Mordecai should be immediately rewarded with a royal parade, and that Haman should see to it! The parade follows as the king commands, and at its conclusion Haman goes home to the scorn and fateful predictions of his wife, and Mordecai returns to his vigil at the king's gate. By this time the second banquet is due to begin and so Haman, in the midst of his misery, has to attend another meal with the king and Esther.

Esther 7 tells the story of the second banquet. Upon sitting down to eat the king once more asks Esther what she wishes from him. Finally she comes to the point: she reveals that there is someone who seeks to kill her and all her people in the king's realm. Enraged at this, the king asks who has laid such plans. When she identifies the culprit as Haman, the king stalks from the table in rage. Haman, for his part, throws himself on Esther's dining couch to beg for her mercy. When the king returns to the banquet hall to see this spectacle, he assumes Haman has resorted to sexual assault as well and so commands Haman's death. At the suggestion of one of the servants, the king has him hung on the very gallows Haman has prepared for Mordecai.

Esther 8–10: The Rise of Mordecai and the Slaughter of the Jews' Enemies

According to Esther 8 the king follows the hanging of Haman by rewarding Esther with Haman's estate, and Mordecai with the royal signet ring Haman once possessed. In turn, Esther sets Mordecai over Haman's house. Seeing her opening, Esther begs the king to reverse Haman's orders with regard to the Jews of the kingdom. The king not only grants her that request, he also commands his scribes to write whatever she requests and put his seal upon it and have it delivered throughout the kingdom. Thus it is that the slaughter of the Jews is forestalled, and in its place Jews in the country of Persia are given the right to slaughter their foes on "a single day throughout all the provinces of King Ahasuerus, on the thirteenth day of the twelfth month, which is the month of Adar" (8:12). The latter date relates to the date of Purim, a sure sign that whatever else this book was intended to do, it most certainly provides a rationale for this Jewish drinking festival (see more below in "Critical Issues"). Because of the decree Mordecai is royally honored, the Jews of the kingdom rejoice, and, so says the book, many become Jews to avoid slaughter.

Esther 9 then relates the slaughter permitted to the Jews of the country and the city. The Jews of the country slaughter for one day — the 13th of Adar — and the Jews of the city are granted, per Esther's request, two days to slaughter their foes, the 13th and 14th of Adar. (As a result the Jews of the country celebrate Purim only one day, while city Jews enjoy a two-day feast!) The chapter closes by noting that Mordecai (and Esther by her assistance) decree the Feast of Purim on the 14th and 15th of Adar to commemorate the defeat of Haman's plan.

Esther 10 concludes the book with remarks on the continued greatness of Ahasuerus (= Xerxes) and the glory of Mordecai.

Critical Issues in Studying the Book of Esther

The Greek Additions to Esther and the differences among the Hebrew text and some Greek texts of the book provide a first area of interest to scholars. Its date and relationship to the historical era in which it is set have also occupied the attention of observers. And its precise connection to the Jewish festival of Purim continues to be an item of interest.

The Texts of the Book of Esther

The Masoretic Text of Esther differs notably from some Greek translations of the book. Most significant are the additions to the Greek text that have "corrected" the absence of references to God in the Masoretic Text. Six additions amounting to an additional 107 verses appear in a number of Greek manuscripts of Esther. The additions follow the "canonical" form of the book. Addition "A" relates a dream of Mordecai and his discovery of the plot against the Persian king. Addition "B" records Haman's edict against the Jews. Addition "C" provides the prayers of Mordecai and Esther. Addition "D" provides the details of Esther's audience with the king. Addition "E" records the king's counter-edict to that of Haman. And Addition "F" gives the interpretation of Mordecai's dream (reported in Addition "A"). Most scholars agree that these six different additions came from widely varying sources, and several may even have been composed first in Hebrew and only later translated into Greek. In any case, the impact of the lot of them is to make the characters in the story more overtly pious and to introduce into the text the person of God in explicit ways.

Another striking aspect of Esther's textual history is the existence of a "Greek Alpha Text" which omits substantial portions of the Masoretic Text (most notably the passages relating the book to Purim) while nonetheless preserving the additions found in other Greek texts of Esther. The question — still very much in dispute — is whether the Alpha Text is a Greek translation of a pre-Masoretic Text form of Esther. Most take the view that the Alpha Text is not a translation of an early form of the book but rather a revision of the Greek tradition. Rendering the question especially difficult to adjudicate is the fact that the Alpha Text is preserved only in five medieval manuscripts.

Eastern stairway of the Apadana (Audience Hall) of Darius I at Persepolis. (Courtesy of the Oriental Institute, University of Chicago)

The Date of the Book of Esther and Its Value as Historiography

Establishing the date of the book of Esther is in part tied to how one settles the question of the Alpha Text. If it is a pre-Masoretic form of the story, the book's development over time must be taken into account in considering its ultimate origin. But if the Alpha Text is merely a later recension of the Greek text, we have only to contend with the Masoretic form to consider the question of dating from the evidence of the content of the book. The latter position is the dominant one, and it is the one we follow here.

A date prior to the Maccabean era, when Jews had substantial reason for hatred of Gentile kings thanks to the Seleucid oppression of the Palestinian community, seems assured since this book takes such a sanguine view of non-Jewish rulers. But the absence of any loanwords from Greek in the Hebrew text suggests an even earlier date, sometime before the smashing success of Hellenization among Jews throughout the ancient world, a success that would have surely shown itself, no matter how remotely, in the language of a work

like Esther. This suggests to many a late Persian period date for the book's origin, an era when a relatively "uncontaminated" form of Hebrew might have still been the norm and when it was quite possible to hold a relatively positive view of Gentile kings, yet to also be wary of their capacity for causing trouble for the Jewish people. Reinforcing this is the observation some make that the Hebrew of the book is most like that of the Chronicler's Work, and its date to around 400 B.C.E. is widely accepted; thus a date sometime in the 300s is not unreasonable.

This raises the question of whether the book of Esther relates anything of historical value. Can we relate the events narrated to any episodes we know from the period? Does it offer some insight on the life of Jews in the Persian Empire far from the homeland of Judea? The answers to these questions depend, of course, on just how far one is willing to go in attributing credence to the veneer of verisimilitude in the narrative. Some have indeed been tempted to grant a great deal of credence to the hints at "historicality," to take for granted that the book is based in real events and real late

Persian practices. However, a simple survey of the story line and a closer look at the nature of the episodes narrated in the book make this view seem rather unlikely. The hyperbole of some of the book's claims (e.g., the half-year party of the king and the king's permission to Jews to slaughter their foes mercilessly for not one, but two days!) makes it less than credible. Its thematic organization — particularly around banquets and questions of loyalty — bespeaks not so much a historical narrative, but a fictionalized, didactic account. The hints it gives that it was composed from several disparate accounts (of Mordecai, of Esther, of Vashti) also undercut any confidence that it is a unified "historical narrative." The names of its key figures also hint at the possibility that the Jewish work relies on earlier Babylonian stories; Mordecai's name echoes that of the Babylonian god Marduk, and Esther's name recalls that of Ishtar, a goddess. Like so many examples of the court tales from Herodotus (and evident in Daniel 1–6), this has all the earmarks of such an instructive tale that sets out not to report history, but to educate and inspire its audience.

The Book of Esther and the Feast of Purim

That the Feast of Purim is not mentioned in the Alpha Text of Esther has raised the possibility for some that the book was not originally tied to the feast, that the connection between the two came only much later. Of course, that position depends on dating the Alpha Text's Hebrew predecessor before the Masoretic Text, a position that is not widely accepted.

Still, even if the book explains Purim from its earliest stage of development, the affiliation between the story and the feast is not as close as one might anticipate, nor is the feast itself particularly religious in character. Ostensibly the name for the feast comes from Hebrew *pur,* related to the casting of lots before Haman to establish the date on which he would see to the destruction of the Jews of the kingdom (3:7). But even that seems only barely tenable as a connection, and some who do accept it have suggested that it was a Persian festival adapted to Jewish use. Add to all of this the observation, made above, that the feast itself is nonreligious — its main purpose according to later tradition was to provide an occasion for drinking well beyond the point of inebriation! — and the link between the text of the book of Esther and the Feast of Purim seems very tenuous at best. It is almost as if a quite independent tale (that itself may have developed from several separate tales; see above) was placed only later in service to justifying the feast.

Theological Themes in the Book of Esther

The first thing to observe about theological themes in Esther is the ostensible absence of them. Famous for its failure to record even the name of God, the book of Esther has long been castigated for its "worldly" character from the days of the rabbis to our own time. However, things are rarely so simple as they seem, and even a quick look at the progress of the story as it appears in the Masoretic Text reveals its essentially theological core. Still, the additions to the Greek text noted above were likely deemed necessary to overcome the oft-noted deficiency; these additions create a second theological perspective in the book.

Theological Themes in the Masoretic Text

That providence is the overriding theme of the Masoretic version of the book is clearly recognizable. Vashti's refusal to dance necessitates a search for a new queen, which in turn leads to Esther's entry into the court of the king, which leads in turn to her favor before Ahasuerus, and so on. Likewise, the coincidence of Mordecai's overhearing the plot against the king and drawing Haman's special attention is what brings Mordecai into the king's presence and makes him privy to Haman's plans and thus able to do such good for the Jewish people. That this is not mere chance but rather the hand of God at work is hinted at by various moments in the text. Mordecai sees it as no matter of chance that Esther is placed next to the king's ear (4:14), and in presuming his certain demise after the tables turned on him Haman's own family seems to acknowledge a power behind Mordecai's people superior to that which Haman might wield (6:13). In short, the book of Esther, very much like another court tale in the Bible, the Joseph story, provides a very significant role for God though hardly mentioning him at all (see, e.g., Joseph's declamation to his fearful brothers, "Even though you intended to do harm to me, God intended it for good, in order to preserve a numerous people, as he is doing today"; Gen 50:20).

Theological Themes in the Additions to the Greek Text

Not all the additions known from the Greek Text of Esther add theological dimension to the work. We rehearse the contributions of those that do.

Addition A 1-11 (set before the events of the first chapter of Hebrew Esther) rehearses a dream in which Mordecai sees two great dragons preparing for war as the enemy nations outfit themselves to destroy a single righteous nation. The latter people cry out to God, and as a result there comes a river of deliverance from God and retribution against the oppressors. Mordecai wakes and considers the dream a foreshadowing of God's plan for Israel. The theological import of this addition hardly requires explanation.

Addition C, which is to be placed after 4:17, when Esther has promised to intercede for Israel, records Mordecai's pious prayer to God in which he explains his obstinate (and potentially devastating) resistance to bowing to Haman. He does not deign to do so, for such an act would violate his sole commitment to the God of Israel. As a consequence, Mordecai prays that God would not ignore the cry of such a faithful people for mercy. Interestingly this passage adds an intercessory element to the book, one that matches the importunate pleading of Mordecai with Esther, and of Esther with the king.

Addition C, best located shortly after Addition B, the text of Haman's edict against the Jews, and just before Esther's potentially deadly uninvited appearance before the king, reports Esther's own intercessory prayer. Echoing Moses' mountaintop appeal to God's sense of reputation when God was inclined to destroy the faithless people (Exod 32:1-14), Esther observes that God is known for keeping his promises to Israel and that, even though the people sinned and perhaps deserved the exile they endured, God could hardly let them be destroyed altogether as Haman planned to so. Thus, she pleads, God should save Israel this time too. As for her, she offers an explanation for her apparent willingness to share a bed with an uncircumcised man: though she abhors the intimacy with the king and regards the royal turban she must wear as polluting as a soiled menstrual rag, her placement is God's chance to save his people, to remain true to his reputation. Such a bold prayer adds more than piety to the Masoretic version of the story. It also reflects its author's appreciation of the traditions found in the Pentateuch — and as we shall see, in the Psalms as well, among other places — of boldness in intercession (cf. Abraham in Genesis 18; Moses in Exodus 32).

Addition D fits after 5:2, the beginning of Esther's audience with the king. In the addition the king reacts at first with rage and Esther, fainting, falls into one of her maids. At that moment God changes the king's mood to one of compassion so that the king leaps forward to gather Esther up and assure her of his mercy. This addition hardly adds much in terms of theological sophistication — it is certainly nothing like Addition C — and seems mostly intended to enhance the entertainment value of the story. Nonetheless, it is notable for its introduction of an active *and named* God in the story.

Addition E comes much later, after 8:12. It offers a record of the decree uttered by Mordecai under royal authority. In essence it decries the willful disregard for the will of the God of Israel exhibited by Haman's earlier decree and urges all to ignore that promulgation in favor of this new one that *is* supported by the omniscient God of Israel. Anyway, argues the decree, the people of Israel are not due the suffering Haman has assigned to them, but rather honor and respect for they are a law-keeping people who give allegiance to the God who is the true director of imperial fates. This addition echoes most closely Addition C, though its form and style are most similar to those of Addition B. In any case, it deepens the text's claim to God's lordship over all human affairs, even the wishes of foreign kings and prime ministers!

Addition F, the last one, follows the conclusion of the Masoretic version of the book. It recalls Mordecai's prophetic dream reported in Addition A and identifies the river as Esther, Mordecai and Haman as the two dragons, and the nations as the foes of Israel who would destroy God's people. The outcome of the dream matches the outcome of Haman's threat to Israel: the would-be evildoers are vanquished and Israel is vindicated by God's own intervention.

All in all, then, the additions work effectively to bring to clarity God's special role in directing the providential sequence of events in the Masoretic Text. What was only hinted at in the Hebrew version of Esther is made clear in the additions to the Greek text. Moreover, especially Esther's prayer before approaching the king adds dimension to the role of the humans in the story as religious individuals, persons motivated by particular theological convictions.

The View of Gentiles and Israelites

In closing it is important to note that a further dominant theme in Esther — one that is not on first sight clearly theological in nature — is the book's estimate of Gentiles and Israelites. Not surprisingly the narrative makes plain a disdain for Gentiles who are hostile to Israel (Haman), but less expected is its relatively gentle treatment of Gentiles such as the king, people who are not by nature hostile, but who are gullibly manipulated into using their power against Israel by her foes. The narrative has no vitriol for such figures, but rather a degree of bemused tolerance. At the same time the narrative regards such figures as even a bit foolish, and harmful only if they lack guidance from one or more of God's own people. As for Israel, without ever saying so even the Masoretic Text's version of the story makes clear God's preferential option for his chosen people. They cannot be overcome by even the most scheming of foes, and this acknowledgement comes not from Israel, but the wife of her greatest enemy in the story (6:13).

Questions for Review and Discussion

1 What attitude does the book of Esther take toward Gentiles, and especially toward the king?

2 Read Esther 2. What does this chapter indicate regarding the character assigned to Jews in this story?

3 On the basis of your reading of Esther 1–2, what are the indications regarding the book's quality as historiography?

Further Reading

Fox, Michael. *Character and Ideology in the Book of Esther.* 2nd ed. Grand Rapids: Wm. B. Eerdmans, 2001.

Larkin, Katrina J. A. *Ruth and Esther.* OTG. Sheffield: Sheffield Academic, 1996.

Levenson, Jon D. *Esther.* OTL. Louisville: Westminster John Knox, 1997.

Crawford, Sidnie White. "Esther." In *ECB,* 329-36.

The Writings

Chapter 20

Introduction to the Wisdom Books

Unlike the Pentateuch or the Historical Books, there is little that holds the so-called Wisdom Books together as a whole in the Old Testament. While some would meet our expectation of "wisdom" books — literature that purveys human insight and instruction — others do not fit this description well at all. Rather than enter now into the debate over just what "wisdom" was as a genre or phenomenon in ancient Israel and early Judaism, in this chapter we provide instead a brief survey of the books included under this heading and then return to the question of wisdom's meaning in light of that quick survey. We follow this with chapters covering each of those books in their own right.

The Wisdom Books of the Old Testament

In the Christian Old Testament five books slip in between Esther, the last of the "historical" narratives, and Isaiah, the first of the prophetic books. They are Job, Psalms, Proverbs, Ecclesiastes, and Song of Songs. They are, as it turns out, quite disparate in nature.

Job is well known to readers. It is a book that begins with the tale of a man who suffers unjustly because of a bet between God and one of his heavenly council, Satan, and continues with the speeches of that man, Job, and

his friends, addressing his dilemma. They produce human insight on the question of apparently innocent suffering in the sight of a good and just God. The book ends with God's reply to Job, and obliquely to his friends, and a curious restoration to Job of all that was taken from him in the test.

Psalms is also well known to readers. It is a collection of hymns — from laments, to prayers for deliverance, to thanksgiving songs, and more — that perhaps served as the hymnbook for some part of ancient Israel and early Judaism. The theological themes its poetry invokes include nearly all of those found throughout the Old Testament, including what we call "wisdom," the valorization of God-given human insight.

Proverbs is to many the most obviously "wisdom" book of the lot. It is what its title suggests: a collection of proverbial sayings on all aspects of human existence. While it does call upon the name of the Lord and connect wise behavior with God's rewards, it is mostly a work that offers human insight and extols its virtues.

Ecclesiastes is a very different cup of tea. It is a collection of reflections of someone who has "tried everything under the sun," only to conclude that it is all vanity. The author announces that there is no gain in anything, and that the best you can do with life is accept the lot you have been given, endure the difficulties, enjoy the good times, and wrap it all up with dignity at the end. This, too, might be considered a sort of human insight, as bleak as it may seem to many readers.

Finally, Song of Songs concludes the collection with perhaps the most anomalous entry. The book is basically a collection of love poems with considerably high erotic content. The songs extol the beauty and handsomeness of a pair of lovers and recount the joys and tribulations they experience in expressing their love to one another. The book is, in a sense, a collection of human insight on the ways of love.

"Wisdom" Defined by the Collection

Now we return only briefly to the question that troubled us at the outset of this brief introduction to the "Wisdom" books: what *is* wisdom?

From the standpoint of genre, little seems obvious. We have narratives, poetic speeches, hymns of various subtypes, proverbial sayings, "observational reports" (in Ecclesiastes), and erotic poetry. In spite of some attempts to define ancient Israelite and early Jewish wisdom from the standpoint of genre, there seems little reason from even this brief survey to embrace any of those. But from the standpoint of content there does seem to be a consistent theme worth considering: human insight. As we shall see, what does seem to hold these together — and you may recall, what seemed to plague the Deuteronomic imagination — is the possibility that the exercise of human insight is the best means of clarifying one's place in the world in God's sight. Sometimes human insight can be God-given (e.g., some wisdom psalms), and sometimes it comes from human experience and observation (e.g., Ecclesiastes). And on still other occasions it is the result of both (e.g., Job). But in all cases human insight as the key to living before God seems to be present. With that simple insight in hand we turn to the books themselves.

Further Reading

Murphy, Roland E. *The Tree of Life: An Exploration of Biblical Wisdom Literature*. 3rd ed. Grand Rapids: Wm. B. Eerdmans, 2002.

Chapter 21

Job

Getting Started

1 Read Job 1–2. How does Job perceive himself at the outset of these two chapters, and how does he respond to his situation at their close?

2 Read Job 3–5. How does Job's attitude in this chapter contrast with his outlook at the end of chapter 2? How might you account for this difference? And how does Eliphaz's response to Job measure up to Job's views? Does Eliphaz remind you of any of the theological perspectives we encountered in the Pentateuch?

3 Read Job 42:1-6. Compare Job's attitude in these verses with the ones he exhibits in chs. 1–2 and 3. How might you account for Job's radically new posture in v. 6 especially, and to which is it more similar, what we see in chs. 1–2 or 3?

Preliminary Comments

The book of Job is certainly one of the best-known books of the Hebrew Bible, if not also in the wider body of world literature. Its tale of a righteous man suffering unjustly as the result of a friendly wager between God and one of his heavenly councilors has long stirred recipients' and readers' imagination *and* indignation. Indeed, the biblical book has provoked more than its share of artistic and literary responses (e.g., William Blake's 21 illustrations for the book of Job and the 1958 stage play in verse, *J.B.,* by Archibald Macleish) and more than a few indignant attempts to overcome its offense in antiquity (see esp. reference to the *Testament of Job* below).

A Walk through the Book of Job

The book of Job begins with a narrative prologue that establishes the peculiar relationships among God, Satan (a member of the heavenly council; see p. 169), and Job. It continues with poetic speeches from Job, his friends, and God, and concludes with a narrative epilogue.

Job 1–2: Narrative Prologue
Often suspected of being a source used by the book's author (see "Critical Issues" below), the narrative prologue sets the stage for the reader's appreciation of the speeches Job and his friends deliver in chs. 3–37. We read in 1:1-5 of Job's boundless wealth in terms of family and possessions (he has seven sons and three daughters, nearly countless livestock) and his extraordinary piety

(he makes sacrifice on behalf of his children and their friends after they have feasted for some time, in case any of them has "cursed God in their hearts" while partying).

Although the text makes no explicit claim that Job attributed his great wealth to his personal righteousness, the following conversation between God and Satan makes plain enough Satan's surmise that is the case. We first read that the "heavenly beings" ("sons of God" in Hebrew) come before the Lord God, and Satan is among them. (Here Satan is not the demon of later Judaism, but rather one of God's heavenly councilors.) When asked by God where he has been, Satan replies that he has been on a walking tour of earth. God uses the occasion to ask if in his journeys Satan has observed Job's righteousness, and Satan answers with his own question: "Does Job fear God for nothing?" Satan then asserts that Job's wealth stems from God's blessing, and that Job would not remain so faithful if it were all taken away. God takes the bait, and permits Satan to destroy Job's wealth and family (1:6-12). And so follows a succession of four messengers announcing to Job that all his livestock has been stolen or destroyed by natural disasters and his servants slain, and that his children, gathered at the eldest brother's house for merrymaking, have been buried in the rubble of the home when it is destroyed by a storm (1:13-19). Job's response is to take on the trappings of a mourner and to praise the Lord God as the provider of all things who therefore requires no justification for taking all away; in this "Job did not sin or charge God with wrongdoing" (1:20-22).

The second chapter opens with a second heavenly council meeting and Job and Satan meeting again, whereupon once again Satan replies to God's query regarding his activities that he has been walking the earth. And again God boasts of Job's righteousness, observing that in spite of his inexplicable bad fortune (caused, says God, by Satan's incitement of him!) he remains faithful to God in all things. Satan's reply is that people will do anything to save themselves; but if Job's own being were afflicted, he would then turn on God. Incited once more by Satan's dare, God gives Satan charge over Job's body so long as he does not slay Job (2:1-6). Thus Satan afflicts Job with oozing sores and bodily suffering so profound that Job is reduced to sitting on his mourner's ash heap, scraping his wounds with a broken shard of pottery (2:7-8). To this Job's wife urges him to admit his loss of integrity and "Curse God and die" (2:9); her meaning, it seems, is that Job must have sinned irreparably against God and that the best he could do for one and all would be to call down upon himself God's final, death-dealing wrath. His response, however, vindicates God's estimate of him once more; he calls his wife foolish and reminds her that God who gives good freely is equally just in

---

Reading Guide to Job
Narrative Prologue (1–2)
Job's Opening Gambit (3)
First Cycle of Speeches (4–14)
Second Cycle of Speeches (15–21)
Third Cycle of Speeches (22–27; 29–31)
Wisdom Poem (28)
Elihu's Speeches (32–37)
God Replies to Job (38–41)
Narrative Epilogue: The Final Gambit Between Job and God (42)

---

dealing out bad (2:10). At this point Job's friends who will soon become unceasingly talkative arrive to mourn loudly for and with him, and then to sit for seven days in silence with their suffering friend (2:11-13).

Job 3: Job's Opening Gambit
The speeches begin with Job's opening lament in ch. 3. He mourns the day of his birth, even the day of his conception. He yearns that that day had never occurred, that time could be reversed; and barring that, he wishes he had died at birth, had been stillborn, that he might never have laid eyes on creation. And since neither fate befalls him, he yearns now to die, and yet not even that is provided him. He concludes his lament with the words, "I have no rest; but trouble comes." As it turns out, the book's author may have been at least a little ironic in this: for the trouble that *does* come is in the speeches of Job's "friends."

Job 4–14: First Cycle of Speeches
The first two cycles of speeches are clear in their structure. First, one of Job's friends speaks and then Job responds, and so on until all three friends have spoken and Job has made his reply to each. As is clear from page 191, the third cycle of speeches violates the pattern established in the first two cycles. There is no obvious speech from Zophar, with a wisdom poem in ch. 28 seemingly taking its place, and much of Job's response in chs. 26–27 sounds more like his friends' arguments than his own. This leads to the suggestion that in 26:1-4 Job interrupts Bildad, allowing him to conclude in 26:5-14. Then Job speaks again in 27:1-6, and 27:7-23 provides Zophar's speech. The wisdom poem is an interruption (see below in "Critical Issues"), and chs. 29–31 offer Job's final reply to his friends.

The general thrust of the speeches in all three cycles — as well as Elihu's speeches in chs. 32–37 — is consistent, so it suffices to summarize the first cycle as the exemplar of what appears in the second and third cycles and in Elihu's speeches. We then review the wisdom poem and survey God's response to Job, Job's final response, and the narrative epilogue to the book.

Job 4–7: Eliphaz and Job Trade Speeches

Eliphaz is the first friend to address Job's condition and Job's initial response to his situation. Eliphaz begins by suggesting that Job's impatience results from a loss of perspective (4:1-6) and then offers what he thinks is the proper view of things: God causes no one to suffer innocently, but rather repays humans according to their deeds and misdeeds (4:7-11). Anyway, humans are never perfect and therefore must endure some suffering as a result of their sins (4:12-21). He goes on to warn Job against anger with God, for it must have its consequences as well (5:1-7). One is better served, suggests Eliphaz, seeking God's mercy (5:8-16), and in any case, suffering must be seen as God's pedagogy of the human soul (5:17-27).

Job replies to Eliphaz with scorn: were God just, the punishment Job endures would be far less, for as it is it outdistances anything Job may have done (6:1-7). But because that is not so, Job repeats his yearning for an end to his suffering even if it were to mean death (6:8-13). As for Eliphaz, Job mocks his reply, comparing such a friend to "freshets that pass away" and other such ephemeral phenomena (6:14-23) and challenging Eliphaz to locate the wrong Job has done to receive such suffering (6:24-30). As for the idea that he should have patience, Job informs Eliphaz that such a task is difficult to accomplish under the weight of such horrific conditions (7:1-6). As if speaking so boldly of his own condition is the trigger to turn to God, Job complains that God should have something better to do than watch the human being every moment of the day to reward and punish. Indeed, complains Job, what does human sin harm God anyway that so much suffering should be inflicted? Are we not but the dust of the earth, unnoticeable to God's greatness (7:7-21).

Job 8–10: Bildad and Job Exchange Speeches

Bildad is the second of Job's friends to make a run at corralling him into agreement that God does not punish people needlessly. Relying chiefly on metaphors from the plant world to argue that nothing is without cause in all creation — and so Job's suffering also cannot be without cause — Bildad breaks no new ground beyond that covered by Eliphaz (8:1-19). Indeed, he too urges Job to repent so that he might be blameless and know once more the joy of God's blessing (8:20-22).

Job's reply to Bildad suggests that he still does not see the need for repentance. Instead he wonders if it were possible to sue God for malfeasance, but (foreshadowing God's own response to Job in chs. 38–41) acknowledges that God's greatness in creation is proof alone that he could not win such a lawsuit (9:1-24). When Job contemplates finally the possibility of setting aside his complaint and going on with life, he doubts that would have any consequence either, assuming instead that God would still pursue him. His only hope, unreal as it may be, would lie in God relinquishing divine power to hear Job's plaint (9:25-35). To this Job adds his argument to God: should a creator take so lightly what he has made, coming against his creation with such unjustified force (10:1-17)? This elicits from Job one more bidding prayer of nonexistence, a song denying his own life (10:18-22).

Job 11–14: Zophar and Job Trade Speeches

Zophar adds little to the words of those who preceded him in speech, apart from employing the notion of wisdom — and God's wisdom in particular — to suggest again Job's foolishness in questioning the justice of God (11:1-12). He goes on to offer instruction to Job on how he might effectively repent and call on God's better judgment of him (11:13-20).

Job's answer to Zophar signals his increasing impatience with the friends' posture: he suggests first that

The Speech Cycles in Job 4–31

First Cycle of Speeches

Chapters 4–5 (Eliphaz)	Job responds:	Chapters 6–7
Chapter 8 (Bildad)		Chapters 9–10
Chapter 11 (Zophar)		Chapters 12–14

Second Cycle of Speeches

Chapter 15 (Eliphaz)	Job responds:	Chapters 16–17
Chapter 18 (Bildad)		Chapter 19
Chapter 20 (Zophar)		Chapter 21

Third Cycle of Speeches

Chapter 22 (Eliphaz)	Job responds:	Chapters 23–24
Chapter 25 (Bildad)		Chapters 26–27
Chapter 28 (Wisdom Poem)		Chapters 29–31

the friends' responses to him actually violate all good wisdom, and that even the animals and plants of the earth and fish of the sea know this, and understand that God is in control of reality (12:1-12). Then in a sarcastic hymn he praises the wisdom and strength that are in God: God's exercise of them exalts humans speedily, but then casts them down just as quickly so that in the end they only "stagger like a drunkard" (12:13-25). From this Job turns to expressing his desire to address God directly (13:1-19). He finally does so, asking first that God draw back long enough that Job might speak his objection without fear, for so long as God is watchful he is without hope of speaking and surviving (13:20–14:6). As for the possibility that he might survive such an encounter, Job rejects the analogy made with plants that revive after destruction, observing that a human's end is just that. He remarks sarcastically that this would be no fun for God, for then he would have no one to plague at every turn, and Job would be free of his sorrow (14:7-17). But even this hope seems vain, for hope itself seems to Job to have been undercut by God (14:18-22). With this mournful claim the first cycle closes and opens into the second, a repetition of the first, not only in basic structure but also more or less in content.

Job 28: The Wisdom Poem

Coming in the place one expects another speech from Zophar, Job 28 is instead a wisdom hymn that only loosely fits its context. Just why it is placed here is not easy to say, but that is not what interests us here. Instead we offer only a sense of the contents of the poem and how it might be seen as fitting with the rest of the book.

The speaker begins by observing the human knack for finding precious stones that cannot be seen by even the most sharp-eyed members of the animal kingdom (28:1-11). Yet wisdom remains completely elusive even to the human eye or grasp, and even Abaddon and Death know not its location (vv. 12-22). Only God knows wisdom's place, for in creating all things and setting out the parameters of the creation God saw it, declared it, and established it. As for humanity's access to wisdom, God declared that for them wisdom is but "fear of the Lord" (vv. 23-28).

As we shall see below in "Theological Themes," this majestic hymn is, though at first glance somewhat dissonant with its surroundings, quite consonant with the book as a whole. One can read it in all seriousness as an exhortation completely in sympathy with the teaching of Job's friends: the human being's proper exercise of wisdom is to acknowledge one thing, that God is Lord and deserving of awe and respect. But it can be heard, as words from the increasingly restive Job (a plausible reading given the lack of any indication that Job has ceased

speaking at the end of ch. 27), to be a sarcastic statement of the self-serving morsel God does permit to humans. As we shall see, the book as a whole manages to evoke both responses, even to license both of them.

Job 38–41: God Replies to Job

So confident is Job as he concludes his speech that he challenges God to meet him in court to settle matters between them (31:35-40). Following the (intrusive) speech of Elihu in chs. 32–37 (for more on this, see "Critical Issues" below), God replies to Job's challenge first with an excoriating list of questions to Job regarding *his* place in making creation what it is. God begins, "Where were you when I laid the foundation of the earth?" (38:4), and never relents in his questioning of Job's insight on what is only God's to know until the end of ch. 40. To this searing "reply" that is little more than a taxonomy of the elements of creation, Job replies at last with humility: he has nothing to say for himself, and so he promises not to press God again.

But this turns out not to be enough for God. In a second speech to Job God begins by observing that only he possesses the power to govern creation, and that without such power Job has no standing in a dispute with God (40:6-14). Then to drive the point home God gives an extended description of symbolic creatures of power and might, Behemoth (40:15-24) and Leviathan (41:1-34), beasts that only God can control: Job would have no hope in such a task, but it is possible for God, for he is the creator even of these destructive forces of nature.

The Final Gambit Between Job and God: Job 42

Job's response to the conclusion of God's speech from the whirlwind is to repeat his penance of 40:3-5, adding this time a highly charged concluding verse: having heard and seen God's majesty, Job finishes with, "therefore I despise myself, and repent in dust and ashes" (42:6). The problem is the preposition "in": it may be understood to indicate that Job remains in his position of mourning, "upon" dust and ashes, but now as an exercise in disinterested piety, awe, and respect for God simply because God is God; it could also mean that Job repents "concerning" dust and ashes, in which case he can be heard to say either that he acknowledges the lesson God has taught him or even that he deigns now to leave his piety behind, perhaps in disgust at God's reply that was no reply. The ambiguity of the phrase can hardly be missed and may well have been intentional; such a move would hardly be out of step with the rest of the book.

Only adding to the ambiguity are the concluding verses, 42:7-17. First, God commands Job's friends to hasten in making sacrifice that Job might intercede for them, for God judges them to have spoken wrongly and Job quite rightly! Job sees their sacrifices and prays for them as God predicted, and, in yet another ironic twist, God hears Job's prayer and spares the friends. Then, in one last quirk to the story, as if to reward Job for his insolence in challenging him, God restores to Job all of his earlier wealth twofold and provides him with new children to replace the ones he had lost.

Critical Issues in Studying the Book of Job

Aside from the central issue of Job's views on God's justice and human suffering (which we treat under "Theological Themes"), the questions of date, related ancient Near Eastern works, and compositional history have dominated study of this remarkable book.

The Date of the Book of Job

There is at least general agreement that Job is best dated sometime between the 7th and 4th centuries B.C.E. A 6th-century date may be thought most likely on the basis of a wide range of evidence. Some see Job's plea that his words be inscribed in stone (19:24) as an awareness of Darius's late-6th-century Behistun Inscription (which was inscribed with lead on stone). Also suggesting a Persian-era date is the language employed to name kings and princes in 3:14-15. And the abundant Aramaisms in Job — Hebrew expressions that reflect the influence of Aramaic, the *lingua franca* of the Persian Empire — also support a later than earlier date. An additional indicator is the use of the definite article with Satan in chs. 1–2; that the Chronicler uses the title as a proper name (without the definite article) suggests Job is earlier than the latter work, and the similar use of the title with a definite article in Zechariah invites close affiliation between Job and that late-6th-century prophet.

Related Ancient World Compositions

The themes of divine fairness and a moral economy governed by principles of retributive justice seen in Job are not unique to the book. Across the ancient world we find works that address these compelling issues, especially the apparent failure of the system when difficulties afflict those who would seem immune from troubles due to their peculiar righteousness. Scholars often suggest loose parallels between the poetic dialogues and several Egyptian texts (e.g., *The Dispute Between a Man and His Ba* [*ANET*, 405-7]; *The Admonitions of Ipuwer* [*ANET*, 441-44]). Others point to the Canaanite Epic of Keret (*ANET*, 142-49) as sharing much in common with the narrative framework of the book of Job. However, works from Mesopotamia are most reminiscent of Job.

Dating perhaps a thousand years earlier than Job is the Sumerian work, *A Man and His God* (*ANET*, 589-91). In it the speaker claims, respectfully, to have been unjustly afflicted, and his god hears his claim sympathetically. More similar to Job is the better-known Babylonian Theodicy (*ca.* 1100 B.C.E.; *ANET*, 601-4). Here the complainant takes up the matter of his god's injustice with a friend, and though their dialogue is without the tantrums thrown by Job, the sufferer does question the righteousness of his god.

It would be overreaching the evidence to claim some direct connection between Job and these Mesopotamian traditions. A rather more likely explanation for the shared themes is the universal human experience explored by these texts. They all contend with the troubling puzzle of inexplicable human suffering that violates the expectations of divine justice. That we find such speculation across cultures and time is hardly surprising, and that it takes the form of a dialogue is also not unexpected. Virtually all human cultures have wondered at such seeming injustices, and the wonderment naturally takes shape as discourse between human beings and between humans and their God or gods.

Compositional History

Scholars once widely held that the narrative framework (Job 1–2; 42:7-17) was a later addition to the poetic core of the book of Job. The argument was that the poetry reflected the longstanding, cross-cultural tradition of considering the injustice of innocent suffering (especially in relation to God; cf. the Babylonian Theodicy, *A Man and His God*), and that to those speeches the narrative framework was only later added. Some subsequent scholarship has reversed that assessment, observing that the narrative framework also has its more ancient parallel (Epic of Keret) and that it is more sensible to imagine dialogues being added to a pre-existing narrative than dialogues that presuppose the elements of the narrative coming first. In addition some observe that the narrative epilogue seems very out of keeping with the rest of the book (see our survey above) and consider it to be of questionable origin relative to the rest of the book. But on none of these speculations exists any wide agreement.

Of course, the origin of Elihu's speeches also comes in for its share of investigation. They clearly interrupt a certain flow to the book, and there is no naming of Elihu in Job apart from the speeches associated with him. At the same time, his speeches cohere well not only with those of the other three friends of Job, but they also foreshadow in part some of what God has to say to Job. This evidence pushes some to favor Elihu's contribution with more positive consideration as an integral part of the work.

This last observation, the see-saw approach to answering the question of which came first, narrative or dialogue, and the questions regarding the relationship of the epilogue to the rest of the book, have led some to set aside such compositional-historical speculation in favor of a wholistic literary-critical approach to the book. These writers are varied in their opinions as to the way in which the present text came to be — some suspect a master editor-author, and others are willing to accept the possibility of compositional growth over time — but they are united in their view that we may only make sense of the book as it stands. And for most of these commentators the theological themes evoked by this complex work are what truly evoke their interest.

Theological Themes in the Book of Job

The book of Job is one of a handful of Old Testament books that unfailingly evokes theological reflection by its recipients, be they scholars or laypeople, believers or unbelievers. As a consequence, the range of theological themes either built into the book or evoked by the book's history of interpretation far outstrip the constraints of the few pages we may devote to the matter. So we focus on just three dimensions of the book's theological richness: what it suggests about the reasons for human piety in relation to God; what it indicates about the way humans relate to one another as everyday theologians; and what it communicates regarding the nature of a lived relationship with the Almighty.

Human Piety toward God

The book of Job — or better, its main character, the man called Job — offers a poignant glimpse into the motivations for piety toward God. By piety we mean the habit of belief in and reverence toward God and concomitant commitment to practices that give expression to that belief and reverence. As the book begins we encounter the tale of Job's great piety toward God and his own great wealth. Although the narrative portion of the text is never explicit that Job understands his riches as God's reward for his piety, Satan, in conversation with God, gives voice to the reader's natural suspicion: Job is pious precisely because he is rewarded for his reverence. Remarkably, even in this exchange God remains noncommittal on the question of the connection between piety and success, wealth and contentment (Job 1:6-12). As for Job's response to the sudden reversal of fortunes, at least within the context of the narrative framework he appears to belie the reader's suspicions and Satan's certainty: his piety persists in spite of his enormous suffering.

But, of course, the astute reader knows by now that Job does not remain long in the posture of the pious sufferer. Once he opens his mouth to speak it becomes abundantly clear that he does, indeed, agree with his friends that God should and does reward the righteous and punish the wicked. In their own ways Job and his friends assert this basic understanding of God — this *theology* — over and over again. The difference between Job and his friends is only in whom they trust to be righteous: the friends assign that quality to God, and Job, knowing himself, argues finally that God lacks that quality and should be called to account for it. In any case, all of them agree that God is constrained by a basic logic of retributive justice. Piety does bring rewards from heaven above.

God's response, though, offers no confidence that such a connection is true in practice. In fact, it offers nothing but the certainty that God is a mighty creator of all things existing and that humans are permitted to understand nothing more than that about God in heaven. God neither denies a commitment to rewarding the pious, nor does God confirm it; God only claims authorship of all things.

Job's well-known response to God appears to be disinterested piety, that is, a continued reverence for and belief in God in spite of what he has (not) learned about God's righteousness. Thus as the speeches draw to a close in 42:1-6 the reader seems to be urged toward embracing a similar view of piety toward God, that it is due to God for no other reason than God is God.

At the last, however, the book offers one more twist that keeps the reader off balance on this question, for just as Job seems to embrace a dizzyingly openhearted approach to piety, God rebukes Job's friends for their views (implying confirmation of Job's new disinterested posture), but goes on to reward Job with double his former wealth and a new family to replace the one he lost! A God committed to retributive justice seems to have made a very peculiar return, censuring some of the firmest believers in that theological perspective but rewarding Job for his boldness. On this note the book concludes, leaving the reader struggling to answer the question, "Does God live by our notions of retributive justice?"

Differing on the Nature of God: Theology as Debate

An often overlooked aspect of the book of Job is the evidence it provides that, rightly understood, theology — reflection on the nature of God — is not so much the systematic reflections of ivory tower intellectuals, but rather the diverse and often conflicting claims about God made by believers who grapple with a world beset by the dualities of joy and sorrow, wonder and dread, prosperity and poverty, war and peace. From the urging of Job's wife that he "curse God and die" to the arguments of Eliphaz, Zophar, and Bildad, to the speechifying of Elihu, to Job's responses to his wife and his friends, this book is filled with claims about the true nature of God, claims that compete vigorously with one another.

To begin, Job's wife is certain of God's retributive justice and equally certain that her husband has brought this misery on himself. Moreover, she also seems confident that God's justice leaves no room for forgiveness, and so she begs Job to end their mutual suffering by offending God once and for all. Job's friends share his wife's insistence on God's commitment to retributive justice, but they reject her view that God does not accept repentance, arguing instead that God is equally dedicated to forgiving those who are meritoriously repentant. Elihu's speech affirms the views of the friends, but he adds the notion that unjust suffering among human beings is only *apparently* unjust inasmuch as it may also be explained as God's pedagogy and discipline. Job, the believer most caught up in the fray, represents in alternating literary personalities a posture of unquestioning (1:20-21; 2:10) and chastened (40:4-5; 42:1-6) devotion to God in spite of all innocent suffering. He also represents the startlingly bold views of someone who believes so firmly in the principle of divine retributive justice as to demand his God's obedience to it when God seems to have violated it (see esp. 31:29-37). Together, these diverse theological views occurring side-by-side in the book of Job testify not only to the fundamentally diverse nature of theology as a product of lived experience, but also to the tensions between perspectives naturally attendant to theology done this way. The book of Job shows that the theology that counts for most believers — ideas about God that arise from the everyday lives of believers — is a "conflict discipline."

Job begs for pity from his friends as he sits in a dunghill before his ruined house. Limbourg Brothers, *Très riches heures du Duc de Berry,* fol 82r (15th century); Accademia, Florence. (Giraudon, ArtResource, NY)

The Book of Job and Life in God's Sight

If nothing else, the book of Job accomplishes this "theological task": it reveals to readers of every generation that life lived in God's sight is most definitely not the perfectly ordered existence popular piety has sought since humanity first conceived of a divine creator and overseer. Instead, the ancient author of this book seems to express for every reader of every age a simple, yet fearsome-to-many truth: life with God is unpredictable, full of mystery and wonder, joy and sorrow, good and evil; life with God evokes as many questions about human experience as it provides answers. At a most human level, Job provides to its readers an experience of this truth and a challenge to live with it in faith and trust, or not. It is worth noting, to close, that a later Jewish pseudepigraphon, the *Testament of Job,* gives ample evidence of the discomfort some felt at the book of Job's openness on the question of God's intentions for creation; this simplest point made by the book, it seems, was and continues to be fearsome indeed.

Questions for Review and Discussion

1 What are some of the reasons for dating the book of Job after the Babylonian Exile? Are those reasons particularly convincing to you? Does the date of the book matter that much to its interpretation and impact on readers?

2 Review the basic perspectives on God's way of being articulated by Job, his friends, his wife, Elihu, and

God. Do you agree with the above discussion that these perspectives do not all agree? Do you think there is any way to reconcile all of these views and attribute to the book a single, overarching theological perspective? If so, what do you think that is?

3 Which of the theological perspectives we have seen outside of the book of Job seem to be targets or of particular interest for this book's author? Does your answer to this question suggest anything about how the author of the book viewed "theology" as a human discipline?

Further Reading

Dell, Katharine J. "Job." In *ECB,* 337-63.

Eaton, J. H. *Job.* OTG. Sheffield: Sheffield Academic, 1985.

Newsom, Carol A. *The Book of Job: A Contest of Moral Imaginations.* Oxford: Oxford University Press, 2003.

van Wolde, E. J., ed. *Job's God.* London: SCM, 2004.

Chapter 22

Psalms

Getting Started

1 Read Psalm 1. How would you describe this psalm? What is its primary interest? Its genre?

2 Read Psalm 44. Answer the same questions you answered for the first question with respect to this psalm.

3 Read Psalm 32. Again, treat the same questions. What do you notice about the varying interests and genres of the psalms?

Preliminary Comments

The book of Psalms is popularly described as "Israel's songbook." While the collection entailed in the book does amount to a songbook on one level, we shall soon see that it is, in fact, several songbooks merged together and that it was not Israel's — or early Judaism's — only psalter, but rather almost certainly one among many competing collections. Moreover, just as the interests and perspectives of religious communities today can be discerned in part from the hymnbooks they use, the book of Psalms most certainly announces

something of the views held by its composers and users.

A Walk through the Book of Psalms

Like the book of Proverbs, Psalms presents certain problems for our usual strategy of surveying in some detail the entire contents of a given biblical book. It hardly bears saying that a treatment of all 150 psalms is beyond the scope of this Introduction. So we satisfy ourselves instead with a survey of the contours of the "Five Books" of Psalms marked out by doxologies at the end of each section (Pss 41:13; 72:18-20; 89:52; 106:48; Psalm 150 serves as the doxology to the entire Psalter) and a further survey of the different psalm genres present in the book.

The Five Books of Psalms

Intriguingly, the 150 psalms included in the biblical psalter are clearly divided into five books: Psalms 1–41; 42–72; 73–89; 90–106; 107–150, suggesting an effort on the part of the final editors of the collection to conform it to a five-part Torah. There is, however, only a little evidence internal to the book of Psalms to indicate when that division was made. The obvious evidence of sub-collections within the book of Psalms (e.g., a collection of "Psalms of Ascent" in Pss 120–134), some of which overlap the boundaries of the five books (e.g., Pss 42–83 all call God *elohim,* and thus get the title the "Elohistic Psalter"), speaks in favor of a later than earlier date for the fivefold division. More powerful evidence of a fairly late date for the division comes from the Dead Sea Scrolls. The Psalms Scroll from Cave 11 is the first piece of the Qumran puzzle that speaks for a fluid collection of psalms well into the last two centuries B.C.E. This impressively preserved scroll encompasses the bulk of the last third of the book of Psalms as we know it, but in a widely differing order. It also contains additional material, including Psalm 151 (known from the Greek translation of Psalms), Psalms 154–155 (known from the Syriac Bible), a poem like Sir 51:13-19, 30, a psalm that repeats 2 Sam 23:1-7, David's last words, and a prose list of "David's compositions" that comes four psalms before the end of the scroll. The second indicator from Qumran that psalters still varied in the last centuries before the turn of the eras is the variations in content and order (in relation to the Masoretic Text) found in seven Cave 4 psalms manuscripts. The late date of these manuscripts makes clear that at least at Qumran the book of Psalms we know was probably only partially formed by the turn of the eras; certainly the fivefold division we know in today's Psalter was not yet clear.

What, then, to make of the fivefold division of the book of Psalms? Various theories have been proposed beyond the simple observation that the structure seems intended at least to mimic the structure of the Torah. For example, some have suggested that the books are meant to relate the fate of the covenant with David and elicit hope for its future. On this reading the first book introduces the covenant (Ps 2), the second book observes its transmission to Solomon (Ps 72), and the third book extends the covenant's benefits to David's descendants in recognition of its provisional failure under David's immediate successors (Ps 89). The fourth book then reflects on the reasons for the covenant's failure, citing especially human weakness (Ps 90) and Israel's disobedience (Pss 105–106), and the fifth book outlines observance of the law as a way back from the Exile (Ps 119), raises hope for God's blessing of Zion (Pss 120–134), and a restoration of God's confidence in the Davidic line (Pss 138–145). The problem with this reading, like virtually all the others that try to impose a unifying structure on the book of Psalms beyond simple symmetry with the Torah, is its failure to account for the wide range of psalms that are included in each book, ones that emphatically *do not* serve the agenda the contemporary reader identifies!

Psalm Types

Since Hermann Gunkel pioneered form criticism in his research on the book of Psalms, one way to survey the contents of the Psalter has been via genre classification. Gunkel sought successfully to defeat the notion that psalms were the expressive residue of very personal, individual expressions of piety. Instead, by showing the psalms could be classified according to a variety of genres and suggesting some possible settings in life *(Sitze im Leben)* for the genres he made a persuasive case for the communal, liturgical, and even nationalistic origin of many of the Psalter's songs. The chief result of Gunkel's work, though, was the development of a new way of classifying and considering the varied songs in the book of Psalms. This remains the case, even if further form-critical analysis by subsequent scholars has generated not only more psalm classifications, but also conflicting and overlapping genre classifications. Moreover, by linking form to function, Gunkel and subsequent form critics have, perhaps quite unwittingly, created a double approach to classification, according to form and/or function. So what follows must be understood as but *one* possible description of the broad categories of psalms contained in the book of Psalms, a description that at times relies on form and at other times on function to distinguish among psalm types.

One of the more prominently represented genres is the "Psalm of Thanksgiving" (e.g., Pss 18, 30, 34, 41, 66, 116, 138). These are almost always explicitly individual songs, but many can also be heard as communal thanksgivings and almost certainly functioned that way for the people using them. Typical elements include a call to thanksgiving (e.g., 118:1) or expression of intent to make thanks (e.g., 30:1); an account of what the psalmist is thankful for, which is oftentimes deliverance from some struggle (e.g., 41:4-10); and the thanksgiving to God (e.g., 30:11-12). That these elements most naturally produce an individual thanksgiving is hardly surprising, and so it should also hardly be surprising that the vast majority of psalms assigned to this category appear to be the speech of single persons (but see also Pss 66–68; 124). That does not mean, however, that they did not function communally. Some clearly entail an individual inviting others to join him in thanksgiving (e.g., 118:2-4), and there are likewise hints that these were intended in some ways for communal ritual use (e.g., 118:20). In other words, it seems hard to deny that no matter their apparent primary locus in the mouth of individuals, the thanksgiving hymns were also widely used for communal events as well.

Closely related to psalms of thanksgiving are psalms of lament, at least inasmuch as the reason for thanksgiving is often deliverance from difficult circumstances

Mosaic of flute player; Caesarea Maritima (5th-6th century c.e.). (Photo by Aaron Levin; courtesy Combined Caesarea Expeditions)

do they always appear in this order.) The difference between individual laments (which are the most numerous single type in the Psalter) and communal laments is obvious: the pleas of single speakers arise from their individual experiences, and communal supplications arise from broadly shared experiences such as war, famine, or exile. Communal laments are also quite common in other parts of the Hebrew Bible, and not unexpectedly inasmuch as a recurring theme of literature especially from the Exile and particular moments after the Exile is an appeal to God for deliverance from the consequences of communal sin (see, e.g., Ezra 9; Nehemiah 9).

Hymns are another psalm genre frequently found (e.g., Pss 8, 19, 29, 33, 65, 67, 96, 100, 103–105, 114, 117, 145–150). Essentially songs of praise, they are quite simple in form: they usually include an opening call to the Lord and/or the (heavenly or earthly) assembly that often states the reasons for the praise (29:1-2; 65:1-2), the song of praise itself (Ps 96), and occasionally a repetition of the opening call (147:20). Again, these may be in a sense individual or communal hymns, although even those that praise God for deeds done for individuals seem to be intended for communal, ritual use. Thus the occasion may be release of the imprisoned and healing of the afflicted (Ps 146) or liberation for the whole people (Ps 149). Hymns also were sung to praise the nature of God or of his creation (Ps 8), and these in particular share much in common with other ancient Near Eastern hymns in praise of deities (see esp. the Egyptian Hymn to Aten, *ANET*, 369-71, and the similar Ps 104). The obvious settings in life for hymns were various occasions in the temple liturgy and later worship in the synagogue.

A broader category of psalms we might label "liturgical" arises less from form than function and often overlaps with categories defined principally by form. That is, although they may differ in *specific* function and in the *particular* elements they exhibit, this broad class of psalms all share in common use in the temple (or perhaps later, synagogue) liturgy (worship service) and associated actions. For example, the "Songs of Ascent" in Psalms 120–134 likely reveal a liturgy that accompanied a family's travel "up" to and arrival at Jerusalem for the

following the appeal that comes in a lament. In fact, a common concluding element in psalms of lament is the promise to give thanks for deliverance; in that way the type just surveyed devolves from the genre we turn to now.

There are clear examples of two kinds of laments in the Psalter, individual (e.g., Pss 3, 5, 13, 22, 26, 39, 51, 59, 70, 88, 120, 141) and communal (Pss 44, 74, 79, 80, 83) laments. Virtually all instances of both types include some or all of the same basic elements. They include: an appeal to God from the speaker to be heard (5:1), a complaint about the psalmist's circumstances (22:1), a confession of sin or claim to blamelessness (Pss 51, 69), an appeal to God for deliverance (83:9-18), description of God's positive response (13:6), and a promise to give (or already an expression of) thanks and praise (59:16-17). (Note that not all of these elements are present in every lament, nor yearly festivals. Likewise, Psalms 15 and 24 accord well with rites of entry into the temple precincts, elements of Psalms 48, 118, and 132 seem related to a processional at the temple, and a few psalms seem to provide the liturgy that accompanied making an offering (e.g., Ps 66).

Royal Psalms represent another category that is defined more by function than form. Psalms 2, 72 and 110, for instance, are clearly intended to accompany the coronation of a king. Psalm 20 prays for a king's victory before battle, and Psalm 21 credits God for the monarch's success. Psalm 45 accompanies a ruler's nuptials. Psalms 89, 101, and 144 are prayers of the king for deliverance and victory and of his own commitment to justice. While these were surely used publicly during the period of the monarchy, they likely also functioned after the failure of the state as means of anticipating liturgically the restoration of the Davidic line and the rule of kings over an independent state.

The last category we describe includes Wisdom and Torah Psalms. Generally scholars list under this dual heading Psalms 1, 19, 37, 49, 73, 112, 119, 127, 128 and 133. These two types can be classified together in part because neither is spoken so much *to* God as *about* God, and also because there is not always agreement as to which are Wisdom or Torah Psalms (e.g., Ps 1 is listed under both headings by different scholars). Generally these are descriptive in nature, with only few prescriptive elements. For example, Psalm 1 *describes* the happy existence of those who take delight in the law of the Lord as a life of meditation well rewarded by God in contrast with the life of "wicked sinners," persons who take the role of scoffers. Similarly, Psalm 19 *describes* the activity of God in creating and giving the Law, and Psalm 133 extols the virtues of peaceful family life. Psalm 49 does include *prescriptive* elements, calling an audience to attention (49:1) and admonishing equanimity in the face of economic imbalance (49:17-20), and Psalm 112:1 calls an audience to "Praise the Lord!" before launching into a more typically descriptive Wisdom Psalm.

Critical Issues in the Studying the Book of Psalms

In part because of the present-day widespread fascination with "spirituality," recent scholarship has been prompted to offer much in the way of studies on the book of Psalms. As a consequence the range of "Critical Issues" has expanded quite a lot in the past years. But once more, space limitations require selectivity on our part. As we saw above, the question of the Psalter's formation has been of considerable interest, and connected with that are the matters of Psalms' textual

history and its place in theories about the formation of the Hebrew Bible canon. A second issue that merits our attention is the function of the Psalter in its origin and subsequent use. Finally, we return to the issue of a possible rationale for the five-book structure of the psalter.

The Book of Psalms from a Text-Critical and Canon Perspective

We start with the simplest aspect of the Psalter's textual complexity, the variations in numbering and content between the Masoretic and Septuagint texts of Psalms. First, Masoretic and LXX Psalms divide some of the individual psalms differently. A chart is helpful in seeing these differences. There is some logic to the arrangement provided in the Septuagint, at least with respect to Psalms 9–10, which are, in fact, a single prayer for deliverance.

We have already drawn attention to the evidence the Dead Sea Scrolls provide for the relatively late formation of the canonical book of Psalms. The Psalms Scroll from Cave 11, the largest and most complete Psalms scroll, alone offers ample grounds for dismissing an early formation of the Psalter's present five-part structure and the stabilizing of the texts we find in the Masoretic and LXX editions. The Cave 11 scroll does preserve much of what would become Books 4 and 5 of the present Psalter, but it embraces substantially more material as well, including four noncanonical psalms and a passage from 2 Samuel 23 (151 A and B, 154, 155, and Sir 51:13-20; 2 Sam 23:1-7, "the last words of David"). Add to this the substantial differences exhibited among several of the many Cave 4 manuscripts of Psalms (4Q83-84, 4Q86-87, 4Q92, 4Q95, 4Q98) and the Scrolls leave little doubt that not only the text of Psalms, but its content as well remained thoroughly fluid up to the turn of the eras.

This leads to discussion of the role of the book of Psalms in the larger canon debate. Some scholars are inclined to treat references in early Jewish and Christian

The Masoretic Text and Septuagint of Psalms Compared

Masoretic Text	Septuagint
Psalms 1–8	Psalms 1–8
Psalms 9–10	Psalm 9
Psalms 11–113	Psalms 10–112
Psalms 114–115	Psalm 113
Psalm 116	Psalms 114–115
Psalms 117–146	Psalms 116–145
Psalm 147	Psalms 146–147
Psalms 148–150	Psalms 148–150
	Psalm 151

Psalms Scroll from Qumran. (Courtesy of the Israel Antiquities Authority)

literature to "the Books of Moses, the prophets, and the psalms [or hymns]" (and similar phrases) not only as very early evidence of a tripartite canon; they also see in the particular use of the word "psalms" or "hymns" evidence that the book of Psalms had reached closure well within the period of the 1st century C.E. (see in particular Luke 24:44; cf. Luke 20:42; Acts 1:20). But a close look at the full range of citations that suggest a tripartite canon around the turn of eras quickly undercuts their value for that claim, suggesting in turn that references to "psalms" or "hymns" must also be understood more broadly than as references to a book, let alone the book of Psalms we know today. In short, the pride of place given to the Psalms in the debate over the formation of the canon of the Hebrew Bible is almost certainly unmerited.

The Function of the Psalter

It is usually assumed that the book of Psalms functioned as the temple's prayer and hymnbook. That may be so at some level, but the many indications we have seen thus far of a rather late closure to the canonical form of the book places that in some question. That is to say, parts of the Psalter we possess in our Bibles surely did play a role in the Second Temple, and may have even been used in the First Temple; but the evidence dictates that we reject any notion that the canonical book of Psalms was used for a long time, if at all, in the Second Temple. Of course, that raises the important question of the Psalter's function in the absence of a temple.

In part one can only speculate on this matter, given an absence of unequivocal evidence one way or the other. Nonetheless, it seems clear that the psalms were used in the synagogue as well as the developing "home and hearth" religion of early Judaism. There is also no doubt that eventually the canonical book of Psalms took its place as the authoritative Psalter for posttemple Jewish liturgical practice. Likewise, as the early Christian community took shape, it too used psalms for worship and certainly also for interpreting the meaning of Jesus. Indeed, on the latter point we note that passages from

the book of Psalms make up the single largest group of citations of an Old Testament book in the New Testament; for example, it is Ps 22:1 that Jesus is given to say by Matt 27:46 (par. Mark 15:34) as he dies on the cross.

So much for the "formal" function of the book of Psalms in its early days. There is certainly more to say on this, though, inasmuch as we learn from early rabbinic and Christian writings that the Psalter's evocation of the richness of human experience also caught the eyes of early commentators. Thus the book not only served formal and informal liturgical contexts, but also very quickly took a prominent place in devotional and theological thought.

This brings us to the current resurgence of interest in the Psalter. While it continues to serve as a rich liturgical resource, it has also come to take a very prominent role in contemporary theological thought and devotional practices. In particular, the relatively new field of "spirituality" has been enriched by Scripture altogether, but by the book of Psalms in particular.

The Five-Part Structure of the Book of Psalms

We have already noted (and rejected) the proposal to explain the division of the Psalter in terms of royal covenantal theology. Two other proposals are worth considering as well.

The first we take up because it once played such an important role in the history of Psalms scholarship. Several scholars suggested in the past that liturgical and lectionary use of the Psalter in the synagogue explains its particular structure. This theory proposed that the portions of the book of Psalms were composed to match the weekly Torah portions laid out in a triennial lectionary cycle. Although this is a very attractive proposal, at least inasmuch as it capitalizes on the certainty that the Psalter was important in the synagogue liturgy, attempts to see the thematic or even lexical correspondences between Torah portions in the weekly lectionary and some portion of the Psalms have been none too successful. Thus this thesis has fallen out of favor.

The other proposal we note is more modest and, for that reason at least, receives perhaps more credit than others. Some observe that psalms often seem to be grouped together on various grounds, for instance, the "Elohistic Psalter" described above. Other groupings form around such simple elements as using the same refrain to begin or end, or to begin and end each psalm. Also, clusters of psalms attributed to David, and even to David on the occasion of a similar event, seem to emerge. From this some conclude that the Psalter grew from disparate smaller collections that had their own logic of cohesion, ranging from the repetition of particular catchwords to the development of a common, general theme. The clear advantage this proposal has is its resistance to forcing the entire Psalter into a totalizing explanation that the evidence simply does not bear. It is a proposal that accepts the near certainty that the Psalter grew from many smaller collections. Of course, it leaves open the precise reason for the formation of a five-part Psalter, although that may be as simple as it seems: an effort to provide a liturgical mirror, no matter how foggy, for the shape of the Torah.

Theological Themes in the Book of Psalms

We noted earlier the recent upsurge of fascination in the book of Psalms. It has generated not only many new critical studies, but also more than a few attempts to circumscribe "the theology of the book of Psalms." Hardly can there be so fruitless an endeavor, for even our brief survey of the book's contents proves the incredible variety of theological themes present in it. This is not surprising; with 150 different entries there is bound to be an amazing breadth of perspectives represented. Another reason to expect a highly textured theological witness is the book's genre; it is a hymnbook, and anyone who participates in a contemporary religious community understands how hymnbooks provide an outlet for the full range of a community's theological self-understandings. Indeed, the Psalms give expression to the full range of theological perspectives we have seen thus far in this Introduction. Even more, the Psalter provides some of the very earliest "reader reports" on the theological perspectives attested to in the Hebrew Bible, adding even more variety to the spectrum of such views already present in the Bible.

To provide some sense of the Psalter's richness we treat "theological themes" under two headings. The first section attends to the way the Psalter appropriates some of the theologies of the Hebrew Bible we have thus far observed and how it begins to reshape them through various interpretive moves. The second section offers our notion of what *does* provide unity to the Psalter in spite of its enormous theological diversity.

The Theologies of the Hebrew Bible in the Book of Psalms

Beginning with the Psalter's use of Deuteronomic theology, we are drawn to a host of psalms, but most particularly to laments. For example, Psalm 28, a prayer for deliverance, exemplifies the psalmists' appropriation of the Deuteronomic tradition of God's election of Israel and subsequent promise of retributive justice for her people and their foes according to their behavior (especially as it relates to the law). But there is already evidence of an interpretive stance relative to the Deuteronomic theology. The psalmist hearkens first to God's promise to deliver Israel from its foes should it fall into their hands through a failure to fulfill covenant obligations (28:1-2; cf. Deut 4:25-31; 1 Kgs 8:46-53). Barely secondary to this in importance is the psalmist's invocation of God's promise in the Deuteronomic tradition to punish evildoers as well: "Repay them [evildoers] according to their work, and according to the evil of their deeds" (28:4-5). Absent from the psalm — and from a great number of the laments — is acknowledgement of the sin against the covenant stipulations which created the difficult conditions Israel faced. The psalmist, in other words, was selective in evoking the Deuteronomic themes.

A second hallmark of the laments' interpretive appreciation of the Deuteronomic tradition is the intensity with which they dwell on God's promise of punishment to the wicked, and the sense of vindication the righteous derive from this.

O God, break the teeth in their mouths;
    tear out the fangs of the young lions, O Lord!
Let them vanish like water that runs away;
    like grass let them be trodden down and wither.
Let them be like the snail that dissolves into slime;
    like the untimely birth that never sees the sun.
Sooner than your pots can feel the heat of thorns,
    whether green or ablaze, may he sweep them away!
The righteous will rejoice when they see vengeance done;
    they will bathe their feet in the blood of the wicked.
People will say, "Surely there is a reward for the righteous;
    surely there is a God who judges on earth." (Ps 58:6-11)

When we turn to the Psalter's evocation of the theology associated with the Yahwist tradition in the Hebrew Scriptures, here too we discover a nuanced appreciation of the antecedent theology. For example, Psalm

47 summons the memory of Abraham and Jacob (47:4, 9) in language that recalls God's unilateral choice of Abraham and his descendants to make of Jacob a great nation called Israel (v. 4, where the word "chose" occurs), a nation to rule over all others (v. 9). The psalmist does not stop, though, at invoking the concentration of promise passages in Genesis 12–15; 32. Rather, he augments these essential elements of the Yahwist tradition with claims for God's kingship over all (47:2-3, 6-8), even using language associated with the enthronement of a king to describe God (v. 5).

Psalms 105–106, certainly meant by the author-editors of the Psalter to be read as a single psalm, also thoroughly exemplify the Yahwist's basic story line from the Ancestral Narrative in Genesis 12–50 to the National Saga in Exodus and Numbers. There can be no doubt that the Yahwist's elementary sense of God's unilateral promise pervades the two psalms. But at the end of Psalm 105 the psalmist explains that God fulfilled his promise of land so that Israel "might keep his statutes and observe his laws" (105:45). The resulting change in mood in Psalm 106 is clear: instead of continuing Psalm 105's celebration of God's promises and their fulfillment, Psalm 106 dwells on the ingratitude of Israel to God after God delivered the people from Egyptian might. Psalm 106:13-39 recalls Israel's rebellion from the shores of the Red Sea to the days of the judges in the land, giving instance after instance from the biblical record of the people's ill regard for the gifts God had bestowed on them. Paired with the final verse of Psalm 105, Psalm 106, at least to v. 39, looks like a wholesale shift to a Deuteronomic perspective. But 106:40-46 belies that assumption as quickly as it forms in the mind of the reader, arguing that in spite of Israel's great sin, when the people cried out to God for relief from their distress, God responded, because "for their sake he remembered his covenant, and showed compassion according to the abundance of his steadfast love" (106:45). With this, third person speech gives way to the second person speech: the psalmist gives voice to the age-old cry, "Save us, O Lord our God, and gather us from among the nations, that we may give thanks to your holy name and glory in your praise" (106:47). In this we learn the status of the psalmist and his audience: they live under the consequences of Israel's rebellion, but they also know God's reputation for mercy, and so they recall it to God and ask for it on their own behalf. The turn to Deuteronomic-style retributive justice is only partial, stepping away from it at the last moment to observe that God relents in punishment according to his covenant (106:45) — which has been established in this psalm to be the promises to the ancestors — and because he is praised by those who are gathered from exile (106:47). Psalm 105 proves that for this psalmist the covenant is the unilateral promise of descendants and land characteristic of the Yahwist tradition (cf. Genesis 12; 15; 32; Exodus 32); but Psalm 106's sensitivity to the Deuteronomistic History and the Yahwist's record of wilderness rebellion is reinforced by the idea that the people shall be gathered from exile to praise God when they cry to him for deliverance (cf. Deut 4:29-31; 1 Kgs 8:46-53). In other words, this two-part psalm manages to reconcile the Yahwist and Deuteronomist in a creative way, yet one that clearly favors the Yahwist's unilateralism.

The Priestly Work's influence can also be seen in the Psalter, even if its most characteristic use is as a foil to other perspectives. This pattern is especially clear in Psalm 50, where the language of temple sacrifice is subverted for use in a plea instead for righteous action, dependence on God as deliverer, and bloodless sacrifices of thanksgiving. The final two verses complete the subversion of the Priestly Writer's language.

> "Mark this, then, you who forget God,
>   or I will tear you apart, and there will be no one to
>   deliver.
> Those who bring thanksgiving as their sacrifice honor me;
>   to those who go the right way
>   I will show the salvation of God" (50:22-23)

The speech of God confirms that God's desire is not for the blood of the goats that are his anyway, but for remembrance and thanksgiving from the human community.

Psalm 51 provides another instance of the Psalter's peculiar posture in relation to the Priestly traditions. This well-known psalm, attributed to David when he was discovered in his adultery with Bathsheba, uses the typical vocabulary of the Priestly Writer, including sin, clean and impure, holy, blood(shed), sacrifice; but it employs that language to say that what God most desires in sacrifice is "a broken and contrite heart" (51:17) and the praise from the lips of the sinner (v. 15). So the psalm appears to echo the sentiments of Psalm 50. Yet the last two verses restore to this psalm (and its predecessor?) an appreciation of the temple cult.

> Do good to Zion in your good pleasure;
>   rebuild the walls of Jerusalem,
> then you will delight in right sacrifices,
>   in burnt offerings and whole burnt offerings;
>   then bulls will be offered on your altar. (51:18-19)

Once more we see that the Psalter does not merely parrot, oppose, or choose to support single theologies of the Hebrew Bible; instead it reshapes them in new and creative ways.

Wisdom theology also makes its presence known abundantly in the Psalms, as we have seen in the listing of "wisdom" psalms above. But here too the psalmists modify the basic theological perspective. In Psalm 73, the psalmist begins with an affirmation of God's justice: "Truly God is good to the upright, to those who are pure in heart" (v. 1). Immediately following this declamation, though, the psalmist professes that he nonetheless observed oppressors prospering and being praised by their neighbors. At this sight the psalmist was both disgusted and envious, inclined to jealousy. Then he describes going into God's sanctuary and remembering the truth of that matter, that in the end God sees to justice for the wicked and the righteous. And with that the psalmist is able to close with an affirmation of the basic notion that God acts with retributive justice, and for that reason he places his trust in God. In other words, a wisdom psalm embraces elements of the Deuteronomic tradition to contend with the recurring difficulty for wisdom traditions, the inequities of the world that belie the notion that following human insight necessarily results in prosperity and honor.

Of course, the David-Zion theology is especially well represented in the Psalter. Not only are the Psalms in large part attributed to David, but we also saw above the considerable number of psalms that entail concern for kingship and the rituals associated with it, many of which are especially linked to the David-Zion theology. Also to consider is the theory that the five books of the Psalter somehow relate to David-Zion theological hopes, disappointments, and renewed hopes. But once more we see that the Psalter does not appropriate a theology without adjusting it in one way or another. For example, Psalm 89 is often paired with 2 Samuel 7 as a "David charter" text, especially because of its direct references to God's promise to David of an everlasting dynasty to follow him. But there is more to the psalm than the promise; entailed in it as well are elements of the creation myth familiar from Genesis 1–2 (89:9-10), and the ancient Near Eastern view of divine kingship pervades the hymn (e.g., 89:27). Present as well is a hint of the Yahwist's theology of God's unilateral love for his chosen (89:28). In other words, while serving as a parade example of the David-Zion theology, in the hands of this psalmist the hymn takes into its orbit even more of the rich traditions of Israel's theological imagination.

Theology as a Daughter of Human Experience: The Unifying Theme of the Psalter

The previous survey of the Psalter's appropriation of the theologies of the Hebrew Bible already points to a possible way of conceiving a unifying element in the Psalter. Time and again we saw that the Old Testament theologies covered thus far in our Introduction had their origins in human experience and reflection on God. Likewise, we have seen that those same theologies bubbled up in the words of the psalmists as responses to real human experiences of joy and sorrow, pain and jubilation, exaltation and depression. Even more, the received theologies were "mixed and matched" to create new, somewhat novel theological perspectives. This simple observation suggests one of the most interesting theological characteristics of the Psalter: it provides ample support for the notion that theology is indeed a daughter of human experience. It does not fall from heaven on high, given as a decree from God above, but it bubbles up from human experience in relationship to God. It is the residue of human reflection on what it means to be human in relationship to God. Still more, the Psalter shows that God uses that human discourse to speak further to humanity, using what has already come to be in the way of theological reflection to reveal yet more of Godself. In this way the Psalter is one of the greatest theological treasures of the Hebrew Bible.

Questions for Review and Discussion

1 What are some of the different kinds of psalms, and what are their basic features?

2 How do the psalms relate the theologies we have seen thus far in this book? What is some of the evidence we cited in favor of this explanation of how the theologies relate to the psalms?

3 What do we mean by the saying, "theology is the daughter of human experience," especially as it relates to the Psalter? What does this general notion suggest about all human attempts to reflect on experience in light of Scriptures' testimony?

Further Reading

Anderson, A. A. *The Book of Psalms,* 2 vols. NCBC. Grand Rapids: Wm. B. Eerdmans, 1981.

Prinsloo, Willem S. "Psalms." In *ECB,* 364-436.

Whybray, R. N. *Reading the Psalms as a Book.* JSOTSup 222. Sheffield: Sheffield Academic, 1996.

Chapter 23

Proverbs

Getting Started

1   Read the headings in Proverbs 1:1; 10:1; 22:17; 25:1; 30:1; 31:1. What do these suggest about the nature of the book of Proverbs as a whole?

2   Read Proverbs 8. Who speaks out here, and what is this character's gender and relationship to God?

3   Sample the sayings in Proverbs 25. Can you identify different kinds — genres — of proverbial speech here? What does this small investigation indicate to you about the nature of proverbial wisdom?

Preliminary Comments

The book of Proverbs is exactly what its title indicates: a collection of short sayings that offer advice or express accepted wisdom as truth. Notoriously, the sayings are organized only very loosely into distinct collections that alone rarely exhibit any thematic or structural coherence. Even the chief exception to this judgment, Proverbs 1–9, displays only modest structural organization. As a consequence, rehearsing in some detail the contents of Proverbs, as we have done for other books

thus far, is not practical. Instead, we discuss in turn each of the collections of sayings contained in Proverbs separately. Our survey will reveal the diversity of material contained in this book, as well as the handful of characteristics that nonetheless make of it a coherent whole.

A Walk through the Book of Proverbs

The main sayings collections in the book of Proverbs are marked out by introductory formulae. Using these "titles" and some other division indicators, we divide the book into the following parts.

Proverbs 1:1-7: Introduction

This section is what might be described as the introduction to the entire book. Like the opening verse of Ecclesiastes, Prov 1:1 establishes Solomon as the author of the book. Verses 2-6 then announce the aim Solomon had in producing the book: it was for the sake of learning and instruction in righteousness and equity, educating the simple and young, and advancing the knowledge of the wise. Proverbs 1:7 then appears as a renewed heading, even a summary of the book as a whole: "The fear of the Lord is the beginning of knowledge; fools despise wisdom and instruction."

Reading Guide to Proverbs
Introduction (1:1-7)
A Father's Wisdom for His Son (1:8–9:18)
Proverbs of Solomon (10:1–22:16)
A Parallel with Wisdom of Amenemope (22:17–24:34)
Other Proverbs of Solomon That the Men of
    Hezekiah Collected (25:1–29:27)
The Words of Agur, Son of Jakeh (30:1-33)
The Words of King Lemuel (31:1-31)

Proverbs 1:8–9:18: A Father's Wisdom for His Son

Proverbs 1:8 marks out yet another new beginning: "Hear, my son [NRSV: child], your father's instruction, and do not reject your mother's teaching." The verse is not only an introductory command, but it also cleverly articulates the agenda of the following nine chapters. The imperative mood of the verb "Hear!" leaves little doubt that the advice that follows is not optional, but compulsory. The identities of the speaker and recipient revealed by the words that follow the command, "my son," reinforce the obligatory nature of the advice offered, for in Israelite antiquity sons were duty bound to respect the wishes and commands of their fathers. Indeed, the Ten Commandments require respect for the parent (Exod 20:12), and the Covenant Code metes out capital punishment to children who strike or curse their fathers (Exod 21:15, 17)! Thus the son is required to pay strict heed to his "father's instruction," which, of course, follows in full detail. Inasmuch as the addressees are invited by the form of address to consider themselves in the role of the son, the thrust of the opening command is clear: "Listen to and heed, oh reader, what is instructed here!"

But notably, the opening command not only establishes the relationship between the words of the text and its recipients as that between a son and a father; it adds that a mother's teaching is also to be held in highest regard. This is a peculiar admonition, at least insofar as the word "mother" is never used again in Proverbs 1–9 apart from 6:20, a verse that is identical to 1:8 with respect to the command not to forsake a mother's teaching (Hebrew *torah*). There is, however, a woman who offers instruction in Proverbs 1–9: Dame Wisdom. She speaks out several times (1:20-33; 8:4-36; cf. 9:4-6) to describe herself with generalized terms for wisdom, insight, and understanding. More substantial are her claims to provide riches and life to those who embrace her. In this way she draws a sharp contrast between herself and the "stranger woman," the "evil woman," the "harlot," the "wife of another," or the "foolish woman" (2:16; 6:24, 26, 29; 7:5; 9:13), all of whose embrace leads to various bad ends, most prominently poverty and death. We will see below in "Critical Issues" that these two feminine figures in Proverbs 1–9 suggest a particular sociohistorical background for this part of the book. For now it suffices to observe that, at least on a straightforward reading, Dame Wisdom seems to play the role of "mother" named in 1:8 and 6:20. Thus the reader is commanded not only to hold fast to the advice offered by the speaker as a son heeds a father's command; he is also required to give heed to the instruction Wisdom offers.

The general idea behind most of Prov 1:8–9:18 is that young men do best by themselves when they direct their passions first toward the pursuit of wisdom, and second toward their own wives, and certainly never toward the various types of difficult women listed above. The persistence of this theme is peculiar to Proverbs 1–9 and invites speculation on its possible larger themes. We return to this in "Critical Issues" below.

Proverbs 10:1–22:16: Proverbs of Solomon

That Proverbs 10:1 begins a new unit is clear from a number of indicators. First, the opening words, "The Proverbs of Solomon," are little more than a title, or label. Second, gone are the imperatives of a father's speech to his son, along with the general focus on seeking wisdom and controlling passions, to be replaced here by the use of distich sentences that state simply the results of observing human experience. A distich is a sentence of two lines which are related to one another as synonymous or antithetical claims, or which work together to provide a synthesis. Examples on page 207 illustrate each of these types.

The shift in tone from Proverbs 1–9 is also obvious. While the father speaking to his son presents his case for a certain way of being, and commands his son to obey his advice, the sentences of 10:1–22:16 are descriptive statements derived from human experience. The *prescriptive* nature of chs. 1–9 gives way to the *descriptive* character of 10:1–22:16. Thus the moral suasion of this collection lies simply in the accuracy of its description of experience, not in any exhortation from their author.

The sentences of 10:1–22:16 address a wide variety of human behaviors. Among others, topics include: the value of human industry (10:4; 12:14, 24; 21:25); the merit of confronting misbehavior rather than letting it pass with a wink and a nod, and correspondingly, of accepting discipline (10:10, 17; 13:1; 15:1; 17:10); the wisdom of avoiding fools (14:7; 17:12); the importance of honesty in business dealings (16:11; 20:10, 23); the worth of a wise child to her parents (10:5; 13:1; 19:13); and the benefit of prudent speech (12:13; 13:3; 14:3; 16:13; 18:20). Repeated emphasis on God's righteousness in judgment reinforces the prescriptive force of the descriptive sayings; indeed, one finds clusters of sayings on the justice of God for the wise and righteous (10:27, 29; 14:26-27; 15:8-9, 25-26; 16:1-9; 19:21, 23; 20:23-24; 21:1-2; 22:2-4). For all of their differences otherwise, this latter emphasis *does* link 10:1–22:16 to chs. 1–9.

Proverbs 22:17–24:34: A Parallel With Wisdom of Amenemope

Although we treat it as a separate unit unto itself, this section of text may be divided into two parts. The first portion is distinguished by a heading ("The words of the wise") and its close affiliation with an Egyptian text, the Wisdom of Amenemope (22:17–24:22). The last part, 24:23-34, also bears a heading ("These also are the words of the wise") and overlaps with 6:6-11.

That there are similarities between Prov 22:17–24:22 and the Wisdom of Amenemope has long been recognized, but there is no agreement on the implications of those similarities for understanding the relationship between the collections of sayings. Some argue that Prov 22:17–24:22 depends directly on the more antique Egyptian text and that this section of Proverbs was intended, as the Wisdom of Amenemope seems to have been, as instruction for young men at court. Others take a more cautious approach, observing that the themes in both works are common to advice regarding how best to live among peers and superiors, such as would be the case for individuals in the royal entourage. Whatever the case, the contrast between this material and what we saw in the previous unit, 10:1–22:16, effectively illustrates the two origins usually posited for much of Proverbs: the family and the court. The sort of folk wisdom that pervades 10:1–22:16 has its natural locus in the mouths of parents for their children, while the

Wisdom of Amenemope, an Egyptian text providing instruction for young men of the royal court and bearing resemblance to Prov 22:17–24:22. (British Museum)

admonition to ascend to courtier status by taking good notes (22:29) and to avoid gluttony at the generous table of the ruler (23:1-3) belongs to the aspiring confidant to prime minister and king. It does not hurt the claim that much of 22:17–24:22 finds its origin in the courtly world that the passage just described, 22:29–23:3, has a close parallel in Wisdom of Amenemope 27:16-17; 23:3-8.

The placement of the trailing portion of this section of text, 24:23-34, is difficult to explain, apart from the heading that seems to mark it out as an appendix to the preceding portion ("These *also* are words of the wise"). Further confusing the question of its placement and raising that of its primary origin and purpose is the peculiar mix of themes it addresses: the value of justice in measuring up the neighbor, advice on how to prepare for the execution of a large undertaking, the uselessness of payback after a slight, and the problem of laziness (the theme that links this section with 6:6-11).

Proverbs 25:1–29:27: Other Proverbs of Solomon That the Men of Hezekiah Collected

The most distinctive characteristic of this collection is the presence of many genuine similitudes, sayings that employ the word "like" at the beginning of one of two balanced elements. For example, 25:12 states, "Like a gold ring or an ornament of gold is a wise rebuke to a listening ear." In addition to an unusual abundance of this type of saying, Proverbs 25–29 is also characterized by a small unit at the beginning that seems to offer further instruction for life in the royal setting (25:2-10) and otherwise by sayings of widely-varying interest and

Examples of Distichs from Proverbs 10:1–22:16

Distich Type	Example
Synonymous	Prov 11:7 When the wicked die, their hope perishes, and the expectation of the godless comes to nothing.
Antithetical	Prov 13:20 Whoever walks with the wise becomes wise, but the companion of fools suffers harm.
Synthetic	Prov 14:27 The fear of the Lord is a fountain of life, so that one may avoid the snares of death.

focus. Although some observe in the last two chapters of this section what they think to be an unusual concentration of sayings related to life on the land (e.g., "Anyone who tills the land will have plenty of bread, but one who follows worthless pursuits will have plenty of poverty" [28:19]), a careful reading of the section suggests otherwise; here, too, the collection's most distinguishing characteristic is its eclectic nature.

Proverbs 30:1-33:
The Words of Agur, Son of Jakeh

The proper division of ch. 30 into parts, indeed, if it should be divided at all, remains a subject of considerable debate. Proverbs 30:1-14 is usually assigned to the "Agur" of the superscription in v. 1, while the organization of the rest of the chapter as a series of numerical sayings indicates its separate nature. However, 30:10-14 is a transitional section inasmuch as the types of undesirable persons listed in it feature as interjections in the numerical sayings of 30:15-33. For now we set aside the question of the unity or disunity of the chapter, to focus on a quick survey of its character as a whole.

Proverbs 30:1-14, ascribed to a person named "Agur," is perhaps best understood as a brief, but highly concentrated challenge to traditional wisdom and piety. It appears to be a dialogue between a rather sharp-tongued questioner who wonders even about the existence of God (30:1-4, 7-9) and a pious respondent who calls the questioner to account (30:5-6, 10). The section concludes with a listing of four types of problematic persons: disrespectful offspring, the falsely righteous, the haughty, and those who are destructive toward others.

Proverbs 30:15-33 follows with a series of numerical sayings — a common form in ancient Near Eastern wisdom traditions — that compare widely disparate phenomena that nonetheless share at least one peculiar trait in common (e.g., widely differing things that are never sated include Sheol, a barren womb, parched earth, and a fire). Interspersed with these numerical sayings are further observations on the four kinds of persons described in 30:11-14.

Proverbs 31:1-31: The Words of King Lemuel

Like Proverbs 30, this chapter also divides into two parts. The first, 30:1-9, amounts not so much to the words of the king, as the superscription suggests, but the instruction of a queen to her son. She warns him from strong drink and passions toward women and encourages him instead to give good wine to those who sorrow and are in distress to provide them some relief. She also calls him to see to justice and righteousness in his rule.

The second part, 30:10-31, is the well-known speech in favor of a good wife. It exalts the woman who devotes her time and energy to the well-being of her husband and children. Its "theological" validation of the good wife comes only belatedly, in v. 31.

Critical Issues in the Study of the Book of Proverbs

The book of Proverbs evokes a variety of critical responses. The substantial differences between the Hebrew text and the Greek translation deserve some attention, as do the questions of authorship and compositional history, date, and attitudes toward women.

The Greek Text of the Book of Proverbs

In addition to the sort of transformations of meaning that normally come with translating a text, the Greek of Proverbs exhibits some other more unusual characteristics. There are substantial additions in the Greek text. In addition to congregating especially at the close of identifiable sections (e.g., 27:24-27), the expansions tend to reflect Hellenistic-style wisdom, suggesting that even as the book was translated further proverbial wisdom (of "foreign" origin!) accrued to it. Also peculiar to the Greek text of Proverbs is rearrangement of material to place what appears to be of foreign origin together in one section (that includes in the following order 22:17–24:22; 30:1-14; 24:23-34; 30:15-33; 31:1-9; 25:1–29:27; 31:10-31). Together these two features not only make Septuagint Proverbs particularly interesting from a text-critical perspective; they also support the idea that Proverbs is a composite document with a compositional history that continued even into the stage of translation. These are significant observations for our next topic.

Authorship and Compositional History

While the book of Proverbs is ascribed to Solomon with its superscription in 1:1, the indicators against the reliability of that claim and in favor of it being a late addition are substantial. First, comparison of the contents of Proverbs with the wisdom that the Deuteronomic tradition ascribes to Solomon hardly favors Solomon's authorship. According to 1 Kgs 4:29-34 his "proverbial" wisdom entailed a capacity to classify and name natural phenomena, hardly the various talents exhibited by the sayings in the book of Proverbs. Second, the variety of headings we observed in our walk through the text thoroughly contradicts the idea that this is a work of Solomon alone. Indeed, the headings suggest that this is a wildly composite work that draws together within its scope a wide range of proverbs collections, some of which were not even Israelite in origin. The ascriptions naming Agur and Lemuel suggest foreign origin, and in any case non-Solomonic authorship, and the collection in 22:17–24:22 that so closely resembles the Wisdom of Amenemope are also strong indicators of the book's composite nature. Finally, that further proverbs were added at the stage of translation and that the translator recognized the separate units clearly enough to reassemble them in a new order also indicate the composite nature of the work.

This of course raises the question of the book's *compositional history.* We may say little about this, though, inasmuch as the aim of proverbial wisdom to be *timeless* ensures the absence of temporal indicators in the book's sayings. And the association of certain sections with known wisdom traditions (e.g., 22:17–24:22 and the Wisdom of Amenemope) also offers little help insofar as those sought their own timelessness as well and thus could have been influential on an Israelite author over several centuries' time. The best we can do in this regard is note what seems most likely to be the youngest collection of proverbs and presume that the compositional history came to a conclusion sometime after that anthology's likely date. This leads to our next topic.

The Date of the Book of Proverbs, and a Word About Function

While virtually everything else regarding the growth history of the book of Proverbs must remain highly speculative at best, the approximate dates of the youngest sections within the book do seem clear to some commentators. For a variety of reasons Proverbs 1–9 is often assigned to the Persian period, not the least of which is the concern that young men not be tempted to associate with a "foreign woman." The wicked woman who appears repeatedly in Proverbs 1–9 is twice called the *'ishshah zarah,* the "stranger woman" (2:16; 7:5). The reference is sometimes understood to be the key to understanding other even more damning names for the *femme fatale* of Proverbs 1–9 (e.g., the *'ishshah zonah,* the "harlot woman" in 6:26): she embodies the non-Israelite women whom some returnee Judeans took as wives in the early Postexilic, Persian period, the women whom Ezra and Nehemiah insisted Judean men divorce and send away for the sake of preserving the land of Israel in Judean hands and defending the emerging culture of early Judaism (Ezra 9–10; Neh 13:23-31). Also, the personification of Wisdom as a feminine figure in Proverbs 8 and 31 (where she is made the flesh-and-blood "good wife and mother") is generally thought to be a late development, perhaps datable no earlier than the Persian period. Thus many conclude that apart from the additions made by the translators of Proverbs into Greek, the book was largely complete sometime in the Persian period.

This last offers an opening to address the possible function of the book of Proverbs, or at least one dimension of its function. That the first nine chapters address the question of how young men in postexilic Judah should behave in their personal conduct so as to best support the survival of the Judean community may be indicative of the book's larger purpose. It almost goes without saying that proverbial wisdom is intended to offer insight on how to live well, even prosperously. But this sort of opening section — paired with the closing section on the good wife — suggests that it is not only about individual success and happiness that Proverbs is concerned. In addition, its advice is meant to cultivate the success of the people of Israel as well. If the wisdom of this book is heeded, not only will individual young men flourish, but the whole of God's people will too. If wives and mothers emulate Wisdom, families will certainly prosper, but so will the entire gathering of families into a single people. On this reading Proverbs is the quintessential work about wisdom as at least one of the keys to Israel's strategy for being God's chosen people in the world.

The Treatment of Women in the Book of Proverbs

The foregoing should help put the lie to readings of Proverbs that unduly highlight its occasionally negative portraits of women. While these are not to be excused as mere ciphers for the foreign threats to identity and communal survival Israel faced in the Postexilic period — the misogyny of some of these sayings *does* reflect some ancient attitudes toward women — they must still be understood as part of a larger agenda that is far less concerned about denigrating the female gender than it is about cultivating a way of being for the entire people of Israel. The time-conditioned, negative attitudes toward women are placed in service of a larger agenda in the book of Proverbs. As such, contemporary readers would be (ironically) quite unwise to take direction from Proverbs in configuring gender relations today. To do so would be a little like reading Paul's Letter to the Galatians as a guide for gauging the character of the inhabitants of present-day Ankara!

Theological Themes in the Book of Proverbs

The "theology" present in the book of Proverbs is, for the most part, quite straightforward: God, or fear of God, is depicted as the font of wisdom, and God in turn favors those who exercise wisdom in their daily dealings. The way this basic theme is articulated varies from section to section in the book, and it is absent from a few parts, and may even be put in question by 30:1-14, but it is nonetheless the dominant message of Proverbs regarding the nature of God. There is more, though. Read in its canonical context, the book of Proverbs also raises the question of the relationship between Torah and Wisdom, and it provides a counterbalance to the very different claims made in Job and Ecclesiastes about the value of human wisdom in God's eyes.

God as Wisdom's Font and Admirer

The first major portion of the book, Proverbs 1–9, is clearest on the point that God is the font of wisdom. Wisdom personified describes herself as the first result of God's creative activity: "The Lord created me at the beginning of his work, the first of his acts of long ago" (8:22; see also 2:6). And the admonition to fear the Lord as the beginning of understanding and insight opens and closes this section of the book (1:7; 9:10). That God admires wisdom and rewards its practice among people — and punishes those who eschew it — is also made clear in this section (3:4, 12, 32). Thus we find here a particular concentration of admonitions to fear the Lord as the foundational act of wisdom, as well as Wisdom's commendation of herself as a pathway to God (3:5, 7; 8:35).

The so-called Proverbs of Solomon in 10:1–22:16 is most consistent in emphasizing the connection between fear of God and wisdom and God's favor for those who exercise insight in their dealings, as well as his disgust for those who do not (10:3; 15:33; 16:3: 16:20; 22:12).

Even the section that so closely resembles the Wisdom of Amenemope possesses the basic theological theme of God's reward for those who fear the Lord in their wisdom. Proverbs 22:17b-19 lays out the rationale for the advice that follows:

> Incline your ear and hear my words, and apply your mind to my teaching; for it will be pleasant if you keep them within you, if all of them are ready on your lips. So that your trust may be in the Lord, I have made them known to you today — yes, to you.

Likewise, the section paralleling the Egyptian text closes with this admonition: "My child, fear the Lord and the king and do not disobey either of them; for disaster comes from them suddenly, and who knows the ruin that both can bring?" (24:21-22).

The "Other Proverbs of Solomon That the Men of Hezekiah Collected" upholds this trend. Mixed in with this section's many proverbial sayings and similitudes are typical admonitions regarding piety toward God in thought and deed: act wisely in mending your enemies' wounds, for in so doing you "heap coals on their heads"

and earn God's reward (25:22); the evil do not understand justice as do the seekers of the Lord (28:5); and the greedy cause strife, but the one who trusts wisely in God is enriched (28:25).

Oddly, it is only in the final section of the book that this basic theme recedes and may even come in for critique. As noted above, in "The Words of Agur" God's very existence seems to be challenged, and if God does live, the idea that God is particularly useful to the faithful and wise seems to be mocked. As for the closing chapter, we hear only that a woman who fears the Lord is to be praised (31:30).

Torah and Wisdom: Foes or Friends?

One might think that Proverbs' very idea that practicing common sense in one's daily life amounts to fear of the Lord and brings God's blessing would be a serious challenge to Torah. After all, keeping God's law as a means of meriting God's blessing is at the heart of "Torah" broadly understood. Indeed, as we saw in our survey of the Deuteronomistic History, this is one way to read the treatment of "human wisdom" by the Deuteronomic writers. Writers who prized the keeping of law, the Deuteronomic writers found themselves compelled to denigrate human wisdom, if only obliquely (see esp. the possible reading of 1 Kgs 3:16-28 offered in Chapter 17). So does Proverbs cast aside God's law?

One might argue from the contents of Proverbs for an affirmative answer to the question that closed the previous paragraph, but it would perhaps be a mistake to do so. First, the word "Torah," though sparse in the book, appears like bookends in significant places at the beginning of the book and near its end (6:23; 28:4, 7, 9) as a standard for all other ways of acting and being. It is as though in its final form the book of Proverbs is made to subject common sense to God's "Torah." It is also perhaps worth noting that near the center of the book we also encounter two of the three occurrences of the word "commandment" (Hebrew *mitzvah*): in 13:13 and 19:16 we hear that those who keep the commandment are blessed. With these things in mind, it seems more likely that one should read Proverbs as wisdom that seeks to supplement and reinforce Torah rather than replace it. The purveyors of this wisdom were not enemies of the law, but rather its friends.

Is Proverbs a Reply to Job and Ecclesiastes?

The question posed in this heading is perhaps a bit misleading. It would almost certainly be a mistake to think that the book of Proverbs was composed *precisely* as a reply to the deep skepticism of Job and Ecclesiastes regarding the power of human wisdom and understanding. But reading once more in the context of the canon as a whole it seems foolish (!) to deny that this is how Proverbs functions. Just as Ecclesiastes makes its strong case for the uselessness of expecting particular good to come from wise action, let alone keeping of the law, Proverbs makes the counterargument, claiming relentlessly that the exercise of God-given human insight can only help one and bring God's blessing. And just as the book of Job argues in its own way against the idea that God is necessarily just in his dealings with humanity, Proverbs asserts unyieldingly (with perhaps the exception of the "Words of Agur") just the opposite. The Hebrew Bible, it seems, allows both perspectives to flourish within its boundaries. But of course, this is not the first time in this Introduction that we have had occasion to observe the "catholicity" of vision inherent in the Bible!

Questions for Review and Discussion

1   How many "parts" are there to the book of Proverbs, and what do they suggest regarding the book's compositional history (and what do we actually know of the date of its composition)?

2   Do the various parts of the book of Proverbs all take the same position on the value of God-given human wisdom? If there are dissenting voices within the book, where are they located, and what do you make of their presence in the book?

3   We have already seen the possibility that Proverbs might be in tension with the emphasis on Torah elsewhere in the Hebrew Bible. Are there other theological perspectives we have come across that might be in conflict, real or interpretive, with the one espoused in Proverbs? Can you cite evidence for this from Proverbs and other books of the Bible?

Further Reading

Clements, Ronald E. "Proverbs." In *ECB*, 437-66.

Clifford, Richard J. *Proverbs*. OTL. Louisville: Westminster John Knox, 1999.

Fontaine, Carole R. *Smooth Words: Women, Proverbs, and Performance in Biblical Wisdom*. JSOTSup 356. London: Sheffield Academic, 2002.

Martin, James D. *Proverbs*. OTG. Sheffield: Sheffield Academic, 1995.

Chapter 24

Ecclesiastes

Getting Started

1 Read Ecclesiastes 1. What is the attitude expressed by this author toward the reality of human experience?

2 Read Ecclesiastes 3. Are the words of the opening poem familiar? Does the language of 3:9-15 surprise you, given your previous knowledge of the poem in the first part of the chapter?

3 Read the closing chapter of Ecclesiastes. Does it contradict in any way what you sensed about its author's view of how the world works from chs. 1 and 3?

Preliminary Comments

The book of Ecclesiastes is truly an enigma in biblical literature. Its rhetoric is some of the best known of the Bible to generations of readers. The refrain "Vanity of vanities" (e.g., Eccl 1:2; 12:8), the dictum "For everything there is a season" (3:1a), and the advice to "eat, drink, and be merry" (e.g., 2:24) all owe their place in common parlance to the book of Ecclesiastes. Yet the book's contents otherwise are little known, let alone understood by people within and outside of Jewish and Christian com-

munities of faith. And, as we shall see, when its rather disconsolate message is heard, one wonders how it could have authored so much of our ordinary speech, let alone found its way into the canon of the Hebrew Bible.

A Walk through the Book of Ecclesiastes

The title "Ecclesiastes" is the Greek translation of a word in the first line of the original Hebrew text: "The words of the Teacher *(Qohelet)*" (Eccl 1:1). Thus another name for the book is the Hebrew word "Qoheleth." As we see below, the meaning of this word is much discussed, and little consensus has emerged on what the title means.

Equally befuddling for readers has been the question of the book's structure. At times appearing to be little more than a random collection of only vaguely related thought units, Ecclesiastes has defied virtually all attempts to make a sensible outline of its contents. Some suggest the repeated refrain "Eat, drink, and be merry" and its rough parallels (2:24-26; 3:12-13, 22; 5:18-19; 8:15; 9:7-10; 11:7-10) provide clues to the proper division of the book's parts; but this soon breaks down upon close examination. Others have suggested that the book is most easily understood as a palindrome (an A′B′C′B′A′ structure) and that this signals the influence of Greek philosophy on the author; but this, too, hardly holds together on close inspection. Indeed, the only clear structural elements appear at the beginning and end of the book. Corresponding to the superscription or "title" in 1:1 is a double epilogue in 12:9-11, 12-14; matching the thematic refrain in 1:2, "Vanity of vanities," is its double in 12:8; and corresponding to the poem that completes the beginning of the book in 1:3-11 is a concluding piece in 11:7–12:7. Between these corresponding structures at the beginning and ending of the book there are few coherent units. What does seem apparent, though, is a gradual, though not entirely consistent, lengthening of units of loosely affiliated material. Thus we divide the book as follows.

Ecclesiastes 1:1-11: Superscription, Refrain, and Opening Poem

The book commences with a superscription not unlike what we see in many of the prophetic books (e.g., Jer 1:1; Hos 1:1; Joel 1:1; Amos 1:1) and in Prov 30:1: "The words of the Teacher, the son of David, king in Jerusalem." The formulaic character of the superscription and the certainly more original use of the term "Teacher" (Hebrew *Qoheleth*) in 7:27; 12:8 leave little doubt among readers that it is a late element which was composed so as to identify the Teacher with Solomon, the traditional purveyor of Israel's wisdom traditions.

Following the superscription is the well-known refrain, "Vanity of vanities, says the Teacher, vanity of vanities! All is vanity" (1:2). This sets the theme of the book, at least insofar as much of what follows attacks the notion that there is meaning in anything one might do in life. Indeed, the word for "vanity" (Hebrew *hebel*) means something akin to "vapor," a transitory entity that is little more than air itself.

The opening poem that follows in 1:3-11 is actually the first part of a speech that, in its present form, is assigned to Solomon. Following the refrain in v. 2, it sets out the first evidence for the premise that all is vanity.

People gain nothing from their labor, and generations come and go, but the earth never changes (vv. 3-4); indeed, the sun maintains a changeless cycle of rising and setting, the wind blows in unchanging patterns, and the streams run to the sea and never fill it up (vv. 5-7). From this the author concludes that "all things are wearisome," "there is nothing new under the sun," and worst of all, passing generations are forgotten by those that follow (perhaps implying that all that was, will be again for lack of human memory of the sameness of all things; vv. 8-11). Together these opening poetic reflections set indelibly the tone of the rest of the book.

Ecclesiastes 1:12–2:26: Solomon's Speech

In 1:12-13 the speaker announces that as king in Jerusalem he set out to understand "all that is done under heaven," only to conclude that it is a sorry business God has given humanity to pursue. Indeed, no effort avails anyone or anything, and this the speaker discovered by seeking and obtaining wisdom, insight, about all there is in creation (1:14-18). Likewise, the pursuit of pure pleasure brings no satisfaction (2:1-11). Realizing this, the speaker returns to wisdom and reports that he understands that wisdom is better than folly, yet the wise and the foolish all come to the same fate, so what use is there in seeking wisdom (2:12-17)? Thus, he concludes, one is left to hate his miserable existence and to realize that whatever he may accomplish in this life is left to the new generation that forgets its forebears and may or may not be wise in its use of the resources passed on (2:18-23). What is left? Given the circumstances, the speaker advises his audience to eat, drink, and be merry when the good times come, to enjoy what little good life yields (2:24-26).

Ecclesiastes 3:1–4:16: God as Master of Time and Its Consequences for Life in the World

This section begins with one of the other well-known sayings from Ecclesiastes: "For everything there is a season, and a time for every matter under heaven" (3:1). The following series of antithetical pairs underscores the poem's opening claim: there is a time to be born and a time to die, a time to plant and a time to harvest, a time to weep and a time to laugh, a time to love and a time to hate, a time for war and a time for peace (vv. 2-8). The irony, writes our author, is that to God we owe this discernible order in creation along with our awareness of it, yet God has withheld from us the capacity to make any advantage of this awareness: the timing for all of these things — birth and death, planting and harvesting, love and hate, war and peace — is determined wholly by God, and we live at the mercy of the patterns God dictates (vv. 9-11). In light of this the author advises his audience once more to eat, drink, and be happy and to take pleasure in toil itself, for God permits such incomplete awareness of the pattern of human existence, not to provide the key to success, but to induce our awe at his majesty (vv. 12-15)! To drive home the pointlessness of trying to decipher the nature of human existence through calculations built from what God does reveal, the author goes on to observe that often where justice and righteousness should prevail by any reasonable standard, wickedness rules instead (v. 16; on the contradictory tenor of v. 17, see "Critical Issues" below). Furthermore, all of this is so because God means to prove to humans that they are no better than animals; both live and die just the same (vv. 18-21). All good that is left to humans, then, is to enjoy what good comes to them in life (v. 22).

The argument of 4:1-16 follows, then, with a certain logical consistency: since the best in human life is to enjoy the good when it comes, everything else we may consider to be worthwhile is relative. Productive work, though its fruits are perhaps to be enjoyed, is done out of envy (vv. 4-6), and those who have no children cannot even count on heirs to enjoy the fruit of their labors (vv. 7-8). Companionship is perhaps a salve for the sorrows entailed in human existence, and it will be of help when trouble is faced, but it too does not overcome the weariness of life (vv. 9-12). And the gaining of a great reputation and the power to lead many only lasts so long as the life of the one who achieves such status; it too evanesces with the passing of the person (vv. 13-16). Thus the dead who face no more such things are better off than the living, and those who have not existed at all are best off (vv. 1-3).

Ecclesiastes 5:1–6:12: On Careful Speech Before God and Officials, and On Wealth

This section hints at one possible way of understanding the author's compositional strategy. We see here loose linkages between elements, as if a thought prompted a new thought, which in turn produced yet another.

The section begins with a reflection on the importance of careful speech before God: one should not be rash in making vows, one should be careful in speaking in ordinary conversation lest one anger God, one should utter dreams and hopes with due regard for the cares their pursuit might bring. In all of this, fear God (5:1-7).

The reflection on the importance of judicious speech then seems to prompt the author to address how one might or might not respond to the oppressive behaviors of an official. The author's advice is to go silent if one sees oppression, for behind that official there is another, and behind that one still another (5:8; we shall see that this is an important indicator of the book's date as well).

Yet, says the author, at least officials are an advantage for a land: "a king for a plowed field" (5:9).

Perhaps this thought of prosperity is what prompts the following, lengthier digression on possessions and wealth (5:10–6:9). First, the author bemoans the way the acquisition of wealth is addictive, giving no rest to those who acquire much, and making those with little yearn for more (5:10-12). And to make matters worse, he observes, when one comes into the world one is without anything and when one leaves it in death one is bereft; and so what gain is there in all the toil (5:13-17)? In the face of this, his advice — resonating throughout the book — is that one enjoy the good one has in life according to one's lot, and let that suffice (5:18-20). This insight prompts a reiteration of the plaint about the futility of effort and acquisition and a reaffirmation of the value of embracing what one has rather than striving after more (6:1-9).

Following is a passage that many treat as a "bridge" text or even as a random thought; it amounts to the claim that God has determined all things already, and so there is no point in human striving, especially since what exists of a life after its passing is unknown to us (6:10-12). We suspect that this is *not* so random, or even a bridge passage, but the overarching thought to summarize the preceding section: all of this advice about accepting one's lot, about judiciousness in acquisitions and enjoying the pleasures of life comes from the most basic assumption of all, that all has been determined already. In that sense, an underlying theme throughout all of Ecclesiastes is the sense that all has been predetermined.

Ecclesiastes 7:1-29: Mocking Wisdom?

This chapter begins with a collection of sayings that seem contradictory to the sentiments expressed thus far in the book (7:1-14). For example, v. 12 states boldly that wisdom is like the protection of money, that it is life-giving. This hardly squares with the notion that all is vanity, including wisdom! Perhaps a clue to this passage lies in the half verse at the end of v. 6: "this also is vanity." Some commentators see in this a globalizing claim against the surrounding sayings from standard wisdom: wisdom itself is, indeed, vanity.

Strengthening this judgment is the shift in tone in the second half of the chapter. After v. 14 the mood begins to shift to the one typical of the rest of the book, so that by v. 15 the author is reflecting once more on the ways normal expectations of justice are perverted by circumstances. The advice that follows is more wisdom like the first part of the chapter, but it is tempered by the observation in v. 15: so don't be too righteous or too wise, too wicked or too foolish (vv. 16-17). Yet even this half of the chapter modulates between traditional wisdom and the more cynical perspective typical of the book as a whole. Thus the best guess is that the author was, indeed, mocking traditional wisdom in a rather random manner. The haphazard approach can hardly be a surprise to recipients of the book, though, as it reflects well the general sentiment expressed by the author otherwise!

Ecclesiastes 8:1–11:6: Collected Reflections on the Futility of Seeking Gain

This long section is often divided into further portions by most commentators. However, what perhaps justifies setting it apart the way we have here is the single consistent theme that is unbroken throughout this section: there is only futility in seeking gain of any kind in life. While earlier sections held to the same theme, portions like ch. 7 interrupted that basic message with slightly different reflections. There is no such interruption of this long unit.

Ecclesiastes 8:1-9 begins the section with a consideration of how one ought to relate to kings. The argument of the section is that there is little point in resisting the will of royalty, as they get their way in time, even if it brings hurt to other people. This leads to one of the book's clearest rejections of retributive justice as a way of imagining the working of the world (8:10-15) and the judgment that seeking "wisdom" of the way God works is also without profit, even for those who claim to be wise (8:16-17).

The litany of observation, bitter conclusion, and in this case, advice, continues in ch. 9. Ecclesiastes 9:1-6 observes different experiences to conclude that the same fate comes to one and all, without regard for merit or wisdom. Thus the writer advises that one does best to enjoy what good comes one's way and to do what one is set to doing by circumstances, for there is no predicting outcomes (and gaining by such predictions; 9:7-12).

Following is an illustration of the futility of trying to gain fame, get ahead, or acquire and exercise wisdom. The author recalls a certain city that was saved from a besieging army by the words of a poor wise man, but just as soon as he had done his great deed, he was forgotten (9:13-15). The author then bemoans the power of

Pool of Solomon at Bethlehem, one of three dating to the Hasmonean period (2nd century B.C.E.), "from which to water the forest of growing trees" (Eccl 2:6). (Phoenix Data Systems, Neal and Joel Bierling)

wisdom to save, but then go unheeded, and recites what appears to be a string of wise sayings, as if to recall something of the poor wise man's instruction to underscore the futility of it (9:16–10:4). Seeming to underscore this simple point again, 10:5-11 lists seriatim the way various "industrial" activities lead to harm to those who engage in them (e.g., the ditchdigger falls into his own pit). By contrast, admits the author, wisdom can be productive, and foolishness is certainly problematic to its practitioner (10:12-15). Likewise, you are better off if your king is independent and powerful and not a vassal to some other power, for to have abundance and power is better than want and weakness (10:16-19). In yet another random, yet curiously related comment, the author adds in 10:20 that one needs to be wary in one's speech when a king is powerful.

As if to draw these reflections to a close, the author argues in 11:1-6 that one does best — perhaps in light of all his observations about the vagaries of existence — simply to "send out your bread upon the waters" to let what may come of it: sow the seed by day, rest by evening, and repeat it all over again, knowing there is nothing more you can do to control your destiny.

Ecclesiastes 11:7–12:8: A Concluding Poem

Corresponding in some degree to the opening poem in 1:3-11, the author offers a final peroration: from the perspective of age the speaker advises the young to take pleasure in what they have when they have it, for the day will come to even those of long years when there will be no more pleasure to be had, when

> the silver cord is snapped,
> and the golden bowl is broken,
> and the pitcher is broken at the fountain, and the wheel broken at the cistern,
> and the dust returns to the earth as it was,
> and the breath returns to God who gave it. (12:6-7)

And with that, one last time the author utters his recurring judgment: "vanity of vanities . . . all is vanity" (12:8).

Ecclesiastes 12:9-14: Epilogue

The close of the book is actually tripartite. First, 12:9-10 mentions the "Teacher" once more, assigning to him more wisdom teaching and the collection of proverbs (suggesting this to be an addition from the same hand that provided other attributions of the book to Solomon). Then, vv. 11-12 offer exhortation to respect the *sayings* of the wise as fixed and firm truths and to distrust all else, since, "of making many books there is no end, and much study is a weariness of the flesh." This is usually taken as an effort to fix the recipient's loyalty to the preceding "insights." Finally, in what many see to be a very late addition by someone deeply troubled by the skepticism of the book, vv. 13-14 affirm God's justice to those who are righteous and those who are wicked and urge, therefore, the keeping of the commandments.

Critical Issues in Studying Ecclesiastes

In addition to the obvious problem of structure, which we addressed already above, questions of authorship, date, provenance, and intention are the most obvious ones to attend the study of this strange book.

Who Wrote Ecclesiastes?

The name given to the author of the book is "Teacher," but the Hebrew of the term, *Qoheleth,* is less clear than the repeated use of that title might indicate (1:1, 2, 12; 7:27; 12:8, 9, 10). It might also mean "Gatherer," or something like that. In any case, the final redactors left little doubt about whom they hoped their audience would see as the reputed author of this wisdom book: 1:1 and 12 refer to the Teacher as, "son of David, king in Jerusalem" and "king over Israel in Jerusalem" respectively; and 12:9 describes him as wise, a teacher of wisdom and collector of proverbs. One suspects the editor protests too much. For as we see below, there is much

to indicate a Ptolemaic era date for the book, making it impossible for Solomon to have written it. But it is not surprising that the book is attributed to Solomon, as we know already that one way to give "wisdom" teaching an authoritative place in Israelite and early Jewish imagination was to assign its origin to the traditional purveyor of wisdom, Solomon (see 1 Kings 3, as well as the Deuteronomic writer's perspective on Solomon's reputation encoded in his account of it).

Who, then, did write the book? We can hardly assign it to any particular person, but we can tell a great deal from the content of the book about the person who did write it. If we trust the author's claims to have tried so many possible ways of gaining pleasure and advantage in life — from education to business to agriculture to pure hedonism! — it seems certain that the author was well off by any ancient standards. The leisure that permitted him to test so many pursuits was likely won only through the possession of great tracts of land worked by his former debtors (who gave their land to him in payment for their debt, but remained on it to work it for him; see the discussions of the sociohistorical context of Isaiah and Amos in Chapters 27 and 34 below).

Where and When Was Ecclesiastes Written?

While there is still some debate on the question, most agree that Ecclesiastes must have been written in Ptolemaic-era Judah. A concrete indicator of the book's Ptolemaic date is the reference in 5:8-9 to tiers and tiers of officials who oversee apparently oppressive governmental policies. As we saw in our historical survey in Chapter 3, the Ptolemies ruled over Palestine for virtually all of the 3rd century B.C.E. Their governmental approach was determined by their adaptation of Pharaonic patterns of government, as they sought mostly to accommodate to those they ruled most directly, the Egyptians. Adding to this their own desire to ensure the greatest return from their imperial holdings while maintaining a socioeconomic status quo that held all in their place, they produced a bureaucracy known in the ancient world for its expansive policies. Certainly high taxation policies supported by an officialdom that saw to the collection of every last obligation in Egypt was little difficulty to the citizenry, given the richness of that land. But in Judah it would have been an enormous burden and would have no doubt created the conditions for one to wonder if God's justice had been permanently subverted, if the logic of seeking one's fate and pursuing it to success promoted by popular Greek philosophy had been overturned. Thus the book's general concern to say that pursuit of change in one's condition is futile has also been taken as an indicator of its date and provenance in Ptolemaic-era Judah.

What Did the Author Intend?

There are different ways to read the evidence of the text on this score. Our "implied author," wealthy as he apparently was, could be seen as very kind *or* very conniving and manipulative in creating this book. He could be viewed as a kindhearted man of wisdom insofar as he advised people who lacked any hope of social and economic mobility (thanks to the socioeconomic and political structures imposed by the Ptolemaic Empire) to accept their lot in life. Rather than trust the "grand old religion" characterized by the Deuteronomic perspective or cast their lot with popular Greek philosophy's suggestion that you could determine your fate and pursue it to success and happiness, our author advised his audience to forego the associated hopes of socioeconomic mobility. Instead, they should simply enjoy the good that came to them in their predetermined life patterns — which they could not decipher if they tried! — and suffer through the evil they endured. On this simple reading the author sounds to be a thoughtful patriarch to his community, a speaker of a harsh, but liberating truth.

A more cynical view of the intentions of this author can also be suggested. Recalling that he must have been a man of leisure, it is important to recall also how he would have come by the time necessary to test out so many patterns of life: he likely had free time because large numbers of people who were once indebted to him had become his landless servants. On this view, for him to say that one should accept one's lot in life, whether it be for good or for ill, seems to be deeply self-serving. Indeed, should those who work his land get the idea that their labor there, or elsewhere, might win them a better place in the world, they might well neglect the duties that made him a rich and leisurely man! On this view, the author's advice to accept one's lot in life — to reject Deuteronomic theology and popular Greek philosophy — is a cynical move to lock into place an economic structure from which only he could benefit.

There is also a much more sanguine view of the author's intention in writing that does not assume his interest in the poor around him at all. Some have suggested that he was writing for other men of leisure like himself, people who also had achieved by some means or another the sort of freedom to test experience that our author seems to have developed. On this view, his book is aimed squarely at those neighbors as friendly advice: I've used my resources and freedom to try it all, only to discover that it does not produce any more pleasure than we have already experienced; so avoid my mistake and embrace what you have in life rather than strive for more.

"The golden bowl is broken, and the pitcher is broken at the fountain" (Eccl 12:6). Late Bronze storage jars at Tell Migne-Ekron. (Phoenix Data Systems, Neal and Joel Bierling)

Theological Themes in Ecclesiastes

Some might wonder if there could be "theological themes" in a book like Ecclesiastes. Yet even if the author had only the most cynical of intentions, our understanding of narrative criticism indicates that an audience encountering the text might still find theological significance. Indeed, reading Ecclesiastes apart from our suspicions about what an original author may have intended, we see that it does make claims about the nature of God and what it means to be human in God's sight.

God's Control Over All Creation

A clearly recurring theme in Ecclesiastes is God's control over all reality. There can be no claiming that the human can know what God intends with his control over creation, but there can also be no denying that God all the same orders all things. The passage that most epitomizes this, of course, is Ecclesiastes 3. But other passages make this same point, perhaps none more pithily than 11:5, "Just as you do not know how the breath comes to the bones in the mother's womb, so you do not know the work of God, who makes everything." God is the maker and controller of all things in creation.

Humanity at the Mercy of God

The contrasting theme to God's control over all things is that of humanity's helplessness before the God of creation. The author seems never to tire of reminding his audience that, while one may ascertain something of God's way with the world, one can never know enough to make any difference from the knowledge. Instead, humanity is fated to live with whatever comes from the hand of God and from the circumstances that befall us day by day. The corollary of this, of course, is that God's reputation for acting with justice toward the righteous and the wicked is in no way to be trusted. The most powerful articulation of this perspective comes in 8:10-14.

> There is a vanity that takes place on earth, that there are righteous people who are treated according to the conduct of the wicked, and there are wicked people who are treated according to the conduct of the righteous. . . . This also is vanity. (v. 14)

We have in this text a profound rejection of the notion of retributive justice, and with it an affirmation of the complete and ultimate helplessness of the human being to shape definitively his or her fate. All rests in the hands of a God whose ways are, in the last analysis, inscrutable.

Enjoying God's Creation

The corollary of this double-edged sword of God's mysteriousness and human helplessness is a simple positive: inasmuch as one cannot "figure God out" or establish one's fate, all that is left in life is to enjoy the good that comes to one. Just as 8:10-14 provides a powerful rejection of retributive justice, 8:15 follows it with the simple advice offered time and again in the book: "So I commend enjoyment, for there is nothing better for people under the sun than to eat, and drink, and enjoy themselves, for this will go with them in their toil through the days of life that God gives them under the sun" (see also 3:12, 22; 5:19; 6:3; 9:9). The book's claim is unmistakable: there *are* good things in creation, and they are there for human enjoyment, so humans should not miss the opportunity to take pleasure in those things. In this sense, Ecclesiastes sponsors — perhaps somewhat ironically, given the most cynical reading of the original author's intention — a sort of "theology of leisure."

Questions for Review and Discussion

1 What is the chief problem facing readers of the book of Ecclesiastes as they seek to make sense of the book as a whole?

2 What are some ways of explaining what an original author may have intended with this strange book?

3 What do we mean by the phrase a "theology of leisure"? How does the book of Ecclesiastes seem to promote such a theology?

Further Reading

Fox, Michael V. *A Time to Tear Down and a Time to Build Up: A Rereading of Ecclesiastes.* Grand Rapids: Wm. B. Eerdmans, 1999.

Jarrick, John. "Ecclesiastes." In *ECB,* 467-73.

Seow, Choon-Leong. *Ecclesiastes.* AB 18C. New York: Doubleday, 1997.

Chapter 25

Song of Songs

Getting Started

1 Read Song of Songs 2:8-17. What sort of relationship is entailed in this poetry? What sort of imagery do the speakers use to describe each other and their relationship?

2 Read Song of Songs 3:1-5. What does the nature of the woman's search and its outcome indicate about the marital status of the couple who dialogue throughout this book?

3 Given these first experiences with Song of Songs, consider also what this book's place in "sacred" Scripture might be.

Preliminary Comments

Song of Songs (also called "Song of Solomon" because he is mentioned in 1:1, 5; 3:7, 9, 11; 8:11-12, or "Canticle of Canticles" according to Latin texts) is tucked in the Christian canon just after Ecclesiastes, the last of the "wisdom" and "poetic" texts that occupy space between Esther and Isaiah. In the Hebrew canon it is usually placed at the head of the "Five Scrolls" (Hebrew *Megil-*

lot: Song of Songs, Ruth, Lamentations, Ecclesiastes, and Esther). Its content often surprises novice readers of the Old Testament, as its vividly sexual love songs are not what most readers expect to find between the covers of the Bible, and as such join many of the other texts we have surveyed thus far that put the lie to many of the more popular notions of what "should" be found in God's word. That it endured skepticism from readers from even its earliest days is evident from the speculation in the Mishnah as to whether it was a sacred text (i.e., whether it "makes the hands unclean"). But any uncertainty then and since was not of much consequence, for in the end the Mishnah's brief debate about the book's sacredness ends with a resounding affirmation of its suitability to God's people Israel (*m. Yad.* 3.5). Likewise, throughout history Jewish and Christian interpreters have been particularly fond of Song of Songs' evocative content. We return especially to the history of interpretation in "Critical Issues" below, but first attend to our usual survey of the book's contents.

A Walk through Songs of Songs

The structure of Song of Songs is not particularly clear to most readers. One has the sense in reading it that it is mostly a rather loose collection of love poems without any real order. But one organizing principle has presented itself to at least one well-known commentator on the book (Roland Murphy; see "Further Reading" below): often the dialogue between two parties, a man and a woman, is broken, and then resumes again. Using that observation as a structuring device yields the following divisions.

Songs of Songs 1:1-6: Introduction

Song of Songs 1:1 is actually a superscription that reads, "The Song of Songs, which is Solomon's." Perhaps this is a late addition that builds from the mention of Solomon elsewhere in the book to give greater credibility to the anonymous collection of love songs. It is, in any case, somewhat ambiguous in that the Hebrew does not actually ascribe the book to Solomon so much as suggest it *belongs to him.* Whether that means the superscript author meant to speak of the book as Solomon's possession or creation is not clear; however it hardly restrained tradition from attributing authorship to him, and even using that as support for the work's authority.

The introduction is the woman's expression of desire for her lover (vv. 2-4) and her self-representation to the "daughters of Jerusalem" (vv. 5-6). In one of the many place references in the book, she likens her own blackness to the "tents of Kedar" and the "curtains of Solomon" (v. 5).

Song of Songs 1:7–2:7:
A Dialogue between the Lovers

The opening verses of this section set the stage for the rest of it: the woman asks the man's location so they might meet, and he responds with a lightly mocking tone (1:7-8). Then follows a give-and-take between the two dialogue partners that amounts to a contest of lovers for the reputation of greatest admirer. It establishes the pervasive pattern in the book of the partners describing

each other and their love for one another with similes and metaphors that involve wildlife and agriculture and entail references to various geographical locales. (Notably, not all of these comparisons may sound as flattering to modern ears as they most likely did to ancient auditors!) The woman says of her lover, "My beloved is to me a cluster of henna blossoms in the vineyards of En-gedi" (1:14); "as an apple tree among the trees of the wood, so is my beloved among men" (2:3). And regarding her own love for the man, she says it is among the women of her acquaintance like "a lily among brambles" (2:2). As for the man, he compares his lover "to a mare among Pharaoh's chariots" (1:9) and equates her eyes with doves and their shared bed and the building housing it with a forest canopy (1:15-17). The section closes with an adjuration of the woman to the daughters of Zion to refrain from stirring up a love such as the one she experiences until "it is ready" (cf. 3:5; 8:4).

Song of Songs 2:8-17:
The Woman Recalls a Visit From Her Lover

In this brief passage the woman recalls a visit from her lover in springtime. Again, animal and agricultural imagery figures prominently in the speeches both partners deliver. The woman recalls the man's arrival, likening him to "a gazelle or a young stag" (2:9), and in his speech to her he observes the signs of spring with references to growing plants and the sound of the turtledove, and he calls his lover "my dove" (and adds, inexplicably, a reference to "little foxes" she should catch for them; vv. 10-15). And in speaking of their mutual embrace she says, "he pastures his flock among the lilies" (v. 16), and closes the section by calling her lover to "be like a gazelle or a young stag" (v. 17).

Song of Songs 3:1-5:
The Woman Addresses the Daughters of Zion

That the addressees of this speech are the daughters of Zion is apparent from the closing verse that repeats the adjuration that first appeared in 2:7. What the woman describes is her fervent, and eventually successful, nighttime search in the city streets for her lover. She reports that when she finally found him, she took him almost by force into the chamber in which her mother conceived her (3:2-4). That this is a report of a dream — it is unclear whether it was sleeping or waking — is clear from v. 1, where she reports that this she saw upon her "bed at night."

Song of Songs 3:6-11:
Sighting a Royal Wedding Procession

In a departure from the direct speech of the two lovers, this section records the observation of a wedding scribe each part of that portion of the female human body: her hair is like a flock of goats, her teeth like shorn ewes, her lips are crimson red, and so on. And just as in the earlier passage, place names figure into this description, inasmuch as the flock of goats descends the slopes of Gilead, the woman's neck is like the tower of David, and her smell is like the scent of Lebanon. The man also describes the impact all this beauty has on him: he hastens to summon his lover, and he admits that his heart is ravished by even a single glance at her.

The second part of the passage is a "garden poem" in which the male describes his companion with horticultural metaphors (4:12-15). The focus of the description is evidently the aspects of the woman that engender life, and the reference at the start to her being "a garden locked" is usually taken to mean that she is chaste (4:12). Finally, the woman speaks, inviting the man to the garden that is hers and to feast there on the fruits of her garden (4:16). The man's response is to accept the invitation, after which a third party exhorts the couple to "Eat, friends, drink, and be drunk with love" (5:1).

Song of Songs 5:2–6:4: The Woman Tantalizes the Daughters of Jerusalem

Once again the woman reports another dream. This time she is apparently ready to retire for the night when her lover arrives and asks to be let into her chamber. She tarries, concerned that she has already settled for the evening, but at his insistence she rises to unbolt the door, and when she does he has gone (5:2-6). Her response is to stage a search like the one she reports in her first dream (3:1-5). This time, though, she not only fails in her hunt, but also is beaten and abused by the sentinels who helped her in her first dream (5:7). Then the woman calls upon the daughters of Jerusalem for help in her search, and in response to their query as to why they should favor *her* with their efforts, she offers another description of her lover's physical delights, which more than arouses the interest of the other women (5:8–6:1). Then, as if to say that the whole request was little more than a ploy intended to give the woman a chance to engender envy in her colleagues, she admits that her lover is in his garden, safe from harm, and committed to her as she is to him (6:2-3).

Song of Songs 6:5-12: The Man Describes His Lover Again and She Visits Him

This soliloquy repeats most of what the man has already said of his lover (see esp. 4:1-11), but he does add the words of queens and concubines who witness her beauty (6:1-10). Oddly, they use the similes of sun, moon, and threatening army with its banners to describe the woman (v. 10). The section closes with the woman

Nahal David waterfall at En-gedi, an oasis known for its vineyards (Song of Songs 1:14). (Phoenix Data Systems, Neal and Joel Bierling)

processional. The presence of armed men accompanying the wedding group, mention of King Solomon by name, and description of a richly-adorned palanquin (portable throne) and a crown assure the reader that this is the wedding party of royalty. Otherwise, the only element of this passage that links it inextricably to the surrounding material is 3:10b-11a, another solemn appeal to the daughters of Zion to come out and see the spectacle.

Song of Songs 4:1–5:1: The Man's Description of the Beauty of His Lover

This passage begins with the man's florid description of his lover and its impact on him (4:1-11). He describes her from her face to her breasts, using similes to de-

describing (in a text that is perhaps corrupt, and thus unclear to most translators) a rendezvous she shared with her lover (vv. 11-12).

Song of Songs 6:13–8:4: Observers Describe the Woman's Beauty

In the first part of this section bystanders bid the woman let them inspect — and not too surprisingly — describe her beauty (6:13–7:5). Using many of the same images from earlier in the book, the people extol the physical attraction of the woman. Notably, though, they use an unusually substantial number of place names in their description, invoking the pools of Hesbon, the gate of Bath-rabbim, the tower of Damascus, and Carmel to paint their portrait of the woman's features.

The male adds his voice to the chorus of praise, injecting into his horticultural description a declaration of his aim to enjoy the fruits of the woman's garden (7:6-9). The woman responds by paying tribute to their mutual commitment, invites the man to a tryst in the fields, and warns the daughters of Jerusalem again to avoid awaking love "until it is ready" (7:10–8:4).

Song of Songs 8:5-14: An Appendix

The book closes with what appear to be several very brief, distinct units, the best known of which is the woman's comparison of love to death and Sheol: just as the latter two are relentless in their pursuit and ultimately victorious, love as strong as theirs cannot be quenched by any force (8:6-7). The book ends with the woman summoning her lover one last time in the same language used in 2:9, 17: he should come "like a gazelle or a young stag upon the mountain of spices" (8:14).

Critical Issues in Studying Song of Songs

There are a variety of textual and literary features that have evoked scholarly interest in this text, especially the question of its genre. Also of interest to recent scholarship has been the history of the book's interpretation.

Literary and Textual Issues

A first literary "issue" is more an observation about the language of the text. The book possesses an unusual number of *hapax legomena,* single occurrences of Hebrew words. Such a concentration of words ensures that the translation we read is at times little more than the result of educated guesses at the meaning of the Hebrew words. This, combined with the repeated use of metaphors and similes, gives the impression of a very ornate writing style and presents fertile ground for those interested in studying classical Hebrew poetry at its apex.

The question of the book's genre is the more contentious literary issue among scholars. While the small genres or forms taken up in the book are evidence enough, just how to classify the Song of Songs as a whole remains a matter of dispute. Some are no more adventurous than to say that it is a single love poem or perhaps a concatenation of similar love poems. At the other end of the spectrum are those who have generated elaborate theories that the book is a drama meant for production in the ancient world. The various speakers in the text have been especially significant in engendering that approach. Still others suggest it is the liturgy for the marriage of deities. No one of these proposals is without problems, and there is no consensus forming around any one of them.

As to textual issues, the most notable element here is the presence of three manuscripts of Song of Songs at Qumran, two of which do not have material that survives in the Masoretic Text. It would be tempting to attribute this to prudishness on the Essenes' part, but the portions missing — as well as those that apparently remained — in these manuscripts offer no support to such an explanation.

The History of Interpretation

From antiquity to the present Song of Songs has evoked more than its share of interpretive interest, in large part because of the desire or need to harness its obviously erotic love poetry for religious or theological purposes. From very early on Judaism read the book as the story of God's relationship with Israel. For this reason it is hardly surprising that among the *Megillot* Song of Songs' festival affiliation is with Passover, a feast of God's special act of liberation for the people Israel. Chiefly under the influence of Origen's landmark interpretation of Song of Songs, Christians have long read the book as the story of God and Christ in relationship with the church and the individual believer. The Targumic tradition is perhaps the most elaborate of the ancient interpreters, though: it reads the whole of the book as an extended allegory of Israel's experience from the Exodus from Egypt to the Exile and Return. As for modern readers, the greatest fascination has been with understanding the poetry in its own right as ancient erotic poetry and in circumscribing the physical descriptions of the lovers in relation to a wider ancient Near Eastern literary tradition that produced a similar descriptive work, called a *wasf.* Also of special interest in recent years has been the striking equation of love and death that comes toward the end of the book.

Theological Themes in Song of Songs

Understandably, it has been an interpretive challenge to establish the theological themes in Song of Songs, inasmuch as we have in the book essentially a collection of erotic poetry. This is not to say that interpreters have been completely stymied in the endeavor; quite the contrary, it has been something of a cottage industry over the centuries, as the foregoing, quick survey of the history of interpretation indicates. That being said, it is important to note that the theological themes we might elicit here are emphatically not *in* Song of Songs, but rather derive from a theological reading of the book. Indeed, this is one of two books in the Hebrew Bible that never uses the name of God (the other being Esther).

Devotion between God and God's People

Both Judaism and Christianity have read the two lovers in Song of Songs as God and God's people, in varying forms. What is remarkable about this approach is its implication for the mutuality of love and devotion between human communities and God. While the more obviously theological portions of the Hebrew Bible reveal an abiding imbalance in the relationship between God and humanity, an imbalance that ranges from slight (e.g., the psalms of thanksgiving and some of the hymns in Psalms) to enormous (e.g., God's unremitting care in the Yahwist traditions for Abraham and his descendants in spite of their unremitting rebellion), reading Song of Songs as a metaphor for the love between God and his people produces a very different portrait: here the love is entirely mutual, in nearly complete balance. The man glories in the goodness of the woman, and the woman reciprocates with the same intensity and devotion. These are equal partners in a profoundly committed relationship. Understood in this way Song of Songs provides a brief, but powerful, alternative to the dominant vision of the way the human community is related to God. It might be utopian in character, but it is present within the canon all the same, prompting a "minority report" on the divine-human relationship that has not been ignored in the history of Judaism and Christianity.

The Alienation between God and Humanity

Having made the foregoing observation about how Song of Songs can be read as a description of God's relationship with humanity, it is necessary to observe further that the man and the woman in the book are nonetheless still clearly alienated from one another in a very significant way: though devoted to one another, they remain unmarried, forced to seek fulfillment of their relationship in secret, required to depend upon the help of third parties in arranging their trysts. In the woman's vision in 3:1-5 she needs the help of the sentinels in the city streets to find her lover, and when she finally lays hold of him, she drags him to her *mother's chamber* to consummate their love. In her second dream the sentinels beat her for her efforts (perhaps because they now realize that she and her lover are not married?), and so she calls upon the daughters of Jerusalem to help her, and then only to observe that her lover is already waiting for her in the secrecy of her garden (5:2–6:4). Outside of the woman's dream world, 7:10–8:4 reports a tryst that also must be kept secret. (Note especially the woman's apparent admission in 8:1 that the couple's relationship is not licit.) All of this evidence indicates that the love poetry that makes up Song of Songs was surely composed to reflect the experiences of a young, unmarried couple deeply enthralled by the power of a new love, compelled by their premarital status to live out their relationship incompletely and largely in secret. Read theologically, this datum affixes a significant dimension to the utopianism we noted above — though mutually enthralled, the relationship enjoyed by the partners remains incomplete, fractured by an insurmountable gulf that inheres in their basic way of being. Thus a telling proviso must be attached to the complete mutuality of devotion entailed in Song of Songs' notion of the human-divine relationship; it is a full mutuality that can exist only in the partners' imagination (the woman's dreams) or apart from the perception of others. It is an idealized, unreal mutuality, even if it is what the couple yearns for and proclaims for themselves. Reality and the ideal do not necessarily match; reality might, in fact, appear to observers to be more like what we understand about this relationship from the rest of the Hebrew Bible.

Related to this is the curious refrain offered by the woman in 2:7; 3:5; 8:4. She urges her compatriots, the "daughters of Jerusalem," not to "stir up or awaken love until it is ready!" Could one hear in this the introduction of an eschatological dimension to the relationship idealized by the love poems? Or is it possible to take this as warning that such an exalted connection to God, though it is the ideal to be sought out, can also be searing in nature? Whatever one's reading of this strange refrain, a theological interpretation of Song of Songs must take it into account.

Questions for Review and Discussion

1   At the outset of this chapter you were asked to consider what place Song of Songs might have in a book of "sacred" Scripture. Might you answer that question differently now that you have read the book

through and encountered the foregoing reflections? Are you persuaded that this book has "theological significance"?

2   Consider again the tension suggested above between Song of Songs' notion of the relationship between God and God's people and the views of the same relationship apparent in the rest of the Hebrew Scriptures. Do you agree with the assessment made here? Can you think of other witnesses in the Bible that either support the view taken here or contradict it?

3   What do you make of the much-ballyhooed connection between love and death articulated in 8:6-7?

How might this be treated from the perspective of a theological reading?

Further Reading

Brenner, Athalya. *The Song of Songs*. OTG. Sheffield: Sheffield Academic, 1989.

Murphy, Roland E. "Song of Songs, Book of." *ABD* 6:150-55.

Pope, Marvin H. *Song of Songs*. AB 7C. Garden City: Doubleday, 1977.

Rogerson, John W. "Song of Songs." In *ECB,* 474-81.

The Prophets

Chapter 26

Introduction to the Prophets

Among the many challenges the books of the Prophets provide to novice Bible readers, perhaps the most vexing is the way they preserve the words of ancient figures in forms edited many years later by people with often very different attitudes than the prophets themselves. For instance, while Jeremiah was clearly a bitter foe of the institutions and power structures of his day, it seems likely that some of the editors responsible for the final form of the book that bears his name were favorable to some of those very institutions he excoriated with his most venomous denunciations! As a result readers have been torn between paying heed to the "true words" of the prophets and listening instead to the whole of the prophetic books that have come down to us. Because we are committed in this Introduction to treating the books of the Bible in their canonical order and form, we will, at least in "walking through the text" and treating "theological themes," favor the final forms of the prophetic books. But we will also clarify for readers what can be known of the historical prophets in our discussion of critical issues associated with each prophetic book. To set the stage for that endeavor we provide in this chapter a few comments on the nature of prophecy in the ancient world, an overview of the prophets as they are thought to have appeared in historical order, and a sampling of some of the unfamiliar genres we encounter in the prophetic books.

Prophets and Prophecy in the Ancient Near East and Israel

Information about prophets and prophecy in the wider ancient Near Eastern world is scant, but we do possess some significant testimony. From the 18th-century B.C.E. royal archives of Mari found in northern Mesopotamia we have evidence of male and female prophets who were called upon to deliver divine messages to the king, usually to promise success in some future endeavor or to warn against actions that might not be successful. Archives from Assyrian kings of the 7th century provide much the same portrait of prophets as servants to the royal house who offer divine assurance of royal success and counsel of care. It is likely that these prophets belonged to distinct classes, guilds, or groups, a fact indicated by the various titles given them in the archival records. In both cases — these are our most important sources of information regarding prophecy in the ancient world — prophets serve kings, not the people as a whole, and their service is to support kings and rarely, if ever, to call them to account or condemn them (see also p. 163).

The named prophets of the Hebrew Bible were "God's heralds" speaking the word of the Lord directly to kings and the people as individual instruments of God. In this they are like their ancient Near Eastern counterparts. But they are different from the Mari and Assyrian prophets as well in several important respects. They were individuals who did not seem to belong to distinct groups, guilds, or classes and even distinguished themselves from them at times; thus we hear Amos say that he is neither a prophet nor a prophet's son (Amos 7:14), and we witness Jeremiah oppose the prophets of his own day repeatedly. Also, the prophets of Israel were more accustomed to speaking words of condemnation to kings than providing oracles of support. And even though it might be only because we possess just the *royal* archives of these other ancient Near Eastern peoples, it is striking that Israel's prophets spoke to the people as a whole just as much as they did to the kings.

One other characteristic of Israelite prophecy, whether it was shared with its ancient Near Eastern counterparts or not, is important to note: Israel's prophets always spoke from and to particular historical contexts. It is impossible to appreciate them as historical figures without an understanding of their historical circumstances. Thus we will pay attention to those realities in our discussion of critical issues associated with studying the books of Israel's prophets.

A Survey of the Prophets according to Historical Order

One prerequisite to understanding the prophets in their historical context is some idea of their actual order of appearance and activity. They are not arranged in the Christian Old Testament according to their chronological order. They include Isaiah, Jeremiah, Ezekiel, Daniel, and the twelve Minor Prophets: Hosea, Joel, Amos, Obadiah, Jonah, Micah, Nahum, Habakkuk, Zephaniah, Haggai, Zechariah, and Malachi. Slipped in after Jeremiah is Lamentations, a book attributed to Jeremiah as his laments on the occasion of Jerusalem's fall to Babylon. The books' present arrangement may be the result of a combination of factors. Size of book certainly was a consideration; the "Major Prophets" Isaiah, Jeremiah, and Ezekiel fall together because they have in common their considerable length, just as the "Minor Prophets" belong together because of their common brevity. Thematic connections may also have been a factor; for example, Obadiah likely follows Amos because at the end of Amos Edom, with which Obadiah is singularly concerned, is mentioned (Amos 9:12). In any case, these books are not arranged according to the chronological order of the prophets for whom they are named.

So what was their historical order of appearance? When answering this question it is helpful to think of Israel's prophets clustering around three critical junctures in Israelite history: the 8th century and the period of Assyria's hegemony; the late 7th and early 6th centuries and the period of the Babylonian Exile; and the late 6th to the 5th centuries and the period of Persian rule over Judah. (For a list of the prophets in canonical order, along with general dates for each, see p. 229 below.)

The books of the Minor Prophets are 12 in number. They receive the moniker "minor" not because of their corresponding prophets' significance relative to Isaiah, Jeremiah, or Ezekiel, but because of the brevity of the books in the collection. The longest is Hosea at 14 chapters, and the shortest is Obadiah at just 21 verses! The collection includes the books listed below (along with a general idea of when the prophecies contained in each of them were announced).

The 8th century B.C.E. saw the first flurry of prophetic activity. Amos and Hosea spoke to the Northern Kingdom of Israel, condemning social injustice, religious apostasy, and royal trust in false powers. At around the same time Isaiah and Micah addressed the Southern Kingdom of Judah on essentially the same range of issues. A counselor to kings, Isaiah advised (with only limited success) royal dependence on God alone in the face of the Assyrian threat. A country prophet, Micah condemned the rich city dwellers and their abuse of the poor people of the land, proclaiming inescapable doom. Both sets of prophets could count on the looming threat of Assyria as evidence of God's displeasure with the people and the kings' choices. As for emphases, while Amos and Hosea used the Exodus story as a leitmotif in their preaching, the southern prophets understandably appealed more vigorously to the tradition of Davidic kingship and to the importance of Zion, Jerusalem.

The next major period in Israelite prophetic activity came with the demise of Assyria and the advent of the Babylonians. Zephaniah may come from the era of Josiah's reforms, for he announces God's decision to spare Judah while destroying other nations for their sins. Nahum reflected on the fall of Assyria in 612, reveling in the empire's demise. And Habakkuk reflected on the rise of Babylon and the certain demise of Judah, raising the question of God's justice in the course of such reflections.

The early career of Jeremiah overlapped with those of Nahum and Zephaniah, but Jeremiah's activity continued into the Babylonian era as well, and so we assign him to the second major turning point in Israelite history. His mission was largely to announce the justice of the impending Babylonian Exile in God's sight and encourage a sensible response to imperial power on the part of the Judean population. He, or a later editor, also envisioned a new day ahead when God would make an unbreakable covenant with the people (Jer 31:31-34). During the Exilic period itself one unnamed prophet

The Prophetic Books of the Old Testament: Their Order and Likely Dates of Composition

(all dates B.C.E.)

Isaiah	second half of 8th century
Jeremiah	late 7th–early 6th centuries
Ezekiel	early 6th century
Daniel	mid-2nd century
Hosea	mid-8th century
Joel	4th century (?)
Amos	mid-8th century
Obadiah	early 6th century
Jonah	5th–4th centuries
Micah	late 8th century
Nahum	late 7th century
Habakkuk	late 7th century
Zephaniah	late 7th century
Haggai	late 6th century
Zechariah	late 6th century
Malachi	second half of 5th century

and two named prophets were active. Ezekiel, a priest from Jerusalem, held forth in Babylon even as Jeremiah's career drew to a close in Judah. Using an abundance of symbolic actions and vision reports, Ezekiel expressed to his fellow exiles the circumstances and reasons for their plight, God's judgment on other nations, and God's plans for Israel's future restoration. Obadiah was the other Exilic-era prophet, and his main concern was to call for vengeance against Edom for the advantage it took of Judah after the Babylonian conquest of 586. An unnamed prophet made additions to the words of the historical Isaiah in the late Exilic period. While the "historical" Isaiah of the 8th century provided much of what we read in Isaiah 1–39, virtually all readers recognize that there is a different hand at work in Isaiah 40–55. As we shall see, there are several clear indications that the author of these chapters was present among the exiled Judeans, not the least of which is his reference to Cyrus of Persia as the Lord's "messiah" who would deliver Israel from exile (Isa 45:1-7). This "prophet" aimed in particular to convince Judeans in exile to return to the homeland when the opportunity came.

After the Exile four more named prophets were active, and one additional unnamed prophet made further additions to the book of Isaiah. Two prophets, Haggai and Zechariah, cooperated to see to the reconstruction of the Jerusalem temple and legitimate priestly governance in the Postexilic period. In fact, the dated prophecies in Haggai and Zechariah 1–8 are arranged in succession using an identical date formula, indicating that they should be read together. Joel is not easily

dated, but appears to be a very late, eschatological prophecy of the "Day of the Lord." Malachi is the name assigned to the last prophetic book in the collection, but it is likely an artifice; the word means "my messenger," and most readers see it as a continuation of the material found in Zechariah 9–14. Thus, as we shall see below, Zechariah 9–14 and Malachi may have been a loose collection of prophetic oracles worked into the anthology so as to provide a 12-part collection.

The remaining prophetic book is not a prophetic book at all. Jonah is actually a novella about a prophet, datable most likely to the Persian period. It was included in the collection perhaps in part to fill out the dozen, and certainly because we hear of a prophet named Jonah in 2 Kgs 14:25.

Forms of Prophetic Speech

The genres one encounters in the prophetic books are often befuddling to modern readers. Many of them simply have no contemporary parallels, leaving the reader without an adequate point of reference for making sense of them. As a result prophetic literature can be quite challenging. To ease the difficulty for readers, if only a little bit, we offer here some examples of the most common prophetic forms of speech.

Oracles, revelations of God's speech, are the basic staple of prophetic speech. Although the precise nature of an oracle can vary widely depending on its content, two kinds dominate: oracles of doom and of salvation. An example of the former comes from Amos 1:9-10 (just one of several successive oracles against the nations surrounding Israel and finally against Israel herself).

> Thus says the Lord:
> For three transgressions of Tyre,
>> and for four, I will not revoke the punishment;
> because they delivered entire communities over to Edom,
>> and did not remember the covenant of kinship.
> So I will send a fire on the wall of Tyre,
>> fire that shall devour its strongholds.

From the same prophet we have an oracle of salvation, limited though its scope of saving may be.

> Hate evil and love good,
>> and establish justice in the gate;
> it may be that the Lord, the God of hosts,
>> will be gracious to the remnant of Joseph. (Amos 5:15)

"Woes" are another frequently-occurring genre in the prophetic books. Isaiah 5:8-10 is a well-known woe against rich landowners who grab ever more property from the poor for themselves.

> Woe, you who join house to house,
> who add field to field,
> until there is room for no one but you,
>   and you are left to live alone
>   in the midst of the land!
> The Lord of hosts has sworn in my hearing:
> Surely many houses shall be desolate,
>   large and beautiful houses, without inhabitant.
> For ten acres of vineyard shall yield but one bath,
>   and a homer of seed shall yield a mere ephah.
>   (Isaiah 5:8-10)

It is worth noting that not all genres in the prophetic books are direct speech forms. Some take the shape of narratives or reports. One of these is the call narrative that appears in several books including Isaiah, Jeremiah, and in Ezekiel. Isaiah's is one of the most striking (Isa 6:1-13).

> In the year that King Uzziah died, I saw the Lord sitting on a throne, high and lofty; and the hem of his robe filled the temple. Seraphs were in attendance above him; each had six wings: with two they covered their faces, and with two they covered their feet, and with two they flew. And one called to another and said:
>
> > "Holy, holy, holy is the Lord of hosts;
> > the whole earth is full of his glory."
>
> The pivots on the thresholds shook at the voices of those who called, and the house filled with smoke. And

I said: "Woe is me! I am lost, for I am a man of unclean lips, and I live among a people of unclean lips; yet my eyes have seen the King, the Lord of hosts!" Then one of the seraphs flew to me, holding a live coal that had been taken from the altar with a pair of tongs. The seraph touched my mouth with it and said: "Now that this has touched your lips, your guilt has departed and your sin is blotted out." Then I heard the voice of the Lord saying, "Whom shall I send, and who will go for us?" And I said, "Here am I; send me!" (Isa 6:1-8)

The prophets could also employ a wide variety of other forms known from other contexts, all in service of conveying God's word as it had been revealed to them to their audiences. For example, wisdom genres appear widely in the speech of Isaiah, and Jeremiah especially favored sermons. As we work our way through the prophets we shall uncover still other forms. For now, though, these few examples should provide a sense of the diverse and uncommon character of prophetic speech forms and offer some basic notion of what to expect. As for the critical issues and theological themes associated with the prophets, these too we leave to the separate chapters on each of the prophetic books that follow.

Further Reading

Blenkinsopp, Joseph. *A History of Prophecy in Israel.* Rev. ed. Louisville: Westminster John Knox, 1996.
Redditt, Paul L. "Introduction to Prophetic Literature." In *ECB,* 482-88.

Chapter 27

Isaiah

Getting Started

1 Read Isaiah 5. What is the mood of this chapter? What seems to be the speaker's judgment on Israel, and especially on its past and prospects for the future?

2 Read Isaiah 40. Do the language and mood of this chapter contrast with that of Isaiah 5? How so? Do these differences suggest anything about the compositional nature of Isaiah?

3 Finally, read Isaiah 56. Consider once again the contrasting character of the language and mood of this passage in relation to those of Isaiah 5 and 56. Again, what do your observations suggest about the makeup of the book of Isaiah?

Preliminary Comments

The book of Isaiah is considered one of the richest collections of theological reflection in all of the Bible, and not surprisingly so. After all, as we see below, it reflects a number of different prophetic voices, each one possessing its own unique emphasis. The first part of the book

preaches condemnation for social injustice and religious apostasy and holds out hope for the future, mostly on the basis of a restored Davidic monarchy. The second part preaches consolation to the disconsolate and restoration of Israel's fortunes along the lines of God's great deeds for the ancestors in ages past. The third part of the book is dominated by a prophetic critique of the restored Israel's failures. And these are only the touch points for each part of the book. It is no surprise, then, that Isaiah was one of the most popular resources for New Testament writers as they constructed their theologies from the story of Jesus and the scriptural resources of the Hebrew Bible.

A Walk through Isaiah

As we observed in the preceding chapter, the book of Isaiah is actually the product of at least three different prophets, one from each of the three major junctures in Israelite history that produced the prophetic literature. It was not always the case, though, that readers understood this about Isaiah as a critical matter. In fact, it was only in 1892 that the scholar Bernard Duhm observed what Christian and Jewish readers had sensed for centuries: that the book of Isaiah could hardly have been authored by a single person. While major parts of Isaiah 1–39 reflect the political realities in Judah during the late 8th century B.C.E., Isaiah 40–55 mentions figures and circumstances Jews experienced only in the late Exilic period, and Isaiah 56–66 mirrors circumstances Jews faced when they returned to Judah under Persian rule in the late 6th century. Thus Duhm posited three books in one: First Isaiah in chs. 1–39, Second Isaiah in chs. 40–55, and Third Isaiah in chs. 56–66. Duhm understood that this division was an oversimplification, and that there is in fact considerable overlap among the three parts of Isaiah; recent study of Isaiah has confirmed that more nuanced observation in many ways. For the sake of simplicity, though, we will treat Isaiah in three steps corresponding to the three basic parts Duhm identified.

First Isaiah: Isaiah 1–39

Isaiah 1–39 may be broken into six parts. Isaiah 1–12 provides biographical and autobiographical prose, sayings, and poetic texts from different periods of the prophet's activity. These are mostly considered to be authentic sayings of the historical Isaiah. Within this section we encounter an opening chapter that touches on nearly all of the themes in the book of Isaiah (and which bears in 1:1 a regnal-formula superscription as we see in a number of other prophetic books, including Hosea and Amos). From announcements of doom as the consequence for religious infidelity and social injustice, to promises of consolation for the repentant, to anticipation of the restoration of Zion's glory, the first chapter has it all. It is as if it was made to be a compendium of the full range of basic themes that dominate the entire book of Isaiah.

Isaiah 2–4 records the prophet's oracles of doom and salvation for Judah and Jerusalem. The section begins with a second superscription like the one in ch. 1, indicating to some a second beginning to the book (although more likely ch. 1 is the sort of "summary statement" we suggested above). In any case, this section begins with a word of hope for the future (2:2-4) that matches Mic 4:1-3, but then launches into a description of the awful realities present in the Judah that Isaiah observed: social injustice, moral chaos, and religious apostasy reigned. In 3:13-15 the Lord indicts Israel as though in a court proceeding, and sentence is pronounced on the people in the form of a condemnation for the "court ladies" of Jerusalem (3:16–4:1). The section closes with an oracle introduced by the words "On that day," a signal of a salvation oracle describing how, once cleansed of her iniquity, Jerusalem will be restored (4:2-6).

Isaiah 5 stands out for its blend of the love song about the vineyard (vv. 1-7) and the following woes (vv. 8-24). The prophet sings of how the Lord planted a vine-

Reading Guide to Isaiah

First Isaiah (1–39)
Biographical and Autobiographical Prose, Sayings, Poetry (1–12)
Oracles Against the Nations (13–23)
Isaiah Apocalypse (24–27)
Oracles of Judgment Against Israel and Judah (and Foes) (28–31)
Poems and Prayers Related to the Coming Age of Judgment (32–35)
Historical Narrative (36–39; cf. 2 Kgs 18:13–20:19)

Second Isaiah (40–55)
Anticipating the Fall of Babylon and the Return (40–48)
The Justice Required of Zion (49–55)

Third Isaiah (56–66)
Welcoming Foreigners to the Temple (56:1-8)
On the Problem of Leadership in Judah (56:9–59:21)
Envisioning the New Zion (60–62)
Assorted Oracles (63:1–66:16)
Foreigners Exalt the Lord (66:17-24)

yard and tended it with loving care, only to see it yield wild and sour grapes. The Lord sought justice in Israel and reaped the opposite in the form of large landholders defrauding their poorer neighbors of their land (vv. 8-10), the rich consuming the goods of the poor (vv. 11-13), and so on. Isaiah cries "Woe!" against Israel for these sins and then announces that God will bring a foe from afar to punish Israel for its sins (vv. 25-30).

Finally in Isaiah 6 we come to the call of Isaiah. Since it is placed after five introductory chapters, one has the sense that what came first was intended to summarize the nature of Isaiah's ministry. This strange call narrative (which we saw in full in the preceding chapter) confirms that, in a sense. In the year that King Uzziah died (742 or 733 B.C.E.) Isaiah finds himself in the heavenly council chambers and fears for his life as he is not clean enough to dwell in the presence of the holy ones; but he is made clean by the heavenly beings (vv. 1-7). Once that is done God announces the need of an emissary, and Isaiah volunteers without knowing the task before him. God accepts his offer and, when Isaiah asks what he is to say, he discovers the difficult truth: he is called to speak unrelenting condemnation against Israel so that nothing of it but a "stump" or "root" remains at the end of it all (vv. 8-13). With that the tenor of the oracles of condemnation tinged with hope for the future that we find in chs. 1–5 becomes clear. This was Isaiah's task.

Isaiah 7–8 provides prophecy set within a particular historical setting. Here we read of Isaiah's intervention into Judean politics on the occasion of the Syro-Ephraimite threat. Syria and Israel had joined forces against the imperial power Assyria and were determined to force Judah to join them in the rebellion. God sends Isaiah to counsel Ahaz, king of Judah, against joining the alliance and to trust in God alone. Isaiah tells Ahaz that he has only to wait and that God will raise up a devout and successful king from the line of David who would assure Judah's fate against the foes (7:14-17), but ominously the last verse hints that Ahaz would not listen and instead bondage to Assyria is to follow, as indeed it did because Ahaz sought help from the empire against Syria and Israel. Thus Isaiah 8 is Isaiah's speech announcing the doom that would follow Ahaz's failed policy.

The Lord planted a vineyard, Israel, and "expected it to yield grapes, but it yielded wild grapes" (Isa 5:1-2). **Vineyard at Lachish.** (Phoenix Data Systems, Neal and Joel Bierling)

Following this event-related prophetic section are several chapters of oracles of doom and salvation in Isaiah 9–12. In a prophecy of a new age and new ruler (perhaps Hezekiah), 9:1-7 is a well-known oracle of salvation promising a child who would become a "Prince of Peace" on the throne of David. But then 9:8–10:4 returns to prophecy of judgment and condemnation for Israel, 10:5-19 describes woe for Assyria for overstepping its role as God's instrument of punishment, 10:20-27 reverts back to hope for a future restoration, and 10:28-34 announces further judgments. But ch. 11 shifts entirely to hope, anticipating the much quoted future peaceful kingdom and its impact on the nations surrounding it. The unit closes with two hymns of praise and thanksgiving to be sung on that day of salvation (ch. 12; on the importance of certain passages in this section for Christian thought, see "Theological Themes" below).

As is typical of the prophetic books, we find also in Isaiah extended sections of oracles against the nations hostile to Israel, interspersed with prophecies of happier days ahead for Israel. Isaiah 13–23 contains nine such oracles. The targets include Babylon (13:1–14:23; 21:1-10), Assyria (14:24-27), Philistia (14:28-32), Moab (15:1–16:14), Syria (17:1-14), Egypt (19:1-15; 20:1-6),

Arabia (21:13-17), Edom (21:11-12), and Sidon (23:1-18). Their scope clearly extends beyond the 8th-century context. Indeed, some of these are Isaiah's own speeches, while others — for example some against Babylon — must have come from later speakers. One that seems certain to have been Isaiah's was that directed against Egypt (20:1-6), a speech delivered perhaps on the occasion of Hezekiah's consideration of an alliance with Egypt in 711.

Isaiah 24–27, often called the "Isaian Apocalypse" because of its proto-apocalyptic contents, anticipate the final end of the earth, and are widely viewed as a late addition to the book of Isaiah because of the apocalyptic elements present in them. Isaiah 24:1-20 describes earth's final downfall and the salvation of a few survivors. The rest of the unit is taken up by prophecy and prayer that anticipate God's defeat of the cosmic powers and restoration of Jerusalem to greatness, the great banquet on Zion (25:6-10), and perhaps even resurrection (26:19). Finally the section closes with a positive renewal of the song of the vineyard (27:2-6; cf. 5:1-7) and references to the restoration of Jacob reminiscent of the Exile.

Isaiah 28–31 returns to the theme of oracles of judgment against Israel and Judah, but the chapters also include woes and predictions of disaster for the great foes Assyria and Egypt. Isaiah 28 is a long oracle against Israel and Judah that concludes with a parable of the good farmer, a defense of God's justice in rendering judgment against the nations. Isaiah 29:1-16 seems to recall the siege of Jerusalem by Sennacherib and its sudden end in Jerusalem's favor, and then suggests that for all of that Israel still did not understand God's intentions. But 29:17-24 closes with another oracle of assurance, invoking in particular Abraham and Jacob and God's promises to them and their responses to God as reasons for hope. This same vacillation between promises of condemnation and restoration appears in chs. 30–31: negotiations with Egypt as a means of self-defense against Assyria are condemned (30:1-7), Israel's record of rejection is even written down (30:8-17), but an oracle of God's promised mercy follows, along with the promised destruction of Assyria (30:18-33). Again Egyptian alliances are condemned (31:1-3), but God's deliverance of the people from Assyria is assured (31:4-9).

Then Isaiah 32–35 shifts the tone again, offering poems and prayers regarding the coming age of judgment and redemption. Isaiah 32 anticipates the ideal of a kingdom ruled by a proper Davidic king: it will be an age when hunger ceases, when nature is restored. But then ch. 33 anticipates a tyrant's attack on Jerusalem, and resolves in anticipation of God's deliverance once more. Isaiah 34 is an oracle against Edom, suggesting its later date, for Edom earned this hatred for helping Babylon defeat Judah. Then finally ch. 35 offers what some call a "link chapter" because it sounds so much like what we find in Isaiah 40–55. Indeed, with its language of restoration and highways in the desert it seems certain to have been the first part of so-called Second Isaiah. What separates it from the rest of Second Isaiah, though, is the Historical Appendix of chs. 36–39.

Isaiah 36–39 is a third-person historical narrative which parallels 2 Kgs 18:13–20:19 (with the exception of 38:9-20, Hezekiah's song of thanksgiving for deliverance). Isaiah 36–37 narrates God's successful intervention on King Hezekiah's behalf against Sennacherib of Assyria when the latter besieged Jerusalem in 701, and Hezekiah followed Isaiah's advice to simply trust in the Lord. Chapter 38 recounts Hezekiah's illness and how he was given respite and longer life because he beseeched the Lord through Isaiah. And ch. 39 relates Isaiah's prediction of the Babylonian Exile when Hezekiah went against the principles of the David-Zion theology and appeased Merodach-baladan of Babylon by giving him payment from the temple treasury. It seems probable that these chapters were inserted after ch. 35 by a

later tradent to underscore the Isaian view that hope for the future lies partly in the realization of the David-Zion theological ideal of a faithful Davidic king like Hezekiah enthroned in Jerusalem, and that failures like the Exile were precipitated by the breakdown of that theology in practice.

Second Isaiah: Isaiah 40–55

Second Isaiah is commonly divided into two parts. Isaiah 40–48 is addressed to Jacob and Israel and anticipates the fall of Babylon and Judah's restoration to the land. Isaiah 49–55 speaks to Zion and Jerusalem and concerns itself with the justice required of the people. Thus it is evidently an exilic work that anticipates Judah's restoration through the agency of Cyrus of Persia, as we shall see.

The first part begins with a passage reminiscent of Isaiah's call in Isaiah 6; this prophet is summoned to speak for God as well (40:1-11). But unlike the Isaiah of the 8th century, this prophet's mission is to speak comfort to God's people, to promise them redemption from the Lord and a new exodus. Then, as if to overcome the objection that Judah's political defeat spoke against God's power, there follows a defense of the Lord as incomparable to anything else as a creator God and indeed, no mere national deity, but God of all the cosmos (40:12-31).

Isaiah 41–48 then defends and elaborates the notion of the new exodus that would entail the movement of Judeans from Babylon back to the land of Judah. Isaiah 41 begins with a challenge to the nations, drawing attention to Cyrus of Persia as one whom God had raised for a special purpose (vv. 1-7). Then we hear for the first time Israel, Jacob and Abraham called "servant" and addressed as the object of God's affection and attention in all of this, the reason for God's action even in Cyrus (vv. 8-20). Correspondingly, God challenges the gods of other lands to be so devoted to their peoples and concludes that in fact such gods do not exist at all (vv. 21-29).

This leads to the first Servant Song in Second Isaiah. Isaiah 42:1-4 (5-9) describes the servant as one who will bring justice to the nations. We will address below in "Critical Issues" the possible identities of the servant. In any case, this song prompts a psalm of praise for what God plans to do (42:10-17), but also a commentary on how the people remain heedless of what God intends due to their historical infidelity (42:18-25). Thus Israel's redemption is said to be God's act alone; not even sacrifice can allow Israel to participate in its own salvation (43:1-28). Thus the people are assured of their salvation (44:1-8, 21-23), while idolatry is condemned (44:9-20).

Following is the Cyrus oracle, God's proclamation

that he has anointed Cyrus of Persia as his "messiah" who will deliver Israel (44:24–45:8), a defense against those who question Cyrus's appointment (45:9-19), and an offer of salvation to the nations through recognition of the sovereignty of the God of Israel (45:20-25).

This leads to a contrast between the gods of Babylon and the God of Israel that denies the existence of the deities of the foreign land (46:1-13) and a description of the end of Babylon (47:1-15). The section closes with a renewed direct address to the people of Israel, calling them to belief in what God plans for them and closing with an appeal to flee Babylon when the time comes for their freedom and redemption, trusting that as Israel once was spared thirst in the desert, this time too they would be cared for by God on their journey home (48:20-21).

The second section of Second Isaiah, chs. 49–55, opens with the second Servant Song (49:1-6). Whoever he is, his role is to be a light to the nations, a beacon to Israel to restore all of its people. Following, 49:7-26 is an announcement of the new exodus and the restoration of Zion: the people who are called to leave Babylon to return to the land of Judah need not worry about the journey or the circumstances they encounter at its end. Thus the Servant may be confident in spite of opposition (50:1-11; vv. 4-11, the third Servant Song), and Israel, trusting in God's history with the ancestors, Abraham and Sarah in particular, can also be assured of future salvation (51:1-8).

Isaiah 51:9-11 then expresses a plea for God's help against the chaos Israel might experience (echoing the imagery of the sea monsters of the deep, Rahab and the dragon), and God responds with assurances and the promise that the cup of wrath Israel once drank from is now handed over to her foes (51:12-23). As a result Jerusalem will be restored in all her glory (52:1-6). To that end a deliverer will come and the Lord will come to Jerusalem (52:7-10); so the people should willingly flee Babylon when their chance comes to do so (52:11-12).

Next we encounter the last Servant Song, which recounts how the servant was bruised for the people's sins, how he suffered greatly for them and bore their shame without complaint, even perhaps unto death. The hymn has the character of a thanksgiving for the servant's offering of himself (52:13–53:12).

Second Isaiah continues then with a description of Zion restored like a spouse or mother. The poem also speaks of this as a new postflood situation, when all things were renewed and a covenant of peace was established (54:1-17). The prophet then appeals to his audience to participate in the restoration and to repent; when they do, even nature will join in the joy of the moment (55:1-13).

Third Isaiah: Isaiah 56–66

Third Isaiah is much more difficult to outline than the other parts of the book. It does seem to have "bookend" pieces, inasmuch as it begins with an oracle that introduces foreigners into the temple and its worship (56:1-8), and it closes with a similar sort of oracle that announces how foreigners will exalt the Lord (66:17-24). Also evident is a description of the New Zion this prophet envisions in chs. 60–62. The portions that vex readers most, though, lie between the bookends and the central section.

Isaiah 56:9–59:21 may generally be described as a section about the problem of leadership in postexilic Judah. In 56:9–57:13 the community's leaders are condemned, especially since the righteous perish unjustly while the wicked prosper and some sort of sorcery has been permitted that entails worship of foreign gods in most reprehensible ways. Following this attack on improper worship are a poem of consolation for the righteous (57:14-21) and a discourse on true and false fasting, apparently aimed at drawing the distinction between the righteous and the wicked (58:1-14). Isaiah 59:1-8 explains why fasting and prayers are ineffectual — the people and their leaders are unjust — and then follow a communal confession of sin and a description of God's judgment to punish and redeem (59:9-21).

The core of Third Isaiah is chs. 60–62. Isaiah 60 describes the glory of the New Zion, Jerusalem restored. Gentiles will flow to the city, foreigners will make sacrifice in the temple, and even some of the Israelites in dispersion will return by the sea. The New Zion will be greater than the one built by Solomon, and the promise of great land and descendants to Abraham will be fulfilled. Isaiah 61:1-4 describes the anointing of the prophet who proclaims this good news, and 61:5-11 extends that news, reaffirming many of the themes from ch. 60. Finally, Isaiah 62 is a description of Zion's destiny from the mouth of the prophet: she will be a crown of beauty, a royal diadem in the hand of God, the thing over which God rejoices. The chapter closes with an echo of 40:1-3, but now as the fulfillment of the call to return to Zion; the city once forsaken will be called "Sought Out" (62:10-12).

Isaiah 63:1–66:16 shifts moods again. The first unit, 63:1-6, describes God's vengeance on Edom for its participation in destroying Judah at the beginning of the Exile. Isaiah 63:7–64:12 continues with a psalm of communal lamentation that seems to have been composed following the Babylonian conquest. Isaiah 65:1-7 provides God's response to the lament, suggesting that he was ready to provide respite but no one sought him out in proper worship, chasing instead after foreign gods with false worship. That not all were committed to the wrong is apparent in 65:8-16, which suggests there was a division in the Jerusalem community between God's servants and the reprobates. What is likely a late insertion follows in 65:17-25; it offers an apocalyptic vision of a future healed of the rifts described in the preceding — and following — material. Thus 66:1-6 continues to describe the divided community. Then, with a literary suddenness that was likely meant to convey a similarly abrupt change in reality, attention turns to the rebirth of Jerusalem and the establishment of a new community (66:7-16). The book closes with the vision of Israel's homecoming to Jerusalem, the service of the Gentiles as declarers of God's glory and servants even in the temple, and the declaration that all flesh shall worship the Lord (66:17-24).

Critical Issues in Studying the Book of Isaiah

Not surprisingly given its length and complexity, a multitude of critical issues have attracted the attention of readers of the book of Isaiah. We must restrict ourselves to but a handful. Although we have treated Isaiah as a three-part book, one of the most important contemporary issues is whether this simple division is accurate. Having admitted that, it is nevertheless also important to address for our readers the social and historical contexts of the three periods that seem to have generated the material in Isaiah. We also address the perennially vexing problem of the identity of the Servant in Second Isaiah.

The Greater Complexity of the Book of Isaiah

While our survey of the contents of Isaiah has more or less upheld the notion that there are three largely distinct parts of the book, some exceptions to the complete division into three were also apparent. For instance, Isaiah 24–27 seems almost certainly to be some of the latest material to have accrued to the book. And ch. 35 seems certainly to have been the original beginning of what continues in Isaiah 40, so-called Second Isaiah. (Others go so far as to say that chs. 33–34 were also part of Second Isaiah as well.) Thus Isaiah 36–39 was, as we noted above, likely inserted late to serve the interests of the David-Zion theology. Apart from this separation of the probable beginning of Second Isaiah from ch. 40, Second Isaiah does seem to hold together well as a distinct unit that reflects the exilic context. But when we come to Third Isaiah we encounter in chs. 60–62 material that echoes Second Isaiah more than it does the rest of chs. 56–66, and we run across at least one late apocalyptic addition in 65:17-25. Still others think that

we can locate in Isaiah 56–66 prophecies from the 8th century as well. Lastly, we note that ch. 1 recapitulates many of the themes of the book as a whole, and chs. 2–5, though almost certainly mostly from Isaiah, also reflect a broader view and come before the actual call of Isaiah. In short, while it seems certain that there were at least three stages in the production of the book of Isaiah, it is not possible to say that the three successive parts to the book entirely reflect those stages. Perhaps the best way to envision the process is as one of two major successive redactions of the original prophet's words and some further, later additions that created a single book of very mixed character.

The Social and Historical Context of the Historical Isaiah

Isaiah the prophet was active from around 740 to 700 B.C.E. While many of the oracles attributed to him may have come from different times during those 40 years, there are three particular periods to which we can attribute his work: the Syro-Ephraimite crisis in 735-734, Hezekiah's brush with an alliance with Egypt in 711, and the Assyrian siege of Jerusalem in 701.

What were the circumstances that Isaiah faced in these years? His prophecies reveal that economic injustice was an issue. The most famous evidence of this is to be found in 5:8-24, where we read of wealthy landholders adding the land of the poor to their own property in payment for debt, the abuse of the resources of the poor by the wealthy for their own entertainment and sustenance, and the subversion of justice in the courts. Isaiah also condemned Israel's reliance on foreign powers (e.g., 20:1-6), but especially so in connection with the faithfulness of Davidic kings. Indeed, he did not appeal to the laws of the Pentateuch to encourage faithfulness and justice, but rather to the promise to David of an eternal dynasty in Jerusalem; if only the descendants of David and the people would trust in that promise from God, all would be well even in the face of the most serious threats.

This would be the focus of each of the three clearly defined moments in Isaiah's ministry. When King Ahaz faced the Syro-Ephraimite alliance in 735-734 Isaiah counseled resistance to the two nations' pressure and independence from Assyria (ch. 7). But Ahaz ignored Isaiah and allied himself with Assyria, prompting Isaiah's promise that Assyria would be God's instrument of punishment for this lack of trust (7:18-25). Seeing Ahaz's failure to trust, Isaiah prophesied the coming of a new king — perhaps Hezekiah — who would trust the Lord and earn the blessings that were promised to such Davidic kings (9:2-7; 11:6-9). Similarly, when Hezekiah was tempted in 711 to ally with Egypt against the rising

Assyrian threat Isaiah graphically called the king to trust not in foreign power but the protection of the Lord (20:1-6). Finally, when the Assyrians besieged Jerusalem in 701 Isaiah 36–37 portrays Isaiah as once again urging Hezekiah to resist any alliances and to trust in the Lord. The result, as we know from our survey of Isaiah, was a miraculous deliverance, a vindication of Isaiah's policy of divine trust.

Yet in spite of these successes, Isaiah understood that Judah was nonetheless fated to be defeated in the end for the overriding faithlessness of her kings. Thus even in his commission we hear that he was called to announce doom and destruction until all that remained was the "stump" of Jesse (ch. 6). Likewise, a recurring theme in his oracles regarding Judah is the anticipation that it would one day be devastated by a foreign power like Assyria, and that its only hope for the future lay in a remnant of the people and a faithful Davidic king who together would be the basis for a renewed, even ideal Israel and Jerusalem (2:2-4; 9:2-7; 11:6-9; 29:17-21).

The Social and Historical Context of Second Isaiah

The prophecies we find concentrated in Isaiah 40–55 (and perhaps 33–35) clearly come from a much later time than the 8th-century world of Isaiah. The key to dating this material is the mention of Cyrus of Persia as God's anointed (45:1). The text clearly understands Cyrus as on the rise and his conquest of Babylon as imminent. From 546 on it was clear to all that Cyrus and Persia were soon to replace the Babylonian king Nabonidus and his empire as the true powers in the Near East. Moreover, everyone knew that Persian policy was to repatriate people exiled from their homelands so that they could cultivate those lands and produce income for the empire. Thus Judeans living in Babylon — by then already for nearly two generations — anticipated the day when they would be invited by a victorious Cyrus to return to Judah to rebuild their temple and its economy so as to produce revenue for Persia.

But therein lay the problem. After two generations most Judeans in Babylon had happily accommodated to their context. They had settled comfortably in the rich and fertile land of Babylon and had even prospered there. It seems certain they had even begun to make a certain peace with the main god of Babylon, Marduk, who after all was worshipped mostly through a single New Year festival and in response provided enormously fertile crops. By contrast, their God required constant faithfulness and had responded to their infidelity with exile from their homeland. They also no doubt saw the clear advantages of the rich farmland of Babylon over the difficult land of Judah, and of the city of

Babylon over the ruins of Jerusalem. (For evidence of the Judeans' success and comfort in Babylon, see our discussion of the Murashu documents in Chapter 3 above.) As for the prospect of making the long journey "home" to Judah, few would have wanted to risk it, for travel in the ancient world was a dangerous undertaking to say the least.

These were the challenges faced by the author of Second Isaiah. His response was evident in our survey of the text above. As for the idea that Marduk was preferable to the God of Israel, Second Isaiah announced for the first time in Israelite history that there was, in fact, but one God alone. Until this time the biblical authors held to a henotheistic view. That is, they understood their God to be the one divinity among the many worthy of worship. Second Isaiah overturned that notion, denying the existence of other gods altogether (41:21-29; 46:1-13). On the difficulty of the trip home to Judah, Second Isaiah announced that God would lead a new exodus more glorious than the first (40:3-5; 41:17-20; 48:20-22; 49:7-13). And to contend with the exiles' preference for the land of Babylon and its capital city, Second Isaiah spoke of God's act of new creation and restoration of Zion (49:14-26), as well as of Babylon's impending doom for overstepping its bounds as God's instrument of discipline for Judah (47:1-15).

What success did Second Isaiah have in encouraging a return? As our survey of the books written in the name of Ezra and Nehemiah proves, some did heed the call to return and rebuild Jerusalem and the temple. But one answer to the question of the Servant's identity suggests that, at least in Second Isaiah's own day, success was limited at best. Recall the tenor of the Servant Songs: the first says he will bring justice to the nations (42:1-6); the second makes of him a light to the nations (49:1-6); the third reveals that for all of his effort he experiences serious opposition (50:4-11); and the last even indicates that he was persecuted and may have been killed for his trouble (52:13–53:12). Some think that the songs are about the prophet himself and that the progression of the songs indicates that his message, which included calling the people to return to Judah, was not all that well received, that perhaps even his fellow Judeans were violently opposed to his call to return. Others suggest Israel was the Servant, and that its mission to the nations brought upon it suffering. The most plausible reading, though, may be to admit that various referents were intended by the author, and that together they were meant to promote the notion that corporate and individual suffering, not national might, would bring to fruition God's plan for salvation.

The Social and Historical Context of Third Isaiah

Last, we address the social and historical context of Third Isaiah. Although it is not true for all of the prophecies in Isaiah 56–66, many of them seem to reflect the postexilic context and some of the frustrations and disappointments experienced by the returnees to Judah. What were those conditions and why were they so difficult?

As the people returned they did not encounter the gloriously renewed Zion Second Isaiah had promised. Instead they found a land long neglected and cities in terrible disrepair. The infrastructures necessary for rebuilding the cities, especially Jerusalem, were in ruins, the temple was little more than a heap of rubble, and the fragmented stepped farmlands had long since been over-cultivated and perhaps never properly rotated. Moreover, the returnees soon came into conflict with "the people of the land," those who had never left, over land possession, temple construction (see Ezra-Nehemiah), and definition of the emerging religious community. To make matters even more complex, it seems certain the land's inhabitants were considerably more diverse than ever before, as refugees from the Babylonian conquests of years before had no doubt also settled in the land. Thus the central issue became one of how order would be restored in these chaotic conditions. From Ezra-Nehemiah we know that it came through the efforts of Persian appointees who ruled in favor of the returnees and who saw to a fairly narrow definition of who counted as the "true Israelites" who could participate in rebuilding Judah.

Some see Third Isaiah as reflecting the views of those who came out on the short end of this struggle to shape the new Judean community. For all of its disorder, Isaiah 56–66 does work out to be roughly a balance of condemnation for the unjust rulers and oppressors and consolation for the righteous who were oppressed. Indeed, it begins with an oracle welcoming the most outcast of all — foreigners and eunuchs — into the temple (56:1-8), and it closes with a similar anticipation of foreigners coming into service of the Lord. In between it offers condemnation for all who have oppressed others — from the leaders of the community (56:9-12) to Edom (63:1-6) — and consolation for those who have suffered (see esp. chs. 60–62). In short, Third Isaiah seems to work as an address to those who were frustrated by the outcome of the reestablishment of Judah, who were marginalized by their neighbors. These may have been the people of the land, and others may have been some who returned but did not for one reason or another meet the standards of the new community's rulers. In any case, the author of Third Isaiah clearly considers his favored audience to be the true heirs to Israel's religion, the true believers, the

ones who "tremble at his [the Lord's] word" (66:5); in time, they will inherit the good, says this author, not the false leaders in the land.

Theological Themes in Isaiah

The theological themes in the book of Isaiah are understandably diverse and naturally reflect something of the tripartite nature of the book. To address all of those themes here is well beyond the scope of an Introduction, and to attempt too cursory a survey risks doing the book an injustice. There is at least one overarching theme, though, that of trusting in the Lord's promises. It was simply worked out somewhat differently by the three parts of the book. We use that common theme and its different manifestations in each of the three parts of Isaiah to organize our reflections on theological themes in Isaiah.

Trust in the Lord in First Isaiah

Isaiah's intense concern for social justice in Judah, though not at first glance a strictly "theological" theme, does deserve some attention before addressing his notion of trust in the Lord. Like earlier prophets of the 8th century we will address below (Amos, Hosea, and Micah), Isaiah saw the practice of official religion without proper regard for social justice as worthy of severe condemnation (see esp. chs. 2–4). This is a theological theme inasmuch as Isaiah made clear the necessary link between true worship and just human action. The first without the second was worthless (1:12-17).

In addition to this, the prophet Isaiah had a single overriding theological claim to make as well: that trust in the Lord's promises to the house of David and to Zion in the face of all difficulties and challenges was the key to Judah's success. Where he saw a failure to trust in God's promises to sustain the faithful Davidic king and to make Zion great and witnessed instead confidence in human power or wisdom (such as Ahaz exhibited in his alliance with Assyria; ch. 7), Isaiah promised doom and destruction. But where he encountered a Davidic king who trusted in the Lord, he announced Judah's success and hope for its future, as was the case with Hezekiah on several occasions (chs. 36–37). Thus Isaiah could announce horrible prophecies of doom for Judah (3:16–4:1) but also envision in its future idyllic times (4:2-6; 9:1-7; 11:1-9), all depending on how the people and their king behaved.

Trust in the Lord in Second Isaiah

Second Isaiah continues the theme of calling for trust in the Lord. However, this author does not base that trust on promises regarding David and Zion, but on the great deeds of God in the Primeval History, on the promises to the ancestors, and on God's actions on behalf of the people in the Exodus from Egypt and the wandering in the wilderness. Echoes of the Exodus become promises of a new exodus from Babylon to Judah. Recollections of God's act of creation at the beginning become announcements of God's new creation in the land of Israel. Even the memory of the flood is evoked to suggest that, just as then God made things new, so God was making things new again for God's beloved people. All God asks of the people

Trust

is trust in these promises, demonstrated in their willing return to Judah to renew their worship there of God and their possession of that land as the land promised them by God. When the people do rely on God's promise and return to the land there will even be a bonus for them: according to Second Isaiah all of creation will recognize in that day that the center of the world, the universe even, is Zion; seeing that the nations will flow to Israel's side to prosper the people and grant them their service. The promises to the ancestors articulated first and most clearly in Gen 12:1-3 would be fulfilled.

Trust in the Lord in Third Isaiah
As we have seen above, Third Isaiah addresses trust in the Lord in a very different way: for this writer those who should trust are the oppressed and troubled, those who have been left aside from what little prosperity and happiness could be gained in the Postexilic era under Persian rule. Through their exclusion from the temple cult and its economy, many were deeply disappointed in the outcome of the return. Third Isaiah's advice to them is to wait for the day when they would be vindicated by God breaking in upon their existence and restoring justice to them. Darkly, God's action on their behalf would be the violent destruction of the oppressors, but on the brighter side, God would also bring to them comfort and consolation quite apart from the destruction of the wicked.

Wadi Ytem in southern Transjordan, a dry brook which, with heavy rainfall, might become a "river in the desert" (Isa 43:19-20). (Denis Baly)

Just as there is a mood of universalism in Second Isaiah, there is a similar mood in Third Isaiah. But here the "universal" extent of God's mercy is, ironically, limited: those who tremble at the word of the Lord can expect, without exception, to know God's special mercy and deliverance. And just as Second Isaiah envisions an international flavor to the embrace of God's vision and God's people, Third Isaiah shares a similar sort of focus. But again, the nations come to serve the elect of God, not the wicked oppressors (see esp. Isaiah 60, where the flow of Gentiles to Zion is envisioned *within* the Book of Consolation).

The Canonical Book of Isaiah and Theology
Even the differences among the three parts of Isaiah on the question of "trust in the Lord" show that this book has its own complex theological witness as a whole. As a consequence, Isaiah in many ways reflects some of the same circumstances we saw with respect to the book of Psalms above: as a composite work arising out of diverse human experiences in the sight of God, it reflects the importance of human experience in engendering theological reflections. It also testifies to the thoroughly

intertwined nature of the theological visions we encounter in the Old Testament. We saw above the echoes of Yahwist theological traditions, as well as sentiments that took into account elements of the Priestly worldview. If we had time and space to explore the theological richness of Isaiah further, we would see additional Old Testament theologies being taken up and developed in the book. But again, we only note this and leave it to readers to take a more complete look at this question with the help of the text of Isaiah and secondary literature on it.

The Book of Isaiah and Christian Thought

As we noted above, the book of Isaiah is quoted very often in the New Testament. It was also very popular among early Christian interpreters of the tradition. The obvious reason for this is the book's enormous collection of theological motifs within its 66 chapters. But another reason, better known to most readers, is the fuel it provided for messianic thought in early Christianity.

Numerous oracles in First Isaiah served early interpreters of Jesus particularly well, as they did other messianic movements in early Judaism. Especially the oracles in Isa 9:2-7; 11:1-3 offered support to the view that a messiah would come from the line of David, whom many saw to be Jesus. Also significant in First Isaiah for early Christian (and Jewish) eschatological imagination was 11:6-9, with its vision of a future peaceable kingdom.

The difficulty in reading the prophecies of First Isaiah as an anticipation of Jesus, of course, was Jesus' fate on the cross. Here too Isaiah provided prophetic foresight to clarify matters among Christian believers. The Servant Songs of Second Isaiah (42:1-9; 49:1-6; 50:1-11 [4-9]; 52:13–53:12) provide prophetic foretelling of the suffering a servant of the Lord would endure on behalf of the people. Especially the final song, with its vivid language of affliction, suffering, and even death

made clear to those who saw in Jesus the promised Messiah the explanation for Jesus' death: it was foretold as an aspect of the Messiah, and its significance was just as the book of Isaiah had foretold; it was a death for the salvation of others.

Again, we must beg our readers' forgiveness in cutting short our discussion of Isaiah's theological significance, and here especially as it pertains to early Christian thought and interpretation of Jesus. In the New Testament section of this Introduction, though, we return to these themes on the appropriate occasions.

Questions for Review and Discussion

1   How many "parts" are there to the book of Isaiah, at least as traditional scholarship has viewed the matter? What did we suggest above, though, about the full complexity of the book's compositional history?

2   What are the differing moods in each of the parts of the book of Isaiah? How do these reflect particular human experiences, specific social and historical contexts?

3   What are some of the theological riches of the book of Isaiah we touched on in this chapter? Take the time to read Isaiah carefully for yourself and create your own list of further theological themes!

Further Reading

Barker, Margaret. "Isaiah." In *ECB*, 489-542.
Blenkinsopp, Joseph. *Isaiah 1–39; Isaiah 40–55; Isaiah 56–66*. AB 19, 19A, 19B. New York: Doubleday, 2000, 2002, 2003.

Chapter 28

Jeremiah

Getting Started

1   Read Jeremiah 8:8-9. What does the prophet say
about the "pen of the scribes" and what the scribes
have done to the law?

2   By contrast, read Jeremiah 11:1-14. Do you recognize
the rhetoric of this speech? Where have you encountered it before?

3   Read Jeremiah 19:1-9. How does the genre of this
material differ from that of the previous two passages
you read? What does the sum of your reading thus far
indicate about the nature of the book of Jeremiah?

Preliminary Comments

Jeremiah is perhaps the prophet best known to us as
a person, thanks in large part to the way he reported
his own ruminations and to his scribe, Baruch, who recorded events in Jeremiah's life. Through these autobiographical and biographical reports Jeremiah has earned
the reputation among readers as a mournful prophet
who expressed without reserve his anguish at fulfilling his role as a servant of the Lord who had little good

news to report to his audiences. Living in the days of
Babylon's hegemony, his task was to announce Judah's
impending doom and expulsion from the land. But Jeremiah was not without hope, for he also looked beyond
the Exile to the day when God would continue with his
people in a new covenantal relationship.

We also note at the outset that the book of Jeremiah,
like that of Isaiah, is composite, or so many assume. As
we shall see in our survey of the book's contents and in
discussing the critical issues associated with its study,
some of the book clearly hails from Jeremiah himself,
some of it is the biography composed by Baruch, and
some is made up of prose sermons that may be attributed either to Jeremiah or possibly to later tradents,
perhaps of a Deuteronomic persuasion.

A Walk through Jeremiah

Structure in Jeremiah is difficult to discern, probably in
large part because the book underwent such a long and
complex compositional history (see "Critical Issues"
below). The following is only a rough outline that we
elaborate more fully below.

Jeremiah 1:1–25:14: Oracles against Judah and Jerusalem

The book is introduced in 1:1-3 with a typical prophetic book superscription.

> The words of Jeremiah son of Hilkiah, of the priests who were in Anathoth in the land of Benjamin, to whom the word of the Lord came in the days of King Josiah son of Amon of Judah, in the thirteenth year of his reign. It came also in the days of King Jehoiakim son of Josiah of Judah, and until the end of the eleventh year of King Zedekiah son of Josiah of Judah, until the captivity of Jerusalem in the fifth month.

Interestingly, this provides Jeremiah with a 40-year ministry, ranging from 627 to 587 B.C.E. Because the ensuing call narrative resonates so clearly with that of Moses and both men had 40-year ministries, some see this as an attempt to assimilate Jeremiah to Moses, or even make of him the "prophet like Moses" promised in Deut 18:15-19.

The call narrative itself (1:4-19) entails God's affirmation that Jeremiah was chosen for service before he was even conceived, Jeremiah's demurral that he is but a child, and the Lord's commissioning of him nonetheless. The call concludes with visions that reveal Jeremiah's task: to announce impending destruction of Judah from the north for its apostasy.

Jeremiah 2:1–4:2 is in some ways an introduction to and summary of the book's larger message. It begins with a fond recollection of Israel's early devotion to God (2:1-3), but then describes Israel's long history of apostasy (2:4-37) in the form of a covenant lawsuit. Israel is indicted for faithlessness toward God and for going after other gods wantonly, with the people being compared even to a "wild ass at home in the wilderness, in her heat sniffing the wind" (2:24). The conclusion of the indictment is a judgment against the people and the promise of exile (2:36-37). But then in 3:1–4:2 the prophet lays out the conditions for repentance and the possibility of return and even offers up a model confession of sin. Jeremiah thus gives voice to both possibilities, unrelenting apostasy leading to doom or repentance and possible salvation.

As if to indicate which possibility he thought more likely — though this was surely a later editorial effort — we hear next in 4:3–6:30 the prophecy of a foe from the north who would serve as God's instrument of punishment. First comes a warning (4:3-4), then a vivid description of the invaders from the north and the devastation they bring to Jerusalem and the land (4:5-31). Then ch. 5 details the sins that merited the punishment, producing a typical litany against religious apostasy, social injustice, and failed leadership. Chapter 6 closes the

section with a renewed description of the approaching foe, further evidence of Jerusalem's sin and defenselessness, and the people's lament at their fate. At the last we hear that the foe comes precisely because Jeremiah diagnosed the people's sin accurately.

Jeremiah 7:1–10:25 then relates the prophet's judgment that Judah's fate was sealed. First, Jeremiah preaches in the temple to announce the impending exile (7:1-15). Then we hear that intercession is futile, as is preaching to change Judah's fate, for Judah's idolatry has been too great and its ears remain too closed (7:16–8:3). The rest of the section is a collection of oracles on the theme of Judah's predetermined fate, an exhortation to prepare for the departure into exile, and a prayer that God's wrathful attention be drawn away to other nations (8:4–10:25). Especially noteworthy in this section is Jeremiah's indictment of some who are clearly purveyors of the written word and who claim to be "wise" because the "law" is with them (8:8-9). Some see in this Jeremiah's hostility toward what might have been the early Deuteronomic movement. Its proponents promoted the keeping of a written law as the means of avoiding the wrath of God, while Jeremiah held up the spoken word of the prophet as the only trustworthy revelation of God's will.

The next major section of Jeremiah is a lengthy collection of rather disparate pieces which together announce the predetermined fate of Judah; most of these pieces are assigned to the periods of Josiah and Jehoiakim's reigns (11:1–20:18). The section begins with a prose sermon that is almost surely a late, perhaps Deuteronomic addition. It explains, after the fact, that exile befell the nation for its worship of other gods and neglect of the covenant that God had made with them (11:1-14, with a poetic addition in vv. 15-17). Next is the first of Jeremiah's six laments (11:18–12:6) followed by God's own lament over Jerusalem (12:7-13) and God's announcement that if Judah's neighbors repent on the occasion of Judah's exile they will be spared upon Judah's restoration (12:14-17). Chapter 13 then records Jeremiah's symbolic use of the tattered loincloth to signal Judah's fate, the allegory of the wine jar, an invitation to repentance, and finally the announcement of the Exile and a description of Jerusalem's shame in the wake of it. Chapter 14 is a lament over Jerusalem's coming defeat and the drought that will accompany the suffering. Notably, a third prohibition of prophetic intercession (14:11-12; see also 7:16; 11:14) is set right in the middle of the lament that was intended to produce a response from God; its placement is undeniable evidence that Judah's fate was irrevocably sealed. Jeremiah 15–16 is yet another extended unit assuring the certainty of Judah's fate. Beginning with a claim that even Moses' and Samuel's intercession would not save the people, this long unit also encompasses Jeremiah's second personal lament (15:10-21) and his symbolic act of remaining single without children to avoid the suffering that would come to families (16:1-9). The unit closes with another (probably post-Jeremiah) reference to the conversion of the nations (16:19-21; see also 10:23-25; 17:12-13; 20:13). Jeremiah 17:1-13 follows with a series of observations on the human heart, proving that while it is blessed when it trusts in God, its inclination is to be devious, while by contrast God's ways are exalted. Jeremiah's third lament follows in 17:14-18, and a late insertion on Sabbath observance concludes ch. 17. Chapter 18 reports the symbolic act of visiting the potter, whose actions are likened to God's making and destroying according to his disposition regarding his creation; the chapter continues by reporting Judah's choice of apostasy and subsequent destruction. The chapter concludes with Jeremiah's fourth personal lament (18:18-23). This lengthy unit closes with a report of Jeremiah's public proclamation of Judah's fate through the breaking of pottery, his subsequent persecution by being placed in the stocks, and his prophecy against his persecutor, Pashhur of the temple police (19:1-20:6), as well as Jeremiah's fifth and sixth laments (20:7-13, 14-18).

Jeremiah 21:1-24:10 provides oracles from the reign of Zedekiah, the son of Josiah who was appointed king over Judah in 597 by the Babylonian conqueror Nebuchadrezzar. The unit begins with an oracle against Zedekiah and Jerusalem for planning a rebellion against Babylon, an oracle that once again promises that Babylon will defeat Jerusalem and Judah utterly (21:1-10). Then follows a series of oracles against the royal house in 21:11-23:8, broken only by what appear to be late additions in 22:1-5 and 23:1-8, oracles offering restoration for repentance. Also noteworthy in this section are the prophecy in 22:24-30 that no descendant of Jehoiachin would rule again (a prophecy that was later reversed, as we shall see, when the image of the cast-off signet ring returns in Hag 2:20-23) and the vision of the baskets of good and bad figs (24:1-10).

This first large portion of Jeremiah concludes with a prophecy from "the fourth year of King Jehoiakim" (25:1; 605 B.C.E.), but that seems likely to have been composed in the Exile as a reflection on the event of the

Exile after the fact. The chapter includes the much interpreted prophecy of 70 years in exile and the promise that the king of Babylon would then be disciplined for his part in disciplining Judah (25:11-12; cf. Zech 1:12; Dan 9:2, 24-27).

Jeremiah 26-45:
Accounts of Jeremiah's Prophetic Ministry
This long section may be divided roughly into five parts. The first, 26:1-29:32, is a series of episodes that contend in particular with true and false prophecy. The second is the "Book of Consolation," chs. 30-31. Jeremiah 32-36 provides more biographical material from Jeremiah's career. Chapters 37-44 record the prophet's suffering before, during, and after Jerusalem's fall, and ch. 45 reports God's commission of Baruch.

Jeremiah 26:1-19 records the second Temple Sermon. Borrowing themes and language from ch. 7, this time Jeremiah speaks conditionally, suggesting that if the people heed his call to repentance they might be spared. They respond that he deserves death for speaking against the temple of the Lord, but Jeremiah replies that he is only speaking the word of the Lord. Recalling the precedent of Micah compelling repentance in Hezekiah by falsely predicting doom, the elders agree that Jeremiah's prophecy should be respected. (Note the contradiction this offers to the Deuteronomic notion that true prophecy is that which comes true [Deut 18:22]!) By contrast, Jer 26:20-24 reports that Uriah, a prophet who spoke the same sort of message, but without official support, was put to death by the king.

The next section, 27:1-28:17, records Jeremiah bearing a yoke to signify the proper posture of Judah in

"Good figs," representing the chosen remnant who would build a new future following the return from exile (Jer 24:1-10). (Phoenix Data Systems, Neal and Joel Bierling)

relation to the king of Babylon. This episode apparently took place in 595-594 when Zedekiah was tempted to join in an alliance against Babylon. Zedekiah heeded Jeremiah's advice, even though a competing prophet Hananiah proclaimed that Jeremiah was wrong and that the yoke of Babylon would be broken — as he broke Jeremiah's wooden yoke — within two years' time. Jeremiah's response to Hananiah was that the wooden yoke would thus be replaced by an iron yoke and that for his misleading prophecy Hananiah would be dead within the year. The unit closes by observing that Jeremiah's prophecy in this last regard was entirely accurate.

The section of true and false prophecy closes with Jeremiah's letter to Babylon warning of a long exile of 70 years and encouraging the deportees to get comfortable in their new home (29:1-23), the response of the prophet Shemaiah from Babylon that Jeremiah's speech was treasonous and deserved punishment (vv. 24-28); and Jeremiah's reply that because of his misleading prophecy none of Shemaiah's descendants would live to see the restoration that God would bring to Judah (vv. 29-32).

The next major section is the Book of Consolation (chs. 30–31). It is a bit of a red herring to suggest that it is from Jeremiah's ministry because much of it appears to have come from later hands, even if it is introduced with a divine command to Jeremiah to record the words in a book, words concerning God's plan to restore Israel and Judah to the land of their ancestors (30:1-4). First Jacob is promised restoration (30:5-11), then Zion and/or Samaria (30:12-24), then Israel as a whole (31:1-6). Then the homecoming of the exiles is foretold as a response to their lament (31:7-20), and the return itself is narrated (31:21-26). Chapter 31 closes with a string of late eschatological promises, the best known of which is assurance that God will one day make a new covenant with the people whereby the law will be written in their hearts and God will "remember their sin no more" (vv. 31-34).

Jeremiah 31:38–33:26 constitutes an appendix to the Book of Consolation that dwells especially on the future of Jerusalem. The framing elements — 31:38-40 and 33:14-26 — are late eschatological passages. Sandwiched between them are two episodes: Jeremiah's purchase of land in Anathoth as a signal of his divinely-inspired confidence that in spite of the impending destruction of Jerusalem God planned to restore Judah in time (32:1-44) and Jeremiah's prophecy that God would rebuild the walls of Jerusalem even after the Babylonian destruction of them (33:1-13).

Chapters 34–36 return to accounts of Jeremiah's activity around the siege of Jerusalem. In 34:1-7 he prophesies the capture of Zedekiah and, in another indication that true — or at least surviving! — prophecy did not always come to pass, Jeremiah also predicts

Zedekiah's peaceful death (cf. 52:8-11). In 34:8-22 we read that Zedekiah manumitted the slaves of Jerusalem, perhaps to assuage the Lord, but when the approach of the Egyptians forced Babylon to temporarily back off he rescinded the order, prompting further condemnation from Jeremiah, who saw in such an act further covenant infidelity. As a contrast Jeremiah in ch. 35 invites Rechabites to drink wine; they refuse in faithfulness to their covenantal obligation to avoid strong drink. Jeremiah's response is to ask the inhabitants of Judah and Jerusalem why, if the Rechabites hold fast to an obligation on the word of their ancestor, they cannot obey the word of the Lord that is at hand in his own speech. And so once more Jeremiah proclaims Jerusalem's impending destruction for its faithlessness but also promises descendants to the Rechabites for their fidelity. The last episode in this unit, ch. 36, recalls the famous incident of Jehoioakim's response to the scroll Jeremiah dictated to Baruch and had him read in the temple. The first reading of the warning speech received a favorable hearing and it was brought before King Jehoiakim. The king's response, though, was to cut it in pieces and burn it, after which Jeremiah commissioned the same scroll (and more) all over again as a signal of the humiliating death the king would experience.

Jeremiah 37–38 describes Zedekiah's temptation to trust that the Egyptian advance would drive off the Babylonians, the arrest of Jeremiah on suspicion of desertion, and Zedekiah's consultation of Jeremiah regarding the proper course of action (ch. 37). In a subsequent episode Jeremiah was cast by enemies into a cistern, saved from it by an Ethiopian eunuch, and consulted once more by a fearful Zedekiah, who then returned Jeremiah to house arrest (ch. 38).

Jeremiah 39:1–40:6 narrates the fall of Jerusalem, the capture of Zedekiah, the slaughter of his heirs before his eyes, his blinding, and his deportation to Babylon, as well as the special favor the Babylonian conquerors showed to Jeremiah. As the episode closes, we read that Jeremiah is freed by the Babylonians and that he joined Gedaliah and the other people who were left in the land.

The next major section, 40:7–44:30, underscores the author's view that the future of Judah lay with the Babylonian exiles, not those who remained behind or fled to Egypt. Jeremiah 40:7–41:18 relates the third rebellion against the Babylonians and the assassination of Gedaliah as the Babylonians' representative. In 42:1–43:7 we read that the rebels then consulted Jeremiah as to what they should do and that they rejected his advice from the Lord to remain in the land, electing instead to flee to Egypt and take Jeremiah and Baruch with them. Jeremiah 43:8–44:30 reports that when in Egypt Jeremiah first committed the symbolic act of burying stones in the entrance of Pharaoh's palace to signal that even there the Judeans were not safe from the Babylonian threat (43:8-13). Then he prophesied against the idolatrous practices of the Jews in the Egyptian diaspora (44:1-14), to which they replied they would do as they pleased in this matter, for their worship of the queen of heaven had brought them prosperity in the past (44:15-19). Jeremiah reminds them that, in fact, such practices brought them exile in the first place and they would suffer still more for their continued apostasy (44:20-30).

This large section closes with God's word to Baruch, dated to 605. In it Baruch is assured that he would survive the tribulations to come.

Jeremiah 25:15-38; 46–51: Oracles against Foreign Nations

The vision reported in 25:15-38 of God commanding that the cup of wrath be handed to all the nations at one time introduced the oracles against foreign nations. It describes in vivid detail the results of God's wrath against the nations. Jeremiah 46–51 actually records the oracles. The targets include Egypt (46:1-28), the Philistines (47:1-7), Moab (48:1-47), Ammon (49:1-6), Edom (49:7-22), Damascus (49:23-27), Kedar and Hazor (49:28-33), Elam (49:34-39), and finally, in one long collection of oracles, Babylon (50:1–51:64). The oracles are, as one would imagine, tailored to the particular character of each nation and its particular offenses against the people or God. Clearly, the greatest vitriol is reserved for Babylon. Indeed, the oracle against Babylon concludes with Jeremiah's command to Seraiah to travel to Babylon and read the scroll against the place, tie a stone to it, and cast it into the Euphrates, saying, "Thus shall Babylon sink, to rise no more, because of the disasters that I am bringing on her" (51:64a). The rest of that verse reads like the conclusion to the book: "Thus far are the words of Jeremiah" (51:64b).

Jeremiah 52:1-34: Historical Appendix

This chapter largely duplicates 2 Kgs 24:18–25:30, although it does add some detail to that account of the end of Judah and the Exile. The fact that the last verses repeat 2 Kgs 25:27-30, Jehoiachin's elevation to the king's table in Babylon in 560, proves the late redaction of the book as a whole.

Critical Issues in Studying Jeremiah

The critical issues associated with studying Jeremiah are fairly obvious to most readers. One that is clear to those familiar with the Greek and Hebrew texts of the book is the substantial difference between those two traditions.

Interior of a Late Bronze Age cistern at Jerusalem. When not storing water, a cistern might serve as a hiding place or prison (Jer 38:6). (Courtesy of the Israel Antiquities Authority)

A question that even casual readers of the English text often pick up on is how best to explain the different kinds of material in the book that include poetic oracles, sermons, and biographical and autobiographical material. A third issue that comes from dealing with the last one is assessing the history and fate of the prophet himself.

The Greek and Hebrew Texts of Jeremiah

When we compare the Greek of Jeremiah with the Hebrew text, the first thing we notice is that the Greek is about one-eighth shorter than the Hebrew of the Masoretic Text. Most of the difference is made up by small differences of little consequence, but the Greek does lack some longer passages as well (e.g., 33:14-26; 52:27b-30). But even more significant is the different placement of the oracles against the nations in the Greek text. What appears as Jeremiah 46–51 in the Masoretic Text follows 25:13 in the Greek text. This effectively makes the Greek text of Jeremiah a book that moves from condemnation for Judah to condemnation for the nations and lastly to words of hope for restoration. Interestingly, this is the shape of Ezekiel, as well as of many of the other prophetic books.

Until the Dead Sea Scrolls were discovered scholars assumed that the Greek text was an abridged (and mildly adjusted) version of the Hebrew text. But one of the manuscripts of Jeremiah found at Qumran (4QJer[b]) reflects the Greek, indicating either that the Greek preserves the older form of the book and the Masoretic Text is an expanded and rearranged version or that both text traditions existed side by side. Which of these options is correct remains a matter of dispute.

The Composition of the Book of Jeremiah

It is not only the text of Jeremiah that causes confusion about its exact makeup; the content itself adds to readers' puzzlement. Our survey already made clear that there are three major kinds of material in the book: autobiographical text mostly in oracular form (including the individual laments), biography, and prose sermons.

It is important to note as well that the differences are not merely formal in character. In terms of intention, the most striking contrast is between the oracles from Jeremiah and some of the prose sermons. While Jeremiah's own oracles are relentless in announcing doom for Judah, the prose sermons make him sound like a Deuteronomic preacher. Indeed, many of them feature exactly the rhetoric we find in Deuteronomy and in the speeches of the Deuteronomistic History.

How do we explain these different kinds of material? The biographical material is easiest to account for: it reflects the work of Baruch or someone like him who recorded and preserved accounts of Jeremiah's ministry. As for Jeremiah's own oracles, these too seem easily enough explained as a genuine record of the prophet's speech. What becomes difficult is reconciling the oracles with the prose sermons. The former are almost completely unrelenting in their announcement of doom, while the latter occasionally hold out hope for salvation if the people turn from their ways to keeping the law. It is this that has demanded explanation.

Some suggest that Jeremiah spoke his oracles of doom prior to the Deuteronomic reform movement, but that when he became aware of its aims he was converted to it and became one of its spokesmen. Thus his prose sermons reflect that change of heart.

Others suggest that Jeremiah's words were taken over by the Deuteronomic writers and adapted, perhaps in Jeremiah's absence after he was taken to Egypt. According to this view, a Deuteronomic writer's aim was to co-opt a competing voice, that of the prophet. While the Deuteronomic writers relied on the written word of the law, the prophet claimed to speak God's true word as an oral proclamation; and while the Deuteronomic writers relied on an established, determined body of discourse, the prophet's mediation of divine speech was completely

unpredictable. It is not hard to imagine that these two modes of discourse may have found themselves in conflict with one another. In fact, 8:8-9 suggests that was indeed the case. As readers will recall from our survey of the text, there Jeremiah condemned "the wise" who say that "the law of the Lord is with us." The basis for the condemnation is that "the false pen of the scribes has made it [the law] into a lie." As a result, says Jeremiah, "the wise shall be dismayed and taken; since they have *rejected the word of the Lord,* what wisdom is in them?" The tenor of Jeremiah's charge is that the "scribes" (perhaps the Deuteronomic writers?) rely on a written word of law and reject the true word of the Lord that is spoken by him and the prophets. The intensity of this hostility can hardly be underestimated. Could it be that the Deuteronomic writers, challenged directly by Jeremiah, commandeered his words in his absence and added to them prose sermons of their own making, thus transforming him into a fellow Deuteronomist?

While still acknowledging the tension between Jeremiah's own oracles and the prose sermons, still others suggest a more peaceable compositional history for the book of Jeremiah. They theorize that Jeremiah's followers appreciated his words, but also came under the influence of the Deuteronomic movement. And so when they gathered and edited the words of their mentor and prophetic hero, they added to them further words reflecting the perspective they had gained by their acquaintance with the Deuteronomic writers.

Yet another approach to the problem of the book's compositional history takes a much less defined view of things, suggesting that at most we can say that it emerged from a "rolling compositional process" whereby varying contributions from different perspectives accrued to what were only a few original words of the historical prophet.

Whatever the case, it is clear that the book of Jeremiah underwent a complex and lengthy compositional history that has resulted in a book that does not always speak with one voice. As such it ends up being in some ways nearly as theologically rich as the book of Isaiah.

The Career of the Prophet

The decision one makes about the compositional history of the book of Jeremiah determines, at least in part, how we understand the career of the prophet. If the first view articulated above is accepted — that Jeremiah essentially converted to the Deuteronomic movement — then his career was essentially two-part and concluded with his alignment with the creators of Deuteronomy and the Deuteronomistic History. If we accept, on the other hand, the view that Jeremiah never wavered from his position of announcing in oral speech the doom that would befall Jerusalem and apostate Judeans — and certainly his final oracles for the Jews of the Egyptian diaspora support this — then his career must be understood as that of an unrelenting foe of the Deuteronomic movement, but one who was co-opted by its adaptation of his words to their own aims. A similar view of his career arises if we accept the view that his followers adapted him to the Deuteronomic worldview, the only difference being that the "takeover" was in this case not hostile so much as a natural outgrowth of later affiliations. Last, if we embrace the "rolling composition" theory we must admit to knowing little or nothing of the prophet's career.

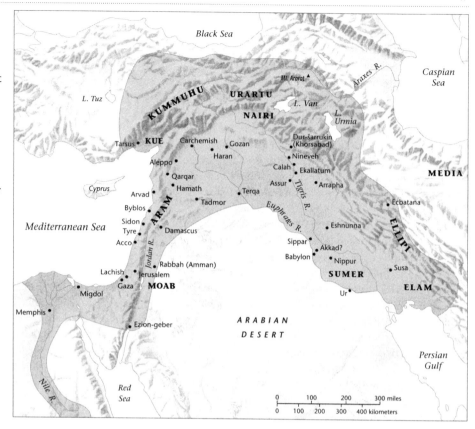

ASSYRIA AND BABYLONIA

One other aspect of Jeremiah as a person that we have until now neglected also deserves attention. The careful reader of the book will have observed that Jeremiah was from a priestly family. This surely entitled him to some ease of life in the Judah of his day, yet he chose — or according to his call, God chose for him — a life of difficult prophecy to his neighbors. He seemed to eschew the privileges he could have enjoyed as a member of the priestly class for the sake of his peculiar mission. However, his status may nonetheless have been a factor on occasion, providing him with highly-placed defenders and advocates in those instances when his foes sought to do him harm. To see the possible significance of Jeremiah's status one has only to observe the fate of Uriah, who preached as Jeremiah did but was unable to survive his foes' opposition (26:20-24).

Theological Themes in Jeremiah

One way to approach the theological themes in the book of Jeremiah is to treat them as they surface in the three different kinds of "theologically expressive" material identified in the book: the prophet's own oracles spoken on behalf of God, the prose speeches that reflect a Deuteronomic perspective, and the prophet's laments.

The Theological Perspective of the Historical Prophet

The prophet Jeremiah understood God in a clear-eyed way: the Lord God is alone the creator of heaven and earth, alone the elector of God's people, alone the judge of that people, and alone their redeemer.

The prophet's understanding of God as a creator is expressed in a beautiful passage, 10:10-13.

> But the Lord is the true God;
>> he is the living God and the everlasting King.
> At his wrath the earth quakes,
>> and the nations cannot endure his indignation.
> It is he who made the earth by his power,
>> who established the world by his wisdom,
>> and by his understanding stretched out the heavens.
> When he utters his voice, there is a tumult of waters in the heavens,
>> and he makes the mist rise from the ends of the earth.
> He makes lightnings for the rain,
>> and he brings out the wind from his storehouses.

The prophet's confidence in God's creative power extends

so far as to suggest that other gods who *did not* act to create would perish from the earth (v. 10b). In this Jeremiah makes a move toward the sort of full-fledge monotheism that we saw in Second Isaiah's approach to contending with the attractiveness of Marduk of Babylon.

Referring to Israel and Jacob with the greatest regularity of all the prophets, Jeremiah confirms the election of the people as God's special possession (2:3; 10:16; 51:19). Just as God is the sole creator of all things, Israel is God's special piece of creation, God's elect. But just so, this special relationship also brings God's judgment against the people in a unique way. While others may act with injustice and infidelity, it is Israel that suffers most intensely for these failures. Indeed, the prophet's mission is to announce to Judah the certainty of God's judgment against Israel through the agency of the Babylonians (1:14-15).

And just as the prophet understood Israel to be under God's judgment, he also foresaw its restoration and return to prosperity (30:18). But before the restoration the prophet foresaw a long period of exile for the people, and so began to develop the first "theology of diaspora."

> Thus says the Lord of hosts, the God of Israel, to all the exiles whom I have sent into exile from Jerusalem to Babylon: Build houses and live in them; plant gardens and eat what they produce. Take wives and have sons and daughters; take wives for your sons, and give your daughters in marriage, that they may bear sons and daughters; multiply there, and do not decrease. But seek the welfare of the city where I have sent you into exile, and pray to the Lord on its behalf, for in its welfare you will find your welfare. For thus says the Lord of hosts, the God of Israel: Do not let the prophets and the diviners who are among you deceive you, and do not listen to the dreams that they dream, for it is a lie that they are prophesying to you in my name; I did not send them, says the Lord.
>
> For thus says the Lord: Only when Babylon's seventy years are completed will I visit you, and I will fulfill to you my promise and bring you back to this place. For surely I know the plans I have for you, says the Lord, plans for your welfare and not for harm, to give you a future with hope. Then when you call upon me and come and pray to me, I will hear you. When you search for me, you will find me; if you seek me with all your heart, I will let you find me, says the Lord, and I will restore your fortunes and gather you from all the nations and all the places where I have driven you, says the Lord, and I will bring you back to the place from which I sent you into exile. (29:4-14)

The Theological Perspective of the Deuteronomic Redactors

While Jeremiah announced God's judgment that Judah was subject to God's wrath for its infidelity and social injustices, the Deuteronomic redactors (excluding for now the other options we entertained above as explanations of some of the prose speeches) made Jeremiah a Deuteronomic preacher.

> At the beginning of the reign of King Jehoiakim son of Josiah of Judah, this word came from the Lord: Thus says the Lord: Stand in the court of the Lord's house, and speak to all the cities of Judah that come to worship in the house of the Lord; speak to them all the words that I command you; do not hold back a word. It may be that they will listen, all of them, and will turn from their evil way, that I may change my mind about the disaster that I intend to bring on them because of their evil doings. You shall say to them: Thus says the Lord: If you will not listen to me, to walk in my law that I have set before you, and to heed the words of my servants the prophets whom I send to you urgently — though you have not heeded — then I will make this house like Shiloh, and I will make this city a curse for all the nations of the earth. (26:1-6)

The rhetoric of the foregoing passage is unmistakable in its Deuteronomic tone. It is also in undeniable conflict with the message of Jeremiah himself: while he left no room for repentance and deliverance from doom at the hands of Babylon, the Deuteronomic redactor at least wanted to suggest the opening was there, so long as the law was observed. Because this was almost certainly a postdestruction redaction, it signals how confident the Deuteronomic tradents were that God operated not by mere whimsy, but according to the standard of the law and retributive justice. To make that perspective dominant they went so far as to "convert" their closest competitor, Jeremiah, the prophet who may himself have called them liars (see 8:8-9)!

The Theology of Jeremiah, the Person

While the historical prophet spoke God's word and communicated a theology "imposed" upon him by God, Jeremiah also had his own, personal theological judgment. It comes to expression in his laments (11:18–12:6; 15:10-21; 17:14-18; 18:18-23; 20:7-13, 14-18). Throughout his laments Jeremiah bemoans what he sees to be not only the injustice committed by others against one another, but also the injustice done to him as a prophet. And his response is not merely to observe the injustices, but to go further and question God regarding the matter, and urge God to give him justice before his enemies. The former sentiment, that God is due some questioning from the prophet, is expressed well in Jeremiah's first lament:

> You will be in the right, O Lord,
>   when I lay charges against you;
>   but let me put my case to you.
> Why does the way of the guilty prosper?
>   Why do all who are treacherous thrive?
> You plant them, and they take root;
>   they grow and bring forth fruit;
> you are near in their mouths
>   yet far from their hearts. (12:1-2)

No sooner, though, than Jeremiah questions the justice of the situation — and of God, by implication — the prophet continues in the very next verse:

> But you, O Lord, know me;
>   You see me and test me — my heart is with you.
> Pull them out like sheep for the slaughter,
>   and set them apart for the day of slaughter. (12:3)

Together these verses capture the theological contribution of the prophet's own laments. He reflects the rich, but often forgotten, tradition in Judaism and Christianity of the faithful calling God to account for what they see to be injustice, but also expressing confidence that God will make right what is wrong. Interestingly, Lamentations, the next book we treat and one attributed by tradition to Jeremiah, ends on a note that is perhaps the least confident on this latter score.

Questions for Review and Discussion

1 What are the three major types of material we find in Jeremiah? What are some of the ways scholars explain the differences among those types of literature?

2 What was Jeremiah's message to the people of Judah regarding their immediate and distant future?

3 How do the prose sermons in Jeremiah compare with the poetic speeches we are confident belonged to the historical figure? How do those sermons compare to the prophet's own laments?

Further Reading

Brueggemann, Walter. *A Commentary on Jeremiah: Exile and Homecoming.* Grand Rapids: Wm. B. Eerdmans, 1997.

Carroll, R. P. *Jeremiah.* OTG. Sheffield: JSOT, 1989.

Diamond, A. R. Pete. "Jeremiah." In *ECB,* 543-616.

Chapter 29

Lamentations

Getting Started

1   Note how many verses each chapter of Lamentations has. What is the common number in all cases?

2   Survey Lamentations 3. What sort of mood does it convey, from beginning to end? Does this poem give voice to a hopeful or hopeless point of view?

3   Note the closing verses of the book of Lamentations. How do they compare with the sentiments expressed in the end of ch. 3?

Preliminary Comments

Like the book of Proverbs, the book of Lamentations is what its title (earned from early rabbinic writings that labeled it *qinot,* "lamentations") suggests: a collection of laments. It is ascribed by the Septuagint translation to Jeremiah, perhaps because of his reputation for weeping (Jer 9:1) and the Chronicler's claim that he wrote laments (2 Chr 35:25); accordingly it is placed in the Septuagint (and in most modern English translations) after the book of Jeremiah. In Jewish tradition it is usually placed among the *Megillot,* the "Scrolls" associated with

festivals (Ruth, Song of Songs, Ecclesiastes, Lamentations, and Esther). The anonymous poems are set in the early days following Babylon's destruction of Jerusalem. The book offers a poignant depiction of the suffering endured there after the crushing blows of the Babylonian conquest. Acknowledging that God seemed to have abandoned the city, the book vacillates between laments tinged with hope for restoration and expressions of nearly complete despair. It is little wonder that in Jewish tradition it was from early on used for mourning rituals and was associated with the 9th of Ab, the day on the Jewish calendar devoted to remembering the destruction of the First and Second Temples, the Bar Kochba revolt, and in time other major experiences of suffering for the Jewish people.

A Walk through Lamentations

The first four chapters of Lamentations are acrostic laments, speeches with 22 verses (or a multiple thereof), with each full verse beginning with one of the 22 letters of the Hebrew alphabet. Although the fifth chapter also has 22 verses, each verse does not begin with successive letters in the Hebrew alphabet. Chapters 1, 2, and 4 are dirges over the city of Jerusalem, ch. 3 is an individual lament, and ch. 5 is a communal psalm of lament like those in Psalms 74 and 79.

Lamentations 1: The City Laments

This chapter divides neatly into two parts: the first half is a description of the suffering of the fallen city (vv. 1-11), and the second half is the city speaking of her own disaster (vv. 12-22). Jerusalem is a woman in this chapter, and to describe the city's fall the author uses images evoking the utmost shame for a woman in the ancient world: not only was she formerly the paramour to more than one suitor, now she is without any of her paramours to comfort her (vv. 2, 6); her children have been taken away captive before her (v. 5); her former riches are gone (v. 7); those who once honored her now only despise her, for they have seen her naked, a source of great shame in the ancient world (v. 8); and she polluted herself with her own menstrual blood, and her sacred boundaries have been violated (vv. 9-10). The double meanings of these references are hard to miss: in their futile attempts to ensure the city's survival Judah's leaders made alliance with one after the other possible suitor nation or king, all of whom abandoned Jerusalem at the last; the city's inhabitants and its remaining treasures have been taken away in exile and its shame has been laid bare for all to see; its inhabitants warred among themselves in the face of external threats, shedding their own blood in the city confines; and the sanctuary itself was invaded and violated by outsiders.

The second half of the chapter already begins in the last part of v. 11, which shifts to first person speech. Now it is the woman-city who speaks. Although she describes in similar terms her downfall and acknowledges her guilt and the justice of God's punishment, she also expresses dismay at the absence of comforters or mercy (vv. 12, 16).

Altogether, then, this chapter sounds the theme repeated in the rest of the book: the difficulty of understanding God's obvious rejection of his chosen city and people. It also establishes the pattern of giving voice to an entire community's concern through the speech of an individual.

Lamentations 2: A Description of Zion's Suffering

Having just made the latter claim for ch. 1, Lamentations 2 departs somewhat from the pattern, providing instead a sustained description of Jerusalem's downfall and its consequences. However, the speech does continue to personify Jerusalem as a woman. The speaker describes her as utterly defeated by her enemies at God's behest; everything, from infrastructure to the city's leaders to its religious figures to its simple people, has been abandoned to destruction and devastation (vv. 1-10).

In v. 11 first person speech resumes, but apparently as the words of the one who observes Jerusalem's devastation; the speaker expresses extreme unease at the sight of Jerusalem's suffering, noting graphically both his or her own physical revulsion at the sight of such suffering, as well as the depth of depravity that provokes such a visceral response. The speaker notes especially how the famine has led to the death of infants at their mothers' dry breasts (v. 12) and the consumption by mothers of their own offspring (v. 20). The result was not only the speaker's horror, but also the taunts and ridicule of passersby and old enemies alike (vv. 16, 22). As for the city herself, all that is left for her to do is cry out in anguish (v. 19).

Lamentations 3: An Individual Lament and Expression of Hope for the Future

This triple acrostic of 66 verses is not only the structural center of the book, but is perhaps also to be read as its ideological and theological center. Spoken this time by a male, the first 20 verses of the chapter are a litany of remorse at having created the circumstances that led to God's merciless attack on him. Then in v. 21 the speaker announces that, for all of the suffering he deserves and endures, there is reason for hope: "The steadfast love of the Lord never ceases, his mercies never come to an end" (3:22). Knowing this, says the speaker, one may endure much suffering and persecution quietly and with patience (vv. 22-39), for "the Lord will not reject forever" (v. 31). The speaker is so confident of God's eventual mercy that he invites others to join him in his anticipatory hope (vv. 40-41) and then leads his people in a prayer of repentance and a plea for deliverance (vv. 42-66). This lengthy prayer is filled with further images of the people's suffering and admissions of guilt and closes with an expression of confidence that God will hear the people's plea (vv. 55-66).

Lamentations 4: More Laments and Regrets over the Fall of Jerusalem

The penultimate chapter resumes the description of Jerusalem's fall and the sins of the people that brought the destruction; it also renews the laments over the suffering endured by the city's inhabitants. Jerusalem's once-golden reputation has dimmed and the treasures of its temple are cast about (v. 1). The children of the city are no better than jackal offspring, going hungry and wandering without direction (vv. 2-4). Those who were once regal die homeless (v. 5). Reiterating the horror recorded in 2:20, we hear that once loving mothers now boil their own children for food (4:10). All of this, says the speaker of the lament, because of the people's rebellion against God and his representatives in their midst (v. 16). In the tradition of relieving some of the tension that comes with defeat, the chapter closes with a taunt for Edom, which participated in plundering Judah: to her the cup of suffering will pass in time as well (vv. 21-22).

Lamentations 5: A Closing Communal Lament

The final chapter appears until its close to hew closely to the lament genre. Giving voice to their lament, it first rehearses in some detail the suffering the people have endured (vv. 1-18). Then, ramping up to the plea for deliverance, the speaker acknowledges God's enduring reign (v. 19). But suddenly the strict adherence to the genre's pattern takes a slight turn with a renewed, and sharply-worded complaint: "Why have you forgotten us completely? Why have you forsaken us these many days?" (v. 20). Genre order is restored and upset again in the closing two verses which may be the most heart-rending words in all of Scripture: "Restore us to yourself, O Lord, that we may be restored; renew our days as of old — unless you have utterly rejected us, and are angry with us beyond measure" (vv. 21-22). Thus the book ends, with this soaring plea that drops back into excruciating uncertainty: the magnitude of Jerusalem's destruction and suffering have, so it seems, the last word in this writer's imagination.

Critical Issues in Studying Lamentations

The book of Lamentations is finding increased scrutiny in recent years, especially from scholars interested in literary approaches to biblical scholarship. As interesting as these developments are, though, space only permits treatment of the more typical concerns raised by the book. The first is its relationship to other ancient Near Eastern lament texts; the second is the question of what sort of person composed this work, and where, when, and why he did so; and the third is the matter of the book's genre and the use of poetic genres within it.

Lamentations and Ancient Near Eastern Lament Texts

For more than 30 years scholarship has recognized the similarities between Lamentations and some particular Sumerian works, as well as to a broader genre found in the Sumerian context. The closest literary parallel is the Lament for Ur, but Lamentations' more general counterpart is the genre "Lament over a ruined city and/or temple" (see *ANET,* 611-19). Both Lamentations and the ancient Sumerian texts entail a dirge over a fallen city and attendant sacred sites, and give voice to the irony that the god associated with cities and sites permitted destruction as punishment for human error. One must be careful not to overinterpret the parallels, however, inasmuch as a similar fate befell more than a few other urban sacred places in antiquity. The "parallels" might be little more than the adaptation of a multicultural genre to an equally multicultural experience.

Authorship, Provenance, Date, and Purpose

In view of the lateness of the attribution and the otherwise external reasons for it, we may reliably set aside the notion that Jeremiah was the author of Lamentations. Likewise, because of the vast differences in the Hebrew of the two books, we can assume that the author(s) of the book of Jeremiah was (were) not the same as the one who composed Lamentations. This leaves us with no specific candidates, but it still leaves open the much more interesting question of what sort of person may have put this small book together. That, however, requires attention to the additional questions of date, provenance, and purpose.

As for date and provenance, there is little argument against the obvious: the book clearly reflects the immediate aftermath of the Babylonian conquest and destruction of Jerusalem, and the intimacy of detail used to describe the situation demands a Jerusalem, or at least Judean provenance. The aim is likewise relatively uncontested: as we have already seen, it is a work consumed with lamenting the fall of Jerusalem and its inhabitants into the hands of the Babylonians and subsequent chaos and disaster and with expressing guarded hope for God's restoration of the city and its people. These accepted notions raise an interesting difficulty for the question of authorship: even if the work was, as seems likely, a composite of several laments, it did take some literary skill to integrate them and conform all but ch. 5 to the acrostic pattern. This is a difficulty precisely because of the context to which Lamentations is assigned, a devastated place in a shockingly distressed era; such contexts are not normally considered the settings inhabited by individuals who might have been able to produce literature like this. Some have suggested an author from the ranks of the priests or cult prophets, but most such elites were surely deported by the opportunistic Babylonians. We can only guess that perhaps a handful of intellectuals were somehow left behind, and to them we must assign this work.

The Genre of Lamentations and Its Use of Poetry

Compounding the consternation of those who find it difficult to imagine an intellectual in early postconquest Judah are the elevated literary characteristics of the book of Lamentations. As described above, Lamentations 1–4 are all full-scale acrostic poems, each having

Lamentation scene on an Eighteenth Dynasty (late fourteenth century B.C.E.) relief from Memphis, Egypt. (Bildarchiv Foto Marburg)

22 stanzas (or a multiple of 22) that begin with the letters of the Hebrew alphabet in order. Not only that, but each of the three lines in every stanza of the threefold acrostic in ch. 3 begins with the alphabet letter assigned to that stanza. So even the acrostic form exhibits here considerable sophistication.

At the level of the book's genre as a whole there is also evidence of erudition. As we saw above, the variations on the lament genre are considerable in the book, evidence of an author who not only grasps the nature of the genre, but also has the capacity to bend it in evocative ways. This is especially the case, and with considerable effect, with the last chapter and its tenuous appeal for God's mercy at the end. Add to this the fact that *only* ch. 5 eschews the basic characteristic of an acrostic — using the letters of the alphabet to start each stanza of the poem — but retains a 22-verse structure, and it seems hard to deny the author-editor of the book considerable literary skill.

There is still more evidence of this writer's skill. While most Hebrew poetry is composed in balanced stichs, since the late 19th century scholars have recognized, with some recent modifications, the widespread use of unbalanced lines in Lamentations. Dubbed the *qinah* meter (after the lament, *qinah* in Hebrew), this is, in fact, known essentially from Lamentations and is restricted to chs. 1–4; once again, ch. 5 is made to stand out.

Altogether, then, the literary characteristics of the book of Lamentations mark it as an extraordinary work, further evidence suggesting its author was no ordinary survivor of the Babylonian conquest.

The Theological Theme in the Book of Lamentations

There is really a single important theological theme in the book of Lamentations, namely reflection on the conundrum of the justice in God's punishment for his sinful, yet chosen people. Interestingly, the book hardly touches on the question of whether the defeat of Jerusalem was a matter of justice from God; the author is convinced that it was just, that God's people had earned the punishment that came to them from God through the agency of the Babylonians. The question that clearly troubled this author, though, was whether or not God's anger was without end. After all, these were his chosen people who called Jerusalem home; this was his chosen place for them to worship him. Surely, hoped our author, God would relent in his wrath and return his people to their place in mercy and forgiveness. And yet, the author asserts that with confidence only in the central ch. 3 and then follows it with a renewed description of the pain and suffering that abided in his own time.

The close of the book, as we have noted above, raises the question of God's mercy again and does not answer with the same confidence expressed in ch. 3. What results is a deeply poignant expression of the entirely human yearning for absolute certainty in the face of a God who allows himself to be known only in part. Even with all the evidence of God's desire for his people, the poet gives voice to the fear that haunts every human heart, the fear that human sin can drive away even this God of mercy. It is not without (happy) irony that this profound expression of anxiety *and* confidence that Lamentations entails was embraced within the canon of the Jewish and Christian Bible: it acknowledges who we are and gives expression to who we know God to be in spite of our fears, a God whose "steadfast love . . . never ceases," whose "mercies never come to an end" (3:22).

Questions for Review and Discussion

1   What is an acrostic, and what are the different ways that genre is represented in the book of Lamentations?

2   Compare the laments in this book (esp. the one in ch. 5) with Psalms 44, 60, or 74. What similarities and differences does your comparison produce?

3   You have seen how we understand the close of the book of Lamentations. Do you agree with that reading? Are there other ways you might construe the close of the book, other theological themes it might evoke other than the one identified above?

Further Reading

Berlin, Adele. *Lamentations.* OTL. Louisville: Westminster John Knox, 2002.

Clines, David J. A. "Lamentations." In *ECB,* 617-22.

Miller, Charles William. "Reading Voices: Personification, Dialogism, and the Reading of Lamentations 1." *Biblical Interpretation* 9 (2001) 393-408.

Salters, Robert B. *Jonah & Lamentations.* OTG. Sheffield: JSOT, 1994.

Chapter 30

Ezekiel

Getting Started

1   Read Ezekiel 1–3. What do you make of the strange imagery in these chapters? How might one explain such visions for the prophet?

2   Read Ezekiel 11:1-12 and ch. 37. How do the moods of these two passages compare? What are the two messages of the prophet?

3   Read Ezekiel 47–48. How do these chapters complement 1–3; 11:1-12; and 37?

Preliminary Comments

In Ezekiel we encounter a prophet famous for his symbolic actions and strange behaviors. Indeed, some of the more adventuresome contemporary interpreters have subjected Ezekiel to psychoanalysis from afar and even accused him of drug use. But what truly sets him apart from the historical figures of Isaiah and Jeremiah, whom we have already treated, are other more salient characteristics of his identity and preaching. First we note that, like Jeremiah, he was from a priestly family, but that for him this identity was far more formative

Located in Babylo

and defining. Second, the locus of his preaching sets him apart: while Jeremiah and Isaiah were active in the land of Israel, like Second Isaiah, Ezekiel was located in Babylon, having arrived there as part of the first deportation in 597 B.C.E. And while the other two prophets announced impending doom, Ezekiel preached not only in anticipation of the final defeat of Jerusalem, but also in the wake of it. As a consequence, he was concerned not only to offer an explanation for the Exile, but also to point the way beyond it. It is also possible that we encounter in the prophecy of Ezekiel the beginnings of "scribal prophecy," that is, prophetic speech that was first written and perhaps only later spoken.

A Walk through Ezekiel

While the details of the book of Ezekiel are fairly complex, the basic outline is clear.

Ezekiel 1–3: *The Call of Ezekiel*

The superscription to the book of Ezekiel arouses its share of interest among interpreters and thus deserves special attention (1:1-3).

In the thirtieth year, in the fourth month, on the fifth day of the month, as I was among the exiles by the river

Chebar, the heavens were opened, and I saw visions of God. On the fifth day of the month (it was the fifth year of the exile of King Jehoiachin), the word of the Lord came to the priest Ezekiel son of Buzi, in the land of the Chaldeans by the river Chebar; and the hand of the Lord was on him there.

In addition to the doubled nature of the superscription, the dates mentioned in it provide substantial interest, particularly the first. Readers have long asked, in the 30th year of what? Some speculate that it is Ezekiel's 30th year, the age at which a priest could take up his duties in the temple (Num 4:3). Others suggest that the first date refers to the time when Ezekiel or his followers wrote down his prophecies relative to when he actually spoke them. Still others propose that the 30 years mark the amount of time since an important event, such as the discovery of the Book of the Law by Josiah in the temple and the beginning of the Deuteronomic reform. The latter possibility has slight help in its favor in the fact that the second part of the superscription refers to 593, the fifth year of Jehoiachin's exile; 30 years before that date puts one within striking distance of the beginning of the Josianic reform, 623. In any case, we do know from the second date the first datable prophecy of Ezekiel, late July 593.

The rest of Ezekiel 1–3 relates Ezekiel's inaugural vision of the heavenly throne-chariot and his call. In 1:4-28 Ezekiel relates the complex image of God's mobile heavenly throne. That Ezekiel was hard put to describe what he saw is evident from the frequent use of the expression "like." "As for the appearance of the wheels and their construction: their appearance was *like* the gleaming of beryl" (1:16). Or again, "When they moved, I heard the sound of their wings *like* the sound of mighty waters, *like* the thunder of the Almighty" (1:24). What is clear is that there are four creatures with four faces — human, ox, lion, and eagle — and four wings each at the center of a storm. Wheels attached to the creatures provided the storm's mode of movement. Stretched over the wings of the creatures was a dome, and on top of that was "something like a throne," and seated above that was "something that seemed like a human form" (1:26). What Ezekiel described in these last words appears to have been God's glory. His response was to fall to his face in awe.

Ezekiel 2–3 then goes on to narrate Ezekiel's call in the presence of this awesome reality. In 2:1–3:11 a spirit enters Ezekiel, calling him "son of man" and commissioning him to speak against the rebellious people of Israel. He is also given a scroll to eat to symbolize the word he will have to speak. According to 3:12-21 Ezekiel then returns into the midst of his people, and after seven days of stunned silence he is addressed by the word of the Lord again to be informed that he has been made a sentinel for the house of Israel (cf. Jer 6:17; Hab 2:1), God's mouthpiece; whatever the Lord gives him to speak he must speak, whether it is warning or woe. The call narrative ends with Ezekiel being symbolically silenced so as to ensure that whatever speech comes from him is the Lord's word (presumably from the scroll), and never his own.

Ezekiel 4:1–24:27: Prophecies of Doom for Judah and Jerusalem

The first part of this long section reports a series of the bizarre symbolic actions God commands of Ezekiel (4:1–5:17). He is to portray the city of Jerusalem on a brick and set up against it model siege works; he is to lie on his left side for 390 days to signal the number of years of Israel's punishment, and 40 days on his right side to signal the number of years of Judah's punishment; while lying on his side he is to prepare and eat the (unpleasant!) food of the besieged and of the exiled; and he is to cut off his own hair, weigh it, cut it, and scatter it to the wind to symbolize the fate of the people of Jerusalem who will suffer terrible things described then by the word of God at the close of the section.

Again, Ezekiel is given the word of the Lord to speak in 6:1–7:27, this time to announce a double prophecy against Israel's idolatrous practices (6:1-14) and to make a series of prophecies of the coming end (7:1-27). The latter collection of oracles provides vivid images of the suffering that will befall Jerusalem for its infidelity.

Ezekiel 8:1–11:25 is a major section, reporting the prophet's well-known temple visions and the departure of God's holiness from Jerusalem. The first episode entails Ezekiel's visionary transport to Jerusalem to see the idolatrous practices in the temple (8:1-18): he witnesses in the temple the idolatrous offering of incense, the worship of Tammuz the Mesopotamian god of vegetation, and the veneration of the sun. Ezekiel then witnesses God's command to his emissaries to go throughout Jerusalem, marking those who have rejected the idolatrous practices and destroying those who engaged in them; Ezekiel pleads for God's mercy, but it is denied and the act is done (9:1-11). Next 10:1-22 narrates in detail the prophet's vision of God's glory rising up from the temple in Jerusalem to depart from it and desert it to its fate; Ezekiel witnesses the throne-chariot traveling to the eastern gate, toward Babylon and the exiles. Ezekiel 11:1-21 provides an interlude in the departure of the Lord from Jerusalem wherein Ezekiel is commanded to speak against the leaders who remain there and plot confidently their own survival. When Ezekiel does speak to them, one dies and Ezekiel begs God again to spare a

[handwritten top margin: What does this have to do with me? Everything --]

---

remnant, to which God responds with an oracle of hope and salvation for Israel through the eventual gathering of the exiles to the land. Then this central section closes by reiterating the departure of God's glory from the city to the east and reporting Ezekiel's return to Babylon (11:22-25).

The next major section, chs. 12–14, entails symbolic actions and oracles condemning the people and the leaders of Israel. In 12:1-16 Ezekiel is commanded to go about with an exile's baggage to signal the fate of Jerusalem, and even to act out elements of the fate of Zedekiah, after which God explains in an oracle the significance of the acts. In 12:17-20 Ezekiel carries out a further symbolic act, eating and drinking while trembling to indicate the way the people of Jerusalem live in dismay at their coming condition. The chapter closes with God speaking through Ezekiel against those who doubt the truth of his word. This leads to a series of oracles against false prophets who denied the impending doom for Jerusalem, and one against the apparent adaptation of Babylonian sorcery by the exiles (13:1-23). Ezekiel 14 closes the unit with the prophet condemning the elders of Israel who seek relief from the judgment already entered and announcing on God's behalf the utter inevitability of judgment against Jerusalem.

Ezekiel 15–17 next presents a string of allegories and metaphors for the judgment that is to come. Ezekiel 15 is the analogy of a useless vine, a reversal of the well-known image from Psalm 80 of Israel as the vine brought from Egypt and planted in the land (see also Isaiah 5, the Song of the Vineyard). Ezekiel 16, infamous for its crude and difficult imagery, provides an allegory of Jerusalem as an unfaithful wife to God who was raised from foundling status to that of honored spouse, but who nonetheless became a whore. Ezekiel 17 offers the allegory of the eagles to tell of Babylon's defeat of Zedekiah after his violation of an oath of fealty to Babylon by allying himself with Egypt. But the chapter closes with a messianic allegory (17:22-24), presaging the more hopeful tenor that comes in the book beginning fully in ch. 33.

Ezekiel 18 is singular in its impact, arguing that no more does God visit upon later generations the punishment for prior generations' sins (cf. Exod 20:5). Instead, says the Lord through Ezekiel's speech, the individual is accountable for his or her own behavior: sin begets punishment, righteousness produces life. As if to illustrate the point, ch. 19 then delivers two funeral dirges for apostate kings of Judah (probably Jehoahaz and Zedekiah), symbolized by two lion cubs who grew to be marauding lions deserving of their violent ends.

Ezekiel 20–24 then provides the final string of oracles, prophecies, allegories, and symbols of the coming judgment against Jerusalem. In one of the dated oracles in the book of Ezekiel (14 August 591), ch. 20 offers a schematic record of Israel's history of rebellion. Ezekiel 21 reports the sword prophecies, using the image of Nebuchadrezzar's sword coming against Jerusalem. Ezekiel 22 offers prophecies against Jerusalem, all Israel, and all the classes of people in the city and the land. Ezekiel 23 records the allegory of the two sisters, Oholah and Oholibah, Samaria and Jerusalem respectively, who, though married to God, went after other suitors — the nations and their gods — and paid the price for their sin in exile. In 24:1-14 God commands Ezekiel to enact the allegory of the pot, the food contents of which are incinerated by the fire below it, just as Jerusalem will be besieged and burnt. Finally, in 24:15-27, after Ezekiel's wife dies God instructs him to mourn without any outward expression as a witness to the people of the way they should mourn the fall of Jerusalem. At the end of this section God tells Ezekiel that when a messenger from fallen Jerusalem reaches him he will be able to speak once more for himself to proclaim a new message (one that turns out to be an oracle of salvation; cf. 33:21-22).

Ezekiel 25–32: Oracles against the Nations

This section serves as the bridge between the doom announced for Judah and Jerusalem in chs. 1–24 and the hope that is expressed in chs. 33–48: Israel's enemies now face their doom, opening the way for Israel's future.

Ezekiel 25 first offers a series of short oracles against Ammon, Moab, Edom, and Philistia for the roles they played in plaguing Israel over the years prior. Then 26:1–28:19 provides an extended series of oracles against Tyre for its gloating over Israel and its anticipation of commercial opportunity with the demise of Jerusalem (something Tyre did not enjoy because Babylon besieged it next). Ezekiel 26 announces that Tyre would be destroyed by Nebuchadrezzar (though in fact the Babylonian did not do so at the end of the siege). Ezekiel 27 offers a dirge over Tyre as a once gloriously successful ship of trade now brought to a sudden and violent end. And Ezekiel 28 reports the oracles against the leader of Tyre, a dirge over the fallen king (that interestingly places him in "Eden, the garden of God"; 28:13), and an oracle against Tyre's near-north neighbor, Sidon. The oracles against the nations close with a long section devoted to Egypt: ch. 29 is an oracle against Pharaoh and a late prophecy (dated to 571, Ezekiel's latest) that Egypt would be Nebuchadrezzar's "wages" in place of Tyre; ch. 30 announces doom for Egypt as a whole; ch. 31 uses the image of a proud and strong cedar to compare Egypt to Assyria, indicating that both fall because of pride and that Pharaoh himself will suffer defeat; and ch. 32 offers a dirge over Pharaoh and a prediction that Egypt would join others defeated by God's wrath in the netherworld.

Ezekiel 33–39: Prophecies of Restoration

In this section Ezekiel turns attention to prophecies setting out the possibility of and terms for restoration. It begins in ch. 33 with God reiterating Ezekiel's role as his mouthpiece. Then God gives Ezekiel the task of announcing God's desire that all should live, and to that end, that each individual who repents for their sins may know restoration (33:1-20). (Recall that ch. 18 established the principle of individual responsibility.) Then suddenly the messenger from fallen Jerusalem arrives and, as promised, Ezekiel's capacity for speech is restored so that he might at last speak for himself again (vv. 21-22). The chapter closes with an oracle indicating that there was already in the wake of the fall a dispute among the exiles and those still in the land about possession of the land (vv. 23-33).

Ezekiel 34 offers another explanation for Israel's plight: its kings, "the shepherds," were negligent in their duties, leaving "the sheep," the people, to be devoured by their enemies. But this state of affairs will be reversed, announces Ezekiel, when a new Davidic ruler more faithful than his predecessors will be placed over Israel and the scattered sheep are gathered together and sorted according to quality. Then peace will reign and the people will live in safety again.

Ezekiel 35–36 begins with a renewed oracle against Edom (35:1-15), but only to epitomize the foes who wrongly took the "mountains of Israel" in the wake of the Babylonian defeat as a contrast to God's new action: against them God moves to restore the land to Israel (36:1-15). The reason for this restoration is given in 36:16-38: it is for God's honor that he restores Israel completely to prosperity and makes it possible for Israel to be faithful anew to the covenant.

This last leads to the well-known vision of the valley of dry bones (37:1-14). Ezekiel is transported to a valley filled with bones and is told by God to prophesy to them that they will take on flesh and skin and have breath in them. As he does so, God gives Ezekiel to say that these are the exiles raised again to life in their own land as God's chosen people. Of course, this is not literal resur-

"O dry bones, hear the word of the Lord" (Ezek 37:4). Bone repository of a First Temple period tomb adjacent to the *Ecole Biblique,* Jerusalem. (Phoenix Data Systems, Neal and Joel Bierling)

rection of the body — that notion would develop only later (with respect to this passage in a reworking of it by a Dead Sea Scroll, 4Q386) — but rather a symbol for the restoration of Israel. God then commands Ezekiel to enact the symbol of two sticks representing Israel and Judah joined as one under one Davidic ruler: with this Ezekiel announces most clearly the recurring theme of God's aim to restore *all* Israel after the Babylonian Exile (37:15-28).

The passage on restoration concludes with the Gog of Magog oracles (chs. 38–39). Some consider these chapters to be secondary. Whatever the case, using the semi-mystical Gog as a cosmic foe against Israel who is defeated triumphantly by God, the passage shows how God will be acknowledged by all nations as sovereign and Israel will be recognized as God's specially protected people. The sequence is clear: in 38:1-16 God attacks Israel; in 38:17-23 God wages war against Gog and his allies, gaining victory over the foe in 39:1-16; as a result 39:17-29 reports that in the apocalyptic sacrificial feast on Gog's flesh and blood God's glory is recognized by all. Not surprisingly, Gog and Magog turn up as Satan and his army in Rev 20:8, and the ghastly feast is appropriated in Rev 19:17-19.

Ezekiel 40–48: The New Temple and the New Land

Whether these chapters came from Ezekiel or later tradents (see "Critical Issues" below), they form a suitable conclusion to the book: they give expression to the ideal relationship between God and Israel for the future toward which Ezekiel's prophecy builds.

The section begins with a lengthy description of the ideal new temple (chs. 40–42). While the details are best left to the text itself, a general outline can be discerned: 40:1-27 describes the temple area and the gates to the temple; 40:28-46 describes the inner gate towers; 40:47–41:4 describes the temple itself; 41:5-15 treats the surrounding chambers and rooms; 41:16-26 relates the interior details of the temple; 42:1-14 depicts the priests' rooms; and 42:15-20 establishes the exterior dimensions of the temple and the corresponding means of distinguishing between holy and common space. The dimensions and accoutrements described in this passage are quite expansive and elaborate and reflect an idealized vision of the temple as the holy place of God. It is, indeed, a paradigmatic temple that Ezekiel envisions here.

With the new temple complete, Ezekiel is next given a vision of the return of God's glory to Jerusalem and the holy place (43:1-12). In this section Ezekiel is told to explain to the people that the temple plan outlined in the prior chapters provides the holiness necessary for God's presence to be restored to the land. Also in this section Ezekiel is told to warn against defiling the temple by mixing with it the burial of kings; its role as God's abode must now be respected, unlike the disrespect given it as a holy place in the preexilic period. Indeed, from this point on the king is referred to no longer by the Hebrew term *melek,* "king," but with *nasi,* "prince." Some suggest this is merely an adaptation of the Priestly language for royalty, but it is curious that Ezekiel uses the Hebrew term for king only in a negative context.

The next major section offers regulations for the sacrificial cult that would operate in the new temple (43:13–46:24). Ezekiel 43:13-27 describes the altar of burnt offerings, constructed much like a Babylonian ziggurat. Chapter 44 provides for the ministers in the temple, famously distinguishing between the Zadokites — who according to this passage remained faithful when the Levites rebelled (Numbers 16) — and the rest of the Levites as priests (vv. 1-16). Because of their special honor in the past the Zadokites (descendants of Aaron's son, Eleazar?) assume the highest duty of altar service, and the rest of the Levites are relegated to temple servant status. But the Zadokites are not without restrictions, as 44:17-27 imposes on them various requirements reflecting in large part the Priestly regulations we saw in Leviticus. Correspondingly, though, 44:28-31 assures the priests a good living, providing to them the bulk of the sacrificial proceeds. Indeed, 45:1-9 provides for the distribution of lands to house the Zadokites, the Levites, and the prince; the mode of distribution makes perfectly clear the ascendancy of the Zadokites, and the

deeding of land to the prince seems intended to limit his agency among God's people! Then follows a series of regulations: weights and measures for offerings (45:10-17); festival regulations (45:18-25); regulations for the offering of the prince (that again constrain his activity in relation to the actions of preexilic kings; 46:1-15); rules restraining the prince from making gifts from anyone's but his own property (46:16-18); and a description of the sacrificial kitchens (46:19-24).

The closing section, chs. 47–48, begins with Ezekiel's vision of the sacred river that flows from the east side of the new temple to give new life and abundance to the otherwise desiccated land; as a result, the place teems with creatures described in language reminiscent of the Priestly Work's rhetoric (47:1-12). This then sets the stage for the establishment of new tribal boundaries and land allotments that even make provision for the aliens who reside among Israel (47:13-23). Ezekiel 48:1-29 provides a more detailed description of the allotments given to each tribe, and vv. 30-35 describe the tribal gates and general dimensions of the new Jerusalem.

Critical Issues in Studying Ezekiel

A number of features in the book of Ezekiel present themselves as matters of critical interest. In addition to the clarity of structure we have already observed in our survey of its contents, a further structuring device seems to have been the inclusion of dates for many of Ezekiel's visions or oracles. These help us establish the time of the prophet's activity and also to consider something of the historical background and character of the prophet. Another feature that demands our attention is the significance of the close relationship the book shares not only with the Priestly tradition, but most especially the Holiness Code (Leviticus 17–26). Also apparent from our survey is the ambiguous relationship between this figure's prophecy and the David-Zion theology. Finally, we must address the relationship between Ezekiel 40–48 and the rest of the book.

Chronology, Historical Background, and the Character of the Prophet

Including the ambiguous mention of the "thirtieth year" in 1:1, there are 15 dates in Ezekiel (1:1, 2; 3:16; 8:1; 20:1; 24:1; 26:1; 29:1, 17; 30:20; 31:1; 32:1, 17; 33:21; 40:1), with the earliest being July 593 (1:2) and the latest March-April 571 (29:17). Thus Ezekiel was one of the deportees from the Babylonian incursion against Judah in 597, and his prophetic career spanned the early part of the exilic experience. It was during these years that the exiles witnessed from a distance the continued rebellion of Judah against Babylonian rule in the form of Zedekiah's misbegotten violation of his oath of loyalty to Babylon and alliance with Egypt. Of course, to effect such a policy entailed worshipping the gods of his allies, and this may account for what Ezekiel saw in the temple when he traveled there to witness the continuing religious apostasy in Jerusalem (ch. 8). It also accounts for the frequent motif of condemning Zedekiah's rebellion (chs. 12; 17; 21). But even more, this date and context for Ezekiel's ministry provide insight on why he addresses those who remained in Judah and his fellow exiles: it seems clear from his prophecies that the rebellious spirit was present not only back in Judah, but also among some of the exiles. Thus we see through Ezekiel's testimony that the early exilic experience was not immediately one of settling into a new land and way of life, but did entail continued hope, false though it may have been, for a restoration of Judah as a nation-state.

We also gain some insight in this way into the prophet himself. While he is best known for his bizarre symbolic actions and nearly cosmic visions, at a more substantive level we learn from this contextualization that he, like Jeremiah, advocated submission to Babylon. But unlike Jeremiah who saw Babylonian domination as the will of God, Ezekiel understood this submission as an expression of loyalty to God alone. This was his concern time and again in his oracles, visions, and symbolic acts, to express for his audience the primacy of loyalty to the one God of Israel.

Ezekiel and the Holiness Code

Some influences on Ezekiel are clear. He was somehow closely related to his contemporary Jeremiah (e.g., he and Jeremiah both use the same proverb about sour grapes [Jer 31:29; Ezek 18:2]), he shared with the Deuteronomic tradition a sense of retributive justice, and his purity and priestly interests highlight the influence of the Priestly tradition on him. But one of the more striking — and puzzling, too — common universes of discourse is the one Ezekiel shares with Leviticus 17–26, the Holiness Code. Not only do they have in common some peculiar turns of phrase not found elsewhere in the Hebrew Bible, more importantly neither distinguishes between ritual and moral law, and they both have notions of the holy and profane wherein the former in particular is expanded apparently beyond the comfort zone of other authors. How do we explain this connection? It seems likely that Ezekiel was familiar at least with the ideas of Leviticus 19–20 and 26 and that otherwise the prophet and the author(s) of the Holiness Code both knew, perhaps independently, a common set of covenant laws (associated perhaps with the Autumn Feast).

Ezekiel and the David-Zion Theology

Another interesting feature of Ezekiel is his ambivalence toward kings. He clearly has it in for Zedekiah, and the funeral dirges for the two lion cubs symbolizing kings suggest that he had low esteem for still other monarchs of Judah. He repeatedly blames aspects of the Exile and Jerusalem's fall on kings, and the new temple and new Jerusalem of chs. 40–48 do not provide a particularly glorious place for the king, who in this material becomes a prince (Hebrew *nasi*). Yet at the same time Ezekiel fondly anticipates the day when God will establish a new, faithful Davidic ruler over a united Israel (34:23-24; 37:22-25). One way to reconcile these two perspectives is by comparison with Isaiah. Isaiah too had low regard for certain Davidic kings — Ahaz in particular — yet at the same time he was a vigorous proponent of the David-Zion theology (e.g., Isa 11:1-9). Likewise, Ezekiel holds Zedekiah in utter disdain, but can still anticipate the day when a Davidic king loyal to God would rule again.

But what does remain troublesome is the language used for the king and the constraints placed on him in Ezekiel 40–48. His reduction to a *nasi* "prince," and the limitations placed on his behavior denote a much lower estimate of the royal office than one might expect from a vigorous advocate of the David-Zion theology. There are two ways to explain this. One is that Ezekiel did hold to the David-Zion theology, but also wanted to constrain it somewhat for the sake of the ascendancy of the temple cult and its hierarchy and for the sake of focusing the people's true and complete loyalty on God. A second explanation depends on how one understands the material in Ezekiel 40–48, our next critical issue.

The Origin of Ezekiel 40–48

Because the material in Ezekiel 40–48 is so different in style and focus from what comes before it, most commentators assign it to a later Priestly author. In that case, the second way of explaining the diminished role and power of the king in Ezekiel 40–48 is clear: it simply reflects a later, diminished appreciation of kings and their proper roles. But one can also argue that for all of their differences, chs. 40–48 still come from Ezekiel himself. Indeed, the section fulfills the promises in 20:40-44 and 37:23-28 that the sanctuary would be restored, 43:1-5 is part of the visions series that entails God's departure and return to Jerusalem, and chs. 38–39 are connected to chs. 40–48 according to the pattern evident in Psalm 48. Also, the vision of the new temple and new Jerusalem in many ways fulfills the thrust of the book as a whole: it moves from punishment for Israel, to punishment for the foes, to restoration, all the time focusing in particular on the sanctity of Jerusalem and the temple; chs. 40–48 are only a fitting conclusion to the sequence. Thus we might say that at least from a recipient's perspective the implied author of Ezekiel 40–48 and the one associated with the rest of the book are one and the same.

Theological Themes in Ezekiel

In terms of theological insights, Ezekiel is perhaps best known for his contribution to an emerging notion of individual responsibility in relation to God. Ezekiel's prophecy entails other themes, though, that reflect the theologies we have seen throughout our Introduction. We turn to a survey of some of these now, along with a discussion of Ezekiel's idea of individual responsibility.

Ezekiel on Individual Responsibility

Ezekiel 18 makes clear this prophet's understanding of individual responsibility in relation to God. The first three verses of the chapter set the theme unequivocally.

> The word of the Lord came to me: What do you mean by repeating this proverb concerning the land of Israel, "The parents have eaten sour grapes, and the children's teeth are set on edge"? As I live, says the Lord God, this proverb shall no more be used by you in Israel. Know that all lives are mine; the life of the parent as well as the life of the child is mine: it is only the person who sins that shall die.

In the following verses, Ezekiel makes clear that retributive justice is the measure by which all shall be judged, but only as individuals. What makes this such an intriguing moment in the development of theological imagination in the Hebrew Bible is its departure from what preceded it. Recall that the Deuteronomic writers shared Ezekiel's devotion to notions of retributive justice; yet they held that the sins of the nation — present, past, and even future — could be held against one and all, without regard for an individual's particular culpability. Indeed, the Deuteronomic tradition eventually assigned so much of the burden for Israel's failure to individual kings that it is impossible to consider that approach to retributive justice as anything but corporate in nature: the sin of just a few, or even of the one, can bring down an entire people! By contrast, Ezekiel makes clear in ch. 18 that neither is the weight of sin transferred from generation to generation, nor are the consequences for one person's sin visited upon others.

Of course, this notion is not only at odds with what we find in other parts of the Hebrew Bible we have surveyed; some would also say that it contradicts human experience. Unjust actions have consequences that reach beyond the actor who commits them, and they do have an impact on generations other than that of the actor. As a consequence, not all have found Ezekiel's claim particularly helpful or convincing.

Ezekiel and Theologies in the Hebrew Bible

While we have made clear Ezekiel's distance from the Deuteronomic writers, it is nonetheless clear that he shared much in common with them as well, most noticeably commitment to the notion that God works with humanity according to principles of retributive justice. He also shares something of the Deuteronomic tradition's ambivalence regarding kings (though in fact the Deuteronomic writers can be viewed as having no ambivalence on this score, reserving only scorn for the office in the final analysis).

Ezekiel also is clearly connected with the Priestly tradition, as we have noted above. His own appreciation of the office, and his affiliation with it, make this connection a natural one to observe in the book. But just as is the case with Ezekiel's appreciation of the Deuteronomic tradition, here too he takes his own way, especially in exalting the Zadokites over the Levites, placing particular blame on the latter for the experience of the Exile and promising them a reduced status in any future temple. Indeed, although the precise significance of Ezekiel's views for understanding the history of the priesthood is still unclear to most readers, it is an important voice in the theology of sacrifice and the priesthood one might try to construct from the Old Testament.

Most clearly Ezekiel is connected with the Holiness Code, and especially its vision for the people's future should they keep the laws of God and maintain their purity in the land. The echoes shared between the vision of two futures for Israel in Leviticus 26 and Ezekiel are well known, and the two texts' concern for purity and holiness is unmistakable. Ezekiel repeats God's determination to "manifest my holiness" among the people Israel with some regularity in a clear parallel to the view of holiness in Leviticus 17–26 (Ezek 20:41; 28:22, 25; 36:23; 38:16, 23; 39:27). Notably, 44:19 and 46:20 seem to reverse this view slightly, suggesting that the holiness carried by the priests should not be communicated to the people. While this may add fuel to those who think Ezekiel 40–48 comes from a different hand than the one that produced the rest of the book, it is also possible to read this as Ezekiel transforming something of the Holiness Code's view of things: under the influence of the Priestly tradition Ezekiel constrains the zeal of the traditions seen in the Holiness Code, suggesting that while God's holiness should be clear to the people, it should nonetheless be reserved in its full experience to the priestly leadership. In any case, we see in this another instance of theologies of the Hebrew Bible being developed and redeployed depending on the context and character of the (implied) authors responsible for the "reconditioning" of Israel's theological imagination.

Finally, it is important to note that Ezekiel, in the end, also goes his own direction theologically in important ways. Perhaps the most important of these new initiatives from Ezekiel, besides the concern for individual responsibility, is the view he offers to parallel the notion of retributive justice. There is not a compelling sense in Ezekiel that it is the law that the people have failed to keep; rather they have worshipped falsely and committed injustices in a general sense that echoes something of the 8th-century prophets' assertion that justice and faithful worship are largely instinctual matters (see Chapter 27 on Isaiah above, and Chapters 32, 34 and 37 below on Hosea, Amos, and Micah, respectively). Thus when the glory of the Lord departs Jerusalem in Ezekiel 8–11 it is because God deems the people's apostasy and injustice to be overwhelming in its weight, and so God exercises God's sovereignty to leave the people to their fate. Likewise, when the people experience shame at the memory of their evil, God returns to Jerusalem and promises their restoration as well. That is, when the people instinctively perceive — and learn from Ezekiel's actions — that they failed their God, God responds again as a sovereign, but this time in mercy.

Questions for Review and Discussion

1 How does Ezekiel understand the fate of Jerusalem to have come to pass? What was it that ultimately permitted the city to experience the conquest of Babylonian armies?

2 What is Ezekiel's view of corporate and individual responsibility? How is this different from and similar to what we encountered in the Deuteronomic Collection?

3 What sort of vision is articulated in Ezekiel 40–48, and how is it understood by scholars in relationship to the rest of the book?

Further Reading

Block, Daniel I. *The Book of Ezekiel.* 2 vols. NICOT. Grand Rapids: Wm. B. Eerdmans, 1997-98.

Goldingay, John A. "Ezekiel." In *ECB,* 623-64.

Greenberg, Moshe. "The Design and Themes of Ezekiel's Program of Restoration." *Interpretation* 38 (1984) 181-208.

McKeating, Henry. *Ezekiel.* OTG. Sheffield: JSOT, 1993.

Chapter 31

Daniel

Getting Started

1 Read Daniel 1. What is the nature of this story? What view of oppressive foreign kings does it take?

2 Read Daniel 10–12. How does this image-filled description of the end time differ in tenor from Daniel 1? Assuming that some of the oppressive figures in these two chapters are foreign kings, how do they compare with the foreign king of Daniel 1? How might an audience respond differently to the vision in Daniel 10–12 after reading the story in Daniel 1?

3 Consider what you understand by the term apocalyptic as you read this chapter and the book of Daniel. How does this encounter with Daniel change that understanding?

Preliminary Comments

In the book of Daniel we encounter the single book-length representative of the apocalyptic genre in the Hebrew Bible. Daniel also stands out for its mix of Hebrew and Aramaic — a trait it shares in any significant way only with Ezra in the Old Testament — and for the fact

that it is likely the youngest book in the collection. In the Christian canon it is included among the Prophets, but notably the Jewish canon places it among the Writings. Indeed, as our survey of it will show, it hardly looks the part of a prophetic book, at least as we have come to know them in Isaiah, Jeremiah, and Ezekiel. Rather, it appears to be a book unto its own, a completely novel literary phenomenon in the Hebrew Bible.

A Walk through Daniel

The book of Daniel divides cleanly into two parts: folktales of Jews in a foreign land and in a foreign king's court (chs. 1–6) and reports of Daniel's apocalyptic visions (chs. 7–12).

Daniel 1–6: Tales of Faithful Jews in a Foreign Court

The opening verses set the time and place of the stories that follow, signaling by their inaccurate dating that these are folktales we are about to encounter, not historiography. The date offered is "the third year of the reign of King Jehoiakim of Judah," when "King Nebuchadnezzar came to Jerusalem and besieged it" and "the Lord let King Jehoiakim of Judah fall into his power" (1:1-2).

The problem, of course, is that King Jehoia*chin*, Jehoia-*kim*'s son, occupied the throne when the Babylonians besieged Jerusalem in 597 B.C.E.; the date suggested by the notice in vv. 1-2 is 606!

The rest of the first chapter introduces the book's heroes and provides their first test. Their Hebrew names are Daniel, Hananiah, Mishael, and Azariah, and they are described as "Israelites of the royal family and of the nobility, young men without physical defect and handsome, versed in every branch of wisdom, endowed with knowledge and insight and competent to serve in the king's palace" (1:3b-4). They are brought into the king's court to be taught the language and literature of the Babylonians and fed with the king's rations (v. 5); this will prepare them to be appropriate courtiers. Moreover, the palace master renames them Belteshazzar, Shadrach, Meshach, and Abednego, respectively.

In 1:8-17 we learn that Daniel, however, refuses to defile himself with the food of the king's table, presumably because it violates his understanding of the Jewish laws of food purity. The palace master, fearing that Daniel and his friends would not fare well and the king would notice and blame him, urges Daniel to eat as he is directed. Daniel proposes a test, that he and his friends be allowed vegetables and water for 10 days, at the end of which the palace master can compare their appearance and wisdom to that of the others who eat the king's rations. The palace master agrees, and at the end of the test, of course, Daniel and his friends "appeared better and fatter than all the young men who had been eating the royal rations" (v. 15), and to them "God gave knowledge and skill in every aspect of literature and wisdom; Daniel also had insight into all visions and dreams" (v. 17). When they are brought before the king the four young men prove to be tenfold wiser than any of the magicians and wise men in the king's employ, and this by God's favor (1:18-21).

The second test of the young men comes in ch. 2, "in the second year of Nebuchadnezzar's reign" (v. 1; 603!). The king has a dream that disturbs him and so he sends for wise men of Babylon and commands that they not only interpret the dream for him, but also actually tell him what he dreamt without a clue from him! The king's wise men understandably respond that such a thing is beyond even the wisest of them (vv. 2-11). The king's response is to decree the execution of the whole lot of them, Daniel and his friends included, for their failure in his service (vv. 12-13). Daniel, though, asks for time to provide the dream and its interpretation, and having his request granted, prays to God for insight; this request too is granted him, and he praises God for it (vv. 14-23). Then Daniel goes before the king and introduces the dream and its interpretation by first confirming that it

> ### *Reading Guide to Daniel*
>
> **Folktales of Jews in a**
> **Foreign King's Court (1–6)**
> > The Four Young Men Refuse the King's Table (1)
> > Daniel Interprets Nebuchadnezzar's Dream (2)
> > The Three Young Men in the Fiery Furnace (3)
> > The Madness of King Nebuchadnezzar (4)
> > Belshazzar's Feast and the Handwriting
> > on the Wall (5)
> > Daniel in the Lions' Den (6)
>
> **Daniel's Apocalyptic Visions (7–12)**
> > The Four Beasts, the "One Like a Human Being,"
> > and the Ancient One (7)
> > The Ram and the Goat (8)
> > Contemplation of Jeremiah's Prophecy
> > and Prayer of Repentance (9)
> > Final Vision: Historical Apocalypse (10–12)

is not for wise men to do this, but that it comes instead from God in heaven (vv. 24-30). The dream, says Daniel, is of a statue with a head of gold, a chest and arms of silver, middle and thighs of bronze, and feet of iron mixed with clay. As the king envisions this, a stone is "cut out, not by human hands" and it strikes the statue at its feet, bringing the whole thing down in pieces; the stone then "became a great mountain and filled the whole earth" (vv. 31-35). As for the dream's interpretation, Daniel shares with the king that his kingdom is the head of gold, and the additional parts down to the feet of iron and clay are succeeding, lesser kingdoms. The stone *qua* mountain is the act of God to bring down the kingdoms and replace them with "a kingdom that shall never be destroyed, nor shall this kingdom be left to another people" (vv. 36-45). To this seemingly unwelcome interpretation the king responds with awe and worship for Daniel's God and grants promotions all around for Daniel and his three friends (vv. 46-49). The identities of the kingdoms in addition to the Neo-Babylonian Empire are not made clear here, but given the rest of the book's contents (esp. chs. 5 and 7) they are surely meant to be Media (silver), Persia (bronze), and Greece (iron and clay), and the division of the fourth is likely a reference to the distribution of the remains of Alexander the Great's empire among his generals. The stone-become-mountain, of course, is Israel (cf. Isa 51:1; Ps 118:22).

The third test is of Shadrach, Meshach, and Abednego, with no mention of Daniel at all (suggesting to some that chs. 2 and 3 had different origins). This time the king erects a huge golden statue that he requires all to bow down to and worship when they hear a musical cue. He decrees that whoever does not worship the statue will be thrown into a fiery furnace (3:1-7). Of course, Daniel's three friends refuse to do this, and Babylonians hostile to them tell the king of their refusal (vv. 12). Brought before the king, the friends' only defense is that their God will deliver them from the furnace if he wishes, but in any case they will not worship the golden statue (vv. 13-18). With that they are thrown into the furnace to be destroyed, yet the fire does not touch them and they are accompanied by a fourth with the appearance of a god. Seeing their miraculous deliverance the king has them removed from the fire, decrees that blasphemy against their God is punishable by death, promotes the three friends in the province of Babylon, and sends a doxology honoring the God of Israel to all Babylon (3:24–4:3).

Daniel 4 recalls the suffering of King Nebuchadnezzar. (It was long suspected that the original version of this tale dealt with Nabonidus, a suspicion supported if not confirmed by a Dead Sea Scroll called the "Prayer of Nabonidus" that observes that king was struck with a disease at Teima.) He has a dream that, though he relates it fully to his diviners, they cannot interpret (vv. 4-7). So he turns again to Daniel and relates the dream of a great tree that shelters the birds and the animals and that is cut down by a "holy watcher" who descends from heaven. The "he" of the dream is then assigned the lot of the animals of the field and the mind of an animal until "seven times pass over him" (vv. 8-18). Daniel's interpretation — offered with some trepidation inasmuch as he hopes for the king's sake that the dream is for others — is that the tree and the one gone mad among the animals are the king, and that he should repent of his sins (vv. 19-27). Indeed, the dream is for the king and he suffers the fate predicted, including coming back to his senses, for which he praises God as one who has nearly converted (vv. 28-37).

The theme of foreign kings being subject to God's will continues in ch. 5, but on a much darker note. Here we learn that King Belshazzar (in actual fact the son of Nabonidus, the last king of the Neo-Babylonian Empire) has a grand feast at which he uses the sacred vessels taken from the temple in Jerusalem as booty (vv. 1-4). As he and his guests make merry, a human hand is seen writing on the wall of the palace in signs indecipherable to the king, but nonetheless terrifying to him. None of his diviners can interpret the writing, even though he promises great rewards to the one who can (vv. 5-9). At the queen's behest he summons Daniel to interpret (vv. 10-16). Refusing the rewards, Daniel tells Belshazzar that for his abuse of the temple vessels he is a dishonor to his father Nebuchadnezzar, who had honored the God of Israel, and that his kingdom is about to be taken from him and divided between the Medes and the Persians. Within the night the king is dead and "Darius the

Mede" receives the kingdom (vv. 17-31). Notably, Darius was not a Mede, but a Persian ruler!

Daniel 6 relates the best-known story from the book, Daniel's encounter in the lions' den. Much a reflection of ch. 3, it begins with officials hostile to Daniel's elevated role devising a way to force the king to punish him (vv. 1-9). When Daniel does not obey the law they get the king to accept that prayer can be made only to the king, and they catch him worshipping his own God and reveal his disobedience to Darius (vv. 10-13). The penalty is to be thrown to the lions, and Darius, with great reluctance, has it enforced on Daniel, for whom Darius prays and fasts (vv. 14-18). Of course, the lions leave Daniel alone, the king learns of his deliverance by the God of Israel, the king has Daniel's accusers and their families fed to the lions instead, and last of all he issues a decree praising Daniel's God (vv. 19-27). As the chapter closes we read that Daniel continues to prosper in Darius' reign, as well as in the reign of Cyrus (who actually preceded Darius; see "Critical Issues" below).

Daniel 7–12: The Apocalyptic Visions

The second half of Daniel differs substantially from the first in terms of its genre. We turn from the tales of Jews in a foreign king's court to four apocalyptic visions in chs. 7, 8, 9, and 10–12. Scholars have developed a very precise definition of the elements included in exemplars of the apocalyptic genre. It entails a narrative in which an otherworldly being reveals heavenly realities to a human recipient; the revelation usually deals with place because it involves a new world beyond or different from this one; and it is time-related in that it anticipates an eschatological judgment, an end-time determination of the fate of nations and individuals. This genre was likely first fully developed in the last few centuries before the turn of the eras, and from early on it came in two types: reports of heavenly journeys or visions, and historical apocalypses. Daniel 7–12 is the latter type. It divides history into major periods and focuses on the end time when God will intervene to reward the righteous and punish the wicked. The situation entailed in chs. 7–12 is also very different from that of the first half of the book. While the tales place Daniel and his friends in the Babylonian Exile (and the ill-defined period associated with "Darius the Mede" and his successor Cyrus!), the visions are about Jerusalem and its fate at a time of severe discrimination against its inhabitants. Indeed, because the visions are so symbolic we depart from our normal procedure here and integrate a "Critical Issue" into the rehearsal of the text, namely an explanation of what the visions refer to in the history of Israel and early Judaism. As we shall see, the evidence indicates that the persecution was that experienced by Jews under Seleucid rule and that the visions were likely composed just as Maccabean revolt got underway.

The first vision is reported in Daniel 7, and it echoes Nebuchadnezzar's dream in ch. 2, but without any of the goodness attributed to the symbolized kingdoms of that vision. Daniel begins by informing the reader that he had the dream vision "in the first year of King Belshazzar of Babylon" (7:1). He testifies that he saw four beasts arise from the sea: a lion with eagle's wings, one that looked like a bear, a leopard with four wings, and finally a fourth to which he gives no name but describes as the most terrifying. The last had 10 horns, three of which fell away to make room for a little one that is particularly hideous (vv. 1-8). Next Daniel sees the heavenly throne room and the Ancient One seated on the throne. The Ancient One judges the last beast and destroys it and disempowers the others (vv. 9-12). Then Daniel sees "one like a human being" presented to the Ancient One on the throne and commissioned to have dominion over the nations (vv. 13-14). No longer the interpreter of dreams, Daniel asks one of the heavenly attendants the meaning of all this. He is told that the beasts are kings and that, though they shall rule for a time, the "holy ones of the Most High shall receive the kingdom forever — forever and ever" (vv. 15-18). As for the fourth beast, the 10 horns are 10 kings that shall arise from a single kingdom, and the last is another king who would offend the Most High but would in the end be defeated (vv. 19-28).

The four beasts, of course, are four kingdoms: the Babylonians, the Medes, the Persians, and the Greeks. The 10 horns are the rulers who succeeded Alexander the Great, and the little hideous horn is Antiochus IV Epiphanes, the Seleucid ruler who persecuted the people of Israel so terribly. The Ancient One in Daniel's vision is God. The only difficult identification is that of the "one like a human being" (or "one like a son of man"). While early Christians interpreted this figure as Christ (thus the use of the phrase "son of man" in the Gospels), the author of the vision surely had someone else in mind. Some suggest the "one like a human being" is the aggregate of faithful Jews, and the term is synonymous with "the holy ones of the Most High" who will receive the kingdom in the last days. In the alternative, the title may refer to an angelic figure, probably the archangel Michael (10:13, 21; 12:1). This seems the more likely of the two readings, since otherwise in the book Daniel refers to angelic beings with the word "man" (8:15; 9:21; 12:6-7). Thus the vision as a whole acknowledges the power of Antiochus to disrupt Jewish life for a time, but it anticipates nonetheless that through the agency of one like Michael the holy ones — the faithful of Israel — will be delivered from their suffering.

Daniel's second vision came two years later (8:1), and like the first report there is first a vision and then an interpretation. The vision itself is of a ram with two horns that at first has its way with all it encounters (vv. 2-4). But then it is attacked violently by a goat with a single horn; the goat prevails, but its single horn is broken and replaced by four others (vv. 5-8). Out of one of the horns comes another horn that grows as high as the heavens, where it casts down some of the stars and tramples them, and even acts against the "prince of the host" and violates the regular burnt offering of his sanctuary. Daniel hears that the transgression will last around three and one-half years (vv. 9-14). Then Daniel is approached by the angel Gabriel, who explains the vision: the ram with two horns represents the kings of Media and Persia, and the male goat is the king of Greece — Alexander — and the four horns that come from him are the kingdoms that follow him. And, says Gabriel, there will be one among them who is most troubling, who will rise against "the Prince of princes" but will nonetheless be defeated by divine agency, not by human hands (vv. 15-27). Once more the vision focuses on Antiochus IV Epiphanes. As noted in the explanation itself, the ram is the Persian Empire and the goat is Alexander the Great. He is struck down in his prime and replaced by four other horns — his successors — from one of which comes the horn that grows to the high heavens, Antiochus. His actions are atrocious violations of God's sanctuary and attacks against its keepers, and even against God himself, but once more the vision closes with the anticipation of heaven-sent vindication for Israel's faithful ones.

Daniel 9 provides a very different kind of revelation. Daniel sets about contemplating the prediction in Jer 25:11-12; 29:10-14 that Jerusalem must suffer 70 years' devastation. His contemplation prompts him to offer a prayer of repentance and supplication like that encountered in Ezra 9 and Nehemiah 9. The prayer is Deuteronomic in its theology: it rehearses the people's history, acknowledges Israel's sin and the righteousness of Jerusalem's suffering, and begs God's mercy apart from the righteousness Israel does not have to offer (9:1-19). As soon as Daniel is finished praying, the angel Gabriel appears to offer an interpretation of the Jeremiah prophecy (vv. 20-23). The 70 years are actually 70 weeks of years, that is, 490 years (which, inaccurately, would place the end of the period in 196 B.C.E.!). Seven weeks will cover the time for the restoration of the temple and its oversight by an anointed one, and 62 weeks of function for the temple will follow. But at the end of that period "an anointed one shall be cut off . . . and the troops of the prince who is to come shall destroy the city and the sanctuary," but his desolation of the sanctuary will in turn be cut off at the end of the 70 weeks (vv. 24-27). Here again, the prophecy focuses on the behavior of Antiochus IV Epiphanes and on assuring the audience that he would not prevail in the long run. The first anointed is likely Joshua, the high priest at the time of the Persian-subsidized restoration of the temple. The second anointed is perhaps Onias III, who was murdered in 171. The "prince to come" is Antiochus, and his desolation of the sanctuary, of course, was his violation of the Jewish temple and his prohibition of Jewish practices. Just as in ch. 8, here too the audience is assured that his power will not endure, that his devastations will cease through divine intervention. What makes ch. 9 particularly interesting is the way the prayer expresses the theology that

Statue of a male goat, which in Daniel's vision (ch. 8) represents Alexander, the "king of Greece." Incense or offering-bowl holder from the "Great Death Pit" at Ur (ca. 2500 B.C.E.). (Trustees of the British Museum)

is most seriously threatened by the realities addressed symbolically by all the visions: the righteous are suffering terribly while the wicked seem to be in control; in the battle between good and evil, evil seems to be winning. Thus the Deuteronomic theology of retributive justice seems to have lost all coherence. But Gabriel's interpretation points to a new possibility — that though things seem out of balance at present, they will not remain that way. Justice will be served, but in God's good time, according to a plan that lay beyond human knowledge, at least until Daniel receives his visions and communicates them! Once known, they offer assurance to those who see their suffering as unjust.

Chapters 10–12 encompass Daniel's final vision. Chapter 10 sets the stage for the vision, which comes in "the third year of King Cyrus of Persia" (535; 10:1) after Daniel had fasted for three weeks. (Fasting as a means of inducing ecstatic experiences was not unknown in the ancient world.) He first sees an angel who is of marvelous appearance and powerful voice and falls helpless before him (10:2-9). The angel, Gabriel, lifts him up and explains that he was delayed in coming to explain the future of Daniel's people for the period of Daniel's fasting because he was contending with the prince of the kingdom of Persia, whom Michael was vying with in his absence (10:10-14). (Throughout the "princes" of each kingdom seem to be angelic counterparts to earthly beings; thus war was waged in heaven as on earth.) Again, Daniel weakens and falls before the angel, and again he is lifted up to receive the heavenly secret of Israel's future that "is inscribed in the book of truth" (10:15–11:1). In 11:2-20 the angel narrates in considerable detail the political intrigues and military engagements of the Ptolemies and Seleucids in relation to Judah and Jerusalem until the rise of Antiochus IV Epiphanes. Throughout the angel refers to the Ptolemies as the "king of the south" and the Seleucids as the "king of the north." This nomenclature continues as the angel next relates in even greater detail the activities of Antiochus IV Epiphanes. He describes Antiochus's meddling with the priesthood in Jerusalem ("the prince of the covenant" in 11:22) and his first attack on Egypt that met with some success (11:21-28). Then in 11:29-39 he describes Antiochus's second expedition against Egypt that Rome halted and the consequences that flowed from that experience for Jerusalem and the sanctuary. Because he was enraged at being repelled, says the angel, "the king of the north" "set up the abomination that makes desolate" in the sanctuary in Jerusalem, even making alliance with some among the Jews who "forsake the holy covenant" (11:30). This refers to Antiochus's establishment of a foreign altar in the temple and to the fact that some Jews agreed with his "Hellenizing" reforms. The response of the "wise" (Hebrew *maskilim;* the same name given to Daniel and his friends in 1:3) will be to stand firm in their faith, falling even to the sword, even though "they shall receive a little help" (11:34; some think this refers to the Maccabean Revolt). Daniel 11:40-45 then narrates a further future in which the king of the south will trigger another confrontation that will in turn elicit a series of other battles culminating in Antiochus's death in the land of Israel. That he did not die there, but rather late in 164 in Persia after an attempted temple robbery, and that the rest of what vv. 40-45 predict did not come to pass help date the vision: it was composed sometime during Antiochus' persecution, but before his death in 164. In any case, Antiochus's defeat is not the end for the apocalyptic vision: 12:1-4 explains that the end comes when Michael the angel shall arise for the deliverance of "everyone who is found written in the book" and the "wise *(maskilim)* shall shine like the brightness of the sky, and those who lead many to righteousness, like the stars forever and ever" (12:3). The vision and the book end with Daniel asking for a time when all these things would come to pass: three options follow, suggesting that as time passed and events did not transpire as anticipated in the vision new calculations were introduced (12:5-13).

Critical Issues in Studying Daniel

The issues raised by the book of Daniel include the date of its composition, the precise nature of the tales told in chs. 1–6, echoes of ancient Near Eastern myths in the book, and the identity of the book's author and his purpose in writing (especially as that pertains to the apocalyptic genre of the book).

The Date of the Book of Daniel

At first glance one might think that Daniel was a product of the Exile. After all, the court tales begin under the rule of Nebuchadnezzar, the Babylonian king responsible for the deportation of Judeans to Babylon in the early 6th century. But as we shall see below, the court tales of chs. 1–6 openly signal to readers that they are folktales, not history, and should therefore not be taken as indication of the book's date of composition. A more obvious indicator of the book's date, though, is the nature of the historical apocalypses we encounter in chs. 7–12. In establishing Daniel's credibility as a visionary of the *author's* and *audience's future,* they time and again assign to him the task of envisioning accurately *his future,* which is the *receiving audience's past.* We call this phenomenon *ex eventu* prophecy, that is, prophecy of an event after its occurrence. It is evident in relatively general terms in the first three visions (chs. 7–9) and in a very specific way

in the last, full-blown historical apocalypse (chs. 10–12). There Daniel's visions of *his future* and the *receiving audience's past* are accurate in detail, but only up to a point. Daniel — or better, the author of the vision — clearly knows of events that we place in late 164, but is unaware of the precise nature of Antiochus's death and the restoration of Judean possession of the Temple Mount at the end of 164. For that reason many date the book to the last part of 164, but before the last month of that year.

Daniel 1–6: History or Exemplary Folktales?

While some readers are wont to make of Daniel 1–6 a historical narrative, the references above to inaccurate dates and titles (e.g., 1:1-2, 21; 5:30) — by no means comprehensive in their scope — make clear that can hardly be the case. In fact, the inaccuracies seem calculated to telegraph the point that these are not stories from history at all, but rather are exemplary folktales about the Jewish experience with Gentile kings. A further indication that these are folktales is the reputation of "Daniel" outside of this book. He is mentioned in Ezek 14:14, 20; 28:3 as an ancient legendary figure and is named also in the Epic of Akhat from Ugarit, suggesting that he was not a historical figure at all, but an ideal type, perhaps a bit like Balaam the prophet (cf. Numbers 22–24; the Deir ʿAlla inscription).

The point the stories make is, in the end, both simple and complex. It is simple in its basic substance: foreign kings are not intrinsically good or bad; rather they are what their behavior makes of them (if not in almost all cases also somewhat dense!). Nebuchadnezzar may have made foolish demands on the Jews and others in his court, and others in their governments may have too easily manipulated him and Darius (chs. 1–3; 6), but in the end, both kings were suitably submissive to the authority of Israel's God (see esp. ch. 4). On the other hand, some foreign kings are simply badly behaved, such as Belshazzar (ch. 5). The good news of the folktales is that God will deal with the wicked kings in due time, and the vision in ch. 2 suggests the view of the author of the folktales that in the end God's rule will prevail. As we shall see, though, the stories' point is a bit more complex when they are wedded to the apocalyptic visions of chs. 7–12 and the historical context those suggest for the book of Daniel as a whole.

Where did these stories come from? At least three things suggest the Eastern Diaspora. First, the sort of wisdom Daniel possesses in being able to interpret dreams — called "mantic wisdom" — is characteristic of the east. The setting in the Babylonian Exile also points to the east. Finally, these are very much "court tales" like the one we encounter in the book of Esther, another book easily assigned to the Eastern Diaspora.

Echoes of Ancient Near Eastern Myth in the Apocalyptic Visions

An often overlooked but intriguing aspect of the apocalyptic visions are the echoes of ancient Near Eastern myths in several of them. The presence of these myths in a book as late as Daniel indicates something of their enduring quality in the Mediterranean world. We cite the two clearest examples of this pattern in Daniel 7–12.

In ch. 7 the image of the four beasts rising from the sea evokes mythic traditions that turn up as early as in the Ugaritic texts in Canaan, but appear also abundantly in the Hebrew Bible. (In fact the pattern of *four* kingdoms is also typical of Greek and still earlier mythic traditions, thus suggesting the artificial insertion of "the Medes" into the sequence as an empire.) In its basic form the myth is of the sea monster, Yamm, challenging the god Baal and being destroyed by him. For instance, Ps 74:14 describes God as breaking the head of Leviathan (i.e., Yamm), and Isa 27:1 looks forward to the day when the Lord will destroy Leviathan, the dragon that is in the sea. The author of Daniel has adapted the myth even further, though. The Ancient One who first appears in 7:9 appears not to be the mythic equivalent of the god Baal who defeats the creatures of the chaotic sea, but rather the high god El of Canaanite religions. The "one like a human being" who comes on the clouds is more likely the rough equivalent to the Baal figure inasmuch as the Ugaritic texts refer to him as a "rider of the clouds." In any case, the entire mythic tradition has been adapted to the author's larger purpose of showing that in the end the beasts that arise from the primeval chaos of the sea are judged and destroyed by the One God, the Ancient One, the God of Israel.

A second instance of reliance on ancient Near Eastern mythic traditions, in part by way of Isaiah 14, appears in Daniel 8. Isaiah 14:12-15 compares the Babylonian king to the Day Star of Canaanite myth, who claims to ascend above all stars but is brought low for his pride. Just so, Daniel 8 depicts Antiochus's assault on the sanctuary as an assault on the heavenly stars and God himself. Again the mythic tradition is put into service for the sake of making clear just who *is* in charge, namely the God of Israel who shall break Antiochus in the end.

The Identity of the Author of the Book of Daniel and His Purpose

Finally, it is necessary to address the possible identity of the author of the book of Daniel and suggest something of his purpose in creating this strange melding of court tales and apocalyptic visions.

As for the author's identity, we are not asking after his name, but rather his religious horizon. What sort of person, as a matter of faith, created this text? A clue is certainly available in the uses of the verbal root "to be prudent, wise" (Hebrew *skl*). Daniel 1:17 tells us that God gave knowledge and skill (Hebrew *haskel*) to Daniel and his friends. Then in 11:33, 35; 12:3 the verb root provides the basis for another substantive, *maskil*, "wise one." We learn that under the violent attack of Antiochus the wise (Hebrew *maskilim* [plural]) shall enlighten some among the people, but they will also be persecuted and killed to be "refined, purified, and cleansed, until the time of the end" (11:33, 35). But when the end does come — when God intervenes to settle once and for all the battle between good and evil — "those who are wise shall shine like the brightness of the sky"; they shall enjoy astral immortality alongside the heavenly angels (12:3). Many speculate that the author of Daniel counts himself among these "wise ones" who apparently passively resisted the "reform" efforts of Antiochus and some Jews, choosing to suffer even death if necessary to uphold their faith. From this we learn a great deal about the author and his kindred: they counted "wisdom" as the insight necessary to cling to one's faith no matter the consequences. They were people of deep devotion who could not be deterred from their faith, even by the violent persecution Antiochus brought against them.

So what was the purpose of this "wise one" in writing the book of Daniel, and especially in bringing together the two disparate parts of the book? One possibility is that with the tales of wildly successful Jews in foreign courts he sought to provoke his audience to reconsider the longstanding tradition that the righteous would be rewarded and the wicked would suffer. Perhaps he sought to provoke them to respond with dismay in the face of the Antiochene oppression, to bring to a head their doubts about the old Deuteronomic system of retributive justice, forcing them to cry out, "How can you tell us such stories in days like these? *Now* the righteous suffer and the apostate prosper!" Then, by moving to the apocalyptic visions, he would have responded to their challenge, demonstrating that the old system still worked, but in a way never before imagined: the reward for righteousness came no longer in the present age as long life and prosperity, but as eternal life in the age to come. In this way the book of Daniel overcame what might have become in time fatal objections to the old Deuteronomic theology and its profound belief in God's justice for all according to their ways.

Of ultimate importance to Daniel's effort to save Deuteronomic-style retributive justice from the junk heap of history was his adaptation of the apocalyptic genre. By taking up this literary phenomenon that includes a heavenly messenger reporting heavenly secrets to an earthly being, and especially secrets about the ultimate disposition of creation (the classic definition of the apocalyptic genre), Daniel is able to place the accuracy of ideas of retributive justice well beyond question. Only history in its fullness — known by the visionary chosen by God — will tell the whole tale. Note that this approach to understanding God's way of working in creation will return to the fore in parts of our Introduction to the New Testament.

Theological Themes in Daniel

Clearly we have already begun to delve into the chief theological theme of the book of Daniel, its peculiar form of adherence to the Deuteronomic traditions. The other theological themes we attend to here are related to this one.

The Justice of God according to the Book of Daniel

As we have already observed, Daniel successfully draws the Deuteronomic tradition back from the brink of practical extinction. By doing so, though, it also ensures that God's reputation for justice remains intact and is even made cosmic in the sense that once Daniel is done with it, it reaches across time and space. Of course, that reputation was under increasing pressure from the time of the Exile on. Not everyone responded to the Deuteronomic explanation of the Exile favorably; not everyone was convinced that the Babylonian defeat of Judah was a just punishment for Israel's apostasy. This was surely so in part because not all who suffered had been unfaithful. Among such devout believers surely the question arose early on: why should all suffer for the sins of a few? In the exilic work of Ezekiel we have seen a way around that problem in the notion of individual responsibility, but that too struggled to make a full and adequate response to the wider suffering of *all* Judah, indeed, *all* Israel. In the Persian-era works of Ezra and Nehemiah we saw a response that simply assigned to those who suffered a lower status, an approach that clung fast, against any evidence to the contrary, to the Deuteronomic perspective. In Ecclesiastes from the Ptolemaic period we saw an author who simply saw no way around the problem, who asserted that there was no divine justice and one should not expect any either. So it is hardly surprising that an author found himself finally compelled in the Seleucid period — in the face of the Antiochene persecution — to deal with this challenge in a new way, in the ultimate way the author of Daniel did: God's justice will be proven in a new age to come, when God establishes a time and a place that confirms his justice for all the cosmos and for all time.

Time in the Book of Daniel

Time may not at first seem to be a theological theme, but it becomes one in the hands of the author of the book of Daniel. By determining that the past and the present and the future were and are and will be governed entirely by divine fiat, the author of Daniel took the step that made God's reach truly cosmic. After his effort — and similar efforts by other apocalypticists like the authors of *1 Enoch,* 4 Ezra, and 2 Baruch — God was not only the Lord of creation and all that is in it, but of the passage of time itself. We see this in several ways throughout the book of Daniel.

This is first apparent in the court tales of Daniel 1–6, at least in their retelling to 2nd-century B.C.E. audiences. By signaling God's responsiveness to the faith of Jews in the long-past Exile — even though they were not certain of it themselves (3:16-18) — the author established the lordship of God over the past. Hearing these stories of the 6th century in the 2nd century, audiences could not miss the implication regarding God's activity in history.

The apocalyptic visions then build on this sense that God is Lord of all time. By putting accurate visions of the people's future from Daniel's perspective — and the past from the audience's perspective — into Daniel's mouth to report as revelations from a heavenly being of heavenly secrets, the author assures his audience's profound recognition of God's control over all of history. Not only did God control events in the present reality of the figures whose stories are told in the first half of the book; God also determined their future and the past of the audience.

The latter recognition — that God controlled history and could communicate its import through a heavenly visionary and a human agent — was foundational, as we have seen, to *ex eventu* prophecy and, now we see, to apocalyptic as a worldview altogether. It was this set of factors that permitted the audience of such a text as this to hear the prophet narrate no longer just their past, but their future as well, and trust that narration: and what was narrated was a story of vindication for them as the righteous of Israel. Thus God's lordship over time was also sovereignty over the fate of creation itself.

Creation and God's Control over It in Daniel

We noted earlier the echoes of ancient Near Eastern creation stories in some parts of the apocalyptic visions of Daniel. This ties in well with what we have just observed, the absolute power the book assigns to God in relation to creation and all that is in it. Not only is God the author of creation, God is also the one who determines its destiny. The imagery invoked by Daniel indicates not only that, but the fact that God's judgment is discerning in weighing his own creation. He is capable of destroying parts of it according to the apocalyptic worldview — indeed, he is not just capable, but desirous of doing so. But again we should note that the apocalyptic vision, at least as it appears in the book of Daniel, is one that bends God's desire to those who understand themselves to be God's righteous people, over against those who lack righteousness.

This last observation leads to a final one regarding Daniel's theological perspective on creation and God's relationship to it. As we have seen, the apocalyptic worldview unflinchingly treats entire portions of creation as hopelessly corrupt: this is the nature of the dualism inherent in most apocalyptic visions. This, too, sets Daniel and its singular representation of apocalyptic in the Old Testament apart: this worldview is unafraid of the implications that stem from suggesting that something of God's good creation was irreparably evil. There *are* hints in Daniel of what is to come — the existence of a separate evil power that is responsible for the corruption of creation — but full development of an embodied evil apart from God was yet to come in Israelite and Jewish imagination (but see p. 170 for a brief history of Satan).

Questions for Review and Discussion

1 How does the book of Daniel divide up easily into two parts? What are the two parts, and how are they related to each other?

2 What is the apocalyptic genre, and how does Daniel evince that genre in its fullest form among all the books of the Old Testament?

3 What is at the heart of the theological vision apparent in Daniel? To which of the theologies we encountered in the Pentateuch is it most closely related?

Further Reading

Collins, John J. *The Apocalyptic imagination: An Introduction to Jewish Apocalyptic Literature.* 2nd ed. Biblical Resource Series. Grand Rapids: Wm. B. Eerdmans, 1998.

———. *Daniel.* Hermeneia. Minneapolis: Fortress, 1993.

Provan, Iain. "Daniel." In *ECB,* 665-75.

Seow, C. L. *Daniel.* Louisville: Westminster John Knox, 2003.

Chapter 32

Hosea

Getting Started

1   Read Hosea 1–3. What is the structure of these three chapters? How do the two narrative portions in chs. 1 and 3 work together with the oracular material in ch. 2?

2   Skim through Hosea 4–11, paying special attention to ch. 11. Do the same for Hosea 12–14, paying special attention once more to the concluding chapter of the section, Hosea 14. Do you notice a pattern? Is it a pattern familiar to you from reading some of the other prophetic books we have encountered?

3   As you read the following chapter, read along in your biblical text as well to assess the ways in which Hosea's marital history early in the book is echoed in the purely oracular material later in the book. What does this loose connection between the biographical and oracular portions of the book indicate about compositional history?

Preliminary Comments

The book of Hosea is perhaps best known for the symbolic marriage God commands its namesake to undertake as testimony to his audience regarding the relationship between God and Israel. God requires Hosea to marry Gomer, a woman with a questionable sexual history, and to name the children he fathers by her in ways symbolic of God's judgment on Israel. However, there is much more to this book, the longest of the Minor Prophets, than Hosea's marriages and his children's identities. Indeed, Hosea's marital history is exhausted in the first three chapters, leaving the last 11 chapters to oracles of the prophet. As we shall see, what truly sets this prophetic book apart, especially from the others produced in the 8th century B.C.E., is the degree to which hope for the future is woven into the fabric of the prophet's speech.

A Walk through Hosea

Chapters 1–3 are a combination of narrative about Hosea's marital history and oracles offering an explanation of their significance. The rest of the book is made up of oracles.

Hosea 1–3: Hosea's Marital History
The book begins with a somewhat stereotypical superscription (1:1; it may be indicative of the Deuteronomic

editing; see "Critical Issues" below). A later editor tells the reader that "The word of the Lord came to Hosea," signaling the divine origin of this prophet's words; there can be no mistaking that these oracles and actions are God's word, that Hosea was but the instrument of God. The superscription goes on to date Hosea's activity to the reigns of Uzziah, Jotham, Ahaz, and Hezekiah of Judah, and of Jeroboam of Israel. Notably the kings of Judah listed indicate that Hosea was active at least from *ca.* 750 to 725 B.C.E., while Jeroboam II ruled only until 746! It seems likely that the editor simply ignored the successors to Jeroboam II, a series of short-lived reigns under increasing duress from Assyria (see the list of Kings of Judah and Israel and their chronology on p. 158). As we shall see, this, among other things, indicates to many readers that the words of Hosea, a prophet to the Northern Kingdom, underwent redaction at the hands of a Judean editor.

Hosea 1:2-9 then records the Lord's arresting instructions to Hosea regarding marriage and child naming. Hosea is instructed to take a "wife of whoredom and have children of whoredom, for the land commits great whoredom by forsaking the Lord" (v. 2). Hosea does so, marrying Gomer and conceiving with her a son, whom God commands Hosea to name Jezreel, after the place where Jehu slew Jezebel and the rest of her family, putting an end to the Omride dynasty (2 Kgs 10:11). The Lord's judgment on the house of Jehu is negative, in spite of the fact that Elisha condoned Jehu's slaughter of the last of the Omrides, and naming the child Jezreel is meant to announce the impending end of that Jehu dynasty (vv. 2-5). Next, Hosea and Gomer bring forth another child, a daughter whom God commands Hosea to name Lo-ruhamah, "Not pitied," to indicate God's attitude toward Israel (v. 6; in a later addition v. 7 adds that Judah will be exempt from this judgment). Finally, the couple bears another son who is named by God Lo-ammi, "Not my people," again to announce God's view of Israel (1:8-9). In what is deemed by most to be another late addition, 1:10–2:1 reverses the judgments rendered by the names of the last two children.

Next 2:2-13 provides a long oracle that develops the marriage metaphor to explain what Israel had done to anger God. The passage begins with the language of a lawsuit. Some have suggested that we have in this oracle a covenant lawsuit, although it is more likely modeled after a divorce proceeding (see further below in "Critical Issues"), especially given the declaration of divorce in v. 2: "Contend with your mother, contend, for she is not my wife and I am not her husband" (cf. Deut 24:1). The imagery in the bill of particulars and announcement of punishment that follow depicts God as a faithful husband, Israel as an adulterous wife, and the gods

---

Reading Guide to Hosea

Hosea's Marital History (1–3)

Rebellion and Restoration (I) (4:1–11:11)
    The Indictment (4:1-3)
    Oracles Announcing Israel's Sin and Punishment (4:4–10:15)
    God's Compassion for Israel and Plan to Restore Her (11:1-11)

Rebellion and Restoration (II) (11:12–14:9)
    Oracles Announcing Israel's Sin and Punishment (11:12–13:16)
    God's Compassion for Israel and Plan to Restore Her (14:1-9)

Israel worshipped in place of the Lord as the wife's lovers. Baal, the Canaanite fertility-god who became particularly popular, is singled out for special attention, and apparently for good reason: Israel had worshipped him using the festivals mandated for honoring the Lord (2:11) with the expectation of receiving in return good crops and agricultural success (v. 12). The punishment that would come to Israel was the destruction of the agricultural abundance the people thought they would win from worshipping Baal.

Hosea 2:14-23, thought by some to be a later addition, announces God's plan to lure Israel back and to begin again with the people as in the days of the people's first entry into the land. Indeed, the Valley of Achor was where Israel first sinned upon entering the land (Josh 7:20-26), but now, said the Lord, it will become "a door of hope" (2:15). Likewise, Israel will turn from Baal — a word that means "lord" or "husband" — to her real "husband," the Lord God (v. 16), and in response God will provide the agricultural produce Israel yearns for (vv. 21-23).

Hosea 3:1-4 closes this first section of Hosea with God instructing Hosea to "love a woman who has a lover and is an adulteress," and he does so by paying a bride price for the woman (v. 1). It is not clear whether he purchases the right to marry Gomer a second time or he marries another woman. Given the symbolism of a renewed relationship between God and Israel the oracle expresses, Gomer seems the most likely candidate. In any case, Hosea is also instructed to avoid intercourse with this woman for a time to signal the period of punishment Israel will have to endure before full restoration takes place.

Hosea 4:1–11:11: Rebellion and Restoration (I)
This lengthy section is a diverse collection of oracles. The editor's organizing principle seems to have been a rather simple repetition of the pattern we have already

seen in other prophetic books: first provide God's indictment of Israel (4:1-3), follow that with a collection of the prophet's oracles announcing Israel's sins and her consequent punishment (4:4–10:15), and conclude with a chapter on God's compassion for Israel and plan to restore her (11:1-11).

Hosea 4:1-3 is a classic indictment. The people of Israel are called to pay heed, "for the Lord has an indictment against the inhabitants of the land" on the basis of Israel's lack of loyalty to God and attendant sins between human beings (vv. 1-2). The consequence is all the land and its human and animalian inhabitants mourn and languish (v. 3). This brief passage sets the stage for the oracles that follow, a long bill of particulars mixed with oracles of doom.

The first oracle (or perhaps collection of related fragments) announces God's charges against Israel's leaders and his decision to stand against them (4:4–5:7). Next, expressing what is a typical concern for Hosea, the oracle in 5:8-14 condemns the foreign alliances Judah and Israel made in the case of the Syro-Ephraimite War. Hosea 5:15–6:11a is an attack on Israel's false repentance, 6:11b–7:12 provides another litany of Israel's sins (especially as they were manifest in faithless foreign alliances), and 7:13-16 is a lament for Israel in the wake of her destruction. Hosea 8 may perhaps be treated as a single oracle that again attacks Israel's foreign policy, linking it this time with religious apostasy as well. Chapter 9 also may have been a single oracle that begins with a graphic anticipation of Israel's dispersion to Egypt and Assyria, continues with an oracle against false prophets (perhaps for their role in encouraging faithless alliances), and concludes with remembrance of Israel's adoption in the wilderness and her eventual rebellion against God and subsequent suffering for it. Hosea 10 observes that as much as Israel prospered in the land she grew ever more disloyal, chasing after other gods and placing kings over herself; these things led to even greater sin and punishment, in contrast with repentance that would have produced righteousness.

Hosea 11 provides a significant shift in tone as well as imagery. Depicting God as a parent and Israel as a child, the oracle describes the relationship between Israel and God as one between a son and his parent. God tenderly called Israel from Egypt, but the more God called to the son, the more the son rebelled; yet God still parented faithfully, hoping for a better response. Because a better response was not forthcoming, the son will soon experience the natural consequences of rebellion — taking the form of exile to Egypt and Assyria — but even so, God will not relent as a loving parent and will in time restore Israel, bringing the wayward one back from the dispersion.

Bronze figurine of a male deity, possibly Baal, found at Shechem (Late Bronze IIA). (Joint Expedition to Shechem; photo L. Ellenberger)

Hosea 11:12–14:9: Rebellion and Restoration (II)

Like the previous section, this one is a loose collection of oracles organized so as to announce first Israel's sin and punishment (11:12–13:16) and then God's will nonetheless to be merciful and redeeming in due time (14:1-9).

The oracles of condemnation are once more rather disparate in nature. Hosea 11:12–12:1 condemns Israel's foreign alliances and once again consigns her to exile in Egypt and Assyria. In 12:2-6 we hear an indictment of Judah, embodied in Jacob with whom God wrestled at the Jabbok (Genesis 32) and whom God met with promise at Bethel (Genesis 35). Hosea 12:7-9 may offer the single surviving example of the prophet's concern for injustice, condemning Israel for a pattern of oppressively acquiring wealth and promising a return to wandering as in the days between the Exodus and the entry into the land. Hosea 12:10–13:3 reports that God's prophets, spurned by Israel, will bring God's destruction just as God used a prophet to lead Israel from Egypt and to guard her; for this sin and for Israel's idolatry the people will be made as ephemeral as the morning dew, chaff that blows away, or smoke that dissipates. Finally, 13:4-16 recalls that God cared for Israel ever since Egypt, but Israel shunned God; as a result Israel will experience God's wrath, and no one, not even kings can save her. (Note that 13:14 is quoted in 1 Cor 15:55 to very different effect!)

Like ch. 11, Hosea 14 provides a reply to the doom announced in the preceding chapters. The prophet calls Israel to return to the Lord God, to reject alliances with Assyria and worship of other gods (vv. 1-3). When that happens God will heal Israel's disloyalty and renew his loving-kindness for the people (vv. 4-8), and it will happen when Israel has the wisdom to see the value of repentance and righteousness (v. 9).

Critical Issues in Studying Hosea

We attend here to two issues related to the study of Hosea. First, as is the case with most of the prophetic books, Hosea underwent an editorial process that makes dating it somewhat more complex than simply ascribing it to the time of the prophet himself. A second crucial issue in studying Hosea has been defining the notion(s) of covenant that appear in it.

Date, Provenance, and Editorial History

While the superscription to the book of Hosea dictates assigning the prophet's activity to the third quarter of the 8th century, there are two reasons to avoid dating the book correspondingly. First, the superscript is plainly a later redaction itself. Indeed, we shall see similar "headings" for several other books among the Minor Prophets, and we have already encountered them in Isaiah and Jeremiah. Because of their common use of the reigns of kings of Israel and Judah to date the activity of the prophets, and because that method of dating events is commonly found in Deuteronomic material, many surmise that an early collection of prophetic books bearing this superscription (including Hosea; see esp. Jeremiah in Chapter 28 above) was assembled and edited by someone related to the Deuteronomic reform movement.

Second, there are several clear instances of "Judean" redaction. While Hosea himself mentions Judah occasionally (e.g., in 5:8-14 his concern with the Syro-Ephraimite War naturally evokes mention of Judah), he was a prophet to Israel. As a result, many of the mentions of Judah and other things unique to the Southern Kingdom are perhaps later redactions from a southern editor of Hosea's prophecy who sought to use the prophet's words as a caution for Judah. For instance, 1:7 is a clearly dislocated, single-verse oracle of salvation for Judah. Likewise, 1:10–2:1 abruptly reverses the claims made in the names of the children of Hosea and speaks of the reunion of Israel *and Judah.* The reference to the Davidic line in 3:5 seems more at home in the mouth of a southerner than a prophet to Israel. And the close of 5:5, "Judah also stumbles with them," introduces an imbalance of content and poetic structure to an oracle otherwise concerned only with Israel. These and other passages have long suggested to readers a late, Judean redaction of the book.

As a result the date we assign to Hosea should perhaps be "manifold." While there are good indications within the book that some of its oracles do come from the third quarter of the 8th century — the Syro-Ephraimite War falls squarely in the middle of that period — the later redactions require a later date, perhaps in the late 7th century, when the Deuteronomic reform was already underway and some of its adherents saw the value in invoking as cautionary words for Judah the speech of the prophets whose announcements of Israel's impending doom came true. Thus we should perhaps view Hosea as a "rolling composition" not unlike one of the perspectives on Jeremiah's composition history; the editorial process began with Hosea's own activity in the 8th century and continued at least until the late 7th century.

The Question of Covenant and the Ancestral and Mosaic Traditions in Hosea

Among the 8th-century prophets Hosea is unique for his apparent awareness of some elements of the Ancestral and Mosaic traditions. He knows a tradition about the fate of two cities by the Dead Sea (11:8), something of Jacob (12:3-4), the notion of Moses as a prophet (2:15;

11:1; 12:13), and Israel's wandering in the wilderness (which he idealizes; 2:14; 9:10; 12:9). This affirms that such traditions were of some antiquity, that they had a home in the north, and that they were held up as constitutive for Israel's existence.

The more vexing question is that of Hosea's awareness of the Sinaitic covenant. Hosea uses the Hebrew word *berit,* usually translated as "covenant" in ways that have suggested to some his awareness of the covenant we read of in the Pentateuchal legislative materials, especially in Deuteronomy. But 2:18 refers to a covenant with the zoological realm and is clearly not the agreement between God and people we know from the Pentateuch. Likewise, the references to covenant in 10:4; 12:1 borrow from the imagery of international treaties, and the agreement violated at Adam according to 6:7 is simply unknown to us and therefore not fairly assigned Pentateuchal status. That leaves the reference to covenant and law (Hebrew *torah*) in 8:1, a verse generally attributed to Deuteronomic redactors of Hosea. As for the references to marriage agreements that use the term "covenant," they are nothing more than references to the contract that existed between marriage partners.

So what are we to make of the similarity of language and sentiment between Hosea and Deuteronomy? The best explanation seems to be that Hosea's rhetoric influenced the Deuteronomic school of thought. This would coincide well with the idea that the reform movement had its origins among northern Levites and came to Judah after the fall of the north. Indeed, some have gone so far as to speculate — without much good foundation — that Hosea was himself a Levite! In any case, it does seem clear that this prophet, afflicted with a tragic marital history, indelibly imprinted religious imagination, including that of the Deuteronomic writers, with his unique depiction of the relationship between God and people.

Theological Themes in Hosea

Hosea's contribution to theological imagination is particularly rich in large part because of his use of such powerful metaphors for God and God's relationship with the people of Israel. He also adds to the Old Testament's witness against relying on anything or anyone else but God for salvation and well-being, including foreign powers and the act of sacrifice in the absence of true trust in God.

God in the Book of Hosea

Hosea's best-known image for God and Israel together is the marriage metaphor. God plays the faithful, tender husband, and Israel is depicted as the wayward wife, unfaithful to her husband. Chapters 1 and 3 provide the "narrative" basis for the metaphor, and ch. 2 especially develops the notion to circumscribe the relationship between God and his people. The imagery in ch. 2 of God, the husband, stripping the faithless wife, Israel, naked and exposing her for all to see (v. 3) is obviously offensive to contemporary sensibilities, but its devastating and unique character must have also had a profound impact on ancient audiences. Conversely, the tenderness of the husband/God in the latter portion of ch. 2 in calling his wife/Israel back and renaming his children more generously must also have had its effect on the audiences that this form of Hosea reached. In any case, Hosea participated in a rich tradition of depicting God as a spouse.

The other most striking image for God in Hosea is that in ch. 11 of a parent caring for his or her son. Here we discover that God called Israel as a son out of Egypt (v. 1), and in spite of Israel's immediate turn to other gods (v. 2), God acted as the devoted parent, cradling his son to heal and comfort him, leading him in love, lifting him in the air to touch cheek-to-cheek, and bending down to feed him (vv. 3-4). Even though after this Israel still went its wayward way, God — being God and not a mortal — did not execute his fierce wrath, acting evermore the role of the parent, loving unstintingly his errant son (v. 9). This imagery also laid the foundation for later understandings of God and God's steadfast devotion to Israel.

Hosea on the Singularity of God as Israel's Salvation

Hosea is relentless in making clear to Israel the view that God alone could provide deliverance from its troubles and its foes. Yet Israel sought refuge in other things that Hosea roundly condemns. The most obvious target of Hosea's criticism is Israel's habit of making alliances with foreign powers to save itself from threats from other nations. The results are broken treaties that endanger Israel (6:7; 10:4; 12:1), the foolish alliance with Assyria in the Syro-Ephraimite crisis (5:8-14), as well as Israel's repeated fruitless appeals to Egypt for help (7:11, 16; 12:1). Instead of trust in human powers, Hosea's prophecy counsels Israel's trust solely in God: the contrast between the call to repentance and trust in God in 10:11-12 and the reality of Israel's apostasy and God's frightening response in 10:13-15 make this clear enough.

Hosea also attacks the priests and the sacrifices they receive from the people of Israel as a false hope that would not elicit God's love without corresponding trust. In 4:4-14 we see Hosea's vitriol for the priests and their willingness to take advantage of the sacrifices offered insincerely, and again in 6:1-6 he mocks the people who rely disingenuously on their sacrifices after blatant rejection of their God for others. In this too Hosea urges his audience to trust solely in the God of Israel for their salvation; but as history tells us, his urgings were without full effect for Israel in the end, and though they served as warnings to Judah, there too the people paid too little heed too late to the admonitions of the prophets.

Questions for Review and Discussion

1   In retrospect, how did you answer questions 1 and 2 in "Getting Started"? Did you successfully anticipate the suggestion that the book of Hosea is the product of editors, not the prophet alone? If not, how might you have read differently to discern that for yourself?

2   How are women depicted in the book of Hosea? Are such typologies in evidence today? Are such typologies acceptable today? If not, what has changed, and what does this mean for the book of Hosea as a sacred, authoritative text?

3   How do the theological themes in Hosea relate to the feminine imagery it uses so widely? Is there a way to read the more difficult feminine imagery in the book in a way that sublimates its harshness to the book's theological aim? Or do the images remain irredeemable?

Further Reading

Davies, Graham. *Hosea.* OTG. Sheffield: JSOT, 1993.

Emerson, Grace I. "Hosea." In *ECB,* 676-85.

Keefe, Alice A. *Woman's Body and the Social Body in Hosea.* JSOTSup 358. Sheffield: Sheffield Academic, 2001.

Seow, C. L. "Hosea, Book of." *ABD* 3:291-97.

Chapter 33

Joel

Getting Started

1   Read through the book of Joel in one sitting. How would you outline the basic elements of this book?

2   In your reading of the book what did you notice about the place of the nations? Do they function differently here than in Isaiah, Jeremiah, or Ezekiel?

3   Did you notice as well the prominent role nature plays in Joel? What role does it play, and how is it put to that use? Who puts it to that use?

Preliminary Comments

The book of Joel is best known for its image of a storm of locusts playing the role of a destroying army (1:1–2:17). But just as there is more to Hosea than the marital history of the prophet in chs. 1–3, there is more to Joel than the locust plague. Most notably Joel provides a long description of the "Day of the Lord" in 2:18–3:21 (= Hebrew chs. 3 and 4) that seems to have undergone two editions, the last perhaps as late as the period after Alexander the Great died and left his kingdom to his bickering generals, the "Diadochoi." As a result of this

compositional history, the book of Joel comes to us as a fascinating mix of an author's memory of a real locust plague mixed with later authors' reflections on the power of God's wrath and blessing for his people.

A Walk through Joel

Joel may be divided into three parts.

Joel 1:1–2:17: The Locust Plague

Joel begins with a superscription (1:1) that is only in part like the one we saw in Hosea. It does make clear that the word of the Lord "came to" Joel, confirming that the prophecy that follows is God's word, not Joel's own, but it does not bear the regnal date formula found at the beginning of Hosea. As we shall see in "Critical Issues" below, this already signals the later date of Joel's composition in relation to Hosea.

Joel 1:2-7 describes in vivid terms the devastation brought by a plague of cutting, swarming, hopping, and destroying locusts, likening them to a nation that behaves as ravaging lions and lionesses. The plague leaves nothing of the agricultural produce of the land, just as lions utterly destroy and consume their prey. Next 1:8-14 records a call to lament. All Israel should join in, for the destruction of the crops has cut off the offerings to God in the temple and left farmers and vintners alike in utter economic ruin. Thus all should put on sackcloth, lament, and take up a holy fast, from the priests to the elders to all the inhabitants of the land. Joel 1:15-20 is the lament itself, commencing with the anxious acclamation that the Day of the Lord is near. The lament goes on to say that while there is no food, no gladness in the temple, no crop in the land, and no stores in the granaries, there are fire in the pastures and the fields and starvation among the animals on the ranch.

Joel 2:1-11 returns to the locust plague to link it with the Day of the Lord. In this way the plague becomes explicitly an act of God. The passage begins with a blast of the ram's horn to alert all the people that the Lord's Day is near, and that it is in this instance a day of danger and destruction (vv. 1-2). The plague of locusts is like charging war-horses, a devouring flame, and an attacking army (vv. 4-5). Led by the Lord himself, the plague makes Eden a wilderness, anguishes the people, disembowels their defenses, and reduces the cosmos itself to a trembling mass (vv. 3, 6-11).

For all of the threat borne in the warning of the Day of the Lord, Joel 2:12-17 still expresses an author's view that repentance among the people will produce a change of heart in God. Thus the passage begins with God calling for fasting, weeping, and mourning as signs of a return to the Lord. The human speaker takes up the cause next, urging his audience to return, for (reciting a classic expression of God's mercy) "the Lord, your God . . . is gracious and merciful, slow to anger, and abounding in steadfast love" (v. 13). Confident of this divine character, all people, from the elderly to the infant at the breast, should take up a fast of repentance, and the priests should pray to the Lord, appealing even to his vanity to gain for one and all salvation.

Joel 2:18-27: God's Response to Israel's Repentance
And so it is that 2:18-27 reports an oracle of salvation that responds to the fast commanded by vv. 12-17. Hearing the people's plea, God responds with pity and grants the land new fecundity and drives out the "northern army" (referring to imperial powers, but recalling also the locust plague). As a result no one, human or animal, should fear, for all is well when God repays Israel for the losses incurred during the plague, when God promises to be present in the people's midst forevermore.

Joel 2:28–3:21: The Coming Cosmic Day of the Lord
This long section of Joel reflects perhaps a later hand, but it most certainly builds on what precedes it. In fact, it begins in 2:28-32 by saying that sometime *after* the

deliverance announced in vv. 18-27 — sometime in the future — God will take the further step of pouring out his spirit on all Israel so that everyone, from the young to the old, will be able to see the future that is coming, the Lord's day of universal judgment. This will be done so that God's people can call on the name of the Lord and be protected from God's destructive wrath at the end of the age.

Indeed, on the Day of the Lord the nations will be gathered for judgment according to their treatment of God's chosen people (3:1-8). Those who abused Israel shall experience a reversal of their fortunes: for example, God will deliver Tyre and Sidon, who sold Judahites into slavery to acquire great wealth, into the hands of the people of Israel only to be sold in turn to the Sabeans for great profit (3:8).

Joel 3:9-17 reports God's challenge to the nations to prepare for the judgment as though preparing for war. To that end, the well-known admonition in Mic 4:3 to make swords into plowshares and spears into pruning hooks is reversed by Joel 3:9-10: God calls the nations to make their farm implements into weapons of war, and the nations are urged to hasten to the "valley of decision" for the Day of the Lord and the judgment it will bring (3:11-15).

As for Israel, the Lord in Zion is a refuge for her on the Day of the Lord, and from that day onward the land of Israel will flow with good fruits and Jerusalem shall be holy, free of the contamination brought by foreigners (3:16-18). By contrast the old enemies Egypt and Edom will be desolated through God's vengeance for Judah and Zion, the Lord's permanent dwelling (3:19-21).

Critical Issues in Studying Joel

Several issues have regularly intrigued scholars in their study of Joel. First is the matter of the book's central image, the locust plague: Is it meant to refer to a natural phenomenon, to war among the nations, or to the Day of the Lord? A second issue, not unrelated to the first, is the date of the book of Joel.

What Did Joel Wish to Address?
Any reader of the book of Joel quickly realizes that it freely mixes the images of a conquering army, a plague

of locusts, a withering drought, and the Day of the Lord. Which of these lies at the heart of the prophet's concern, and how are these images related?

Scholars have developed a variety of answers to this question. Perhaps the best is that the prophet observed a drought that in turn brought in its wake a plague of locusts. He then used the image of that horrible experience to speak metaphorically of prior, present, and future encounters with hostile nations and their armies and in turn of God's judgment against Judah and the nations on the Day of the Lord. In this way, the prophet capitalized on devastating natural phenomena the people of Judah were all too familiar with to convey the equally destructive power of foreign armies, also well known among the people of Judah. Together, both *familiar* realities provided experiential reference points for the prophet's ultimate concern, to describe the Day of the Lord that brings judgment to the iniquitous in Judah and among the nations and exaltation to the faithful among God's chosen people.

When Was the Book of Joel Written?

The question of the date of the book is widely disputed. This is largely because its predominant focus on ecological phenomena instead of historical events sharply reduces internal indicators of date, as does the vagueness of the book's few references to nations and events. Another of the book's features that makes dating it such a vexing endeavor is the strong possibility that it was composed in two stages, with 1:1–2:27 coming first and 2:28–3:21 coming second. Nonetheless, an emerging consensus is that Joel is in its entirety a postexilic composition.

Several reasons support the latter judgment. First, the absence of the regnal formula at the beginning suggests composition at a time when kings ruled no more over the people and there was little or no anticipation of a return to kingship. The book also contains occasional clear references to the Exile and the restoration to Judah (3:2, 7). Also, especially the warrior hymn of ch. 3 incorporates postexilic, "protoapocalyptic" material like that found in Zechariah 9–14 and Isaiah 24–27. Likewise, the accusation that Tyre, Sidon, and Philistia sold Judeans into slavery recalls the Greek practice that began only in the Persian period. On the other hand, missing is any mention of king or court, even where the people are called to repentance; this too is an indicator of the Postexilic period when the monarchy no longer existed. And among the many echoes of other Scripture in Joel, 2:31b incontestably repeats Mal 4:5b.

Theological Themes in Joel

As in so many other prophetic books, the central theme in the book of Joel is that of God's relationship to Israel and the nations. What Joel brings to this topic that sets the book apart is the centrality of the image of the Day of the Lord, and especially the varying notions of that future event. Also constitutive for a theological appreciation of the book is its evocation of nature as an instrument of God's punishing wrath.

The Nations in Joel

Joel was completed at a time when the notion of the nations serving as God's instrument of punishment for Israel had perhaps diminished in its usefulness. The long history of struggle under foreign, and particularly imperial, oppression no doubt had dulled the utility of that motif: how could God have intended such a relentless exploitation of the nations in this capacity? Thus, while 1:1–2:17 — perhaps the oldest, even preexilic portion of the book — does seem to merge a foreign nation (maybe Assyria) with the locust plague that comes against Israel for her sins, when we turn to the depiction of the nations in the later portions of the book they are only the recipients of God's wrath for their abuses of God's people. Thus we see in this postexilic prophetic book an important shift in conceiving the relationship between God and the nations: less and less do they serve as instruments of God's wrath against Israel, and more and more are they the targets of that wrath.

The Day of the Lord in Joel

In the book of Joel we encounter a profound exposition of the Day of the Lord that comes close to — but does not reach — apocalyptic proportions. Among other things, the absence of an otherworldly emissary to a human recipient as well as the essentially this-worldly outcome of the Day of the Lord (it does not seem to entail a new spatial or temporal realm) assure the nonapocalyptic character of the book's genre as well as its nonapocalyptic outlook. Nevertheless, the depth of description assigned to the Day of the Lord makes of it for some readers a "protoapocalyptic" book, a precursor in form and function (if not also date) to the full form of apocalyptic we saw in Daniel.

Nature in Joel

The use of nature imagery in the form of the locust plague is striking for its harshness and, even more so, for the fact that it is God, the author of nature itself, who uses it to such gruesome and troubling ends. In fact, this is not the only place, let alone the first or last occasion, in the Hebrew Bible that God employs nature to work woe. But the concentrated form of it here makes it a particularly striking example and one worthy of note, for together with the other motifs already cited it produces a striking portrait of God among the prophetic books.

God in Joel

The portrait of God that emerges from the book of Joel as a result of its depiction of the Day of the Lord, the nations, and nature is one of a Deity who exercises complete sovereignty over those things he creates. God's might in the poetry of the book of Joel is unquestioned and unwavering. As in Ezekiel where God could exercise sovereignty to abandon Jerusalem to its fate, in Joel God seems to go even a distance more in employing the elements of creation to punish and work woe. Just as in Ezekiel God can exercise sovereignty to renew and rebuild the people and Jerusalem, so also in Joel God uses the same power that destroys to renew and protect Israel in the face of the devastation visited upon the nations.

Questions for Review and Discussion

1   What is the "Day of the Lord" and how does it function in the book of Joel?

2   Recalling the "Getting Started" questions, what role do nature and the nations play in Joel, and what do their uses signal about the book's conception of God?

3   What do we mean by the term "protoapocalyptic," and how does it figure into our understanding of the book of Joel?

Further Reading

Barton, John. *Joel and Obadiah.* OTL. Louisville: Westminster John Knox, 2001.

Gelston, Anthony. "Joel." In *ECB,* 686-89.

Hiebert, Theodore. "Joel, Book of." *ABD* 3:873-80.

Simundson, Daniel J. *Hosea, Joel, Amos, Obadiah, Jonah, Micah.* Nashville: Abingdon, 2005.

Chapter 34

Amos

Getting Started

1   Read Amos 1:1. What information regarding the date of Amos's activity does this superscription provide?

2   Read Amos 5:1–6:14. What sort of practices does Amos seem to condemn in this passage?

3   Read Amos 9:11-15. How does the tone of this prophecy differ from that of the material you read from chs. 5 and 6?

Preliminary Comments

The book of Amos has the reputation of focusing in particular on the social injustices committed by the elite of the Northern Kingdom (Israel) in the middle of the 8th century B.C.E. While this was a primary focus of the prophet, his critique was also directed against associated religious practices of those northern elites. Indeed, Amos could not have addressed social injustices and avoided religious practices, for the two were inextricably tied together in ancient Israel. Thus only when we take into account both dimensions of this prophet's speech do we come to an understanding of him and his book.

A Walk through Amos

Like Joel, the book of Amos is divisible into three major parts.

Amos 1–2: Oracles against the Nations

Like Hosea, Isaiah, and Jeremiah (and other prophetic books we will address later), the report of Amos's speech begins with a superscription that includes a regnal dating formula. Amos prophesied to Israel "in the days of King Uzziah of Judah and in the days of King Jeroboam son of Joash of Israel, two years before the earthquake" (1:1). This places Amos in the latter portion of the first half of the 8th century, perhaps in the decade 760-750.

The same verse also tells us that Amos was a "shepherd of Tekoa." As we see below, this professional designation for Amos has puzzled more than a few commentators. What is nonetheless apparent is the fact that he lived in the Southern Kingdom of Judah, but was elected to speak to the Northern Kingdom of Israel. One should keep this in mind in reading the following series of oracles against the nations that culminates in a tirade against Israel itself!

Amos introduces the oracles with the bold announcement that the "Lord roars from Zion, and utters his voice from Jerusalem; the pastures of the shepherds wither, and the top of Carmel dries up" (1:2). The geographical markers in this charge should not go unnoticed: God speaks from the heart of the Southern Kingdom — Jerusalem — to devastate the north, signified by Carmel. In any case, then follow oracles against Damascus (1:3-5), Philistia (1:6-8), Tyre (1:9-10), Edom (1:11-12), Ammon (1:13-15), Moab (2:1-3), Judah (2:4-5), and finally Israel itself (2:6-16). Each oracle is introduced with the statement, "For three transgressions . . . and for four, I will not revoke the punishment." The thrust of the formulaic phrase is that God's decision to punish the nations for their wrongs is final. The most striking thing about this set of oracles, though, is the way it surely built credibility for Amos, the southerner, as he addressed a crowd of northerners. Moving from condemnation for one enemy of Israel to another, Amos must have won for himself an increasingly enthusiastic audience, and assuming that the oracle against Judah is from Amos (and not a later editor; see "Critical Issues" below), the throng of auditors might even have cheered out loud at the prospect of their most despised enemy facing defeat. But then he turned his attention to Israel itself, condemning its citizenry for corrupting justice and oppressing the poor in order to feed their idolatrous practices (2:6-8) and disdaining God's great deeds and servants provided on their behalf (2:9-12). For their sin the people of Israel faced a terrible day of reckoning ahead (2:13-16).

Amos 3–6: Oracles Against Israel's Injustice and Apostasy

This series of oracles takes careful note of Israel's sins so as to condemn them roundly. The first oracle, ch. 3, begins with a reminder that Israel was God's elect (vv. 1-2). Then follows a series of rhetorical questions regarding the irresistible conclusion from certain kinds of evidence. Where two walk together there must be agreement; when a lion roars in the forest it must have caught prey; when a bird falls to a snare on the ground there must have been a trap for it (vv. 3-5). Likewise, proclaims Amos, if the warning trumpet is blown in the city the people fear, if disaster befalls a city God is at work, and if the Lord has spoken, fear among the people and prophecy from God's chosen ones are inevitable (vv. 6, 8; v. 7, as we see below in "Critical Issues," is surely a later addition). Amos 3:9-11 then reports what the chosen one has to say: the enemies of Israel are summoned to Samaria to assail it for its oppression, violence, and robbery of its own citizens. The aftermath of this attack will be a plundered and destroyed Israel, symbolized by the fragmentary remains of one of the couches used by the rich as they reclined at their outlandishly expensive banquets (v. 12). The chapter closes with God testifying that, indeed, on that day of reckoning he will attack in

---

Reading Guide to Amos

Oracles against the Nations (1–2)
Oracles against Israel for Social Injustice
   and Religious Infidelity (3–6)
More Oracles of Doom for Israel
   and a Hopeful Vision (7–9)

---

particular the accoutrements of the elite's idolatrous and wastrel practices, breaking down the altars of Bethel and destroying the ostentatious buildings that housed the rich in their costly apostasies (vv. 13-15).

Amos 4 moves to an even more explicit linkage between Israel's excesses and false religion. Calling them "cows of Bashan" (a breed known for its extraordinary fatness), v. 1 denounces even the wives of the wealthy for their demands upon their husbands for good drink and sustenance (who likely had to oppress their poor farmer tenants to obtain such items). As a result, says Amos, they will be led away bound through the city's broken walls after Israel's enemy (likely Assyria) defeats her as God's punishment (vv. 2-3). In the meantime, Amos mockingly invites the elites to continue with their empty worship of the God of Israel at Bethel and Gilgal, insisting that their sacrifices in the wake of such injustices are nothing but further transgressions against the Lord (vv. 4-5). To indicate how stubborn this people was, Amos recalls that God tried before to discipline Israel: he caused famine, he made crops fail and towns and cities suffer drought, he visited various plagues on Israel's agricultural complex, and he sent violent foes into their midst, and still they did not turn from their wicked ways (vv. 6-11). Thus the oracle concludes with God announcing his intention to bring all of the same upon Israel again, apparently in a final display of anger and of his utter sovereignty over all creation (vv. 12-13).

The last part of this middle section is 5:1–6:14. It is a collection of fragmentary oracles that further describe the socioeconomic injustices and related religious apostasy of Israel (e.g., 5:10-13, 21-27; 6:4-7), the destruction that shall come to Israel to punish her for these sins (e.g., 5:2-3, 8-9, 16-17), and the resulting devastation that will follow (e.g., 6:9-10). One of the most significant passages in this long section is Amos's woe oracle for those who look forward to the "Day of the Lord": because of Israel's great sin, what was to be a day of vindication will be instead a day of great suffering and disappointment, of darkness and gloom (5:18-20). With only a few words Amos establishes a tradition of reversing the Day of the Lord to work against God's own people, a tradition we already saw carried on in Joel.

Amos 7–9: Visions of God's Judgment and a Prophecy of Restoration

The first part of this section is a series of three judgment visions. The first vision entails judgment by locusts, the second judgment by fire, and the third judgment by the measure of a plumb line (7:1-9). Altogether the series signals the failure even of prophetic intercession for Israel. In spite of Amos's pleading in 7:2, 5, the last vision assures readers that in the final analysis God will execute judgment against Israel in spite of the prophet's pleas.

The next unit, 7:10-17, is a biographical interlude that reports Amos's encounter with the priest of the sanctuary at Bethel, Amaziah. Amaziah sends word of Amos's prophecy of death for King Jeroboam and exile for all Israel and then urges Amos to cease his prophecy in Israel and go home to speak there instead. Amos's blunt reply to Amaziah's exhortation is famous: first he rejects the title of prophet and then reports God's commission of him as a prophet of doom to the kingdom of Israel. God's command was irresistible in spite of Amos's own reluctance to preach.

A fourth vision follows in 8:1-3. This time Amos sees a basket of summer fruit (Hebrew *qayits*). In a play on words, the Lord goes on to say to Amos that the end (Hebrew *qets*) has come upon Israel and that the temple songs will become wailing at the multiplication of dead bodies. The rest of ch. 8 announces the consequences attendant to the hastening conclusion of Israel's existence: those who oppress the needy shall be judged and suffer for their unforgettably horrible deeds, feast will turn to mourning, songs to lamentation, a famine of God's very presence through the word will befall the land, and the rich young men and women shall faint from thirst (vv. 4-14).

Amos 9:1-6 opens the closing chapter with the fifth and final vision. This time Amos sees the Lord appear at the shrine in Bethel, where its destruction is carried out and its users and personnel are scattered and slaughtered to the very last one of them. The vision closes with a hymn acknowledging God's sovereign power over creation itself. The chapter continues with the Lord answering those who think themselves immune from such fates as those Amos predicts because they are God's chosen, brought out of Egypt by his special favor: as it turns out, others are led from place to place by God, so Israel has no special privilege even in this (vv. 7-10).

The book concludes with a belatedly hopeful passage, one that is deeply dissonant with the rest of the book. Amos 9:11-15 is an oracle of restoration, an anticipation of the day when the fallen "booth" of David (implying the Exile) shall be raised again, the people's fortunes will be restored, and their land will be abundant again.

Critical Issues in Studying Amos

The book of Amos has been fertile ground for scholarly disputes and speculation. We survey only two of those issues. The first has to do with the book's compositional history, with debate swirling around the degree to which we may reliably assign part or all of the book to Amos himself. The second issue is the question of the precise practices condemned by the prophet.

The Compositional History of the Book of Amos

To any careful reader of Amos it is plain that the dominant message of the work is one of condemnation for Israel. Relentlessly Amos predicts the end of Israel for the sins of its elite, describing their fate in some of the most vivid terms encountered in the Hebrew Bible (e.g., 4:1-3). Seeing the consistency of this theme, most have concluded that the historical Amos was a remorseless preacher of doom.

But precisely that conclusion raises questions about a number of passages in the book. Indeed, 5:4, 6, 14-15; and 9:11-15 provide unusual respite from Amos's otherwise calamitous notions regarding the future. The first two passages urge auditors to seek the Lord and live, and the last passage clearly presumes the failure of the Davidic line and nonetheless looks forward to its restoration and the renewal of Israel under its banner. The first two passages echo the rhetoric of Deuteronomy and are widely understood to be Deuteronomic redactions of Amos. Editorial interventions of a Deuteronomic hand are also apparent in 3:7, which uses the characteristically Deuteronomic phrase "his servants the prophets" (cf. 2 Kgs 17:23; 21:10; 24:2), and the superscription that dates Amos's prophecy with a regnal formula (cf. Isa 1:1; Jer 1:1-3; Hos 1:1). This may have been part of a larger effort by the Deuteronomic writers to "co-opt" the prophets, such as we saw already in the editorial history of Jeremiah. As for the last editorial addition, it seems quite likely that 9:11-15 comes from the Postexilic period, when it was feasible — if only remotely — to yearn for a restored Davidic line over the land of Israel. On this reading the book of Amos went through at least two redactional stages before it took its present form.

Of course, some object to this view on the composition history of the book of Amos. Most notably, Shalom Paul insists that the entirety of the book comes from the mouth of the 8th-century prophet himself. Such an argument is often thought to be very difficult to make, especially with regard to 9:11-15; yet it has its proponents.

What Did Amos Condemn?

Amos's social critique is intense and sharply honed, even more so perhaps than most readers realize. We attend two of Amos's targets here, and note also his con-comitant attack on the religious practices of Israel.

One target is evident in 6:4-7. In this passage we hear that some in Israel "lie on beds of ivory" while they "eat lambs from the flock, and calves from the stall" and "drink wine from bowls, and anoint themselves with the finest oils." This is commonly understood to describe a *marzeach,* a feast associated with the cult of the dead. Those who had the leisure to undertake such feasts were almost surely the landed elite, who, like those con-demned in Isaiah 5, had achieved their wealth by taking land from the poor in payment for debts owed; thus they relied not on their own labor, but that of their poor neighbors. In turn, if they were to eat "lambs from the flock" or "calves from the stall," they had to dispossess the same poor neighbors who raised flocks and herds! The depth of Amos's disgust with these rich elites is quite understandable.

Amos also repeatedly condemns the perversion of justice accomplished by the more affluent of the commu-nity. For example, 4:1 (the oppressive "cows of Bashan"), 5:7 (woe to "you who turn justice to wormwood"), 10 ("They hate the one who reproves in the gate"), and 12b ("you who . . . push aside the needy in the gate") reflect Amos's concern that the powerful are stealing justice from the poor in property and other sorts of disputes. Even more obvious is the oracle in 8:4-6 that condemns again the falsification of fairness by the rich and power-ful against the poor and weak in judgments of disputes.

But Amos was not content just to condemn the social injustices of the powerful; he also calls them to account for their (consequently) false religiosity. In particular, we read in 4:4-5 the prophet's taunt of those who worship with tithes and offerings of leavened bread. After having indicted the same people for their oppression of the poor in 4:1-3, the implication is that God is unmoved by piety that seeks to cover over social injustice. Indeed, in 5:21-24 the prophet announces God's disgust for the "festivals" and "solemn assemblies," "burnt offerings and grain offerings," and "offerings of well-being of . . . fatted animals" provided by the powerful. Instead of receiving these gifts of homage, Amos says that God will instead "let justice roll down like waters, and righteous-ness like an ever-flowing stream."

Theological Themes in Amos

The key theological theme in the book of Amos is its linkage of faith with social justice. Closely related to that double emphasis is Amos's reconfiguring of the "Day of the Lord" as a day of judgment on faithless and unjust Israel.

Ivory carving of a sphinx in a thicket, typical of the wealth and luxury assailed by Amos (3:15; 6:4) and showing Syrian and Egyptian influence. (Courtesy of the Israel Antiquities Authority)

Social Justice and Religious Practice

The well-known clarion call from Amos after giving voice to God's antipathy toward Israel's sacrifices, "But let justice roll down like waters, and righteousness like an ever-flowing stream" (5:24), epitomizes the book's sensibilities regarding religious — that is ritual, cultic, or sacrificial — practices and social justice. While the God who speaks through Amos never rejects right wor-ship, to be of any use it must nonetheless be accompa-nied by just action toward the neighbor, and especially the less powerful neighbor. Indeed, where such justice is lacking, no amount of ritual action will have a positive impact on God's regard for the offering agent; instead it will only deepen God's ire against the offenders.

As a result of this sort of reasoning in Amos, we derive from the book some of the most powerful biblical testi-mony regarding worship and its relationship to *praxis* in the world. But we also often miss the full nuance of Amos's argument. Readers often take Amos's prophetic speech to mean that God rejects so-called "empty ritual" altogether in favor of social action. Rather, he gives voice to the view that ritual action which connects the human to God does have its place — its essential place — in the divine-human equation, but such action becomes empty if the grounding in the divine does not also produce in the human community a desire to make it the best it can be, the most just it can be. Likewise, just behavior does not replace ritual action; it merely fulfills the potential ritual action engenders.

The Day of the Lord in Amos

In our survey of Joel we have already seen an instance of making the "Day of the Lord" a day of wrath. Amos is the first prophet we have evidence for having done that.

The concept of the impending "Day of the Lord" provides the background for the book's oracles altogether. In 1:2 (cf. Joel 3:16) the "Lord roars from Zion," and in 5:18 Amos speaks a woe over those who desire that day. Throughout the book it is announced as the day when God will execute judgment against Israel through the agency of the Assyrian emperor and his army. It will not be the day of light, glory, and vindication tradition anticipated, but rather a day of darkness, gloom, and shame for Israel, *precisely* because of the nation's elites who abuse their power to oppress the poor and worship God emptily. The indictment earned by social injustice and empty worship assures a Day of the Lord all would rue.

Thus it is that, apart from the handful of (probably Deuteronomic) calls to "seek the Lord and live," to "seek good and not evil," and the concluding verses

anticipating a restored Davidic line, the book of Amos is considered to be one of the most relentlessly gloomy collections of prognostications. Amos announces the wrath of God in ways not soon forgotten.

Questions for Review and Discussion

1   Where was Amos from, and to which kingdom did he preach?

2   What were the two concerns of Amos in his preaching, and how do they show up in the speeches preserved from Amos?

3   What is the relationship between the two central topics addressed in the prophecy of Amos?

Further Reading

Carroll R., M. Daniel. "Amos." In *ECB,* 690-95.

King, Philip J. *Amos, Hosea, Micah: An Archaeological Commentary.* Philadelphia: Westminster, 1988.

Paul, Shalom M. *Amos.* Hermeneia. Minneapolis: Fortress, 1991.

Chapter 35

Obadiah

Getting Started

1   Read Obadiah completely and make an outline of the text.

2   What are the themes of this little book? Where have you seen at least one of them before?

3   Who is Edom, and what is Edom's relationship to Esau in this work?

Preliminary Comments

This, the briefest book in the Old Testament, is dated to the Exile by its clear knowledge of the fall of Judah, Jerusalem, and the First Temple. Its principal concern is to announce judgment on Edom for its participation in pillaging Judah and Jerusalem in the wake of the Babylonian conquest. Like Joel and Amos, it places the concept of the Day of the Lord at the center of its proclamation.

A Walk through Obadiah

Amounting to only 21 verses, Obadiah is barely long enough to require division into a Reading Guide. All the same, there is a sense that vv. 1-14 amount to an an-

nouncement of judgment against Edom, while vv. 15-21 gradually, and then completely, shift the focus to the vindication of Judah, indeed of the greater Israel of old.

Obadiah 1-14: Against Edom

The superscription to this little book is simply, "The vision of Obadiah." The brevity of the introduction and the fact that the name attached to the book means "servant of the Lord" have suggested to some that this is simply an anonymous oracle that was for some reason (perhaps to fill out the 12?) assigned a separate prophetic title so as to serve as a stand-alone work.

Whatever the origin of the oracle, its focus is clear: Edom, unjust despoiler of Israel, deserves punishment. Verses 1b-4 announce God's intention to make Edom least among the nations, to bring it down from its aerie-like heartland (perhaps a place close to the later city of Petra). Then vv. 5-7 taunt Edom by noting its own despoilage at the hands of its former friends; notably the prophet calls Edom "Esau" in v. 6, reminding the reader that Judah and Edom were meant to be allies too, originating as they did from the twins Jacob and Esau. But vv. 8-11 assure the reader that there was never any such alliance of any consequence. Instead, because of the violence Edom did to its brother Jacob in the time of the Babylonian conquest, only shame shall come to Esau before Jacob. Edom should never have stood against his brother, and now, says the prophet, Edom must pay (vv. 12-14).

Obadiah 15-21: Vindication for All Israel

Echoing the theme already well known from Joel and Amos, v. 15 announces the nearness of the Day of the Lord, the time when Edom will suffer the consequences of its actions and all Israel will be vindicated. Signaling the author's vision of a restored and united kingdom serving as God's instrument of vengeance against Edom on this Day of the Lord, v. 18 announces that "the house of Jacob shall be a fire, the house of Joseph a flame, and the house of Esau stubble." Verses 19-21 draw the oracle to a close, predicting Israel's eventual possession of nearly the entire Levantine region, including, of course, "Mount Esau" and its kingdom.

Critical Issues in Studying Obadiah

The central critical issues attached to study of Obadiah center around its relationship to other anti-Edom oracles in the prophetic corpus (e.g., Amos 1:11-12; Isaiah 34; Ezekiel 35) and to Lam 4:21-22, but most of all to Jer 49:7-22.

It is noted that Obad 1-4 closely reflects Jer 49:14-16 and Obad 5-6 matches with Jer 49:9-10. This closeness has suggested to some dependence between the two works of some sort, but perhaps a better way to conceive of the relationship is through shared source material. This in turn — along with the other anti-Edom oracles — suggests that there was a known collection of oracles against Edom for her violation of Judah at the time of the Babylonian Exile, a collection editors could easily draw on in making their own works.

Related to this last observation is the suspicion that even this short book is composite. Verses 1-4 certainly seem to provide a distinct oracle, but these have been integrated into the remaining material through v. 14 to make a new whole. In turn vv. 15-18 may be seen as separate from vv. 19-21, the true oracle of salvation. Here too it appears that somewhat disparate source material has been woven together to create a new composition. It is the thematic focus of the work as a whole, a piece of lit-

erature achieved from perhaps quite disparate sources, that gives Obadiah its theological significance.

Theological Themes in Obadiah

While the consensus is that the book of Obadiah came into existence in the Exilic era, its positing of Edom's destruction for its opposition to Judah and its anticipation of a restored united Israel under God's watchful presence suggest its theological value beyond that historical moment and the book's superficial expression of a "hate Edom" theology. As a whole the work announces God's fierce protection of God's chosen, even to the extent of punishing decisively on the Day of the Lord those who have afflicted Israel. At the same time it announces God's favor for all Israel, a favor so enduring that God will remember Israel even after she has been divided and dispersed by Assyria and Babylon and overcome by Edom. Thus the short book not only embodies the particular ill regard in which Judahites held Edom — Esau — but also the author's confidence that, no matter the enemy, God will always come to the aid of all Israel to restore her to the fullness God established for her at the beginning of time.

Questions for Review and Discussion

1 How does the concept of the Day of the Lord in Obadiah compare with its use in Amos and Joel?

2 Why does Edom come in for such criticism from the author of Obadiah?

3 How does the portrait of God in Joel compare with the portrait that emerges from a reading of Obadiah?

Further Reading

Barton, John. *Joel and Obadiah.* OTL. Louisville: Westminster John Knox, 2001.
Ben Zvi, Ehud. *A Historical-Critical Study of the Book of Obadiah.* BZAW 242. New York: de Gruyter, 1996.
Gelston, Anthony. "Obadiah." In *ECB,* 696-98.

Chapter 36

Jonah

Getting Started

1 Recall what you already know of the story of Jonah. Does what you already know of the book match with what you have come to know prophetic books to be from our study so far?

2 Read Jonah 2. How does this passage match with what you know of the book of Jonah already, and with what we have already seen with respect to the prophetic books?

3 As you read the book of Jonah and the accompanying chapter consider your preconceptions about the book. How are your views changed by this experience?

Preliminary Comments

The book of Jonah, though placed among the Minor Prophets, is in fact a mixture of fable, satire, and folktale that as a whole is perhaps best described as a novella. Here we find none of the genres characteristic of the other prophetic books: no oracles against Israel or foreign nations, no oracles of salvation, and no full-fledged call narratives. The only true claim this book has to a place among the prophetic books is the fact that its main character, Jonah, is named as a prophet who advised Jeroboam II in a conflict with Syria (2 Kgs 14:25). Thus instead of a prophetic book we have a two-part tale that features a reluctant prophet, his unwilling conversion of foreigners to faith in the God of Israel, and a demonstration of God's mercy for the whole breadth of creation.

A Walk through the Book of Jonah

A Reading Guide to Jonah divides the book into two parts. Chapters 1–2 recount the command to Jonah to preach to Nineveh, his flight from the task that leads to the conversion of a boatload of pagans, and his prayerful sojourn in the belly of a great fish. Chapters 3–4 record God's renewed command to Jonah that he preach repentance to Nineveh, his still-reluctant effort on that account, and his prayerful stay atop a hillside overlooking Nineveh where he hopes in vain for the city's destruction (and hears God's judgment on his attitude).

Jonah 1–2: From Joppa Toward Tarshish to the Belly of the Fish

The book begins with words reminiscent of those we find at the beginning of other prophetic books: "Now the word of the Lord came to Jonah son of Amittai" (1:1). But after God's announcement of the specific commission to go to Nineveh to preach repentance (1:2) the book never once again resembles the other prophetic books. In any case, we first learn in 1:3 that Jonah has no intention of following the command of the Lord. Indeed, why would he? Nineveh was the capital of Assyria, Israel's age-old enemy, and in the eyes of the book's readers in the Postexilic period (see "Critical Issues" below for the dating of the book), that city's inhabitants deserved nothing better than the treatment its armies gave to Israel in 721 B.C.E.: total annihilation. Jonah signals assent to this perspective by buying passage on a boat from Joppa to Tarshish, a place that lies in the opposite direction from Nineveh. Jonah 1:4-6 reports that God sends a storm to foil Jonah's attempt to escape his calling, but that Jonah's response to the storm is to descend to the hold of the ship and sleep while the pagan sailors beseech their gods for help. But Jonah's respite is brief, for he is soon called from the hold by the ship's captain to entreat his God as well. When the sailors cast lots to see whose behavior among them has led to their troubles, the lot falls to Jonah, and the sailors realize that his flight from the Lord is the reason for the storm (1:7-10). After resisting Jonah's entreaties that they cast him into the sea to save themselves, they pray for forgiveness from Jonah's God and do as he commands them, whereupon they make sacrifice to the God of Jonah in place of their own gods (1:11-16). For his part, having accidentally converted a boatload of pagans, Jonah is swallowed by a great fish, and he lingers in its belly for three days and nights (1:17). Within the fish Jonah prays to God a hymn of thanksgiving for God's mercy to those who beseech him (2:1-9), a curious choice of genres for a man caught in the digestive tract of a sea creature, but as it turns out a very fitting choice as it expresses Jonah's worst fear, that God does seek to redeem all those who beseech him, Nineveh included, should it so come to pass. After his hymn, God causes the fish to spew Jonah out upon the beach.

Jonah 3–4: From the Shore to Nineveh to the Hilltop Outside Nineveh

After picking himself up off the beach, Jonah hears God's call a second time, and this time Jonah obeys

Phoenician galley ship. Assyrian stone relief. (ca. 1350–612 B.C.E.; British Museum). (Erich Lessing/Art Resource, NY)

(3:1-4). The result of his preaching in Nineveh over the course of three days is the city's repentance in sackcloth, from the king to the animals of the city, and the city's hope that God will see their repentance and spare them God's wrath (3:5-9). Their repentance, as it turns out, is effective: God turns away from wrath to mercy, just as Jonah's prayer in the fish anticipated; Nineveh is spared (3:10).

In the face of this remarkable turn of events, Jonah says aloud what the reader already knows: that he fled to Tarshish because he knew that God is "gracious . . . and merciful, slow to anger and abounding in steadfast love," and thus even Nineveh, great enemy that she was to Israel, could be spared if repentant (4:1-2). Seeing this, Jonah confesses further his desire to die rather than see this conversion of Nineveh, to which God responds, "Is it right for you to be angry?" (4:3-4). Jonah's affirmative answer to the question comes in the form of his retreat to east of the city to watch from there for the destruction he wishes upon Nineveh (4:5). As he waits God causes a plant to grow to provide Jonah shade from the heat of the sun. But the next day God sends a worm to attack the shade plant and kill it so that Jonah will suffer the heat, a circumstance that prompts Jonah to wish for a second time that he might die rather than suffer such heat (4:6-8). To Jonah's plea to die God responds by asking Jonah to consider the comparison between Jonah's passion for a plant that comes and goes in a day's time and God's compassion for the people of Nineveh who are equally a creation of God as the plant: should God not be concerned about Nineveh if Jonah is concerned about a plant?

Critical Issues in Studying Jonah

There is wide consensus on when Jonah was written, where it comes from, and what the sociohistorical background was for its particular argument.

Dating the Book of Jonah

The evidence weighs heavily in favor of dating Jonah to the Postexilic period. Few doubt that Second Isaiah influenced the imagination of this author, as did Jeremiah; thus the book must have been composed sometime after the middle of the 6th century. The evidence of the text's language is somewhat ambiguous, but most think it favors a postexilic, Persian-period date. But perhaps most compelling as evidence of its postexilic date is the concern of the book to address — even satirize — those within Judah who saw self-isolation and rejection of the other as the proper responses to non-Jewish neighbors. One thinks especially of the views espoused in Ezra and Nehemiah regarding marriage between Jewish men and non-Jewish women, views developed in the Postexilic period. Seen in this light, Jonah can even be understood as a response to such reforms in postexilic Judah.

The Provenance of the Book

This question is settled largely by the consensus on the date of the book. The proper locus for the sort of concerns expressed here is the land of Israel in the Postexilic period, a time and place where one would especially have been compelled to entertain questions of association or nonassociation. While Jews of the Diaspora hardly had choices in the matter of association, their brothers and sisters in Judah did, especially given Persian sponsorship of their control over the region. Thus the debate about how best to respond to non-Jewish neighbors was likely to have been significant in postexilic Judean life. The book of Jonah appears to be a contribution to that debate.

The Sociohistorical Background for the Debate over Relationships between Jews and Non-Jews

Why, precisely, was the question of how to relate to non-Jewish neighbors an issue of discussion in postexilic

Judah? As we noted in our chapter on the historical context of the Bible's development, Persian-period Judah was a significantly pluralistic context. Because of pressure exerted by the dying Neo-Babylonian Empire on other regions nearby, Judah had experienced a substantial inflow of refugees and immigrants during the Exilic period. In addition, it seems certain that the Judeans left behind by the Babylonian conquerors were influenced by their new and diverse co-inhabitants of the land. Thus when Persia defeated Babylon and returned Judeans in exile to their ancestral land, these "returnees" found a culturally, religiously, and socially complex community. In addition, the returnees were permitted by their Persian patrons to dictate the terms of life in the land, at least insofar as their governance produced adequate revenues for the empire, especially through collection of levies through the agency of the temple cult. As a consequence the question of how to respond to the diversity of religious and cultural perspectives in Judah was critical: should the participants in this renewed tax-producing, empire-satisfying temple cult be enlarged to include all Judeans, or should it be restricted to only those who were deemed by the community leadership orthodox enough in their practice and pure enough in their bloodlines? It is against this backdrop that one is able to make the best sense of the book of Jonah.

Theological Themes in Jonah

There can be no doubt that the chief theme in Jonah is the mercy of God for all of God's creation. A subsidiary theme is a polemic against those who would, by contrast, presume to dictate the proper recipients of God's mercy.

The Mercy of God in Jonah

As noted above, the author of the book of Jonah includes a refrain that was surely very familiar to his audience: God is "gracious . . . and merciful, slow to anger, and abounding in steadfast love" (4:2; cf. Exod 34:6; Neh 9:17; Ps 86:5; Joel 2:13). That Jonah gives voice to the refrain almost regretfully hardly undercuts the book's central theme that God seeks to provide mercy to all creation. There is much else in the book that reinforces that theme. Jonah's prayer in the belly of the fish (ch. 2) gives the book's first unequivocal articulation of that perspective. By singing a hymn of thanksgiving under such desperate circumstances, Jonah signals his (later grudging) certainty that God will rescue those who ask for deliverance. But even before that, recipients of the book are alerted to Jonah's — and the author's — confidence that God is merciful. Told to preach to Israel's old enemy, the Assyrians, Jonah books passage on a ship going in the opposite direction! If he were not certain of God's mercy but rather of God's wrath, he would have most certainly rushed to Nineveh to deliver the bad news and see its outworking in their midst. Jonah's ticket stub for travel to Tarshish was proof already that he, more than anyone else, understood God's abounding and steadfast love.

A Polemic against Isolationists

The flipside of the coin that bears the sign of God's mercy is the niggardly outlook of some in postexilic Judah. The book's satire on such folks and their perspective constitutes a second theological theme articulated in the book of Jonah: God's rejection of the human tendency to hoard for itself the good news of God's saving mercy. The satire is consistent throughout the book. Fleeing God's will to convert the enemy and confident of God's steadfastness, Jonah tries to frustrate God's plan and only manages in the process to accidentally convert a boatload of pagans to the worship of the God of Israel (ch. 1)! When Jonah is faced with certain death, he calls upon the mercy that he would withhold from others, knowing that it will be given to him as surely as the sun will rise on each new day. Even when he finally executes his assigned task of being the mouthpiece for God's intentions, when everything in him tells him that God will succeed where he wanted God to fail, he still waits hopefully for the destruction of the other, not its salvation. Not getting what he wants, he absurdly wishes to die rather than see God give freely to others what God gave to him without justification. To top it all off, his theological imagination is so puny that when God teaches him the lesson of God's tender care for all creation through the life and death of the shade plant, all he can do is wish again to die.

It is tempting to see in Jonah little more than a stinging indictment of the "hater of the other," a figure we can laugh at and ridicule as wrongheaded. But this is perhaps the most sophisticated theological aspect of this little book: as readers we are lured into Jonah's mistake by the satire; we are reminded that we are all just like him, impulsively vilifying the other. But, says Jonah himself from the belly of the fish, we can thank God for his mercy even for those who alienate themselves from God through fear and hatred of the other. Thus in the end the book of Jonah says to one and all, God is indeed "merciful, slow to anger, and abounding in steadfast love." This was most assuredly a powerful claim in postexilic Judah as the people faced the experience of settling into a new and challenging world.

Questions for Review and Discussion

1   How did your preconceptions about the book of Jonah change as a result of your reading?

2   What are the likely date and purpose of the book of Jonah?

3   How does Jonah compare with the other prophetic books we have looked at? What are some of the possible reasons this tale found its way into the prophetic collection?

Further Reading

Ben Zvi, Ehud. *Signs of Jonah: Reading and Rereading in Ancient Yehud*. JSOTSup 367. Sheffield: Sheffield Academic, 2003.

Gunn, David. "Jonah." In *ECB*, 699-702.

Salters, Robert B. *Jonah and Lamentations*. OTG. Sheffield: JSOT, 1994.

Chapter 37

Micah

Getting Started

1   How does Micah characterize the rulers and leaders of Israel? In what ways are they deemed responsible for the doom that faces the people?

2   What is Micah's attitude toward city dwellers and country folk? Are there passages that are especially indicative of his attitude?

3   What sort of future does the book of Micah envision for Israel? Is it all doom, or are there rays of hope expressed by the book? If so, what are they?

Preliminary Comments

Micah, a contemporary of Isaiah (though perhaps a few years younger), shared the intense feelings of Isaiah regarding social injustice and idolatry in Israel and Judah. However, what sets him and the book composed in his name apart from Isaiah and First Isaiah are his rural roots. While Isaiah spoke as a citizen of Jerusalem and even a confidant of the kings of Judah, Micah was an observer looking into the capital city and the royal circle from the outside. Thus his critique is less tempered than

Isaiah's, his distaste for the city, the kings, and their ways much more intense. Likewise, he was famously able to announce not only the fall of Judah, but with particular boldness the destruction of Jerusalem as well (3:9-12). And yet, for all of that the book that bears Micah's name is also one of the more hopeful of the prophetic books preserved in the canon; but as we shall see, this is thought by most not to result from Micah's own speech, but from the work of his editors.

A Walk through Micah

After the superscription in 1:1, Micah divides into four distinct portions.

Micah 1:1–3:12: Threats Against Samaria and Jerusalem

Micah 1:1 records a familiar superscription, dating the prophet's activity to the reigns of Jotham, Ahaz, and Hezekiah of Judah. It also puts us on notice that this is a rural prophet, coming from the little town of Moresheth about 20 miles southwest of Jerusalem. We also hear that Micah spoke not only against Judah, but Israel as well.

Micah 1:2-7 opens the book with an oracle of doom

that depicts God as a divine warrior, descending to earth to wage war against the wicked and unjust. Remarkably, Micah signals the depth of God's poor regard for all Israel by naming not only Samaria as a false place of worship, but Jerusalem as well, calling it nothing more than a "high place" (v. 5). For their iniquities both cities will be laid waste, and nature itself will wreak havoc on the kingdoms (vv. 4, 6).

Micah then uses the next section (1:8-16) to lament the fate of specific places, producing a series of puns (clear in Hebrew, but not in English) on the names of those loci (vv. 10-15). First, though, the prophet declares that he will go barefoot and naked as a sign of mourning for the soon-to-be-devastated cities (vv. 8-9). Thus the section closes fittingly with a call to the inhabitants of the two nations to make themselves bald, another aspect of the mourning rite.

Micah 2:1-11 offers a sustained indictment of Israel's social injustices. Echoing Isa 5:8-12 and Amos 8:4, the first two verses of ch. 2 indict the practice of the rich taking land in payment for debt. Because of this injustice God plans a punishment that will bring down the haughty and reduce them to wailing and lamentation. God will take away from them the power to "cast the line by lot," to acquire title to new lands (2:3-5). Micah then castigates the prophets who preached weal in the face of woe and cautions those who spoke the truth (vv. 6, 11; cf. Isa 30:10; Amos 2:12), expressing as well a further indictment of those who dispossess the poor of their land and well-being (vv. 7-10). Announcing quite suddenly on the heels of this stinging denunciation a future restoration of the remnant of Israel, vv. 12-13 seem to be a clear example of exilic or postexilic editing.

Micah 3 is devoted to indicting the officials who have overseen the plundering of the land by the elites and to announcing in the bitterest terms the inevitable destruction of their capital cities. Verses 1-4 take on the rulers of the nations, accusing them of nothing short of cannibalism and promising them nothing but God's wrath. Verses 5-8 then attack the prophets who speak words of assurance and comfort in the face of all the evidence to the contrary, promising them also a day of reckoning to come. The chapter closes with Micah offering up one

last blistering attack on rulers, prophets, and priests, mocking their confidence in God's favor, and finally promising that Zion itself will be plowed under, made into nothing more than a heap of ruins (vv. 9-12). (Note that the long wait for the fulfillment of this last prophecy famously had to be explained by Micah's successor in Jer 26:18-19 as the result of Hezekiah's repentance in response to Micah's words of warning.)

Micah 4:1–5:15: Proclaiming Israel's Restoration and Glorious Future

This lengthy section is thought by many to come from someone other than Micah. (For more on that question see "Critical Issues" below.) Whatever its origin, it constitutes one of the best-known parts of this book.

Micah 4:1-5 looks forward to Jerusalem's adoration by all the nations as the one true place to worship the one God, the God of Israel. Reiterating Isa 2:2-4, vv. 1-3 include the anticipated declaration of all peoples that they should flow to Zion like living waters to embrace the one God and that they will one day turn their weapons of war into farming implements to join in the labor of making the promised land produce its fruit. Micah 4:6-8 expresses the breadth of God's embrace, declaring that even the lame and cast off will be included in this new kingdom of which Jerusalem will be the crown jewel. In 4:9–5:1 the prophet contrasts the present suffering from imperial attacks (including Babylon in v. 10!) with the glory to come in Israel's restoration. The passage closes, however, on a negative note, observing that for the time being even the ruler of Judah is under constraint, subjected to the rod of the oppressor (5:1).

The closing admission in the prior section is the prompt for the famous prophecy of a shepherd king for Jerusalem (5:2-6; cf. the New Testament texts that read the prophecy as anticipation of Jesus, Matt 2:6; John 7:40-43). Born in Bethlehem (cf. Gen 35:19; Ruth 4:11; 1 Sam 17:12), this king will tend the nation as a shepherd tends a flock, and he will defend against the ravaging Assyrians, should they come against the nation. After such an aggression against the kingdom the remnant will be a blessing to those who favor it and a despoiling lion to those who assail it (5:7-9; cf. Gen 12:2-3; Gal 3:8). When all is concluded, God will end war for Israel by destroying the tools of battle altogether, purify the land of idolatrous practices, and carry out vengeance against those who opposed Israel (5:10-15).

Micah 6:1–7:7: Renewed Oracles of Doom, Denunciations, and Laments over Israel

This new collection of complaints against Israel opens with an exemplar of the (covenant) lawsuit genre (6:1-8). Playing the role of God's attorney, the prophet summons

Israel, saying the Lord has an indictment for his people (vv. 1-2). Then the prophet reports God's complaint, asking how Israel could be so errant in view of his actions on their behalf in bringing them from Egypt through the leadership of Moses, Aaron, and Miriam (Exodus 13–15) and in making Balaam speak only blessing when he was commanded by Balak to curse Israel (Numbers 22–24). Then using their own words the prophet mocks the pseudo-penitents' sacrificial offerings (6:6-7), and, echoing Hos 6:6, Amos 5:24, and Isa 7:9; 30:15, he explains to them that what God wants from them instead is what they seem unwilling to give: justice, love of kindness, and humility before the Lord.

Micah 6:9-16 follows, declaring a kind of punishment for Israel in light of the judgment rendered in the lawsuit: because of their intolerable corruption of justice and their oppression of the weak and poor (vv. 9-12), as well as their following in the ways of the Northern Kingdom and its capital (v. 16a), the inhabitants of Jerusalem shall suffer hunger, thirst, loss of wealth, and crop failure in spite of their abundance (vv. 13-15), and they shall be the object of ridicule for God's true followers (v. 16b).

Micah 7:1-7 concludes this section with a renewed indictment of the nation's leaders, this time taking in even the best among them as well, suggesting that they are all akin to enemies laying in wait to ambush the unsuspecting with acts of injustice (vv. 2-3) or to brier patches and thorn hedges, impediments to those who would bear good fruit (v. 4). Micah's advice to the wise under such circumstances is to trust no one, not even your spouse or your child, your mother or your father or your in-laws. Look instead to the Lord and await his salvation (vv. 5-7).

Micah 7:8-20: God's Favor for Israel and Contempt for Her Enemies

The book of Micah closes with a startlingly positive prophecy. The section begins with a warning to the nations who have been used by God to humble Israel: do not gloat, for although Israel suffers rebuff under their rule, the nations will in turn be shamed by God (7:8-10). When that time comes, Jerusalem will be refortified in expanded form, and the old foes Assyria and Egypt will come to make obeisance, for their own lands will be fruitless on account of their misdeeds (vv. 11-13).

The prophet then calls upon God to act as a shepherd for the people, to restore them to good pastures of old, and to show them the marvels of the days of the escape from Egypt so that the nations cease their taunting and become as the unclean things, despised and full of dread for the God of Israel (vv. 14-17). Seeing this, the prophet observes that there is no god like the God of Israel who is merciful and compassionate (cf. Jonah 4:2; Exod 34:6; Neh 9:17; Ps 86:5; Joel 2:13). The prophet

concludes by addressing God directly, saying unequivocally that God will forgive sins and show faithfulness to Jacob and Abraham's descendants because of God's oath to them in the days of old (Gen 12:1-3; 15:1-21; cf. Exod 32:7-14).

Critical Issues in Studying Micah

In the case of Micah the standard critical issues of "who, when, and where" are somewhat complicated by the book's obvious editorial history. Few dispute the notion that 4:1–5:15 and 7:8-20 are in whole or in part from later hands. Also, 6:1–7:7 may just as easily have come from another prophet as from Micah. As a consequence, it is necessary to address first the issues associated with the book's compositional history. Then we turn to the standard critical issues.

The Compositional History of the Book of Micah

Scholars have long accepted the authenticity of Micah 1:1–3:12 as the prophet's own words, with the exception of 2:12-13, which does seem to reflect the exilic experience. But when attention turns to 4:1–5:15, the positive tone of most of it, and especially its favor for the line of David, have alerted careful readers to the possibility that it is not Micah's own speech. The prophet hardly can be seen as a fan of the monarchy, and his nearly unrelenting message of doom in chs. 1–3 seems impossible to reconcile with the upbeat vision of chs. 4–5. Thus many attribute this section entirely to exilic and postexilic authors. However, there are some indications that the core of these two chapters is from Micah. Depending on whether one allows Isaiah to have uttered Isa 2:2-4, quotation of it in 4:1-3 could be a sign of Micah's hand since he was a younger contemporary of the other prophet. Certainly the prophecy of strong defense against Assyria in 5:5-6 is suggestive of Micah's time, not the Exilic or Postexilic era. Thus it seems more likely that 4:1–5:15 is an "expanded Micah" accomplished by later editors of an existing testimony from the prophet himself.

The argument about 6:1–7:7 centers on the degree to which its content meshes with the certain Micah material in 1:1–3:12. The references to the Exodus and its major characters (6:3-4) and to Balak and Balaam (6:5) are startling inasmuch as Micah shows no evidence otherwise of knowing of the "national saga" we find in Exodus and Numbers. The well-known refrain in 6:8 to do justice, love kindness, and walk humbly with God is so reminiscent of Amos, Hosea, and Isaiah that some see it as a "stock phrase" from the prophetic tradition that could have been voiced by any prophet, let alone Micah. Other such indicators have led many to suspect the authenticity of this section. For all of that, though, nearly all commentators also agree that however one settles this question, the themes of the section are consonant with those sounded in Micah 1:1–3:12.

Finally, 7:8-20 is widely treated as postexilic in origin. Indeed, it echoes themes familiar from Psalm 137 and Isaiah 40–66, works widely believed to come from the Babylonian and Persian periods. The book's closing exhortation to God that he remember the oath sworn to the ancestors bespeaks a unilateralism not evident at all in the undoubtedly authentic Micah text of 1:1–3:12, a unilateralism that is nonetheless characteristic of some postexilic theological imaginations (e.g., Jonah).

Who Wrote the Book of Micah? When and Where?

It should be plain from the preceding section that the question of who wrote this book is complex and admits of no single answer. Micah himself surely contributed a substantial portion (most of 1:1–3:12 and perhaps parts of 4:1–7:7), though not as the written word, but as his oral speech delivered in the 8th century B.C.E. Subsequently followers of the prophet, or simply folks who appreciated his message, put some of his words into writing, and in the process added more oral material from other prophets, material that was coherent with Micah's speech and with their own time and conditions. Micah 6:1–7:17 may have developed under such circumstances. At a still later date — probably in the Exile and the Postexilic period — additional material was added to ch. 2 (vv. 12-13) and to the rest of the book to address the experience of exile and return and the disappointments and hopes entailed in both realities. Such additional material is most obvious in 7:8-20, but portions of 4:1–7:7 may also come from this period too.

The matter of where this book came together is also not so easy to settle. Certainly Micah was a Judean, and his earliest followers were also sure to be residents of the region as well. But the exilic additions to the book may just as easily have been inserted by exiles in Babylon as persons who remained in Judah (although the higher level of literacy among the exiles favors that locus). The postexilic additions seem certain to have been made in Judah, inasmuch as they reflect concerns for a restored Jerusalem.

Theological Themes in Micah

Because of its long compositional history, Micah is exceptionally rich in theological perspectives for such a brief book. Among the themes we touch on here are Micah's unstinting condemnation of social injustice, particularly as it was manifest in urban settings, and the book's expansive and diverse affirmation of God's steadfast mercy.

Micah on Social Injustice

As noted at the outset of our treatment of Micah, this prophet's aim in condemning social injustices in Israel was far broader than that of Isaiah or Amos, or even Hosea. The other 8th-century prophets were quick to condemn the lack of righteousness they discerned in leaders and economic elites. But Micah's critique takes on a slightly different edge inasmuch as he focuses so consistently on the two locations, Jerusalem and Samaria. His view of injustice locates a good deal of it in urban settings, whereas by contrast the rural people are not so guilty and can even be seen as the victims of the city dwellers' avarice (see, e.g., 2:3-5). That is not terribly surprising in that the wealthy landholders who grew rich by taking possession of real estate in payment for debt almost certainly sought safety in the city from those they treated so poorly in the land. In any case, as a consequence of this somewhat dichotomous (and probably equally inaccurate) assessment of the source of nearly all oppression, the prophetic concern for social justice has often been taken as God's favor for the "simple people" of the land over against the city dwellers and their (costly) sophistication.

Affirming God's Steadfast Mercy

While the historical Micah was clearly engaged in a vigorous campaign to announce doom for the oppressors in Israel and Judah, the book of Micah is nonetheless characterized by some of the most clearly hopeful passages from the 8th-century prophets. We see this especially in 4:1–5:15 and 7:8-20, along with the fragment in 2:12-13. Particularly significant is the breadth of the foundations for hope. In 5:2-6 we encounter a hope for the future that hinges on the emergence of a messianic king from Bethlehem, apparently a future Davidic ruler. But in 7:18-20 the good of the eschatological future lies in the fulfillment of God's promises to the ancestors, Abraham and Jacob. Two more disparate bases for future hope could hardly be named.

Another profound aspect of God's mercy in the book of Micah is the quality of the future envisioned by its author(s). Micah 4:1-3, echoing Isa 2:2-4, looks forward to the day when war will be no more and weapons will be made into farm implements. Like Third Isaiah, the author also anticipates the self-subjection of the peoples to Israel's rule (5:7-8) and their dismay at their previous oppression of Israel (7:16-17). In all, then, the book's vision of the future is expansively hopeful in ways few of the other 8th-century prophets' books are.

Questions for Review and Discussion

1 How does Micah's prophetic speech match up with the oracles offered by his 8th-century counterparts Isaiah, Micah, and Hosea?

2 What roles did you learn cities and rural settings to play in Micah? How is this important in setting his oracles apart from his 8th-century counterparts?

3 What is the nature of this book's compositional history? Is it any more complex than that of most of the other prophetic books we have treated, and if so, what makes it so complex?

Further Reading

Ben Zvi, Ehud. *Micah.* FOTL XXIB. Grand Rapids: Wm. B. Eerdmans, 2000.

King, Philip. *Amos, Hosea, Micah: An Archaeological Commentary.* Philadelphia: Westminster, 1988.

Rogerson, John W. "Micah." In *ECB,* 703-7.

Chapter 38

Nahum

Getting Started

1 Read through Nahum and try to record an outline of its development.

2 What nation is the object of God's wrath in this brief prophetic book? Which nation is conspicuous by its absence as a target of God's wrath, especially given our experience of the preceding prophetic books?

3 In regard to the last question, which prophetic book is this one most like of those we have read to this point?

Preliminary Comments

This brief book, like Obadiah, is limited in its scope to condemnation of a foreign nation. Dating to some-time around the defeat of Nineveh (613 B.C.E.), Nahum stands in sharp contrast to the book of Jonah by either anticipating or describing with relish the fall of the mighty imperial power's renowned city Nineveh. As such the book strikes a rather solitary, triumphalist theme.

A Walk through Nahum

A Reading Guide to Nahum divides into two clear por-tions. After a title for the book in 1:1, 1:2–2:2 encom-passes a hymn to the divine warrior and oracles of doom for Nineveh interspersed with declamations concerning the advantage Judah gains from Assyria's demise. The remainder of the book, 2:3–3:19, describes in vivid terms the ruin of Nineveh.

Nahum 1:1–2:2: A Hymn to the Divine Warrior and Prognostications of Nineveh's Doom

The superscription in 1:1 is brief and unfortunately at points rather opaque in its terms. The verse reads, "An oracle concerning Nineveh," and further describes what follows as "the book of the vision of Nahum of Elkosh." From this we learn that what follows is a single oracle — a claim that is only partly true, as the book contains in fact several oracles — and that Nahum, the one who spoke the oracle, received it as a vision. We also learn that Nahum is from Elkosh. Regrettably, the location of Elkosh is unknown.

The hymn to the divine warrior follows in 1:2-9. The first part of the hymn, 1:2-3a, is a striking revision of the classic description of God provided in Exod 34:6-7 (and, among others, in Jonah 4:2!). The Lord *is* slow to anger, but when he does grow angry, he is "jealous and avenging," "wrathful," quick to take "vengeance on his adversaries" and to "rage against his enemies"; and though he is long patient, he is also "great in power" and "will by no means clear the guilty." On the basis of this substantial remodeling of the divine personality, Nahum launches into a description of what God's wrath entails: God uses nature itself to reshape the world to the detriment of his enemies (1:3b-5; cf. 2 Sam 22:8-16 and Ps 18:7-15). As a result they cannot stand before his anger, which is like fire for them but a stronghold for those he favors (1:6-8a). As a consequence God can be trusted to make a full end of his adversaries, so why plot against such a formidable power (1:8b-9)?

The remainder of the first half of the book is a series of oracles that alternate between predictions of doom for Nineveh and words of exaltation for Judah at the prospect of its deliverance from Assyrian vassalage. Nahum 1:10-11, 14; 2:1 are three brief oracles announcing God's judgment against Nineveh and Assyria and the impending doom that the empire and its crown jewel could anticipate. By contrast, 1:12-13, 15; 2:2 predict Judah's freedom from Assyrian oppression; especially notable is the language of 1:15, which, invoking "the feet of one who brings good tidings, who proclaims peace," is echoed in Isa 40:9 and even more explicitly in Isa 52:7.

Nahum 2:3–3:19: The Devastation of Nineveh

This part of the book begins with a dramatic description of the offensive against Nineveh (2:3-9). A terrifying sight, the warriors of God are clothed in blood-red, the same color as their shields, and their chariots and horses glisten and bristle with the metal accoutrements of war. They dash through the city and its squares like lightning, mustering the surprised and disoriented officers to battle (2:3-5). As a consequence, the waters of the Tigris River's tributary, the Khosr, overflow dangerously into the city, threatening even the palace; thus the city is evacuated as it floods and the conquerors plunder its treasures (2:6-9).

Nahum interrupts the account of the sack of Nineveh with a taunt. Satirizing the way of the lion, the symbol of the Assyrian Empire (see p. 300 for a relief displaying the lion of Assyria), 2:10-13 announces that even lions quake at the appearance of God's hosts. Even though the lion has secured plenty for his pride and filled his den with riches, God will cut off the prey from the lion of Assyria, leaving it destitute, unable anymore to announce conquests and success.

The account of the sack of Nineveh concludes in 3:1-3. Describing the aftermath of victory over Nineveh, the prophet's vision continues with a "woe" for Nineveh. Her booty is so rich that the plundering army can hardly see to the end of it, and as they continue to dominate the city,

all one can see and hear are the sounds of the "military machine" (horses and chariots and the soldiers they carry) and the heaps of bodies almost as endless as the city's booty.

The remainder of the book is a series of taunts against Nineveh in the wake of her destruction. Nahum 3:4-7 likens Nineveh to a prostitute, describing in painful detail her public shaming (cf. Ezekiel 16; 23:1-4). Next 3:8-13 recalls the Assyrian defeat of the Egyptian capital Thebes in 663, announcing that Nineveh is no better or stronger and that therefore she too will befall the horrible fate her own armies inflicted on the Egyptian city. Then 3:14-17 mocks the greatness of Nineveh and her legendary military and commercial might: she might prepare for the attack of her foes, but it will be of no use, for her armies are like plagues of locusts and grasshoppers, ravaging for a time, but evanescing quickly when their time is up. The book closes with the prophet making a taunt over Nineveh that almost takes on the tone of a lament, only to conclude with unmitigated joy at the city's fall: her leaders are asleep and her people are dispersed, there is no balm for the affliction Nineveh endures, and at that the peoples clap for joy, seeing the oppressor oppressed.

Critical Issues in Studying Nahum

The traditional questions of date, place, and authorship are mildly contested in the study of the book of Nahum. Also of interest is the degree to which this book expresses God's wrath for non-Israelites and completely sidesteps critique of Israel and Judah, a factor that suggests Nahum, whoever he may have been, was somehow connected to court prophecy.

The Date, Provenance, and Authorship of Nahum

The date of the book is, in general terms, not difficult to determine. As noted above, the oracles of Nahum clearly presuppose the imminence of Nineveh's fall, or its recent destruction. Thus a date around 613 is assured. But is this a book that anticipates that event or recalls it? Obviously the placement of Nahum on one or the other side of that event is determined by how one assesses the book's rhetoric. There is, in fact, little agreement on the issue since Nahum gives little indication one way or the other. The remaining anxiety is that the prophecy was announced and recorded at a much later date for several conceivable alternative contexts as an expression of God's allegiance to Israel over all other foes. There is no way, however, to be certain that this was not the case.

The book's provenance is likewise relatively clear if it is dated close to the events it reports, but less obvious if we accept the possibility that it may have been com-

Assyrian king Ashurbanipal hunting lions, which were common to the region and survived there until the nineteenth century c.e. Alabaster relief from Ashurbanipal's palace at Nineveh. (Trustees of the British Museum)

posed much later for a different context. Assuming that it was related closely to the fall of Nineveh, its composition in Judah seems certain. Beyond that, though, there is the problem of the hometown of the prophet. He is reported to be from "Elkosh" (1:1), a locus completely unknown to modern readers. On this matter too we are forced to remain uncertain.

As for the book's authorship, some are naturally suspicious of the very existence of the prophet to whom the words of the book are attributed. His name, Nahum, means "comfort" or "comforter," hardly a surprising moniker for a prophet who delivers an oracle assuring Israel of God's just revenge against Nineveh and vindication of God's chosen. Adding to the suspicion about the prophet's identity — indeed, his existence apart from a literary construct — is the mysterious character of the hometown he is given by the superscript. As a consequence we must remain uncertain on this matter as well.

The Social Location of the Prophet

Whoever was responsible for the oracles in the book of Nahum, one thing can be said for certain: he did not follow the pattern of the earlier prophets in condemning not only foreign nations, but the people of Israel as well. This figure has no corrective to offer to Israel, only vitriol for Nineveh and its horrifically brutal imperial policies. This observation has given cause to suspect that the book records the speeches of a "court prophet," someone who was in the employ of the king and his governmental structure. If this is so, "Nahum" stands in sharp contrast to Isaiah, Jeremiah, Micah, Hosea, and Amos. Indeed, many of them seemed inclined to criticize such

prophets as the one seemingly responsible for the book of Nahum! Jeremiah's conflict with Hananiah in Jeremiah 28 is the classic expression of this sort of tension between "official prophets" and the unaffiliated figures we encounter in persons like Jeremiah or Amos.

Theological Themes in Nahum

The divine personality who emerges from the book of Nahum is in some respects quite unusual in relation to the God presented by the other preexilic prophetic works we have surveyed. Here God's emotions are strong — and violent in their expression — and even God's mercy for Israel seems framed largely in terms of aggression toward those who have violated Israel. Thus the God who rises from the pages of the book of Nahum is unusually one-sided, an executor of violent and final justice without much regard for nuance and with none for mercy.

It is worth noting that this sharply defined portrait of the divine did not languish on the pages of this book, never to appear again in Jewish or Christian imagination. It turns up again in early Jewish and Christian apocalyptic and is especially evident in Revelation 17–18, where the fall of Rome is regarded with the same sort of glee we find in the words of Nahum.

Questions for Review and Discussion

1   What was the nature of Assyrian imperial policy that made it such a tempting target for Nahum's vitriol?

2   When do we think this book was composed, and why was its author engaged in the issues addressed by the oracles it contains?

3   What sort of theology arises from a reading of Nahum? Is it counterbalanced by any of the other prophetic books we have read thus far?

Further Reading

O'Brien, Julia M.. *Nahum, Habakkuk, Zephaniah, Haggai, Zechariah, Malachi.* Nashville: Abingdon, 2004.

Robertson, O. Palmer. *The Books of Nahum, Habakkuk, and Zephaniah.* NICOT. Grand Rapids: Wm. B. Eerdmans, 1990.

Rogerson, John. "Nahum." In *ECB,* 708-710.

Habakkuk

Getting Started

1   Read Habakkuk 1:2–2:5. How might you characterize this passage from the standpoint of its genre? Who are the characters featured in this passage, and what is the nature of their relationship?

2   Notice the language of Habakkuk 2:4. Does this verse echo anything you know from the New Testament?

3   Read Habakkuk 3. How does this passage relate thematically to 1:2–2:5? Is there consonance of dissonance between the two passages?

Preliminary Comments

Habakkuk was active between Josiah's death and the first conquest of Judah by the Neo-Babylonian Empire (609 to 597 B.C.E.). He was a contemporary of Jeremiah. Habakkuk agreed with the better-known prophet that Babylon was God's chosen instrument for punishing Judah and that Babylon would in time receive its due recompense from God as well. But Habakkuk differed from Jeremiah in also giving voice to the sure and certain complaint of many in Judah: "Is this experience just? Where is God's justice?" God's response is that all will be balanced in the end and that in the meantime the "righteous live by faith" in God's promises.

A Walk through Habakkuk

A Reading Guide to Habakkuk divides it into a superscription (1:1), a dialogue between the prophet and God (1:2–2:5), five taunting woes against Babylon (2:6-20), and a poem that gives voice to the reason for hope in the face of the impending catastrophe that looms over Judah (ch. 3).

Habakkuk 1:1–2:5: A Dialogue between God and the Prophet

The dialogue between God and the prophet is divisible into two parts: 1:2-11 and 1:12–2:4. The first part begins with the prophet laying out his complaint in unequivocal terms: "O Lord, how long shall I cry for help, and you will not listen?" (1:2a); how long will "the wicked surround the righteous?" (1:4b). Assuming that the wicked of whom Habakkuk speaks are fellow Judahites, the divine reply in 1:5-11 is only partly good news: God will arouse the Babylonians as an instrument of punishment for the wicked. The description of the advancing Babylonian forces recalls the language other prophets used to describe the former imperial power, Assyria. The armies of Babylon are fierce, their horses are swifter than leopards, their horsemen fly like eagles on the make, and they fear no power. They will bring down the wicked through their wholesale destruction of Judah.

The second part of the dialogue begins with Habakkuk's response to the divine reply: it is not in any way satisfactory! Describing first God's eternal and steadfast character which ordinarily assures believers of God's opposition to treachery and injustice, the prophet observes that nonetheless present circumstances suggest God is in fact unconcerned about the suffering of the righteous at the hands of those who are wicked (1:12-13). It is as if God has made people like the fish of the sea, ready for harvest by avaricious fisherman. Thus the enemy has his way with God's righteous ones, exulting in his conquests as a fisherman rejoices in his catch (1:14). There is no end to the enemy's conquests without mercy (1:15-17). Demanding therefore an explanation of the uncertainty of God's justice, Habakkuk takes up his post to await God's answer to his complaint (2:1). God's answer comes quickly: the prophet should write plainly for all to see that at the appointed time God will make right what seems wrong; that in the meantime the righteous should live by their faith in the steadfastness of the God of Israel (but see "Critical Issues" below for further discussion of this key phrase); and that the arrogant wicked ones of the present will receive their own just reward as well (2:2-5).

Habakkuk 2:6-20: Five Taunting Woes

The mood of the oracles shifts from this give-and-take between God and the prophet to woes directed against the nations. It seems likely that not all of the woes are attributable to Habakkuk; some were certainly uttered by other prophets against other nations than Babylon (e.g., Assyria, and perhaps the Macedonians), and their diversity suggests that the book underwent redaction at a time later than the prophet's own activity. In any case, they give broader expression to the prophet's disdain for oppressors, evident already in his dialogue with God in 1:2–2:5.

After an introduction that makes clear the woes are equally taunts (v. 6a), the first woe begins with language directed against economic oppressors (vv. 6b-7), hearkening back to the prophet's concern for injustice committed between members of a single nation-state. But as the woe concludes in v. 8 it is quite apparent that the greed condemned in vv. 6b-7 applies to a nation in its relationship with other nations. The same may be said with varying degrees of accuracy of the second, third, and fourth woes in vv. 9-11, 12-14, and 15-17. Each begins by condemning avarice, violence, or drunkenness that is costly to one's neighbor and then (more

or less) "globalizes" the image to apply the charges to nations, not individuals or communities. The final woe, though, focuses on a different theme, that of idolatry (vv. 18-19). It ridicules those who worship stone or wood deities as deluded fools. The concluding verse of the unit states, on the other hand, the positive to the negative of idolatry (v. 20): "the Lord is in his holy temple; let all the earth keep silence before him!"

Habakkuk 3:1-19: The Prayer of Habakkuk

The prayer of Habakkuk is less an oracle than a psalm that the final editors likely imported as a source, a suggestion supported by the liturgical instruction that marks the beginning of it (3:1). It begins fully in vv. 2-3a with the description of the divine warrior and his origin from the south (a vestige of earliest Israelite imagination, paired perhaps with the sense that the people and their God came up from the south after the Exodus; cf. Deut 33:2; Judg 5:4; Ps 68:7-8). It continues in vv. 3b-7 to describe the effect of the divine warrior on nature, a sure sign of his power. The poem next offers a lengthy description of the Lord's defeat of the enemies of the divine (vv. 8-15). Again, images from nature are used to communicate the power of the divine warrior: his anger is directed against rivers and sea (opponents of the divine warrior in Canaanite myth), he causes the mountains to writhe at the sight of him, and the sun and moon respond to the Divine in acts of honor. In the end the enemy is defeated utterly. The psalm concludes with the prophet acknowledging his own awe at the prospect of the divine warrior's intervention (v. 16) and an expression of confidence that, even though present circumstances might still fall short of what is hoped for, he is certain of God's justice in the end (vv. 17-19a). In a further indication that the psalm was a source for the book's editors is the closing liturgical instruction, "To the choirmaster: with stringed instruments" (v. 19b).

Critical Issues in Studying Habakkuk

In addition to the question of the book's date and provenance, surely the most compelling to the modern reader's imagination is the meaning of the heart of God's response to Habakkuk in 2:4. As we see below, the grammatical problems associated with the verse raise questions that remain largely unresolved.

The Date and Provenance of the Book of Habakkuk

While the range of proposals for the book's date has in the past been quite considerable, more recently a consensus has justifiably formed around a date in the early period of the Neo-Babylonian Empire. Along with the general tone of the book, the reference to Chaldeans in 1:6 is the primary evidence in favor of a Neo-Babylonian date, and the concern to address the impending onslaught of Babylonian power suggests the later part of Josiah's reign or, more likely, that of Jehoiakim or Jehoiachin. The location for the book seems obvious: Jerusalem and, more generally, Judah. The prophet's concern for the fate of Judah is evident especially in 2:1-5 and ch. 3.

Habakkuk 2:4: What Does It Really Mean?

While Habakkuk 2:4 was unequivocally clear to St. Paul as he wrote to the Romans and the Galatians (Rom 3:28; 5:1; Gal 2:16; 3:11, 24; see, by contrast, Jas 2:24), the Hebrew of the text leaves some confusion as to its original intent. The first half of the verse, "Look at the proud!" uses a difficult word for "proud" — indeed a *hapax legomenon* (single occurrence in the Hebrew Bible) — and the verse is imbalanced, providing no corresponding fate for the "proud" to the one assigned to the righteous, that they would live (by faith). For all of that, it seems most likely, given the passage that follows in 2:5-20, that the "proud" refers to Babylon, the "righteous" to Judah, and that the fate of the proud would be to fall (in time).

Theological Themes in Habakkuk

The singular theme of this book is the "balance" of God's judgment in favor of the people of Judah, God's chosen. While the prophet gives voice to the fact that God uses Babylon as a tool to chastise Judah, he also makes bold to question the justice of this. For his trouble he receives a reply that makes clear, in spite of the difficulties with 2:4, God's plan is ultimately to vindicate Judah. Thus the picture of God's justice in the book

is "balanced," much as it is throughout the prophetic corpus, between delivering punishment to the people for their disobedience and working weal for them as God's chosen.

Yet what sets Habakkuk apart, perhaps, is the boldness of the prophet's claim against God. He has no hesitation in questioning God's justice to evoke the answer he receives. That courageous move also permits this book another distinction, that of providing perhaps the most concentrated expression of the recurring prophetic notion of God's justice.

Questions for Review and Discussion

1   What is the evidence that Habakkuk was active in the Neo-Babylonian period? Without the mention of Chaldeans in 1:6, what alternatives might there be to this date?

2   How would you compare Habakkuk with the figure we became acquainted with in the book of Job?

3   Why do we suggest that the book of Habakkuk is a particularly concentrated expression of prophetic views of God's justice?

Further Reading

Gelston, Anthony. "Habakkuk." In *ECB*, 710-14.

O'Brien, Julia M. *Nahum, Habakkuk, Zephaniah, Haggai, Zechariah, Malachi*. Nashville: Abingdon, 2004.

Robertson, O. Palmer. *The Books of Nahum, Habakkuk, and Zephaniah*. NICOT. Grand Rapids: Wm. B. Eerdmans, 1990.

Chapter 40

Zephaniah

Getting Started

1   Read Zephaniah 1:1–2:3. What is the theme of this section of text, and where have you encountered it before in our survey of the prophetic books?

2   Read Zephaniah 2:4-15. How is this passage similar to material in Amos?

3   What do the passages you read to answer the first two questions indicate about the date of this work, especially given your experience so far with other prophetic books?

Preliminary Comments

Another very brief prophetic book, Zephaniah is notable especially for its evocation of the Day of the Lord theme, as well as for its series of oracles against the nations that parallels a similar pattern in Amos 1:2–2:16. Probably datable to the early part of Josiah's reign, some of the book anticipates the Deuteronomic reforms.

A Walk through Zephaniah

A Reading Guide to Zephaniah divides it into three major portions: 1:1–2:3 invokes the theme of the Day of the Lord; 2:4-15 announces oracles against the nations, concluding with Israel; and 3:1-20 turns first to an oracle against Jerusalem and then to oracles of salvation.

Zephaniah 1:1–2:3: Superscription and the Day of the Lord

The genealogy of the prophet that begins the superscription to this book (1:1) is somewhat complex, but perhaps necessarily so, as its author seems intent on ensuring the reader's awareness that Zephaniah is a descendant of Hezekiah, a reforming king of Judah. After the genealogy the superscription concludes with the regnal formula we have seen at the beginning of other prophetic books (a formula that may indicate, as noted earlier, that these were gathered together by a Deuteronomic collector). The regnal formula in this case sets the prophet in the reign of Josiah, conspicuously the next reforming king of Judah after Hezekiah!

The ensuing section, 1:2-6, is not explicitly connected to the Day of the Lord; but inasmuch as 1:7-18 embraces two oracles of the Day of the Lord, it seems a good bet that the destruction envisaged in these verses can be connected, at least from a recipient's perspective, to the Day of the Lord. In any case, the devastation predicted by this oracle is utter and complete, using the cosmic language of the creation narrative in Gen 1:2, 20-26. In fact, it describes an exact reversal of what God accomplished in creation, undoing the making of humans, animals, birds, and fish.

Zephaniah 1:7-13 next describes the Day of the Lord as an act of sacrifice on God's part: he will seek out the transgressors in the various parts of Jerusalem — particularly officials, given the language of the passage — and offer them up, attacking especially those who attribute to God no real power to shape their destiny in any way (v. 12b). A second oracle pertaining to the Day of the Lord follows in 1:14-18, likening it to divine warfare that brings utter and complete annihilation.

The section closes with a call to repentance (2:1-3) that at first glance seems to echo Deuteronomic language we also saw in such texts as Amos 5:4. However, the Hebrew verb for "seek" here is different from the one that typically appears in Deuteronomic texts, so it is not so clear that we have in this text clear evidence of a Deuteronomic redaction (to go along with the superscription).

Zephaniah 2:4-15: Oracles against the Nations

In a manner very similar to what we find in Amos 1:2–2:16, Zephaniah gathers together oracles against a series of nations. The people west of Judah — the Philistines of Gaza, Ashkelon, Ashdod, Ekron — are named first as ones to be dispossessed by a "remnant of the house of Judah" (2:4-7). In vv. 8-11 attention turns to the people east of Judah, including the Transjordanian people of Moab and Ammon. A single verse treats a single people to the south, the Ethiopians (v. 12), and in the final oracle against a foreign nation Assyria and its capital city, Nineveh, come in for the most extended prediction of destruction (vv. 13-15). While this series of oracles lacks the poetic structure that governs the one in Amos 1:2–2:16 ("for three and for four . . ."), it does match Amos's care in moving rather methodically around the environs of Judah.

Zephaniah 3:1-20: An Oracle against Jerusalem and Oracles of Salvation

Just as Amos turned attention to Israel at the end of his series of oracles against the nations surrounding the Northern Kingdom, Zephaniah, having completed the circuit around Judah, delivers an oracle condemning Jerusalem (3:1-8). Zephaniah condemns the city for its failure to trust in God and for the injustice of the officials of the city, including judges, prophets, and priests (vv. 1-5). He announces God's previous assistance to Judah and Jerusalem and the failure of the people to respond with respect

Khirbat al-Mudayna al-'Aliya, Iron I site on the eastern frontier of ancient Moab, surrounded by a huge defensive wall and tower. Periodically in conflict with Judah, Moab was at the time of Zephaniah a vassal of Assyria. (Photo by Reuben G. Bullard, Jr.; courtesy Bruce Routledge, Moab Marginal Agricultural Project)

and honor for God, and so reports God's plan to pour out his anger and indignation on the errant (vv. 6-8).

As soon as the oracle against the people is complete, the mood of the books shifts radically to speak of salvation and renewal. After disciplining the people, says Zephaniah, God plans on restoring them in marvelous ways. The oracle begins by announcing the removal of the rebels from Judah's midst and the exaltation and consolation of the remnant that was faithful (vv. 11-13). Following is a song that revels in God's vindication of Israel; in it God acts as king and warrior to deliver and protect the people (vv. 14-18a). The book closes with what is likely a postexilic addition (on this, see "Critical Issues" below) that anticipates the return of exiles to Judah (vv. 18b-20).

Critical Issues in Studying Zephaniah

The identity of the prophet, to which the complicated superscription draws particular attention, is one issue that has fascinated scholars (although without any definitive outcome, as we see below). The date of the book and the elements that seem to contradict that date — and so suggest a compositional history that extends beyond the prophet himself — have also drawn their share of attention. Finally, we have already noted in passing a further interesting feature, the echoes of Amos in Zephaniah, a feature that points toward the possibility of a "master" redactor of the Minor Prophets.

Identity of the Prophet and Date, Provenance, and Composition of the Book

The idea that Zephaniah is from royalty is suggested by the genealogy that opens the book in 1:1a. Tracing the prophet's lineage back to a Hezekiah suggests to some readers the reforming king known from 2 Kings 18–20 and the book of Isaiah. However, even though the name is unusual, it seems certain that the editor or Zephaniah himself would have acknowledged explicitly his royal lineage. That some Hebrew manuscripts of the book read Hilkiah where the majority read Hezekiah does not help much. Thus in the final analysis it seems best to admit that we do not know much more about the prophet's identity than what the genealogy and the content of the book suggest.

The superscription plainly sets the prophecy in the days of Josiah's reign. As for when in his reign the prophet was active, the condemnation of officials of various sorts in 3:3-5 indicates the pre-reform period of Josiah's rule. At the same time, some elements of Zephaniah's own thought are reminiscent of Deuteronomic reforms, suggesting either later redaction of the book or perhaps Zephaniah's own sympathies with that perspective. Indeed, we already saw in Chapter 11 that Deuteronomy and its basic theological outlook were almost certainly known, and perhaps even promoted by some adherents, well before Josiah instituted his reforms. Zephaniah may have been a sympathizer with the incipient movement. This suggests not only a Josianic-era date, but it adds substance to the otherwise obvious indications of a Jerusalem provenance.

Having said all of that regarding date and provenance, it is still necessary to acknowledge the presence of some passages that strongly indicate a compositional history for the book that extends beyond Josiah's reign. Most obvious are the last three verses of the book that anticipate an ingathering of exiles and return to Judah. The first motif recalls Isa 58:6 and the second echoes Isa 62:10. Thus, like many of the other prophetic books we have covered, this one too seems to have undergone at least some editorial adjustments from later hands.

Echoes of Amos in Zephaniah

While we already know that the repetition of elements of one prophetic book in another is not all that unusual (e.g., Mic 2:1-2 recalls Isa 5:8-12 and Amos 8:4), the echoes of Amos in Zephaniah are striking. We noted already the cycle of oracles against the nations in 2:4-15 that follows a similar geographical pattern established in Amos 1:2–2:16. In addition, 2:1-3, like Amos 5:4-6, 14-15, calls abruptly for repentance, only to return nearly as quickly to themes of judgment that eventually lead to condemnation for Judah. These are striking resemblances. Yet there are also substantial differences, just as one would expect given that we are dealing with two different prophets. All the same, the similarities leave some justification for wondering if Zephaniah knew the book of Amos. But more likely, the similarities point to a late redactor of the Minor Prophets who, where the opportunity presented itself, shaped the works of the individual prophets in ways that echo one another. We shall have occasion to return to this possibility as we draw our survey to a close in examining Haggai and Zechariah 1–8, as well as Malachi as the last book in the collection.

Theological Themes in Zephaniah

We need say little more about Zephaniah's theological import than to recall the work of his near contemporary, Habakkuk. Like the latter prophet, Zephaniah acknowledges the righteousness of God's wrath for Judah due to its leaders' injustice and impurity. Also like Habakkuk, Zephaniah understands the way God uses the nations to serve his purposes but also disciplines them in time. Finally, like Habakkuk, Zephaniah understands God's justice to be balanced in favor, ultimately, of the chosen people: after their just punishment, God will restore them through the faithful remnant to greatness and favor.

Questions for Review and Discussion

1   How does Zephaniah use the theme of the Day of the Lord in his prophetic speech? How is this similar to and different from other uses of the Day of the Lord in prophetic traditions we have encountered?

2   What are the similarities between Zephaniah and Amos, and how might we best account for them? What do they suggest about the Minor Prophets as a collection of books?

3   What sort of theology arises from a reading of Zephaniah? How is it similar to any prophetic books we have already encountered?

Further Reading

Gelston, Anthony. "Zephaniah." In *ECB*, 715-17.

O'Brien, Julia M. *Nahum, Habakkuk, Zephaniah, Haggai, Zechariah, Malachi*. Nashville: Abingdon, 2004.

Robertson, O. Palmer. *The Books of Nahum, Habakkuk, and Zephaniah*. NICOT. Grand Rapids: Wm. B. Eerdmans, 1994.

Chapter 41

Haggai

Getting Started

1 Begin by reading all of Haggai. What does your reading indicate was the issue the prophet sought to address?

2 Can you tell from the book whether the prophet was successful in getting the people to respond to his request?

3 In Haggai 2:20-23 the prophet seems to be responding to another concern separate from the one he addresses throughout the rest of the book. Can you make out what concern among the people he was addressing with this brief oracle?

Preliminary Comments

Haggai is a small book, but the impact of its words was measurably significant in its day: they helped bring to completion the construction of the Second Temple. As such Haggai, and the closely related material in Zechariah 1–8 (see Chapter 42), reveal a sharp refocusing of the prophetic office in the Postexilic period. While prophets from the 8th century to the Exile were

regularly critics of the temple cult and its personnel and of secular officials, these prophets were allies of the sacerdotal officials and their institutions and partners in securing the good governance of Judah as a Persian imperial holding.

A Walk through Haggai

The book of Haggai consists of five sections dated by day, month, and year in the reign of Darius of Persia, placing the oracles in 520 B.C.E. (cf. Zech 1:1, 7; 7:1).

Haggai 1:1-11: Oracle of Judgment against the People

The first oracle, dated to "the second year of King Darius, in the second month, on the first day of the month" (August 520), acknowledges the troubled conditions the returnees experienced in postexilic Judah (1:5-6, 9-11). The description reads like a financial analyst's sketch of a depressed agrarian economy: people work hard for a harvest that is undercut by natural disaster and brings such insufficient return that hunger and thirst persist, and inflation is so robust that those who earn wages feel as though their pockets have holes. The oracle also explains the cause of all of this: it is God's displeasure at the people's failure to rebuild the temple while they are quite content to expend large sums to build their own "paneled" houses (vv. 2-4, 7-8). The reference to paneled houses is telling: it suggests very labor-intensive construction, thus the expenditure of considerable sums at least among the economic elites, those whose capital would have been required to support the temple building project.

Haggai 1:12-15a: The People's Response
Next we hear that the prophet was successful. His admonition brought action from the people as a whole, and especially from two key returnees: Zerubbabel, the heir of David, and Joshua, the heir to the high priesthood. Together they apparently were key to overseeing and promoting the temple's reconstruction with satisfactory results. Note that this oracle's date comes at its conclusion in 1:15a.

Haggai 1:15b–2:9: Oracle of Encouragement
This oracle came in October 520, probably during the Festival of Booths. Haggai is called to announce to Zerubbabel, Joshua, and all the people that even if the new temple (or its beginnings — it is unlikely that it was completed by this time with an August start!) seemed but a shadow of the first temple, God would see to it in time that the promises made so long ago would be fulfilled: through God's intervention the treasures of the nations would flow to the temple and fill it with splendor so that its glory would exceed even that of Solomon's temple.

Haggai 2:10-19: A Further Oracle of Encouragement
This passage begins with another date formula (December 520) and a request for a legal ruling from the priests regarding the communicability of holiness and impurity: the answer Haggai receives indicates that only impurity is transferable from one object to another, thus even consecrated things contacted by impure things become impure by touch (2:10-14). It seems possible that Haggai is making an oblique objection to those who remained uncertain about the temple's reconstruction, arguing instead that the reconsecrated open-air altar on the temple site (cf. Ezra 3:1-7) was sufficient for their

use. In the alternative, the reference to "this people" and the impurity of their sacrifices in v. 14 may focus this critique on those who had remained in Judah during the Exile, whose religious practices were rejected by the Persian-authorized returnees. (For more on this, see "Critical Issues" below.)

In any case, the passage continues with Haggai observing that ever since the laying of the new foundation stone for the temple (cf. Ezra 3:10-13) the local economy had improved considerably, proving Haggai's opening argument that God's disappointment in the people's failure to rebuild the temple was the cause of their suffering (2:14-19).

Haggai 2:20-23: Oracle of Salvation
The closing oracle came on the same day as the preceding oracle. Haggai is instructed to speak to Zerubbabel to tell him that God will one day intervene in history to restore Zerubbabel to the throne of David and to eliminate all opposition — the Persians and their imperial policy — to such an event. In announcing this Haggai articulates a reversal of Jeremiah's outburst against Jehoiachin, saying that God would remove him from power as a signet ring from his hand (Jer 22:24-30); in restoring Zerubbabel the signet ring will be replaced, and the Davidic line will be restored.

Critical Issues in Studying Haggai

The questions of when this book was created, who wrote it, and why it was composed are easily answered: the oracles were delivered in 520 by the prophet Haggai (named in Ezra 5:1; 6:14), largely in order to see to the temple's reconstruction. Issues worthier of our consideration include explaining why the temple's reconstruction could have been delayed so long and what Haggai's true attitude toward the royal line was, given Persian policy against subject peoples enjoying monarchic rule.

Why Was the Temple Not Yet Rebuilt in 520?
When one remembers that the people had begun to return to Judah beginning in 538 and that Persian imperial policy required the construction of a temple, sacrifice in it, and thereby the collection of adequate revenues for the empire, it is surprising that in 520 Haggai is still required to exhort the community to undertake the construction effort. How could the people have delayed so long?

One factor that delayed the temple's reconstruction was surely the conflict between the returnees and the people who had remained in the land. We learned from

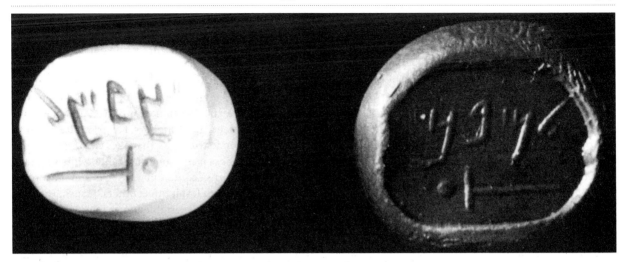

Ezra 4:1-5; Neh 4:7-8 that there was some tension between the parties, with the returnees rejecting the help of the remnant in the land because they were unclean by virtue of their syncretistic practices that developed over the period of the Exile. This discord apparently led to obstructionism on the part of some in regard to rebuilding efforts. It is also possible that some among the returnees who possessed the resources necessary for rebuilding were more interested in spending their resources on themselves; indeed, 1:4 seems to say just that. Still others may have seen the temple's restoration as fiscal foolishness, as it would provide a place from which the priests could work more effectively in collecting their portions of sacrifices made at the reconsecrated altar and gathering the taxes the Persian Empire required of Judah to permit its continued religious autonomy.

But why did Persia not descend upon Judah to correct what must have seemed a very serious problem relative to revenue collections? As it turns out, the empire was embroiled in its own difficulties that essentially made it possible for lands on the periphery of the imperial holdings to be lax, even rebellious, with little consequence. After Cyrus passed from the scene one of his more notable successors, Cambyses, took the throne in 529. Because Cambyses' domestic policies in the empire's homeland offended the nobility upon whom emperors relied for legitimacy, Cambyses was compelled to remain at home for much of his reign to guard against a *coup d'etat*. When he finally did venture out in 522 to act as an imperial power should — to expand his holdings — he was murdered and his rule overthrown at home, leading to chaos throughout the empire and full-scale rebellion by the peoples it had subjugated. Only when Darius rose to power and began violently and quite successfully to put down the revolts in 521 did it seem absolutely necessary for subject

Seal "belonging to Mibneh," and impression (Shechem, late 8th–early 7th century B.C.E.). A seal might be worn as a signet ring to symbolize political authority. (Joint Expedition to Shechem; photo L. Ellenberger)

peoples to play by the imperial rules. Thus it seems likely that Judeans finally had a sense of urgency about the temple's reconstruction that had been lacking for a variety of reasons until then.

Haggai on The Restoration of the Davidic Monarchy

Haggai 2:20-23 is often read as proof that Haggai was a proponent of restoring the Davidic monarchy. Indeed, in reversing Jeremiah's prophecy that God would remove Jehoiachin as a "signet ring," he does anticipate Zerubbabel's elevation to the throne. However it is also plainly the case that Haggai sees this as an act of God; the first person speaker who will cause cosmic changes to overthrow other powers in favor of Zerubbabel's rule is God. Thus Haggai does not anticipate human action to bring about the rule of a king, but awaits — and encourages awaiting — the intervention of God to make that happen. On this reading Haggai supports the restoration of the monarchy, but only according to God's will, not the will of the people who might wish it to happen sooner. This prepares nicely for the innovation Zechariah sought to establish, a transfer of secular power over Judah to priests, in keeping with Persian imperial policy.

Theological Themes in Haggai

The theological themes in the book evolve from Haggai's desire to see to the rebuilding of the temple.

Because he uses the troubled economy in postexilic Judah as evidence of God's displeasure over the failure to rebuild the temple, and in doing so attributes to God the wrathful use of natural forces, Haggai especially reinforces the notions of God's retributive justice and God's special control over nature, topics well known from Deuteronomy and the larger Deuteronomic tradition. Because he reflects the interests and perspectives of the returning priestly class, he gives expression to the Priestly theological perspective as well.

Haggai and the Deuteronomic Tradition

In his eagerness to compel communal compliance with respect to reconstructing the Jerusalem temple, Haggai was more than willing to bring the longstanding Deuteronomic tradition of God's retributive justice to bear. In 1:1-6 he cites the people's preoccupation with their own paneled homes as the cause of God's displeasure and concomitant prevention of economic prosperity. In 1:7-11 Haggai sharpens the attack, observing that God expresses his annoyance by restraining nature's assistance in bringing bounty from the land. Likewise, because the people have resumed their efforts on behalf of the temple, Haggai observes that God has already begun to restore the land's prosperity (2:18-19). These passages recall not only the general Deuteronomic favor for God's retributive justice but also the specific traditions in Deuteronomy especially that refer to God's use of nature to afflict the faithless. For example, the Deuteronomic curses in Deut 28:38-44 play especially on God's control over nature as a tool for dealing with those who fail in their covenant obligations. In all of this Haggai evinces his appreciation of what we know to be the Deuteronomic tradition and what he surely knew as the book of Deuteronomy and perhaps also the history that upholds its theological perspective, the Deuteronomistic History in Joshua to 2 Kings.

Haggai and the Priestly Tradition

At the same time, Haggai's obvious affiliation with the temple and its officials mark him out as an early proponent of the postexilic Priestly theology. Especially telling is the ruling he requests and receives from the priests. Their understanding of holiness and impurity echoes the Priestly tradition we observed in Genesis, Exodus, Leviticus, and Numbers. For example, the complex legislation in Numbers 19 makes clear the Priestly view that holiness is not communicable, while impurity — especially corpse contamination — is and must be carefully dealt with lest it infect others. Just so, Haggai's deep interest in reestablishing a temple building to house the priests and serve as their base of operations betrays his close affiliation with Priestly theology and its larger religious imagination.

Questions for Review and Discussion

1   What was Haggai's principal concern, and was he successful in evoking the people's response to his pleas?

2   What was Haggai's view of the recurring hope for a restoration of Davidic rule, and how did he express that view?

3   How does Haggai's vision reflect any of the theological perspectives we have already identified in the Old Testament?

Further Reading

Meyers, Carol L., and Eric M. Meyers. *Haggai, Zechariah 1–8*. AB 25B. Garden City: Doubleday, 1987.

Petersen, David. *Haggai and Zechariah 1–8*. OTL. Philadelphia: Westminster, 1984.

Rogerson, John W. "Haggai." In *ECB*, 718-20.

Chapter 42

Zechariah

Getting Started

1   Survey Zechariah 1–8, noting especially the date formulas that introduce the oracles. How do these link this part of Zechariah to the book of Haggai?

2   Read Zechariah 6:9-15 carefully. What does this oracle suggest was Zechariah's chief concern?

3   Survey Zechariah 9–14. Does this material appear different in tone at all from the first part of Zechariah and the book of Haggai? If so, what differences do you notice?

Preliminary Comments

As we see below, Zechariah is actually at least two, if not three, different works. The first part reports the dated oracles of Haggai's colleague and contemporary, Zechariah (cf. Ezra 5:1; 6:14). The rest of the book reflects much later circumstances in postexilic Judah. What holds the book together is focus on the postexilic world.

A Walk through Zechariah

As noted Zechariah divides into two to three parts.

Zechariah 1–8: Dated Oracles of the Prophet Zechariah

The first oracle, 1:1-6, is dated to 520 B.C.E., perhaps after Haggai's last oracle. In what seems to many to be a redundant speech, Zechariah reminds the people of their failure to heed the "former prophets" and that as a result God has judged them harshly. But the speech is not redundant, since it sets the stage now for a new set of warnings and an exhortation to heed them, lest a similar fate befall the people.

The second oracle is actually a set of visions in 1:7–6:15 that involve an interpreting angel and the prophet (as well as some related material). The set is dated to the early months of 519 (1:7). The first vision is of a horseman on patrol over the earth and the announcement of the return of weal to Jerusalem (1:7-17). The second vision of four horns and four smiths (1:18-21) alludes to four great powers that oppress the people (the horns) and the foes who smash those powers (the smiths). The third vision is of a surveyor who measures Jerusalem for its complete reconstruction, using dimensions echoing those provided in Ezekiel 40–48 (2:1-5).

Intervening between the third and fourth vision is a separate oracle that urges exiles to return from all their places of dispersion to the Promised Land, for God prepares to afflict the nations for their oppression and bring others to the people's side as fellow believers in the Lord God (2:6-13).

The visions resume in 3:1-10. Here the prophet sees a person, rather than having a vision interpreted to him by the angelic guide. In this case, the prophet witnesses the appearance of the high priest, Joshua, in the heavenly court. Satan, one of the heavenly councilors, accuses Joshua of being impure (see p. 170 for a survey of Satan in the Old Testament). The response of the angel of the Lord is to have Joshua stripped of his "filthy" (dung-covered!) garments and reclothed in priestly garments, but also a "turban." The Hebrew word for turban, *tsanif*, occurs only a few times in the Hebrew Bible, as a simple headband for a man (Job 29:14) or women (Isa 3:23), but also as a king's crown (Isa 62:3; see also Sir 11:5; 47:6; in Sir 40:4 it appears in reference to a priest). The ambiguity of the term, its absence in other descriptions of priestly garments and its occurrence in a work that was likely nearly contemporary with Zechariah (Third Isaiah) is suggestive. Add to that the vision's closing words of the angel of the Lord where he mysteriously refers to the advent of the "Branch," a Davidic figure (3:8; see Isa 11:1), and one is set to wondering if perhaps the priest is being invested with a new sort of authority, akin to that provided ordinarily to kings. Moreover, earlier in the vision the angel of the Lord grants Joshua access to the heavenly council (3:7), also a royal privilege in light of ancient Near Eastern notions of divine kingship.

The following vision in 4:1-14 advances the developing case for heightened power in priestly hands. The prophet is shown a 49-candlepower lampstand, suggesting the surplus of blessing that comes with the arrangement about to be introduced (one normally expects a 7-candlepower lamp). Next to the lampstand are two olive trees that represent Zerubbabel, the returnee heir of David, and Joshua, the high priest, and from them comes the oil that fuels the lamp. Zerubbabel is named as the founder and builder of the temple. Then the angel closes the vision with the solemn words, referring to the two olive trees, "These are the two anointed ones who stand by the Lord of the whole earth" (v. 14).

The sixth vision, in 5:1-4, is of a flying scroll of huge dimensions, the significance of which is not particularly clear. That it contains only prohibitions of theft on one side and of swearing falsely on the other side suggests to some that the purpose of such great space is that the words can be read by anyone. Others note that the dimensions are those of the porch in Solomon's temple (1 Kgs 6:3); what the significance of that might be is equally unclear. In any case, the scroll travels about as a sort of "account settler," entering the homes of thieves and those who bear false witness in order to consume them.

The seventh vision is much less opaque (5:5-11). A woman named "Wickedness" travels in a basket out of Judah and to Babylon. The implication is clear: God purifies the Promised Land and pollutes the old oppressor of God's people.

The final vision, recalling the first, is of four chariots pulled by unusually colored horses (6:1-8). The chariots seem to reflect God's emissaries who patrol the earth with God's power, and one in particular is assigned to take up residence in "the north country," Babylon, again as a sign of God's control.

After the final vision comes a historical appendix in 6:9-15. It records Zechariah communicating God's instructions to the leaders of the returnee community to make a crown of silver and gold. It is placed on the head of Joshua, the high priest, and he is called the Branch and the builder of the temple

Lampstand *(menorah)*, with shophar and incense shovel, stone relief from the Byzantine-period synagogue at Qatzrin in the Golan Heights. (Phoenix Data Systems, Neal and Joel Bierling)

(contradicting the fifth vision in 4:1-14). Then, however, the text mentions a "priest by his throne" and "peaceful understanding between the two" (6:13). As for the crown, it is apparently removed and placed in the care of the community leaders. There are many difficulties in this passage, not the least of which is the fact that the Hebrew text actually reads throughout "crowns," not "crown" in the singular. Likewise, the mention of "two of them" in v. 13 puzzles most interpreters. Some have drawn from these hints the conclusion that the original text included Zerubbabel (and that he was granted a crown as well) and has somehow fallen out of the text. Another possibility, of course, is that the passage marks the transfer of royal authority to the priest Joshua and a second crown was held in reserve for the would-be king who otherwise is unmentioned. There were certainly reasons, as we shall see, for avoiding any overt mention of a royal pretender under the watchful eyes of Persian rulers.

Zechariah 7 contains a priestly reply to a question about fasting in the fifth and seventh months, namely whether the people should continue to do so as they did during the Exile. The answer comes in the form of language recalling that of the 8th-century prophets, who pointed out that ritual without proper intent is useless and that indifference to God only produces God's wrath. Chapter 8 then shifts in mood to express the promises of God to Jerusalem, suggesting, as does much of the book, that it is only through God's action that weal can return to the people of restored Judah.

Zechariah 9–14: Two Oracles
As we noted above, the last part of Zechariah stands separately from chs. 1–8. This part divides further into two titled oracles in chs. 9–11 and 12–14.

The first oracle is a collection of poetic speeches about the Day of the Lord. Its theme echoes what we have seen already in Amos, Joel, and Obadiah, to name a few. Included are oracles against Israel's neighbors (9:1-8), a prediction of a coming king (9:9-10; the inspiration for Matt 21:5-7), a passage about revenge for Judah against its enemies (9:11-17), a chapter on how the people are restored by God from their dispersion among the nations and their experiences of oppression (10:1-12), a promise that tyrants should one day fall (11:1-3), and an oracle about a failed shepherd of the people who is replaced by God's choice of a good shepherd (prophet) (11:4-17).

Zechariah 12–14 begins with the title that marked the beginning of ch. 9: "an oracle." Like chs. 9–11, this material is quite disparate, although the unifying theme seems to be the advent of the Day of the Lord. Zechariah 12:1–13:6 indicates that Jerusalem will express regret over its sin and be cleansed of its idolatry. Then follows

a separate oracle that is messianic in character (13:7-9); it speaks of the shepherd being smitten for the sake of the sheep (and quite naturally turns up in the Gospels at Matt 26:31 and Mark 14:27). The book then concludes with a long description of a final war and victory for God and God's people and the vindication of Jerusalem (14:1-21). The language of this section is evocative of a wide range of passages from earlier portions of the Hebrew Bible.

Critical Issues in Studying Zechariah

Clearly a most pressing issue for scholars has been the relationship between Zechariah 1–8 and 9–14. Also of interest to us is the attitude in Zechariah 1–8 toward priests and royalty.

The Relationship between Zechariah 1–8 and 9–14
As we noted above, Zechariah 1–8 is best read in conjunction with Haggai. The two oracle headings in 1:7 and 7:1 are identical in form to those that we saw in Haggai, and a prominent theme treated by Zechariah, the proper power of priests, is a natural follow-up to the concerns expressed in Haggai that the temple be rebuilt. Both initiatives responded to the Persian Empire's demand that priests have charge over imperial territories and that there be operating cultic centers where exchange could take place and taxes could be collected.

Zechariah 9–14, on the other hand, seems much later and seems to reflect some of the later frustrations with disappointed hopes in postexilic Judah. It is also more closely tied to the last book of the Old Testament, Malachi, inasmuch as the superscription for that book is identical with the heading given to Zechariah 9–11 and 12–14: "an oracle." Thus some speculate that Zechariah was originally but chs. 1–8 and that the remaining material somehow belongs with Malachi. We shall return to this in our brief treatment of Malachi to follow. In any case, the relationship between the two parts of Zechariah seems clear: they are, indeed, two *separate* parts.

Priests and Kings in Zechariah 1–8
We noted in our survey of Zechariah 1–8 that several passages contend with the question of priests and Davidic heirs in postexilic Judah. The first, 3:1-10, seems already to hint at increased power for the high priest in the Postexilic period: invested with a turban that may be royal in its implications and given access to the heavenly council, Joshua certainly seems to take on royal traits in this passage. Chapter 4, with the vision of two

olive trees next to the lampstand, and the decree that Zerubbabel, heir of David, would see to the rebuilding of the temple, suggests a certain sharing of power and a peculiarly royal responsibility for the temple, the home of the priests. But then, to confuse matters even more, 6:9-15 recounts the creation of a crown (or crowns?) and the placement of a crown on Joshua's head, with no mention of Zerubbabel. Moreover, Joshua is called the "Branch," a messianic title apparently given to Zerubbabel in ch. 4, and Joshua is deemed the rebuilder of the temple, again contrary to ch. 4.

Together these confusing elements have prompted some to suspect that Zerubbabel was included in 6:9-15 and that he was proposed as a new Davidic ruler of Judah, but when Persian imperial attention made this a dangerous prospect, he was expunged from the text. The problem is that there is no real textual evidence for this view; instead we must rely on our speculation about why the text appears as it does and *insert* Zerubbabel where it is no longer is!

An alternative view is that, while the details remain murky, the three passages work to legitimate for the returnees priestly rule in place of royal rule. Those who still yearned for an independent Judah under the firm guidance of a Davidic king surely were tempted by Zerubbabel's presence, and may even have resented the power granted to the high priest by Persian policy. Thus Zechariah's visions and historical reports confirm that God is in league with Persian policy, that God wishes the people to submit to sacerdotal governance. It is even possible to read the plural "crowns" in 6:9-15 as a concession to those who yearned for a Davidide to return to power: the second crown was for the future king, and it would be there when the time was ripe (cf. Hag 2:20-23).

Theological Themes in Zechariah

Like Haggai, Zechariah seems clearly rooted in Deuteronomic and Priestly traditions. Also like Haggai, the prophet had to contend with David-Zion theology and its abiding power over the people's imagination. We have already addressed the latter topic, and so we treat here the other two in quick order. We also address the implications of the two books, Haggai and Zechariah 1–8, for understanding the religious life of the postexilic Judean community.

Deuteronomic and Priestly Influences on Zechariah?

All of Zechariah, not just chs. 1–8, is imbued with an appreciation of the power of God's retributive justice. Clearly, wide-ranging aspects of chs. 1–8 are based on an appreciation of that theological perspective, and

the use of the Day of the Lord in chs. 9–14 leaves little doubt about that section's embrace of the theme. More interesting is the degree to which the Priestly tradition, as we know it from the Pentateuch, was influential on this author. The vesting of Joshua in Zechariah 3 echoes Leviticus 8, but not exactly so, and the general interest in priestly power never leads to a naming of Aaronites as the privileged altar priests. As a result, one is left with the sense that Zechariah and the Priestly Writer shared common interests but were not necessarily writing and speaking from the very same fund of traditions and thought patterns.

The Temple-Centered World of Haggai and Zechariah

Our survey of these two prophets' work should leave little doubt about where religious practice and theological imagination were concentrated in postexilic Judah: in the temple and its priestly leadership. The implications of this intense focus on the power of the priesthood and the centrality of the temple certified that postexilic Judaism would express itself in many ways through ritual. Liturgy, the "work of the people" through the agency of the priests, was central. Thus we can imagine that the old question of whether practice engenders belief or belief engenders practice came to be pertinent for these people, as it remains pertinent for present generations of Jews and Christians. New Testament developments prove that the question was on people's minds.

Questions for Review and Discussion

1 What is the relationship between Haggai and Zechariah 1–8? What is the relationship between Zechariah 1–8 and 9–14?

2 What theological trends from earlier in the Hebrew Bible are evident in Zechariah? Do they appear across both parts of the book?

3 What was the consequence for religion and theology of the postexilic concentration on the temple and the priesthood?

Further Reading

Meyers, Carol L., and Eric M. Meyers. *Haggai, Zechariah 1–8*. AB 25B. Garden City: Doubleday, 1987.

Petersen, David. *Haggai and Zechariah 1–8*. OTL. Philadelphia: Westminster, 1984.

Rogerson, John W. "Zechariah." In *ECB*, 721-29.

Chapter 43

Malachi

Getting Started

1   Read through Malachi, observing its chief concern. What do you see that to be?

2   How does Malachi's central concern relate to those taken up in Haggai and Zechariah 1–8?

Preliminary Comments

As we noted in the previous chapter, the book of Malachi begins with the same title that we find beginning Zechariah 9–11 and 12–14. In spite of that close connection, though, the theme of Malachi is more closely related to the interests of Haggai and Zechariah 1–8. But here we encounter no rosy outlook on the temple and the power of sacrifice to make things right with God, nor do we find a loving embrace of priests and their leadership. Malachi sees, instead, horrible corruption in these and condemns it roundly, for in the final analysis he *does* share with Haggai and Zechariah a deep appreciation of the power of sacrifice, the temple, and the priesthood to support the good of the people.

A Walk through Malachi

Appearing at times rather disparate, Malachi does possess some unifying themes evident even in a brief outline of its contents.

Malachi 1:1-5: Superscription and Opening Speech

The book opens with a superscription that repeats the simple title, "an oracle," that appears in Zech 9:1; 12:1. Then vv. 2-5 answers the plaintive question from the people, "How have you loved us?" with God reminding them of the favor shown to Jacob over Esau. This small section participates in the larger tradition of "damning Edom" for the sake of Judah. The author argues quite simply that the histories of Judah's fate and Edom's fate should make clear God's favor for the people.

Malachi 1:6–2:16: The Infidelity of Priests and Laity

The first part of this section, 1:6–2:9, is a long attack on corrupt priests. They pollute the sacrifices and the altar in the Lord's temple by replacing the pure beasts brought by worshippers with blind and lame creatures from the temple flocks. As a result, their efforts on behalf of laypeople only offend God. Thus the Lord decides to eradicate the priests, smearing the dung of their offering on their faces that they might suffer its fate, to be burned outside the city gates in the local garbage dump (Exod 29:14). Then the prophet recalls the Lord's covenant with Levi, the father of the priestly line, echoing Num 25:10-13 and Deut 33:8-11, to show how the current priesthood has violated the covenant not only in impure sacrifice, but also in false instruction. Then 2:10-16 explicitly addresses marriage outside the community and divorce, but most think that, following the previous passage on the infidelity of the priests, this one refers also to the people's apostasy; just as the religious leaders are unfaithful to God, the laity are too.

Malachi 2:17–3:5: The Coming Day of Judgment

Malachi 2:17–3:5 then announces the coming of judgment, which will be ushered in by a messenger (3:1; see also Matt 11:10; Mark 1:2; Luke 1:17, 76) who will also refine the "descendants of Levi," apparently to purify the priesthood for a return to proper sacrifice. With that in place, God will at last draw near for judgment. The targets of God's wrath will include adulterers, those who swear falsely, those who oppress hired laborers, the widow, and the orphan and mistreat the sojourner, and last of all, those who do not trust the Lord. The last may be a cover term for other assorted sins.

Malachi 3:6–4:3: The Double-Sided Nature of God's Judgment, Twice Over

This section is normally divided differently. However, we see in it a twice-repeated double-sided description of God's judgment. In 3:6-7 the theme is set: from the beginning the children of Jacob have rebelled, yet not perished, so, says God, "Return to me, and I will return to you." Then 3:8-12 provides the first double-sided description of God's judgment. It begins with a question from the people, "How are we robbing you [God]?" God replies that their robbery comes in their failure to make a full tithe and complete offerings. The challenge that follows is that they should make a test of God's pledge to return to them if they return to God by fulfilling their tithes and offerings; then they will see the windows of heaven overflow with blessing as proof of God's steadfastness.

The second double-sided description of God's

judgment in 3:13–4:3 also begins with a question, "How have we spoken against you?" God repeats to the people their own claim that it is vain to serve God, that no profit comes from keeping his commandments. To this some who revered the Lord respond by recording themselves in a book as the ones who *do* trust God to respond to the faithful, and God announces that he will spare them on the day of judgment.

The section closes with a description of the day of judgment that entails the death of the wicked and the joy of the righteous (4:1-3). Together with 3:6-7 this passage serves to bracket the two double-sided descriptions of God's judgment.

Malachi 4:4-6: The Promise of a Forerunner

The book concludes with an admonition to remember the statutes and ordinances given through Moses, so that when Elijah comes to announce the day of judgment he will be able to turn the hearts of all people that they might escape judgment and curse.

Critical Issues in Studying Malachi

There are two issues we wish to address here. The first has to do with the place of Malachi in relation to Zechariah 9–14 and within the Minor Prophets as a whole. The second is the book's treatment of the priesthood, and in particular the notion of a covenant with Levi.

Malachi, Zechariah 9–14, and the Twelve

We have noted several times now that the book of Malachi and Zech 9:1; 12:1 all begin with the same single word, "an oracle" (Hebrew *massaʾ*). This has led some to suspect that Zechariah 9–14 and Malachi belonged together at one time and that for some reason Malachi was stripped away from its original locus to create a separate prophetic book. Further indication that this might be the case comes from the name of the prophet, Malachi. The word means simply, "my messenger," a rather prosaic personal name for a prophet! Some suspect that the name was created only to permit the formation of a separate book from Zechariah 9–14.

But why would anyone have undertaken such a strange surgical procedure on the biblical text? The answer most often given is that it accomplished for the creators of the Minor Prophets what their collection of prophetic books could not accomplish itself: division into 12 books to match the number of the tribes of Israel. Having said that, and admitting the attractiveness of the proposal on some levels, one is hard pressed to see other strong evidence of a similar interest in forming the collection of the Minor Prophets. Nor is it particularly clear why someone saw it necessary to match the number of tribes with the number of smaller prophetic books, especially since there are still three other prophetic books to contend with. Thus in the end we are left only to speculate on the meaning of these curious circumstances.

Attitudes toward the Priesthood in Malachi

Two passages in particular, 1:6–2:9 and 3:1-5, raise questions about this book's view of the priesthood. The first passage, as we have seen, is a long attack on the priests for their impurity and in particular their pollution of the people's sacrifices. In critiquing the priests Malachi reminds them of the covenant with Levi. We can only infer this covenant from a variety of passages. In Deut 33:8-11 Moses blesses the line of Levi with covenantal language and speaks of the instructional role of Levites as does Mal 2:6. The reference to a covenant of life and well-being in 2:5 also echoes Num 25:12-13, where God gives Phinehas (an Aaronite, if also a Levite!) a promise of eternal priesthood for his zeal on behalf of the Lord. We may also mention Jer 33:21 and Neh 13:29, which refer to covenants with Levites. All of these may have been in the speaker's mind when he made this claim. In any case, the reference to *Levi* — not *Aaron* or *Zadok,* the more common monikers for temple priests in the Persian period — suggests an antiquarianism on the prophet's part. The *true* and *good* priesthood is the *original* priesthood (over against Aaronites and/or Zadokites?).

The second passage of interest here is 3:1-5. The messenger who comes to prepare God's way for judgment "will sit as a refiner and purifier of silver, and he will purify the descendants of Levi and refine them like gold and silver, until they present offerings to the Lord in righteousness" (3:3). The reiteration of the title "descendants of Levi" is striking, and the focus of the messenger on preparing them in particular is even more arresting. The implication, of course, is that the prophet saw in the Levitical priesthood the people's salvation: with the offering of pure and upright sacrifice restored, the people's return could be assisted, if not also ensured.

Altogether, then, the evidence in the book of Malachi points toward an elevated view of the *Ur*-priest Levi and his true descendants and a desire to see them replace the corrupt priesthood that is, after all, assimilated to the dung of its sacrifices and its fate (2:3). It is well worth noting the echoes of Exod 32:25-29 in this passage. Recall that there the Levites were the ones who proved themselves zealous for the Lord, over against the obvious lack of purity exhibited by Aaron in the golden calf episode. Likewise, we would be remiss not to note that in later Jewish literature, from the Dead Sea Scrolls to the *Testaments of the Twelve Patriarchs,* there is a consistent theme of exalting Levi and his genuine descendants as the model of the priesthood. Malachi unquestionably participates in that tradition.

Theological Themes in Malachi

Two theological themes deserve attention here. First, we treat the mixture of Deuteronomic and Priestly thought in this short book. Second, we address its "theology of worship."

Deuteronomic and Priestly Thought in Malachi

While some of the language typical of the Deuteronomic and Priestly strands in the Pentateuch is present in Malachi, their influence is felt more clearly in the mood of the book as a whole. There can be no question that Malachi buys into the basic notion of a Deuteronomic outlook, that God rewards the righteous and punishes the wicked. The repeated emphasis in Malachi on God's judgment and the importance placed on being prepared to experience it assure us of this. What adds nuance to this emphasis is the significance attached to proper sacrifice as a component of being prepared and to the role pure priests play in ensuring proper sacrifice. This is a Priestly contribution to the theological imagination of Malachi. What this rather simple mixture of perspectives demonstrates is the degree to which the theological strands we have identified in the Hebrew Bible were *known* even before the Bible's closure as a canon and the fact that those strands had begun already to meld together in how they were received and reused. We would be foolish to think that the author of Malachi identified the perspectives united here as "Deuteronomic" or "Priestly." Rather, they were surely encountered together in the emerging Pentateuch, and from there they began to work together in the theological imagination of a Jew in Persian-period Judah.

The Theology of Worship in Malachi

Malachi is certainly not alone in the Old Testament in giving expression to a particular theology of worship, but it is perhaps of particular significance as the "final word" in the Old Testament canon.

While it would be tempting to see the theology of worship in this book as rather mechanical — pure sacrifices offered by pure priests produce good results for the worshippers — there is more to the story. Particularly, Malachi's anger against the priests for replacing pure offerings with blind and lame beasts from the temple flock (1:8) bespeaks a more sophisticated vision. What is at stake here is not reward and punishment, but rather simple contact with God above. The sacrifice of a pure offering draws God's attention to the worshipper and places the Deity and the human in touch with one another. To undercut that at all is what Malachi objects to so vehemently. The theology of worship here, then, is not just about "gift exchange" and benefits, but also using the experience of worship to come into communion with God. Malachi sets a standard that is respected often in the New Testament and in other early Jewish and Christian literature.

Questions for Review and Discussion

1   What, in retrospect, do you think was Malachi's chief concern? How does that relate Malachi to Haggai and Zechariah 1–8?

2   What are the theological influences on Malachi? How do you think they shaped his theology of worship as we just described it?

Further Reading

Carroll R., M. Daniel. "Malachi." In *ECB,* 730-35.

Hill, Andrew E. *Malachi.* AB 25D. Garden City: Doubleday, 1998.

Petersen, David L. *Zechariah 9–14 and Malachi.* OTL. Philadelphia: Westminster, 1995.

Chapter 44

Apocrypha, Pseudepigrapha, and Other Early Jewish Writings

Forming the Canon of the Old Testament / Hebrew Bible

Getting Started

1   Using a Bible that contains the Apocrypha or Deuterocanonicals, consult the table of contents. What are the names of the books that we have not covered so far in our study of the Old Testament?

2   What are some of the genres of the books that you identified in answering the last question?

Preliminary Comments

The books we have covered thus far — all part of the canon of the Old Testament or Hebrew Bible — do not include a further collection of books revered among Roman Catholics: the Apocrypha, or Deuterocanonicals. Beyond those books, still other Jewish texts from the ancient world vied at one time or another for a place of authority in religious imagination. In the following pages we simply name and introduce briefly the books of the Apocrypha and some of these other texts, which we call Pseudepigrapha.

The Apocrypha (or Deuterocanonicals)

The books of the Apocrypha as they appear in the Roman Catholic canon include Tobit, Judith, 1 and 2 Maccabees, Wisdom of Solomon, Ecclesiasticus, and Baruch (with the Letter of Jeremiah as ch. 6). There are also additions to Daniel and Esther. (We leave aside the Prayer of Manasseh and 1 and 2 Esdras, which appear as an appendix after the New Testament in Roman Catholic Bibles.)

Tobit is a Jewish novella from perhaps the 3rd century B.C.E. Set in the "Assyrian exile," the book tells the tale of a faithful Jew, Tobit, who nonetheless experiences terrible misfortune, only to see those difficulties overcome by the faithful action of his son, Tobias, who is assisted by God's angelic emissary, Raphael. Tobit is a story rich in implications for Jews living under threat, in foreign places, and in the context of faithful families.

Judith, composed sometime during Hasmonean rule, tells the story of a woman from the tiny Israelite town of Bethulia who was able to bring down the Assyrian army through a combination of faithfulness to her own traditions and deceit and treachery against the Assyrians.

1 Maccabees was likely written sometime in the late 2nd century B.C.E. during the Hasmonean period. It relates the early days of the Maccabean Revolt and its successes under several of the Maccabees. Although purporting to be a history of Maccabean/Hasmonean rule, it also clearly works very hard to show the soundness of the Maccabees' roots in Israelite and Jewish tradition.

2 Maccabees also rehearses something of the Maccabean Revolt, but it focuses in particular on the fortunes of the temple in Jerusalem, ending its account in 161 B.C.E. when the temple was once more firmly in Jewish hands and renewed in its activities. The book is usually dated to the end of the 2nd or the beginning of the 1st century B.C.E.

Judith with the Head of Holofernes, Hendrik Goltzius (ca. 1577). Judith, a wealthy and devout widow from Bethulia, deceives and beheads the chief general of Nebuchadnezzar's army. (Rijksmuseum Amsterdam)

Wisdom of Solomon is usually assigned to the Egyptian diaspora, perhaps Alexandria, and it dates to the 1st century B.C.E. and reflects a massive attempt to contend with the possibility of a "natural theology." It is clearly written to encourage an audience to remain firm in their traditions in spite of challenges from their non-Jewish neighbors. The author employs a wide range of Greek conventions and philosophical notions, but mostly to affirm the abiding benefit of Jewish faith in the face of pressures to conform to other options.

Ecclesiasticus, or *Wisdom of Ben Sira,* was composed by a Jewish school master in Jerusalem sometime before 180 B.C.E. His book was subsequently translated into Greek by his grandson around 130. The book resembles Proverbs because of its dominant genre — the proverbial saying — but it differs from the biblical book in assembling sayings in thematic groups. The author espouses a rather conventional wisdom that sees sensible action, guided by the Torah, as provoking God's blessings.

Baruch was probably composed sometime after the middle of the 2nd century B.C.E., although it is set in the Babylonian Exile and purports to be the words of Jeremiah's scribe of the same name. The first part of the book is a historical introduction (that is highly inaccurate!) and a corporate confession of sin for use by Jews making sacrifice at the remains of the altar in Jerusalem. The second part of the book is a pair of poems, one in praise of Wisdom and the other an address to Jerusalem regarding restoration. Its focus on confession of sin and restoration suggests Baruch was meant in large part to assist Jews suffering oppressive conditions. Appended to Baruch is the Letter of Jeremiah, a sermon against idolatry.

The *Additions to Esther,* usually interspersed throughout the biblical book in Catholic Bibles, come from the Greek tradition of Esther where various pious elements were added to the book, perhaps to overcome its otherwise apparently "secular" character (see Chapter 19 above). *Additions to Daniel* include at the end of ch. 3 a *Prayer of Azariah* and a *Song of the Three Jews.* The stories of *Susanna* and *Bel and the Dragon* appear as chs. 13 and 14 of the book of Daniel.

Pseudepigrapha, Dead Sea Scrolls, and the Writings of Josephus and Philo

In addition to the Apocrypha, still other Jewish texts from antiquity survive to this day, in spite of not having been included in the biblical collection. We call these Pseudepigrapha more out of habit than as a matter of accurate description. The term means "false writings" and implies something negative about these texts. In fact, the better way to define them is "noncanonical Jewish religious texts" from the "biblical era" (meaning the period during which the Old *and* New Testaments were composed). There can be no doubting that many of these works vied for inclusion in authoritative collections and might even have become part of the canon, given different circumstances in antiquity. As such they are not that different from what we have in the Old Testament and thus merit our attention as further evidence of Jewish religious imagination in the years of that religion's early development. We describe here only two of these, and we choose them in large part because they were apparently used as authoritative texts by a particular Jewish community, the Essenes (to whom we return below in our survey of the Dead Sea Scrolls).

Jubilees is a "retelling" of the biblical story, from creation to the escape of the people from Egypt and Pharaoh's army. It is a record of a revelation Moses received on Mount Sinai that augments the biblical account of Genesis and Exodus, focusing in particular on establishing a jubilee-based chronology of world history and placing in the ancestral period the origin of some of the Mosaic law, as well as other legal stipulations not otherwise known from the Torah. Most agree that *Jubilees* was composed sometime around the middle of the 1st century B.C.E. and that it may have been intended, among other things, to combat what some perceived to be a diminishing emphasis on Torah piety in the Hasmonean age. If the number of manuscripts of *Jubilees* found among the Dead Sea Scrolls (more than 20) is any indicator of its importance to that community, it was likely an authoritative text for the Essenes, the people of the scrolls (on the Dead Sea Scrolls and the Essenes, see p. 14 above, and further in Chapter 46 below).

1 Enoch is another Jewish text that did not make it into any contemporary canonical collection of Old Testament/Hebrew Bible books, but which nonetheless was deeply important to various Jews in antiquity, especially the Essenes. A vast apocalyptic work, *1 Enoch* is, in fact, a collection of five booklets dating from at least the 3rd to the 1st century B.C.E. The booklets are themselves composite and range from a "Book of the Watchers" (chs. 1–36), which depends in great part on the tradition of Gen 6:1-4, to "parables" of Enoch (chs. 37–71), to an "astronomical" book that deals with the calendar from the perspective of the heavenly bodies (chs. 72–82), to dreams of Enoch (chs. 83–90) and an "admonition" or "epistle" of Enoch (chs. 91–105). Two appendices, chs. 106–107 and 108, are added to the last booklet but are probably secondary. The attraction of this work for the Essenes — and surely other Jews of antiquity — was its revelation of heavenly secrets regarding the past, present, and future as God sees time

relative to the fate of God's chosen people, and especially the most righteous of God's chosen ones. In this sense it is one of the most important pieces of apocalyptic literature from early Judaism that remains to us.

The substantial manuscript evidence for both of them in the Dead Sea Scrolls suggests that *1 Enoch* and *Jubilees* were quite popular among the Essenes. But the Essenes kept still other texts, in addition to manuscripts of all the biblical books (except for Esther and Nehemiah, which may simply have perished with the passage of time and damage to the scrolls). They composed many of their own texts, among which we number the *Community Rule* or *Manual of Discipline,* a "charter document" for the community that provides the rules for living as an Essene and a particularly clear statement of the community's vision of reality, one that is highly dualistic and deterministic in character. Another text from Qumran from this category — which we label "sectarian" because they are texts the *sect* created — is the *War Scroll,* a vision of the battle between the forces of evil and the powers of God at the end of days. The *War Scroll* lays out the battle plans for that final war and reveals how angelic and earthly beings participate in the pitched conflict, one that resolves in favor of God's chosen. Yet another example of sectarian literature is the *Damascus Document,* another "community rule," but one that seems intended more for Essenes who do not live in separate community, but among other Jews.

In addition to sectarian and "biblical" texts, the Essenes also kept and/or produced much of the pseudepigrapha we already knew before the discovery of the Scrolls in 1947, including, as noted, *1 Enoch* and *Jubilees.* They also had manuscripts of Tobit and other books of the Apocrypha. The Essenes also preserved otherwise unknown "pseudepigrapha." These are works that scholars do not assign to the Essenes themselves, but that also have not appeared otherwise among the manuscripts that survive from antiquity and in the collections of various religious groups, who out of antiquarian or religious interests held on to ancient Jewish works like *1 Enoch* and *Jubilees.* These include such texts as *Aramaic Levi,* a document that apparently begins with a recollection of Genesis 34 where Levi and his brother Simeon violently avenge the rape of their sister, Dinah. It goes on to narrate Levi's prayer to God regarding the pollution in creation, the appointment of Levi to the priesthood in a heavenly vision and by his own father's commission, as well as instructions for sacrifice, a record of Levi's life history, and a speech by Levi in praise of wisdom. The exaltation of Levi in this work is indicative of the community's interest in a pure, renewed priesthood. Another text from this collection of "previously unknown pseudepigrapha" is *Pseudo-Jubilees,* which retells portions of Genesis and Exodus in ways that build on, but also expand, the *Jubilees* retelling of the same events. It should be noted that not all scholars agree that these and other such texts are necessarily "previously unknown pseudepigrapha" merely preserved by the Essenes. It is also possible that they are texts the Essenes composed themselves without inserting a great deal of their own peculiar language and thought that are so evident in the clearly "sectarian" texts.

The significance of the Dead Sea Scrolls from our perspective is the light they cast on a kind of Judaism that was present in the days of early Judaism and Christianity. From the Scrolls we learn a great deal about how Jews understood themselves in the days of Jesus and the beginnings of Judaism and Christianity as sister religions. The same can be said of the works of two other writers we cover here, Philo and Josephus.

Philo was a Jewish philosopher active during the 1st century C.E. in Alexandria. His extensive writings reflect an interest in clarifying the place of Judaism in the Greek world and, in particular, demonstrating the power of the Jewish vision in relation to the hegemony of the Greek vision. In essence Philo goes to great lengths to show the comparability — and perhaps superiority — of Jewish thought, the Torah itself, with Greek philosophy. For that reason his works present a terrific resource for examining the way at least one Jew negotiated being a Jew in a Hellenistic world. Indeed, his writings were almost exclusively focused on "exegeting" the Torah in light of Greek thought.

Josephus also casts important light on the era of early Judaism and Christianity. He was a Jewish historian who, after surrendering to the Romans in the war between Rome and the Jews (66-70 C.E.), became a sort of apologist for Judaism to the Romans. He wrote his *Jewish Antiquities,* a retelling of substantial portions of the biblical account, to provide a version of the biblical story more "accessible" to Roman literary and ideological sensitivities. He also wrote a book on the war between Rome and the Jews in which he had participated (*Jewish War*) to provide Rome with a more sanguine view of the role of most Jews in that sequence of events. In addition, Josephus wrote other apologetic works that have come down to us. Taken together his writings provide further insight on the way some Jews were imagining themselves in light of the emerging biblical traditions, especially as they faced the tensions of Roman rule.

Although this treatment of Jewish literature outside of the Old Testament has been all too brief, it should give our readers a sense of the flavor of these texts and of how they cast important light on the development of early Judaism, and even Christianity as well. A quick look back at even the few we covered here also shows their importance for demonstrating the very early practice of depending on the traditions that did make it into Jewish and Christian Bibles. But that observation raises a new question: just how did the books of the Hebrew Bible come to be accepted as canonical?

Column VIII of the Manual of Discipline from Qumran Cave 1. (John C. Trever)

Forming the Canon of the Old Testament/Hebrew Bible

While Chapter 63 in this book treats the formation of the New Testament canon at length, we devote briefer attention here to the canonization of the Old Testament/Hebrew Bible. (For a brief discussion of the meaning of the term "canon," see p. 9 in Chapter 2 above.) That should not be taken as evidence that the issue of the canon of the "First Testament" is much less complex than that of the "Second Testament." Quite the contrary, it is our admission that the issue is vastly *more* complex and that very little can be known with certainty regarding it!

Part of the reason the canon formation of the

Old Testament is so complex is its possession by two faiths. It is one thing to speak of the canon of the Old Testament and yet another thing again to speak of the canon of the Jewish Scriptures. As we saw in Chapter 2 above, the canons of Jews and Christians differ in their content and organization. Moreover, there are differences among the canons of various Christian communities as well. Thus the very question "Which canon?" is the first complicating factor in addressing this question.

More vexing to researchers, though, is the paucity of clear evidence for the canon formation process in the case of the Hebrew Bible/Old Testament. While Chapter 63 in this book rehearses a relative wealth of evidence from the early Christian period for the formation of the New Testament canon, rarely do we find such clear indicators from the ancient world regarding the formation of the Old Testament or the Hebrew Bible. As we see below, there are many passing references in ancient texts that have inspired much speculation on the matter, but very little solid evidence to go on. Only very late do we find Jewish and Christian writers giving us *lists* of books that are considered authoritative enough to be counted as "closed collections" to which nothing can be added and from which nothing can be taken. Before those lists, there are only hints on which scholars have built several theories. We turn now to a survey of the hints and the theories as a way of giving students some insight on this complex problem.

Indications of an Emerging Canon of the Hebrew Bible

Already within the period entailed by the completion of the books that *are in the Bible* we see the Torah beginning to exercise its influence on later religious imagination. Think only of how Second Isaiah of the Exilic era seems to have been influenced by the Yahwist traditions we know from the Pentateuch, or of the power the Deuteronomic and Priestly traditions held over the postexilic prophets Haggai, Zechariah, and Malachi. But the most frequently cited piece of evidence that the Torah had begun to take definitive shape and to influence the religious views of early Judaism is Ezra's famous declaration of the Torah to the people according to Nehemiah 8–9. Some go so far as to speculate that what Ezra read aloud was the Pentateuch as we have it now, more or less. Moreover, this same theory holds that the reading of the Torah — and essentially its elevation to canonical status — was mandated by the Persian governing authority as proof that the community had a "constitutional document" upon which all its members could agree. While this may not be the full extent of the story — and we most certainly cannot be sure due to the

paucity of evidence that remains to us — the account in Nehemiah 8–9, in any case, shows the emerging power of what we know as the Pentateuch.

Recalling also our discussions of "interpretive motifs" in the books of the Pentateuch, readers probably already see the further, obvious indications that a "canon" of the Torah was emerging very early on, well before the rise of the early Christian movement. The range of interest in elucidating the Pentateuch is also testimony to its emerging power. For instance, we saw a fascination with addressing such small, passing matters as the juxtaposition of two commandments in Lev 19:3, to "revere your mother and father and keep my Sabbaths" (see "Theological Themes" in Chapter 9), to a concern to meet head on the larger problems posed to the theological and moral imagination by such an account as the near-sacrifice of Isaac in Genesis 22 (see "Theological Themes" in Chapter 7). Moving beyond such specific instances, we also saw above that the major pseudepigrapha that contended for "canonical" status were themselves derivative of the Pentateuch in one way or another *(1 Enoch; Jubilees).*

As a consequence of these various indications most accept a relatively early date for the "scripturalization" of the Torah. That is to say, perhaps as early as the 5th century, and certainly by the late 4th and early 3rd centuries B.C.E., what we know as the Pentateuch or Torah had emerged as a sacred text, religious literature with authority over its readers and recipients. It functioned as "scripture" for people of faith. This is *not to say* that the Torah had achieved canonical status in the fullest sense of being set in all of its parameters.

We do not find such early, clear evidence that the Prophets, former or latter, or the Writings achieved scriptural status, let alone canonical status. One way to understand this, perhaps, is to view those books as "ancillary" to the Torah; as a consequence they did not serve as bases for exegesis and rewriting themselves, but only as aids to that process. Indeed, if we were to take a closer look at *Jubilees* we would see some evidence for this sort of "synoptic" reading of the Torah with other emerging books of the Bible.

This brings us to the famous, though ultimately ambiguous, earliest indicators of a tripartite canon. One of these is to be found in the Prologue to the Wisdom of Ben Sira (written by the author's grandson around 130 B.C.E.; see above).

> Many great teachings have been given to us through *the Law and the Prophets and the others that followed them,* and for these we should praise Israel for instruction and wisdom. Now, those who read the scriptures must not only themselves understand them, but must also as

lovers of learning be able through the spoken and written word to help the outsiders. So my grandfather Jesus, who had devoted himself especially to the reading of *the Law and the Prophets and the other books of our ancestors,* and had acquired considerable proficiency in them, was himself also led to write something pertaining to instruction and wisdom, so that by becoming familiar also with his book those who love learning might make even greater progress in living according to the law.

The two references to "the Law and the Prophets" and a third, less clearly defined category of books, have prompted some scholars to suggest that already in the second century B.C.E. there was a fully-formed tripartite canon such as we have in the Hebrew Scriptures today. But of course, the grandson provides no listing of the books he understood as belonging to the categories he names, nor does he say anything about the closed or open nature of the collections.

Similar sorts of references appear in a Dead Sea Scroll (4QMMT C 9-12) and a variety of other nonbiblical texts like those described above (2 Macc 2:13-14; Philo, *Contempl.* 3.25-28; *Mos.* 2.37-40; Luke 24:44; Josephus, *C. Ap.* 1.37-43; *4 Ezra* 14:22-48). But only in the 6th- to 7th-century C.E. Babylonian Talmud do we find an unequivocal *listing of books,* and then only a listing with no explicit provisions for exclusion or inclusion: *b. B. Bat.* 14b-15a reports that "Our Rabbis taught that the order of the prophets is Joshua and Judges, Samuel and Kings, Jeremiah and Ezekiel and the Twelve." The *baraita* also gives an order for the books of the Writings that places Chronicles last, after Ezra and Nehemiah. Interestingly, the passage is at pains to address the Prophets and the Writings but assumes the Torah's order to be known, suggesting that as late as the 7th century C.E. Jews were still wrestling over the order and list of books to be included in a *canon.* Otherwise it is hard to imagine why someone would have felt compelled to report this information!

Altogether, then, the evidence for the complete formation of a *canon* of the Hebrew Bible/Old Testament suggests it was a long and very open process, the contours of which we ultimately may never fully grasp.

Theories Regarding the Origin of the Hebrew Bible/Old Testament Canons

Not all would agree with our concluding statement to the previous section. Thus there has been no shortage of attempts to address the question of the Hebrew Bible's canonization. For the sake of simplicity, we suggest that there are two basic perspectives on this matter. Some, defining canon broadly as a *collection of authoritative*

("scriptural") texts, and relying in large part on the early references to a (supposedly) tripartite canon we listed above, argue for an early determination of the collection. Others, defining canon narrowly as a *fixed, closed collection of books,* argue that the collection remained open and fluid well into the early centuries of the Common Era.

Representatives of the first approach include Sid Leiman and Roger Beckwith. They assert that the 6th-7th century C.E. passage in *b. B. Bat.* 14b-15a reflects the division and ordering of the biblical books implied by the 2nd-century B.C.E. reference to "the law, the prophets, and the other books of our ancestors" in the Prologue to the Wisdom of Ben Sira (and they cite and discuss as supporting their views most of the other passages listed above).

The second approach to canon is exemplified in the work of Julio Trebolle, Eugene Ulrich, and James VanderKam. Holding to the narrower definition of canon as a *fixed, closed collection of texts,* these scholars see no clear evidence in the list of passages relied upon by Leiman and Beckwith for canon. Quite the contrary, they also observe the textual fluidity of the books that became the Bible among the Dead Sea Scrolls, as well as other signs that the Bible's precise shape remained undetermined, and conclude that the process leading to a closed, fixed collection of books continued for a very long time, well into the first part of the Common Era.

What is there to settle the difference between these two positions? Clearly, how one defines "canon" determines in part which view is preferred, and in that sense the two positions may not be so far apart, were they to share a common understanding of canon in the first place. But for our purposes, it is more important to note that the abiding disagreement merely confirms the fluidity of the question and the murkiness of the evidence. In the end, the most one can say reliably is that a long, involved process, far more complex than the limited evidence permits us to understand, eventually produced a closed, fixed collection of books called "Bible" among Jews and Christians. Yet the very fact that interpretation of those books began before their formation into a narrowly defined canon and continues to this day somewhat obviates the whole question anyway. Because people of faith continue to reflect on their relationship with God in light of *Scripture,* the *canon* is continually *reopened* to new vistas! As we turn to the New Testament now in our Introduction, it is worth noting that in some important respects this is exactly what it is, a rereading of many of the Scriptures of early Judaism in light of a singular event in human and divine history, the appearance of Jesus Christ, his teaching, and his death and resurrection.

Further Reading

Beckwith, Roger. *The Old Testament Canon of the New Testament Church and Its Background in Early Judaism.* Grand Rapids: Wm. B. Eerdmans, 1985.

Feldman, Louis H. *Josephus's Interpretation of the Bible.* Berkeley: University of California Press, 1998.

Harrington, Daniel J. *Invitation to the Apocrypha.* Grand Rapids: Wm. B. Eerdmans, 1999.

Leiman, Sid Z. *The Canonization of the Hebrew Scripture: The Talmudic and Midrashic Evidence.* 2nd ed. Hamden: Archon, 1991.

Schenk, Kenneth. *A Brief Guide to Philo.* Louisville: Westminster John Knox, 2005.

Trebolle, Julio. "A 'Canon Within a Canon': Two Series of Old Testament Books Differently Transmitted, Interpreted and Authorized." *RevQ* 19 (2000) 383-99.

Ulrich, Eugene. "The Notion and Definition of Canon." In *The Canon Debate,* ed. Lee Martin McDonald and James A. Sanders, 21-35. Peabody: Hendrickson, 2002.

VanderKam, James C. "Authoritative Literature in the Dead Sea Scrolls." *DSD* 5 (1998) 382-402.

———. *An Introduction to Early Judaism.* Grand Rapids: Wm. B. Eerdmans, 2001.

———, and Peter Flint. *The Meaning of the Dead Sea Scrolls.* San Francisco: HarperSanFrancisco, 2002.

Framework for Reading the New Testament

Chapter 45

Content and Origin of the New Testament Writings

Getting Started

1 Review the table of contents for the Old Testament in your Bible, and recall the general outlines of this story line and the genres that are present in the Old Testament.

2 List the 27 books of the New Testament. Refer to a Bible that has a brief introduction preceding each book and note one aspect that is distinctive of each book.

3 Identify some of the traditions within your school. What is their function and purpose?

Preliminary Comments

Christians divide the Bible (from Greek *biblos,* "book") into two parts: those books that arose from the faith community of God's chosen people, Israel, and those that arose from the faith community of the early Christian followers of Jesus. These two parts are referred to as the Hebrew Scriptures and the New Testament. Our in-depth examination of the Hebrew Scriptures in the first part of this study has provided an indispensable founda-

tion for turning now to a study of the New Testament writings. It is not possible to read the New Testament writings without a solid understanding of the Hebrew Scriptures because they provide the foundation and the context out of which they emerged.

Before examining the New Testament writings, we need to give attention to the following issues that will enable us to read these writings responsibly:

- the content of the New Testament;
- the political, social, philosophical, and religious contexts of the New Testament;
- the principles necessary for the interpretation of the New Testament;
- an understanding of the nature of a Gospel.

The Diversity of the New Testament World

The world out of which the New Testament arose was every bit as diverse as ours. Jesus and the apostles emerged from the religious context of a very diverse Judaism with groups vying to represent the true heart of their religion. Since the time of Alexander the Great (330 B.C.E.), the spread of Greek thought, language, and culture had fostered a common worldview. Yet, the people of the Roman Empire continued to search for something new, for new ways of imagining the world and its relations to the Divine. Even within early Christianity no one perspective dominated. Distinct attempts were made in different centers to capture the picture of Jesus and his message. The way Christians in Rome (as seen from the Gospel of Mark) imaged the figure of Jesus was decidedly different from the way Christians in Ephesus (as seen from the Gospel of John) did. This awareness helps us realize the richness within the New Testament that gives a beauty to the diversity of the traditions behind its composition. The aim of this study will be to try to open up and appreciate this rich diversity.

Contents of the New Testament

The New Testament writings can be divided into three major literary genres: narratives, letters, and an apocalypse. These books are not arranged chronologically, but rather according to their literary genres. Since the Gospels contain the teaching and ministry of Jesus, they are placed at the beginning, occupying a position similar to that which the Torah held in the canon of the Hebrew Bible.

A major principle of interpretation is to identify the type of text one is reading and to interpret that text according to the characteristics of that genre. Attention will be given to this in more depth in Chapter 48 when we examine the nature of a Gospel.

Narratives (5)

The four Gospels, Matthew, Mark, Luke, and John, all conform to the literary form of a narrative. When we read these writings, we do so through the lens of a narrative. The Acts of the Apostles is another New Testament narrative, being the second volume of the Gospel of Luke. While Luke's Gospel was a narrative presenting Jesus' ministry and the message of salvation that he proclaimed, the Acts of the Apostles narrates how this message of salvation is continued in the ministry and preaching of Jesus' followers, the Apostles.

Letters (21)

The most common literary genre in the New Testament is the letter. Twenty-one letters are found in our New Testament, whereas in the Hebrew Scriptures not a single book can be classified as such (although there are brief letters recorded in the context of some of the books). These writings are to be interpreted according to the genre of a letter as communications from a leader of the Christian community to a community or communi-

The 27 New Testament Writings	
Gospels	4
Synoptic Gospels: Matthew, Mark, Luke, John	
Acts of the Apostles	1
Letters	
Pauline Letters	14
Missionary Letters (6)	
1 and 2 Thessalonians	
1 and 2 Corinthians	
Galatians	
Romans	
Captivity Letters (4)	
Philemon	
Philippians	
Colossians	
Ephesians	
Pastoral Letters (3)	
1 and 2 Timothy	
Titus	
Hebrews (1)	
General Letters	7
James	
1 and 2 Peter	
1, 2 and 3 John	
Jude	
Revelation	1
Total:	27

ties with which he was connected. As we shall see, Paul started the phenomenon of writing to Christian communities that he had founded to instruct them further in the Christian faith and to correct difficulties that had arisen within those communities. Paul is responsible for writing seven letters (Romans, 1 and 2 Corinthians, Galatians, Philippians, 1 Thessalonians, and Philemon). A further six letters (2 Thessalonians, Colossians, Ephesians and the Pastoral letters [1 and 2 Timothy, Titus]) emerge from the hand of Paul's followers. They wrote in Paul's name after his death to communities that Paul had founded. Their aim was to remind them of Paul's teaching and to correct problems in the way in which Paul would have written had he been alive. Finally, the Letter to the Hebrews was also attributed to Paul in the tradition of the church, even though it did not bear his name.

Besides the writings attributed to Paul, seven more letters are attributed to other leaders within the Christian community such as Peter, James, John, and Jude. In a way similar to Paul's correspondence, they write to communities that were associated with them to instruct them and to correct problems within their communities.

Apocalypse (1)

The book of Revelation is the only example in the New Testament of an apocalyptic writing. This literary genre was very popular in the period between the two testaments. It is also found in the Hebrew Scriptures, where the book of Daniel is a good representative. Revelation was written by a Christian prophet, John, who had been exiled to the island of Patmos (off the coast of Ephesus) because of his adherence to the word of God (Rev 1:9-11). To understand this writing we have to interpret it according to the characteristic features of apocalyptic writing. Written in very symbolic language, it can be understood only by those who are part of the community. It gives the assurance that God is in control of history and that ultimately God will triumph over the forces of evil.

The Language, Text, and Translation of the New Testament

The world of Jesus was, as we have noted, a very diverse world which is reflected in the languages that were used in that environment. Aramaic was the spoken language of the ordinary Jewish people, a language they had adopted from the time of the Babylonian Exile onwards (587-538 B.C.E.). Hebrew was the language of worship, the language in which the sacred books of Judaism were written. Hebrew was studied in the synagogue, and children were instructed in it so that they would be able to read their Sacred Scriptures in the liturgy. Greek became the language of the ancient world after the conquests of Alexander the Great. In Palestine, particularly Galilee, Greek was widely used. Latin was the language of the conquerors, the Romans. Its usage at the time of Jesus was restricted to official correspondence. Most Romans, however, preferred to speak Greek, which was considered the language of the educated. Given the context of Jesus and his early followers, we can presume that they would have spoken Aramaic among themselves, that they were conversant with Greek coming from Galilee,

Authorship

The concept of authorship in the New Testament is very different from our understanding of an author today. Many people today show great concern and anxiety when a scholar says that a certain book was not written by the person to whom the book is attributed. For example, while the Letter to the Ephesians says "From Paul, an apostle of Christ Jesus by the will of God . . ." (Eph 1:1), most scholars would argue that Paul could not have written it because the style, vocabulary, and thoughts that it addresses reflect a period of time much later than the time of Paul. The solution is to realize that the way in which we conceive of an author today is not the same as it was in the ancient world. To expect that people living 2,000 years ago must conform to our ways and understanding of things is arrogant on our part. We must be respectful of the fact that peoples in the past had equally valid ways of doing things that differed remarkably from our ways.

In the ancient world, a writing would be attributed to a person in the sense that his authority was invoked for the writing. For example, in the instance of 2 Thessalonians one can see a disciple of Paul using Paul's name even though Paul had long since died, to settle a problem in the way in which Paul would have addressed it had he still been alive. Invoking Paul's authority would have reminded the readers of Paul's teaching and authority. Further, in the ancient world it was considered

a mark of respect by students to attribute their work to the teacher from whom they had acquired their learning. In the mind of the writer, invoking the name of some great teacher was not seen as fraudulent, but rather as a mark of respect that acknowledged the authority and learning of the teacher. It is against this background that we are to understand many of the attributions of authorship in the New Testament.

This was not a phenomenon found only in the New Testament writings. We see this as something that had long been a practice in the Hebrew Bible. Many of the psalms are attributed to David, while the Song of Songs is attributed to Solomon. In the tradition, David was the great lyricist, and it was natural that the book of Psalms should be associated with him, while his son Solomon was revered for his wisdom, insight, and learning. Consequently, many of the so-called wisdom books bear his name. The same process is observable in the world of ancient Greece and Rome.

To say that a writing may not have been physically written by Paul in no way calls into question the truth of Scripture, or its inspiration, or the importance of the writing itself. It simply draws our attention to a world that has a different understanding of the role of an author. In the final analysis, it actually gives a greater importance to Paul and the other apostles to whom writings are also attributed as the authorities behind the writings.

and that they would have a familiarity with Hebrew as their language of worship. Latin would probably have remained unfamiliar to them since its usage was limited to the conquerors. We can see this multilingual dimension reflected in the placard that was raised above Jesus' cross announcing his offense: "'Jesus of Nazareth, the King of the Jews' . . . and it was written in Hebrew, in Latin, and in Greek" (John 19:19-20). Presumably the reference to Hebrew would be to Aramaic.

Outside Palestine the Hebrew Scriptures had been translated into Greek in Alexandria, Egypt, in the course of the 3rd century B.C.E. This Greek translation came to be known as the Septuagint (see p. 14 for a full description). The early Christians used this Greek translation of the Hebrew Scriptures when they preached and wrote their own letters and Gospels. The type of Greek used was the language spoken in the eastern part of the Roman Empire. It was not as refined as the classical Greek of the great Athenian philosophers and poets, but it was the common language (hence it was called *koine* or common Greek). The vast majority of Christians in the second half of the 1st century C.E. must have been Greek-speaking, since all their writings were composed in Greek.

The original New Testament writings have long since been lost. What remains are copies of these writings. In fact, we possess more than 5,000 Greek manuscripts containing all or parts of the New Testament. From an examination of these manuscripts and using very careful principles of scientific textual analysis, scholars have produced a Greek text of the New Testament that forms the basis today for all translations made into the vernacular.

The Emergence of the New Testament Writings

Oral Traditions
The concept of tradition helps us understand more clearly the process out of which the New Testament writings emerged. As its name implies, tradition (from Latin *tradere*, "to hand on") refers to the passing on from one group to another the customs, beliefs, and values of that group to ensure the continued identity between the two.

In the ancient world about 90 percent of people were illiterate. This is not a judgment made on their intellectual abilities. It is a reminder that the people of the ancient world belonged to oral societies where reading and writing were reserved to elite groups such as the scribes within the framework of Judaism. A positive consequence of the lack of reading and writing skills is that people developed techniques for the memorization and the handing on of what was important for them, especially their sacred writings. Jesus never wrote anything.

The Mission of the Disciples
The Synoptic Gospels show Jesus forming a group of followers around him whom he instructs in his teaching and then sends out to act in like manner. For example, the Gospel of Luke paints the picture in this way:

"Then Jesus called the twelve together and gave them power and authority over all demons and to cure diseases, and he sent them out to proclaim the kingdom of God and to heal. He said to them, 'Take nothing for your journey, no staff, nor bag, nor bread, nor money — not even an extra tunic. Whatever house you enter, stay there, and leave from there. Wherever they do not welcome you, as you are leaving that town shake the dust off your feet as a testimony against them.' They departed and went through the villages, bringing the good news and curing diseases everywhere." (Luke 9:1-6; see also Mark 6:7-13; Matt 10:5-15; Luke 10:1-12)

However, the Gospel of Luke (Luke 4:16-21) presents a narrative of Jesus reading from his sacred texts in the context of a synagogue service.

The world of Judaism was somewhat different from the wider Mediterranean world in the sense that reading their Sacred Scriptures was an essential feature of their religion. All Jewish males had to be able to read their sacred writings in the synagogue. Hence they received an education enabling them to do this.

In the world of early Christianity, the memory of Jesus of Nazareth was at first preserved orally. When the early

The Calling of the Apostles Peter and Andrew, Duccio di Buoninsegna (1308/1311). (National Gallery of Art, Washington — Samuel H. Kress Collection)

The Beatitudes

Matthew 5:3-12	Luke 6:20-23
Blessed are the poor in spirit, for theirs is the kingdom of heaven.	Blessed are you who are poor, for yours is the kingdom of God. (v. 20b)
Blessed are those who mourn, for they will be comforted. (v. 21b)	Blessed are you who weep now, for you will laugh.
Blessed are the meek, for they will inherit the earth.	
Blessed are those who hunger and thirst for righteousness, for they will be filled.	Blessed are you who are hungry now, for you will be filled. (v. 21a)
Blessed are the merciful, for they will receive mercy.	
Blessed are the pure in heart, for they will see God.	
Blessed are the peacemakers, for they will be called children of God.	
Blessed are those who are persecuted for righteousness' sake, for theirs is the kingdom of heaven.	
Blessed are you when people revile you and persecute you and utter all kinds of evil against you falsely on my account. Rejoice and be glad, for your reward is great in heaven, for in the same way they persecuted the prophets who were before you.	Blessed are you when people hate you, and when they exclude you, revile you, and defame you on account of the Son of Man. Rejoice in that day and leap for joy, for surely your reward is great in heaven; for that is what their ancestors did to the prophets. (vv. 22-23)

Christians gathered together to celebrate their sacred meals, they remembered and passed on the sayings and teachings of Jesus of Nazareth. Recording these memories in writing only occurred decades later. Even when these memories were placed in writing, the oral characteristics of the Jesus movement did not cease. It continued side by side with the oral memory and tradition.

Jesus formed the center of a community of disciples who were empowered with a mission similar to his own, a ministry of preaching and healing. The preaching of Jesus' followers began during his ministry and continued after his death and resurrection (see Matt 28:16-20; Mark 16:15-18; Luke 24:44-49). A tradition began of handing on a message that conformed to Jesus' command: "Repent, for the kingdom of heaven has come near" (Matt 4:17). The disciples' preaching focused on two aspects of the tradition, namely Jesus' sayings and deeds. It aimed at remaining faithful to Jesus' ministry while at the same time adapting it to new situations arising within the communities.

Fidelity to Jesus' teaching was one dimension of the Jesus tradition, as can be observed in Paul's preaching. Since he was not an eyewitness to Jesus' ministry, Paul identifies the tradition as one of the sources (but not the only one) from which he received his material (see p. 334). In this way Jesus' message endured and continued through the ongoing preaching of Jesus' followers.

Adaptation of the message to the context of the situation of the hearers was another clearly observable dimension of the Jesus tradition. Note how Matthew and Luke reproduce the Beatitudes (Matt 5:3-12; Luke 6:20-23).

Matthew and Luke show evidence of adapting the Beatitudes to their own situations. However, there is a voice or a spirit to which they both bear witness and to which they endeavor to remain true. This is how tradition operates. The Gospel writers endeavor to remain faithful to the spirit or the voice of Jesus' message or teaching. This is not done through a verbatim memorization of what Jesus said, but rather an adaptation of his message to new situations by retelling it in new ways and new forms. The prime concern for the tradition that is passed on is fidelity to the religious truth.

Our 21st-century vision of the world is very different from that of other centuries. We have a strong historical consciousness and tend to equate truth with our notion of what is historical. For the people of biblical times, however, the stress was on the religious message. The aim in the transmission of the message and story of Jesus of Nazareth was to preserve its religious and moral truth.

During the first decades after Jesus' death, there was no reason to put anything down in writing since this was an oral culture. The disciples were content with handing on their message through personal interaction either through one-on-one contact or through public preaching. When they gathered in someone's home to pray (much in the same way that Jews prayed in their synagogue worship) and to celebrate the memory of Jesus' last meal, his followers kept his memory alive. These early communities had the vivid expectation that Jesus would return within their own lifetime. Belief in the imminent expectation of Jesus' return (his second coming or, as the early Christians referred to it, the parousia [from a technical Greek word referring to the "arrival or visit" of an important official or general]) was one of the early tenets of their faith. (See the interesting controversy that Paul is called upon to settle in 1 Thess 4:13-18.)

Written Documents

The first writings of the New Testament made their appearance in the mid 50s and early 60s C.E. The Apostle Paul was responsible for this. He responded energetically to situations that came to his attention regarding communities that he had founded. Writing letters to them was one way in which he could show his pastoral concern and keep in contact with the congregations, instruct them deeper in his message, and solve problems that had arisen since he had left them. Paul's dominant concern was with the present, namely to resolve present conflicts. However, as time went on Paul's letters were passed on to other communities in the region. This happened particularly among the churches that Paul had founded. It became important for them to obtain other letters Paul had written to neighboring communities. This desire is expressed at the end of the letter to the Colossians (Col 4:16).

The appearance of the Gospels started around the time of the destruction of the city of Jerusalem (70 C.E.) and in the decades following. As the original followers of Jesus dispersed and died, the oral preservation of Jesus' memory was threatened. The apostles were the immediate link between the second generation Christians and the person of Jesus. With the passing of the apostles, some form of record was needed to preserve their oral preaching. This gave an impetus for the production of certain collections. An examination of the four Gospels shows that a passion narrative (an account of the suffering, death, and resurrection of Jesus as a fulfillment of the Scriptures) must have originally stood behind them. By drawing on the Hebrew Scriptures, the followers of Jesus made sense of his death. They did so ultimately by reaching back into their Sacred Scriptures to illustrate the significance of what had happened to Jesus.

Written collections of parables, sayings of Jesus, miracle stories, as well as controversy stories all lie behind the written composition of our present Gospels.

We will examine in greater detail and depth later the sources our Gospel writers used in composing their Gospels (see Chapter 48). The four Gospels arose from these written traditions along with those traditions still circulating orally. Mark's Gospel is judged to be the first Gospel to be written. Mark clearly shows his genius because he started something that would be imitated by others. The Passion Narrative forms the basis for his development and also the way in which he has made use of the collections of parables, sayings, and miracles that were available.

The purpose of the Gospel writers was twofold: to preserve Jesus' memory and teaching as well as to provide an aid and instruction for their communities so that Jesus' teaching would speak to them decades after Jesus' death. Once again the twofold characteristics of tradition are evident here: fidelity to Jesus' memory and adaptation to the new context of those communities for whom they were writing.

The Gospel of Matthew was probably written a decade and a half later and the Gospel of Luke shortly thereafter together with his sequel, the Acts of the

Paul as a Recipient of Tradition

On several occasions Paul acknowledges his debt to the tradition:

"Now I would remind you, brothers and sisters, of the good news that I proclaimed to you, which you in turn received, in which also you stand, through which also you are being saved, if you hold firmly to the message that I proclaimed to you — unless you have come to believe in vain.

"For *I handed on to you* as of first importance what *I in turn had received*: that Christ died for our sins in accordance with the scriptures, and that he was buried, and that he was raised on the third day in accordance with the scriptures, and that he appeared to Cephas, then to the twelve. Then he appeared to more than five hundred brothers and sisters at one time, most of whom are still alive, though some have died. Then he appeared to James, then to all the apostles." (1 Cor 15:1-7)

"For I received from the Lord what *I also handed on to you,* that the Lord Jesus on the night when he was betrayed took a loaf of bread, and when he had given thanks, he broke it and said, 'This is my body that is for you. Do this in remembrance of me.' In the same way he took the cup also, after supper, saying, 'This cup is the new covenant in my blood. Do this, as often as you drink it, in remembrance of me.' For as often as you eat this bread and drink the cup, you proclaim the Lord's death until he comes." (1 Cor 11:23-26)

Time Chart for the Emergence of the New Testament Writings

30		Jesus	
40			
		Oral Traditions	
50			
	Paul's seven		
60	genuine letters		
70			
		Mark	
			James
80		Matthew	
90	2 Thessalonians		
	Colossians	Luke-Acts	
	Ephesians		
	Pastorals		
	Hebrews		
		John	
100		Revelation	
		Letters	
			1 Peter
			Jude
110			
120			2 Peter

Apostles, which traces the spread of the message of Jesus throughout the Roman Empire. The Gospel of John was the last to make its appearance toward the end of the 1st century. It is a very different Gospel because John uses traditions independent from the Synoptics. The concern of these Gospel writers is with handing on the moral truth and religious message of Jesus of Nazareth in a way that speaks to the needs and concerns of their own communities.

Finally, other writings make their appearance. We have already noted how disciples of Paul wrote letters to the communities that Paul had founded (2 Thessalonians, Colossians, Ephesians, and the Pastoral Let-

ters) long after his death in order to challenge them to remain faithful to his teachings and to correct emerging problems within those communities in the manner in which Paul would have done. Other letters also arose invoking the authority of other important Christian leaders. The letters of 1 and 2 Peter, James, and Jude are all associated with some of the most important leaders of early Christianity coming from the hands of disciples or followers of these Christian leaders.

A distinctive writing emerged at the end of the 1st century, namely the book of Revelation which, as we have seen, belongs to the apocalyptic genre. A crisis of persecution in Asia Minor at the end of the 1st century appears to be the context and impetus for the production of this writing (see Chapter 62).

Putting It All Together

This survey of the emergence of the writings of the New Testament shows that the development of these books spanned almost a century. While no one can give an exact date for Jesus' death, scholars generally agree on a time around 30 C.E. This means that the first writings to emerge, those of Paul, appeared some 20 to 25 years later. Our four Gospels appeared only some 40 to 60 years after Jesus' death (between 70 and 90). The last writing of the New Testament, probably 2 Peter, appeared around 110. One can at least say that by the year 120 all the books of the New Testament had been written. However, a further issue needs to be examined. Although these writings had been written by 120, it took a much longer time for all of them to be acknowledged as sacred writings carrying an authority for the believing community. This issue is complicated by the fact that many other writings made their appearance at the same time. The 27 New Testament books were not the only writings to have been written during that first century after Jesus' death. The story of how and why these 27 writings were finally accepted will be addressed at the end of this study in Chapter 63.

Questions for Review and Discussion

1 Prepare a talk that you would give explaining how the New Testament writings are based on the preaching and teaching of Jesus.

2 Discuss the differences between narratives and letters, the two major literary types of writings in the New Testament.

Further Reading

The following books are invaluable tools for consulting articles related to New Testament topics and themes:

Evans, Craig A., and Stanley E. Porter, eds. *Dictionary of New Testament Background.* Downers Grove: InterVarsity, 2000.

Freedman, David Noel, ed. *The Anchor Bible Dictionary.* 6 vols. New York: Doubleday, 1992.

———, Allen C. Myers, and Astrid B. Beck, eds. *Eerdmans Dictionary of the Bible.* Grand Rapids: Wm. B. Eerdmans, 2000.

Chapter 46

Political, Social, and Religious Context of the New Testament World

Getting Started

1 On a map of the Mediterranean Basin identify where the following countries are located today: Israel, Palestine, Egypt, Greece, and Rome.

2 Work out the distances from Jerusalem to Cairo, Athens, and Rome.

Preliminary Comments

Our study of the Hebrew Bible has provided an excellent entry into the world of the New Testament, especially religiously and culturally. To understand the New Testament writings we must know what the world of Jesus and his followers was like in all its dimensions. In this chapter we will sketch a picture of the political situation in Palestine and the Roman Empire at the time of Jesus and the birth of the New Testament. We will also look at what life (the social situation) was like for people who heard the message of Jesus. Finally, we will examine the religious situation throughout the empire among Jews and pagans alike.

Political Context of the New Testament Era

Roman Occupation of Judea (63 B.C.E.)

The New Testament era is framed against the background of Rome's domination of the Mediterranean and in particular its rule of Palestine. From 67 to 63 B.C.E. rivalry between two Hasmonean brothers (John Hyrcanus II and Aristobulus II) for control of Judea became progressively more intense. In 63 B.C.E. the Roman general Pompey, traveling in the East, endeavored to extend Rome's power. John Hyrcanus II appealed to Pompey for assistance in defeating his brother Aristobulus II, who had proclaimed himself high priest and king of Judea. This gave Pompey the opportunity to intervene in Judea. He entered Jerusalem and the temple and established Roman control over the territory of Judea. He appointed John Hyrcanus II high priest and local governor with Antipater II (the ruler of the southern territory of Idumea) as his advisor and helper. Both were answerable to the governor of Syria. Judea now formed part of the larger Roman province of Syria, and the people of Judea had to pay a heavy annual tax. The Jews lost the independence they had gained under the Maccabees and Hasmoneans (167-63 B.C.E.).

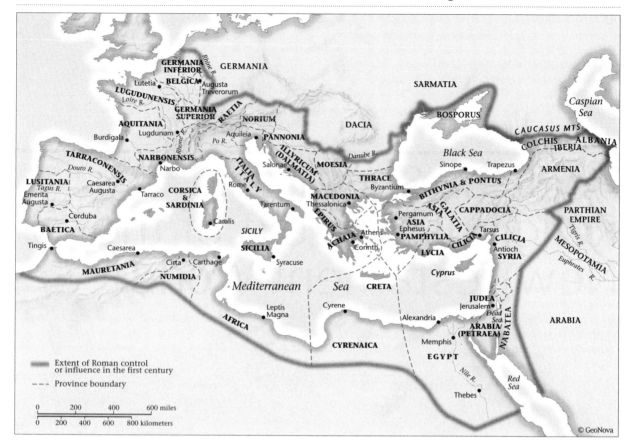

THE ROMAN EMPIRE IN THE 1ST CENTURY C.E.

Civil War between Pompey and Julius Caesar (49-47 B.C.E.)

In 49 B.C.E. the two most powerful generals, Pompey and Julius Caesar, struggled to assume sole power over Rome's emerging empire. Both came to Egypt, where the Egyptians under the leadership of Cleopatra slaughtered Pompey (48). Julius Caesar was besieged at the port of Alexandria (47). Antipater II showed ingenuity by sending troops to Caesar's aid, and as high priest Hyrcanus II urged the Jews in Egypt (of which there was a sizable number) to support Caesar. This help turned the tide. Caesar rewarded Antipater and the Jews for their assistance, without which he would have been defeated. Antipater was appointed ruler of all Jewish territory and made a Roman citizen. The Jewish tax was reduced and the Jewish religion declared to be a *religio licita* (a recognized religion) throughout the Roman world. The importance of this status for the Jewish religion ought not be underestimated. It meant that they could practice their religion unhindered. This favored status lasted for many years.

Herod the Great (37-4 B.C.E.)

On the death of his father Antipater II, Herod was made vassal king *(rex socius)* of Judea by the Roman Senate, and in July 37 B.C.E. he entered Jerusalem. After the death of Cleopatra, Octavian (the future Augustus Caesar) expanded Herod's territory in 30 B.C.E. to include the whole of Palestine. Herod was a great enthusiast of Greek and Roman culture and embarked on enormous building projects both inside and outside his territory. Within his kingdom he rebuilt the ancient city of Samaria, which had been destroyed in 108, renaming it Sebaste after the Roman emperor (*Sebastos* is Greek for Augustus). He rebuilt the port city of Strato's Tower, renamed as Caesarea Maritima (also in honor of the emperor). There he built a palace, a theater, an amphitheater (whose ruins can be seen today), and a temple in honor of Augustus. However, in Jerusalem he undertook his most extensive projects, including a palace for himself and a fortress that overlooked the temple, called the Antonia. He enlarged the Jerusalem temple to twice its former size by constructing retaining walls and filling in the land around the temple area. The rebuilding of the temple began in 20 and was consecrated in 11 B.C.E. although its decoration was not fully completed until 63 C.E. (seven years before its eventual destruction by the Romans). Herod's reconstruction of the temple was driven more by political than religious motives. He hoped that this action would gain support from the populace, but that never happened. They always resented the fact that he was not fully Jewish.

Afraid of losing power, Herod constructed a number of fortresses around his borders: Machaerus (east of the Dead Sea where John the Baptist was imprisoned), the Herodium (south of Bethlehem), and Masada (west of the Dead Sea). Herod's final years were marked with bitter cruelty and violence. Fearing numerous plots to oust him, he murdered a number of his own sons. While Matthew's account of the killing of the male children of Bethlehem is not mentioned outside the New Testament, it certainly does conform to this picture of Herod as a cruel tyrant. Herod died on 1 April 4 B.C.E. Since Jesus had been born during Herod's rule, his birth would be prior to 4 B.C.E., probably around 6 B.C.E.

An assessment of Herod shows that economically and politically he achieved much for the land of Palestine. Herod's loyal support of Rome brought great benefits for the country. and his building projects restored work and industry. Yet because Herod's family originated from Edom or Idumaea, whose population had been forced to become Jews in 100 B.C.E., the Jewish populace considered him to be half-Jewish and resented his rule as that of a foreigner.

The Successors of Herod the Great

On Herod's death Augustus divided the territory among his three sons. He abolished the kingship in order to satisfy the Jews.

- Archelaus (4 B.C.E.–6 C.E.) was appointed ethnarch over the territories of Judea, Samaria, and Idumea. He was a tyrant and was eventually banished by Augustus Caesar to southern Gaul. His territory was then ruled directly by Roman prefects or procurators.
- Herod Antipas (4 B.C.E.–39 C.E.) was appointed tetrarch over Galilee and Perea. His rule was also unpopular. He is the Herod that the New Testament refers to the most. He had John the Baptist executed (Mark 6:14-29). Jesus called him "the fox" (Luke 13:31-32). He met with Jesus before his crucifixion (Luke 23:6-12).
- Herod Philip II (4 B.C.E.–34 C.E.) was appointed tetrarch over the northwestern territories of Trachonitis, Gaulanitis, and Paneas. Not much is known about his rule. He built the city of Caesarea Philippi

---

Titles for rulers within the Roman Empire

Ethnarch: Ruler of a nation or a people (from Greek ethnos, "nation")

Tetrarch: Ruler of a fourth part of a territory. A lesser title than ethnarch.

Prefect: Governor of an imperial province. A later title for this office was procurator.

All rulers remained subject to the authority of Rome.

(named after himself and the Roman emperor). Jesus went into this territory when he visited the villages of Caesarea Philippi (Mark 8:27).

These rulers provide the political context for Jesus' ministry. In Galilee where Jesus grew up and conducted most of his ministry, Herod Antipas was the ruler. In Jerusalem where Jesus spent the last days of his life, Roman prefects were in charge — at the time of Jesus' trial and death Pontius Pilate (26-36 C.E.) was the prefect.

Direct rule of Judea by Roman prefects came to an end in 41 C.E. Herod Agrippa I (39-44 C.E.), a grandson of Herod the Great, had taken over the territories of his uncles Philip and Antipas in 39. He was a good friend of the Roman emperor Claudius (41-54), who added the territory of the Roman prefects, Judea and Samaria, to his realm. Assuming the title of vassal king, Agrippa ruled a territory equal in size to that of his grandfather and gained the respect of the Jewish leaders. Acts 12 reports his persecution of Christians whereby he executed James, the son of Zebedee, and imprisoned Peter.

Control of the whole of Palestine reverted again to direct Roman rule under seven Roman prefects (44-66 C.E.) because of the early death of Herod Agrippa I in 44. This was a period of growing unrest, as is seen from the rise of the *sicarii* (from Latin *sica,* "dagger," referring to those who carried a dagger concealed under their cloaks, the equivalent of modern terrorists), the *Zealots* (spiritual heirs of the Maccabees, who had an intense zeal for the protection of the Law at all costs), and finally an uprising against the Romans.

The Jewish War against the Romans (66-73 C.E.)

The insurgency broke out under the Roman prefect Gessius Florus (64-66 C.E.) who had been instructed by the Emperor Nero to obtain 17 gold talents from the temple treasury. In 66 when the Jews protested, Florus ordered the cavalry to charge, killing thousands. The Jews revolted. The Roman general Vespasian was entrusted with quelling the revolt. In 69 he was acclaimed Roman emperor and left his army under the control of his son,

Titus. Swiftly the Roman forces gained control over the whole of Palestine with the exception of Jerusalem and the fortresses around the Dead Sea. In 70 the Roman forces captured Jerusalem and destroyed the temple. The Arch of Titus that stands in the Roman Forum today was built to commemorate the Roman triumph.

With the fall of Jerusalem the war was practically over. The fortresses on the Dead Sea, such as Masada, were captured by 73. Palestine became a province of the emperor, ruled directly by Roman forces, and the Jewish nation ceased to exist. With the destruction of the temple the nature of Israel's religion changed forever. The sacrifices that the Law of Moses prescribed could no longer be offered at the temple. The Jews attempted a second revolt in

Triumphal Arch of Titus in Rome celebrating the destruction of Jerusalem in 70 C.E. (Robert Harry Smith)

132-135, but it was quickly suppressed by the Emperor Hadrian, who built a temple to the Roman god Jupiter on the place where Herod's magnificent temple once stood. Having lost their homeland, the Jewish people were scattered throughout the world.

Social Context of the New Testament Era

An examination of life under the Romans is equally important for understanding the New Testament writings. From the time of Alexander the Great (336-323 B.C.E.) the process of hellenization (from Greek *hellenizein,* "to live as a Hellene [or Greek]") had spread throughout the Mediterranean world. Alexander had begun his conquests with the noble idea of unifying the world through Greek culture. This process of hellenization continued over the centuries following his death. Yet while people adopted Greek dress, customs, and sport, many aspects of Eastern cultures influenced the Greek world in its turn, particularly in the realm of religion.

The Roman Empire as heir to the Hellenistic world thrived on the unity that had been created through the use of a common language and culture. The Romans even adopted most aspects of Greek religion to the extent that Roman and Greek gods came to be identified with each other. For this reason we refer to "the Greco-Roman world."

At the time of Jesus' birth most Jews throughout the Roman Empire spoke Greek and lived in centers dominated by Greek culture. Their Sacred Scriptures had been translated into Greek in Egypt (see Septuagint on page 14). Their world outside Palestine was very different from the one painted by the books of their Sacred Scriptures. It was this outside world that Paul and the early Christian missionaries encountered when they spread the gospel message beyond the borders of Palestine.

The Greeks had a great zest for knowledge. Not only did they leave behind a language that had the vocabulary and tools necessary for expressing and investigating knowledge in every field of human interest (such as medicine, philosophy, and science), but they also left behind a culture that expressed itself permanently with tangible monuments found in art, literature, and architecture, to name but a few.

The influence of Hellenism was largely experienced in the city. A Greek city was walled around with an *agora* (or marketplace) in the center. Throughout the city one would observe buildings such as theaters, amphitheaters, temples, aqueducts, and gymnasiums. Most often a temple, dedicated to the god of the city, dominated the city, as can be seen in Athens.

Anthropologists refer to this Mediterranean society as largely a peasant or agrarian society structured around

Roman Emperors during the New Testament Era

The Julio-Claudian Dynasty

(Trustees of the British Museum)

Augustus Caesar (Octavian; 27 B.C.E.–14 C.E.). The first emperor of the Roman Empire. An effective administrator, he replenished the treasury and established efficiency in government. Peace (the famous Pax Romana) prospered throughout the empire. Travel in the empire was greatly increased through the elimination of piracy on the Mediterranean Sea. The network of Roman roads made communication and travel possible between all parts of the empire. Jesus was born (Luke 2:1-7) during Augustus's rule.

Tiberius (14-37 C.E.). The stepson of Augustus who furthered his policies well. He was disliked by the ordinary citizens because he refused to contribute to the "bread and games" (a way previous rulers had tried to bribe support from the people). He ruled during the life and ministry of Jesus (Luke 3:1 speaks of the beginning of John the Baptist's ministry) and appointed Pontius Pilate as prefect of Judea (26-36) during whose administration Jesus was crucified.

Caligula (37-41 C.E.). A great-grandson of Augustus. His rule was a disaster and he spent the whole treasury that Augustus had accumulated. Caligula was mad with power and introduced the concept of emperor worship, which would have repercussions for Christians for centuries to come. He insisted that he be addressed as a god and ordered that a statue of himself be erected in the temple of Jerusalem. Fortunately for the Jews, Caligula was assassinated by his bodyguards before the governor of Syria was forced to carry out this decree.

Claudius (41-54 C.E.). Caligula's uncle, appointed emperor by the Senate. He was physically frail, but one of the most learned men in Rome. His rule was highly successful. Paul began his missionary activity and letter-writing during this time. Acts 18:2 mentions that Claudius ordered all the Jews in Rome to leave. This account is supported by the Roman historian Suetonius's report that Claudius ordered Jews out of Rome because of a riot that had been started by a certain Chrestus (Christus?). Acts 11:28 also speaks of a severe famine occurring during his rule. Roman writers mention a number of serious famines during this period. Claudius was poisoned by his fourth wife, Agrippina.

(American School of Classical Studies)

Nero (54-68 C.E.). The son of Agrippina. A ruthless ruler, he poisoned his stepbrother Britannicus because he was suspicious of him and had his mother, Agrippina, his wife, as well as his closest friends, Seneca and Burrus, murdered. In 64 Rome was devastated by a fire, for which Nero blamed the Christians. Both Peter and Paul were put to death in Rome during this time. Nero eventually committed suicide while traveling in the East.

The Year of the Four Caesars (69 C.E.). Unrest throughout the empire led to a succession of emperors: **Galba** (68-69), **Otho** (69), **Vitellius** (69). Finally, the general **Vespasian** was acclaimed emperor and restored stability to the empire (69-79).

power and privilege. At the top echelons of Roman society was the ruling class made up of the emperor and the senators, as well as the aristocratic rulers in the different provinces. This group would make up about 1 to 2 percent of the population. Their wealth grew as did their power.

The retainer class made up about 5 percent of the population. Comprised of priests, tax collectors, and bureaucrats, they served the ruling class by carrying out their wishes. Below this group were the merchants and artisans. The largest population group (about 75 percent) comprised the peasants, who were mainly farmers and day laborers.

Slaves were also a common element of this agrarian society. People were taken into slavery through wars or through poverty. Many educated slaves served as teachers, accountants, or secretaries for the wealthy elite.

The family created the most important bonds and relationships in the ancient world. Within the family was a hierarchy of roles, with the father as head of the family. The man's role was exercised in the public and political spheres, while the woman's role was in the private sphere of the home.

Three unique features of this world are important to note:

- Patron-client relationships: To succeed in this type of society one had to have support from the more powerful or the wealthy. A patron offered protection and favors for his/her client, while a client in return

The Flavian Dynasty

Vespasian (69-79 C.E.). A general who began to quell the Jewish uprising. On becoming emperor he left the war in the hands of his son Titus. Vespasian provided peace and prosperity for the empire.

(Collection of Gleason L. Archer)

Titus (79-81 C.E.). Son of Vespasian, he crushed the Jewish uprising.

Domitian (81-96 C.E.). Judged a tyrant by both Christian and Roman writers. His desire for emperor worship and his persecution of Christians provided the context for the book of Revelation.

The Adoptive and Antonine Dynasty

Nerva (96-98 C.E.). Appointed emperor by the Senate because Domitian left no heir.

Trajan (98-117 C.E.). Nerva's son and heir. An effective administrator, he issued rules that resulted in the persecution of Christians. The letter of Pliny the Younger (a governor in Asia) was written at this time describing this persecution in Asia Minor.

Hadrian (117-138 C.E.). A distant relative of Trajan. The second Jewish Revolt broke out under Bar Kochba (132-135), and Hadrian expelled all Jews from Jerusalem. He built Aelia Capitolina, a Gentile city, over the city of Jerusalem.

Antoninus Pius (138-161 C.E.). Adopted son of Hadrian.

Marcus Aurelius (161-180 C.E.). Adopted son of Antoninus Pius. Known as the philosopher-emperor.

would offer support and loyalty to the patron. Many of the relationships described in the New Testament can be understood against this framework. (See, e.g., Jas 2:1-7, where a rich man enters the assembly.)

- Honor and shame: These values permeated every aspect of society. Honor is the value that one holds of oneself as well as one's value in the eyes of others. A person has this honor through birth or can acquire this honor. It was vital to maintain one's honor — a loss of honor brought shame.
- Limited-goods society: People believed that there was a limited supply of all the good things of life. This meant that people could extend their own goods only

at the expense of others. Most people were concerned about preserving what they had, which meant preserving the status quo.

This description reveals that the world of the 1st century C.E. was very different from our own 21st-century world. It is vital that we bear this in mind when we read the texts of the New Testament and try to understand where the differences lie.

Philosophical World of the New Testament Era

The current philosophies of the New Testament era exerted an enormous influence both on the way in which the early Christians expressed their message and on how they countered much of the thinking that influenced their congregations. The word "philosophy" (derived from Greek *philos,* "lover or friend," and *sophia,* "wisdom," thus "lover of wisdom") embraces the search for true knowledge of the world and of oneself. The origins of philosophy in Greece can be traced to the 7th century B.C.E. By the 5th century, Athens had become a thriving center for philosophical inquiry. Many great thinkers attracted students to Athens, and the schools of philosophy that developed around them helped to perpetuate their philosophy.

Socrates (ca. 469-399 B.C.E.)

Socrates was the first of the great Athenian philosophers. He attracted many followers, who in turn became extremely influential after his death. His method (the Socratic method) consisted in questioning everything that was traditionally accepted as obvious or true. This aroused concern and eventually anger among those whose beliefs were subjected to scrutiny. Socrates was eventually put to death on the charge of corrupting the youth of Athens. Like Jesus, Socrates did not commit his message to writing, so it was left to his disciples. Consequently, it is difficult to distinguish clearly where Plato's thought differs from that of Socrates, just as it is often difficult to identify where the message of Jesus is to be distinguished from that of writers such as Mark, Matthew, Luke, or John.

Platonism

Plato (427-347 C.E.) was the most famous of Socrates' students. In his writings, Plato constructed dialogs with Socrates as the central character. Through his ability to ask the right questions, Socrates leads the inquirer to discover the answer.

A number of Plato's insights were to have an enduring legacy on the future understanding of the world and the individual search for truth. He taught a dualism that accepted the existence of two worlds: the world in which we live and the true, invisible world. The material world consists of shadows that point to and reflect the true world above. We see a world of shadows made up of multiple reflections of the true, invisible world that contains their true image. For example, the real world contains one idea (or "form") of beauty that is eternal and perfect, whereas in our world of shadows there are hundreds of reflections of beauty, but none is ever able to express beauty fully. The contrast between the one and the multiple is fundamental in distinguishing between the two worlds.

Our human bodies belong to this material world where they experience change and ultimately death. Our souls, however, come from the invisible world and return to that world at death. The purpose of life is to prepare the soul to be freed from the prison house of the body so that it can return to the world above from which it came. The philosopher's task was to educate others in the eternal values (such as beauty and truth) and so prepare their souls for an escape from this material world and a return to the world above.

Plato's thought influenced the Hellenistic world to such an extent that it became an essential ingredient of the worldview, much like the air we breathe is central to life and yet we seldom consciously pay attention to it. While Platonism had started to wane by the time of Jesus, it nevertheless continued to exert an important influence on Christian teachers, especially in the years after the New Testament. The Letter to the Hebrews reflects Plato's worldview very closely and can only be understood against that background. The writer used the contrast between the two worlds, the spiritual and the material, in order to describe the relationship between the Hebrew Scriptures and the New Testament or between events of the past that were fulfilled in Christ. Just as there were many sacrifices in the past, now there is only one sacrifice in the person of Christ (Heb 10: 11-12).

Stoicism

Stoicism took its name from Greek *stoa*, the "colonnaded porch" where its founder Zeno (333-263 B.C.E.) taught in Athens. Compared with Platonism which was dualistic (believing in two worlds), Stoicism was monistic at its core (the universe is one). Divine reason or the Logos (Greek "word or reason") guided the whole universe. A spark of the divine Logos was within every person. If persons lived according to that Logos, they were obeying their nature and would find happiness and tranquility in life. Since emotions and passions were a distortion of true nature, people had to learn to control or overcome their emotions. To achieve this aim the Stoics taught a system of moral values that included self-sufficiency, tranquility, and the natural rights of all people (including slaves and women) as well as detachment from all things including suffering and wealth. At the time of Paul and the early Christians, Stoicism had become one of the major philosophies influencing the ethical life of the Greco-Roman world. Some famous Stoics were Seneca (a contemporary of Paul) and the Roman emperor Marcus Aurelius (161-180 C.E.). The prologue of John's Gospel refers to Jesus as the Logos, the Word of God (a term not found in the Hebrew Scriptures). Paul's statements at times tend to echo Stoic thoughts: "Not that I am referring to being in need; for I have learned to be content with whatever I have" (Phil 4:11).

Epicureanism

The teachings of Epicurus (342-270 B.C.E.) in Ephesus provided the foundations for this philosophy. He built on the scientific views of another philosopher, Democritus (460-370), who had taught an atomic theory whereby the world was composed of tiny invisible particles (called atoms) and empty space. The nature of the atoms was to coalesce, forming objects for a time, then disintegrating and forming again in other objects. This happens with everything in the universe including humans. Using these views, Epicurus drew out their logical consequences for an ethical way of life. Among the consequences the following are the most significant:

- Death is not to be feared, because at death these atoms simply disintegrate and reform.
- The gods are not to be feared, because all things are determined by the chance grouping of atoms.
- The major aim in life was the avoidance of pain and the attainment of pleasure.

This last point has caused much misunderstanding. The common perception is that Epicureanism sought and promoted inordinate pleasure. Epicurus, however, was no hedonist. He believed in the gods and appealed to common sense as the basis for truth: be true to one's feelings. Groups of Epicureans formed together in which they lived out their philosophy and practiced their values, especially friendship and care for one another. A number of Roman poets were Epicureans, including Lucretius (95-51 B.C.E.) and Horace (65-8 B.C.E.).

Cynicism

Cynicism dates back to another of Socrates' students, Antisthenes (ca. 446-366 B.C.E.). The Cynics did not teach an attitude that distrusts the sincerity of others, as cynicism is understood today. Instead they taught that virtue was the only good, achieved through self-control. Cynics were wandering preachers, moving from town to town, challenging people regarding the values that directed their lives, such as the search for fame, fortune, and power. They were a countercultural movement challenging their hearers to adopt a more authentic life that freed them for true happiness. They led a very ascetic life, begged for food, and wore a very distinctive dress: a short cloak with a purse and staff. Some scholars see their wandering preaching and way of dress similar to the lifestyle of Jesus and his disciples (see Luke 10:1-12). However, a closer examination of Luke's description shows that while the Cynics carried a purse, bag, and sandals, the disciples of Jesus did not — a deliberate way of distinguishing the wandering followers of Jesus from the Cynics! The Cynics used the Socratic method of asking questions and developed a literary device in arguing with an imaginary opponent, called a "diatribe," which included the elements of a discourse containing rhetorical questions. Many of Paul's letters show this characteristic style. The Cynics used lists of virtues and vices in their teaching. This was also a characteristic feature of Paul's letters (Gal 5:19-23).

Philo (20 B.C.E.–50 C.E.)

Philo was a wealthy hellenized Jew from Alexandria in Egypt. His extensive writings are extremely important. Influenced by the Greek philosophical schools, he endeavored to explain the Hebrew Scriptures by using thought patterns that the Greco-Roman world would understand. Platonism's concept of two worlds and the soul's descent into the body enabled him to interpret the Hebrew Scriptures in an allegorical way. Scholars debate whether Philo's writings influenced the New Testament directly or whether the commonalities between them were attributable to the world out of which they both stem. It is indisputable that the thought process of the Letter to the Hebrews embraces Platonism as a framework for interpreting the Hebrew Scriptures. The concept of the Logos in the prologue of John's Gospel also finds an echo in Philo's usage of the concept.

The Religious World of the New Testament Era

The Greco-Roman Religious World

A consideration of the pagan religious world of the 1st century C.E. is important for the study of the spread of Christianity throughout the Roman Empire. The life and message of Jesus and his ministry occurred within the context of the religious world of Judaism in Palestine. However, a study of the pagan religions has relevance because after Jesus' death his message was proclaimed to the wider Greco-Roman world. It is necessary to understand how those hearers or readers heard that message according to their context and religious background. Paul's preaching (and that of the other Christian missionaries) was to people with a pagan worldview that embraced the existence of numerous gods and goddesses. Given this context, Paul's hearers would at first appropriate the message within the context of the familiar. For example, Paul and Barnabas were mistaken for the gods Hermes and Zeus when they preached in Lystra during their first missionary journey (Acts 14:8-18).

Traditional Greco-Roman Mythology

The greatest difference between the religious world of Greece and Rome and that of Judaism lies in their understanding of the divine. Judaism is a monotheistic religion (belief in one God), while the Greco-Roman religions were polytheistic (belief in many gods). While the religions of Greece and Rome began independently of each other, by the 1st century C.E. the two religious traditions had fused together so that there was very little difference between them. Since the culture and language of Greece had dominated the world, it is natural that the Greek religion exerted the greatest influence in transforming the Roman religion. The major difference originally separating the Greek and Roman gods was that the Roman gods and goddesses did not have sexual relationships. Consequently, no genealogies could be constructed indicating relationships among the deities.

Greek religious mythologies influenced the wider Hellenistic world, but indigenous Roman rituals and cults were never adopted by the rest of the Roman Empire. Perhaps this was because Rome was originally one city-state that grew into the administrative seat of the empire. As such its religious rituals and customs were simply one among numerous other city-states that already had attained a unity and common vision through the spread of Hellenistic culture.

The Greek city-states had myths associated with their history and foundation. Consequently, certain gods and goddesses were venerated within that city. Temples were erected to them, special festivals were celebrated in their honor, and rituals were conducted even daily as a way of honoring and appeasing the gods and goddesses.

Mystery Religions

The term "mystery religion" refers to a form of religious experience among groups of worshippers (Greek *mystes,* "one initiated") who believed that through their secret initiation rituals *(mysterion)* they were able to experi-

Greco-Roman Gods and Goddesses — The Twelve Olympians

Although the Greeks worshipped numerous gods and goddesses, their major gods and goddesses were believed to live on Mount Olympus in Greece.

In the early 2nd century B.C.E. Quintus Ennius grouped certain Roman gods and goddesses by identifying them with their Greek counterparts and called them the "united gods."

The fourteen dieties listed below were reduced to a canon of twelve Olympians. Hestia is removed from the list (her home is the family hearth as well as the temple hearth). Hades is also removed since his home is not on Mount Olympus, but the Underworld.

Greek male gods	Function	Roman male gods
Apollo	God of sun, music, and poetry	Apollo
Ares	God of war	Mars
Dionysus	God of wine and of ecstacy	Bacchus
Hades	God of the realm of the dead	Pluto
Hephaestus	God of fire	Vulcan
Hermes	God of speech; messenger of the gods	Mercury
Poseidon	God of the sea and earthquakes	Neptune
Zeus	Supreme god: order and justice	Jupiter

Greek female gods	Function	Roman female gods
Aphrodite	Goddess of love and beauty	Venus
Artemis	Goddess of the moon, hunting, and chastity	Diana
Athena	Goddess of wisdom	Minerva
Demeter	Goddess of corn	Ceres
Hera	Goddess of marriage	Juno
Hestia	Goddess of the hearth	Vesta

ence the life of the gods. The early Christian preachers would have to compete with these new religious movements in order to bring people to accept Christ. A major difference with early Christianity was that the mystery religions did not make social demands on their hearers, hence no personal morality was stressed. Attention here will be given to two of the most popular 1st-century C.E. mystery religions, the Eleusinian mysteries and the mysteries of Mithras.

The Eleusinian mysteries developed from a festival that celebrated agricultural fertility. The background to the observance was the myth about Hades, who carried off into the place of the dead Persephone, the daughter of the goddess Demeter (goddess of corn and agriculture). Demeter's rage at this caused a drought on the earth, depriving humans of food and gods of sacrifices. Zeus dispatched Hermes to Demeter with a compromise. Persephone was allowed to return to her mother, but she had to spend one-third of every year with Hades (the four months when the land is dry and unproductive). With time, initiation into the Eleusinian mysteries became a celebration and participation in the mystery of life, death, and rebirth for the initiates.

The mysteries of Mithras originated in Persia, and the cult was very popular among Roman soldiers. In the 3rd century C.E. it became the state religion of Rome. Women were excluded from participation. Information about this cult is gleaned from carvings found in caves (called *Mithraeum*) where their rituals took place. Mithras was worshipped as the sun-god, who was born on December 25 (the winter solstice) and was visited by shepherds. He later sacrificed a bull (the zodiac sign of Taurus), and from this bull's blood came new life. Initiates had to go through seven stages of initiation, each under the protection of a planetary god. These seven stages were a preparation for the eventual salvation that the initiate would experience at death when the soul moved through seven planetary stages to the place from which it originated. Every Mithraeum had a central statue of Mithras slaying a bull. One can note many similarities with the rituals of Christianity: December 25 was taken over by Christians to celebrate the birth of God's Son on earth, while baptism and common meals were two features that Mithraism and Christianity held in common.

The Emperor Cult

The cult of the Roman emperor traces its origins to Alexander the Great, on whom many of the cities of the East bestowed divine honors. Subsequent rulers were afforded similar honors and worship. In Egypt at the end of the 3rd century B.C.E. their rulers (the Ptolemies, descendants of Alexander the Great's general Ptolemy) were worshipped as divine from the moment they became king. In the 1st century C.E. Augustus refused to accept divine honors during his lifetime, but they were bestowed on him at his death and temples were erected in his name. Also during the 1st century C.E. Caligula demanded that statues portraying him as divine should be set up throughout the empire. Domitian named himself "Lord and God," an action that infuriated Christians as can be seen from the book of Revelation. In the 2nd century the issue of worship of the emperor became a very serious matter leading to the persecution of those Christians who refused to participate. Pliny the Younger (governor of the Roman province of Bithynia in Asia Minor in 110 C.E.) used the willingness or refusal to offer wine and incense before a statue of the emperor as a test to see who was a Christian and who was not: those who refused were persecuted.

The Jewish Religious World

Our study of the Hebrew Bible has laid a firm foundation for understanding the New Testament writings against their background within the religious world of Judaism. One additional feature is noted by the Jewish historian Josephus in his description of the religious world of his time: "At this time there were three schools of thought among the Jews, which held different opinions concerning human affairs; the first being that of the Pharisees, the second that of the Sadducees, and the third that of the Essenes" (*Ant.* 13:171; in *Ant.* 18.23 Josephus speaks of a "fourth philosophy" which was led by Judas the Galilean, a revolutionary, and his offspring).

Josephus's words lead the reader to view Judaism at the time of the birth of Christianity not as a monolithic entity, but rather as diverse whereby the traditions of Israel were handed on and lived out in the 1st century C.E. in a number of different ways. To a certain extent the analogy of Christianity today can speak to this reality. Christianity is not a monolithic entity, but comprises many different groups, or denominations, that interpret Christian traditions in different ways, each claiming to be true to Jesus' spirit and to those writings that record his message. We will endeavor to show in our study of the New Testament writings that the early Christians were just as diverse in handing on Jesus' message.

In this light Second Temple Judaism at the time of the birth of the New Testament was equally diverse. These different groups within 1st-century C.E. Judaism interpreted their traditions in surprisingly diverse ways.

We need to caution that our knowledge of these groups is limited. When Josephus explains them, he is doing so for a Roman readership and consequently simplifies what was a much more complicated and nuanced situation.

Sadducees

Our knowledge of the Sadducees is very limited. Some scholars say their name derives from the Hebrew word for "the righteous ones." Others say it derives from Zadok, a priest at the time of Solomon (1 Kgs 1:26). The Sadducees were the officiating priests at the temple of Jerusalem, supporting their claim to this exclusive function from the words of Ezekiel: "These are the descendants of Zadok, who alone among the descendants of Levi may come near to the Lord to minister to him" (Ezek 40:46). The high priests came from their group and served as representatives of the people before the foreign rulers. This gave them a political status and importance as the wealthy aristocracy of the land of Palestine. They would naturally want the status quo to continue unhindered.

The Sadducees (just as the Samaritans) accepted only the first five books of Moses as their Sacred Writings. They upheld the free will of the individual to make choices. Through the exercise of free will humankind (not God) is responsible for evil. The Sadducees rejected the Pharisees' understanding of the Oral Law. They also rejected concepts that had become central to the Pharisees' vision of their religion, such as belief in the resurrection of the dead and belief in angels.

Pharisees

The Pharisees were essentially lay people. Their name is probably derived from the Hebrew word meaning "the separated ones," although we do not know to what this separation actually refers. They were first mentioned in the 2nd century B.C.E., originally as involved in conflicts with the Maccabees and the Sadducees. As time progressed their role was largely restricted to preserving their interpretation of their Israelite traditions. After the destruction of the Jerusalem temple they became leaders in the synagogues.

For the Pharisees the Hebrew Scriptures included the Torah, the Prophets, and the Writings. In addition they also accepted the Oral Law, the interpretations given by the Jewish rabbis to the Torah in applying it to new situations over the course of time. This Oral Law was ultimately contained in the Mishnah (written around 200 C.E.) and later in the Talmud (around 400). The Pharisees "built a fence around the Law" by applying the Torah to the daily lives of the Jews, enabling them to live faithfully in new and changing situations.

The Pharisees, the scholars of the Law, were referred to as rabbis ("teachers"). Two important rabbis, Hillel and Shammai, lived during the 1st century C.E., and their interpretations have been preserved in the Talmud. Shammai offered a stricter interpretation of the Law, while Hillel was more open. Hillel offered a teaching that was very close to the golden rule of Jesus. Regarding the essence of the Law, Hillel said: "Do not do to your neighbor what is hateful to yourself. This is the entire Torah. All the rest is commentary."

The Pharisees also accepted belief in resurrection and in angels. The Gospels often present Jesus in conflict with the Pharisees, but it is possible that the Gospels reflect more their own situation in Galilee after the destruction of Jerusalem in 70 C.E. The Pharisees did not tie the religion of Israel exclusively to the temple or the land; instead their interpretation of the Law centered on the application of the Law to one's daily life. As such they were able to give a direction to Judaism that enabled it to survive into future centuries without the presence of the temple. Judaism today owes its survival and heritage to the work and interpretation of the Pharisees.

Essenes

The Essenes' importance for the study of the New Testament lies in the fact that they provide us with an illustration of one way in which Judaism was being lived and interpreted at the time of Jesus. The writings of the New Testament make no reference to the Essenes. There are, however, some similarities in the writings of the Dead Sea Scrolls and in the New Testament, especially in the use of similar vocabulary. Common expressions such as "sons of light and sons of darkness" are found both in the Dead Sea Scrolls and in the Gospel of John. While some scholars argue that Jesus originated from the Essenes, no evidence has been produced to support such a theory. In fact, the lifestyle of Jesus was very different from that of the Essenes. They were a "withdrawal group," while Jesus spent his ministry directly involved with sinners and those whom the Law rejected.

The Fourth Philosophy

Josephus refers to the "fourth philosophy," which seems to embrace some political activists around the time of the death of Herod the Great. Following Herod's death, two leaders incited a revolt which was quickly put down. In 6 C.E. Judas the Galilean caused further unrest through his opposition to taxes that had been imposed. While this group is not to be seen as directly continuing to the *sicarii* and the Zealots of the 60s C.E., what they did hold in common was their zeal for fidel-

ity to the Jewish Torah. They strenuously opposed the Roman occupation, even to the extent of using violence as a means to withstand against it. In this they were certainly heirs to the heritage of the Maccabees, who gained independence through the sword.

Putting It All Together

This understanding of the religious world of Judaism at the time of the emergence of the New Testament helps to explain many aspects of the New Testament, particularly the way the different Gospel writers portray Jesus' interaction with the various Jewish groups. For example, the controversy between Jesus and the Sadducees regarding the question of the resurrection of the dead (Mark 12:18-27) is understandable when one realizes that the Sadducees did not believe in resurrection. When Paul was brought before the Sanhedrin (the Jewish council, made up of Pharisees and Sadducees), he aligned himself with the Pharisees, exploiting the religious tensions between the Pharisees and Sadducees by acknowledging his belief in the resurrection of the dead (Acts 23:6-10).

The picture painted in the Gospels of the different religious groups at the time of Jesus is colored by two aspects. The Gospels present the narrative from the perspective of Jesus and his followers. They are written from situations of conflict which imply that a one-sided picture of the opponents has emerged. The Gospel narratives also reflect the period post-70 C.E., with the result that some of the opposition current at the time of the Gospels' composition is being read back into Jesus' life and ministry.

As a teacher Jesus fits well into this context, offering yet another insight and interpretation of Israel's traditions. In addition to the Sadducees, Pharisees, Essenes, Zealots, Sicarii, and the Fourth Philosophy, there is as well Jesus and his followers, each in their own way claiming to be true to the heart of Israel's traditions.

Only two groups survived the destruction of the temple and the land in 70 C.E., the Pharisees and Jesus' followers. The two great religions of Judaism and Christianity owe their origins to those fateful events: Judaism is heir to the legacy of the Pharisees, while Christianity is heir to Jesus' heritage.

Questions for Review and Discussion

1 What are some of the major similarities and differences between the world of Jesus and ours?

2 Prepare a talk on one of the ancient religions or philosophies. What interests you about it?

Further Reading

Freyne, Sean. *Galilee from Alexander the Great to Hadrian, 323 B.C.E. to 135 C.E.* Wilmington: Michael Glazier, 1980.

Malina, Bruce J. *The New Testament World: Insights from Cultural Anthropology.* Rev. ed. Louisville: Westminster/John Knox, 1993.

———. *Windows on the World of Jesus: Time Travel to Ancient Judea.* Louisville: Westminster/John Knox, 1993.

Turcan, Robert. *The Cults of the Roman Empire.* Oxford: Blackwell, 1996.

Chapter 47

Interpreting the New Testament

Getting Started

1 Read the opening chapter of the Gospel of Mark. Then examine chapters 3 and 4 in the Gospels of Matthew and Luke.

2 What are some of the similarities that you note among these three Gospels? Are you able to deduce anything from these observations?

Preliminary Comments

Chapter 4 of this Introduction provides a survey of different approaches and methods of interpretation with regard to the Bible that have been employed over the course of the centuries, and in particular with regard to the Old Testament. This chapter will focus on two methods of interpretation that have been most useful in providing insight into the New Testament texts, namely the historical-critical method and narrative criticism. We will use these two methods exclusively in our examination of the New Testament books. They provide the best entry into these writings and make it possible to attain the clearest understanding of these New Testament texts.

The Historical-Critical Methods of Interpretation

From the Renaissance onwards, historical consciousness permeated the human mind in an inescapable way, influencing every discipline of study including that of the Bible. To read an ancient text like the Bible meant reading it in the historical context of its time and worldview. This involved adopting tools that would enable one to read the biblical text against that background. Naturally, this initially generated fear among believers, for it was felt that these historical approaches undermined the very foundation of the faith. But, one of the great contributions of historical-critical methods has been to bring the believer to a realization of the difference between the message contained in the biblical writings and the way in which that message is expressed, the worldview in which that message is incarnated.

In searching for the biblical message, it is incumbent upon the student of the Bible to situate the Bible's worldview in its difference, in its strangeness. This involves examining the context from which the New Testament texts emerged and the issues and questions they grappled with, issues very often strange and foreign to our present world.

Scholars have applied the term "historical-critical"

to a wide diversity of meanings embracing a variety of methods that at times almost renders the term meaningless. However, a strict interpretation of the term refers to a number of approaches that have built one upon another, four of which we describe below.

Textual Criticism

Like Old Testament text criticism, New Testament textual criticism aims at establishing as far as possible the most reliable reading of the Greek text of the New Testament through the investigation of the thousands of manuscripts containing parts of the texts that have come down to us over the course of the centuries. Since we do not possess the original copies of any of the biblical manuscripts, textual criticism endeavors to establish as accurately and objectively as possible what that original text looked like.

Obviously, it is impossible to reconstruct the original text with absolute certainty. Textual critics attempt to provide the most probable text that can be reconstructed at present from the available manuscripts. This reconstructed text has been called the "critical text" since it is the result of applying a host of objective principles and criteria to produce a text that is commonly agreed upon by scholars. Such a critical Greek text, in the case of the New Testament, is accompanied by an apparatus of footnotes which draw attention to the decisions that scholars have made based on the different readings available from the manuscripts.

Source Criticism

With the importance given to historical consciousness in the 18th and 19th centuries, historical questions were asked of the biblical documents as well. One of the fundamental issues that immediately became evident was the presence of sources behind the biblical writings. As we have seen in Chapter 5, the first five books of the Bible were at one time identified by the Documentary Hypothesis as being composed from four basic sources. In the New Testament, a critical study of the Gospels also revealed the use of sources. Matthew and Luke were seen to use the Gospel of Mark as their basic source together with another source, identified as Q (from German *Quelle,* "source"), that consisted mainly of Jesus' sayings.

Not only did the source critics identify these various sources lying behind the biblical writings, they also endeavored to reconstruct them. Attention will be given to Gospel source criticism when we examine the question of the Synoptic Problem later in this chapter.

Form Criticism

As we saw in the introduction to Old Testament form criticism, this method pays close attention to the

---

Textual Criticism Illustrated

A good example of the results of textual criticism can be seen in the passage of the Lord's Prayer in Matthew's Gospel in the NRSV. While text criticism obviously is dealing with the Greek reading of the text, we are able to see the results of this in our own English editions. The ending of the prayer in Matt 6:13 reads: "And do not bring us to the time of trial, but rescue us from the evil one." A footnote in the NRSV reads: "Or *from evil.* Other ancient authorities add, in some form, *For the kingdom and the power and the glory are yours forever. Amen.*" This indicates that the ancient manuscripts preserve different readings concerning the ending of the prayer. Textual critics have concluded according to their criteria that the original ending of the prayer in Matthew's Gospel did not contain the familiar words: "For the kingdom and the power and the glory are yours forever. Amen."

---

smaller units (called "forms") which comprise the text. Form critics endeavor to get behind the body of the text and its sources to these units that ultimately went to make up the source or text. These units are classified according to their type or form which is always expressed in a similar structure. For example, the controversies of Jesus were all told using a similar structure. Examine the question about paying taxes to Caesar and the question about the resurrection (Mark 12:13-17, 18-27). You will notice that a common structure lies behind them. Other forms that we can identify in the Gospels are parables, miracle stories, sayings, infancy narratives, and a passion narrative. The categorization into the various literary forms is highly technical. All that we intend is to draw attention to some of these classifications.

Form criticism aims at reaching behind the Gospels to reconstruct the oral tradition behind the written text. The various forms that have been identified are seen as vestiges of the oral tradition itself. In the final analysis form criticism is an attempt to trace the history of the development and handing on of the various forms, particularly in the course of their oral transmission. This entails identifying the situation, or *Sitz-im-Leben* (a German expression for the context or "life situation" within the community), that gave rise to the particular form and its developing transmission. It is a study of the handing on of the traditions within the context of the community. Source criticism is invaluable in helping us to get behind the written texts to a period that predates the Gospels of Matthew and Luke by one to two decades (i.e., to around the years 60 to 70 C.E.). Form criticism turns its attention to the years between the death of Jesus and the composition of the Gospels (from the

Ending of the Gospel of Luke in Codex Sinaiticus (fourth century c.e.). (Institute for New Testament Textual Research, Münster/Westphalia)

community in mind for whom they addressed a specific message, and so they were actually creative theologians. Perhaps it would be better to refer to this branch of criticism as "author criticism," since the aim is to discover the contributions that the redactor made to the inherited material. In the course of our studies we will pay a great deal of attention to this "author criticism," for it will be our scope to discover the theological vision of each of the Gospels. We will attempt to understand what exactly that vision was, and how and why the Gospel writers changed their sources in order to communicate that vision of Jesus and his message.

Redaction criticism is based upon the final text of the Gospel, the text that we have in front of us today. As such it is predominantly a literary approach. Today, however, most biblical scholars have moved beyond redaction criticism to study in more depth the Gospels as literary documents.

mid-30s until the 60s). Scholars attempt to see why the believing communities remembered and handed on these specific aspects of the tradition as well as how and why changes were brought into the tradition.

Redaction Criticism

Form criticism deals with establishing and examining the units and forms that the Evangelists had available in the composition of their Gospels. Redaction criticism studies how the writers of the Gospels creatively used and molded this material they inherited. The name "redaction criticism" comes from German *Redakteur,* which literally means an editor. However, the task of the Gospel writers embraces much more than simply the work of an editor. They used the sources, the forms, and the oral traditions that had come down to them in composing their narratives. This was much more than just "cut and paste," since they brought a depth of theological meaning and direction to the material at hand. Each of the Gospel writers had a distinct vision of Jesus, a specific group or

The Synoptic Problem

The three Gospels of Matthew, Mark, and Luke are called the Synoptic Gospels. Synoptic comes from two Greek words, *syn,* "with," and *horao,* "to perceive with the eye, to notice," so the term means "seeing with the same eyes." Because of their close similarities, the first three Gospels are often printed in parallel columns, creating what is termed a "synopsis" or "harmony" of the Gospels. In this way one can take a comprehensive view of Jesus' ministry in all three Gospels ("seeing his ministry with the same eyes").

An interesting question emerges when the Synoptic Gospels are examined closely. On the one hand, there are very close similarities in the three Gospels, particularly in the way in which they are structured. On the other hand, there are notable differences between them. So the question emerges: "How does one account for this mixture of similar and dissimilar material in these three Gospels?" This is the Synoptic Problem or question.

The Synoptic Problem Illustrated

In the history of interpretation the application of the historical-critical methods outlined above has proved extremely helpful in providing solutions to the Synoptic Problem. Before examining solutions, however, we shall illustrate the problem clearly by looking at the content, arrangement, and details within these three Gospels.

Content

Similarities among these Gospels are immediately evident when one notes that the words and deeds of Jesus are to a large extent basically the same. A statistical examination reveals the following:

- Mark has 661 verses, while Matthew has 1,068 and Luke 1,149.
- Matthew has 606 of Mark's verses (only 55 verses of Mark are not found in Matthew).
- Luke has 320 of Mark's verses (of the 55 verses of Mark which Matthew does not have, Luke has 24 new verses).

This means that only 31 verses in Mark do not occur in Matthew and Luke.

Dissimilarities are also evident. Some events are narrated by two of the Evangelists, while other events occur in only one Gospel. For example, Matthew and Luke give an account of Jesus' birth, whereas Mark does not mention it. All three Gospels mention Jesus' temptations, although only Matthew and Luke describe the actual three temptations (but in a different order).

Arrangement

Similarities appear in the outline of Jesus' ministry as presented in each of the Gospels:

- John the Baptist preaches in the desert where Jesus is baptized.
- After his temptation Jesus begins his public ministry of preaching and healing.
- Most of Jesus' activity is centered in Galilee and the surrounding areas.
- Jesus journeys to Jerusalem where he is crucified, and the accounts end with his resurrection.

Dissimilarities in the structure of the Gospels are also striking. Matthew groups the sayings of Jesus into five great discourses. Luke constructs a long travel narrative of Jesus' journey to Jerusalem (9:51–19:27) where he places these sayings of Jesus.

Details

Similarities are found in the striking agreements in Greek vocabulary or style. This is remarkable if one real-

izes that Jesus taught in Aramaic, while the Gospels were written in Greek.

There are notable *dissimilarities* with small details. See, for example, the placard that was erected over the cross of Jesus:

- "This is Jesus, the King of the Jews." (Matt 27:37)
- "The King of the Jews." (Mark 15:26)
- "This is the King of the Jews." (Luke 23:38)

Solutions Proposed

St. Augustine's Solution

Until the 18th century the commonly accepted solution to this problem was the one that had been proposed by St. Augustine (354-430 C.E.). He taught that the Gospels were written by those whose names they bear and in the sequence in which they appear in the Bible: Matthew (an apostle) wrote first; Mark (a disciple of Paul the Apostle) was the next writer, who produced an abbreviated form of Matthew; Luke (also a disciple of Paul) wrote his Gospel next using both Matthew and Mark; finally, John (another apostle, known as "the Beloved Disciple") wrote his Gospel using the three Synoptic Gospels, but producing a different type of Gospel, a "Spiritual Gospel." The similarities were explained through the literary dependence of the Gospels on each other. Augustine attributed the differences to the personality of each author.

This solution does not resolve all the difficulties, raising a number of serious questions. John is so different from the other Gospels that it cannot claim a literary dependence upon them. Further, Mark is not a summary of Matthew, as there are so many essential features that are missing: there is no account of the Sermon on the Mount, Jesus' birth, resurrection, or postresurrection appearances.

The Griesbach Hypothesis

In the late 18th century Johann Griesbach (1745-1812) proposed another solution. He argued that Mark was written after Matthew and Luke and that it was an abbreviation of both Gospels. This theory is still supported by a small number of scholars today. However, most scholars are convinced that Mark was the first Gospel to have been written and became the source for Matthew and Luke's Gospels. This is the heart of the next theory, the Two-Document Hypothesis.

The Two-Document Hypothesis

This solution to the Synoptic Problem has become the most widely accepted view in biblical scholarship as it helps to explain most of the difficulties in the relationship among the Gospels. It was first proposed in the 19th century and arose from the use of the historical-critical methods outlined above. Source criticism lies at the heart of this theory, explaining the similarities and differences between the Synoptic Gospels on the basis of written sources that were used. The Gospels were analyzed from a literary perspective in order to discover those sources.

In presenting this view, an understanding of the way in which the Gospels emerged came to light. In Chapter 45 we painted a picture of the growth and development of all the New Testament writings that conformed to the insights gained from this theory. In what follows we will flesh out in greater depth what we argued earlier. The following five stages in the production of the Synoptic Gospels have been proposed from this literary analysis.

The first stage comprised oral traditions.
Everything in Jesus' world was oral. He taught openly but never committed anything to writing. His disciples continued his ministry of teaching and preaching in an oral way over the next 40 years (from Jesus' death (ca. 30 C.E.) to the appearance of Mark (ca. 70 C.E.). The preaching of the gospel of Jesus by his disciples is known as the *kerygma* (Greek "proclamation, preaching"). At first this kerygma was entirely in Aramaic since the early Christians all came from Judaism and lived in Palestine. With the passage of time missionaries such as the Apostle Paul spread the message within the Roman Empire in Greek-speaking areas. Not only did the message now have to be translated into another language, *koine* Greek, but it also had to be adapted to new needs and circumstances of the hearers. Much study has been done in more recent times by anthropologists and linguists concerning the use of oral traditions in oral cultures around the world. This has helped draw analogies with the oral culture of nascent Christianity. While the stories about Jesus and his sayings were considered to be authoritative, the very nature of an oral society resulted in a variation in the way in which these sayings and stories were transmitted. These variations were also facilitated through the translation from Aramaic to Greek. We can see this in the wording of the placard placed over the cross of Jesus mentioned above (Matt 27:37; Mark 15:26; Luke 23:38).

Form criticism contributed greatly toward understanding the oral transmission of the sayings and stories about Jesus within this oral society. As indicated above, form critics argued that the written Gospels emerged from numerous originally oral forms (or genres) including conflict stories, pronouncement stories, parables, and sayings.

The second stage comprised short written compilations.
Collections were made from the oral preaching and the forms used when preaching, producing compila-

tions such as a passion narrative, sayings of Jesus, Jesus' parables, and his miracles. These were written to preserve the memories of the apostles as well as for catechetical purposes. From examining Matthew and Luke scholars have identified material that is not found in Mark but is common to both these Gospels. Scholars have concluded that this common material is derived from a written compilation of the sayings and teachings of Jesus that is referred to as the *Q document or source,* as noted above. No text or copy of the Q document has been found, but it has been reconstructed using source criticism from those passages that are common to Matthew and Luke and distinct from Mark. Q was originally composed in Greek.

This common material comprises about 250 verses in total and contains some of the most well-known teachings or sayings of Jesus. The Q document contains practically no narrative. Instead it presents a series of Jesus' sayings (very similar to the Gospel of Thomas which was discovered in 1945). These sayings are recorded chiefly in the sermons in Matthew and the journey of Jesus to Jerusalem in Luke.

The third stage was the composition of the Gospel of Mark.
In examining the final stages of Gospel development, scholars have turned to redaction criticism to explain their composition. As we have indicated, redaction criticism is concerned with identifying the author's (redactor's) contribution in putting together the sources that were used. The redactor does not slavishly copy his sources; instead he assembles them and reinterprets them according to his theological perspective.

Mark is attributed with the first attempt to produce a written synthesis of Jesus' teaching and deeds. In doing so, he invented the Gospel genre. Writing around 70 C.E. Mark used the oral traditions that had come down to him as well as some of the short written collections that already existed (such as a grouping of the parables; see Mark 4). He transformed the oral *kerygma* into a narrative focusing upon the suffering, cross, and death of Jesus. His theological focus differed from that of the Q document with its interest centered on Jesus' teaching. That Mark was the first to do this can be seen from the following considerations:
- From a statistical viewpoint: Only 31 verses in Mark are not found in Matthew or Luke. Mark is also the shortest of the three Gospels. It is a principle of linguistic criticism that the shortest document is generally the original text.
- From a consideration of Mark's vocabulary: Mark was written in Greek by someone whose mother tongue was not Greek, probably Aramaic. His

A Q Passage: The Lament over Jerusalem

A good example of a Q passage can be seen in Jesus' lament over Jerusalem (Matt 23:37-39; Luke 13:34-35). Although the exact correspondences have to be identified from the Greek text, the NRSV translation provides a good illustration of the closeness of the two passages.

Matt 23:37-39	Luke 13:34-35
"Jerusalem, Jerusalem, the city that kills the prophets and stones those who are sent to it! How often have I desired to gather your children together as a hen gathers her brood under her wings, and you were not willing!	"Jerusalem, Jerusalem, the city that kills the prophets and stones those who are sent to it! How often have I desired to gather your children together as a hen gathers her brood under her wings, and you were not willing!
See, your house is left to you, desolate.	See, your house is left to you.
For I tell you, you will not see me again until you say, 'Blessed is the one who comes in the name of the Lord.'"	And I tell you, you will not see me until the time comes when you say, 'Blessed is the one who comes in the name of the Lord.'"

Scholars maintain that Luke preserved better than Matthew the sequence of the passages and sayings in the Q source. This explains why they indicate Q passages by the Lukan chapter and verse preceded by the designation Q. For example, the above passage is designated as Q 13:34-35.

sentence structure is Aramaic/Hebrew as can be seen from the way he joins his sentences and clauses with the Greek word *kai* ("and"). This is the typical form of sentence construction in Hebrew, but not in Greek. An examination of the same passages in Matthew and Luke shows that they have corrected Mark's "barbaric" Greek and expressed it in good Greek.

- Mark tends to be repetitious while Matthew and Luke have simplified Mark. A good illustration of this can be seen from the following example:

That evening, at sundown, they brought to him all who were sick or possessed with demons. (Mark 1:32)

That evening they brought to him many who were possessed with demons. (Matt 8:16)

As the sun was setting, all those who had any who were sick with various kinds of diseases brought them to him. (Luke 4:40)

The fourth stage was the composition of the Gospel of Matthew.

About a decade after Mark (ca. 80 C.E.) Matthew appeared. A literary examination shows that Matthew has incorporated around 90 percent of Mark into his Gospel. In addition, Matthew used the Q document (also used by Luke) to stress Jesus' teachings. Matthew produced an enlarged edition of Mark with a theological focus upon Jesus as teacher. At the same time Matthew's Gospel

contained material that was known only to him, referred to as *Special M (Matthew)*. In an attempt to show Jesus as Israel's true teacher who was greater than Moses, Matthew introduced five major sermons into the structure of Mark's Gospel. These five speeches would remind readers of the five books of the Torah.

The fifth stage saw the composition of the Gospel of Luke and the Acts of the Apostles.

Written in the early 90s C.E., Luke's Gospel incorporated about half of Mark together with the Q document. Scholars maintain that Luke has preserved better than Matthew the sequence of the passages and sayings in Q. Like Matthew, Luke incorporated into his narrative information that was available only to him. This material is referred to as *Special L (Luke)*. Not only did Luke produce another Gospel with the intention of demonstrating that Jesus was the Universal Savior, he also added a sequel, the Acts of the Apostles, to show how the salvation brought by Jesus is extended by his followers to the rest of the world.

The Two-Document Hypothesis Illustrated

A passage occurring in all three Synoptic Gospels is referred to as the triple tradition. Scholars also speak of Markan priority, in that Mark is judged to have been written first and that Matthew and Luke used Mark as their primary source. A good example of the triple tradition occurs in the opening chapters of Jesus' ministry. Mark begins with three events: the preaching of John the Baptist (1:1-8), the baptism of Jesus (1:9-11) and Jesus' temptation (1:12-13). Matthew and Luke preserve the exact same sequence of events: preaching of John (Matt 3:1-12; Luke 3:1-20), baptism of Jesus (Matt 3:13-17; Luke 3:21-22) and the temptation of Jesus (Matt 4:1-11; Luke 4:1-13).

The narrative about the proclamation of John the Baptist (Mark 1:1-8; Matt 3:1-12; Luke 3:1-20) illustrates this *triple tradition* clearly. (Compare the passages in the English synopsis on p. 357.) We can make the following observations about these texts:

- Mark's Gospel opens with the narrative of the proc-lamation of John the Baptist. John is mentioned only after the quotation from Isaiah. Matthew introduces John the Baptist right at the beginning of the nar-rative. Luke situates the events within a historical framework. Both Matthew and Luke have two chap-ters on the birth of Jesus that precede this event.
- Mark, in opening his Gospel narrative, has joined together two quotations from two different proph-ets and identifies them both as coming from the prophet Isaiah! The first part of the quotation (Mark 1:2) comes from the prophet Malachi: "See, I am sending my messenger to prepare the way before me . . ." (Mal. 3:1). The second part comes from Isa 40:3. Matthew recognizes this error and corrects it by reproducing the passage from Isaiah alone. Luke also corrects the error of Mark, but continues with the quotation from Isa 40:3 because it suits the theme of his Gospel, namely a focus on the meaning of a jour-ney. It indicates that Luke has the text of the prophet open in front of him.
- In Mark, John's audience consists of "people from the whole Judean countryside and all the people of Jerusalem" (1:5). For Luke, John is simply speaking to the crowds. The fact that Matthew alone men-tions the Pharisees and Sadducees shows that he must have a particular interest in them. The rest of Matthew proves this to be the case; the Pharisees are Jesus' chief opponents in his Gospel. This shows an important insight into how the Gospels developed. When Matthew was written (a decade after the de-struction of Jerusalem), the temple no longer existed and the nation of Israel was going through a crisis of faith. "Where were they to worship?" "How were they to worship?" The Pharisees answered the challenge by stressing fidelity to the traditions of their past. The sanctification of the people's everyday life was now paramount, with the result that stress was placed upon the types of food they ate and how they dealt with foreigners. The Pharisees saw Jesus' followers as their chief opponents because Christians were also proclaiming a particular way of life that was true to Israel's traditions.

- A quick look at Matthew and Luke shows that they have many similarities between them (which are missing from Mark), for example, the reference to the speech of John: "You brood of vipers" (Matt 3:7; Luke 3:7). While Mark's John foretells that Jesus will baptize with the Holy Spirit, Matthew and Luke's John adds the reference to baptizing with the Holy Spirit *and with fire* (Matt 3:11; Luke 3:16), and they go on to describe in graphic detail the impending judgment and destruction that his fire will bring. This argues for the view that in constructing their narratives Matthew and Luke must have been using a common source (Q). This is known as the double tradition.

The Two-Document Hypothesis (the two documents being the Gospel of Mark and the Q Source) implies that whenever a passage occurs in all three Synoptic Gospels, Matthew and Luke must have found it in Mark. Where Luke and Matthew have a passage in common that does not occur in Mark (such as the Lord's Prayer in Luke 11:2-4; Matt 6:9-13) we assume that they used the common source Q. Central to this view is Markan priority: Mark is the central document used by Matthew and Luke to which is added the Q source. Similarities stem from using these same sources, while differences come from the use of sources known only to one Evan-gelist (such as Special M and Special L).

While not all scholars accept the Two-Document Hy-pothesis, it still remains the most widely held solution to the Synoptic Problem. A few scholars have proposed much more complicated views that postulate that the Gospels went through numerous editions. In this Introduction we accept the Two-Document Hypothesis and use it as our working hypothesis. However, we do acknowledge that the reality probably was more compli-cated than we have envisaged.

Narrative Criticism as a Method of Interpreting the New Testament

Although the historical-critical methods are still the most widely used methods in interpreting the New Testament, other literary methods have been gaining importance in recent scholarship. For example, the speech act theory of communication applies the three elements of author, text, and reader to bring deeper ap-preciation and understanding in reading the Bible. Nar-rative criticism takes seriously the nature of the Gospels as narratives, and interpreting them in this way leads to a deeper appreciation and understanding of these texts. We will consider some elements of this method that lead to an appreciation of the Gospels and apply them briefly to the Gospel of Mark by way of illustration and introduction to Mark itself.

The actual author and the implied author.

In Chapter 1 we drew attention to the distinction between the actual author and the implied author of a text. As we noted, the implied author is the vision of the author that we deduce from the text itself. For example, for the Gospel of John we envision an implied author who is meditative, reflecting upon events, and for Matthew, a person at home in the world of Judaism. The implied author is accessible to the reader only through the text. (Page 3 illustrates the relationship between the reader, text, and author.)

The actual reader and the implied reader.

Reading the text provides insight into the reader for whom the text was written. For example, a Gospel text may focus on issues important to Jews, suggesting that the author was writing for Jewish people (or at least Jewish Christians). The reader that we construct from the text is the implied reader. We can distinguish then three levels of readers: the first-time reader, the implied readers, and present-day readers.

For example, in Luke 1:1-4 the reader is addressed as Theophilus, either a real person (a real reader) or, symbolically, Christian believers (literally, "beloved of God"). The implied reader may be someone who is not an eyewitness to the beginnings of the Christian movement but who desires a reliable account of those events and Jesus' message. Paul's letters, although not narratives, offer good examples of implied readers. From 1 Cor 10:17 we can form a mental image of concerns among his Corinthian readers as well as Paul's perspective on the disputes.

The narrator.

The narrator is the voice that the implied author uses to guide the reader through the narrative and to tell the story. In general, the New Testament narratives are told by third person narrators, although some examples of first person narrators do exist. For example, Luke begins: "I too decided, after investigating everything carefully from the very first . . ." (Luke 1:3). In Acts the narrator is presented as Paul's companion on some of his missionary journeys; e.g., Acts 16:11). Most often, however, the narrator speaks in the third person and is outside the narrative, with the advantage that the narrator knows everything related to the story.

An examination of the Gospel of Mark provides the following characteristics illustrating how the narrator functions in a narrative.

- Mark's narrator has total knowledge. Opening with the words, "The beginning of the good news of Jesus Christ, the Son of God" (Mark 1:1), he states his intention of telling the story about Jesus Christ. In narrating this account he demonstrates insights into characters and events that only he knows. The narrator has total insight and understanding into what is happening in the story and the ability to impart this information to the reader.

- Mark's narrator projects the thoughts and feelings of the characters. For example, Mark shows Jesus' frustration with the disciples on many occasions. In calming the storm at sea Jesus says to his disciples: "Why are you afraid? Have you still no faith?" (4:40). The feelings of the disciples are also noted: When James and John request Jesus to give them places of authority in his kingdom, Mark comments: "When the ten heard this, they began to be angry with James and John" (10:41). This technique enables the reader to see the story from the narrator's point of view and to know what other characters are thinking. This is not possible for a character within the story.

- Mark's narrator often makes brief comments to help the reader understand the special significance of certain events. When Jesus speaks about the "desolating sacrilege set up where it ought not to be," the narrator comments, "let the reader understand" (13:14), underscoring the special significance of what has been said. Parenthetical remarks in 7:3-4 explain the purification customs of Jews. On seven occasions the narrator translates for the sake of the reader the meaning of Aramaic words used in the narrative (e.g., "Talitha cum," "Little girl, get up!" in 5:41; see also 3:17; 7:11, 34; 14:36; 15:22, 34).

The purpose of these techniques is to establish a relationship with the reader. The reader comes to trust the narrator's perspective and accepts the judgments that are made in the course of the narrative. This is well demonstrated in the way the various characters are presented. The narrator introduces Jesus at the very beginning of the Gospel as "Christ, the Son of God," a perspective reinforced throughout the narrative. Jesus is the one whom the reader has learned to trust. By contrast the narrator presents the Jewish authorities in a negative light and the reader learns to distrust them. Finally, the disciples are portrayed as vacillating. In the beginning the narrator introduces them favorably through their immediate response to Jesus' request: "Follow me" (1:17). As the narrative progresses, the narrator shows the disciples failing to understand who Jesus is, and they desert Jesus. In the ultimate analysis, the reader sees the story as the narrator does and

Synoptic Chart of the Preaching of John the Baptist (Matt 3:1-12; Mark 1:1-8; Luke 3:1-20)

Matthew 3:1-12

¹In those days John the Baptist appeared in the wilderness of Judea, proclaiming, ²"Repent, for the kingdom of heaven has come near." ³This is the one of whom the prophet Isaiah spoke when he said,

"The voice of one crying out in the wilderness:
'Prepare the way of the Lord, make his paths straight.'"

⁴Now John wore clothing of camel's hair with a leather belt around his waist, and his food was locusts and wild honey. ⁵Then the people of Jerusalem and all Judea were going out to him, and all the region along the Jordan, ⁶and they were baptized by him in the river Jordan, confessing their sins. ⁷But when he saw many Pharisees and Sadducees coming for baptism, he said to them, "You brood of vipers! Who warned you to flee from the wrath to come? ⁸Bear fruit worthy of repentance. ⁹Do not presume to say to yourselves. 'We have Abraham as our ancestor'; for I tell you, God is able from these stones to raise up children to Abraham. ¹⁰Even now the ax is lying at the root of the trees; every tree therefore that does not bear good fruit is cut down and thrown into the fire.

¹¹I BAPTIZE YOU WITH WATER FOR REPENTANCE, BUT ONE WHO IS MORE POWERFUL THAN I IS COMING AFTER ME; I AM NOT WORTHY TO CARRY HIS SANDALS. HE WILL BAPTIZE YOU WITH THE HOLY SPIRIT AND FIRE. ¹²His winnowing fork is in his hand, and he will clear his threshing floor and will gather his wheat into the granary; but the chaff he will burn with unquenchable fire."

Mark 1:1-8

¹The beginning of the good news of Jesus Christ, the Son of God. ²As it is written in the prophet Isaiah, "See, I am sending my messenger ahead of you, who will prepare your way; ³the voice of one crying out in the wilderness: 'Prepare the way of the Lord, Make his paths straight.'"

⁴John the baptizer appeared in the wilderness, proclaiming a baptism of repentance for the forgiveness of sins. ⁵And people from the whole Judean countryside and all the people of Jerusalem were going out to him, and were baptized by him in the river Jordan, confessing their sins. ⁶Now John was clothed with camel's hair, with a leather belt around his waist, and he ate locusts and wild honey. ⁷He proclaimed, "THE ONE WHO IS MORE POWERFUL THAN I IS COMING AFTER ME; I AM NOT WORTHY TO STOOP DOWN AND UNTIE THE THONG OF HIS SANDALS. ⁸I HAVE BAPTIZED YOU WITH WATER; BUT HE WILL BAPTIZE YOU WITH THE HOLY SPIRIT."

Luke 3:1-20

¹In the fifteenth year of the reign of Emperor Tiberius, when Pontius Pilate was governor of Judea, and Herod was ruler of Galilee, and his brother Philip ruler of the region of Ituraea and Trachonitis, and Lysanias ruler of Abilene, ²during the high priesthood of Annas and Caiaphas, the word of God came to John son of Zechariah in the wilderness. ³He went into all the region around the Jordan, proclaiming a baptism of repentance for the forgiveness of sins, ⁴as it is written in the book of the words of the prophet Isaiah,

"The voice of one crying out in the wilderness:
'Prepare the way of the Lord, make his paths straight.
⁵Every valley shall be filled, and every mountain and hill shall be made low, and the crooked shall be made straight, and the rough ways made smooth;
⁶and all flesh shall see the salvation of God.'"

⁷John said to the crowds that came out to be baptized by him, "You brood of vipers! Who warned you to flee from the wrath to come? ⁸Bear fruits worthy of repentance. Do not begin to say to yourselves. 'We have Abraham as our ancestor': for I tell you, God is able from these stones to raise up children to Abraham. ⁹Even now the ax is lying at the root of the trees; every tree therefore that does not bear good fruit is cut down and thrown into the fire."...

"I BAPTIZE YOU WITH WATER; BUT ONE WHO IS MORE POWERFUL THAN I IS COMING; I AM NOT WORTHY TO UNTIE THE THONG OF HIS SANDALS. HE WILL BAPTIZE YOU WITH THE HOLY SPIRIT AND FIRE. ¹⁷His winnowing fork is in his hand, to clear his threshing floor and to gather the wheat into his granary, but the chaff he will burn with unquenchable fire."

adopts the same perspective through the trust the narrator has built up in the reader.

Putting It All Together

We shall use the approaches of historical criticism and narrative criticism throughout our study of the New Testament writings. Employing both methodologies in interpreting the books of the New Testament will provide an understanding of these writings that moves beyond a subjective interpretation and firmly roots the interpretation in a fidelity to the text.

Questions for Review and Discussion

1 Cut out the same story from two different newspapers. Compare the two articles and try to discern the sources that they used. Can you identify the view-point of each writer as well as what had been omitted from each article?

2 Examine the account of the temptation of Jesus in the Gospels of Luke and Matthew (Luke 4:1-13; Matt 4:1-11). Identify what is similar and what is different. What sources do you think they were using?

Further Reading

Funk, Robert W., ed. *New Gospel Parallels.* Vol. 1: *The Synoptic Gospels.* Philadelphia: Fortress, 1985.

Havener, Ivan. *Q: The Sayings of Jesus.* Good News Studies 19. Wilmington: Michael Glazier, 1987.

Powell, Mark Allan. *What Is Narrative Criticism?* GBS. Minneapolis: Fortress, 1990.

Rhoads, David M., Joanna Dewey, and Donald Michie. *Mark as Story: An Introduction to the Narrative of a Gospel.* 2nd ed. Minneapolis: Fortress, 1999.

The Synoptic Gospels

Chapter 48

What Is a Gospel?

Getting Started

1 List your favorite TV programs.

2 Organize them into similar groups or genres.

3 What are the characteristics that identify a program as belonging to one particular genre?

Use of the Word "Gospel"

The English word "gospel" comes from Anglo-Saxon *Godspell,* meaning "good tidings" or "good news." It translates Greek *euangelion.* In the New Testament this word refers to the good news preached by Jesus that God's kingdom is at hand: "Now after John was arrested, Jesus came to Galilee, proclaiming the good news *(euangelion)* of God, and saying, 'The time is fulfilled, and the kingdom of God has come near; repent, and believe in the good news *(euangelio)*'" (Mark 1:14-15).

Background
The background for the New Testament word "gospel" *(euangelion)* can be traced back to both the Jewish and the Greco-Roman worlds. In the Hebrew Bible the verb "to announce good news" or "to bring good news" occurs in the prophet Isaiah. For example, the messenger announces the good news of Israel's redemption from exile: "Get you up to a high mountain, O Zion, herald of good tidings; lift up your voice with strength, O Jerusalem, herald of good tidings, lift it up, do not fear" (Isa 40:9; see also 41:27; 52:7; 61:1).

Luke 4:16-19 presents Jesus taking up the words of Isa 61:1-2 to announce his ministry in terms of the good news: "The Spirit of the Lord is upon me, because he has anointed me to bring good news to the poor. He has sent me to proclaim release to the captives and recovery of sight to the blind, to let the oppressed go free, to proclaim the year of the Lord's favor."

The Greco-Roman world also demonstrates a usage of the word "gospel" *(euangelion).* A famous inscription found at Priene (dated to 9 B.C.E.) honors Augustus Caesar (27 B.C.E.–14 C.E.) as the one whom the gods sent into the world to bring Roman peace *(pax Romana)* and salvation to humanity. Augustus brings "good news" to the world through the events of his life. The first announcement of "good news" occurred at his birth. Consequently, Augustus's birthday is referred to as the beginning of "good news" for the whole world.

Both these worlds, Jewish and Greco-Roman, provided a source for the early Christians to give expression to the message Jesus came to proclaim. Jesus' proclamation not only fulfilled the role of Isaiah's prophecy in regard to the restoration of Zion as well as the expectations the world placed in the salvation brought by Augustus Caesar, but it also far surpassed them. In order to illustrate the fuller understanding and meaning of this word "gospel" we will trace the way in which the respective New Testament writers used the term and provide a few examples. We begin with Paul, since his are the first writings to have appeared and they show the earliest usage of this word within the Christian world.

Paul's Use of the Term

Although the word "gospel" is connected with the writings of Matthew, Mark, Luke, and John, Paul uses the noun more than any other New Testament author. He uses the phrase "the gospel of God" (Rom 1:1; 15:16; 2 Cor 11:7), "the gospel of Christ" (Rom 15:19; 1 Cor 9:12; 2 Cor 9:13; 10:14; Phil 1:27; 1 Thess 3:2), and "the gospel of his Son" (Rom 1:9). The first phrase usually refers to the origin of the gospel, namely God ("the gospel from God") while the last two point to the content of the gospel, namely Jesus ("the gospel about Christ or about his Son"). In Rom 1:1-6 and 1 Cor 15:1-8 Paul gives his most detailed descriptions of the gospel.

In Rom 1:1-6 Paul refers to "the gospel of God" as the message of salvation that has its origin in God. It was promised before through the prophets. Its content is Jesus, who is both God's Son (as demonstrated through the resurrection from the dead) and human (belonging to the Jewish people in that he is descended from the line of David). The importance of this message for Paul's readers is that they have received grace and faith from Jesus.

In 1 Cor 15:1-8 Paul speaks of the "good news that I proclaimed to you." This gospel is the message of salvation that Paul preached. Its content focuses on the belief that Jesus died, was buried, was raised on the third day, and appeared to many witnesses. The importance for the readers is that they have received this message "through which also you are being saved" (v. 2).

The Evangelists' Use of the Term

Among the Evangelists only Mark and Matthew use the noun "gospel." Mark begins his account with the words: "The beginning of the good news of Jesus Christ, the Son of God." Here the term does not describe the literary genre of Mark's work, but the content of his message, namely, that Jesus is the Christ, the Son of God. In this regard Mark is similar to Paul. For Mark, the gospel refers first of all to the message Jesus preached: "Jesus came to Galilee, proclaiming the good news of God" (Mark 1:14-15). It also indicates the preaching about

Jesus where Mark equates the gospel with the person of Jesus: "For those who want to save their life will lose it, and those who lose their life for my sake, and for the sake of the gospel, will save it" (8:35).

Matthew, unlike Mark, always qualifies the noun. He speaks about "the good news of the kingdom" (Matt 4:23; 9:35; 24:14) by which he means the gospel whose content is the kingdom of God, preached first by Jesus. He also speaks of "this good news proclaimed in the whole world" (26:13), implying that the message of salvation preached by Jesus continues to be preached by the church.

Luke uses the verb in both his Gospel and the Acts of the Apostles to mean "to announce the message of salvation" (see Luke 4:18-19).

Use of the Term from the Second Century Onwards

Examination of the New Testament writings shows that the noun "gospel" did not refer to a type of written literature. Instead, it denoted the oral message that captures God's salvific activity in Jesus Christ on behalf of humankind. Only in the middle of the 2nd century C.E. did the plural form "Gospels" come to refer to the writings of the Evangelists. Justin Martyr (who died in 165) writes that the "the Apostles in their memoirs, which are called Gospels, have handed down what Jesus ordered them to do" (1 Apol. 66.3).

Besides the four canonical writings of the New Testament, this title was also given to a number of extracanonical writings that have come to light in more recent times. We refer to only two examples:

In the Gospel of Thomas the term occurs only at the end of the writing: "The Gospel according to Thomas." The book itself, however, which may have been composed as early as the end of the 1st century, gives its title and the name of its author at the beginning: "These are the secret sayings which the living Jesus spoke and which Didymos Judas Thomas wrote down." This title identifies this work as a compendium of sayings.

The Gospel according to Mary is a title that appears only in the margins of that writing. However, the term "gospel" does appear in its text: "he (Jesus) greeted them all, saying: '. . . For the Son of man is within you. Follow after him! Those who seek him will find him. Go then and preach the *gospel* of the kingdom. Do not lay down any other rules beyond what I appointed for you.'" Here the gospel is the message which the disciples have to proclaim.

Making Sense of the Data

The above survey of the word "gospel" in both the New Testament and extrabiblical texts indicates a twofold

stage of development in usage and identification. In the first stage, embracing the period of the New Testament writings, the word "gospel" or "good news" referred to the oral preaching of the message of salvation begun by Jesus and continued by his disciples. The message preached by Jesus was about the kingdom, while the message continued by the disciples was about Jesus, who came to establish the kingdom. In this first stage, gospel was never used to refer to a written work.

A second stage in the usage of the word occurred from the end of the 2nd century C.E. onwards. For the first time "Gospel" referred beyond the oral proclamation of Jesus and his followers to those writings that record that proclamation. The identification of writings as "the Gospel according to Matthew, or Mark, or Luke, or John" begins. But, the canonical Gospels are not the only writings identified as gospels. Other writings that did not make their way into the New Testament canon are also identified in this way.

An examination of the writings outside the New Testament is very revealing for understanding the meaning of "Gospel." The Gospel of Thomas, for example, is a sayings collection of Jesus' words — it is not a narrative as are the canonical Gospels. This shows that the term "gospel" is not used to refer to a type of writing,

The beginning of the Gospel of Mark and a portrayal of Mark writing (eleventh century). (Department of Rare Books and Special Collections, The University of Michigan Library)

but rather to the content of the writings, the message of salvation that Jesus and his disciples preached.

In transmitting the oral message of salvation into writing, the writers had to decide how they were to express this gospel message. In other words, what type (genre) of writing they were going to use. Mark began the written process and opted for a narrative form to express this gospel message of salvation. The other canonical writers imitated Mark in continuing to use this narrative form. Some writers outside the New Testament chose very different forms to express this message, such as sayings collections (the Gospel of Thomas and the Q source) or miracle collections (the first 12 chapters of the Gospel of John depend on a "Book of Signs" as their source).

Our survey leads us to suggest the following definition. "Gospel" refers to any writing that continues to hand on the message of salvation preached by Jesus and interpreted by his followers. This indicates that a gospel is not a genre but rather the message of salvation related to Jesus of Nazareth that is expressed in written form through the use of whatever genre the writer chose in order to communicate this message.

Literary Genre of the Canonical Gospels

Concept of Genre

In literature no text exists on its own, but is always classified together with other texts that have definite characteristics in common, a class or group known as a literary genre. The attempt to determine the genre of a particular writing is extremely important for interpretation because the conventions associated with its genre help the reader understand that piece of literature. For example, if one understands the rules and codes that are used in poetry, by applying them in reading one will be better able to understand a particular poem. However, to read a novel as though it were a historical treatise would apply the wrong codes and conventions to the novel and one would end up with a false interpretation and understanding.

Traditionally, the study of literature has identified three principal literary genres, namely poetry (or lyric composition), narrative (or epic composition), and drama. Largely derived from the writings of the Greek philosopher Aristotle, this classification still has enormous value for understanding a particular writing.

Within each genre are obviously many subgenres. For example, narrative texts can be grouped or classified either by their form or their content.

An epic is a subgenre of narrative texts that are classified based on form. It generally has a lofty style, with a narrative that is long and flowing. Every culture possesses epic narratives recording their traditions relating to historical or legendary events from their past. The most famous epics are the *Iliad,* which records the siege of Troy, and the *Odyssey,* focusing on the journeys of the hero Odysseus. Biography is a subgenre of narrative that is classified according to content. Biography aims at giving an overarching narrative of a person's life that includes not just what a person did, but also a person's character as well as background and context.

How Does This Apply to the Canonical Gospels?

The canonical Gospels demonstrate all the characteristics of the main genre of narrative texts. From the perspective of content they resemble the subgenre of biography, in that the focus is upon Jesus of Nazareth, especially with regard to his teaching. More particularly, we see these Gospels as influenced by biographical works of their own time. There is no doubt that the epics of Homer influenced the Gospel narratives, but the

---

Classification of Narrative Texts into Subgenres

Classification based on form

Epic

Fable

Fairy tale

Essay

Novel

Classification based on content

Biography

Science fiction

Historical novel

Psychological novel

---

biographical works of the Hebrew Bible had far greater impact. For example, the German scholar Klaus Baltzer suggests that Mark was influenced by the biographies of the Hebrew prophets for the outline of his narrative on Jesus. Mark opens his account with a description of Jesus' baptism (not his birth), which is seen as a call to his mission (similar to the call of the prophets such as in Isaiah 6). Mark then narrates how Jesus carried out his mission of preaching and of healing, in the same way that the prophetic books record the prophet's preaching and deeds. The account of Jesus' suffering and death that occupies almost half of Mark's Gospel is akin to the accounts of the sufferings of the prophets in the course of their ministry (see esp. Jeremiah). This comparison to prophetic biographies helps us to understand why so little is narrated about the life and character of Jesus. As with the prophets, the focus is on Jesus' mission, which entails the preaching of God's kingdom.

We have already shown how the elements of author, text, reader, and narrator apply to the Gospels. Some further characteristics are important for understanding the Gospels as narratives, namely their setting, characters, and plot:

- The setting of a narrative provides the background necessary for an understanding of what happens in the story. The general setting of the Gospel narratives is the land of Palestine, but one needs to pay close attention to the specific location. Whenever a narrator elaborates the setting it is to make the story come alive or to provide further explanation of the events.
- The characters are the actors in the story. Details given about these characters are important, since it is their activities that produce the plot. Not only individuals may be characters, but also groups such as the disciples or the religious leaders.
- The plot is the way in which the events of the narrative have been arranged. This has not occurred

haphazardly, but according to a particular design in the narrator's mind. The core of the plot revolves around a main conflict (or a number of conflicts) that tends toward some form of solution. In reading a narrative it is important to note the various conflicts that emerge.

We now turn to the Gospels, using narrative criticism to gain a deeper appreciation of these writings. The three fundamental elements of author, text, and reader are present. However, we need to keep in mind the understanding of these terms according to the world of the 1st century C.E., as the methods of historical criticism have shown. Behind the author we need to see a long history of oral transmission by which the stories about Jesus were handed on (and orally molded) and eventually put into writing. The Gospel writers Matthew, Mark, Luke, and John did not write an account of the life and ministry of Jesus Christ on their own, but relied heavily on stories that were circulating orally in their communities. By the same token, the first readers of the text were actually hearers: it was read to them, since most people at that time were not literate. In this way the text retained its oral nature. As readers of the Gospels today, an awareness of their oral nature will unlock much about them.

Questions for Review and Discussion

1   Comment upon the following definition of the term "Gospel": "A Gospel refers to any writing that continues to hand on the message of salvation preached by Jesus and interpreted by his followers."

2   Explain to a friend why an understanding of the genre of the canonical Gospels should matter.

Further Reading

Burridge, Richard A. *What Are the Gospels? A Comparison with Greek-Roman Biography.* 2nd ed. BRS. Grand Rapids: Wm. B. Eerdmans and Livonia: Dove, 2004.
Koester, Helmut. "The Term 'Gospel.'" In *Ancient Christian Gospels: Their History and Development,* 1-48. Philadelphia: Trinity Press International, 1990.

Chapter 49

The Gospel of Mark

Getting Started

Read the Gospel of Mark in one sitting. Then answer the following questions:

1 List the main events in the narrative.

2 Which event do you consider to be the most important of all the events?

3 How does the Gospel begin?

4 How does the Gospel end?

5 What struck you as you read the narrative (or what had you not noticed in previous readings of the Gospel)?

Preliminary Comments

Mark's Gospel is a narrative that begins with John the Baptist heralding the arrival of the Messiah and ends at Mark 16:8 with the empty tomb. As such it forms a unity. However, some things militate against appreciating this unity. Although chapter divisions can be traced as early as the 4th century C.E., division of the text into verses first occurred in printed editions only in the 16th century. Although this was an important development, the result was to break the narrative into sections that sometimes distort its unity. For example, in 9:1 a new chapter begins with a verse that really belongs to what precedes it. A further hindrance to the unity of the Gospel is its use in the liturgy where sections of the Gospel are read independently of their context, with the result that passages tend to be treated as entities in their own right apart from the author's larger purpose in the complete Gospel.

Mark was the first to produce a narrative of the life and ministry of Jesus and to use the traditions related to Jesus to address his specific community. Other writers would imitate Mark's narrative approach to speak to their own distinctive communities.

Every narrative consists of numerous events brought into conjunction to produce a plot or story line that is propelled forward by means of conflict. In shaping his Gospel, Mark demonstrates originality in weaving together independent traditions to form a narrative about Jesus that leads inevitably to the cross. The heart of the conflict within Mark's Gospel relates to Jesus' identity and the nature of his message. Who is Jesus, and what is his role in God's plan?

A Walk through the Gospel of Mark

Mark 1:1-13: Overture in the Desert

At the outset, Mark expresses Jesus' identity as the Christ, the Son of God (1:1). In the course of the Gospel, Mark leads the reader to understand more clearly what this means. From the beginning the reader knows exactly who Jesus is. The characters in the story, however, only grasp this identity progressively and slowly.

Mark's narrative shows God in control of what is to unfold. God initiates the whole process, as the opening prophecy from Isa 40:3 declares. God's plan that had been progressively revealed in the course of Israel's history is now about to unfold.

Mark gives no details about Jesus' origins or background. His focus is upon Jesus' ministry. John the Baptist is the first character to be introduced. His task is to prepare the way for the one who is to come by proclaiming a message of repentance. At the moment of Jesus' baptism, his identity is proclaimed by the Father: "You are my Son, the Beloved; with you I am well pleased" (v. 11).

These opening verses present the reader with an understanding of Jesus' identity as God's Son. Filled with the Spirit, he can carry out the Father's plan. The initial struggle that he endures is a prelude to what he will experience in the rest of his ministry. Satan's temptation is an attempt to deflect Jesus from his mission. The presence of the wild beasts and the angels in v. 13 contrasts the danger to which Jesus is subjected (the wild beasts) with God's protecting power (the angels) ever present to him in this danger.

Mark 1:14–8:21: Ministry in Galilee

The Theme of Jesus' Preaching (1:14-15)

Mark begins by presenting succinctly the theme of Jesus' message: "The time is fulfilled, and the kingdom of God has come near; repent, and believe in the good news" (1:15). The Gospel of Mark proclaims that God's kingdom (or "God's rule," "God's reign") is about to begin, just as the prophet Isaiah announced in the opening verses: God's plan is about to unfold.

Mark 1:16-20: Call of the First Disciples

Jesus initiates a call to two groups of brothers, Simon (Peter) and Andrew, James and John, "to follow him." They unhesitatingly leave their occupation, family, and associates to go with Jesus. The term "to follow" becomes symbolic for discipleship. For Mark it deliberately conjures up the image of journeying with Jesus.

Mark 1:21–3:6: Conflict with the Religious Authorities

The first hint of conflict emerges in Jesus' first miracle

Reading Guide to the Gospel of Mark

Overture in the Desert (1:1-13)

Ministry in Galilee (1:14–8:21)
   Theme of Jesus' Preaching (1:14-15)
   Call of the First Disciples (1:16-20)
   Conflict with the Religious Authorities (1:21–3:6)
   Jesus Appoints the Twelve (3:13-19)
   Jesus Teaches in Parables (4:1-41)
   En Route to Caesarea Philippi (5:1–8:21)

En Route to Jerusalem (8:22–10:52)
   Healing the Blind (8:22-26)
   Peter Acknowledges Jesus to Be the Messiah
      (8:27–9:1)
   The Transfiguration (9:2-8)
   Further Predictions of Jesus' Death (9:30-32;
      10:32-34)
   Healing Bartimaeus (10:46-52)

Jesus in Jerusalem (11:1–13:37)

The Conflict Reaches a Climax: The Suffering and Death of Jesus (14:1–16:8)
   Conflict with Authorities (14:1–15:38)
   Roman Centurion's Confession (15:39)
   The Role of Women Disciples in the Narrative
      (15:40–16:8)

---

in 1:21-28. When Jesus teaches in the synagogue at Capernaum, his authority as teacher is contrasted with that of the scribes. This foreshadows the deeper conflict that is going to break out in the next chapter between Jesus and the Jewish religious leaders.

But a conflict on another level is also evident in this passage. Jesus' very first miracle involves the expulsion of "an unclean spirit" that acknowledges Jesus to be "the Holy One of God," showing that the supernatural realm is able to identify Jesus for who he really is. This begins Jesus' struggle with those forces of evil that are opposed to the establishment of God's kingdom. In expelling the demon, Jesus shows that his power transcends the world of evil. Jesus, however, commands the demon to "be silent" (1:25) before he expels it. Here begins a theme that becomes more and more conspicuous throughout the narrative and one that puzzles the reader. Why does Jesus go out of his way to maintain a secret about his identity? In 1:44 Jesus commands the leper to "say nothing to anyone." A reason for this silence will be discovered later at Peter's confession of Jesus (8:30).

In 2:1–3:6, the conflict with the religious authorities takes center stage. Above all, they object to the following claims that Jesus makes:

Jesus dares to forgive sins, a claim that occurs in the context of one of Jesus' first miracles (2:1-12). The power

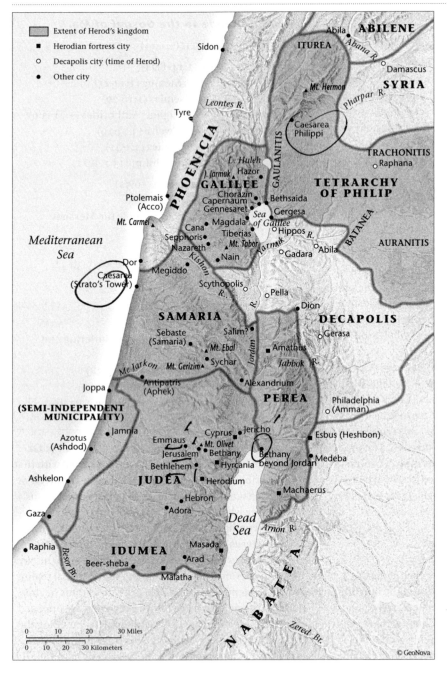

PALESTINE IN THE 1ST CENTURY C.E.

Son of Man, is "lord even of the sabbath" (2:28). Here Jesus claims authority to interpret the Jewish laws and, in this instance, how the Sabbath law is to be implemented: "The sabbath was made for humankind, and not humankind for the sabbath" (2:27). Because his actions and teaching are so contrary to what they were used to, the Jewish authorities conclude that Jesus' healings could not have come from God. They must be the work of Satan.

Mark provides a further account of Jesus healing on the Sabbath (3:1-6). The outcome of this event highlights the religious leaders' hostility toward Jesus. Mark comments: "The Pharisees went out and immediately conspired with the Herodians against him, how to destroy him" (3:6).

Mark 3:13-19: Jesus Appoints the Twelve

An important stage in Jesus' ministry occurs with his choice of disciples. This action sets up two distinctive groups: those outsiders (including the Pharisees and the Jewish authorities) who do not accept nor understand him and those insiders (the Twelve) whom he instructs more deeply in his message. This division between insiders and outsiders will become clearer as Jesus' ministry unfolds.

to forgive sins belongs to God alone. Israel obtained God's forgiveness through the temple with its various rituals and sacrifices. Jesus now claims for himself what the temple system solely endeavored to do. Consequently, the authorities accuse Jesus of blasphemy (2:7).

Jesus justifies his actions on the Sabbath (2:23-28). When the disciples pick grain on the Sabbath, the authorities accuse them of "doing what is not lawful on the sabbath" (2:24). In response, Jesus says that he, the

Mark 4:1-41: Jesus Teaches in Parables

The distinction between insiders and outsiders already becomes clearer in this chapter. In the Jewish world, a parable was part of figurative speech (a *mashal*) that the rabbis used to clarify something difficult to understand. By means of a story and referring to familiar things, an understanding of the unfamiliar would emerge. The Gospels of Matthew and Luke present Jesus using parables to elucidate his teaching especially about the kingdom of God. Mark's usage, however, is different

The Rule of God

Jewish future hopes looked forward to one final act of God that would establish God's rule for all time. The rule of God in Mark's narrative, however, has reinterpreted this by breaking it into two phases. The first stage begins with Jesus' teaching and his miracles of healing. In Jesus' life and ministry, God's rule is experienced. The second phase looks to the future, to the final establishment of God's rule in its fullness through the final breaking in of God's power at the end of time.

The First Phase in Jesus' Ministry

Here God's rule is hidden. Only those who have been given insight into its mystery can understand: "To you has been given the secret of the kingdom of God, but for those outside, everything comes in parables; in order that 'they may indeed look, but not perceive, and may indeed listen, but not understand; so that they may not turn again and be forgiven'" (4:11-12).

Jesus reinforces this mystery by always talking in parables. Right up to the end of the story, Jesus keeps his identity a secret. Conflict develops between those who accept God's rule and those who oppose it. This is the heart of the plot of Mark's Gospel.

The Final Phase of God's Rule at the End of Time

Only toward the end of his ministry in Mark's Gospel does Jesus begin to speak about the final establishment of God's rule. The Son of Man will come in the clouds to bring together God's chosen ones (13:26). God will establish God's rule in power.

A reversal of fortunes will occur. Those who have used their human power to enrich themselves and to suppress others will find their fortunes reversed: they will be condemned. Those who lost their lives for Jesus and his message will be the greatest in his kingdom.

Mark's Gospel believes that this final phase is imminent. At this stage all conflicts will be resolved.

in that here Jesus uses parables rather to confuse and confound those who are the outsiders (4:11-12).

Chapter 4 culminates with the miracle of the calming of a storm (4:35-41). Here we, as readers, gain insight into the beginning of another conflict: the relationship and commitment of the disciples to Jesus. Since the disciples are in the privileged position of insiders, we expect that they had gained a deeper insight into his person and message. However, in this episode we are suddenly surprised to learn that this is not the case. Caught in the midst of a storm on the Sea of Galilee, they are terrified. In panic they awaken Jesus, who calms the storm and then reprimands them for their fear (4:40). Their lack of faith is the central issue here. As insiders

instructed in the secrets of the kingdom, they should have placed their faith in Jesus. For the first time we realize that the disciples have not really grasped who Jesus is. This is the heart of the conflict that develops between Jesus and the disciples: a struggle for faith in the identity of Jesus. At the outset (1:1), Mark showed that his central focus was to bring his readers to an understanding of who Jesus is. Through the help of the narrator, the reader has grasped this, but surprisingly those closest to Jesus have failed to understand who he is and have failed to commit themselves to him. This event provokes the decisive question that needs to be asked: "Who then is this, that even the wind and the sea obey him?" (4:41).

Mark 5:1–8:21: En Route to Caesarea Philippi

For Mark the geographical setting of the Sea of Galilee is significant. While the western shore was Jewish territory, the eastern shore was largely Gentile territory. Consequently, when Jesus sails from one side of the lake to the other, Mark consciously portrays Jesus moving between his own people and the Gentiles. In 5:1-20 Jesus crosses the lake into Gentile territory (note the herd of 2,000 swine) where he heals a person possessed by demons. Analogous to the Roman legions that took possession of the land of Palestine, this man is oppressed by the forces of evil (as suggested by his name, Legion; v. 9). Jesus heals him, showing once again his triumph over the forces of evil. At the end of this episode, Jesus sends this man out to proclaim among his own people what has happened. This is in sharp contrast to other occasions where Jesus instructs people to keep quiet (1:44). The explanation for this action lies in the setting. Since Jesus is in Gentile territory, the misconceptions about him are not applicable. The man goes out to spread the news about what Jesus has done.

Oral Traditions

A further area of concern between Jesus and the Pharisees emerges in 7:1-23, where the religious leaders show concern for Jesus' disregard for their oral traditions. In this account, Mark refers to the Jewish tradition of washing the hands before eating. Contact with those who were not Jewish was thought to make a person unclean, and a ritual, such as the washing of hands, was one means of purification. These traditions were essential to the Jewish community as they helped to preserve the identify of their culture, while at the same time maintaining their relationship with the all-holy God. When Jesus eats a meal with tax collectors, the authorities see him associating with those who are "unclean." This shocks them because it represents a total disregard for their traditions.

Having crossed the lake again into Jewish territory (5:21), Jesus performs two more miracles: the healing of a woman who has suffered for 12 years from hemorrhages, and the raising to life of a 12-year old girl (5:21-43). Mark's story-telling technique is very striking here. The healing of the woman is imbedded within the story of the healing of the young girl. The miracles of Jesus are works of God's power challenging and overthrowing Satan's power. As such, they are clear indications of Jesus' identity.

Overall the section 5:1–8:21 draws attention to Gentile responses in faith to Jesus. We have already seen the response of Legion (5:1-20). There is also the remarkable exchange between Jesus and a Syro-Phoenician woman (7:24-30) who seeks healing for her daughter. Despite Jesus' initial rejection, she perseveres in her faith and her daughter is healed.

Contrasted with these responses is the rejection of Jesus by his own people in Nazareth (6:1-6): "And he was amazed at their unbelief" (v. 6). The conflict with the Pharisees and the scribes also intensifies (7:1-23). However, the narrator draws our attention to the disciples' lack of faith. After narrating two accounts of the multiplication of bread (6:30-44 and 8:1-10, in Jewish and Gentile territory, respectively), Mark shows that the disciples are still preoccupied with having no bread (8:14-21). Jesus shows his frustration with them: "Do you not yet understand?" (v. 21).

Mark 8:22–10:52: En Route to Jerusalem
Healing the Blind (8:22-26)

This central section opens and closes with an account of Jesus healing a blind person (8:22-26; 10:46-52). This illustrates Mark's technique of giving direction to the whole section by using two common poles for the reader to use in relating the material. In the first encounter at Bethsaida, Jesus brings a blind man to sight in two successive stages. At first he sees only dimly: "I can see people, but they look like trees, walking" (8:24). In a similar way throughout this section Jesus struggles to bring the disciples to understanding and faith in him.

Peter Acknowledges Jesus to Be the Messiah (8:27–9:1)

Peter's confession at Caesarea Philippi marks the turning point of the Gospel. Having come to the northernmost part of the land, Jesus asks his followers, "Who do people say that I am?" (8:27). Jesus is intent on leading his followers to a deeper awareness of who he is. Not satisfied with their answer that he is viewed as a great prophet, Jesus pushes the disciples to disclose their understanding. True to form, Peter acts as spokesperson for the group and acknowledges, "You are the Messiah" (8:29).

It appears that for the first time one of the disciples has grasped Jesus' identity. Jesus again warns the disciples, as he has done previously, not to speak to anyone about this (8:30). He uses this opportunity to instruct his followers more fully about his mission and identity. For the first time in the narrative he tells them that the Son of Man (referring to himself) is to suffer and die and after three days he will rise again (v. 31). Peter is most perturbed at this talk and starts to remonstrate with Jesus. Jesus responds by telling Peter that he is seeing things from a human perspective and not through the eyes of God.

At issue here are the different understandings that Jesus and Peter have regarding the Messiah. The Psalms of Solomon, dating to the middle of the 1st century B.C.E., illustrate how the people of Jesus' time viewed the expected Messiah: God's Anointed One would establish God's rule on earth by reversing the political fortunes of the people of Israel and overthrowing the oppressive Roman rule. This is the concept Peter has in mind when he says to Jesus, "You are the Messiah." But this is not Jesus' understanding of his own role or task. While his ministry is directed toward the establishment of God's rule, the focus is not on a political overthrow through powerful force. Instead, the focus rests with the call to enter into a relationship with God where the values of justice, peace, and concern for all are dominant and where God is in control. Jesus establishes this rule of God through the paradox of suffering and death. In effect, Jesus says to Peter and the other disciples: "I am not a political conquering Messiah, but rather, I am a Messiah who suffers, dies, and through resurrection brings life to humanity."

This episode provides a clearer insight as to why Jesus constantly told people to keep quiet about him. Jesus distanced himself from those political aspirations and hopes that were associated with the concept of Messiah. If people hailed him as Messiah, his ministry would not have lasted very long. The Romans would soon have intervened to remove a potential political threat as they had done many times in the past. In correcting Peter's notion of Messiah, Jesus uses the opportunity to give his ministry a new understanding, one that embraces suffering and death willingly.

Without doubt this is a turning point in the narrative. Jesus now journeys toward Jerusalem, where his ministry will ultimately culminate in suffering and death. While the disciples still struggle to grasp Jesus' true identity and mission, he instructs them on the values they must embrace (8:34–9:1). Following Jesus entails accepting the cross, just as Jesus did. Willingness to lose one's life for Jesus' sake will ultimately bring salvation. Their lives must show a willingness to remain faithful to Jesus even in the face of death. Jesus envisages martyrdom for himself and for those who follow him.

The Transfiguration (9:2-8)

Mark situates the account of the transfiguration after the first prediction of Jesus' death and resurrection. Its purpose is to clarify Jesus' identity for his followers and to strengthen them for that time when Jesus is arrested and put to death. Appearing together with Moses and Elijah, Jesus shows how the two great representatives of the past, the Law and the Prophets, lead to him. As happened at the baptism, a voice from heaven proclaims Jesus to be the Son of God (9:7). Again the reader perceives Jesus' identity clearly. The disciples' response, however, is one of incomprehension. As they descend the mountain, the disciples continue to show their lack of understanding as they discuss among themselves Jesus' speech about this rising from the dead. While we, the readers, are clear about who Jesus is and what is to happen to him, Mark points out that at every turn the disciples fail to understand.

The Transfiguration, Duccio di Buoninsegna (1311; National Gallery, London). Jesus stands before the apostles Peter, John, and James and flanked by the prophets Moses and Elijah. (ArtResource, NY)

Further Predictions of Jesus' Death (9:30-32; 10:32-34)

When Jesus again speaks about his impending death in 9:30-32, Mark comments that the disciples "did not understand what he was saying and were afraid to ask him." Instead, as they journey along the road (vv. 33-37), they have been arguing about who is the greatest among them. This makes perfect sense in the context of the disciples' hopes that Jesus, as Messiah, would free Israel from her enemies and bring about Israel's independence under God's rule. Jesus' talk about his death prompts them to wonder who would take charge of this movement once Jesus has gone. The disciples still think in terms of power and political liberation.

Jesus' response draws attention again to values that are in sharp contrast to those of the disciples. To be a follower of Jesus means emulating Jesus, whose foundational value is not status and power, but service. Using a

little child, the lowest on the hierarchical level of society, Jesus shows that a follower must seek to embrace first of all those whom society considers the least important.

On a third occasion Jesus speaks about his death (10:32-34). The disciples' response is again important (vv. 35-45). James and John ask Jesus to let them sit on his right and left hand when he establishes his kingdom. These seats were reserved for those who would share in a king's power. In effect James and John were asking that when Jesus did establish his political kingdom, they be made his most powerful associates.

As his previous response, Jesus draws attention to the values his followers should embrace. Speaking metaphorically of his death as a baptism, he tells them that they also will share in his death through their own deaths. The values of the kingdom contrast sharply with those of society: the most important virtue is not one that seeks positions of power and places of prestige, but rather one that aims at service. Using himself as an example, Jesus says that his mission has been "not to be served but to serve, and to give his life a ransom for many" (10:45). Symbolically, Jesus shows that his death will bring about the spiritual liberation of those associated with him.

In recounting this journey to Jerusalem Mark reveals much more about Jesus, his mission, and what it means to be his follower. Through the conflict with his disciples we, as readers, gain a deeper understanding, but they remain locked into their preconceived ideas. These conflicts show that a disciple is someone who is willing to embrace the cross of suffering and death (8:34; 10:38-39) and whose life is characterized above all else by service (9:35; 10:43-45).

Healing Bartimaeus (10:46-52)
The narrative of the journey to Jerusalem culminates with another healing of a blind person, Bartimaeus. Looking back, the passage frames the section that begins with the first miracle of the healing of the blind man at Bethsaida (8:22-26). It invites the reader to reflect on the previous material that focuses on the three predictions of Jesus' death and resurrection. Whereas we the readers have understood that Jesus' mission would be carried out through suffering and death, the disciples, however, continue to remain blind to the true meaning of Jesus' messiahship.

This passage also looks forward to the future. The blind Bartimaeus calls upon Jesus as "the Son of David," a true messianic acknowledgement. Jesus performs this miracle without instructing him to keep quiet as he has done in the past. The reason for this change emerges from what follows: Jesus is about to enter Jerusalem, and the end of his life is swiftly approaching. Given that framework, Jesus' actions are viewed as messianic.

Mark 11:1–13:37: Jesus in Jerusalem
The plot reaches a climax with Jesus' entry into Jerusalem (11:11). He appears in the role of a triumphant Messiah, who enters the city on a donkey fulfilling the prophecy of Zech 9:9. Mark shows the reader that while Jesus is indeed the fulfillment of the hopes of the past, ultimately this triumphant figure will be humiliated in death.

Jesus enters the temple precincts (11:15-19) and chases out the money-lenders and those selling animals for sacrifice. This event is a challenge to the heart of Judaism and alienates above all the Sadducees, for whom the temple was a source of power, wealth, and influence. Further, quoting the prophet Isaiah, Mark's Jesus proclaims the temple "a house of prayer for all the nations" (Isa 56:7). Jesus, unlike the Sadducees, extends God's kingdom to embrace the Gentiles. Previously, as was shown, Jesus has performed miracles of healing and exorcism among the Gentiles, showing that his ministry is not confined to the world of Judaism. God's rule embraces all peoples.

Chapter 13 has Jesus looking into the future, offering admonitions on the end of the world. Jesus opens this sermon by foreseeing the destruction of the temple and the city. By means of apocalyptic language and imagery, Jesus issues a call for watchfulness. For Mark's Jesus, the end of the world is expected soon, and Mark wishes to encourage his readers to persevere and to be watchful (13:32-37).

Mark 14:1–16:8: The Conflict Reaches a Climax: The Suffering and Death of Jesus
Conflict with Authorities (14:1–15:38)
Throughout these events Jesus appears as the one who is in control. In the high priest's interrogation, Jesus acknowledges quite openly that he is the Messiah, "the Son of the Blessed One" (14:61-62). Viewed in this light, Jesus determines his own fate, volunteering the information needed to convict him. The sentence of death is carried out by the Roman authorities. With Jesus' death, the conflict is resolved and the authorities think they have won. They have, however, been instruments in carrying out God's plan. The final scene of the empty tomb brings about a complete reversal: the one who was put to death is now the Risen One. God's plan has won the day.

The Roman Centurion's Confession (15:39)
The Gospel of Mark opens with the narrator announcing his intention of showing that Jesus is both Messiah and Son of God. The conflicts to which we have drawn attention have revolved around the misunderstanding of the authorities and the disciples concerning Jesus as Messiah. But Mark wishes to develop the understanding about Jesus even further. Jesus is not just Messiah, but also Son of God. Jesus is openly proclaimed as Son of God by the voice from heaven on two occasions: the baptism and the transfiguration (1:11; 9:7). Finally, at the moment of Jesus' death, a Roman centurion proclaims Jesus as God's Son: "Truly this man was God's Son!" It is to this confession that the Gospel has brought the reader. There is real irony here as a Gentile is the first to make this confession of faith.

Conflict with the Disciples
The second major conflict in Mark involves the disciples' struggle in realizing Jesus' identity. In Jesus' last meal with his followers on the night before his death, Jesus points to this struggle: one of them will betray him (14:18); they will "all become deserters" (14:27); and Peter will deny him three times (14:30). To this Peter replies: "Even though I must die with you, I will not deny you" (14:31).

The disciples are unable to carry out their pledge to remain true to Jesus. Judas betrays him. Then, in the course of the night vigil in the garden of Gethsemane, Jesus' three closest disciples, Peter, James, and John, all fall asleep (14:32-42). When Jesus is arrested, they flee (14:50). Finally, Peter denies Jesus (14:66-72).

The Role of Women Disciples in the Narrative (15:40–16:8)

After the disciples' desertion, the narrative suddenly focuses on another group of followers whose presence the reader had not previously noticed. A group of women disciples show that they understand far better than those male disciples what it means to be a follower of Jesus. In the final two chapters, three episodes depict the women's role as central and significant: they witness to the death, burial, and resurrection of Jesus.

The women disciples witness Jesus' death (15:40-41). In introducing these "watching women," the narrator makes a number of very significant observations:

- *They are not from Jerusalem.* The narrator pointedly says that they were from Galilee.
- *They follow Jesus.* Note that Jesus' first call in 1:16-20 was the invitation to follow him. The Greek verb for "to follow" implies more than just physical following: it demands some degree of commitment. The women are specifically identified in this way as disciples. Now that the male disciples had deserted Jesus, true discipleship falls upon these "watching women." As such they witness his death.
- *They serve Jesus.* The Greek verb *diakonein,* translated here by "provided for him," means "to serve." Mark has in mind more than just providing a meal for Jesus. Service is the true hallmark of discipleship, something that the male disciples failed to understand. In 9:35 when the disciples were arguing about who was the greatest in the kingdom, Mark comments, "(Jesus) said to them, 'Whoever wants to be first must be last of all and servant of all.'" Later, after James and John request to share in the power of Jesus' kingdom, Jesus replies, "Whoever wishes to become great among you must be your servant" (10:43).

Note that at the beginning of the narrative (in the episode of the healing of Simon's mother-in-law in 1:31) as well as here at the end (15:41) Mark emphasizes women who have served Jesus. While Jesus had to correct the male disciples' understanding of discipleship, the women disciples have understood from the beginning that to be a disciple means that one must embrace

service to others. By choosing the verbs "to follow" and "to serve," the narrator wishes to emphasize that the women are to be seen in the role of true disciples.

Three women are named among "the group looking on": Mary Magdalene, Mary the mother of the younger James and of Joses, and Salome. Just as the inner circle of male disciples comprised three men, Peter, James, and John, so does the inner circle among the many women disciples (v. 40). Mark presents them as an alternative to the three men of the former inner circle. As the watching group, their role in the narrative is to witness to the death of Jesus.

The women disciples witness Jesus' burial (15:47). Their role as witness continues in this scene: "Mary Magdalene and Mary the mother of Joses saw where the body was laid." The narrator has subverted the normal structures of society.

The women disciples witness to the resurrection (16:1-8). The narrative ends with the same group of women going to the tomb to anoint Jesus' body. While in the previous scenes they were passive onlookers, now they become active agents. This scene brings the reader back to the opening scene of the Passion Narrative where another woman anoints Jesus. The whole Passion Narrative is "included" between these two scenes of women anointing Jesus.

The first anointing scene at Bethany (14:3-9) is situated between the plot of the religious authorities to arrest Jesus (vv. 1-2) and Judas Iscariot's agreement to betray him (vv. 10-11). An unnamed woman serves Jesus by preparing him for burial (v. 8). Her action shows an understanding of discipleship that the male disciples lack: she is the first to show an awareness of Jesus' mission that would lead to death. The Markan Jesus raises her to the position of the true disciple, one who seizes an opportunity for service: "Wherever the good news is proclaimed in the whole world, what she has done will be told in remembrance of her" (vv. 8-9). Where else in the Markan narrative do any followers of Jesus receive such endorsement for their actions?

It is against this background that the final scene of the women in 16:1-8 is to be interpreted. They too come to anoint Jesus' body. Like the woman at Bethany, they come to do what they can for Jesus — in this lies their *diakonia* (their service). Their discipleship shows they follow Jesus and serve him to the end.

The women come to anoint Jesus' body, but discover that "he has been raised; he is not here" (16:6). The young man at the tomb instructs them to tell the disciples and Peter that "he is going ahead of you to Galilee;

there you will see him, just as he told you" (v. 7; see 14:28). The reference to Galilee is significant: the Gospel message began in Galilee, so a return to Galilee would bring the Gospel full circle.

Making Sense of the Ending

The final verse of Mark comes as a surprise to the reader (16:8). Unnerved by the events at the tomb, the women are unable to carry out the young man's instructions, running away in fear. On this note the Gospel ends.

Just as the male disciples deserted Jesus, now the women disciples do the same. This sudden departure of the women in fear should not be judged too harshly as it leaves the narrative open for the reader to supply an ending. By sharing in the omniscience of the narrator, the reader is presented with a challenge. Will the reader grasp the true meaning of discipleship? How will the reader respond?

In the course of the narrative, the narrator has already provided an understanding of a future beyond the final scene of 16:8. Mark 13 presents Jesus showing his disciples that ultimately they too would share in a discipleship that will involve betrayal and suffering (vv. 9-13). Reading back through the narrative, the reader is led to understand that the fear that grips the male and female disciples is something temporary. Ultimately they will overcome their paralysis and fear. In line with the message of the Scriptures, one sees that God's plans ultimately do triumph despite the human frailties of the characters in the biblical story.

The narrative, with its open ending, becomes a challenge to action. The disciples have the privilege of being the initial insiders in the narrative. The male disciples relinquish this position to the women disciples, who in their turn relinquish it to the reader. The narrator shares his omniscience with the reader and in this way the reader receives a wider perception of the whole unity of the narrative.

The role of the women disciples at the empty tomb enables the story of Mark's Gospel to live on. The narrator reaches across time to the reader to continue the story. The power of Mark's Gospel consists, not in the information that it communicates to the reader, but in what it challenges the reader to do. The narrative on discipleship starts with the simple injunction: "Follow me" (1:17). The women disciples show that this following leads to the cross and the grave. But discipleship leads beyond the grave through the power of the resurrection. "How do we follow?" This is the question addressed to every reader of Mark's narrative. If they follow as true disciples, they too are promised that beyond the cross lies the resurrection.

Critical Issues in Studying Mark

When and Where Was the Gospel of Mark Written?

Some clues emerge from the Gospel that help to suggest a probable context for its origin.

- *The destruction of the temple and Jerusalem.* Many

Different Endings for the Gospel of Mark

A cursory glance at the end of Mark in most Bibles will show a number of different endings proposed for the narrative. These possibilities arise from a comparison of the numerous ancient manuscripts that have come down to us from the earliest centuries. From these manuscripts three possible endings for the Gospel have emerged:

Mark 16:1-8: *This is the shortest ending and is found in the most ancient manuscripts. The Gospel concludes with the women disciples at the empty tomb. There they are instructed to go to the male disciples and announce that Jesus is going ahead to Galilee where he will meet them. Instead of following out this command, they run away and say nothing to anyone. The Gospel ends on a note of fear.*

Mark 16:1-9: *This is called "the shorter ending." One verse has been added as an attempt to bring the narrative to a satisfactory conclusion. In effect, it reverses what v. 8 said. It claims that the women did indeed tell the disciples about their experiences at the tomb and*

became missionaries to spread the gospel message to "east and west."

Mark 16:1-20: *The "longer ending" is found in the majority of authoritative manuscripts. For this reason it is included in the Roman Catholic canon and is referred to as "the canonical ending." To a large extent it draws on the endings of Matthew and Luke in order to provide a well-rounded conclusion to Mark that includes a further appearance of Jesus to his followers and their experience of his Ascension.*

These different endings point to an uncertainty in the early church as regards the original ending of the Gospel. In what follows I shall argue that 16:1-8 makes perfect sense as the original ending of Mark. Failure to understand this ending led to the addition of material based upon the other Gospels. This is not to say that the canonical ending does not have a value. It has been accepted by the church as part of the canon and is a wonderful witness to the missionary dimension of Christianity.

scholars argue that the way in which Jesus speaks about the destruction of the temple reflects recent experiences of Jews and Christians in 70 C.E. with the Roman destruction of Jerusalem. The disciples' statement in 13:1-2 is seen as a reminder to readers after the war that Jesus had warned of the fate of the city's great buildings: "Not one stone will be left here upon another; all will be thrown down." Later in this discourse Jesus clearly alludes to the readers that they could interpret these events for themselves: "But when you see the desolating sacrilege set up where it ought not to be (let the reader understand) . . ." (v. 14).

- *Persecution of Jesus' disciples.* Jesus envisages a situation after his death where his disciples also experience persecution and death. When James and John ask to share in his kingdom, Jesus tells them that they will indeed share in his suffering and death (10:39). This points to a setting where the readers themselves are experiencing persecution. Mark writes to this situation and uses the example of Jesus, who gave his own life as a ransom. His life led inexorably to the cross and death. For the disciples, to follow Jesus meant that it would lead ultimately to the cross in their lives. One of the first major experiences of persecution for Christians was Nero's persecution in Rome, where the two great leaders of early Christianity, Peter and Paul, met their deaths between 64 and 67 C.E.

From the above, scholars point to three possible contexts for the appearance of Mark's Gospel.

- Rome. The traditional viewpoint has been that Mark's Gospel arose in Rome shortly after the deaths of Peter and Paul during Nero's persecution. Clement of Alexandria at the end of the 2nd century C.E. argues for this viewpoint. This certainly conforms to the picture painted above of a context where the hearers/readers are experiencing persecution. This would place the Gospel somewhere around 70. The use of Latinisms in the Gospel adds further support to this view of Rome as its place of origin.
- Palestine/Syria. This is a more recent view that takes seriously the graphic description of the destruction of the temple and the city of Jerusalem. The hardship endured during the Roman war provides the context for these descriptions. Just as the Jews suffered enormously through the devastation of their sacred temple and city, so too did those Christians who still lived in Palestine.
- Alexandria. Given that the earliest manuscripts of Mark have come from Egypt and that a Secret Gospel of Mark circulated there at the end of the 2nd century,

The Use of Latinisms in Mark

Mark uses such Latin words as *legio* ("legion," 5:9); *denarion* ("denarius," 6:37; 12:15; 14:5); *kentyrion* ("centurion," 15:39); and Greek *hodon poiein* in 2:23 (which conforms to Latin *iter facere,* "to make one's way"). Finally, the coin referred to in 12:42 (Latin *quadrans*) is significant. Mark explains the meaning of Greek *lepta duo,* "two small copper coins," as "worth a penny *(kodrantes),*" which would be familiar to his readers while the former would not. This Roman coin did not circulate in the East, but was in use only in the western part of the Roman Empire. This is a strong argument that the readers are in Rome and Mark is referring to their currency.

some scholars have proposed Alexandria as the original home for this writing. However, from what we know of Alexandria at this time, persecution and suffering are not experiences that belong to that context.

Of all these possibilities, the traditional view of Rome around 70 C.E. fits the best. As we shall see below, Mark's audience is clearly Gentile, and in particular Mark seems to show a special concern for Rome (e.g., the important role of the centurion who first acknowledges Jesus as the Son of God; 15:39).

Who Were the First Hearers/ Readers of the Gospel of Mark?

As we have already shown, Mark uses a number of Latinisms. Further, his Gospel includes seven Aramaic phrases that are translated into Greek (see p. 377), more than any of the Gospels, which shows that Mark's readers knew Greek but did not understand Aramaic. This would exclude an audience that had come from the world of Judaism and indicates that Mark's audience was made up of Gentile Christians. Further support derives from the fact that Mark had to explain Jewish customs to his audience (see, e.g., 7:1-5. where Mark explains Jewish purifications before meals).

Who Is the Author of Mark?

"The Gospel according to Mark" is a title added at the close of the 2nd century to distinguish it from other writings of a similar nature. The first references to Mark as the author of this Gospel come from Papias (ca. 70-125), a bishop of Hierapolis and a chronicler of early Christianity, who is quoted by the church historian Eusebius (ca. 260-339).

Traditionally, Mark has come to be associated with the references to a John Mark in the Acts of the Apostles (Acts 12:12, 25; 13:13; 15:37-39). Other New Testament writings refer to someone named Mark. Two references to Mark occur in the Pauline tradition (neither makes reference to his other name, John) (Col 4:10; Phlm 24). Further reference to a Mark occurs in 1 Pet 5:13, where the author sends greetings to the readers from "my son Mark."

While it is impossible to say whether all these references refer to one and the same person, tradition has tended to melt them together into a synthesized whole. John Mark originated from Jerusalem: his Jewish name (John) and Hellenized Roman name (Mark) show that he was at home in both the Jewish and Greek worlds. As a cousin of Barnabas, he became an associate of Paul and Barnabas during their first missionary journey. There was a falling-out between Mark and Paul. Later, toward the end of Paul's life, they reconciled and Mark became Paul's companion in Rome, where he was associated with both Paul and Peter at the end of their lives.

This Gospel's authority stems from the preaching and teaching of the two foremost apostles of the early church, Peter and Paul. Since the ancient traditions often have some basis in historical reality, it seems plausible to accept that the writer of this Gospel was a John Mark whose authority was derived from these two figures. Because Mark's Gospel comes indirectly from the two greatest of the apostles it meets unquestionably one of the key requirements for canonicity.

The Style of Mark

At first glance Mark's use of the Greek language appears to be poor. He ignores the use of subordinate clauses, preferring to join his sentences by means of the word "and" (Greek *kai*). The best explanation is that Mark seems to be thinking in Hebrew and writing in Greek. Hebrew uses the word "and" (the "*waw* consecutive") to

join sentences, whereas Greek uses subordinate clauses and conjunctions. In addition, Mark has a very limited Greek vocabulary of some 1,270 words.

Nevertheless, Mark is a very skillful author. For example, he uses a technique known as "inclusion" *(inclusio)* whereby a section is framed by two similar events. For example, Mark frames the heart of the Gospel (the travel journey to Jerusalem, 8:27–10:45) between two events narrating Jesus' healing the blind. In 8:22-26 Jesus heals the blind man at Bethsaida and in 10:46-52 he heals the blind Bartimaeus. The significance of these miracles emerges from their context as frames for the central section of the Gospel, where the disciples continue to remain spiritually blind, unable to see who Jesus is despite his teaching during the course of this journey.

Another technique in the Gospel is the "sandwiching of events," where two events are described, with one event sandwiched between another. A good example of this occurs in 5:21-43. Mark begins by describing how Jairus came to Jesus begging him to heal his sick daughter. Mark interrupts this narrative by introducing another miracle in the middle of this episode (vv. 24b-34), in which Jesus responds to a woman troubled by hemorrhages for 12 years.

One more significant stylistic technique is the use of geography to structure the Gospel. The diagram on p. 377 shows clearly how the outline of the Gospel follows a geographical framework. Beginning in the desert of Judea with the baptism, Jesus then moves to Galilee, where he continues his ministry in the region around the sea of Galilee. Jesus then goes north to the borders of Palestine and into the region of Caesarea Philippi. The narrative reaches a climax when Peter acknowledges Jesus to be the Messiah. Having corrected Peter's understanding by showing that his own messiahship embraces suffering and death, Jesus then journeys toward Jerusalem, where his ministry culminates in death and resurrection.

Theological Themes in the Gospel of Mark

Two main theological themes permeate Mark's Gospel. The first relates to Jesus' identity. From the outset Mark wants the reader to know that it is his intention to lead the reader into a discovery that Jesus is the Messiah, the Son of God. At the same time Mark also wants the reader to understand these implications for the disciples. Discipleship embraces following Jesus along the way to the cross. In tracing the plot of the Gospel, attention has already been drawn to these two themes. In revisiting them here, the purpose will be to draw out their significance for the reader.

Aramaic Words in Mark

3:17: In listing the 12 special disciples, Mark notes the nickname given to two of them: "Boanerges, that is, Sons of Thunder."

5:41: Reporting the healing of a little girl, Mark writes: "[Jesus] took her by the hand and said to her, 'Talitha cum,' which means, 'Little girl, get up!'"

7:11-12: In a dispute with the Pharisees about their traditions, Jesus remarks: "But you say that if anyone tells father or mother, 'Whatever support you might have had from me is Corban' (that is, an offering to God) — then you no longer permit doing anything for a father or mother."

7:34: Mark records Jesus' actions in curing a deaf man: "Then looking up to heaven, he sighed and said to him, 'Ephphatha,' that is, 'Be opened.'"

14:36: In the Garden of Gethsemane just prior to his arrest, Jesus prays: "Abba, Father, for you all things are possible."

15:22: The place where Jesus is crucified is identified in Aramaic: "Golgotha (which means the place of a skull)."

15:34: At his death, Jesus cries out: "'Eloi, Eloi, lema sabachthani?' which means, 'My God, my God, why have you forsaken me?'"

Who Is Jesus?

Messiah

Mark opens his Gospel with a straightforward acknowledgment of Jesus as Messiah and Son of God (1:1), providing the reader with clear insight into Jesus' identity.

Scholars use the term "messianic secret" to describe a theme in Mark's narrative in which Jesus consistently instructs people to keep quiet about his miraculous powers (1:44; 3:10-12; 5:42-43; 7:36-37; 8:30; 9:9). This technique of concealing Jesus' messiahship stems from Mark's need to show that Jesus' identity differs radically from the hopes and expectations of his own people. The popular view of the coming Messiah was a political figure who would liberate Israel from Roman rule. If Jesus had endorsed this identification, he would have been involved in a political movement or uprising similar to others of that time.

When questioned by the high priest about his identity, Jesus did not hesitate in acknowledging that he was the Messiah (14:61-62). This open admission occurred on the eve of his death. In this death people will come to understand the true nature of his messiahship: that he is the one who has come to suffer and die and through

this bring salvation to humanity: "not to be served but to serve, and to give his life a ransom for many" (10:45).

Son of Man

Jesus used the title "Son of Man" to identify himself. It occurs some 14 times in Mark. The Hebrew Scriptures provide little help in determining exactly what is meant by this phrase. It occurs often in the book of the prophet Ezekiel (see, e.g., Ezek 24:2). The NRSV translates Hebrew *ben 'adam* as "Mortal," which captures the meaning very succinctly, designating the humanity, the mortality of the prophet. In many ways, this is exactly what Mark wants the title to capture in reference to Jesus. Mark's picture of Jesus draws attention to Jesus' humanity more than any of the other Gospels. His Jesus has clear emotions: he gets angry (3:5); he gets tired (4:38); he sighs (8:12) and spits (7:33); he is disappointed (9:19). Fear grips him on the eve of his death (14:34), and on the cross he cries out to the Father with the feeling of abandonment (15:34). Mark presents Jesus as fully human, and the title "Son of Man" is meant to capture this.

This phrase refers to more than just Jesus' humanity. In the book of Daniel it takes on another perspective, that of an apocalyptic figure who would come at the end of time. Daniel sees a vision of someone like "a son of man" (NRSV "human being") coming on the clouds of heaven and having divine authority (7:13-14). This Son of Man is variously interpreted. Many consider it to be a collective term that refers to the faithful people of Israel. Over time, it acquired an individual understanding that referred to a celestial individual who would establish God's kingdom. A popular collection of writings at the time of Jesus, the book of 1 Enoch, has a long section (the Similitudes or Parables in chs. 37–71) in which the Son of Man features quite prominently. His role was to rescue God's people from the domination of tyrannical powers and at the end of time exercise judgment on humanity.

Mark uses the term "Son of Man" in three distinctive ways:

1. The earthly, human Son of Man, who has power to forgive sins (2:10) and is Lord of the Sabbath (2:28).

Geographical Development of Mark

Opening in the desert of Judea (1:1-13)

Ministry in Galilee (1:14–8:26)

Confession at Caesarea-Philippi (8:27–9:1)

Journey to Jerusalem (9:2–10:52)

Death in Jerusalem (11:1–16:8)

The Baptism, Elimo Philipp Njau. (Society for the Propagation of the Gospel, London)

2. The apocalyptic Son of Man, who will come in glory (8:38; 14:62) at the end of time (13:26).

3. The suffering Son of Man (8:31), who will be betrayed (14:41) and killed (9:31), giving his life "a ransom for many" (10:45), and who will rise from the dead (9:9-12).

The first two uses of this term are found in the tradition. This is the way the Son of Man was understood in the books of Ezekiel, Daniel, and 1 Enoch: it refers to the humanity of this figure and also looks forward to an apocalyptic role in the future whereby he will establish God's kingdom through judgment. What is distinctive about this figure in Mark (and in the other Synoptic Gospels) is that it also refers to Jesus' role as the one who must suffer and die before he can exercise the role of heavenly king and judge. It captures the very essence of Jesus' mission: through suffering and death he brings about God's kingdom.

Son of God

By this title, Mark indicates Jesus' identity in relationship to God. Having designated Jesus as God's Son for the reader at the outset of the narrative, Mark draws attention to this identity on three important occasions.

- This special relationship to the Father is proclaimed first at Jesus' baptism when a voice from heaven announces: "You are my Son, the Beloved; with you I am well pleased" (1:11). The voice from heaven recalls two texts from the Hebrew Scriptures: Ps 2:7, a psalm sung at the coronation of Israel's kings as God's adopted sons ("today I have begotten you"); and Isa 42:1, God's chosen servant ("I have put my spirit upon him; he will bring forth justice to the nations"). This unique relationship between God and Jesus is characterized by the love the Father has for his Son.
- At his transfiguration a voice from heaven again identifies Jesus as "my Son, the Beloved" (9:7). This occurs at the turning point of the Gospel as Jesus heads toward Jerusalem and death. Its purpose here is to give the disciples an unambiguous understanding of Jesus' identity as God's Son.
- At the end of the Gospel a centurion confesses: "Truly this man was God's Son!" (15:39).

These three confessions provide the reader with a clear realization of Jesus' true identity and mission. As Son of God, Jesus is the beloved servant who carries out the Father's will (1:11); he shares the glory of the Father and is the climax of God's revelation (9:7); and finally Jesus dies for humanity, and it is his death that reveals who he truly is (15:39).

What Is Discipleship?

The following characteristics highlight the values and the attitude that a follower of Jesus must embrace.

Taking Up the Cross

The essence of discipleship lies in following Jesus through suffering and service. The heart of Mark's Gospel is Jesus' journey to Jerusalem (8:27–10:52). Along this way Jesus instructs his followers about what it means to be his follower: "If any want to become my followers, let them deny themselves and take up their cross and follow me . . ." (8:34-35). To follow Jesus is to accept

Son of God

The declaration of Jesus as God's Son at his baptism has been interpreted in many different ways. One early interpretation led to one of the first heresies within early Christianity, known as Adoptionism or Docetism. According to this view, Jesus was fully human from the moment of his conception, but his divine nature overshadowed him only at the moment of his baptism. The significance of the baptism for Jesus lies in God's adoption of this human, Jesus, as God's son from that moment onwards. Mark does not speculate nor say anything about Jesus' nature and activity prior to his baptism. It may be that such interpretations were common in the early church, and this may have provided the impetus for Matthew and Luke to begin their Gospels with a clear statement on the divinity of Jesus from the moment of his conception.

the initial call that Jesus addresses to Peter, Andrew, James, and John (1:16-20). They respond by leaving everything to follow him. This response of "journeying" with Jesus remains the essence of discipleship. It is a following that leads to the cross.

Service

Not only do Jesus' disciples follow him on the path of suffering and death, they also follow him by embracing his values. Chief among these is the call to service: "For the Son of Man came not to be served but to serve, and to give his life a ransom for many" (10:45). Service remains the hallmark of a disciple. Jesus challenges his companions to rethink their own values through an overarching commitment to service. While they focus exclusively upon themselves and their own ambitions, he shows that their concern should rather be for the other and the other's needs (9:35).

Watchfulness

Discipleship also entails watchfulness, as cautioned in the sermon on the destruction of Jerusalem and the end of time: "Beware, keep alert; for you do not know when the time will come" (13:33-37). Mark preserves the hope in an expectation of the return of Jesus (the *parousia*) in the not too distant future. Reflecting the views of the time, this period of waiting is a period of intense danger, especially of apostasy whereby false prophets will lead the faithful astray (13:21-22).

Putting It All Together

Mark presents the disciples in such a way that the reader discovers what characteristics a true follower of Jesus must embrace. At the same time the reader is aware that those first followers of Jesus struggled and often failed to live up to the challenge. By means of negative examples the reader sees how not to act in following Jesus. Mark writes for readers who are all too human, who know what the struggles of life entail. To them Mark offers the challenge and the comfort that the suffering Son of Man will come again in glory. Discipleship embraces the journey of following Jesus in suffering and service, knowing that followers are imitating Jesus in all they do. The open ending of the Gospel challenges the reader to take up the cross and follow Jesus.

Questions for Review and Discussion

1 In what way is Peter's confession of Jesus as Messiah in Mark 8:27–9:1 the turning point in the narrative?

2 Do you think that the empty tomb is an effective ending for Mark's Gospel?

3 What does the Gospel of Mark reveal about the future of the disciples?

Further Reading

Evans, Craig A. "Mark." In *ECB,* 1064-1103.

Kingsbury, Jack Dean. *Conflict in Mark: Jesus, Authorities, Disciples.* Minneapolis: Fortress, 1989.

Rhoads, David M., Joanna Dewey, and Donald Michie. *Mark as Story: An Introduction to the Narrative of a Gospel.* 2nd ed. Minneapolis: Fortress, 1999.

Tolbert, Mary Ann. *Sowing the Gospel: Mark's World in Literary-Historical Perspective.* Minneapolis: Fortress, 1989.

Chapter 50

The Gospel of Matthew

Jesus, The Teacher

Getting Started

1 Read the following passages from the Gospel of Matthew: 5:1–7:29; 10:1-42; 13:1-52; 18:1-35; 24:1–25:46.

2 Write a paragraph on each of these sections identifying their main theme.

Preliminary Comments

Matthew's Gospel contains some of the most well-known passages in the New Testament, such as the Sermon on the Mount, the Beatitudes, the form of the Lord's Prayer that Christians recite today, the story of the Magi. The position of Matthew's Gospel at the beginning of the New Testament is also significant because it forms a bridge between the Old and New Testaments. The most Jewish of all the Gospels, Matthew portrays Jesus as the fulfillment of the Jewish Torah and draws out his significance for his community.

Our examination of the Synoptic Problem showed that Matthew used Mark's Gospel as one of his major sources. Consequently, the basic content of his Gospel remains very close to that of Mark. In comparing Matthew with Mark's narrative, you will notice a number of major differences. Matthew presents Jesus as a teacher who delivers five important sermons in the course of the narrative. Matthew brought together Jesus' teaching from his sources by molding it together into five well-developed sermons in order to portray Jesus as the teacher who fulfills Israel's hopes. Further significant differences with Mark's Gospel occur in the opening and closing of Matthew's Gospel. Matthew begins his narrative with a focus on Jesus' birth. At the conclusion of his narrative, Mark's description of the women running away in fear is replaced with Jesus' appearance to his followers as a proof that he is alive.

A Walk through the Gospel of Matthew

In this walk through Matthew we intend to focus on what is distinctive in this Gospel without repeating what Matthew holds in common with Mark.

Matthew 1:1–2:23: The Infancy Narrative
Matthew begins with the account of Jesus' birth. We immediately get a sense of the author's intentions and concerns. His Gospel opens in Greek with the words *"Biblos geneseos"* (1:1), which means literally "the record of the generations." Matthew intends to provide

The Significance of the Number Fourteen

Hebrew, as other ancient languages such as Greek and Latin, did not have our system of Arabic numerals. They signified numerical values through the letters of their own alphabets. Every letter of the alphabet had a specific value that was not arbitrary, but always held that value. We frequently see this at the end of movies where dates appear using the Latin alphabet. For example: L = 50; C = 100; M = 1000, and so forth.

The importance of the number fouteen in Matthew's genealogy can be understood against this background. In Hebrew the name of David (written as *dwd*) adds up to fourteen. In Hebrew the letter *d* has the value of 4, while the letter *w* has the value of 6. Hence, the name David would have the value of (*dwd*) 4+6+4 = 14.

In this way Matthew draws attention to the fact that Jesus is the descendent of David. As Son of David he is unquestioningly the Messiah.

a list of Jesus' ancestors similar to the Old Testament genealogical records of the great figures of Israel's past. This phrase could also be an allusion to the first book of the Hebrew Bible, named *Genesis* in the Septuagint (the Greek translation of the Old Testament). In this sense Matthew envisages the story of Jesus as a new beginning, a new creation.

The genealogy (1:2-17) is constructed around three sets of 14 generations. Matthew wishes to show that God has laid clear plans in the course of history for the coming of the Messiah.

While Matthew's genealogy traces Jesus' lineage through the male side, four women are deliberately singled out (Tamar, Rahab, Ruth, and Uriah's wife [Bathsheba]). The first three women were not Israelites, and Bathsheba's husband was not an Israelite. From the outset Matthew introduces one of the major themes of his Gospel. While Jesus' message was first preached exclusively to the Jews, it would ultimately be addressed to the Gentiles (non-Jews), who would give it a welcome reception. God's plan is realized despite these irregular unions (Tamar [Genesis 38], Rahab [Joshua 2], Ruth [Ruth 3], and Bathsheba [2 Samuel 11]). This paves the way for the extraordinary nature of Jesus' birth described in the opening chapter.

As in Luke 1, Matthew shows that Jesus was born through the power of the Holy Spirit ("the child conceived in her is from the Holy Spirit" [1:20]). A new creative action of God gives birth to the Messiah as the fulfillment of God's plan. This opening chapter defines very clearly Jesus' identity as the son of David, the Mes-

Reading Guide to the Gospel of Matthew

Introduction: The Birth of Jesus, the Messiah (1:1–2:23)

Part One: John the Baptist and the Sermon on the Mount (3:1–7:29)

Narrative: John's Preaching and Baptism
Jesus' Temptation and the Beginning of His Teaching in Galilee

Sermon: The Sermon on the Mount (5:1–7:29)

Part Two: Ministry in Galilee (8:1–10:42)

Narrative: Jesus Continues Preaching and Healing in Galilee
Nine miracles Are Recorded and Jesus Calls a Group to Follow Him

Sermon: The Mission Sermon (10:1-42)

Part Three: Opposition to Jesus' Teaching in Galilee (11:1–13:52)

Narrative: John the Baptist Inquires about Jesus
Jesus' Conflict with the Religious Leaders about the Sabbath

Sermon: The Parable Sermon (13:1-52)

Part Four: Jesus' Vision of the Church (14:1–18:35)

Narrative: Continued Controversies with Jewish Groups such as the Pharisees
Death of John the Baptist

Sermon: Sermon on the Church (18:1-35)

Part Five: Journey to and Entry into Jerusalem (19:1–25:46)

Narrative: Jesus Foretells His Death a Third Time
Jesus Enters Jerusalem and Cleanses the Temple

Sermon: Eschatological Discourse (24:1–25:46)

Conclusion: The Passion Narrative and the Resurrection (26:1–28:20)

The Last Supper
Jesus' Arrest and Trial before Jewish and Roman Courts
Crucifixion and Death
Burial and a Guard Placed at the Tomb
Resurrection Appearances

siah who is God's presence among humanity, "Emmanuel . . . God is with us" (1:23).

The second chapter draws the reader's attention to the child's destiny. Wise men (magi or astrologers) from the East come seeking the child. Following the signs of the heavens, they conclude that this child is destined to become king of the Jews (2:1-12). King Herod fears the child as a potential threat to his rule. He orders the slaughter of all children in Bethlehem two years old and younger. Matthew's narrative has painted a sharp contrast between the Gentiles who come seeking the king of the Jews and the Jewish authorities who refuse to believe. This contrast foreshadows the ultimate outcome of the Gospel narrative where the Jewish authorities hand Jesus over for crucifixion to the Romans, while a Roman centurion at the crucifixion confesses: "Truly this man was God's Son!" (27:54). This opening scene is a prelude to an important insight of the Gospel: how the message that was first intended for the Jews was embraced by the Gentile world.

A number of Old Testament allusions lie behind this narrative: Herod's massacre of the innocents parallels Moses' birth, where the Pharaoh endeavored to kill all the male Hebrew children (Exod 1:8–2:25). Another Old Testament figure also appears in the background of this passage, Joseph. The Joseph of Genesis and Joseph, the guardian of Jesus, are interpreters of dreams, and both go down to Egypt. Matthew focuses his birth narrative around Joseph, while Luke narrates the story almost from Mary's point of view.

In the course of his narration Matthew has used five quotations from the Greek translation of the Hebrew Scriptures (Matt 1:23 = Isa 7:14; Matt 2:6 = Mic 5:2 and 2 Sam 5:2; Matt 2:15 = Hos 11:1; Matt 2:18 = Jer 31:15; and Matt 2:23 = Isa 4:2?). His purpose was to show that God's plan was fulfilled in Jesus' birth. Matthew's way of interpreting the Bible was in line with the way in which people of his time interpreted their Scriptures. They saw that every word had an inspired meaning. In presenting an interpretation, the focus was on the word and not on the context in which the word appeared. Matthew interprets his sacred writings in the way a scholar of his time did.

The Five Sermons

First Sermon: The Sermon on the Mount (5:1–7:29)
This sermon is Matthew's most significant construction. The Sermon on the Mount has been described as "a design for life in the kingdom." The figure of Moses lies clearly in the background. Like Moses, Jesus goes up a mountain to deliver to humanity a compendium of ethical instruction (5:1). In the ultimate analysis Jesus brings Moses' instruction to fulfillment (5:17).

The Sermon opens with a series of nine Beatitudes (5:3-12) or blessings that are bestowed on different categories of people. The poor, meek, peacemakers, sorrowful, merciful, persecuted are those who uniquely enjoy God's blessings. Luke also has a Sermon (Luke 6:17-49), but it contains only four beatitudes. A compari-

son of both accounts shows that Matthew has tended to spiritualize the blessings more: for example, "poor in spirit," "hunger and thirst for righteousness," as well as extending the blessings to the merciful, pure in heart, peacemakers.

Matthew's Jesus goes on to indicate his role as the fulfillment of the Law or Torah (5:17-48). He upholds the Jewish Torah, as an expression of God's will for God's people. His role is not to do away with the Law, but to bring people to a deeper understanding of that Law: "Do not think that I have come to abolish the law or the prophets; I have come not to abolish but to fulfill" (5:17). In a series of six antitheses Jesus shows how his fulfillment of the Law entails going beyond an external obedience to the Law to the inner heart of what lies behind the Law. As such Jesus' interpretation makes the biblical Torah more penetrating for the human heart: "You have heard that it was said . . . But, I say to you . . ." Jesus prohibits not only killing, but also anger; not only adultery, but also lust. He goes further by repudiating some interpretations of the past: "You have heard that it was said, 'An eye for an eye and a tooth for a tooth'" (5:38). This is known as the Law of Talion (or retribution). This law is found at the heart of the Torah (Exod 21:23-25; Lev 24:19-20; Deut 19:21). In a society where there was no police force, it was a very positive law. While justice was considered to be retributive, one could not exact justice beyond the offense. Jesus, however, rejects such an approach and challenges his followers to give up any desire to seek revenge. Jesus points to a way that leads beyond the cycle of violence to one that looks for alternatives that deal with the situation through the law of love.

These antitheses reach a climax by extending the law of love to everyone, including one's enemies (5:44). Matthew's Jesus shows that the law of love of neighbor (Lev 19:18) was meant to embrace even enemies. Again Jesus demands more from his hearers, a "higher righteousness" than the scribes and Pharisees (5:20). Throughout this sermon Jesus speaks with an authority that not only parallels that of Moses, but also goes beyond it.

Jesus calls on his hearers to imitate God in all their actions. Just as the Father sends rain and sun on all, good and evil alike, so believers must show love for all without distinction and without limit: "Be perfect, therefore, as your heavenly Father is perfect" (5:48).

In the rest of the sermon Jesus continues to map out a way of life for his followers:

- through the reinterpretation of the religious practices of his day: almsgiving, prayer, and fasting (6:1-18);
- through exclusive trust and devotion to God (6:19-34);
- through the treatment of others (7:1-12).

Outline of Chapter 13

(1) Parable of the Sower (13:1-9)

Purpose of Parables (13:10-17)

Explanation of the Sower Parable (13:18-23)

(2) Parable of the Weeds (13:24-30)

(3) Parable of the Mustard Seed (13:31-32)

(4) Parable of the Yeast (13:33)

Use of Parables (13:34-35)

Explanation of the Weeds Parable (13:36-43)

(5) Parable of the Treasure (13:44)

(6) Parable of the Pearl (13:45-46)

(7) Parable of the Net (13:47-53)

Second Sermon: The Mission Sermon (10:1-42)

Matthew names the 12 disciples in this context (10:2-4). Significantly, these 12 disciples are instructed: "Go nowhere among the Gentiles, and enter no town of the Samaritans, but go rather to the lost sheep of the house of Israel" (10:5-6). According to Matthew their preaching and healing mission is directed exclusively to the people of Israel, as was Jesus' mission (15:24). Only at the end of the Gospel does Jesus send the disciples out to the Gentiles (28:19). In this way Matthew presents a progressive development of the Gospel preaching starting with Israel and later being extended to the Gentiles. This is different from the other Gospels, which see a ministry to the Gentiles during Jesus' life. See, for example, Luke's Jesus, who sends the disciples ahead of him into Samaria to prepare the way (Luke 9:52-56).

Matthew 10:16-23 describes the hostile reaction the disciples will face in the course of their mission. It seems that Matthew reflects conditions that his own community was experiencing in their proclamation of the gospel. He shows his habit of bringing together Jesus' words with a commentary that reflects the situation of his own readers.

Words of encouragement (10:24-33) follow this discussion of persecution. Matthew's Jesus reminds them that their lives are in God's hands: "So do not be afraid; you are of more value than many sparrows" (10:31). Trust in God should enable the disciples to withstand the pressures and divisions that arise as a result of commitment to Jesus (10:34-39). The disciples are given the assurance that God is present with them in their healing and preaching ministry. Welcoming the disciples is tantamount to welcoming Jesus; and welcoming Jesus is

The Nature of a Parable

Jesus' characteristic way of teaching is through parables. To construct his parables Jesus drew on the agricultural world of his hearers. For us who come from a technologically-orientated society, some of these images create difficulties. Even for those who come from a rural world, many of the customs of that world are also puzzling. To understand them we need to know the world of that time.

The word "parable" comes from the Greek word *parabole,* indicating a wise saying, a figure of speech. In reference to the New Testament it refers to a short story (or an example) that is told in order to convey a message by means of a comparison. Ultimately two things are being compared for a purpose.

Jesus tells a story in which different aspects of God's kingdom are highlighted by means of a comparison. The "kingdom of God" basically refers to "the rule or reign of God." It refers to a relationship that has been established between God and humanity and how God exercises God's power for those in this relationship. As we have noted, it is both a present and a future reality.

Matthew always speaks of "the kingdom of heaven" rather than 'kingdom of God," showing his Jewish sensitivity. In order to uphold the commandment that said, "You shall not make wrongful use of the name of the Lord your God" (Exod 20:7), the Jews avoided using the divine name. Instead they would use circumlocutions to refer to God: heaven is one of these circumlocutions.

Scholars make a distinction between a parable and an allegory. Both are figures of speech where a story is told and a comparison drawn from that story. The difference is that a parable conveys only one point in the comparison; it has only one message. In the allegory, every detail in the story is significant and communicates a message. In Matthew 13 we can see this distinction clearly: in the parable of the Weeds (vv. 24-30) Jesus tells a parable, but in vv. 36-43 the interpretation turns it into an allegory where every detail is significant: "The one who sows the good seed is the Son of Man; the field is the world . . ." (vv. 37-38).

tantamount to welcoming God, the Father. Their mission is to extend God's grace to everyone.

Third Sermon: The Parable Sermon (13:1-58)

This sermon in Matthew 13 contains seven parables. Matthew has used Mark 4 as the basis for this sermon, but has brought together a number of other parables in order to present a more encompassing teaching of Jesus on the kingdom.

Interior of the fourth-century c.e. synagogue at Capernaum. (Phoenix Data Systems, Neal and Joel Bierling)

Matthew divides this sermon into two parts: the first is addressed to the crowds (13:1-35), the second to the disciples in a house (13:36-53). The parable of the Sower and its interpretation show how this parable was transformed into an allegory. This probably occurred when Jesus' followers adapted the parable to the situation of their audience. In the interpretation, an emphasis is placed on the different difficulties and obstacles that believers encounter when handing on the word. In the parable of the Weeds and its interpretation, we have the same transformation from a parable into an allegory (13:24-30, 36-43). The concern lies on the separation between good and evil, a separation reserved for the end time.

Particularly noteworthy in this chapter is the response of the disciples to Jesus' teaching. Unlike Mark where the disciples struggle to understand Jesus and his teaching, the disciples in Matthew's Gospel do understand. This emerges clearly at the conclusion to this sermon (see 13:51-52) where Jesus asks them: "'Have you understood all this?' They answer, 'Yes.'" The final parable in this section concerns the master of the household who brings out new and old treasure from his house. Those who follow Jesus are like scribes who have been trained for the kingdom: in Jesus' teaching they recognize that in the *newness of his revelation* Jesus interprets for them the *past revelation* that came through Moses. Jesus is the one who makes it possible for them to understand the past. The disciples respond to this positively.

Fourth Sermon: The Church (18:1-35)

Here Matthew uses traditional Jesus sayings found in his sources to instruct his own community. This chapter operates on two levels. It can be read on the surface level of the ministry of Jesus and on the deeper level of instructions directed to Matthew's own community.

The sermon opens with a discussion on greatness in the kingdom of God (18:1-5). In the kingdom, the value of humility is most important because life in God's kingdom acknowledges dependence on and trust in God's power. That is why a little child is held up for emulation.

The instructions on church discipline and the law of forgiveness (vv. 15-22) strive to bring Jesus' teaching to life within the community. Matthew's Jesus gives the community the right to ostracize members who refuse to change their ways. Peter's sevenfold offer of forgiveness is in fact a generous offer. But Jesus takes the opportunity to show the true nature of his forgiveness. "Seventy-seven" times is Jesus' response to Peter, which shows the infinite quality that forgiveness requires. The final parable in this chapter on the Unforgiving Servant (vv. 23-35) develops this further by calling forth divine judgment on those who refuse to forgive.

The highlight of the sermon is Jesus' promise to remain with his followers: "For where two or three are gathered in my name, I am there among them" (v. 20). This reminds the reader of the theme of God's abiding presence with the community at the beginning of the

Gospel: "'and they shall name him Emmanuel,' which means, 'God is with us'" (1:23) and at the end: "And remember, I am with you always, to the end of the age" (28:20). The whole Gospel is included between these two statements about Jesus as God's abiding presence among God's people.

Final Sermon: Eschatological Discourse (24:1–25:46)
This long speech on the end times owes its inspiration to Mark 13. It opens with the disciples asking about the destruction of the temple and the end of the age. Jesus continues to warn them not to be led astray (24:4). The hallmark of the chapter is the spirit of watchfulness, since no one knows the day when the Son of Man will return (24:37-51): "Therefore you also must be ready, for the Son of Man is coming at an unexpected hour" (v. 44). This section culminates in the parable of the Judgment of the Nations (25:31-46). What is so striking about this parable is Jesus' challenge to his hearers to embrace a lifestyle that is very different from that of the scribes and Pharisees. His followers are to embrace an ethos of concern for the least members of society: they must pay attention to the poor and lowly rather than the rich and powerful.

Matthew 26:1–28:20: The Passion Narrative and the Resurrection
Matthew's narrative on Jesus' death and resurrection follows Mark's account very closely. At the same time, Matthew has introduced a number of aspects that conform to his interests and theology.

- Judas: Matthew adds details that embellish Judas's betrayal. Matthew alone states that Judas was paid 30 pieces of silver for betraying Jesus (26:14-16). The details surrounding Judas's death (27:3-10) are referred to as fulfilling the prophet Jeremiah (Jer 32:6-15), while the actual price of 30 pieces of silver comes from Zechariah (Zech 11:12-13).
- A warning dream: Pilate's wife warns her husband not to have anything to do with "that innocent man" after she has received a dream (27:19). It reminds the reader of the warning dreams that occurred in the infancy narrative.
- The end times: When Jesus died not only was the veil of the temple torn in two, but "the earth shook, and the rocks were split. The tombs also were opened, and many bodies of the saints who had fallen asleep were raised" (27:51-52). Matthew uses images that describe the end times. Just as heavenly signs marked Jesus' birth, so Jesus' death also embraces cosmic events. Jesus' death dramatically changed the world in its relationship with God.

- Roman guards at the tomb: In an attempt to prevent Jesus' disciples from stealing the body, Roman soldiers are posted at the tomb (27:62-66; 28:11-15). After the resurrection these soldiers are bribed to say that his disciples did in fact steal the body. Matthew is undoubtedly using this narrative to counter the Jewish leaders of his time who were attacking the Christian belief in the resurrection.
- Resurrection appearance (28:16-20): In the Gospel of Mark Jesus promises that after his resurrection he will go ahead of his disciples to Galilee (Mark 14:28; 16:7). Matthew continues this tradition by having the risen Jesus appear to them on a mountain in Galilee (28:16). The reappearance of the theme of a mountain is significant. The mountain is the place where God's revelation occurs: it reminds the reader of Jesus' revelation in the Sermon on the Mount (5:1) and of God's revelation to Moses on Mount Sinai (Exod 19:3). Jesus' sending his disciples out to teach and baptize all the nations reverses the command to go only to "the lost sheep of the house of Israel" (10:5-6). This outreach to the Gentiles must reflect what is already happening in Matthew's community. Many Gentiles must be making inroads into their community. The baptismal formula "in the name of the Father and of the Son and of the Holy Spirit" must reflect the baptismal custom of Matthew's community. This shows a further development within the early Christian church: the original baptismal ritual included a baptism in the name of Jesus (see, e.g., Acts 10:48: "So he ordered them to be baptized in the name of Jesus Christ"). The ritual developed to incorporate all three persons. Finally, the risen Jesus gives them the assurance that he will be with them "to the end of the age" (28:20). As we noted above, this is an inclusion with the opening of the Gospel, where Jesus is identified in the words of the prophet Isaiah as "Emmanuel: God is with us" (1:23). The presence of God will continue in the community of those who believe in Jesus.

Critical Issues in Studying Matthew

Use of Sources
Matthew used the Gospel of Mark as his basic source. While Mark was directed to a Gentile audience, Matthew's intention was to rewrite this Gospel for a community largely made up of Christian Jews. Matthew's style is very different from that of Mark. He wrote in a very polished Greek and tended to improve on Mark. The picture of Jesus in Matthew downplays the human characteristics that Mark had painted. Compare, for example, the description of the woman with a hemorrhage

Example of Matthew's Editing of Mark

The Baptism of Jesus

Mark 1:9-11

In those days Jesus came from Nazareth of Galilee and was baptized by John in the Jordan. And just as he was coming up out of the water, he saw the heavens torn apart and the Spirit descending like a dove on him. And a voice came from heaven, "You are my Son, the Beloved: with you I am well pleased."

Matthew 3:13-17

Then Jesus came from Galilee to John at the Jordan, to be baptized by him. John would have prevented him, saying, "I need to be baptized by you, and do you come to me?" But Jesus answered him, "Let it be so now; for it is proper for us in this way to fulfill all righteousness." Then he consented. And when Jesus had been baptized, just as he came up from the water, suddenly the heavens were opened to him and he saw the Spirit of God descending like a dove and alighting on him. And a voice from heaven said, "This is my Son, the Beloved, with whom I am well pleased."

Matthew preserved Mark's basic text. He inserted a dialogue between Jesus and John about Jesus' baptism by John. This dialogue is Matthew's creation. He tried to answer a question that puzzled his community: If Jesus was without sin, as his followers came to believe, then why was he baptized with John's baptism of repentance? Matthew constructs this narrative to answer that question. Matthew's Jesus replies that he accepts baptism because it is part of God's plan. The use of the word "righteousness" here is characteristic of Matthew's vocabulary.

in Mark 5:21-43 and Matt 9:18-26. You will notice that Matthew avoids mentioning that Jesus did not know who touched him and he leaves out the disciples' judgment that Jesus had asked a stupid question.

Into this framework provided by the Gospel of Mark, Matthew introduced the sayings source Q that was well suited to his purpose because of its Jewish character. In using Q, Matthew rearranged it to fit into the five basic sermons that he constructed. In addition to Mark and Q, Matthew had his own special material, referred to by scholars as Special M. This is information known only to Matthew. We see this especially in the opening chapters of the Gospel.

A characteristic feature of Matthew's Gospel is his use of Old Testament quotations throughout the Gospel. This is very evident in the first two chapters, where he uses these quotations to support the episode that he narrated (see 1:23; 2:5-6, 15, 17-18, 23).

Matthew's use of Old Testament quotations has led some scholars to argue that he created these stories on the basis of these quotations. But when you examine these episodes carefully, you see that it is hard to imagine how the quotation could simply have generated the story. It makes more sense to see these accounts as coming to Matthew from his sources. To these Matthew added a quotation since it was his deliberate intention to show that Jesus is the Messiah who fulfills the expectations of the past.

The author should not be seen as simply using scissors and paste to construct his narrative. He rewrote the narrative giving his own theological focus on Jesus, the

disciples, and the community. He had a much more developed understanding of Jesus, the community, and the end times. The narrative that Matthew ultimately produced was to become the most popular of the Gospels in the early church.

Who Is the Author of the Gospel of Matthew?

The earliest reference we have to the authorship of this Gospel comes from Papias (ca. 70-125 C.E.), as recorded by the historian Eusebius (260-339) in his *Ecclesiastical History* (3:39.16): "Matthew collected the oracles *(logia)* in the Hebrew language, and each interpreted them as best he could." Papias claims that Matthew wrote the "oracles of Jesus" in Hebrew. The view that the Gospel of Matthew (as we have it today) was originally written in Hebrew (or Aramaic) and later translated into Greek is difficult to uphold from a scholarly point of view. An examination of the canonical Gospel shows that it was written in Greek, and the language and style are certainly not those of a translation from another language.

This does not mean that Papias is completely wrong. He was writing about four decades after the composition of Matthew so may have known the tradition related to this Gospel. The problem lies with our interpretation of what Papias says. Papias clearly speaks about "the oracles." He is not referring to the Gospel, but rather the tradition of the "sayings" *(logia)* that lie behind the Gospel of Matthew.

We can bring this information together in this way: An unknown writer who was not an eyewitness originally wrote the Gospel of Matthew in Greek, relying on sources

Antioch of Syria (Antakya, Turkey), location of the first Christian church outside Jerusalem. (Phoenix Data Systems, Neal and Joel Bierling)

such as Mark and Q. The name Matthew was associated with the sayings tradition which the author used. Since the Gospel relied heavily on the tradition of Jesus' sayings, it ultimately took its name from them and gave it its authority. We will continue to speak of the author of the Gospel as Matthew, but it is to be understood as referring to the unknown disciple who composed this Gospel based on the traditions of Matthew.

From an examination of the Gospel itself, we can say that this unknown writer was a Christian Jew writing for a community of Christians who had come from Judaism. This is seen from his use of the Septuagint, the parallels he draws between Jesus and Moses, that Jesus is the Son of David, how Jesus is the fulfillment of the Law or Torah, and the controversies with the Jewish religious leaders, especially the Pharisees. The Gospel shows an author who knows the world and thought of Judaism really well.

Who Are the First Readers of This Gospel?
Our examination of Matthew's Gospel has indicated two interesting phenomena.

- Matthew's Gospel has a predominantly Jewish focus with the intention of showing the relationship of Jesus to the world and beliefs of Judaism. The Gospel breathes the thought and world of Judaism. Further, Matthew's Jesus understands his mission as directed

exclusively to his own people: "I was sent only to the lost sheep of the house of Israel" (15:24). His sending out of the disciples was directed in like manner exclusively to the people of Israel: "Go nowhere among the Gentiles" (10:5).

- On the other hand, Matthew's Gospel also embraces an outreach to the Gentiles. We have already observed how the story of the Magi at the opening of the Gospel sets the stage whereby the gospel message is rejected by the Jewish authorities and embraced by seekers from the Gentile world. The Gospel ends with Jesus sending forth his followers to make disciples of all nations (28:19-20).

Reflecting on these aspects, scholars have proposed the following scenario for the origin of this Gospel. It emerges from a Christian community that was predominantly Jewish, hence we would call it a Christian Jewish community. The strongly anti-Pharisaic attitude in this Gospel would be explained from the context of the world of Judaism immediately after the destruction of Jerusalem and the Temple in 70 C.E. The only religious groups to survive those horrendous events were the Pharisees and the followers of Jesus.

The Gospel of Matthew emerges against that background. It reflects a community of followers of Jesus who were struggling with the Pharisees for the heart and

Comparison of Matthew with Hebrew Bible Texts

Matthew quotes the Greek translation (the Septuagint) of the Old Testament at least 60 times, while he alludes to it on more than 100 occasions. Here is a selection of some of Matthew's quotations to show how they compare with the Hebrew Bible texts:

Matthew (Septuagint)

"Look, the virgin shall conceive and bear a son,
    and they shall name him Emmanuel." (1:23)

"And you, Bethlehem, in the land of Judah,
    are by no means least among the rulers of Judah;
    for from you shall come a ruler
    who is to shepherd my people Israel." (2:6)

"Out of Egypt I have called my son." (2:15)

"A voice was heard in Ramah,
    wailing and loud lamentation,
    Rachel weeping for her children;
    she refused to be consoled,
    because they are no more." (2:18)

"He will be called a Nazorean." (2:23)

"One does not live on bread alone,
    but by every word that comes from the mouth
    of God." (4:4)

Hebrew Bible

Look, the young woman is with child and shall bear a
    son, and shall name him Immanuel. (Isa 7:14)

But you, O Bethlehem of Ephrathah,
    who are one of the little clans of Judah,
    from you shall come forth for me
    one who is to rule in Israel,
    whose origin is from of old,
    from ancient days. (Mic 5:2)

When Israel was a child, I loved him,
    and out of Egypt I called my son. (Hos 11:1)

A voice is heard in Ramah,
    lamentation and bitter weeping.
    Rachel is weeping for her children;
    she refuses to be comforted for her children,
    because they are no more. (Jer 31:15)

A shoot shall come out from the stump of Jesse, and a
    branch (*netser*) shall grow out of his roots. (Isa 11:1)

He humbled you by letting you hunger, then by
    feeding you with manna, with which neither you
    nor your ancestors were acquainted, in order to
    make you understand that one does not live by
    bread alone, but by every word that comes from
    the mouth of the Lord. (Deut 8:3)

soul of Judaism. Each group was claiming to be the true interpreter of and heir to the traditions of Israel's past. This explains why it is important for Matthew's Gospel to present Jesus as the fulfillment of the Law.

A decade after the destruction of Jerusalem Matthew's community experienced a new phenomenon. The numbers of Gentiles entering their community increased dramatically. Matthew uses his Gospel to show that this outreach to the Gentiles is in conformity with Jesus' intentions and spirit. The acceptance of Gentiles into their community is part of God's plan to bring salvation to the nations of the world. This direction would set the stage for the emergence of two separate religions: Judaism (from the followers of the Pharisees) and Christianity (from the followers of Jesus). The Gospel of Matthew is a beautiful record of this initial transformation.

Where would the community of Matthew be located? Many scholars suggest the city of Antioch because it was one of the very few early Christian centers where the makeup of the community was predominantly Jewish Christian. One would date this Gospel to around 80.

Theological Themes in the Gospel of Matthew

Virginal Conception

Matthew 1:18-25 speaks of the virginal conception of Jesus. Matthew's main interest here is to show that Jesus is divine, that he is God's Son. Some modern scholars tend to question the virginal conception, arguing that this belief is a Christian adaptation of a pagan myth where the gods are seen to beget humans. However, one of the clearest differences with these accounts is that Matthew is speaking about a virginal conception, not divine sexual intercourse, as was the case with the pagan gods. Further support for the virginal conception is its attestation in two independent sources, Matthew and Luke. This surely shows a tradition that predates either

"Land of Zebulun, land of Naphtali, on the road by the sea, across the Jordan, Galilee of the Gentiles — the people who sat in darkness have seen a great light, and for those who sat in the region and shadow of death light has dawned." (4:15-16)	"In the former time he brought into contempt the land of Zebulun and the land of Naphtali, but in the latter time he will make glorious the way of the sea, the land beyond the Jordan, Galilee of the nations. The people who walked in darkness have seen a great light; those who lived in a land of deep darkness — on them light has shined. (Isa 9:1-2)
"He took our infirmities and bore our diseases." (8:17)	"Surely he has borne our infirmities and carried our diseases; yet we accounted him stricken, struck down by God, and afflicted. (Isa 53:4)
"Here is my servant, whom I have chosen, my beloved, with whom my soul is well pleased. I will put my Spirit upon him, and he will proclaim justice to the Gentiles. He will not wrangle or cry aloud, nor will anyone hear his voice in the streets. He will not break a bruised reed or quench a smoldering wick until he brings justice to victory. And in his name the Gentiles will hope." (12:18-21)	"Here is my servant, whom I uphold, my chosen, in whom my soul delights; I have put my spirit upon him; he will bring forth justice to the nations. He will not cry or lift up his voice, or make it heard in the street; a bruised reed he will not break, and a dimly burning wick he will not quench; he will faithfully bring forth justice. He will not grow faint or be crushed until he has established justice in the earth; and the coastlands wait for this teaching. (Isa 42:1-4)
"'Eli, Eli, lema sabachthani?' that is, 'My God, my God, why have you forsaken me?'" (27:46)	"My God, my God, why have you forsaken me? Why are you so far from helping me, from the words of my groaning?" (Ps. 22:1)

of the two Gospels. From a theological perspective it is supported for Protestants by a belief in the authority and the inerrancy of Scripture while for Catholics it is supported by church tradition.

Anti-Semitism

The hostile statements made by Matthew against the Pharisees and the Jews in particular (esp. ch. 23) have given rise in past centuries for a strongly anti-Semitic attitude. This is an illustration of what happens when the biblical text is read independently of its social context. Matthew's Gospel must be seen to emerge from a situation of conflict within the Jewish community. Both the Pharisees and the followers of Jesus are struggling with each other for the heart of Judaism. A writing emerging from such a hostile environment would portray its opponents in a very negative light. Further, Matthew tends to paint the Pharisees in the light of those who possess qualities that he does not want his community to adopt. They become his foils for showing what characteristics they should avoid if they are to be true followers of Jesus. The tragedy is that sometimes Christians have read these statements as accurate descriptions of all the Jew-

ish people. That is unfair, especially since Matthew and his community considered themselves to be the heirs of Judaism.

Jesus the Teacher Fulfills the Law

As we have indicated above, in composing his Gospel Matthew was concerned with a twofold reality: the relationship of the teaching of Jesus to the traditions of Israel and the fact that many Gentiles had accepted the message of Jesus.

Matthew's starting point was to present Jesus as the Teacher (the Rabbi) who upheld the true traditions of Israel. The following statement captures the very essence of all that Jesus did and said: "Do not think that I have come to abolish the law or the prophets; I have come not to abolish but to fulfill" (5:17). Jesus claimed for himself the authority to interpret the traditions of Israel's past as contained in the "law and the prophets" (a phrase used to refer to Israel's Sacred Scriptures). The Law specifically refers to the Torah, the expression of God's will for God's people that is found in the first five books of the Hebrew Scriptures. Jesus' statement claimed authority to give the biblical Torah the rightful understanding and interpretation. This "fulfillment" meant that Jesus took a hard look at the traditions of Israel's past and made a distinction between those traditions that truly were an expression of God's will for God's people and those that were not.

In the Sermon on the Mount, after his statement on fulfilling the Law, Jesus goes on to give his own understanding and interpretation of the laws through a sustained contrast: "You have heard that it was said . . . but I say to you . . ." (5:21-48). Jesus does not contradict the teaching of the Law. Instead, he calls on his followers to adhere to the Law in a much more intense way. He tells them that they are to abide by the Law more fully than even the Jewish religious leaders were doing: "For I tell you, unless your righteousness exceeds that of the scribes and Pharisees, you will never enter the kingdom of heaven" (5:20). By the word "righteousness" Matthew embraces the concept of "moral action according to God's will." Jesus challenges his followers to ensure that the way they lead their lives must be according to God's will (discovered in the Torah, the biblical Law). They must be dedicated to doing God's will more intensely than even the religious leaders of that day. In the antitheses of Matthew (5:21-48), Jesus asks his followers to abide by the intention and the spirit, rather than giving a mere legalistic adherence to the Law.

Jesus' fulfillment of the Law culminates in the simple command to love God and to love one's neighbor as oneself (22:34-40). Matthew's Jesus presents his teaching on the centrality of the spirit of love in response to the question of a lawyer (one who belongs to the Pharisee party, an expert in interpreting the Jewish Law). When Jesus concludes this statement on the importance of loving God and neighbor, he says: "On these two commandments hang all the law and the prophets" (22:40). This statement is significant because it draws the reader's attention back to Jesus' saying in the Sermon on the Mount that he has come not to abolish the Law and the prophets, but to fulfill them. Here Jesus shows in the clearest way how he fulfills the Law. He brings people to realize that the fullest understanding of the intention of the Law is contained in the law of love. Love should be the dominant motive in all that one does in order to carry out God's will as envisaged by the Law.

The fulfillment of the Law looks beyond the confines of Israel to embrace all humanity. God's revelation through Israel was not meant to be isolationist or exclusive, but rather it was a revelation intended ultimately for all people. Since Matthew's community has experienced many Gentiles joining it, Matthew interprets this as a clear fulfillment of God's plan. This is what God intended from the very beginning in choosing Israel as God's chosen nation. In this sense Jesus truly is "the fulfillment of the law and the prophets."

Discipleship

The negative picture of the disciples so characteristic of Mark's Gospel is transformed by Matthew into a very positive one. This change emanates from Matthew's image of Jesus: he is a rabbi with students (the disciples) around him. As students, the disciples absorb Jesus' teaching faithfully throughout the Gospel. At the end they can go out and continue Jesus' ministry of teaching (28:19-20). Because the disciples could effectively carry out Jesus' mission only if they first understood Jesus' teaching clearly, Matthew's Jesus instructs them on every possible occasion.

The purpose of their mission is to make disciples (Greek *matheteuein,* 28:19; see 13:52; 27:57). Jesus sees his followers in the role of scribes who have been trained in the ways of the kingdom: "Therefore every scribe who has been trained *(matheteutheis)* for the kingdom of heaven is like the master of a household who brings out of his treasure what is new and what is old" (13:52). Their training conforms to the essence of Jesus' teaching on his fulfillment of the Law.

Peter receives a prominent place in Matthew's treatment of the disciples and is featured much more positively than in Mark, taking on the role of the one who represents the other disciples. Jesus endorses Peter's confession of him as Messiah with a special blessing (16:17) and identifies Peter as the "rock (on which) I will build my church" (v. 18). When Jesus promises Peter the power of "binding and loosing," he uses images that refer in a Jewish context to making legal decisions regarding the Law. This same power is entrusted in 18:18 to the community of disciples. Consequently, Jesus presents Peter's role as intimately bound up with the community. He is representative of the community.

The whole Gospel is directed toward instructing the community on the nature of discipleship. Matthew's Gospel has been described as "a handbook" for the community on how to lead their lives. The five sermons are orientated toward this instruction. This is the only Gospel that uses the term "church" (Greek *ekklesia,* 16:18; 18:17) for the Christian community, a term that was popular in the Pauline world for the assembly of Christian believers.

Throughout the sermons the word "brother" is used in the Greek text (5:22, 24, 47; 18:15, 21, 35), but this is not meant to be understood in the restrictive sense of referring only to males. Hence the NRSV translates it correctly as "brother and sister" in order to designate the disciples who are living in close relationship with one another and with God. The bottom line for all members of Matthew's community is that they are all equal; they are all "brothers and sisters." Discipleship begins a new life for the members of Matthew's community. They share in the community's life in an equal way.

Teaching, then, is the fundamental mission of a disciple according to Matthew's Gospel. Within the community the disciples instruct new members or help those members whose faith is weak. This task of teaching is carried out in the spirit of "brotherly equality." Jesus sums up the qualities and attitudes demanded of a disciple: "But you are not to be called rabbi, for you have one teacher, and you are all students. And call no one your father on earth, for you have one Father — the one in heaven. Nor are you to be called instructors, for you have one instructor, the Messiah. The greatest among you will be your servant. All who exalt themselves will be humbled, and all who humble themselves will be exalted" (23:8-12).

While Matthew's Gospel is a narrative about Jesus, his focus remains with his own community. Through the story of Jesus and his disciples Matthew addresses his own community. The disciples in Matthew's Gospel become models for the life of every believer who is called to discipleship in the sense of being a student who learns Jesus' teachings and passes them on to others.

Questions for Review and Discussion

1 How does Matthew's infancy narrative help the reader understand the significance of the person of Jesus? What does it contribute to our understanding of Jesus and his mission?

2 Explain the meaning of Matthew's use of the following terms: righteousness; fulfillment; church.

3 Discuss the difference between Matthew's and Mark's understanding of discipleship.

Further Reading

Carter, Warren. *Matthew: Storyteller, Interpreter, Evangelist.* Rev. ed. Peabody: Hendrickson, 2004.

Overman, J. Andrew. *Matthew's Gospel and Formative Judaism: The Social World of the Matthean Community.* Minneapolis: Fortress, 1990.

Powell, Mark A. *God with Us: A Pastoral Theology of Matthew's Gospel.* Minneapolis: Fortress, 1995.

Saldarini, Anthony J. "Matthew." In *ECB*, 1000-63.

Senior, Donald. *What Are They Saying about Matthew?* Rev. ed. New York: Paulist, 1996.

[handwritten note:] F Dale Bruner Two Volume Commentary on Matthew

Chapter 51

Luke-Acts (1): The Gospel of Luke

Jesus: The Savior of the World

Getting Started

1 The first two chapters of the Gospel of Luke serve as an overture to the Gospel. What are some of the themes that appear there and continue through the rest of the Gospel?

2 Explain the following aspects of Jesus' first sermon in Luke 4:16-30. How does the quotation of Isa 61:1-2 summarize the mission of Jesus? Who are Elijah and Elisha? Why do the people react so violently to Jesus' message? In what way does their response foreshadow the destiny of Jesus?

Preliminary Comments

The Gospel of Luke and the Acts of the Apostles are two volumes of one work. This unity of Luke-Acts is seen from an examination of the language, style, thought, and above all the theological vision that emerges from both narratives. The opening of both volumes immediately establishes a close connection. In both Luke 1:1-4 and Acts 1:1-2 the author speaks in the first person singular ("I") and indicates how he went about writing the narrative. Both volumes are addressed to Theophilus.

The second volume deliberately connects to the thought of the first by summarizing it briefly.

The Gospel of Luke together with the Acts of the Apostles comprises about one quarter of the entire New Testament. This alone shows their importance. In addition, the Gospel has captured the popular imagination of Christians throughout the ages: the angels heralding the birth of Jesus to the shepherds in the fields; the parables of the Prodigal Son and the Lost Coin; and the journey of the disciples to Emmaus are scenes that are vividly imprinted on the minds of every generation of Christians.

Luke's historical vision is analogous to that of the Deuteronomist in the Hebrew Bible who traced a narrative of Israel's history from the entry into the promised land under Joshua to the destruction of that land under the Babylonians (see Chapter 12 for an overview of the Deuteronomic Collection). Luke also writes a theological, historical narrative that traces the birth of a new religious movement in Palestine to its spread throughout the Roman world until it reaches the capital of Rome (61 C.E.). Luke imitates the historians of his day in constructing this narrative. He situates Jesus of Nazareth at the center of history by dividing history into three time periods: that of Israel, Jesus, and the church. The first volume, the Gospel, opens with the narrative about John

Reading Guide to the Gospel of Luke

Prologue (1:1-4)

The Infancy Narrative (1:5–2:52)
- Birth and Circumcision of John the Baptist and Jesus (1:5–2:40)
- Jesus' Boyhood (2:41-52)

Preparation for Jesus' Public Ministry (3:1–4:13)
- Preaching of John the Baptist
- Baptism and Temptation of Jesus

Ministry in Galilee (4:14–9:50)
- First Sermon at Nazareth and Rejection (4:14-30)
- Healing Miracles and Call of First Disciples (4:31–5:16)
- Controversies with Authorities (5:17–6:11)
- Choosing of the Twelve and Sermon on the Plain (6:12-49)
- Further Miracles and Parables (7:1–8:56)
- Mission of the Twelve (9:1-6)
- Feeding of 5000 and the Identity of Jesus (9:7-50)

Travel Narrative: Journey to Jerusalem (9:51–19:27)
- The Heart of the Gospel: The Disciples Are Trained in Jesus' Teaching

Ministry in Jerusalem (19:28–21:38)
- Jesus' Entry into Jerusalem and Cleansing of the Temple (19:28–21:4)
- Eschatological Discourse on Fate of Jerusalem and the End Time (21:5-38)

Passion and Resurrection Narrative (22:1–24:53)
- Passion and Crucifixion of Jesus (22:1–23:56)
- Resurrection of Jesus (24:1-53)
- Empty Tomb (24:1-12)
- Appearance on Road to Emmaus (24:13-35)
- Appearance in Jerusalem (24:36-49)
- Ascension into Heaven (24:50-53)

the Baptist as the last of Israel's prophets, who prepares the way for the Messiah, Jesus. This first volume concentrates on the ministry of Jesus, who brought salvation to all humanity. Luke develops his theological and historical vision in the second volume, the Acts of the Apostles, with the Apostles continuing Jesus' ministry. Luke's theological focus is not on the *parousia,* the return of Jesus (as in the Gospel of Mark), but on the enduring present activity of the Christian church in handing on this salvation of Jesus.

The above considerations help to explain the approach adopted in this and the following chapter. Most introductions to the New Testament tend to keep these two works separate, remaining true to their sequence in the New Testament. We believe that such an approach misses the beauty of the theological vision that Luke wishes to share with his reader. Consequently, we shall treat the Gospel and Acts together as they were intended to be read, as one major work in two volumes.

Our approach to both the Gospel of Luke and the Acts of the Apostles will again employ the methodology of narrative criticism, with the focus on the unfolding of the plot and how the narrator communicates his specific vision to the reader. At the same time, as with the Gospel of Matthew, redaction criticism will also help to focus on Luke's special contribution to this narrative story that he inherited from Mark, his basic source.

A Walk through the Gospel of Luke

Luke 1:1-4: Prologue

Luke's opening differs dramatically from Mark, who begins by stating his purpose: namely, that Jesus is the Christ, the Son of God (Mark 1:1). Luke, while presuming the existence of other accounts, writes a narrative that conforms to the rules of Hellenistic literature and rhetoric and provides a deeper reflection upon everything about which the reader has already been instructed.

Close examination of 1:1-4 yields a number of important points:

- The narrator says that he depends on those who "were eyewitnesses and servants of the word" (v. 2). Perhaps a better translation would be: "the original eyewitnesses who became ministers of the word." This is a double description of Jesus' disciples as eyewitnesses who eventually became ministers of the word. Luke speaks as a second-generation Christian, carefully marking his distance from the "events" and "the eyewitnesses of the word."
- Theophilus is mentioned again in the introduction to the second volume, Acts, but he is otherwise unknown. There is no reason to doubt that the author is dedicating his composition to a real person. The text indicates that he is a recent convert: "so that you may know the truth concerning the things about which you have been instructed." The meaning of his name also gives rise to a symbolic interpretation. *Theophilus* comes from Greek *theos,* "God," and *philos,* "beloved or friend"; hence the name can stand for Christian readers who are indeed "beloved of God."
- These events have a note of fulfillment in that they belong to a past and a present which are not unrelated to what God has promised in the Old Testament. Luke sees the ministry of Jesus as a fulfillment of the hopes

and promises of the past. The narrator gives an assurance that what is now being taught in the narrator's own day has firm roots in the person of Jesus.

Luke 1:5–2:52: The Infancy Narrative

In narrating the account of Jesus' birth, Luke uses the technique of parallelism prominent in both the Gospel and Acts. He parallels the annunciation and the births of John and Jesus in order to highlight the superiority of the birth of Jesus.

Only the Gospel of Luke records John's birth. The account is reminiscent of many narratives in the Hebrew Bible where a childless couple receives the blessing of a child. However, Luke uses a parallel description to contrast the births of John and Jesus. John's conception and birth is in line with the Hebrew Bible's narratives of births to elderly parents. Jesus' birth is on another level — it is a birth to a virgin through the creative power of the Holy Spirit. John belongs to the world of the past; Jesus begins a new age: "The law and the prophets were in effect until John came; since then the good news of the kingdom of God is proclaimed, and everyone tries to enter it by force" (16:16).

Jesus' birth is preceded by an account of the annunciation to Mary by the angel Gabriel. In her response Mary shows her openness to the acceptance of God's plan despite not understanding what it entails.

Luke uses another literary technique found in his sources. He introduces speeches into the mouths of his characters to capture the essence of their feelings at that specific time and to communicate an understanding of the event. In the infancy narrative, Luke introduces a number of hymns that have the same function as speeches: Mary's song (*Magnificat,* 1:46-55); Zechariah's song (*Benedictus,* 1:67-79); the angels' song (*Gloria in excelsis,* 2:13-14); and Simeon's Prayer (*Nunc dimittis,* 2:28-32). Quite probably these hymns originated in the worshipping community. Stylistically, they closely resemble Jewish hymns that have been discovered from that period, especially among the Dead Sea Scrolls. Luke has adapted them to fit his narrative. Mary's Song, the *Magnificat,* is very similar to Hannah's prayer in 1 Sam 2:1-10.

Only Luke has an episode from Jesus' youth: the account of the 12-year-old child in the temple (2:41-52). At issue is Jesus' identity as God's Son: "Did you not know that I must be in my Father's house?" (v. 49). This affirmation provides a bridge between the infancy narrative and the adult ministry of Jesus. In the infancy narrative Jesus is identified as God's Son. In the opening scene of Jesus' ministry, his baptism, he is also clearly proclaimed as God's Son: "You are my Son, the Beloved; with you I am well pleased" (3:22).

The Parallel Structure of Luke 1–2

The first two chapters can be briefly outlined in this way:

The Annunciations
to Zechariah (1:5-25)
to Mary (1:26-38)
Visit of Mary to Elizabeth — song of Mary (1:39-56)

The Births
of John — circumcision — song of Zechariah (1:57-80)
of Jesus — circumcision — song of Simeon (2:1-40)
Visit of Jesus and family to the temple (2:41-52)

Through the narrative of the birth of John and Jesus, Luke introduces several themes that will develop throughout the rest of the two volumes. These two chapters may be compared to an overture to a concert: the important themes are first introduced, then developed fully throughout the narrative.

In these opening chapters, the narrator shows how God's promises in the past are now brought to fulfillment in Jesus' birth. This fulfillment centers upon God's promise of the gift of salvation that comes through Jesus and begins in the very heart of Israel: Jerusalem and the temple.

This salvation not only looks to the past and the fulfillment of its hopes, it also looks to the future and the extension of this salvation to the wider world. The backdrop of Luke-Acts is the Roman Empire. Luke introduces the context of Jesus' birth by identifying Augustus as the emperor who orders a census to be taken up throughout the world. Later, Luke introduces the ministry of John the Baptist by situating it within the framework of the Roman world: "In the fifteenth year of the reign of Emperor Tiberius, when Pontius Pilate was governor of Judea, and Herod was ruler of Galilee" (3:1). Simeon foretells the universalism of this salvation when he encounters the child Jesus as "a light for revelation to the Gentiles" (2:32). When Luke traces

---

Jesus' Birth (Luke 2:1-40; Matt 2:1-23)

A comparison of Luke's account of Jesus' birth (2:1-40) with that of Matthew (2:1-23) reveals a number of interesting points. In Luke Jesus' birth occurs in a stable in Bethlehem, while in Matthew it occurs in a house. Luke introduces poor shepherds who come to visit the child, while Matthew has Eastern astrologers following a star to find the king of the Jews. In Luke the child and his family go to the temple where Jesus is recognized as the salvation for all peoples, while in Matthew the child and his family escape to Egypt. This contrast shows how each writer has presented the narrative to conform to the message he wishes to convey to his readers.

Jesus as Savior

The Gospel of Mark presents Jesus as the suffering Messiah, while Matthew sees him as the Teacher. For Luke, Jesus is the Savior of the world. On two occasions Luke stresses that the name of the child is Jesus (1:31; 2:21), a name that means "Yahweh is salvation."

Notice the frequent reference to salvation in these chapters:

- Mary's song: "My soul magnifies the Lord, and my spirit rejoices in God my Savior." (1:47)
- Zechariah's song: "He has raised up a mighty savior for us in the house of his servant David." (1:69)
- The announcement to the shepherds: "I am bringing you good news of great joy for all the people: to you is born this day in the city of David a Savior, who is the Messiah, the Lord." (2:10-11)
- Simeon in the temple: "Master, now you are dismissing your servant in peace, according to your word; for my eyes have seen your salvation, which you have prepared in the presence of all peoples, a light for the revelation to the Gentiles and for glory to your people Israel." (2:29-32) This is a true summary of the significance of Jesus' ministry: salvation is to be extended to the Gentiles as well as to Israel.
- Anna in the temple: "At that moment she came, and began to praise God and to speak about the child to all who were looking for the redemption of Jerusalem." (2:38)

Jesus' genealogy (3:23-38), he presents Jesus as the "son of Adam, son of God" (v. 38). Whereas Matthew situates Jesus in the context of the world of Judaism by presenting Jesus as the son of the fathers of the Jewish nation, Abraham and David, Luke presents Jesus as the Savior of the world by situating him as a descendent of the father of humanity, Adam.

Connected to the theme of salvation is the significance of the temple and the city of Jerusalem in the narrative of Luke-Acts. For Second Temple Judaism the temple was the place of God's presence among God's people. There God distributed salvation to the chosen people. It was their sacred space where they maintained their bonds with their God. Luke begins his Gospel with Zechariah officiating as a priest offering sacrifices to God. The Gospel opens in the heart of the religious world of Judaism. Jesus comes to this world with the purpose of transforming it.

Luke 3:1–4:13: Preparation for Jesus' Public Ministry

As with the Gospels of Mark and Matthew, Luke begins the narrative of Jesus' public ministry with an account of John's proclamation and Jesus' baptism. Mark is clearly his source, but Luke adds a number of distinctive aspects. John's proclamation is situated in "the fifteenth year of the reign of Emperor Tiberius" (3:1). The baptism provides the occasion for Jesus' identification as God's Son. This is further supported in the genealogy, which traces Jesus back to Adam, "son of God" (3:38).

In this section we note as well the importance given to the Spirit. In response to Jesus' prayer at his baptism, the Spirit descends upon him. Acts will present a parallel account of the Apostles gathered together after Jesus' ascension when the Spirit comes down upon them while at prayer.

The same Spirit leads Jesus into the wilderness to be tempted. Here Luke uses the Sayings Source, Q. The major difference between Luke's version and Matthew's lies in the sequence of the temptations, where the order of the second and third temptations is reversed. Luke's final temptation (at the pinnacle of the temple) conforms to his concern with the theological significance of Jerusalem. At the end of the episode Luke comments: "When the devil had finished every test, he departed from him until an opportune time" (4:13). That opportune time comes at the end of the Gospel narrative when Jesus' passion and death are viewed as a struggle against the forces of evil: "Then Satan entered into Judas called Iscariot, who was one of the twelve; he went away and conferred with the chief priests and officers of the temple police about how he might betray him to them" (22:3-4). Ultimately the gift of God's salvation must entail the destruction of the forces of evil that are opposed to God. This occurs through Jesus' resurrection.

Luke 4:14–9:50: Ministry in Galilee

Jesus' Rejection in His Home Town of Nazareth (4:14-30)

Luke's introduction to Jesus' ministry in Galilee is highly significant. He takes an event that Mark and Matthew present later in Jesus' ministry and situates it at the outset of the ministry in order to anticipate Jesus' final rejection in Jerusalem. Luke uses it further to set out Jesus' identity and some of the major themes of his Gospel.

Luke reports that Jesus reads from Isa 61:1-2, a passage that captures the heart of Jesus' ministry and which he endorses as a summary of his mission. Jesus' task is to proclaim the good news especially to those who are the outcasts of society: the poor, the captives, the blind, the oppressed. His words declare the fulfillment of the promises made by God in the period of Israel and relate precisely to the ministry that he is beginning. Today demarcates the period of Jesus from the period of Israel and the period of the church. In the perspective of Luke, the period of the church is the period of salvation.

What Jesus proclaimed about himself and the kingdom is now continued in the apostolic preaching. Luke looks back on the Christ-event and maintains that what happened then continues to be effective for people. Paul proclaims that Jesus "was handed over to death for our trespasses and was raised for our justification" (Rom 4:25). Luke puts it this way: "God has made him both Lord and Messiah, this Jesus whom you crucified" (Acts

> **Three Time Periods in Luke's Salvation History**
>
> Israel → Jesus → Church

2:36; see also 4:10). Both Luke and Paul have a backward glance, looking at something achieved for humans at a moment in history that precedes us and our generation. Luke, with his concern for salvation-history, prefers to relate the period of Jesus to the fulfillment of God's promises in Isa 61:1-2.

The response to Jesus' sermon is anything but positive (4:23-30). The scene enables the reader to see Jesus as the Spirit-anointed messiah and prophet. His claim to fulfill the hopes of the past today elicits a rejection which foreshadows Jesus' ultimate destiny and anticipates a difficult path ahead. In referring to Elijah and Elisha, Jesus shows that he stands in the line of those prophets who failed to find acceptance among their own people. The people of Nazareth foreshadow the response of those who in the rest of Luke-Acts refuse to accept Jesus' message. The references to Elijah and Elisha also give a justification for the mission to the Gentiles. Just as those prophets were sent to people outside their own nation, so too Jesus' ministry will extend beyond Israel's borders. The extension of this mission is a consequence of the rejection of his own people.

This incident at Nazareth alerts the reader at the beginning of Jesus' ministry to his spirit-filled, messianic, and prophetic identity. He proclaims this good news of God's salvation today. It also shows the reader what to expect in the response that is generated to the person and message of Jesus. Some reject this message. The Jesus who is filled with the Spirit foreshadows his followers, who will also be filled with the Spirit. Just as Jesus experienced rejection from his own people, so those who follow him will experience a similar rejection.

Luke's Sermon on the Plain (6:17-49)

A comparison of Luke's Sermon on the Plain with Matthew's Sermon on the Mount reveals that both rely on the common Sayings Source Q, but Luke's version is much shorter. The list of beatitudes is also significant. Luke has only four beatitudes (vv. 20-21) addressed directly to the hearer/reader and focusing on material concerns (poverty, hunger, mourning, persecution), while Matthew has nine beatitudes that focus on spiritual aspects (Matt 5:3-12).

In addition to the beatitudes, Luke has four woes (vv. 24-25) that envisage a reversal of fortunes in the future for those who have everything. Without doubt both the beatitudes and woes capture the central theme of Jesus' message: a concern for the poor and marginalized in society. In these verses Jesus gives expression to the prophetic words that prompted his first sermon in Nazareth.

Luke 9:51–19:27: Travel Narrative: Journey to Jerusalem

The opening verse sets the direction for this narrative section: "When the days drew near for him to be taken up, he set his face to go to Jerusalem" (9:51). For Luke, Jesus' ministry embraces a journey to Jerusalem (9:52-53; 13:22; 17:11). He prepared the reader for this when he first introduced John the Baptist (ch. 3). There he uses the quotation from Isa 40:3 (which he found in his source, Mark) and extends it by adding v. 4, which refers to a path being constructed in the wilderness. In the narrator's mind this is a foreboding of the theme of Jesus' long journey to Jerusalem to bring salvation to humanity. Within the travel narrative the reference to "road" or "way" occurs at 9:57 and 18:35. Elsewhere, it is found at 19:36; 20:21; and 24:32. In this travel section, Luke expands a journey to Jerusalem that was in his source, Mark, by introducing material that he found in the Sayings Source Q and his own Special Source L.

The concept of a journey was also central in Luke's background and culture. The most significant event in Israel's history was their liberation from Egypt and their wanderings for 40 years in the desert, during which they encountered their God who formed them into a people. The most important narratives for the Greeks and Romans were the *Iliad*, the *Odyssey*, and the *Aeneid*, in which the theme of a journey was highly significant. For example, in the journeys of Odysseus and Aeneas one sees how they encountered their gods and carried out their mission.

On this journey the narrator shows Jesus training those whom he had selected to follow him to become ministers of the word who will continue his mission after he has ascended to the Father. In a sense this training serves as the basis for what the author has assured Theophilus at the beginning of the narrative. A number of passages are distinctive to the Gospel of Luke and help to illustrate this theme.

Only Luke records the mission of the seventy (10:1-12). In the Torah seventy is the number of all the nations of the earth. Luke's readers would undoubtedly take this as pointing to the mission to the Gentiles. Shortly after the mission of the seventy, Luke narrates the well-known parable of the Good Samaritan (10:25-37). The parable is situated in the context of a dialogue between Jesus and a lawyer. In response to Jesus' questions, the lawyer identifies the twofold arms of the law of love (love of God [Deut 6:5] and love of neighbor [Lev 19:18]) as the essence for a moral life. Jesus develops this parable in reply to the lawyer's further question: "Who is my neighbor?" In an unexpected way Luke introduces a Samaritan as the hero of the story. The priest and Levite pass by, thinking the person is dead. They are obeying their Torah laws which state that by touching a corpse one becomes unclean, which would make them unable to carry out their priestly duties in the temple. The Samaritan ignores both the ethnic divide that separates him from the Jews as well as the purity rules and responds to the injured person as "my neighbor." In this story Jesus shows that love for another transcends ethnic and religious boundaries.

In the course of this journey Jesus' training centers on the correct attitudes toward wealth and riches. The Sermon on the Plain already showed Jesus' particular concern for the poor of society. Nowhere does Luke condemn riches as such, but he does challenge a certain attitude to wealth. In two parables special to his Gospel: the parable of the Rich Fool (12:13-21) and Lazarus and the Rich Man (16:19-31), Jesus shows the futility of spending every effort on acquiring wealth. At the conclusion to the parable of the Rich Fool, God responds: "'You fool! This very night your life is being demanded of you. And the things you have prepared, whose will they be?' So it is with those who store up treasures for themselves but are not rich toward God" (12:20-21). Jesus teaches his followers to go further by embracing a lifestyle that reaches out to the outcasts of society. Luke's parable of the Great Dinner (14:15-24; compare Matt 22:1-14) deliberately focuses on the invitation being extended to the outcasts of society: "Go out at once into the streets and lanes of the town and bring in the poor, the crippled, the blind, and the lame'" (14:21). Jesus' followers embrace Jesus' ethos in the opening chapters of Acts, where they hold all things in common, selling their possessions and distributing the proceeds to those in need (Acts 2:44-45).

Luke's Jesus also expands his disciples' horizon regarding their image of God. The parable of the Prodigal Son (15:11-32) is in reality a parable that illustrates the all-encompassing and forgiving love of the father toward his two children. God's love reaches out to those who have turned their backs on his love (the younger son), as well as to those who expect God to act according to human standards (the elder son). The character of God's love emerges as an unconditional love that embraces all without distinction. The father's reaction to the younger son is a remarkable image that speaks to today's Christian of this unlimited love: "While he was still far off, his father saw him and was filled with compassion; he ran and put his arms around him and kissed him" (15:20).

Luke 19:28–21:38: Ministry in Jerusalem

The narrative of Jesus' long journey culminates in Jerusalem, where most of the activity centers on the temple area. Jesus enters the city in a kingly way and once again encounters the opposition of the forces of evil. These events lead to his arrest and death. Of significance in this narrative is the emphasis that Luke brings to bear on his source, Mark. Whereas Mark's narrative was far more apocalyptic and expected the *parousia* soon, Luke places the end of time in the distant future (21:9).

Luke 22:1–24:53: Passion and Resurrection Narrative

Luke follows his source, Mark, closely and adds his own theological understanding of the events. Luke presents Jesus undergoing two trials. The first is *the Jewish trial* (22:66-71) before the Jewish Sanhedrin, or Council, who question Jesus about being the Messiah and Son of God. Jesus refuses to answer directly because they would not believe. Since the authorities cannot convict Jesus on charges of blasphemy, they accuse him before Pilate of political charges. In the *Roman trial* (23:1-25) Jesus is charged with "perverting our nation, forbidding us to pay taxes to the emperor, and saying that he himself is the Messiah, a king" (23:2). Luke's narrator continually implies that Pilate considers Jesus to be innocent. The same is true regarding Herod Antipas, to whom Pilate sends Jesus when he learns that he is from Galilee (23:6-12). Pilate unequivocally expresses his belief in Jesus' innocence: "I have examined him in your presence and have not found this man guilty of any of your charges against him. Neither has Herod, for he sent him back to us. Indeed, he has done nothing to deserve death" (23:13-17). Ultimately Pilate gives in and hands Jesus over to be crucified (23:25).

Luke introduces some important changes in reporting Jesus' crucifixion, allowing his theology to emerge more clearly. The theme of forgiveness is dominant in the final words of Jesus. He prays for his executioners: "Father, forgive them; for they do not know what they are doing" (23:34). He extends forgiveness to the criminal who asks for it: "Truly I tell you, today you will be with me in Paradise" (23:43). This promise exemplifies God's generosity as portrayed in the parable of the Prodigal Son. Finally, Luke changes the final words of Mark's Jesus, which express a desperate feeling of abandonment, to words of confidence and trust in the Father as Jesus hands over his spirit: "Father, into your hands I commend my spirit" (23:46).

Jesus ultimately triumphs over death through his resurrection. Luke differs from Mark by narrating a number of appearances to his disciples which he situates in and around Jerusalem. Luke returns the narrative to the place where it all began, Jerusalem. The first appearance is to two disciples on the way from Jerusalem to Emmaus (24:13-35). Here the theme of a revelation taking place in the course of a journey occurs again. Jesus explains the meaning of the events that have occurred as a fulfillment of God's promises in the past. In Acts, Jesus' followers would make a similar appeal to Scripture to explain their message to their hearers. In the breaking of the bread they recognize Jesus' presence. This foreshadows the eucharistic meals that the followers of Jesus would later share together.

A final appearance occurs in Jerusalem. Jesus again turns to the Hebrew Scriptures to explain the meaning of the recent events, that the Messiah would suffer and rise from the dead, "and that repentance and forgiveness of sins is to be proclaimed in his name to all nations, beginning from Jerusalem'" (24:45-49). Jesus' followers are to become ministers of that same word and to extend the salvation that Jesus brought to the rest of the world. The narrative concludes with Jesus' ascension to heaven (24:50-53).

In a sense the journey of Jesus to Jerusalem has been more than just a journey to a city; it is Jesus' journey to God. The period of Jesus has come to a conclusion. The

The Prodigal Son amid the Swine, engraving by Albrecht Dürer (ca. 1496). (Trustees of the British Museum)

disciples return to Jerusalem to await the outpouring of the Spirit when the period of the church will begin. From Jerusalem they will begin their ministry to the ends of the earth. The book of Acts narrates how the followers of Jesus, gifted by the promised Holy Spirit, journey from Jerusalem to the ends of the earth (Acts 1:8).

Critical Issues in Studying Luke

Use of Sources

The Gospel indicates that the author consulted both written and oral sources (1:3). As with the Gospel of Matthew, Luke's basic source was Mark. Luke preserves Mark's basic story line that moves progressively according to this geographical structure:

- Judean ministry (John the Baptist and Jesus' baptism and temptation)
- Galilean ministry

Road to Emmaus, with nearby monastery at Latrun commemorating Jesus' postresurrection appearance to the disciples. (Phoenix Data Systems, Neal and Joel Bierling)

- Travel narrative to Jerusalem
- Ministry in Jerusalem
- Passion and resurrection in Jerusalem.

Luke uses this geographical structure, but expands it in three places, to bring across his own theological perspective:

The beginning: Whereas Mark opens with John the Baptist, Luke adds the infancy account. This narrative functions like an overture in which the themes that are important throughout his work are first introduced, such as that of universal salvation.

The middle: Luke expands Mark's journey to Jerusalem from just over two chapters (Mark 8:27–10:52) to 10 chapters (9:51–19:27). Here he introduces material that he obtained from his Sayings Source Q and Special Source L (referring to material special to Luke) with the intention of providing Jesus' instruction on what it means to be a disciple.

The end: Mark ends with an open narrative about the women running away, leaving the reader with many unanswered questions. The Gospel of Luke answers those questions. The narrator records how Peter went to the tomb to ascertain for himself the veracity of the women's report. Further there is the memorable account of the two disciples encountering the risen Jesus on the road to Emmaus. The narrative ends with the ascension.

Who Is the Author?

The author of the Gospel of Luke and the Acts of the Apostles is one person. Ancient sources from around the end of the 2nd century C.E. attribute this writing to Luke, one of Paul's companions. The New Testament tells us that Luke was a physician who remained faithful to Paul and was with him in his final imprisonment (Col 4:14; 2 Tim 4:11; Phlm 24).

From an examination of the Gospel itself we can infer a certain amount of knowledge about the author. He says very clearly in the prologue that he was not an eyewitness — he had to rely on sources and the witness of others. In other words, he was a second- or third-generation Christian. Of all the Evangelists, Luke has the best command of the Greek language. In fact his stylistic usage in the opening verses is highly revealing. These verses show a close connection to contemporary literature of the Greco-Roman world. A Jewish historian, Josephus, living at approximately the same time as Luke, wrote a two-volume work, *Against Apion*. The prologues of this work and of Luke-Acts show striking similarities.

- Both are addressed to an honorable patron: "Most excellent Theophilus" in Luke-Acts and "Most excellent Epaphroditus" in Josephus.
- Both divide their work into two volumes, with the second volume referring back to the first.
- Both aim at instructing all who want to know the truth.
- Both give insight into the reason for writing the work and express briefly how the writer intends to go about illustrating the argument.

In drawing attention to the similarities between Luke-Acts and Josephus, we are not arguing that Luke knew Josephus or vice versa. That simply cannot be shown. What it does show is that Luke uses a style that conforms to the historical narratives of his own day, of which Josephus is one specific example. The author, Luke, is undoubtedly a well-educated person who writes his narrative employing the literary conventions of his day and age. His method of constructing speeches which he puts on the mouths of his characters to capture their thought and argument is also characteristic of the writings of contemporary Greek and Roman historians. Luke also uses the Septuagint, the Greek translation of the Hebrew Bible. This usage is reflected not just in the quotations that he renders but also in the use of its style.

From all this we conclude that the writer is an unknown second-generation Christian. He was a highly-educated person who composed a historical narrative using the Greek literary styles of his time. While he himself was Greek, he had a detailed knowledge of the Hebrew Scriptures and compiled a narrative that takes its place alongside the great epics of classical literature.

The Narrator of Luke-Acts

Not only does the author of Acts describe the Gospel as his "first book" and succinctly describe its contents ("all that Jesus did and taught"), he dedicates it to the same Theophilus (Acts 1:1-2). Practically all scholars agree on the common authorship of these two New Testament writings; modern studies of the language, style, and the theological preoccupations of the two works support this view.

Acts includes a further series of passages where the narrator speaks in the first person plural: the so-called "we sections" (Acts 16:10-17; 20:5-15; and 21:1-18; 27:1-28:16). Here the change from the third person in the rest of the narrative to the first person plural suggests that the author wishes to present the narrator as at times a companion of Paul.

This has led many to conclude that the author did indeed accompany Paul. One view sees these passages as part of a diary that the author later used in composing Acts. However, an examination of Acts' picture of Paul raises some serious questions. Acts does not mention any of Paul's letters. If we only had Acts to rely upon, we would not know that Paul was a letter-writer. Is it possible for someone who was Paul's companion (particularly at those times when Paul was supposed to have written most of his letters) to be unaware of them?

Further, the picture drawn of Paul in his letters is of someone at the center of controversy in the church, whereas in Acts the picture is very different. Paul is presented as living a very harmonious life with the other apostles, especially Peter and James.

The problem and its solution lie in returning to our consideration of the communication process whereby the author uses a narrator to tell the story. One cannot immediately conclude that the narrator of Luke-Acts is identical to the author. One should rather see the "we sections" as a literary device. Notable as well, these sections always occur in the context of a sea voyage, whether from Troas to Philippi, or from Caesarea to Rome. Examples of such fictional accounts of sea voyages are found in ancient Hellenistic writings as a literary device used to stress the authenticity of the narration and to show that the traveler was under the guidance of the gods. The same literary device is used in the narrative of Acts — Paul's voyages are under the guidance of the Spirit and conform to the carrying out of God's plan.

Documents dating from the end of the 2nd century reflect a tradition in the early church identifying the author with Luke, an associate of Paul, who was not an eyewitness to the events. This Luke is referred to on a few occasions in the New Testament.

It makes little difference to the interpretation of the Gospel or Acts whether one can establish that its author was the traditional Luke, a sometime companion of Paul, even a physician. What is important is the text of Luke's Gospel and what it may say to Christians, regardless of the identity of its author. For the sake of convenience, we refer to the author as Luke, without making any claims to his identity. However, it is vital to recognize that the two writings have a common author.

Who Are the First Readers of This Gospel?

Since Luke used Mark as a source, his Gospel must have been written well after 70 C.E. when Mark's Gospel had become known and used throughout the Christian world. Further evidence to support a date after 70 comes from Luke's description of the destruction of Jerusalem (21:20-24) that indicates a detailed knowledge of that event.

Most scholars would date Luke-Acts in the late 80s, but there is much discussion about where the Gospel was written and who were the first recipients of this work. Undoubtedly, the readers are Gentile, Greek-speaking Christians whom the writer wants to strengthen in their faith. It would make sense to see this work addressed to those areas where Paul had preached the Gospel. Because of the emphasis in Acts 16:6-10 on the Spirit's impulse in bringing the message to Europe, many scholars see the likely area for the first readers as the churches in Greece. In this sense the recipients of this work are not one single Christian community, but probably a much larger area comprising many Christian churches or centers.

Theological Themes In Luke

Jesus as Savior of the World

This is the main theme of Luke's Gospel, as evident from the many references to salvation in the opening two chapters. According to Luke the salvation that Jesus brings humanity is one that touches every dimension of their lives. It is a deliverance from every form of evil, whether spiritual, material, political, etc. Jesus' encounters with people are an extension of the salvation he offers them. His conflict with the powers of evil is ultimately a struggle in which the devil opposes God's gift of salvation. Through Jesus' resurrection the power of evil is ultimately conquered. This salvation looks to the past, to the fulfillment of the hopes of Israel, and to the future, to its extension to the world of the Gentiles.

The Centrality of Jerusalem

The Gospel opens in the temple of Jerusalem with Zechariah performing his priestly duties (1:5). It closes with the disciples returning to Jerusalem and the temple after Jesus' ascension, "and they were continually in the temple blessing God" (24:53). In narrating the ministry of Jesus, Luke develops Jesus' journey to Jerusalem (9:51–19:27). Acts opens in Jerusalem, where the Apostles are awaiting the fulfillment of Jesus' promise of the gift of the Spirit.

The significance of Jerusalem is related to the theme of salvation. For the Jewish people, Jerusalem is that sacred place where God's salvation was extended to their people through God's presence in the temple. The Gospel begins where God's salvation is operative, and Luke shows that it is Jesus' task now to replace that salvation (2:30-32). His long journey to Jerusalem prepares the way for this replacement. Through his death and resurrection in Jerusalem, Jesus shows that he, not the temple, will bring salvation to the world. The tearing of the temple curtain at the moment of Jesus' death is symbolic of this transfer of the place of salvation from the temple to the person of Christ (23:45).

Acts opens in Jerusalem with Jesus' farewell mission to his disciples: "But you will receive power when the Holy Spirit has come upon you; and you will be my witnesses in Jerusalem, in all Judea and Samaria, and to the ends of the earth" (Acts 1:8). Beginning in Jerusalem, the place where Jesus brought salvation to humanity, his followers now extend that salvation to the ends of the earth.

The Role of the Holy Spirit

Luke-Acts presents the Spirit playing an important role throughout. The Spirit moves in John the Baptist "even before his birth" (1:15), and his parents, Elizabeth and Zechariah are both "filled with the Holy Spirit" (1:41, 67). Mary conceives through the power of the Spirit (1:35). Jesus begins his ministry through the power of the Spirit. He is baptized by the Spirit (3:22) and led into the wilderness by the Spirit to be tempted (4:1). He begins his ministry of preaching (4:14) and healing (v. 18) "filled with the power of the Spirit." The foundation of the church at Pentecost (Acts 2:1-13) and the spread of the Christian mission are guided by the power of the Spirit (13:1-3).

The Role of Women

Women appear more frequently in Luke's Gospel than any of the other Gospels. Their importance is already clear in the opening chapters. Luke records Jesus' birth from Mary's point of view, while Matthew records the birth from Joseph's perspective. Elizabeth (1:39-58) and Anna (2:36-38) are important characters in the infancy narrative. Other important women are the widow of

Balancing Men and Women Narratives

Men	Women
Naaman the leper (4:27)	Widow of Zarephath (4:25-26)
The centurion's servant (7:1-10)	Widow of Nain's son (7:11-17)
Men of Nineveh (11:32)	Queen of the South (11:31)
Man with the Lost Sheep (15:3-7)	Woman and the Lost Coin (15:8-10)
Two men in a bed (17:34)	Two women grinding (17:35)
Pharisee and the Tax Collector (18:10-14)	Widow and the Unjust Judge (18:2-8)

Nain (7:11-17), Martha and Mary (10:38-42), and Mary Magdalene (24:10). When Luke narrates parables, he balances ones involving men with others involving women (e.g., the parable of the Woman and the Lost Coin [15:8-10] as well as the widow who demands justice [18:1-6]).

Concern for the Poor

The infancy narrative foreshadows a special interest in and concern for the poor that operates throughout Luke-Acts. Jesus is born in a stable (2:7), in contrast to Matthew's picture of his birth in a house (Matt 2:11). The first to receive the news of Jesus' birth are poor shepherds (2:8-14). In the Beatitudes Luke addresses the material needs of the poor (6:20), in contrast to Matthew's focus on spiritual poverty (Matt 5:3). Some of the best known of Luke's parables focus on the contrast between poverty and riches, for example, the account of the poor man Lazarus and an unnamed rich man (16:19-31).

In Acts Luke paints a picture of the early church where the faithful share all things in common (Acts 4:32-37) and one of the first organizational structures was intended to help the poor (6:1-6).

Importance of Prayer

In Luke's Gospel Jesus is truly a person of prayer. He prays at all the decisive moments in his life: he prays at his baptism (3:21); before he chooses the Twelve he spends the night in prayer (6:12); in the garden of Gethsemane the theme of prayer dominates (22:39-46). His disciples see him at prayer and ask that he teach them how to pray (11:1-4). Finally, two parables are devoted to the theme of prayer: the friend who comes at midnight

(11:5-13) and the widow who beseeches the judge for justice (18:1-8).

Acts portrays the church gathered together in prayer on a number of occasions: it is one of the most distinctive marks of that early community (2:46-47). While they are gathered for prayer at the very beginning, the Holy Spirit descends on them (2:1-3).

Praise and Joy

Luke's Gospel opens and closes with praise given to God, hence creating an inclusion. Characteristic of the opening chapters are the numerous hymns and songs of praise that emanate from the various characters. Mary (1:46-55), Zechariah (1:67-79), and Simeon (2:28-32), all burst out praising and thanking God for what God has done for them. The Gospel closes on a note of praise: "and they were continually in the temple blessing God" (24:53).

Discipleship

Luke's presentation of discipleship reveals the diversity of those called to follow Jesus, whose message embraces everyone. An open hospitality is extended to all: tax collectors, sinners, women. In Luke's account of the call of Peter (5:1-11), the first requirement for discipleship is acknowledgement of unworthiness: "Go away from me, Lord, for I am a sinful man" (5:8). The call involves a mission. To carry out this mission "they left everything and followed him" (5:11). In Mark's version (Mark 1:16-20), they leave their nets, whereas in Luke the emphasis is on leaving everything.

The role of women disciples in following Jesus receives considerable attention. Mary, the mother of Jesus, features prominently in the opening chapters and shows her openness and response to God's call to be the mother of the Messiah. She does not fully understand everything, but she reflects on the events, "treasuring all these things in her heart" (2:51). Mary demonstrates one of the important characteristics of a disciple, namely hearing the word and responding to it with an openness that allows God to lead.

The narrative of Jesus' journey to Jerusalem reveals the particular values required of a disciple. Among these are the attitudes toward wealth and riches (12:22-34) and the importance given to love of God and neighbor

(10:29-37). The examples of Martha and Mary (10:38-42) express two approaches to discipleship: Martha represents the disciple involved in activity, while Mary represents the contemplative disciple. In praising Mary's approach, Jesus stresses that establishment of a relationship with God is of paramount importance (10:41-42).

Ultimately, the disciples are prepared to continue Jesus' work in spreading the good news of salvation to the ends of the earth. During Jesus' ministry they are sent out on a mission (10:1-12) which prepares them for the task once Jesus has left. The Acts of the Apostles becomes a necessary second volume showing how Jesus' followers carry out his intention.

Questions for Review and Discussion

1   Discuss Luke's image of Jesus. What view of Jesus' teaching does Luke wish to stress?

2   Why is Jerusalem so significant for the Gospel of Luke?

3   Luke's Jesus shows a concern for those marginalized by society. Do you think that concern for the poor of society is sufficiently recognized by today's Christians?

4   Examine one of Jesus' parables in Luke's Gospel that you think really challenges today's Christians.

Further Reading

Balch, David L. "Luke." In *ECB,* 1104-60.

Conzelmann, Hans. *The Theology of St. Luke.* New York: Harper & Row, 1960.

Fitzmyer, Joseph A. *The Gospel According to Luke.* 2 vols. AB 28, 28A. New York: Doubleday, 1981, 1985.

Powell, Mark Allan. *What Are They Saying about Luke?* New York: Paulist, 1989.

Selvidge, Marla J. *Daughters of Jerusalem.* Scottsdale: Herald, 1987.

Chapter 52

Luke-Acts (2): The Acts of the Apostles

The Apostles Continue Jesus' Mission

Getting Started

1 Read Acts 1–2: the origin of the church. How do these chapters set the stage for the rest of the narrative?

2 Read Acts 9:1-22 (the call of Paul): Does Paul's call reflect the call of any of the prophets of the Hebrew Scriptures? What mission is Paul given?

Preliminary Comments

The Acts of the Apostles describes the origins of the Christian church and how the first followers continue Jesus' mission. As we have indicated, the key to interpreting this writing is to see it as a continuation of the narrative of the Gospel of Luke. The theological vision of the writer needed this second volume to show how God's salvation continues to be spread throughout the world.

The title Acts (or Deeds) of the Apostles was given to this writing long after its composition. A popular genre of the time was called Acts, in which a writer would narrate the deeds of a famous person, for instance, the Acts of Hannibal. However, our writing does not aim to tell the deeds of the apostles. Although the names of the 11 apostles are carefully recorded in the beginning

(1:12-14) and great pains are taken to replace the traitor Judas with the election of Matthias (vv. 15-26), the only apostles whose deeds are actually referred to are Peter, John, and later Paul. John's role in the narrative is very brief: he is not mentioned after the first few chapters. Peter also disappears from the scene in ch. 12, only to emerge briefly in ch. 15. Paul becomes the dominant force in the narrative from ch. 13 onward, yet the narrative suddenly ends with Paul in prison. Nothing further is said about his fate. If the purpose of this narrative were to describe the deeds of the apostles, it would surely have narrated what happens to those leaders of the Christian movement.

Acts 1:8 expresses the purpose of this narrative very succinctly. The writer depicts the risen Jesus instructing his followers on how they are to continue his mission. Through the power of the Spirit their ministry begins in Jerusalem and spreads stage-by-stage from Jerusalem, the mother church, to outer Judea and Samaria (8:1, 5, 26), Caesarea (8:40), Galilee (9:31), Damascus (9:2), Phoenicia, Cyprus, and Syrian Antioch (11:19), the Roman provinces of Cilicia, Galatia, Asia, Macedonia, and Achaia, and finally to Rome itself (23:11; 28:14), "the ends of the earth" (1:8).

Acts concludes with Paul in Rome under house arrest. Just as the Gospel of Mark ends with unfinished business, so does Acts. The questions remain: What happened to Paul? Was he put to death? If not, what happened to him? The narrator is not interested in such questions; he wants to show that the instruction of Jesus at the ascension has been fulfilled. With the arrival of Paul in Rome the message of salvation has been preached to "the ends of the earth." In a sense Acts, as Mark, remains an open book, in that it appeals to the reader to continue Paul's activity by spreading the gospel message. Just as the reader is invited into the story of the Gospel of Mark, so the reader is challenged by the Acts of the Apostles to become a participant in the drama of God's salvation.

A Walk through the Acts of the Apostles

As with our approach to Mark, Matthew, and Luke, we read Acts from the perspective of narrative criticism, whereby we focus on the unfolding of the plot and how the narrator communicates his specific vision to us, the readers.

Acts 1:1-26: Introduction
to the Ministry of the Church

The narrator connects this writing to the previous work, the Gospel of Luke. He addresses Theophilus, to whom the first volume was dedicated, and summarizes the Gospel's contents very succinctly (1:1-2). This deliberate continuity emphasizes for the reader that this work must be read as a sequel to Luke, part of a larger whole, the narrative of Luke-Acts.

Over the course of 40 days the risen Jesus appears to his followers. This 40-day period symbolizes the 40 years that the Israelites wandered through the desert, during which they discovered they were God's people and realized the care and love God had for them. These 40 days remind the reader that Jesus was alive and was with his disciples for a limited time after his death. During his appearance they came to a deeper understanding of their mission through Christ's presence among them.

Jesus' commission to the disciples in 1:8 provides the structure for the book of Acts. The disciples await the fulfillment of this promise in Jerusalem. The place of Judas is taken by the choice of Matthias (1:21-26). Since nothing is mentioned about Matthias in the rest of the narrative, the importance of his selection lies in the fact that the number of 12 disciples is reconstituted. Just as Jesus began his work of reconstituting God's people through the selection of 12 disciples, so the followers of Jesus show their task of continuing this work.

Acts 2:1-5:42: Mission in Jerusalem
Pentecost and Peter's Sermon (2:1-36)
The account begins with God's action that sets the stage

Reading Guide to the Acts of the Apostles

Introduction to the Ministry of the Church (1:1-26)
> Mission of the Apostles and Their Witness to the Ascension (1:1-11)

Mission in Jerusalem (2:1-5:42)
> Pentecost and Peter's Sermon (2:1-36)
> Mission of the Apostles within Jerusalem (3:1-5:42)

Mission from Jerusalem to the Rest of Palestine (6:1-12:25)
> Choice of the Seven to Help the Apostles (6:1-7)
> Death of Stephen and the Conversion of Saul (6:8-9:43)
> Missionary Activity of Peter (10:1-11:18)
> Believers Flee Persecution (11:19-12:25)

Paul's Missionary Journeys to Asia Minor and Europe (13:1-21:16)

Paul's Mission to Rome (21:17-28:31)
> Paul's Arrest in Jerusalem, Imprisonment in Caesarea (21:17-23:35)
> Paul before Governors and Kings in Caesarea (24:1-26:32)
> Paul's Last Journey to Rome (27:1-28:31)

---

for the unfolding of the rest of the narrative. At the Feast of Pentecost, the Spirit came down upon the apostles, anointing them to become ministers who spread the gospel message. The Jewish Feast of Pentecost (Greek "50th") was celebrated 50 days after the Feast of Passover. Originally an agricultural feast, this feast came to be associated with God's giving of the Law and making a covenant with the Israelites at Sinai. The descent of the Spirit as tongues of fire is colored by the symbolism in the Sinai account, where God's presence is accompanied by thunder and lightning. Philo (a Jewish scholar in Alexandria during the 1st century C.E.) adds to the description of that scene by saying that angels took what God said to Moses in private and carried it out on tongues to give to all the people. In Acts the symbols of the wind and the tongues of fire show that God is present renewing the covenant with the people.

The narrator painstakingly identifies those who witnessed the events in Jerusalem as "Parthians, Medes, Elamites, and residents of Mesopotamia, Judea and Cappadocia, Pontus and Asia, Phrygia and Pamphylia, Egypt and the parts of Libya belonging to Cyrene, and visitors from Rome" (2:9-10). This list depicts them as representatives of the whole of humanity, symbolizing that the gospel is to be preached to the four corners of the earth. The opening chapters establish the main theme of the whole work: the gospel message of salvation being brought to all humanity.

Luke's Gospel begins its account of Jesus' public ministry with his baptism and the descent of the Spirit. In like manner the narrative of Acts opens with the descent of the Spirit on Jesus' followers. Just as Jesus' ministry was empowered by the Spirit, so now the same Spirit is operative in his successors to bring the message of salvation to all.

Peter's long Pentecost speech is typical of the speeches in Acts in vocabulary and style. The author, Luke, does not reproduce the actual, historical words of the speaker; rather he constructs these speeches in a style similar to the Hellenistic writers of his time in order to convey the major themes of the narrative. Peter interprets the events of Pentecost (2:15-21) as a fulfillment of a prophecy of Joel, who foretold that God's Spirit would be poured out upon all humanity (Joel 2:28-32). Following his sermon Peter implores his hearers to repent *(metanoia)*, which requires a dramatic change of heart (v. 38).

The narrator portrays the fellowship of the Jerusalem community in idealistic terms (2:43-47): believers sell their possessions and share all things in common so that any in need are cared for. Dramatically, Luke shows the first Christians creating a community that remains true to Jesus' message on discipleship expressed in the call of the rich ruler (Luke 18:18-30).

Mission of the Apostles within Jerusalem (3:1–5:42)

Luke paints a progressively deepening opposition between the apostles and the religious authorities in Jerusalem. The Sadducees show a strong antagonism to this new movement. A well-respected Pharisee, Gamaliel, defends the apostles: "If this plan or this undertaking is of human origin, it will fail; but if it is of God, you will not be able to overthrow them — in that case you may even be found fighting against God!" (5:38-39).

Acts 6:1–12:25: Mission from Jerusalem to the Rest of Palestine

Choice of the Seven to Help the Apostles (6:1-7)

Despite the picture drawn earlier of a community united in heart and mind (4:32), the narrator shows tension within the community between the Hellenists (Greek-speaking Jews influenced by Greco-Roman culture) and the Hebrews (Aramaic-speaking Jews who wanted to hold on to their Jewish culture in an uncontaminated way). Both groups had accepted the following of Jesus, but their cultural background still continued to influence them.

The tensions were more than just cultural. Theological differences arose regarding the place of the temple

in Jewish life. The immediate followers of Jesus were all "Hebrew Christians" who continued to worship in the temple. However, the "Hellenist Christians" had come to regard temple worship as no longer valid (as can be seen from Stephen's speech; 7:48-50).

Tensions between the two groups surface in the daily distribution of food. The Twelve settle the dispute by appointing seven men who are to care for the daily distribution of the food for the Hellenist Christians. The growth of the Christian community necessitated the development of some form of structure to accommodate this. The followers see this development as part of Christ's will in that the Spirit guides them in the appointment of the Seven (6:6).

Death of Stephen and the Conversion of Saul (6:8–9:43)

Opposition between the followers of Jesus and the religious authorities intensifies and sets the stage for the dispersal of these followers beyond Jerusalem as the risen Jesus has foretold. Stephen, one of the seven, arouses opposition with his teaching about the place of the temple. He is brought before the Sanhedrin (the Jewish council) and accused of speaking "blasphemous words against Moses and God" (6:11). In particular he is accused of saying that Jesus will destroy the temple.

Stephen delivers a sermon in his defense (although he does not answer the charges leveled against him). It is an intriguing speech, much longer than any of the speeches of Peter and Paul in Acts. Luke composed it to communicate a theological vision of how God's chosen people continually resisted those whom God raised up. Both Joseph and Moses were opposed by their own people. Even the temple is seen by Stephen as an act of opposition to God because God is not meant to be confined to a house built by humans (7:48-49). Stephen's speech culminates in a tirade against his hearers whom he accuses of putting the Righteous One, Jesus, to death (7:51-53).

Stephen's final charge so angers his hearers that they seize him and stone him to death. Technically, only the Romans could pass and carry out a death sentence. Here, however, we have the spontaneous reaction of a crowd angered by what they judged to be blasphemy. The Romans turn a blind eye, considering this to be an internal Jewish religious matter.

Two important points emerge from this account. The narrator describes Stephen's death in terms closely resembling Jesus' death in Luke's Gospel. Both Jesus and Stephen pray for forgiveness for their executioners (Luke 23:34; Acts 7:60). At the moment of death both Jesus and Stephen commit their spirit to the Lord (Luke 23:46; Acts 7:59). Not only is Stephen the first martyr, but he becomes an example for all future Christian martyrs. Following Stephen's death a persecution breaks out against Christians. While the Twelve remain in Jerusalem, many of Jesus' followers scatter outside Jerusalem. For the narrator, this is significant as it marks the beginning of the spread of Christianity as the risen Jesus had proclaimed (1:8).

Second, the narrator draws attention to an important figure in the background: "a young man named Saul. . . . And Saul approved of their killing him" (7:58–8:1). This Saul was to become the greatest advocate in the spread of the Christian movement!

The call of Saul (9:1-31) must surely be the most important event in the history of early Christianity and marks a turning point for the movement. We can see the importance this call has for the narrator in that he reports it two more times (22:6-21; 26:9-23). Paul also refers to his call in his own writings (Gal 1:13-17). The theological implications are significant. Jesus' address: "Saul, Saul, why do you persecute me?" (9:4) lays the ground for Paul's understanding of the unity between the believer and the risen Christ. It will become the basis for his teaching on the body of Christ.

Just as the Hebrew prophets were called for a specific mission, so was Paul: "he is an instrument whom I have chosen to bring my name before Gentiles and kings and before the people of Israel" (9:15). Saul becomes the instrument to extend the message of salvation to the Gentile world. For this reason, it is better to speak about Paul's call rather than his conversion. Conversion implies the idea of changing from one religion to another. This is not what happened to Paul. Paul interpreted his religious traditions in the new light of Jesus' resurrection. Paul's religious experience of the risen Jesus enabled him to view his own traditions anew, and his call directed him toward communicating that understanding to the Gentiles.

Missionary Activity of Peter (10:1–11:18)
Luke marks the conversion of a Roman centurion, Cornelius, as another milestone in the spread of the Christian message. Significantly, he shows that Peter (the apostle to the Jews) is the one who first opens up the Christian message to the Gentile world and so gives authority to the Gentile mission. Peter experiences a vision that declares all foods clean, erasing the basic Jewish distinction between pure and impure. The symbolism extends further: the separation that had been made between those who were circumcised and those that were not is no longer operative. All foods and all peoples are acceptable to God. This dream gives Peter divine authentication for baptizing Cornelius and his household. The Christian message is not the exclusive property of those

who have been circumcised. Further authentication for Peter's actions appears through the Spirit descending on those present, who then start speaking in tongues (10:45-47).

Believers Flee Persecution (11:19–12:25)
After Stephen's death, the Hellenists or Greek-speaking Christians flee Jerusalem and settle in Phoenicia, Cyprus, and Antioch (11:19), where they are quite successful in bringing many Gentiles into the Christian movement. When the leadership in Jerusalem hears about it, they send Barnabas (a Greek-speaking Jewish Christian from Cyprus) to Antioch to investigate. Barnabas sees the work of the Spirit in the large numbers joining the movement and brings Paul from his hometown of Tarsus to help with the new missionary thrust (vv. 25-26).

The first part of Acts climaxes with Herod Agrippa I's persecution of the Christians. He puts James (the son of Zebedee) to death and imprisons Peter (12:2-3). Peter escapes (vv. 6-11) and leaves Jerusalem for "another place" (v. 17). He sends word to James ("the brother" of the Lord), the leader of the Jerusalem church. Herod himself dies suddenly (44 C.E.), and Luke interprets his death as a divine judgment. His message is clear: those who attack God's people will meet divine punishment (vv. 23). A tone of triumph draws this section to a conclusion: "But the word of God continued to advance and gain adherents" (v. 24). Then, after completing their mission, Barnabas and Saul return to Jerusalem along with John, who is also called Mark.

Acts 13:1–21:16: Missionary Journeys of Paul to Asia Minor and Europe
Luke devotes the second part of Acts to describing the journeys of Paul and his companions as they extend the message of salvation throughout Asia and Europe. The church of Antioch takes the initiative (13:1-3). In the context of a liturgical celebration of worship and fasting, they understand that the Spirit wants Barnabas, Paul, and John Mark to be sent out. The community lays

hands on them and sends them forth. Barnabas is mentioned first in this list, indicating that he is the leader of the group.

First Missionary Journey (13:3–14:28 [46-49 C.E.])

The narrator describes the journey in graphic detail. Barnabas, Paul, and John Mark set out for the island of Cyprus. They preach throughout the island, moving from Salamis to Paphos. An encounter with a false prophet, Bar-Jesus (or Elymas), shows that their struggle is not just with earthly forces and draws a parallel to the struggle that Peter experiences in preaching the message in Samaria when he encounters the opposition of Simon Magus (8:9-24).

From Cyprus they sail to Asia Minor and arrive in Perga of Pamphylia (13:13). The reference to "Paul and his companions" now presents him as the leader of the missionary group. A dispute arises between Paul and John Mark, resulting in the latter leaving the mission to return to Jerusalem. No reason is given for the dispute, but it was to have serious repercussions later when Paul sets out on his second journey. At that point Barnabas wants John Mark to accompany them again, but Paul refuses to allow someone who abandoned them once to rejoin them (15:37-39).

From Perga they travel to Pisidian Antioch (a different Antioch from the one in Syria). Luke's description of Paul's missionary activity in Antioch is almost a blueprint for his future ministry. Paul first seeks out the Jewish synagogue where he preaches on the Sabbath. It was customary in the Sabbath service to invite a learned visitor to give the sermon to the congregation (13:16-41). The structure of Paul's sermon is similar to those of Peter: reference to the Hebrew Scriptures as witness to God's plan; the fulfillment in the ministry of Jesus; appeal to accept Jesus; and the forgiveness that his death and resurrection offer. Despite the Jews' initial favorable reaction to the message, Paul is forced to direct his attention to the Gentiles. This will become paradigmatic for Paul's ministry — outreach to the Gentiles always occurs only after a rejection by the Jews.

Jewish hostility increases, so Paul and Barnabas move to Iconium (13:51–14:5) where they encounter an almost identical experience. Large numbers become believers, but strong opposition and an attempt to stone them force Paul and Barnabas to move on to another city, Lystra (14:5-7). Paul heals a man lame from birth, which recalls a similar healing by Peter in 3:1-10. Both Peter and Paul are shown to possess Jesus' healing power in their ministries. In this way they continue both Jesus' preaching and his healing ministry. The Greeks in Lystra are so impressed with Paul's miraculous activity that they welcome him as a manifestation of the god Hermes and Barnabas as the representation of Zeus. Although the crowds try to offer them sacrifice, Paul convinces them that are mere mortals (14:15). Finally, Jews arrive from Antioch and Iconium and stir up the crowds against them: Paul is stoned, dragged out of the city, and taken for dead (v. 19).

From Lystra they move to a neighboring town, Derbe, where they make many converts (14:20-21). A famous convert, Gaius of Derbe, will later accompany Paul on his third missionary journey (20:4). They return home from Derbe and retrace their steps visiting the believers that they have left behind in Lystra, Iconium, Antioch, and Perga (14:21-28). From the seaport of Attalia the two companions set sail for Antioch, where they lay forth the success of what God has done in their mission (14:27).

The narrator has described the spread of the gospel in great detail. The significance of this first church-sponsored mission lies in the large numbers of Greeks who have come to accept the gospel preached by Paul and Barnabas. This message has found a foothold in Asia Minor, and Paul has emerged as an important leader in the context of this early Christian movement, placed on a par with the very first disciples of Jesus.

The Jerusalem Council (15:1-35)

The narrative pauses to draw attention to the results of the missionary endeavors of Paul and Barnabas: the addition of large numbers of believers from the Gentile world. This prompts intense discussion regarding the relationship between the believer and the Jewish Torah. The issue did not arise when the vast majority of believers in Jesus came from the world of Judaism. But now large centers have developed in Asia Minor, where believers have no connection with the roots of Judaism. Two main approaches arise toward the new converts from the Gentile world. The Judaizers or circumcision party (Christian Jews) demand that all believers abide by all the stipulations of the Mosaic Law. For converts from the Gentile world this would involve circumcision and the observance of all the Jewish dietary rules. Paul represents a second approach, arguing that Christ has freed the believer from the stipulations of the Jewish Law and, consequently, Gentiles who become Christians are no longer bound by circumcision and the Jewish dietary laws.

Paul discovers that those belonging to the circumcision party are undermining what he has accomplished and are causing confusion among his newly formed communities. As a consequence, the church at Antioch sends Paul and Barnabas to Jerusalem to resolve the matter (15:1-3). We have two accounts of this conference: one from 15:1-35, the other from Paul's letter to

PAUL'S FIRST JOURNEY

portrayed by Paul in Galatians as a highly conservative person, Luke shows him as a moderate who requires only a few specific laws from the Gentile Christians.

The decision is as follows: Gentile Christians do not have to undergo circumcision in order to become Christians. They are freed from all the requirements of the Mosaic Law except for four laws that require that they abstain from: meat offered to idols; eating meat with blood in it; eating strangled animals (that were not ritually killed); incestuous unions (Greek *porneia* is translated in many different ways, but its meaning is exact: it refers to attempted marriages of an incestuous nature).

These requirements (vv. 19-21) are in effect what the Mosaic Law asked of all Jews, and those Gentiles who were living among Jews (Leviticus 17–18). The decision is communicated by letter to the church at Antioch and brought there by delegates chosen by the Council. It is also seen to be the decision of the Holy Spirit (v. 28). For the narrator this is a significant event in the growth of the Christian movement: it shows the acceptance of Gentile converts as full members of the Christian community and what is required of them.

Second Missionary Journey (15:36–18:22 [49-52 C.E.])
Luke returns to focus on the spread of the Christian message through Paul's journeys. Paul decides to visit the churches he has founded in Asia Minor. This time he takes Silas as his companion because of a disagreement with Barnabas over taking John Mark who had deserted them during the first journey. Galatians 2:12-13 gives another insight into the dispute: Paul notes that in the controversy over observing food laws, Barnabas was also influenced by those of the "circumcision faction."

Paul and Silas visit the new churches in Asia Minor and make an important convert in the person of Timothy (16:1-3) who joins them on the mission. They travel to Troas where Paul has a dream of a Macedonian

the Galatians (Gal 2:1-10). However, there are many discrepancies among them. The contexts in which these accounts were written were very different. Galatians was written around 54/55 C.E., some five years after the Council of Jerusalem (49). Memories of the disputes are fresh in Paul's mind, while some of the issues still continue. On the other hand, Acts was written in the mid-80s, long after the matter had been resolved. Consequently, the narrator avoids the conflicts and hostilities and shows a simple record of a resolution that became the approach of the Christian church.

In this narrative four voices are dominant: Paul, his adversaries (the circumcision party), Peter, and James. Paul's account in Galatians gives the picture from his viewpoint. He was not going to give an inch, and he convinced the Jerusalem leadership to support his position. The narrator of Acts wishes to emphasize the unity among the church leaders: Paul's statement is actually the shortest. Peter gives testimony to what the Holy Spirit has done in the conversion of the household of Cornelius: that is sufficient justification for seeing God's hand in the entry of the Gentiles to membership in the body of Christ. James, the leader of the church in Jerusalem, provides the decisive answer. Despite being

PAUL'S SECOND JOURNEY

the message: his imprisonment as well as his Roman citizenship.

From Philippi Paul moves on to Thessalonica (17:1-9) and Beroea (vv. 10-15), where he encounters a similar acceptance by some and strong opposition from others. Forced to flee, he ultimately arrives in Athens, the cultural capital of the ancient world (vv. 16-34). As usual Paul discusses with the Jews in the synagogue. He also engages the Greeks in the marketplace. Intrigued by his preaching, some Greek thinkers bring Paul to the Areopagus (a hill where the council of Athens used to meet). Luke's construction of this sermon is a masterpiece. As any good speaker, Paul tries to connect with his audience. He begins by praising them for their religious sensi-

inviting him to preach the message in Macedonia (16:4-10). Paul interprets this as God directing the mission to cross over into Europe. It is a highly significant moment in the course of early Christianity because it brings the message to the shores of Europe and shapes the future course of the faith. Notice that the "we" narrative begins at Troas (16:10) and carries over to the events in Philippi (v. 17), where the narrative reverts to the third person.

The first Christian church established by Paul in Europe is Philippi (16:11-40). The city had few Jews since there was no synagogue. Lydia gives Paul hospitality, and he uses her house as the base for his operations. He expels a demon from a slave-girl, an action that angers her owners who lose a lucrative source of income. Paul is thrown into prison after being beaten. That night an earthquake breaks open the prison gates (a reminder of Peter's escape), but Paul refuses to flee. This so impresses the prison guard that he and his family are baptized. In the morning Paul reveals his Roman citizenship; he and Silas are released and asked to leave the city. In this account we have everything that is representative of Paul's ministry: the welcome as well as the opposition that he evokes. The narrator shows how Paul uses every opportunity to foster the spread of

tivity, "how extremely religious you are in every way" (v. 22). This is despite Luke's earlier comment that Paul was upset at the many pagan images he had observed in the city (v. 16). Paul then endeavors to lead his hearers to his way of thinking. He starts with their altar "to an unknown god" (v. 23), whom Paul now identifies with the one God who created the heavens and the earth. He even quotes some of their poets and philosophers to show how they point to this one God of the universe: "For 'In him we live and move and have our being'; as even some of your own poets have said, 'For we too are his offspring'" (17:28). But when Paul speaks of Jesus' resurrection from the dead, his audience rejects him. Up to that point Paul's sermon is truly effective, showing both how his and their understanding of God connect. But their philosophical understanding of the world makes it impossible for them to accept belief in a resurrection of the body. For the Greeks the human being is made up of body and soul. The body, being material, is evil and acts as the prison house of the soul. Life's aim is to be freed from this material world (the world of shadows) and to attain the real world (see Plato's allegory of the prisoners in the cave.) Paul's concept that we human beings will continue to exist in

PAUL'S THIRD JOURNEY

the afterworld with a body makes no sense to his audience. Normally people accepted or rejected Paul's message. In this case they are indifferent to what he says (v. 32). In this sermon, Luke uses Paul to give a depth of vision on the understanding of God as the creator of the universe, of the unity of the human race, and the centrality of the resurrection for belief.

From Athens, Paul moves on to Corinth where he achieves better success (18:1-17). The city of Corinth was situated between two ports, Lechaeon and Cenchraea, along a busy sea route. The city was economically prosperous and attracted people from all over the Mediterranean basin. Corinth had a reputation as a morally degenerate city: "to live as do the Corinthians" was a common expression indicating a morally bad life. Paul stays in Corinth for 18 months (v. 11), longer than he has spent so far on his journeys. His stay here is significant because it provided him with the opportunity to write a number of letters. The first letter to the Thessalonians was his first writing and was an attempt to instruct a community that he had founded a few weeks earlier in aspects of the Christian faith about which they were unsure, including issues related to the resurrection. In Corinth, Paul meets up with Aquila and Priscilla, two believers who have recently come from Rome, having been expelled by Claudius when he drove out all Jews from the city in 49 C.E. They are tentmakers, the same trade as Paul. Finally, the Jews bring Paul before the proconsul Gallio, who dismisses their charges of promoting worship "in ways that are contrary to the law" as of no interest to him because he considers them to be of an internal religious nature (vv. 12-16).

Paul leaves Corinth with the intention of returning home to Antioch by sea (18:18-22). He travels with Aquila and Priscilla as far as Ephesus. They remain there while Paul promises to return again later. Paul lands at the port of Caesarea in Palestine, goes up to Jerusalem to

Temple of the Olympian Zeus at Athens, with the Acropolis in the background. (Nicholas Wolterstorff)

PAUL'S JOURNEY TO ROME

greet the church (v. 22), and returns to Antioch to report to them because they had initially sponsored this missionary journey. In tracing the details of Paul's journey, the narrator shows how the gospel message has moved beyond Asia Minor to find a firm foothold in Europe. Throughout the description the narrator demonstrates how the Spirit is guiding the progress and direction of these journeys. The commission of the risen Jesus to his followers continues to be implemented.

Athena temple on the acropolis at Lindos, Rhodes, overlooking St. Paul's Bay. (Phoenix Data Systems, Neal and Joel Bierling)

Third Missionary Journey (18:23–21:16 [53-58 C.E.]) Luke continues to focus on the spread of the gospel with a description of Paul's third and final missionary journey. He shows Paul's apostolic concern for the churches which he has founded. In Ephesus an important event has occurred during Paul's absence (18:24-28). Aquila and Priscilla instruct a certain Apollos, a learned man from Alexandria, in the fullness of the Christian message. Apollos then sets out for Corinth, where he becomes an influential figure in that church. When Paul arrives in Ephesus (19:1-20), he encounters a number of disciples of John the Baptist whom he teaches about the Holy Spirit and brings to a full understanding of Jesus. Paul spends three years in Ephesus (20:31), the longest time spent in any church. From an examination of Paul's writings, we see that he conducted an important letter-writing career during this period. However, Acts does not mention this.

From Ephesus, Paul travels to Macedonia, where he spends three months, probably in Corinth (20:3).

Paul returns home by sea, setting sail from Philippi. At Miletus on the west coast of Asia Minor, Paul invites the elders from Ephesus to join him. Paul's speech is very touching because he tells them he will not see them again. Again the narrator uses a speech to bring across his interpretation of the events; premonitions and prophecies of Paul's future arrest are made throughout the return voyage. Paul lands at Caesarea and travels to Jerusalem, where he is warmly welcomed (21:15-17).

Paul's third journey has ended. The narrator has shown how over a period of some 15 years Paul has established thriving Christian centers throughout Asia Minor and Greece in fulfillment of the mission entrusted him as the apostle to the Gentiles.

Acts 21:17–28:31: Paul's Mission to Rome

Paul's arrest in Jerusalem sets in motion the completion of Jesus' commission to the disciples to preach the gospel "to the ends of the earth" (1:8). The narrator goes to great trouble to show that Paul's arrest and the subsequent events are not because of any threat to Rome, but rather because of religious disputes with the Jewish leadership (23:26-30). After being kept in prison in Caesarea for two years (58-60), Paul exercises his rights as a Roman citizen and appeals to the emperor to hear his case (25:10-12).

After an arduous sea voyage to Rome that includes being shipwrecked at Malta (27:27–28:10), Paul eventually arrives in Rome, where he is kept for a further two years under house arrest (61-63). Paul continues to evangelize despite his situation. The narrative ends with Paul awaiting trial before the Roman emperor. Nothing is said about the outcome of the trial (28:30-31).

From a Jewish perspective Rome is certainly the "ends of the earth." From another perspective the gospel message must continually be preached afresh, for there is always somewhere else to spread the word. In this way the ending of the narrative of Acts is most fitting. By not completing the story, the reader is challenged to become like Paul, someone who continues to extend the gospel everywhere. The open ending reaches across time to the reader with the challenge to participate in this commission to spread the good news ever further.

Critical Issues in Studying the Acts of the Apostles

The previous chapter considered the authorship, readership, and date of Luke-Acts. Here we shall pay attention to other issues related specifically to Acts itself.

Luke's Artistry

Parallelism is a key stylistic and theological device the author uses throughout Acts. We have already seen in the Gospel of Luke how the author tells the story of the annunciations and births of John and Jesus in a parallel way. In Acts he uses the same feature here to show that the early Christians continue Jesus' mission and ultimately that God's hand is in the plan that is unfolding in the lives of Jesus and his followers.

The role of the Spirit is decisive in both volumes. The Spirit comes down upon Jesus at his baptism, and in the power of the Spirit Jesus goes forth to preach. At the opening of Acts, the Spirit comes down upon the apostles, and in the power of the Spirit they exercise their ministry. As with the ministry of Jesus, the ministry of Peter and Paul is characterized by two features: preaching and miraculous acts of healing.

The life of Paul parallels the life of Jesus in a dramatic way. Besides a teaching and a healing ministry, Paul's mission experiences rejection similar to that of Jesus. He is put on trial, scourged on a number of occasions, and imprisoned. In all these sufferings, Paul rejoices because he understands them as sharing in the sufferings of Christ.

A key characteristic of Acts is the dominant place that speeches hold in the narrative. They occupy about one quarter of the whole account. As we have noted, this use of speeches reveals Luke's literary heritage. By means of these speeches, Luke develops his themes more fully and stresses above all the theological issues central to his plan.

Historicity of Acts

This study has focused on Luke's abilities as a narrator who constructs his account in an extraordinarily gifted literary and stylistic way to communicate a theological vision to his readers. In undertaking our walk through the book, we have been intent on remaining faithful to the development and unfolding of the narrative itself. But, how historical is this writing? Scholars are divided on this issue. We have already seen one instance of a discrepancy between Paul and Acts on the details relating to the Council of Jerusalem. However, Luke's reference to events and his knowledge of the world of that time certainly lend credence to his account. He must be judged according to the standards of his own world and in terms of his own purpose. Conforming to the style of a Greek historian of his time, Luke has produced a narrative that uses his sources and traditions to communicate a theological vision.

Paul and the Collection for the Poor

The letters of Paul give further insight into his concern for the poor, supplementing the account in Acts. After James gives the final decision at the Council of Jerusalem, in addition to the agreement as regards what laws the Gentile Christians should embrace, Paul notes: "They asked only one thing, that we remember the poor, which was actually what I was eager to do" (Gal 2:10). Paul also notes in his letters that throughout his missionary journeys he takes up a collection for the poor in Jerusalem. At the end of his Letter to the Romans written during his third missionary journey, Paul expresses his wish to visit them, but says he must first return to Jerusalem with the funds for the poor, "for Macedonia and Achaia have been pleased to share their resources with the poor among the saints at Jerusalem" (Rom 15:25-26). Paul refuses support for himself from the communities that he establishes or visits. Instead, he urges them to show concern for the poor. Taking up a collection for the poor in Jerusalem would also be a way of showing the unity of the Christian communities. Just as every Jew contributed an annual tax to the temple in Jerusalem and in this way showed their identity as Jews bonded by God's presence in the temple, so Paul uses the collection for the poor in Jerusalem as a similar way of maintaining that bond among the communities.

Theological Themes in the Acts of the Apostles

Universal Salvation

We have already commented extensively on the major theme that unites the Gospel of Luke and the Acts of the Apostles: God's salvation, prepared for in the past, is brought by Jesus and now extended to the whole world. This theme unfolds through the symbolism of Jerusalem, which operates as the goal to which the Gospel moves and the point from which Acts starts.

The hopes of Israel had been for the reestablishment of God's kingdom. Luke shows an awareness of these hopes. When Jesus and the disciples journey toward Jerusalem, their expectations are that the kingdom will be established soon (Luke 19:11). At the opening of Acts in Jerusalem, again the expectation of the imminent establishment of God's kingdom is in the minds of the disciples: "Lord, is this the time when you will restore the kingdom to Israel?" (1:6). Jesus' reply is to show them that the vision is far vaster; it goes beyond the simple establishment of God's kingdom in Israel. Yes, on the one hand, Jesus has come to bring fulfillment to past hopes. That is why the gift of the Spirit is communicated to them in Jerusalem. Pentecost is a renewal of God's covenant with God's people. The choosing of a successor, Matthias, to replace Judas and so preserve the symbolic group of Twelve, is a graphic way of showing God's reconstitution of God's people as the 12-tribe kingdom.

On the other hand, Jesus' mission was to enlarge those hopes and visions to embrace all humanity. When the followers of Jesus receive the gift of the Spirit, they are commanded to go out from Jerusalem and spread the gospel message of salvation to all humanity. All are invited to become members of this kingdom. No barriers exclude anyone from membership. Luke continues to show the message being embraced by women, the poor, Gentiles, slaves: a message of salvation that is universal in its embrace and spatial in its outreach "to the ends of the earth."

Other Dominant Themes

The themes already indicated in the Gospel of Luke continue to weave their way through this narrative. Some additional emphases occur in Acts:

- The shift of the message of salvation from the Jews to the Gentiles. The proclamation is always addressed first to the Jews, but when they reject it the address is made to the Gentiles, who by and large respond positively.
- Gentiles do not need to become Jews first. Those who accept Jesus' message are freed from the dietary obligations of Judaism as well as circumcision for males.
- There is a harmony in the Christian church that is guided by the Spirit. The leadership is always open and attentive to the workings and guidance of the Spirit.
- The age of the parousia lies in the remote future. It is no longer imminent. Instead, believers are living in the age of the church, which prepares them for life in the present.

Discipleship

The Way

Luke gives the reader insight into how this group of followers understood themselves. The earliest term used to identify them is "the Way" (9:2; see also 19:23; 22:4; 24:14, 22), a designation that truly captures the uniqueness of this movement. It connects back to the life and ministry of Jesus, which Luke records as a journey to Jerusalem and ultimately to God. The followers of Jesus also see their lives as ultimately a journey to God, hence all they do is influenced by the goal toward which their journey tends. On this journey God is present, as seen in the constant references to the presence of the Spirit leading Paul and his companions on their journeys.

Values for This Journey

Acts proposes a number of values that identify the believer as belonging to the Way.

Concern for the poor dominates the lifestyle of those early Christian communities: "All who believed were together and had all things in common; they would sell their possessions and goods and distribute the proceeds to all, as any had need" (2:44-45; see also 4:34-37). This concern finds further expression with the appointment of the Seven, whose responsibility it was to see to the distribution of food among the Hellenist Christians (6:1-6).

Prayer and worship are other key aspects of the Christian community's life in Acts. Luke describes the apostolic community immediately after the ascension of Jesus as "constantly devoting themselves to prayer" (1:14). While they are praying the Holy Spirit descends upon them (2:1-13). On the release of the apostles Peter and John from prison, the community offers praise for God's goodness and appeals to God for the gift of boldness in proclaiming the message (4:24-31).

Witness and testimony to the resurrection are key characteristics of an apostle. Acts 1:8 sets God's plan in motion by constituting them as witnesses "to the ends of the earth." Becoming "a witness with us to his resurrection" is one of the qualifications Peter sets forth for the one who is to replace Judas (1:21-22). The apostles' testimony is given through sermons and preaching as well as through the witness of their lives. Above all they imitate the life of Jesus through their own suffering. In Acts the verb "to bear witness" (Greek *martyrein*) occurs frequently. It is from this Greek verb that our word "martyr" is derived, since a martyr is someone who gives witness through death.

A consequence of this open public witness is that the followers of Jesus experience persecution, suffering, and even death. Stephen is the prime example of one whose witness ends in the imitation of Jesus' death. Paul's life too is marked by rejection and persecution. He endures hardships with joy, knowing he is sharing in Christ's

sufferings. This spirit of rejoicing in the midst of hardships is clearly evident in Paul's experience in Philippi. Luke notes that after his arrest and imprisonment there, "about midnight Paul and Silas were praying and singing hymns to God" (16:25).

Boldness is a quality that accompanies this ability to bear witness. When Peter and John are arrested, the members of the Jewish council note their "boldness"; realizing "that they were uneducated and ordinary men, they were amazed and recognized them as companions of Jesus" (4:13). Acts ends by drawing attention to the importance of this virtue: Paul lived in Rome "two whole years at his own expense and welcomed all who came to him, proclaiming the kingdom of God and teaching about the Lord Jesus Christ with all *boldness* and without hindrance" (28:30-31). The source of this boldness lies in the belief of the power of Jesus and the presence of his Spirit empowering them.

Questions for Review and Discussion

1 Illustrate how Acts 1:8 summarizes the narrative structure of the book.

2 What is your assessment of Luke as a writer?

3 What do you consider to be the major insight that Luke-Acts has contributed to an understanding of Christianity?

Further Reading

Pervo, Richard I. *Luke's Story of Paul*. Minneapolis: Fortress, 1990.

Powell, Mark Allan. *What Are They Saying about Acts?* New York: Paulist, 1991.

Richter Reimer, Ivoni. *Women in the Acts of the Apostles: A Feminist Liberation Perspective*. Minneapolis: Fortress, 1995.

Squires, John T. "Acts." In *ECB*, 1213-67.

The Letters of Paul

Chapter 53

Paul: Apostle to the Nations

Getting Started

1   What is your impression of Paul from prior experience, either in reading the Bible on your own or as part of a faith community? What is his personality? Is he someone you might like to have at your home BBQ?

2   Again, given your prior experience, how do you understand Paul in relationship to Jesus and the traditions about Jesus we encountered in the chapters on the Gospels?

Preliminary Comments

From the New Testament perspective, Paul is the most influential person, after Jesus, in the origin and spread of Christianity. Thirteen of the New Testament letters are attributed to him. Over the course of the centuries the Letter to the Hebrews has also been counted among Paul's writings. The Acts of the Apostles devotes half its narrative to Paul's missionary activities. Not only did Paul bring Jesus' message beyond the confines of the Jewish world and incarnate it into the Greco-Roman world, but his interpretation of Jesus' message became the authoritative understanding, influencing every major appropriation in the course of Christianity's two-thousand-year history.

Paul initiated a writing movement within the circles of Jesus' followers that produced an authoritative record of the apostolic community's beliefs and spurred others on to produce their own written documents. In this introductory chapter on Paul we will give an overview of his life, outline the classification and format of his letters, and briefly examine his theology. Finally, we will present an appreciation of Paul in the context of his world and the future course of Christianity.

Overview of Paul's Life

The only sources for our information about Paul come from the Acts of the Apostles and Paul's own letters. In studying Acts, we saw that the writing's main thrust was to present a theological vision of Christianity's spread from Jerusalem to Rome ("the ends of the earth" [Acts 1:8]). Paul was the main protagonist in the spread of Jesus' message to the heart of the Roman Empire. In discussing the narrator of Luke-Acts, we noted some gaps in the narrative of Acts, namely that there was no mention of Paul's activity as a letter-writer. This has led

The "street called Straight," major east-west corridor *(cardo maximus)* of Damascus, where Ananias greeted Paul (Acts 9:11). (B. K. Condit)

someone in his 50s. During the 1st century C.E. Jews usually had two names, one Hebrew and one Roman (or Greek). Paul *(Paulus)* was a Roman name and Saul a Hebrew name (the most famous Saul was the first king of Israel).

In his letter to the Philippians, Paul gives a beautiful summary of his Jewish roots: "circumcised on the eighth day, a member of the people of Israel, of the tribe of Benjamin, a Hebrew born of Hebrews; as to the law, a Pharisee; as to zeal, a persecutor of the church; as to righteousness under the law, blameless" (Phil 3:5-6). Acts adds to this information that Paul was born in Tarsus, the capital of Cilicia: "a citizen of an important city" (Acts 21:39). By birth Paul was a Roman citizen (Acts 16:37-38; 22:25-29). He could owe his citizenship either to his family or to the city of Tarsus.

Paul was a Hellenized Jew, educated in his hometown of Tarsus. His native tongue was undoubtedly Greek. He learned to use the rhetorical skills in reading and writing Greek that the education of that day would provide. This education would have given him an understanding of the philosophical and ethical views of the great Greek thinkers and rhetoricians. Without doubt he must have known about the Stoic, Epicurean, and Cynic thought of his day. He also would have studied the Hebrew Scriptures as well as their Greek translation (the Septuagint). Probably in Tarsus Paul learned the trade of tentmaker (Acts 18:3). Scholars are divided as regards what that trade entailed. The traditional view is that Paul worked with skins, involving all aspects of a trade dealing in leather goods. Other scholars suggest some type of weaving, since it was also customary to make tents out of woven cloth. Growing up in the Diaspora meant that Paul also knew the Gentile world well. This enabled him to speak and work among the Gentiles, not as a stranger but as one who truly understood their way of life.

Paul identifies himself also as a Pharisee (Phil 3:5). Acts acknowledges this (26:4-5), although it probably goes too far in suggesting that Paul was educated by Gamaliel (22:3), an influential rabbi in Jerusalem from 20 to 50 C.E. Paul's letters do not imply that he was in Jerusalem during the time of Jesus' ministry or death (26-30). As a Pharisee, Paul would have been trained in the importance of the Torah and the oral Law, and he must have been able to read and write Hebrew and Aramaic (see Acts 21:40; 22:2; 26:14). All this indicates that Paul, who was educated in Tarsus, came to Jerusalem in his early 20s to study the Torah shortly before Stephen's death.

some scholars to distrust Acts and what it says about Paul historically. However, such a conclusion is itself unhistorical. The author of Luke-Acts may not have been Luke and may have had only a vague knowledge of Paul's activity; nevertheless there is too much agreement between Paul and Acts regarding Paul's life and mission for one to disregard the information in Acts about Paul. For this reason, we shall use what Acts tells us about Paul, but in a critical way.

Paul the Pharisee

Neither Paul nor Acts tells us when Paul was born. We would estimate his birth somewhere around 8 C.E. Acts 7:58 introduces Paul for the first time at the stoning of Stephen and says that Paul was "a young man." In his letter to Philemon Paul describes himself as "an old man" (v. 9), which in that time would probably describe

Paul's Call and Acceptance of Jesus

Paul notes that he was a Torah-observant Jew who zealously protected his traditions by persecuting Jesus' followers (Gal 1:13-14; Phil 3:6). While Paul never says why he was so antagonistic toward them, we can surmise that it was because they claimed Jesus as Messiah. For Paul, the Pharisee, such a profession was tantamount to blasphemy. Jews of the 1st century C.E. envisioned the expected Messiah as a powerful figure who would establish God's kingdom on earth. Yet Jesus was anything but a mighty ruler: a wandering teacher of humble origins, he was executed by the Romans as a common criminal. For Paul, such claims for messiahship would deny the very hopes and expectations of his Jewish roots and traditions. Further, Paul's reading of the Hebrew Scriptures gave an added interpretation to the crucifixion of Jesus. Writing later to the Galatians, Paul quotes Deut 21:23: "Cursed is everyone who hangs on a tree" (Gal 3:13). As a Pharisee, Paul would have interpreted Jesus' death as a punishment and curse by God. His zeal led him to try to eradicate this dangerous interpretation of his traditions by persecuting Jesus' followers (Gal 1:23).

Everything changed dramatically with Paul's experience on the road to Damascus. The one who had tried to destroy the Jesus movement became its most forceful adherent. Both Acts and Paul testify to Paul's change as coming from a divine encounter with the risen Jesus (Acts 9:1-9; Gal 1:13-17). Without doubt this made Paul realize that the "curse of the cross" was not the end of Jesus — he was alive and blessed by God. It took Paul time to make sense of this experience. He writes that after this event he went off to the deserts of Arabia for three years (Gal 1:17-18). During which time he brought his belief in the risen Lord to bear upon his Jewish traditions and made sense of them in the light of the resurrection. Belief in the cross and resurrection was to become the central tenet of Paul's new faith.

Chronology for Paul's Life

None of Paul's letters is dated. The only way to give a time frame for his writings and activities is by correlating them with events from external history that can be dated with a certain amount of accuracy. Four dates are significant in constructing a chronology of Paul's life: Herod Agrippa I's death in 44 C.E. (Acts 12:20-23); the expulsion of the Jews from Rome by the Roman emperor Claudius in 49 (18:2); the proconsul Gallio in Corinth in 50/51-52 (18:12-17); and the Roman governor of Judea, Felix, in 58-60 (23:23–24:26).

Reading a Pauline Letter

The ancient Greco-Roman world has left behind hundreds of manuscripts containing personal correspondence dealing with business or family matters as well as

Proposed Chronology for Paul's Life

Traditional Dates	Event
6 B.C.E.	Jesus' birth
8 C.E. (?)	Paul's birth
36	Call/Conversion by risen Christ
36-39	In Arabia (three years)
39	First visit to Jerusalem after Damascus event
39-44	Stay in Tarsus and Cilicia
44-45	Antioch
46-49	First missionary journey: from Antioch to Cyprus and southern Asia Minor; return to Antioch
49	Council of Jerusalem
49-52	Second missionary journey: from Antioch, through southern Asia Minor, Galatia, Macedonia, Corinth (wrote 1 Thess); return to Jerusalem and Antioch
53-58	Third missionary journey: from Antioch through Asia Minor, Galatia to Ephesus (three-year stay: imprisonment? [wrote Gal, Phil, Phlm, 1 Cor]). Further travels to Europe: Macedonia and Corinth (wrote 2 Cor, Rom); return to Jerusalem
58-60	Arrest in Jerusalem; imprisoned two years in Caesarea
60-61	Sea journey to Rome
61-63	Roman imprisonment (two years)
64	Death in Rome under Nero Caesar

more formal communications discussing such topics as friendship and morality (e.g., the Roman Stoic philosopher Seneca [died 65 C.E.], *Letters on Morality*). This correspondence shows a more or less standard formula that was adopted for writing letters in the ancient world. A study of Paul's letters reveals that he remains faithful to this format when communicating with his communities.

Format of a Pauline Letter

The standard ancient Greco-Roman letter comprised four parts: (1) the opening formula; (2) the thanksgiving; (3) the message or body; and (4) the final greetings. Paul used this format in composing his letters.

- Opening Formula: This comprises a sentence containing three elements: the name of the sender, those who are addressed, and a short greeting. The name of the sender is placed at the beginning of the letter (not at the end as is our custom). Often a short phrase identifies the sender's authority. The addressees in Paul's context are generally those communities or churches who receive the letter. The short greeting reflects the context of the letter. For example, in the Jewish world the greeting is simply "Peace" (Hebrew *shalom*), while in the Greco-Roman context it is "Greetings" (Greek *chairein*; Latin *ave*). Paul customarily joins the two greetings together ("Grace and Peace"). This twofold greeting (unique in the ancient world) is significant because it shows Paul's awareness that his communities originate from the cultural worlds of both Judaism and Hellenism.

  Paul and Timothy, servants of Christ Jesus. To all the saints in Christ Jesus who are in Philippi, with the bishops and deacons: Grace to you and peace from God our Father and the Lord Jesus Christ. (Phil 1:1-2)

- Thanksgiving: In Greco-Roman letters an expression of thanks *(eucharistein)* follows the opening formula. The writer thanks the gods for assistance received or gives thanks for some human aid. Paul uses this formula of thanksgiving to introduce some of the important themes of his letters. For example, in the opening thanksgiving section of the Letter to the Philippians (Phil 1:3-11) Paul introduces the theme of gratitude, giving thanks for their fidelity to the faith that he has handed onto them. Not all letters include such a detailed expression. For example, it is lacking in the letter to the Galatians. This may be because Paul was irate about what was happening in the Galatian communities and so jumped immediately into the discussion.

- Message or Body of the Letter: This is the heart of the letter and usually comprises two parts: a doctrinal section that concentrates on explaining the teaching of the Christian message and an ethical or hortatory section that gives instructions for the way believers are to lead their lives. These sections are not necessarily distinct, but often interact with each other. One of Paul's basic methods is to derive the ethical from the doctrinal teaching. Scholars use the phrase "the imperative flows from the indicative" to capture the idea that the way a believer acts depends upon what he or she believes. While the body of Paul's letters often embrace many chapters (Romans and 1 Corinthians are the longest, comprising some 16 chapters each), the Greco-Roman letter was generally much shorter, comprising generally only about a chapter (similar in length to Philemon, 2 and 3 John, and Jude).

- Final Greetings: Today we would refer to this as the signature. If the letter was being dictated, the sender would often pen a greeting in his own hand. In Galatians Paul adds: "See what large letters I make when I am writing in my own hand!" (Gal 6:11). Often Paul adds further news about himself or emphasizes advice that would be followed by a final blessing: "The grace of the Lord Jesus Christ be with your spirit" (Phil 4:23).

Dispatch of the Letter

After the letter had been written either on papyrus or parchment, it was rolled up, sealed, and the address placed on the outside. Letters had to be delivered by someone designated for this task. Wealthy families had slaves to perform this task. Paul usually entrusted his letters to individuals well known to the communities concerned: Timothy, for example, brought 1 Corinthians (16:10); Titus was entrusted with 2 Corinthians (8:16-24); Epaphroditus (who came from Philippi) brought Philippians (2:25); and Tychicus was the bearer of Colossians (4:7-8) and Ephesians (6:21).

Composition of the Letter

The ancient world adopted different methods for writing a letter. One could write the letter oneself, dictate it word for word to another, communicate the sense of the letter while leaving the actual composition to a scribe, or simply entrust the writing to a scribe without communicating its contents.

An examination of Paul's letters reveals that Paul probably dictated his letters word for word to a scribe. While Paul seems to have used different scribes in the writing of his letters, their similar style and language can only be attributed to the fact that Paul must have dictated them. There is evidence that Greco-Roman scribes employed some form of shorthand to take down a dictated letter. As we mentioned, at the conclusion to most of Paul's letters he indicates that he has taken up the pen to conclude the letter with his own personal greetings (see 1 Cor 16:21; Phlm 19; Gal 6:11). One of the strongest arguments for not including Colossians, Ephesians, 2 Thessalonians, and the Pastorals among the authentic letters of Paul is that their language, style, and thought are widely different from those letters genuinely acknowledged as Paul's.

Classifying Paul's Letters

While 13 New Testament letters bear Paul's name, scholars usually classify them into three groups: authentic

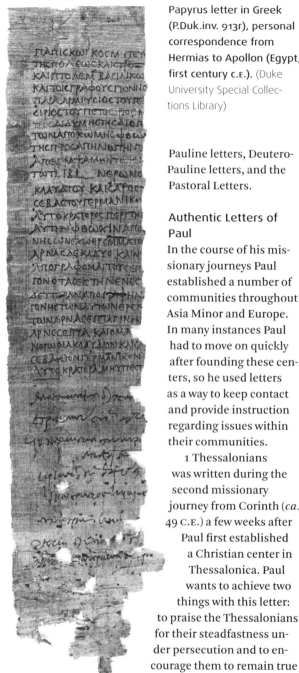

Papyrus letter in Greek (P.Duk.inv. 913r), personal correspondence from Hermias to Apollon (Egypt, first century c.e.). (Duke University Special Collections Library)

Pauline letters, Deutero-Pauline letters, and the Pastoral Letters.

Authentic Letters of Paul

In the course of his missionary journeys Paul established a number of communities throughout Asia Minor and Europe. In many instances Paul had to move on quickly after founding these centers, so he used letters as a way to keep contact and provide instruction regarding issues within their communities.

1 Thessalonians was written during the second missionary journey from Corinth (*ca.* 49 c.e.) a few weeks after Paul first established a Christian center in Thessalonica. Paul wants to achieve two things with this letter: to praise the Thessalonians for their steadfastness under persecution and to encourage them to remain true to the faith he has entrusted to them. At the same time he tries to correct certain false ideas that are circulating in the community relating to Jesus' second coming. Many of the Thessalonians are confused about what would happen to those who have died before Christ returns. Paul puts their minds at rest by assuring them that everyone will be raised, whether or not one is alive at the time of the Lord's return.

The letters to the Corinthians were written during the third missionary journey (53-58). In all Paul wrote four letters to the Corinthians during this journey, of

which only two exist today. 1 Corinthians was written from Ephesus and deals with practical problems within the Corinthian community. It also answers many questions the community addressed to Paul in a letter. Paul answers each of these questions at length, such as the Christian attitude toward sex, the eating of meat offered to idols, the correct celebration of the Eucharist, and the understanding of the resurrection. In each case Paul uses the opportunity to develop his understanding of the Christian message. 2 Corinthians was written after Paul had left Ephesus and was traveling through Macedonia en route to Corinth. Since his opponents had rejected his authority to teach, Paul defends his ministry as an apostle and develops a noteworthy teaching on the nature of ministry.

Philippians was also written from Ephesus during the third missionary journey and indicates that during this period he was in prison. This is a very personal letter expressing great joy in the fidelity of the Philippians to the Gospel message as well as Paul's joy at being able to share in Christ's sufferings. Paul presents Jesus as the true example of service and humility.

Philemon is also a letter from prison written from Ephesus at the same time as Philippians during the third missionary journey: "Paul, a prisoner of Christ Jesus" (v. 1). A slave, Onesimus, had escaped and had come to Paul in Ephesus. Paul sends him back to the slave owner, Philemon. This short letter is one of the finest testimonies to forgiveness in the entire New Testament.

Galatians was written from Corinth during Paul's third missionary journey (*ca.* 57). Exactly who the readers are has been greatly disputed by scholars. This letter is largely written to counter the inroads of certain groups such as the Judaizers (those Christians who

Paul's Letters

Authentic Letters (7)
   1 Thessalonians
   1 Corinthians
   2 Corinthians
   Philippians
   Philemon
   Galatians
   Romans

Deutero-Pauline Letters (3)
   Colossians
   Ephesians
   2 Thessalonians

Pastoral Letters (3)
   1 Timothy
   2 Timothy
   Titus

wanted Jesus' followers to maintain their bonds with the Jewish faith), who considered Paul's message to be a distortion of the original Christian message. For them salvation was only possible for those who maintained their Jewish roots. They demanded that the large numbers of Gentile converts who had adopted the Christian faith through Paul's preaching should become Jews first of all and embrace all the requirements of the Torah. These attacks gave Paul the opportunity to work out for the first time his understanding of freedom from the Torah and the total efficacy of the salvific work of Jesus Christ (5:1).

Romans was written from Corinth during the third missionary journey (*ca.* 57) and is undoubtedly Paul's greatest letter. Paul writes to Christians in Rome, introducing himself and preparing them for his projected visit. Because this letter does not arise out of the context of controversies, Paul is able to give a calm presentation of his theological views and to highlight the central tenets of his gospel. The central theme of this letter is expressed in this way: "For I am not ashamed of the gospel; it is the power of God for salvation to everyone who has faith, to the Jew first and also to the Greek. For in it the righteousness of God is revealed through faith for faith; as it is written, 'The one who is righteous will live by faith'" (1:16-17).

Deutero-Pauline Letters

A study of the letters to the Colossians, Ephesians, and 2 Thessalonians, particularly from the perspective of their style, vocabulary, and thought, gives rise to the conclusion that someone other than Paul was responsible for them. This person (or maybe a number of people), a "second Paul" (hence the term *deutero,* "second"), was a student of Paul, steeped in his thought, who wrote to communities with whom Paul had been associated in order to resolve issues that had arisen in those centers. He (or they) wrote in Paul's name to remind the readers of Paul's authority and to indicate what Paul would have taught them had he been alive. As we have noted previously, this was an acceptable and common procedure within the ancient world which gave renewed attention and support to the authority of important teachers such as Paul.

Colossians is written to the community at Colossae, a city of Asia Minor. A problem has arisen that is undermining the community's belief in the position of Christ. Writing in the name of Paul toward the end of the 1st century, the writer endeavors to present a picture of Christ as the only redeemer, the only savior and center of worship who guides and directs the universe: "He is the image of the invisible God, the firstborn of all creation; for in him all things in heaven and on earth were

created, things visible and invisible, whether thrones or dominions or rulers or powers — all things have been created through him and for him" (1:15-16).

While the letter is entitled "to the Ephesians," the orginal text bears no such designation and lacks reference to any specific community. Instead, it seems to have been sent as a type of "encyclical" passed around from community to community in Asia Minor. This letter addresses the same issues as the letter to the Colossians, but in a more intense way. Using the name and authority of Paul, the writer shows that God had a plan from the beginning to bring together the whole creation in Christ: "With all wisdom and insight he has made known to us the mystery of his will, according to his good pleasure that he set forth in Christ, as a plan for the fullness of time, to gather up all things in him, things in heaven and things on earth" (1:8-10).

Not all scholars agree that 2 Thessalonians is a Deutero-Pauline letter. Since it is hard to harmonize its thoughts with the first letter to the Thessalonians, we prefer to treat it as a letter written by someone other than Paul after his death. The issues of the resurrection and the second coming of Jesus continue to cause problems in the community, and the writer uses Paul's authority to remind them of the essence of Paul's teaching. Some believe that the day of the Lord is at hand and have given up working. The writer shows them that this is not the case and gives criteria by which they can judge when that day is to come. The writer instructs them on the need to work, with Paul as an example: he worked as a tent-maker when he was with them and did not rely upon them for support (3:8).

Pastoral Letters

These letters are presented as written by Paul to Timothy and Titus, pastors (Latin *pastores,* "shepherds") or leaders of the Christian communities. They intend to offer Paul's companions instruction on how to carry out their pastoral role of leadership within their communities. The context presumes a period much later than Paul's where a more developed structural organization of the Christian communities had emerged. Added to this, the language and style of these writings are very different from Paul's authentic letters. Because of their similarity in style and language, they are judged to have been written by the same person toward the close of the 1st century. These three writings call on Paul's authority to outline the qualities that leaders within the Christian community should exercise.

1 Timothy is written to one of Paul's closest associates, Timothy. The writer defends the church against the inroads of false teachers into the Christian communities. The heresies that the writer has in mind seem to

be an early form of Christian Gnosticism. The Gnostics proclaimed the ability to communicate a special type of secret knowledge regarding the origin of the world and the way in which one came to salvation. The writer's instructions concern Christian leadership and represent an attempt to organize the community to deal with these new threats.

2 Timothy continues to strengthen the leadership of the Christian communities against the perceived threats that false teachers posed to the traditional teachings. Hence, the figure of Paul plays an important role in reminding the readers about the foundation of their faith.

Titus is a further description of the qualities that a leader must have. It also provides the ethical guidelines that members of the Christian community must embrace in dealing with one another. Its content is very similar to 1 Timothy, except that it lays greater stress on what one should believe.

Theological Themes in Paul's Letters

We will focus on theological themes in the universally accepted seven letters of Paul. The Deutero-Pauline and Pastoral letters clearly show a development in thought and a change in context from the world of Paul.

Paul never worked out a system of theology that would integrate everything into his view of God, Jesus, and humanity. His letters address practical, concrete situations of communities that were struggling in their awareness of the Christian message and in their adherence to Christ. To understand Paul's thought one has first to understand the circumstances that he addresses in each church for these dictate what Paul considers and how he responds. Consequently, Paul's seven letters do not contain the entirety of his theological vision. Rather, they contain those elements that Paul judged his communities needed to hear at that moment. In this brief overview we will pay attention to three central aspects of Paul's faith which will be helpful in reading the letters against the background of the situation that gave rise to that particular writing.

The Foundation of Paul's Belief:
The Crucifixion and Resurrection of Jesus

The opening of Paul's first letter to the Corinthians gives clear expression to this perspective. He contrasts the approaches of his own people, the Jews, and of the pagans or Greeks to the views of Jesus' followers toward salvation: "For the message about the cross is foolishness to those who are perishing, but to us who are being saved it is the power of God" (1 Cor 1:18). For Paul, Jews rely upon the convincing power of signs and Greeks on

human wisdom, while Jesus' followers rely upon Christ crucified, "Christ the power of God and the wisdom of God" (1:23-24).

We mentioned earlier that Paul, the Pharisee, would have experienced difficulties with the Christian proclamation of the crucified Christ. In the Letter to the Galatians, he quotes Deut 21:23: "Cursed is everyone who hangs on a tree" (Gal 3:13). Paul's personal experience of the risen Christ challenges him to see the crucifixion of Jesus in a new light. While the Hebrew Scriptures portray God's curse resting on the one who was crucified, Paul also sees them teaching that God will ultimately vindicate the righteous Servant, who suffers and dies on behalf of the sins of human beings (Isa 52:13–53:12). Consequently, Paul explains the curse as one that was directed, not at Jesus, but at us. This gives rise to an interpretation of Jesus' death that has influenced Christian theology ever since: Jesus bore the curse of our sins, atoning for sin by dying upon the cross. For Paul, Jesus' resurrection is a demonstration of God's action in accepting Jesus' death on behalf of humanity: it is the greatest triumph of God's righteousness. The central dimension of the faith of Jesus' followers rests for Paul on the crucifixion and resurrection. His letters attempt to explain more fully the implications of these events, not just intellectually, but more especially ethically, namely how believers should lead their lives.

Righteousness of God and
Justification of the Sinner

The concepts of righteousness and justification have been at the heart of the disputes within Christianity since the 16th century. It is important to get beyond the denominational squabbles that have beset Christianity for five hundred years and strive to obtain clarity about what Paul himself is saying.

Paul speaks frequently about "the righteousness (Greek *dikaiosyne*) of God." In this phrase he focuses on God's activity in bringing about humanity's salvation: "But now, apart from law, the righteousness *(dikaiosyne)* of God has been disclosed, and is attested by the law and the prophets, the righteousness of God through faith in Jesus Christ for all who believe" (Rom 3:21-22). In Jesus' death and resurrection God has worked salvation; salvation is God's action. The consequence is that those who believe attain justification *(dikaiosis)* or are justified *(dikaioun)*. Jesus' death and resurrection bring those who believe into a relationship with God whereby they are accounted as "justified," innocent or freed from all sin or guilt. The distinction drawn by Protestants, who interpret this acquittal before God as one where God declares that people are now justified, and Catholics, who argue that this acquittal involves a total transformation of the nature of the human being, was not really on Paul's radar screen. It was a nuance to which Paul had not given attention. What is important is that Paul stresses the salvific actions of God ("righteousness") in bringing people into relationship with God and the consequences of that action ("justification") in the lives of believers.

Paul's Attitude to Jews and Greeks in the Context of God's Salvific Action

For Paul the liberating power of faith in Christ has transformed God's relationship with the human race. Paul's message of the gospel is directed to both Jews and Greeks (the two groupings that Judaism of his day used to designate the whole human race) to see how this transformation occurred within their own religious context.

> For I am not ashamed of the gospel; it is the power of God for salvation to everyone who has faith, *to the Jew first* and *also to the Greek.* For in it the righteousness of God is revealed through faith for faith; as it is written, "The one who is righteous will live by faith." (Rom 1:16-17)

For the Jewish people the Torah (the Law) was the expression of God's will for how God's people should lead their lives. It was the single most important aspect of the relationship between God and God's people. After becoming a follower of Jesus, Paul viewed the Torah in a new light. His central critique of the Torah is that it usurped the place that Jesus should occupy in the plan of salvation. Intended to be a guide to how God's chosen people should lead their lives in their covenant relationship with God, the Torah prepared the way for Jesus: "But now that faith has come, we are no longer subject to a disciplinarian" (Gal 3:23-25). Paul sees that salvation and justification came through faith in Jesus Christ. Justification is not something earned by good actions of obedience to the stipulations of the Torah. The Torah brings with it a knowledge of sin, of what is right and what is wrong, but it does not bring about the means of enabling people to carry out what they are instructed to do. Knowledge without empowerment means that one continues to wallow in sin (Rom 7:7-12). Faith in Jesus Christ liberates one from the power of sin and the Torah. It empowers one to lead life in conformity to God's will: "We know that our old self was crucified with him so that the body of sin might be destroyed, and we might no longer be enslaved to sin. . . . So you also must consider yourselves dead to sin and alive to God in Christ Jesus" (Rom 6:6-11).

Paul saw his mission as directed to bringing the gospel message to the pagan world (the Greeks, or Gentiles,

as he refers to them). Again reflecting upon his own Scriptures, Paul understood that God's plan had always included bringing the Gentiles into relationship with God. In the promises that God directed to Abraham, God said that "in you all the families of the earth shall be blessed" (Gen 12:3). The prophets also looked forward to the future when God's blessings would include the Gentiles (Isa 42:1). Paul saw these promises fulfilled in the person of Jesus Christ.

For Paul, the death and resurrection of Jesus has universal implications. All peoples, whether Jew or Gentile, have the possibility of coming into relationship with God through faith in Christ Jesus. Neither Jew nor Gentile earns this relationship: only faith in the risen Christ brings one into that right relationship. The consequence of all this is that in the risen Christ all former distinctions have passed away: "There is no longer Jew or Greek, there is no longer slave or free, there is no longer male and female; for all of you are one in Christ Jesus. And if you belong to Christ, then you are Abraham's offspring, heirs according to the promise" (Gal 3:28-29).

Importance of Paul's Theology

Of all the figures within the world of early Christianity, Paul is the one from whom we have the largest body of material, and hence we are able to construct a more comprehensive theology. These three aspects of Paul's thought (the crucifixion and resurrection of Jesus, the righteousness and justification of the sinner, and the universality of the salvific action of Jesus) will help us understand Paul's letters more easily. Nowhere does Paul actually give a detailed explanation of the terms that he uses nor the thought that he embraces. He presupposes an understanding in his readers. As personal communications from Paul to individual communities, these letters are not difficult to understand provided one can fill in many of the gaps that exist through an understanding of the background to the events leading up to their writing.

None of the great developments within the history of Christian thought has occurred without a debt to Paul's thought. The Christian movement that began within the world of Judaism with Jesus of Nazareth met world civilization for the first time in the preaching and teaching of Paul of Tarsus. As a Jewish rabbi, his training gave him the ability to understand the Hebrew Scriptures as pointing to the person and work of Jesus as part of God's plan for humanity. As a Greek, his training in rhetoric and philosophy gave him the ability to present Jesus' message in a language and in a way that people from the Hellenistic world would understand. In Paul's missionary activity and in his writings, the words that were addressed at the time of his call on the road to Damascus were fulfilled: "He is an instrument whom I have chosen to bring my name before Gentiles and kings and before the people of Israel" (Acts 9:15).

Questions for Review and Discussion

1   Examine 1 Corinthians and show how the format of an ancient letter is expressed in this writing.

2   Why is it important to know something about the historical context that formed the background to the letters of Paul?

3   Why is Paul important for the history of Christianity?

Further Reading

Dunn, James D. G. *The Theology of Paul the Apostle.* Grand Rapids: Wm. B. Eerdmans, 1998.

Murphy-O'Connor, Jerome. *Paul, the Letter-Writer: His World, His Options, His Skills.* GNS 41 Collegeville: Liturgical, 1995.

Neyrey, Jerome H. *Paul, In Other Words: A Cultural Reading of His Letters.* Louisville: Westminster/John Knox, 1990.

Puskas, Charles B., Jr. *The Letters of Paul: An Introduction.* GNS 25. Collegeville: Liturgical, 1993.

Roetzel, Calvin J. "Paul." In *EDB*, 1016-20.

Chapter 54

1 Thessalonians

Paul's Correspondence with a Young Church

Getting Started

1 Read Paul's first letter to Thessalonica. List the characteristics of the readers of this letter.

2 Describe Paul's main concerns in writing to the Thessalonians. How does he encourage them?

Preliminary Comments

Our treatment of Paul's letters will follow the same method adopted when reading the Gospels. We will conduct a brief walk through the letter itself, from which we will draw out critical issues and theological themes that are important for Paul's thought. We need to introduce a further dimension at the beginning that will enhance the understanding of the letter. We cannot read independently of the life-situation for which it was written and out of which it emerged. Neither can the letter be understood without knowing something about the needs of the community itself. For this reason we will briefly examine the background to the letter in the introductory observations.

This first letter to the Thessalonians is Paul's earliest writing to have survived. Consequently, it is the oldest

New Testament document. Here we get an insight into Paul's earliest thought before he gave expression to themes he developed later related to the justification of the sinner through faith.

Background Information

In the course of the second missionary journey (49-52 C.E.) Paul, together with Silas and Timothy, made the significant move from Asia Minor (modern Turkey) to Macedonia (northern modern Greece) where they proclaimed the gospel message. Paul moved throughout Greece evangelizing the cities of Philippi, Thessalonica, Beroea, Athens, and Corinth (where he spent 18 months). The Acts of the Apostles notes that Paul and his companions came to Thessalonica after having been forced to leave Philippi (Acts 16:39–17:1). Paul remarks that they "had already suffered and been shamefully mistreated at Philippi" (1 Thess 2:2). It is not clear how long Paul and his group stayed in Thessalonica. Acts presents a summarized version of their stay, which embraced preaching for three Sabbaths in the synagogue (17:2) and then in the house of Jason (vv. 5-9), after which they had to leave the city suddenly because of disturbances in the Jewish community. However, from Paul's own writings

In the thanksgiving section (1:2-10) Paul is more expansive than in his other letters. He gives thanks to God for this community and continues to remember them in his prayers (v. 2). They demonstrate they are a community of faith, hope, and love (v. 3). In reflecting on his initial preaching in Thessalonica, Paul sees that the people responded because the power of the Holy Spirit was working through his preaching (vv. 4-5). Their response to the gospel brought with it persecution as well as joy that they could suffer in imitation of the Lord and of Paul. Their faith response has become legendary among the Christians of Macedonia and Achaia and even beyond (v. 8). Paul praises two dimensions of this response: the way the Thessalonians offered Paul hospitality, which set an example to be imitated by other communities, and the way in which they turned from the worship of idols to worship the living God (v. 9).

it seems that his stay in Thessalonica was a little longer. He mentions in 1 Thess 2:9 how hard he worked among them: "You remember our labor and toil, brothers and sisters; we worked night and day, so that we might not burden any of you while we proclaimed to you the gospel of God." When Paul later writes to the Philippians, he thanks them for their gifts while he was in Thessalonica (Phil 4:16). All this suggests a more prolonged stay.

The forced departure from Thessalonica prompts Paul to write this letter out of pastoral concern for the community. He takes the opportunity of his extended stay in Corinth to write, noting that he has been separated from them "for a short time" (1 Thess 2:17) and that he is extremely concerned about them. Since Paul himself is unable to return to them ("but Satan blocked our way" [2:18]), he decides to send Timothy from Athens to see what has been happening in Thessalonica (3:1-5). Timothy later returns to Paul in Corinth, where he assures Paul of their faith and how they long to see him again (3:6). In joyful response to this news and out of a concern to instruct them further in some aspects of the Christian faith, Paul writes this letter.

A Walk through 1 Thessalonians

1 Thessalonians 1:1-10:
Opening Formula and Thanksgiving
Paul adapts the form of a Greco-Roman letter to his own needs. As the first of his letters, it is an experiment in writing a Christian letter. Paul will develop this approach further in his later letters. While Silvanus and Timothy are included among the senders of the letter (1:1), Paul is the actual one responsible for it, as can be seen from his referring to himself in the first person singular (3:5; 5:27). In addressing the letter "to the church of the Thessalonians," Paul intends it to be read when the Christians gather together to worship.

1 Thessalonians 2:1-12:
Paul's Ministry in Thessalonica
Paul opens the body of the letter with a reference to his visit in Thessalonica where he was openly embraced. This contrasts sharply with his reception in Philippi (2:2). Paul defends his ministry among the Thessalonians by clarifying his motives in preaching among them (v. 3). He understands that his mission was directed by God, and he carries it out, not to please himself or his hearers, but to please God (v. 4). Paul's preaching is not motivated by greed or for seeking praise from others. He notes

The City of Thessalonica
Thessalonica was the capital of the Roman province of Macedonia and was situated on the famous Via Egnatia, a Roman highway running east and west across the Roman Empire. Named after Alexander the Great's half-sister, Thessalonica was a city with a rich and varied religious heritage that reflected the diversity of its population. Archaeology has demonstrated that the Roman emperor was worshiped here: Julius Caesar was acknowledged as a god during the 1st century C.E., which marks the beginnings of the imperial cult, or emperor worship. The Roman goddess Roma was worshiped there, as well as other gods, many of them from the eastern part of the empire, including Serapis, Isis, Zeus, Asclepius, Aphrodite, Demeter, and Dionysus. Archaeologists have discovered two different synagogues within the city, one for Jews, another for Samaritans. Paul's Letter to the Thessalonians reflects this religious background: "For the people of those regions report about us what kind of welcome we had among you, and how you turned to God from idols, to serve a living and true God" (1:9)

that he and his helpers never claimed support from the community, even though they were entitled to it (v. 7). Note that Paul refers to himself and his fellow helpers as "apostles," which shows that the term embraces more than just the 12 disciples of Jesus. It refers to all those who have been sent to preach the gospel message.

Paul uses two striking images from family life to describe his ministry among them. He compares himself and his companions to a nursing mother who takes care of her children with tenderness and love (v. 7). He also likens them to a father who encourages and pleads with his children to lead their lives in a way "worthy of God" (vv. 11-12). Paul earns his own keep through his trade as a tent maker. In this way he shows that he does not want to burden anyone (v. 9). One can imagine Paul working in his shop while at the same time using the occasion to preach to those around him.

1 Thessalonians 2:13-16: Further Thanksgiving

Paul again thanks God that the Thessalonians accepted his preaching for what it really was: the word of God (2:13). Now he also gives thanks for their steadfast endurance in the face of persecution (v. 14). The Thessalonian Christians are seen to have suffered at the hands of their pagan neighbors in a way similar to the persecution that the Christian communities of Judea suffered at the hands of the Jews (v. 14). It is important to understand what Paul intends when he says "the Jews, who killed both the Lord Jesus and the prophets" (vv. 14-15). Paul is himself a Jew and always proud of that fact (Rom 11:1). He is not condemning the Jewish people as an entire race. As the Gospels show, it is *some* Jews, particularly the leaders, who were responsible for Jesus' death, just as *some* Jews were responsible for the death of the prophets.

1 Thessalonians 2:17–3:5:
Paul's Intention to Visit Again

This passage shows the intense bonds that exist between Paul and the community of Thessalonica. Paul uses the image of a family to describe his present relationship with them, speaking of himself and his companions as being made "orphans" (2:17) because they have been separated from the Thessalonians. He says that he wanted to return to visit them many times, but was prevented from doing so by Satan (v. 18). What exactly Paul refers to we do not know. He identifies the faith of this community as the reason he will be able to rejoice and exult when the Lord Jesus returns (v. 19). His intense concern for the Thessalonians prompts Paul while in Athens to send Timothy to them to find out what is happening and also to "strengthen and encourage" their community (3:2). Paul understands that persecution and

Triumphal arch of the emperor Galerius on the Via Egnatia, Thessalonica, glorifying the Roman victory over the Persians. (B. K. Condit)

suffering are part of the lot of a follower of Jesus so they should not be surprised when it happens (v. 4).

1 Thessalonians 3:6-13: Timothy's Report to Paul

Timothy returns to Paul in Corinth where he reports about the Thessalonians' endurance and faith, for which Paul gives thanks to God. Their faith gives Paul encouragement in the midst of his persecutions and sufferings (3:7). Here we see the reciprocal nature of the strengthening of faith. Just as Paul's faith has strengthened the Thessalonians, now the faith of the Thessalonians is strengthening Paul.

At this point in the letter Paul turns to instruct the community in aspects of the gospel message that he feels they need to hear. Probably he has heard from Timothy that there are dimensions of the Christian faith that need to be developed (v. 10). Paul concludes this section with a prayer in which he asks that God will enable him to visit the Thessalonian community again. He addresses this prayer to "our God and Father himself and our Lord Jesus" (v. 11) and prays that the people's love for each other and for everyone will be increased (v. 12).

1 Thessalonians 4:1-12:
Instructions on How to Lead Their Lives

Paul now instructs the Thessalonians regarding their moral life. His advice is given "in the Lord Jesus" (4:1), so that it comes not simply from Paul but from the Lord's spokesperson. Possibly in response to Timothy's report, Paul begins his instructions with negative vices (vv. 3-8) that should be avoided. The list is one Paul has taken from a traditional list of vices as used to present moral instruction in the Greco-Roman world. A Christian is to avoid sexual immorality, passion, and impurity (a similar list is found in Col 3:5). God wills the people's sanctification, so they are to eschew all impurity that will lead away from holiness (4:7). Indeed, the Holy Spirit has been given to them so that they can increase in holiness. Paul then gives positive instructions (vv. 9-12) to increase and deepen the people's love for one another. This love should be reflected in a quiet life and the ability to mind their own affairs and continue to work so that they do not need to depend upon others for support (vv. 11-12).

1 Thessalonians 4:13–5:11:
Instructions on the Parousia

In this passage Paul presents his central teaching, which arises from certain concerns or questions of the Thessalonians. Part of the essence of the Christian faith is that the Lord will come unexpectedly, like a thief in the night (5:2; see also Matt 24:42-44). It seems that Paul and other Christians at this time believed that the return of Christ would happen soon, in their own lifetime. The logical question was what would happen to those who have already died. Paul responds that all will share in Christ's resurrected life: "We who are alive, who are left until the coming of the Lord, will by no means precede those who have died" (4:15). Paul describes the return of Christ in language reminiscent of the celebration of a Roman triumph when the victorious general returned to his city: all the inhabitants went out to meet him along the road to welcome his return. "Then we who are alive, who are left, will be caught up in the clouds together with them to meet the Lord in the air; and so we will be with the Lord forever" (v. 17).

The unexpected return of the Lord should not be a source of fear, but of hope and expectation. Through baptism, Christians become "children of light" (5:5)

who belong to the day and are equipped with the virtues of faith, love, and hope (v. 8; see also 1:3). Once again it is the resurrection of Jesus that provides the certain hope: "For God has destined us not for wrath but for obtaining salvation through our Lord Jesus Christ, who died for us, so that whether we are awake or asleep we may live with him" (vv. 9-10).

1 Thessalonians 5:12-22:
Instructions on Church Life

This final list of instructions captures the essence of the life of a follower of Jesus. It draws attention chiefly to how Christians interact with one another: concern and love for the other should be what directs their actions.

1 Thessalonians 5:23-28: Final Greetings

Paul concludes the letter with a prayer reminding the Thessalonians that their ability to carry out these exhortations and instructions comes from God and the Lord Jesus: God is the one who sanctifies them, and Jesus enables them to remain faithful (5:23-24). After exhorting the people to pray for him, Paul instructs them to have this letter read to all the brothers and sisters (v. 27). This may imply that there was more than one house church in Thessalonica. Finally, Paul concludes with a blessing which will become customary in his other letters: "The grace of our Lord Jesus Christ be with you" (v. 28). He probably took these blessings from their use in the worship of the communities.

Critical Issues in Studying 1 Thessalonians

The Position of 2:13-16 in the Letter

One of the basic questions that scholars raise about 1 Thessalonians is whether 2:13-16 was part of Paul's original letter or whether it had been added later. Those who think that it had been added by a later editor argue that the way in which the Jews are referred to here is uncharacteristic of Paul's view of the Jews in his other letters. The phrase "the Jews, who killed both the Lord Jesus and the prophets," (2:15) is contrary to Paul's vision that sees "the rulers of this age" (1 Cor 2:8) responsible for Jesus' death. The further anti-Semitic statements that the Jews "have constantly been filling up the measure of their sins" and that "God's wrath has overtaken them at last" (1 Thess 2:16) are also judged as contrary to Paul's hope, expressed throughout his other letters, that in the end "all Israel will be saved" (Rom 11:26).

As indicated above in the brief commentary on 2:13-16, these arguments need not militate against the presence of this passage in Paul's original letter. All the manuscripts that we possess contain this passage in this context. Conjectures as to whether something belongs or should be changed in a text must always be based upon the evidence of the manuscripts, not on preconceived ideas. Paul's concern here in 1 Thessalonians is not with all Jews, but only with those who are in Thessalonica. In 2 Cor 11:24 Paul does speak about Jews who persecuted him. Further, when one reads Rom 11:26 in its context, Paul's vision emerges far more clearly: "I want you to understand this mystery: a hardening has come upon part of Israel, until the full number of the Gentiles has come in. And so all Israel will be saved" (vv. 25-26). In this perspective Paul would see those Jews in Thessalonica who are persecuting him as representing those upon whom God's wrath ("a hardening," Rom 11:25) has come. It is quite understandable that these Jews, who have been attracting many Gentiles to their faith, would become angry when Paul draws those same Gentiles away to accept his message of the risen Christ. This passage then is not to be seen as anti-Semitic or a rejection of all Jews in general. Paul is concerned with one particular group who are hostile to him, and he sees them in the context of his wider vision of God's plan of salvation where some Jews would reject Jesus and his message. But Paul always holds out the hope that in the end "all Israel will be saved."

Neither Paul, nor the Gospel writers, can be used to argue a perspective, as has been done tragically in the past history of Christianity, that all Jews are responsible for Jesus' death. The New Testament puts it clearly that the civil authorities were the ones who were responsible and that the religious authorities threatened by the implications of Jesus' teaching collaborated with them. All the early followers of Jesus were Jewish, which resulted in tensions arising within the world of Judaism itself: tensions between the Jewish followers of Jesus and those who rejected his message. When antagonisms arose, they must be read in this context as a struggle within the heart of Judaism itself.

Enduring Importance of 1 Thessalonians

As we have indicated, this letter is the earliest New Testament writing to survive. In writing 1 Thessalonians, Paul was not aware that he was starting a literary movement that would ultimately flower forth into the production of a body of literature that would be authoritative for Christian believers through the centuries. He was reacting to a concrete situation arising within a community a few months old in the Christian faith, and as a pastor he wanted to nourish and protect that faith. The enduring quality of the letter is that it sets forth for Christians of every generation the basic dimensions of their faith. Looking at the opening verses of the letter, first and foremost are references to God the Father, the Lord Jesus Christ, and the Holy Spirit (1:3-5); Paul lists virtues of faith, hope, and love as core virtues for the Thessalonians (v. 3), and these remain the cardinal virtues for all Christians. What Paul stresses for the Thessalonians resonates as the same faith that Christians profess today. The first Letter to the Thessalonians is to be treasured as both a remarkable testimony to the faith of early Christianity and a mirror for the way in which Christianity has remained true to that heritage.

Theological Themes in 1 Thessalonians

The main focus of 1 Thessalonians is what is termed apocalyptic eschatology, a particular perspective concerned with the end of all things. Based on Greek *eschaton,* meaning "last or end," and *logos,* "word," eschatology is "a word about the end." Paul's faith as reflected here in 1 Thessalonians can be briefly summarized in this way: Jesus is the Christ, the Son of God, whom God has raised from the dead. This risen Jesus will soon return to the earth as a judge and will free his followers from their suffering and persecution. The return of Jesus is referred as the *parousia* (Greek "coming, arrival, advent"). A similar expectation occurs in the Sayings Source Q that lies behind the Gospels of Matthew and Luke.

The earliest evidence we have, then, for the first Christians' understanding about the future was an expectation that Jesus would return soon to judge the world and to vindicate his faithful followers. Both Paul's earliest letters and the Sayings Source Q present this common vision. With time this expectation would shift when Jesus had not returned and Christians were forced to realize that Jesus had never said when he would return. The immediate return of Jesus was seen to be the wishful expectation of his followers.

Paul goes further in his description of the future return of Jesus. He uses imagery that is particularly at home in the world of his time: "with a cry of command . . . the archangel's call . . . the sound of God's trumpet . . . (we) will be caught up in the clouds together . . ." (4:16-17). All these images are typical of a genre of literature very common in that day, namely apocalyptic literature (Greek *apokalypsis,* from the verb "to uncover, to make known, to reveal," is the opening word of the book of Revelation). An apocalypse endeavors to look behind the events in the world to the real spiritual causes that lie behind them.

When Paul speaks about the return of Jesus and the end time, he employs an apocalyptic eschatology that

Apocalyptic Worldview

Present age	(God intervenes)	Future age
Evil		Good
Suffering		Reward of the faithful
Trials		Punishment of evil

looks at the end of history and sees it from the context of the spiritual causes and struggles that surround it. Paul's writings are by no means apocalypses, but his worldview does embrace that of his time. He shares with this vision the belief that there are two ages: the present age and the age to come. In 1 Thessalonians Paul is of the conviction that this age will come to an end soon. He also believes that he will be alive when this happens ("we who are alive, who are left until the coming of the Lord," 4:15). However, Paul adds a new insight into this traditional apocalyptic worldview. The death and resurrection of Jesus inaugurated the end of this present age. For Paul the end of the age has already begun, but it has not yet fully arrived. Christians were eagerly expecting the return of Jesus who would bring the fulfillment of the end. For this reason Paul urges his hearers/readers to lead their lives in a way that conforms to the message of Jesus in preparation for his return. Christians live in the period between the first coming of Jesus (already) and his return (not yet). To describe the final coming of Jesus Paul uses, as we have indicated, images borrowed from this apocalyptic worldview. Paul's entire first letter to the Thessalonians centers around two poles: Jesus' death and resurrection and the eager expectation of his future return. Christians live between these two poles. Their lives are influenced by Jesus' death and resurrec-tion and their moral focus is guided by Jesus' life and teaching as they prepare themselves for his return to share in the future age.

Questions for Review and Discussion

1   Imagine you were in Thessalonica in 51 C.E. What do you think the response of the readers would have been to this letter?

2   List the basic beliefs that Paul holds as part of the faith that he passes on to the Thessalonians.

3   Examine Paul's references to the Holy Spirit in this letter. Write a comprehensive paragraph that expresses Paul's understanding of the Holy Spirit.

Further Reading

Gaventa, Beverly Roberts. "Thessalonians, First letter to the." In *EDB,* 1298-99.

Jewett, Robert K. "1 Thessalonians." In *ECB,* 1413-22.

———. *The Thessalonian Correspondence: Pauline Rhetoric and Millenarian Piety.* Philadelphia: Fortress, 1986.

Koester, Helmut. "I Thessalonians — Experiment in Christian Writing." In *Continuity and Discontinuity in Church History,* ed. F. Forrester Church and Timothy George, 33-44. Leiden: Brill, 1979.

Malherbe, Abraham J. *Paul and the Thessalonians: The Philosophic Tradition of Pastoral Care.* Philadelphia: Fortress, 1987.

Chapter 55

1 and 2 Corinthians

Challenges Facing a Young Church

Getting Started

1   Read 1 Corinthians. Identify the issues that were problems for the Corinthian church, and explain in one sentence how Paul resolves the challenges.

2   Read 2 Corinthians. Briefly describe how Paul defends his role as an apostle. Why do you think Paul needed to do this?

Preliminary Comments

Paul's contact with the city of Corinth extended over a period of eight years. He knew this community well because he had spent 18 months there during his second missionary journey. While we have two letters to the Corinthians in our New Testament, there is evidence that Paul wrote to them on at least two other occasions. Our two letters give an invaluable insight into Paul's life, thought, and feelings. They also give the reader an entry into the struggles of an early Christian community living out its Christian way of life in the context of a culture that promoted very different values. As you read through these letters, you will discover passages that are real gems: for example, the passages on love and on the res-

urrection in 1 Corinthians 13 and 15, respectively, and the autobiographical descriptions of Paul's sufferings as an apostle (2 Cor 11:16-33).

Background Information

Corinth was a city that controlled an isthmus (a narrow four-mile wide strip of land surrounded by water on both sides) connecting the mainland of Greece to the southern Peloponnesian peninsula. Corinth was within walking distance of two ports situated on the Aegean and the Ionian (Adriatic) Seas. Strategically it was very important, as it controlled access between the peninsula and the Greek mainland. At the same time the two ports gave access to the western and eastern parts of the Mediterranean.

Archaeology has shown that Corinth was inhabited for four thousand years. In 146 B.C.E. the Romans destroyed the city. A century later in 44 B.C.E. Julius Caesar rebuilt it as a Roman colony. When Paul first visited (50/51-52 C.E.), Corinth was a very cosmopolitan city with people from throughout the Roman Empire. The Greek gods were worshipped here, as were the Egyptian gods Isis and Serapis. The Isthmian games were held every alternate year (including 51, when Paul was there),

---

Reading Guide to 1 Corinthians

Opening Formula (1:1-3)

Thanksgiving (1:4-9)

Body (1:10–16:18)

    Divisions within the Community (1:10–4:21)

    Problems within the Community and Questions
        from the Community: Lawsuits, Sexual
        Behavior, Food, Eucharist (5:1–11:34)

    Issues Relating to Gifts and Charisms (12:1–
        14:40)

    The Resurrection (15:1-58)

    Information from Paul: Travel Plans and Praise
        for Certain People (16:1-18)

Final Greetings (16:19-24)

---

although they were not as prestigious as the Olympian Games in the eyes of the wider world.

Corinth had acquired a bad reputation in the Mediterranean world as a city of immorality. Some historicans dispute whether this charge was justified, attributing responsibility for ruining Corinth's image to Athens, the cultural center of the ancient world and obviously a rival to Corinth. The Athenian poet Aristophanes used the verb "Corinthianize" as a reference to engaging in sexually licentious activity. Others report that Corinth hosted a thousand priestesses of the goddess Aphrodite (Venus) who were in essence sacred prostitutes. These cultural dimensions of the city could explain many of the challenges that the Christian community of Corinth faced and which Paul addressed in his letters.

1 Corinthians

It is important to begin with a survey of what we know of Paul's contact with Corinth prior to writing 1 Corinthians. A series of texts provide the evidence.

Acts 18:1-17 speaks about Paul's first contact with Corinth in 50/51-52 C.E., when he came there from Athens on his second missionary journey. Paul stayed with the tentmakers Aquila and Priscilla, who had recently come from Rome. According to his custom, he first preached to the Jews, then concentrated his message on the Gentiles. The names mentioned in 1 Cor 16:15-18 (see also Rom 16:21-23) show that the Christian community comprised both Jewish and Gentile converts (probably the Gentile Christians were in the majority). After he had spent 18 months in Corinth, the local Jews brought Paul before the tribune Gallio. However, viewing their accusations as an internal squabble about the Jewish law,

Gallio refused to get involved and released Paul. Paul left Corinth with his companions Aquila and Priscilla.

Acts 18:24-28 notes that between Paul's first and second visits to Corinth a certain Apollos, a Jew from Alexandria, met Priscilla and Aquila, who explained "the Way of God" to him and then sent him off to Corinth. He must have been well received by a certain segment of the Corinthian Christian community because Paul speaks out against the formation of factions among believers there. This was one of the impulses leading Paul to write this letter.

In 1 Cor 5:9 Paul notes that he had already written one letter to Corinth, but this letter has not survived. It deals, as Paul notes, with instructions "not to associate with sexually immoral persons."

In 1:11 (and 11:18) Paul says that while in Ephesus, where he spent three years during his third missionary journey, he has heard news from "Chloe's people" telling of divisions within the Corinthian community.

1 Corinthians 7:1 also notes that the Corinthians had written to Paul with a number of questions. This letter was probably in response to the letter that Paul had already sent them (5:9).

1 Corinthians was written from Ephesus (16:8) around 56/57 to answer the questions that the Corinthians had raised in their letter and to further resolve other issues

Shops lining the marketplace of Corinth. Larger than the Forum at Rome, the *agora* was the glory of Roman Corinth. (Ewing Galloway)

of concern to Paul. Although it is called 1 Corinthians, it is in fact the second letter that Paul wrote them.

A Walk through 1 Corinthians

1 Corinthians 1:1-9:
Opening Formula and Thanksgiving

Paul includes Sosthenes in the opening of this letter. However, the letter clearly presents Paul as the author (4:14). This is probably the same Sosthenes, "the official of the synagogue" (Acts 18:17), who was beaten when Gallio refused to hear Paul's case. Paul's thanksgiving praises God for the grace (Greek *charis*) they have received so that they "are not lacking in any spiritual gift" (1:7).

1 Corinthians 1:10–4:21:
Divisions within the Community

The first issue Paul addresses was one reported to him by Chloe's people (1:11) concerning disunity within the community. Members of the community were giving allegiance to different leaders: "'I belong to Paul,' or 'I belong to Apollos,' or 'I belong to Cephas,' or 'I belong to Christ'" (1:12). For Paul, the problem is that preachers are "God's servants, working together" (3:9). The promotion of human leaders causes disunity within the community and takes away from the role that Christ and God play within the growth of the Christian community, "God's field, God's building" (3:9).

Paul also gives insight into the social composition of the community. Most of the Corinthian Christians were from the lower levels of society: not many were "wise by human standards," powerful, or of noble birth (1:26).

Paul's argument ultimately concerns the lack of understanding regarding his central message, the gospel of the death and resurrection of Jesus Christ (1:18-25). For the world the message of salvation through the cross is a stumbling block and pure foolishness (v. 23), yet for the believer it is "Christ the power of God and the wisdom of God" (v. 24). Paul develops the theme of God's true wisdom in chs. 2–4. His attack on human wisdom is not to be seen as a rejection of human reason. Instead, Paul is countering those Corinthians who assert a special understanding or wisdom that others do not have. This wisdom lays claim to a superiority that further divides the community into those who are well educated ("the wise") and those who are not ("foolish" according to human standards). Contrasted to this human wisdom is the wisdom of God. God's wisdom appears foolishness to humans because God brings salvation through the cross of Jesus. This is the wisdom that Paul preaches in order to lay a solid foundation which is Jesus Christ (3:11).

Paul goes on to stress that believers are God's temple

where, as the Israelites believed, God's spirit dwells (3:16-17). Yet Paul cautions the Corinthians not to be pretentious, ironically contrasting their response to the faith with that of the apostles: "We are fools for the sake of Christ, but you are wise in Christ" (4:10).

1 Corinthians 5:1–11:34:
Problems within the Community and Questions

Turning from the issue of divisions within the community, Paul addresses a number of other concerns specific to this community and which continue to threaten its unity.

Incest (5:1-13)

Paul responds with alarm to the report of a man sexually involved with his stepmother (5:1-13). This is something that would not be accepted even in a pagan community, so much more should it be rejected by a Christian community. Paul had preached the freedom of the believer in Christ, but this did not mean that the Christian no longer had moral laws or could act just as he/she liked. Paul counters with instructions that focus primarily on responsible sexual conduct. When Paul says that this man should be excommunicated, he is concerned with defining the boundaries of the Christian community. Those who do not allow their actions to conform to the faith of the community are to be excluded because, like leaven, their deeds will permeate the entire community and in time destroy it (v. 8).

Lawsuits before Pagan Courts (6:1-11)

Paul continues to define the boundaries of the Christian community. The standards of the Christian community are not to be defined by the pagan world. Hence members are not to turn to pagan courts to settle disputes but rather should settle them among themselves (6:1-8). Paul further distances Christian standards from those of the pagan world through his list of vices that are to be avoided (vv. 9-11).

Sexual Permissiveness (6:12-20)

"All things are lawful for me" (6:12) is a slogan the Corinthian Christians use to justify their behavior, arguing for total sexual freedom. Paul counters that "not all things are beneficial." One must ensure that choices made do not result in becoming slaves to what has been chosen. To give free expression to sexual impulses is not true freedom: instead it results in becoming enslaved by lusts and desires. From a theological perspective, Paul sees every Christian as part of the body of Christ (v. 15) and a temple of the Holy Spirit (v. 19). Since intercourse involves a union between two partners, intercourse with a prostitute destroys the union that already exists between a believer and Christ.

Directions concerning Marriage (7:1-40)

Paul turns from matters Chloe's people had raised to reply to questions posed by the letter the Corinthians had written him (7:1). In what follows Paul uses the phrase "now concerning" as a way of introducing his response to a new issue (7:1, 25; 8:1; 12:1; 16:1, 12). The first topic Paul addresses is marital relationships. In the previous section he reacted against a moral philosophy, libertinism (6:12-20), which held that ethically one could act however one liked: everything was permissible! Now Paul addresses exactly the opposite moral position, asceticism, which held that every form of bodily pleasure or happiness should be avoided. It seems that in Corinth some married Christians had adopted a sexual asceticism by rejecting sexual intercourse with their spouse.

Paul's teaching here must also be understood against the background of his apocalyptic eschatology, namely his belief that the end of the world was imminent ("the appointed time has grown short," 7:29). Because Paul believes that Jesus is to return soon and that the world will come to an end, he concludes logically that people should retain their current status: whether Jew or Greek (vv. 17-20), slave or free (vv. 21-24), married or unmarried (vv. 25-35).

Starting with the Corinthians' statement that "It is well for a man not to touch a woman" (v. 1), Paul proceeds to examine the implications. While abstinence from sexual relations may be considered a good thing, Paul gives two situations where it is important to have sexual relations. Within the context of marriage, abstinence could lead to the lack of self-control and the seeking of sex outside of marriage (vv. 2-7). Further, Paul says those who are single ("the unmarried and the widows," v. 8) and cannot practice self-control should marry even though he would like everyone to be as he is, namely single and practicing abstinence (vv. 8-9).

Turning to those who are married, Paul considers the issue of divorce. He begins by referring to the command regarding divorce and remarriage (vv. 10-11). While Jesus had in mind the context of Judaism where the two partners were Jewish, Paul has in mind the Greco-Roman world and the situation where one of the partners is not a believer and wishes to separate. Clearly Paul has no command from the Lord (v. 12) in this regard, so he gives his own instructions that allow the "unbelieving" partner to separate (or divorce) in this context (vv. 12-16).

In the rest of the chapter (vv. 17-40) Paul shows how his worldview is dominated by an apocalyptic eschatology that determines his ethical instructions. His basic teaching is that everyone should remain in the state in which they are now because the end of the world is soon approaching (v. 31).

Ethical Context of Corinth

Both extremes of libertinism and asceticism referred to in this letter reflect the moral context of Corinthian society. As we have noted, many Corinthians indulged in sexual libertinism through enjoying the services of the thousand prostitutes in the religious temples. Others had adopted the opposite perspective of asceticism by refusing all forms of sexual pleasure. This dual approach of libertinism and asceticism reflects a larger number of philosophical streams evident in Greek society at that time and in particular that of Corinth. Among these was an early form of Gnosticism, a type of proto-Gnosticism. In the writings of Paul we see aspects that would become central issues in later Gnosticism. For example, one's true nature is not at home in the material world, which is considered evil: hence a driving force in moral action would be rejection of the world and its pleasures. We also note the importance that Paul attributes to the concept of wisdom *(gnosis),* which he discusses in chs. 1-2. Further, a strong debate had been raging for more than a century between Cynic and Stoic philosophers over the place of marriage within society. The Cynics rejected marriage, while the Stoics looked upon marriage as one of the stable and necessary dimensions of civic life.

Further support for the influence of these philosophers on Paul's thought comes from his style of argumentation. When Paul says, "It is well for a man not to touch a woman" (7:1), he is in effect arguing as did the Cynics, namely making a statement and then proceeding to discuss or examine it. This pattern of argumentation is called a diatribe.

Eating Meat Sacrificed to Idols (8:1-13; 10:23–11:1)

One of the challenges facing the early Christians was how they interacted with the pagan society in which they lived. The issue that Paul debates here, namely eating meat sacrificed to idols, was certainly problematic. Meat sold in the marketplace often came from sacrifices that had been offered in the pagan temples. Such meat would have been forbidden in the context of the Israelite tradition, and the decision of the Jerusalem Council (Acts 15:29) included it among its brief list of things Gentile Christians should avoid. What were Christians to do if invited to a pagan friend's house for a meal and the meat came from the marketplace? Could they accept an invitation to a banquet held at a pagan temple where the meat had recently been sacrificed? These are practical issues of concern to the Corinthian Christians.

Paul's answer rests upon the firm belief that since only one God exists and the pagan gods do not, the whole question about meat offered to idols is really a

Equality in the Roles of Men and Women

Paul's thought is often criticized for being patriarchal in the sense that he views the world solely from the male perspective and that the woman's role was always subservient to that of the man. Without doubt Paul was living in a male-dominated society and was very much a product of his time. However, it is worth noting the equality to which Paul gives expression when he does discuss the roles of men and women within this chapter.

	Men		Women
7:2	Each man should have his own wife		Each woman her own husband
7:3	The husband should give to his wife her conjugal rights		Likewise the wife to her husband
7:4	Likewise the husband does not have authority over his own body, but the wife does		For the wife does not have authority over her own body, but the husband does
7:5	Do not deprive one another except perhaps by agreement for a set time		Do not deprive one another except perhaps by agreement for a set time
7:11	The husband should not divorce his wife	7:10	The wife should not separate from her husband
7:12	If any believer has a wife who is an unbeliever, and she consents to live with him, he should not divorce her	7:13	If any woman has a husband who is an unbeliever, and he consents to live with her, she should not divorce him
7:14	For the unbelieving husband is made holy through his wife		The unbelieving wife is made holy through her husband
7:15	But if the unbelieving partner separates, let it be so; in such a case the brother or sister is not bound		But if the unbelieving partner separates, let it be so; in such a case the brother or sister is not bound
7:16	Husband, for all you know, you might save your wife		Wife, for all you know, you might save your husband
7:32-33	The unmarried man is anxious about the affairs of the Lord, how to please the Lord; but the married man is anxious about the affairs of the world, how to please his wife	7:34	The unmarried woman and the virgin are anxious about the affairs of the Lord, so that they may be holy in body and spirit; but the married woman is anxious about the affairs of the world, how to please her husband

nonissue. Yet out of respect for the conscience of others it might be necessary to refrain from eating such meat (10:28). This decision follows logically from Paul's opening words: "We know that 'all of us possess knowledge.' Knowledge puffs up, but love builds up" (8:1). While knowledge may be correct, it can also make one feel superior. Knowledge should always defer to love: in other words, one's freedom should be restricted out of concern or love for a fellow member of the Christian body. Paul generalizes this position when concluding this discussion: "So whether you eat or drink, or whatever you do, do everything for the glory of God. Give no offense to Jews or to Greeks or to the church of God, just as I try to please everyone in everything I do, not seeking my own advantage, but that of many, so that they may be saved" (10:31-33). While the issue of eating meat sacrificed to

idols is not one that Christians struggle with today, nevertheless concern for the conscience of another should always be an issue to which Christians give attention.

Paul Defends His Role as an Apostle (9:1-27)

This is one of the gems of this letter. Paul defends his right to be considered an apostle: "Have I not seen Jesus our Lord? Are you not my work in the Lord?" (9:1). In other words, experiencing the risen Christ and carrying out his missionary command are the two hallmarks of an apostle.

Paul provides insight into the life of an apostle in the early church. Apostles were supported by the communities they established and among whom they worked (vv. 4-5). They might also be accompanied by a wife (and children) whom the communities would support. But while Paul upholds an apostle's right to this support (vv. 8-12), neither he nor Barnabas used it. Instead, Paul supported himself through his work as a tentmaker. In this way others could not attribute false motives to his actions (e.g., accusing him of preaching for the sake of making money). Paul offers a wonderful insight into his heart and motivations: "I have become all things to all people, that I might by all means save some. I do it all for the sake of the gospel, so that I may share in its blessings" (vv. 22-23). Finally, he employs images taken from athletics (vv. 24-27), drawing on the Isthmian games held at Corinth every two years in order to illustrate how he himself has struggled and worked tirelessly as a missionary in order to bring the Corinthians to Christ.

Community Worship (10:1–11:34)

Paul sheds light on a number of aspects of worship in this early Christian community. His understanding of the effects of celebrating the eucharistic meal is that those who participate in this liturgy become one body with Christ (10:17). Therefore, one cannot share in the sacrifice to pagan idols because it is in effect a sharing with demons (v. 20). A Christian cannot participate both in sacrifices to idols (demons) and in the table of the Lord (v. 21).

In 11:1-16 Paul deals with an issue that reflects his 1st-century cultural context, whether one should cover the head when praying. This was an intensely debated issue in the Greek and Roman worlds. Arguing that women should cover their heads, Paul uses the creation story to present a social hierarchy: God is the head of Christ, Christ the head of man, and man the head of woman (v. 3). From this Paul deduces that the man is the image of God, hence his head should not be covered, whereas the woman is the image of man, so she should have hers covered. It is difficult for us to understand the logic in this argument. It seems as though Paul himself was not convinced of his logic, because he ends by saying: If you want to continue discussing this point, forget it: our custom here in the Corinthian churches is the same as in all the other Christian centers and we will not deviate from it (v. 16). Ultimately, Paul retreats to an argument from authority!

Finally, Paul considers the celebration of the Lord's Supper, or Eucharist (11:17-34). He is unhappy with what is happening in Corinth. Just as Jesus celebrated the gift of his body and his blood in the context of a meal, so the Corinthians continue to celebrate a meal then followed by a remembrance of what Jesus did at that Last Supper (vv. 24-26). However, at these observances the wealthy are eating and drinking to their hearts' content while the poor eat nothing (v. 21). For Paul, the celebration of the Lord's Supper is meant to be a celebration of the unity of the community, not a cause for division. In effect Paul's solution is: "Stay at home if you want to eat and drink!" This is one of the first indications of a separation between an ordinary meal and the sacred meal of the Eucharist.

What is invaluable in this discussion is Paul's description of the eucharistic narrative that was recited in celebrating the meal. This is the earliest document that we have regarding the institution of the Eucharist by Jesus. While Paul's letter is dated to around 57 C.E., the tradition behind it is obviously more ancient because Paul is simply quoting what has been handed on to him (11:23). While the Gospel records also rely upon traditions that have been handed on to them, all date from the late 60s and later.

1 Corinthians 12:1–14:40: Gifts and Charisms

Chapters 12 and 14 focus on the issue of charisms, while ch. 13 appears to interrupt the discussion with a beautiful hymn on love. We shall discuss this hymn in below in "Theological Themes in 1 Corinthians." The Corinthian church has experienced an ecstatic abundance of religious phenomena, identified as gifts of the Spirit or charisms: utterances of wisdom and knowledge, faith, gifts of healing, working of miracles, prophecy, discernment of spirits, speaking in tongues, and the interpretation of tongues (12:8-10). Similar expressions of religious enthusiasm were well known in the Hellenistic religious world. Paul stresses that the Corinthians should never forget the purpose of these gifts, namely for building up the community, the body of Christ ("for the common good," v. 7). His use of the image of a body to describe the relationship among the members of the Christian communities and Christ is one of the theological gems of this letter. In the Greco-Roman world it was common to compare the state to a human body (see Livy, *From the Founding of the City,* 2.32:9-12). For Paul this image stresses the unity, equality, and importance of every member of the community.

In ch. 14 Paul restricts his attention to two gifts with which the Corinthians had become enamored, speaking in tongues and prophecy. Speaking in tongues *(glossolalia)* refers to the experience of speaking in an ecstatic way with words that are unintelligible both to the person speaking and to those present. This is not to be confused with the event of Pentecost, where the Holy Spirit descended on the apostles and everyone present could understand because they heard in their own language. Examples of ecstatic speech are known from the wider Greco-Roman world, especially among the mystery religions. Paul reminds his hearers/readers that, while he speaks more than any of them in the gift of tongues, yet "in church I would rather speak five words with my mind, in order to instruct others also, than ten thousand words in a tongue" (vv. 19).

1 Corinthians 15:1-58: The Resurrection

The resurrection of the dead is a further issue dividing the community. Paul asks quite bluntly: "How can some of you say there is no resurrection of the dead?" (15:12). The very proof for resurrection is evidenced from the fact that Christ has been raised from the dead, based on the testimony of eyewitnesses: Peter, James, the Twelve, the apostles, five hundred brothers, and even Paul himself. Paul in effect says: "If you want proof of the risen Christ, these individuals will testify because they have seen Jesus Christ alive" (vv. 3-9). Just as with Paul's treatment on the Eucharist (11:23-26), so here Paul relies upon traditional material that has come down to him.

Paul then draws out the implications of Jesus' resurrection for the lives of Christians. Believers will also share in the resurrection in the future age. This discussion is prompted by the 1st-century cultural and social context. The Greek philosopher Plato taught that the body was the prison house of the soul, implying that the purpose of existence in this material world was to liberate the soul from the prison of the body. Consequently, for the Greeks the notion of a body living on after death would appear to be a contradiction. Paul grounds the Christian belief on the resurrection of Jesus himself (v. 12). This belief affects Christians in two ways: first, the Christian who has been baptized into Christ has been baptized into his death and resurrection. In other words, the believer already participates in the resurrection of Jesus: it influences him/her in the present.

But Jesus' resurrection also has an influence on the future: it guarantees that all Christians are to be raised from the dead (vv. 20-34). Jesus is the first fruits of those who have died (v. 20), but after him come all who belong to Christ (v. 23). Paul uses the image of Adam to show how Christ influences humanity. Just as the sin of one man, Adam, brought sin into the world and affected every human being, so too Jesus' death and resurrection affect all humanity.

A further question concerns the Corinthians: "With what type of body will I rise?" (v. 35). When arguing for the resurrection of the dead, Paul had been taking on the Greco-Roman world. Now he turns his attention to Jewish/Hebrew objections and stresses the transformation that occurs in the resurrected body. Paul teaches that in the resurrection of the dead a transforming power adapts the body to suit the new world in which it finds itself (vv. 35-58). Using the analogy of a seed being sown in the ground, Paul shows how a seed has to die in order to burst forth as a new plant. So with the Christian: he/she dies, and what is corruptible is sown in the ground only to spring forth through the power of the risen Christ into something new (vv. 42-49). The physical body is transformed into a spiritual body. Paul can only describe this spiritual body by saying what it is not. In closing his treatment on the resurrection, Paul stresses that death has now lost its sting because of Jesus' victory over death (vv. 54-57).

1 Corinthians 16:1-18: Information from Paul

Paul concludes the body of the letter with a reference to the collection that he wants taken up for the poor in Jerusalem (16:1-4) and a discussion of his future travel plans (vv. 5-12). He also offers praise for various people.

1 Corinthians 16:19-24: Final Greetings

Paul's final greetings are typical of all his correspondence. He sends greetings from the churches and people around him. He mentions Aquila and Prisca (Priscilla) who are now in Ephesus, but who had previously been associated with him in Corinth (Acts 18:2). Paul takes up the pen himself and writes a final prayer that had become standard in the time of the Jesus movement in Palestine: "Our Lord, come! (16:22), *Marana tha* in Aramaic (see Rev 22:20).

Critical Issues in Studying 1 Corinthians

Unity and Integrity of the Letter

One of the common disputes in studying Paul's letters concerns whether they are a compilation of a number of letters or whether they were originally a unity. The question is further posed regarding whether some passages had been added at a later stage (integrity). Our position is that the unity and integrity of each of Paul's letters should be presumed. Too often resort is made to hypotheses that destroy the unity because certain things do not conform to the preconceived ideas of the scholar! In this study of 1 Corinthians we have treated the letter as a unity and find no reason to presume that passages were added later, thus destroying its integrity.

There are three places where some scholars argue for the insertion of passages into the text in the course of transmission of this letter:

Chapters 9 and 10 are seen to break the discussion on meat offered to idols that commences in 8:1-13 and then continues in 10:23–11:1. While it is true that the sequence of thought is interrupted with Paul's discussion on his role as an apostle, this does not mean that his thought should always be judged to be as consistent as a reader of the 21st century would demand. There is no reason why in the course of writing a letter, Paul would not digress and return to a topic later. This would

The Resurrected Body (15:46-49)

Physical body	Spiritual Body
Perishable	Imperishable
Weakness	Power
Physical	Spiritual
Image of man of earth	Image of man of heaven

be particularly the case if Paul were dictating to a scribe, a procedure especially evident in 1 Corinthians. In his discussion on the divisions in the church in 1:10-17, Paul says he is glad that he has not baptized anyone in the Corinthian community so that no one can claim allegiance to him on that basis and split the community (vv. 14-15). Then he suddenly remembers that there was in fact someone else whom he had baptized, so he adds as an afterthought: "I did baptize also the household of Stephanas; beyond that, I do not know whether I baptized anyone else" (v. 16). One can almost imagine Paul walking up and down dictating this letter, then suddenly remembering something and needing to correct it. In v. 17 he then returns to his argument: "For Christ did not send me to baptize."

Some scholars also see Paul's discussion on love in ch. 13 as a later insertion into the text because it interrupts the instruction on spiritual gifts. However, Paul presents love as the greatest of the gifts, and he does mention a number of other gifts in this short chapter (faith, tongues, and prophecy). There is no reason to exclude it from Paul's original letter because it undoubtedly adds to the focus on gifts and helps to put them into a context.

Finally, many scholars view 14:34-36 as a later insertion into the text. The arguments here are weightier than for the other passages indicated. This passage speaks about a woman's place in public worship, contending that women should not speak in such a context (vv. 34-35). Some scholars argue that this passage was inserted later to restrict the role of women in liturgical celebrations. Modern social scientists draw attention to the strict division within ancient society between public and private space. A man's space was in the public arena, while a woman's was the home, the private space. A further argument is that this passage interrupts the flow of thought and contradicts what Paul had instructed earlier when he acknowledged that women do in fact pray and prophesy in the Corinthian church (11:5). Nevertheless, we think it is still arbitrary to exclude this passage on the basis of a preconceived idea that at the end of the 1st century a change took place in public Christian worship restricting a woman's role. It seems more likely that the customs of society were at play right from the beginning in early Christian worship whereby the public

and private roles of men and women were respected and upheld, particularly in the Greco-Roman communities.

Our main argument against later insertions comes from the state of the Greek text itself. There is no evidence that these passages were ever challenged in any of the earliest manuscripts we possess. All these passages are found in the location that we have them today. When ancient manuscripts witness to the omission of certain passages (such as the different witnesses to the ending of the Gospel of Mark or the account of the woman caught in adultery in John 8:1-11), we have every right to conclude that these passages are from a later date. Until such textual evidence is produced, it is best to remain with the established text at hand.

Baptism on Behalf of the Dead

A real puzzle emerges when Paul briefly mentions a custom of accepting baptism on behalf of the dead (15:29). Explanations of this single verse are legion. It is a good reminder that our knowledge of the early Christian community is limited. The written record deals with controversial issues in the community. Paul does not mention customs that were generally agreed upon, even though they may have been central to the life and worship of the community. Rather than offer a conjecture, it is best simply to acknowledge that we do not know.

Theological Themes in 1 Corinthians

Sexuality

Paul's teaching regarding sexuality must be understood against the cultural background of the world in which he is preaching and teaching. Paul tries to weave a straight path between two excesses that were particularly noteworthy in 1st-century C.E. Hellenistic society. On one side were those (such as the proto-Gnostics) who argued that since only the spiritual nature of the human being was important, it did not matter what one did with one's body. On this philosophical basis, they argued for total sexual freedom. On the other side were those (the ascetics) who argued that every form of sexual expression was evil and must be totally rejected. Paul does not want to fall into either extreme.

What emerges strikingly from our walk through the letter is the equality that Paul stresses between man and woman in marriage. Our examination of ch. 7 draws attention to the way Paul shows that what is attributable to the man in marriage is likewise attributable to the woman. It is certainly a high point in a reflection on marriage.

Paul's ethical teaching on sexuality is guided by his principle that the place for the expression of sexuality is in the context of marriage: "To the unmarried and the widows I say that it is well for them to remain unmarried as I am. But if they are not practicing self-control, they should marry. For it is better to marry than to be aflame with passion" (7:8-9). Paul is firmly convinced that the end of the world and the return of Christ are to occur soon and so advises that it is better for people to remain as they are. This advice is given not to place a burden on his community, but rather to help them be free from anxiety in preparing for the coming of the Lord (7:32-33).

Paul's reference to sexual relations between males occurs in the context of a catalog of vices: "Do you not know that wrongdoers will not inherit the kingdom of God? Do not be deceived! Fornicators, idolaters, adulterers, male prostitutes, sodomites, thieves, the greedy, drunkards, revilers, robbers — none of these will inherit the kingdom of God" (6:9-10). Three terms here have a sexual reference: fornicators, male prostitutes, sodomites. It is important to recognize that Paul wrote in Greek and that it is sometimes difficult to capture the exact meaning of words when translated into another language. We must also understand these words in the context of Paul's world as well as how he used them in the context of his letter. "Fornicators" translates Greek *pornoi.* Later in this chapter Paul condemns "fornication" (*porneia,* v. 18). By this he intends indulging in sexual relations with prostitutes, particularly the famous sacred temple prostitutes in Corinth. This is not the only practice that Paul condemns. In 5:1 he speaks about "sexual immorality" *(porneia,)* referring here to incest: the man who was having sexual relations with his stepmother. Applying all this to 6:9, what Paul has in mind with his reference to "fornicators" *(pornoi)* is a condemnation of all who engage in egregious sexual immorality, although he does not clearly define what that entails.

The next two words Paul uses are more difficult to describe: "male prostitutes" and "sodomites" (NRSV; Greek *malakoi* and *arsenokoitai,* respectively). Greek *malakoi* (lit., "soft") refers to those who are effeminate. In Greco-Roman usage this was a technical term for those boys or male slaves who played the feminine role in a sexual relation with an adult male. Greco-Roman society saw nothing shameful about an adult male having sexual relations with a male youth. While the NRSV translation ("male prostitutes") may capture an aspect of this word, much more is intended here. It shows that Paul is distancing himself from contemporary culture by condemning an activity that embraces either pederasty or male prostitution.

Greek *arsenokoitai* (lit., "those who go to bed with males") is a much more definite word. It harks back to the prohibition of Lev 18:22: "You shall not lie with a male as with a woman" (see also 20:13). Paul refers to

this activity again at the beginning of the Letter to the Romans: "Men committed shameless acts with men and received in their own persons the due penalty for their error" (Rom 1:27). From this discussion it appears that Paul rejects both pederasty and sexual relationships between people of the same sex (male with male, female with female).

The question arises as to how to understand this in today's society. It is important to note that Paul can only speak from his own context. The terms "homosexual" or "homosexuality" are modern words never used by Paul or in his world. Our modern knowledge of human psychology, biology, and the like has progressed vastly since Paul's time. Consequently, it is not possible simply to transpose what Paul says in the 1st-century context (where he is addressing very specific issues) to a vastly different 21st-century world in which different issues are at play. Needless to say, Paul's teaching on this issue has provoked much study and discussion.

Love

Chapter 13, often described as "a hymn to love," contains one of the most beautiful descriptions of love in the entire Bible. Paul's hymn falls into three stanzas. In the first (13:1-3), he situates his discussion within the context of the gifts of the Spirit. For Paul, love is essentially a gift, the greatest of the gifts (v. 13). In the second stanza (vv. 4-8a), he personifies love and describes it in terms of the present, of what it does: "Love is patient; love is kind; love is not envious. . . . Love never ends." The Hebrew mind operates in terms of concrete action, whereas the Greek mind is more abstract, describing the essence of things. Paul does not describe love in abstract, philosophical terms, but rather uses numerous verbs in a decidedly concrete Hebrew way to provide images that evoke action. In the final stanza (vv. 8b-13), he contrasts the present with the future in order to show that while all things will pass away, "faith, hope, and love abide, these three; and the greatest of these is love" (v. 13).

Paul's understanding of love can be seen from an examination of the Greek word *agape.* While English has only one word for "love," Greek has three *(philia, eros, agape),* each with a specific nuance. *Philia* refers to "brotherly love, or friendship" and captures the bonds that exist among humans. *Eros* connotes the "ardent desire or fondness for something" and implies the movement from myself to another viewed as the object of my love. Finally, *agape* indicates the bestowing of love on another. God is the supreme example of *agape* love because God's love aims at communicating something outside of God and is not looking to receive anything in return. While *eros* is concerned with the reception of love from another, *agape* wishes to communicate love.

The noun *agape* was seldom used in classical Greek literature; it seems that the early Christians chose that noun precisely because of its infrequent usage so that they could describe the unique concept of love that Jesus taught. Every tradition of early Christianity stresses this concept of *agape* love. Paul himself captures the selfless notion of *agape* love later when he says: "God proves his love for us in that while we still were sinners Christ died for us" (Rom 5:8).

The Cross and Resurrection

At the beginning of 1 Corinthians Paul shows that the theological foundation for his faith and message rests on Jesus' death and resurrection. He is unashamed of this message, which clearly defines the faith of Jesus' followers and separates them from Jews and Gentiles: "For the message about the cross is foolishness to those who are perishing, but to us who are being saved it is the power of God" (1:18). While Jews rely on the power of signs to convince and Gentiles on the power of wisdom, Jesus' followers rely upon the cross (vv. 22-25).

At the end of the letter Paul returns to the centrality of resurrection for his message. Chapter 15 is one of the most powerful testimonies to belief in the resurrection: "If Christ has not been raised, then our proclamation has been in vain and your faith has been in vain" (v. 14). Paul is not content with simply stressing the belief that Jesus is risen; he wishes to show that this belief brings both present and future consequences for the believer. He explains the resurrected body through the analogy of a seed that needs to die in order to become a tree or plant. Paul's is the first attempt to develop a "theology of the resurrection" that speaks to Jews and Gentiles alike. This will be imitated by Christians throughout the centuries as they try to communicate the meaning of the resurrection for their own situation.

2 Corinthians

Paul's Contact with Corinth between 1 and 2 Corinthians

While in Ephesus, Paul wrote 1 Corinthians in 56/57 C.E. In early 57 Timothy came to Corinth (Acts 19:21-22) after Paul's letter had arrived and found that the situation had deteriorated. He returned to Paul in Ephesus to report the situation.

Paul then makes a quick, "painful visit" (2:1) to Corinth. This is Paul's second visit to Corinth (the first was when he established the church in his second mis-

---

> ### Reading Guide to 2 Corinthians
>
> **Opening Formula** (1:1-2)
>
> **Thanksgiving** (1:3-11)
>
> **Body** (1:12–13:10)
>   The Crisis between Paul and the Corinthians (1:12–7:16)
>   The Collection for Jerusalem (8:1–9:15)
>   Paul Defends His Apostolic Authority (10:1–13:10)
>
> **Final Greetings** (13:11-13)

sionary journey (Acts 18:1-17). Someone causes Paul pain (2:5-11), so Paul leaves and returns to Ephesus.

In Ephesus Paul writes another letter to Corinth which he describes as written "out of much distress and anguish of heart and with many tears" (2:4). This letter (the third that Paul wrote them) has been lost. Titus brings this letter to Corinth (7:6-8).

Paul leaves Ephesus and crosses over into Macedonia, staying perhaps at Philippi. In late 57 Titus returns to Paul in Macedonia (7:6) with the good news that the Corinthians have changed their attitude and are sorry for causing him distress (vv. 9-15).

Paul immediately writes to the Corinthians to share his joy at the change in relationship. This is our 2 Corinthians (Paul's fourth letter to them). He sends it again with Titus and two other "brothers" (8:16-24).

Paul again visits Corinth (his third visit; see 12:14; 13:1-2). He returns home on his third missionary journey, taking with him the collection for the poor in Jerusalem.

A Walk through 2 Corinthians

2 Corinthians 1:1-11:
Opening Formula and Thanksgiving

Paul again uses the traditional Greco-Roman format of a letter. Here he extends the opening formula to include a wider audience: "To the church of God that is in Corinth, including all the saints throughout Achaia" (1:1). In his thanksgiving Paul speaks about the hardships he has endured in Asia, probably in Ephesus where he spent three years (vv. 8-9).

2 Corinthians 1:12-7:16:
The Crisis between Paul and the Corinthians

Paul's Previous Relationship with Corinth (1:12–2:13)
Paul had visited Corinth and planned to return (1:16). His visit from Ephesus turned out to be a "painful visit" (2:1). So, Paul decides not to return as the visit would be

fruitless and would probably result in creating more tensions. Instead, he writes a letter "out of much distress and anguish of heart" (v. 4). The cause of many of the problems in Corinth stem from an unnamed individual. Inspired by Paul's letter, the Corinthians change their attitude and punish the person who caused Paul so much heartache. Paul shifts from demanding justice to extending mercy to the one who has offended him (v. 7). This gives insight into Paul's pastoral approach, where he balances the demands of justice with mercy. After leaving Ephesus in 57, Paul goes to Troas where he has great success in preaching the Gospel message (v. 12).

The *bema,* a platform for public oration and the administration of justice, in the *agora* at Corinth. Constructed in 44 c.e., it is likely the place where Paul was brought before the tribune Gallio. (Phoenix Data Systems, Neal and Joel Bierling)

Paul's Ministry (2:14–7:16)

Paul defends his ministry against his opponents. He needs no letter of recommendation, since the Corinthians are his "letter" testifying to his ministry among them (3:2). Paul contrasts his work with that of Moses (3:12-18). While Moses put a veil over his face when he spoke with the Israelites, Paul argues that when one turns to the Lord the veil is uncovered because the Spirit is at work revealing the Scriptures (3:16-17). The Gospel he preaches is unveiled except for those whose eyes have been blinded by the powers of darkness of this world (4:3-4). Paul always attributes his success to God, not to himself (4:7). In his life Paul reflects the ministry of Jesus, "always carrying in the body the death of Jesus, so that the life of Jesus may also be made visible in our bodies" (4:10).

2 Corinthians 4:16–5:10 is a beautiful celebration of what it is to live by faith, not by sight (5:7). Paul does not lose heart because the future life is far more glorious than the present. The Spirit is the guarantee of what is to come. Paul sees his life and ministry as accountable to the Lord (5:10) and so is not afraid because he knows that the Lord is aware of his sincerity and integrity. In 5:16-21 Paul shows the depths of his insight into the nature of ministry. Jesus' mission was one of reconciliation, and he has given to Paul the task of continuing that same ministry of reconciliation (5:18-19). Paul describes his work as a sharing in that of Christ (6:1), and he urges the Corinthians to allow God's grace to bear fruit among them. In describing his ministry (6:4-10) Paul recounts the hardships he has endured in carrying out that task.

Just as Paul has opened up his heart to them, he begs the Corinthians to open their hearts to him (6:11-13).

In 6:14–7:1, which appears to be a digression in Paul's train of thought, he shows that the problems of concern to him have not been fully resolved in Corinth. Paul reminds the Corinthians that as a community they are "the temple of the living God" (6:16); they live in a relationship with God as their Father and are God's sons and daughters (v. 18). This identity should separate them from the pagan world of idols. The closing paragraph (7:5-16) abounds with the vocabulary of joy and rejoicing: "not because you were grieved, but because your grief led to repentance" (v. 9).

2 Corinthians 8:1–9:15: The Collection for Jerusalem

In these two chapters Paul organizes the collection for the poor of Jerusalem. Here he imitates the custom of the Jews in the Diaspora who used to send an annual temple tax to Jerusalem. Paul holds up the Macedonians as examples of generous giving for the Corinthians to imitate (8:1-5) as well as Jesus Christ: "though he was rich, yet for your sakes he became poor, so that by his poverty you might become rich" (8:9). In ch. 9 Paul extends his appeal to include the Christians of the whole province of Achaia (of which Corinth is capital). Chiding them to honor their pledge to contribute, he tells them that when he was speaking about the collection in

Macedonia he had held them up as examples of generosity (9:1-5). Paul provides a theological and scriptural justification for his appeal for money (vv. 6-15). This passage is among the most memorable in the letter and reflects Jesus' teaching on the use of talents. "God loves a cheerful giver" (v. 7) has become a proverb. God gives generously to the believer, so believers in turn must imitate God in their actions. By showing concern for the poor, they reflect God's generosity (v. 13).

2 Corinthians 10:1–13:10: Paul Defends His Apostolic Authority

Paul's tone changes dramatically. The previous two chapters were optimistic about the response of the Corinthians to his request for help with the collection. Now Paul shows uncertainty as he speaks of his impending third visit. In ch. 10 he defends his apostolic authority and argues against the accusations made by those who were opposed to him. Paul's intent is to exercise his ministry in a way that builds up and does not destroy (10:8). He refers to those who are undermining his teaching and ministry as "false apostles" (11:13).

In order to defend himself, Paul indulges in some boasting which he would rather not do (11:16-21). This boasting concerns what the Lord has done through him. He offers an extensive description of his apostolic ministry and the trials and hardships he has had to endure (vv. 21-33). This testimony provides insight into Paul's feelings, weaknesses, and strengths. He reports that he has been imprisoned, flogged, stoned, shipwrecked, hungry, thirsty, without food, cold, and naked (vv. 23-29)—all of which he has endured for the sake of spreading the gospel among the churches. Paul makes a second boast about the visions and revelations he has experienced from the Lord (12:1-7). This testimony shows that he was a mystic with an intimate relationship with the Lord. In order that Paul might not become proud in these experiences, the Lord has given him "a thorn . . . in the flesh" (12:7). What exactly this suffering entails we do not know, but Paul sees it as a reminder of his own humanity and vulnerability. In his suffering, Paul recognizes the power and strength of God ("My grace is sufficient for you, for power is made perfect in weakness"; v. 9), and this leads him to acknowledge that "whenever I am weak, then I am strong" (v. 10).

2 Corinthians 13:11-13: Final Greetings

Paul concludes the letter in his usual abrupt way. He reasserts his desire that they listen to his words and change their way of life, and he prays that they will live together in peace and overcome their divisions. His final Trinitarian blessing is the most extensive that Paul ever wrote and continues to be used in Christian liturgies today: "The grace of the Lord Jesus Christ, the love of God, and the communion of the Holy Spirit be with all of you" (13:13).

Critical Issues in Studying 2 Corinthians

Unity and Integrity of the Letter

Of all Paul's letters, 2 Corinthians is the one whose unity scholars have questioned the most. This has resulted in hypotheses that view 2 Corinthians as a compendium of between two and five separate letters! As mentioned in the study of 1 Corinthians, suggestions that view Paul's letters as sewing together a number of independent letters should not be made too quickly. Only when strong arguments favor such a theory should one have recourse to it. The discussion is very complex and so many different solutions have been proposed that it is impossible (and also confusing) to address all of them. We therefore refer to only one section in the letter for which strong arguments contend that it derives from independent letters, namely chs. 10–13.

Paul's tone changes dramatically when he begins ch. 10. The news that Titus reported to Paul (7:5-7) was such that it appeared that all the problems between Paul and Corinth had been resolved. However, in these four chapters Paul adopts a harsh tone and his opponents continue to criticize him. Of the many explanations accounting for this change in tone, we shall mention two. One views chs. 10–13 as part of another letter, independent from 2 Corinthians, written in another context and added to the ending of 2 Corinthians. After Paul wrote chs. 1–9, new difficulties arose with the arrival of the "super-apostles" in Corinth undermining Paul's teaching and so he was forced to write this letter to reestablish both his teaching and his authority.

A second suggestion contends that these chapters were originally part of the same letter as chs. 1–9. At the end of ch. 7 Paul had concluded the issues regarding those who had openly defied his authority and had embarrassed him. They had been dealt with by the Corinthians, and Paul was happy with the outcome. Beginning with ch. 10 Paul now faced a widening problem concerning those whom he calls the super-apostles (11:5). While Paul had resolved the previous issue, he now needed to focus on this group and to draw the attention of the Corinthian Christians to them.

Paul's transitions from one section to another do not always flow smoothly; perhaps it is better to say that he tends to jump from one theme or thought to another rather quickly. Consequently, it becomes somewhat arbitrary to argue that a change in tone is an indicator for the existence of an earlier letter. In support of the unity

Paul and the Super-Apostles

Super-Apostles	Paul
Hebrews, Israelites, descendants of Abraham	Hebrew, Israelite, descendant of Abraham (11:22)
Ministers of Christ	Minister of Christ (11:23)
Great powers	Worked signs, wonders, and miracles in Corinth (12:11-12)
Spiritual experiences	Taken up to the third heaven, sees things about which he cannot speak (12:1-4)
Build on Paul's foundation	Builds upon no one (10:15)
No endurance of suffering or persecution	Testifies to enduring suffering and persecution (11:23-29)
Supported by Corinthians	Accepts no money for himself from Corinth (12:16-18)
Need letters of recommendation	Needs no such letters: the Corinthians are his letter of recommendation (3:1-2)

of 2 Corinthians and these two sections, one can point to similarities in the way Paul describes his opponents and the super-apostles. In the end, arguments favoring the unity of this writing seem to be the strongest, and consequently there is no need to resort to hypotheses.

While the issue about the integrity and unity of 2 Corinthians continues to intrigue scholars, in the final analysis what is important for most readers is to understand what Paul intends to communicate. Generally speaking, the reader views shifts in tone as stemming from Paul's change in subject matter and the different strategies of rhetoric that he uses to communicate his thought.

Who Are the Super-Apostles?

While it is difficult to identify precisely the "super-apostles" (11:5; 12:11), it is possible to characterize them generally from Paul's description in chs. 10–13. They were Jewish Christians who had recently come to Corinth and boasted about their great powers.

The super-apostles were like other groups opposed to Paul, such as the Judaizers of Phil 3:2-11. They endeavored to undermine Paul's ministry both in what he did and what he taught. Further, they were a group who showed that they were in awe of their positions of power. In many ways this opposition was fortuitous since it gave Paul the opportunity to reflect more fully on the central tenets of his belief. Without opposition to the resurrection of Jesus, to the Eucharist, and to his ministry, we would never have obtained Paul's reflections and insights into these central issues.

Theological Themes in 2 Corinthians

Paul's Ministry as an Apostle

Paul's autobiographical descriptions of his ministry as an apostle are among the most poignant of all his writings. A picture of Paul emerges from his description of his endurance as a missionary. This description far surpasses anything that the Acts of the Apostles was able to paint about Paul's ministry. In everything Paul gives glory to God and Jesus for the power that has sustained him. Paul's attitude to suffering and his weakness shine through his whole ministry. Not only does he see his suffering as an opportunity to share in the sufferings of Christ "so that the life of Jesus may also be made visible in our bodies" (4:10), he also sees his suffering as a way to trust in Christ's power to overcome his weakness (11:16-33).

Paul's ministry is also strengthened through his ecstatic experiences (12:1-4). He reports being taken up to heaven where he saw things that he cannot share (12:1-4). Acts gives a glimpse of this dimension in recording Paul's call, conversion, and commissioning to bring the message to the Gentiles (Acts 9:1-19). However, here in 2 Corinthians Paul shows that this mystical aspect of his ministry was far deeper and more significant than otherwise realized.

Besides the suffering that came from persecution and the perils of his travels, Paul's ministry is characterized as well by bearing a physical suffering that he endured constantly, "a thorn in the flesh" (12:7). Instead of reacting against it, Paul shows the Corinthians that there is a value in persevering and accepting suffering. Its value comes from Christ's grace that is bestowed in weakness, enabling one to endure. One's strength ultimately comes from the Lord: "For whenever I am weak, then I am strong" (v. 10).

While Paul's descriptions of his own life and ministry are significant, their real importance lies in the fact that they become a paradigm not just for the Corinthians, but for every reader. In human weakness Christ's power is evident and the believer is called upon to trust when Christ's "power is made perfect in weakness" (12:9).

Finally, Paul characterizes his work as a "ministry of reconciliation" (5:18), akin to that of Christ: "In Christ God was reconciling the world to himself" (5:19). In sharing in Jesus' ministry, Paul has the task of continuing this ministry by appealing to others to "be reconciled to God" (v. 20).

Spiritual Renewal

The imagery that Paul uses in this letter enables him to provide a glimpse into his expectations regarding the future world. In 1 Corinthians Paul spoke about putting on a "spiritual body" after death (1 Cor 15:44). Paul develops his thought further in this letter by indicating that here and now believers are already preparing the spiritual bodies in which they will be fully clothed at death. In the afterlife God will replace this earthly "tent" with a house that has not been made by human hands, one that will last forever (2 Cor 5:1). In the present life, believers groan intensely, desiring to receive this new life (v. 4). The Spirit has been given them as a guarantee that they will inherit what God has prepared (v. 5). In union with Christ through the power of the Spirit the believer becomes a new creation: "Everything old has passed away; see, everything has become new!" (v. 17).

Questions for Review and Discussion

1   1 Corinthians 15 is the oldest text that we have on the resurrection of Jesus. Compare what Paul says about the resurrection with what the Gospels have to say (Matt 28:1-10; Mark 16:1-8; Luke 24:1-12; John 20:1-10). Note the agreements or disagreements. Why are there these similarities or differences?

2   What ethical advice does Paul stress in 1 Corinthians? Do you agree or disagree with what Paul has to say? Is it relevant for today?

3   Describe how your idea of Paul and his ministry has developed or changed from reading 2 Corinthians.

4   List the accusations that were made against Paul by his opponents according to 2 Corinthians. For example: Paul vacillates (2 Cor 1:17).

Further Reading

Barclay, John. "2 Corinthians." In *ECB,* 1353-73.

Barton, Stephen C. "1 Corinthians." In *ECB,* 1314-52.

Fitzgerald, John T. "Corinthians, Second Letter to the." In *EDB,* 283-85.

Murphy-O'Connor, Jerome. *St. Paul's Corinth: Text and Archaeology.* 3rd ed. Collegeville: Liturgical, 2002.

Richardson, Peter. "Corinthians, First Letter to the." In *EDB,* 281-83.

Talbert, Charles H. *Reading Corinthians: A Literary and Theological Commentary on 1 and 2 Corinthians.* Rev. ed. Macon: Smyth & Helwys, 2002.

Witherington, Ben, III. *Conflict and Community in Corinth: A Socio-Rhetorical Commentary on 1 and 2 Corinthians.* Grand Rapids: Wm. B. Eerdmans, 1995.

Chapter 56

Philippians and Philemon

Two Letters of Friendship from Prison

Philippians

Getting Started

1 Read Paul's Letter to the Philippians. List the times that Paul uses words for joy or rejoicing.

2 In one page describe Paul's relationship with the Philippians.

Preliminary Comments

Four letters situate Paul in the context of prison (Philippians, Philemon, Colossians, and Ephesians). In this chapter we consider the first two letters, Philippians and Philemon; we will examine the other two (Colossians and Ephesians) separately since most scholars doubt whether Paul wrote them. Philippians is one of Paul's most intimate letters as it reveals the depth of his affection for the Christians of Philippi. Theologically, it presents a magnificent reflection on the person of Jesus Christ.

Background Information

Philippi, an important city in the Roman province of Macedonia, was situated on the Via Egnatia, the Roman highway that crossed the empire from east to west. It lay 10 miles inland from the sea and depended heavily on trade and commerce that passed from the sea along this highway. Established *ca.* 356 B.C.E. by Philip II of Macedon, the father of Alexander the Great, it came under Roman rule in 168. In 42 B.C.E. Brutus and Cassius (the assassins of Julius Caesar) were defeated here by Mark Antony and Octavian (the future Augustus Caesar). When Octavian later defeated Mark Antony at the battle of Actium in 31 B.C.E., it became a military colony where retired Roman soldiers were settled.

Paul established his first European church in this city during the course of his second missionary journey (49-52 C.E.; see Acts 16:11-15; Phil 4:15). Lydia, a rich woman involved in the purple goods industry, became a Christian and invited Paul and his companions to use her house as their headquarters. When Paul exorcised a slave girl, her masters were annoyed because they lost a great source of income! Paul and Silas were arrested, flogged, and thrown into prison (see also 1 Thess 2:2). When an earthquake hit the jail, Paul and Silas refused to escape, and this action led to the conversion of the jailer. Paul revealed his Roman citizenship, which caused the magistrates to apologize for the way they had treated Roman citizens. Paul and Silas left the city and went to Thessalonica. Paul returned here twice in the course of his third missionary journey (Acts 20:1-2; 20:6). This account describes the important role that women played both in Philippi and in the transmission of the Christian message. It clearly reflects the social situation of the Roman city, Philippi, at that time.

The church of Philippi was very different from other churches that Paul had founded up to this point. It was largely a Gentile Christian church and no major problems developed there. The Philippians' adherence to the faith that Paul had preached was a source of great joy to Paul (1:3-4). A major reason for writing was to thank them for their concern and for the gifts they had sent Paul in Thessalonica and Corinth (4:18; see vv. 15-16; 2 Cor 11:9). This friendly relationship between Paul and Philippi explains why it is the most joyful of all his letters. Words for "joy and rejoicing" occur more than 16 times in this brief letter.

A Walk through Philippians

Philippians 1:1-11:
Opening Formula and Thanksgiving
Paul includes Timothy as co-author of the letter, but he does so out of respect. In 1:3 Paul writes in the first person singular, and he later refers to Timothy in the third person (2:19-24). Paul addresses this letter "to all the saints in Christ Jesus" (1:1), a common designation for believers: they are called to be holy through their union with Christ Jesus. He also mentions specifically those who have leadership roles in the community ("the bishops and deacons").

Paul thanks God for the Philippian believers (vv. 3-8). He opens with a tone of joy that endures throughout the letter. Paul is grateful for the way in which they have remained true to the faith he brought them as well as for their continued concern. He prays that their love may continue to "overflow" and that they will have the spiritual insight to know how to act (vv. 9-11).

Philippians 1:12–3:1:
News and Instructions for the Community
Paul's Personal Situation (1:12-26)
Paul testifies that there is a positive side to his imprisonment: it has helped to spread the gospel (1:12-18). Even the "imperial guard" has come to recognize that his imprisonment stems from his loyalty to Christ. Many Christians have been emboldened because of Paul (v. 14). Others were preaching to enhance their own pres-

---

Reading Guide to Philippians

Opening Formula (1:1-2)

Thanksgiving (1:3-11)

Body (1:12–4:20)

News and Instructions for the Community (1:12–3:1)
  Paul's Personal Situation (1:12-26)
  Instructions to the Community (1:27–2:18)
  Paul's Future Plans (2:19–3:1)

Paul's Example for the Path to Salvation (3:2–4:9)
  Beware of the Judaizing Danger (3:2-11)
  Strive toward the Goal (3:12–4:1)
  Virtues of Harmony, Joy, and Peace (4:2-9)

Paul's Gratitude for the Philippians' Help (4:10-20)

Final Greetings (4:21-23)

---

tige, but Paul says the motives are unimportant: what is vital is that the message of Christ is preached (v. 18).

Paul reflects on the possible outcome of his imprisonment (vv. 19-26): he will either be put to death or be released ("remain in the flesh," v. 24). While Paul would rather die to be with Christ (v. 23), he judges that Christ wants him to continue to live and spread the gospel message (v. 25).

Instructions for the Community (1:27–2:18)
Paul exhorts the Philippians to steadfastness (1:27-30), harmony (2:1-2), humility (vv. 3-11), and obedient selflessness (vv. 12-18). The core of this advice is the striking liturgical hymn to Christ (vv. 6-11). Paul appeals to the Philippians to imitate Jesus' life: through humiliation Jesus received exaltation. They too will come to the resurrection if they, like Jesus, are willing to humble themselves.

Paul's Future Plans (2:19–3:1)
Paul plans to send Timothy to Philippi soon (2:19-23) and also hopes to visit there when he is released (v. 24). The Philippians have sent Epaphroditus to care for Paul in his imprisonment, but Epaphroditus falls ill and Paul has to send him back. Paul explains that Epaphroditus has not deserted but has carried out his task despite his illness.

Philippians 3:2–4:9:
Paul's Example for the Path of Salvation
Beware of the Judaizing Danger (3:2-11)
Paul's tone of joy changes dramatically in the opening passage of this section, where he warns about those Christian Jews (the Judaizers) who want Christians to

continue to adhere to all the stipulations of Jewish Law. They demand that Christians who come from the world of paganism become Jews first (through circumcision for males) and abide by the Jewish food regulations. The Judaizers were Paul's arch opponents, which explains his anger. In defense of his interpretation of the Christian message, Paul boasts first of all about his Jewish roots, which give him authority to speak about Jewish customs. He speaks of his rejection of Jewish privileges, how he turned from legalism to a faith in Christ, and how he has himself died with Christ and looks forward to sharing in Christ's resurrection.

Striving toward the Goal (3:12–4:1)

Paul urges the Philippians to remain firm and not forget their future hope of glory (4:1). Using his own example (3:17), he shows them how to lead their lives in this present world. Paul further urges them to avoid a lifestyle that concentrates on an exclusive enjoyment of bodily desires ("their god is the belly," v. 19). Instead, they must remember that they are citizens of heaven (v. 20) and that Christ will return to transform our human bodies into the likeness of his own glorified body (v. 21).

Virtues (4:2-9)

Paul exhorts the Philippians to live out the virtues of harmony, joy, and peace. He challenges two women from the congregation to make up their differences, as their falling out is the cause of disharmony in the community (4:2-3).

Philippians 4:10-20:
Paul's Gratitude for the Philippians' Help

Paul demonstrates how much he appreciates the Philippians' assistance in the past as well as now in prison. It is not his custom to accept aid for himself; however, their generosity will be rewarded by the Lord.

Philippians 4:21-23: Final Greetings

Paul sends greetings from himself and Timothy, as well as from those who are with him, "especially those of the emperor's household" (4:22). Paul concludes as usual by invoking the blessing of the Lord Jesus (v. 23).

Critical Issues in Studying Philippians

Two important issues have received much attention among scholars. These issues relate to the letter's origin and unity. We shall focus on the main aspects of the issues involved and offer a perspective on what appear to be the strongest arguments.

Origin and Date of the Letter

Paul provides the following information about himself and his situation: He is in prison (1:7, 13, 17) and Timothy is with him (1:1; 2:19-23). Members of the "praetorian (or 'imperial') guard" [1:13]) are watching him. These are either soldiers belonging to the emperor stationed in Rome or those belonging to a provincial governor (as in Acts 23:35). Christians among the "emperor's (or 'Caesar's') household" are present with him when he writes this letter (4:22). This term designates officials in the employment of the emperor, whether in Rome or throughout the empire. Paul indicates that he may be put to death (1:19-21), yet he also hopes that he will be freed (vv. 24-25) and that he will come to visit the Philippians soon (2:24).

While Paul has been in prison much communication has circulated between Philippi and Paul. When they first learn of his imprisonment, the Philippians send Epaphroditus to care for him (4:15-18). Epaphroditus falls ill so Paul sends him home to Philippi with this letter to explain what has happened (2:25-30). Paul intends to send Timothy soon (vv. 19-23) and hopes to come to them soon when he is released (v. 24).

Since Paul does not state where he is, the question arises: What location would best suit the above information about Paul's context? Three possibilities arise:

Rome (61-63 c.e.)

Paul's captivity in Rome (which was more like a house arrest) at the end of his life (Acts 28:16-31) is the traditional location for his writing this letter. The "imperial guard" (1:13) is identified as the emperor's guard in Rome, while "those of the emperor's household" (4:22) are understood as converts in the imperial palace in Rome. The major difficulty in situating Paul in Rome stems from Paul's description of his contact with Philippi while he is in prison. The distance from Rome to Philippi is 700 miles (along the Via Egnatia), 900 miles by ship along the west coast of Italy and up the east coast of Greece. Such a formidable trip would take many months. Multiplying that by the number of times people and information moved between Paul and Philippi, as indicated above, would present an obstacle to situating Paul in Rome.

Caesarea (58-60 c.e.)

Paul was arrested in the Jerusalem temple at the end of his third missionary journey (Acts 21:27-36). When Paul's nephew discovered a plot to assassinate him, he reported it to the tribune who transferred Paul to the governor's headquarters in Caesarea (Acts 23:12-35). There he remained until he appealed to have his case heard by the emperor and was sent to Rome. The view that Paul wrote this letter from Caesarea has not received much support because its contents do not agree with what is known of Paul's imprisonment here. In the letter Paul hopes to be released soon, and he assures the Philippians that he will visit them on his release. Paul's situation in Caesarea was desperate, and because he felt he had no hope of being released, he had to appeal to the emperor. Further, the same problem of distance raised against the Roman hypothesis would also apply here. Caesarea is some 1,000 miles from Philippi by sea and would require a journey of many months. Again, the frequent contacts between Philippi and Caesarea would render the possibility even more unlikely.

Traditional site of Paul and Silas's imprisonment at Philippi (Acts 16). (Phoenix Data Systems, Neal and Joel Bierling)

Ephesus (54-56 C.E.)

This relatively recent proposal seems to offer the best solution to the evidence. While Acts makes no specific mention of an imprisonment during Paul's three years in Ephesus, it does speak of a riot when some of his traveling companions were brought before the magistrate there (Acts 19:21–20:1). Paul reports in 2 Cor 6:5; 11:23 that he had endured "far more imprisonments," which implies that the imprisonments that Acts mentions (Caesarea and Rome) are not the only times Paul was in prison. Paul also mentions in 1 Cor 15:32 that he had to fight with "wild animals at Ephesus" when his life was threatened, a figurative description which nevertheless suggests that Paul was in prison. Further, 2 Cor 1:8-10 mentions the "affliction we experienced in Asia; for we were so utterly, unbearably crushed that we despaired of life itself." Consequently, an imprisonment in Ephesus would best suit the Letter to the Philippians. The distance between Ephesus and Philippi by sea is *ca.* 400 miles, which would require a trip of only a couple of weeks. Paul's struggle with the Judaizers would also fit better into the context of his third journey rather than a later period. As the letter indicates, Paul also planned to visit Philippi (2:24), which is in fact what he did on his release from Ephesus (Acts 20:1).

The most plausible conclusion is to see this letter originating in Ephesus somewhere between 54 and 56.

Unity of the Letter

As mentioned previously, it has been a hobby of scholars to dissect Paul's correspondence and try to discover other letters out of which the seven authentic letters were composed. We argue, though, that presumption for the unity of Paul's letters should be maintained unless strong arguments militate against it. The major concern about the unity of Philippians stems from ch. 3, where Paul's tone changes dramatically from joy (in the rest of the letter) to harsh condemnation of the Judaizers. This is not sufficient reason to take the chapter as evidence of a separate letter of Paul. As indicated previously, Paul's letters were largely dictated, and so his thoughts tend to jump suddenly from one point to another. We can imagine that while writing to the Philippians in a joyful spirit, he is aware of some dangers that threaten his beloved community and so he takes the opportunity to warn them.

Paul Tells the Philippians to Imitate Him (3:17)

For a modern reader this sounds self-promoting and somewhat arrogant. However, in the context of the Greco-Roman world the most common method of teaching ethics was to refer to examples of people who demonstrated in their lives the virtues (or vices) that the teacher wished to exemplify. Moral teachers did not consider it inappropriate to refer to themselves as illustrations for the values that they wished to communicate to their students.

Theological Themes in Philippains

Hymn to Christ (2:5-11)

This passage contains the most insightful theological reflection in the whole letter and is one of the most poetic passages of all Paul's writings. This was an early Christian hymn sung in honor of Christ that Paul has adopted for his letter. The NRSV captures its literary genre well by translating it in the format of a hymn.

The New Testament refers to Christians singing "psalms, hymns, and spiritual songs to God" (Col 3:16; see also Eph 5:19; Acts 16:25). The earliest reference to Christianity found among pagan writers also notes that they used to sing "a hymn to Christ as a God" (Pliny the Younger, *Letter X to Trajan,* 10.96-97). While we do not possess a collection of these hymns and songs such as the book of Psalms, nevertheless throughout the New Testament there is evidence of early Christian writers using these hymns in their own works. On some occasions they are clearly delineated by the writer as a hymn (e.g., Rev 4:8, 10-11; and the songs in the Infancy Gospel of Luke). On other occasions the songs are woven into the text itself with no clear acknowledgement that they were being used. Among the more important hymns that scholars have identified in Paul's writings are Phil 2:6-11; 1 Cor 13; Rom 11:33-36; Col 1:15-20; Eph 5:14; 1 Tim 3:16; 2 Tim 2:11-13.

If Paul wrote Philippians *ca.* 56 C.E., and if he was using a hymn already being used in Christian worship, this Hymn to Christ could date back to the early 40s, providing insight into the earliest understanding that the Christians had of the person of Christ and his relationship to God.

The first part of the hymn concentrates on the self-humiliation of Jesus Christ as a servant (2:6-8). Paul refers to the person of Christ who "was in the form of God"; that is, he was understood to possess that quality associated with the manifestation of God in the Hebrew Bible (v. 6). Yet he did not look upon this equality with God as something to be exploited, but was willing to let go of it ("emptied himself") and took on the human form of a "slave" or "servant," in the biblical sense of one dedicated to carrying out God's will (v. 7). By accepting the human condition as one obedient to the will of God, he also accepted the obedience of death, which is an essential aspect of the human condition (v. 8). However, he went even further to experience a death that is the ultimate of humiliation: death on a cross. The humiliation of Jesus Christ has moved progressively downward from equality with God, to subservient obedience in becoming man, then to further humiliation in death, and finally death on the cross.

The second part concentrates on the exaltation of Christ (2:9-11). Responding to his obedience, God reaches into the depths of Jesus' death and exalts him to God's right hand, giving him "the name that is above every name." In the biblical world a name gives expression to the essence of a person's being and captures the fullness of that person (v. 9). The whole universe now bends in worship of Jesus Christ (v. 10) and acknowledges him as Lord (v. 11), the title in the Hebrew Bible for God. Jesus Christ is proclaimed by all creation as Lord, equal to God.

The context in which Paul uses this hymn is very significant. He is not intent on philosophizing about Jesus, nor about giving a doctrinal teaching about the nature of Jesus. Paul is concerned that the life of Jesus must be imitated by his followers. In introducing this hymn into his letter, Paul writes: "Let the same mind be in you that

---

Hymn to Christ Jesus (2:6-11)

Scholars have divided the hymn of Phil 2:6-11 into different stanzas. The following reconstruction is one attempt to conform as closely as possible to its content and thought. It contains two sections each with three stanzas in which the mystery of Jesus Christ is presented through the structure of passing from humiliation to exaltation.

The Humiliation of Christ (2:6-8)
Christ Jesus who, though he was in the form of God,
    did not regard equality with God
    as something to be exploited,
But emptied himself,
    taking the form of a slave,
    being born in human likeness.
And being found in human form,
    he humbled himself
    and became obedient
    to the point of death —
    even death on a cross.

The Exaltation of Christ (2:9-11)
Therefore God also highly exalted him
    and gave him the name
    that is above every name,
So that at the name of Jesus
    every knee should bend,
    in heaven and on earth and under the earth,
And every tongue should confess
    that Jesus Christ is Lord,
    to the glory of God the Father.

was in Christ Jesus" (v. 5). The humble obedience of Jesus Christ provides the example that his followers should emulate. Rather than searching for and holding on to their importance, they should be willing to make themselves less for the sake of others and work for their good. It is a self-sacrificing love that Paul seeks to present in holding up Jesus Christ for emulation. Just as Jesus passed from humiliation to exaltation, so will it be with his followers. Just as God the Father raised Jesus up in the depths of his humiliation, so too will God the Father exalt Jesus' followers who in their lives willingly accept humiliation for the sake of others. The path to salvation is like that of Jesus: to empty oneself and to become obedient to God's will.

Friends and Enemies

Among the important topics that ancient philosophers and writers examined frequently was the concept of friendship. The famous orator, Cicero, wrote an important treatment, *On Friendship,* in which he called a friend "a second self" (21:80). Philippians can also be considered a letter of friendship since it captures beautifully Paul's relationship to the Philippian community, to Timothy and Epaphroditus. Paul's joy abounds in the friendship that is displayed in the way in which he praises his friends.

Alongside the praise of friends in the ancient world went the condemnation of enemies. It is not surprising that Paul introduces ch. 3 on the dangers and evils of the Judaizers by warning his friends, the Philippians, about these people and trying to protect them from the inroads they are making into their community. Paul's language is harsh: "Beware of the dogs!" (3:2), employing a term of derision for people who were not circumcised. Paul is being ironical here because he is attacking the same people (the Judaizers) that he encountered in Galatia who demanded that all those from the pagan world who accepted Jesus as the Messiah should be circumcised and abide by the dietary stipulations of the Jewish Torah.

Philemon

Getting Started

1   Read the letter to Philemon. List the main characters together with the phrases that Paul uses to describe them.

2   Do you see any significance in the use of these descriptions?

Background Information

The Letter to Philemon is different from the other genuine letters of Paul in two ways. The shortest of Paul's letters (only 25 verses), it is closer to Greco-Roman letters, which were usually able to fit onto one sheet of papyrus (see also 2 and 3 John and Jude). Also, it is addressed to an individual (Philemon), not a community. But this is not a private letter; it has a distinct public nature. Philemon is probably the leader of a house church, and the mention of so many other names gives it a public quality in that it is intended to be read in this church.

The first question to be addressed is the location of Philemon and those around him. A way toward a solution is to note several similarities with the Letter to the Colossians. Eight of the 10 individuals mentioned in Philemon are mentioned in Colossians as well: Timothy, Archippus, Onesimus, Epaphras, Mark, Aristarchus, Demas, and Luke. In particular the references in Colossians to Onesimus (Col 4:9) and Archippus (v. 17) situate these people with Colossae. If, as we contend, Colossians was written long after Paul's death, this would imply that the writer of Colossians was using a tradition that connected Archippus and Onesimus with Colossae and would support the view that Philemon also was from Colossae.

The question of when and where Paul wrote this letter is similar to the discussion above relating to Philippians. Paul states that he is a prisoner (vv. 1, 9, 10, 13, 23). The three possibilities for his imprisonment remain Rome, Caesarea, and Ephesus. As with Philippians, Paul indicates that he expects to be released soon and will visit Philemon on his release (v. 22). Paul's expectation does not match his situation in Rome or Caesarea where he was facing possible execution. Further, the distance between Ephesus and Colossae is only about 100 miles, and it would be logical to imagine that when Onesimus ran away from his master he would have come to this large city.

A Walk through Philemon

Philemon 1-7: Opening Formula and Thanksgiving

Paul and Timothy write to their "dear friend and coworker" Philemon, a slaveowner, as well as to "our sister" Apphia, "our fellow soldier" Archippus, and the community that gathers to worship in Philemon's house. Philemon is probably a wealthy person and the patron of a house church in Colossae. In the thanksgiving section (vv. 4-7) Paul praises Philemon's faith and love.

> ### *Reading Guide to the Letter to Philemon*
> **Opening Formula** (vv. 1-3)
>
> **Thanksgiving** (vv. 4-7)
>
> **Body** (vv. 8-22)
>   Paul's Plea for Onesimus (vv. 8-16)
>   Expansion of the Plea (vv. 17-22)
>
> **Final Greetings** (vv. 23-25)

Philemon 8-16: Plea for Onesimus

In prison Paul becomes Onesimus's "father" and Onesimus becomes his "child" (v. 10) in Christ. He has been tremendously helpful to Paul in prison, although previously he had been useless to Philemon (v. 11). Paul is actually making a pun on the name of Onesimus, which means "useful" in Greek. He continues this pun in v. 20: "Let me have this *benefit* (Greek *onaimen*) from you." Paul does not command Philemon to do anything, instead he appeals to him. He would have liked to keep Onesimus with him in Ephesus, but Paul is careful to respect Philemon's rights and sends Onesimus back (vv. 13-14) with the plea that he accept him back "no longer as a slave but more than a slave, a beloved brother" (v. 16).

Philemon 17-22: Paul Expands His Plea

Paul promises to pay for anything that Onesimus owes Philemon. Some scholars think that Onesimus might have stolen something when he fled from Philemon. Paul reminds Philemon that he owes him his obedience and he is confident that he will do more than Paul requests. To conclude, Paul tells Philemon of his intention to visit him when released and asks him to prepare for that visit.

Philemon 23-25: Final Greetings

Paul sends greetings from himself, Epaphras, Mark, Aristarchus, Demas, and Luke. He ends in his usual manner with a blessing.

Critical Issues in Studying Philemon

The most discussed question regarding this letter is slavery and Paul's failure to condemn this institution. To understand this issue it is necessary to view slavery within the context of the 1st century C.E. In that period people became slaves, not because of color or race, but because they had been captured in war, sold into debt, born to slave parents, or captured by slave hunters. The social status of a slave depended upon that of the owner. In many cases slaves were better educated than their masters. Slaves could be teachers, doctors, property managers — all of which services benefited the master.

The most difficult form of slave life was experienced by those who worked in mines or as rowers on ships.

Paul was a product of his time and one cannot expect him to view slavery as the inhuman practice we regard it today. Slavery was part of the status quo and as such he accepted it. Further, Paul had an apocalyptic eschatological perspective, expecting the end of the world and the return of Christ to occur soon. This is why he advised the Corinthians regarding marriage: "In whatever condition you were called, brothers and sisters, there remain with God" (1 Cor 7:24). For Paul, whether or not one was a slave at the time of one's call was immaterial (1 Cor 7:21-23). It was more important to be a "slave" of Christ. In union with Christ one gained new status where there is "no longer slave or free . . . for all of you are one in Christ Jesus" (Gal 3:28).

Theological Themes in Philemon

Why is this short letter in the New Testament? This question is often raised by those who expect a condemnation of slavery and do not find it. The importance and value of Philemon lies in its presenting the most beautiful appeal to forgiveness in the entire New Testament. The message of Jesus Christ centered upon the gift of forgiveness, whereby God the Father forgives sinners and welcomes them back with open arms (see the parables in Luke 15 of the Lost Sheep, the Lost Coin, and the Prodigal Son). In this letter Paul does not command forgiveness, but he appeals to the slaveowner to recognize that Onesimus has become a brother in Christ. He challenges him to move beyond what society demands, to forgive the slave, and receive him back.

Paul's challenge to Philemon rests upon his own relationship with the man. He calls him "our dear friend" (v. 1) and demonstrates feelings of friendship toward him throughout the letter. As we noted in discussing the Letter to the Philippians, friendship was prized highly in the ancient world. According to Euripides, a Greek dramatist of the 5th century B.C.E., friends were "one soul" (*Orestes,* 1046). They looked on reality in the same way and held the same values. Given this context, Paul reminds Philemon that, since he should share the same values as Paul himself, their friendship would demand that he extend forgiveness to Onesimus.

Questions for Review and Discussion

Philippians

1 What autobiographical details does Paul give the reader in Philippians?

2 What are the main reasons that led Paul to write Philippians? Base your answer upon your reading of the letter itself.

Philemon

3 What are Paul's intentions in Philemon?

4 How do you think Onesimus responded to the letter?

Further Reading

Philippians

Craddock, Fred B. *Philippians.* Interpretation. Atlanta: John Knox, 1985.

Martin, Ralph P. *Carmen Christi: Philippians 2:5-11 in Recent Interpretation and in the Setting of Early Christian Worship.* Rev. ed. Grand Rapids: Wm. B. Eerdmans, 1983.

———. *Philippians.* Rev. ed. NCBC. Grand Rapids: Wm. B. Eerdmans, 1980.

Osiek, Carolyn. "Philippians, Letter to the." In *EDB,* 1049-50.

Wanamaker, Charles A. "Philippians." In *ECB,* 1394-1403.

Philemon

Barth, Markus, and Helmut Blanke. *The Letter to Philemon.* ECC. Grand Rapids: Wm. B. Eerdmans, 2000.

Hooker, Morna D. "Philemon." In *ECB,* 1447-50.

Lewis, Lloyd A. "An African American Appraisal of the Philemon-Paul-Onesimus Triangle." In *Stony the Road We Trod,* ed. Cain Hope Felder, 232-46. Minneapolis: Fortress, 1991.

Soards, Marion L. "Philemon, Letter to." In *EDB,* 1046-47.

Chapter 57

Galatians and Romans

Paul's Gospel

Paul's Letters to the Galatians and the Romans focus on the essence of the Christian faith. They do this in two very different ways. Galatians is the earlier of the two letters, written in the heat of an argument. Romans is devoid of controversy, and Paul is able to present his understanding of the faith calmly. Since both writings deal with very similar issues, we examine them together to show the development of Paul's thought.

Galatians

Getting Started

1 Read the Letter to the Galatians. What do you discover about Paul in this letter?

2 Note the controversy between Paul and Peter. What do you think it is all about?

Preliminary Comments

The essence of the dispute between Paul and his opponents centers on the role the Law plays in the path to salvation. Paul's opponents taught that Jesus' followers (whether they came from the world of Judaism or the pagan world) still needed to fulfill the requirements of the Jewish Torah. For Paul, this is a denial of the role and position of Jesus Christ. The path to salvation comes through faith in Jesus Christ, not in obedience to the stipulations of Jewish Law. Faith in Jesus Christ has set us free. That is why some scholars have referred to Galatians as "the letter of Christian freedom."

Galatians witnesses to the struggle the early Christians experienced in reconciling Jesus' teaching with that of their Jewish traditions. Because Paul's views won out in this dispute and his writings are in the New Testament, one tends to forget that Paul's opponents were as equally sincere and convinced of their understanding of the meaning of Jesus Christ. For new converts to Christianity, it was obviously a confusing time.

Background Information

Paul writes this letter "to the churches of Galatia" (1:2). Where exactly these churches are situated is one of the critical issues that must be addressed before we read the letter. Scholars are divided in their answers: (1) the central region of Asia Minor, around modern Ankara

THE TWO GALATIAS

Reading Guide to Galatians

Opening Formula (1:1-5)
Body (1:6–6:10)

Polemic: Paul's Strong Defense of the Gospel (1:6–4:31)
The Issues of the Adversaries (1:6-10)
Paul Defends His Gospel (1:11–2:14)
The Core of Paul's Gospel (2:15-21)
Arguments in Defense of Paul's Gospel (3:1–4:31)

Ethical Exhortation to Keep Their Freedom in Christ (5:1–6:10)

Final Greetings (6:11-18)

in Turkey; or (2) the southern coastal region of Asia Minor.

The Northern Galatian Theory

The traditional view, held by most scholars, is that Paul was writing to churches in the central region of Asia Minor near Ancyra, modern Ankara, Turkey. Supporters of this view argue that the name Galatia refers to the area where the original inhabitants, Galatians (Gauls or Celts), had lived. Arguments in support of this location are based on Paul's calling them "Galatians" (Greek *Galatai,* 3:1), in an ethnic sense. The Acts of the Apostles does not describe Paul's missionary activity in this region, but one must remember that Acts does not give a comprehensive account of everything Paul did. Further, it is possible to see in some references his probable work in this area: "They (Paul, Silas, Timothy)

went through the region of Phrygia and Galatia, having being forbidden by the Holy Spirit to speak the word in Asia" (Acts 16:6).

The Southern Galatian Theory

Supporters of this view understand the name Galatia as a reference to the Roman province of Galatia (the southern coastal region of Asia Minor). In 25 B.C.E. the last king of the Galatians died, and Rome enlarged the original northern territory of the Galatians to incorporate the southern region as well, as far as the Mediterranean Sea. It included cities such as Pisidian Antioch, Iconium, Lystra, and Derbe. Acts 13–14 describes Paul visiting these cities during his first missionary journey. The Southern Galatian theory would date the letter shortly after Paul's visit during his second missionary journey *ca.* 50 C.E.

While arguments support both possibilities, the Northern Galatian theory (the ethnic use of the term Galatia) has more support. This theory would place the letter during Paul's third missionary journey, probably from Ephesus. Paul's three-year stay there (54-57) would have made it possible for him to hear news about other missionaries undermining his message in that region, thus prompting his energetic response. Consequently, we would date the letter ca. 54/55.

A Walk through Galatians

Galatians 1:1-5: Opening Formula

Paul begins with a defense by identifying himself as an apostle (1:1), one sent on a mission by Jesus Christ and God the Father. He sends greetings in general from "all the members of God's family who are with me" (v. 2). His greetings summarize his gospel of freedom (vv. 3-5). Paul's response to his opponents' attacks is one of anger; hence this is the only one of Paul's existing letters that lacks the traditional thanksgiving!

Galatians 1:6–4:31: Polemic: Paul's Strong Defense of His Gospel

The body of the letter falls into two distinct parts: a polemical section in which Paul issues a strong defense of his gospel message (1:6–4:31) and an ethical part in which he exhorts his readers to uphold their freedom (5:1–6:10).

The Issue and the Adversaries (1:6-10)

Paul shows how surprised he is to learn that the Galatians are deserting the gospel that he had preached. He curses anyone who preaches a different gospel (1:8).

Paul Defends His Gospel (1:11–2:14)

This section conforms to the rhetoric used in a court defense *(apologia)*. One can almost imagine Paul as the defendant in the case, the missionaries in Galatia as the accusers, and the Galatians as the judge! Paul gives three arguments to support his understanding of the gospel.

1. Divine call to become an apostle to the Gentiles (1:11-24). Paul describes his call and subsequent events. After then spending three years in Arabia, he makes a brief visit to Jerusalem where he meets Cephas (Peter) and James. From there he moves to Syria and Cilicia (Tarsus, his hometown).

2. The Jerusalem Council (2:1-10). Support for Paul's gospel comes as well from the agreement that he reached with the leaders of the community in Jerusalem, James, Cephas (Peter), and John, 14 years after his call. Acts 15 gives a somewhat different account of these events. According to Paul the outcome of this meeting was a compromise with "the pillars" of the church (v. 9): Paul's mission was to the Gentiles, while Peter's was to the Jews. Those from the Gentile world who became followers of Jesus were not required to be circumcised. Finally, Paul is asked to "remember the poor, which was actually what I was eager to do" (v. 10).

3. The Antioch dispute (2:11-14). Paul recounts how he stood up to Peter (and those who came from James, v. 12). He criticizes the hypocrisy of Peter, who stopped sharing meals with Gentile believers. In a sense this foreshadows what was happening among the Galatians with the arrival of those who wanted believers to continue Torah observance.

The Core of Paul's Gospel (2:15-21)

This is the heart of Paul's letter as well as his gospel. Paul uses the concept of justification (Greek *dikaiosyne*) derived from a legal context to express God's dealings with human beings. From Paul's perspective all humans are sinners and deserve God's judgment and punishment. But instead of condemning humanity, God extends mercy to those who have faith in Jesus Christ. This is God's great gift or grace. This gift comes not through obedience to works of the Torah but through faith in Christ. Paul opposes those who place their trust in "works of the Torah" because they are relying upon themselves (self-righteousness) to earn salvation, whereas salvation is a gracious gift (v. 21).

Arguments in Defense of Paul's Gospel (3:1–4:31)

Paul makes six arguments from experience and Scripture to defend his gospel.

1. The gift of the Spirit (3:1-5). Paul refers to the Galatians' experience. They received the Spirit when Paul preached among them — it did not come from doing the works of the Torah.

2. The evidence of Scripture (3:6-14). Referring to the example of Abraham, Paul shows how Abraham was justified not by works but because he believed. God also promised that all the nations of the earth would be blessed in Abraham. Likewise, the Gentiles who believe are justified by their faith, not by doing works of the Law nor by being circumcised.

3. The purpose of the Torah (3:15-29). Paul sees the Torah as preparing the way for Christ. He compares the Torah to a "disciplinarian" (the slave who takes care of a child and leads that child to school). It was intended to lead one to Christ, but once Christ has come the purpose of the Torah has been fulfilled (vv. 25-26).

4. Freedom from slavery to the elements of the world (4:1-11). Paul again speaks to the Galatians' experience. Their knowledge of God frees them from the slavery they experienced in their former lives. Why do they want to return to slavery?

5. The experience of friendship (4:12-20). The Galatians were Paul's friends. How can Paul's accusers turn the Galatians against him so quickly?

6. The allegory of Hagar and Sarah (4:21-31). In contrast to the way in which Paul's opponents interpret this allegory, Paul shows that Hagar, the slave woman, represents those who refuse to accept the message of Jesus and remain slaves of the Torah. By contrast, Sarah, the free woman, represents those who are made free through faith in Christ.

Galatians 5:1–6:10: Ethical Exhortation to Keep Their Freedom in Christ

In the second part of the body of this letter Paul turns to ethical exhortation. His theme is: "For in Christ Jesus neither circumcision nor uncircumcision counts for anything; the only thing that counts is faith working through love" (5:6). Paul encourages the Galatians to live by the Spirit, not by the flesh, and presents lists of vices (vv. 16-21) and virtues (vv. 22-26) to illustrate the life they must lead and what they must avoid.

Galatians 6:11-18: Final Greetings

Paul takes up the pen and writes in his own hand summarizing his gospel: "For neither circumcision nor uncircumcision is anything; but a new creation is everything!" (6:15). His sufferings bear witness to his share in Christ's sufferings. These "marks of Jesus branded on my body" (v. 17) outshine the marks of circumcision. In his usual style Paul concludes with a final blessing (v. 18).

Critical Issues in Studying Galatians

Relationship between Acts 15 and Galatians 2:1-14

This relationship has been a source of much scholarly examination. As noted in our discussion of the Acts of the Apostles, there are certainly discrepancies between these two accounts. However, the contexts in which they were written were very different and each passage must be understood within that setting. Galatians was written *ca.* 54/55, some five years after the Council of Jerusalem (49). Paul has very clear memories of the disputes, and some of the issues still continue. Acts, however, was written in the mid-80s, long after the matter had been resolved. Consequently, Luke presents a simple record of a resolution that was to become the practice of the Christian church.

Who Are Paul's Opponents in Galatia?

Scholars have advanced many proposals. The evidence of the letter itself supports the view that Jewish Christian missionaries came into the Galatian communities and argued that Gentile believers had to be circumcised and abide by the stipulations of the Torah. They are the same group that Paul encountered in Philippi and Corinth, called Judaizers: Jewish Christians who held that Jesus' followers had to remain within the world of Judaism.

Theological Themes in Galatians

Paul and the Law

Throughout his ministry Paul wrestled with the relationship of Jesus' followers to the Jewish Torah. His central message is that Christ was the fulfillment of the Torah and that believers were set free from obedience to it. For Paul, the issue concerned Christ's role in salvation. Through Jesus' death and resurrection believers have been freed from the curse that the Torah brings (3:13). Justification comes through faith in Jesus Christ, not through performing works of the Law. The essence of the distinction between these two ways of life rests upon whether one trusts in what Christ has done or whether one relies upon oneself to work one's own salvation.

The Equality of All in Christ

"There is no longer Jew or Greek, there is no longer slave or free, there is no longer male and female; for all of you are one in Christ Jesus" (3:28). The equality of which Paul speaks is one that comes through union with Christ. He does not mean a social equality, but a theological unity that he expresses elsewhere through the images of the body of Christ (1 Cor 12:12-31) as well as the wild olive branches grafted onto the vine of Israel (Rom 11:17-24).

"The Faith of Jesus Christ"

Traditionally this phrase has been understood as the Christian's faith *in* Christ (an objective genitive). A recent proposal regards the phrase as a subjective genitive, namely the faith *of* Jesus Christ, his faithfulness to the will and plan of his Father. This faithfulness of Jesus led to his death and resurrection and brought about justification for the sinner. The two proposals are not necessarily exclusive: both are essential in the plan of God's justification. The believer must place trust in what Christ has accomplished. At the same time, Jesus' fidelity to the plan of his Father is essential in the process of justification. Both dimensions emerge in 2:16: "And we have come to *believe in Christ Jesus,* so that we might be justified by *the faith of Jesus Christ.*" (see NRSV footnote).

Romans

Getting Started

1 Read the Letter to the Romans. Note some of the important teachings that Paul stresses.

2 Paul uses a number of quotations from the Hebrew Scriptures. List some of them.

Preliminary Comments

Paul's Letter to the Romans is his longest and the last of his "genuine" letters to have survived. Without doubt it is Paul's most important writing because it contains a wonderful synthesis of his basic teaching. It is also the most significant and influential writing in the history of Christianity. Over the course of the centuries this letter has inspired Christian thinkers in seeking to communicate their understanding of Christianity to a new generation of believers. For St. Augustine, Romans was the inspiration behind his conversion to Christianity, and he based his teaching on grace and sin upon his reflections on this letter. At the time of the Protestant Reformation in the 16th century, Romans was the source for Martin Luther's teaching on justification by faith and John Calvin's reflections on predestination. In the 20th century the Protestant theologian Karl Barth produced a monumental commentary on Romans.

Background Information

Paul did not found the church in Rome. We do not know the exact origins of the Christian community in the capital of the Roman Empire, but evidence indicates that Christians were here early on. The narrator of Acts of the Apostles notes that present in Jerusalem at the time of the first Pentecost were "visitors from Rome" (Acts 2:10). This probably reflects a more theological than historical purpose. Nonetheless, it shows that in the perception of early Christianity the message of salvation had reached this community early.

Ancient inscriptions and writings reveal a large Jewish presence in the Roman capital. In his *Life of Claudius* (25.4) the Roman historian Suetonius writes that in 49 C.E. the emperor Claudius "expelled the Jews from Rome because of their constant disturbances incited by Chrestus." Some scholars suggest that Suetonius, a pagan historian, inaccurately reproduced the name *Chrestus* for *Christus!* This could imply the presence of Christians in Rome at this time and that the disturbances in Rome could have arisen from tensions between Jews and the Jewish followers of Jesus.

The emperor Nero (54-68) revoked Claudius's edict with the result that many of those Jews and Christians who had been expelled returned *ca.* 54. Paul wrote this letter a few years later while in Corinth during his third missionary journey (in the winter of 57/58).

While it is not possible to assign one specific motive for writing this letter, it is probably the result of a number of reasons. Paul intended to visit Rome on his way to Spain, so he took the opportunity to introduce himself and his thought to this community. Because the letter was not prompted by specific issues or problems (as with his other letters), Paul was able to present his essential message calmly and precisely.

A Walk through Romans

Romans 1:1-15: Opening Formula and Thanksgiving

Paul expands his usual opening with a summary of the gospel (1:1-6) so he might instantly connect with his readers, who would recognize the essence of their own faith. In the thanksgiving section (vv. 8-15), he acknowledges how their faith echoes throughout the world and then sets out the purpose of the letter: his intention of visiting them and sharing his faith. However, he is mindful that he is preaching in a church he has not founded, so he expresses his desire that they mutually strengthen each other's faith.

Romans 1:16–11:36: Doctrinal Issues

The body of the letter divides into two parts: doctrinal issues (1:16–11:36) and ethical matters (12:1–15:13).

The Forum in Rome. The oldest of the city's public squares, it comprised a complex of open spaces and government buildings, temples, and shops. (Paul Achtemeier)

Righteousness of God Revealed through the Gospel (1:16–4:25)

The first doctrinal section reflects on God's righteousness which is revealed through the gospel. It opens with a statement of Paul's theme and his understanding of the gospel message (1:16-17): the righteousness (Greek *dikaiosyne*) of God and justification by faith. Paul uses language taken from the legal system. By the "righteousness of God" he understands God's action of pardoning believers for their sins because of their faith in Jesus Christ. God is merciful and just and pardons the Jew first, then the Gentile because of their faith in Jesus Christ.

Turning first to God's judgment of the Gentiles (1:18-32), Paul argues that they were able to come to a knowledge of God through the created world. They refused to acknowledge God and this led to idolatry (v. 23) and to depraved behavior that was against one's nature (vv. 24-32).

In 2:1-11 Paul uses the style of a diatribe in which he speaks to an imaginary Jew whom he accuses of a false sense of superiority. If Jews act the same as the Gentiles, they too are deserving of punishment. Reward or punishment will be meted out to people in the future according to their deeds: to the Jews first, whom God

will judge according to their fidelity to the Law, and then to the Gentiles, whom God will judge according to their hearts and conscience (2:5-16). The only requirement for justification is faith in Jesus Christ. Faith in Christ and not works of the Law is the important thing (3:27-31).

In 4:1-25 Paul uses the example of Abraham to illustrate and support his argument that faith justifies. He bases his position on Gen 15:6: that "Abraham believed God, and it was reckoned to him as righteousness" (4:3; see also Gal 3:6). Two chapters later in Genesis, God introduces circumcision as a requirement for the covenant (Gen 17:11-12). Since Abraham's faith came before that requirement, Paul concludes that faith comes before circumcision and is more important in the path to justification before God. Abraham is the father of all who believe, those who have not been circumcised as well all those who have (4:11-12). Paul's argument proceeds in the way a rabbi of the time would have argued, taking the phrase "it was reckoned to him as righteousness" (v. 22) as applicable not just to Abraham but also to Abraham's descendants (v. 24). Paul concludes with a return to his thesis: "It will be reckoned to us who believe in him who raised Jesus our Lord from the dead, who was handed over to death for our trespasses and was raised for our justification" (vv. 24-25).

Salvation for Those Justified by Faith (5:1–8:39)

Justification by faith brings with it peace with God, who pours the Holy Spirit into the hearts of believers (5:1-5). Before the coming of Jesus, humanity was in need of justification and reconciliation. The cross of Christ showed God's immense love: "while we still were sinners Christ died for us" (5:8), bringing justification and reconciliation with God. Paul does not lose sight of his apocalyptic expectations: although the believer has already been reconciled to God, the believer has not yet been saved. Salvation is awaited in the future return of Christ: "For if while we were enemies, we were reconciled to God through the death of his Son, much more surely, having been reconciled, will we be saved by his life" (5:10).

Paul turns to another example, Adam, to show how all humanity sinned before God (5:12-21). He contrasts the actions of Christ and those of Adam: Just as the actions of one person, Adam, resulted in sin and death for all humanity, so those of one person, Christ, resulted in salvation and life for all (v. 18). Paul sees humanity divided into two groups: those who are in Adam (in sin) and those who are in Christ (under grace) (v. 19).

For Paul a new member shares in Christ's life and death through baptism, and in 6:1-11 he explains the spiritual consequences of baptism. Using imagery taken from the baptism ritual (v. 4), Paul stresses that the old self was crucified with Christ, was buried with him (by going down into the baptismal water) and then, just as Christ was raised from death by the Father, they were raised to new life (symbolized by rising from the baptismal font). Once again Paul distinguishes between the present situation and that which is to come. Believers have already shared in the death and resurrection of Christ, but they await the future hope of glory when they shall be united to Christ in the fullness of his resurrection (v. 8).

In ch. 7 Paul reflects on the meaning of the Mosaic Law. As a faithful Jew, Paul sees the Law as God's greatest gift which communicates knowledge of God's will. Fidelity to it will bring the fullness of God's blessings. However, Paul's reflections lead him to the conviction that the Law is unable to accomplish what it was intended to do. He presents a monologue with a very personal and insightful reflection on his own interior life (vv. 7-25), which is in fact representative of the struggle of every human: "I do not understand my own actions. For I do not do what I want, but I do the very thing I hate" (v. 15). Paul experiences an interior struggle between what he knows to be right (the Law), and the evil tendencies within him leading him astray. The Law is unable to resolve that struggle. Instead it is the power of grace that comes to him from Jesus Christ that liberates him.

Having shown the limitations of the Law, Paul reflects upon life led in the Spirit (8:1-39). The believer becomes an adopted child of God, able to call on God in the words of Jesus as "Abba! Father!" (v. 15). Life is led now in the Spirit, but it also gives a future hope of glory for which the creation groans in labor pains (v. 22).

God's Election of Israel (9:1–11:36)

This third doctrinal section considers God's choice of Israel in the context of God's plan of salvation for all humanity. The real problem for Paul is this: If Israel is God's chosen nation, how is it possible that the people of Israel have now rejected Christ? He is adamant that God's promises have not failed. God did foresee both the rejection of the Israelites and the call of the Gentiles. Paul continues to stress that salvation is for all. It is useless to seek salvation simply through one's deeds or through deeds of the Law. Throughout this section Paul quotes extensively from the Hebrew Scriptures to illustrate his argument.

Paul concludes that God has not rejected the people of Israel (11:1). Throughout their history the majority failed, yet God saved a remnant (vv. 2-10). The "stumbling" of Israel at the moment has the positive effect that salvation has now been offered to the Gentiles (vv. 11-12). Paul sees a divine plan here: the people of Israel have rejected Jesus, which has made it possible for the

Gentiles to accept Jesus and become part of Abraham's descendants through faith. But in the end, all Israel will be saved (vv. 25-32). Verses 33-36 conclude this section with a beautiful hymn praising the mind of God: "To him be the glory forever. Amen" (v. 36).

Romans 12:1–15:13: Ethical Matters

Since this ethical discourse follows the long theological section, Paul is in effect saying that what God has done for believers in the person of Christ (chs. 1–11) should now evoke a response on behalf of the hearers/readers (12:1–15:13). In 12:1-8 Paul introduces his well-known imagery of the body of Christ: there is one body yet many members with different gifts "according to the grace given to us" (v. 6).

Chapter 13 reflects on the attitude of the Christian toward the state (vv. 1-7). Paul recommends that those who are followers of Christ respect their allegiance to the civil authorities. He calls the Christians in Rome to be model citizens and to pay their taxes. Paul follows with a reference to the law of love (following the teaching of Jesus) which encapsulates all the other commandments (vv. 8-10).

Romans 15:14-33: Paul's Travel Plans

The body of the letter concludes with a reference to Paul's travel plans. He speaks with pride of his missionary activity and "what Christ has accomplished through me to win obedience from the Gentiles, by word and deed" (v. 18). Paul mentions his hope of going on to Spain (vv. 24, 28) after visiting Rome. His present plans are to take the collection that had been generously given by the communities in Achaia and Macedonia to the poor in Jerusalem. Paul concludes with a request for the Romans to pray for him and ends with a blessing for them (v. 33).

Romans 16:1-27: Final Greetings

This chapter contains a word of recommendation for Phoebe (vv. 1-2). We will discuss below its position in the letter. Paul greets 26 people, many of whom he names. We know only of a few of them from Acts and Paul's other letters. The closing (vv. 21-23) contains greetings from other Christians at Corinth as well as a greeting from Tertius, the scribe.

Critical Issues in Studying Romans

Unity and Integrity of the Letter

The Chester Beatty Papyrus II ($\mathfrak{P}$46, *ca.* 200 C.E.) contains a Letter to the Romans with only 15 chapters. This has led many scholars to postulate that originally Romans had only 15 chapters and that ch. 16 was actually a separate letter of recommendation on behalf of Phoebe. They view this letter as addressed to Ephesus and in the course of its transmission, being such a short letter, it was copied at the end of Romans and with time taken to be part of that letter. A further argument is that in Romans Paul is writing to a community whom he has never met. Why then would he include so many references to people in the final chapter? It would make more sense to see ch. 16 as written to a church that Paul knew.

However, these arguments are not totally persuasive. While 𝔓46 does not include ch. 16 as part of the Letter to the Romans, the textual evidence among ancient manuscripts for its position as part of the letter is very strong. The list of individuals to whom Paul sends greetings may be his way of connecting with people he knew within a strange community. Having been singled out by name, they could testify to the community on Paul's behalf and introduce and recommend him. The existence of the letter without ch. 16 may represent an attempt in the course of the transmission to give Romans the spirit of a general letter. By removing the final chapter with all its references to specific people, Romans then was not associated with any particular community and hence might have a more universal flavor.

Theological Themes in Romans

Righteousness of God and Justification of the Sinner

This is the major theme that weaves its way throughout the letter. Since Romans sets forth Paul's basic understanding of God and humanity's relationship with God, his view of righteousness and justification occupies center stage. No other letter considers this thought so fully. Romans 3:9-31 gives the most comprehensive reflection on the concept of righteousness.

The word "righteousness" (Greek *dikaiosyne*) is applied to God, who works the salvation of humanity (3:21-22). The word originates in the context of the legal system and captures the idea of human beings brought before the judgment seat of God, where God acquits them and shows his graciousness. In this context Paul argues that all humans are sinners: "What then? Are we any better off? No, not at all; for we have already charged that all, both Jews and Greeks, are under the power of sin" (v. 9). The death of Jesus on the cross brought the sinner justification, which was communicated through the faith of the believer: "They are now justified by his grace as a gift, through the redemption that is in Christ Jesus, whom God put forward as a sacrifice of atonement by his blood, effective through faith" (vv. 24-25).

Paul uses the term "justification" (Greek *dikaiosis*) to express the effect of God's gift of righteousness on the sinner. In judgment God has acquitted the sinner, not because of anything the sinner has done, but because of what God's Son has done (5:10-11). Faith in Jesus Christ is the central factor that brings the sinner into relationship with Jesus, and through his acceptance of the gift of God's righteousness the sinner is justified. This gift is open to all people: Jew as well as Greek.

The Concept of Original Sin (5:12-21)

At the time of Paul there was much speculation on the Genesis account of Adam and his influence on the human race. In the Hellenistic world many myths dealt with the origins of humanity. One such myth spoke about a "First Man" who fell from the region of light and entered the material world, becoming head of the human race. In Alexandria, Egypt, the Jewish philosopher Philo (*ca.* 20 B.C.E.–50 C.E.) reflected on the two creation stories in Genesis (1:1–2:4a; 2:4b-25) against the philosophic background of his world. He saw in the first creation account the First Man, Adam, created in God's image as the perfect being, and he identified him with Divine Wisdom, God's Son. In the second creation account he saw the description of the Second Adam, the man of clay, the one who fell and sinned.

In both the Hellenistic and Jewish worlds a connection was made between sin and death. The writer of the 2nd-century B.C.E. book of Sirach says: "From a woman sin had its beginning, and because of her we all die" (Sir 25:24). The Jewish work *4 Ezra* (*ca.* 100 C.E.) speaks of evil growing in the human heart and leading to death: "For an evil heart has grown up in us, which has alienated us from God, and has brought us into corruption and the ways of death, and has shown us the paths of perdition and removed us far from life — and that not just a few of us but almost all who have been created!" (*4 Ezra* 7:48; trans. Bruce M. Metzger, in *OTP*, 1:538).

While it is difficult to prove that Paul ever knew any of the above writings, they reflect the common thought of both the Hellenistic and Jewish worlds of the 1st century C.E. Paul's starting point was the person of Christ, and he came to read Genesis in the light of Christ and the interpretations of Genesis circulating in his world. Paul is above all concerned with the grace that Christ brought to the human race, a gift open to all. To contrast this gift of grace for all through Christ, Paul turns to the Adam narrative, where one person, Adam, brings sin and death for the human race through his act of disobedience: "Therefore just as one man's trespass led to condemnation for all, so one man's act of righteousness leads to justification and life for all" (5:18).

Paul never uses the terminology of "original sin." It

was only in drawing on four centuries of Christian reflection on this passage of Romans that Augustine (354-430 C.E.) ultimately constructed a theology of original sin in opposition to Pelagius (*ca.* 354–418), who denied original sin and argued that everything was innately good. Augustine argued that through sin Adam fell from an original state of grace, and through human generation this state of alienation from God was passed on to every human born into this world. Augustine's view triumphed and became an established doctrine within the Roman Catholic church (see the Council of Trent, "Decree on Original Sin" Session 5, 17 June 1546).

Paul's Attitude to the State (Romans 13)

At the time of Paul there were no nation-states as we understand them today. Rather, the Roman Empire encompassed provinces comprising very diverse peoples and a complex arrangement of governance. Paul speaks in 13:1-7 about obedience to "governing authorities" (v. 1) whose power came from God. Consequently, every person should be subject and obedient to them: "Whoever resists authority resists what God has appointed, and those who resist will incur judgment" (13:2). In particular one shows obedience to rulers by paying taxes to them (vv. 6-7).

This passage has been variously interpreted over the course of time. It has led to a very submissive attitude toward authority and leaders as divinely appointed. But does Paul teach that a Christian must obey civil authority unquestioningly? Again Paul must be seen in the context of his world as well as that of the rest of the New Testament writings. He was writing at a time when the Roman emperors were promoting peace throughout the empire. There were no persecutions against Christians, who could worship unhindered. But the situation was to change a few decades later with persecutions initiated under Nero Caesar (54-68) and later under Domitian (81-96). The book of Revelation (written during the time of Domitian) shows a markedly different attitude to authorities. Rome is compared to Babylon and portrayed as corrupt and evil (Rev 18:1-24).

Consequently, Paul's teaching on obedience to authorities must be interpreted against its context. It must not be transposed into very different situations where the authorities have betrayed the power given them by God. Paul is not advocating a "blind obedience." He just does not envisage a different situation.

Questions for Review and Discussion

Galatians

1 What is the role of Law in Paul's thought in Galatians?

2 Discuss Paul's use of family and adoption images in Galatians.

Romans

3 Summarize Paul's major theological views as portrayed in Romans. Which do you consider to be the most important?

4 What does Paul's ethical teaching in Romans have to say to a person of the 21st century?

Further Reading

Galatians

Cousar, Charles B. *Galatians.* Interpretation. Atlanta: John Knox, 1982.

Gaventa, Beverly R. "Galatians." In *ECB,* 1374-84.

Matera, Frank J. "Galatians, Letter to the." In *EDB,* 476-78.

Romans

Heil, John Paul. *Paul's Letter to the Romans: A Reader-Response Commentary.* New York: Paulist, 1987.

Reumann, John. "Romans." In *ECB,* 1277-1313.

Robinson, John A. T. *Wrestling with Romans.* Philadelphia: Westminster, 1979.

Chapter 58

Deutero-Pauline Letters, Pastoral Letters, Hebrews

Paul's Heritage

Pseudonymity

In Chapter 45 we discussed the concept of authorship with regard to Paul's writings. The ancient world did not have a problem in attributing writings to a specific writer even though he/she did not actually write them. Today such attribution would be considered forgery or plagiarism. The ancients considered it a mark of respect to use the authority of their teacher from whom they had derived their knowledge. The term pseudonymity designates this practice. A pseudonymous writing is one that is falsely attributed to a well-known person. This is not to be confused with an anonymous writing, which is without a name.

In addition to Paul's seven genuine letters already examined are six pseudonymous writings, judged to have been written after Paul's death by a disciple invoking his authority. These are the Deutero-Pauline ("second Paul") letters, 2 Thessalonians, Colossians, and Ephesians, and the Pastoral Letters, 1 and 2 Timothy and Titus. In addition, tradition attributes the Letter to the Hebrews to Paul, although he is never named in this writing.

2 Thessalonians

Getting Started

1 Read the Second Letter to the Thessalonians. What do you discover about Paul in this letter?

2 Can you notice any differences with the First Letter to the Thessalonians? Compare 1 Thess 5:1-11 and 2 Thess 1:5-12.

Preliminary Comments

Although we are convinced that Paul did not write the Deutero-Pauline letters, in examining them we will refer to the author as Paul for simplicity's sake without intending to imply that Paul was the actual author.

A Walk through 2 Thessalonians

In the **opening formula** (1:1-2) and **thanksgiving** (1:3-12), Paul praises the Thessalonians for their steadfastness in the midst of persecution and affliction. He expresses the expectation that God will reward those who are persecuted. In transition to the body of the letter Paul prays that God will make them worthy of God's call (vv. 11-12).

The **body of the letter** (2:1–3:15) begins with a discussion on the delay in the Parousia (2:1-12). Paul exhorts the readers not to be excited by reports that the day of the Lord is already here (v. 2) because the signs that are to come first have not taken place: the rebellion and the revelation of the lawless one (vv. 3-4). Someone is restraining the lawless one in the present time (vv. 6-7).

In 2:13-17 Paul thanks God for choosing the Thessalonians for salvation. They are to remain firm in the traditions Paul taught them.

The writer offers advice on how to respond to the delay in the coming of the Lord (3:1-15). Many Thessalonians have concluded that because the coming of the Lord is soon there is little reason to work. The writer commands that "anyone unwilling to work should not eat" (v. 10) and gives himself as an example of someone who labored "night and day, so that we might not burden any of you" (v. 8). A further instruction regards those who fail to heed his instructions: "Have nothing to do with them" (v. 14).

The **final greetings** (3:16-17) contain an autobiographical conclusion similar to those of Paul's genuine letters.

Critical Issues in Studying 2 Thessalonians

Is Paul the Writer of 2 Thessalonians?

Until the 18th century the traditional view was that Paul wrote this letter shortly after 1 Thessalonians. Today the majority of scholars deny Paul's authorship. On the one hand, the similarities between 1 and 2 Thessalonians are striking. The opening of both letters is practically identical. The themes are very close: the need for suffering and the apocalyptic expectation that gave direction to all Paul's thought.

On the other hand, the dissimilarities between 1 and 2 Thessalonians are also striking. The style of 2 Thessalonians is more elaborate and more formal than the direct personal and informative style of 1 Thessalonians. When the writer concludes the letter with a greeting in his own hand, he adds: "This is the mark in every letter of mine" (3:17), suggesting the existence of a number of letters by Paul. Since 1 Thessalonians was Paul's first letter, 2 Thessalonians must have been written long afterwards when Paul had written many more letters!

The strongest reason for rejecting Paul's authorship comes from the development of thought regarding the expectation of the Parousia. For 2 Thessalonians the end is no longer imminent: it has been delayed. A period of time must separate the two writings for this development to have occurred.

On the strength of all these arguments the most logical conclusion is that this letter is pseudonymous, written after Paul's death at Rome in 64 C.E.

Date and Purpose of the Letter

Following the above arguments, it seems appropriate to date this letter toward the end of the 1st century C.E. 2 Thessalonians implies that the readers are experiencing severe hardships (1:4, 6, 7). This suits the period when under the emperor Domitian (81-96) Christians suffered their second persecution by the Roman state.

This letter was written after Paul's death by a second-generation disciple who knew Paul's thought well. Writing in the name of Paul to a community that the apostle had founded, he reminds the hearers/readers of Paul's teachings and at the same time encourages them not to expect the immediate arrival of the Lord.

Theological Themes in 2 Thessalonians

God's Judgment

A major theme of 2 Thessalonians is that God's judgment will bring reward for those persecuted for their faith and punishment for the persecutors (1:5-10). This theme is typical of apocalyptic writings, evident especially in Revelation (Rev 16:5-7). The descriptions here resemble the struggle described in Revelation 20. The writer embraces the typical apocalyptic worldview of a dualistic struggle between the powers of good and evil. The lawless one is the representative of Satan, Jesus the representative of God. When Jesus returns, their conflict will result in Jesus' victory (2 Thess 2:8).

The Necessity and Value of Human Work

Because of their apocalyptic expectations some Christians had given up work and were relying on others for support. The writer strongly disapproves (3:10). As in the other Pauline letters, the readers are urged to imitate Paul's example of working to earn his keep without relying upon support from the communities.

Colossians

253 26/325
25,3 +1 238

Getting Started

1 Read the Letter to the Colossians. What do you learn about Paul in this letter?

2 What does this letter teach about Jesus Christ?

Preliminary Comments

The city of Colossae was a center of commerce and textile production, situated in the Lycus River valley in Phrygia (the interior region of Asia Minor, modern Turkey) about 100 miles west of Ephesus. Located nearby were two other important cities, Hierapolis (renowned for its hot springs) and Laodicea (also a commercial and textile center). Christian churches were established in all three cities (4:13-17), but there is no evidence that Paul had ever preached there (2:1). The writer tells the Colossians to pass this letter on to the Laodiceans and to read another one that he had sent to Laodicea (4:16), suggesting that these three churches were closely connected.

The letter presents Paul as the writer (1:1; 4:18). From prison (1:24; 4:3, 18) he sends it by means of Tychicus, "a faithful minister, and a fellow servant in the Lord" (4:7-9).

A Walk through Colossians

The **opening formula** (1:1-2) identifies Paul as the sender together with Timothy. The letter is addressed "to the saints and faithful brothers and sisters in Christ." "In Christ" is an important Pauline concept that grounds the community's life in Jesus' saving action. The **thanksgiving** (1:3-14) praises God for their faith in Jesus, their hope in the promise of a future life, and their love for one another. In response to Epaphras's report, Paul continues to pray "that you may be filled with the knowledge of God's will" (v. 9). The prayer reminds them that the source for bearing good fruit is God's power.

The first part of the **body** (1:15-2:23) presents **doctrinal teaching**. It opens with a hymn praising the supremacy of Christ (1:15-20). Christ is the image of God who brings reconciliation between God and humanity (v. 20). Paul reminds the Colossians that they were formerly alienated from God, but all this changed through

> **Reading Guide to Colossians**
>
> **Opening Formula** (1:1-2)
>
> **Thanksgiving** (1:3-14)
>
> **Body** (1:15-4:6)
>
>   **Doctrinal Teaching** (1:15-2:23)
>   Hymn in Praise of the Supremacy of Christ (1:15-20)
>   Paul's Apostolic Ministry (1:21-2:5)
>   The Preeminence of Christ versus Human Traditions (2:6-23)
>
>   **Moral Exhortations** (3:1-4:6)
>
> **Final Greetings** (4:7-18)

the death of Jesus, who makes them "blameless" before God (vv. 21-22). An account of Paul's apostolic ministry (1:21-2:5) reveals how he communicated the mystery of God's plan to the Gentiles. This mystery is "Christ in you" (1:27): Christ has come to dwell in the lives of the Gentiles. In Christ is contained all the fullness of knowledge and wisdom (2:3).

Paul contrasts Christ's preeminence with human traditions (2:6-23). He states clearly that the full nature of the divinity dwells in the person of Christ, and believers share in that fullness because he is the head (vv. 9-10). As such they are freed from powers of the universe through Christ's death (vv. 12-15).

The second section of the body of the letter features **moral exhortations** developed from the foregoing reflections (3:1-4:6). As individuals and as a community, believers have been raised with Christ and freed from slavery to the powers of the universe. They should use their freedom to set their minds on the spiritual reality (3:1-4). Paul employs the image of changing clothes to describe the life that Christians are called to lead: they are to put off certain vices (vv. 5-9) and put on special virtues (vv. 12-17). Paul offers a typical Hellenistic listing of vices and virtues. He was also influenced by the social stratification of that world and adapted the traditional "household codes" to encourage the community to conform his readers' family relationships to the conventions of the time (3:18-4:1).

The **final greetings** (4:7-18) name several people with whom Paul associates his greetings (eight are mentioned in the Letter to Philemon; note the references to Onesimus, Mark and "Luke, the beloved physician"). "Grace be with you" is an abbreviation of the traditional liturgical blessing: "The grace of our Lord Jesus Christ be with all of you" (see 1 Thess 5:28; 2 Thess 3:18).

Critical Issues in Studying Colossians

Is Paul the Writer of Colossians?

The majority of modern scholars contend that Paul did not write this letter. The following observations are important:

- The vocabulary of Colossians is distinctive: 25 words are not found in Paul's other letters while 34 do not appear elsewhere in the New Testament.
- The style is also distinctive: the sentences are long and laborious; note that in the Greek text 1:9-20 (11 verses) is one sentence and 2:9-15 (six verses) is also one sentence.
- Many of Paul's central themes are absent here, such as righteousness and the Law.
- Many theological themes are a development on previous ideas: for example, Jesus is the image of God (2 Cor 4:4), the true visible manifestation of God (Col 1:15). Others are new ones not found in Paul's genuine letters: Christ is the head of the body, the church (1:18). In Paul's genuine letters the resurrection is something hoped for in the future (Rom 6:5), while in Colossians believers are already raised in Christ (2:13; 3:1).

These arguments cumulatively point to someone other than Paul as the author, yet the similarities with Paul's genuine letters point to a writer intimately familiar with his thought and message. The church writer Ignatius (died in 110) knows of this letter, which suggests that it was written prior to 100, probably in the early 80s. The close identification between the characters in Philemon and Colossians shows that the writer knew and used that letter, and it is likely the letters had the same place of origin: Ephesus. Colossians was likely written after Paul's death by one of his disciples, a member of a school of Paul's followers who wished to preserve Paul's heritage and protect the Colossians from false teachers.

Colossians 3:18–4:1: The Household Codes

The New Testament contains a number of lists of rules for the Christian household (e.g., Eph 5:21–6:9; Titus 2:1-10; 1 Tim 2:1-2, 8-15 and 5:1-2; 6:1-2; 1 Pet 2:13–3:12). In the Hellenistic world, lists of duties (referred to by

scholars as "household codes") were drawn up regarding authorities, parents, brothers, sisters, husbands, wives, children, business associates. In the Christian sphere, the need for such guidelines developed in those communities situated in the midst of the Gentiles. Christians also wanted to show their Gentile neighbors that they too were honorable members of society, trustful citizens, and so adopted similar lists or household codes that reflect their unique values. Paul encouraged his communities to embody responsible family relationships and presents these household codes within the framework of the Christian message patterned on his principle of the Lordship of Jesus over all.

A major difficulty with these household codes concerns their interpretation. These admonitions were expressed within the context and conventions of the 1st century C.E. How then do we understand these admonitions in a 21st century that is socially and culturally very different from the world of the New Testament? Basically two answers are given: (a) Some scholars argue that since these instructions are part of the Bible, God's word, they are to be accepted literally in the exact way in which they are expressed. They are as normative as the Ten Commandments. (b) Other scholars distinguish between the underlying point of these codes and the way in which they are presented. By these admonitions Paul is encouraging wives to be good wives and husbands to be good husbands. He does this in terms of the structure and stratification of his own society. We endorse this

Site of ancient Colossae. Originally situated at a junction of the main route from Ephesus to the Euphrates, the city lost its commercial role to Laodicea and Hierapolis when the road to Pergamum was moved to the west. (Phoenix Data Systems, Neal and Joel Bierling)

second approach as it conforms to the norms of biblical interpretation that always strive to separate the message from the way in which it is packaged.

Theological Themes in Colossians

The Exalted Christ

As in Phil 2:6-11, the writer uses a hymn from the liturgy to express his understanding of the person of Christ (1:15-20). In this passage the hymn deals with Christ's position in relation to creation and redemption.

"He is the firstborn of all creation" (1:15). This refers to Christ's supremacy, his preeminence in relation to all creation. Just as the Father and the Spirit were involved in the creation, so was Christ. All things in the universe were created through him and for him. He also holds all things together: the entire universe is in his control. Moreover, Christ is "the head of the body, the church" (v. 18a). This is a development over the thought of 1 Corinthians, where Paul refers to the body of Christ as the community of believers, but he does not regard Christ as the head of the body. The concept of head expresses the notion of superiority, preeminence, and control.

"He is the firstborn from the dead" (1:18b). The second part of the hymn refers to Christ's relationship to redemption. He is the first one to experience the resurrection from the dead. Because God's presence dwells in him in the fullest way possible (v. 19), he is able to bring about reconciliation ("making peace") among all things through his death on the cross. This reconciliation has universal application.

The Opponents in Colossae

Much has been written in an attempt to identify Paul's opponents at Colossae, but no unanimity has been reached. The members of the Christian community there were believers who had come from the world of the Gentiles (1:21, 27). Paul uses the hymn to Christ in order to counteract the views of the opponents: Christ is preeminent to everything in the universe. His use of such words as "wisdom," "knowledge," and "fullness" in reference to the person of Christ is deliberate because these are terms that the opponents adopted to support their perspectives.

This has led many scholars to propose that the opponents' views resembled a movement known as proto-Gnosticism or pre-Gnosticism, the early stages of a religious phenomenon that would be widespread and highly influential from the 2nd century C.E. on. This religious movement promised its adherents a secret knowledge that offered them salvation.

In the hymn, the writer portrays Christ as "the

firstborn of all creation; for in him all things in heaven and on earth were created, things visible and invisible, whether thrones or dominions or rulers or powers" (1:15-16). The author warns against those false teachers who situated powerful intermediaries between God and the material world. These "elemental spirits" had to be appeased through the knowledge of what observances to keep such as "festivals, new moons, or sabbaths" (2:16). The writer of Colossians rejects these views by proclaiming that Christ is preeminent and superior to everything in the heavenly realm. Christ is the one to offer true knowledge and salvation, a knowledge that is unavailable to these false teachers.

Ephesians

Getting Started

1   Read the Letter to the Ephesians. What does this letter tell us about Paul?

2   What is the main idea contained in this letter?

Preliminary Comments

There are many provoking questions concerning this letter. The reference in the opening formula to the saints "in Ephesus" is suspect as it is missing in some of the best and most ancient manuscripts. As with 2 Thessalonians and Colossians, this letter was not written by Paul, but by a disciple some decades after Paul's death (see below).

A Walk through Ephesians

In the **opening formula** (1:1-2) Paul addresses the saints who are faithful in Christ Jesus. The original text lacks the specific designation "in Ephesus." While the address could refer to Christians anywhere, the mention of Tychicus at the end of the letter (6:21) indicates Christian centers where Paul had been active, namely western Asia Minor.

The writer enlarges the traditional thanksgiving section by including a *blessing (1:3-14)* that leads into the *thanksgiving (1:15-23)*. The blessing uses liturgical language similar to Jewish blessings and proclaims Christ's place in God's plan of salvation. God destined believers for salvation through God's Son, Jesus, whose

---

Reading Guide to Ephesians

Opening Formula (1:1-2)

Blessing and Thanksgiving (1:3-23)

Body (2:1-6:20)

    Doctrinal Issues: The One Body of Christ, the Church (2:1–3:21)

    By Grace Believers Are Saved through Faith in Christ (2:1-10)

    Jews and Gentiles Are Reconciled in Christ (2:11-22)

    Paul's Ministry to the Gentiles (3:1-12)

      Prayer for the Readers and Doxology (3:13-21)

    Ethical Matters (4:1–6:20)

    Exhortations for Unity of Faith and the Church (4:1–5:20)

    Household Code (5:21–6:9)

    The Armor of God against Evil (6:10-20)

Final Greetings (6:21-24)

---

death brought redemption, forgiveness of sins, and grace (vv. 5-7). This leads into Paul's prayer of thanksgiving to God for the faith and love of the readers. God's plan of salvation culminates in Christ, the head of the church, his body (vv. 22-23).

The **body** of the letter begins with a discussion of **doctrinal issues** (2:1–3:21). Here Paul reflects on the one body of Christ, the church. By grace believers are saved through faith (2:1-10). In the body of Christ Jewish and Gentile believers are reconciled together (2:11-22). The readers, "Gentiles by birth" (v. 11), have been "brought near by the blood of Christ" (v. 13). Paul uses different metaphors to describe their new relationship: members of "the household of God" (v. 19) and part of a building with the apostles and prophets for its foundation and Jesus Christ as the cornerstone (v. 20). This building grows into a holy temple where God dwells (vv. 21-22).

In 3:1-12 Paul refers to his ministry among the Gentiles directed toward bringing them to knowledge of God's plan: a mystery that has been hidden and only now made known that "the Gentiles have become fellow heirs, members of the same body, and sharers in the promise in Christ Jesus through the gospel" (v. 6). This leads into a prayer (3:13-19) that the readers may be strengthened by the power of God's Spirit and come to know Christ's love. The section ends with a doxology, a hymn of praise to God and Christ Jesus (3:20-21).

The second part of the body, **ethical exhortations** (4:1–6:20), applies Paul's teaching to the lives of his readers. Paul reminds them that God has chosen them to be holy and blameless (4:1; see 1:4). Therefore they

must lead a life of unity in the Spirit (4:3) which reflects the "one Lord, one faith, one baptism, one God and Father of all" (vv. 5-6). The new life they have received means that they cannot continue to live according to the old ways (4:17-24). Paul's description reflects the transformation that occurs in the ritual of baptism: "You were taught to put away your former way of life . . . and to clothe yourselves with the new self" (vv. 22-24). He spells out the rules for this new life (4:25–5:2). This instruction further develops through the use of a catalog of vices (5:3-7) and virtues (vv. 8-20) so characteristic of Hellenistic moral instruction.

The moral instructions continue with a household code (5:21–6:9) similar to Col 3:18–4:1. Combined here are the images of the church as the body of Christ and as the bride of Christ (5:30-33). The readers are called to "reverence for Christ" (5:21). Christ's position is the norm that influences relationships within the household: unity and obedience are the two fundamental virtues.

Paul's final instructions are inspired by the imagery of putting on armor and setting off to war (6:10-20). The struggle Paul has in mind is with "the cosmic powers of this present darkness," " the spiritual forces of evil in the heavenly places" (v. 12). The command to "put on the whole armor of God" (v. 11) is again a reminder of the baptismal ritual.

In the **final greetings** (6:21-24) Paul mentions Tychicus, who will tell the readers everything that is happening to Paul (just as he did in Col 4:7). Paul's blessing is for those who have "an undying love for our Lord Jesus Christ" (6:24).

Critical Issues in Studying Ephesians

Who Are the Recipients of This Letter?

The addressees of this letter remain a mystery. As noted, the phrase "in Ephesus" is lacking in the most ancient manuscripts, such as $\mathfrak{P}$46 (Chester Beatty Papyrus II, *ca*. 200 C.E.) and the 4th-century Codices Sinaiticus and Vaticanus. This is the least personal of all Paul's letters. Yet, Paul had spent three years in Ephesus (54-57; Acts 20:31). One would expect that he would have referred to some members of that community as well as some details about their personal situations. Apart from a brief reference to Paul's imprisonment and to Tychicus (6:20-21), there are no references to individuals or events. Further questions arise as to why Paul says: "I have heard of your faith" (1:15) when in fact he had worked in the community and knew it intimately. Finally, the impression gained from reading Ephesians is that the readers of this letter were Gentile Christians (2:11). No mention

Parallel Texts in Colossians and Ephesians

Col 4:7-8
Tychicus will tell you all the news about me; he is a beloved brother, a faithful minister, and a fellow servant in the Lord. I have sent him to you for this very purpose, so that you may know how we are and that he may encourage your hearts.

Eph 6:21-22
So that you also may know how I am and what I am doing, Tychicus will tell you everything. He is a dear brother and a faithful minister in the Lord. I am sending him to you for this very purpose, to let you know how we are, and to encourage your hearts.

Col 3:12-13
As God's chosen ones, holy and beloved, clothe yourselves with compassion, kindness, humility, meekness, and patience. Bear with one another and, if anyone has a complaint against another, forgive each other.

Eph 4:1-2
I therefore, the prisoner in the Lord, beg you to lead a life worthy of the calling to which you have been called, with all humility and gentleness, with patience, bearing with one another in love.

Col 3:16-17
Let the word of Christ dwell in you richly; teach and admonish one another in all wisdom; and with gratitude in your hearts sing psalms, hymns, and spiritual songs to God. And whatever you do, in word or deed, do everything in the name of the Lord Jesus, giving thanks to God the Father through him.

Eph 5:18-20
. . . but be filled with the Spirit, as you sing psalms and hymns and spiritual songs among yourselves, singing and making melody to the Lord in your hearts, giving thanks to God the Father at all times and for everything in the name of our Lord Jesus Christ.

is made of Jews anywhere in the letter. This would not agree with the picture of Acts 19:1-10 that shows Paul's ministry in Ephesus embracing both Jews and Gentiles.

Some scholars have proposed that Ephesians was in reality a circular letter written to communities founded by Paul in Asia Minor. It has also been suggested that the place in the opening formula where traditionally a church was mentioned was left blank for the individual church to supply its own name. This would account for those manuscripts that do bear the inscription "To the saints who are in Ephesus" because they would come from Ephesus, while Marcion's reference "to the Laodiceans" would originate in Laodicea.

Is Paul the Author of Ephesians?
At least 90 words in Ephesians are not found in the undisputed letters of Paul. While Paul does use some unique words in his writings, the number in this letter is striking. Another stylistic characteristic of Ephesians is its use of long, involved sentences, even more so than found in Colossians. For example, in the original Greek text the passages 1:15-23; 3:1-6; and 4:11-16 are each a single sentence. To make sense of these verses in English, translators usually divide them into multiple sentences. This is very different from the style of Paul's genuine letters. As regards the thought of Ephesians, concepts found in Paul's other letters such as body, fullness, mystery, reconciliation take on a different and more developed understanding.

Finally, the relationship of Ephesians to Colossians is also worth noting. One third of the words in Colos-

sians are found in Ephesians. In addition, between one third and one half of the verses in Ephesians have verbal parallels in Colossians.

The relationship between Ephesians and Paul's genuine letters is also interesting. Ephesians seems to have drawn on all seven genuine letters. When Paul wrote Romans, after writing to the Galatians, he referred to similar themes and issues, but he did not simply draw directly and verbally on what he had written before. For this reason most scholars conclude that the use of both Paul's genuine letters and Colossians must have been by someone other than Paul who deliberately used their language and themes.

We conclude that Ephesians arises from one of Paul's disciples, a member of a group who continued to reflect and hand on Paul's teaching as new situations and concerns developed within those communities Paul had founded. It would make sense to see these disciples (or "school") situated in Ephesus, and the early 90s would be the most feasible date for Ephesians. This letter is known to Ignatius (ca. 110), who mirrors 5:25-29 in his Letter to Polycarp.

The Literary Character of Ephesians
Ephesians is not a typical letter. Unlike Paul's genuine letters, which were written to resolve problems in communities he had established, this writing mentions neither concrete issues nor individuals — which is highly surprising given Paul's missionary activity in Ephesus.

Instead, our writer celebrates Paul's thought and

the accomplishments since his death. He shows that Paul's vision of unity within the Christian community ("no longer Jew or Greek, . . .slave or free, . . .male and female," Gal 3:28) has brought forth fruit. In Ephesians crises and divisions are behind. What Paul had seen as an ideal, our writer celebrates as reality. Consequently, this writing draws attention to and celebrates this unity as the culmination of Paul's thought and teaching. To consider it either a "circular letter" sent to all the Pauline churches or as an introduction to a collection of Paul's letters is a valid understanding of this writing.

Theological Themes in Ephesians

The dominant theme of this letter is the concept of the church. Ephesians uses the word "church" (Greek *ekklesia*) nine times to refer to the universal church (1:22; 3:10, 21; 5:23, 24, 25, 27, 29, 32). In his genuine letters Paul refers to the church in the sense of the local community that gathers together in someone's house, a house church. In Colossians the word occurs four times: twice for the universal church (1:18, 24) and twice for the local church (4:15, 16). Ephesians then shows the end of a development in the concept from local church to universal church.

In describing the universal church, the writer of Ephesians uses a number of images or metaphors. The most significant is that of the body. As in Colossians (Col 1:18, 24), Christ is the head of the body (Eph 1:22; 5:23). The writer extends this concept even further and gives it a cosmic role. As head, Christ has been placed over all things in the universe, "far above all rule and authority and power and dominion" (1:21). Christ is also the fullness of the church, "which is his body, the fullness of him who fills all in all" (1:23).

Further descriptive of the relationship between Christ and the church is the church as the bride of Christ (5:22-33): "Christ loved the church and gave himself up for her" (v. 25). Christ's death makes the church holy and without blemish so he can present the church to himself as a pure and holy bride (v. 27). Among allusions to rituals within the Christian community, the bride is washed clean and made holy (v. 26), a reference to baptism. The bridal image also captures the ideal relationship between husband and wife.

The church is also the temple of the Lord (2:21-22), the place where God dwells among humanity. Built upon the foundation of the apostles and prophets with Christ as the cornerstone, the structure "grows" into the household of God (vv. 19-21).

The unity of the church is exemplified in the mystery of Christ, which brings about the unity of Jews and Gentiles in the body of Christ (3:4-6). Paul endeavored hard to achieve this unity during his journeys and letters. Ephesians shows how decades later this unity has been realized.

The Pastoral Letters

Getting Started

1   Read 1 and 2 Timothy and Titus. What does each of these letters say about Paul?

2   Write a one-page summary of the advice that the writer gives to Timothy and Titus in these letters.

Preliminary Comments

1 and 2 Timothy and Titus are called the Pastoral Letters (from Latin *pastor* "shepherd"). Like a shepherd who cares for his sheep, these letters offer Paul's advice to two of his young associates, Timothy and Titus, who had accompanied him on his missionary journeys.

Timothy is associated with Paul in the Acts of the Apostles and in many of his letters. Acts recounts

Colonnaded road at Ephesus, once lined with shops, leading from the harbor to the theater. (Phoenix Data Systems, Neal and Joel Bierling)

Timothy joining Paul and Silas on the second missionary journey (Acts 16:1-5). He is "the son of a Jewish woman who was a believer; but his father was a Greek" (16:1). According to 2 Tim 1:5, his mother was Eunice and his grandmother, Lois. Paul had Timothy circumcised, not because Paul believed it was necessary for salvation, but because their mission took them first to the Jews and he wanted Timothy to be accepted within the context of the Jewish community.

In the letters, Timothy is mentioned together with Paul as author (1 Thess 1:1; 2 Thess 1:1; 2 Cor 1:1; Phil 1:1). Paul gives details of his associations with Timothy in his ministry to the churches. For example, Paul sent Timothy to Thessalonica from Athens on the second missionary journey to find out the state of the community (1 Thess 3:1-5) and to report back (v. 6). Paul also planned to send Timothy from Ephesus to Corinth on his third journey to remind them of his teaching (1 Cor 4:17; 16:10-11). He also planned to send Timothy to Philippi from Ephesus so he could report back about the community (Phil 2:19-24). 1 Timothy situates Timothy in Ephesus as its leader (1 Tim 1:3).

1 and 2 Timothy tell us that Timothy has a close relationship to Paul: "my loyal child" (1 Tim 1:2); "my beloved child" (2 Tim 1:2). He is young (1 Tim 4:12). The gift of leadership has been given him by the laying on of hands by the elders or presbyters (4:14). He has been frequently ill (1 Tim 5:23). All this can be reconciled with information in Acts and Paul's letters. The writer of 1 Timothy adds further that Paul left Timothy behind in Ephesus when he went off to Macedonia (1:3) and he hopes to return soon to Ephesus to see Timothy (3:14-15).

Titus also was Paul's coworker. While Acts does not mention him, Paul's letters (especially Galatians and Corinthians) do. He accompanied Paul on his visit to Jerusalem 14 years after Paul's conversion. He was a Gentile convert (Gal 2:1-3). Paul entrusted Titus with organizing the collection in Corinth (2 Cor 8:5-6, 16-24). After Paul's "painful visit" (2 Cor 2:1) to Corinth, he sent Titus to them, and he returned to tell Paul that the problems had been resolved (7:6-16). The Letter to Titus situates him as the leader in Crete (1:5).

1 Timothy

A Walk through 1 Timothy

In the **opening formula** (1:1-2) the writer identifies himself as Paul, an apostle chosen by God. A thanksgiving

---

> **Reading Guide to 1 Timothy**
>
> **Opening Formula** (1:1-2)
>
> **Thanksgiving** (None)
>
> **Body** (1:3–6:19)
>
> > **Attack on False Teachers** (1:3-20)
> >
> > **Church Leadership Functions: Part 1** (2:1–3:16)
> > Ordering of Worship and Role of Women (2:1-15)
> > Instructions to Bishops/Overseers (3:1-7)
> > Instructions to Deacons (3:8-13)
> > The Mystery of Our Religion (3:14-16)
> >
> > **Attack on Ethics of False Teachers** (4:1-10)
> >
> > **Church Leadership Functions: Part 2** (4:11–6:19)
> > Encouragement to Timothy as Teacher (4:11–5:2)
> > Instructions for Widows (5:3-16)
> > Instructions for Elders/Presbyters (5:17-25)
> > Instructions for Slaves (6:1-2)
> > False Teaching and True Riches (6:3-10)
> > Instructions for Timothy (6:11-19)
>
> **Final Greetings** (6:20-21)

section so typical of Paul's letters is missing because the writer is anxious to deal with a most urgent matter, the false teachers (1:3-20). It is not clear exactly what their beliefs were. They probably belonged to an early form of Gnosticism because the writer speaks about their preoccupation with "myths and endless genealogies that promote speculations" (v. 4). They also had strong Jewish connections because Paul refers to the Torah in vv. 8-9.

The **body** of the letter contains two sections that deal with church order (2:1–3:16 and 4:11–6:19). The first part (2:1–3:16) deals with the role of women, bishops/overseers, and deacons within the community. Paul begins the code with the obligation of offering prayers for kings and for those in authority (2:1-2). He speaks about the role of men (2:8) and women (2:9-15) in the worshipping community. This passage has caused great controversy in interpretation. It forbids women "to teach or to have authority over a man" (v. 12) and reflects the patriarchal mentality characteristic of 1st-century C.E. Greco-Roman society.

Paul considers the role and functions of the "bishop/overseer" within the community (3:1-7). Throughout this study of the Pastoral Letters, we have deliberately refrained from referring to the "office" of bishop or others but speak rather of their function or leadership role. What is stressed here is not a status, but a function of leadership. Paul draws the qualities from the Hellenistic ethical philosophical lists of his time. The bishop/overseer is to be "temperate, sensible, respectable, hospitable, an apt teacher" (v. 2). In 3:8-13 he discusses the similar qualifications for deacons. Verse 11 mentions "women (deacons)" whose qualifications embrace seriousness, temperance, fidelity. Unfortunately, nothing is explained about the service that either the male or female deacons perform. This section ends with a beautiful hymn defining the mystery of our religion, namely the person of Jesus Christ (3:16).

In 4:1-10 the writer again turns attention to the threat of false teachers, comparing their ethics and that of a true "servant of Christ Jesus" (v. 6): "they forbid marriage and demand abstinence from foods, which God created" (v. 3).

The second part of the church order codes (4:11–6:19) begins with an exhortation to Timothy listing the qualities for which Timothy must strive: he must "set the believers an example in speech and conduct, in love, in faith, in purity" (4:12). In particular he is to be concerned about the reading of Scripture as well as the teaching within the community (v. 13). He then gives instruction for three other groups within the house church:

- Widows (5:3-16): In listing their qualifications the writer implies that widows at the time of this letter might serve a particular function within the church. These widows must be older than 60 years, married only once, and have no dependent children (vv. 9-10). Their lives must have attested that they had "washed the saints' feet, helped the afflicted, and devoted herself to doing good in every way" (v. 10). These widows would be cared for from the common funds (Acts 6:1).
- Elders (5:17-25): In Acts and the Letter to Titus the term "elder/presbyter" (Greek *presbyteros*) was used interchangeably with "bishop/overseer" *(episkopos)*. Here the writer considers the qualities of the elder/presbyter separately from those of bishop/overseer examined earlier (3:1-7), implying a distinction between the two groups. Apparently by the time of 1 Timothy all bishops were elders, but not all elders were bishops. The elders' task was above all preaching and teaching (v. 17).
- Slaves (6:1-2): As in the household codes, slaves are to honor their masters in the context of the church. Once again the writer simply reflects the status quo of his society and is not presenting an authoritative endorsement of the institution of slavery for all time.

The body of the letter ends with further instructions for Timothy (6:3-16). He is also to instruct the rich to be ready to do good and to share their wealth (6:17-19).

In the **final greetings to Timothy** (6:20-21), the writer again warns against the false teachers and pleads with him to avoid their so-called knowledge (v. 20). The reference to knowledge (Greek *gnosis*) perhaps indicates that the false teachers belonged to an early form of Gnosticism.

2 Timothy

A Walk through 2 Timothy

The **opening formula (1:1-2)** is similar to 1 Timothy. As with Paul's genuine letters, 2 Timothy contains a **thanksgiving (1:3-5)**, where the writer praises God for Timothy's faith. It is a very personal tribute, mentioning the Jewish faith of Lois (Timothy's grandmother) and Eunice (his mother).

The **body of the letter (1:6–4:18)** begins with a plea to Timothy to witness based on Paul's example (1:6–2:13). Paul challenges Timothy to allow the power of the Spirit to be rekindled (1:6). He invites Timothy to share in the suffering he is experiencing in prison and not to be ashamed of it (v. 8). He also pleads that Timothy hold fast "to the standard of sound teaching that you have heard from me" (v. 13). Paul shows a certain isolation in his imprisonment and feels that many have turned away from him, being drawn away by false teachers (v. 15). Three images that are traditional in Paul's writings (soldier, athlete, farmer [2:3-6]) show that only by doing one's work will one reap reward. Finally, 2:11-13 is a hymn to Christ taken from the liturgy, placed here as a reminder to Christ Jesus' example and influence on the lives of believers.

The faithful must avoid the teaching and example of false teachers (2:14–3:9). The life of a good minister contrasts with the type that the false teachers present. They are "wrangling over words" (2:14), delight in "profane chatter" (v. 16), and teach that "the resurrection has already taken place" (v. 18). Again Paul lists vices (3:1-5) to be avoided in what are now considered "the last days" (v. 1).

In contrast to that of the false teachers, Paul presents his own example and teaching for Timothy to follow (3:10–4:18). He highlights the role of Scripture in the community as "inspired by God," "useful for teaching, for reproof, for correction, and for training in righteousness" (3:16). Turning to his personal situation, Paul gives one of the most memorable statements about his life's work as a minister of Christ (4:6-8). In what is very much like his last will and testament, he compares himself to an athlete who competes in order to gain "the

Reading Guide to 2 Timothy

Opening Formula (1:1-2)

Thanksgiving (1:3-5)

Body (1:6–4:18)

Plea to Witness; the Example of Paul in Prison (1:6–2:13)

Avoid the False Teachers (2:14–3:9)

The Example of Paul; Paul's Situation (3:10–4:18)

Final Greetings (4:19-22)

crown of righteousness" (v. 8) that will be awarded on the last day.

Paul turns to very practical matters and reveals much about his situation and his attitude. He invites Timothy to come and visit him soon (4:9). His associates all having left to minister elsewhere, only Luke remains with him (v. 11). Paul requests Timothy to bring him what he needs: his cloak, books, and parchments (v. 13). As always Paul places confidence and trust in the Lord who "will rescue me from every evil attack" (v. 18).

The letter concludes with the usual **final greetings** (4:19-22) which include greetings from a number of Paul's co-workers.

Titus

A Walk through Titus

The **opening formula** (1:1-4) uses the customary elements of Paul's genuine letters, but here the style is more formal and developed. As with 1 Timothy this letter contains no **thanksgiving**. Instead, the author proceeds with the **body of the letter** (1:5–3:11) to speak about the issues that concern him. He first addresses leadership functions within the church (1:5-9), the issue that is paramount in all the Pastoral Letters. Paul implies that he had left Titus behind in Crete to organize the churches there. He delineates the qualities of elders/bishops (Greek *presbyteroi/episkopoi*). It appears that the elders and bishops are one and the same in this letter, whereas 1 Timothy indicates a development with the two groups representing different functions. The description of the bishop's qualifications here is similar to that in 1 Tim 3:1-7: he is to be "blameless . . . upright, devout, and self-controlled" (1:7-8).

Paul's next theme is false teaching (1:10-16). Again it is difficult to reconstruct what these teachers are promoting. The problems seem to be the same ones that

concern the two letters to Timothy arising from early forms of Gnosticism.

In 2:1–3:7 Paul refers to the moral behavior expected of members of the community. Again these norms are similar to the household codes. They are to regulate relationships among the members and flow from "sound doctrine" (2:1) that Titus is urged to teach. Paul stresses guidelines of behavior for various groups within the Christian community: older men (2:2), older women (v. 3), young women (vv. 4-5), younger men (vv. 6-8), and slaves (vv. 9-10). Their way of life should provide an example for others to imitate (v. 7).

A further attack on false teaching (3:8-11) concludes the body of the letter. The readers are encouraged not to engage in senseless discussion that gets nowhere. They are to avoid anything that would lead to dissention within the community.

The letter closes with **final greetings** (3:12-15) in which the writer gives personal notes and details hard to harmonize with the picture of Paul that Luke has presented in Acts. "Grace be with all of you" (v. 15) implies that more than just Titus is reading this letter!

Critical Issues in Studying the Pastoral Letters

Who Is the Writer of These Letters?

Since the 18th century the Pauline authorship of these three letters has been universally challenged to such an extent that today most scholars argue that the writer could not have been Paul. Their arguments are based on the following observations:

- The Muratorian Canon (*ca.* 180 C.E.) demonstrates that the Pastoral Letters had been accepted as authoritative before the end of the 2nd century: ". . . one to Titus, two to Timothy for the sake of affection and love. . . ." The first reliable evidence we have for the Pastoral Letters comes from the letter of Polycarp to

Reading Guide to Titus

Opening Formula (1:1-4)

Thanksgiving (None)

Body (1:5–3:11)

Church Functions (1:5-9)

Attacks on False Teaching (1:10-16)

Exhortation to Correct Behavior; Household Codes (2:1–3:7)

Further Attacks on False Teaching (3:8-11)

Final Greetings (3:12-15)

- the Philippians, where 4:1 shows a familiarity with 1 Tim 6:10 and 6:7. Since Polycarp's letter was written *ca.* 120, the Pastorals must have preceded this date.
- Nearly 40 percent of all the words in the Pastorals are not found elsewhere in the letters of Paul, and almost half of these do not occur again in other New Testament writings.
- The style of the Pastorals differs remarkably from that of Paul's letters. It is much more peaceful and reflective than Paul's argumentative style, resembling more the style of 1 Peter.
- The biographical information about Paul in these letters cannot be coordinated with what is known about Paul from Acts prior to Paul's imprisonment in Rome. If these letters came from Paul, they would argue for another missionary journey after his imprisonment from 64 to 67.
- The church leadership functions presumed by these letters show a development beyond the time of Paul's ministry. Titus reveals a double leadership in the church of presbyters/bishops and deacons. This is similar to the twofold division of the Didache (15:1), written *ca.* 100, and 1 Clement (42:4-5; 44:4-5), *ca.* 95. 1 Timothy implies a threefold leadership role of bishop, presbyter, and deacon (see the letters of Ignatius of Antioch, *ca.* 110).

From these considerations it is best to conclude that the Pastoral Letters were written after Paul and after the Letters to the Colossians, Ephesians, and 2 Thessalonians. Certainly, the author must stand in Paul's tradition, being more likely a third generation member of this school or tradition.

When Were the Pastoral Letters Written?

If one accepts that the Pastoral Letters are pseudonymous, how are the autobiographical references to be understood? The form of 2 Timothy is very much like Paul's last will and testament. One would see it being written shortly after Paul's death by someone who knew Paul and was associated with him during the end of his life. This means that the biographical details in this letter are largely historical and have been used to present a witness of the apostle for future generations, a challenge to continue Paul's work so that the gospel message continued to spread. Titus and 1 Timothy would be written much later toward the end of the 1st century in imitation of 2 Timothy in order to speak to the crises of their own day by using Paul's authority.

The Pastoral Letters point to a development in leadership functions within the church. 2 Timothy makes no mention of the functions of bishop, elder, or deacon. Titus, however, mentions both elders/presbyters and

bishop (singular), yet draws no distinction between the two groups — they seem to exercise the same function as is indicated by their inclusion in the same paragraph (Titus 1:5-9). Finally, in 1 Timothy the functions of bishop/overseer (singular; 1 Tim 3:1-7) and elders/presbyters (plural; 1 Tim 5:17-22) are discussed separately. From this we propose the following scenario: Since 2 Timothy makes no mention of specific functions of leadership in the community, we would situate it earlier than the other Pastoral Letters. Titus makes no distinction in functions between bishops and presbyters, while 1 Timothy presumes a separation of functions or roles. This suggests that Titus preceded 1 Timothy in composition. We postulate then that the Pastoral Letters were written in the sequence of 2 Timothy, Titus, then 1 Timothy. The canonical order is based solely upon length of the writing, not on chronology.

How Are the References to Timothy and Titus to be Understood?

Still unresolved are a number of issues. What about Timothy and Titus? Were they still alive when these letters were written? Or did these letters use their names simply as a way of speaking to the church decades later? This would indicate that not only is the authorship pseudonymous but the addressees are pseudonymous as well.

Theological Themes

Ecclesial Vision of These Letters

The Pastoral Letters presume church communities structured similarly to the pattern of families within the Greco-Roman world. The church is the household of God (1 Tim 3:15) to whom God gives life. This new household of God includes old and young women, old and young men, slaves, as well as various leadership roles such as bishops/overseers, elders/presbyters, and deacons.

The daily life of believers is intimately connected to their life of worship (1 Tim 2:10). They become "a people of (God's) own who are zealous for good deeds" (Titus 2:14). The writer applies the typical household codes of his society to the church as the household of God. Specific behaviors are required of each group within this household.

The leadership functions exercised within the early Christian communities are somewhat difficult to identify. We can attempt to make sense of them in the following way:

Within the context of the Jewish world, elders/presbyters (Greek *presbyteroi*) were an essential feature in the synagogue, and from them the early Jewish Christian communities developed this function. They were men older either in age or in faith. Their task was to work together as a group within the community in order to give it direction and to care for the beliefs and the moral lives of the community.

There are no references in the genuine Pauline letters to elders/presbyters. We note that Paul's communities were largely charismatic communities where the members had been gifted by the Spirit to exercise ministries as apostles, teachers, prophets, and evangelists (1 Cor 12:27-31). The Letter to the Philippians points to a developing form of leadership referred to as "bishops/overseers (Greek *episkopoi*) and deacons" (Phil 1:1). Bishops/overseers was a term used widely in a secular sense within the Hellenistic world for someone who acts as "protector or as a patron." With time it was used to refer to people who exercised official functions with various responsibilities.

The Value of Scripture

2 Timothy contains one of the most important statements about Scripture in the Bible: "All scripture is inspired by God and is useful for teaching, for reproof, for correction, and for training in righteousness" (3:16). The Scriptures referred to are the Hebrew Bible. At this stage the Christian Scriptures were still in the process of being written, and it would take another two centuries before they would universally be considered as Sacred Writings. For 2 Tim 3:16 their nature as Scripture means that they are inspired, that God has "breathed life into them" and this life is communicated to those who read them. Their purpose is to teach and to preserve the faith of the community. This text together with 2 Pet 1:20-21 would be the object of theological reflections in later centuries in an attempt to explain inspiration.

The Letter to the Hebrews

Getting Started

Read the Letter to the Hebrews. Note all the allusions that the writer makes to the Hebrew Scriptures.

Preliminary Comments

We have examined Paul's seven genuine letters, the three Pseudo-Pauline Letters, and the three Pastoral Letters. Church tradition considered a further writing, called simply "To the Hebrews," as Paul's 14th letter. For this reason we examine this writing in this chapter under Paul's heritage. The earliest traditions come from the Eastern church at the end of the 2nd and beginning of the 3rd centuries C.E. Clement of Alexandria (*ca.* 150-215) argued that Paul wrote this letter but did not mention his name because many Jews were hostile to him. Origen (*ca.* 185-254, also from Alexandria) questioned whether it was written by Paul, saying, "But who wrote the letter, God really knows." Nevertheless, in the East the view of Paul as the author became universally accepted. While the Western church was more skeptical about Paul's authorship, the authority of Augustine and Jerome argued for its inclusion in the canon in the late 4th century. This writing was universally accepted as written by Paul from the 4th until the 16th century, when Martin Luther questioned its authorship and suggested that Apollos (1 Cor 1:12; 3:4-6, 22; Acts 18:24-28) was its author.

The title "To the Hebrews" does not appear in the original text, but was added later. It is first found in The Chester Beatty Papyrus II, $\mathfrak{P}$46, undoubtedly the best manuscript of Paul's letters, dated *ca.* 200. The early church probably gave it this title because its contents focus exclusively on Jesus' superiority over Jewish practices and institutions.

The usual features of a letter are absent from this writing. There is no opening formula: the writer does not identify himself, nor does he say who the readers are. Further, there is no thanksgiving section that normally follows the opening formula. Instead, the writer begins immediately with his central focus on God's Son. Throughout the writing are very few references to the context of the readers. The only epistolary feature of this writing is found at the conclusion, where a brief greeting is appended (13:24-25).

The writer characterizes his writing as "a word of exhortation" (13:22) and encourages the readers to remain true to their faith commitment. Some scholars have suggested that we view this work as a literary sermon, which really does capture its genre. Like the speeches of Cicero that were first delivered orally, then later refined and put in writing, our author has delivered this sermon in a liturgical context and it has been committed to writing with the intention of being read again in the liturgy.

Because it is not a letter, but rather a sermon, we shall refer to this writing simply as "Hebrews." Instead of speaking about the writer or the author, we shall refer to the preacher to capture its nature as a sermon.

Reading Guide to Hebrews

The Position of Christ (1:1–10:18)

    Prologue (1:1-4)

    Superiority of Jesus as God's Son (1:5–4:13)

    Superiority of Jesus' Priesthood (4:14–7:28)

    Superiority of Jesus' Priestly Work (8:1–10:18)

Exhortations Derived from the Previous Arguments (10:19–13:17)

Epilogue and Conclusion (13:18-25)

A Walk through Hebrews

This writing divides into two main parts: the first considers the position of Christ (1:1–10:18), while the second (10:19–13:17) draws out the consequences of this understanding of Christ for its hearers/readers.

The Position of Christ (1:1–10:18)

Prologue (1:1-4)

The preacher contrasts two periods of revelation: in the past God spoke through many prophets, but now God speaks through God's only Son. He sets the stage for his basic theme, the superiority of Jesus to everything that has gone before. God has appointed Jesus as "heir of all things" (1:2).

Superiority of Jesus as God's Son (1:5–4:13)

The prologue refers to the superiority of God's Son. This section begins by arguing Jesus' superiority to the angels (1:5–2:18), underscored by a series of quotations from the Hebrew Scriptures. God declared Jesus to be his Son, rather than the angels, who are God's servants. Providing practical application of this doctrinal discussion, the preacher warns the hearers to take seriously the salvation that Jesus has mediated (2:1-4).

The preacher continues his argumentation: Jesus' superiority over those who were God's intermediaries in the past 3:1–4:13). He is "the apostle and high priest of our confession" (3:1). Moses, the great Lawgiver, was faithful over God's house as God's servant, but Jesus was faithful as God's Son. The preacher urges his hearers to imitate Jesus' faithfulness and not be like the Israelites, who because of their disobedience wandered through the wilderness and were ultimately refused entry into the Promised Land. He encourages them to strive to attain the heavenly rest by obedience, "so that no one may fall through such disobedience as theirs" (4:11).

Superiority of Jesus' Priesthood (4:14–7:28)

The preacher now considers the superiority of Jesus' priesthood (4:14–7:28) over the priesthood of the past:

"Since, then, we have a great high priest who has passed through the heavens, Jesus, the Son of God, let us hold fast to our confession" (4:14). Because he was also human, Jesus, as the heavenly high priest, is able to sympathize with our weaknesses; he was tested in every way that we are, yet he is without sin (v. 15). Jesus did not choose this role for himself, but was appointed by God to be the people's representative and became "the source of eternal salvation for all who obey him" (5:9).

In ch. 7 the preacher considers the argument for the superiority of Jesus' priesthood. He shows that Jesus' priesthood is like the priesthood of Melchizedek, by taking two texts from the Hebrew Bible that speak about Melchizedek: "The Lord has sworn and will not change his mind, 'You are a priest forever according to the order of Melchizedek'" (Ps 110:4). To this he adds his reflections on Gen 14:17-20, which shows Melchizedek's superiority to the Levitical priesthood of Israel. Since nothing is said in Genesis about Melchizedek's ancestry, he concludes that he was a priest forever (7:3). The preacher argues that the person who receives a tithe is greater than the one who gives it. In this sense the Levitical priests were greater than the Israelites because they received tithes from them, and they paid in turn tithes to Melchizedek through their ancestor Abraham. This shows that Melchizedek is greater than the Levitical priests; his priesthood is greater than theirs.

In 7:11-28 the preacher argues that Jesus' priesthood was not in the line of the Levitical priesthood. Instead, it was similar to that of Melchizedek. The Levitical priests were many, and they died (a sign of imperfection). Jesus' priesthood is one and remains forever (vv. 23-24). The Levitical priests offered many sacrifices, but Jesus offered only one: an eternal sacrifice (v. 27). Jesus has been declared to be an eternal priest like Melchizedek according to Ps 110:4. The Levitical priesthood has now been abrogated because Jesus exercises a priesthood that continues forever, and he offers a sacrifice that happened once, but has effects for all (vv. 26-27).

Superiority of Jesus' Priestly Work (8:1–10:18)

The preacher draws attention to various aspects of Israelite religion to show the superiority of Jesus' work. His reasoning is based upon Platonic thought, whereby earthly things are viewed as copies or shadows of the one true reality in the heavenly realm. In 8:5 the preacher quotes Exod 25:40, where God orders Moses to build a tabernacle according to the heavenly tabernacle that God showed him. This means that the earthly tabernacle is a shadow of the real heavenly tabernacle. Jesus' ministry surpasses that of the Hebrew Bible because he exercises a ministry in heaven where the true tabernacle is (8:2).

Jesus also establishes a new covenant that fulfills the prophecies of Jer 31:31-34: "In speaking of a 'new covenant,' he has made the first one obsolete. And what is obsolete and growing old will soon disappear" (8:13). In ch. 9, the preacher compares the death of Jesus and the ritual surrounding the Day of Atonement. Just as the high priest went once a year into the holy of holies with the blood of goats and bulls, Jesus enters once and for all into the heavenly sanctuary with his own blood (vv. 1-10). There Jesus ratifies the new covenant and appears "in the presence of God on our behalf" (v. 24). His was the most perfect sacrifice, and as such it is offered only once, not year after year as with the high priest on the Day of Atonement (v. 28).

In 10:1-18 the preacher reiterates the superiority of Jesus' sacrifice. That sacrifices had to be performed over and over again in the Levitical priesthood shows they were unable to take people's sins away. Jesus did away with all these sacrifices and offered only one sacrifice, once and for all (v. 12). The people's sins are taken away, and there is no longer need for further offerings for sin.

Exhortations Derived from the Previous Arguments (10:19–13:17)

The preacher assures his hearers that they are capable of entering the heavenly sanctuary with Jesus and that they should approach that sanctuary with confidence (10:19-25). Consequently, he calls on them to remain faithful and encourage others in doing good deeds. Chapter 11 is one of the most powerful passages in the New Testament and the culmination of his sermon, whereby he reflects on the nature of faith. He begins with a definition of faith: "the assurance of things hoped for, the conviction of things not seen" (11:1). From the Hebrew Bible he provides a long list of examples of people who demonstrate a faith that relies upon God's future promises. However, despite their great faith they did not receive what they hoped for. They had to wait for God's promises to be fulfilled in us because "God had provided something better so that they would not, apart from us, be made perfect" (v. 40). Again the preacher remains true to his contrast between the old and the new dispensations.

After these examples of past heroes of faith, the preacher turns to the present and urges his hearers to persevere in their own faith. "Since we are surrounded by so great a cloud of witnesses . . ." (12:1), they must keep their eyes on Jesus, "the pioneer and perfecter of our faith" (v. 2).

Epilogue and Conclusion (13:18-25)

The sermon concludes in the style of a letter. The preacher asks his hearers to pray for him and he gives a blessing (13:20-21). He tells them about Timothy's release from prison (v. 23) and sends greetings from himself and "those from Italy" (v. 24).

Critical Issues in Studying Hebrews

Who Is the Author?

The author does not name himself. Most scholars now reject the traditional view of Paul as author for the following reasons:

- The style of the writing: This work is anonymous, which is contrary to Paul's custom of identifying himself. Paul also uses the format of a Greco-Roman letter, whereas the only characteristics of a letter here are the concluding greetings. This is also a cleverly structured work that develops progressively, unlike Paul's style that at times jumps backward and forward.
- The writing contains many ideas and expressions that do not appear in Paul's letters. Most significant is that of the priesthood of Jesus. Connected with this concept are ritual ideas such as purification and perfection that are also absent from Paul's thought.
- Many concepts that are central to Paul's letters do not occur in this writing, such as the body of Christ (Rom 12:1-8). Paul also speaks of Christ's death in terms of reconciliation and justification, ideas foreign to this writing.
- The author states that he received his understanding of the gospel message from others, not from the Lord (2:3). Paul was very strong about the fact that he had received the message directly from the Lord.

As a result, it is hard to consider Paul as the author. If we examine the writing itself closely, the following aspects emerge regarding the implied author:

- He has a good Jewish background, as seen from his knowledge and use of the Hebrew Bible and Jewish institutions such as the temple (or tabernacle), sacrifices, and priesthood. He deals with them in detail in order to show that Jesus is superior to them all. A Gentile Christian would have presented Jesus in very different terms.
- Culturally, he betrays an Alexandrian background. The Jews in Alexandria had embraced Greek culture and philosophy. The most famous Jewish Alexandrian at that time was the philosopher Philo, who was influenced by Plato's thought, and the thought of Hebrews bears close affinities to that of Plato and Philo. The writer contrasts the visible-earthly-shadowy world

of the Hebrew Scriptures to the invisible-heavenly-real world of the New Testament. For example, the multiple sacrifices of the Hebrew world are a shadow of the one sacrifice of Jesus; the priests of the Hebrew Bible are shadows of Jesus, the perfect priest. Further, the author of Hebrews applies an allegorical interpretation of the Hebrew Scriptures similar to that used by Philo, whereby new meanings are derived from details of the text. This is clearly seen in the reference to and interpretation of Melchizedek.

- The Greek of this writing is among the best in the New Testament. Whenever the author quotes from the Hebrew Scriptures, he does so from the Septuagint (the Greek translation).

This examination shows that the implied author of this work was someone at home in the world of both the Jew and the Greek. A Christian Jew from Alexandria would be the best candidate. Many conjectures have been proposed, including Barnabas, Luke, Stephen, and Apollos, all of which have arguments in their favor. Indeed, Apollos (the candidate of Martin Luther) would fit best: he was a Jew, who spoke Greek, a native of Alexandria, "an eloquent man, well versed in the scriptures" (Acts 18:24). However, in the final analysis it is still conjecture, and it is best to say that we do not know.

Who Are the Recipients?
The title "To the Hebrews" is found first in the Chester Beatty papyrus 𝔓46 (*ca.* 200). While the writing does not offer many details about the hearers, it does appear that the writer has a particular community in mind. In the final chapter he mentions that he has visited them before and hopes to see them again (13:19, 23).

Traditionally this text has been viewed as addressed to Jewish Christians. Supporting this contention are its references to Jewish institutions such as sacrifice, the temple, and the priesthood. The numerous quotations from the Hebrew Scriptures as well as the arguments for the superiority of Jesus support a Jewish Christian audience. However, most scholars today do not restrict this writing in such an exclusive sense. The reference to the Hebrew Scriptures does not demand a detailed knowledge of them by the hearers. In fact, the hearers should recognize Plato's worldview whereby two spheres are contrasted: the world of the Hebrew Scriptures and that of Jesus Christ. It would make more sense to see this writing addressed to Gentile Christians with some Jewish Christians among them.

More recently scholars have proposed strong arguments for situating the hearers in Rome. The earliest evidence for this letter comes from references in *1 Clement* (*ca.* 95) and the *Shepherd of Hermas* (*ca.* 140), both of which emanated from Rome. The conclusion to the writing also mentions that greetings are being sent by those from Italy (13:24). It would seem strange that the writer would mention their origin unless they were sending greetings home.

As regards the date of this writing, its use by Clement of Rome shows that it was written before 95. The author is a second-generation Christian (2:3), so it could not have been written before 70. A date between 80 and 90 would appear to be the most feasible.

Theological Themes

The Position of Jesus Christ
The central theme of this writing is Jesus' superiority, especially in regard to the world and religion of the Hebrew Scriptures. This perspective has both positive and negative consequences. Positively, the preacher gives his hearers reasons for their belief. He reminds them of who they are, what they have accepted, and why they should remain true and faithful. He upholds the uniqueness and significance of Jesus for his hearers/readers. The challenge is to preserve this uniqueness. Negatively, such a perception might inspire the attitude that "We're better than you!" whereby Christians see themselves superior to those outside their community.

The writing also presents a clear perspective on Jesus, placing special stress on his humanity. While Jesus is Son of God, the writer also stresses his humanity, showing that Jesus fully understands our experiences because he has lived through them himself. He is able to sympathize with our human plight. There is one big difference: Jesus is without sin (4:15).

Jesus the Eternal High Priest
The high priesthood of Jesus is another major theme. It culminates in the understanding that in heaven Jesus offers an eternal sacrifice to the Father. This concept of Jesus is surprising, given the picture presented of him in the Gospels. There Jesus is clearly a layperson who is very critical of temple worship. However, the vision of this writing can be seen as a theological development from Jesus' opposition to the temple and the Levitical priesthood. Jesus comes to replace the worship and priesthood of Israel with one centered on himself.

Certain parallels have been noted between the figure of Melchizedek in the Dead Sea Scrolls and this presentation in Hebrews. In the Scrolls Melchizedek is portraited as a heavenly being who appears at the end of history as leader of the heavenly armies. He will overcome the powers of evil, and he functions in the way the high priest functions on the Day of Atonement.

All this indicates that at the time of Hebrews many Melchizedek traditions were circulating. The preacher is aware of some of them and uses them to give expression to Jesus' role, not just as the fulfillment of Israel's past hopes, but rather as one who replaces them and is superior to the past dispensation.

Interaction between Christianity and Culture

Hebrews offers a tremendous example of how to transpose belief in Jesus and his significance into the thought patterns of another culture. Hebrews shows how Jesus is understood within the context of Judaism as well as in the framework of Alexandrian, Platonic, and Hellenistic thought. Taking the traditions that had been handed down to him (2:3), the preacher reflects on them and gives them a new expression in terms of the thinking and traditions that were familiar to his hearers.

The preacher offers an important paradigm for Christians of every age. Christians today need to take seriously this approach by beginning with a clear understanding of the traditions of their own faith that have been passed down to them by former generations. They are challenged to give expression to this belief by means of the language, philosophy, and thought patterns of their own world. As the Christian thinker Anselm (*ca.* 1033-1109) expressed it: "*Fides quaerens intellectum* (Faith seeking understanding)."

Questions for Review and Discussion

2 Thessalonians

1   Identify all the references to Jesus in 2 Thessalonians. What is the writer saying about Jesus through these references, and how would you compare this to 1 Thessalonians?

2   What does 2 Thessalonians teach about the final coming of Jesus?

Colossians

1   Present a brief argument that either defends or opposes Paul as author of this writing.

2   List the people referred to by name in this letter. What does the writer say about them? Where else do they occur in the New Testament? (Refer to a concordance of the New Testament for assistance.)

Ephesians

1   What is the relationship between the Letter to the Colossians and the Letter to the Ephesians? Support your argument with examples from the letters.

2   What are some of the challenges the writer presents to his readers in the ethical section of this letter?

The Pastoral Letters

1   List the job descriptions and qualifications needed for the functions of bishop, presbyters, and deacons as they are described in Titus and 1 Timothy.

2   Identify three passages in these letters that you find memorable. Why do they appeal to you?

To the Hebrews

1   Why do think the writer wants to express Jesus as superior to the traditions of Israel?

2   List sayings that you find in this writing that are in usage today in the religious language of Christianity.

Further Reading

2 Thessalonians
Collins, Raymond F. *Letters That Paul Did Not Write: The Epistle to the Hebrews and the Pauline Pseudepigrapha*. Good News Studies 28. Wilmington: Michael Glazier, 1988.
Gaventa, Beverly Roberts. "Thessalonians, Second Letter to." In *EDB*, 1299-1300.
Jewett, Robert K. "2 Thessalonians." In *ECB*, 1423-27.

Colossians
Hay, David M. "Colossians, Letter to the." In *EDB*, 270-71.
Hooker, Morna D. "Colossians." In *ECB*, 1404-12.
Schweizer, Eduard. *The Letter to the Colossians*. Minneapolis: Augsburg, 1982.

Ephesians
Gundry-Volf, Judith M. "Ephesians, Letter to the." In *EDB*, 411-13.
Marshall, I. Howard. "Ephesians." In *ECB*, 1385-93.
Schnackenburg, Rudolf. *Ephesians*. Edinburgh: T. & T. Clark, 1991.

Pastoral Letters

Fiore, Benjamin. *The Function of Personal Example in the Socratic and Pastoral Epistles.* AnBib 105. Rome: Pontifical Biblical Institute, 1986.

Perkins, Pheme. "Pastoral Epistles." In *ECB,* 1428-46.

Pervo, Richard I. "Pastoral Epistles." In *EDB,* 1014-15.

Young, Frances M. *The Theology of the Pastoral Letters.* New Testament Theology. Cambridge: Cambridge University Press, 1994.

Hebrews

D'Angelo, Mary Rose. "Hebrews." In *The Women's Bible Commentary,* ed. Carol A. Newsom and Sharon H. Ringe, 2nd ed., 455-59. Louisville: Westminster/John Knox, 1998.

Evans, Louis H. *Hebrews.* Preacher's Commentary 33. Nashville: Thomas Nelson, 1985.

Thiselton, Anthony C. "Hebrews." In *ECB,* 1451-82.

Thompson, James W. "Hebrews, Epistle to the." In *EDB,* 568-70.

The Johannine Tradition

Chapter 59

The Gospel of John

Jesus the Son of God

Getting Started

1 Read the Gospel of John. How is Jesus portrayed in this Gospel?

2 Note five major differences between John and the Synoptics.

3 Note the seven miracles that John narrates in the Gospel.

Preliminary Comments

The Gospel of John is very different from the Gospels of Matthew, Mark, and Luke. The differences arise because John's traditions and sources are independent of those behind the Synoptic Gospels. The Gospel of John is usually symbolized by means of the picture of an eagle. Just as an eagle soars in the sky and then swoops down and appears to hover, so John's Gospel reaches great heights in its portrayal of Jesus as the Son of God by reflecting and drawing out the significance of Jesus' ministry (see, e.g., the account of the multiplication of bread). While the Synoptic Gospels only describe the miracle (Matt 14:13-21; Mark 6:30-44; Luke 9:10-17), John's Jesus

explains the significance of the miracle in great detail (6:1-71).

Our path through the Gospel of John will endeavor to highlight the main themes that trace their way through the Gospel as well as its distinctive message, picture of Jesus, and concept of discipleship.

A Walk through John

John 1–12: The Book of Signs: Jesus Reveals Himself

Jesus Reveals Himself to His Disciples (1:1-51)
John's Gospel opens with a hymn to the Incarnate Word (1:1-18). The human Jesus is identified with the heavenly Word (Greek *Logos*). *Logos* as a designation for Jesus is unique to the Gospel of John. As the Word made flesh among us, Jesus makes known to those who accept him the "power to become children of God" (v. 12). After this prologue has set the ultimate context for Jesus as the divine Word come down from heaven, John opens with the ministry of John the Baptist as witness to Jesus, the Lamb of God, an image that foreshadows Jesus' sacrificial death on behalf of humanity (vv. 19-34). The call of the first disciples in John is very different from that of the Synoptics. According to John, they were initially

Reading Guide to the Gospel of John

Book of Signs: Jesus Reveals Himself (1–12)

Jesus Reveals Himself to His Disciples (1:1-51)

First Two Signs: From Cana to Cana (2:1-4:54)
Changing Water to Wine (2:1-12)
Cleansing of the Temple (2:13-25)
Nicodemus and Being Born Again (3:1-36)
Samaritan Woman and the Water of Life (4:1-45)
Healing of an Official's Son (4:46-54)

Jesus Replaces the Feasts of Israel (5:1-10:42)
Sabbath: Jesus Heals on Sabbath (5:1-47)
Passover: The Bread of Life (6:1-71)
Tabernacles: The Light of the World (7:1–10:21)
Dedication: "The Father and I are one" (10:22-42)

Jesus Raises Lazarus and Subsequent Events (11:1–12:50)
Raising of Lazarus: The Life of the World (11:1-44)
Plot to Kill Jesus (11:45-57)
Mary Anoints Jesus (12:1-50)

Book of Glory: Jesus Returns to the Father (13–21)
Last Supper and Farewell Discourses (13:1–17:26)
Jesus' Passion and Death (18:1–19:42)
Jesus' Resurrection (20:1-31)
Empty Tomb and Appearances of Jesus (20:1-29)
First Ending to the Gospel (20:30-31)
Epilogue (21:1-25)
Appearance by Sea of Galilee (21:1-23)
Second Ending to Gospel (21:24-25)

of overflowing wine: "The time is surely coming, says the Lord, when the one who plows shall overtake the one who reaps, and the treader of grapes the one who sows the seed; the mountains shall drip sweet wine, and all the hills shall flow with it" (Amos 9:13). Through this sign Jesus establishes his ministry as inaugurating the messianic age.

Cleansing of the temple (2:13-25).
Jesus has moved from Galilee to Jerusalem. Notice how the location in John's Gospel often shifts between Galilee and Jerusalem. Another major shift occurs when John transposes the narrative of the cleansing of the temple from the end of Jesus' ministry to the beginning. By this change of location John shows at the outset that Jesus had come to replace the temple. True worship is now centered, not in a building, but in his person: "Destroy this temple, and in three days I will raise it up. . . . But he was speaking of the temple of his body" (vv. 19-21). This is an important theme of John's Gospel: Jesus replaces Jewish institutions such as the temple and the Jewish feasts.

Jesus' discourse with Nicodemus (3:1-21).
John develops Jesus' sayings through the literary device of a discourse. At the heart of these discourses were sayings (e.g., "God is spirit, and those who worship him must worship in spirit and truth"; 4:24) or actions (e.g., the miracle of the multiplication of bread; 6:1-14) that provide opportunity to reflect and develop Jesus' teaching in detail.

The key to this discourse between Jesus and Nicodemus, a leading Pharisee, is 3:3: "Very truly, I tell you, no one can see the kingdom of God without being born from above." The phrase "from above" has a twofold meaning in Greek *(anothen)*: "from above" or "again." Nicodemus understands the reference as "being born again" (which is impossible physically) while Jesus understands it as being born "from above" by means of water and the spirit. A characteristic feature of John's Gospel is Jesus' use of misunderstanding to develop his message. The essence of the Jewish religion lay in their natural birth as God's chosen people. The essence for Jesus lay in a rebirth by the Spirit. In this way Jesus replaces another foundation central to the Jewish religion.

In the context of this discourse Jesus presents the first of three sayings related to the Son of Man being lifted up: "No one has ascended into heaven except the one who descended from heaven, the Son of Man. And just as Moses lifted up the serpent in the wilderness, so must the Son of Man be lifted up, that whoever believes in him may have eternal life" (vv. 13-15; see 8:28; 12:32-34; see also Mark 8:31; 9:31; 10:33). This refers first of all to

disciples of John the Baptist before being called to follow Jesus at the Jordan River. The disciples identify Jesus by various titles: Rabbi, Son of God, and King of Israel. Jesus' invitation to discipleship is straightforward: "Come and see" (v. 39). A follower is one who comes and lives with Jesus.

The First Two Signs: From Cana to Cana (2:1-4:54)

Changing water to wine (2:1-12).
In contrast to the numerous miracles in the Synoptic Gospels, John has chosen seven that communicate a sign value, rather than an expression of the dynamic power present in the person of Jesus. The first sign, changing water into wine in the context of a wedding, represents the tremendous abundance of God's revelation and wisdom now beginning in Jesus' ministry. The prophets spoke of a future hope in terms of the imagery

being lifted up on the cross. But Jesus also points beyond that to his ascension and being lifted up to heaven. The life of Jesus is intended to move beyond the cross to his return to the Father. Only then can Jesus send the gift of the Spirit proclaimed in this discourse. The theology of John's Gospel centers on the vision of the Word having come down from heaven and then returning to heaven.

The witness of John the Baptist (3:22-36).

John the Baptist plays an important role in John's Gospel. The prologue calls him a witness (1:6-9, 14-18), and the public ministry opens with John's testimony to Jesus as the Lamb of God (vv. 19-34). Using wedding imagery, the Baptist compares himself to the friend of the bridegroom who rejoices greatly at the bridegroom's wedding. The symbolism is based on John's understanding of Jesus as the bridegroom who is coming for his bride, Israel. John rejoices: "He must increase, but I must decrease" (3:30).

Jesus' discourse with the Samaritan woman (4:1-45).

The Samaritans were descendants of the inhabitants of the Northern Kingdom, Israel, and pagan peoples whom the Assyrians had brought into the territory to repopulate it after the destruction of Israel in 721 B.C.E. Consequently, their religion was a mixture of the teachings of Moses as well as pagan ideas. They accepted only the first five books of the Hebrew Bible and did not accept the Jerusalem temple as their center of worship. Instead, their temple was on Mount Gerizim. When Jesus sits down at the well beside the Samaritan woman and asks her for a drink of water, he is breaking two major customs of his society — talking with a woman in public and associating with Samaritans. Jesus uses the situation of needing water to bring his conversation to a higher spiritual level where he speaks of "living water" that comes from above (4:13-14). Jesus presents himself as the living water and teaches that true religion is centered not on a place, but on worship "in spirit and in truth" (v. 23). For John's Gospel the important aspect of a believer is that he or she gives witness to Jesus: first John the Baptist is a witness, and now this Samaritan becomes a witness to the pagan world around her.

Healing of an official's son (4:46-54).

Jesus' second sign, the gift of life to a boy, again takes place at Cana. It is the culmination of the previous chapters whereby Jesus has spoken to Nicodemus about the gift of new life and to the Samaritan woman of the gift of living water that would well up to eternal life. Now we have the realization of the gift of life in this boy's miraculous healing.

Jesus Replaces the Feasts of Israel (5:1–10:42)

In the previous section Jesus has shown that his mission is to replace Jewish institutions such as the temple with worship centered on himself. The focus now turns to Jesus as the replacement of the Jewish feasts. The theme of life continues to unfold in this section.

Sabbath (5:1-47).

The third of Jesus' signs occurs by the Sheep Gate at a pool, Bethzatha, with five porticoes (5:2). By healing a cripple, Jesus shows that he continues God's life-giving work on the Sabbath: "My Father is still working, and I also am working" (5:17). The climax of this sign is Jesus' claim to equality with the Father (vv. 19-21), a theme he continues to develop in the rest of the discourse. Jesus claims four witnesses who point toward him and his

Pool of Bethzatha at Jerusalem, associated with healing in biblical times. (W. S. LaSor)

work: the Baptist, Jesus' own works, the Father, and the Scriptures (vv. 31-47).

Passover (6:1-71).

The fourth of Jesus' signs occurs at the time of the second Passover. This is the only miracle to occur in all four Gospels (Matt 14:13-21; Mark 6:30-44; Luke 9:10-17). The miracle of the feeding of 5000 represents Jesus' task to give the world spiritual nourishment. John's narration of this episode reminds the reader of the institution of the Eucharist at the Last Supper in the Synoptic Gospels. John uses the word "to give thanks" (Greek *eucharisteo*, v. 11) to refer to the blessing of the bread; then Jesus distributes the bread as he did at the Last Supper.

Following the account of the multiplication of the bread, Jesus performs his fifth sign, walking on water (vv. 16-24). Here Jesus demonstrates his power over the forces of nature. The focus of this sign is on the declaration "It is I; do not be afraid" (v. 20). "It is I" should really be translated: "I AM," a reference to the name that God reveals to Moses at the burning bush (Exod 3:14). Without doubt Jesus is claiming his equality with God by identifying himself with God's sacred name.

In explaining the significance of the multiplication of bread, Jesus shows that he gives eternal nourishment: "I am the bread of life. Whoever comes to me will never be hungry, and whoever believes in me will never be thirsty" (6:35). Jesus identifies himself as the eucharistic food that nourishes life.

Tabernacles (7:1-10:21).

The eight-day Feast of Tabernacles celebrated at the beginning of the wine harvest was a very joyful occasion. The ritual included a daily procession to the temple bringing water from the pool of Siloam as an offering while the whole area of the court of women was bathed in torchlight. Two elements central to this feast become the focus of these chapters: water and light. By giving these features a new significance, Jesus shows that he replaces this Jewish feast. Jesus himself is the life-giving water and the light of the world.

The replacement theme continues in Jesus' claim: "I am the light of the world" (8:12). Once again Jesus uses an "I AM" saying, speaking in the manner of God of the Hebrew Scriptures. John draws further attention to Jesus' claim to speak in this way at the end of ch. 8: "'Very truly, I tell you, before Abraham was, I am.' So they picked up stones to throw at him" (vv. 58-59). The narrator draws attention to the fact that Jesus' audience looks on this as blasphemous.

Jesus' sixth sign (9:1-12), the healing of the man born blind, is further illustration of the replacement theme. As the light of the world, Jesus grants sight to a man blind from birth. For Jesus, this miracle is an opportunity to show God's work in the world (v. 3) and also an opportunity to show the different responses to God's work. Reactions to this sign mirror the various levels of belief: ranging from hostility (some of the Pharisees: "This man is not from God" [v. 16]); to reluctance to admit God's working (the parents: "We know that this is our son, and that he was born blind; but we do not know how it is that now he sees" [vv. 20-21]); to the confession of the man born blind: "If this man were not from God, he could do nothing" (v. 33).

Dedication (10:22-42).

The Feast of Hanukkah (Dedication) celebrates the rededication of the temple during the Maccabean war for independence (164 B.C.E.). The replacement theme emerges here as well when Jesus claims: "The Father and I are one" (10:30) and that he has been sanctified by the Father (v. 36). While the feast celebrates the consecration of the temple, Jesus replaces it through his own consecration.

Jesus Raises Lazarus and Subsequent Events (11:1-12:50)

The raising of Lazarus from the dead is Jesus' seventh and final sign (11:1-44). This miracle becomes the catalyst for drawing together the opposition against Jesus that culminates in his arrest and death (vv. 45-53). The Jewish concern is described in the words of the high priest Caiaphas that have become immortal: "You know nothing at all! You do not understand that it is better for you to have one man die for the people than to have the whole nation destroyed" (vv. 49-50).

The central aspect of this sign is Jesus' ability to grant life. Just as he can bring someone back to physical life, so Jesus has the ability to grant eternal life. Jesus shows that the gift of eternal life is not just reserved for the end of time, but rather is a gift believers receive now through their belief in Jesus. A key characteristic of John's Gospel is its focus on the present. Eschatology is that belief and teaching related to the end time. This teaching can be viewed from two perspectives: that of the end time when Jesus returns to establish his kingdom (an apocalyptic, future-orientated eschatology) or the present when God is active in our world through the person of Jesus (a realized eschatology). The Gospel of John presents a realized eschatology which distinguishes him radically from the future apocalyptic eschatology of the Synoptic Gospels.

Two episodes (with parallels in the Synoptic Gospels) follow the account of the raising of Lazarus. The first is the anointing at Bethany (12:1-11; see Mark 14:3-9; Matt

26:6-13). John gives a few more specific details as coloring to a common tradition that obviously lies behind all the accounts. He names the woman as Mary, and it occurs "six days before the Passover" (v. 1). As with the Synoptics, John uses the event as an acted prophecy looking forward to Jesus' burial. The second account is Jesus' triumphant entry into Jerusalem (vv. 12-19; see Mark 11:1-10; Matt 21:1-11; Luke 19:28-40). These episodes mark the end of Jesus' public ministry and prepare the reader for the next major part of the Gospel which sets the stage for Jesus' death and resurrection.

John 13–21: The Book of Glory: Jesus Returns to the Father

The Last Supper and the Farewell Discourses (13:1–17:26)

"Now before the festival of the Passover, Jesus knew that his hour had come to depart from this world and go to the Father" (13:1). These words present the central theme of the next eight chapters, Jesus' return to the Father. The death of Jesus is not the focus or the climax in these chapters. Instead, his death is one stage in his return to the Father.

The Last Supper (13:1-38).

The narration of the Last Supper is significantly different from the Synoptic account. John does not narrate the institution of the Eucharist, but instead reflects upon the significance of this event in the context of the multiplication of bread (ch. 6). Here John provides an account of Jesus washing the feet of his disciples. This action becomes a sign of service, an example for his followers to imitate, and points to his own death (13:14-15). As with the Synoptics, Jesus foretells Peter's denial and Judas's betrayal.

The Farewell Discourses (14–17).

These chapters are a masterpiece. John has brought together from his traditions sayings of Jesus that were originally in different contexts and presents them as a unified teaching of Jesus on the eve of his death. The voice of Jesus appears to speak as though from heaven and addresses not just his immediate followers, but disciples of all ages and places. In many ways the literary form of these chapters resembles that of a farewell testament in which an important figure bids farewell to his close associates: e.g., Moses' final blessing to the Israelites (Deuteronomy 33), David (2 Sam 23:1-7), Paul (Acts 20:17-38; 2 Tim 3:1–4:8), and the *Testaments of the Twelve Patriarchs*. Distinctive characteristics of these testaments can be observed here: the awareness of an imminent departure (13:33); the request to his hearers to be faithful to his message and example (14:15) as

well as to remain in unity and peace after his departure (17:21-23; 14:27).

An important theme in these chapters is the promise of a successor to take Jesus' place. Jesus promises to send the Paraclete (the advocate, counselor, comforter) who is the "Spirit of truth" (14:16-17). His task is to lead the disciples to a deeper understanding of all that Jesus has taught them (14:16-17, 25-31; 16:5-11, 13-15). Jesus fulfills this promise on his Resurrection day when he breathes on his followers and says to them: "Receive the Holy Spirit" (20:22).

Another key feature of these discourses is the appeal to abide in Jesus. The image of the vine and the branches is a memorable figure of speech: "I am the vine, you are the branches. Those who abide in me and I in them bear much fruit, because apart from me you can do nothing" (15:5). Jesus presents a mystical union of the believer with God: "As you, Father, are in me and I am in you, may they also be in us, so that the world may believe that you have sent me (17:21).

John's Gospel is distinctive in its ethical focus. It does not deal with specific or concrete ethical issues as do the Synoptics. The only ethical command in the Gospel is the "love commandment," "love one another as I have loved you" (15:12). Jesus presents it as a new commandment and his farewell gift to his followers (13:34). For Jesus, the newness stems from the imitation of Jesus' love: "No one has greater love than this, to lay down one's life for one's friends" (15:13). It is a love that is self-sacrificing to the extent of death.

The final discourses culminate in what has been called "the High Priestly Prayer of Jesus" (17:1-26). It opens with a focus on himself: he prays for glory, that he will return to that state he had before he became human (vv. 1-5). Next he prays for his disciples (vv. 6-19), that they will be protected from the hostile world in which they live and will remain faithful to Jesus' message. Finally, he prays for all future believers (vv. 20-26), that they may continue to remain in the unity that exists between the Father and Jesus "so that they may be one, as we are one" (v. 22).

Jesus' Passion and Death (18:1–19:42)

While the account of Jesus' passion and death is similar to the Synoptic account, a number of details are surprisingly different. For John, the Last Supper occurs on the day before Passover (for the Synoptics it is on Passover itself). Jesus dies on the cross at the same time that the Passover lambs are being slaughtered in the temple. This is a symbolic way of showing Jesus as the sacrificial Lamb of God dying on behalf of humanity's sins, as announced at the opening of the Gospel by John the Baptist (1:29).

The scene of Jesus' death also differs from the Synoptics. Among those present at the foot of the cross are Jesus' mother and "the disciple whom Jesus loved" (19:25-27). Jesus gives them to each other in a symbolic way of establishing a community of believers who are related to him. The final words of Jesus differ in each of the Gospels: in John Jesus exclaims: "It is finished" (v. 30). This brings to a conclusion the work the Father has given him to accomplish.

John describes the piercing of the side of Jesus in a dramatic way to highlight the meaning of Jesus' death. The blood and water that flow from his side symbolize the gift of saving life that emanates from his death. Jesus himself had spoken about rivers of living water flowing from his side (7:38-39). This life-giving water, which symbolizes the Spirit, is poured upon his followers at his death. In the early church, Christian thinkers such as Augustine interpreted the references of blood and water as symbols of the Christian sacraments of baptism and Eucharist that come from Jesus' death.

Jesus' Resurrection (20:1-31)

John skillfully narrates four scenes that depict different levels or reactions of belief to the risen Jesus.

- Peter and the Beloved Disciple run to the empty tomb (vv. 1-10). The Beloved Disciple, seeing the cloths lying in the empty tomb (v. 5), is the first to believe and comes to faith before he actually sees the risen Jesus.
- Mary Magdalene sees the risen Jesus but mistakes him for the gardener (vv. 11-18). She only recognizes him when he calls her by name (see 10:14-16), and through his call Mary comes to believe.
- On Easter night Jesus appears in the room where 10 of the disciples have taken refuge (vv. 19-23). After breathing the Spirit on them (a gift he had promised would come from his death; 16:5-11), Jesus sends them forth to continue his own mission (v. 21).
- Absent when Jesus appeared to the others, Thomas says he will only believe if he were to physically touch Jesus (vv. 24-29). A week later, Jesus appears to all the disciples (including Thomas). Thomas then confesses his belief in words that present the deepest belief in Jesus: "My Lord and my God" (v. 28). This confession produces an inclusion with the opening verse of the Gospel, where John declared that "the Word was with God and the Word was God" (1:1).

The first edition of the Gospel probably ended here at ch. 20 with the author's statement of purpose (vv. 30-31). John declares that he has selected his material from traditions that were available to him with the dis-tinct purpose of bringing people to belief in Jesus as the Messiah, the Son of God, and that through this belief his readers will come to eternal life.

Epilogue (21:1-25)

Most scholars consider ch. 21 to be a later addition coming from further traditions circulating within the community of the Beloved Disciple. The editor adds two scenes to emphasize concerns for his community.

- Verses 1-14 describe a miraculous catch of fish (see Luke 5:1-11). The Beloved Disciple is the first to recognize the risen Lord. The catch of fish is symbolic of the mission the disciples are to perform: their task is to bring all peoples to belief in Jesus. Ancient zoology taught that there were 153 types of fish. Just as the disciples caught every type of fish (v. 11), so the risen Jesus is sending his disciples out to bring all peoples into union and belief in him.
- Verses 15-23 recount the restoration of Peter to the believing community. His threefold profession of love in Jesus parallels his threefold denial earlier. Jesus gives Peter the role of shepherd of the flock. The flock is still Jesus' flock ("my sheep"), but Peter is to care for it to the extent of being willing to lay down his life for it (vv. 18-19). Undoubtedly, the editor is reflecting Peter's actual dying a martyr's death.

Attention then turns to answer a problem that had arisen within the community of the Beloved Disciple. Many believed that Jesus had taught that the Beloved Disciple would not die before Jesus' return, but it seems that this disciple had indeed died, thus provoking a crisis. The editor uses this account to show that Jesus had never foretold that the disciple would not die.

In a second conclusion to the Gospel (vv. 24-25), the editor again identifies the Beloved Disciple as the faithful witness for the tradition behind the Gospel (see 19:35). The readers can be sure because his testimony is true. The editor also notes that there were many other "signs" that Jesus did that have not been written down. In fact, so many other traditions continue to circulate about Jesus that it would be impossible to write down everything that he did and taught (v. 25).

Critical Issues in Studying John

Comparison with the Synoptic Gospels

A comparison of the Gospel of John with the Synoptics shows that its narrative is very different, yet a number of close similarities do occur.

Similarities with the Synoptics

John and the Synoptics share the following similarities as regards content (a selective list):

- The ministry of John the Baptist (1:19-34; Matt 3:1-17; Mark 1:1-11; Luke 3:1-22)
- The cleansing of the Temple (2:13-25; Matt 21:12-17; Mark 11:15-19; Luke 19:45-48)
- The multiplication of bread (6:1-14; Matt 14:13-21; Mark 6:30-44; Luke 9:10-17)
- Jesus walks on water (6:16-21; Matt 14:22-33; Mark 6:45-52)
- Anointing of Jesus (12:1-8; Matt 26: 6-13; Mark 14:3-9)
- The Passion and Resurrection (18:1–21:25; Matt 26:47–28:20; Mark 14:43–16:8; Luke 22:47–24:53)

John and Mark both present events in the same sequence in one section: the multiplication of bread (6:1-14; Mark 6:30-44), the walking on water (6:16-21; Mark 6:45-52), and the confession of Peter (6:67-69; Mark 8:27-29).

Both John and Luke speak of Jesus' friends Martha and Mary (11:1-45; Luke 10:38-42), both state that Judas was possessed by Satan (13:2, 27; Luke 22:3), and both

mention the presence of two angels at Jesus' tomb (20:12; Luke 24:4).

These similarities are so few that it does not argue for John's knowledge of any of the Synoptic Gospels. They do show that some traditions were known to John that were also part of the Synoptic traditions.

Dissimilarities with the Synoptics

Content

John has no account of Jesus' birth; instead, he presents a hymn to the pre-existence of the word. He does not describe Jesus' baptism: the role of the Baptist is to witness to Jesus, not to baptize him. The account of the temptation by Satan in the wilderness is absent, and there are no accounts where Jesus exorcises demons. Jesus' miracles focus not on his struggle with the forces of evil, but rather with their symbolic nature. Of the seven signs in John, only two (the multiplication of bread and the walking on the sea) are common to the Synoptics. John has no account of the institution of the Eucharist during Jesus' Last Supper; he transposes it to fit into an account of the multiplication of bread. There is no agony in the Garden, and Jesus' death on the cross is described very differently. John does not record a cry of despair on the cross as in Mark; instead Jesus declares that he has accomplished the work the Father had given him to do.

Structure

Characteristic of John's Gospel is Jesus' use of discourses to engage different characters and groups, such as Nicodemus (ch. 3) and the Samaritan woman (ch. 4). John has built up these discourses around events or sayings in Jesus' ministry to draw out more clearly the significance of the person of Jesus. A careful look at John 6 will show how John has used the miracle of the multiplication of bread to draw out the meaning of Jesus as the bread of life for the world.

Sources

The differences arise because John had very different sources at his disposal. He did not know Mark or Q, the two sources at the foundation of the Synoptic Gospels. Instead, a source lies behind his chs. 1–12 that scholars have called "the Signs Source"

The Crucifixion, Matthias Gruenewald, central panel from the Isenheim Altarpiece (ca. 1515; Musée d'Unterlinden, Colmar, France). (Erich Lessing/ ArtResource, NY)

because seven signs are the foundation of this section. The witness of the Beloved Disciple also seems to be an important source for the traditions recorded in this Gospel (21:24).

Aim and vision

The Gospel of John has a very distinct theological vision. It pictures Jesus as the Son of God who comes down from the Father and who is returning to the Father. The focus shifts from Jesus' death to his return to the Father. The intention is not to supplement details omitted by the Synoptics. Instead, the author brings his sources together to accomplish the aim expressed in the original ending to the Gospel: "so that you may come to believe that Jesus is the Messiah, the Son of God, and that through believing you may have life in his name" (20:31). For the Synoptics the central theme of Jesus' message was the kingdom of God, a term found only twice in John's Gospel. John's aim, however, is to arouse belief that Jesus is the Son of God who as the Messiah fulfills the past and as Son reveals the Father to humanity. Through such belief his readers are assured of the gift of eternal life.

Chronology

The broad outline of Jesus' ministry in John's Gospel is similar to the Synoptics: a ministry of healings and preaching in Galilee that culminates in arrest, crucifixion, and resurrection in Jerusalem. Within these broad strokes, John shows significant differences in the sequence of events and their chronology. Among the most striking differences are the following:

- In the Synoptic Gospels, Jesus traces a straight geographical path from Galilee (where most of his ministry was situated) toward Jerusalem, where he dies. In John, Jesus moves backward and forward from Jerusalem to Galilee.
- Jesus celebrates only one Passover in the Synoptics, while in John he celebrates three (2:13; 6:4; 11:55). This leads the reader of John to see Jesus' ministry as lasting at least three years (while the impression given in the Synoptics is that his ministry was less than a year).
- The Synoptics begin Jesus' ministry after John the Baptist has been imprisoned, while in John's Gospel Jesus and the Baptist exercise a baptism ministry simultaneously (3:22–4:3).
- Most noticeable is the cleansing of the temple. In John this occurs at the outset of Jesus' ministry (2:13-21), where it defines his role of replacing the Jewish institutions. In the Synoptics, this event occurs in Jesus' final week in Jerusalem and acts as the catalyst for his arrest.

- In the Synoptic Gospels the final meal that Jesus celebrates with his disciples is a Passover meal. John, however, presents Jesus' meal occurring on the evening before Passover. According to John, when Jesus dies on the cross, the paschal lambs are being slaughtered in the temple. This is the preparation day for the Passover (13:1, 29; 18:28; 19:14). Certainly, John is emphasizing the theological significance of Jesus' death as the Lamb of God whereby his death replaces the Passover feast. Many scholars think that John's scenario is the more historical given that it would be impossible for Jesus' arrest, trial, and crucifixion to occur on the actual Feast of Passover, the most sacred time for the Jews. It makes more sense if these events occurred just prior to Passover as John notes.

Authorship and Composition

The oldest manuscript that can be identified with a Gospel is one housed in the John Rylands Library in Manchester, England. Dated to the first half of the 2nd century, this fragment contains John 18:31-33, 37-38. Many witnesses to the text of John have been discovered in Egypt, showing that it was widely known there (e.g., Papyrus 𝔓66, dated *ca.* 200, contains the entirety of the Gospel). Yet despite its popularity in Egypt, the Gospel did not originate there.

Irenaeus (*ca.* 120-202), an important 2nd-century church leader, identifies John, the Beloved Disciple, as the author of this Gospel. This John, he claimed, lived in Ephesus and died *ca.* 98 during the reign of the emperor Trajan. As with the other Gospels, this tradition seems to have taken hold in the 2nd century with the purpose of defending the authority behind the writing, rather than establishing its actual writer.

The Gospel itself does not identify the writer, although editorial comments associate authorship with the Beloved Disciple. At the foot of Jesus' cross is "the disciple whom he loved" (19:26), an eyewitness to the crucifixion (v. 35). In ch. 21, an appendix to the Gospel, the editor claims that this Beloved Disciple is the one who has written these things, and "his testimony is true" (v. 24). This figure appears for the first time in the final meal with Jesus, where he reclines next to Jesus and acts as Peter's spokesman, asking Jesus who will betray him (13:21-29). When Jesus is arrested, the Beloved Disciple helps Peter gain access to the courtyard of the high priest, with whom he was acquainted (18:15-18). The Beloved Disciple is the only male disciple at the cross, and Jesus entrusts the care of his mother to him (19:26-27). Symbolically, the Beloved Disciple becomes the son of Jesus' mother and in this way brother to Jesus.

On Easter morning, the Beloved Disciple arrives first

at Jesus' tomb, but allows Peter to enter ahead of him. He is the first to believe that Jesus has been raised from the dead (20:2-10) and also the first to recognize the risen Jesus when the disciples are fishing on the Sea of Galilee (21:4-7). In the final chapter, Peter's future death is foretold, while Jesus refuses to speculate on the Beloved Disciple: "If it is my will that he remain until I come, what is that to you?" (21:22). If the Beloved Disciple had actually died, it may have caused a crisis in the community, and so the editor corrects the implication that the Beloved Disciple would not die.

Who is this Beloved Disciple? Some scholars accept the traditional interpretation that identifies him with John, the son of Zebedee and brother of James. Others see the Beloved Disciple as a symbol for the ideal or perfect disciple. Most plausibly, he was a minor disciple during Jesus' ministry who was neither one of the Twelve nor an apostle. Because he exercised such a small role in Jesus' ministry he is unimportant for the Synoptic tradition. However, he did become the founder of a community out of which the Fourth Gospel emerged, and as an eyewitness was responsible for those traditions that developed within the context of that community.

John 21:20-24 and 19:35 give the impression that this Beloved Disciple was responsible for writing this Gospel. He could, however, be the source behind the tradition that is at the basis of the Fourth Gospel. It seems more likely that the writer was a disciple of this Beloved Disciple, molding the tradition that he had received into the form that made its way into the Gospel. Then at a later stage another editor added the final chapter.

The above description shows that John's Gospel had a long and complicated history of composition. Central to the development of this Gospel is its situation within a community. Three figures are important within this community:

- The Beloved Disciple, an eyewitness to Jesus' ministry, who founded the community and whose preaching and teaching were the source for the traditions that emerged.
- The Evangelist, a disciple of the Beloved Disciple, was the real literary genius who crafted this Gospel on the basis of the traditions and reflections that had developed over the course of many decades.
- The final editor added more traditions and material to the first edition of the Gospel in order to resolve a number of issues that had developed within the community.

Time and Place
The Gospel of John was written toward the end of the

1st century, as supported by the existence of a fragment from the early 2nd century. The identity of the community responsible for this Gospel remains uncertain. Ephesus, Antioch in Syria, and Alexandria all have had support among scholars. However, we can offer a few observations about this community.

The Fourth Gospel shows a greater knowledge of Palestinian geography than does any of the other Gospels. For example, the Gospel knows of the pool of Bethzatha (5:2) and Siloam (9:7), Solomon's portico in the temple (10:23), as well as the place of Bethany (11:18). We have also seen its awareness of the Jewish feasts and institutions.

Much of the Gospel's thought shows familiarity with expressions and ideas popular within the Qumran community. Like that community, John's Gospel shows a strong tendency to draw contrasts such as light (a symbol of truth) and darkness (evil) as a way of capturing the opposition between the Gospel community and the rest of the world. Jesus, the light of the world, has overcome the darkness of the world. His followers are "sons of light" as opposed to the "sons of darkness." This does not mean that the Gospel of John was actually familiar with or associated with the Qumran community. Rather, the thought of the Gospel must have developed within a community familiar with and at home in a Palestinian environment that shared its common matrix of thought.

Despite this detailed knowledge of Jewish traditions and its familiarity with Palestine, the Gospel of John also shows that a parting of the ways had occurred between the followers of Jesus and Judaism. References to believers being driven out of the Jewish synagogues (9:22, 34-35) reflect a situation where Judaism was defining its boundaries and expelling the followers of Jesus. Between 85 and 90 the rabbis at Jamnia included among the benedictions recited in the synagogue a declaration that those who held different opinions were to be cursed. This could be the backdrop to the Gospel of John and would account for the hostility directed within the Gospel toward "the Jews."

Theological Themes in John

Jesus, the Divine Son, Reveals the Father
The prologue presents the context for understanding Jesus. He is "the Word (who) became flesh and lived among us" (1:14). Jesus is the Word who has come from the Father to make the Father known.

This concept of "the Word" (Greek *Logos*) as it is used in John's Gospel derives from two sources. The first comes from the Greek world where Logos was a philosophical concept of Stoic philosophers referring to cosmic reason that orders and pervades the universe and is accessible to the human mind. The aim of all human life was to ensure that every action conforms to reason. The human being must strive to live in harmony with the universal Logos. For the Greeks, the Logos also referred to that creative power that had structured the world out of chaos. A second source is the Hebrew wisdom tradition that reflects upon Sophia (the Greek word for wisdom), the personification of Divine Wisdom who acted alongside God as God's agent in the creation of the world. The reflections on Divine Wisdom go beyond creation to give expression to God's communication of revelation to humanity (see Sirach 24; Wis 6:12–9:18; Prov 8:22-36).

The Greek and Hebrew traditions come together in the writings of the great Jewish philosopher Philo, who lived in Alexandria in Egypt *ca.* 20 B.C.E.–50 C.E. For Philo the Logos was the image of God, a true reflection of God. It also served as the model or ideal for God's creation of the cosmos and was the instrument through which creation was effected. In Philo's description, the Logos was God's first creation. Thereafter, the Logos brought everything else into being.

John's use of the term Logos in the prologue reflects these two traditions as they had come together in Philo's thought. Jesus is that heavenly Sophia which has come down to earth, becoming flesh in the person of Jesus as the incarnation of God's creative Wisdom and Reason. Jesus of Nazareth is that Logos which speaks the word of God and reveals God intimately and fully.

The very concept of the Word captures the idea of communicating knowledge of God. The prologue ends with the statement that reinforces this task of making God known: "It is God the only Son, who is close to the Father's heart, who has made him known" (1:18). This sets the scene for the entire Gospel and all that Jesus does throughout this book. As the Son of God, Jesus has come from the Father, abides in the Father, and reveals himself as the only way to the Father. The purpose of this revelation of the Father is to bring people into a relationship as children of the Father (1:12) who are the heirs of eternal life (3:16).

The most dramatic way in which this Gospel speaks of the relationship of Jesus to the Father and demonstrates his role as the divine Son who reveals the Father comes from Jesus' use of the phrase "I am," where Jesus appropriates for himself the way in which God speaks in the Old Testament. Jesus makes a clear claim to divinity by speaking in the manner of God and makes himself equal to God. Any Jewish audience would immediately understand the claims Jesus was making.

Jesus is the one who has come down from heaven (1:9; 3:19; 9:39; 11:27; 12:46; 16:28; 18:37). As the one whom the Father has sent, Jesus reveals the Father and the way to eternal life. He challenges those who encounter him to a decision for or against him. In the second half of the Gospel Jesus is set on his return to the Father. His death is one stage in that return to glory. However, he promises his followers the gift of the Paraclete, who will continue to guide and direct them.

John's Gospel uses many titles to describe Jesus. In addition to the Word, the opening chapter refers to Jesus as the Lamb of God (1:36), Rabbi (v. 38), and Messiah (v. 41). All of these are understandable against a Jewish background. When Jesus is put to death, he dies at the same time that the paschal lambs are being slaughtered in the temple for the Feast of Passover. In this way Jesus is seen to replace Passover. As rabbi, Jesus is indeed the teacher, who brings the word of the Father to humanity as "the way, and the truth, and the life" (14:6).

Discipleship

The call to discipleship in John's Gospel is above all a call to respond to Jesus in faith; a call to believe in Jesus as the one sent by the Father. The consequences of this faith decision are immense. The disciple is called to witness to his/her belief in a hostile world and as a consequence will experience hardships and persecution. The intent of the account of the healing of the blind man expelled from the synagogue because of his belief in Jesus (ch. 9) is to strengthen those readers who themselves are facing expulsion and hardships on account of their faith.

Disciples are also called to share in the love and unity that exists between the Father and the Son. This is one of the main themes in the Farewell Discourses. Disciples will share in that love between the Father and the Son if they in turn show love for one another (14:21-24; 16:27). As already noted, a distinctive feature of John's Gospel compared with the Synoptics is the lack of instruction on ethics. In the Synoptics, Jesus is embroiled in numerous controversies with the Jewish authorities related to issues concerning everyday affairs: taxes, divorce, marriage, Sabbath observance. None of these feature in John's Gospel. Here the important ethical requirement is love. A further reason why John considers specific ethical instruction unnecessary is that believers are guided by the Paraclete, the Spirit of truth, who "will guide you into all the truth" (16:13). John's Gospel bears witness to a community totally dependent upon the guidance of the Paraclete-Spirit to help them to know how to act. In this sense it is a very charismatic community.

Another key aspect of discipleship is witnessing. The disciples continue the role of witnesses that ultimately emanates from God: The Father witnesses to the Son (12:28), and the Son's whole life witnesses to the Father. Once Jesus has departed, the Paraclete bears witness to

Jesus (16:7-15). John the Baptist's task is to bear witness to Jesus (1:32). In this long line of witnesses the disciples' task is to continue to witness to Jesus.

The author portrays the characters in the Gospel in such a way that they show that discipleship involves a response in faith to Jesus. These individuals show the different possible faith responses: in a sense they operate as though on a trajectory from total unbelief to total belief.

- Although Judas Iscariot, the betrayer, had been one of Jesus' intimate circle of disciples, he really was not one of Jesus' own. He was preoccupied with material possessions (12:4-6). His greatest sin was allowing Satan to lead him astray: "Satan entered him!" (13:27) and he handed Jesus over to the Jewish authorities. Judas is an example for all who first believe and then fall away, succumbing to the power of Satan.
- Nicodemus (3:1-21; 19:39) seeks out Jesus at night (3:2). He is attracted to Jesus and his message and wants to find out more, but he does not want anyone else to know and so comes in the stealth of night. At the end of the narrative together with Joseph of Arimathea he brings a large amount of spices to anoint the body of Jesus as Jewish ritual required. Nicodemus is an example of those who are attracted to Jesus but find it difficult to take the final step of full commitment.
- Thomas (20:24-29) is the example of a believer whose faith rests upon signs (v. 25). On seeing the risen Jesus he makes the ultimate confession: "My Lord and my God!" (v. 28). The author uses the example of Thomas to instruct the readers that they, unlike Thomas, must come to belief not through seeing but through the power of the Spirit leading them to Jesus. The risen Jesus illustrates this through the blessing: "Blessed are those who have not seen and yet have come to believe" (v. 29).
- The Beloved Disciple is the example of the true believer (the exact opposite of Judas). The first specific reference to him in the Gospel occurs in the context of the Last Supper: "One of his disciples — the one whom Jesus loved — was reclining next to him" (13:23). The NRSV fails to capture the depth that the author intended. Literally, this verse should read: "was reclining on the bosom of Jesus," recalling the description of the relationship between Jesus and the Father in the prologue: "It is God the only Son, who is close to the Father's heart, who has made him known" (1:18; lit., "in the bosom of the Father"). The closeness of the disciple to Jesus is reflective of the closeness of Jesus to the Father.
- A further incident that reflects this disciple's faith occurs in his appearance at the foot of the cross with

Jesus' mother (19:25-27). He is the one disciple who has remained true until the end. In giving him to his mother and his mother to the Beloved Disciple, Jesus presents him as a paradigm for all disciples: they are all called to be part of Jesus' family in a spiritual sense. The Beloved Disciple is the first to believe in the resurrection of Jesus. When he saw the empty tomb "he saw and believed" (20:8). He is also the first to recognize the risen Jesus at the Sea of Tiberias (21:7). The author uses this disciple as a model of what a disciple should be. Above all, love for Jesus characterizes this disciple, and it is this love that enables him to believe and to see with the eyes of faith where others are unable.

Many other characters appear in John's narrative, and each says something about the nature of belief in Jesus. The characters have a special function for the author in that they provide an opportunity to show the qualities of a faith commitment to Jesus.

Other Theological Themes

A number of key ideas are specific to the Gospel of John, symbols that help to capture a deeper awareness of Jesus' significance.

- The Word who is God (1:1) came into the world as the light of the world (8:12), "the true light, which enlightens everyone " (1:9). This light has come to overcome the darkness of the world. In a way similar to the thought of Qumran, the symbolism of light and darkness refers to two moral principles that struggle for domination over humanity. Depending upon their response, people are either children of light or children of darkness.
- Life is John's favorite theme. The purpose of his Gospel was to communicate life: "so that you may come to believe that Jesus is the Messiah, the Son of God, and that through believing you may have life in his name" (20:31). This life, or more correctly, this eternal life as John names it, is first of all the life of God which the Son possesses from the Father (5:26). One reason the Son became human was to communicate life to humanity (10:10). This life is attained through belief (3:16), and the power of the Spirit communicates this gift of life to humanity (6:63).
- Love is the virtue that unites the Father, the Son, and believers. Love comes from the Father and is communicated through the Son to all disciples. The Father loves the Son above all because of the Son's willingness to lay down his life (10:17). The Son's obedience to the Father shows the depths of his love for him (14:31). The Son shows the depths of his love for his

The Seven Signs in John's Gospel

Changing water into wine (2:1-11)

Healing of an official's son in Cana (4:46-54)

Healing of a cripple (5:2-9)

Feeding of the 5000 (6:1-14)

Walking on water (6:16-21)

Healing the blind man (9:1-12)

Raising Lazarus from the dead (11:1-44)

followers because he gives up his life on their behalf (15:13). The disciple is called to follow Jesus' example. The only commandment that Jesus gives his followers is that of love: "that you love one another as I have loved you" (15:12).

- The noun "faith" never occurs in John's Gospel. Instead, John uses the verb "to believe," showing preference for action rather than speculation. John also uses the verb in a special way, always accompanied with the preposition "in." For John, one always believes in a person, not in something. This shows an active commitment to a person, the person of Jesus: "This is the work of God, that you believe in him whom he has sent" (6:29).
- Scholars believe that among the sources that John used to compile his Gospel was a source that contained a narrative of Jesus' miracles identified as the Signs Gospel.
- While we use the term "miracle" (from Latin *miraculum,* "something to be wondered at") to refer to the mighty deeds of Jesus, this is not how the Gospels describe them. The Synoptic Gospels use the Greek word *dynamis,* which means "an act of power." The Gospel of John, on the other hand, uses the Greek *semeion* ("sign") or *ergon* ("work"). This shows in John a distinctive theology regarding Jesus' mighty works.

When the Synoptics describe these deeds of Jesus as "acts of power," they envisage an on-going struggle between the kingdom of Satan and the kingdom of Jesus. These actions were Jesus' chief assault on Satan's power. That is why in the Synoptics so many of the mighty

deeds of Jesus involve the expulsion of demons (e.g., Matt 12:28).

John's Gospel presents Jesus' actions as having a symbolic function and so he names them "signs." When Jesus heals the official's son, it points to Jesus as the one from whom spiritual life emanates. When Jesus raises Lazarus to life, it is a sign that Jesus is the one who grants the gift of eternal life. All these actions point beyond themselves to a deeper spiritual reality. John further speaks of these actions as "works," indicating that Jesus' ministry is a continuation of God the Father's work in the world, a work that began with creation and reached a climax in the Israelites' exodus from slavery in Egypt.

Questions for Review and Discussion

1   Examine three important characters in the Gospel of John and show how John uses them as examples for different types of belief in the person of Jesus.

2   Examine one of the "signs" in the Gospel in detail. Show how this functions as a sign in the Gospel.

3   How does the picture of Jesus in John's Gospel differ from the picture of Jesus presented by the Synoptics? Which of the images of Jesus in the four Gospels appeals to you most and why?

Further Reading

Brodie, Thomas L. *The Quest for the Origin of John's Gospel: A Source-Oriented Approach.* New York: Oxford University Press, 1993.

Brown, Raymond E. *The Community of the Beloved Disciple.* New York: Paulist, 1979.

Koester, Craig R. "John, Gospel of." In *EDB,* 723-25.

Schneiders, Sandra M. "Women in the Fourth Gospel and the Role of Women in the Contemporary Church." *BTB* 12 (1982) 35-45.

Scott, J. Martin C. "John." In *ECB,* 1161-1212.

Chapter 60

The Letters of John

Getting Started

1 Read 1 John. List the similarities that you observe with the Gospel of John, as well as the differences.

2 Read 2 and 3 John. What issues are addressed in the three Letters of John?

Preliminary Comments

The first letter of John shows striking similarities with John's Gospel, though there are also many differences in language and style. Our examination will show that the writer probably comes from the same school or circle of tradition ("the Johannine community") as the author of the Gospel. The opponents of the three letters differ from the opponents of the Gospel in that they are not Jews (as in the Gospel) but believers who have left John's community and are interpreting the Gospel in a very different way from the author of the letters and his community. We will deal in more detail with the background to these three writings after examining the content of each letter.

1 John

A Walk through 1 John

1 John 1:1-4: Prologue
Although this writing is referred to as a letter, it does not have any of a letter's characteristic features. It imitates the opening of the Gospel of John with a prologue that speaks about the Word of life (1:1). The word is the announcement of eternal life that Jesus made visible and possible for believers to share.

1 John 1:5–3:10: Walk in the Light of God
The word "message" (Greek *angelia*) is a marker used twice in this letter to divide this writing into two parts (1:5; 3:11) which imitate the two parts of the Gospel of John (1–12; 13–21). The writer begins the first part with the call to imitate God. Since God is light, the believer is called to walk in the light (1:5-7). The world is divided into light and darkness: God is light; darkness is evil. The Christian has fellowship with God if he/she keeps the commandments. This is similar to the Farewell Discourses of the Gospel, where union with God entails keeping the commandments.

The author considers sin and the importance of acknowledging one's sinfulness (1:8–2:2). To say that one is sinless is to make God out to be a liar (1:10). Forgiveness comes through Jesus (1:7), whose blood offers "the atoning sacrifice for our sins" (2:2) and the sins of the world. The author presents Jesus as the Paraclete ("advocate"; 2:1) who pleads our cause before the Father.

1 John stresses the need to keep the commandments if one wishes to know God (2:3-11). This is an "old" commandment in the sense that believers have been instructed in it since the beginning of their conversion (v. 7). The writer issues a strong denunciation of the world (2:12-23) as the place where the evil one lives (v. 14). The idea of a struggle with the evil one leads to a warning against the antichrist (vv. 18-27). Those who are against (anti-) Christ are those "who went out from us" (v. 19). Anointing with the Spirit enables believers to stand firm in the truth in which they have been instructed (v. 20).

The Gospel of John pays little attention to the return of Christ (the Parousia). By contrast, for 1 John it is an essential theme (2:28–3:3). If one is united with Jesus now in the present, one need fear nothing in the future. The writer calls the readers to abide in Christ (2:28). The Father's love is celebrated by the fact that believers become "the children of God" (3:1). As God's children in the present, believers are being prepared for the future: "When he is revealed we will be like him, for we will see him as he is" (3:2).

1 John 3:11–5:12: Love One Another

In the previous part the author proclaims the *angelia* ("message") in terms of light because God is light. Now the writer calls the readers to walk as children of the God of love. The essence of the commandments is to believe that Jesus is the Christ, the only Son of God, and to love one another (3:11-24). Jesus Christ came in the flesh as the Son of God. Those who do not believe this belong to the world (4:1-6). God loved first and "sent his Son to be the atoning sacrifice for our sins" (4:10). In response believers should love one another (v. 11). Faith and love are inextricably bound together: those who believe that Jesus is the Christ are begotten as children of God (5:1). If believers love God, they will love those who are begotten by God, namely the children of God (v. 2). This part concludes in 5:6-12 by stressing that the main witness

to Jesus is the Spirit, who is present in the Christian through baptism. The Spirit is a most effective witness. Through his indwelling within the believer, the Spirit becomes part of the believer and witnesses to Jesus as the Son of God. Acceptance of this witness to Jesus is the means to eternal life (5:12).

1 John 5:13-21: Conclusion

Just as the Gospel of John ends with a statement of purpose (John 20:31), so this writing ends with a similar statement of intent: "I write these things to you who believe in the name of the Son of God, so that you may know that you have eternal life" (5:13). The ending is without the characteristic features of a letter. It concludes with three statements proclaiming "We know" (vv. 18-20) in which the dualism between God and the world again culminates in opposition. "We know" that those who are born of God do not sin, and the evil one is unable to touch them because they are protected by God (v. 18). "We know" that we are God's children, while the world is under the dominion of the evil one (v. 19). "We know" that the Son of God has come and that we abide in him (v. 20). 1 John culminates in a profession of belief in Jesus as the Son of God and the gift of eternal life, just as the Gospel did: "He is the true God and eternal life" (v. 20).

2 John

A Walk through 2 John

In the **opening formula** (vv. 1-3) the sender calls himself the "elder" (or presbyter) and identifies the receivers as "the elect lady and her children," a symbolical reference to a sister community of the Johannine community. The elder's authority is acknowledged and respected.

The **body of the letter** (vv. 4-11) opens with an expression of joy: the elder praises the members of the community to whom he writes for "walking in the truth" (v. 4).

The message is a warning against the "antichrist," the deceivers, who teach that Jesus Christ did not come as a human being (v. 7). The elder urges the readers not to accept such deceivers into their homes, for to do so would be to participate in the evil that they are perpetrating (vv. 10-11).

The elder sends **final greetings** (vv. 12-13) not just from himself, but also from members of his community.

3 John

A Walk through 3 John

The **opening formula** (vv. 1-2) identifies very briefly the writer as the elder and the receiver as a certain Gaius. The elder expresses concern for the health of Gaius as well as for his spiritual well-being.

The **body of the letter** (vv. 3-12) opens with an expression of joy (vv. 3-4) as did 2 John. The elder tells Gaius that some friends have testified to how he, Gaius, is walking in the truth. This gives the elder great joy.

The elder tells Gaius, who has a reputation for hospitality, to receive the missionaries whom he has sent from his community. Gaius is to give them assistance and then send them on their way. The elder notes how he has already written to the church in this connection, but a certain Diotrephes has refused to offer them hospitality and refuses to acknowledge the elder's authority (v. 9). Diotrephes not only spreads false charges against the elder, but also forbids members of his community to help those missionaries coming from him and even goes so far as to expel from the church anyone who assists them (v. 10). The elder commends to Gaius Demetrius, presumably one of the missionaries whom he is sending (v. 12). In a sense 3 John serves as a letter of recommendation for Demetrius.

Final greetings (vv. 13-15) are sent from the friends in the elder's church to the friends in Gaius's church.

Critical Issues in Studying the Letters of John

Authorship of 1, 2, and 3 John

2 and 3 John are identical in letter format. Both claim to be written by "the elder" ("presbyter"). Although 1 John does not have the format of a letter, it does have some close similarities with 2 John. Compare, for example, "For this is the message you have heard from the beginning, that we should love one another" (1 John 3:11) with "I ask you, not as though I were writing you a new commandment, but one we have had from the beginning,

> **Reading Guide to 3 John**
>
> **Opening Formula** (1-2)
>
> **Body** (3-12)
>   Expression of Joy (3-4)
>   Message (5-12)
>
> **Final Greetings** (13-15)

let us love one another" (2 John 5). The same writer ("the elder") is judged to be responsible for all three letters.

Examination of the relationship between the Gospel of John and 1 John shows many similarities in both style and vocabulary. We noted in the walk though the letter that the structure of 1 John is based upon the structure of the Gospel. At the same time, there are also some surprising differences between the two writings:

- While the term *Logos* appears in both writings (and nowhere else in the New Testament), the meaning of this term is different in each writing. In the Gospel it refers to Jesus as the Incarnate Word of God, while in 1 John it emphasizes the message of the word of life (1 John 1:10).
- In the Gospel Jesus is the light, while in 1 John God is light.
- In the Gospel the focus is on realized eschatology, in that eternal life is a gift presently experienced by believers. In 1 John the focus is on future eschatology, whereby reference is made to the Parousia when the believer is called to account (1 John 2:28).

Because of these differences, the same author cannot be claimed for all four writings. However, their similarities suggest that they emerge from the same environment or context, probably from the same community that reflected upon Jesus' message. One disciple within that community was responsible for the Gospel while another was responsible for the letters. We have already distinguished three different figures behind the Gospel: the Beloved Disciple as the source of the traditions on which the community was founded, the Evangelist who put those traditions into writing, and the final editor who was responsible among other things for the final chapter, ch. 21. To this we add a fourth disciple, the writer of the letters.

The letters would have been composed after the writing of the Gospel. If the Gospel was written *ca.* 90 C.E., then one would see the letters being written *ca.* 100.

Occasion for Writing the Letters

The opponents of the community have changed between the Gospel and the letters. In the Gospel the antagonists are the Jews, and at the time of composition Jesus' followers are being expelled from the synagogues (see John 9). However, in the letters the opponents are former members of the community who have left (1 John 2:19).

Those who left the community differ from the writer of 1 John and the community itself on two essential aspects:

- Christology: Since 1 John strongly emphasizes belief in Jesus as the Christ, the Son of God who came in the flesh, we can conclude that those who left the community refused to acknowledge this (1 John 4:2-3). The author calls them "antichrists" (2:18).
- Morality: The writer of 1 John attacks the opponents because they claim to be without sin (1:8, 10; 3:4-6). They profess the ability to act in any way they please and that whatever they do has no relevance to their relationship to God as God's children.

It is difficult to identify this group that had left the Johannine community. They show similarities with later forms of Gnosticism, such as the Docetists, who taught that the Christ descended upon Jesus at baptism and left him before his death. What seems central to this group is that their interpretation of the Gospel of John is not in harmony with the way in which the community interprets it. Those who left read the Gospel to say that salvation comes though faith in Jesus and that the death of Jesus has no salvific value.

1 John seeks to give an authentic interpretation of the Gospel of John and to say: this is the way in which the Gospel has been understood by the Johannine community and those responsible for it. As such, 1 John is not a letter, but a "covering introduction" to the Gospel.

2 John is an attempt to warn another Johannine community that some of those who had left their community were about to come to them to propagate their views. The elder warns them not to let these false teachers into "the house" (2 John 10).

3 John is an appeal to a certain Gaius to show hospitality to missionaries sent by the elder.

Theological Themes in the Letters of John

These three letters provide insight into how a tradition is being interpreted. Both the members of the Johannine community and those who have left it give allegiance to the Gospel of John. However, each group interprets it differently and uses the Gospel to support its viewpoint. The essence of their dispute lies with the understanding of the person of Jesus Christ. Against the attacks of those who have left the community, the elder shows the importance he attributes to the salvific value of Jesus' death contrary to the views of the opponents who only stress Jesus' entrance into the world. These letters show how the early Christians struggled to give expression to the theological significance of the person of Jesus. Only through these struggles did they come to a deeper awareness and appreciation of Jesus' work. The greatest contribution of the tradition stemming from the Gospel of John and upheld by the letters is the unique role that Jesus exercises in the life of believers and its salvific value.

Another important theological insight in these letters is the importance given to the role of the Spirit. The Johannine community is led by the Spirit. It is the highest authority in that community. The elder shows the need for the testing of spirits, for discerning between the "spirit of the antichrist" and the "Spirit of God" (1 John 4:1-3). Both those in the elder's community and those who have left it appeal to the Spirit in support of their own interpretations. They had no way to control the divisions, and tragically the Johannine community soon disappeared from the scene of Christianity.

Questions for Review and Discussion

1 What contribution do you think these letters make to Christian thought by their inclusion in the New Testament?

2 What do these three letters teach about the person of Jesus Christ?

Further Reading

Brown, Raymond E. *The Churches the Apostles Left Behind*. New York: Paulist, 1984.

Culpepper, R. Alan. *1 John, 2 John, 3 John*. Atlanta: John Knox, 1985.

Hobbs, Herschel H. *The Epistles of John*. Nashville: Thomas Nelson, 1983.

Painter, John. "1, 2, and 3 John." In *ECB*, 1512-28.

Rensberger, David. "John, Letters of." In *EDB*, 725-26.

General Letters and Revelation

The General Letters

Preliminary Comments

The New Testament letters are generally divided into two groups: the letters associated with Paul (his authentic letters, the disputed letters, the Pastoral Letters, as well as Hebrews) and the General Letters (James, 1 and 2 Peter, Jude, 1, 2, and 3 John).

In the Eastern church the General Letters are known as the Catholic Letters, catholic in the sense of universal since they were addressed to the wider church. In the Western church they are called the Canonical letters because they were approved for use in the church's liturgy.

In Athanasius's list of New Testament writings (367 C.E.; see p. 528) the General Letters are placed immediately after the Gospels and the Acts of the Apostles and before Paul's letters. This same sequence appears in many canons or lists of New Testament writings, and in fact it appears to be the traditional order. Before the invention of printing, the order varied greatly, especially the sequence of books within each group. Almost all Greek manuscripts have the General Letters immediately following Acts. The basis for this is attribution of the General Letters to the great apostles, Peter, James, John, and Jude, while Paul's letters are by someone who came after them, "the least of the apostles" (1 Cor 15:9).

We have already considered the three letters of John. In this chapter we will examine the remaining four General Letters: James, 1 and 2 Peter, and Jude.

James

Getting Started

Read the Letter of James. What ethical advice does James offer his readers?

A Walk through the Letter of James

The writer uses the traditional **opening formula** of a letter (1:1), although he omits the characteristic final greetings. He introduces himself simply as "James, a servant of God and of the Lord Jesus Christ" and identifies his readers as "the twelve tribes in the Dispersion," indicating that they live outside Palestine. They are Jewish Christians whom James sees as the beginning of the fulfillment ("the first fruits of God's creatures," 1:18) of

> ### Reading Guide to James
>
> **Opening Formula** (1:1)
>
> **Introduction to Themes of the Letter** (1:2-27)
>
> **Body** (2:1–5:6)
> > Avoid Partiality: Rich and Poor (2:1-13)
> > Be Doers of the Word (2:14-26)
> > Speech and the Tongue (3:1-12)
> > Call to Friendship with God (3:13–4:10)
> > Do Not Speak Evil against One Another (4:11-12)
> > Arrogance of the Rich (4:13–5:6)
>
> **Conclusion** (5:7-20)

all the promises God made to Israel about the reconstitution of God's 12-tribe kingdom.

In place of a thanksgiving section characteristic of Paul's letters, James has an **introductory section** introducing themes he will develop in the course of this writing (1:2-27). Using an introductory formula of joy (vv. 2-11), he addresses three themes: suffering is to be accepted joyfully since testing leads to perfection (vv. 2-4); God is the giver of all gifts, especially wisdom (vv. 5-8); and the contrast between rich and poor (vv. 9-11). James uses a second introductory formula of blessedness (1:12-27) to introduce another group of themes: endurance under testing leads to eternal life (vv. 12-18); the readers are to be doers of the word (vv. 22-25) and must be careful in speech (v. 26); and true religion entails a concern for the poor (v. 27).

The **body of the letter** (2:1–5:6) takes up the themes mentioned in the introductory section. James opens with a call to avoid partiality, especially between rich and poor (2:1-13). Discrimination on the basis of wealth cannot be reconciled with faith in Jesus Christ. James gives an example from their "synagogue" whereby the rich are honored and the poor shunned. His challenge to the accepted values of his world applies to every generation to reevaluate their treatment of the poor. This conforms to Jesus' teaching that the poor are promised the inheritance of the kingdom (v. 5; see Matt 5:3). James further reminds his readers of the importance of the "royal law" ("You shall love your neighbor as yourself," v. 8), a law of love that should guide every dimension of life.

James next calls his readers to be "doers of the word," to put faith into action (2:14-26). Faith on its own without works is dead. James uses the style of a Greek diatribe to illustrate his point, presenting an example reminiscent of Jesus' parable of the Judgment of the Nations (vv. 15-17; Matt 25:31-46). For further support James turns to the Scriptures (vv. 21-26). Abraham's faith was put into action through deeds: "You see

that faith was active along with his works, and faith was brought to completion by the works" (v. 22). The prostitute Rahab also illustrates James's theme (v. 25); the hospitality she gave Israel's spies in Jericho is worthy of imitation. Christian communities should act in like manner by receiving church representatives!

Addressing the theme of speech and the tongue (3:1-12), James begins with a reminder that "all of us make many mistakes" (v. 2). He uses a multiplicity of images to construct a picture of evil that is perpetrated by speech. His climax is pessimistic: "No one can tame the tongue — a restless evil, full of deadly poison" (v. 8). The tragedy of the uncontrolled tongue is that we use it both to bless God and to curse our neighbor who is "made in the likeness of God" (v. 9).

James's ethical advice culminates in his call to choose friendship with God over friendship with the world (3:13–4:10). He contrasts two lifestyles: one directed by earthly wisdom which is "unspiritual, devilish" (3:14-16); the other directed by divine wisdom that comes down from above and is "pure, peaceable, gentle, willing to yield, full of mercy and good fruits" (vv. 17-18). He challenges the reader to live according to God's wisdom, not the world's. Friendship with God cannot coexist with friendship with the world (4:4). This is the letter's central message: friendship with the world means enmity with God. James calls on the reader to submit to God and to resist the devil (vv. 7-8).

Returning to the theme of controlling speech, James cautions, "Do not speak evil against one another" (4:11-12). Here he equates slander and judgment. By slandering another, one usurps God's role as the true Lawgiver: "So who, then, are you to judge your neighbor?" (v. 12).

In the final section of the body James castigates the arrogance of the rich (4:13–5:6). He offers examples of two groups who seek friendship with the world: rich merchants (4:13-17) and rich landowners (5:1-6). James condemns the merchants for making their plans without reference to God: "Instead you ought to say, 'If the Lord wishes, we will live and do this or that'" (4:15). The rich landowners have defrauded the laborers of their just daily wage (5:4), lived lives of luxury and pleasure (v. 5), and "condemned and murdered" the righteous poor (v. 6). In all these actions, they fail to realize God's concern for the poor.

The letter **concludes** (5:7-20) without the usual epistolary format. James exhorts his readers to patience in the time of suffering (vv. 7-11) as they wait for "the coming of the Lord" (vv. 7-8). He admonishes them not to resort to taking oaths (v. 12) because in a Christian community one's word should be one's honor. James reminds the readers that in every situation they should turn to God in prayer (vv. 13-18). The letter concludes

The General Letters

503

with an exhortation to bring back those who have wandered from the truth (vv. 19-20). Concern for others has been a consistent feature throughout the letter, and it culminates here with a call to bring back one's brother or sister into friendship with God.

Critical Issues in Studying James

The Author of This Letter

The writer identifies himself as "James, a servant of God and of the Lord Jesus Christ" (1:1). James (Greek *Iakobos*) was a popular name in Israel since it was the name of the Hebrew patriarch Jacob, the father of the twelve tribes of Israel. Many people bear the name James (or Jacob) in the New Testament world. Among these are James, the son of Zebedee, apostle and brother of John (Mark 1:19); James, the son of Alphaeus, also an apostle (3:18); and James, the Lord's brother (Gal 1:19).

Does the writer wish to identify himself with one of these people named James? In the opening formulas of their letters Paul and Peter always identify themselves in their role as apostles. Our writer identifies himself, not as an apostle, but as "a servant." This is a typically biblical term defining the relationship between God and God's people (God's servants). It is used to refer to Jesus (Phil 2:7) and also as a title for Christian leaders, for example, "a servant of Jesus Christ" (Rom 1:1) or "servant of Christ" (Gal 1:10). Because the writer identifies himself as a servant, rather than apostle, we can exclude the two apostles (James, the son of Zebedee, and James, the son of Alphaeus) as authors. Further, since James, the son of Zebedee, was martyred by Herod Agrippa I in 44 C.E., this letter could not have been written so early. Consequently, the only leader that can be identified with the author of this letter is James, the brother of the Lord and leader of the Jerusalem church. He was an important figure at the Council of Jerusalem in 49 (Acts 15) and was leader of the Jerusalem church until his martyrdom in 62. He was also mentioned by the contemporary Jewish historian Josephus.

The implied author that emerges from the text is someone equally at home in the spheres of Judaism, Hellenism, and early Christianity. His knowledge of Judaism is innate. He makes extensive usage of the Hebrew Scriptures and shows a strong reliance upon Jewish thought such as the Law and wisdom. At the same time he shows an excellent knowledge of the Greek language, its style and composition. Many Greek words not found elsewhere in the New Testament occur in this letter and the author's use of the Greek diatribe is impressive. Finally, the implied author is at home in

the world of early Christianity. Although the name of Jesus Christ is only mentioned twice in this whole letter (1:1; 2:1), much of his thought relies upon sayings of Jesus, especially the Sermon on the Mount.

From this, we can make the following conclusions: The writer clearly identifies himself with James the brother of the Lord and leader of the church in Jerusalem. However, a literary analysis of the letter shows that the Greek is of such superior quality that it is impossible to imagine someone from Galilee being able to produce this writing, even if a secretary were helping him. The thought of this writing appears to belong to the early stages of the Christian movement: Christian places of worship referred to as "synagogues" (2:2); a close association with the sayings of Jesus as reflected in the Gospels of Matthew and Luke; lively expectation of the coming of the Lord (5:7-8).

Consequently, it would be best to suggest that this writing was written shortly after the death of James by a disciple who wanted to see that his work endured. Using the teachings and sayings of James, the writer wrote in James's name to Jewish Christians outside Palestine, urging them, just as James would have had he been alive, to remain true to their friendship with God and avoid friendship with the world.

"Brother of the Lord"

This term is highly debated, and agreement is very difficult if not impossible. Theological considerations tend to influence the historical considerations, while the exact designations of "brother and sister" in Western societies today tend to mask the imprecision found in other cultures. Consequently, the best understanding that would remain faithful to the New Testament world is to see the term referring to someone belonging to the family of Jesus, understood in the wider sense of a social network without trying to give it any further precision.

The Readers of This Letter

The writer identifies his audience as "the twelve tribes in the Dispersion" (1:1). The reference is best understood in relationship to Israel's hope for the restoration of her 12-tribe kingdom. This expectation laid the foundation for the preaching of John the Baptist and Jesus. When Jesus says to the Syro-Phoenician woman that he "was sent only to the lost sheep of the house of Israel" (Matt 15:24), he is putting his mission into this context of restoring the kingdom.

In opening the letter in this way, James shows that his mission continues that of Jesus. James's readers are the first fruits (1:18) of this new kingdom. The reference to "the Dispersion" in this context adds further precision. The readers form part of the beginning of the reconstituted kingdom of God outside Palestine. They are Jewish Christians, heirs to the promises God made to God's people in the Hebrew Scriptures. They see these promises now being fulfilled in their communities comprised of followers of Jesus of Nazareth. Consequently, it is best to see the Letter of James addressed to a number of Jewish Christian communities spread outside Palestine, one of which was Antioch in Syria.

Theological Themes in James

The most important characteristic of the Letter of James is the connection it maintains with Israel's traditions. James shows, as no other New Testament writing does, that the heritage of Jesus' followers is rooted within Israel's religion. The letter exudes the atmosphere of the world of the Hebrew Scriptures. Not only does he quote from the Hebrew Scriptures, but the writer also appropriates key theological concepts. The concept of the 12-tribe kingdom now being inaugurated in the sphere of James's Jewish Christian communities illustrates well this adoption of Israel's traditions.

The theology of the letter remains at home in the context of ancient Judaism. God is the Lawgiver, the Father of lights, the one who is to come at the end of the world to judge and reward humanity. The letter contains only two references to Jesus Christ, and they do not reflect on the person or mission of Jesus (as did Paul throughout his letters).

James is a practical letter which outlines the type of life a member of the kingdom of God must lead. God is creating a new social order, "the first fruits of God's creatures" (1:18). James's ethical instructions define the boundaries of these communities. Two distinctive characteristics define them. First, everyone is treated equally, with no place for discrimination on the basis of wealth or any other form of partiality. Second, the letter continues the central concern of the Hebrew Scriptures for the poor. James stands in the prophetic tradition of giving voice to the poor and marginalized within society. He re-echoes Jesus' promise that the poor will become heirs of the kingdom (2:5; Matt 5:3) and champions the concerns of the poor by condemning the injustices they experience (2:1-7) and the rich landowners for exploiting the wages of laborers (5:1-6). His condemnations were not meant to change the rich, but rather to assure his readers, who are poor, that God is on their side and does hear their cries for help.

1 Peter

Getting Started

Read 1 Peter. Write a paragraph on the value that 1 Peter assigns to suffering.

Preliminary Comments

Peter is one of four names for the same person in the New Testament. He is also called Symeon in Acts 15:14 and 2 Pet 1:1; Simon (the Greek form of Symeon) in the Gospels; and Cephas (a transliteration of the Aramaic word for "rock") once in the Gospel of John (1:42) and four times each in 1 Corinthians and Galatians. The English name Peter comes from the Greek *Petros* ("rock"), which translates the Aramaic *Cephas*).

The New Testament provides the following information about Peter. He was the "son of Jonah" (Matt 16:17); married (Mark 1:30 and par.); had a brother, Andrew (Mark 1:16 and par.). He was always placed first in the lists of the Twelve and acted as their spokesperson. He denied Jesus, but his relationship with Jesus was restored through the resurrection (John 21:15-19). In Acts, he was a leader of the church in Jerusalem, but left to become a missionary to the Jews. He was held in great respect in Antioch and fell into controversy with Paul. He died a martyr in Rome *ca.* 64 (1 *Clement* 5:1-7 mentions that both Peter and Paul were put to death in Rome and were considered to be "the greatest and most righteous pillars of the church."

A Walk through 1 Peter

In the **opening formula** (1:1-2) the writer follows the traditional Greco-Roman form of a letter. He identifies himself as "Peter, an apostle of Jesus Christ." We will discuss later how this reference is to be understood, but for now we will refer to the author as Peter. He identifies his readers as "the exiles of the Dispersion in Pontus, Galatia, Cappadocia, Asia, and Bithynia." "Exiles of the Dispersion" is a technical term for Jews living outside their homeland, Palestine. However, Peter is writing not to Jews, but to Christian churches in these Roman provinces of Asia Minor. He uses this phrase not literally as in the Letter of James, but metaphorically for Christians as exiles in that they are living outside their homeland, heaven. He names these Roman

<table>
<tr><td>

Reading Guide to 1 Peter

Opening Formula (1:1-2)

Body (1:3–5:11)
    Identity and Values of the Christian (1:3–2:10)
    Christian Life in a Gentile World (2:11–3:12)
    Meaning of Suffering for a Christian (3:13–5:11)

Final Greetings (5:12-14)

</td></tr>
</table>

provinces in the direction someone who was carrying this letter would travel. Finally, Peter sends greetings.

The first part of the **body** of the letter deals with the identity and values of a Christian (1:3–2:10). In place of the usual thanksgiving common to Paul's letters, Peter opens with a section that blesses God for the great gift of salvation granted those readers who became Christians from the pagan world (1:3-12). He stresses the value of the faith that has been handed on to them. Long ago the prophets foretold the salvation for which they now hope (v. 10). They should look upon the sufferings they are enduring now as an opportunity to witness to the "genuineness of your faith" (v. 7).

Peter calls the readers to lead lives of holiness (1:13-25), referring to the exodus when the Israelites in the desert are called to imitate God: "You shall be holy, for I am holy" (v. 16). Christians too are called to be different from the world, to take their values, not from the world, but from God. Peter reminds his readers that they were ransomed by the blood of Christ, "like that of a lamb without defect or blemish" (v. 19), a clear reference to the Jewish Passover.

Because of the saving work of Jesus, believers have become a holy priesthood (2:1-10). Christians (both Jewish and pagan by origin) must consider themselves "a chosen race, a royal priesthood, a holy nation, God's own people" (v. 9). These words are taken from the establishment of God's covenant at the time of the exodus (see Exod 19:5-6), indicating that Christians have inherited God's promises to the Israelites. Above all, Christians are "God's people." Using further quotations from the prophet Hosea, Peter reminds the readers that they were originally separated from God, but now they have become part of God's people (v. 10).

The second section of the body (2:11–3:12) deals with Christian life in a Gentile world, focusing on the ethical conduct of God's people. The readers must consider themselves "aliens and exiles" (2:11) in this present world since their true homeland is heaven (1:1). In 2:13–3:12 Peter uses the literary form of the household code to instruct his readers (see the discussion of Col 3:18–4:1 and Eph 5:21–6:9 above). He calls on his readers to adopt a special attitude toward civil authorities

(2:13-17). He goes on to discuss the attitude of slaves toward their masters (vv. 18-25); of wives and husbands toward each other (3:1-7); and finally the attitude that members of the church should have one for another (vv. 8-12). In stressing these codes, Peter hopes that the witness of their lives will attract others from the wider pagan society to join their communities.

The third section of the body (3:13–5:11) considers the meaning of suffering for Christians. The Christian is to have confidence in the midst of suffering (3:13-17). Peter reminds the readers of the example of the sufferings of Jesus (vv. 18-22), whose death was that of "the righteous for the unrighteous, in order to bring you to God" (v. 18).

Christians are also to lead lives that avoid sin (4:1-11). Their lives are different from those of their pagan neighbors. Peter offers a list of vices (4:3), similar to those that Paul used (Rom 1:29-31). These vices were associated with pagan feasts. Now they are Christians, they have separated themselves from such celebrations (1 Pet 4:4).

Peter invites his readers to see their sufferings as a share in Christ's sufferings (4:12-19), which calls for rejoicing. Since Peter was a witness to the suffering of Christ and shared in his glory (5:1), he urges his fellow elders to care for the community entrusted to their care (vv. 2-4). Using the image of Christ the Shepherd, he urges them to be true shepherds caring eagerly for their flock.

Peter closes the body of the letter with a set of final exhortations (5:5-9). He urges the readers to humble themselves (vv. 5-6), to place their anxieties upon God (v. 7), and to be watchful (v. 8). The motivation for their conduct is: "Like a roaring lion your adversary the devil prowls around, looking for someone to devour" (v. 8). A doxology (5:10-11) offers the promise that God will "restore, support, strengthen, and establish" them in all the sufferings they experience.

The **final greetings (5:12-14)** are traditional. Silvanus is either the one who brought this letter or the one who wrote it on Peter's behalf. Greetings are sent from the church in Rome (identified as "Babylon") as well as "my son Mark."

Critical Issues in Studying 1 Peter

The Author of 1 Peter

The implied author identifies himself with Peter, the apostle (1:1); he was witness to Christ's sufferings and shares in his glory (5:1). He is an elder, who speaks with authority. Further, the implied author knows and quotes from the Hebrew Scriptures. He also knows and employs the Greco-Roman expression of morality through household codes and lists of vices.

Identification of the implied author with Peter, the

apostle and leader of the Twelve, fits with the image of Peter as reported in the rest of the New Testament. However, two serious problems question this identification. First, the Greek of 1 Peter is among the best in the New Testament, which would make it unlikely for a fisherman from Galilee to have written it. Second, much of the thought in this letter bears similarity to Paul's theology. For example, 1 Peter uses expressions common in Paul, such as "in Christ" (3:16: 5:10, 14). Also 1 Peter stresses the centrality of the saving death and resurrection of Jesus, a key theme in Paul's writings.

The best solution is to view the letter in a similar relationship to Peter as the Deutero-Pauline letters are to Paul. The arguments against Peter physically writing this letter are convincing. However, since Peter's authority is claimed very strongly in this letter, it points to one of his disciples being responsible for writing it shortly after Peter's death (64). The symbolization of Rome as "Babylon" (5:13) implies the destruction of Jerusalem by Rome in 70 C.E. (just as Babylon had destroyed Jerusalem in 587 B.C.E.) Consequently, this letter probably stems to one of Peter's disciples in Rome shortly after 70 C.E. He was assisted by Silvanus and Mark (5:12-13), two disciples intimately associated with Paul and whose contributions would account for the Pauline influences in this letter.

The Readers of This Letter

The address to "exiles in the Dispersion in Pontus, Galatia, Cappadocia, Asia, and Bithynia (1:1) names Roman provinces in northern, central, and western Asia Minor. We do not know of any missionary activity of Peter in this region. Nevertheless, the letter invokes his authority, showing the great regard in which he was held in these regions. It is possible that after Peter's death, when problems emerged in those regions, a disciple of Peter wrote to that region where Peter's authority was well respected to resolve certain issues and give encouragement in the way Peter would have had he been alive.

Theological Themes in 1 Peter

Many theological themes emerge in this letter that show why it is included in the canon of the New Testament. Its description of the dignity of the Christian has led some scholars to conjecture that the letter originated as a baptismal homily. 1 Peter is a wonderful theological testament to the meaning of Christian suffering as a sharing in the sufferings, death, and resurrection of Jesus.

Peter's theological reflection on Jesus' death is intriguing and has some important implications. The letter speaks about the aftermath of Jesus' death on two occasions. In 3:18-19 Peter says: "He was put to death in the flesh, but made alive in the spirit, in which also he went and made a proclamation to the spirits in prison." He paints a picture of Jesus after his death going to the place of the dead and there proclaiming his victory over sin and death. Then, in 4:6 Peter continues with the same image: "For this is the reason the gospel was proclaimed even to the dead, so that, though they had been judged in the flesh as everyone is judged, they might live in the spirit as God does." Again, Peter shows the influence of Jesus' death on those who have died, no matter where or when.

The implications are important. Christians believe that salvation comes only through the person of Christ. But the natural question arises: What happens to those who lived before Christ's coming or who have through no fault of their own never heard of Christ and his message? Peter provides a possible answer. The death of Jesus is not limited. When Jesus died upon the cross, the effects of his death reached beyond time and place. The image of Jesus preaching to the dead (4:6) expresses in an amazing way how the grace of Christ's death touches even the dead and makes it possible for them to share in God's kingdom.

2 Peter

Getting Started

Read both the letters of 2 Peter and Jude. Note the similarities that you find between these two letters.

A Walk through 2 Peter

The only feature of a letter appears in the **opening formula (1:1-2)**. The writer identifies himself as "Symeon Peter, a servant and apostle of Jesus Christ." The readers are mentioned in general terms as "those who have received a faith as precious as ours." The opening greetings are similar to those in 1 Peter and in Jude.

The **body of the letter (1:3–3:16)** has two parts. Forgoing the typical thanksgiving, the writer proceeds immediately to issues of concern to him. He begins with exhortations to moral virtue (1:3-15), reminding his readers of God's promise that they will be "participants of the divine nature" (v. 4). He challenges them to remain firm in the call the Lord has given him. The writer lists certain qualities or virtues to strive for: faith, goodness, knowledge, self-control, endurance, godliness, mutual affection, love. He speaks in a manner that implies that he is about to die.

In the second part of the body Peter defends the traditional belief in the second coming (Parousia) of Jesus against his opponents (1:16–3:16).

- Peter's preaching is based not on "cleverly devised myths," but on eyewitness experiences such as the transfiguration when God testified to Jesus as his own Son (1:16-19).
- The Hebrew prophets were divinely inspired to prophesy concerning the coming of the Lord (1:20-21). No prophecy is a matter of personal interpretation, but rests upon a community interpretation.
- The false teachers in their midst are similar to the false prophets of the Hebrew Scriptures (2:1-10). Peter shows how in the past God punished the wicked. He draws on the letter of Jude for his illustrations.
- Their false teaching leads them to embrace immoral lives which are more like that of animals than humans (2:11-22). Peter compares his opponents to a dog that returns to its own vomit!
- The center of the false teachers' doctrine is the denial of the coming of Christ (3:1-10). "Where is the promise of his coming?" (v. 4) is a way of saying: "He is not going to come!" The opponents deny his coming from experience: the world has never changed and consequently will not change. To this Peter answers with many arguments: the creation occurred simply by God's word (v. 5); the world was destroyed by water at God's word (v. 6); the world will be destroyed again at the end by fire at God's word (v. 7). For Peter, the coming of Christ has been delayed as a sign of God's patience in that God hopes that more people will repent (v. 9).
- Because the world is going to end in a conflagration, Peter's readers should be paying attention and "leading lives of holiness and godliness" (3:11-13).
- Peter appeals to the writings of Paul (3:14-16). At this time the church is making a collection of Paul's letters (v. 16) and they are being considered Sacred Scripture (v. 16). In effect, the writer says that the readers can rely on this teaching regarding the com-

ing of Christ because both Paul and Peter testify to it as the traditional faith of the Christian communities.

The letter concludes without the usual final greeting but with a final **exhortation and doxology** (3:17-18). The readers are forewarned not to be led astray but to grow in the knowledge of the Savior Jesus Christ.

Critical Issues in Studying 2 Peter

The Relationship of 2 Peter and Jude

This is the most important issue to be examined in this letter as it has implications for understanding 2 Peter and for dating this writing. Almost all of the Letter of Jude is included within 2 Peter. Of the 25 verses in Jude, 19 can be found in 2 Peter in one form or another.

An examination of the two writings reveals these connections:

- 2 Pet 1:1-2 is similar to Jude 1-2
- 2 Pet 2:3-18 is similar to Jude 4-16
- 2 Pet 3:2-3 is similar to Jude 17-18
- 2 Pet 3:14, 18 is similar to Jude 24-25

It appears that 2 Peter borrowed from Jude for a number of reasons. The Letter of Jude can be understood well without 2 Peter, but 2 Peter needs Jude to give a clearer understanding of what is said. For example, 2 Pet 2:11 refers to angels bringing a slanderous judgment. Jude 9 alludes to Michael the Archangel contending with Satan about Moses' body, a reference to an apocryphal story circulating at the time in the *Assumption of Moses*. Later 2 Peter omits another apocryphal quotation from Jude 14-15 which quotes *1 En* 1:9. It makes more sense to see 2 Peter deliberately excluding these quotations from apocryphal writings than for Jude to have inserted them deliberately. Finally, it is more logical that the longer writing (2 Peter) would borrow from the shorter one (Jude) than vice versa.

The Author of 2 Peter

The writer says that he is "Symeon Peter, a servant and apostle of Jesus Christ" (1:1). He claims to have witnessed the transfiguration of Jesus (1:16-18) and refers to the first letter of Peter (3:1). The implied author makes more of a connection with the apostle than does 1 Peter! Nevertheless, some strong points argue against the identification of Peter as the implied author:

- Comparison with the Letter of Jude has shown that 2 Peter must have been written after Jude. This indicates that 2 Peter is a late writing.

A relief representation of Peter crucified upside-down; Rome. (W. S. LaSor)

- The writer belongs to the second generation of Christians (*for ever since our ancestors died,* 3:4).
- Paul's writings have become a collection and considered Sacred Scripture. This could only happen many decades after Paul's death (*ca.* 67).
- Concern for the second coming of Christ was not an issue for 1 Peter. Hence, this writing must come from a stage long after 1 Peter and be written by a different author (as the style and language also indicate).

These points indicate that this writing could have been written neither by the Apostle Peter nor by the disciple who wrote 1 Peter. Its context betrays a period at the end of the 1st and beginning of the 2nd centuries. It certainly does not reflect a time either prior to or shortly after 64.

The author's deliberate connection with the Apostle Peter makes it best to see this writing coming from a disciple of Peter (but a disciple different from that of 1 Peter and writing much later) who uses Peter's authority in areas where Peter was held in high regard in order to overcome false teachings undermining the traditional

Christian faith. In this way he reminds his readers of Peter's teaching, especially on this issue of the coming of Christ. It would probably have been written somewhere between 100 and 120.

The Readers of This Letter

"To those who have received a faith as precious as ours" (1:1) is a very general address. Since the author refers back to 1 Peter (3:1), the readers are probably in the same vicinity as the readers of the first letter. They also hold Paul's letters with great authority. The region of Asia Minor is the logical place to situate them.

The Form of 2 Peter

The opening address is the only feature of a letter in the whole writing. It lacks a thanksgiving section, the closing formula of final greetings, and contains no personal references to individuals. Instead, it resembles the form of a testament, a characteristic literary genre found often in the biblical writings. A testament presents an important character bidding farewell to his closest associates. He speaks about his death and offers advice and exhortations to those who remain behind, preparing them for the difficulties that lie ahead. In the Hebrew Scriptures, Moses offers a testament in Deuteronomy 29–31, as does Joshua in Joshua 23–24, and the 12 Patriarchs in the apocryphal *Testaments of the Twelve Patriarchs*. Christian writings include the farewell discourses of Jesus in John 13–17 and of Paul in Acts 20:18-38. Even 2 Timothy can be seen to belong to this literary form.

In this context 2 Peter is to be viewed as a testament. Prior to his death, Peter reminds his readers of everything he has taught them. He uses this literary form to urge Christians to remain true to the traditional faith and to warn them about impending dangers that Peter had foreseen.

Theological Themes in 2 Peter

2 Peter is clearly the last writing of the New Testament and gives insight into how Christian tradition and thought had developed by the beginning of the 2nd century. In this sense it is extremely valuable. It illustrates above all how concern for the second coming of Christ continued to remain an issue within the Christian community.

The letter shows that disputes were settled by appealing to the traditional faith of the apostolic community. Some scholars have argued that 2 Peter distorted the traditional faith by overstressing adherence to doctrines that could only be interpreted by the apostolic leaders. Such an argument is in fact itself a distortion of 2 Peter because it reads into this writing issues that come from a post-Enlightenment rejection of authority and tradition. Instead, 2 Peter gives witness to a desire within early Christian communities to remain faithful to what had been handed on through the apostolic witnesses. It provides insight into the necessity of remaining connected to the Christian tradition and avoiding distortions both in belief and in morality that lead away from Jesus' teachings.

This writing appeals to the authority of both Peter and Paul. Fidelity to both apostolic witnesses is vital in remaining true to the traditional faith. By referring to the writings of Paul, 2 Peter acknowledges indirectly the importance of the Pauline perspective as well.

The inspiration of Scripture is another important theological legacy of 2 Peter. The writings of the communities of Israel and of the early Christian apostles arose under the guidance of God's Spirit: "no prophecy of scripture is a matter of one's own interpretation, because no prophecy ever came by human will, but men and women moved by the Holy Spirit spoke from God" (1:20-21). Peter does not explain how this happens, but emphasizes that this body of writings owes its origin to God's inspiration. By including those of Paul (3:16) it ultimately gives rise to the understanding that the Christian writings have a status equal to the Hebrew Scriptures because of God's inspirational activity.

Jude

A Walk through Jude

In the **opening formula (vv. 1-2)** the writer identifies himself as "Jude, a servant of Jesus Christ and brother of James." He refers to the readers generally as "those who are called, who are beloved in God the Father and kept safe for Jesus Christ," and ends by sending greetings.

The writer begins by describing the **occasion for the letter (vv. 3-4)**. While preparing to write to them, he hears about some people who have entered the community and are distorting the teaching that they have previously received. Accordingly, he warns his readers about them.

The **body of the letter** opens with three examples from the Hebrew Scriptures of how God punished the wicked in the past (vv. 5-10), intended here as a warning not to abandon the faith.

- God punished those Israelites he had taken out of Egypt because of their complaints against God (v. 5)

> **Reading Guide to Jude**
>
> **Opening Formula** (1-2)
>
> **Occasion for the Letter** (3-4)
>
> **Body** (5-23)
>   Examples of the Punishment for Disobedience (5-10)
>   More Examples of Punishment (11-13)
>   Prophetic Warnings (14-19)
>   Purpose of the Letter (20-23)
>
> **Doxology** (24-25)

- God punished the angels who came down to earth seeking women (v. 6)
- Sodom and Gomorrah were punished because they "indulged in sexual immorality and pursued unnatural lust" (v. 7)

Jude says that he will leave the judgment to God just as the archangel Michael did when he contended with the devil over Moses' body (vv. 8-10).

The writer adds three further examples of God's punishment (vv. 11-13): Cain, Balaam, and Korah. These examples of Israelite leaders who led the people astray serve as warnings to the present community not to be led astray by the false teachers.

Jude shows how these false teachers had been foretold by the prophets and apostles (vv. 14-19). He refers to the example of Enoch, who was taken up to heaven (Gen 5:23-24), by quoting from the apocryphal *1 Enoch:* "See, the Lord is coming with ten thousands of his holy ones" (v. 14). Consequently, these teachers can be assured that God's punishment lies ahead.

The body of the letter ends with the purpose for writing (vv. 20-23). Jude wishes to build up the readers' faith (v. 20). He encourages them to pray in the Spirit, to keep themselves in God's love and trust in Christ's mercy (v. 21). As in the Letter of James, the readers are encouraged to show concern for those "who are wavering" (v. 22).

The letter culminates without personal greetings but with a **doxology** in praise of God through Jesus Christ (vv. 24-25).

Critical Issues in Studying Jude

The Author of Jude

The name Jude (Greek *Judas*) was common in New Testament times. The author deliberately identifies himself with James, "the brother of the Lord" (see Matt 13:55:

"Are not [Jesus'] brothers James and Joseph and Simon and Judas?").

The picture of the implied author that emerges from this letter shows the writer has an excellent knowledge of Greek. Twenty-two Greek words in this very short letter are found only here in the New Testament. Jude also gives the impression that he belongs to a generation after that of the apostles (vv. 17-18).

Consequently, the writer cannot be identified with Jude, the brother of James. Instead, we view the writing as coming from a second-generation Christian. As with Peter's letters and the Deutero-Pauline letters, this writer uses Jude's authority to resolve problems arising within certain areas of the Christian community. The "brothers of the Lord" were important people within the context of the early church, and his identification with James gives him the authority he needs for this writing.

The Readers of This Letter

The letter contains a very general address (v. 1). Its contents imply that the readers have an excellent knowledge of the Hebrew Scriptures and also value apocryphal writings. The letter is also written in excellent Greek. These are the same characteristics attributed to the readers of James. Consequently, this letter is seen to be sent to readers outside Palestine in the regions of Antioch and Syria. A letter bearing the authority of James and of Jude would hold great significance in those regions.

The Use of Noncanonical Sources

This brief letter shows evidence of the use of noncanonical writings. Jude knows and refers to a legend about the burial of Moses that was found in the *Assumption of Moses,* and he quotes from *1 Enoch.*

The use of these apocryphal writings has caused concern for some scholars over the centuries. They argue that if Jude is an inspired writing, it would not have quoted from noninspired works. This is a fallacious argument. In Acts, Luke presents Paul quoting from Greek writings outside the Jewish tradition (Acts 17:28). By quoting these extrabiblical sources, neither Jude nor Luke's Paul is trying to give them an authoritative status. They are simply referring to something that has a beauty or truth and is well known by the readers.

Theological Themes in Jude

This brief emergency letter lays an important stress upon the value of one's heritage and past traditions. For 21st-century readers the references and allusions that Jude makes are foreign and extremely difficult to understand or follow. However, for readers of Jude's

world, they would be immediately understood. He shows a depth of understanding and appreciation for all the heroes (both positive and negative) of their past and uses these examples to speak to his present. Jude wishes to illustrate that the past does give direction to the present and that one can rely upon God's protection, mercy, and justice. He uses negative examples as illustrations of God's justice and punishment in order to encourage his readers to withstand the inroads of the false teachers. The letter illustrates that Scripture can illuminate the readers' imagination by showing how people have responded to God in the past and how the reader can respond in like manner.

Questions for Review and Discussion

James

1 What contribution does the Letter of James make to the thought and life of Christianity?

2 Can you note any differences between the thought of James and the thought of Paul?

1 Peter

1 Why would some scholars consider 1 Peter to come from a baptismal homily?

2 What contribution do you think 1 Peter makes to Christian life and morality?

2 Peter

1 What does 2 Peter have to say about the coming of Christ (the Parousia) and the end of the world?

2 What is the value of having 2 Peter in the canon of the New Testament?

Jude

What does Jude say about the false teachers? Why is he so concerned about them?

Further Reading

James

Bauckham, Richard. "James." In *ECB,* 1483-92.

Chester, Andrew, and Ralph P. Martin. *The Theology of the Letters of James, Peter, and Jude.* Cambridge: Cambridge University Press, 1994.

Hartin, Patrick J. *The Spirituality of Perfection: Faith in Action in the Letter of James.* Collegeville: Liturgical, 1999.

Maynard-Reid, Pedrito U. *Poverty and Wealth in James.* Maryknoll: Orbis, 1987.

Tamez, Elsa. *The Scandalous Message of James: Faith without Works Is Dead.* Rev. ed. New York: Crossroad, 2002.

Watson, Duane F. "James, Letter of." In *EDB,* 670-71.

1 Peter

Brown, Raymond E., Karl P. Donfried, and John H. P. Reumann, eds. *Peter in the New Testament: A Collaborative Assessment by Protestant and Roman Catholic Scholars.* Minneapolis: Augsburg, 1973.

Davids, Peter H. "Peter, First Letter of." In *EDB,* 1036-38.

Elliott, John H. *1 Peter.* AB 37B. New York: Doubleday, 2000.

Stanton, Graham N. "1 Peter." In *ECB,* 1493-1503.

2 Peter and Jude

Bauckham, Richard. *Jude and the Relatives of Jesus in the Early Church.* London: T. & T. Clark, 2004.

McKnight, Scot. "2 Peter." In *ECB,* 1504-11.

———. "Jude." In *ECB,* 1529-34.

Osburn, Carroll D. "Jude, Letter of." In *EDB,* 750-51.

———. "Peter, Second Letter of." In *EDB,* 1039-41.

Chapter 62

The Book of Revelation

Getting Started

Read Revelation 1–3. Make a comparative list of the angel's praise and blame for each church.

Preliminary Comments

The book of Revelation (often mistakenly called "Revelations"), also known as the Apocalypse, takes its name from its opening Greek word, *apokalypsis.* In our study of the book of Daniel we discussed the concept of apocalyptic and apocalypse in detail. We shall apply what we have already observed to this writing, which is probably the most misunderstood and misused book in the whole Bible.

Over the centuries political anarchists and antigovernment groups have used this book to support their ideologies (e.g., David Karesh). Artists have also found in this book a rich source of imagery. At the time of the millennium, the book of Revelation evoked enormous feelings and concern. Fundamentalist Christians interpreted many of the symbols as prophecies of imminent gloom and disaster, but nothing happened!

Faced with such varied interpretations that continue to attach to this book, it is important in our final study to use what we have learned throughout this course in

order to attain a responsible reading of this writing. Because of its difficulty, we will first address a number of background issues before examining the contents of the book.

The Literary Genre of the Apocalypse

Scholars define an apocalypse as a literary work, usually written in the form of a narrative, which presents a revelatory vision that a seer has received, sometimes through the mediation of an angel who transports the seer on a journey to show the vision or explain it. Although it is a literary presentation, the testimony of the seer being transported into an altered state of consciousness must not be ignored.

A study of extrabiblical apocalypses shows that it is difficult to attribute common characteristics to all since not every category applies to each one. A look at some of the features found in other apocalypses will show how closely this writing is to them and will help us understand the book of Revelation more fully.

The elements mentioned above in our definition of an apocalypse are clearly evident in Revelation:

Narrative

The writing is narrative in form, with the seer, John, describing his revelatory experiences. One unique feature is that it is not meant to be read as a linear narrative in which each scene builds upon the previous one, ultimately climaxing in the final chapter. Instead, the reader must read each vision as an entity in its own right, each drawing from and building upon the other.

Visions

The foundation for the book is a series of visions John receives and which the angel helps him interpret. These revelatory experiences occur in an altered state of consciousness. When he wishes to communicate his experience of these visions to his readers/hearers, he can only do it through symbolic language.

Mediation of an Angel

Revelation, true to the context of Judaism in John's day, presents God as distant from the world. God can only communicate with the help of angels, God's messengers and intermediaries between God and humanity.

Journey through the Skies

John's journey forms the background for all the visions. He is "in the spirit" (1:10), and the angel takes him to various places where he experiences God's presence and message.

In addition to these characteristics the following elements are also central features in apocalyptic literature and especially in the book of Revelation.

Symbolism and Symbolic Language

Explanation of the symbols in this book must begin from within John's own context, namely, from the Hebrew Scriptures and the Greco-Roman context (never from our world!). To express his revelatory experiences and visions, John turns to the Hebrew Scriptures: of the 404 verses in Revelation, 278 have connections with the Hebrew Scriptures. Among the common symbols that occur are the following:

- Animals: The Roman Empire is symbolized as a *beast:* "And the beast that I saw was like a leopard, its feet were like a bear's and its mouth was like a lion's mouth" (13:2).
- Colors: *White* is a symbol of victory: "Then I saw heaven opened, and there was a white horse! Its rider is called Faithful and True, and in righteousness he judges and makes war" (19:11).
- Objects: A *crown* signifies victory (2:10); *eyes* symbolize knowledge (4:6); *horns* speak of power (13:1); the *Lamb* is a symbol of Christ (5:6).
- Numbers: *Four* represents the four cardinal directions (north, south, east, west); *twelve* was the astrological symbol for the zodiac, as well as for the 12 tribes of Israel and the 12 apostles of Jesus. The

importance of the number *seven* is derived from the lunar calendar: a quarter of a month (the time between full moons) is seven days. Consequently, seven became central to configuring the whole pattern of life. The Babylonians organized their whole calendar around the number seven (seven days in one week), and for the Israelites the seventh day became the Sabbath, the day of rest. Seven is the most important symbol in the book of Revelation. It appears some 54 times: there are seven stars (1:16), seven letters to seven churches (chs. 2–3), seven seals (6:1–8:2), seven trumpets (8:6–11:15), seven bowls of wrath (16:1-17). Seven became the symbol for completeness and per-

St. John the Evangelist at Patmos, Hans Burgkmair the Elder (1505; Alte Pinakothek, Munich). (Scala/ ArtResource, NY)

fection. In contrast, *six* (one less that seven) became the symbol of imperfection, for evil. *One thousand* indicates a multitude.

Pseudonymity

Apocalypses of this period were usually pseudonymous works, attributed to a hero from the past who prophesied historical events from his time down to that of the readers. While Christian tradition has usually associated this writing with John, the Beloved Disciple and author of the Gospel of John, scholars today question this identification almost universally (see "Critical Issues in Studying Revelation"). Other apocalypses situate the seer in the distant past, but the author of Revelation is present at the time of the readers and speaks directly to them.

Persecution

Another feature of many apocalypses is their context of persecution. Revelation shows that John of Patmos and his readers have faced persecution and expect much more. This theme weaves its way throughout the writing.

While Revelation shows that the persecution experienced by the followers of Jesus came from both Jews and Gentiles, fear of a Roman persecution was certainly strongest among the Christians of Asia Minor. Generally, Roman society and the emperors were tolerant toward new religious movements, especially from the East. Since the time of Julius Caesar, the Jews had been accorded special status as a "lawful religion" *(religio licita)*. Even after their failed war of independence (66-70 C.E.) they were allowed to continue worshipping their own God (although their temple tax now went to pay for the temple of Jupiter Capitolinus in Rome as punishment for their uprising). Roman thinking first grouped Christians together with the Jews, but over time the differences between the two became more apparent and the protections afforded the Jewish religion were no long applied to the followers of Jesus.

The question of honoring the Roman emperor as a god was a matter of ultimate concern to Christians. In the eastern part of the empire, the peoples were culturally enthusiastic about worshipping the emperor as a god since this was part of a heritage where Pharaohs and kings were acknowledged as gods. In Rome and the western empire many of the emperors were hesitant in encouraging this.

The picture of a constant state-sponsored persecution of Christians over the first four hundred years of Christianity is a historical fallacy. Only four major state persecutions of Christians occurred during this time. The first Roman persecution of Christians occurred under Nero Caesar (54-68).

Evidence indicates continuing persecutions of Chris-

The Symbolic Number of the Beast

"This calls for wisdom: let anyone with understanding calculate the number of the beast, for it is the number of a person. Its number is six hundred sixty-six." (13:18)

The beast referred to here is the first beast from the sea that demands worship from all the inhabitants from the earth. Those who refuse are persecuted. John says that the reader can figure out who the beast is because the letters of his name add up to 666. Throughout history, attempts have been made to identify the beast with various people, such as the Pope, Hitler, Ronald Reagan, and even Bill Gates! Most of these suggestions say something about those making the identifications. It also shows the fallacy in the method of interpretation. To find out who this person is, the interpreter should start not with the present world or one's own presuppositions, but rather with the world of John.

Most scholars see this beast as Nero Caesar. John's contemporaries did not use arabic numerals for mathematic and arithmetic calculations as we do today. Instead, they used the letters of their alphabet as their numeric symbols. These letters always had the same value. For example, we know from watching the credits of movies how the letters of the Latin alphabet had certain values: L = 50; C = 100; M = 1000, and so on. The Hebrew alphabet also used letters for numbers. The name Neron Caesar, when transliterated from Hebrew, gives the letters NRON CSR. Giving these letters the numerical value they hold in Hebrew produces the following result:

N + R + O + N + C + S + R

50 + 200 + 6 + 50 + 100 + 60 + 200 = 666

tians throughout Asia Minor. In 112 Pliny, the Roman governor of Bithynia (northern Asia Minor), wrote to the emperor Trajan (98-117), asking advice on how to deal with Christians. Pliny told Trajan that he asked those accused three times if they were Christians, and, if they continued to admit it, he condemned them to death. Those who said they were not and offered sacrifices he would release. Trajan endorsed Pliny's approach. Pliny also indicates that he had inherited this approach, showing that such persecution of Christians had been occurring before Trajan's rule.

The persecution referred to in the book of Revelation comes from the Roman state and concerns worship of the emperor (13:4, 12-17; 16:2; 19:20). The use of Babylon (18:1-24) as a symbol for the city of Rome is significant. Jerusalem had been destroyed by Babylon in 587

B.C.E. and again by Rome in 70 C.E. For this symbolism to be effective, Revelation would have to have been written sometime after Jerusalem's second destruction.

Revelation uses a code name for the Roman emperor responsible for the present persecution of Christians: "let anyone with understanding calculate the number of the beast, for it is the number of a person. Its number is six hundred sixty-six" (13:18). We argued above that this refers to the emperor Nero (see p. 514). Nero had committed suicide, but according to a legend circulating in the eastern part of the empire (referred to as *Nero redivivus,* "Nero returned to life"), he did not die but was restored to life and would return to rule again over the

References to Persecution in Revelation

1:9 I, John, your brother who share with you in Jesus the persecution and the kingdom and the patient endurance, was on the island called Patmos because of the word of God and the testimony of Jesus.

2:10 (To the church of Smyrna): Do not fear what you are about to suffer. Beware, the devil is about to throw some of you into prison so that you may be tested, and for ten days you will have affliction. Be faithful until death, and I will give you the crown of life.

2:13 (To the church of Pergamum): I know where you are living, where Satan's throne is. Yet you are holding fast to my name, and you did not deny your faith in me even in the days of Antipas my witness, my faithful one, who was killed among you, where Satan lives.

3:10 (To the church of Philadelphia): Because you have kept my word of patient endurance, I will keep you from the hour of trial that is coming on the whole world to test the inhabitants of the earth.

6:9-11 When he opened the fifth seal, I saw under the altar the souls of those who had been slaughtered for the word of God and for the testimony they had given; they cried out with a loud voice, "Sovereign Lord, holy and true, how long will it be before you judge and avenge our blood on the inhabitants of the earth?" They were each given a white robe and told to rest a little longer, until the number would be complete both of their fellow servants and of their brothers and sisters, who were soon to be killed as they themselves had been killed.

17:6 "And I saw that the woman was drunk with the blood of the saints and the blood of the witnesses to Jesus."

18:24 "And in you was found the blood of prophets and of saints, and of all who have been slaughtered on earth."

empire. John of Patmos puts it: "the beast that had been wounded by the sword and yet lived" (13:14).

While Nero was the first emperor to persecute Christians, his actions were limited to Rome. Domitian was the first emperor to encourage worship of himself as a god in the eastern part of the empire. He also encouraged his subjects to refer to him as "our Lord and God" *(Dominus et Deus),* the same terms Christians used for Christ. Domitian ruled as an absolute monarch. According to the Roman historian Suetonius, his final years were ones of terror. He put to death everyone who opposed him. Eventually he was assassinated by a conspiracy that involved his own wife, Domitia. Various Christian writers speak of Domitian's rule as a time of fear and persecution for Christians, especially in the East.

We can conclude that this apocalypse was written toward the end of Domitian's rule (90-96) during the period that Christians were being forced to participate in worship of the emperor and the pagan gods. Domitian was seen to fulfill the Nero legend in that he was identified with *Nero redivivus* ("Nero returned to life"). Early church writers are supportive of this context for Revelation (Irenaeus [*ca.* 120-202], Clement of Alexandria [*ca.* 150-215], Origen [*ca.* 185-254], Eusebius [*ca.* 260-339], and Jerome [*ca.* 340-420]).

A Walk through Revelation

Revelation 1:1-3: The Prologue
The writing is identified as "the revelation of Jesus Christ" that God has given through an angel to John, who now communicates it to the reader. The first of seven beatitudes occurs in v. 3. The blessing is for those who read and hear the words of this prophecy. This shows that the writing is meant to be read aloud in the context of worship.

Revelation 1:4–3:22:
Letters to the Seven Churches
Revelation opens with the characteristics of a letter (1:4-5). The author uses the brief Greco-Roman formula in which he identifies himself simply as John and the readers as "the seven churches that are in Asia." To them he sends "grace and peace" from God "who is and who was and who is to come" (v. 4; see Exod 3:14) and from Jesus Christ, "the faithful witness, the first-born of the dead and the ruler of the kings of the earth" (v. 5). Not only does this section contain seven letters, but the whole apocalypse is framed within the context of a letter sent to the seven churches of Asia Minor. The book ends with a brief final greeting (22:21).

An inaugural vision (1:9-20) sets this writing within its true context. John reports that what appears here is the consequence of a religious experience: "I was in the spirit on the Lord's day" (v. 10). In this altered state of consciousness, he is instructed to write what he experiences to the seven churches. The seer has been transported beyond the world of everyday reality to experience the divine. John communicates this experience through symbols and the imagery of the Hebrew Scriptures.

Letters to seven churches (2:1–3:22) follow this vision, showing that this writing is primarily directed to them and their 1st-century context. The seven churches — Ephesus, Smyrna, Pergamum, Thyatira, Sardis, Philadelphia, and Laodicea — are situated on a circular

Nero's Persecution of Christians

But all human efforts, all the lavish gifts of the emperor, and the propitiations of the gods, did not banish the sinister belief that the conflagration was the result of an order. Consequently, to get rid of the report, Nero fastened the guilt and inflicted the most exquisite tortures on a class hated for their abominations, called Christians by the populace. Christus, from whom the name had its origin, suffered the extreme penalty during the reign of Tiberius at the hands of one of our procurators, Pontius Pilatus, and a most mischievous superstition, thus checked for the moment, again broke out not only in Judaea, the first source of the evil, but even in Rome, where all things hideous and shameful from every part of the world find their centre and become popular. Accordingly, an arrest was first made of all who pleaded guilty; then, upon their information, an immense multitude was convicted, not so much of the crime of firing the city, as of hatred against mankind. Mockery of every sort was added to their deaths. Covered with the skins of beasts, they were torn by dogs and perished, or were nailed to crosses, or were doomed to the flames and burnt, to serve as a nightly illumination, when daylight had expired.

Nero offered his gardens for the spectacle, and was exhibiting a show in the circus, while he mingled with the people in the dress of a charioteer or stood aloft on a car. Hence, even for criminals who deserved extreme and exemplary punishment, there arose a feeling of compassion; for it was not, as it seemed, for the public good, but to glut one man's cruelty, that they were being destroyed.

Tacitus, *The Annals*, 15:44. *Complete Works of Tacitus*, ed. Alfred John Church and William Jackson Brodribb (repr. Mineola: Dover, 2006).

Reading Guide to the Book of Revelation

Prologue (1:1-3)

Letters to the Seven Churches (1:4–3:22)

First Cycle of Visions and Revelatory Experiences (4:1–11:19)
   God and the Lamb (4:1–5:14)
   Opening of the Seven Seals (6:1–8:2)
   The Seven Trumpets (8:3–11:19)

Second Cycle of Visions and Revelatory Experiences (12:1–22:5)
   The Woman, Dragon, Beasts, and the Lamb (12:1–14:20)
   Seven Plagues and Seven Bowls of God's Wrath (15:1–16:21)
   The Judgment of Babylon (17:1–19:10)
   Final Victory and Vision of the Heavenly Jerusalem (19:11–22:5)

Epilogue, Admonitions, and Final Blessing (22:6-21)

route that someone would travel when delivering this writing. The letters are all structured similarly, though some are longer than others. Jesus begins each letter with the words "I know," and either praise or condemnation follows. All end with a call to remain faithful and to listen to what the Spirit is telling the churches. The churches face many challenges: losing the love they used to have (Ephesus); compromising in belief and morality (Pergamum, Thyatira); persecution (Smyrna, Philadelphia [these two churches receive no condemnation, only praise]); complacency (Sardis); and being lukewarm (Laodicea).

Revelation 4:1–11:19: First Cycle of Visions and Revelatory Experiences

The book of Revelation falls easily into two sections. Chapter 4 opens with reference to an open door: "After this I looked, and there in heaven a door stood open!" (v. 1). At the end of ch. 11 God's temple is opened (11:19). These act as markers around which the various visions are grouped.

God and the Lamb (4:1–5:14)

John's vision focuses first on God (ch. 4) and then on the Lamb (ch. 5). His experience of God is expressed through the imagery of the Hebrew Scriptures: the description of God in terms of gems is dependent upon Ezek 1:26-28; the four living creatures come from Ezek 1:4-13; 10:18-22; God as the Holy One is from Isa 6:3. God holds a scroll that is perfectly sealed ("with seven seals"), written on both sides (5:1). No one is worthy to open the seals except "the Lion of the tribe of Judah, the Root of David" (5:5). A surprise emerges: John expects to see a Lion; instead, he sees a Lamb that has been slain (v. 6). This shows symbolically how Jesus has transformed the messianic hopes. The Jews expected a powerful kingly Messiah (the Lion); instead Jesus came, bringing salvation in gentleness, kindness, and sacrifice (the Lamb). A hymn is sung celebrating Jesus' death and the ransom he won by his blood. From this liturgical language, the hearer/reader sees the early Christians worshipping Jesus in the same way they worship God. Their liturgy shows that for them Jesus is divine, equal to the Father.

Opening of the Seven Seals (6:1–8:2)

The Lamb now opens the sealed scroll. The first four seals depict the four horsemen of the Apocalypse (6:1-8), with imagery drawn from Zech 6:1-5. John's description could also be influenced by contemporary events, such as the Parthian attacks on the Romans. The white horse symbolizes conquest; the red horse, slaughter; the black horse with the scales in the rider's hands, famine; and the pale green horse (the color of a rotting corpse), death. These disasters are God's judgments on the world, the consequences for misusing the power that God has given humanity. God does not intentionally cause war, famine, and death, but they are the natural consequences of what happens when God's moral laws are ignored. Wars inevitably lead to famines, and famines bring death.

The fifth seal (6:9-11) shifts focus to the souls of the martyrs that are under the altar in the heavenly sanctuary. They demand that God's justice be meted out upon those who have shed their innocent blood, but they are encouraged to be patient until the full number of martyrs has been completed. The sixth seal (6:12-17) resumes God's punishments against those who are evil. Here John again borrows symbols from the Hebrew Scriptures: the sun turns black and the moon turns to blood (Joel 2:31); the sky rolls up like a scroll (Isa 34:4). These are not intended as literal predictions, but rather to emphasize the terror facing a world that refuses to change.

Before describing the seventh seal, John narrates two visions that offer consolation (7:1-17). In the first vision Christ embraces those who come from the house of Israel. Angels hold back the four winds from wreaking havoc upon the earth until God's elect have been sealed on their foreheads: 144,000 of those sealed (vv. 4-8): 12 thousand from each of the 12 tribes of Israel shows completeness. In the second vision (vv. 9-17), the outreach is to the nations of the world who are incorporated into the community of the redeemed. The eschatological peace of God's presence is described beautifully in vv. 16-17.

The Seven Trumpets (8:3–11:19)

The opening of the seventh seal prepares the way for the sounding of seven trumpets and the punishments that will follow them. The blowing of the trumpets is preceded by a half-hour silence (8:1). Initially four trumpets are mentioned (8:6-12) unleashing the hail, the sea turned to blood, the star called "Wormwood," the darkening of the heavenly bodies. John derives this imagery from the plagues of Egypt (Exod 7:14–12:50). Just as God delivered his people from Egypt, so the new people of God will be delivered from these plagues. Since only one third is affected in each plague, this is not the totality of God's judgment.

Before the blowing of a fifth trumpet, an eagle announces three woes on humanity. Each woe is embodied in the next three trumpet blasts or disasters (8:13). The fifth trumpet (first woe) unleashes a plague of locusts from "the bottomless pit" (9:1-12). The sixth trumpet (second woe) announces the invasion of a force of cavalry from the East (9:13-21). Again the description is of a vision, not real events. What is seen in a vision is a symbol of reality. The seer draws the attention of the hearer/reader to the meaning contained in the symbol. In reading the book of Revelation, the hearer/reader strives to capture the meaning, not the symbol itself.

Just as after the sixth seal, so at the end of the sixth trumpet blast the narrator interrupts the narrative to relate two visions that prepare for the seventh trumpet. These two interludes force the hearer/reader to wait in expectation for what is to come: it is a dramatic literary device. In the first of these visions (10:1-11), John sees "another mighty angel" (v. 1; see 5:2) coming down with a "little scroll open in his hand" (v. 2). This scroll is different from the scroll of 5:1-14. It contains a message which at first is pleasant to the taste, but then becomes sour (10:10). This symbolizes how God's message of salvation brings joy ("honey"), while its consequences bring suffering and judgment ("bitter"). John is commanded to prophesy to "many peoples and nations and languages and kings" (v. 11).

The second vision in this interlude (11:1-14) is one of the most difficult passages in the whole book. Two witnesses prophesy that the woes will be limited to 42 months (three and one-half years [11:2-3; see Dan 7:25; 12:7] or one half of seven years!).

The first section of the book ends with the sounding of the seventh trumpet (11:15). No description of judgment or destruction follows. Instead, the heavens break out in songs of praise to God celebrating the victory and the coming of God's kingdom: "The kingdom of the world has become the kingdom of our Lord and of his Messiah, and he will reign forever and ever" (v. 15). The next section will return to the beginning and continues to reflect on God's rule of the world and humanity's response. It is a good illustration that the visions of the book of Revelation are not to be read as linear accounts detailing charts of what is to occur, but as self-contained visions inviting the hearer/reader to enter into the meaning of the visions rather than to seek a blueprint for future events.

Revelation 12:1–22:5: Second Cycle of Visions and Revelatory Experiences

The Woman, Dragon, Beasts, and the Lamb (12:1–14:20)

The first part of Revelation opened with an inaugural vision. In a similar way this part begins with a series of visions. Their purpose is to introduce characters who are at the heart of the rest of the book: the dragon and the two beasts.

The vision of a woman clothed with the sun, with the moon under her feet, and 12 stars on her head (12:1-18) draws on both biblical and extrabiblical legends. Here it echoes the dream of Joseph (Gen 37:9): these symbols

The Four Horsemen, woodcut from *The Apocalypse* by Albrecht Dürer (1496/1498). Death, Famine, Pestilence, and War trample their victims. (Rosenwald Collection, © 2000 Board of Trustees, National Gallery of Art, Washington)

refer to his father (Jacob), his mother, and his brothers (the sons of Jacob, the ancestors of the tribes of Israel). Taken together this symbolizes the people of Israel. Among the religions of the ancient world is also evidence of a legend of a sky-goddess who is pregnant and pursued by a many-headed monster. Using these myths John presents an image of a woman (Israel) bringing forth a male child (the Messiah). The dragon (a symbol of Satan) tries to destroy the Messiah (the child). There ensues a struggle between the woman, her offspring (the church), and the dragon. God will protect them in this struggle.

The next vision (13:1-10) is of the first beast from the sea. This beast is given power by the dragon, the source of all evil, Satan. The beast's description comes from the symbolism of Dan 7:2-28. Most scholars see the beast representing the Roman Empire, which at the time of John was perceived as the embodiment of evil because of its promotion of emperor worship. John's account appears to reflect the legend of *Nero redivivus* ("Nero returned to life") who was to return to assume power: "One of its heads seemed to have received a death-blow, but its mortal wound had been healed" (v. 3).

A further vision (13:11-18) presents the picture of a second beast from the earth. This beast "exercises all the authority of the first beast on its behalf, and it makes the earth and its inhabitants worship the first beast, whose mortal wound had been healed" (v. 12). This second beast symbolizes those who work on behalf of the Roman emperors (the first beast) by promoting emperor worship. It refers especially to the governors of the Roman provinces. As indicated previously, the reference to the number 666 most likely points to the emperor Domitian as a *Nero redivivus.*

The next, consoling vision (14:1-5) of the Lamb and the 144,000 reassures the hearers/readers that they will survive the persecutions of the dragon and the two beasts.

The vision of three angels (14:6-13) is "a call for the endurance of the saints" (v. 12). The first angel announces good news for all; the second announces the fall of Babylon (symbol of Rome); while the third promises divine judgment on all who continue to worship the beast.

The last vision in this series (14:14-20) sees the Son of Man reaping the harvest and executing judgment.

Seven Plagues and Seven Bowls of God's Wrath (15:1–16:21)

The narrator has presented a number of parallel portraits of God's control of the world, each giving a different insight into this rule. Through the symbols of seven plagues contained in seven bowls, John underscores the intensity of the struggle of God's faithful with the world.

Before the plagues are poured out, John sees a vision of the heavenly realm where Moses' victory song is sung, proclaiming that God is victorious over the nations. They will all worship God and acknowledge God's justice (15:3-4). This assures the hearer/reader that in the final struggle the victory will be God's. Again John uses the plagues of Egypt to describe God's judgment of the world. These seven plagues "are the last, for with them the wrath of God is ended" (v. 1). Revelation 16:16 speaks of the final battle at a place "that in Hebrew is called Har-magedon" ("Mountain of Megiddo"; also known as Armageddon) where numerous ancient battles had been fought.

The Judgment of Babylon (17:1–19:10)

In the ancient world and in the Bible cities are often described as women. Here John portrays Babylon as a prostitute. The reference to "seven mountains" (17:9) is indicative of Rome's seven hills. The depth of Rome's abominations emerges in the reference to her persecution of Christians under Nero: "the woman was drunk with the blood of the saints and the blood of the witnesses to Jesus" (v. 6). Following the destruction of the city, described in graphic detail in ch. 18, heaven rejoices at Rome's downfall (19:1-10). The hymn speaks of the marriage of the Lamb and his bride (19:7-8), which foreshadows the culmination of this book.

Final Victory and the Vision of the Heavenly Jerusalem (19:11–22:5)

John depicts Jesus as a great warrior on a white horse at the head of the armies of heaven; he is "King of kings and Lord of lords" (19:16). John's vision sees the beast from the sea and the beast from the earth (the false prophet) overthrown and cast into "the lake of fire that burns with sulfur" (v. 20). Chapter 20 introduces a theme found only in Revelation, one that has given rise to innumerable interpretations: the thousand-year reign of Christ. Satan (the dragon) alone remains, and he is shut up in "the bottomless pit" (v. 1) for a thousand years, while Christ and his martyrs rule on earth. At the end of this thousand-year period, Satan is let loose to deceive the nations (v. 7). However, the devil is thrown into the lake of fire where the beasts had been thrown, and there "they will be tormented day and night forever and ever" (v. 10).

A new heaven and a new earth now emerge (21:1–22:5). A new Jerusalem comes down from heaven to earth like a bride prepared to meet her husband (21:1-2; see 19:9). God will dwell among humanity, and all the limitations of humanity will be removed: no more death, tears, mourning, crying, pain (21:4). Using images taken from the opening chapters of Genesis, John describes the new Jerusalem with a river flowing from the throne of God watering the tree of life (22:1-5).

Revelation 22:6-21:
Epilogue, Admonitions, and Final Blessing

John's literary skill is evident in these final verses. He returns to themes mentioned in the beginning of the book, affirming the genuineness of his revelatory visions (22:6 and 1:10-11), identifying his book as a prophecy (v. 7 and 1:3), and giving instructions for it to be read aloud in the churches (v. 18 and 1:3). "These words are trustworthy and true" (v. 6) remind the hearer/reader of what John said at the beginning: the veracity of his visions relies upon God (1:1), Jesus, and the angel whom Jesus sent as mediator (v. 16; see 1:1) He instructs the hearers/readers not to add or subtract anything from this book (vv. 18-19). Finally, John endorses one of the oldest prayers of the Christian church: "Amen. Come, Lord Jesus!" (v. 20; see 1 Cor 16:22). Since the book of Revelation was being sent as a letter to the churches of Asia Minor, the seer concludes with the usual final greetings: "The grace of the Lord Jesus be with all the saints. Amen" (v. 21). While so many disturbing images and symbols pervade the pages of this narrative, the seer ends with visions that give comfort, hope, and reassurance.

Critical Issues in Studying Revelation

The Author

On four occasions the author identifies himself as John (1:1, 4, 9; 22:8). Since he does not identify himself any farther, he must have expected that his hearers/readers would immediately know who he was. From the mid-2nd century the author was identified with John, the son of Zebedee, the presumed writer of the Fourth Gospel. In the Western church, Justin Martyr (died ca. 165) and Irenaeus of Lyons (died ca. 202) make this identification. The Eastern church hesitated in making this identification. Dionysius of Alexandria (died 265) made a careful study of the style, grammar, and vocabulary of the book and concluded that it could not have been written by the same author as the Fourth Gospel, but by another John whom he referred to as "John the Elder."

A literary examination shows that the author's native language was not Greek, but more probably Aramaic. The Greek of Revelation is among the poorest in the New Testament, with numerous examples showing an Aramaic influence. John's vision was firmly shaped by the destruction of Jerusalem in 70, and an apocalyptic worldview was central to his whole theological perspective. He has a personal awareness of the situation of the churches of Asia Minor.

upward until its focus rests upon the heavenly Jerusalem. In this way the writer is able to present his message from several perspectives, giving different insights into the same reality of God's rule.

In presenting a reading guide to the book of Revelation for our walk through this writing, we have endeavored to remain true to the writing without imposing a preconceived structure upon it. By focusing on the distinctive visions one is able to see the various sections and the message that emerges from each.

The Aegean island of Patmos, place of exile for Roman political prisoners and site of John's visions. (Nicholas Wolterstorff)

From this internal and external evidence scholars have suggested that the author was a Jewish Christian prophet named John who escaped from Palestine just prior to the Jewish War of Independence in 66 and came to Ephesus and then was exiled to Patmos. From there he addressed the churches of Asia Minor as a prophet who had been granted a revelatory experience and message to interpret present events according to God's mind.

Structure of the Book

As a Jewish Christian apocalyptic prophet, the author focuses on God's rule and the coming of Christ at the end times to establish God's kingdom. In presenting the series of visions that form the heart of this apocalypse, he adopts a structure that is cyclical rather than linear. The book contains a series of parallel sections that are entities in their own right. Woven together with other parallel sections, each vision develops a deepening understanding of God's rule and coming kingdom. Consequently, the book is not to be read from ch. 1 through ch. 22 in a linear way as though it were offering a blueprint of every successive event that is to occur. Rather, each section is to be taken in its own right and understood as a unity. Taken together with all the other sections, they present an ever-deepening insertion into the mystery of God's rule. The sections come together much like a spiral revolving in an ever-progressing form

Principles for Interpretation of the Book

The book of Revelation has been and continues to be a source for some of the strangest interpretations. Most of these reflect the presuppositions of the interpreter rather than the book itself. In the course of the above discussion, certain pointers for a responsible reading of this writing have emerged.

- The literary genre of the book is an apocalypse. Fidelity to the nature of an apocalypse is essential in interpreting this writing.
- Revelation emerges from a time of persecution at the end of the 1st century C.E. The interpreter seeks to explain the book and particularly its symbols from the context of its own world, which is rooted in the traditions of the Hebrew Scriptures and the cultural heritage of the Greco-Roman world.
- Revelation appeals to the imagination of the hearer/reader. Every book of the Bible is distinct in that it appeals to some dimensions of the human person more than to others. For example, the Letter to the Romans appeals to the intellect while the New Testament hymns appeal to our emotions.
- The book forms a unity, but the sections within it are to be understood in a parallel (rather than a linear) way. Like flashlights that illuminate various sections of a room, so these sections throw distinctive light upon different aspects of the reality of God's rule.
- The book of Revelation has two main divisions (chs. 1–11 and 12–22). These two sections reveal the

intensity and an ever-deepening of John's revelatory experiences.

- Since Revelation roots its symbols in the Hebrew Scriptures, it must be interpreted in harmony with the teachings of the rest of the Scriptures.

Fidelity to these insights will enable the hearer/reader to approach the book of Revelation with more confidence, and a responsible understanding of this writing will result.

Theological Themes in Revelation

Millenarianism or the
Thousand Year Rule (20:4-6)

The three verses of 20:4-6 represent the only place in the entire Bible that speaks about a thousand-year reign of Christ, yet they have provoked an intense discussion over the course of the centuries. The Latin word *millennium* means a thousand years, hence the term millenarianism is used to refer to interpretations related to this thousand-year reign. The picture presented here is that at the end of time those faithful followers of Christ who had not worshipped the beast would be the first to come to life and reign with Christ for a thousand years. The rest of the dead would only come to life after the thousand-year period had passed.

The origins of this thought are traced back to the messianic hopes of Israel. Originally, the prophets taught that one day God would intervene to establish again the earthly kingdom of David through his Messiah: "On that day I will raise up the booth of David that is fallen, and repair its breaches, and raise up its ruins, and rebuild it as in the days of old" (Amos 9:11). However, some apocalyptic passages in the Hebrew Scriptures appear to be more pessimistic and look forward to God's victory at the end of time without speaking about the restoration of the earthly kingdom of David: "Now the Lord is about to lay waste the earth and make it desolate" (Isa 24:1).

Some intertestamental writings tend to bring these two expectations together. For example, in *4 Ezra* 7:28 (end of the 1st century C.E.), God brings the evil age to an end and the Messiah is to rule for four hundred years. After this come the judgment and the resurrection. In the *Ascension of Isaiah* 4:14-17, after Beliar has ruled (as an anti-Christ) for 1,333 days the Lord will cast Beliar into Gehenna. A period of rest follows, after which they will all be taken up into heaven.

1 Corinthians 15:23-28 also presents a sequence of events: The resurrection of Christ occurs first, then those who belong to Christ. Then, those who belong to

Christ will rule with Christ until he has conquered all. Finally, Christ hands over the kingdom to his Father.

In the history of interpretation, Rev 20:4-6 has been interpreted in one of two ways: either literally or symbolically. Those who read this passage in a literal way form different schools of thought:

- Postmillennialists maintain that Christ will come only after the thousand years have occurred.
- Premillennialists argue that Christ will come before the thousand years begin.

However, one can also read 20:4-6 symbolically. In the intertestamental examples mentioned above, the length of time assigned to the rule of the Messiah varies greatly. This reinforces the understanding that the main aim of the book of Revelation is not to forecast a blueprint for the future, but rather to use symbols to express and to enhance the message of God's rule over the world. Consequently, we think that the two phases describing the establishment of God's kingdom are not meant to be read as a literal pattern of what is to occur, but rather as two symbolic ways in which John, the seer, expresses the same message: God's victory over evil will be effective and complete, no matter what forces are opposed to God. The central message conveyed is that Christ will return; he will destroy evil and the forces opposed to God and will establish God's kingdom.

Encouragement and Admonition

The main theological theme of the book of Revelation is hope. John, the seer, is not preoccupied with a timetable (as so many interpreters of this book tend to be). Instead, he wishes to communicate that God is ruler of the world and will ultimately overcome all the forces of evil to establish his kingly rule. This rule will bring to an end the suffering and persecution that God's people are experiencing. In offering hope to his hearers/readers, John encourages them to persevere in steadfast adherence to Jesus Christ. John also warns those who are tempted to worship the beast that abandoning their first love will result in judgment and eternal punishment. Believers face a stark choice: remain faithful and you will attain a blessed reward; abandon Christ and he will abandon you to the eternal judgment.

"Blessed are those who wash their robes, so that they will have the right to the tree of life and may enter the city by the gates" (22:14). This final beatitude brings together the role of Christ and of the believer on the path to salvation. The work of Jesus Christ, the Lamb that has been slain, is the foundation on which the believer's salvation rests. The Lamb who was slain opened the seals and carried out God's plan perfectly. However, the Lamb's death and the offer of salvation require a response from believers. They are to wash their robes "in the blood of the Lamb" (7:14). Believers must accept what the Lamb has won for them. This is the heart of Jesus' message in the Gospels and its interpretation in Paul's letters. In its own way the book of Revelation reflects this central New Testament belief. Salvation is won through the blood of the cross of Christ. This salvation is offered to be accepted or to be rejected. The choice bears with it eternal consequences. Those who accept the gift of the white garment eagerly await the new heaven and the new earth and cry with expectation: "Come, Lord Jesus!" (22:20).

Questions for Review and Discussion

1 What contribution do you see the book of Revelation making to the thought and life of Christianity?

2 Read the description of the dragon and the first and second beasts in ch. 13. Show how the author has used the characteristics of apocalyptic writing in this chapter to convey his message.

Further Reading

Collins, Adela Yarbro. *Crisis and Catharsis: The Power of the Apocalypse*. Philadelphia: Westminster, 1984.

Metzger, Bruce M. *Breaking the Code: Understanding the Book of Revelation*. Nashville: Abingdon, 1993.

Pilch, John J. *What Are They Saying about the Book of Revelation?* New York: Paulist, 1978.

Stuckenbruck, Loren T. "Revelation." In *ECB*, 1535-72.

Chapter 63

The Canon of the New Testament

Preliminary Comments

As we saw in Chapter 44 above, the question of the origin of the Old Testament canon is quite complex and remains shrouded in mystery, thanks to a paucity of evidence and difficulty interpreting the evidence we do have. The situation is somewhat different with regard to the New Testament canon. We have more, clearer evidence to help us here and so can say more with confidence.

Concept of Canon

Today all Christians, whether Roman Catholic, Orthodox, or Protestant, agree on which books comprise the New Testament. However, it took more than three centuries for Christians to reach agreement on the canon of Scripture, the list of books that constitute the sacred writings of Christianity. The word canon (in Greek, originally "a straight rod") designates a rule or standard by which something can be measured (see p. 9 and Chapter 44 above). Christians first used this word in the 2nd century C.E. for a "canon of faith" or the standard of beliefs that Christians held. A secondary usage developed to designate those books that reflected that standard of faith. By extension the term refers to the list of sacred

books that are considered authoritative and normative for the Christian faith.

For our consideration of the New Testament canon we can use this definition: "The list of those writings that the believing community has accepted as holding an authoritative role for the life and belief of their community." As such they are considered Sacred Writings (Latin *Scripturae*). The canon of Scripture ensures that the beliefs and moral vision of Christians continue among future generations in a faithful and authentic way. The original ending of the Gospel of John reflects this vision very well: "These are written so that you may come to believe that Jesus is the Messiah, the Son of God, and that through believing you may have life in his name" (John 20:31). The writer shows that his intention was to deepen his readers' faith and to hand on that faith to future generations.

The New Testament writings are the founding documents of Christianity, operating much as does the Constitution of the United States. A group can call itself Christian only if it adheres to the same writings, believes the same teachings, and expresses the same moral vision as found in these 27 New Testament writings. Just as all new laws passed by generations of Americans should adhere to the vision of the Constitution, so the belief and actions of every Christian group should conform to these founding documents.

Situation at the Beginning of the Second Century C.E.

The Sacred Scriptures of Jesus and his disciples were the Torah, the Prophets, and the Writings. The first indications that Jesus' followers began to look on writings other than the Hebrew Scriptures as authoritative can be seen within the New Testament writings themselves. In Col 4:16 the author, writing in Paul's name, addresses his readers: "And when this letter has been read among you, have it read also in the church of the Laodiceans; and see that you read also the letter from Laodicea." This passage shows that Paul's letters were viewed as significant, not just for the church or community to whom they were sent, but for the wider Christian communities. A process had begun whereby writings from a particular situation were seen to transcend that context and to have universal application. The passage from Colossians shows that Christians were eager to hand on Paul's writings and to acquire other letters that he had written. The suggestion that believers at Colossae should also read a letter that had been written to the Laodiceans indicates that many other letters had been written in those early years of Christianity by Paul or his disciples, although these have disappeared from history.

Further insight into the views of early Christianity regarding their sacred writings comes from 2 Pet 3:15-16: "So also our beloved brother Paul wrote you according to the wisdom given him, speaking of this as he does *in all his letters*. There are some things in them hard to understand, which the ignorant and unstable twist to their own destruction, as they do *the other scriptures*." Writing in the name of Peter in the early decades of the second century, the author implies that there was a collection or group of Paul's letters. This would be the natural culmination of what Colossians had indicated. Even more remarkable is the attitude adopted toward Paul's writings. They were placed on the same level as "the other scriptures," the Hebrew Scriptures. Paul's letters were considered "sacred writings" with the same authority as those of the Law, the Prophets, and the Writings.

This was a remarkable step. The early Christians probably arrived at this perspective as a consequence of their liturgical practices. For example, the occasion when Christians would have heard Paul's letters read would have been when the community gathered together to worship. Early Christian worship was based upon the Jewish synagogue service. Among the significant elements of that service was the reading of their sacred texts, the Law and the Prophets, following a continuous, cyclical schedule. After these readings someone would deliver a sermon explaining and applying the text to the lives of the hearers. Justin Martyr, writing *ca.*

Justin Martyr's Description of a Christian Sunday Service

On the day which is called Sunday we have a common assembly of all who live in the cities or in the outlying districts, and the memoirs of the Apostles or the writings of the Prophets are read, as long as there is time. Then, when the reader has finished, the president of the assembly verbally admonishes and invites all to imitate such examples of virtue. Then we all stand up together and offer up our prayers, and, as we said before, after we finish our prayers, bread and wine and water are presented. He who presides likewise offers up prayers and thanksgivings, to the best of his ability, and the people express their approval by saying "Amen." The Eucharistic elements are distributed and consumed by those present, and to those who are absent they are sent through the deacons. . . . Sunday, indeed, is the day on which we all hold our common assembly because it is the first day on which God, transforming the darkness and [prime] matter, created the world; and our Savior Jesus Christ arose from the dead on the same day. For they crucified Him on the day before that of Saturn, and on the day after, which is Sunday, He appeared to His Apostles and disciples, and taught them the things which we have passed on to you also for consideration.

1 Apology, 67, trans. Thomas B. Falls. Saint Justin Martyr (Washington: Catholic University of America Press, 1965), 106-7

155, gives an interesting account of a Christian Sunday celebration:

This is the earliest record detailing a Christian liturgical celebration. Justin is intent on defending Christian practices against pagan attacks that accused Christians of vile actions during their worship services. His defense (or Apology, as the title of the work indicates) describes the various liturgical practices, especially the Sunday Eucharist. His reference to "the memoirs of the Apostles or the writings of the Prophets" indicates that the early Christian community did have a collection of books of apostolic origin that were judged to have a status equal to those of the Hebrew Bible. By reading the apostolic writings simultaneously with the Law and the Prophets, the hearers began to consider them to have the same authority for their faith and moral vision.

Many Other Books Appear

Besides the present 27 New Testament writings, other books emerged over the course of the next few centuries which appeared to have a similar purpose and literary form to those of the New Testament writings. This gave rise to the question: "What writings should be identified as authoritative for the Christian communities?" In what follows we present an overview of some of these writings to provide insight into the very diverse world of early Christianity.

Apostolic Fathers

The term Apostolic Fathers designates a group of early Christian writers from the period immediately following the apostles (*ca.* 95 to 150). Leaders of various Christian churches continued the epistolary practice of apostles such as Paul, Peter, and John of writing to churches to explain the Christian faith more fully and to correct, admonish, and encourage their hearers.

Among the writings of the Apostolic Fathers, the following are the more significant:

- Clement, a bishop of the church in Rome, wrote to Corinth *ca.* 95. Like Paul who wrote to Corinth decades earlier, Clement tried to settle the problem of factions within the community. He wrote with the intention of restoring peace and harmony to the community.
- Ignatius, the third bishop of Antioch (according to the church historian Eusebius), journeyed under guard as a prisoner from Antioch to Rome, where he was put to death *ca.* 110 under the emperor Trajan. In the course of this journey, he wrote seven letters. From Smyrna he wrote four letters of encouragement to the churches of Ephesus, Magnesia, Tralles in Asia, and one to Rome. In an astonishing plea, he asked his readers not to make any representations on his behalf to deprive him of the crown of martyrdom. At Troas, he wrote a further three letters to the churches of Philadelphia and Smyrna, as well as to Bishop Polycarp of Smyrna. These letters are a wonderful testimony to the depth of faith and love of a Christian leader during the first part of the 2nd century.
- Polycarp, a bishop of Smyrna, was martyred *ca.* 155. While he is reported to have written a number of letters, only one is extant, to the Philippians. Ignatius had visited Philippi en route to Rome. When the Christians in Philippi requested that he send a collection of Ignatius's letters, Polycarp sent those in his possesson and added a covering letter warning against certain dangers.
- *Shepherd of Hermas* (probably written between 140 and 155) was a very popular writing, regarded in some Christian churches as having sacred authority. It is a religious allegory that addresses the question of sin after baptism. A view circulating in some

Christian circles taught that if Christians sinned after baptism there was no possibility of forgiveness, even for those who repented. *Hermas* rejects this view and stresses the possibility of forgiveness (though this repentance could occur not more than once!).

- The *Didache* (Greek, "teaching") or *The Teaching of the Twelve Apostles* was a manual of early Christian ritual and moral instruction. While a number of early Christian writers mentioned it, the first manuscript was only rediscovered in 1873 in a library in Constantinople. This book was probably written *ca.* 100 and shows similarities with traditions found in the Gospel of Matthew, particularly the Sermon on the Mount. Some scholars situate it within the same context as that Gospel, namely the church in Antioch. Its main concern is with Christian liturgical and ritual practices at the end of the 1st century C.E., including baptism, fasting, prayer, and the celebration of the Eucharist. The purpose is to establish a certain uniformity in liturgical celebrations.

Nowhere do the Apostolic Fathers claim an authority for their writings equal to that of the writings of the

The Didache

7 ¹But with respect to baptism, baptize as follows. Having said all these things in advance, baptize in the Name of the Father and of the Son and of the Holy Spirit, in running water. ²But if you do not have running water, baptize in some other water. And if thou cannot baptize in cold water, use warm. ³But if thou hast neither, pour water on the head three times in the name of the Father and Son and Holy Spirit. ⁴But both the one baptizing and the one being baptized should fast before the baptism, along with some others if they can. But command the one being baptized to fast one or two days in advance.

8 ¹And do not keep your fasts with the hypocrites. For they fast on Monday and Thursday; but you should fast on Wednesday and Friday. ²Nor should you pray like the hypocrites, but as the Lord commanded in his gospel, you should pray as follows: "Our Father in heaven, may your name be kept holy, may your kingdom come, may your will be done on earth as in heaven. Give us today our daily bread [Or: the bread that we need; or: our bread for tomorrow]. And forgive us our debt, as we forgive our debtors. And do not bring us into temptation but deliver us from the evil one [Or: from evil]. For the power and the glory are yours forever." ³Pray like this three times a day.

Bart D. Ehrman, ed. and trans., *The Apostolic Fathers*, vol. 1. Loeb Classical Library 24 (Cambridge, Mass.: Harvard University Press, 2003), 429-30

The Gospel of Thomas

The Gospel of Thomas is a collection of some 114 sayings that are generally introduced by the phrase, "Jesus said." These sayings consist of many forms: proverbs, wisdom sayings, parables, eschatological sayings, as well as rules for the community. This Coptic document was translated originally from Greek. Fragments of the Gospel written in Greek were discovered at the beginning of the 20th century but were only identified as belonging to the Gospel of Thomas when it was discovered in this Coptic form. Since these Greek fragments come from a manuscript written before 200 c.e., this points to the existence of the Gospel of Thomas in Egypt at the end of the 2nd century.

The Gospel of Thomas bears witness to a long process of transmission. It probably originated in Syria at the beginning of the 2nd century, using traditions similar to but independent of the canonical Gospels. When the form and words of individual sayings in the Gospel of Thomas are compared with similar sayings in the New Testament, Thomas almost always witnesses to an earlier form of the traditional saying. This indicates that some of the traditions used by the Gospel of Thomas were as ancient as those behind the New Testament Gospels. Changes occurred through the influence of context in the course of transmission. One can see evidence of the influence of Gnostic circles in Egypt on some of the sayings, giving a stronger emphasis to wisdom interpretation (see, e.g., the final saying, 114).

A Selection from the Sayings of the Gospel of Thomas

Prologue

These are the secret sayings that the living Jesus spoke and Didymos Judas Thomas recorded.

1. And he said, "Whoever discovers the interpretation of these sayings will not taste death."
2. Jesus said, "Let one who seeks not stop seeking until one finds. When one finds, one will be disturbed. When one is disturbed, one will marvel, and will reign over all."
3. Jesus said, "If your leaders say to you, 'Behold, the kingdom is in heaven,' then the birds of heaven will precede you. If they say to you, 'It is in the sea,' then the fish will precede you.

"Rather, the kingdom is within you and it is outside you. When you know yourselves, then you will be known, and you will understand that you are children of the living Father. But if you do not know yourselves, then you dwell in poverty, and you are the poverty."
4. Jesus said, "The person old in days will not hesitate to ask a little child seven days old about the place of life, and that person will live. For many of the first will be last, and will become a single one."
5. Jesus said, "Know what is before your face, and what

is hidden from you will be disclosed to you. For there is nothing hidden that will not be revealed."
7. Jesus said, "Blessed is the lion that the human will eat, so that the lion becomes human. And defiled is the human that the lion will eat, and the lion will become human."
70. Jesus said, "If you bring forth what is within you, what you have will save you. If you do not have that within you, what you do not have within you [will] kill you."
71. Jesus said, "I shall destroy [this] house, and no one will be able to build it."
73. Jesus said, "The harvest is large but the workers are few, so beg the lord to send out workers to the harvest."
74. He said, "Lord, there are many around the drinking trough, but there is nothing in the well."
75. Jesus said, "There are many standing at the door, but those who are alone will enter the wedding chamber."
76. Jesus said, "The kingdom of the Father is like a merchant who had a supply of merchandise, and then found a pearl.

"That merchant was prudent; he sold the merchandise and bought the single pearl for himself. So also with you, seek his treasure that is unfailing, that is abiding, where no moth comes to consume and no worm destroys."
77. Jesus said, "I am the light that is over all things. I am all: from me all came forth, and to me all attained. Split a piece of wood; I am there. Lift up the stone, and you will find me there."
110. Jesus said, "Let one who has found the world, and has become wealthy, renounce the world."
111. Jesus said, "The heavens and the earth will roll up in your presence, and whoever is living from the living one will not see death." Does not Jesus say, "Whoever has found oneself, of that person the world is not worthy?"
112. Jesus said, "Woe to the flesh that depends on the soul. Woe to the soul that depends on the flesh."
113. His disciples said to him, "When will the kingdom come?"

"It will not come by watching for it. It will not be said, 'Behold, here,' or 'Behold, there.'

"Rather, the kingdom of the Father is spread out upon the earth, and people do not see it."
114. Simon Peter said to them, "Let Mary leave us, for females are not worthy of life."

Jesus said, "Behold, I shall guide her to make her male, so that she too may become a living spirit resembling you males. For every female who makes herself male will enter the kingdom of heaven."

John Kloppenborg, Marvin W. Meyer, Stephen J. Patterson, and Michael G. Steinhauser, *Q-Thomas Reader* (Sonoma: Polebridge, 1990), 129-55

The Infancy Gospel of Thomas

More than idle curiosity drove the imagination of early Christians to produce the kind of stories recorded here. These accounts emerge from a desire to protect the traditional faith that Jesus was both divine and human from those Gnostics who were undermining that belief. For example, one group, known as the Docetists (from Greek *dokein,* "to appear"), claimed that Christ only appeared to be a real human being but in fact was not. Other Gnostics distinguished between Jesus and the Christ. While Jesus was a real live human being, the divine Christ only came upon and entered the human Jesus at the moment of his baptism. This same divine Christ left the human Jesus before his death, so that it was only the human Jesus that died.

To counter such views infancy gospels arose whereby Jesus was portrayed as fully human and fully divine from the moment of his birth. These narratives try to capture in an imaginative way what the child Jesus would have been like with divine powers.

Most scholars see the various infancy gospels emerging during the 2nd century C.E. Some scholars have dated the Infancy Gospel of Thomas from *ca.* 125.

Selections from the Infancy Gospel of Thomas

1. I, Thomas the Israelite, announce and make known to you all, brothers from among the Gentiles, the mighty childhood deeds of our Lord Jesus Christ, which he did when he was born in our land. The beginning is as follows.

2. ¹When this boy Jesus was five years old he was playing at the crossing of a stream, and he gathered together into pools the running water, and instantly made it clean, and gave his command with a single word. ²Having made soft clay he moulded from it twelve sparrows. And it was the sabbath when he did these things. And there were also many other children playing with him. ³When a certain Jew saw what Jesus was doing while playing on the sabbath, he at once went and told his father Joseph, "See, your child is at the stream, and he took clay and moulded twelve birds and has profaned the sabbath." ⁴And when Joseph came to the place and looked, he cried out to him, saying, "Why do you do on the sabbath things which it is not lawful to do?" But Jesus clapped his hands and cried out to the sparrows and said to them, "Be gone!" And the sparrows took flight and went away chirping. ⁵The Jews were amazed when they saw this, and went away and told their leaders what they had seen Jesus do.

3. ¹Now the son of Annas the scribe was standing there with Joseph; and he took a branch of a willow and with it dispersed the water which Jesus had collected. ²When Jesus saw what he had done he was angry and said to him, "You insolent, godless ignoramus, what harm did the pools and the water do to you? Behold, now you also shall wither like a tree and shall bear neither leaves nor root nor fruit." ³And immediately that child withered up completely; and Jesus departed and went into Joseph's house. But the parents of the boy who was withered carried him away, bemoaning his lost youth, and brought him to Joseph and reproached him, "What kind of child do you have, who does such things?"

J. K. Elliott, ed., *The Apocryphal New Testament,* rev. ed. (Oxford: Clarendon, 1993), 75-76

apostles. While it is difficult to establish exactly what writings were known or which ones were considered to be authoritative, Polycarp shows he had a collection of Paul's writings as well as a knowledge of the Gospels of Matthew and Luke from which he quotes (although he never refers to them by the term Gospel). He clearly acknowledges an authority for these writings that is lacking in other documents.

Gnostic Writings

Gnosticism (from Greek *gnosis,* "knowledge") was an influential movement within the first four centuries of early Christianity. In fact, many movements identified as Gnostic arose during this period. What was distinctive about them was the attempt to explain the Christian and Jewish traditions by means of philosophic speculation originating in Greek thought, particularly that of Plato.

The Gnostics claimed to possess a secret knowledge only available to those initiated into their movement through specific rituals. They interpreted the Genesis accounts of creation of the world and humanity by means of philosophical and mythological speculation. Their secret knowledge gave insight into the origins of both the heavenly and material realms. All things ultimately originated from the one true God who was totally spirit, totally unknown, and unknowable. This divine Being produced offspring, other divine spirits, who in turn produced their own offspring. Consequently, a whole divine spiritual realm emerged at different levels removed from the divine Spirit. One of these divine beings (or "aeons") named in some texts *Sophia* (Greek, "wisdom") exceeded her position and so fell from the divine world. The material world was created by an evil creator, emanating from the fall of this heavenly being.

The Gnostics believed that a spark of the divine was imprisoned within them. Their struggle was to liberate this spark from its prison house within the material world and return to the divine sphere. An extensive literature developed within Gnostic circles to instruct believers more deeply in the secrets and to communicate the means by which they could overcome the powers of evil and ultimately return to God's realm. Salvation consisted in the spark that had come from the divine, and the purpose of life for the Gnostics was to attain passage back to the realm of God. The person of Christ gives the clearest illustration of this rhythm of descent from and return to the divine.

Certain early traces of Gnostic thought can be found already in the later writings of the New Testament, such as Colossians and Ephesians. However, this movement within Christianity truly began to flourish only toward the second half of the 2nd century. This provoked a strong reaction from those who saw the Gnostics distorting the traditional faith of Christianity. Among the opponents of the Gnostics were Irenaeus of Lyons (France), Hippolytus and Justin Martyr (both from Rome), all writing at the end of the 2nd century. They are referred to as the Apologetic Fathers (from Greek *apologia,* "defense"). Justin Martyr wrote two Apologies in which he defended the Christian faith against charges made against it.

Until 1945 the only knowledge of these Gnostic writers came secondhand from their opponents, the Apologetic Fathers, who quoted them simply to refute them. In 1945 an entire Gnostic library was discovered buried in a 6-foot jar at Nag Hammadi, on the eastern bank of the Nile River in Upper Egypt. This library consisted of some 52 treatises written in Coptic dating from *ca.* 400. Among these writings are the Apocryphon of James, the Gospel of Truth, the Dialogue of the Savior, and the Acts of Peter and the Twelve Apostles. The Gospel of Thomas is the best known of these Nag Hammadi discoveries. These are among the most precious discoveries related to the New Testament made in the past century. From these writings we gain insight into the diversity of thought that was evident within early Christianity.

Apocryphal Books

The term apocrypha (from Greek *apokrypto,* "to hide, to keep secret") refers to those books excluded from the canon of Scripture. Originally, it designated those writings that Christians judged did not express the essence of the Christian faith; hence they could not act as an authority for faith and action and should be kept hidden. The above Gnostic writings would belong to this group of writings. In a very graphic way the burial of the Nag Hammadi texts in a jar in the ground illustrates this desire to hide those writings that were considered to be a danger to the faith of the universal church.

Among the apocryphal writings are a number of infancy gospels that focus attention on the hidden years of Jesus. The Infancy Gospel of Thomas describes Jesus as a youth of five or six years old. The Protevangelium of James reports the birth and life of Mary, the mother of Jesus. Many Acts also appeared, such as the Acts of Peter, Paul, John, and Thomas, that describe the apostles' travels, their miracles, and above all their deaths. These writings actually belong to the literary genre of novel. They attempt to fill out details relating to the life of Jesus, his mother, and the apostles, particularly in those areas where little is said in the Gospels. They all became extremely popular in the early church, as can be seen from the numerous copies that have come down to us over the centuries.

Search for Agreement on a Canon

As a result of all these writings the problem arose: Just what books constitute an authority that witnesses to the true Christian faith? It was to take Christians three centuries to arrive at a consensus.

Marcion

Marcion was the first to raise the question about the contents of a canon. He was a wealthy shipowner from the East who came to Rome *ca.* 140 where he held views that led to his excommunication by the church of Rome. Marcion was very anti-Judaic and proposed a belief in two Gods. The God of the Jews and of the Hebrew Scriptures was seen as the creator God, a God of anger and justice, while Jesus was the agent of the Superior God of love of the New Testament. Marcion rejected the whole of the Hebrew Scriptures. He went even further, examining the Christian writings and accepting or rejecting various books according to his anti-Judaic stance. Marcion divided the writings into two groups:

- The Evangelicon, which accepted only the Gospel of Luke. In Rom 2:16 Paul speaks of "my Gospel," and Marcion took this as a reference to Luke.
- The Apostolicon, in which he accepted 10 of Paul's letters (excluding the Pastoral Letters). Marcion placed Galatians at the beginning since he perceived that it was hostile to Judaism. In it Paul contrasts works of the Law with life led under Christ. Ephesians he called the Letter to the Laodiceans.

Marcion realized that a list of authoritative writings was essential for defining the identity and faith of any group. His importance lies not in the actual list of books that he named as the authority to which Christians should adhere; his solution was flawed by his prejudiced hostility toward Judaism. Rather, Marcion is important because he unknowingly forced the church to grapple with this question over the next two centuries as it tried to achieve agreement on the composition of the canon of Scripture.

Muratorian Canon

An Italian scholar, Ludovico Antonio Muratori (hence the name of the document), discovered a canon, or list of books, as a fragment in a library in Milan and published it in 1740. This is the second oldest canon that we possess. The fragment itself was produced in the 8th century by a scribe who was extremely careless in copying the original manuscript. While much debate centers on the date and place of the original text, most scholars date it to the second half of the 2nd century in Rome.

The fragment is more than just a list of books; it also contains brief information on the various books of the New Testament. As a fragment, it begins in the middle of a sentence and also ends abruptly. Its first reference is to "the third book of the Gospel, that according to Luke." Consequently, one can presume that mention of the Gospels of Matthew and Mark must have preceded the reference to Luke. John follows, with a reference to his epistles. Thirteen letters of Paul are cited. No mention is made of Hebrews, 1 and 2 Peter, and James. The fragment also accepts the book of Revelation as well as a Revelation of Peter. One surprising note is that it considers the apocryphal book of Wisdom to be a canonical New Testament writing. Finally, it comments that the Shepherd of Hermas may be read but is not canonical because it was composed only recently and was not written by an apostle.

This canon gives insight into the views regarding the list of sacred writings of one center of early Christianity (probably the church of Rome) toward the end of the 2nd century. From the Muratorian Canon we gain the impression that two conditions were important for a book to be considered part of the canon:

- It must be accepted by all the Christian churches and used in their liturgy.
- It must come either directly or indirectly from an apostle.

Eusebius

Eusebius, bishop of Caesarea (*ca.* 260-339), was the first great historian of the Christian church. In his *Ecclesiastical History* he devotes attention to the history of the Christian Bible. Building on the work of another early Christian scholar, Origen (*ca.* 185-254), Eusebius divided the apostolic writings into four categories:

- Those universally accepted. He includes the four Gospels, 14 letters of Paul (including Hebrews), 1 Peter, 1 John, Acts, and Revelation.
- Those more or less accepted: "disputed yet familiar to most people in the church." Among these he mentions the Letters of James, Jude, 2 Peter, and 2 and 3 John.
- Those rejected. Here he enumerates the Acts of Paul, the Shepherd of Hermas, the Apocalypse of Peter, the Epistle of Barnabas, the Teachings of the Apostles.
- The fictions of heretics: writings put forward under the name of apostles to promote the teachings of heretics. Among them are the Gospels of Peter and Thomas.

While Eusebius's list appears somewhat confused and inconsistent at times, he does show that he has tried to give an accurate account of the current state of affairs. The emperor Constantine commissioned him *ca.* 332 to produce 50 manuscripts of the Bible in order to foster religious unity and uniformity throughout his empire. Eusebius entrusted the task to trained scribes and ultimately sent "magnificent and elaborately bound volumes" to the emperor. These 50 volumes would exercise an important influence in the production of future copies of the New Testament in the Eastern church.

Athanasius

In 367, according to his yearly custom, Bishop Athanasius wrote an Easter letter to his churches in Alexandria. Replying to a request to list all the authoritative Christian writings, Athanasius acknowledges 27 books as canonical. This is the first documentation where the 27 New Testament books are listed together and described as the only holy books. Athanasius further forbids the use of any apocryphal books alongside these writings. He also notes that the *Didache* and the *Shepherd of Hermas* were used for catechetical purposes. While some disputes continued to arise, Athanasius's letter gives expression to an ever deepening view within the early church that only these 27 books are to be accepted as canonical. Consensus around this view quickly began to solidify in the various centers of the church, namely the Syrian, Greek, and Western church. By the end of the 4th century, all Christians acknowledged their canonical status.

Theological Observations

The church took three centuries to reach an agreement that only these 27 books are authoritative. The production of the canon was not the result of one or two people imposing a view upon the rest of Christianity. Instead, it grew out of a common consensus gradually emerging among Christian communities scattered throughout the ancient world.

Four factors were largely responsible for the acceptance of writings as part of the corpus of Sacred Scripture alongside those of the Hebrew Bible:

• Universal usage in the liturgy: The liturgy was the place where other writings (alongside those of the Hebrew Scriptures) were first considered sacred texts. This context conferred upon them an equal authoritative status. Certain centers obviously exercised more importance than others, given their association with the early church. Antioch was responsible for the preservation of the traditions of the Gospel of Matthew. The churches of Asia Minor, especially the church at Ephesus, were responsible for the preservation of the writings of Paul and John, while the church at Rome played a large hand in the preservation of the Gospel of Mark and probably Romans and Hebrews as well.

• Apostolic origin, direct or indirect: The authority of an apostle was deemed extremely important for the acceptance of certain writings. This conforms to the notion of canon as an authority of faith. The testimony of the early witnesses to the message of Jesus is seen to be preserved in their body of writings. Since concern for a canon shows the desire to maintain a standard of faith, what better standard could there be than those writings that came from those early witnesses? While the apostle may not have physically written the text, the name connected to the writing shows that the intent was to speak in the name and spirit of that apostle. Hence, the letters of Paul, Peter, and James are readily accepted as part of the canon. Other writings such as Mark (viewed as a disciple of Peter) and Luke-Acts (the writer Luke is seen to be a companion of Paul) were accepted because of their apostolic associations. The book of Revelation was at first connected to the Apostle John; when this identification began to be questioned, its place in the canon was also questioned. The Letter to the Hebrews gained acceptance through its reputed identification with Paul. Apostolic connection was not sufficient on its own to win authoritative status, however, as can be seen from the fact that many other writings bore the signature of an apostolic figure but failed to win acceptance. It needed to be viewed in conjunction with other criteria.

• Conformity with the standard of faith: Since the term canon originally referred to the standard of beliefs that Christians held, the question emerged: "Does this writing reflect the faith that comes from the apostles?" This accounted for the rejection of the Gnostic writings, even though most of them bore the name of apostolic witnesses. The Gospel of Thomas and Gospel of Peter were rejected for precisely these reasons: they were used and interpreted in the context of Gnostic communities that did not reflect the traditional faith. While many of the traditions in these writings may have gone back to the early stages of the church, the way in which they were being used and the new traditions that had been incorporated into them made their rejection inevitable.

• From a theological viewpoint: Christians see the acceptance of these 27 books as part of Sacred Scripture not simply from a historical point of view, as outlined above. They also see their final recognition as part of the influential guiding hand of the Spirit. Just as the Acts of the Apostles testifies to the guidance of the Spirit in the preaching and transmission of the message of Jesus, so this same Spirit guides the commission of this message to writing. The Spirit continues to guide the church in recognizing and accepting those books as Sacred Scripture. From a Christian theological viewpoint, the church did not establish the canon: rather, the church gave recognition to that canon which had emerged through the inspiration of the Spirit. This conforms to Jesus' promise of sending another Paraclete: "When the Spirit of truth comes, he will guide you into all the truth; for he will not speak on his own, but will speak whatever he hears, and he will declare to you the things that are to come" (John 16:13).

Questions for Review and Discussion

1   What is the significance of the following for the canon of the New Testament?

> Marcion
>
> The Muratorian Fragment
>
> The Easter Letter of Athanasius

2   Examine the selection of early Christian writings provided above from the Didache and the Infancy Gospel of Thomas and answer the following questions:

> What was the purpose for each writing?
>
> What would have been the effect on church thought and teaching if such books were to have been officially approved and read authoritatively in church?

Further Reading

Brown, Raymond E. *An Introduction to the New Testament.* ABRL. New York: Doubleday, 1996.

Dunn, James D. G. *Unity and Diversity in the New Testament: An Inquiry into the Character of Earliest Christianity.* 2nd ed. Philadelphia: Trinity Press International, 1990.

Metzger, Bruce M. *The Canon of the New Testament: Its Origin, Development, and Significance.* Oxford: Clarendon, 1987.

Chapter 64

Quest for the Historical Jesus

For the first eighteen hundred years of Christianity it was generally assumed that the picture presented of Jesus by the Gospel writers was an exact portrayal of the person of Jesus. In our studies, particularly of the Gospels, we have seen that each Gospel provides a very different image of Jesus. It is clear that the Gospel portraits of Jesus are not exact videocamera records, as it were, of the actual Jesus. In fact, one has to respect three essential stages in the production of the Gospel portraits of Jesus. Stage one would embrace the historical person, Jesus, his preaching and teaching in Aramaic among the people of Palestine. Stage two represents the way in which that preaching is handed on, primarily orally, by the followers of Jesus through their own ministry of preaching and teaching, largely now in Greek throughout the wider Greco-Roman world. Already a transformation is occurring by which Jesus' message is transmitted in another language and in another culture. Stage three features the transformation of the preaching of Jesus' followers into writing with the production of the Gospels, which speak to the communities of their writers, each presenting a distinct portrait of Jesus and his message. So the question emerges: Is it possible to probe behind the Gospels, to move from stage three back to stage one of the process, in order to be able to arrive at the actual, or "historical," Jesus?

The Search for the Jesus of History

The first attempt to separate the theological portraits of Jesus from the Jesus of history began at the time of the Enlightenment in the 18th century when human reason and historical consciousness were seen as central to understanding the human condition. The same historical methods and principles that were used to study ancient writings were now applied to the Bible. Hermann Samuel Reimarus (1694-1768) was among the first scholars who tried to separate out a picture of Jesus that was distinct from that of Christ developed by the Gospels. His work was published after his death in 1778. The portrait of Jesus that he reconstructed was that of a Jewish revolutionary who failed in his attempt to overthrow Roman occupation and was executed by the Romans. The picture of Christ that emerged in the Gospels was a fictional reconstruction made by Jesus' followers who had stolen his body and then claimed that he had been raised from the dead. While Reimarus and those who followed him claimed that their research was based upon historical principles and methods, it was also determined by major presuppositions that excluded the divine from the investigation.

Over the course of the next century many scholars continued to apply the historical methods of their age to a study of the Gospels. Source criticism was a major method directing their investigations. Heinrich Julius Holtzmann (1832-1910) argued strongly that Mark was the first Gospel to be written. Johannes Weiss (1863-1914) situated Jesus within the context of his own world, namely 1st-century Palestine, and presented him as a prophet who preached a message about the end time (an "eschatological prophet").

Albert Schweitzer (1875-1965) marks a pivotal moment in historical biblical scholarship. His work, *The Quest of the Historical Jesus: A Critical Study of Its Progress from Reimarus to Wrede* (German 1906; English 1910), was to set a direction for and influence scholarship over the next hundred years. Schweitzer examined the studies made during the previous century and concluded that they said more about the people making the study than about the person of Jesus—that although they claimed to work historically, their own presuppositions influenced their investigations. His starting point was that of Weiss, in which Jesus was viewed as an eschatological prophet. For Schweitzer most previous scholarship had failed to recognize this dimension of Jesus' apocalyptic conviction that he was the prophet, God's Messiah, come to inaugurate God's kingdom through his death. Yet because this kingdom failed to materialize, Schweitzer evaluated Jesus' life and death as that of a misguided failure!

Rudolf Bultmann (1884-1976) was without doubt the most important New Testament scholar to take up the challenges left by Schweitzer. He embraced a decided pessimism regarding what could be ascertained about the Jesus of history, arguing that the majority of the traditions about Jesus in the Gospels are largely the creation of the early faith community. This community used their own worldview and mythology to portray Jesus as a divine figure who came down from heaven to reveal a message that was in effect timeless. Bultman's own theological vision provided the foundation for his approach in that he maintained that faith need not be founded upon history. It was the challenge set by the Gospel picture of Jesus that was essential. Just as Jesus presented a challenge to the people of his own day, so people today must make a similar existential decision of faith and an ethical commitment to Jesus' universal message.

Many of Bultmann's own students were responsible for highlighting the implications that his approach had posed. Ernst Käsemann, in a lecture delivered in 1953 ("The Problem of the Historical Jesus"), showed that the essential problem opened up by Bultmann was that if there was no connection between the Jesus of history and the Christ of the Gospels, then Christianity was based upon myth. He argued that there had to be a connection: the Christ of faith must be rooted in the Jesus of history. Käsemann and others sought to establish criteria by which one could discern the historical aspects contained in the Gospel narratives.

Continuing Quest for the Historical Jesus

Many different approaches to the historical Jesus have emerged in more recent scholarship. First are those who stress the essential Jewishness of Jesus. Most renowned among these scholars is E. P. Sanders, who sees Jesus' message as that of an eschatological prophet who preached that God's judgment was imminent. Sanders envisions Jesus and his followers much like the Essenes who were preparing themselves for the breaking into history of God's rule and judgment. Sanders accepts that the basic outline of Jesus' life was essentially historical, and he places great stress on Jesus' cleansing of the temple, which was seen in terms of Jesus' expectation that God was going to destroy the temple and inaugurate a new kingdom.

Other scholars endeavor to portray Jesus as a political activist. From a study of sociology some scholars, such as Gerd Theissen, argue that Galilee and Judea were contexts in which revolt against the Romans was fomenting. In this setting Jesus and his followers, through their wandering lifestyle and countercultural message, would appeal to those who were advocating opposition to the Romans.

Other scholars interpret Jesus as a wisdom teacher. The work of the Jesus Seminar fits largely into this perspective. The Seminar is a group of some one hundred scholars whose aim is to establish the authentic sayings and deeds of Jesus by using a set of commonly accepted criteria. One of the main criticisms of this group is their method of deciding upon what are and what are not authentic Jesus sayings or deeds. These scholars vote democratically on what they consider to come from Jesus by using color-coded beads. A red bead indicates the acceptance of a saying as undoubtedly coming from Jesus; a pink one lessens the certainty to a probability; a grey one accepts that the ideas probably came from Jesus although the words did not; and finally, black indicates that Jesus definitely did not say that. A further aspect of the approach of the Jesus Seminar has been to popularize their research; the color-coded method of voting certainly has caught media attention.

Evaluation of This Ongoing Search

As can be seen from the attempts over the past two to three hundred years to construct a picture of the Jesus of history, the results have not been very successful. Only very minimal agreement has been reached. This brief overview has also shown how varied and different are the pictures of the historical Jesus that have emerged. In many ways the observation of Schweitzer continues to apply: the constructs of scholars reflect more their own reality and presuppositions than the historical reality! This is a sober reminder that a Jesus who is presented in terms that are attractive to our world is probably being clothed too much in the scholar's own clothes. It acts as a warning that one presentation of the historical Jesus by a scholar will never and can never capture the essence of the person of Jesus.

Nevertheless, such investigations are important. They are not to be seen as a threat to Christian belief, as some responses to the above theories sometimes claim. Christian faith needs good historical research to be able to separate the essential from the culturally- and time-bound. The historical, sociological, and anthropological research that has gone into studies on the historical Jesus has opened up more clearly the context of the world out of which Jesus originated. The picture of Jesus as a 1st-century peasant Jew has certainly become much clearer, and the reader is able to understand the person and teaching of Jesus more concretely.

While consensus may not have formed on one encompassing, universal picture of the historical Jesus, a certain degree of agreement regarding the general pattern of Jesus' life has emerged. He was born during the rule of Herod the Great in Judea and grew up in Nazareth. He was baptized by John and began proclaiming a message about God's kingdom that was countercultural and championed the poor and outcasts of society. Jesus' lifestyle was that of an itinerant preacher who was accompanied by a varied group of followers.

Given Jesus' healings and the large crowds that followed him, speculation arose that Jesus was the expected Messiah. Such hopes would have prompted reaction from the Romans, who would have considered Jesus as just another troublemaker fomenting opposition to their rule. The crucifixion of Jesus under Pontius Pilate is understandable in the context of that period. It is also supported by two historians of the time, Josephus and Tacitus. Jesus' followers, who accepted him as the Messiah, would never have invented his crucifixion as it was not part of current messianic interpretation of the Hebrew Scriptures. The continuation of Jesus' legacy is attributable to his followers' conviction that he was alive. Their belief in the transforming power of the risen Christ gave them the impetus and strength to continue his preaching about the kingdom of God, not just in Palestine but throughout the Greco-Roman world.

Questions for Review and Discussion

1   In what way do the different theological pictures of Jesus presented by the four Gospel writers make it difficult to determine the historical picture of Jesus?

2   What is the picture of Jesus that you take with you as a result of this study of the New Testament?

Further Reading

Carlson, Charles E.. "Jesus Christ." In *HBD,* 510-23.

Meier, John P. *A Marginal Jew: Rethinking the Historical Jesus.* 3 vols. ABRL. New York: Doubleday, 1991-2001.

Witherington, Ben, III. *The Jesus Quest: The Third Search for the Jew of Nazareth.* 2nd ed. Downers Grove: Inter-Varsity, 1997.

Wright, N. T. *Jesus and the Victory of God.* Minneapolis: Fortress, 1996.

Index

Words defined in the glossary and otherwise not addressed in substantive ways in the rest of the Introduction are not included in the index. If you do not find a word in the Index, consult the Glossary.